Fodor's

FOURTEENTH EDITION

New

Japan

The complete guide, thoroughly up-to-date

Packed with details that will make your trip

The must-see sights, off and on the beaten path

What to see, what to skip

Mix-and-match vacation itineraries

City strolls, countryside adventures

Smart lodging and dining options

Essential local do's and taboos

Transportation tips, distances and directions

Key contacts, savvy travel tips

When to go, what to pack

Clear, accurate, easy-to-use maps

Books to read, videos to watch, background essays

Fodor's Travel Publications, Inc.
New York • Toronto • London • Sydney • Auckland
www.fodors.com/

Fodor's Japan

EDITOR: Stephen Wolf

Editorial Contributors: Robert Andrews, Diane Durston, Nigel Fisher, Kiko Itasaka, Dawn Lawson, Jared Lubarsky, David Miles, Michael O'Connell, Simon Richmond, M. T. Schwartzman (Gold Guide editor), Holly Thompson, James Vardaman, Simon Winchester, Sara Wood

Editorial Production: Janet Foley, Melissa Klurman

Maps: David Lindroth, *cartographer*; Steven K. Amsterdam, *map editor*

Design: Fabrizio La Rocca, *creative director*; Guido Caroti, *associate art director*; Jolie Novak, *photo editor*

Production/Manufacturing: Mike Costa

Cover Photograph: Brian Lovell/Nawrocki Stock Photo

Copyright

Special Sales

CONTENTS

Maps

ON THE ROAD WITH FODOR'S

WE'RE ALWAYS THRILLED to get letters from readers, especially one like this:

It took us an hour to decide what book to buy and we now know we picked the best one. Your book was wonderful, easy to follow, very accurate, and good on pointing out eating places, informal as well as formal. When we saw other people using your book, we would look at each other and smile.

Our editors and writers are deeply committed to making every Fodor's guide "the best one"—not only accurate but always charming, brimming with sound recommendations and solid ideas, right on the mark in describing restaurants and hotels, and full of fascinating facts that make you view what you've traveled to see in a rich new light.

About Our Writers

Our success in achieving our goals—and in helping to make your trip the best of all possible vacations—is a credit to the hard work of our extraordinary writers.

Longtime Kyōto resident **Diane Durston** is the author of *Old Kyōto: A Guide to Traditional Shops, Restaurants, and Inns* and *Kyōto: Seven Paths to the Heart of the City*. A frequent lecturer on Kyōto history, crafts, culture, and urban preservation in Japan, she now lives in the Pacific Northwest.

A resident of Tōkyō, **Jared Lubarsky** has lived in Japan since 1973. He has worked for cultural exchange organizations and taught at public and private universities. He still ponders the oddities of Japanese culture and still wonders why the signs that advise you not to ride elevators during an earthquake are posted *inside* the elevators.

Much of this book was updated by **Nigel Fisher,** the writer and publisher of "Voyager International," a newsletter on world travel. His particular interests are in telling his readers about art, about divine places to stay, and about the most delicious food. He has traveled extensively in Japan for more than 20 years.

David Miles has been involved with things Japanese since he first went solo to Japan in 1986 at the age of 16. After taking degrees in Japanese and Asian Studies at Georgetown University, David wrote for English language magazines in Japan and traveled and lived throughout Honshū and Kyūshū. He is currently working on a television program for broadcast throughout Japan.

Michael O'Connell left his job as a public relations executive in New York City to travel through Asia, settling down in Sapporo, Hokkaidō Prefecture, in 1993. He contributes articles to national daily newspapers, edits a magazine covering Hokkaidō, and has written travel guides on Sapporo and the 1998 Nagano Winter Olympics.

Simon Richmond has written on food, culture, travel, and politics from Tasmania to Tōkyō to Waterloo. His numerous credits include the *Sydney Morning Herald* and Tokyo's *Nihon Keizai Shimbun*. After a stint as editor of the Kansai edition of *Time Out* magazine, he once again hit the road as a freelancer, traveling and writing throughout Japan and Asia.

Tennessee-born **James Vardaman** wrote the guidebook *In and Around Sendai* and co-authored *Japanese Etiquette Today* and *Japan from A to Z: Mysteries of Everyday Life Explained*. He has been professor of English at Surugadai University in Saitama Prefecture and worked as a translator. This year he deftly revamped our Tōhoku chapter based on his broad knowledge of the region.

Simon Winchester is the Asia-Pacific editor of *Condé Nast Traveler*. In his numerous dips in Japanese hot springs, he has reached *yudedako* (*see* his essay on hot springs *in* Chapter 2) more than once.

We'd also like to thank Marion Goldberg, Hiroko Tani, and the New York staff of the Japan National Tourist Organization (JNTO); the JNTO Tōkyō staff, especially Mihoko Suzuki; Ryokichi Tada and Irene Jackson of Japan Airlines; NorthWest Airlines; Mr. Kimoto of the Prince Hotel Group; and John Tedford of Japan Railways.

New This Year

Because of outstanding contributions from all of our writers this year, *Fodor's Japan (14th Edition)* is hands down the best guide to the country that we have ever published. We have ambitiously set out to make the book as helpful as possible in introducing you to Japan, or helping you get to know the country even better, as the case may be. You'll come across four signs of this.

The first is the Japanese Cultural Primer, which will answer questions that you might have about *geisha,* Shintō beliefs, or the close-knit quality of Japanese society, as well as provide basic information on the country's crafts, the varieties of culinary experience, and the apparent obsession with hot springs.

The other three innovations have to do with the Japanese language. If you don't know Japanese, learning even a few words will illuminate the meanings of place-names throughout the country. For that purpose we have added short glossaries to each chapter. Knowing these words will also help when you go to ask directions from a Japanese local—being able to ask for the *eki* instead of the train station, or *Himeiji-jō* instead of Himeiji Castle—will touch off an immediate spark of understanding and act as a bridge between you and whomever you address. We have also added accent marks, called macrons, and hyphens to relevant Japanese words to make meanings clearer and long words less baffling. Both of these changes will help you pronounce the words more correctly, which is no small feat.

On the Web, check out Fodor's site (www.fodors.com/) for information on major destinations around the world and travel-savvy interactive features. The Web site also lists the 80-plus stations nationwide that carry the *Fodor's Travel Show,* a live call-in program that airs every weekend. Tune in to hear guests discuss their wonderful adventures—or call in to get answers for your most pressing travel questions.

How to Use This Book

Organization

Up front is the **Gold Guide,** an easy-to-use section divided alphabetically by topic. Under each listing you'll find tips and information that will help you accomplish what you need to in Japan. You'll also find addresses and telephone numbers of organizations and companies that offer destination-related services and detailed information and publications.

Chapters in *Fodor's Japan* are arranged by region, starting with Tōkyō and proceeding west to Kyushu before ending up in the country's northern reaches of Tōhoku and Hokkaidō. Each city chapter begins with an Exploring section subdivided by neighborhoods; each subsection recommends a walking tour and lists sights in alphabetical order. Each regional chapter is divided by geographical area; within each area, towns are covered in logical geographical order, and attractive stretches of road and minor points of interest between them are indicated by the designation *En Route.* Within town sections, all restaurants and lodgings are grouped together.

Each chapter begins with a glossary of key words to help you get the most out of reading this book—and to aid in navigating among the Japanese with tidbits of the language. Chapter itineraries follow, with recommendations of what to visit in the time you have; you can mix and match those from several chapters to create a complete vacation. Then come the exploring, dining, lodging, nightlife and the arts, shopping, and sports sections. The A to Z section that ends each chapter covers getting to the city or region and getting around it. There are also helpful contacts and resources in the A to Z sections.

Our new Japanese Cultural Primer, Chapter 2, serves as an introduction to the country's craft traditions, religion, society, cuisine, and bathing in hot springs. There is also a chronology of Japanese history and an extensive recommended reading section. And at the end of the book you'll find a traveler's glossary of key Japanese words and phrases.

Icons and Symbols

★   Our special recommendation
✕   Restaurant
🏨   Lodging establishment
✕🏨   Lodging establishment whose restaurant warrants a special trip
🐤   Good for kids (rubber duckie)
☞   Sends you to another section of the guide for more information
✉   Address
☎   Telephone number
🕐   Opening and closing times

✉ Admission prices (those we give apply to adults; substantially reduced fees are almost always available for children, students, and senior citizens)

Numbers in white and black circles that appear on the maps, in the margins, and within the tours correspond to one another.

Dining and Lodging

The restaurants and lodgings we list are the cream of the crop in each price range. Price charts appear in the Pleasures and Pastimes section that follows each chapter introduction.

Hotel Facilities

We always list the facilities that are available—but we don't specify whether they cost extra: When pricing accommodations, always ask what's included. In addition, assume that all rooms have private baths unless otherwise noted.

Restaurant Reservations and Dress Codes

Reservations are always a good idea; we note only when they're essential or when they are not accepted. Book as far ahead as you can, and reconfirm when you get to town. Unless otherwise noted, the restaurants listed are open daily for lunch and dinner. We mention dress only when men are required to wear a jacket or a jacket and tie. Look for an overview of local habits in the Gold Guide and in the Pleasures and Pastimes section that follows each chapter introduction.

Credit Cards

The following abbreviations are used: **AE,** American Express; **DC,** Diners Club; **MC,** MasterCard; and **V,** Visa.

Don't Forget to Write

You can use this book in the confidence that all prices and opening times are based on information supplied to us at press time; Fodor's cannot accept responsibility for any errors. Time inevitably brings changes, so always confirm information when it matters—especially if you're making a detour to visit a specific place. In addition, when making reservations be sure to mention if you have a disability or are traveling with children, if you prefer a private bath or a certain type of bed, or if you have specific dietary needs or other concerns.

Were the restaurants we recommended as described? Did our hotel picks exceed your expectations? Did you find a museum we recommended a waste of time? If you have complaints, we'll look into them and revise our entries when the facts warrant it. If you've discovered a special place that we haven't included, we'll pass the information along to our correspondents and have them check it out. So send us your feedback, positive *and* negative: e-mail us at editors@fodors.com (specifying the name of the book on the subject line) or write the Japan editor at Fodor's, 201 East 50th Street, New York, New York 10022. Have a wonderful trip!

Karen Cure
Editorial Director

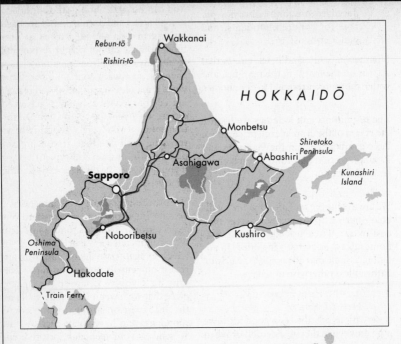

HOKKAIDŌ

Rebun-tō
Rishiri-tō
Wakkanai
Monbetsu
Shiretoko Peninsula
Asahigawa
Abashiri
Kunashiri Island
Sapporo
Noboribetsu
Kushiro
Oshima Peninsula
Hakodate
Train Ferry

N

Oki Islands
Matsue
Tottori
Tsushima
Hagi
Yamaguchi
Hiroshima
Iki Island
Fukuoka
Okayama
Kōbe
Ōsaka
Goto Islands
Matsuyama
Takamatsu
Seto Nai-kai
Awaji Island
Wakayama
Beppu
Tokushima
Oita
Nagasaki
Aso
Uwajima
Kōchi
Kii Peninsula
Amakusa Islands
Kumamoto
SHIKOKU
Shimoda
Shimo-Koshiki Island
KYŪSHŪ
Kagoshima
Miyazaki
Kuchinoerabu Island
Yaku Island
Tanega Island

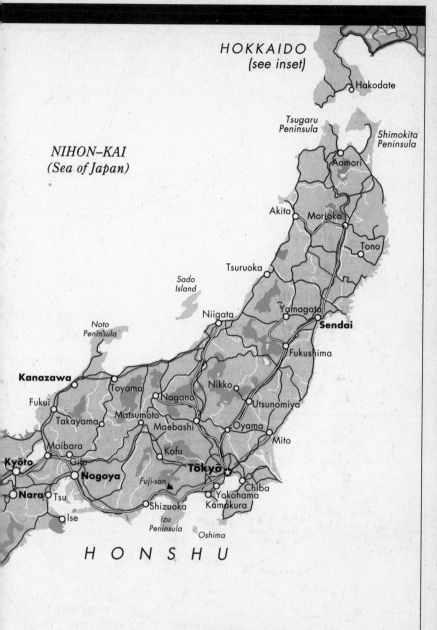

HOKKAIDO
(see inset)

Hakodate

Tsugaru
Peninsula

Shimokita
Peninsula

NIHON–KAI
(Sea of Japan)

Aomori

Akita

Morioka

Tono

Tsuruoka

Sado
Island

Yamagata

Niigata

Sendai

Noto
Peninsula

Fukushima

Kanazawa

Toyama

Nikko

Fukui

Nagano

Utsunomiya

Takayama

Matsumoto

Maebashi

Oyama

Kyōto

Maibara

Kofu

Mito

Gifu

Tōkyō

Nagoya

Fuji-san

Chiba

Nara

Tsu

Yokohama

Shizuoka

Kamakura

Ise

Izu
Peninsula

Oshima

H O N S H U

P A C I F I C   O C E A N

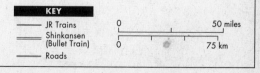

KEY

JR Trains

Shinkansen
(Bullet Train)

Roads

0 ____ 50 miles

0 ____ 75 km

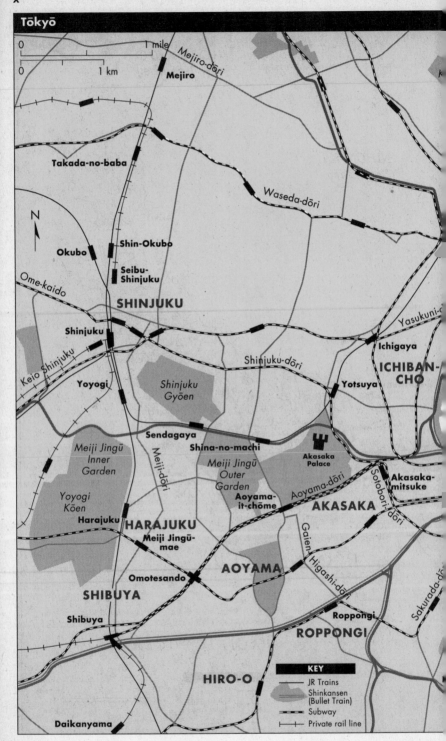

Tōkyō

0 — 1 mile
0 — 1 km

N

Mejiro-dōri
Mejiro

Takada-no-baba

Waseda-dōri

Okubo
Shin-Okubo
Seibu-Shinjuku

Ome-kaido

SHINJUKU

Shinjuku

Keio Shinjuku

Yoyogi

Shinjuku Gyōen

Shinjuku-dōri

Yasukuni-d...

Ichigaya

ICHIBAN-CHO

Yotsuya

Sendagaya
Shina-no-machi

Meiji Jingū Inner Garden

Meiji-dōri

Meiji Jingū Outer Garden

Akasaka Palace

Aoyama-it-chōme

Aoyama-dōri

Sotobori-dōri

Akasaka-mitsuke

AKASAKA

Yoyogi Kōen

Harajuku

HARAJUKU

Meiji Jingū-mae

AOYAMA

Gaien Higashi-dōri

Sakurada-d...

SHIBUYA

Omotesando

Shibuya

Roppongi

ROPPONGI

HIRO-O

Daikanyama

KEY

— JR Trains
═ Shinkansen (Bullet Train)
▪━▪ Subway
┼─┼ Private rail line

World Time Zones

Numbers below vertical bands relate each zone to Greenwich Mean Time (0 hrs.).
Local times frequently differ from these general indications,
as indicated by light-face numbers on map.

Algiers, **29**

Anchorage, **3**

Athens, **41**

Auckland, **1**

Baghdad, **46**

Bangkok, **50**

Beijing, **54**

Berlin, **34**

Bogotá, **19**

Budapest, **37**

Buenos Aires, **24**

Caracas, **22**

Chicago, **9**

Copenhagen, **33**

Dallas, **10**

Delhi, **48**

Denver, **8**

Djakarta, **53**

Dublin, **26**

Edmonton, **7**

Hong Kong, **56**

Honolulu, **2**

Istanbul, **40**

Jerusalem, **42**

Johannesburg, **44**

Lima, **20**

Lisbon, **28**

London
(Greenwich), **27**

Los Angeles, **6**

Madrid, **38**

Manila, **57**

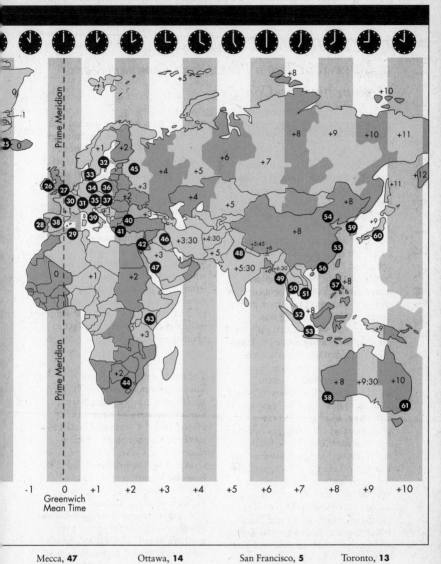

-1 0 +1 +2 +3 +4 +5 +6 +7 +8 +9 +10
Greenwich
Mean Time

Mecca, **47**
Mexico City, **12**
Miami, **18**
Montréal, **15**
Moscow, **45**
Nairobi, **43**
New Orleans, **11**
New York City, **16**

Ottawa, **14**
Paris, **30**
Perth, **58**
Reykjavík, **25**
Rio de Janeiro, **23**
Rome, **39**
Saigon (Ho Chi Minh
City), **51**

San Francisco, **5**
Santiago, **21**
Seoul, **59**
Shanghai, **55**
Singapore, **52**
Stockholm, **32**
Sydney, **61**
Tokyo, **60**

Toronto, **13**
Vancouver, **4**
Vienna, **35**
Warsaw, **36**
Washington, D.C., **17**
Yangon, **49**
Zürich, **31**

SMART TRAVEL TIPS A TO Z

Basic Information on Traveling in Japan, Savvy Tips to Make Your Trip a Breeze, and Companies and Organizations to Contact

A

ADDRESSES

Broken down into single elements, Japanese addresses are very simple. The following is an example of a typical Japanese address: 6-chōme 8-19, Chūō-ku, Fukuoka-shi, Fukuoka-ken. In this address the "chōme" indicates a precise area (a block, for example), and the numbers following "chōme" indicate the building within the area (buildings aren't always numbered sequentially in a row—numbers may have been assigned when a building was erected). You will find that only local police officers and postmen in Japan seem to be familiar with the area defined by the chōme. Sometimes, instead of a "chōme," "machi" (town) is used. "Ku" refers to a ward (a district) of a city, "shi" refers to a city name, and "ken" indicates a prefecture, which is roughly equivalent to a state in the United States. It is not unusual for the prefecture and the city to have the same name, as in the above address. There are a few geographic areas in Japan that are not called ken. One is Hokkaidō. The other exceptions are greater Tōkyō, which is called Tōkyō-to, and Kyōto and Ōsaka, which are followed by the suffix "-fu"—Kyōto-fu, Ōsaka-fu.

Not all addresses will conform exactly to the above format. Rural addresses, for example, might use "gun" (county) where cities have "ku" (ward).

It is important to note that often even Japanese people cannot find a building based on the address alone. If you get in a taxi with an address written down, do not assume the driver will be able to find your destination. Usually, people provide very detailed instructions or maps to explain their exact locations. A common method is to give the location of your destination in relation to a major building or department store.

Note: At press time, we learned that postal codes were to change throughout Japan in February 1998 from a three-numeral-plus-two number (such as 415-19) to a three-numeral-plus-four number (such as 415-1927). With no time to spare, and with an assurance from the Japan National Tourism Organization that we wouldn't be steering you wrong, we decided to render all postal codes with the three-numeral prefix only, which will still work to get your letters to Japan effectively. Keep in mind that the postal code change has most effect in rural areas: Allow a few more days for your letters to get to country towns.

AIRPORTS

The major gateway to Japan is Tōkyō's **Narita Airport** (NRT). To alleviate the congestion at Narita, **Kansai International Airport** (KIX) opened in 1994 outside of Ōsaka to serve the Kansai region, which includes Kōbe, Kyōto, Nara, and Ōsaka. A few international flights use **Fukuoka Airport,** on the island of Kyūshū; these include Northwest flights from Honolulu and flights from other Asian destinations. **Chitose Airport,** outside of Sapporo on the northern island of Hokkaidō, handles some international flights, though at present these are mostly nonscheduled flights. Most domestic flights serving Tōkyō use **Haneda Airport.**

Tōkyō's **Narita Airport** is 80 km (50 mi) northeast of the city and serves the majority of Japan's international flights. There is a departure tax of ¥2,040, which is waived for children under two and transit passengers flying out the same day as their arrival. Japan Airlines (JAL) and United Airlines are the major carriers between North America and Narita; Northwest, American Airlines, and All Nippon Airways (ANA) also link North American cities with Tōkyō. JAL, Cathay Pacific, Virgin Atlantic Airways, and British Airways fly between Narita and Great Britain; JAL, United Airlines, and Qantas fly between Narita and Australia; and JAL and Air New Zealand fly between Narita and New Zealand.

Narita Terminal No. 2 has two adjoining wings, north and south. When you arrive, your first task should be to convert your money into yen; you'll need it for transportation into Tōkyō. In both wings, money exchange counters are located in the wall between the customs inspection area and the arrival lobby. In the shopping-restaurant area between the two wings is the Japan National Tourist Organization's Tourist Information Center, where you can get free maps, brochures, and other information. Directly across from the customs area exits at both terminals are the ticket counters for Airport Limousine Buses to Tōkyō. *See* Tōkyō A to Z *in* Chapter 3 for information on the one-to two-hour trip from the airport to Tōkyō proper.

If you plan to skip Tōkyō and center your trip on Kyōto or central or western Honshū, **Kansai International Airport** is the airport to use. Built on reclaimed land in Ōsaka Bay, it is laid out vertically. The first floor is for international arrivals; the second floor is for domestic departures and arrivals; the third floor has shops and restaurants; and the fourth floor is for international departures. A small Tourist Information Center (☎ 0724/56–6025) on the first floor of the passenger terminal building is open daily 9–5. Major carriers are British Airways, Canadian Airlines, Japan Airlines, and Northwest Airlines. The trip from KIX to Kyōto takes 75 minutes by JR train; to Ōsaka it takes 45–70 minutes. *See* Chapters 7 and 9 for more information.

Flying time is 13¾ hours from New York, 12¾ hours from Chicago, 9½ hours from Los Angeles, and 11–12 hours from the United Kingdom. Japan Airlines' new GPS systems allow a more direct routing, which reduces its flight times by about 30 minutes. Flying on the eastbound route, because of tail winds, knocks about 45 minutes of the flight.

➤ AIRPORT INFORMATION: **Narita Airport** (☎ 03/3639–6126). **Kansai International Airport** (☎ 0724/55–2500). **Fukuoka Airport** (☎ 092/451–3917). **Chitose Airport** (☎ 0123/23–0111). **Haneda Airport** (☎ 03/3201–7111).

AIR TRAVEL

MAJOR AIRLINE OR LOW-COST CARRIER?

Most people choose a flight based on price, but there are other issues to consider. Major airlines offer the greatest number of departures; smaller airlines—including regional, low-cost, and no-frill airlines—usually have a more limited number of flights daily. Major airlines have frequent-flyer partners, which allow you to credit mileage earned on one airline to your account with another. Low-cost airlines offer a definite price advantage and fewer restrictions, such as advance-purchase requirements. Safety-wise, low-cost carriers as a group have a good history, but **check the safety record before booking** any low-cost carrier; call the Federal Aviation Administration's Consumer Hotline (☞ Airline Complaints, *below*).

INTERNATIONAL CARRIERS

➤ MAJOR AIRLINES: **American** (☎ 800/433–7300). **All Nippon Airways** (☎ 800/235–9262). **Canadian Airlines** (☎ 800/426–7000). **Continental** (☎ 800/525–0280). **Delta** (☎ 800/221–1212). **Japan Airlines** (☎ 800/525–3663). **Korean Air** (☎ 800/223–1155). **Northwest** (☎ 800/225–2525). **Thai Airways International** (☎ 800/426–5204). **United** (☎ 800/241–6522).

➤ FROM THE U.K.: **All Nippon Airways** (☎ 0171/355–1155). **British Airways** (☎ 0345/222–111). **Japan Airlines** (☎ 0171/408–1000). **Korean Air** (☎ 0800/413–000). **Lufthansa** (☎ 0345/737–747). **Swissair** (☎ 0171/434–7300). **Thai Airways International** (☎ 0171/499–9113).

➤ WITHIN JAPAN: **All Nippon Airways** (✉ 3-6-3 Irifune-chō, Chūō-ku, Tōkyō, ☎ 03/5489—8800). **Japan Airlines** (✉ 5-37-8 Shiba, Minato-ku, Tōkyō, ☎ 03/5489–2111).

DOMESTIC CARRIERS

➤ MAJOR AIRLINES: **All Nippon Airways** (☎ 03/5489–8800). **Japan Airlines** (☎ 03/5489–2111). **Japan Air System** (☎ 03/3438–1155).

GET THE LOWEST FARE

The least-expensive airfares to Japan are priced for round-trip travel. Major airlines usually require that you **book far in advance and stay at least seven days** and no more than 30 to get the lowest fares. Ask about "ultrasaver" fares, which are the cheapest; they must be booked 90 days in advance and are nonrefundable. "Supersaver" fares are a little more expensive; they require only a 30-day advance purchase. Remember that penalties for refunds or scheduling changes are stiff for international tickets, usually about $150. International flights are also sensitive to the season: **plan to fly in the off-season** for the cheapest fares. If your destination or home city has more than one gateway, **compare prices to and from different airports.** Also price flights scheduled for off-peak hours, which may be significantly less expensive.

To save money on flights from the United Kingdom and back, **look into an APEX or Super-PEX ticket.** APEX tickets must be booked in advance and have certain restrictions. Super-PEX tickets can be purchased at the airport on the day of departure—subject to availability.

DON'T STOP UNLESS YOU MUST

When you book, **look for nonstop flights** and remember that "direct" **flights stop at least once.** International flights on a country's flag carrier are almost always nonstop; U.S. airlines often fly direct. Try to **avoid connecting flights,** which require a change of plane. Two airlines may jointly operate a connecting flight, so ask if your airline operates every segment—you may find that your preferred carrier flies you only part of the way.

USE AN AGENT

Travel agents, particularly those who specialize in finding the lowest fares (☞ Discounts & Deals, *below*), can be helpful when booking a plane ticket. When you're quoted a price, **ask your agent if the price is likely to get any lower.** Good agents know the seasonal fluctuations of airfares and can usually anticipate a sale or fare war. However, waiting can be risky: The fare could go *up* as seats become scarce, and you could wait so long

that your preferred flight sells out. A wait-and-see strategy works best if your plans are flexible, but if you must arrive and depart on certain dates, don't delay.

CHECK WITH CONSOLIDATORS

Consolidators buy tickets for scheduled flights at reduced rates from the airlines, then sell them at prices that beat the best fare available directly from the airlines, usually without advance restrictions. Sometimes you can even get your money back if you need to return the ticket. Carefully read the fine print detailing penalties for changes and cancellations, and **confirm your consolidator reservation with the airline.**

➤ CONSOLIDATORS: **United States Air Consolidators Association** (✉ 925 L St., Suite 220, Sacramento, CA 95814, ☎ 916/441–4166, ℻ 916/441–3520).

AVOID GETTING BUMPED

Airlines routinely overbook planes, knowing that not everyone with a ticket will show up, but sometimes everyone does. When that happens, airlines ask for volunteers to give up their seats. In return these volunteers usually get a certificate for a free flight and are rebooked on the next flight out. If there are not enough volunteers the airline must choose who will be denied boarding. The first to get bumped are passengers who checked in late and those flying on discounted tickets, **so get to the gate and check in as early as possible,** especially during peak periods.

ENJOY THE FLIGHT

For more legroom, **request an emergency-aisle seat**; don't, however, sit in the row in front of the emergency aisle or in front of a bulkhead, where seats may not recline.

If you don't like airline food, **ask for special meals when booking.** These can be vegetarian, low-cholesterol, or kosher, for example.

Some carriers have prohibited smoking throughout their systems; others allow smoking only on certain routes or even certain departures from that route, so **contact your carrier regarding its smoking policy.**

COMPLAIN IF NECESSARY

If your baggage goes astray or your flight goes awry, complain right away. Most carriers require that you file a claim immediately.

➤ AIRLINE COMPLAINTS: U.S. Department of Transportation **Aviation Consumer Protection Division** (✉ C-75, Room 4107, Washington, DC 20590, ☎ 202/366–2220). **Federal Aviation Administration (FAA) Consumer Hotline** (☎ 800/322–7873).

B

BUS TRAVEL

Japan Railways (JR) offers a number of overnight long-distance buses that are not very comfortable but are inexpensive. You can use Japan Rail Passes on these buses. City buses are quite convenient, but **be sure of your route and destination,** because the bus driver will probably not speak English. Some buses have a set cost from ¥120 to ¥180, depending on the route and municipality, in which case you board at the front of the bus and pay as you get on. On other buses, cost is determined by the distance you travel. You take a ticket when you board at the rear door of the bus; it will bear the number of the stop at which you boarded. Your fare is indicated by a board with rotating numbers at the front of the bus. Under each boarding point, indicated by a number, the fare will increase the farther the bus travels.

JR runs buses in some areas that have limited rail service. Remember, these buses are covered by the JR Pass, even if some JR seat reservation clerks seem to think otherwise.

➤ BUS LINES: **Japan Railways** (☎ 03/3423–0111).

➤ GENERAL INFORMATION: **Tōkyō Bus Transportation Association** (☎ 03/3379–2442).

BUSINESS HOURS

General business hours in Japan are 9–5 weekdays. Many offices are also open at least half of the day on Saturday but are generally closed on Sunday.

Banks are open 9–3 weekdays and 9–noon on the first and last Saturdays of the month. They close on Sunday.

Department stores are usually open 10–7 but close one day a week, which varies from store to store. Other stores are open from 10 or 11 to 7 or 8.

C

CAMERAS, CAMCORDERS, & COMPUTERS

Always **keep your film, tape, or computer disks out of the sun.** Carry an extra supply of batteries, and **be prepared to turn on your camera, camcorder, or laptop** to prove to security personnel that the device is real. Always **ask for hand inspection of film,** which becomes clouded after successive exposure to airport x-ray machines, and **keep videotapes and computer disks away from metal detectors.**

Fluorescent lighting, which is used a lot in Japan, will give photographs a greenish tint. You can counteract this discoloration with an FL filter.

➤ PHOTO HELP: **Kodak Information Center** (☎ 800/242–2424). *Kodak Guide to Shooting Great Travel Pictures,* available in bookstores or from **Fodor's Travel Publications** (☎ 800/533–6478; $16.50 plus $4 shipping).

CUSTOMS

Before departing, **register your foreign-made camera or laptop with U.S. Customs** (☞ Customs & Duties, *below*). If your equipment is U.S.-made, call the consulate of the country you'll be visiting to find out whether the device should be registered with local customs upon arrival.

CAR RENTAL

Rates in Tōkyō begin at $87 a day and $437 a week a for an economy car with unlimited mileage. This does not include tax, which is 5% on car rentals. Reservations in the U.S. should be made at least a week in advance.

➤ MAJOR AGENCIES: **Budget** (☎ 800/527–0700, 0800/181181 in the U.K.). **Hertz** (☎ 800/654–3001, 800/263–0600 in Canada, 0345/555888 in the U.K.). **National InterRent** (☎ 800/227–3876; 01345/222525 in the U.K., where it is known as Europcar InterRent).

INTERNATIONAL DRIVER'S PERMITS

In Japan your own driver's license is not acceptable. You need an International Driver's Permit; it's available from the American or Canadian automobile association, or, in the United Kingdom, from the Automobile Association or Royal Automobile Club (☞ Auto Clubs *under* Driving, *below*).

CUT COSTS

To get the best deal, **book through a travel agent who is willing to shop around.**

Also **ask your travel agent about a company's customer-service record.** How has it responded to late plane arrivals and vehicle mishaps? Are there often lines at the rental counter, and, if you're traveling during a holiday period, does a confirmed reservation guarantee you a car?

NEED INSURANCE?

When driving a rented car you are generally responsible for any damage to or loss of the vehicle. You also are liable for any property damage or personal injury that you may cause while driving. Before you rent, **see what coverage you already have** under the terms of your personal auto-insurance policy and credit cards.

BEWARE SURCHARGES

Before you pick up a car in one city and leave it in another, **ask about drop-off charges or one-way service fees,** which can be substantial. Note, too, that some rental agencies charge extra if you return the car before the time specified on your contract. To avoid a hefty refueling fee, **fill the tank just before you turn in the car,** but be aware that gas stations near the rental outlet may overcharge.

CHILDREN & TRAVEL

CHILDREN IN JAPAN

Be sure to plan ahead and **involve your youngsters** as you outline your trip. When packing, include things to keep them busy en route. On sightseeing days try to schedule activities of special interest to your children. If you are renting a car don't forget to **arrange for a car seat** when you reserve. Most hotels in Japan allow children under a certain age to stay in their parents' room at no extra charge, but others charge them as extra adults; be sure to **ask about the cutoff age for children's discounts.**

BABY-SITTING

Some very expensive Western-style hotels and resort hotels have supervised playrooms where you can drop off children. The baby-sitters, however, are unlikely to speak English. Child-care arrangements can be made through the concierge, but some properties require up to a week's notice.

FLYING

As a general rule, infants under two not occupying a seat fly at greatly reduced fares and occasionally for free. If your children are two or older **ask about children's airfares.**

In general the adult baggage allowance applies to children paying half or more of the adult fare. When booking, **ask about carry-on allowances for those traveling with infants.** In general, for babies charged 10% of the adult fare you are allowed one carry-on bag and a collapsible stroller, which may have to be checked; you may be limited to less if the flight is full.

According to the FAA it's a good idea to use safety seats aloft for children weighing less than 40 pounds. Airlines, however, can set their own policies: U.S. carriers allow FAA-approved models but usually require that you buy a ticket, even if your child would otherwise ride free, since the seats must be strapped into regular seats. Airline rules vary regarding their use, so it's important to **check your airline's policy about using safety seats during takeoff and landing.** Safety seats cannot obstruct any of the other passengers in the row, so get an appropriate seat assignment as early as possible.

When making your reservation, **request children's meals or a free-standing bassinet** if you need one; the latter are available only to those seated at the bulkhead, where there's enough legroom. Remember, however, that bulkhead seats may not have their own overhead bins, and there's no storage space in front of you—a major inconvenience.

CONSUMER PROTECTION

Whenever possible, **pay with a major credit card** so you can cancel payment if there's a problem, provided that you can provide documentation. This is a good practice whether you're buying travel arrangements before your trip or shopping at your destination.

If you're doing business with a particular company for the first time, **contact your local Better Business Bureau and the attorney general's offices** in your state and the company's home state, as well. Have any complaints been filed?

Finally, if you're buying a package or tour, always **consider travel insurance** that includes default coverage (☞ Insurance, *below*).

➤ LOCAL BBBs: **Council of Better Business Bureaus** (✉ 4200 Wilson Blvd., Suite 800, Arlington, VA 22203, ☎ 703/276–0100, FAX 703/525–8277).

CUSTOMS & DUTIES

When shopping, **keep receipts** for all of your purchases. Upon reentering the country, **be ready to show customs officials what you've bought.** If you feel a duty is incorrect, appeal the assessment. If you object to the way your clearance was handled, get the inspector's badge number. In either case, first ask to see a supervisor, then write to the port director at the address listed on your receipt. Send a copy of the receipt and other appropriate documentation. If you still don't get satisfaction, you can take your case to customs headquarters in Washington.

ENTERING JAPAN

Japan is strict about bringing firearms, pornography, and narcotics into the country. Anyone caught with drugs is liable to be detained, deported, and refused reentry into Japan. Certain fresh fruits, vegetables, plants, and animals are also illegal. Nonresidents are allowed to bring in duty-free: (1) 400 cigarettes or 100 cigars or 500 grams of tobacco; (2) three bottles of alcohol; (3) 2 ounces of perfume; (4) other goods up to ¥200,000 value.

ENTERING THE U.S.

You may bring home $400 worth of foreign goods duty-free if you've been out of the country for at least 48 hours and haven't already used the $400 allowance or any part of it in the past 30 days.

Travelers 21 and older may bring back 1 liter of alcohol duty-free. In addition, regardless of your age, you are allowed 200 cigarettes and 100 non-Cuban cigars. (At press time, a federal rule restricting tobacco access to persons 18 years and older did not apply to importation.) Antiques, which the U.S. Customs Service defines as objects more than 100 years old, enter duty-free, as do original works of art done entirely by hand, including paintings, drawings, and sculptures.

You may also send packages home duty-free up to $200 worth of goods for personal use, with a limit of one parcel per addressee per day (and no alcohol or tobacco products or perfume worth more than $5); label the package PERSONAL USE, and attach a list of its contents and their retail value. Do not label the package UNSOLICITED GIFT, or your duty-free exemption will drop to $100. Mailed items do not affect your duty-free allowance on your return.

➤ INFORMATION: **U.S. Customs Service** (inquiries, ✉ Box 7407, Washington, DC 20044, ☎ 202/927–6724; complaints, Office of Regulations and Rulings, 1301 Constitution Ave. NW, Washington, DC 20229; registration of equipment, ✉ Resource Management, 1301 Constitution Ave. NW, Washington, DC 20229, ☎ 202/927–0540).

ENTERING CANADA

If you've been out of Canada for at least seven days you may bring in C$500 worth of goods duty-free. If you've been away for fewer than seven days but more than 48 hours, the duty-free allowance drops to C$200; if your trip lasts 24–48 hours, the allowance is C$50. You may not pool allowances with family members. Goods claimed under the C$500 exemption may follow you by mail; those claimed under the lesser exemptions must accompany you.

Alcohol and tobacco products may be included in the seven-day and 48-hour exemptions but not in the 24-hour exemption. If you meet the age

SMART TRAVEL TIPS / THE GOLD GUIDE

requirements of the province or territory through which you reenter Canada you may bring in, duty-free, 1.14 liters (40 imperial ounces) of wine or liquor *or* 24 12-ounce cans or bottles of beer or ale. If you are 16 or older you may bring in, duty-free, 200 cigarettes and 50 cigars; these items must accompany you.

You may send an unlimited number of gifts worth up to C$60 each duty-free to Canada. Label the package UNSOLICITED GIFT—VALUE UNDER $60. Alcohol and tobacco are excluded.

➤ INFORMATION: **Revenue Canada** (✉ 2265 St. Laurent Blvd. S, Ottawa, Ontario K1G 4K3, ☎ 613/993–0534, 800/461–9999 in Canada).

ENTERING THE U.K.

From countries outside the European Union, including Japan, you may import, duty-free, 200 cigarettes or 50 cigars; 1 liter of spirits or 2 liters of fortified or sparkling wine or liqueurs; 2 liters of still table wine; 60 milliliters of perfume; 250 milliliters of toilet water; plus £136 worth of other goods, including gifts and souvenirs.

➤ INFORMATION: **HM Customs and Excise** (✉ Dorset House, Stamford St., London SE1 9NG, ☎ 0171/202–4227).

CUSTOMS, MANNERS, & ETIQUETTE

Propriety is an important part of Japanese society. Many Japanese expect foreigners to behave differently and are tolerant of faux pas, but *they* are pleasantly surprised when people acknowledge and observe their customs. The easiest way to ingratiate yourself with the Japanese is to take time to learn and respect Japanese ways.

It is customary to **bow upon meeting someone.** The art of bowing is not simple; the depth of your bow depends on your social position in respect to that of the other person. Younger people, or those of lesser status, must bow deeper in order to indicate their respect and acknowledge their position. Foreigners are not expected to understand the complexity of these rules, and a basic nod of the head will suffice. Many Japanese

are familiar with Western customs and will offer their hand for a handshake.

Do not be offended if you are not invited to someone's home. Most entertaining among Japanese is done in restaurants or bars. It is an honor when you are invited to a home; this means that your host feels comfortable and close with you. If you do receive an invitation, bring along a small gift—a souvenir from your country is always the best present, but food and liquor are also appreciated. Upon entering a home, **remove your shoes in the foyer and put on the slippers that are provided** (in Japan, shoes are for wearing outdoors only). It is important to have socks or stockings that are in good condition.

DINING

Japanese restaurants often provide a small hot towel called an *oshibori.* This is to wipe your hands but not your face. You may see some Japanese wiping their faces with their oshibori, but generally this is considered to be in bad form. When you are finished with your oshibori, do not just toss it back onto the table, but fold or roll it up. If you are not accustomed to eating with chopsticks, ask for a fork instead. When taking food from a shared dish, do not use the part of the chopsticks that have entered your mouth to pick up a morsel. Instead, use the end that you have been holding in your hand.

DOING BUSINESS

As Japan's role in the global economy expands, the number of business travelers to Japan increases. Although many business practices are universal, certain customs remain unique to Japan. It is not necessary to observe these precepts, but Japanese will always appreciate it if you do.

In Japan, *meishi* **(business cards) are mandatory.** Upon meeting someone for the first time, it is common to bow and to proffer your business card simultaneously. Although English will suffice on your business card, it is better to have one side printed in Japanese (there are outfits in Japan that will provide this service in 24 hours). In a sense, the cards are simply a convenience. Japanese sometimes have difficulty with Western names, and referring to the cards is helpful. Also, in a society where hierarchy matters, Japanese like to know job titles and rank, so it is useful if your card indicates your position in your company. Japanese often place the business cards they have received in front of them on a table or desk as they conduct their meetings. Follow suit, and do not simply shove the card in your pocket.

The concept of being fashionably late does not exist in Japan; it is extremely important to **be prompt for both social and business occasions.** Japanese addresses tend to be complicated (☞ Addresses, *above*), and traffic is often heavy, so allow for adequate travel time. Most Japanese are not accustomed to using first names in business circumstances. Even workmates of 20 years' standing use surnames. Unless you are sure that the Japanese person is extremely comfortable with Western customs, it is best to **stick to last names and use the honorific word - san after the name,** as in *Tanaka-san* (Mr. or Mrs. Tanaka). Also, respect the hierarchy, and as much as possible address yourself to the most senior person in the room.

Don't be frustrated if decisions are not made instantly. Rarely empowered to make decisions, individual business-people must confer with their colleagues and superiors. Even if you are annoyed, don't express anger or aggression. Losing one's temper is equated with losing face in Japan.

A separation of business and private lives remains sacrosanct in Japan, and it is best not to ask about personal matters. Rather than asking about a person's family, it is better to **stick to neutral subjects in conversation.** This does not mean that you can only comment on the weather but rather that you should be careful not to be nosy.

Because of cramped housing, again, many Japanese entertain in restaurants or bars. It is not customary for Japanese businessmen to bring wives along. If you are traveling with your spouse, do not assume that an invitation includes both of you. You may ask if it is acceptable to bring your spouse along, but remember that it is awkward for a Japanese person to say no. You should pose the question carefully, such as: "Will your [wife or husband] come along, too?" That will avoid the need for a direct, personal refusal.

Usually, entertaining is done over dinner, followed by an evening on the town. Drinking is something of a national pastime in Japan. If you would rather not suffer from a hangover the next day, do not refuse your drink—sip, but keep your glass at least half full. Because the custom is for companions to pour drinks for each other, an empty glass is nearly the equivalent of requesting another drink. Whatever you do, **don't pour your own drink, and if a glass at your table happens to be empty, show your attentiveness by filling it for your companion.**

A special note to women traveling on business in Japan: Remember that although the situation is gradually changing, most Japanese women do not have careers. Many Japanese businessmen do not yet know how to interact with Western business-women. They may be uncomfortable, aloof, or patronizing. Be patient and, if the need arises, gently remind them that, professionally, you expect to be treated as any man would be.

D
DINING

Food, like many other things in Japan, is expensive. Eating at hotels and famous restaurants is costly; however, you can eat well and reasonably at standard restaurants that may not have signs in English. Many less-expensive restaurants have plastic replicas of the dishes they serve displayed in their front windows, so you can always point to what you want to eat if the language barrier is insurmountable. A good place to look for moderately priced dining spots is in the restaurant concourse of department stores, usually on the bottom floor.

In general, Japanese restaurants are very clean (standards of hygiene are very high). The water is safe, even when drawn from a tap. Most hotels have Western-style rest rooms, but restaurants may have Japanese-style toilets, with bowls recessed into the floor, over which you must squat.

THE GOLD GUIDE / SMART TRAVEL TIPS

For more information on food and dining in Japan, *see* The Discreet Charm of Japanese Cuisine *in* Chapter 2.

DISABILITIES & ACCESSIBILITY

TIPS & HINTS

When discussing accessibility with an operator or reservationist, **ask hard questions.** Are there any stairs, inside *or* out? Are there grab bars next to the toilet *and* in the shower/tub? How wide is the doorway to the room? To the bathroom? For the most extensive facilities meeting the latest legal specifications, **opt for newer accommodations,** which are more likely to have been designed with access in mind. Older buildings or ships may offer more limited facilities. Be sure to **discuss your needs before booking.**

➤ COMPLAINTS: **Disability Rights Section** (✉ U.S. Dept. of Justice, Box 66738, Washington, DC 20035-6738, ☎ 202/514–0301 or 800/514–0301, FAX 202/307–1198, TTY 202/514–0383 or 800/514–0383) for general complaints. **Aviation Consumer Protection Division** (☞ Air Travel, *above*) for airline-related problems. **Civil Rights Office** (✉ U.S. Dept. of Transportation, Departmental Office of Civil Rights, S-30, 400 7th St. SW, Room 10215, Washington, DC 20590, ☎ 202/366–4648) for problems with surface transportation.

TRAVEL AGENCIES & TOUR OPERATORS

The Americans with Disabilities Act requires that travel firms serve the needs of all travelers. That said, you should note that some agencies and operators specialize in making travel arrangements for individuals and groups with disabilities.

➤ TRAVELERS WITH MOBILITY PROBLEMS: **Access Adventures** (✉ 206 Chestnut Ridge Rd., Rochester, NY 14624, ☎ 716/889–9096), run by a former physical-rehabilitation counselor. **Hinsdale Travel Service** (✉ 201 E. Ogden Ave., Suite 100, Hinsdale, IL 60521, ☎ 630/325–1335), a travel agency that benefits from the advice of wheelchair traveler Janice Perkins. **Wheelchair Journeys** (✉ 16979 Redmond Way, Redmond, WA 98052, ☎ 425/885–2210 or 800/313–4751), for general travel arrangements.

DISCOUNTS & DEALS

Use common sense and **compare all your options before making a choice.** A plane ticket bought with a promotional coupon may not be cheaper than the least expensive fare from a discount ticket agency. For high-price travel purchases, such as packages or tours, keep in mind that what you get is just as important as what you save. Just because something is cheap doesn't mean it's a bargain.

LOOK IN YOUR WALLET

When you use your credit card to make travel purchases you might get free travel-accident insurance, collision-damage insurance, and medical or legal assistance, depending on the card and the bank that issued it. American Express, MasterCard, and Visa provide one or more of these services, so **get a copy of your credit card's travel-benefits policy.** If you are a member of the American Automobile Association (AAA) or an oil-company-sponsored road-assistance plan, always **ask hotel or car-rental reservationists about auto-club discounts.** Some clubs offer additional discounts on tours, cruises, or admission to attractions. And don't forget that auto-club membership entitles you to free maps and trip-planning services.

DIAL FOR DOLLARS

To save money, **look into "1-800" discount reservations services,** which use their buying power to get a better price on hotels, airline tickets, even car rentals. When booking a room, always **call the hotel's local toll-free number** (if one is available) rather than the central reservations number—you'll often get a better price. Always ask about special packages or corporate rates.

When shopping for the best deal on hotels and car rentals **look for guaranteed exchange rates,** which protect you against a falling dollar. With your rate locked in you won't pay more even if the price goes up in the local currency.

➤ AIRLINE TICKETS: ☎ 800/FLY–4–LESS.

➤ HOTEL ROOMS: **Steigenberger Reservation Service** (☎ 800/223–5652). **Travel Interlink** (☎ 800/888–5898).

SAVE ON COMBOS

Packages and guided tours can both save you money, but don't confuse the two. When you buy a package your travel remains independent, just as though you had planned and booked the trip yourself. Fly-drive packages, which combine airfare and car rental, are often a good deal.

JOIN A CLUB?

Many companies sell discounts in the form of travel clubs and coupon books, but these cost money. You must use participating advertisers to get a deal, and only after you recoup the initial membership cost or book price do you begin to save. If you plan to use the club or coupons frequently you may save considerably. Before signing up, find out what discounts you get for free.

➤ DISCOUNT CLUBS: **Entertainment Travel Editions** (✉ 2125 Butterfield Rd., Troy, MI 48084, ☎ 800/445–4137; $23–$48, depending on destination). **Great American Traveler** (✉ Box 27965, Salt Lake City, UT 84127, ☎ 800/548–2812; $49.95 per year). **Moment's Notice Discount Travel Club** (✉ 7301 New Utrecht Ave., Brooklyn, NY 11204, ☎ 718/234–6295; $25 per year, single or family). **Privilege Card International** (✉ 237 E. Front St., Youngstown, OH 44503, ☎ 330/746–5211 or 800/236–9732; $74.95 per year). **Sears's Mature Outlook** (✉ Box 9390, Des Moines, IA 50306, ☎ 800/336–6330; $14.95 per year). **Travelers Advantage** (✉ CUC Travel Service, 3033 S. Parker Rd., Suite 1000, Aurora, CO 80014, ☎ 800/548–1116 or 800/648–4037; $49 per year, single or family). **Worldwide Discount Travel Club** (✉ 1674 Meridian Ave., Miami Beach, FL 33139, ☎ 305/534–2082; $50 per year family, $40 single).

DRIVING

It is possible for foreigners to drive in Japan with an international driver's license, and though few select this option, it is becoming more popular. (To obtain a license, contact your country's major auto club; ☞ *below.*) Major roads are sufficiently marked in the Roman alphabet, and on country roads there is usually someone to

ask for help. However, it's a good idea to **have a detailed map with towns written in** *kanji* **(Japanese characters) and** *romaji* **(Romanized Japanese).**

In Japan, people **drive on the left.** Speed limits vary, but generally the limit is 80 kph (50 mph) on highways, 40 kph (25 mph) in cities.

Driving along the Tōkyō–Kyōto–Hiroshima corridor and in other built-up areas of Japan is not advisable. Trains and subways will get you to your destinations faster and more comfortably. Roads are congested, gas is expensive (about ¥140 per liter, or $6.25 per gallon), and highway tolls are exorbitant (tolls between Tōkyō and Kyōto amount to ¥9,250). In major cities, parking is a nightmare.

That said, a car can be the best means for exploring the rural parts of Japan. Consider taking a train to those areas where exploring the countryside will be the most interesting and renting a car locally for a day or even half a day.

➤ AUTO CLUBS: In the United States, **American Automobile Association** (AAA, ☎ 800/564–6222). In the United Kingdom, **Automobile Association** (AA, ☎ 0990/500–600), **Royal Automobile Club** (RAC, ☎ 0990/722–722 for membership, 0345/121–345 for insurance).

E

ELECTRICITY

To use your U.S.-purchased electric-powered equipment, **bring a converter and adapter.** The electrical current in Japan is 100 volts, 50 cycles alternating current (AC) in eastern Japan, and 100 volts, 60 cycles in western Japan; the United States runs on 110-volt, 60-cycle AC current. Wall outlets in Japan accept plugs with two flat prongs, like in the United States, but do not accept U.S. three-prong plugs.

If your appliances are dual-voltage, you'll need only an adapter. Don't use 110-volt outlets, marked FOR SHAVERS ONLY, for high-wattage appliances such as blow-dryers. Most laptops operate equally well on 110 and 220 volts and so require only an adapter.

F

FERRY TRAVEL

Ferries connect most of the islands of Japan. Some of the more popular routes are from Tōkyō to Tomakomai or Kushiro in Hokkaidō; from Tōkyō to Shikoku; and from Tōkyō or Ōsaka to Kyūshū. You can **purchase ferry tickets in advance** from travel agencies or before boarding. The ferries are inexpensive and are a pleasant, if slow, way of traveling. Private cabins are available, but it is more fun to travel in the economy class, where everyone sleeps in one large room. Passengers eat, drink, and enjoy themselves, creating a convivial atmosphere.

FESTIVALS

Because festivals offer a unique glimpse into Japanese culture and traditions, you should **consider dates and places for festivals when you are planning your trip.** *See* Festivals and National Holidays *in* Chapter 1, and contact the nearest branch of the Japan National Tourist Organization for specific festival dates (☞ Visitor Information, *below*).

G

GAY & LESBIAN TRAVEL

It is no small feat to orient yourself as a gay or lesbian traveler to Japan's gay nightlife. Forget about gay restaurants, cafés, even bookstores that sell more than "adult" books. A few words about the Japanese attitude toward homosexuality will help you thrive while in Japan. Because Japan does not have the religious opposition to homosexuality that the West does, the major barrier that continues to suppress gay lifestyle in Japan is the Confucian duty to continue the family line, to bring no shame to the family, and to fit into Japanese society. What this spells for lesbian and gay travelers is a seemingly small amount of establishments that cater to a gay clientele. There *are* bars, karaoke lounges, discos, "snacks" (a type of bar), hostess bars, host bars, and drag king/queen bars—the trick is finding them. Even the gay district of Tōkyō, Shinjuku 2-chōme (a 15-minute walk west of Shinjuku Station) will leave you wondering if you've found the place or not. When you get there,

look for people who live in the area, particularly Westerners, and approach them. The Japanese would never broach the subject except, perhaps, at the end of a night of drinking. In fact, it is a bad idea to broach the subject with a Japanese: It will cause much awkwardness, and the response will be nowhere near as sophisticated as it has become in the West. All of this said, homosexuality (as an interest but not a life choice) is more accepted in the realm of human expression than it is in the West. This all sounds quite discouraging, but in actuality, Japan can prove to be an outlet of immense freedom for gays if you are successful in making friends in Tōkyō, the Kansai area (Kyōto–Ōsaka–Kōbe), and Hiroshima.

➤ IN TŌKYŌ: **International Gay Friends** (☎ 03/5693–4569) is one gay meeting group. **Occur Help Line** (☎ 03/3380–2269) sets aside different days of the month for women or men. **Out in Japan** magazine is available at Tower Records.

➤ GAY- & LESBIAN-FRIENDLY TRAVEL AGENCIES: **Advance Damron** (⊠ 1 Greenway Plaza, Suite 800, Houston, TX 77046, ☎ 713/850–1140 or 800/695–0880, FAX 713/888–1010). **Club Travel** (⊠ 8739 Santa Monica Blvd., West Hollywood, CA 90069, 310/358–2200 or 800/429–8747, FAX 310/358–2222). **Islanders/Kennedy Travel** (⊠ 183 W. 10th St., New York, NY 10014, ☎ 212/242–3222 or 800/988–1181, FAX 212/929–8530). **Now Voyager** (⊠ 4406 18th St., San Francisco, CA 94114, ☎ 415/626–1169 or 800/255–6951, FAX 415/626–8626). **Yellowbrick Road** (⊠ 1500 W. Balmoral Ave., Chicago, IL 60640, ☎ 773/561–1800 or 800/642–2488, FAX 773/561–4497). **Skylink Women's Travel** (⊠ 3577 Moorland Ave., Santa Rosa, CA 95407, ☎ 707/585–8355 or 800/225–5759, FAX 707/584–5637), serving lesbian travelers.

GUIDES

The Japan National Tourist Organization (JNTO) sponsors a Good-Will Guide program in which local citizens volunteer to show visitors around their hometowns; this is a great way to have contact with Japanese people. These are not professional guides; they usually volunteer both because they enjoy welcoming foreigners to their town and because they want to practice their English. The services of Good-Will Guides are free, but you should pay for their travel costs, their admission fees, and any meals you eat with them while you are together. To participate in this program, **make arrangements for a Good-Will Guide in advance through JNTO** in the United States or through the tourist office in the area where you want the guide to meet you. The program operates in many areas, including Tōkyō, Kyōto, Nara, Nagoya, Ōsaka, and Hiroshima.

H
HEALTH

MEDICAL PLANS

No one plans to get sick while traveling, but it happens, so **consider signing up with a medical-assistance company.** Members get doctor referrals, emergency evacuation or repatriation, 24-hour telephone hot lines for medical consultation, cash for emergencies, and other personal and legal assistance. Coverage varies by plan, so **review the benefits carefully.**

➤ MEDICAL-ASSISTANCE COMPANIES: **International SOS Assistance** (✉ Box 11568, Philadelphia, PA 19116, ☎ 215/244–1500 or 800/523–8930; ✉ 1255 University St., Suite 420, Montréal, Québec H3B 3B6, ☎ 514/874–7674 or 800/363–0263; ✉ 7 Old Lodge Pl., St. Margarets, Twickenham TW1 1RQ, England, ☎ 0181/744–0033). **MEDEX Assistance Corporation** (✉ Box 5375, Timonium, MD 21094-5375, ☎ 410/453–6300 or 800/537–2029). **Traveler's Emergency Network** (✉ 3100 Tower Blvd., Suite 1000B, Durham, NC 27707, ☎ 919/490–6055 or 800/275–4836, FAX 919/493–8262). **TravMed** (✉ Box 5375, Timonium, MD 21094, ☎ 410/453–6380 or 800/732–5309). **Worldwide Assistance Services** (✉ 1133 15th St. NW, Suite 400, Washington, DC 20005, ☎ 202/331–1609 or 800/821–2828, FAX 202/828–5896).

I
INSURANCE

Travel insurance is the best way to **protect yourself against financial loss.**

The most useful policies are trip-cancellation-and-interruption, default, medical, and comprehensive insurance.

Without insurance you will lose all or most of your money if you cancel your trip, regardless of the reason. It's essential that you **buy trip-cancellation-and-interruption insurance,** particularly if your airline ticket, cruise, or package tour is nonrefundable and cannot be changed. When considering how much coverage you need, look for a policy that will cover the cost of your trip plus the nondiscounted price of a one-way airline ticket, should you need to return home early. Also **consider default or bankruptcy insurance,** which protects you against a supplier's failure to deliver.

Medicare generally does not cover health-care costs outside the United States, nor do many privately issued policies. If your own policy does not cover you outside the United States, **consider buying supplemental medical coverage.** Remember that travel health insurance is different from a medical-assistance plan (☞ Health, *above*).

Citizens of the United Kingdom can buy an annual travel-insurance policy valid for most vacations during the year in which it's purchased. If you are pregnant or have a preexisting medical condition, make sure you're covered.

If you have purchased an expensive vacation, particularly one that involves travel abroad, comprehensive insurance is a must. **Look for comprehensive policies that include trip-delay insurance,** which will protect you in the event that weather problems cause you to miss your flight, tour, or cruise. A few insurers sell waivers for preexisting medical conditions. Companies that offer both features include Access America, Carefree Travel, Travel Insured International, and Travel Guard (☞ *below*).

Always **buy travel insurance directly from the insurance company;** if you buy it from a travel agency or tour operator that goes out of business you probably will not be covered for the agency or operator's default, a major risk. Before you make any purchase, **review your existing health**

and home owner's policies to find out whether they cover expenses incurred while traveling.

➤ TRAVEL INSURERS: In the United States, **Access America** (✉ 6600 W. Broad St., Richmond, VA 23230, ☎ 804/285–3300 or 800/284–8300), **Carefree Travel Insurance** (✉ Box 9366, 100 Garden City Plaza, Garden City, NY 11530, ☎ 516/294–0220 or 800/323–3149), **Near Travel Services** (✉ Box 1339, Calumet City, IL 60409, ☎ 708/868–6700 or 800/654–6700), **Travel Guard International** (✉ 1145 Clark St., Stevens Point, WI 54481, ☎ 715/345–0505 or 800/826–1300), **Travel Insured International** (✉ Box 280568, East Hartford, CT 06128-0568, ☎ 860/528–7663 or 800/243–3174), **Travelex Insurance Services** (✉ 11717 Burt St., Suite 202, Omaha, NE 68154-1500, ☎ 402/445–8637 or 800/228–9792, FAX 800/867–9531), **Wallach & Company** (✉ 107 W. Federal St., Box 480, Middleburg, VA 20118, ☎ 540/687–3166 or 800/237–6615). In Canada, **Mutual of Omaha** (✉ Travel Division, 500 University Ave., Toronto, Ontario M5G 1V8, ☎ 416/598–4083, 800/268–8825 in Canada). In the United Kingdom, **Association of British Insurers** (✉ 51 Gresham St., London EC2V 7HQ, ☎ 0171/600–3333).

L

LANGUAGE

Communicating in Japan can be a challenge. This is not because the Japanese don't speak English but because most of us know little, if any, Japanese. It is worthwhile to **take some time before you leave home to learn a few basic words,** such as where (*doko*), what time (*nan-ji*), bathroom (*o-te-arai*), thanks (*arigatō gozaimasu*), excuse me (*sumimasen*), and please (*onegai shimasu*).

English is a required subject in Japanese schools, so most Japanese study English for nearly a decade. This does not mean that everyone *speaks* English. Schools emphasize reading, writing, and grammar. As a result, many Japanese can read English but can speak only a few basic phrases. Furthermore, when asked "Do you speak English?" many Japanese will, out of modesty, say no, even if they

do understand and speak a fair amount of it. It is usually best to simply ask what you really want to know slowly, clearly, and as simply as possible. If the person you ask understands, he or she will answer, or perhaps take you where you need to go. If that person does not understand, try someone else.

Although a local may understand your simple question, he or she cannot always give you an answer that requires complicated instructions. For example, you may ask someone on the subway how to get to a particular stop, and he may direct you to the train across the platform and then say something in Japanese that you do not understand. You may discover too late that the train runs express to the suburbs after the third stop; the person who gave you directions was trying to tell you to switch trains at the third stop. To avoid this kind of trouble, **ask more than one person for directions every step of the way.** You can avoid that trip to the suburbs if you ask someone *on* the train how to get to where you want to go. Also, remember that politeness is a matter of course in Japan, and that the Japanese won't want to lose face by saying that they don't know how to get somewhere. If the situation gets confusing, **bow, say *arigatō gozaimashita*** ("thank you" in the past tense), **and ask someone else.** Even though you are communicating on a very basic level, misunderstandings can happen easily.

Traveling in Japan can be problematic if you don't read Japanese. Before you leave home, **buy a phrase book** that shows English, English transliterations of Japanese (*romaji*), and Japanese characters (*kanji* and *kana*). You will read the *romaji* to pick up a few Japanese words and match the kanji and kana in the phrase book with characters on signs and menus. When all else fails, ask for help by pointing to the Japanese words in your book.

Learning Japanese is a major commitment. Japanese writing alone consists of three character systems: *kanji*, characters borrowed and adapted from China centuries ago, which represent ideas; and two forms of *kana*—hiragana and katakana—which represent sounds. Hiragana is used to write some Japanese words, verb inflections, and adjectives; katakana is used for foreign words, slang expressions, and technical terms. There are two sets of 47 kana and more than 6,000 kanji, although most Japanese use fewer than 1,000 kanji. This is more than a tourist can learn in a short stay, so you will find yourself scanning your surroundings for *romaji,* which is easier to interpret.

The most common system of writing Japanese words in Roman letters is the modified Hepburn system, which spells out Japanese words phonetically and is followed in this book.

For information on pronouncing Japanese words, notes on how we are rendering Japanese words in this guide, and a list of useful words and phrases, turn to An English-Japanese Traveler's Vocabulary at the end of this book.

Note: There is some disagreement over the use of gai-jin (literally "outside person") as opposed to *gai-koku-jin* (literally "outisde country person"), because the former has negative echoes of the days of Japanese isolationism. In the 17th and 18th centuries, when the Japanese had contact only with Dutch traders, Westerners were called *buttā-kusai* (literally "stinking of butter"—obviously a derogatory term. Gai-koku-jin, on the other hand, has a softer, more polite meaning, and many Westerners in Japan prefer it because it has no xenophobic taint.

We have chosen to use the word gai-jin instead of gai-koku-jin to translate the word "foreigner" for two reasons. First, it is commonly used in books written by Westerners who have lived in Japan, and as such it has wider recognition value. Second, as Japan becomes more global—especially its younger generation—gai-jin is losing its negative sense. Many Japanese use gai-jin as the one word they know to describe non-Japanese, and most often mean no offense by it.

So if children giggle and point at the "gai-jin-san," know that it is meant with only the kindest fascination. And if you feel that extra politeness is appropriate, use gai-koku-jin with colleagues whom you respect—or with whoever might be using gai-jin a bit too derogatorily.

CHAPTER GLOSSARIES

At the beginning of each chapter you will find a glossary of words that will appear elsewhere in the chapter untranslated. Getting to know these Japanese words will help you if you need to ask directions from a non-English speaker. Even among Japanese who know English, using Japanese words whenever possible—*eki,* for example, which means train station—will make getting around that much easier.

LODGING

Overnight accommodations in Japan run from luxury hotels to *ryokan* (traditional inns) to youth hostels and even capsules (☞ Hotels, *below*). Western-style rooms with Western-style bathrooms are widely available in large cities, but in smaller, out-of-the-way towns it may be necessary to stay in a Japanese-style room.

RYOKAN

If you want to sample the Japanese way **spend at least one night in a ryokan** (inn). Usually small, one- or two-story wooden structures with a garden or scenic view, they provide traditional Japanese accommodations: simple rooms in which the bedding is rolled out onto the floor at night.

Ryokan vary in price and quality. Some older, long-established inns cost as much as ¥80,000 per person, whereas humbler places that are more like bed-and-breakfasts are as low as ¥5,000. Prices are per person and include the cost of breakfast, dinner, and tax. Some inns will allow you to stay without having dinner and lower the cost accordingly. However, this is not recommended, because the service and meals are part of the ryokan experience.

It is important to **follow Japanese customs in all ryokan.** Upon entering, **take off your shoes,** as you would do in a Japanese household, and put on the slippers that are provided in the entryway. A maid, after bowing to welcome you, will escort you to your room, which will have tatami (straw mats) on the floor and will probably be partitioned off with shōji (sliding paper-paneled walls). Remove your slippers before entering your room; you should not step on the tatami with either shoes or slippers. The room will have little furniture or decoration—perhaps one small low table and cushions on the tatami, with a long, simple scroll on the wall. Often the rooms overlook a garden.

Plan to arrive in the late afternoon, as is the custom. After relaxing with a cup of green tea, have a long, hot bath. In ryokan with thermal pools, you can take to the waters anytime, although the doors to the pool are usually locked from 11 PM to 6 AM. In ryokan without thermal baths or private baths in guest rooms, guests must stagger visits to the one or two public baths. Typically the maid will ask what time you would like your bath and fit you into a schedule. In Japanese baths, washing and soaking are separate functions: wash and rinse off entirely, and then get in the tub. Be sure to keep all soap out of the tub. Because other guests will be using the same bathwater after you, it is important to observe this custom. After your bath, change into a *yukata*, a simple cotton kimono, provided in your room. Do not feel abashed about walking around in what is essentially a robe—all other guests will be doing the same.

Dinner, included in the price, is served in your room at smaller and more personal ryokan; at larger ryokan, especially the newer ones, meals will be in the dining room. After you are finished, a maid will discreetly come in, clear away the dishes, and lay out your futon. In Japan *futon* means bedding, and this consists of a thin cotton mattress and a heavy, thick comforter. In summer, the comforter is replaced with a thinner quilt. The small, hard pillow is filled with grain. The less expensive ryokan (under ¥7,000 for one) have become slightly lackadaisical in changing the sheet cover over the quilt with each new guest; feel free to complain (in as inoffensive a way as possible, of course, so as not to shame the proprietor). In the morning, a maid will gently wake you, clear away the futon, and bring in your Japanese-style breakfast. If you are not fond of Japanese breakfasts, which often consist of fish, pickled vegetables, and rice, the staff will usually be able to rustle up some coffee and toast.

Because most ryokan staffs are small and dedicated, it is important to be considerate and understanding of their somewhat rigid schedules. Guests are expected to arrive in the late afternoon and eat around 6. Usually the doors to the inn are locked at 10, so plan for early evenings. Breakfast is served around 8, and checkout is at 10.

A genuine traditional ryokan with exemplary service is exorbitantly expensive—more than ¥30,000 per person per night with two meals. Many modern hotels with Japanese-style rooms are now referring to themselves as ryokan, and though meals may be served in the guests' rooms, they are a far cry from the traditional ryokan. There are also small inns claiming the status of ryokan, but they are really nothing more than bed-and-breakfast establishments where meals are taken in a communal dining room—for an additional fee—and service is minimal. In lesser-priced inns, which run from ¥5,000 for a single room to ¥7,000 for a double, tubs are likely to be plastic rather than cedarwood and small rooms might overlook a street rather than a garden. Rooms will have tatami straw mat floors, futon bedding, and a scroll and/or flower arrangement in its rightful place. JNTO offers a publication listing some of these.

Bear in mind that **not all inns are willing to accept foreign guests** because of language and cultural barriers. This makes calling ahead for a room important, so that you can be sure to get one. Also, top-level ryokan expect even new Japanese guests to have introductions and references from a respected client of the inn, which means that you, too, might need an introduction from a Japanese for very top level ryokan. On the other side of this issue, inns that do accept foreigners without introduction may be treated as "cash cows," which means giving you cursory service and a lesser room. When you reserve a room, try to have a Japanese make the call for you, or if you know Japanese, it will convey the idea that you understand the customs of staying in a traditional inn.

➤ INFORMATION: **Japan Ryokan Association** (✉ 1-8-3 Maru-no-uchi,

Chiyoda-ku, Tōkyō, ☎ 03/231–5310) or the JNTO (☞ Visitor Information, *below*).

MINSHUKU

Minshuku are private homes that accept guests. Usually they cost about ¥5,000 per person, including two meals. Although in a ryokan you need not lift a finger, **don't be surprised if you are expected to lay out and put away your own bedding in minshuku.** Meals are often served in communal dining rooms. Minshuku vary in size and atmosphere; some are private homes that take in only a few guests, while others are more like no-frill inns. Some of your most memorable stays could be at a minshuku, as they offer a chance to become acquainted with a Japanese family and their hospitality.

➤ INFORMATION: **Japan Minshuku Association** (✉ 1-29-5 Takadanobaba, Shinjuku-ku, Tōkyō, ☎ 03/3232–6561).

TEMPLES

You can also arrange accommodations in Buddhist temples. JNTO has lists of temples that accept guests. A stay at a temple generally costs ¥3,000–¥9,000 per night, including two meals. Some temples offer instruction in meditation or allow you to observe their religious practices, while others simply offer a room. The Japanese-style rooms are very simple and range from beautiful, quiet havens to not-so-comfortable, basic cubicles. Either way, temples provide a taste of traditional Japan.

HOME VISITS

Through the Home Visit System, travelers can get a sense of domestic life in Japan by visiting a local family in their home. The program is voluntary on the homeowner's part, and there is no charge for a visit. It is active in many cities throughout the country, including Tōkyō, Yokohama, Nagoya, Kyōto, Ōsaka, Hiroshima, Nagasaki, Sapporo, and others. To make a reservation, **apply in writing for a home visit at least a day in advance** to the local tourist information office of the place you are visiting. Contact the Japan National Tourist Organization (JNTO) (☞ Visitor Information, *below*) before leaving for Japan for more information on the program.

HOTELS

Full-service, first-class hotels in Japan are similar to their counterparts all over the world, and because many of the staff speak English, these are the easiest places for foreigners to stay. They are also among the most expensive.

Business hotels are a reasonable alternative. These are clean, impersonal, and functional. All have Western-style rooms that vary from small to minuscule; service is minimal. However, every room has a private bathroom, albeit cramped, with tub and hand-held shower, television (with Japanese-language channels), telephone, and a hot-water thermos. Business hotels are often conveniently located near the railway station. The staff may not speak English, and there is usually no room service.

Designed to accommodate the modern Japanese urbanite, the capsule hotel is a novel idea. The rooms are a mere 3½ ft wide, 3½ ft high, and 7¼ ft long. They have an alarm clock, television, and phone, and little else. Capsules are often used by commuters who have had an evening of excess and cannot make the long journey home. Although you may want to try sleeping in a capsule, you probably won't want to spend a week in one.

INEXPENSIVE ACCOMMODATIONS

JNTO publishes a listing of some 200 accommodations that are reasonably priced. To be listed, properties must meet Japanese fire codes and charge less than ¥8,000 per person without meals. For the most part, the properties charge ¥5,000–¥6,000. These properties welcome foreigners (many Japanese hotels and ryokan do not like to have foreign guests because they might not be familiar with traditional-inn etiquette). Properties include business hotels, *ryokan* (☞ *above*) of very rudimentary nature, *minshuku* (☞ *above*), and pensions. It's the luck of the draw whether you choose a good or less-than-good property. In most cases, rooms are clean but very small. Except in business hotels, shared baths are the norm, and you will be expected to have your room lights out by 10 PM.

Many establishments on the list of reasonably priced accommodations—and many that are not on the list—can be reserved through the nonprofit organization **Welcome Inn Reservation Center.** Reservation forms are available from your nearest JNTO office (☞ Visitor Information, *below*). The center must receive reservation requests at least one week before your departure to allow processing time. If you are already in Japan, JNTO's Tourist Information Centers (TICs) at Narita Airport, downtown Tōkyō, and Kyōto can make immediate reservations for you at these Welcome Inns.

➤ RESERVATIONS: **Welcome Inn Reservation Center** (✉ International Tourism Center of Japan, Kotani Bldg., 2nd floor, 1-6-6 Yuraku-chō, Chiyoda-ku, Tōkyō 100, ☎ 03/3580–8353, ℻ 03/3580–8256).

LODGING PRICES

Outside of cities and major towns, most lodgings quote prices on a per-person basis with two meals, exclusive of service and tax. If you do not want dinner at your hotel, it is usually possible to renegotiate the price. Stipulate, too, whether you wish to have Japanese or Western breakfasts, if any. Throughout this guide, price categories assigned to all hotels reflect the cost of a double room with private bath and no meals. However, when you make reservations at a noncity hotel, you will be expected to take breakfast and dinner at the hotel—that will be the rate quoted to you unless you specify otherwise.

APARTMENT & VILLA RENTALS

If you want a home base that's roomy enough for a family and comes with cooking facilities, **consider a furnished rental.** These can save you money; however, some rentals are luxury properties, economical only when your party is large. Home-exchange directories list rentals (often second homes owned by prospective house swappers), and some services search for a house or apartment for you (even a castle if that's your fancy) and handle the paperwork. Some send an illustrated catalog; others send photographs only of specific properties, sometimes at a charge. Up-front registration fees may apply.

➤ RENTAL AGENTS: **Property Rentals International** (✉ 1008 Mansfield Crossing Rd., Richmond, VA 23236, ☎ 804/378–6054 or 800/220–3332, ℻ 804/379–2073).

M

MAIL

The Japanese postal service is very efficient. Although numerous post offices exist in any given city, it is probably best to use central post offices located near the main train station, because the workers speak English and can handle foreign mail. Some of the smaller post offices are not equipped to send packages.

Post offices are open weekdays 8–5 and Saturday 8–noon. Some of the central post offices have longer hours, such as the one in Tōkyō, located near Tōkyō Eki (train station), which is open 24 hours, year-round. Most hotels will supply stamps and mail your letters and postcards, usually with no "service fee."

It costs ¥110 to send a letter by air to North America and Europe. An airmail postcard costs ¥70. Aerograms cost ¥90.

RECEIVING MAIL

To get mail, **have parcels and letters sent poste restante at the central post office in major cities;** unclaimed mail is returned after 30 days. American Express offices, located in all major Japanese cities, are other good places to have mail sent.

➤ AMEX OFFICES: **American Express** (✉ Halifax Building, 16-26 Roppongi 3-chōme, Minato-ku, Tōkyō).

MONEY

The unit of currency in Japan is the yen (¥). There are bills of ¥10,000, ¥5,000, and ¥1,000. Coins are ¥500, ¥100, ¥50, ¥10, ¥5, and ¥1. Japanese currency floats on the international monetary exchange, so changes can be dramatic. At press time the exchange rate was about ¥124 to the U.S. dollar, ¥90 to the Canadian dollar, and ¥182 to the pound sterling.

ATMS

Before leaving home, **make sure that your credit cards have been programmed for ATM use in Japan.** Note that Discover is accepted mostly in the United States. Local bank cards often do not work overseas or may access only your checking account; **ask your bank about a MasterCard/ Cirrus or Visa debit card,** which works like a bank card but can be used at any ATM displaying a MasterCard/ Cirrus or Visa logo. These cards, too, may tap only your checking account; check with your bank about its policy.

➤ ATM LOCATIONS: **Cirrus** (☎ 800/ 424–7787). A list of **Plus** locations is available at your local bank.

COSTS

Japan is expensive, but there are ways to cut costs. This requires, to some extent, an adventurous spirit and the courage to stray from the standard tourist paths. One good way to hold down expenses is to **avoid taxis** (they tend to get stuck in traffic anyway) and **try the inexpensive, efficient subway and bus systems**; instead of going to a restaurant with menus in English and Western-style food, go to places where you can rely on your good old index finger to point to the dish you want, and **try food that the Japanese eat** (☞ Dining, *above,* and The Discreet Charm of Japanese Cuisine *in* Chapter 2).

A cup of coffee costs ¥350–¥600; a bottle of beer: ¥350–¥1,000; a 2-km taxi ride: ¥600 (¥840 in Tōkyō); a McDonald's hamburger: ¥340; a bowl of noodles: ¥700; an average dinner: ¥2,500; a double room in Tōkyō: ¥9,000–¥34,000.

CURRENCY EXCHANGE

For the most favorable rates, **change money at banks.** Although fees charged for ATM transactions may be higher abroad than at home, Cirrus and Plus exchange rates are excellent, because they are based on wholesale rates offered only by major banks. You won't do as well at exchange booths in airports or rail and bus stations, in hotels, in restaurants, or in stores, although you may find their hours more convenient. To avoid lines at airport exchange booths, **get a small amount of local currency before you leave home.**

➤ EXCHANGE SERVICES: **International Currency Express** (☎ 888/842–0880 on the East Coast or 888/278–6628 on the West Coast for telephone

orders). **Thomas Cook Currency Services** (☎ 800/287–7362 for telephone orders and retail locations).

TRAVELER'S CHECKS

Whether or not to buy traveler's checks depends on where you are headed. **Take cash if your trip includes rural areas** and small towns, traveler's checks to cities. If your checks are lost or stolen, they can usually be replaced within 24 hours. To ensure a speedy refund, buy your checks yourself (don't ask someone else to make the purchase). When making a claim for stolen or lost checks, the person who bought the checks should make the call.

P

PACKING FOR JAPAN

Because porters can be hard to find and baggage restrictions on international flights are tight, **pack light.** What you pack depends more on the time of year than on any dress code. For travel in the cities, pack as you would for an American or European city. At more expensive restaurants and nightclubs, men will usually need to wear a jacket and tie, and women will need a dress or skirt. Wear conservative-colored clothing at business meetings. Casual clothes are fine for sightseeing. Jeans are as popular in Japan as they are in the United States and are perfectly acceptable for informal dining and sightseeing.

Although there are no strict dress codes for visiting temples and shrines, **you will be out of place in shorts or immodest outfits.** For sightseeing, leave sandals and open-toe shoes behind; you'll need sturdy walking shoes for the gravel pathways that surround temples and fill parks. Make sure to bring comfortable clothing that isn't too tight to wear in traditional Japanese restaurants, where you may need to sit on tatami-matted floors. For beach and mountain resorts, pack informal clothes for both day and evening wear.

Japanese do not wear shoes in private homes or in any temples or traditional inns. Having shoes you can quickly slip in and out of is a decided advantage. Take some wool socks along to help you through those shoeless occasions.

THE GOLD GUIDE / SMART TRAVEL TIPS

If you're a morning coffee addict, **take along packets of instant coffee.** All lodgings provide a thermos of hot water and bags of green tea in every room, but for coffee you'll either have to call room service (which can be expensive) or buy very sweet coffee in a can from a vending machine. If you're staying in a Japanese inn, they probably won't have coffee, and it may be hard to find in rural areas.

Although sunglasses, sunscreen lotions, and hats are readily available, you're better off buying them at home, because they're much more expensive in Japan. It's a good idea to carry a couple of plastic bags to protect your camera and clothes during sudden cloudbursts.

Take along small gift items, such as scarves or perfume sachets, to thank hosts (on both business and pleasure trips), whether you've been invited to their home or out to a restaurant.

Bring an extra pair of eyeglasses or contact lenses in your carry-on luggage, and if you have a health problem, **pack enough medication** to last the entire trip or have your doctor write you a prescription using the drug's generic name, because brand names vary from country to country. It's important that you **don't put prescription drugs or valuables in luggage to be checked**: it might go astray. To avoid problems with customs officials, carry medications in the original packaging. Also, don't forget the addresses of offices that handle refunds of lost traveler's checks.

LUGGAGE

In general, you are entitled to check two bags on flights within the United States and on international flights leaving the United States. A third piece may be brought on board, but it must fit easily under the seat in front of you or in the overhead compartment.

If you are flying between two foreign destinations, note that baggage allowances may be determined not by piece but by weight—generally 88 pounds (40 kilograms) in first class, 66 pounds (30 kilograms) in business class, and 44 pounds (20 kilograms) in economy. If your flight between two cities abroad *connects* with your transatlantic or transpacific flight, the piece method still applies.

Airline liability for baggage is limited to $1,250 per person on flights within the United States. On international flights it amounts to $9.07 per pound or $20 per kilogram for checked baggage (roughly $640 per 70-pound bag) and $400 per passenger for unchecked baggage. Insurance for losses exceeding these amounts can be bought from the airline at check-in for about $10 per $1,000 of coverage; note that this coverage excludes a rather extensive list of items, which is shown on your airline ticket.

Before departure, **itemize your bags' contents** and their worth, and label the bags with your name, address, and phone number. (If you use your home address, cover it so that potential thieves can't see it readily.) Inside each bag, **pack a copy of your itinerary.** At check-in, **make sure that each bag is correctly tagged** with the destination airport's three-letter code. If your bags arrive damaged or fail to arrive at all, file a written report with the airline before leaving the airport.

PASSPORTS & VISAS

Once your travel plans are confirmed, **check the expiration date of your passport.** It's also a good idea to **make photocopies of the data page**; leave one copy with someone at home and keep another with you, separated from your passport. If you lose your passport, promptly call the nearest embassy or consulate and the local police; having a copy of the data page can speed replacement.

U.S. CITIZENS

All U.S. citizens, even infants, need only a valid passport to enter Japan for stays of up to 90 days.

➤ INFORMATION: **Office of Passport Services** (☎ 202/647–0518).

CANADIANS

You need only a valid passport to enter Japan for stays of up to 90 days.

➤ INFORMATION: **Passport Office** (☎ 819/994–3500 or 800/567–6868).

U.K. CITIZENS

Citizens of the United Kingdom need only a valid passport to enter Japan for stays of up to six months.

➤ INFORMATION: **London Passport Office** (☎ 0990/21010) to find out fees and documentation requirements and to request an emergency passport.

S
SENIOR-CITIZEN TRAVEL

To qualify for age-related discounts, **mention your senior-citizen status up front** when booking hotel reservations (not when checking out) and before you're seated in restaurants (not when paying the bill). Note that discounts may be limited to certain menus, days, or hours. When renting a car, **ask about promotional car-rental discounts,** which can be cheaper than senior-citizen rates.

➤ EDUCATIONAL TRAVEL PROGRAMS: **Elderhostel** (☒ 75 Federal St., 3rd floor, Boston, MA 02110, ☎ 617/426–8056).

SHOPPING

Despite the high value of the yen and the high price of many goods, shopping is one of the great pleasures of a trip to Japan. You may not find terrific bargains here, but if you know where to go and what to look for, you can purchase unusual gifts and souvenirs at reasonable prices. In particular, **don't shop for items that are cheaper at home**; Japan is not the place to buy a Gucci bag (electronics, too, are generally cheaper in the U.S.). Instead, **look for things that are Japanese-made** for Japanese people and sold in stores that do not cater primarily to tourists.

Don't pass up the chance to purchase Japanese crafts. Color, balance of form, and absolutely superb craftsmanship make these items exquisite and well worth the price you'll pay. That means that some craft items are quite expensive. For example, Japanese lacquerware carries a hefty price. But if you like the shiny boxes, bowls, cups, and trays and consider that quality lacquerware is made to last a lifetime, the cost is justified. Be careful, though: Some lacquer items are made from a pressed-wood product rather than solid wood, and only experts can tell the difference. If the price seems low, it probably means the quality is low, too.

For more information on Japanese crafts, *see* Chapter 2.

STUDENTS

To save money, **look into deals available through student-oriented travel agencies.** To qualify you'll need a bona fide student ID card. Members of international student groups are also eligible.

➤ STUDENT IDS & SERVICES: **Council on International Educational Exchange** (☒ CIEE, 205 E. 42nd St., 14th floor, New York, NY 10017, ☎ 212/822–2600 or 888/268–6245, FAX 212/822–2699), for mail orders only, in the United States. **Travel Cuts** (☒ 187 College St., Toronto, Ontario M5T 1P7, ☎ 416/979–2406 or 800/667–2887) in Canada.

➤ HOSTELING: **Hostelling International—American Youth Hostels** (☒ 733 15th St. NW, Suite 840, Washington, DC 20005, ☎ 202/783–6161, FAX 202/783–6171). **Hostelling International—Canada** (☒ 400-205 Catherine St., Ottawa, Ontario K2P 1C3, ☎ 613/237–7884, FAX 613/237–7868). **Youth Hostel Association of England and Wales** (☒ Trevelyan House, 8 St. Stephen's Hill, St. Albans, Hertfordshire AL1 2DY, ☎ 01727/855215 or 01727/845047, FAX 01727/844126). Membership in the United States is $25; in Canada, C$26.75; in the United Kingdom, £9.30.

In Japan: **Japan Youth Hostel Association** (☒ Hoken Kaikan, 1-1 Ichigaya-Sadohara-chō, Shinjuku-ku, Tōkyō, ☎ 03/3269–5831).

T
TAXES

HOTEL

A 5% federal consumer tax is added to all hotel bills. Another 3% local tax is added to the bill if it exceeds ¥15,000. You may **save money by paying for your hotel meals separately** rather than charging them to your bill.

At first-class, full-service, and luxury hotels, a 10% service charge will be added to the bill in place of individual tipping. At the more expensive ryokan, where individualized maid service is offered, the service charge will usually be 15%. At business hotels, minshuku, youth hostels, and economy inns, no service charge will be added to the bill.

THE GOLD GUIDE / SMART TRAVEL TIPS

SALES

There is an across-the-board, nonrefundable 5% consumer tax levied on all sales. Since the tax was introduced in 1989, vendors have either been absorbing the tax in their quoted retail prices or adding it on to the sale. Before you make a major purchase, inquire if tax is extra.

A 5% federal consumer tax is added to all restaurant bills. Another 3% local tax is added to the bill if it exceeds ¥7,500. At the more expensive restaurants, a 10%–15% service charge is added to the bill. Tipping is not the custom.

TAXIS

Taxis are an expensive way of getting around cities in Japan. The first 2 km (1 mi) cost about ¥620 (¥840 in Tōkyō), and it is ¥90 for every additional 370 meters (400 yards). If possible, avoid using taxis during rush hours (8 AM–9 AM and 5:30 PM–6:30 PM).

In general, it is easy to hail a cab: Do not shout or wave wildly—simply **raise your hand if you need a taxi.** Japanese taxis have automatic door-opening systems, so **do not try to open the taxi door.** Stand back when the cab comes to a stop—if you are too close, the door may slam into you. When you leave the cab, do not try to close the door; the driver will use the automatic system. Only the curbside rear door opens. A red light on the dashboard indicates an available taxi, and a green light indicates an occupied taxi.

Drivers are for the most part courteous, although sometimes they will balk at the idea of a foreign passenger because they do not speak English. Unless you are going to a well-known destination such as a major hotel, it is advisable to **have a Japanese person write out your destination in Japanese.** Remember, there is no need to tip.

TELEPHONES

The country code for Japan is 81. When dialing a Japanese number from outside of Japan, drop the initial 0 from the local area code.

CALLING HOME

You can make international calls from the many green phones that have gold plates indicating, in English, that the telephone can be used for these calls. There are three Japanese companies that provide international service: KDD (001), ITJ (0041), and IDC (0061). Dial: company code + country code + city/area code and number of your party. KDD offers the clearest connection, but is also the most expensive. Telephone credit cards are especially convenient for international calls. For operator assistance in English on long-distance calls, dial 0051.

Before you go, **find out the local access codes** for your destinations. AT&T, MCI, and Sprint long-distance services make calling home relatively convenient. If you find that the access number is blocked in your hotel room, ask the hotel operator to connect you. If the hotel operator balks, ask for an international operator, or dial the international operator yourself. One way to improve your odds of getting connected to your long-distance carrier is to travel with more than one company's calling card (a hotel may block Sprint, for example, but not MCI). If all else fails, call your phone company collect in the United States or call from a pay phone in the hotel lobby.

➤ TO OBTAIN ACCESS CODES: **AT&T** Direct (☎ 800/435–0812). **MCI** WorldPhone (☎ 800/444–4141). **Sprint** International Access (☎ 800/877–4646).

PAY PHONES

Pay phones are one of the great delights of Japan. Not only are they conveniently located in hotels, restaurants, and on street corners, but pay phones, at ¥10 for three minutes, have to be one of the few remaining bargains in Japan.

Telephones come in three styles: pink, red, and green. Pink phones, for local calls, accept only ¥10 coins. Most red phones are only for local use, but some accept ¥100 coins and can be used for long-distance domestic calls. Domestic long-distance rates are reduced as much as 50% after 9 PM (40% after 7 PM). Green phones take coins and often accept what are known as telephone cards—disposable cards of fixed value that you use up in increments of ¥10. Telephone cards, sold in vending machines, hotels, and a variety of stores, are tremendously convenient, because you will not have to search for the correct change.

Tipping is not common in Japan. It is not necessary to tip taxi drivers, or at beauty parlors, barber shops, bars, and nightclubs. A chauffeur for a hired car will usually receive a tip of ¥500 for a ½-day excursion and ¥1,000 for a full-day trip. Porters charge fees of ¥250–¥300 per bag at railroad stations and ¥200 per piece at airports. It is not customary to tip employees of hotels, even porters, unless a special service has been rendered. In such cases, a gratuity of ¥2,000 or ¥3,000 should be placed in an envelope and handed to the staff member discreetly.

TOUR OPERATORS

Buying a prepackaged tour or independent vacation can make your trip to Japan less expensive and more hassle-free. Because everything is prearranged you'll spend less time planning.

Operators that handle several hundred thousand travelers per year can use their purchasing power to give you a good price. Their high volume may also indicate financial stability. But some small companies provide more personalized service; because they tend to specialize, they may also be more knowledgeable about a given area.

A GOOD DEAL?

The more your package or tour includes, the better you can predict the ultimate cost of your vacation. Make sure you know exactly what is covered, and **beware of hidden costs.** Are taxes, tips, and service charges included? Transfers and baggage handling? Entertainment and excursions? These can add up.

If the package or tour you are considering is priced lower than in your wildest dreams, **be skeptical.** Also, **make sure your travel agent knows the accommodations** and other services. Ask about the hotel's location, room size, beds, and whether it has a pool, room service, or programs for children, if you care about these. Has

your agent been there in person or sent others you can contact?

BUYER BEWARE

Each year consumers are stranded or lose their money when tour operators—even very large ones with excellent reputations—go out of business. So **check out the operator.** Find out how long the company has been in business, and ask several agents about its reputation. **Don't book unless the firm has a consumer-protection program.**

Members of the National Tour Association and United States Tour Operators Association are required to set aside funds to cover your payments and travel arrangements in case the company defaults. Nonmembers may carry insurance instead. Look for the details, and for the name of an underwriter with a solid reputation, in the operator's brochure. Note: When it comes to tour operators, **don't trust escrow accounts.** Although the Department of Transportation watches over charter-flight operators, no regulatory body prevents tour operators from raiding the till. You may want to protect yourself by buying travel insurance that includes a tour-operator default provision. For more information, *see* Consumer Protection, *above.*

It's also a good idea to choose a company that participates in the American Society of Travel Agent's Tour Operator Program (TOP). This gives you a forum if there are any disputes between you and your tour operator; ASTA will act as mediator.

➤ TOUR-OPERATOR RECOMMENDATIONS: **American Society of Travel Agents** (☞ Travel Agencies, *below*). **National Tour Association** (✉ NTA, 546 E. Main St., Lexington, KY 40508, ☎ 606/226–4444 or 800/755–8687). **United States Tour Operators Association** (✉ USTOA, 342 Madison Ave., Suite 1522, New York, NY 10173, ☎ 212/599–6599, FAX 212/599–6744).

USING AN AGENT

Travel agents are excellent resources. In fact, large operators accept bookings made only through travel agents. But it's a good idea to **collect brochures from several agencies,**

SMART TRAVEL TIPS / THE GOLD GUIDE

because some agents' suggestions may be influenced by relationships with tour and package firms that reward them for volume sales. If you have a special interest, **find an agent with expertise in that area**; ASTA (☞ Travel Agencies, *below*) has a database of specialists worldwide. Do some homework on your own, too: Local tourism boards can provide information about lesser-known and small-niche operators, some of which may sell only direct.

SINGLE TRAVELERS

Prices for packages and tours are usually quoted per person, based on two sharing a room. If traveling solo, you may be required to pay the full double-occupancy rate. Some operators eliminate this surcharge if you agree to be matched with a roommate of the same sex, even if one is not found by departure time.

GROUP TOURS

Among companies that sell tours to Japan, the following are nationally known, have a proven reputation, and offer plenty of options. The classifications used below represent different price categories, and you'll probably encounter these terms when talking to a travel agent or tour operator. The key difference is usually in accommodations, which run from budget to better, and better yet to best.

➤ SUPERDELUXE: **Abercrombie & Kent** (⊠ 1520 Kensington Rd., Oak Brook, IL 60521-2141, ☎ 630/954-2944 or 800/323-7308, FAX 630/954-3324). **Travcoa** (⊠ Box 2630, 2350 S.E. Bristol St., Newport Beach, CA 92660, ☎ 714/476-2800 or 800/992-2003, FAX 714/476-2538).

➤ FIRST CLASS: **Japan & Orient Tours** (⊠ 3131 Camino Del Rio North, No. 1080, San Diego, CA 92108, ☎ 619/282-3131 or 800/377-1080, FAX 619/283-3131). **Orient Flexi-Pax Tours** (⊠ 630 3rd Ave., New York, NY 10017, ☎ 212/692-9550 or 800/545-5540, FAX 212/661-1618). **Pacific Bestour** (⊠ 228 Rivervale Rd., River Vale, NJ 07675, ☎ 201/664-8778 or 800/688-3288, FAX 201/722-0829). **Pacific Delight Tours** (⊠ 132 Madison Ave., New York, NY 10016, ☎ 212/684-7707 or 800/221-7179, FAX 212/532-3406). **TBI Tours** (⊠ 787 7th Ave., Suite 1101,

New York, NY 10019, ☎ 212/489-1919 or 800/223-0266).

PACKAGES

Like group tours, independent vacation packages are available from major tour operators and airlines. The companies listed below offer vacation packages in a broad price range.

➤ AIR/HOTEL: **Japan & Orient Tours** (☞ Groups, *above*). **Pacific Bestour** (☞ Groups, *above*). **Pacific Delight Tours** (☞ Groups, *above*). **United Vacations** (☎ 800/328-6877).

➤ FROM THE U.K.: **British Airways Holidays** (⊠ Astral Towers, Betts Way, London Rd., Crawley, West Sussex RH10 2XA, ☎ 01293/723-171). **Creative Tours** (⊠ 1 Tenterden St., 2nd floor, London W1R 9AH, ☎ 0171/495-1775). **Japan Travel Bureau** (⊠ 95 Cromwell Rd., London SW7 4JT, ☎ 0171/663-6161). **Kuoni Travel** (⊠ Kuoni House, Dorking, Surrey RH5 4AZ, ☎ 01306/742-222, FAX 01306/744-222).

THEME TRIPS

➤ ADVENTURE: **Wilderness Travel** (⊠ 801 Allston Way, Berkeley, CA 94710, ☎ 510/548-0420 or 800/368-2794, FAX 510/548-0347).

➤ CUSTOM PACKAGES: **Absolute Asia** (⊠ 180 Varick St., 16th floor, New York, NY 10014, ☎ 212/627-1950 or 800/736-8187).

➤ LEARNING: **Earthwatch** (⊠ Box 9104, 680 Mount Auburn St., Watertown, MA 02272, ☎ 617/926-8200 or 800/776-0188, FAX 617/926-8532), for research expeditions.

TRAIN TRAVEL

Riding Japanese trains is one of the pleasures of travel in the country. They are efficient and convenient, and they run frequently and very much on time. The Shinkansen (bullet train), one of the fastest trains in the world, connects major cities north and south of Tōkyō. It is only slightly less expensive than flying but is in many ways more convenient because train stations are more centrally located than airports. On the main line that runs west from Tōkyō, there are three types of Shinkansen. The *Nozomi* makes the fewest stops, which can cut off as much as an hour from long cross-country trips; it is the only Shinkansen on which you cannot use a JR Pass. The *Hikari* makes just a few more stops than the Nozomi. The *Kodama* is the equivalent of a Shinkansen local, making all stops along the Shinkansen lines. The same principle of faster and slower Shinkansen also applies on the line that runs north from Tōkyō to Morioka, in the Tōhoku region.

Other trains, though not as fast as the Shinkansen, are just as convenient and substantially cheaper. There are three types of train services: *futsū* (local service), *tokkyū* (limited express service), and *kyūkō* (express service). Both the tokkyū and the kyūkō offer a first-class compartment known as the Green Car.

Because there are no porters or carts at train stations, and the flights of stairs connecting train platforms can turn even the lightest bag into a heavy burden, it is a good idea to **travel light when getting around by train.** Savvy travelers often have their main luggage sent ahead to a hotel that they plan to reach later in their wanderings. Good to know as well is that every train station, however small, has luggage lockers, which cost about ¥300 for 24 hours.

➤ INFORMATION: **JR Hotline** English-language information service (☎ 03/3423–0111).

PURCHASING TICKETS

Many travelers assume that rail passes guarantee them seats on the trains they wish to ride. Not so. If you are using a rail pass, there is no need to buy individual tickets, but you should **book seats ahead.** This guarantees you a seat and is also a useful reference for the times of train departures and arrivals. You can reserve up to two weeks in advance or just minutes before the train departs. If you fail to make a train, there is no penalty and you can reserve again.

Seat reservations for any JR route may be made at any JR station except those in the tiniest villages. The reservation windows or offices, *midori-no-madoguchi,* have green signs in English and green-striped windows. If you are traveling without a Japan Rail Pass, there is a surcharge of approximately ¥500 (depending

upon distance traveled) for seat reservations, and if you miss the train you'll have to pay for another reservation. When making your seat reservation, you may request a no-smoking or smoking car. Your reservation ticket will show the date and departure time of your train as well as your car and seat number. On the platform, you can figure out where to wait for a particular train car. Notice the markings painted on the platform or on little signs above the platform; ask someone which markings correspond to car numbers. If you don't have a reservation, ask which cars are unreserved. Sleeping berths, even with a rail pass, are additional. Nonreserved tickets can be bought at regular ticket windows. There are no reservations made on local service trains. For traveling short distances, tickets are usually sold at vending machines. A platform ticket is required if you go through the wicket gate onto the platform. The charge is ¥140 (in Tōkyō and Ōsaka, the tickets are ¥120).

Most clerks at train stations know a few basic words of English and can read Roman script. Moreover, they are invariably helpful in plotting your route. The complete railway timetable is a mammoth book written only in Japanese; however, you can **get an English-language train schedule from the Japan National Tourist Organization** (JNTO) that covers the Shinkansen and a few of the major JR Limited Express trains. JNTO's booklet *The Tourist's Handbook* provides helpful information about purchasing tickets in Japan.

RAIL PASSES

If you plan to travel extensively by rail, **get a Japan Rail Pass,** which offers unlimited travel on Japan Railways (JR) trains. It is possible to purchase one-, two-, or three-week passes. A one-week pass is less expensive than a regular round-trip ticket from Tōkyō to Kyōto on the Shinkansen. **You must obtain a rail pass voucher prior to departure for Japan** (they are not obtainable in Japan), and the pass must be used within three months of purchase. The pass is available only to people with tourist visas, as opposed to business, student, and diplomatic visas.

When you arrive in Japan, you must exchange your voucher for the Japan Rail Pass. You can do this at the Japan Railways (JR) desk in the Arrivals Hall at Narita Airport or at the JR stations of major cities. When you make this exchange, you determine the day that you want the rail pass to begin—and, accordingly, when it ends. You do not have to begin travel on the day that you make the exchange. Pick the starting date to maximize the pass's use. The Japan Rail Pass allows you to travel on all JR-operated trains (which cover most destinations in Japan), but not lines owned by other companies. It also allows you to use buses operated by Japan Railways. You can make seat reservations without paying a fee on all trains that have reserved-seat coaches, usually the long-distance trains. The Japan Rail Pass does not cover the cost of sleeping compartments on overnight trains (called blue trains), nor does it cover the newest and fastest of the Shinkansen trains, the Nozomi, which make only one or two stops on longer runs. The pass covers only the Hikari Shinkansen, which make a couple more stops than the Nozomi, and the Kodama Shinkansen, which stop at every station along the Shinkansen routes.

Japan Rail Passes are available in coach class and first class (Green Car), but most people find that coach class is more than adequate. A one-week pass costs ¥28,300 coach-class, ¥37,800 first-class; a two-week pass costs ¥45,200 coach-class, ¥61,200 first-class; and a three-week pass costs ¥57,700 coach-class, ¥79,600 first-class. Travelers under 18 pay lower rates.

Note: Rail Passes cannot be purchased in Japan.

➤ INFORMATION: **Japan Railways Group** (✉ One Rockefeller Plaza, Suite 1622, New York, NY 10020, ☎ 212/332–8690).

➤ BUYING A PASS: Contact a travel agent or **Japan Airlines** (✉ JAL; 655 5th Ave., New York, NY 10022, ☎ 212/838–4400), **Japan Travel Bureau** (✉ JTB; 810 7th Ave., 34 floor, New York, NY 10019, ☎ 212/698–4900

or 800/223–6104), or **Nippon Travel Agency** (✉ NTA; 111 Pavonia Ave., Suite 217, Jersey City, NJ 07310, ☎ 201/420–6000 or 800/682–7872). JAL, JTB, and NTA also have bureaus in other major U.S. cities.

TRAVEL AGENCIES

A good travel agent puts your needs first. Look for an agency that has been in business at least five years, emphasizes customer service, and has someone on staff who specializes in your destination. In addition, **make sure the agency belongs to the American Society of Travel Agents** (ASTA). If your travel agency is also acting as your tour operator, *see* Buyer Beware in Tour Operators, *above.*

➤ LOCAL AGENT REFERRALS: **American Society of Travel Agents** (ASTA, ☎ 800/965–2782 24-hr hot line, FAX 703/684–8319). **Alliance of Canadian Travel Associations** (✉ 1729 Bank St., Suite 201, Ottawa, Ontario K1V 7Z5, ☎ 613/521–0474, FAX 613/521–0805). **Association of British Travel Agents** (✉ 55–57 Newman St., London W1P 4AH, ☎ 0171/637–2444, FAX 0171/637–0713).

TRAVEL GEAR

Travel catalogs specialize in useful items, such as compact alarm clocks and travel irons, that can **save space when packing.** They also offer dual-voltage appliances, currency converters, and foreign-language phrase books.

➤ MAIL-ORDER CATALOGS: **Magellan's** (☎ 800/962–4943, FAX 805/568–5406). **Orvis Travel** (☎ 800/541–3541, FAX 540/343–7053). **TravelSmith** (☎ 800/950–1600, FAX 800/950–1656).

U

U.S. GOVERNMENT

The U.S. government can be an excellent source of inexpensive travel information. When planning your trip, **find out what government materials are available.**

➤ ADVISORIES: **U.S. Department of State** (✉ Overseas Citizens Services Office, Room 4811 N.S., Washington, DC 20520); enclose a self-addressed, stamped envelope. Interactive hot line (☎ 202/647–5225, FAX 202/647–3000). Computer bulletin board (☎ 301/946–4400).

➤ PAMPHLETS: **Consumer Information Center** (✉ Consumer Information Catalogue, Pueblo, CO 81009, ☎ 719/948–3334) for a free catalog that includes travel titles.

V
VISITOR INFORMATION

For information before you go, contact the **Japan National Tourist Organization** (JNTO). When you get there, call or stop by one of the **Tourist Information Centers** (TIC) for information on western or eastern Japan; use the **Japan Travel-phone**; and, for recorded information 24 hours a day, call the **Teletourist** service.

➤ JAPAN NATIONAL TOURIST ORGANIZATION (JNTO): **U.S.: New York:** (✉ 1 Rockefeller Plaza, Suite 1250, New York, NY 10020, ☎ 212/757–5640); **Chicago:** (✉ 401 N. Michigan Ave., Chicago, IL 60601, ☎ 312/222–0874); **San Francisco:** (✉ 360 Post St., Suite 601, San Francisco, CA 94108, ☎ 415/989–7140); **Los Angeles:** (✉ 624 S. Grand Ave., Suite 1611, Los Angeles, CA 90017, ☎ 213/623–1952). **Canada: Toronto:** (✉ 165 University Ave., Toronto, Ontario M5H 3B8, ☎ 416/366–7140). **U.K.: London** (✉ Heathcoat House, 20 Savile Row, London W1X 1AE, ☎ 0171/734–9638). **Japan:** Tōkyō (✉ 6-6 Yuraku-chō 1-chōme, Chiyoda-ku, ☎ 03/502–1461); **Kyōto** (✉ Kyōto Tower Bldg., Higashi-Shiokoji-chō, Shimogyo-ku, ☎ 075/371–5649).

➤ TOURIST INFORMATION CENTERS (TIC): **Tōkyō:** (✉ Tōkyō International Forum, 3-5-1 Maru-no-uchi, Chiyoda-ku, ☎ 03/3201–3331; ✉ Terminal Bldg., Narita Airport, Chiba Prefecture, ☎ 0476/32–8711). Kyōto: (✉ Kyōto Tower Building, Higashi-Shiokoji-chō, Shimogyo-ku, ☎ 075/371–5549).

➤ JAPAN TRAVEL-PHONE: **Eastern Japan** (☎ 0088/22–2800). **Western Japan** (☎ 0088/22–4800).

➤ TELETOURIST SERVICE: Tōkyō (☎ 03/3201–2911).

W
WHEN TO GO

The best seasons to travel to Japan are spring and fall, when the weather is at its best. In the spring, the country is warm, with only occasional showers, and flowers grace landscapes in both rural and urban areas. The first harbingers of spring are plum blossoms in early March; *sakura* (cherry blossoms) follow, beginning in Kyūshū and usually arriving in Tōkyō by mid-April. Summer brings on the rainy season, with particularly heavy rains and mugginess in July. Fall is a welcome relief, with clear blue skies and beautiful foliage. Occasionally a few surprise typhoons occur in early fall, but the storms are usually as quick to leave as they are to arrive. Winter is gray and chilly, with little snow in most areas. Temperatures rarely fall below freezing.

For the most part, the climate of Japan is temperate and resembles that of the East Coast of the United States. The exceptions are the subtropical southern islands of Okinawa, south of Kyūshū, and the northern island of Hokkaidō, where it snows for several months in the winter and is pleasantly cool in the summer.

To avoid crowds, **do not plan a trip for times when most Japanese are vacationing.** For the most part, Japanese cannot select when they want to take their vacations; they tend to do so on the same holiday dates. As a result, airports, planes, trains, and hotels are booked far in advance. Many businesses, shops, and restaurants are closed during these holidays. Holiday periods include the few days before and after New Year's; Golden Week, which follows Greenery Day (April 29); and mid-August at the time of the Obon festivals, when many Japanese return to their hometowns.

CLIMATE

➤ FORECASTS: **Weather Channel Connection** (☎ 900/932–8437), 95¢ per minute from a Touch-Tone phone.

What follows are the average daily maximum and minimum temperatures for major cities in Japan.

TŌKYŌ

Jan.	46F	8C	May	72F	22C	Sept.	78F	26C
	29	− 2		53	12		66	19
Feb.	48F	9C	June	75F	24C	Oct.	70F	21C
	30	− 1		62	17		56	13
Mar.	53F	12C	July	82F	28C	Nov.	60F	16C
	35	2		70	21		42	6
Apr.	62F	17C	Aug.	86F	30C	Dec.	51F	11C
	46	8		72	22		33	1

KYŌTO

Jan.	48F	9C	May	75F	24C	Sept.	82F	28C
	35	2		56	13		68	20
Feb.	53F	12C	June	82F	28C	Oct.	74F	23C
	32	0		66	19		53	12
Mar.	59F	15C	July	93F	34C	Nov.	62F	17C
	40	4		72	22		46	8
Apr.	65F	18C	Aug.	89F	32C	Dec.	53F	12C
	44	7		74	23		33	1

FUKUOKA

Jan.	53F	12C	May	74F	23C	Sept.	80F	27C
	35	2		57	14		68	20
Feb.	58F	14C	June	80F	27C	Oct.	74F	23C
	37	3		68	20		53	12
Mar.	60F	16C	July	89F	32C	Nov.	65F	18C
	42	6		75	24		48	9
Apr.	62F	17C	Aug.	89F	32C	Dec.	53F	12C
	48	9		75	24		37	3

SAPPORO

Jan.	29F	− 2C	May	60F	16C	Sept.	72F	22C
	10	−12		40	4		51	11
Feb.	30F	− 1C	June	70F	21C	Oct.	60F	16C
	13	11		50	10		40	4
Mar.	35F	2C	July	75F	24C	Nov.	46F	8C
	20	− 7		57	14		29	− 2
Apr.	51F	11C	Aug.	78F	26C	Dec.	33F	1C
	32	0		60	16		18	− 8

1 Destination: Japan

LIFE: A PERFORMING ART

IT WAS ONE BRIEF SCENE in a movie that first drew me to Japan: Kenji Mizoguchi's version of the classic medieval revenge tale, *The Forty-Seven Loyal Rōnin*.

The lord Asano has committed an unpardonable offense against the shogunal government, and is ordered to commit ritual suicide. His castle stands forfeit, his clan is dissolved, and his retainers must descend to the unthinkable status of rōnin: men without land or master. There is, however, an honorable alternative. They can refuse to surrender the castle, and die in its defense.

A young man of lesser rank appears at the castle gates and begs permission to take part. The clan steward refuses him—the honor of such a death is above his station—and the young man falls to the ground in despair.

"This," I said to myself, "is as far from my life as anything can get." And off I went to Japan.

Life in the United States is a perpetual invitation to move one's boundaries—a constant stream of advertisements for something more you should want, something other you could become. Here, by contrast, was a culture in which you might have one definitive encounter with the limits imposed on your life. "*This* is what you are; to this you may aspire. To *that* you may not." If the encounter happens to knock you to the ground, it also, paradoxically, sets you free. It focuses you—you see the boundaries for what they are. The space inside is yours to fill in the best way you can.

The inherited class distinctions of Asano's day are long gone. Modern Japan is a social democracy—or its own version of one—where more than 80% of the people regularly describe themselves to government pollsters as "middle class." What imposes the limits in Japan today is education. Basic literacy is virtually universal, which is no mean accomplishment when literacy requires you to know two syllabic alphabets of 50 characters each as well as some 1,800 ideograms, some of which are composed of 20 strokes or more, just to read a newspaper. Seven of every 10 young Japanese go on from the six years of compulsory education to high school. About half the high school graduates go on from there to junior colleges, universities, and specialized vocational schools.

One's place in the world reveals itself early. Attend good schools, work hard, and you can pass the exams for the good schools farther up the ladder. Graduate from a top university, and you can reasonably look forward to a job in a prestigious company (better still, in government service), a good marriage, the admiration of your peers, and a comfortable retirement. Graduate from a less respected school, and you revise your hopes accordingly. To this, you may aspire. To that, you may not.

You are bounded as well, in Japan, by all the affiliations—voluntary and otherwise—that draw you into the fabric of everyday life: clubs at school, PTA, neighborhood associations, unions and federations, and amateur and professional societies for every imaginable human endeavor. The *Zenkoku Dantai Meibō*, a national register of public and private organizations, runs to 516 pages and some 4,500 entries. You are what you belong to—and belong you must: Your membership in an organization authenticates whatever it is you do. Nothing will mystify a Japanese more about you than the idea that you might want to do something purely on your own, or that you would make any serious claim on their attention—a business appointment, for example—representing no one but yourself.

Your affiliations bind you as well into a network of personal relations—*oyabun* to *kobun* (boss to subordinate), *sensei* to *seito* (teacher to student), *sempai* to *kohai* (older to younger member)—that follows you the rest of your life, defining even the levels of language you should and should not use. Put two old schoolmates together at a reunion: family men with grown children, established in their respective careers, who may not have seen each other in 20 years. They fall immediately into a pattern of behavior determined solely by which of them joined the high school baseball team ahead of the other. Your affiliations make you a meaningful member of society, because they let other people know what they can expect of you, and vice versa.

OF ALL THE GENERALIZATIONS I know about Japan, this one explains the most: The Japanese do not like surprises. They take inexhaustible delight in things new and different, especially from other cultures. But for the unprecedented, for sudden changes in the structure of everyday life, they have little taste. Nobody here plays practical jokes, however harmless. Nobody just drops in on anybody else, however close the acquaintance. Loudspeakers on trains announce every station well in advance, and even tell you on which side of the car the doors will open. The nonrefundable "key money"—usually two months' rent— that tenants must pay their landlords for the privilege of signing a lease, usually puzzles newcomers to this country. The function of the custom is clear enough: It discourages people from suddenly deciding to move.

Similarly, in the workplace, the core of the Japanese wage system is the bonus: a fixed multiple of one's basic salary, paid out twice a year. This regularity tells banks and travel agencies, automobile and household appliance makers exactly when most people in the country will have large lumps of discretionary income in their pockets—and how much.

In enterprises large and small, managers hold endless rounds of discussions, called *nemawashi,* with unions, with other managers, and with customers and suppliers before making even the tiniest changes to the way they do business. Every foreigner who has spent time here has a story about something perfectly reasonable he tried to accomplish that ended in frustration. Chances are, the only reason it went wrong was because he failed to make sure that the Japanese involved could see it coming a long way off.

Of course, there are exceptions to all this. Like any society, Japan has its share of mavericks and adventurers, but it is a small share, quite incidental to the real strengths and achievements of the culture. One of those strengths—ask anyone who has ever attended a conference here, or taken a package tour—is efficiency. Let the task be well defined, dispose the people working on it in due hierarchy, and the Japanese will bring it off with astonishing grace, every detail in place, every contingency provided for. Distaste for the unexpected can be a weakness, but it is also a strength. Predictability makes Japan an orderly society—one of the safest in the world—where it's possible to accept, even welcome, the limits on one's mobility.

Where in the West can you find substantial numbers of people living in the same place, making the same livelihoods, for five and six generations? If there are fewer and fewer such people every year in Japan, there are still enough to provide the society with an ethos: a sense of focus, of craftsmanship, of pride in what they do.

PREDICTABILITY ENTAILS, as well, a preoccupation with surfaces. Everything that charms and delights visitors to this country—the exquisite design of a traditional garden, the choreography of Kabuki, the artistry of a Japanese meal, the elegance with which a sales clerk will wrap even the simplest souvenir—all betray that abiding concern with form and presentation.

As foreigners, we are casual beneficiaries of all this, somewhere outside of the web of relationships and affiliations that turn the wheels of life in Japan. Why then do the Japanese treat visitors so well? Because our relationship is so clearly defined: we are Guests, and they know how their society expects them to play Host. The sense of life as a performing art—which in the West we lost in the great wars of this century—has remained part of the fabric of postwar Japan. It is another of the binding paradoxes that can set you free: You might not be able to get too personal with any Japanese host, but the beauty in playing your role has a dignity that is timeless.

— Jared Lubarsky

NEW AND NOTEWORTHY

The yen swings. The late 1990s saw it climb from the high nineties to ¥120 to the U.S. dollar and above, which brought prices more in line with what you'd expect from traveling in Europe. Given also that the Japanese National Tourist Office assists in providing information on economical travel and a reservation service for budget hotels, it is now easier than ever to counter some of the high costs of traveling in Japan. At the same time, with the Japanese economy veering toward the precipice over which other Asian countries fell in late 1997, the Japanese are showing more signs of welcoming *gai-jin* (foreigners) on holiday.

Hotels awakened at last to the fact that they had been pricing themselves out of the reach of mere mortals and began offering attractive special rates for package tours. It's even possible these days to walk in off the street and demand a discount at many of the better big-city hotels. Rents for commercial real estate are sharply lower, making it possible for new Western-style restaurants with popular pricing strategies to open in the heart of Tōkyō and Ōsaka.

The excitement of Nagano's **XVIII Winter Olympics** (in the so-called Japan Alps), held between February 7 and 22, 1998, has now passed. An estimated 3,000 athletes and team officials participated in seven sports for a total of 64 events. Nagano City was the center for the Games and the location of the Olympic Village, the main media center, and the ice rinks, as well as the opening and closing ceremonies. The Nordic and Alpine events took place west of Nagano City in the Hakuba area and in the foothills of the Japan Alps.

As a result of the games, a new **Shinkansen** (bullet train) line runs between Tōkyō and Nagano. This *Hokuriku* Shinkansen branches off of the Jōetsu line, which runs from Tōkyō north to Niigata, at Takasaki. Another Shinkansen extension also is up and running. The route links Morioka, formerly the end of the Shinkansen line north

from Tōkyō, with Akita on the northwest coast of the Tōhoku region.

Four years of intense negotiations—so secret at times that they were referred to as "**nontalks**"—led to an early-1998 U.S.–Japan accord liberalizing air travel between the two countries. This means that American, Continental, Delta, and All Nippon Airways will be allowed to collectively add some 90 weekly flights to their trans-Pacific schedules. In the next two years, US Airways and TWA will also be able to add flights to Japan. Look for increased service from Chicago, Dallas, Atlanta, Houston, and Newark.

Compared to what they were before the opening of a second terminal building in 1992, arrival and departure procedures at Tōkyō's **Narita International Airport** are pleasant and lightning fast, although using this facility in mid-July through August or in March, when the largest numbers of Japanese take vacations abroad, can still be a harrowing experience. The construction of two new runways at Narita has been held up for years by land acquisition problems—a small coalition of local farmers continue to refuse the government the necessary land for completion. Meanwhile, the airport is operating at close to peak capacity, and this can often mean a shortage of berths for incoming planes. Arriving passengers—especially on foreign carriers—frequently have to board transfer buses to shuttle from distant parking spaces to the main building.

And after huge cost overruns and extensive delays—building on landfill in Ōsaka Bay was trickier than contractors anticipated—the new **Kansai International Airport** (KIX) is up and running. It is used primarily for international flights, though there are connecting domestic flights to Japan's major metropolitan areas. (Ōsaka's Itami Airport continues to handle most of the region's domestic flights.) KIX serves the entire Kansai region, alleviating the congestion of Tōkyō's airports and allowing you to save a few hours on the train from Tōkyō if you decide to skip the capital and center your trip on Kyōto. Keep in mind that exorbitant landing fees (the highest in the world) have limited the number of carriers that fly into KIX.

WHAT'S WHERE

Tōkyō

A state-of-the-art financial marketplace, a metropolis of exquisite politeness, a city that is frustratingly large yet has astonishing beauty in its small details—these are a few of the myriad ways Tōkyō can be described, and all contain at least a grain of truth. Ultimately, it is the sum of its districts and neighborhoods—among them Ueno, Asakusa, Ginza, Tsukiji, Shibuya, and Shinjuku. Although daunting in its sheer size, Tōkyō is, in fact, extremely easy to negotiate: virtually anyplace you're likely to visit is within a five-minute walk of a train or subway station, and all station stops are marked in English.

Side Trips from Tōkyō

Nikkō, Kamakura, Mt. Fuji—each of these must-sees is within a couple of hours of the great metropolis. You will either love or hate Toshō-gū, the shrine that is the centerpiece of Nikkō, but most agree on the grandeur of that city's natural beauty. Kamakura, capital of Japan for more than a century, has a splendid legacy of historic and cultural sights. And no matter how many photographs or artistic renderings of Mt. Fuji you have seen, the perfect symmetry and supreme majesty of this dormant volcano will fill you with awe when you get a glimpse of the real thing.

The Japan Alps

Soaring mountain peaks, slices of traditional Japan, delightful natural color from spring's flowering trees through summer's alpine wildflowers to the kaleidoscopic hues of autumn, and superb hiking and skiing make this central alpine block one of the finest districts in the country. West along the Nihon-kai, Kanazawa is as enjoyable a city as you'll find in Japan, and the Chūbu region's coastal scenery on islands and peninsulas perfectly balances a turn through the mountains.

Kyōto

Kyōto is a cross-section of 11 centuries of Japan's history—including the present. Its hundreds of temples and shrines and its gardens have tremendous allure, for gaijin *and* Japanese. Add to that traditional shopping districts and intriguing local foods and you come up with some of the best reasons to travel to Japan.

Nagoya, Ise-Shima, and the Kii Peninsula

Nagoya is Japan's fourth largest city, an industrial metropolis whose appeal is, admittedly, limited. Prospects change dramatically as you head south of the city to Ise-Shima National Park and the highly venerated Grand Shrines of Ise. Circling the Kii Peninsula will take you past magnificent marine scenery, coastal fishing villages and resorts, and Mt. Yoshino-san, with perhaps the finest springtime display of sakura (cherry blossoms) in Japan. Then, inland, the mountaintop monastery of Kōya-san looms almost as large as myth with its 123 temples.

Nara

Nara's parks, ancient temples, and traditional shops and restaurants make it one of Japan's quintessential old cities. It might not have the volume of sacred sights that Kyōto does—or all of its concrete and steel—but Nara's shrines and parks are among the country's finest. The fact that it exists in the midst of Japan's overbuilt industrial corridor makes Nara's restful quality that much more precious.

Ōsaka

Japan's "Second City" in terms of industry, commerce, and technology—after Tōkyō, naturally—Ōsaka is known for its bunraku puppet theater, its superb restaurants, and its dynamic spirit. It may not be the window to Japan's past that Kyōto and Nara are, but it is that much better a place to see what moves the country today.

Kōbe

Kōbe is unique in Japan for its blending of European and Japanese influences both in its architecture and in the attitudes of the inhabitants. For these reasons, it is often the choice of residence for many Westerners, who would rather not deal with the bustle and crowding of more expensive Ōsaka.

Western Honshū

The two coasts of Western Honshū make for very different experiences of Japan. The industrial San-yō strip on the Inland Sea does have its attractive cities, most notably Kurashiki, as well as Hiroshima, and the nearby Miyajima, a small island whose vermilion *torii* (gate) rises famously out of the water. The more remote northern San-in region has a slower pace, and the mountainside town of Tsuwano, coastal Matsue, and coastal points in between make great escapes from the overdevelopment of the modern world.

Shikoku

The smallest of Japan's four main islands, Shikoku rests neatly beneath Western Honshū across the Seto Nai-kai (Inland Sea), connected to Honshū by a remarkable chain of bridges. Rugged east–west mountain ranges halve Shikoku, where you will be treated more as a welcome foreign emissary than as an income-bearing tourist. Perhaps that reflects on the Japanese Buddhists who still come to make religious pilgrimages to the island's 88 sacred temples as they have done for centuries.

Kyūshū

The relatively quiet island of Kyūshū, which hangs like a tail off the south end of Honshū, has a mild climate, lush green countryside, hot springs, and eerie volcanic formations. Its cities are mostly free of skyscrapers and filled with sights of historical and cultural significance.

Tōhoku

Tōhoku is, undeservedly, one of Japan's least-visited areas. Almost a world apart from the Japan of the Tōkyō–Ōsaka corridor, Tōhoku is one of the best places to take in rural Japan, high-country plateaus and volcanic lakes, and mountainside temples. Summer here is refreshingly cool, and the sensational August festivals held in the cities of Akita, Aomori, Hirosaki, and Sendai offer a convenient excuse for a trip to the north.

Hokkaidō

Hokkaidō is Japan untamed. It can be said about the rest of Japan that cities dominate the countryside—not so in Hokkaidō. Its cities and towns are outposts of modern urban humanity that wild mountains, virgin forests, sapphire lakes, and surf-beaten shores keep at bay. Hokkaidō is Japan's last frontier, and the attitudes of the inhabitants are akin to those of the pioneers of the American West—or of any last places.

PLEASURES AND PASTIMES

Bathing

Partly because of the importance of purification rites in Shintō, Japan's ancient indigenous religion, the art of bathing has been a crucial element of the culture for centuries. Baths in Japan are as much about pleasure and relaxation as they are about washing and cleansing. Traditionally, communal bathhouses served as centers for social gatherings, and even though most modern houses and apartments have bathtubs, many Japanese still prefer the pleasures of communal bathing—either at *onsen* (hot springs; ☞ *below*) while on vacation or in public bathhouses in their own neighborhoods.

Japanese bathtubs themselves are different from those in the West—they're deep enough to sit in upright with (very hot) water up to the neck—and the procedures for using them are quite different as well. They are for soaking, not washing: Soap must not get into the bathwater. How is this accomplished? Before taking the plunge, you sit on a stool in a special area outside the tub that is equipped with faucets or shower hoses and a floor drain. There you wash with soap and rinse thoroughly in preparation for entering the tub. The water in the tub is as hot as the body can endure, and the reward for making it past the initial shock of the heat is the pleasure of a lengthy soak in water that does not become tepid.

Many hotels in major cities offer only Western-style reclining bathtubs, so to indulge in the pleasure of a Japanese bath you'll need to stay in a Japanese-style inn or find a public bathhouse. The latter are clean, hygienic, and easy to find. Japanese bath towels, which are typically called *taoru* (ta-o-ru), are available for a fee at onsen and bathhouses. They are no more than hand-towel size, and they have three functions: covering your privates (and breasts in mixed bathing), washing before you bathe and scrubbing while you bathe (if desired), and drying off (wring them out hard and they will dry you quite well). If you want a larger towel to dry yourself off, you will have to bring one along.

Beaches

For a country that consists entirely of islands, Japan has surprisingly few good beaches. Those accessible from Tōkyō, around Kamakura and the Izu Peninsula, are absolutely mobbed all summer long. The beaches of Kyūshū and Shikoku are less crowded, more pleasant, and have clear blue water. The country's best beaches are on the subtropical Ryūkyū Islands, which include Okinawa. But bear in mind that many Japanese find it less expensive to fly to Hawaii than to go to the Ryūkyū.

Bēsubōru (Baseball)

It is fair to say that baseball is as much a national pastime in Japan as it is Stateside. If you're a fan—and perhaps even if you aren't—you'll probably want to take in a game in Japan: The way the Japanese have adopted and adapted this Western sport makes it a fascinating and easy-to-grasp microcosm of both their culture and their overall relationship to things Western. The team names alone—the Orix BlueWave and the Chiba Lotte Marines, for example—have an amusing appeal to Westerners accustomed to such monikers as the Yankees and the Indians, and the fans' cheers are different and chanted more in unison than in U.S. ballparks. But a lot is familiar, too. Two non-Japanese players are allowed on each team; past and future American superstars, Kevin Mitchell and Cecil Fielder, to name two, have played besuboru. Tōkyō Dome at Kōraku-en is the place to see pro ball in the big city.

Bicycling

With its narrow roads and largely mountainous terrain, Japan does not offer ideal conditions for long cycling trips. It can be feasible, inexpensive, and delightful to see the sights in some towns by bicycle, however. Where this is the case, there are bicycle-rental shops near the main railway station, as in Kanazawa, Takayama, and Hagi. One region that is flatter and less trafficked than most of Japan is the San-in coast of Western Honshū (☞ Chapter 11). You can do some serious cycling on some of the remote islands, such as Sado, on the Sea of Japan, and Iki, off the coast of Kyūshū. Wherever you ride, don't forget that cars drive on the left side of the road in Japan.

Dining

Japanese food is not only delicious and healthy but also aesthetically pleasing—in fact the aesthetic experience of food is of utmost importance to the Japanese. Even the most humble box lunch (*bentō*) from a railway station or on a train will have been created with careful attention to color combinations and overall presentation.

This guide's regional chapters discuss local specialties in detail, and the Japanese are very proud of their local specialties—from Kyōto's *kaiseki ryōri* (elaborate, multi-course set meals) to the Japan Alps region's use of mountain vegetables and tasty local miso. For an introduction to the delights of Japanese cooking, turn to Diane Durston's "The Discreet Charm of Japanese Cuisine" in Chapter 2, A Japanese Cultural Primer. The English–Japanese Traveler's Vocabulary, at the end of this guide, includes names of food items in Japanese characters.

Language

As difficult as it can be, learning Japanese is also a delight. For basic points on the language, *see* Language *in* the Gold Guide and An English–Japanese Traveler's Vocabulary at the end of this book.

Onsen (Hot Springs)

No doubt the Japanese love of bathing has something to do with the hundreds of *onsen* (natural hot springs) that bubble out of their volcanic island. Many onsen are surrounded by resorts, ranging from overlarge Western-style hotels to small, humble inns; all are extremely popular among Japanese tourists. Traditionally the curative value of hot-spring water was strongly emphasized. Add to that today's need to get away from the frantic pace of life and relax. At resorts, onsen water is usually piped in to hotel rooms or large, communal indoor baths. And some onsen have *rotenburo* (year-round open-air baths) where you can soak outdoors in the midst of a snowy winter landscape. Some of the best-known spas near Tōkyō are at Atami, Hakone, Ito, and Nikkō; in Kōbe, at Arima; in Kyūshū, at Beppu and Unzen; and in Hokkaidō, at Noboribetsu.

Shopping

Japan's *depāto* (pronounced "deh-*pah*-to, meaning department stores) have to be seen to be believed—from their automaton-like white-gloved elevator operators to their elaborate wrapping of even the most humble purchase. Items made by every international designer you can name sit alongside the best of traditional Japanese arts and crafts items, and most have at least two basement levels devoted entirely to the selling of food, from international grocery fare to ready-to-eat Japanese delicacies and everyday menu items. Everything mentioned below is likely to be available in at least one major urban depāto.

Items made of *washi*—hand-molded paper— are one of the best buys in Japan. Delicate sheets of almost-transparent stationery, greeting cards, money holders, and wrapping paper are available at traditional crafts stores, stationery stores, and department stores. Small washi-covered boxes (suitable for jewelry and other keepsakes) and pencil cases are also strong candidates for gifts and personal souvenirs.

At first glance, the ceramics displayed in Japan seem priced for a prince's table. Doubtless some are, but if you keep shopping you can find reasonably priced functional and decorative items that are generally far superior in design to what is available at home. If you don't go to pottery villages such as Hagi and Arita, look in department stores, where the selection is vast and there are items priced for every budget. Sale items are often amazingly good bargains. Vases, sake sets consisting of one or two small bottles and a number of cups, and chopstick rests all make good gifts.

Printed fabric, whether by the yard or in the form of finished scarves, napkins, tablecloths, or pillow coverings, is another item worth purchasing in Japan. The complexity of the designs and the quality of the printing make the fabric, both silk and cotton, special. *Furoshiki*—square pieces of cloth used for wrapping, storing, and carrying things—make great wall hangings.

For a view of how the middle class manages its daily shopping, head to one of the shopping arcades that are often an extension of urban and suburban train or subway stations. Everything—clothes, stationery, books, CDs, electronic goods, food, housewares—is sold in these arcades, which can be madhouses during the evening rush hour.

Markets are another way to get closer to everyday Japanese life. The warrens of shops outside of Tōkyō's fish market in Tsukiji are full of interesting wares. Kyōto's Nishikōji market and its monthly Tō-ji and Kitano Tenman-gū markets are essential experiences. Takayama's Asa-ichi (morning market) is another must for items of local interest.

Skiing

Japan's mountains are beautiful and snowy in winter, with very good skiing conditions. Many ski areas are near natural hot springs, so you can end a chilly day on the slopes with a hot soak. The most popular ski areas are around central Honshū's Nagano, site of the 1998 Winter Olympics; in northern Honshū at Mt. Zao; and in Hokkaidō at Jozankei (in Sapporo) and Daisetsuzan National Park (in the central part of the island).

But be forewarned: The major drawback of skiing in Japan is crowds, especially on weekends and holidays. The slopes can become more heavily packed with people than snow, and trains and highways leading to the ski areas are also congested. If you're set on skiing in Japan, try to go on a weekday or head for Hokkaidō during a nonholiday period.

Sumō

If baseball can be called Japan's modern national pastime, surely sumō is its traditional national pastime, and it remains tremendously popular, even at 2,000 years old. A Shinto-style roof is hung from the ceiling over a circular clay ring in which two enormous wrestlers face off. After various preliminary rites, some of which involve tossing handfuls of salt into the ring to symbolize purification, the actual wrestling begins. A match ends when any part of a wrestler's body (other than the soles of his feet) touches the ground or he is pushed out of the ring. Wrestlers wear only a loincloth-type garment and have slick topknot hairstyles. Six 15-day tournaments are held each year; they run live at sold-out stadiums seating around 10,000 people, and millions more watch on television. The match-ups are shown on huge screens in major train stations and elsewhere—if a tournament is under way while you're in Japan, you'll know it. Tickets can be difficult to obtain, but it's definitely worth a try. If you go, buy the more expensive seats, both because they give you a better view of the action and because they include a bag full of a generous amount of food and sumō-theme souvenirs, such as a tea or sake set whose cups feature drawings of the major wrestlers.

FODOR'S CHOICE

Temples and Shrines

⭐ **Sensō-ji, Tōkyō.** A walk through the grounds of this temple in the heart of traditional Tōkyō's Asakusa district can feel like a journey back in time to its Edo-period heyday, and you can pick up great traditional souvenirs in the surrounding arcades.

⭐ **Hase-dera, Kamakura.** The main attraction here is Japan's largest carved wooden statue, a 30-ft-tall image of the bodhisattva Kannon. But it is the haunting sight of seemingly endless rows of statues of Jizō—the bodhisattva associated with the souls of miscarried, stillborn, and aborted children—that will stay with you after seeing this temple overlooking the sea.

⭐ **Ise Jingū, Ise Peninsula.** The austere beauty of the Grand Shrines of Ise is especially intriguing in light of the fact that the Inner Shrine is completely rebuilt every 20 years.

⭐ **Byōdo-in, Uji, Kyōto.** The Phoenix Hall of this villa turned temple southeast of the city center is one of Japan's finest religious buildings—it's even memorialized on the back of the ¥10 coin. The hall's main icon is an elegant wooden Buddha carved in the 11th century.

⭐ **Kiyomizu-dera, Kyōto.** There is a splendid panorama of the city from the cliffside main hall of this spacious temple complex.

⭐ **Hōryū-ji, Nara.** Japan's oldest temple compound houses one of the country's best collections of Buddhist art. Its 7th-century masterpieces are a vivid testimony to the remarkable variety of artistic traditions that came here from Korea and China at the time.

⭐ **Itsukushima Jinja, Miyajima.** Itsukushima's iconic vermilion *torii* (gate) is strikingly situated in Hiroshima Bay, between the tiny island of Miyajima and the main island.

Parks and Gardens

⭐ **Shinjuku Gyō-en, Tōkyō.** Renowned for its cherry blossoms in April and its chrysanthemums in November, this 150-acre public park and landscape garden is a virtual oasis of quiet green set in one of Tōkyō's most frenetic areas.

⭐ **Kenroku-en, Kanazawa.** A remarkable collection of varied miniature landscapes, this garden has been justifiably designated by the Japanese as one of their country's three most beautiful.

⭐ **Sankei-en, Yokohama.** The many varieties of trees and flowers here ensure that something will be blooming—or changing color—at virtually any time of year. The historic buildings transported here, including a teahouse and a farmhouse, add to the natural beauty.

⭐ **Ginkaku-ji, Kyōto.** This tranquil temple has two beautiful gardens: One provides changing perspectives on a pond, flowers, and trees as you stroll through it; the other is a dry garden with two dazzling sand shapes for quiet contemplation.

⭐ **Katsura Rikyū (Detached Villa), Kyōto.** The loveliness of this vast estate's numerous gardens and rustic teahouses makes the advance planning required to gain permission for a visit worthwhile.

⭐ **Nara Kōen (park), Nara.** Don't let the greedy tame deer (they'll eat even paper right out of your hand) deter you from a visit to this sprawling park, where many of the city's famed temples and shrines, and its national museum and historic botanic garden, reside.

Sights

⭐ **Tsukiji Market, Tōkyō.** If you arise early enough (i.e., considerably before 6:30 AM) to watch 90 percent of the fish consumed in Tōkyō being auctioned off, you are in for a truly memorable experience—but if you sleep in, don't hesitate to stop by later in the day for the great shopping for tea, pickles, baskets, and crockery.

⭐ **Fuji-san.** Believe it or not, one sighting of the elegant profile of the country's highest mountain and de facto national symbol repays many times over the time and money spent to travel to Japan.

⭐ **Geisha, Gion district, Kyōto.** Although their numbers have dwindled significantly in this century, in the evenings these traditional female entertainers still hurry down alleys to appointments in this Kyōto neighborhood, sparkling white *tabi* (socks) peeking out from under their richly brocaded kimono.

⭐ **Torchlight Nō, Heian Jingū, Kyōto.** Nō—the world's oldest extant professional theater—is special wherever you see it, but particularly so when the performance is staged outside, often on shrine or temple grounds, by the light of a bonfire.

⭐ **Daibutsu (Great Buddha), Todai-ji, Nara.** This colossal gilt-bronze image, built in the 8th century and restored after damage several times subsequently, is housed in what is thought to be the world's largest wooden structure.

⭐ **Atomic Bomb Dome and Peace Flame, Hiroshima.** The only building left unreconstructed in the city where an atomic weapon was first deployed against human beings is a poignant and sobering sight, as is the Peace Flame, which will not be extinguished until all of the world's nuclear weapons have been dismantled.

Restaurants

⭐ **Inakaya, Tōkyō.** Sit around a U-shape counter and watch cooks in traditional dress charcoal-grill a delectable array of vegetables, seafood, beef, and chicken. They'll serve your skewered choices direct from the pit on an 8-ft-long paddle. $$$$

⭐ **Attore, Tōkyō.** Although some Westerners find it hard to believe—much less accept—some of the world's best Italian food is to be had in Tōkyō; the cream of the crop is served here. $$–$$$$

⭐ **Heichinrou, Tōkyō.** Sample first-rate Cantonese food while taking in a spectacular view of Hibiya Park and the Imperial Palace at this branch of one of Yokohama Chinatown's oldest and best restaurants. $$$

⭐ **Sasashu, Tōkyō.** This *izakaya* (traditional drinking establishment) stocks Japan's finest sake—and serves the best food to accompany it; the house specialty is charcoal-broiled salmon steak brushed with sake and soy sauce. $$$

⭐ **Farm Grill, Tōkyō.** California-style cuisine meets Tōkyō yuppies in this vast, minimally decorated space; the portions are generous, the prices reasonable, and the menu innovative. $–$$

⭐ **Yagenbori, Kyōto.** The city's best traditional *kaiseki* cuisine is attractively presented on beautiful handmade ceramics in this teahouse in the heart of the geisha district. $$$

⭐ **Sagano, Kyōto.** The subtle, delicate flavor of tofu—which is nowhere better than it is in Kyōto—simmered in savory broth is intensified by the gorgeous natural surroundings of this Arashiyama district retreat. $$

⭐ **Omen, Kyōto.** Noodle dishes are one way to eat exceptional local food and keep costs down. Omen's atmosphere and house specialty won't make you feel like you're sparing anything but yen. $

⭐ **Kanawa Restaurant, Hiroshima.** Hiroshima prides itself on its melt-in-your-mouth oysters; savor them on this restaurant-on-a-barge with river views. $$

⭐ **Shikairo, Nagasaki.** The specialties of the house are *champon*—a tasty noodle dish created in this very restaurant—and Fukien Chinese cuisine, but the menu is nearly as extensive as this restaurant's seating capacity of 1,500. $–$$

Hotels

⭐ **Four Seasons Hotel Chinzan-so, Tōkyō.** The million dollars or so that it reputedly cost to complete each guest room here is evident in every inch of the large rooms, as well as in the lavish lobby. $$$$

⭐ **Palace Hotel, Tōkyō.** The staff of this stately, deluxe retreat across the moat from the Imperial Palace is particularly helpful and professional. $$$$

⭐ **Sawanoya Ryokan, Tōkyō.** The welcoming owners of this popular low-budget spot make visitors of all nationalities feel at home in the traditional Tōkyō neighborhood of Ueno. $

⭐ **Yamaku, Takayama.** A cross between a ryokan and a minshuku (the higher- and lower-end traditional inns), Yamaku provides the best of a Japanese inn—an old wooden building, tatami-mat rooms, large public baths, and meals—affordably in one of Japan's most enchanting towns. $–$$

★ **Tawaraya, Kyōto.** Subdued traditional beauty and modern comforts blend seamlessly at this lodging of choice of kings, queens, presidents, and dictators. *$$$$*

★ **Hirota Guest House, Kyōto.** An English-speaking professional guide operates this gem, a restored sake storehouse south of Kyōto's Imperial Palace. *$*

★ **Sakaya, Beppu, Kyūshū.** Meals prepared in a hot spring–heated backyard oven are included in the reasonable rates charged for accommodations in this beautiful old wooden building. *$*

GREAT ITINERARIES

Planning a trip to Japan can be mind-boggling. There are so many temples and hot springs to visit that they fade into a blur. Trying to figure out whether to spend an afternoon or a day in a place like Kurashiki can throw a wrench into your San-yō coast planning. What *is* the best division of days and nights between Kyōto, Nara, and a stay in one of the Kōya-san monasteries? And is it okay to skip Tōkyō on a first trip to Japan? (The answer is yes.)

Each chapter in *Fodor's Japan* contains itineraries through the cities and regions that it covers. The following itineraries combine sights from various chapters to suggest ways of approaching a trip through Japan. Two areas that we haven't covered below are Hokkaidō and Kyūshū. Short and long itineraries for these islands appear in their individual chapters.

If you intend to travel a lot by train, it is best to get a Japan Rail Pass, which you must purchase outside of Japan (☞ Train Travel *in* the Gold Guide).

Introduction to Traditional Japan (One Week)

Like every other nation, Japan has some sights that are more famous than others. These sights tend to be in the major cities. The following itinerary covers the barest, surface-scratching minimum in modern Tōkyō and glorious Nikkō; the temples and shrines of Kamakura, the power center of Japan's first shogunate; the temples of classical Kyōto; and Nara, Japan's first

permanent capital. For more depth, you will need two weeks at least.

Day 1: Arrive in Tōkyō. Flights from the United States tend to arrive in the late afternoon, which means that it is early evening by the time you reach your hotel in downtown Tōkyō.

Day 2: Visit the major Tōkyō sights or shops that appeal to you. Two of the following would be possible if you move fast: the temples and museums in Ueno Kōen, Ginza's department stores, the fish market and everyday shops in Tsukiji, the smaller shops in Asakusa, or the Imperial Palace grounds (☞ Chapter 2). Arrange to spend your evening in one or two of the nighttime districts, such as Roppongi or Shinjuku, or try to see a Kabuki, Nō, or Bunraku performance (☞ Chapter 3).

Day 3: Spend another day in Tōkyō or head to the picturesque Chūsen-ji (temple) in Nikkō either on your own or with a tour, bearing in mind that you might want to avoid its crowds in high season (☞ Chapter 4). Return to Tōkyō for evening pleasures.

Day 4: Visit Kamakura on your own, traveling from Tōkyō by train. If there is time left in the day, stop on the way back to Tōkyō to visit Yokohama (☞ Chapter 4).

Day 5: Take one of the morning Shinkansen from Tōkyō to Kyōto (☞ Chapter 7). Visit the sights in the Eastern District (Higashiyama) in the afternoon and take in the Gion District in the evening.

Day 6: In the morning visit more Eastern District sights and in the afternoon visit Western District sights. If you are in the city on the 25th of the month, don't miss Kitano Tenman-gū market.

Day 7: Cover Central Kyōto in the morning, including Tō-ji market, if you're in town on the 21st of the month, and take a train to Nara (☞ Chapter 8) in the afternoon to see the elegant temples and Daibutsu (Great Buddha) of Nara Kōen. Return to Kyōto after dinner.

Day 8: Return to Tōkyō via Kyōto and head straight to Narita Airport.

An Extended Introduction to Japan (Two Weeks)

Two weeks are obviously better than one in Japan. Covering the same ground as the one-week itinerary of Japan, this itinerary also includes some of the Japan Alps, Hiroshima, and the Seto Inland Sea. If you want to add a day between Takayama and Kanazawa, consider spending a night in a traditional farmhouse in the rural village of Ogi-machi.

Days 1–4: Same as above in Tōkyō (☞ Chapter 3).

Day 5: Take the train to Nagano and visit Zenkō-ji (temple). Continue by train to Matsumoto and visit Karasu-jō, the Japan Folklore Museum, and the Japan Ukiyo-e Museum (☞ Chapter 6).

Day 6: Travel via Kamikochi to Takayama, one of Japan's best-preserved traditional cities.

Day 7: Head to the Asa-ichi (morning market); then see other Takayama sights before taking a train via Toyama to Kanazawa in the late afternoon.

Day 8: Kanazawa has also preserved many of its traditional buildings, and it is one of the country's finest cities. Take in what sights you can before catching the late-afternoon train to Kyōto (☞ Chapter 7).

Day 9: Visit Kyōto's Eastern District (Higashiyama) and in the evening enjoy the Gion District.

Day 10: Spend the morning at Katsura Detached Villa in southwestern Kyōto; then head up to Arashiyama to visit the Western District sights, such as the famous Kinkaku-ji, Temple of the Golden Pavilion.

Day 11: Cover central Kyōto in the morning, including Tō-ji market, and northern Kyōto in the afternoon.

Day 12: Take a train to Nara in the morning. Take in the temples and museums of Nara Kōen before lunch and consider heading out to Western Nara to see Tōshōdai-ji or Hōryū-ji (temples) there (☞ Chapter 8). Have dinner in Nara and stay the night or head back to your Kyōto lodging.

Day 13: Travel by train through Ōsaka to Himeji to visit its remarkable castle (☞ Chapter 11). Continue on to Okayama and reach historic Kurashiki by early afternoon.

Day 14: Leave Kurashiki by train in time to reach Hiroshima for lunch. Visit the Peace Memorial Park and Museum and then take the train and ferry to Miyajima, with the glorious vermilion *torii* in the bay, and spend the night on-island.

Day 15: Return to Narita Airport in Tōkyō in the morning.

City and Country: Tōkyō and Tōhoku

The contrast of city and country in Japan can almost make you feel like a time traveler. Tōhoku certainly has its modern cities—though a far cry from Tōkyō—but the mountainside *Risshaku-ji* (temple) of Yamadera and the farm community of Tōno can send you spinning back a century or more. There are also places where you can cross the tracks of the 17th-century poet-monk Bashō's celebrated *Narrow Road to the Deep North*. In eight days, four in Tōkyō, four in Tōhoku, you can still have time to head back south and west to finish your two-week trip in Kyōto and Nara.

Days 1–4: Get your feet on the ground in Tōkyō and spend all of your time in the city. Be sure to take in the spectacles of sumō and the Tsukiji fish market. See Ueno's museums and temples, the Ginza's *depāto,* Asakusa's specialty shops, and the nightlife of Roppongi or Shinjuku (☞ Chapter 3).

Days 5–8: Take a Shinkansen north to Yamagata, and then spend the afternoon at the rural pottery town of Hirashimizu or head up to the mountainside Zaō Onsen for a relaxing thermal bath. Spend the next day at Yamadera. Overnight in or near Sendai, and then continue north to the Tōno Basin, stopping at the gorges of Hiraizumi if you like on the way. Pick up a bicycle in Tōno to explore the countryside, and take a look at the folk village. The area is full of interesting folklore and related sights.

Instead of starting with Yamadera, you could head straight for Tōno, spend a day or two there, then move on to Tazawa-ko (lake) and Nyuto Onsen to hike among alpine wildflowers and soak in thermal baths. Return south along the west coast, stopping at Haguro-san, one of the three revered mountains of the sacred Dewa-san range. Like the Yamadera experience, the climb past cedars, waterfalls, and small shrines is remarkable.

City and Country 2: Kyōto and the San-in Coast

The old capital makes for a very different experience of urban Japan. Yes, Kyōto is a modern city with plenty of concrete, but its traditionalism is undeniable. Likewise the San-in coast. Harder to reach because mountains separate it from the rest of the country, the San-in has a blessedly slower pace than most of Japan. The difficulty it poses is slower transportation, which means spending more time on trains. The payoff is seeing a very hospitable part of Japan that few Westerners do.

Days 1–4: Four days in Kyōto will allow plenty of time to see the eastern, central, and western city sights and get in a visit to one of the Imperial villas. Don't forget about the markets—the daily Nishiki-kōji and the monthly Tō-ji and Kitano Tenman-gū markets—crafts shopping, and a Kabuki or Gion Corner performance (☞ Chapter 7).

Days 5–9: Take a train to Kinosaki and begin your trek along the San-in coast. Stay around Kinosaki or Kundani and bask in its relaxing contrast with Kyōto's urbanity. Next morning move on to Matsue and revered Izumo Taisha (shrine) to take in the coast's cultural life. Stay in the area for two days. On the morning of the fourth day, take a train to the mountain town of Tsuwano or to the coastal pottery and temple city of Hagi at the west end of the coast for the rest of your time in the San-in.

To round out this itinerary, finish up with a few days on the San-yō coast—in Hiroshima, Miyajima, Kurashiki, and Himeji (☞ Chapter 11)—or on the less-traveled island of Shikoku (☞ Chapter 12).

FESTIVALS AND NATIONAL HOLIDAYS

Matsuri (festivals) are very important to the Japanese, and a large number are held throughout the year. Many of them originated in folk and religious rituals and date back hundreds of years. Gala matsuri take place annually at Buddhist temples and Shinto shrines, and many are associated with the changing of the seasons. Most are free of charge and attract thousands of visitors as well as locals. For the big three festivals of Kyōto (the Gion, Jidai, and Aoi festivals), hotel bookings should be made well in advance. That said, the same applies to almost all holiday times in Japan, whether nationally or locally.

In most cases, matsuri below are elaborated upon in the relevant chapters of this guide, especially when local history is involved. To find out specific matsuri dates, contact the Japan National Tourism Organization (☞ Visitor Information *in* the Gold Guide).

When national holidays fall on Sundays, they are celebrated on the following Mondays. Museums and sights are often closed the days after these holidays.

traditional kimono, and many people visit shrines and hold family reunions. Although the day is solemn, streets are often decorated with pine twigs, plum branches, and bamboo stalks.

JAN. 15➤ **Adults' Day** honors those who have reached the voting age of 20.

FEB.➤ During the first week, more than 300 pieces of ice sculpture, some huge, populate the **Sapporo Snow Festival,** bringing some 2 million people to the city to see them.

FEB.➤ Asahikawa's **Ice Festival** is a smaller counterpart to Sapporo's, with more of a country-fair atmosphere.

FEB. 11➤ **National Foundation Day** celebrates accession to the throne by the first emperor.

FEB. 13–15➤ Akita (in Tōhoku) City's **Namahage Sedo Festival** enacts in public a ritual from nearby Oga of threatening "good-for-nothings": Men in demon masks carrying buckets and huge knives issue dire warnings to loafers.

attractions are booked solid—is *not* a good time to visit Japan.

MAY 3➤ **Constitution Memorial Day.** This day commemorates the adoption of the Japanese constitution.

MAY 5➤ **Children's Day.** Families with little boys display paper or cloth carp on bamboo poles outside the house or a set of warrior dolls inside the home.

MAY 15➤ Dating back to the 6th century, the **Aoi Festival,** also known as the Hollyhock Festival, is the first of Kyōto's three most popular celebrations. An "imperial" procession of 300 courtiers starts from the Imperial Palace and makes its way to Shimogamo Shrine to pray for the prosperity of the city. Today's participants are local Kyōtoites.

MAY➤ The **Sanja Festival,** held on the third weekend of May at Tōkyō's Asakusa Jinja, is the city's biggest party. Men, often naked to the waist, carry palanquins through the streets amid revelers. Many of these bare bearers bear the tattoos of the Yakuza, Japan's Mafia.

SPRING

MAR. 21 (OR 20)➤ **Vernal Equinox Day** celebrates the start of spring.

APR. 29➤ **Greenery Day.** The first day of **Golden Week**—when many Japanese take vacation, and hotels, trains, and

SUMMER

JUNE➤ On Miyajima near Hiroshima, the lunar calendar determines the timing of three stately barges' crossing of the bay to the island's shrine for the **Kangen-sai Festival.**

WINTER

JAN. 1➤ **New Year's Day** is the "festival of festivals" for the Japanese. Some women dress in

JULY 16–17➤ The **Gion Festival,** which dates back to the 9th century, is perhaps Kyōto's most popular festival. Twenty-nine huge floats sail along downtown streets and make their way to Yasaka Shrine to thank the gods for protection from a pestilence that once ravaged the city.

JULY 24–25➤ Ōsaka's **Tenjin Festival** is a major event, with parades of floats and nighttime fireworks and processions of 100-plus lighted vessels on the city's canals.

AUG.➤ The first week's dreamlike **Neputa Festival,** held in the Tōhoku city of Hirosaki, finds nightly processions of floats, populated with illuminated paintings of faces from mythology, through the streets.

AUG. 3–7➤ The **Nebuta Festival** in northern Tōhoku's Aomori noisily celebrates an ancient battle victory with a nighttime parade of illuminated floats.

AUG. 5–7➤ At Yamagata's **Hanagasa Festival,** in southern Tōhoku, celebrants dance through the streets in local costume among floats. Food and drink are on hand for spectators.

AUG. 6–8➤ Sendai's **Tanabata** celebrates two legendary astrological lovers with a theatrical rendition of their tale, and city residents decorate their streets and houses with colorful paper and bamboo streamers.

AUG. 13–16➤ During the **Obon Festival,** a time of Buddhist ceremonies in honor of ancestors, many Japanese take off the entire week to travel to their hometowns—try to avoid travel on these days.

AUG. 16➤ For the **Daimonji Gozan Okuribi,** huge bonfires in the shape of *kanji* characters illuminate five of the mountains that surround Kyōto. The most famous is the "Dai," meaning big, on the side of Mt. Daimonji in Higashiyama (Kyōto's eastern district). Dress in a cool *yukata* (cotton robe) and walk down to the banks of the Kamogawa to view this spectacular summer sight, or catch all five fires from the rooftop of your hotel downtown or a spot in Funaoka-yama or Yoshida-yama parks. There are Bon dances as well as the floating of lanterns in Arashiyama (the western district).

AUG.➤ Another loud Tōkyō blowout, the **Kanda Festival** is all about taking the Kanda shrine's gods out for some fresh air in their *mikoshi* (portable shrines)—not to mention drinking plenty of beer and having a great time.

AUTUMN

SEPT. 15➤ **Respect for the Aged Day.**

SEPT. 23 (OR 24)➤ **Autumnal Equinox Day.**

OCT. 10➤ **Health-Sports Day** commemorates the Tōkyō Olympics of 1964.

OCT. 22➤ Kyōto's **Jidai Festival,** the Festival of Eras, features a colorful costume procession of fashions from the 8th through 19th centuries. The procession begins at the Imperial Palace and winds up at Heian Shrine. More than 2,000 Kyōtoites voluntarily participate in this festival, which dates back to 1895.

OCT. 22➤ For the **Kurama Fire Festival,** at Kurama Shrine, there is a roaring bonfire and a rowdy portable shrine procession that makes its way through the narrow streets of the small village in the northern suburbs of Kyōto. If you catch a spark, it is believed to bring good luck.

NOV. 3➤ **Culture Day,** a fairly new holiday, encourages the Japanese to cherish peace, freedom, and culture, both old and new.

NOV. 23➤ **Labor Thanksgiving Day** is recognized by harvest celebrations in some parts of the country.

DEC. 23➤ **The Emperor's Birthday.**

DEC. 27➤ The first day of the weeklong New Year celebrations. Travel is *not* recommended.

2 A Japanese Cultural Primer

Crafts

Ritual and Religion

Theater and Dramatic Personae

Society and Silliness

The Discreet Charm of Japanese Cuisine

The Springs of Ecstasy

Japan at a Glance: A Chronology

Books and Videos

SOME ASPECT OF JAPANESE CULTURE is bound to have led you to pick up this book and contemplate a trip to Japan. Perhaps it was the warm aroma of grilled *unagi sushi* or a steaming bowl of *nabeyaki udon*. It could have been the rustle of a *kimono* or the ancient crackle on a piece of *shino* pottery. Or maybe it was the quiet allure of a haiku by Bashō quoted in something that you read about Japan.

Whether or not one of these sparked your interest, no doubt one or more elements of Japanese culture will make your trip unforgettable. In the course of the transworld culture warp you're bound to experience when you set foot on *terra Japonica*, some of the topics below might be useful for getting your bearings.

CRAFTS

Calligraphy
Calligraphy in Japan arrived around 500 AD with Buddhism and its emphasis on writing. By 800, the *kana* of Japanese language—the two alphabets, if you will—began to be artistically written as well. The art of calligraphy lies not only in the creative execution of the characters, as in Western calligraphy, but also in the direct expression of the artist's personality and message. Thick, heavy splotches or delicate, watery lines should be viewed first without respect to their meaning as creative forms displaying emotion. Then, the meaning should come to the fore, adding substance to the emotion.

Like all traditional arts in Japan, there are various schools and styles of calligraphy—five in this case—each with more or less emphasis on structure and expression. The Chinese exported the *tenshō* (primitive "seal style") and *reishō* (advanced primitive, "scribe's style") to Japan with written Buddhist scripture. The Japanese developed three other styles: *sōshō* (cursive writing), the looser *gyōshō* (semicursive "running style"), and *kaishō* (block, or standard style). The first two demonstrate the Japanese emphasis on expression to convey an impromptu, flowing image unique to the moment—retouching and

erasing is impossible. Kaishō has since developed into carved calligraphy on wood—either engraved or in relief—and the traditional stamp art seen at temples and in print. Avant-garde styles now popular, which are difficult even for Japanese to read, can seem the most interesting to foreigners as an art form. You'll see this style in many traditional restaurants.

Go to visitor centers if you would like to try out a brush, and unless you insist on a famous calligrapher's work, most Japanese can write something interesting for you on a decorative board found at most art stores. Reading: *The Art of Japanese Calligraphy,* by Yujiro Nakata.

Ceramics
With wares that range from clean, flawlessly decorated porcelain to rustic pieces so spirited that they almost breathe, Japanese pottery has its share of enthusiasts and ardent collectors for good reason. This century, it has had significant influence on North American ceramic artists. The popularity of Raku firing techniques, adapted from those of the famous Japanese pottery clan of the same name, is one example.

Japanese ceramic styles are defined regionally. Arita *yaki* (ceramic ware from Arita on Kyūshū), Tobe yaki, Kutani yaki, and Kyōto's Kyō yaki and Kiyomizu yaki are all porcelain ware. True to the nature of porcelain—a fine-particled, delicate clay body—these styles are either elaborately decorated or covered with images. Stoneware decoration tends to have an earthier, but no less refined, appeal, befitting the rougher texture of the clay body. Mashiko yaki's brown, black, and white glazes are often applied in patters. Celebrated potter Shōji Hamada (1894–1978) worked in Mashiko.

Other regional potters use glazes on stoneware for texture and coloristic effects—mottled, crusty Tokoname yaki; speckled, earth-toned Shigaraki yaki made near Kyōto; and the pasty, white or blue-white Hagi yaki are alive with the surface and depth of their rustic glazes. Bizen yaki, another stoneware, has no liquid glaze applied to its surfaces. Pots are buried in ash, wrapped in straw, or colored in the firing process by potters' manipulation of kiln conditions.

Unless your mind is set on the idea of kiln-hopping in pottery towns like Hagi, Bizen, and Arita, you can find these wares in Kyōto and Tōkyō department stores. If you do go on a pilgrimage, call local kilns and tourist organizations to verify that what you want to see will be open and to ask about yearly pottery sales, during which local wares are discounted. Reading: *Inside Japanese Ceramics,* by Richard L. Wilson.

Lacquerware

Japanese lacquerware has its origins in the Jōmon period (10,000–300 BC), when basic utensils were coated with lacquer resin made from tree sap. By the Nara period (710–794) most of the techniques we recognize today were being used. For example, *maki-e* (literally, "sprinkled picture") refers to several different techniques that use gold or silver powder in areas coated with liquid lacquer. In the Azuchi-Momoyama period (1568–1600), lacquerware exports made their way to Europe. The following Edo period (1603–1868) saw the broadening of the uses of lacquer for the newly prosperous merchant class.

The production of lacquerware starts with the draining, evaporation, and filtration of sap from lacquer trees. Successive layers of lacquer are carefully painted on basketry, wood, bamboo, woven textiles, metal, and even paper. The lacquer strengthens the object, making it durable for eating, carrying, or protecting fragile objects, such as fans. Lacquer ware can be mirror-like if polished; often the many layers may have inlays of mother-of-pearl or precious metals inserted between coats, creating a complicated design of exquisite beauty and delicacy. The best places to see lacquer ware are Hōryū-ji in Nara—the temple has a beautiful display—and Wajima on Shikoku. Expensive yet precious lacquerware remains one of the most distinctive and highest-quality crafts of Japan.

Textiles

The topic of textiles is invariably linked to the history and nature of kimonos and costumes, which offered the best opportunity for weavers, dyers, and designers to exhibit their skills. Remember that both Buddhism and Confucianism helped to create the four castes in Japan: samurai, Buddhist clerics, farmers, and townspeople (merchants and artisans) in descending order of importance. Courtesans and actors often slipped through the cracks and thus were exempt from the targets of the sumptuary laws that reinforced these strata by making certain types of dress illegal for lower castes. Outer appearance helped to identify social rank and maintained order. Styles of embroidery and decoration and sumptuous clothing changed legal status in reaction to social upheavals and the eventual rise of the merchant class.

The various types of kimono—Japanese traditional dress attire is unisex in cut—are made from flat woven panels that provide the most surface for decoration. While Western clothing follows the body line in a sculptural way, the Japanese use of fabric is more painterly and has little concern for body size and shape. No matter the wearer's height or weight, a kimono is made from one bolt of cloth cut and stitched into four panels and fitted with a collar. When creating kimono, or the Buddhist clerics' *kesa* (a body wrap), no fabric is wasted. Shintō's emphasis is evident in the importance of natural fabrics, as the way of the gods was always concerned with purity and defilement.

Regional designs are the rule in textiles. Kyōto's heavily decorated Nishijin Ori is as sumptuous as Japanese fabric comes. Okinawa produces a variety of stunning fabrics, and both Kyōto and Tōkyō's stencil dyeing techniques yield intricate, elegant patterns. The most affordable kimono are used kimono—which can be nearly flawless or in need of minor stitching. Kyōto's flea markets are a good venue for this. Also look for lighter weight *yukata* (robes), *obi* (sashes), or handkerchiefs from Arimatsu, near Nagoya, for example. Good places to see fabrics are Kyōto's Fuzoku Hakubutsukan (Costume Museum), Nishijin Orimono (Textile Center), and the Tōkyō National Museum, which displays garments of the Edo period.

Papermaking

Papermaking and shōji (paper screens) are a unique and beautiful Japanese creation that are surprisingly affordable, unlike other traditional crafts. *Washi,* Japanese paper, can have a translucent quality that seems to argue against its amazing durability. Shintō's usage of paper as a decorative symbol in shrines—probably due to its purity when new—gives an added importance to the already high esteem the Japanese hold for paper and the written word. Paper is a symbol of *kami* (god), and the process to make it requires an almost ritualistic sense. Usually, the inner bark of the paper mulberry is used, but leaves, ropelike fibers, even gold flake can be added in the later steps of the process for a dramatic effect. The raw branches are steamed, and bleached by exposure to cold or snow. The fibers are boiled with ash lye and subsequently rinsed. After chopping and beating the pulp, it is soaked in a starchy taro solution, and the textures or leaves are added for decoration. A screen is dipped in the floating fibers, and when the screen is pulled up evenly, a sheet of paper is formed. Amazingly, wet sheets when stacked do not stick together.

The best places to view the papermaking process are Kurodani, near Kyōto, Mino, in central Japan, and Yame, near Kurume. Different parts of Japan specialize in different products. Gifu is known for its umbrellas and lanterns, Nagasaki for its distinctive kites, and Nara for its calligraphy paper and utensils. A light, inexpensive and excellent gift, Japanese paper is a handicraft you can easily carry home as a souvenir.

— David Miles

RITUAL AND RELIGION

Tea Ceremony

The tea ceremony was formalized by the 16th century under the patronage of the Ashikaga shōguns, but it was the Zen monks of the 12th century who started the practice of drinking tea for a refresher between meditation sessions. The samurai and tea master Sen-no-Rikyū elucidated "the Way," the meditative and spiritual aspect of the ceremony, and is the most revered figure in the history of tea. For samurai, the ceremony appealed to their ideals and their sense of discipline, and diversions in time of peace were necessary. In essence, tea ceremony is a spiritual and philosophical ritual whose prescribed steps and movements serve as an aid in sharpening the aesthetic sense.

Tea ceremony has a precisely choreographed program. Participants enter the teahouse or room and comment on the specially chosen art in the entryway. The ritual begins as the server prepares a cup of tea for the first patron. This process involves a strictly determined series of movements and actions, common to every ceremony, which includes cleansing each of the utensils to be used. One by one the participants slurp up their bowl of tea, then eat the sweet cracker served with it. Finally, comments about the beauty of the bowls used are exchanged. The entire ritual involves contemplating the beauty in the smallest actions, focusing their meaning in the midst of the impermanence of life.

The architecture of a traditional teahouse is also consistent. There are two entrances: a service entrance for the host and server and a low door that requires that guests enter on their knees, in order to be humbled. Tea rooms often have a flower arrangement or piece of artwork in the alcove, for contemplation and comment, and *tatami* (grass mat) flooring. Though much of the process will seem the same wherever you experience the ceremony, there are different schools of thought on the subject. The three best-known schools of tea are the Ura Senke, the Omote Senke, and the Musha Kōji, each with their own styles, emphases, and masters.

There can be highly formal ceremonies with kaiseki meals and "thick tea," which last for hours, but most Japanese tea ceremonies are less formal "thin teas," accompanied by a sweet, for a small, intimate group. For tea enthusiasts, the first tea of the year is a significant ceremony, as are most Japanese New Year events.

Most experiences of tea that you will have will be geared toward the uninitiated: The tea ceremony is a rite that requires methodical initiation by education. If you don't go for instruction before your trip, keep two things in mind if you attend or are invited to a tea ceremony: First, be in the right frame of mind when you enter the room. Though the tea ceremony is a pleasant event, some people take it quite seriously, and boisterous behavior beforehand is frowned upon. Instead, make conversation that enhances a mood of serenity and invites a feeling of meditative quietude. Second, be sure to sit quietly through the serving and drinking—controlled slurping is expected—and openly appreciate the tools and cups afterward, commenting on their elegance and simplicity. This appreciation is an important final step of the ritual. Above all, pay close attention to the practiced movements of the ceremony, from the art at the entryway and the kimono of the server to the folding of the cleansing cloth and the quality of the utensils. Reading: *The Book of Tea,* by Kakuzo Okakura; *Cha-no-Yu: The Japanese Tea Ceremony,* by A. L. Sadler.

Buddhism

Buddhism in Japan grew out of a Korean king's symbolic gift of a statue of Shaka—the first Buddha, Prince Gautama—to the Yamato Court in AD 538. The Soga clan adopted the foreign faith and used it as a vehicle for changing the political order of the day. After battling for control of the country, the Soga clan established themselves as political rulers and Buddhism took permanent hold of Japan. Shōtoku Taishi, the crown prince and regent during this period, sent the first Japanese ambassadors to China, which inaugurated the importation of Chinese culture, writing, and religion in Japan. Since that time, several eras in Japanese history have seen the equation of consolidating state power with promulgating Buddhist influence and building temples. By the 8th century AD, Japanese Buddhism's six schools of thought were well established, and priests from India and Persia came for the ceremonial opening of Todai-ji (temple) in Nara. Scholars argue that the importation of architectural styles and things Buddhist in this period may have had more to do with the political rather than religious needs of Japanese society. Likewise, the intertwining of religion and state and the importation of foreign ideas had undeniably political motivations during the Meiji Restoration and Japanese colonial expansion early this century. And the use of foreign ideas continues to be an essential component of understanding the social climate in Japan today.

Three waves in the development of Japanese Buddhism followed the religion's Nara-period (710–784) florescence. In the Heian period (794–894), Esoteric Buddhism was introduced primarily by two priests who studied in China: Saichō and Kūkai. Near Kyōtō, Saichō established a temple on Mt. Hiei—which makes it the most revered mountain in Japan after Mt. Fuji. Kūkai established the Shingon sect of Esoteric Buddhism on Mt. Kōya, south of Nara. It is said that he is still in a state of meditation and will be until the arrival of the last bodhisattva (Buddhist messianic saint, *bosatsu* in Japanese). In Japanese temple architecture, Esoteric Buddhism introduced the separation of the temple into an interior for the initiated and an outer laypersons' area. This springs from Esoteric Buddhism's emphasis on *mikkyō* (secret rites) for the initiated.

Amidism was the second wave, and it flourished until the introduction of Zen in 1185. Its adherents saw the world emerging from a period of darkness, during which Buddhism had been in decline, and asserted that salvation was offered only to the believers in Amida, a Nyorai (Buddha), an enlightened being. Amidism's promise of salvation and its subsequent versions of heaven and hell earned it the appellation "Devil's Christianity" from visiting Christian missionaries in the 16th century.

The influences of Nichiren and Zen Buddhist philosophies pushed Japanese Buddhism in the unique direction it heads today. Nichiren (1222–1282) was a monk who insisted that repetition of the phrase "Hail the Miraculous Law of the Lotus Sutra" would bring salvation, the Lotus Sutra being the supposed last and greatest sutra of Shaka. Zen Buddhism was attractive to the samurai class's ideals of discipline and worldly detachment and thus spread throughout Japan in the 12th century.

Japanese Buddhism today, like most religions in Japan, plays a minimal role in the daily life of the average Japanese. Important milestones in life provide the primary occasions for religious observance. Most Japanese have Buddhist burials. Weddings are usually in the Shintō style; recently, ceremonial references to Christian weddings have crept in, added for romantic effect. (This mixing of religions may seem strange in the West, but it is wholly acceptable in Japan and other Asian countries.) Outsiders have criticized the Japanese for lacking spirituality, and it is true that many Japanese don't make some kind of religious observance part of their daily or weekly lives. That said, there is a spiritual element in the people's unflinching belief in the group and Japaneseness circles around very spiritual issues.

For more information on religious and political history, statuary manifestations of bosatsu and the Buddha, and architectural styles, consult *Buddhism, A History,* by Noble Ross Reat, and *Sources of Japanese Tradition,* by Tsunoda, De Bary, and Keene.

Shintō

One thing to remember about Shintō—literally, "the way of the kami (god)"—is that it does not preach a moral doctrine or code of ethics to follow. It is a form of animism, nature worship, based on myth and rooted to the geography and holy places of the land. Fog-enshrouded mountains, pairs of rocks, primeval forests, and geothermal activity are all manifestations of the *kami-sama* (honorable gods). For many Japanese, the Shintō aspect of their lives is simply the realm of the kami-sama, not attached to a religious framework as it would be in the West. In that sense, the name describes more a way of thinking than a religion.

Shintō rites that affect the daily lives of Japanese today are the wedding ceremony, the *matsuri* (festivals), and New Year's Day. The wedding ceremony uses elaborate, colorful kimono for the bride and a simple, masculine *happi* (short coat) worn over a *furisode*-style (literally, "swinging sleeves") robe for the groom. The number three is significant, and sake, of the fruits of the earth from the gods, is the ritual libation.

The neighborhood shrine's annual matsuri is a time of giving thanks for prosperity and of the blessing homes and local businesses. *O-mikoshi,* portable shrines for the gods, are enthusiastically carried around the district by young local men. Shouting and much sake drinking are part of the celebration.

New Year's Day entails visiting an important local shrine and praying for health, happiness, success in school or business, or the safe birth of a child in the coming year. A traditional meal of rice cakes and sweet beans is served in stacked boxes at home, as part of a family time not unlike those of traditional Western winter holidays.

Like Buddhism, Shintō was used throughout Japanese history as a tool for affirming the might of a given ruling power. The Meiji Restoration in 1868 effected this pose to reclaim the emperor's sacred right to rule and to wrest control from the last Tokugawa shōgun. Today shrines are more visited for their beauty than for their spiritual importance, though there is no denying the ancient spiritual pull of shrines like the Ise Jingū, south of Nagoya.

— David Miles

THEATER AND DRAMATIC PERSONAE

Nō

Nō is a dramatic tradition far older than Kabuki; it reached a point of formal perfection in the 14th century and survives virtually unchanged from that period. Where Kabuki was Everyman's theater, Nō developed for the most part under the patronage of the warrior class. It is dignified, ritualized, and symbolic. Many of the plays in the repertoire are drawn from classical literature or tales of the supernatural, and the texts are richly poetic. Some understanding of the plot of each play is necessary to enjoy a performance, which moves at a nearly glacial pace—the pace of ritual time—as it is solemnly chanted. The major Nō theaters often provide synopses of the plays in English.

Where the Kabuki actor is usually in brightly colored makeup derived from the Chinese opera, the principal character in a Nō play wears a carved wooden mask. Such is the skill of the actor, and the mysterious effect of the play, that the mask itself may appear expressionless until the actor "brings it to life," at which point the mask seems to express a considerable range of emotions. As in Kabuki, the various roles of the Nō repertoire all have specific costumes—robes of silk brocade with intricate patterns that are works of art in themselves. Nō is not a very *accessible* kind of theater: Its language is archaic; its conventions are obscure; and its measured, stately pace can put even Japanese audiences to sleep.

In Tōkyō, as a contrast to the rest of the city, Nō will provide an experience of Japan as an *ancient,* sophisticated culture. In Kyōto, the outdoor performances of Nō, especially *Takigi* Nō, held outdoors by firelight on the nights of June

1–2 in the precincts of the Heian Shrine, are particularly memorable.

Somewhat like Kabuki, Nō has a number of schools, the traditions of which developed as the exclusive property of hereditary families. Note that *kyōgen* are shorter, lighter plays that are often interspersed in between Nō performances and are much more accessible than Nō. Consider taking advantage of opportunities to see kyōgen rather than Nō.

Kabuki

Kabuki emerged as a popular form of entertainment by women dancing lewdly in the early 17th century; before long, it had been banned by the authorities as a threat to public order. Eventually it cleaned up its act, and by the latter half of the 18th century it had become Everyman's theater par excellence—especially among the townspeople of bustling, hustling Edo. Kabuki had music, dance, and spectacle; it had acrobatics and sword fights; it had pathos and tragedy and historical romance and social satire. It no longer had bawdy beauties—women have been banned from the Kabuki stage since 1629—but in recompense it developed a professional role for female impersonators, who train for years to project a seductive, dazzling femininity. It had—and still has—superstars and quick-change artists and legions of fans, who bring their lunch to the theater, stay all day, and shout out the names of their favorite actors at the stirring moments in their favorite plays. Edo is now Tōkyō, but Kabuki is still here, just as it has been for centuries. The traditions are passed down from generation to generation in a small group of families; the roles and great stage names are hereditary. The Kabuki repertoire does not really grow or change, but stars like Ennosuke Ichikawa and Tamasaburo Bando have put exciting, personal stamps on their performances that continue to draw audiences young and old. If you don't know Japanese, Tōkyō's Kabuki-za (theater) has superb simultaneous English translation of its plays available on headphones. Reading: *The Kabuki Guide*, by Masakatsu Gunji.

Bunraku

The third major form of traditional Japanese drama is Bunraku puppet theater. Itinerant puppeteers were plying their trade in Japan as early as the 10th century.

Sometime in the late 16th century, a form of narrative ballad called *joruri*, performed to the accompaniment of a three-string banjo-like instrument called the *shamisen*, was grafted onto their art, and Bunraku was born. The golden age of Bunraku came some 200 years later, when most of the form's great plays were written and the puppets themselves evolved to their present form—so expressive and intricate in their movements that they require three people at one time to manipulate them. Puppeteers and narrators, who deliver their lines in a kind of high-pitched croak from deep in the throat, train for many years to master this difficult and unusual genre of popular entertainment. Puppets are about two-thirds human size and are large enough to cover the puppeteers underneath them. Elaborately dressed in period costume, each puppet is made up of interchangeable parts—a head, shoulder piece, trunk, legs, and arms. For example, various puppet heads are used for roles of different sex, age, and character, and a certain hairstyle will indicate a puppet's position in life.

Each puppet is operated by three puppeteers, who must act in complete unison. The *omozukai* controls the expression on the puppet's face and its right arm and hand. The *hidarizukai* controls the puppet's left arm and hand along with any props that it is carrying. The *ashizukai* moves the puppet's legs. This last task is the easiest. The most difficult task belongs to the omozukai. It takes about 30 years to become an accomplished expert. A puppeteer must spend 10 years as ashizukai, a further 10 as hidarizukai, and then 10 years as omozukai. These master puppeteers not only skillfully manipulate the puppets' arms and legs but also roll the eyes and move the lips so that the puppets express fear, joy, and sadness. The spiritual center of Bunraku today is Ōsaka. Periodically there are performances in Tōkyō in the small hall of the National Theater.

Geisha

Because the character for "gei" in "*geisha*" stands for arts and accomplishments ("sha" in this case means person), the public image of geisha in Japan is one of high status. Geisha are not, as is thought in the West, prostitutes. To become a geisha, a woman must perfect many talents. She must have grace and a thorough mastery of etiquette. She should have an accomplished singing voice and dance beautifully. She needs to have a finely tuned aesthetic sense—with flower arranging and tea ceremony—and should excel at the art of conversation. In short, she should be the ultimate companion.

These days, geisha are a rare breed. They numbered a mere 10,000 in the late 1980s, as opposed to 80,000 in the 1920s. This is partly due to the increase of bar hostesses—who perform a similar function in nightclubs with virtually none of a geisha's training—not to mention the refinement and expense it takes to hire a geisha. Because she is essentially the most personal form of entertainer, the emphasis is on artistic and conversational skills, not solely on youth or beauty. Thus the typical geisha can work to an advanced age.

Geisha will establish a variety of relations with men. Besides maintaining a dependable amount of favorite customers, one might choose a *danna,* one man for emotional, sexual, and financial gratification. The geisha's exercise of choice in this matter is due partly to the fact that wages and tips alone must provide enough for her to survive. Some geisha marry, most often to an intimate client. When they do they leave the profession.

A geisha typically starts her career as a servant at a house until 13. She continues as a *maiko* (dancing child) until she masters the requisite accomplishments at about 18. Before World War II, full geisha status was achieved after a geisha experienced a *mizuage* (deflowering ceremony), with an important client of the house.

Maiko must master the shamisen and learn the proper hairstyles and kimono fittings. They are a sight to see on the banks of the Kamo-gawa in the Gion district of Kyōto, or in Shimbashi, Akasaka, and Ginza in Tōkyō. Today, geisha unions, restaurant unions, and registry offices regulate the times and fees of geisha. Fees are measured in "sticks"—generally, one hour—which is the time it would take a stick of *senkō* (incense) to burn.

Sumō

This centuries-old national sport of Japan is not to be taken lightly—as anyone who has ever seen a sumō wrestler will testify. Indeed, sheer weight is almost a prerequisite to success. Contenders in the upper ranks tip the scales at an average of 350 pounds, and there are no upper limits. There are various techniques of pushing, grappling, and throwing in sumō, but the basic rules are exquisitely simple: Except for hitting below the belt (which is all a sumō wrestler wears) and striking with a closed fist, almost anything goes. Get thrown down, or forced out of the ring, and you lose.

There are no free agents in sumō. To compete, you must belong to a *heya* (stable) run by a retired wrestler who has purchased that right from the Japan Sumō Association. Sumō is very much a closed world, hierarchical and formal. Youngsters recruited into the sport live in the stable dormitory, doing all the community chores and waiting on their seniors while they learn. When they rise high enough in tournament rankings, they acquire servant-apprentices of their own.

Tournaments and exhibitions are held in different parts of the country at different times, but all stables in the Sumō Association—now some 30 in number—are in Tōkyō. Most are clustered on both sides of the Sumida River nerar the green-roofed *Kokugikan* (National Sumō Arena), in the areas called Asakusabashi and Ryōgoku. When wrestlers are in town in January, May, and September, you are likely to see some of them on the streets, cleaving the air like leviathans in their wood clogs and kimonos. *See* Around Tōkyō *in* Chapter 3 for tournament details.

— Jared Lubarsky and David Miles

SOCIETY AND SILLINESS

It is impossible to summarize the life of a people in brief. Still, there are a few fascinating points about the Japanese that are nonetheless important to mention, even if only in passing.

The Japanese communicate among themselves in what Dr. Chie Nakane, in his *Japanese Society* (1972), calls a "vertical society." In other words, the Japanese constantly vary the way they speak with each other according to the sex, family and educational background, occupation and position, and age of the speakers. Japanese grammar reflects this by requiring different verbs for different levels of inter-action. Since it is necessary for individu-als to vary the way they speak according to the person, they are always consider-ing the levels of the people around them. In a crowded country, this means that the Japanese are often wondering what other people are thinking—often in an effort to gauge where they belong them-selves. This constant consideration toward other members of their group makes the Japanese keen readers of other people's emotions and reactions.

Where much of the West—the United States in particular—has shed nearly every-thing but wealth as an indicator of posi-tion in society, the Japanese maintain concepts of social order that have feudal echoes, as in the ideas of *uchi* and *soto*. Uchi refers to the home, the inside group, and ultimately, Japan and Japaneseness. Soto is everything outside. Imagine uchi being a set of concentric rings, where the most central group is the family, the next is the neighborhood or extended family, then the school, company, or association, then the prefecture, the family of compa-nies, or the region in which they live, and finally, Japan itself. Japanese verb forms are more casual within the various uchi, as opposed to the more polite forms for those "outside." Interestingly enough, the "gai" in the Japanese word for foreigner, *gai-jin*, is the same character as soto. Soto—not belonging—is an undeniable barrier for non-Japanese. Translated into feeling, being the "other" can be frus-trating and alienating. At the same time, it makes instances of crossing the bound-ary into some level of uchi that much more precious.

Despite the belief that the American pres-ence after World War II was what built Japan, it is more correctly the sense of tribe or group the Japanese have utilized to their advantage since the Meiji Restora-tion that really created modern Japan. In the West we might have trouble with what we see as a lack of individuality in Japa-nese society, but we tend to ignore the sense of togetherness and joy that comes from a feeling of homogeneity. We might also miss any number of subtleties in in-terpersonal communication because we are wholly unaccustomed to them. It can take a lifetime to master the finer points of Japanese ambiguities, but even a basic appreciation of shades of meaning and the Japanese vigilance in maintaining the tightness of the group helps to see the beauty of this different way of life.

This beauty might be that much more pre-cious in the face of change. With more of the younger generation traveling and liv-ing abroad, women especially, the group mentality and its role in supporting the Jap-anese socioeconomic structure are erod-ing rapidly.

You're bound to notice that the Japanese are extremely fond of animation, and they use it in communicating ideas and in ad-vertising far more than we do in the West. So you'll see the anthropomorphizing of garbage cans, signage, and even huge, cute-squid telephone booths. The Japanese also seem to lead the world in the production of multipurpose-less gadgets that astound and delight, if only for a minute or two. If this is your thing, don't miss the shops in downtown Ōsaka, or Harajuku and Shibuya in Tōkyō, because you'll never find these things anywhere else. Some of them are expensive—the mooing cow clock that wakes you up with "Don't-o suleepu yo-ah lie-foo eh-way" looks hardly worth more than $10 but is nearly four times that, if you can even find one available; and the "waterfall sounds" player for shy women using the toilet can run up to $300.

There are reams of books and articles on Japanese English—and how they use and abuse it—but the topic might not come to mind until you set foot in Japan. Through-out the country, on billboards and in stores, on clothes, bags, hats, and even on cars, baffling, cryptic, often side-splitting English phrases leap out at you in the midst of your deepest cultural encoun-ters. For example: "Woody goods: We have a woody heart, now listen to my story." What could this possibly mean? Did it make sense in the original Japanese?

Alas, friends and family might not get why you find funny English so hilarious, without a first-hand encounter with some-thing like "Cream Soda" earnestly printed on a bodybuilder's T-shirt—or a fashion catalog that cryptically asserts "optimistic sunbeam shines beautifully for you." These tortured meanings are no doubt a com-pliment to the ascendancy of the English language, which on the world popular-culture stage is, in whatever form, chic and cool. You might find that on a heavy day of temple viewing, funny English might be the straightest path toward *satori* (enlightenment).

The latest obsessions in Japan can take a long time to get rolling, but when they do they can take over the country. And Japanese homogeneity makes for a certain lemming quality that is utterly intriguing when it comes to observing fads. Take the wild popularity of Tamagotchi, the world's first "virtual pet." It requires periodic feeding, walks, and affection—every two to four hours. Its makers wanted kids to learn responsibility, for if you neglect Tamagotchi, it dies (yes, there's even a Web site graveyard for dead Tamagotchi). This techno-obsession's international success just goes to show how adept the Japanese are at catering to the world's unrecognized needs.

Whatever the fad is when you're in Japan, make a note of it and try to remember the Japanese name or words associated with it. When you try to pronounce them, Japanese friends and colleagues will be immensely humored and impressed. Such is the intensity of fads that they act as barometers of the atmosphere of Japan at any given time.

— David Miles

THE DISCREET CHARM OF JAPANESE CUISINE

Leave behind the humidity of Japan in summer and part the crisp linen curtain of the neighborhood *sushi-ya* some hot night in mid-July. Enter a world of white cypress and chilled sea urchin, where a welcome *oshibori* (hot towel) awaits your damp forehead and a master chef stands at your beck and call. A cup of tea to begin, a tiny mound of ginger to freshen the palate, and you're ready to choose from the colorful array of fresh seafood on ice inside a glass case before you. Bite-size morsels arrive in friendly pairs. A glass of ice-cold beer. The young apprentice runs up and down making sure everyone has tea—and anything else that might be needed. The chef has trained for years in his art, and he's proud, in his stoic way, to demonstrate it. The *o-tsukuri* (sashimi) you've ordered

arrives; today the thinly sliced raw tuna comes in the shape of a rose. (Is it really your birthday?) The fourth round you order brings with it an unexpected ribbon of cucumber, sliced with a razor-sharp sushi knife into sections that expand like an accordion. The chef's made your day. . . .

Red paper lanterns dangling in the dark above a thousand tiny food stalls on the back streets of Tōkyō . . . To the weary Japanese salaried man on his way home from the office, these *akachochin* (red lanterns) are a prescription for the best kind of therapy known for the "subterranean homesick blues," Japanese style: one last belly-warming bottle of sake, a nerve-soothing platter of grilled chicken wings, and perhaps a few words of wisdom for the road. Without these comforting nocturnal way stations, many a fuzzy-eyed urban refugee would never survive that rumbling, fluorescent nightmare known as the last train home.

And where would half of Japan's night-owl college students be, if not for the local *shokudo,* as the neighborhood not-so-greasy spoon is known? Separated at last from mother's protective guidance (and therefore without a clue as to how an egg is boiled or a bowl of soup is heated), the male contingent of young lodging-house boarders put their lives in the hands of the old couple who run the neighborhood café. Bent furtively over a platter of *kare-raisu* (curry and rice) or *tonkatsu teishoku* (pork cutlet set meal), these ravenous young men thumb through their baseball comics each night, still on the road to recovery from a childhood spent memorizing mathematical formulas and English phrases they hope they'll never have to use.

Down a dimly lit back street not two blocks away, a geisha in all her elaborate finery walks her last silk-suited customer out to his chauffeur-driven limousine. He has spent the evening being pampered, feasted, and fan-danced in the rarefied air of one of Tōkyō's finest *ryōtei*. (You must be invited to these exclusive eateries—or be a regular patron, introduced years earlier by another regular patron who vouched for your reputation with his own.) There has been the most restrained of traditional dances, some shamisen playing—an oh-so-tastefully suggestive tête-à-tête. The customer has been drinking the very finest sake, accompanied by a succession of exquisitely presented hors d'oeuvres—what amounts to a seven-course meal in the end is the formal Japanese haute cuisine known as *kaiseki*. His grapes have all been peeled. If it were not for his company's expense account, by now he would have spent the average man's monthly salary. Lucky for him, he's not the average man.

On a stool now, under the flimsy awning of a street stall, shielded from the wind and rain by flapping tarps, heated only by a portable kerosene stove and the steam from a vat of boiling noodles, you'll find neither tourist nor ptomaine. Here sits the everyday workingman, glass of *shōchū* (a strong liquor made from sweet potatoes) in sun-baked hand, arguing over the Tigers' chances of winning the Japan Series as he zealously slurps down a bowl of hot noodle soup sprinkled with red-pepper sauce—more atmosphere, and livelier company than you're likely to find anywhere else in Japan. The *yatai-san,* as these inimitable street vendors are known, are an amiable, if disappearing, breed.

Somewhere between the street stalls and the exclusive ryōtei, a vast culinary world exists in Japan. Tiny, over-the-counter restaurants, each with its own specialty—from familiar favorites, such as tempura, sukiyaki, or sushi, to exotic delicacies, like *unagi* (eel) or *fugu* (blowfish)—inhabit every city side street. Comfortable, country-style restaurants abound, serving a variety of different *nabemono,* the one-pot stew dishes cooked right at your table. There are also lively neighborhood *robatayaki* grills, where cooks in *happi* coats wield skewered bits of meat, seafood, and vegetables over a hot charcoal grill as you watch.

A dozen years ago, sukiyaki and tempura were exotic enough for most Western travelers. Those were the days when raw fish was still something a traveler needed fortitude to try. But with *soba* (noodle) shops and sushi bars popping up everywhere from Los Angeles to Paris, it seems that—at long last—the joy of Japanese cooking has found its way westward.

There *is* something special, however, about visiting the tiger in his lair—something no tame circus cat could ever match. Although tours to famous temples and scenic places can provide important historical and cultural background material, there is nothing like a meal in a local restaurant—be it under the tarps of the liveliest street stall or within the quiet recesses of an elegant Japanese inn—for a taste of the real Japan. Approaching a platter of fresh sashimi in Tōkyō is like devouring a hot dog smothered in mustard and onions in Yankee Stadium. There's nothing like it in the world.

The Essentials of a Japanese Meal

As exotic as it might seem, the basic formula for a traditional Japanese meal is simple. It starts with soup, followed by raw fish, then the entrée (grilled, steamed, simmered, or fried fish, chicken, or vegetables), and ends with rice and pickles, with perhaps some fresh fruit for dessert, and a cup of green tea. As simple as that, almost.

An exploration of any cuisine should begin at the beginning, with a basic knowledge of what it is you're eating: Rice, of course—the traditional staple. And seafood—grilled, steamed, fried, stewed, or raw. Chicken, pork, or beef, at times—in that order of frequency. A wide variety of vegetables (wild and cultivated), steamed, sautéed, blanched, or pickled, perhaps—but never overcooked. Soybeans in every form imaginable, from tōfu to soy sauce. Seaweed, in and around lots of things.

The basics are just that. But there are, admittedly, a few twists to the story, as could be expected. Beyond the raw fish, it's the incredible variety of vegetation used in Japanese cooking that still surprises the Western palate: *take-no-ko* (bamboo shoots), *renkon* (lotus root), and the treasured *matsutake* mushrooms (which grow wild in jealously guarded forest hideaways and sometimes sell for more than $60 apiece), to name but a few.

Tangy garnishes, both wild and domestic, such as *kinome* (leaves of the Japanese prickly ash pepper tree), *mitsuba* (trefoil, of the parsley family), and *shiso* (a member of the mint family) are used as a foil for oily foods. The more familiar-sounding ingredients, such as sesame and ginger, appear in abundance, as do the less familiar—*wasabi* (Japanese horseradish), *uri-ne* (lily bulbs), *ginnan* (ginko nuts), and *daikon* (gigantic white radishes). Exotic? Perhaps, but delicious, and nothing here bites back. Simple? Yes, if you understand a few of the ground rules.

Absolute freshness is first. According to world-renowned Japanese chef Shizuo Tsuji, soup and raw fish are the two test pieces of Japanese cuisine. Freshness is the criterion for both: "I can tell at a glance by the texture of their skins—like the bloom of youth on a young girl—whether the fish is really fresh," Tsuji says in *The Art of Japanese Cooking*. A comparison as startling, perhaps, as it is revealing. To a Japanese chef, freshness is an unparalleled virtue, and much of his reputation relies on his ability to obtain the finest ingredients at the peak of season: fish brought in from the sea this morning (not yesterday) and vegetables from the earth (not the hothouse), if at all possible.

Simplicity is next. Rather than embellishing foods with heavy spices and rich sauces, the Japanese chef prefers his flavors au naturel. Flavors are enhanced, not elaborated; accented rather than concealed. Without a heavy dill sauce, fish is permitted a degree of natural fishiness—a garnish of fresh red ginger will be provided to offset the flavor rather than to disguise it.

The third prerequisite is beauty. Simple, natural foods must appeal to the eye as well as to the palate. Green peppers on a vermilion dish, perhaps, or an egg custard in a blue bowl. Rectangular dishes for a round eggplant. So important is the seasonal element in Japanese cooking that maple leaves and pine needles will be used to accent an autumn dish. Or two small summer delicacies, a pair of freshwater *ayu* fish, will be grilled with a purposeful twist to their tails to make them "swim" across a crystal platter and thereby suggest the coolness of a mountain stream on a hot August night.

That's next: the mood. It can make or break the entire meal, and the Japanese connoisseur will go to great lengths to find the perfect yakitori stand—a smoky, lively place—an environment appropriate to the occasion, offering a night of grilled chicken, cold beer, and camaraderie. To a place like this, he'll take only friends he knows will appreciate the gesture.

Atmosphere depends as much on the company as it does on the lighting or the color of the drapes. In Japan, this seems to hold particularly true. The popularity of a particular *nomiya*, or bar, depends entirely on the affability of the *mama-san*, that long-suffering lady who's been listening to your troubles for years. In fancier places, mood becomes a fancier problem, to the point of quibbling over the proper amount of "water music" trickling in the basin outside your private room.

Culture: The Main Course

Sipping coffee at a sidewalk café on the Left Bank, you begin to feel what it means to be a Parisian. Slurping noodles on tatami in a neighborhood soba shop overlooking a tiny interior garden, you start to understand what it's like to live in Japan. Food, no matter which country you're in, has much to say about the culture as a whole.

Beyond the natural dictates of climate and geography, Japanese food has its roots in the centuries-old cuisine of the Imperial Court, which was imported from China—a religiously formal style of meal called *yusoku ryōri*. It was prepared only by specially appointed chefs, who had the status of priests in the service of the emperor, in a culinary ritual that is now nearly a lost art. Although it was never popularly served in centuries past (a modified version can still be found in Kyōto), much of the ceremony and careful attention to detail of yusoku ryōri is reflected today in the formal kaiseki meal.

Kaiseki Ryōri: Japanese Haute Cuisine

Kaiseki refers to the most elegant of all styles of Japanese food available today, and *ryōri* means cuisine. With its roots in the banquet feasts of the aristocracy, by the late 16th century it had developed into a meal to accompany ceremonial tea. The word kaiseki refers to a heated stone (*seki*) that Buddhist monks placed inside the folds (*kai*) of their kimonos to keep off the biting cold in the unheated temple halls where they slept and meditated.

Cha-kaiseki, as the formal meal served with tea (*cha*) is called, is intended to take the edge off your hunger at the beginning of a formal tea ceremony and to counterbalance the astringent character of the thick green tea. In the tea ceremony, balance—and the sense of calmness and well-being it inspires—is the keynote.

The formula for the basic Japanese meal derived originally from the rules governing formal kaiseki—not too large a portion, just enough; not too spicy, but perhaps with a savory sprig of trefoil to offset the bland tōfu. A grilled dish is served before a steamed one, a steamed dish before a simmered one; a square plate is used for a round food; a bright green maple leaf is placed to one side to herald the arrival of spring.

Kaiseki ryōri appeals to all the senses at once. An atmosphere is created in which the meal is to be experienced. The poem in calligraphy on a hanging scroll and the flowers in the alcove set the seasonal theme, a motif picked up in the pattern of the dishware chosen for the evening. The colors and shapes of the vessels complement the foods served on them. The visual harmony presented is as vital as the balance and variety of flavors of the foods themselves, for which the ultimate criterion is freshness. The finest ryōtei will never serve a fish or vegetable out of its proper season—no matter how marvelous a winter melon today's modern greenhouses can guarantee. Melons are for rejoicing in the summer's bounty . . . period.

Kaiseki ryōri found its way out of the formal tearooms and into a much earthier realm of the senses when it became the fashionable snack with sake in the teahouses of the geisha quarters during the 17th and 18th centuries. Not only the atmosphere but the Chinese characters used to write the word *kaiseki* are different in this context; they refer to aristocratic "banquet seats." And banquets they are. To partake in the most exclusive of these evenings in a teahouse in Kyōto still requires a personal introduction and a great deal of money, though these days many traditional restaurants offer elegant kaiseki meals (without the geisha) at much more reasonable prices.

One excellent way to experience this incomparable cuisine on a budget is to visit a kaiseki restaurant at lunchtime. Many of them offer *kaiseki bentō* lunches at a fraction of the dinner price, exquisitely presented in lacquered boxes, as a sampler of their full-course evening meal.

Shōjin Ryōri: Zen-Style Vegetarian Cuisine

Like an overnight stay in a Buddhist temple, *shōjin ryōri* is the Zen-style vegetarian cuisine. In traditional Japanese cuisine, the emphasis is on the natural flavor of the freshest ingredients in season, without the embellishment of heavy spices and rich sauces. This probably developed out of the Zen belief in the importance of simplicity and austerity as paths to enlightenment. Protein is provided by an almost limitless number of dishes made from soybeans—such as *yu-dōfu*, or boiled bean curd, and *yuba*, sheets of pure protein skimmed from vats of steaming soy milk. The variety and visual beauty of a full-course shōjin ryōri meal offer new dimensions in dining to the vegetarian gourmet. *Goma-dōfu*, or sesame-flavored bean curd, for example, is a delicious taste treat, as is *nasu-dengaku*, grilled eggplant covered with a sweet *miso* sauce.

There are many fine restaurants (particularly in the Kyōto area) that specialize in shōjin ryōri, but it's best to seek out one of the many temples throughout Japan that open their doors to visitors; here you can try these special meals within the actual temple halls, which often overlook a traditional garden.

Sushi, Sukiyaki, Tempura, and Nabemono: A Comfortable Middle Ground

Leaving the rarefied atmosphere of teahouses and temples behind, an entire realm of more down-to-earth gastronomic pleasures waits to be explored.

Sushi, sukiyaki, and tempura are probably the three most commonly known Japanese dishes in the Western world. Restaurants serving these dishes are to be found in abundance in every major hotel in Japan. It is best, however, to try each of these in a place that specializes in just one.

An old Japanese proverb says "*Mochi wa mochi-ya e*"—if you want rice cakes, go to a rice-cake shop. The same goes for sushi. Sushi chefs undergo a lengthy apprenticeship, and the trade is considered an art form. Possessing the discipline of a judo player, the *itamae-san* (or "man before . . . or behind . . . the counter," depending on your point of view) at a sushi-ya is a real master. Every neighborhood has its own sushi shop, and everyone you meet has his or her own secret little place to go for sushi.

The Tsukiji Fish Market district in Tōkyō is so popular for its sushi shops that you usually have to wait in line for a seat at the counter. Some are quite expensive, while some are relatively cheap. "Know before you go" is the best policy; "Ask before you eat" is next.

Among the dozens of kinds of sushi available, some of the most popular are *maguro* (tuna), *ebi* (shrimp), *hamachi* (yellowtail), *uni* (sea urchin), *anago* (conger eel), *tako* (octopus), and *awabi* (abalone), and *akagai* (red shellfish). The day's selection is usually displayed in a glass case at the counter, which enables you to point at whatever catches your eye.

Tempura, the battered and deep-fried fish and vegetable dish, is almost certain to taste better at a small shop that serves nothing else. The difficulties of preparing this seemingly simple dish lie in achieving the proper consistency of the batter and the right temperature and freshness of the oil in which it is fried.

Sukiyaki is the popular beef dish that is sautéed with vegetables in an iron skillet at the table. The tenderness of the beef is the determining factor here, and many of the best sukiyaki houses also run their own butcher shops so that they can control the quality of the beef they serve. Although beef did not become a part of the Japanese diet until the turn of the century, the Japanese are justifiably proud of their notorious beer-fed and hand-massaged beef (e.g., the famous Matsuzaka beef from Kōbe, and the equally delicious Omi beef from Shiga Prefecture). Such a meal certainly is a splurge, but no one should pass up an opportunity to try a beef dinner in Japan.

Apart from sukiyaki and beef, *shabu-shabu* is another possibility, though this dish has become more popular with tourists than with the Japanese. It is similar to sukiyaki in that it is prepared at the table with a combination of vegetables, but it differs in that shabu-shabu is swished briefly in boiling water, while sukiyaki is sautéed in oil and, usually, a slightly sweetened soy sauce. The word *shabu-shabu* actually refers to this swishing sound.

Nabemono, or one-pot dishes, are not as familiar to Westerners as the three mentioned above, but the variety of possibilities is endless, and nothing tastes better on a cold winter's night. Simmered in a light, fish-base broth, these stews can be made of almost anything: chicken (*tori-nabe*), oysters (*kaki-nabe*), or the sumō wrestler's favorite, the hearty *chanko-nabe* . . . with something in it for everyone. Nabemono is a popular family or party dish. The restaurants specializing in nabemono often have a casual, country atmosphere.

Bentō, Soba, Udon, and Robatayaki: Feasting on a Budget

Tales of unsuspecting tourists swallowed up by money-gobbling monsters disguised as quaint little restaurants on the back streets of Japan's major cities abound in these days of the high yen. There are, however, many wonderful little places that offer excellent meals and thoughtful service—and have no intention of straining anyone's budget. To find them, you must not be afraid to venture outside your hotel lobby or worry about the fact that the dining spot has no menu in English. Many restaurants have menus posted out front that clearly state the full price you can expect to pay. (Some do add on a 10% tax, and possibly a service charge, so ask in advance.)

Here are a few suggestions for Japanese meals that do not cost a fortune and are usually a lot more fun than relying on the familiar but unexciting international fast-food chains for quick meals on a budget: *bentō* (box lunches), *soba* or *udon* (noodle) dishes, and the faithful neighborhood *robatayaki* (grills), ad infinitum.

The Bentō. This is the traditional Japanese box lunch, available for takeout everywhere, and usually comparatively inexpensive. It can be purchased in the morning to be taken along and eaten later, either outdoors or on the train as you travel between cities. The bentō consists of rice, pickles, grilled fish or meat, and vegetables, in an almost limitless variety of combinations to suit the season.

The basement levels of most major department stores sell beautifully prepared bentō to go. In fact, a department-store basement is a great place to sample and purchase the whole range of foods offered in Japan: Among the things available are French bread, imported cheeses, traditional bean cakes, chocolate bonbons, barbecued chicken, grilled eel, roasted peanuts, fresh vegetables, potato salads, pickled bamboo shoots, and smoked salmon.

The *o-bentō* (the "o" is honorific) in its most elaborate incarnation is served in gorgeous, multilayered lacquered boxes as an accompaniment to outdoor tea ceremonies or for flower-viewing parties held in spring. Exquisite *bentō-bako* (lunch boxes) made in the Edo period (1603–1868) can be found in museums and antiques shops. They are inlaid with mother-of-pearl and delicately hand-painted in gold. A wide variety of sizes and shapes of bentō boxes are still handmade in major cities and small villages throughout Japan in both formal and informal styles. They make excellent souvenirs.

A major benefit to the bentō is its portability. Sightseeing can take you down many an unexpected path, and you need not worry about finding an appropriate place to stop for a bite to eat—if you bring your own bentō. No Japanese family would ever be without one tucked carefully inside their rucksacks right beside the thermos bottle of tea on a cross-country train trip. If they do somehow run out of time to prepare one in advance—no problem—there are hundreds of wonderful options in the form of the beloved *eki-ben* ("train-station box lunch").

Each whistle-stop in Japan takes great pride in the uniqueness and flavor of the special box lunches, featuring the local delicacy, sold right at the station or from vendors inside the trains. The pursuit of the eki-ben has become a national pastime in this nation in love with its trains. Entire books have been written in Japanese explaining the features of every different eki-ben available along the 26,000 km (16,120 mi) of railways in the country. This is one of the best ways to sample the different styles of regional cooking in Japan and is highly recommended to any traveler who plans to spend time on the Japan Railway trains (☞ Regional Differences, *below*).

Soba and Udon. Soba and udon (noodle) dishes are another life-saving treat for stomachs (and wallets) unaccustomed to exotic flavors (and prices). Small shops serving soba (thin, brown buckwheat noodle) and udon (thick, white-wheat noodle) dishes in a variety of combinations can be found in every neighborhood in the country. Both can be ordered plain (ask for *o-soba* or *o-udon*), in a lightly seasoned broth flavored with bonito and soy sauce, or in combination with things like tempura shrimp (*tempura soba* or *udon*) or chicken (*tori-namba soba* or *udon*). For a refreshing change in summer, try *zaru soba,* cold noodles to be dipped in a tangy soy sauce. *Nabeyaki-udon* is a hearty winter dish of udon noodles, assorted vegetables, and egg served in the pot in which it was cooked.

Robatayaki. Perhaps the most exuberant of inexpensive options is the robatayaki (grill). Beer mug in hand, elbow-to-elbow at the counter of one of these popular neighborhood grills—that is the best way to relax and join in with the local fun. You'll find no pretenses here, just a wide variety of plain, good food (as much or as little as you want) with the proper amount of alcohol to get things rolling.

Robata means fireside, and the style of cooking is reminiscent of old-fashioned Japanese farmhouse meals cooked over a charcoal fire in an open hearth. It's easy to order at a robatayaki shop, because the selection of food to be grilled is lined up behind glass at the counter. Fish, meat, vegetables, tōfu—take your pick. Some popular choices are *yaki-zakana* (grilled fish), particularly *karei-shio-yaki* (salted and grilled flounder) and *asari saka-mushi* (clams simmered in sake, Japanese rice wine). Try the grilled Japanese *shiitake* (mushrooms), *ao-to* (green peppers), and the *hiyayakko* (chilled tōfu sprinkled with bonito flakes, diced green onions, and soy sauce). Yakitori can be ordered in most robatayaki shops, though many inexpensive drinking places specialize in this popular barbecued chicken dish.

The budget dining possibilities in Japan don't stop there. **Okonomiyaki** is another choice. Somewhat misleadingly called the Japanese pancake, it is actually a mixture of vegetables, meat, and seafood in an egg-and-flour batter grilled at your table, much better with beer than with butter. It's most popular for lunch or as an after-movie snack.

Another is **kushi-age,** skewered bits of meat, seafood, and vegetables battered, dipped in bread crumbs, and deep-fried. There are many small restaurants serving only kushi-age at a counter, and many of the robatayaki serve it as a sideline. It's also a popular drinking snack.

Oden, a winter favorite, is another inexpensive meal. A variety of meats and vegetables slowly simmered in vats, it goes well with beer or sake. This, too, you may order piece by piece (*ippin*) from the assortment you see steaming away behind the counter, or *moriawase,* in which case the cook will serve you up an assortment.

Sake: The Samurai Beverage

With all this talk about eating and drinking, it would be an unforgivable transgression to overlook Japan's number one alcoholic beverage, *sake* (pronounced *sa-kay*), the "beverage of the samurai," as one brewery puts it. The ancient myths call this rice wine the "drink of the gods," and there are more than 2,000 different brands produced throughout Japan. A lifetime of serious scene-of-the-crime research would be necessary to explore all the possibilities and complexities of this interesting drink.

Like other kinds of wine, sake comes in sweet (*amakuchi*) and dry (*karakuchi*) varieties; these are graded *tokkyū* (superior class), *ikkyū* (first class), and *nikkyū* (second class) and are priced accordingly. (Connoisseurs say this ranking is for tax purposes and is not necessarily a true indication of quality.)

Best drunk at room temperature (*nurukan*) so as not to alter the flavor, sake is also served heated (*atsukan*) or with ice (*rokku de*). It is poured from *tokkuri* (small ceramic vessels) into tiny cups called *choko*. The diminutive size of these cups shouldn't mislead you into thinking you can't drink too much. The custom of making sure that your drinking companion's cup never runs dry often leads the novice astray.

Junmaishu is the term for pure rice wine, a blend of rice, yeast, and water to which no extra alcohol has been added. Junmaishu has the strongest and most distinctive flavor, compared with various other methods of brewing, and is preferred by the sake *tsu,* as connoisseurs are known.

Apart from the *nomiya* (bars) and restaurants, the place to sample sake is the *izakaya,* a drinking establishment that serves only sake, usually dozens of different kinds, including a selection of *jizake,* the kind produced in limited quantities by small regional breweries throughout the country.

Regional Differences

Tōkyō people are known for their candor and vigor, as compared with the refined restraint of people in the older, more provincial Kyōto. This applies as much to food as it does to language, art, and fashion. Foods in the Kansai district (including Kyōto, Nara, Ōsaka, and Kōbe) tend to be lighter, the sauces less spicy, the soups not as hardy as those of the Kantō district, of which Tōkyō is the center. How many Tōkyōites have been heard to grumble about the "weak" soba broth on their visits to Kyōto? You go to Kyōto for the delicate and formal kaiseki, to Tōkyō for sushi.

Nigiri-sushi, with pieces of raw fish on bite-size balls of rice (the form with which most Westerners are familiar), originated in the Kantō district, where there is a bounty of fresh fish. *Saba-sushi* is the specialty of landlocked Kyōto. Actually the forerunner of nigiri-sushi, it is made by pressing salt-preserved mackerel onto a bed of rice in a mold.

Every island in the Japanese archipelago has its specialty, and, within each island, every province has its own *meibutsu ryōri,* or specialty dish. In Kyūshū, try *shippoku-ryōri,* a banquet-style feast of different dishes in which you eat your way up to a large fish mousse topped with shrimp. This dish is the local specialty in Nagasaki, for centuries the only port through which Japan had contact with the West.

On the island of Shikoku, try *sawachi-ryōri,* an extravaganza of elaborately prepared platters of fresh fish dishes, which is the specialty of Kōchi, the main city on the Pacific Ocean side of the island. In Hokkaidō, where salmon dishes are the local specialty, try *ishikari-nabe,* a hearty salmon-and-vegetable stew.

The Bottom Line

There are a couple of things that take some getting used to. Things will be easier for you in Japan if you've had some experience with chopsticks. Some of the tourist-oriented restaurants (and, of course, all those serving Western food) provide silverware, but most traditional restaurants in Japan offer only chopsticks. It's a good idea to practice. The secret is to learn to move only the chopstick on top rather than to try to move both chopsticks at once.

Sitting on the floor is another obstacle for many, including the younger generation of Japanese to whom the prospect of sitting on a cushion on tatami mats for an hour or so means nothing but stiff knees and numb feet. Because of this, many restaurants now have rooms with tables and chairs. The most traditional restaurants, however, have kept to the customary style of dining in tatami rooms. Give it a try. Nothing can compare with a full-course kaiseki meal brought to your room at a traditional inn. Fresh from the bath, robed in a cotton kimono, you are free to relax and enjoy it all, including the view. After all, the carefully landscaped garden outside your door was designed specifically to be seen from this position.

The service in Japan is usually superb, particularly at a *ryōri-ryokan,* as restaurant-inns are called. A maid is assigned to anticipate your every need (even a few you didn't know you had). "*O-kyakusan wa kamisama desu*" (the customer is god), as the old Japanese proverb goes. People who prefer to dine in privacy have been known to say the service is too much.

Other problems? "The portions are too small," is a common complaint. The solution is an adjustment in perspective. In the world of Japanese cuisine, there are colors to delight in, and shapes, textures, and flavors are balanced for your pleasure. Naturally, the aroma, flavor, and freshness of the foods have importance, but so do the dishware, the design of the room, the sound of water in a stone basin outside. You are meant to leave the table delighted—not stuffed. An appeal is made to all the senses through the food itself, the atmosphere, and appreciation for a carefully orchestrated feast in every sense of the word—these, and the luxury of time spent in the company of friends.

This is not to say that every Japanese restaurant offers aesthetic perfection. Your basic train-platform, stand-up, gulp-it-down noodle stall ("eat-and-out" in under six minutes) should leave no doubts as to the truth of the old saying that "all feet tread not in one shoe."

In the end, you'll discover that the joy of eating in Japan lies in the adventure of exploring the possibilities. Along every city street, you'll find countless little eateries specializing in anything you can name—and some you can't. In the major cities,

you'll find French restaurants, British pubs, and little places serving Italian, Chinese, Indian, and American food, if you need a change of pace. In country towns, you can explore a world of regional delicacies found nowhere else.

There is something for everyone and every budget—from the most exquisitely prepared and presented formal kaiseki meal to a delicately sculpted salmon mousse à la nouvelle cuisine, from skewers of grilled chicken in barbecue sauce to a steaming bowl of noodle soup at an outdoor stall. And much to the chagrin of culinary purists, Japan has no dearth of international fast-food chains—from burgers to spareribs to fried chicken to doughnuts to 31 flavors of American ice cream.

Sometimes the contradictions of this intriguing culture—as seen in the startling contrast between ancient traditions and modern industrial life—seem almost overwhelming. Who would ever have thought you could face salad with lettuce, tomatoes, and seaweed . . . or green-tea ice cream? As the famous potter Kawai Kanjiro once said, "Sometimes it's better if you don't understand everything. . . . It makes life so much more exciting."

Manners

- Don't point or gesture with chopsticks. Licking the ends of your chopsticks is rude, as is taking food from a common serving plate with the end of the chopstick you've had in your mouth.

- There is no taboo against slurping your noodle soup, though women are generally less boisterous about it than men.

- Pick up the soup bowl and drink directly from it, rather than leaning over the table to sip it. Take the fish or vegetables from it with your chopsticks. Return the lid to the soup bowl when you are finished. The rice bowl, too, is to be picked up and held in one hand while you eat from it.

- When drinking with a friend, don't pour your own. Take the bottle and pour for the other person. He will in turn reach for the bottle and pour for you. Japanese will attempt to top your drink off after every few sips.

- Japanese don't pour sauces on their rice in a traditional meal. Sauces are intended for dipping foods lightly, not for dunking or soaking.

- Among faux pas that are considered nearly unpardonable, the worst perhaps is blowing your nose. Excuse yourself and leave the room if this becomes necessary.

- Although McDonald's and Häagen-Dazs have made great inroads on the custom of never eating in public, it is still considered gauche to munch on a hamburger (or an ice cream cone) as you walk along a public street.

— Diane Durston

THE SPRINGS OF ECSTASY

If you're new to Japan, you might be astounded with the popularity of thermal baths in Japan. It begins to seem like the only way for a town to hope to bring in Japanese tourists is to have an *onsen*. In one sense, that is a geological coincidence. Top to bottom, the Pacific Rim boils with volcanic activity, from Hokkaidō to Hawaii to New Zealand. Quite naturally, the Japanese have developed a subculture around one of the more manageable manifestations of this powerful resource. We'll let Simon Winchester say the rest:

Of all the many and varied degrees of the sublime to which the modern Japanese may aspire, none quite compares with that known as *yudedako*. The word means, quite simply, boiled octopus, and Japanese of all ages and both sexes will journey for miles and search for days for the perfect place to become one.

They do so for the simple reason that the attainment of yudedako is—so everyone from Hokkaidō to Okinawa is led to believe from birth—a triumphal final step on the road to perfect physical health. It is an absolute essential for anyone ever hoping to achieve personal sobriety and mental serenity. It helps if you want to achieve marital harmony, to enjoy lifelong freedom from constipation and boils, to secure happiness, to have a clear skin and the faultless functioning of your sexual equipment, and to be rewarded with whatever else constitutes

the Shinto equivalent of earthly Nirvana.

And the best, indeed the only place in which to become like a boiled octopus, where yudedako is to be found (in exchange for a paltry sum in folding money), is that most hallowed of Japanese institutions, the hot spring, the *onsen*—of which, a cursory look at a good Japanese map will display, there are very, very many. The country, fissured from end to end with the cracks and crannies that are the geophysical consequence of being sited on a line of volcanoes, positively wheezes with steam and water. It gushes and sprays almost everywhere, in forest and glade, on meadowland and mountaintop. There are hot springs up in the snowfields. There are others on which float bananas and melon-size oranges. A mad-Ludwig look-alike has channeled one into a mountainside cable car, so you can steam as you fly. Monkeys will chatter and steal your towel from springs down south, while melting icicles will drip into boiling waterfalls up in Hokkaidō. Some waters are naturally bloodred and scented with hibiscus, while others are milky white with suspended sulfur—and smell understandably vile.

There are hundreds of them, in every prefecture, on every offshore island, even (hidden in office buildings and beside cinemas) in cities that have been built, incautiously, above the very fault lines themselves. And to all these superheated hollows flock the inhabitants of the empire in a ceaseless stream of enthusiasm. Small industries—in some towns, very large industries indeed—have sprung up around the onsen to cater to the needs of those who would plunge and soak and steam themselves in the *ofuro,* or baths. Some bath lovers confess to being ofuro-holics, and it's said that there are clinics set up to cater to their excess. "Their passion for hot bathing is proverbial, and no other people in the world take such pride in their sanitary arrangements," as a Government Railway Guide put it 50 years ago.

Modern lyricists go further. To understand the Japanese, they chorus, there is only one True Way: You must bathe with them. Go on in, they urge—the water's fine. Become a boiled octopus, and discern in your personal conversion alongside them their true nature, their inner soul—the *kokoro,* as the language has it, of the mysterious people of Nippon.

Why not indeed? Well, one reason many Westerners—*gai-jin*, as the Japanese rather smoothly call everyone who is not one of them—prefer not to take time out to go bathing in Japan is the understanding that you have to, er, take all your clothes off. *In front of them*. And you *know* they will stare at your body, quite probably finding it a good deal less lovely than their own. They may even laugh or snigger behind their hands.

Furthermore, there are stories of terrible Asian protocols involved in bathing—a series of unwritten and unspoken rules known by every Japanese from conception, the careless breaking of any of which would result in the most frightful retribution. "What if I drop the soap in the ofuro?" is a typical fear. And so most innocent wanderers through Japan, invited to go bathing, prefer to stay snug inside their Hiltons and their Tokyus, mumbling excuses about the nearest onsen being too far, their schedule being too tight, or their being quite clean enough anyway, and thanks very much for asking.

I am not an ofuroholic, nor do I entirely hold to the view that the Japanese are an enigmatic master race knowable only by those who watch them wash. But on the other hand, hot-spring bathing, I have discovered, is enormous fun, and in certain places at certain times it can be truly memorable, the stuff that dreams are made on. So, in the fond hope that others may share the enthusiasm, what follows is a brief illustration of what to do and how to do it and, to a very limited extent, where.

In my case, my first bath was taken at a place in eastern Kyūshū called Yufu-in; and while there are scores of other springs well within the purview of Tōkyō and Ōsaka and Kyōto, readily accessible to the timorous or the city-bound, it is to Yufu-in I will journey, since its memory lingers most poignant.

It was an autumn morning. I caught the Shinkansen from Tōkyō westward to Hakata and was thus hurled in hyperdrive between Honshu and Kyūshū, arriving at the vast station of Shin-Hakata at the predicted split second. A quick scurry along platforms, down flights of granite stairs, along passageways bright with colored neon and robotic salesgirls and the *Blade Runner* twitterings of computer-generated messages, then up more granite stairways to where, slightly dusty and forlorn, stood a country train!

This was an antique that had old leather and fur where the Shinkansen had polished steel and ripstop nylon, and it creaked and swayed as it moved out over the switches. And while the bullet train had vanished bloodlessly into tunnels and darted through arrow-straight cuttings, this old dear rumbled arthritically around curves and over trestle bridges, up and ever upward until it was in the heart of the hills, where the maple trees brushed the windows and the waterfalls splashed the carriage walls. The divine wind—the infamous *kamikaze* that had once scattered Kublai Khan's fleet in Hakata Bay—may have blown stiffly down at sea level: Up here it was still, and clouds stood unmoving by the mountaintops.

The stations slipped by. Moderate-size cities such as Futsukaichi and Kurume, where they make patterned cloths and rubberware. Small towns beside river crossings, with pottery factories and paper mills. And then little clusters of houses—Era and Bungomori and Bungo-Nakamura—where I first spied the telltale signs of seismic waters. In the pine forests behind each hamlet there were wisps of steam rising into the still air, like New York avenues at night and Con Edison is at work, so rural Japan is a place of steam, hissing and bubbling out of the very earth.

And then the train eased into Yufu-in and creaked to a halt on a curve. It was warm, and there was a smell of creosote and pine tar, and a hint of sulfur in the air. After a few moments the train pulled away, and the station yard fell silent but for the cawing of a pair of crows high up in a tree. An old lady stepped from the shade, nudged me, and pointed to a crowd of bicycles for rent; ¥500 until nightfall, she suggested. I handed over the notes, she handed me a map, and on a cycle frame 10 sizes too small I wobbled off into town.

The woman had drawn crosses on the chart to indicate the best baths, but I had a guide with me, a young secretary from Fukuoka who hadn't been to an onsen for weeks and had said she was happy to swap her linguistic expertise for an hour or two of soaking. And so the pair of us headed south along a country lane, bound for a *ryokan*—a Japanese inn—called Kozenin.

There seemed to be no one about. The small dining room stood quite empty except for a stuffed boar standing by a table. But a wood fire smoldered quietly in an open grate, and a discreet cough brought an ancient attendant from behind a screen. She bowed low many times, and there was some conversation from which I caught only the word *furo*, then many *dōmo arigato gozaimashita* and much more low bowing and smiling. Then the two of us were handed *yukata*—cotton dressing gowns—and a pair of tiny squares of tie-dyed cloth called *furoshiki*. We walked outside again, down a graveled path through a small grove of pines, before coming to a pair of doors set in a plane-tree palisade. "A *rotemburo*," Yoko whispered. "Open-air pool. We're lucky."

My *kanji* is poor at the best of times, but I have become accustomed to the fact that the ideograph of "men" looks a sight more complicated than that for "women." So I pointed at what I thought was my door, Yoko grinned her assent, and we went our separate ways.

Inside was a changing room: flagstones worn smooth by centuries of use, stripped-oak walls, a few old iron hooks, a hand pump, some bamboo hand-dippers, half a dozen tiny stools with commodelike openings on top, and a wooden box filled with bars of industrial-strength soap. Beyond, all I could see was steam rising from the surface of what seemed a long and pretty lake that reached deep into the forest. This was the *rotemburo* itself; other springs at Yufu-in might be indoors, but this one was in as natural a setting as its Shinto gods had decreed. I could hear the gurgling of water running into it along bamboo gutters. It was all very peaceful and—mercifully—there seemed to be no one around.

I slipped off my yukata and put it on a hook. For a few seconds, and lest anyone should be lurking, I held my *taoru* ("*ta-o-ru*," towel), with studied casualness, in the approximate area that is always fuzzed-out in Japanese sex films. Then I pumped water into the hand-dipper, took a bar of Lifebuoy, carried my stool down to the edge of the lake, and began to scrub.

This, I had been told, was crucial. Wash and scrub and soap and scrape every square millimeter of your body until not one molecule of grubbiness remains. And this I did, pummeling myself ruthlessly, determined to get it right. "How you doing?" shouted Yoko from behind her bamboo curtain. I replied, breathlessly, that I was doing all I should be doing, and it seemed to be going well.

"Not a drop of soapy water in the bath!" she warned, and I baled and sluiced frantically as one small trickle of foaming liquid seemed to course its errant way toward the steam. But most onsen seem to have been designed by hydraulic architects of some skill: It would take a clumsy fellow indeed to get soapy water into the ofuro, so many and so effective are the little dams of stone erected everywhere as a precaution. The only way to pollute the bath is to get into it unbathed, unrinsed, or, heaven forfend, while holding and planning to use the soap itself. And that you never, never do. As Yoko, in one final reminder, called out.

"Ready?" she then asked. And I heard a splash and a sudden gasp of pleasure. She was in.

Now came the difficult bit. I was clean as a new pin, my skin tingled from the spring water, every atom of saponified glycerin long gone. I dropped my taoru completely and walked across smooth humps of granite to the edge. I dipped my toe into the steaming bath. The water was hot, indeed, but at the same time so extraordinarily soft that there seemed no pain in going farther. I stepped onto a rock slab, gasped at the slight shock, then walked forward to a deeper slab. The water rose steadily about me until it was waist-deep.

"Come on!" urged Yoko, who was, quite unashamedly, watching the entire performance. I could see her now through the mist, her head and shoulders just above the water that beached and lapped against the swell of her breasts. The outline of her body below was refracted out of any recognition too precise for decency.

The only way to retain my own dignity as she watched was to submerge, and so I pitched forward and down and sat as gently as I could on a convenient boulder. Yoko was a few feet away. I smiled at her and she smiled back. She touched my toe with one of hers, then moved toward me slightly and began to massage my foot with both of her naked legs. I closed my eyes and, content and warm and blanketed in the pleasing softness of the water, began to think of paradise.

When I opened my eyes—perhaps 5 or 10 minutes later—I was looking up at the deep blue sky. It was framed by dozens of maple trees, their leaves brilliant red and yellow after the first frosts of autumn. Once in a while one would dislodge, then drop and float, curling in the heat, on the surface of the bath. The air above the pool was cooler now—it was late afternoon, the sun was dipping behind Yufu-san (Mt. Yufu), and flocks of birds were flying back to their nests.

The bath steamed even more vigorously in the cool of the gloaming, and the bamboo runnels carrying the source water from the springs seemed to froth with new energy. Sitting beneath one of these proved a scalding reminder of what high temperature is all about: Yoko sat gaily beneath one for a good minute and then shouted triumphantly: "*Yudedako!*" I looked over at her; she had turned a bright red, like—well, just like a boiled octopus, though minus half a dozen arms. And as I looked down I seemed to be going the same way.

So out we climbed, she careless of the looks, me still taking care to avoid the gazes of the few children who had come in while I dozed. But none of them seemed more than mildly curious; no one seemed to mind, let alone to giggle. "*Hadaka to hadaka no tsukiai*" ("Relationships between naked people are honest relationships"), they say—bathing friends are the best of friends, the bath becomes a great equalizer, no one is more curious than he should be, no one ever behaves such as to spoil the enjoyment of any other bather, no one is embarrassed nor causes embarrassment.

And in that particular sense the bath is Japan, and the lyricists are right. For the manners of the Japanese, lately so corrupted in the cities and by the boardrooms, seem to revert to their impeccable type in the unalloyed egalitarianism of the onsen. Here, rank and title, riches and power, are stripped away with the clothes: There is no way to tell if the body lolling beside you belongs to the boss of Mitsubishi, to an ambassador, to a pauper, to a mendicant priest. With rank neither claimed nor recognized, each bather offers to the other an equal degree of respect and regard.

Then again, a man is well aware in a mixed-sex bath—like this one in Yufu-in—that naked women are all about him, yet the eroticism this induces is only of the mildest form, and all is diminished by the perfect decorum. For above all, decorum and studied delight rule the protocols of bathing—you seek pleasure from the waters, and you ensure that those about you are allowed to seek it too. Small wonder so few psychiatrists find employment in Japan. The onsen to which the Japanese repair each week or each month or every six months seem marvelous devices for purging the soul of envy and anxiety and stress, as well (it is claimed) as for curing all known ills, cleansing the liver and the brain, ensuring potency and attractiveness, long life—and wealth of spirit, if not necessarily of pocket.

And thus we spent the remainder of that autumn evening. We emerged from the first bath, toweled ourselves briskly dry, and cycled to another, and another, until it got too dark to see and we feared we might miss the last train. We sampled iron springs with red water; we found silky-smooth alkali springs that gushed forth *unagi*, or "eel water"; and Yoko knew of a tiny *harinoyu*, or "needle bath," which felt like immersing into a tub filled with small and very hot hedgehogs, and yet was much more pleasant than it sounds.

But in Yufu-in there were no mud baths nor radioactive sand baths, no seaside baths, not a single bath in a cable car, nor any of the astonishingly hot *atsu-yu*, where men with paddles slap at the water to try to keep it from boiling, and where there are Bath Masters to make sure you stay only for the three minutes needed to attain yudedako, and not a fatal second longer. For all these delights I had to wait for other places, other springs.

We caught the train at 10, having dined before a log fire and drunk deep of hot sake and Sapporo beer. The cycle lady was still there, waiting in the starlight, and she smiled as we climbed aboard the old train. She said something to Yoko as we left, and both women laughed. I asked what it was. "The *gai-jin* looks younger," said Yoko. "A very young boiled octopus. Very good, don't you think? Very good."

— Simon Winchester

JAPAN AT A GLANCE: A CHRONOLOGY

10,000–300   Neolithic Jōmon hunting and fishing culture leaves richly decorated pottery.

AD 300   Yayoi culture displays knowledge of farming and metallurgy imported from Korea.

after 300   The Yamato tribe consolidates power in the rich Kansai plain and expands westward, forming the kind of military aristocratic society that was to dominate Japan's history.

ca. 500   Yamato leaders, claiming to be descended from the sun goddess, Amaterasu, take the title of emperor.

538–552   Buddhism, introduced to the Yamato court from China by way of Korea, complements rather than replaces the indigenous Shintō religion.

593–622   Prince Shōtoku encourages the Japanese to embrace Chinese culture and has Buddhist temple Hōryū-ji built at Nara in 607. (Its existing buildings are among the oldest surviving wooden structures in the world.)

Nara Period
710–784   Japan has first permanent capital at Nara; great age of Buddhist sculpture, piety, and poetry.

Fujiwara or Heian (Peace) Period
794–1160   The capital is moved from Nara to Heian-kyō (now Kyōto), where the imperial court is dominated by the Fujiwara family. Lady Murasaki's novel *The Tale of Genji*, written c. 1020, describes the elegance and political maneuvering of court life.

Kamakura Period
1185–1335   Feudalism enters, with military and economic power in the provinces and the emperor a powerless, ceremonial figurehead in Kyōto. Samurai warriors welcome Zen, a new sect of Buddhism from China.

1192   After a war with the Taira family, Yoritomo of the Minamoto family becomes the first shōgun; he places his capital in Kamakura.

1274, 1281   The fleets sent by Chinese emperor Kublai Khan to invade Japan are destroyed by typhoons, praised in Japanese history as *kamikaze,* or divine wind.

Ashikaga Period
1336–1568   The Ashikaga family assumes the title of shōgun and settles in Kyōto. The Zen aesthetic flourishes in painting, landscape gardening, and tea ceremony. Nō theater emerges. The Silver Pavilion on Ginkaku-ji in Kyōto, built in 1483, is the quintessential example of Zen-inspired architecture. The period is marked by constant warfare but also by increased trade with the mainland. Ōsaka develops into an important commercial city, and trade guilds appear.

1467–1477   The Ōnin Wars that wrack Kyōto initiate a 100-year period of civil war.

1543   Portuguese sailors, the first Europeans to reach Japan, initiate trade relations with the lords of western Japan and introduce the musket, which changes Japanese warfare.

1549–1551   St. Francis Xavier, the first Jesuit missionary, introduces Christianity.

Momoyama Period of National Unification

1568–1600 Two generals, Nobunaga Oda and Hideyoshi Toyotomi, are the central figures of this period. Nobunaga builds a military base from which Hideyoshi unifies Japan.

1592, 1597 Hideyoshi invades Korea. He brings back Korean potters, who rapidly develop a Japanese ceramic industry.

The Tokugawa Period

1600–1868 Ieyasu Tokugawa becomes shōgun after the battle of Sekigahara. The military capital is established at Edo (now Tōkyō), which shows phenomenal economic and cultural growth. A hierarchical order of four social classes—warriors, farmers, artisans, then merchants—is rigorously enforced. The merchant class, however, is increasingly prosperous and effects a transition from a rice to a money economy. Merchants patronize new, popular forms of art: Kabuki, haiku, and the ukiyo-e school of painting. The life of the latter part of this era is beautifully illustrated in the wood-block prints of the artist Hokusai (1760–1849).

1618 Japanese Christians who refuse to renounce their foreign religion are persecuted.

1637–1638 Japanese Christians massacred in the Shimabara uprising. Japan is closed to the outside world except for a Dutch trading post in Nagasaki harbor.

1853 U.S. Commodore Matthew Perry reopens Japan to foreign trade.

The Meiji Restoration

1868–1912 Opponents of the weakened Tokugawa shogunate support Emperor Meiji and overthrow the last shōgun. The emperor is "restored" (with little actual power), and the imperial capital is moved to Edo, which is renamed Tōkyō (Eastern Capital). Japan is modernized along Western lines with a constitution proclaimed in 1889; a system of compulsory education and a surge of industrialization follow.

1902–1905 Japan defeats Russia in the Russo-Japanese War and achieves world-power status.

1910 Japan annexes Korea.

1914–1918 Japan joins the Allies in World War I.

1923 The Great Kantō Earthquake shakes Tōkyō and Yokohama.

1931 As a sign of growing militarism in the country, Japan seizes the Chinese province of Manchuria.

1937 Following years of increasing military and diplomatic activity in northern China, open warfare breaks out (and lasts until 1945); Chinese Nationalists and Communists both fight Japan.

1939–1945 Japan, having signed anti-Communist treaties with Nazi Germany and Italy (1936 and 1937), invades and occupies French Indochina.

1941 The Japanese attack on Pearl Harbor on December 7 brings the United States into war against Japan in the Pacific.

1942 Japan's empire extends to Indochina, Burma, Malaya, the Philippines, and Indonesia. Japan bombs Darwin, Australia. U.S. defeat of Japanese forces at Midway turns the tide of the Pacific war.

1945 Tōkyō and 50 other Japanese cities are devastated by U.S. bombing raids. The United States drops atomic bombs on Hiroshima and Nagasaki in August, precipitating Japanese surrender.

1945–1952 The American occupation under General Douglas MacArthur disarms Japan and encourages the establishment of a democratic government. Emperor Hirohito retains his position.

1953 After the Korean War, Japan begins a period of great economic growth.

1964 Tōkyō hosts the Summer Olympic games.

late 1960s Japan develops into one of the major industrial nations in the world.

mid-1970s Production of electronics, cars, cameras, and computers places Japan at the heart of the emerging "Pacific Rim" economic sphere and threatens to spark a trade war with the industrial nations of Europe and the United States.

1989 Emperor Hirohito dies.

1990 Coronation of Emperor Akihito. Prince Fumihito marries Kiko Kawashima.

1992 The Diet approves use of Japanese military forces under United Nations auspices.

1993 Crown Prince Naruhito marries Masako Owada.

1995 A massive earthquake strikes Kōbe and environs. Approximately 5,500 people are killed and 35,000 injured; more than 100,000 buildings are destroyed.

Members of a fringe religious organization carry out a series of poison-gas attacks on the transportation networks of Tōkyō and Yokohama, undermining, in a society that is a model of decorum and mutual respect, confidence in personal safety.

1997 The deregulation of rice prices and the appearance of discount gasoline stations marks a turn in the Japanese economy toward genuine privatization. These small indications constituted a major break from traditional price control policies that supported small merchants and producers.

BOOKS AND VIDEOS

Books

The incredible refinement of Japanese culture has produced a wealth of astonishing literature. Yet where, in the face of thousands of books, should you begin? If you are a newcomer to the subject of Japan, start with Pico Iyer's *The Lady and the Monk,* which will charm you through the first five phases of stereotypical infatuation with Japan and leave you with five times as many insights. Then read Seichō Matsumoto's *Inspector Imanishi Investigates,* a superb detective novel that says volumes about Japanese life (make a list of characters' names as you read to keep them straight). As fearsome a topic as it is, the atomic bombing of Hiroshima, as told by John Hersey in his *Hiroshima,* is essential reading both about Japan and about our century. The book is utterly engrossing both as a human story and for what it tells of the Japanese in particular.

Fiction and Poetry

The great classic of Japanese fiction is the *Tale of Genji*; Genji, or the Shining Prince, has long been taken as the archetype of ideal male behavior. The novel was written by a woman of the court, Murasaki Shikibu, around the year 1000. If the

1,000-plus-page complete edition is too daunting, there is an abridged version as well. From the same period, Japan's Golden Age, *The Pillow Book of Sei Shonagon* is the stylish and stylized diary of a woman's courtly life.

The Edo period is well covered by literary translations. Howard Hibbett's *Floating World in Japanese Fiction* gives an excellent selection with commentaries. The racy prose of late-17th-century Saikaku Ihara is translated in various books, including *Some Final Words of Advice* and *Five Women Who Loved Love.*

Modern Japanese fiction is more widely available in translation. One of the best-known writers among Westerners is Yukio Mishima, author of *The Sea of Fertility* trilogy, among many other works. His books often deal with the effects of postwar Westernization on Japanese culture. Two superb prose stylists are Junchirō Tanizaki, author of *The Makioka Sisters, Some Prefer Nettles,* and the racy 1920s *Quicksand*; and Nobel Prize winner Yasunari Kawabata, whose superbly written novels include *Snow Country* and *The Sound of the Mountain.* Kawabata's *Thousand Cranes*, which uses the tea ceremony as a vehicle, is an elegant page-turner. Jiro Osaragi's *The Journey* is a lucid, entertaining rendering of the clash of tradition and modernity in postwar Japan. Also look for Natsume Sōseki's charming *Botchan* and delightful *I Am a Cat.*

Other novelists and works of note are Kobo Abe, whose *Woman in the Dunes* is a 1960s landmark, and Shusaku Endō, who brutally and breathlessly treated the early clash of Japan with Christianity in *The Samurai.*

There are no less-interesting novelists at work in Japan today. Fumiko Enchi's *Masks* poignantly explores the fascinating public-private dichotomy. Hiroki Murakami's *Wild Sheep Chase* is a wild ride indeed; his short stories are often bizarre and humorous, with a touch of the science-fictive thrown in for good measure. Along with Murakami's books, Banana Yoshimoto's *Kitchen* and other novels are probably the most fun you'll have with any Japanese fiction. Kōno Taeko's *Toddler-Hunting* and Yūko Tsushima's *The Shooting Gallery* are as engrossing and well crafted as they are frank about the burdens of tradition on Japanese women

today. Nobel Prize winner Kenzaburo Ōe's writing similarly explores deeply personal issues, among them his compelling relationship with his disabled son.

Haiku, the 5-7-5 syllable form that the monk Matsuo Bashō honed in the 17th century, is the flagship of Japanese poetry. His *Narrow Road to the Deep North* is a wistful prose-and-poem travelogue that is available in a few translations. But there are many more forms and authors worth exploring. Three volumes of translations by Kenneth Rexroth include numerous authors' work from the last 1,000 years: *One Hundred Poems from the Japanese, 100 More Poems from the Japanese,* and *Women Poets of Japan* (translated with Akiko Atsumi). Each has notes and brief author biographies. *Ink Dark Moon,* translated by Jane Hirshfield with Mariko Aratani, presents the remarkable poems of Ono no Komachi and Izumi Shikibu, two of Japan's earliest women poets. The Zen poems of Ryokan represent the sacred current in Japanese poetry; look for *Dew Drops on a Lotus Leaf.* Other poets to look for are Issa, Buson, and Bonchō. Two fine small volumes that link their haiku with those of other poets, including Bashō, are *The Monkey's Raincoat* and the beautifully illustrated *A Net of Fireflies.*

Another way into Japanese culture is riding on the heels of Westerners who live in Japan. The emotional realities of such experience are engagingly rendered in *The Broken Bridge: Fiction from Expatriates in Literary Japan.*

Travel Narratives

Two travel narratives stand out as superb introductions to Japanese history, culture, and people. Donald Richie's classic *The Inland Sea* recalls his journey and encounters on the fabled Seto Nai-kai. Leila Philip's year working in a Kyūshū pottery village became the eloquent *Road Through Miyama.*

History and Society

Fourteen hundred years of history is rather a lot to take in when going on a vacation, but two good surveys make the task much easier: Richard Storry's *A History of Modern Japan* (by modern, he means everything post-prehistoric) and George Sansom's *Japan: A Short Cultural History.* Sansom's three-volume *History of Japan* is a more exhaustive treatment.

If you are interested in earlier times, Ivan Morris's *The World of the Shining Prince* uses diaries and literature of the time to reconstruct life in the ancient city of Heian (Kyōto) from 794 to 1192. It should be required reading for anyone wishing to tour old Kyōto. *The Culture of the Meiji Period*, by Irokawa Daikichi, covers Japan's 19th-century encounters with the West. Oliver Statler's *Japanese Inn* deals with 400 years of Japanese social history.

Yamamoto Tsunetomo's *Hagakure* (*The Book of the Samurai*) is an 18th-century guide of sorts to the principles and ethics of the Way of the Samurai, written by a Kyūshū samurai. Dr. Junichi Saga's *Memories of Silk and Straw: A Self-Portrait of Small-Town Japan* is his 1970s collection of interviews with local old-timers in his hometown outside of Tōkyō. The accounts are illustrated by Saga's father. Few books get so close to the realities of everyday life in early-modern rural Japan. Elizabeth Bumiller's 1995 *The Secrets of Markio* intimately recounts a very poignant year in the life of a Japanese woman and her family.

The Japanese have a genre they refer to as *nihon-jin-ron*, or studies of "Japanese-ness." Western-style studies of the Japanese way of life in relation to the West also abound. Perhaps the best is Ezra Vogel's *Japan As Number One: Lessons for America*. A fine study of the Japanese mind is found in Takeo Doi's *The Anatomy of Dependence* and Chie Nakane's *Japanese Society*. Edwin O. Reischauer's *The Japanese* and his more recent *The Japanese Today* are general overviews of Japanese society that have of late received criticism for oversimplifying the character of Japanese life and for whitewashing the U.S. role in postwar Japan.

Harel van Wolferen's *The Enigma of Japanese Power* is an enlightening book on the Japanese sociopolitical system, especially for diplomats and businesspeople intending to work with the Japanese. Roland Barthes's impressionistic *Empire of Signs*, though dated by some events he recalls, contains keenly observant vignettes on topics like costume, theater, and the planning of Tōkyō. And as a sounding of the experience of his years in the country, Alex Kerr's *Lost Japan* examines the directions of Japanese society past and present. This book was the first written by a foreigner ever to win Japan's Shinchō Gakugei literature prize.

Religion

Anyone wanting to read a Zen Buddhist text should try *The Platform Sutra of the Sixth Patriarch*, one of the Zen classics, written by an ancient Chinese head of the sect and translated by Philip B. Yampolsky. Another Zen text of high importance is the *Lotus Sutra*; it has been translated by Leon Hurvitz as *The Scripture of the Lotus Blossom of the Fine Dharma: The Lotus Sutra*. Stuart D. Picken has written books on both major Japanese religions: *Shintō: Japan's Spiritual Roots* and *Buddhism: Japan's Cultural Identity*. William R. LaFleur's recommended *Karma of Words: Buddhism and the Literary Arts in Medieval Japan* traces how Buddhism affected medieval Japanese mentality and behavior.

Art, Architecture, and Crafts

A wealth of literature exists on Japanese art. Much of the early writing has not withstood the test of time, but R. Paine and Alexander Soper's *Art and Architecture of Japan* remains a good place to start. A more recent survey, though narrower in scope, is Joan Stanley-Smith's *Japanese Art*. Dore Ashton's *Noguchi East and West* looks at one of the 20th century's finest sculptors.

The multivolume *Japan Arts Library* covers most of the styles and personalities of the Japanese arts. The series has volumes on castles, teahouses, screen painting, and wood-block prints. A more detailed look at the architecture of Tōkyō is Edward Seidensticker's *Low City, High City*. Kazuo Nishi and Kazuo Hozumi's *What Is Japanese Architecture?* treats the history of Japanese architecture and has examples of buildings you will actually see on your travels.

Crafts and individual artisans are covered in the following well-illustrated books: *Japan Crafts Sourcebook*, on a comprehensive host of crafts and where to find them in Japan; *Inside Japanese Ceramics*, on traditions and techniques; *Shōji Hamada*, on one of Japan's most revered potters; the excellent *A Basketmaker in Rural Japan*, based on a Smithsonian exhibition, about a traditional itinerant Kyūshū artisan and rural life on the island; and *The Living Traditions of Old Kyōto*, which covers everything from bamboo work to the making of rice cakes.

Language

There is an overwhelming number of books and courses available for studying Japanese. *Japanese for Busy People* teaches not with grammar as its basis, but real conversational situations. With it you will also learn the two syllabaries, *hiragana* and *katakana*, and rudimentary *kanji* characters. To augment your study of kanji, look for P. G. O'Neill's *Essential Kanji* and Florence Sakade's *Guide to Reading and Writing Japanese*.

Videos

The Japanese film industry has been active since the early days of the medium's invention. A limited number of Japanese films, however, have been transferred to video for Western audiences, and even these may be hard to locate at your local video store. Many Japanese movies fall into two genres: the *jidai-geki* period-costume films and the *gendai-geki* films about contemporary life. Period films often deal with romantic entanglements, ghosts, and samurai warriors, as in *chambara* "swordfight" films. Movies set in more recent times often focus on lower- to middle-class family life and the world of gangsters.

Western viewers have typically encountered Japanese cinema in the works of Japan's most prolific movie directors, Kenji Mizoguchi, Yasujiro Ozu, and Akira Kurosawa. Mizoguchi's career spanned a 34-year period beginning in 1922, and three of his finest films investigate the social role of a female protagonist in feudal Japan: *The Life of Oharu* (1952), *Ugetsu* (1953), and *Sanchō the Baliff* (1954). Ozu directed 54 films from 1927 to 1962; most of his movies explore traditional Japanese values and concentrate on the everyday life and relationships of middle-class families. Among his best work are *Late Spring* (1949), *Early Summer* (1951), *Tōkyō Story* (1953), and *An Autumn Afternoon* (1962).

Kurosawa, who began directing movies in 1943, is the best-known Japanese filmmaker among Western audiences. His film *Rashōmon* (1950), a 12th-century murder story told by four different narrators, brought him international acclaim and sparked world interest in Japanese cinema. Among his other classic period films are *Seven Samurai* (1954), *The Hidden Fortress* (1958), *Yojimbo* (1961), *Red Beard* (1965), *Derzu Uzala* (1975), and *Kagemusha* (1980). The life-affirming *Ikiru* (1952) deals with an office worker dying of cancer. *High and Low* (1963), about a kidnapping, was based on a detective novel by Ed McBain. Two of Kurosawa's most honored films were adapted from Shakespeare plays: *Throne of Blood* (1957) based on *Macbeth*, and *Ran* (1985), based on *King Lear*.

Another director in the same generation as Mizoguchi and Ozu was Teinosuke Kinugasa, whose *Gate of Hell* (1953) vividly re-creates medieval Japan. *The Samurai Trilogy* (1954), directed by Hiroshi Inagaki, follows the adventures of a legendary 16th-century samurai hero, Musashi Miyamoto. A whole new group of filmmakers came to the forefront in postwar Japan, including Kon Ichikawa, who directed two powerful antiwar movies, *The Burmese Harp* (1956) and *Fires on the Plain* (1959); and Masaki Kobayashi, whose samurai period film *Harakiri* (1962) is considered his best work. In the late '60s and '70s several new directors gained prominence, including Hiroshi Teshigahara, Shohei Imamura, and Nagisa Oshima. Teshigahara is renowned for the allegorical *Woman in the Dunes* (1964), based on a novel by Kōbe Abe. Among Imamura's honored works are *The Ballad of Narayama* (1983), about the death of the elderly, and *Black Rain* (1989), which deals with the atomic bombing of Hiroshima. Oshima directed *Merry Christmas, Mr. Lawrence* (1983), about a British officer in a Japanese prisoner-of-war camp in Java during World War II.

Other Japanese filmmakers worth checking out are Yoshimitsu Morita, Juzo Itami, and Masayuki Suo. Morita's *The Family Game* (1983) satirizes Japanese domestic life and the educational system. Itami won international recognition for *Tampopo* (1986), a highly original comedy about food. His other films include *A Taxing Woman* (1987), which pokes fun at the Japanese tax system, and *Mimbo* (1992), which dissects the world of Japanese gangsters. Suo's *Shall We Dance?* (1997) is a bittersweet comedy about a married businessman who escapes his daily routine by taking ballroom dance lessons.

3 Tōkyō

A state-of-the-art financial marketplace, a metropolis of exquisite politenesses, a city that is monstrously large yet has astonishing beauty in its details—these are a few of the myriad ways to describe Tōkyō, and all contain at least a grain of truth. Ultimately, in its ultra-modern speed and its smattering of old-Japanese haunts, Tōkyō is the sum of its districts and neighborhoods—among them Ueno, Asakusa, Ginza, Tsukiji, Shibuya, and Shinjuku.

By Jared
Lubarsky

TŌKYŌ: Of all major cities in the world, it is perhaps the hardest to understand, to feel comfortable in, and to see in any single perspective. To begin with, consider the sheer, outrageous size of it. Tōkyō incorporates 23 wards, 26 smaller cities, seven towns, and eight villages—altogether sprawling 88 km (55 mi) east to west and 15 mi north to south. The wards alone enclose an area of 590 square km (228 square mi), which in turn houses some 8.5 million people. More than 2 million of these residents pass through Shinjuku Station, one of the major hubs in the transportation network, every day.

It's staggering to think what the population density would be if Tōkyō went up as well as out. Mile after mile, houses rise only one or two stories, their low uniformity broken here and there by the sore thumb of an apartment building. Space, that most precious of commodities, is so scarce that pedestrians have to weave in and around utility poles as they walk along the narrow sidewalks. Begin with that observation, and you discover that the very fabric of life in this city is woven of countless, unfathomable contradictions.

Tōkyō is a state-of-the-art financial marketplace, where billions of dollars are whisked electronically around the globe every day in the blink of an eye—and where automatic teller machines shut down at 7 PM. (The machines levy a service charge of ¥105 for withdrawals after 6 PM and on weekends.) It's a metropolis of exquisite politenesses, where uniformed department store staff bow you in and out of the elevators—and where a man in the subway will push an old woman out of the way to get a seat. A city of astonishing beauty in its small details, Tōkyō also has some of the ugliest buildings on the planet and generates more than 20,000 tons of garbage a day. It installed its first electric light in 1833 yet still has hundreds of thousands of households without a bathtub.

Life was simpler here in the 12th century, when Tōkyō was a little fishing village called Edo (pronounced *eh*-doh), near the mouth of the Sumida River on the Kantō Plain. The Kantō was a strategic granary, large and fertile; over the next 400 years it was governed by a succession of warlords and other rulers. One of them, Dōkan Ōta, built the first castle in Edo in 1457. That act is still officially regarded as the founding of the city, but the honor really belongs to Ieyasu (ee-eh-*ya*-su), the first Tokugawa shōgun, who arrived in 1590. When the civil wars of the 16th century came to an end, Ieyasu was the vassal of Generalissimo Hideyoshi Toyotomi, who gave him the eight provinces of Kantō in eastern Japan in exchange for three provinces closer to Kyōto—the imperial capital and ostensibly the seat of power. Ieyasu was a farsighted soldier; the swap was fine with him. In place of Ōta's stronghold, he built a mighty fortress of his own—from which, 10 years later, he was ruling the whole country.

By 1680, there were more than a million people here, and a great city had grown up out of the reeds in the marshy lowlands of Edo Bay. Tōkyō can only really be understood as a *jō-ka-machi*—a castle town. Ieyasu had fought his way to the shogunate, and he had a warrior's concern for the geography of his capital. Edo-jō (Edo Castle) had the high ground, but that wasn't enough; all around it, at strategic points, he gave large estates to allies and trusted retainers. These lesser lords' villas would also be garrisons, outposts on a perimeter of defense.

Farther out, he kept the barons he trusted least of all. Ieyasu had won the Battle of Sekigahara (1600), which made him shōgun, only because someone had switched sides at the last moment; he controlled the barons who might one day turn against him by bleeding their treasuries. They were required to keep large, expensive establishments in Edo; to contribute generously to the temples he endowed; to come and go twice a year in great pomp and ceremony; and, when they returned to their estates, to leave their families—in effect, hostages—behind.

All this, the Edo of feudal estates, of villas and gardens and temples, lay south and west of Edo-jō. It was called the Yamanote—the Bluff, the "uptown." Here, all was order, discipline, and ceremony; every man had his rank and duties. (Very few women were within the garrisons.) Almost from the beginning, those duties were less military than bureaucratic. Ieyasu's precautions worked like a charm, and the Tokugawa dynasty enjoyed some 250 years of unbroken peace, during which nothing very interesting ever happened uptown.

But the Yamanote was only the demand side of the economy: Somebody had to bring in the fish, weed the gardens, weave the mats, and entertain the bureaucrats during their time off. To serve the noble houses, common people flowed into Edo from all over Japan. Their allotted quarters of the city were jumbles of narrow streets, alleys, and culs-de-sac in the low-lying estuarine lands to the north and east. Often enough, the land wasn't even there when it was assigned to them; they had to *make* it by draining and filling the marshes. (The first reclamation project in Edo dates to 1457.) The result was Shita-machi—literally the "down-town," the part below the castle, which sat on a hill. Bustling, brawling Shita-machi was the supply side: It had the lumberyards, markets, and workshops; the wood-block printers, kimono makers, and moneylenders. The people here gossiped over the back fence in the earthy, colorful Edo dialect. They supported the bathhouses and the Kabuki theaters, had fireworks festivals, and went to Yoshiwara—a walled and moated area on the outskirts of Edo where prostitution was licensed—making Shita-machi the biggest licensed brothel quarter in the world. The *Edokko*—the people of Shita-machi—haven't changed much. Their city and its spirit have survived, while the great estates uptown are now mostly parks and hotels.

The shogunate was overthrown in 1867. The following year, emperor Meiji moved his court from Kyōto to Edo and renamed it Tōkyō: Eastern Capital. By now the city was home to nearly 2 million people, and the geography was vastly more complex than before. The broad divisions of Yamanote and Shita-machi remained. The Imperial Palace still provided a point of reference, a locus for the heart of the city, but Tōkyō defied such easy organization. As it grew, it became not one but many smaller cities, with different centers of commerce, government, entertainment, and transportation. In Yamanote rose the department stores, office buildings, and public halls that made up the architecture of an emerging modern state. The workshops of Shita-machi multiplied, some of them to become small jobbers and family-run factories. Still, there was no planning, no grid. The neighborhoods and subcenters were worlds unto themselves, and a traveler from one was soon hopelessly lost in another.

The firebombings of 1945 left Tōkyō, for the most part, in rubble and ashes. Out of that chaos of destruction and death, the rational order of cities like Kyōto, Barcelona, or Washington would seem to present sensible models. But they did not. Tōkyō reverted to type. It became once again an aggregation of small towns and villages. Author Donald Richie has described them as "separate, yet welded to the texture of the metropolis itself." One village was much like any other; the nucleus was always the *shōten-gai,* the shopping arcade. Each arcade had

Tōkyō Overview (Boxes Refer to Detail Maps)

N

Ōji

Toshima-en

Ikebukuro

YŪRAKUCHŌ LINE

Meiji-dōri

Mejiro

Takada-no-baba

Okubo

TŌZAI LINE

Ōme-kaidō

Tama Dōbutsu Kōen
Shinjuku

Shinjuku

TŌEI SHINJUKU LINE

Yoyogi

Seibu-Shinjuku

Shin-Okubo

Shinjuku

MARU-NO-UCHI LINE

Shinjuku Gyo-en

Sendagaya

Shinjuku-dōri

Tōkyō

Totsuya

Ichigaya

Yasukuni-dōri

Waseda-dōri

ARAKAWA LINE

Zōshigaya

Mejiro-dōri

Higashi-Ikebukuro

Ōtsuka

MARU-NO-UCHI LINE

Nakasendō TŌEI MITA LINE

Shinobazu-dōri

Rikugien Gardens

Koishikawa Botanical Gardens

Meiji-dōri

Tōkyō Expwy No.5

Kōraku-en

Tōkyō Dome

Hakusan-dōri Ave.

Hongo-dōri

Kasuga-dōri

CHIYODA LINE

Nishi-Nippori

Nippori

Asakura Sculpture Gallery

Meiji-dōri

Showa-dōri HIBIYA LINE

Ueno

Uguisudani

Ueno

Ueno Kōen

Suido-bashi

Iida-bashi

Ocha-no-mizu

Jimbō-chō

Akihabara and Jimbō-chō

Kanda

Akihabara

Okachi-machi

Kiyosu-bashi-dōri

Asakusa-dōri GINZA LINE

Kappa-bashi-dōri

Asakusa

TŌEI ASAKUSA LINE

Expwy No. 6

Kura-mae-dōri

Asakusa-bashi

Tōkyō Exwy No.1

Tōkyō Exwy

Kokugikan (National Sumo Area)

Ryogoku

Tōkyō Expwy No.7

TŌEI SHINJUKU LINE

Tōkyō

Imperial Palace

Nihombashi, Ginza, and Yūraku-chō

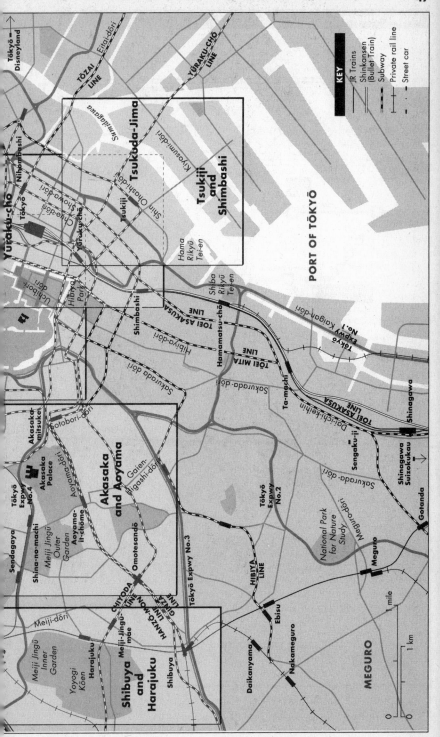

47

KEY
JR Trains
Shinkansen (Bullet Train)
Subway
Private rail line
Street car

Tōkyō Disneyland

TŌZAI LINE
Eitai-dōri
Sumidagawa

YŪRAKU-CHŌ LINE

Yūraku-chō

Tsukuda-Jima

Nihombashi
Tōkyō

Chūo-dōri
Shōwa-dōri
Yūraku-chō

Kiyosumi-dōri

Shin Ōhashi-dōri

Tsukiji

Tsukiji and Shimbashi

Hama Rikyū Tei-en

Uchibori-dōri
Hibiya Park

Shimbashi

Shiba Rikyū Tei-en

PORT OF TŌKYŌ

TOEI ASAKUSA LINE
Hibiya-dōri

Hamamatsu-chō
TOEI MITA LINE

Sakurada-dōri

Sakurada-dōri

Tōkyō Expwy No.1
Kaigan-dōri

Akasaka-mitsuke
Sotobori-dōri

Ta-machi

Dai-ichi-keihin

TOEI ASAKUSA LINE

Shinagawa

Tōkyō Expwy No.4

Akasaka Palace
Aoyama-dōri

Gaien-Higashi-dōri

Akasaka and Aoyama

Sengaku-ji

Shinagawa Suizokukan

Sendagaya

Shina-no-machi

Meiji Jingū Outer Garden

Aoyama-it-chōme

Omotesandō

Tōkyō Expwy No.2

National Park for Nature Study

Gotanda

Tōkyō Expwy No.3

CHIYODA LINE

GINZA LINE
HANZŌ-MON LINE

HIBIYA LINE

Meguro-dōri

Sakurada-dōri

Meguro

Meiji-dōri

Meiji Jingū-mae

Harajuku

Ebisu

Daikanyama

Meiji Jingū Inner Garden

Yoyogi Kōen

Shibuya and Harajuku

Shibuya

Nakameguro

MEGURO

1 mile
1 km
0
0

## 48

Tōkyō Subway

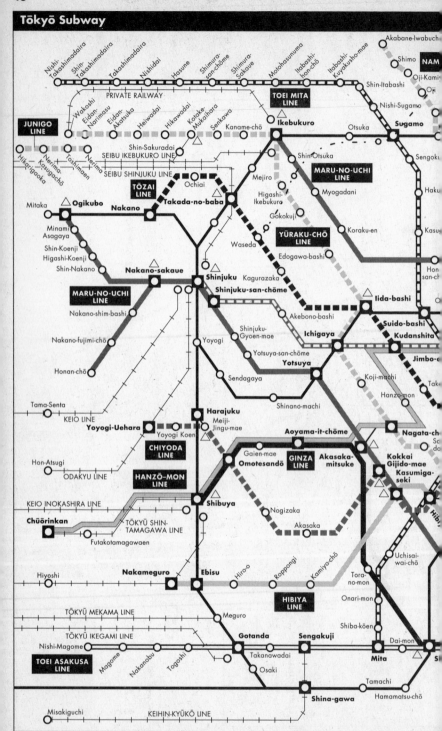

Nishi-Takashimadaira
Shin-Takashimadaira
Takashimadaira
Nishidai
Hasune
Shimura-san-chōme
Shimura-Sakaue
Motohasunuma
Itabashi-hon-chō
Itabashi-Kuyakusho-mae
Shin-Itabashi
Akabane-Iwabuch
Shimo
NAM
Oji-Kami-
Oji
Nishi-Sugamo

PRIVATE RAILWAY
TOEI MITA LINE
Otsuka
Sugamo
Sengoku

JUNIGO LINE
Wakoshi
Eidan-Narimasu
Eidan-Akatsuka
Heiwadai
Hikawadai
Kotake-Mukaihara
Senkawa
Kaname-chō
Ikebukuro
Hakui
Kasu

Hikarigaoka
Nerima-kasugachō
Toshimaen
Nerima
Shin-Sakuradai
SEIBU IKEBUKURO LINE
SEIBU SHINJUKU LINE
Shin-Ōtsuka
MARU-NO-UCHI LINE
Mejiro
Myogadani
Gokokuji
Koraku-en

Ochiai
TŌZAI LINE
Takada-no-baba
Higashi-Ikebukuro

Mitaka
△ **Ogikubo**
Nakano
Waseda
YŪRAKU-CHŌ LINE
Edogawa-bashi
Hon-san-ch

Minami Asagaya
Shin-Koenji
Higashi-Koenji
Shin-Nakano
Nakano-sakaue
Kagurazaka
Iida-bashi

Shinjuku
Shinjuku-san-chōme
Akebono-bashi
Suido-bashi

MARU-NO-UCHI LINE
Nakano-shim-bashi
Shinjuku-Gyoen-mae
Ichigaya
Kudanshita
Jimbo-

Nakano-fujimi-chō
Yoyogi
Yotsuya-san-chōme
Koji-machi
Take

Honan-chō
Yotsuya
Hanzo-mon

Tama-Senta
Sendagaya
KEIO LINE
Shinano-machi

Harajuku
Meiji-Jingu-mae
Yoyogi-Uehara
Yoyogi Koen
Aoyama-it-chōme
Nagata-ch
Sa
do

CHIYODA LINE
Gaien-mae
GINZA LINE
Akasaka-mitsuke
Kokkai Gijido-mae
Kasumiga-seki

Hon-Atsugi
HANZŌ-MON LINE
Omotesandō
ODAKYU LINE

KEIO INOKASHIRA LINE
△ **Shibuya**
Nogizaka

Chūōrinkan
TŌKYŪ SHIN-TAMAGAWA LINE
Akasaka
Hibi

Futakotamagawaen

Hiyoshi
Nakameguro
Ebisu
Hiro-o
Roppongi
Kamiyo-chō
Uchisai-wai-chō

TŌKYŪ MEKAMA LINE
Tora-no-mon

TŌKYŪ IKEGAMI LINE
Meguro
HIBIYA LINE
Onari-mon

Nishi-Magome
Magome
Nakanobu
Togoshi
Gotanda
Sengakuji
Shiba-kōen
Dai-mon

TOEI ASAKUSA LINE
Takanawadai
Mita
△

Osaki
Tamachi

Misakiguchi
KEIHIN-KYŪKŌ LINE
Shina-gawa
Hamamatsu-chō

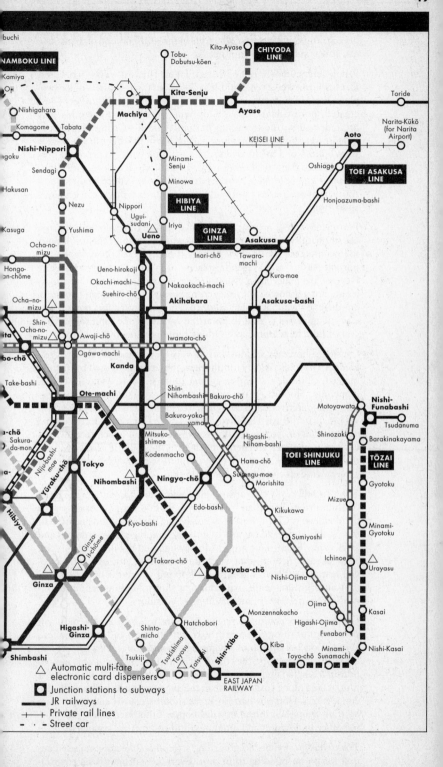

buchi

NAMBOKU LINE

Kamiya

Oji

Nishigahara

Komagome — Tabata

ogoku

Nishi-Nippori

Sendagi

Hakusan

Nezu

Kasuga

Yushima

Ocha-no-mizu

Hongo-an-chōme

Ocha–no-mizu

Shin-Ocha-no-mizu

ita

bo-chō

Take-bashi

a-chō
Sakura-da-mon

Niju-bashi-mae

a

Hibiya

Shimbashi

Tobu-Dobutsu-kōen

Kita-Senju

Machiya

Minami-Senju

Minowa

Nippori

Ugui-sudani

Ueno

Iriya

HIBIYA LINE

GINZA LINE

Ueno-hirokoji

Okachi-machi

Suehiro-chō

Nakaokachi-machi

Akihabara

Awaji-chō

Iwamoto-chō

Ogawa-machi

Kanda

Ote-machi

Shin-Nihombashi

Bakuro-chō

Bakuro-yoko-yama

Mitsuko-shimae

Kodenmacho

Tokyo

Nihombashi

Ningyo-chō

Edo-bashi

Kyo-bashi

Yūraku-chō

Ginza-It-chōme

Takara-chō

Ginza

Higashi-Ginza

Shinto-micho

Tsukiji

Tsukishima

Toyosu

Tatsumi

Shin-Kiba

Hatchobori

Kayaba-chō

Kita-Ayase

CHIYODA LINE

Ayase

Toride

Aoto

Narita-Kūkō
(for Narita Airport)

KEISEI LINE

Oshiage

TOEI ASAKUSA LINE

Honjoazuma-bashi

Asakusa

Inari-chō

Tawara-machi

Kura-mae

Asakusa-bashi

Higashi-Nihom-bashi

Hama-chō

Sujangu-mae

Morishita

Kikukawa

Sumiyoshi

TOEI SHINJUKU LINE

Nishi-Ojima

Monzennakacho

Higashi-Ojima

Funabori

Kiba

Toyo-chō

Minami-Sunamachi

Motoyawata

Shinozaki

Mizue

Ichinoe

Ojima

Nishi-Funabashi

Tsudanuma

Barakinakayama

TŌZAI LINE

Gyotoku

Minami-Gyotoku

Urayasu

Kasai

Nishi-Kasai

EAST JAPAN RAILWAY

△ Automatic multi-fare electronic card dispensers

◨ Junction stations to subways

—— JR railways

+—+ Private rail lines

- · - Street car

a butcher, a grocer, and a rice dealer. It had a mat maker, a barber, and a pinball parlor. And it had a florist and a bookstore—sometimes two of each. You could live your whole life in the neighborhood of the shōten-gai. It was sufficient to your needs.

People seldom moved out of these villages. The vast waves of new residents who arrived after World War II—about three-quarters of the people in the Tōkyō metropolitan area today were born elsewhere—just created more villages. Everybody who lived in one knew his way around, and so there was no particular need to name the streets. Houses were numbered not in sequence but in the order in which they were built. No. 3 might well share a mailbox with No. 12. And people still take their local geography for granted—the closer you get to the place you're looking for, the harder it is to get coherent directions. Away from main streets and landmarks, even a taxi driver can get hopelessly lost.

Fortunately, there are the *kōban:* small police boxes, or substations, usually with two or three officers assigned to each of them full time, to look after the affairs of the neighborhood. These kōban are one important reason for the legendary safety of Tōkyō: On foot or on white bicycles, the police are a visible presence, covering the beat. (Burglaries are not unknown, but street crime is very rare.) You can't go far in any direction without finding a kōban. The officer on duty knows where everything is and is glad to point the way. Like the samurai-bureaucrat of Edo, he seldom has anything more pressing to do.

Outsiders, however, seldom venture very far into the labyrinths of residential Tōkyō. Especially for travelers, the city defines itself by its commercial, cultural, and entertainment centers: Ueno, Asakusa, Ginza, Roppongi, Shibuya, Harajuku, and Shinjuku. Megaprojects to develop the waterfront and the Ebisu area in the 1980s and 1990s added yet others to the list. The attention of Tōkyō shifts constantly, seeking new patches of astronomically expensive land on which to realize its enormous commercial energy. Even with the collapse of the speculative bubble in 1992, you can't buy a square yard anywhere in the city's central wards for much less than $35,000.

Tōkyō is still really two areas, Shita-machi and Yamanote. The heart of Shita-machi, proud and stubborn in its Edo ways, is Asakusa; the dividing line is Ginza, west of which lie the boutiques and department stores, the banks and engines of government, the pleasure domes and swell cafés. Today there are 12 subway lines in full operation—a 13th is under construction—that weave the two areas together. Another special feature of Tōkyō's geography is found where the lines intersect: vast underground malls, with miles of shops, boutiques, and restaurants in fluorescent-lit, air-conditioned corridors.

On the surface, confusion reigns, or seems to. Tōkyō is the most impermanent of cities, constantly tearing itself down and building anew. Whole blocks disappear overnight. The next day, a framework of girders is already rising on the empty lot. It's virtually impossible now to put up a single-family house in the eight central wards of the city; a plot of land alone costs more than the average person will earn in several lifetimes. Home owners live in the suburbs, usually an hour or more by train from their jobs. Only developers can afford land closer in— for office buildings, condominiums, and commercial complexes.

Tōkyō has no skyline, no prevailing style of architecture, no real context for a new building to fit into. Every new project is an environment unto itself. World-famous architects like Isozaki Arata, Maki Fumihiko, and Kurokawa Kishō revel in this anarchy, and so do the designers of neon signs, show windows, and interior spaces. The kind of creative energy you find in Tōkyō could flower only in an atmosphere where there are virtually no rules to break.

Not all of that is for the best. Many of the buildings in Tōkyō are merely grotesque, and most of them are supremely ugly. In the large scale, Tōkyō is not an attractive city. Neither is it gracious, and it is certainly not serene. The pace of life is wedded to the one stupefying fact of population: Within a 36-km (20-mi) radius of the Imperial Palace live almost 30 million souls, all of them in a hurry and all of them ferocious consumers. They live in a city that went from rubble to dazzling affluence in a generation. And even as they are very sure of what they have accomplished, they are terribly uncertain about who they are. They consume to identify themselves—by what they wear, where they eat, and how they use their leisure time.

Tōkyō is a magnet. Money—enormous amounts of it—is of course the great attractor, and it is always looking for new ways of turning itself over. The great collapse of 1992 left Japan's banks sitting on trillions of dollars of bad debt, and the economy has yet to recover, but the Japanese remain among the world's foremost consumers—not merely of things but of culture and leisure. Everything shows up here, sooner or later: van Gogh's *Sunflowers,* the Berlin Philharmonic, Chinese pandas, Mexican food. Even the Coney Island carousel is here—lovingly restored to the last gilded curlicue on the last prancing unicorn, back in action at an amusement park called Toshima-en.

Now the magnet is drawing you. What follows is an attempt to chart a few paths for you through this exciting, exasperating, movable feast of a city.

Tōkyō Glossary

Key Japanese words and suffixes in this chapter include *-bashi* (bridge), *bijutsukan* (art museum), *-chō* (street or block), *-chōme* (street), *chūō* (central, as in Chūō-dōri, Central Street), *daimyō* (feudal lord), *-den* (hall), *depāto* ("deh-*pah*-to," department store), *dōri* (avenue), *eki* (train station), *gai-jin* (foreigner), *-gawa* (river), *-gū* (Shintō shrine), *guchi* (exit), *ike* (ee-*keh,* pond), *-in* (Buddhist temple), *izakaya* (pub), *-ji* (Buddhist temple), *-jima* (island), *jinja* (Shintō shrine), *jingū* (Shintō shrine), *-jō* (castle), *kita* (north), *kōen* ("ko-en," park), *-ku* (section or ward), *kūkō* (airport), *machi* (town), *matsuri* (festival), *minami* (south), *-mon* (gate), *sake* ("*sa*-keh," rice wine), *-shi* (city or municipality), *shinkansen* (bullet train, literally "new trunk line"), *shita* (lower, downward), *torii* ("*to*-ree-ee," gate), *-ya* (shop, as in hon-ya, bookshop), *yama* (mountain), *Yamanote* (the hilly part of town).

Pleasures and Pastimes

Depending on your point of view, Tōkyō has more than 400 years of history—or barely 50. What survives here of the old—temple architecture, performing arts, traditions of craft and design—may not compare to what you find in Kyōto, but the rewards of Tōkyō's museums and theaters are undeniable. What's new is relentlessly so: Tōkyō is an affluent mass market for the latest products and designs, services and amusements—an unbeatable place to shop and party.

Dining

The Japanese are more cautious than they were a decade ago about expense account entertaining, but wining and dining are still crucial in cementing the all-important personal contacts that make the wheels of business, and government, turn. It's still standard practice for Tōkyō's white-collar legions to work late, unwind with their colleagues in a favorite restaurant, and catch the last train home. Single working women (and their dates), bearers of most of the city's discretionary income, flock to whatever new bars and restaurants the magazines have declared in fashion. At last count, there were more than 187,000 places in Tōkyō to take a thirst or an empty stomach—the range of options is astonishing. Tōkyō is, in many ways, a stubbornly provincial city, but whatever the rest of the world has pronounced good eventually makes its way here. It's hard to think of a national cuisine of any prominence that goes unrepresented.

Some of those choices can be hideously expensive. For every budget-buster, however, there are any number of bargains—good cooking of all sorts, at prices ordinary travelers can afford. The options, in fact, go all the way down to street food and *yakitori* (Japanese-style chicken kebab) joints under railroad trestles, where many Japanese go when they have to spend their own money. Food and drink, incidentally, are safe wherever you go.

Performing Arts

Japan is justly proud of its music, dance, and theater traditions, which are quite unique: Unless you happen to catch one of the infrequent (and expensive) performances of a company on tour abroad, you'll never really see the like of Kabuki, Nō, or Bunraku anywhere else.

Kabuki has been pleasing audiences from all walks of life in Japan for more than 300 years; it's the kind of theater—a combination of music, dance, and drama, with spectacular costumes and acrobatics, duels and quick changes and special effects thrown in—that you can enjoy without understanding a word the actors say. Nō, on the other hand, is an acquired taste. A ritual masked drama that has remained virtually unchanged since the 14th century, Nō moves at a stately—nay, glacial—pace, to music and recitation utterly different from anything Western. Bunraku is Japan's puppet theater, like Kabuki a popular entertainment form, but with roots in the western part of the country. The puppets themselves are so expressive and intricate in their movements that each one requires three people to move it around on stage.

Three theaters in Tōkyō present Kabuki, including the landmark Kabuki-za, first built exclusively for that purpose in 1925. Four traditional "schools," each with its own performance space, specialize in Nō; there is also a National Nō Theater, and—on rare occasions—night performances by torchlight in the courtyards of temples. Bunraku is not given as often in Tōkyō as it is in Ōsaka, but if there's a performance anywhere in town during your stay, it's decidedly worth seeing.

Local aficionados will insist that sumō wrestling is not merely a sport but an ancient religious rite. Barely clad contestants square off in a dirt ring about 15 ft in diameter and charge straight at each another; the first one to step out of the ring, or touch the ground with anything but the soles of his feet, loses. None of that happens, however, without ceremonial processions of ranking wrestlers, referees and functionaries in gorgeous costumes, and warm-up rituals elaborately choreographed. It's a great show, and the Tōkyō tournaments (one each in early January, mid-May, and mid-September) are not to be missed.

Shopping

In the late 1990s, upscale consumer goods in Tōkyō—designer clothing, cultured pearls, home electronics—spiraled down from the insanely expensive to the merely costly. Fashions by internationally known designers like Issey Miyake, Rei Kawakubo, Hanae Mori, Yōji Yamamoto, Hiroko Koshino, and Kansai Yamamoto are priced more reasonably in Tōkyō's boutiques and depāto than they are abroad.

Among things more traditionally Japanese, good buys include pottery, fabrics, folk-craft objects in wood and bamboo, cutlery, lacquerware, and hand-made paper. You'll find regional specialties from all over Japan, amounting to an enormous range of goods to choose from. The selections in conveniently located arcades, and the crafts sections of major depāto, make one-stop shopping easy.

EXPLORING TŌKYŌ

The distinctions of **Shita-machi** (literally down-town, to the north and east) and **Yamanote** (just as literally uptown, to the south and west) have shaped the character of Tōkyō since the 17th century and will guide you as you explore the city. At the risk of an easy generalization, it might be said that downtown has more to *see*, uptown more to *do*. Another way of putting it is that Tōkyō north and east of the Imperial Palace embodies more of the city's history, its traditional way of life, whereas the fruit of modernity—the glitzy, ritzy side of contemporary, international Tōkyō—generally lies south and west.

We've divided the city into 10 exploring sections, six in Shita-machi—starting in central Tōkyō with the Imperial Palace District—and four uptown in Yamanote. It can be exhausting to walk from one part of Tōkyō to another—you'll look in vain for places outdoors just to sit and rest en route—and bus travel can be particularly tricky. Fortunately, no point on any of these itineraries is very far from a subway station, and you can use the city's efficient subway system to hop from one area to another, to cut a tour short, or to return to a tour the next day. The areas as we've divided them are not always contiguous—Tōkyō is too spread out for that—but they generally border each other to a useful degree. As you plan your approach to the city, by all means skip parts of an area that don't appeal or combine parts of one tour with those of another in order to get the best of all worlds.

Great Itineraries
You need three days just to take in the highlights of Tōkyō and still have time for some shopping and nightlife. With four or five days, you can explore the city in greater depth, wander off the beaten path, and appreciate Tōkyō's museums at leisure. Eight days would allow for day trips to the scenic and historical sights nearby (☞ Chapter 4).

IF YOU HAVE 3 DAYS
Start *very* early (why waste your jet lag?) with a visit to the **Tsukiji Fish Market** while it's still in high gear; then use the rest of the day for a tour of the **Imperial Palace** and environs. Spend the next morning at Buddhist **Sensō-ji** in Asakusa, and from there take the special tour bus to **Ueno Park** for an afternoon with its many museums, vistas, and historic sites. Start your last day with a morning stroll through the **Ginza** and explore its fabled shops and depāto; in the afternoon, see the Shintō **Meiji Jingū** and take a leisurely walk through the nearby **Harajuku** and **Omotesandō** fashion districts to the **Nezu Institute of Fine Arts**—a perfect oasis for your last impressions of the city.

IF YOU HAVE 4 OR 5 DAYS
Follow the itinerary above, and add to it (or punctuate it with) a morning of browsing in **Akihabara,** Tōkyō's electronics discount quarter, visiting the nearby Shintō **Kanda Myōjin** as well. Spend the afternoon on the west side of Shinjuku, Tōkyō's 21st-century model city; savor the view from the observation deck of architect Kenzō Tange's monumental **City Hall**; and cap off the day with a walk through the greenery of **Shinjuku Gyō-en.** The luxury of a fifth day would allow you to fill in the missing pieces that belong to no particular major tour:

the Buddhist **Sengaku-ji** in Shinagawa, the old Yanaka quarter and its **Asakura Sculpture Gallery,** a tea ceremony, or any of the shops that haven't yet managed to stake a claim on your dwindling resources. See a sumō tournament, if there's one in town; failing that, you could still visit the **National Sumō Arena** in the Ryōgoku district, and some of the sumō stables in the neighborhood.

IF YOU HAVE 8 DAYS

With a week or more, you can make Tōkyō your home base for a series of side trips (☞ Chapter 4). After getting your fill of Tōkyō, take a train out to **Yokohama,** with its scenic port and Chinatown. A bit farther afield but still easily accessible by train, **Kamakura** was the 12th-century military capital of Japan. The **Daibutsu** (Great Buddha) of the **Kōtoku-in Temple** is but one of the National Treasures of art and architecture here that draw millions of visitors a year. For both Yokohama and Kamakura, an early morning start will allow you to see most of the important sights in a full day and make it back to Tōkyō by late evening. As Kamakura is the most popular of excursions from Tōkyō, avoid the worst of the crowds by making the trip on a weekday. Still farther off, but again an easy train trip, **Nikkō** is where the founder of the Tokugawa shogunal dynasty is enshrined. **Tōshō-gū** is a monument unlike any other in Japan, and the picturesque **Lake Chūzen-ji** is in a forest above the shrine. A full two full days, with an overnight stay, would allow you an ideal, leisurely exploration of both. Or go see Mt. Fuji in person.

When to Tour Tōkyō

The best of all possible times to be in Tōkyō are early to mid-April, in cherry blossom time—though two or three days of chill and rain will sometimes come and dampen the enjoyment—and the second half of May. Next best are late September and October. Avoid the rainy season, from late June through mid-July, if you can, and only come in August knowing that you'll get blasted with heat and high humidity. Because mid-August is also one of the few periods when the Japanese themselves can take vacations—the others being the two or three days before and after New Year's and the first week of May—reservations are at a premium for planes, trains, and hotels.

Imperial Palace District

Kōkyo, the Imperial Palace, occupies what were once the grounds of Edo-jō. The first feudal lord here, a local chieftain named Ōta, was assassinated in 1486, and the castle he built was abandoned for more than 100 years. When Ieyasu Tokugawa chose the site for his castle in 1590, he had two goals in mind. First, it would have to be impregnable; second, it would have to reflect the power and glory of his position. He was lord of the Kantō, the richest fief in Japan, and would soon be shōgun, the military head of state. The fortifications he devised called for a triple system of moats and canals, incorporating the bay and the Sumida River into a huge network of waterways that enclosed both the castle keep (the stronghold, or tower) and the palaces and villas of his court—in all, an area of about 450 acres. The castle had 99 gates (36 in the outer wall), 21 watchtowers (of which three are still standing), and 28 armories. The outer defenses stretched from present-day Shimbashi Station to Kanda. Completed in 1640 and later expanded, it was at the time the largest castle in the world.

The walls of Edo-jō and its moats were made of stone from the Izu Peninsula, about 96 km (60 mi) to the southwest. The great slabs were brought by barge—each of the largest was a cargo in itself—to the port of Edo (then much closer to the castle than the present port of Tōkyō is now), and hauled through the streets on sledges by teams of 100 or more men. Thousands of stonemasons were brought from all over the country to finish the work. Under the gates and castle buildings, the blocks of stone are said to have been shaped and fitted so precisely that a knife blade could not be slipped between them.

The inner walls divided the castle into four main areas, called *maru*. The *hon-maru*, the principle area, contained the shōgun's audience halls, his private residence, and, for want of a better word, his seraglio: the *ō-oku*, where he kept his wife and concubines, with their ladies-in-waiting, attendants, cooks, and servants. The shōgun's concubines came and went. At any given time, as many as 1,000 women might be living in the ō-oku. Intrigue, more than sex, was its principal concern, and tales of the seraglio provided a rich source of material for the Japanese literary imagination. Below the hon-maru was the *ni-no-maru*, where the shōgun lived when he transferred his power to an heir and retired. Behind it was the *kita-no-maru*, the northern area, now a public park; south and west was the *nishi-no-maru*, a subsidiary fortress.

Not much of the Tokugawa glory remains. The shogunate was abolished in 1868, and in Emperor Meiji's move from Kyōto to Edo, which he renamed Tōkyō, Edo-jō was chosen as the site of the Imperial Palace. Many of its buildings had been destroyed in the turmoil of the restoration of the emperor, others fell in the fires of 1872, and still others were simply torn down. Of the 28 original *tamon* (armories), only two survived. The present-day Imperial Palace is open to the public only twice a year: on January 2 (New Year's) and December 23 (the Emperor's Birthday), when many thousands of people assemble under the balcony to offer their good wishes to the imperial family. In 1968, to mark the completion of the current palace, the area that once encompassed the hon-maru and ni-no-maru was opened to the public as the Imperial Palace East Garden. There are three entrance gates—Ōte-mon, Hirakawa-mon, and Kita-Hane-bashi-mon. You can easily get to any of the three from the Ōte-machi or Takebashi subway station.

Numbers in the text correspond to numbers in the margin and on the Imperial Palace map.

A Good Walk

A good place to start is **Tōkyō Eki** ①. The Ōte-machi subway stop (on the Chiyoda, Maru-no-uchi, Tōzai, Hanzōmon, and Tōei Mita lines) is a closer and handier connection, but the old redbrick Tōkyō Eki building is a more compelling place. (The **Tōkyō Station Hotel,** incidentally, which wanders along the west side of the building on the second and third floors, serves a fairly decent breakfast for ¥1,500.) Leave the station by the Maru-no-uchi central exit, cross the street in front at the taxi stand, and walk up the broad divided avenue that leads to the Imperial Palace grounds. To your left is Maru-no-uchi, to your right Ōte-machi: You are in the heart of Japan, Incorporated—the home of its major banks and investment houses, its insurance and trading companies. Take the second right, at the corner of the New Maru-no-uchi Building; walk two blocks, past the gleaming, brown marble fortress of the Industrial Bank of Japan, and turn left. Ahead of you, across Uchi-bori-dōri (Inner Moat Avenue) from the Palace Hotel, is the **Ōte-mon,** one of three entrances to the **Imperial Palace East Garden** ② (Kōkyo Higashi Gyo-en).

56

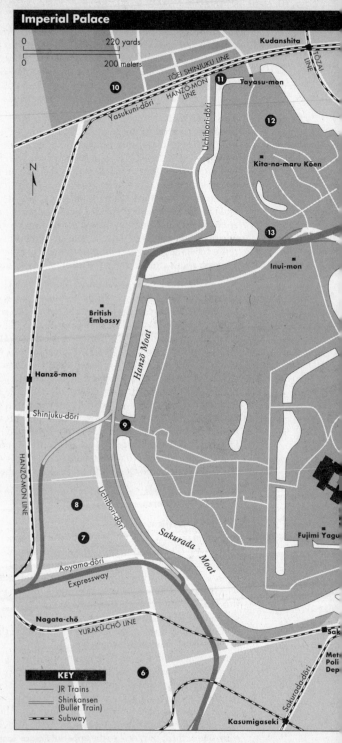

Imperial Palace

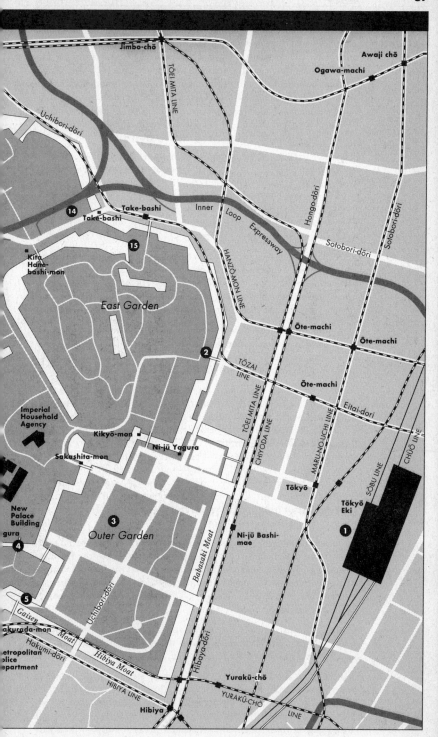

Jimbo-chō

Awaji chō

Ogawa-machi

TŌEI MITA LINE

Uchibori-dōri

Inner Loop Expressway

Hongo-dōri

Sotobori-dōri

Sotobori-dōri

14 Take-bashi

Take-bashi

HANZŌMON LINE

15

Kita-Hane-bashi-mon

East Garden

Ōte-machi

Ōte-machi

2

TŌZAI LINE

Ōte-machi

Eitai-dōri

TŌEI MITA LINE

CHIYODA LINE

MARUNOUCHI LINE

SŌBU LINE

CHŪŌ LINE

Imperial Household Agency

Kikyō-mon

Ni-jū Yagura

Sakashita-mon

Tōkyō

Tōkyō Eki

1

New Palace Building

gura

3

Outer Garden

Ni-jū Bashi-mae

4

Uchibori-dōri

Babasaki Moat

5

Gaisen

akurada-mon

Moat

Hakumi-dōri

Hibiya-dōri

Hibiya Moat

etropolitan olice epartment

HIBIYA LINE

Yurakū-chō

YURAKŪ-CHŌ

Hibiya

LINE

Turn right as you leave the East Garden. Where the wall makes a right angle, you will see the **Tatsumi,** or **Ni-jū Yagura** (Double-Tiered Watchtower), one of three surviving watchtowers on the original fortifications. Here the sidewalk opens out to a parking lot for tour buses and the beginning of a broad promenade. In the far corner to your right, where the angle of the wall turns again, is the **Kikyō-mon,** a gate used primarily for deliveries to the palace. (Short and prestigious indeed is the roster of *Go-yōtashi*—Purveyors to the Imperial Household.) At the far end of the parking lot is **Sakashita-mon,** the gate used by the officials of the Imperial Household Agency itself.

From here to **Hibiya Kōen,** along both sides of Uchi-bori-dōri, stretches the concourse of the **Imperial Palace Outer Garden** ③. This whole area once lay along the edge of Tōkyō Bay. Later, the shōgun had his most trusted retainers build their estates here. These in turn gave way to the office buildings of the Meiji government. In 1899 the buildings were relocated, and the promenade was planted with the wonderful stands of pine trees you see today.

Walk along the broad gravel path to **Ni-jū Bashi** ④ (Two-Tiered Bridge) and the **Sei-mon** (Main Gate). Ni-jū-bashi makes its graceful arch over the moat here from the area inside the gate. The building in the background, completing the picture, is the **Fushimi Yagura,** built in the 17th century. It is the last of the three surviving original watchtowers.

Continue on the gravel walk past the Sei-mon, turn right, and pass through the **Sakurada-mon** ⑤. Before you do, turn and look back down the concourse: You will not see another expanse of open space like this anywhere else in Tōkyō.

Across the street as you pass through the gate is the beginning of Sakurada-dōri. World-renowned architect Kenzō Tange's **Metropolitan Police Department** building is on the north corner. The older brick buildings on the south corner belong to the **Ministry of Justice.** Sakurada-dōri runs through the heart of official Japan; between here and Kasumigaseki are the ministries—from Foreign Affairs and Education to International Trade and Industry—that compose the central government. They inhabit, however, what are surely the most uninteresting buildings, architecturally, of any government center in the world and thus should not tempt you to waver from your course. Turn right and follow the moat as you walk up the hill.

Ahead of you, where the road branches to the left, you will see the squat pyramid of the **National Diet Building** ⑥, which houses the Japanese Parliament. Bear right as you follow the moat to the five-point intersection where it curves again to the north. Across the street are the gray stone slabs of the **Supreme Court** ⑦. This and the **National Theater** ⑧ next door are worth a short detour.

Cross back to the palace side of the street. At the top of the hill, on your right, a police contingent guards the road to the **Hanzō-mon** ⑨, and, beyond it, the new Imperial Palace.

North along the Hanzō Moat is a narrow strip of park; facing it, across the street, is the **British Embassy.** Along this western edge of his fortress, the shōgun kept his personal retainers, called *hatamoto,* divided by *ban-chō* (district) into six regiments. Today these six ban-chō are among the most sought-after residential areas in Tōkyō, where high-rise apartments commonly fetch ¥100 million or more.

At the next intersection, review your priorities again. You can turn right and complete your circuit of the palace grounds by way of the **Inui-**

mon, or you can continue straight north to the end of Uchi-bori-dōri to **Yasukuni Jinja** ⑩, the Shrine of Peace for the Nation.

If you do go to Yasukuni Jinja, **Tony Roma's**—just past the intersection on the west side of Samban-chō—is a good, moderately priced place for charcoal-broiled spare ribs.

Leave Yasukuni Jinja the way you came in, cross the street, turn left, and walk down the hill. The entrance to **Chidori-ga-fuchi Kōen** ⑪ is about 50 yards from the intersection, on the right. The green strip of promenade is high on the edge of the moat, lined with cherry trees. Halfway along, it widens, and opposite the **Fairmont Hotel** a path leads down to the **Chidori-ga-fuchi Boathouse.** Beyond the boathouse, the promenade leads back in the direction of the Imperial Palace.

If you have the time and stamina for a longer tour, retrace your steps from the boathouse, leave the park the way you came in, turn right, and continue down the hill to the entrance to **Kita-no-maru Kōen,** the **Tayasu-mon.** This is one of the largest and finest of the surviving masu gates to the castle. Inside, you come first to the octagonal **Nippon Budōkan** ⑫, site of major rock concerts and martial arts contests.

Opposite the main entrance to the Budōkan, past the parking lot, a pathway leads off through the park, back in the direction of the palace. Cross the bridge at the other end of the path, turn right, then right again before you leave the park on the driveway that leads to the **Kōgeikan** ⑬, in which collections are devoted to works of traditional craftsmanship by the great modern masters.

Return to the park exit and cross the street to the palace side. Ahead of you is the **Inui-mon.** This gate is used primarily by members of the imperial family and by the fortunate few with special invitations to visit the palace itself. A driveway here leads to the Imperial Household Agency and the palace. A bit farther down the hill is the **Kita-Hane-bashi-mon,** mentioned earlier as one of the entrances to the Imperial Palace East Garden.

At the foot of the hill is **Take-bashi**—the name means Bamboo Bridge, but the original construction has, of course, long since given way to reinforced concrete. Here, depending on your reserves of time and energy, you might want to cross the street to see the collection of modern Japanese and Western work in the **Tōkyō Kokuritsu Kindai Bijutsukan** ⑭. On the palace side of Take-bashi is the finely reconstructed **Hirakawa-mon** ⑮, the East Garden's third entrance, which will complete the loop on this walk. From here, follow the moat as it turns south again around the garden. In a few minutes you will find yourself back at Ōte-mon, tired, perhaps, but triumphant.

TIMING

The Imperial Palace area covers a lot of ground—uphill and down—and even in its shorter versions the walk includes plenty to see. Allow at least an hour for the East Garden and Outer Garden of the palace itself, and another if you've booked a guided tour of the Supreme Court. Distances have a way of getting longer as you go; plan to visit Yasukuni Jinja after lunch and spend at least an hour there. The Yūshūkan and Kōgeikan museums are both small and should engage you no more than half an hour each, but the modern art museum will repay a more leisurely visit—particularly if there's a special exhibit. Set your own pace, but assume that this walk will take you a full day, one way or another.

Avoid Mondays, when the East Garden and museums are closed; the East Garden is also closed on Fridays. In July and August, heat will make the palace walk grueling—bring hats and parasols, and carry a bottle of water.

Sights to See

⑪ Chidori-ga-fuchi Kōen. High on the edge (*fuchi* means edge) of the Imperial Palace moat, this park is pleasantly arrayed with cherry trees. Long before Edo-jō was built, there was a lovely little lake here, which Ieyasu Tokugawa incorporated into his system of defenses. Now you can rent a rowboat at **Chidori-ga-fuchi Boathouse**, roughly in the middle of the park, and explore it at your leisure. The park entrance is near Yasukuni Jinja, west and downhill from the corner of Yasukuni-dōri and Uchi-bori-dōri. ☎ *03/3234–1948.* 🚣 *Boat rentals ¥200 for 30 mins.* ☉ *Tues.–Sun. 9:30–4:30 (July and Aug. to 5:30); closed Dec. 16–Feb. 28. Subway: Hanzō-mon and Tōei Shinjuku lines, Kudanshita.*

⑨ Hanzō-mon. The house of the legendary Hattori Hanzō was once at the foot of this small wooden gate. Hanzō was the leader of the shōgun's private corps of spies and infiltrators—and assassins, if need be. They were the menacing, black-clad *ninja,* perennial material for historical adventure films and television dramas. The house is a minute's walk east from the subway. *Subway: Hanzō-mon Line, Hanzō-mon.*

⑮ Hirakawa-mon. The approach to this gate crosses the only wooden bridge that spans the moat. The gate and bridge are reconstructions, but Hirakawa-mon is especially beautiful, looking much as it must have when the shōgun's ladies used it on their rare excursions from the seraglio. Hirakawa-mon is the north gate to the East Garden, southeast of Take-bashi. *Subway: Tōzai Line, Take-bashi.*

② Imperial Palace East Garden. The entrance to the East Garden is the ☞ **Ōte-mon**, once the main gate of Ieyasu Tokugawa's castle. In lieu of paying an admission fee, you will collect a plastic token at the office on the other side of the gate. The bloodcurdling shrieks and howls you may hear on your left as you walk up the driveway are harmless. They come from the National Police Agency *dōjō* (martial arts hall). The hall was built in the Taishō period (1912–25) and is still used for *kendō* (Japanese fencing) practice. On the right is the Ōte Rest House, where for ¥100 you can buy a simple map of the garden.

There was another gate at the top of the driveway, where feudal lords summoned to the palace would descend from their palanquins and proceed on foot. The gate itself is gone, but two 19th-century guardhouses survive, one outside the massive stone supports on the right and a longer one inside on the left. The latter was known as the **Hundred-Man Guardhouse**, and this approach was defended by four shifts of 100 soldiers each. Past it, to the right, is the entrance to what was once the *ni-no-maru*, the "second circle" of the fortress. It is now a grove and garden, its pathways defined by rows of rhododendrons manicured to within an inch of their lives, with a pond and a waterfall in the northwest corner. At the far end of the ni-no-maru is the **Suwa Tea Pavilion,** an early 19th-century building relocated here from another part of the castle grounds.

The steep stone walls of the *hon-maru* (the "inner circle"), with the Moat of Swans below (the swans are actually in the outer waterways), dominate the west side of the garden. Halfway along, a steep path leads to an entrance in the wall to the upper fortress. This is **Shio-mi-zaka,** which translates roughly as "Briny View Hill," so named because in the Edo period one could see the ocean from here.

Nothing remains on the broad expanse of the hon-maru's lawn to recall the scores of buildings that once stood here, connected by a network of corridors. But you can see the stone foundations of the castle keep at the far end of the grounds. As you enter, turn left and explore the wooded paths that skirt the perimeter. There is shade and quiet, and benches are available where you can sit, rest your weary feet, and listen to bird songs. In the southwest corner, through the trees, you can see the back of the **Fujimi Yagura,** the only surviving watchtower of the hon-maru; farther along the path, on the west side, is the **Fujimi Tamon,** one of the two remaining armories.

The foundations of the keep make a platform with a fine view of **Kita-no-maru Kōen** and the city to the north. The view must have been even finer from the keep itself. Built and rebuilt three times, it soared more than 250 ft over Edo. The other castle buildings were all plastered white; the keep was black, unadorned but for a golden roof. In 1657 a fire destroyed most of the city. Strong winds carried the flames across the moat, where it consumed the keep in a heat so fierce that it melted the gold in the vaults underneath. The keep was never rebuilt.

To the left of the keep foundations, there is an exit from the hon-maru that leads northwest to the **Kita-Hane-bashi-mon** gate. To the right, another road leads past the **Toka Music Hall,** an octagonal tower faced in mosaic tile, built in honor of the empress in 1966, down to the ni-no-maru and out of the gardens by way of the northern ☞ **Hi-rakawa-mon.** If you decide to leave the hon-maru the way you came in, through the Ōte-mon, stop for a moment at the rest house on the west side of the park before you surrender your token and look at the pairs of before-and-after photographs along the wall—taken about 100 years apart. In the 1870s, much of the castle was in astonishing disrepair, and the warriors of the Hundred-Man Guardhouse were a trifle ragtag. The imperial seat, and the city around it, have acquired a little prosperity since then. ✉ *Free.* ☉ *Sun., Tues.–Thurs., Sat. 9–3; closed Dec. 25–Jan. 5. Subway: Ōte-machi stop.*

3 **Imperial Palace Outer Garden.** When the office buildings of the Meiji government were moved from this area in 1899, the whole expanse along the east side of the palace was turned into a public promenade and planted with stands of pine. The Outer Garden affords the best view of the castle walls and their Tokugawa-period fortifications: ☞ **Ni-jū Bashi** and the Sei-mon, the 17th-century Fujimi Yagura watchtower, and the ☞ **Sakurada-mon.** Surely the most photographed spot on any visitor's itinerary, this corner of the park is traditionally the starting point for local joggers to begin their 5-km (3-mi) run around the palace. Sei-mon is open only on January 2 and December 23, when the public is allowed inside to offer holiday greetings to the imperial family. *Subway: Chiyoda Line, Ni-jū Bashi-mae.*

13 **Kōgeikan** (Crafts Gallery of the National Museum of Modern Art). Built in 1910, the Kōgeikan was once the headquarters of the Imperial Guard. It is a rambling redbrick building, Gothic Revival in style, with exhibition halls on the second floor. The exhibits are all too few, but many of the craftspeople represented here—masters in the traditions of lacquerware, textiles, pottery, and metalwork—have been designated by the government as Living National Treasures. The most direct access to the gallery is from the Take-bashi subway station on the Tōzai Line. Walk west and uphill about 10 minutes, on the avenue between Kita-no-maru Kōen and the Imperial Palace grounds; the entrance will be on the right. ✉ *1-1 Kita-no-maru Kōen, Chiyoda-ku,* ☎ *03/3211-7781.* ✉ *¥420 (includes admission to National Museum of Modern Art); additional fee for special exhibitions.* ☉ *Tues.–Sun. 10–5. Subway: Hanzō-mon and Tōei Shinjuku lines, Kudanshita.*

❻ **National Diet Building.** This chunky pyramid houses the Japanese Parliament. Completed in 1936 after 17 years of work, it is a building best contemplated from a distance. On a gloomy day, it might well have sprung from the screen of a German expressionist movie. Exiting at Kokkai-Gijidō-mae on the Maru-no-uchi Line will place you in front of the building. *Subway: Maru-no-uchi Line, Kokkai-Gijidō-mae.*

❽ **National Theater** (Kokuritsu Gekijō). Like the Supreme Court, Hiroyuki Iwamoto's 1966 National Theater building was a design competition winner. The result was a rendition in concrete of the ancient *azekura* (storehouse) style, best exemplified by the 8th-century Shōsōin Imperial Repository in Nara. The large hall seats 1,746 and presents primarily Kabuki theater, ancient court music, and dance. The small hall seats 630 and is used primarily for Bunraku puppet theater and traditional music. ✉ *4-1 Hayabusa-chō, Chiyoda-ku,* ☎ *03/3265–7411. Ticket prices vary considerably depending on performance. Subway: Hanzōmon Line, Hanzōmon.*

★ **❹** **Ni-jū Bashi** (Two-Tiered Bridge). This is surely the most photogenic spot on the grounds of the former Edo-jō, which you can approach no closer than the head of the short stone bridge called the **Sei-mon Sekkyō.** Cordoned off on the other side is the **Sei-mon** (Main Gate), through which ordinary mortals may pass only on January 2 and December 23. The guards in front of their small, octagonal, copper-roof sentry boxes change every hour on the hour—alas, with nothing like the pomp and ceremony of Buckingham Palace. Ni-jū Bashi arcs over the moat from the area inside Sei-mon. In the background, the **Fushimi Yagura** watchtower makes for a picturesque backdrop. The bridge is a minute's walk north of the subway; follow the Imperial Palace moat to the courtyard in front of the gate. *Subway: Yūraku-chō Line, Sakurada-mon.*

⓬ **Nippon Budōkan.** With its eight-sided plan based on the Hall of Dreams of Hōryū-ji in Nara, the Budōkan was built as a martial arts arena for the Tōkyō Olympics of 1964. It still hosts tournaments and exhibitions of jūdō, karate, and Japanese fencing, as well as concerts. Tōkyō promoters are fortunate in their audiences, who don't seem to mind that the ticket prices are exorbitant, the acoustics are unforgivable, and the overselling is downright hazardous. From the Kudanshita subway stop, walk west uphill toward Yasukuni Jinja; the entrance to Kitano Maru Kōen and the Budōkan is a few minutes' walk from the station, on the left. ✉ *2-3 Kitano Maru Kōen, Chidoya-ku,* ☎ *03/3216–5100. Subway: Hanzō-mon and Tōei Shinjuku lines, Kudanshita.*

Ōte-mon. This gate is the main entrance to the Imperial Palace East Garden. In former days it was the principal gate of Ieyasu Tokugawa's castle. The so-called *masu* (box) style was typical of virtually all the approaches to the shōgun's impregnable fortress: The first portal leads to a narrow enclosure with a second and larger gate beyond, offering the defenders inside a devastating field of fire upon any would-be intruders. Most of the Ōte-mon was destroyed in 1945 but was rebuilt in 1967 on the original plans. The outer part of the gate, however, survived. *Subway: Ōte-machi stop.*

❺ **Sakurada-mon** (Gate of the Field of Cherry Trees). Sakurada-mon is another *masu* gate. By hallowed use and custom, the small courtyard between the portals is where joggers warm up for their 5-km (3-mi) run around the palace—many will already have passed you. Jogging around the palace is a ritual that begins as early as 6 AM and goes on throughout the day, no matter what the weather. Almost everybody runs the course counterclockwise. Now and then you may spot someone going the opposite way, but rebellious behavior of this sort is frowned upon in Japan. *Subway: Yūraku-chō Line, Sakurada-mon.*

❼ Supreme Court. Designed by Shinichi Okada, the Supreme Court building was the last in a series of open architectural competitions sponsored by the various government agencies charged with the reconstruction of Tōkyō after World War II. Its fortresslike planes and angles speak volumes for the role of the law in Japanese society—here is the very bastion of the established order. Okada's winning design was one of 217 submitted. Before the building was finished, in 1968, the open competition had generated so much controversy that the government did not hold another one for almost 20 years. Guided tours are normally offered only to Japanese student groups but can sometimes be arranged for others in May and October. ⊠ *4-2 Hayabusa-chō, Chiyoda-ku,* ☎ *03/3264–8111 for public relations office (Kōhōka) for permission to visit inside. Subway: Hanzō-mon Line, Hanzō-mon.*

⓮ Tōkyō Kokuritsu Kindai Bijutsukan (National Museum of Modern Art). Founded in 1952 and moved to its present site in 1969, the museum mounts a number of major exhibitions of 20th-century Japanese and Western art throughout the year. The second through fourth floors house the permanent collection, which includes the painting, prints, and sculpture of Rousseau, Picasso, Tsuguji Fujita, Ryūzaburo Umehara, and Taikan Yokoyama. ⊠ *3 Kita-no-maru Kōen, Chiyoda-ku,* ☎ *03/3214–2561.* ☞ *¥420 (includes admission to Kōgeikan [Crafts Gallery]); additional fees for special exhibitions.* ☉ *Tues.–Thurs. and weekends 10–5, Fri. 10–8. Subway: Tōzai Line, Take-bashi.*

❶ Tōkyō Eki (Tōkyō Station). The work of Kingo Tatsuno, one of Japan's first modern architects, Tōkyō Eki was completed in 1914. Tatsuno modeled his creation on the railway station of Amsterdam. The building lost its original top story in the air raids of 1945, but it was promptly repaired. More recent plans to tear it down entirely were scotched by a protest movement. Inside, it seems to be in a constant state of redesign and renovation, but the lovely old facade remains untouched. The best thing about the place is the **Tōkyō Station Hotel,** which wanders along the west side on the second and third floors; the windows along the corridor look out over the station rotunda. The hotel's frosted glass, flocked wallpaper, and heavy red drapes have seen better days—but you couldn't ask for more central accommodations. ⊠ *1-9-1 Maru-no-uchi, Chiyoda-ku,* ☎ *03/3231–2511.*

❿ Yasukuni Jinja (Shrine of Peace for the Nation). Founded in 1869, Yasukuni Jinja is dedicated to the approximately 2.5 million Japanese who have died since then in war or military service. Since 1945, Yasukuni has been the periodic focus of passionate political debate, given that the Japanese constitution expressly renounces both militarism and state sponsorship of religion. Even so, hundreds of thousands of Japanese come here every year, simply to pray for the repose of friends and relatives they have lost. For gai-jin, Yasukuni affords insight into the Japanese historical consciousness available nowhere else.

The shrine is not one structure but a complex of buildings that includes the **Main Hall** and the **Hall of Worship,** both built in the simple, unadorned style of the ancient Shintō shrines at Ise, and the **Yūshūkan** museum of documents and war memorabilia. There is also a **Nō theater,** and, in the far western corner, a sumō-wrestling ring. Both Nō and sumō have their origins in religious ritual, as performances offered to please and divert the gods. Sumō matches are held at Yasukuni in April, during the first of its three annual festivals.

Pick up a pamphlet and simplified map of the shrine in English from the guard station on the right as you enter. Just ahead of you, in a circle on the main avenue, is a statue of Masujiro Omura, commander of the imperial forces that subdued the Tokugawa loyalist resistance to the new Meiji government in 1868. From here, as you look down the avenue to your right, you see the enormous steel outer *torii* of the main entrance to the shrine at Kudanshita; to the left, there is a bronze inner torii that was erected in 1887. (These Shintō shrine arches are normally made of wood and painted red.) Beyond the inner torii is the gate to the shrine itself, with its 12 pillars and chrysanthemums—the imperial crest—embossed on the doors.

None of the displays in the Yūshūkan are identified in English, although in some cases the meanings are clear enough. Rooms on the second floor house an especially fine collection of medieval swords and armor. Perhaps the most bizarre exhibit is the *kaiten* (human torpedo) on the first floor—it is the submarine equivalent of a kamikaze plane. The kaiten was a black cylinder about 50 ft long and 3 ft in diameter, with 3,400 pounds of high explosives in the nose and a man in the center, squeezed into a seat, who peered into a periscope and worked the directional vanes with his feet. It was carried into battle on the deck of a ship and launched against the enemy. On its one-way journey, a kaiten had a maximum range of about 8 km (5 mi).

If time permits, turn right as you leave the Yūshūkan and walk past the other implements of war (cannons, ancient and modern; a tank, incongruously bright and gay in its green-and-yellow camouflage paint) arrayed in front of the pond at the rear of the shrine. There is, unfortunately, no admittance to the teahouses on the far side, but the pond is among the most serene and beautiful in Tōkyō, especially in spring, when the irises are in bloom. ⊠ *3-1-1 Kudankita, Chiyoda-ku,* ☎ *03/ 3261–8326.* 🎫 *¥200.* ☾ *Museum Mar.–Oct., daily 9–5; Nov.–Feb., daily 9–4:30; closed Dec. 28–31. Grounds generally 9–9. Subway: Hanzō-mon and Tōei Shinjuku lines, Kudanshita.*

NEED A
BREAK?   The specialty at the moderately priced **Tony Roma's,** as it is in this chain's umpteen locations, is charcoal-broiled spare ribs. It is on the west side of Uchi-bori-dōri north of the British Embassy, at the intersection straight west of Inui-mon. ⊠ *1 Samban-chō, Chiyoda-ku,* ☎ *03/3222–3440.* ☾ *Daily noon–3 and 5–11.*

Akihabara and Jimbō-chō

This is it: the greatest sound-and-light show on earth. Akihabara is a merchandise mart for anything—and everything—that runs on electricity: block after block of it, with a combined annual turnover well in excess of ¥30 trillion. Here you'll find microprocessors, washing machines, stereo systems, blenders, television sets, and gadgets that beep when your bath water is hot. Wherever you go in the world, if people know nothing else about Japan, they recognize the country as a cornucopia of electronics equipment and household appliances. About 10% of what Japan's electronics industry makes for the domestic market passes through Akihabara.

Just after World War II there was a black market here, around the railroad station, where the Yamanote Line and the crosstown Sōbu Line intersect. In time, most of the stalls were doing a legitimate business in radio parts, and in 1951 they were all relocated in one dense clump under the tracks. Retail and wholesale suppliers prospered there in less-than-peaceful coexistence as they spread out into the adjacent blocks and made the area famous for cut-rate prices.

No visitor to Tōkyō neglects this district; the mistake is to come here merely for shopping. Akihabara may be consumer heaven, but it is also the first stop on a walking tour through the general area known as Kanda—where the true *Edokko*, the born-and-bred Tōkyōites of the old town, claim their roots—to the bookstalls of Jimbō-chō. In a sense, this tour is a journey through time: It's a morning's walk from satellite broadcast antennas to the hallowed precincts of the printed word.

Numbers in the text correspond to numbers in the margin and on the Akihabara and Jimbō-chō map.

A Good Walk

Start at the west exit of the JR Akihabara Station. (There's also a stop nearby on the Hibiya subway line, but the JR provides much easier access.) Come out to the left after you pass through the wicket, into the station square, turn right, and walk to the main thoroughfare. Ahead of you on the other side of the street you'll see the **LAOX** ⑯ building, one of the district's major discount stores.

Before you get to the corner, on the right is a little warren of stalls and tiny shops that cannot have changed an iota since the days of the black market—except for their merchandise. Wander through the narrow passageways and see an astonishing array of switches, transformers, resistors, semiconductors, printed circuit cards, plugs, wires, connectors, and tools; the labyrinth is especially popular with domestic and foreign techno mavens, the people who know—or want to know—what the latest in Japanese electronic technology looks like from the inside.

If you turned left at the corner and crossed the small bridge over the Kanda-gawa, you would soon come to the **Kōtsū Hakubutsukan** ⑰— a detour you might want to make if you have children in tow. If not, turn right at the corner and walk north on Chūō-dōri. Music blares at you from hundreds of storefronts as you walk along; this is the heart of the district. Most larger stores on the main drag have one floor— or even an entire annex—of products for the foreign market, staffed by clerks who speak everything from English to Mandarin to Portuguese. Prices, of course, are duty-free (don't forget to bring your passport. By far the biggest selections are to be found at rival stores **Yamagiwa and Minami** ⑱. Yamagiwa is just past the second intersection, on the right, and Minami is at the far end of the block.

At Minami, cross the street, continue north to the Soto Kanda 5-chōme intersection (there's an entrance to the Suehiro-chō subway station on the corner), and turn left on Kura-mae-bashi-dōri. Walk about five minutes—you will cross one more intersection with a traffic light— and in the middle of the next block you will see a flight of steps on the left, between two new brick buildings. Red, green, and blue pennants flutter from the handrails. This is the back entrance to **Kanda Myōjin** ⑲.

Leave the shrine by the main gate. The seated figures in the alcoves on either side are its guardian gods; carved in camphor wood, they are depicted in Heian costume, holding long bows. From the gate down to the copper-clad torii on Hongo-dōri is a walk of a few yards. On either side are shops that sell the specialties famous in this neighborhood: pickles, miso, and sweet sake laced with ground ginger. On the other side of the avenue you will see the wall and wooded surrounds of **Yūshima Seidō** ⑳ Confucian shrine.

Cross Hongo-dōri and turn left, following the wall downhill. Turn right at the first narrow side street, and right again at the bottom; the en-

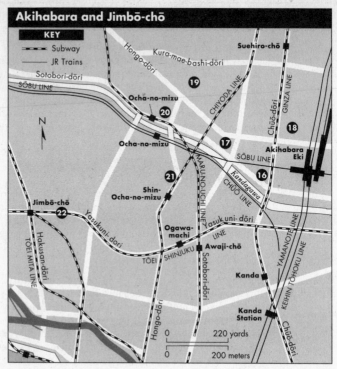

trance to Yūshima Seidō is a few steps from the corner. Japan's first museum and its first national library were built on these grounds; both were soon relocated. As you walk up the path, you will see a statue of Confucius on your right; where the path ends, a flight of stone steps leads up to the main hall of the shrine—six times destroyed by fire, each time rebuilt. The last repairs date to 1954. The hall could almost be in China: Painted black, weathered and somber, it looks like nothing else you are likely to see in Japan.

Retrace your steps, turn right as you leave the shrine, and walk along the continuation of the wall on the side street leading up to **Hijiri-bashi** (Bridge of Sages), which spans the Kanda-gawa at Ocha-no-mizu Station on the JR Sōbu Line. Cross the bridge—you're now back on Hongo-dōri—and ahead of you, just beyond the station on the right, you'll see the dome of the Russian Orthodox **Nikolai Cathedral** ㉑.

Continue south to the intersection of Hongo-dōri and Yasukuni-dōri. Surugadai, the area to your right as you walk down the hill, is a kind of fountainhead of Japanese higher education: Two of the city's major private universities—Meiji and Nihon—occupy a good part of the hill. Not far from these are a score of elite high schools, public and private. In the 1880s, several other universities were founded in this area. They have since moved away, but the student population here is still enormous. Nihon Daigaku (Japan University) alone accepts some 16,000 freshmen a year to its undergraduate program.

Students are not as serious as they used to be. So sayeth every generation, but as you turn right on Yasukuni-dōri, you encounter palpable proof. Between you and your objective—the **bookstores of Jimbō-chō** ㉒—are three blocks of stores devoted almost exclusively to electric guitars, records, travel bags, skis, and skiwear. The bookstores begin at the intersection called Surugadai-shita and continue along Yasukuni-dōri for about 450 yards, most of them on the south (left) side of the street. This area is to print what Akihabara is to electronics.

What about that word processor or CD player you didn't buy at the beginning of your walk because you didn't want to carry it all this way? No problem. There's a subway station (Tōei Mita Line) at the Jimbō-chō main intersection; go one stop north to Suidō-bashi, transfer to the JR Sōbu Line, and five minutes later you're back in Akihabara.

TIMING

Unless you do a lot of shopping, this walk should take you no more than a morning. Cultural landmarks are few, and you can explore them thoroughly in half an hour each. Getting from place to place will take up much of your time. Keep in mind that most stores in Akihabara do not open until 10 AM. Weekends draw hordes of shoppers, but crowds thin out a bit Sunday, when the four central blocks of Chūō-dōri are closed to traffic and become a pedestrian mall.

Sights to See

㉒ Bookstores of Jimbō-chō. For the ultimate browse through art books, catalogs, scholarly monographs, secondhand paperbacks, and dictionaries in most known languages, the hon-ya (bookstores) of Jimbō-chō are the place. A number of the antiquarian booksellers here carry not only rare typeset editions but also woodblock-printed books of the Edo period and individual prints. At shops like **Isseido** (⊠ 1-7 Kanda Jimbō-chō, Chiyoda-ku, ☎ 03/3292–0071) and **Ohya Shōbō** (⊠ 1-1 Kanda Jimbō-chō, Chiyoda-ku, ☎ 03/3291–0062), it is still possible to find a genuine Hiroshige or Toyokuni print—if not in the best condition—at an affordable price. The area is home as well to wholesalers, distributors, and many of Japan's most prestigious publishing houses. The bookstores run for a quarter mile on Yasukuni-dōri beginning at the Surugadai-shita intersection. *Subway: Jimbō-chō on the Tōei Shinjuku and Tōei Mita lines.*

⑲ Kanda Myōjin. This shrine is said to have been founded in 730 in a village called Shibasaki, where the Ōte-machi financial district stands today. In 1616 it was relocated, a victim of Ieyasu Tokugawa's ever-expanding system of fortifications. The present site was chosen, in accordance with Chinese geomancy, to afford the best view from Edo Castle and protect it from evil influences. The shrine itself was destroyed in the earthquake of 1923, and the present buildings reproduce in concrete the style of 1616. Ieyasu preferred the jazzier decorative effects of Chinese Buddhism to the simple lines of traditional Shintō architecture. This is especially evident in the curved, copper-tile roof of the main shrine and in the two-story front gate.

Three principle deities are enshrined here: Daikoku, Ebisu, and Taira no Masakado. Daikoku looks after the well-being of farming and fishing villages. Ebisu is the god of success in business, family prosperity, and happy marriages. Taira-no-Masakado was a 10th-century warrior whose contentious spirit earned him a place in the Shintō pantheon: He led a revolt against the Imperial Court in Kyōto, seized control of the eastern provinces, declared himself emperor—and in 940 was beheaded for his rebellious ways. The townspeople of Kanda, contentious souls in their own right, made Taira-no-Masakado a kind of patron saint, and even today—oblivious somehow to the fact that he lost—they appeal to him for victory when they face a tough encounter.

Some of the smaller buildings you see as you come up the steps and walk around the main hall contain the *mikoshi*—the portable shrines that are featured in one of Tōkyō's three great blowouts, the **Kanda Festival.** (The other two are the Sannō Festival of the Hie Shrine in Nagata-chō and the Sanja Festival of the Asakusa Jinja.) The essential shrine festival is a procession in which the gods, housed for the occasion in their mikoshi, pass through the streets and get a breath of fresh air. The Kanda Festival began in the early Edo period. Heading the procession then were 36 magnificent floats, most of which were destroyed in the fires that raged through the city after the earthquake of 1923. The floats that lead the procession today move in stately measure on wheeled carts, attended by the priests and officials of the shrine in Heian-period (794–1185) costume. The mikoshi, some 70 of them, follow behind, bobbing and weaving, carried on the shoulders of the townspeople. Shrine festivals like Kanda's are a peculiarly competitive form of worship: Piety is a matter of who can shout the loudest, drink the most beer, and have the best time. The festival takes place in odd-numbered years. Kanda Myōjin is west on Kuramae-bashi-dōri, about five minutes from the Suehiro-chō stop on the Ginza Line. ⊠ *2-16-2 Soto Kanda, Chiyoda-ku,* ☎ *03/3254–0753.*

⟨ 🖑 ⟩ ⑰ **Kōtsū Hakubutsukan** (Transportation Museum). This is a fun place to take children. Displays explain the early development of the railway system and include a miniature layout of the rail services, as well as Japan's first airplane, which lifted off in 1903. To get here from the JR Akihabara Eki, cross the bridge on Chūō-dōri over the Kanda-gawa and turn right at the next corner. ⊠ *1-25 Kanda Sudachō, Chiyoda-ku,* ☎ *03/3251–8481.* 🎟 *¥310.* ⊗ *Tues.–Sun. 9:30–4:30.*

⑯ **LAOX.** Of all of the discount stores in Akihabara, LAOX has the largest and most comprehensive selection, with four buildings in this area—one exclusively for musical instruments, another for duty-free appliances—and outlets in Yokohama and Narita. Shop here for cameras, watches, and pearls. ⊠ *1-2-9 Soto Kanda, Chiyoda-ku,* ☎ *03/3255–9041.* ⊗ *Daily 10–7:30. JR Akihabara Eki.*

㉑ **Nikolai Cathedral.** Formally, this is the Holy Resurrection Cathedral. The more familiar name derives from its founder, St. Nikolai Kassatkin (1836–1912), a Russian missionary who came to Japan in 1861 and spent the rest of his life here propagating the Orthodox faith. The building, planned by a Russian engineer and executed by a British architect, was completed in 1891. Heavily damaged in the earthquake of 1923, the cathedral was restored with a dome much more modest than the original. Even so, it endows this otherwise featureless part of the city with the charm of the unexpected. ⊠ *4-1 Surugadai, Kanda, Chiyoda-ku,* ☎ *03/3295–6879.* 🎟 *Free.* ⊗ *Tues.–Sat. 1–4. Subway: Chiyoda Line, Shin-Ocha-no-mizu.*

⑱ **Yamagiwa and Minami.** These rival giants have whole floors devoted to computer hardware, software, fax machines, and copiers; Yamagiwa has a particularly good selection of lighting fixtures, most of them—alas—for 220 volts. ⊠ *Yamagiwa: 4-1-1 Soto Kanda, Chiyoda-ku,* ☎ *03/3253–2111;* ⊗ *Weekdays 10:30–7:30, weekends 10–7:30.* ⊠ *Minami: 4-3-3 Soto Kanda, Chiyoda-ku,* ☎ *03/3255–3730;* ⊗ *Weekdays 10:30–7, weekends 10–7. JR Akihabara Eki.*

⑳ **Yūshima Seidō.** The origins of this shrine date back to a hall for the study of the Chinese Confucian classics that was founded in 1632. The original building was in Ueno, and its headmaster was Hayashi Razan, the official Confucian scholar to the Tokugawa government. The shogunal dynasty found these Chinese teachings—with their emphasis on obedience and hierarchy—attractive enough to make Confucianism a kind of state ideology. Moved to its present site in 1691, the hall became an academy for the ruling elite. In a sense, nothing has changed: In 1872 the new Meiji government established the country's first teacher training institute here, and that, in turn, evolved into Tōkyō University—the graduates of which still make up much of the ruling elite. ✉ *1-4-25 Yūshima, Bunkyō-ku,* ☎ *03/3251–4606.* ☜ *Free.* ☉ *Fri.– Wed. 9:30–5. Subway: Maru-no-uchi Line, Ocha-no-mizu.*

Ueno

Japan Railways' Ueno Eki is Tōkyō's Gare du Nord: the gateway to and from Japan's northeast provinces. The single most important fact of Japanese life since the 17th century has been the pull of the cities. Since 1883, when the station was completed, it has served as a terminus in the great migration from the villages, of people in pursuit of a better life.

Ueno was a place of prominence long before the coming of the railroad. When Ieyasu Tokugawa established his capital here in 1603, it was merely a wooded promontory, called Shi-no-bugaoka (the Hill of Endurance), overlooking the bay. The view was a pleasant one, and Ieyasu gave a large tract of land on the hill to one of his most important vassals, Takatora Toda, who designed and built Edo-jō. Ieyasu's heir, Hidetada, later commanded the founding of a temple on the hill. Shi-no-bugaoka was in the northeast corner of the capital. In Chinese geomancy, the northeast approach required a particularly strong defense against evil influences.

That defense was entrusted to Tenkai (1536–1643), a priest of the Tendai sect of Buddhism and an adviser of great influence to the first three Tokugawa shōguns. The temple he built on Shi-no-bugaoka was called Kanei-ji, and he became the first abbot. The patronage of the Tokugawas and their vassal barons made Kanei-ji a seat of power and glory. By the end of the 17th century, it occupied most of the hill. To the magnificent Main Hall were added scores of other buildings—including a pagoda and a shrine to Ieyasu—and 36 subsidiary temples. The city of Edo itself expanded to the foot of the hill, where Kanei-ji's main gate once stood. And most of what is now Ueno was called *Mon-zen-machi*: "the town in front of the gate."

The power and glory of Kanei-ji came to an end in just one day: April 11, 1868. An army of clan forces from the western part of Japan, bearing a mandate from Emperor Meiji, arrived in Edo and demanded the surrender of the castle. The shogunate was by then a tottering regime; it capitulated, and with it went everything that had depended on the favor of the Tokugawas. The Meiji Restoration began with a bloodless coup.

A band of some 2,000 Tokugawa loyalists assembled on Ueno Hill, however, and defied the new government. On May 15, the imperial army attacked. The Shōgitai (loyalists), outnumbered and surrounded, soon discovered that right was on the side of modern artillery. A few survivors fled; the rest committed ritual suicide—and took Kanei-ji with them—torching the temple and most of its outbuildings.

The new Meiji government turned Ueno Hill into one of the nation's first public parks. The intention was not merely to provide a bit of greenery but to make the park an instrument of civic improvement and to show off the achievements of an emerging modern state. It would serve as the site of trade and industrial expositions; it would have a national museum, a library, a university of fine arts, and a zoo. That policy continued well into the present era, with the building of further galleries and concert halls—but Ueno is more than its museums. The Shōgitai failed to take everything with them: Some of the most important buildings in the temple complex survived or were restored. The "town in front of the gate" is gone, but here and there, in the narrow streets below the hill, the way of life is much the way it was 100 years ago.

Numbers in the text correspond to numbers in the margin and on the Ueno map.

A Good Walk

The best way to begin is to come to Ueno on the JR Yamanote Line and leave the station by the *kōen-guchi* (park exit) on the upper level. Directly across from the exit is the **Tōkyō Bunka Kaikan** (☞ the Arts, *below*), designed by architect Maekawa Kunio and completed in 1961. This is one of the city's major venues for classical music, often booked for visiting orchestras and concert soloists. The large auditorium seats 2,327 and the smaller one 661.

Opposite the Bunka Kaikan on the right is the **Kokuritsu Seiyō Bijutsukan** ㉓. The Rodins in the courtyard—*The Gate of Hell, The Thinker,* and the magnificent *Burghers of Calais*—are authentic castings from Rodin's original molds. Just behind the Seiyō is the **Kokuritsu Kagaku Hakubutsukan** ㉔, and beyond that is a broad street that cuts through the park. Turn left on this street and you come almost immediately to the **Tōkyō Kokuritsu Hakubutsukan** ㉕. Here you should plan to spend some time, even if you are not overly fond of museums: it is one of the world's great repositories of East Asian art and archaeology.

Turn to the left as you leave the museum, walk east, and turn left again at the first corner. The building across the road on your right is the **Jigen-dō,** a memorial hall to Abbot Tenkai, who was given the posthumous title of Jigen Daishi (Great Master of the Merciful Eye). The six bronze lanterns in front, with their dragon faces, are especially fine.

At the end of the road that passes Jigen-dō, turn left again and walk along the back of the museum. To your right is the **cemetery** of Kanei-ji. Several Tokugawa shōguns had their mausoleums here. These were destroyed in the air raids of 1945, but the gate that led to the tomb of the fourth shōgun, Ietsuna, remains. At the end of the road, in the far northwest corner of the park, is **Kanei-ji** ㉖ itself. Behind the temple is the ornately carved gate to what was the mausoleum of Tsunayoshi, the fifth shōgun—famous in the annals of Tokugawa history for his disastrous fiscal mismanagement and his *Shōrui Awaremi no Rei* (Edicts on Compassion for Living Things), which, among other things, made it a capital offense for a human being to kill a dog.

Come out again through the main gate of the temple, and take the first right turn; this puts you on the road that circles the park. Walk south. If you take the first right turn off this road you will soon come to the **Tōkyō University of Arts Exhibition Hall** ㉗ on the left. Farther south along the road, you come to the broad street that runs through the center of the park. Turn left on it, return to the entrance of the Tōkyō Kokuritsu Hakubutsukan, and cross the street to the long esplanade with its reflecting pool. At the opposite end, the path to the right brings you to the **Tōkyō Metropolitan Art Museum** ㉘ with its small but impressive permanent collection of modern Japanese painting.

Return to the south end of the esplanade and you will see a sign for the entrance to the **Ueno Zoo** ㉙. Opened in 1882, the zoo gradually expanded to its present 35 acres. The original section on the hill was connected to the one below, along the edge of **Shinobazu Pond** ㉚ by a bridge and a monorail. The process of the zoo's expansion somehow left within its confines the five-story **Kanei-ji Pagoda.** Built in 1631 and rebuilt after a fire in 1639, the 120-ft pagoda is painted vermilion and

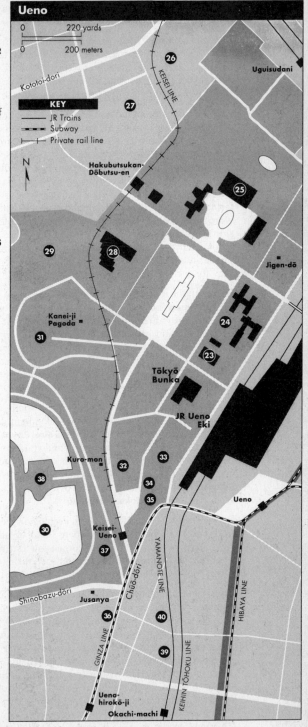

Ueno

0 220 yards
0 200 meters

KEY
— JR Trains
⋯ Subway
⊢⊣ Private rail line

N

Kototoi-dōri

KEISEI LINE

Uguisudani

Hakubutsukan-Dōbutsu-en

Jigen-dō

Kanei-ji Pagoda

Tōkyō Bunka

JR Ueno Eki

Kura-mon

Ueno

Keisei-Ueno

Shinobazu-dōri Jusanya

Chūō-dōri

YAMANOTE LINE

HIBAYA LINE

GINZA LINE

KEIHIN TŌHOKU LINE

Ueno-hirokō-ji

Okachi-machi

has a copper roof on the top level. Most gai-jin find it a bit out of keeping with the bison cages next door.

A much better view of the pagoda is from the path that leads to **Tōshō-gū** ㉛—the shrine to the first Tokugawa shōgun, Ieyasu. Return to the esplanade and follow the sign to Tōshō-gū until you see a small police substation; just beyond it, on a narrow path, the entrance to the shrine is marked by a stone torii that was built in 1633.

After looking around the excellent Tōshō-gū, retrace your steps to the police substation, turn right, and follow the avenue south. Shortly you will see a kind of tunnel of red-lacquered torii, in front of a small **shrine to Inari**, a Shintō deity of harvests and family prosperity. Shrines of this kind are found all over the downtown part of Tōkyō, tucked away in alleys and odd corners, always with their guardian statues of foxes—the mischievous creatures with which the god is associated. A few steps farther, down a small road that branches to the right, is a **shrine to Sugawara Michizane** (854–903), a Heian-period nobleman and poet worshiped as the Shintō deity Tenjin. Because he is associated with scholarship and literary achievement, Japanese students visit his various shrines by the hundreds of thousands in February and March to pray for success on their college entrance exams.

Return to the main road and continue south. You will see on your left the **Kuro-mon** (black gate), a replica of one that once stood at the entrance to the entire Kanei-ji complex. Built in the early 17th century, it was the main gate of the Kokuritsu Hakubutsukan until it was moved to this site in 1937. The bullet holes in it were made during the battle for Ueno Hill in 1868. Through the gate and up the stone steps, **Kiyomizu Kannon-dō** ㉜ is one of the important temple structures that survived the Meiji-Tokugawa battle of 1868.

Leave Kiyomizu by the front gate, on the south side. As you look to your left, you will see a two-story brick administration building, on the other side of which is the **Ueno-no-Mori Royal Museum** ㉝. After a stop in the museum, continue south and you soon come to where the park narrows to a point. Two flights of steps lead down to the main entrance on Chūō-dōri. Before you reach the steps, on the left is the **Shōgitai Memorial** ㉞ and, a few steps away, with its back to the gravestone, the **statue of Takamori Saigō** ㉟.

Leave Ueno Kōen and walk south, keeping on the west side of Chūō-dōri until you get to the corner where Shinobazu-dōri comes in on the right. About a block beyond this corner, you'll see a building hung with banners; this is **Suzumoto** ㊱, a theater specializing in a traditional narrative comedy called *rakugo*.

Turn right at the Shinobazu-dōri intersection and walk west. A few doors from the corner is **Jusan-ya** (☞ Shopping, *below*), a nearly three-century-old family-run shop that sells handmade boxwood combs. Directly across the avenue is an entrance to the grounds of Shinobazu Pond; just inside, on the right, is the small black-and-white building that houses the **Shita-machi Museum** ㊲. Japanese society in the days of the Tokugawa shōguns was rigidly stratified. In Tōkyō—then called Edo—the common people lived "below the castle," most of them in long, single-story tenements called *nagaya*, one jammed up against the next along the narrow alleys and unplanned streets of Ueno and the areas nearby. They developed a unique culture and way of life—which the Shita-machi Museum presents superbly.

From in front of the museum, a path follows the eastern shore of Shinobazu Pond. On the island in the middle of it is **Benzaiten** ㊳, a shrine for the matron goddess of the arts. You can walk up the east side of the embankment to the causeway and cross to the shrine. Then cross to the other side of the pond, turn left in front of the **boathouse,** and follow the embankment back to Shinobazu-dōri. Off to your right as you walk, a few blocks away and out of sight begin the precincts of Tōkyō University, the nation's most prestigious seat of higher learning, alma mater to generations of bureaucrats. Turn left as you leave the park, and walk back in the direction of the Shita-machi Museum.

When you reach the intersection, cross Chūō-dōri and turn right; walk past the ABAB clothing store and turn left at the second corner: At the end of this street is **Tokudai-ji** ㊧, a temple over a supermarket, and the bustling heart of **Ame-ya Yoko-chō Market** ㊵. There are more than 500 little shops and stalls in this market, which stretches from the beginning of Shōwa-dōri at the north end to Ōkachi-machi at the south end. Ōkachi-machi means Ōkachi Town, and the *ōkachi* were the "honorable infantry," the samurai of lowest rank in the shōgun's service.

From here, follow the JR tracks as you wander north. In a few minutes, you will find yourself back in front of Ueno Station.

TIMING

Exploring Ueno can be one excursion or two: an afternoon of cultural browsing or a full day of discoveries in one of the great centers of the city. The best day to come is Thursday, when the Treasure Hall of the Tōkyō Kokuritsu Hakubutsukan is open; plan an hour or two for the museum as a whole. At a brisk pace, you can see most of what's worth seeing at Kanei-ji and Tōshō-gū in half an hour each. Ueno out of doors is no fun at all in February or the rainy season of late June to mid-July. In April the cherry blossoms of Ueno Kōen are glorious.

Sights to See

㊵ **Ame-ya Yoko-chō Market.** The history of Ame-ya Yoko-chō (often shortened to Ameyoko) begins in the desperate days immediately after World War II. Ueno Station had survived the bombings—virtually everything around it was rubble—and anyone who could make it here from the countryside with rice and other small supplies of food could sell them at exorbitant black-market prices. One thing not to be had in postwar Tōkyō at any price was sugar. Before long, there were hundreds of stalls in the black market selling various kinds of *ame* (confections), most of them made from sweet potatoes. These stalls gave the market its name: Ame-ya Yoko-chō means Confectioners' Alley.

Shortly before the Korean War, the market was legalized, and soon the stalls were carrying a full array of watches, chocolate, ballpoint pens, blue jeans, and T-shirts that had somehow been "liberated" from American PXs. In years to come, the merchants of Ameyoko diversified still further—to fine Swiss timepieces and French designer luggage of dubious authenticity, cosmetics, jewelry, fresh fruit, and fish. The market became especially famous for the traditional prepared foods of the New Year, and during the last few days of December, as many as half a million people crowd into the narrow alleys under the railroad tracks to stock up for the holiday. ✉ *Ueno 4-chōme, Taitō-ku.* ⊙ *Most shops and stalls 10–7. JR Ueno Eki.*

㊳ **Benzaiten.** Perched in the middle of Shinobazu Pond, this shrine is for the goddess Benten. She is one of the Seven Gods of Good Luck, a pantheon that emerged sometime in the medieval period from a jumble of Indian, Chinese, and Japanese mythology. As matron goddess of the arts, she is depicted holding a lute-like musical instrument called a *biwa.* The shrine, with its distinctive octagonal roof, was destroyed in the bombings of 1945. The present version is a faithful copy. You can rent rowboats and pedal boats at a nearby boathouse. *Boathouse:* ☎ 03/ 3828–9502; ⊘ *Daily 10–6; rowboats ¥600 for 1 hr, pedal boats ¥600 for 30 mins. JR Ueno Eki; Keisei private rail line, Keisei-Ueno Eki.*

㉖ Kanei-ji. In 1638 the second Tokugawa shōgun, Hidetaka, commissioned the priest Tenkai to build a temple on Shi-no-bugaoka Hill in Ueno to defend his city from evil spirits. Tenkai turned for his model to the great temple complex of Enryaku-ji in Kyōto, established centuries early on Mt. Hiei to protect the imperial capital. The main hall of Tenkai's temple, called Kanei-ji, was moved to Ueno from the town of Kawagoe, about 40 km (25 mi) away, where he had once been a priest; it was moved again, to its present site, in 1879, and looks a bit weary of its travels. ⊠ *1-14-11 Ueno Sakuragi, Taitō-ku,* ☎ *03/3821–1259.* 🎟 *Free; contributions welcome.* ⊘ *Daily 8:30–5. JR Ueno Eki, kōen-guchi.*

㉜ Kiyomizu Kannon-dō (Kannon Hall). This National Treasure was a part of Abbot Tenkai's grand attempt to echo in Ueno the grandeur of Kyōto, but the echo is a little weak. The model for it was Kyōto's magnificent Kiyomizu-dera, but where the original rests on enormous wood pillars over a gorge, the Ueno version merely perches on the lip of a little hill. And the hall would have a grand view of **Shinobazu Pond**—which itself was landscaped to recall Biwa-ko (Lake Biwa), near Kyōto—if the trees in front of the terrace were not too high and too full most of the year to afford any view at all. The principal Buddhist image of worship here is the Senjū Kannon (Thousand-Armed Goddess of Mercy). Another figure, however, receives greater homage. This is the Kosodate Kannon, who is believed to answer the prayers of women having difficulty conceiving children. If their prayers are answered, they return to Kiyomizu and leave a doll, as both an offering of thanks and a prayer for the child's health. In a ceremony held every September 25, the dolls that have accumulated during the year are burned in a bonfire. ⊠ *1-29 Ueno Kōen, Taitō-ku,* ☎ *03/3821–4749.* 🎟 *Free.* ⊘ *Daily 9–5. JR Ueno Eki, kōen-guchi.*

☝ ㉔ Kokuritsu Kagaku Hakubutsukan (National Science Museum). This conventional natural history museum has everything from dinosaurs to moon rocks on display, but it offers relatively little in the way of hands-on learning experiences. Kids seem to like it anyway—but otherwise this is not a place to linger if your time is short. ⊠ *7-20 Ueno Kōen, Taitō-ku,* ☎ *03/3822–0111.* 🎟 *¥420; additional fees for special exhibitions.* ⊘ *Tues.–Sun. 9–4. JR Ueno Eki, kōen-guchi.*

㉓ Kokuritsu Seiyō Bijutsukan (National Museum of Western Art). Along with castings from the original molds of Rodin's *Gate of Hell, The Burghers of Calais,* and *The Thinker,* the wealthy businessman Matsukata Kojiro acquired some 850 paintings, sketches, and prints by such masters as Renoir, Monet, and Cézanne. He kept the collection in Europe. The French government sent it to Japan after World War II—Matsukata left it to the country in his will—and it opened to the public in 1959 in a building designed by Swiss-born architect Le Corbusier. Since then, the museum has diversified a bit; more recent acquisitions include works by Reubens, Tintoretto, El Greco, Max Ernst, and Jackson Pollock. ⊠ *7-7 Ueno Kōen, Taitō-ku,* ☎ *03/3828–5131.* 🎟 *¥420; additional fee for special exhibitions.* ⊘ *Tues.–Thurs. and weekends 9:30–4:30, Fri. 9:30–6:30. JR Ueno Eki, kōen-guchi.*

㉚ Shinobazu Pond. Shinobazu was once an inlet of Tōkyō Bay. When the area was reclaimed it became a freshwater pond. The abbot Tenkai, founder of ☞ **Kanei-ji** on the hill above the pond, had an island made in the middle of it, on which he built ☞ **Benzaiten** for the goddess of the arts. Later improvements included a causeway to the island, embankments, and even a race course (1884–93). Today the pond is in three sections. The first, with its famous lotus plants, is a sanctuary for about 15 species of birds, including pintail ducks, cormorants, great egrets, and grebes. Some 5,000 wild ducks migrate here from as far away as Siberia, sticking around from September to April. The second section, to the north, belongs to Ueno Zoo; the third, to the west, is a small lake for boating.

During the first week of June, the path is lined on both sides with the stalls of the annual All-Japan Azalea Fair, a spectacular display of flowering bonzai shrubs and trees. Nurserymen in *happi* (workmen's) coats sell a variety of plants, seedlings, bonsai vessels, and ornamental stones. ⊠ *Shinobazu-dōri, Taitō-ku.* 🎫 *Free.* ☉ *Daily sunrise–sunset. Keisei private rail line, Keisei-Ueno Eki; JR Ueno Eki, kōen guchi.*

★ ㉝ **Shita-machi Hakubutsukan** (Shita-machi Museum). Shita-machi ("The Town Below the Castle") lay originally between Ieyasu's fortifications on the west and the Sumida River on the east. As it expanded, it came to include what today constitute the Chūō, Taitō, Sumida, and Kōtō wards. During the Edo period, some 80% of the city was allotted to the warrior class and to temples and shrines. In Shita-machi—the remaining 20% of space—lived the common folk, who made up more than half the population. The people below the castle were hardworking, short-tempered, free-spending, and quick to help a neighbor in trouble. And they were remarkably stubborn about their way of life, which as a result retained most of its character well into the modern period. Shita-machi Museum preserves and exhibits what remained of that way of life as late as 1940.

The two main displays on the first floor are a merchant house and a tenement, intact with all their furnishings. This is a hands-on museum: You can take your shoes off and step up into the rooms. On the second floor are displays of toys, tools, and utensils, which were donated, in most cases, by people who had grown up with them and used them all their lives. There are also photographs of Shita-machi and video documentaries of craftspeople at work. Occasionally various traditional skills are demonstrated, and you are welcome to take part. The space in this don't-miss museum is used with great skill, and there's even a passable brochure in English. ⊠ *2-1 Ueno Kōen, Taitō-ku,* ☎ *03/3823-7451.* 🎫 *¥200.* ☉ *Tues.–Sun. 9:30–4:30. Keisei private rail line, Keisei-Ueno Eki; JR Ueno Eki, kōen-guchi.*

㉞ **Shōgitai Memorial.** Time seems to heal wounds very quickly in Japan. Only six years after they had destroyed most of Ueno Hill, the Meiji government permitted the Shōgitai to be honored with a gravestone, erected on the spot where their bodies had been cremated. Descendants of one of the survivors still tend the memorial. *JR Ueno Eki, kōen-guchi; Keisei private rail line, Keisei-Ueno Eki.*

㉟ **Statue of Takamori Saigō.** As chief of staff of the Meiji imperial army—the army that the Shōgitai had died defying—Takamori Saigō (1827–77) played a key role in forcing the surrender of Edo and overthrew the shogunate. Ironically, Saigō himself fell out with the other leaders of the new Meiji government and was killed in an unsuccessful rebellion of his own. The sculptor Takamura Kōun's bronze, made in 1893, sensibly avoids presenting him in uniform. *JR Ueno Eki, kōen-guchi; Keisei private rail line, Keisei-Ueno Eki.*

㊱ **Suzumoto.** Originally built around 1857 for Japanese comic monologue performances called *rakugo,* and since rebuilt, Suzumoto is the oldest theater operation of its kind in Tōkyō. A rakugo comedian does not stand up to ply his trade: He sits on a purple cushion, dressed in a kimono, and tells stories that have been handed down for centuries. The storyteller has only a fan for a prop; he plays a whole cast of characters, with their different voices and facial expressions, by himself. The audience may have heard his stories 20 times already, and still laughs in all the right places. There is no English interpretation, and even for the Japanese themselves the monologues are difficult to follow, filled with puns and expressions in dialect—but don't let that deter you. For a slice of traditional pop culture, rakugo at Suzumoto is worth seeing, even if you don't understand a word. The theater is on Chūō-dōri, a few blocks north of the Ginza Line's Ueno Hirokō-ji stop. You can also take the red double-decker tour bus from Asakusa and get off in front of the theater. ✉ *2-7-12 Ueno, Taitō-ku,* ☎ *03/3834–5906.* 💴 *¥2,500.* 🕐 *Continual performances daily noon–4:30 and 5–8:50.*

㊴ Tokudai-ji. This is a curiosity in a neighborhood of curiosities: a temple on the second floor of a supermarket. Two deities are worshiped here. One is the bodhisattva Jizō, and the act of washing this statue is believed to help safeguard one's health. The other, principal image is that of the Indian goddess Marishi, a daughter of Brahma, usually depicted with three faces and four arms. She is believed to help worshipers overcome various sorts of difficulties and to prosper in business. Among the faithful visitors to Tokudai-ji, naturally, are the merchants of ☞ **Ame-ya Yoko-chō.** ✉ *4-6-2 Ueno, Taitō-ku. JR Yamanote Line, Ōkachi-machi Eki or Ueno Eki.*

★ ㉕ Tōkyō Kokuritsu Hakubutsukan (Tōkyō National Museum). A complex of four buildings grouped around a courtyard, this is one of the world's great repositories of East Asian art and archaeology. The building on the left is the **Hyōkeikan,** the oldest and smallest of the four. Completed in 1909, it has only nine exhibition rooms, all devoted to archaeological objects. Look especially for the flamelike sculpted rims and elaborate markings of Middle Jōmon–period pottery (c. 3500–2000 BC), so different from anything produced in Japan before or since. Also look for the terra-cotta figures called *haniwa,* unearthed at burial sites dating from the 4th to the 7th century. The figures are deceptively simple in shape and mysterious and comical at the same time in their effects.

Behind the Hyōkeikan is a two-story building called the **Hōryū-ji Hōmotsukan** (Treasure Hall), which is open only on Thursdays. In 1878 the 7th-century Hōryū-ji in Nara presented 319 works of art in its possession—sculpture, scrolls, masks, and other objects—to the Imperial Household. These were later transferred to the National Museum, and in 1964 the Treasure Hall was built to house them. If at all possible, schedule your visit to the museum on Thursday, but bear in mind that these works of wood and paper are more than 1,000 years old. If the weather is too hot or wet, the hall may not be open.

The central building in the complex, the **Honkan,** was built in 1937 and houses Japanese art exclusively: paintings, calligraphy, sculpture, textiles, ceramics, swords, and armor. The more attractive **Tōyōkan,** on the right, completed in 1968, is devoted to the art of other Asian cultures. Altogether, the museum has some 87,000 objects in its permanent collection, with several thousand more on loan from shrines, temples, and private owners. Among these are 84 objects designated by the government as National Treasures. The Honkan rotates the works on display several times during the year; it also hosts two special exhibitions a year, April–May and October–November, that feature important collections from foreign museums. These, unfortunately, can be an ordeal: The lighting in the Honkan is not particularly good, the explanations in English are sketchy at best, and the hordes of visitors make it impossible to linger over a work you especially want to study. ⊠ *13-9 Ueno Kōen, Taitō-ku,* ☎ *03/3822–1111.* 🎫 *¥420.* ☉ *Tues.– Sun. 9:30–5. JR Ueno Eki, kōen-guchi.*

㉘ Tōkyō Metropolitan Art Museum. There are three floors of galleries here. The museum displays its own collection of modern Japanese art on the lower level and rents out the remaining spaces to various art institutes and organizations. At any given time, there will be at least five different exhibitions in the building: work by promising young painters, for example, or new forms and materials in sculpture or modern calligraphy. Completed in 1975, the museum was designed by Maekawa Kunio, who also did the nearby Metropolitan Festival Hall. ⊠ *8-36 Ueno Kōen, Taitō-ku,* ☎ *03/3823–6921.* 🎫 *Permanent collection free; fees vary for other exhibits (usually ¥300–¥800).* ☉ *Daily 9–5; closed 3rd Mon. of month. JR Ueno Eki, kōen-guchi.*

㉗ Tōkyō University of Arts Exhibition Hall. The collection here has some interesting works, several of which are designated National Treasures, but it is not actually a museum. The exhibitions on display are intended primarily as teaching materials for courses in the school curriculum. At press time, the hall was closed, its reopening date yet to be determined. ⊠ *12-8 Ueno Kōen, Taitō-ku,* ☎ *03/3828–6111.* 🎫 *Free.* ☉ *Open to public weekdays 10–4 during school yr, mid-Apr.–mid-July, and Sept.–mid-Dec. JR Ueno Eki, kōen-guchi.*

★ **㉛ Tōshō-gū.** Ieyasu, the first Tokugawa shōgun, died in 1616 and the following year was given the posthumous name Tōshō Daigongen (The Great Incarnation Who Illuminates the East). The Imperial Court declared him a divinity of the first rank, thenceforth to be worshiped at Nikkō, in the mountains north of his city, at a shrine he had commissioned before his death. That shrine is the first and foremost Tōshō-gū. The one here in Ueno dates from 1627. Miraculously, it survived the disasters that destroyed most of the other original buildings on the hill—the fires, the 1868 revolt, the 1923 earthquake, the 1945 bombings—making it one of the few early Edo-period buildings in Tōkyō.

The path from the stone entry arch to the shrine itself is lined with 200 *ishidoro* (stone lanterns). Another stone lantern, inside the grounds, is more than 18 ft high—one of the three largest in Japan. This particular lantern is called *obaketoro* (ghost lantern) because of a story connected with it: It seems that one night a samurai on guard duty slashed at the ghost—*obake*—that was believed to haunt the lantern; his sword was so good it left a nick in the stone, which can still be seen. Beyond these lanterns is a double row of bronze lanterns, presented by the feudal lords of the 17th century as expressions of their piety and loyalty to the regime; the lanterns themselves were arrayed in the order of the wealth and ranking of their donors. On the left, before you reach the shrine, is the **Peony Garden,** where some 200 varieties bloom from the end of May into early June. The garden's entrance fee is ¥800; it is open daily 9:30–4:30, January–February and April–May.

The Tōshō-gū, like its namesake in Nikkō, is built in the ornate style called *gongen-zukuri*; it is gilded, painted, and carved with motifs of plants and animals. The carpentry of roof supports and ceilings is especially intricate. The shrine and most of its art are National Treasures. The first room inside is the **Hall of Worship;** the four paintings in gold on wood panels are by Tan'yū, one of the famous Kano family of artists who enjoyed the patronage of emperors and shōguns from the late 15th century to the end of the Edo period. Tan'yū was appointed *goyō eshi* (official court painter) in 1617. His commissions included the Tokugawa castles at Edo and Nagoya as well as the Nikkō Tōshō-gū. The framed tablet between the walls, with the name of the shrine in gold, is in the calligraphy of Emperor Go-Mizuno-o (1596–1680). Other works of calligraphy are by the abbots of Kanei-ji. Behind the Hall of Worship, connected by a passage called the *haiden*, is the sanctuary, where the spirit of Ieyasu is enshrined.

The real glories of Tōshō-gū are its so-called **Chinese Gate,** which you reach at the end of your tour of the building, and the fence on either side. Like its counterpart at Nikkō, the fence is a kind of natural history lesson, with carvings of birds, animals, fish, and shells of every description; unlike the one at Nikkō, this fence was left unpainted. The two long panels of the gate, with their dragons carved in relief, are attributed to Hidari Jingoro—a brilliant sculptor of the early Edo period whose real name is unknown (*hidari* means "left"; Jingoro was reportedly left-handed). The lifelike appearance of his dragons has inspired a legend. Every morning they were found mysteriously dripping with water. Finally it was discovered that they were sneaking out at night to drink from the nearby Shinobazu Pond, and wire cages were put up around them to curtail this disquieting habit. ⊠ *9-88 Ueno Kōen, Taitō-ku,* ☎ *03/ 3822–3455.* 🎫 *¥200.* ⊙ *Daily 9–sundown. JR Ueno Eki, kōen-guchi.*

㉝ Ueno-no-Mori Royal Museum. Although the museum has no permanent collection of its own, it makes its galleries available to various groups, primarily for exhibitions of modern painting and calligraphy. ⊠ *1-2 Ueno Kōen, Taitō-ku,* ☎ *03/3833–4191. JR Ueno Eki, kōen-guchi.*

㉙ Ueno Zoo. The zoo houses some 900 different species, most of whom look less than enthusiastic about being here. First built in 1882 and several times expanded without really modernizing, Ueno is not among the most attractive zoos in the world. On the other hand, it does have three giant pandas (their quarters are near the main entrance). You might decide it's worth a visit on that score alone. On a pleasant Sunday afternoon, however, upwards of 20,000 Japanese are likely to share your opinion; don't expect to have a leisurely view. ⊠ *9-83 Ueno Kōen, Taitō-ku,* ☎ *03/3828–5171.* 🎫 *¥500.* ⊙ *Tues.–Sun. 9:30–4. Keisei private rail line, Hakubutsukan Dōbutsu-en Eki.*

Asakusa

In the year 628, so the legend goes, two brothers named Hamanari Hikonuma and Takenari Hikonuma were fishing on the lower reaches of the Sumida River when they dragged up a small, gilded statue of Kannon—an aspect of the Buddha worshiped as the goddess of mercy. They took the statue to their master, Naji-no-Nakamoto, who enshrined it in his house. Later, a temple was built for it in nearby Asakusa. Called Sensō-ji, the temple was rebuilt and enlarged several times over the next 10 centuries—but Asakusa itself remained just a village on a river crossing a few hours' walk from Edo.

Then Ieyasu Tokugawa made Edo his capital and Asakusa blossomed. Suddenly, it was the party that never ended, the place where the free-spending townspeople of the new capital came to empty their pockets. For the next 300 years it was the wellspring of almost everything we associate with Japanese popular culture.

The first step in that transformation came in 1657, when Yoshiwara—the licensed brothel quarter not far from Nihombashi—was moved to the countryside farther north: Asakusa found itself square in the road, more or less halfway between the city and its only nightlife. The village became a suburb and a pleasure quarter in its own right. In the narrow streets and alleys around Sensō-ji, there were stalls selling toys, souvenirs, and sweets; there were acrobats, jugglers, and strolling musicians; there were sake shops and teahouses—where the waitresses often provided more than tea. (The Japanese have never worried much about the impropriety of such things; the approach to a temple is still a venue for very secular enterprises of all sorts.) Then, in 1841, the Kabuki theaters—which the government looked upon as a source of dissipation second only to Yoshiwara—moved to Asakusa.

Highborn and lowborn, the people of Edo flocked to Kabuki. They loved its extravagant spectacle, its bravado and brilliant language. They cheered its heroes and hissed its villains. They bought wood-block prints, called *ukiyo-e*, of their favorite actors. (*Ukiyo* means "the floating world" of everyday life; *e* means picture. The style's zenith was in the 18th and 19th centuries, and it is still being practiced.) Asakusa was home to the Kabuki theaters for only a short time, but that was enough to establish it as *the* entertainment quarter of the city—a reputation it held unchallenged until World War II.

When Japan ended its long, self-imposed isolation in 1868, where else would the novelties and amusements of the outside world first take root but in Asakusa? The country's first photography studios appeared here in 1875. Japan's first skyscraper, a 12-story mart called the Jū-ni-kai, was built in Asakusa in 1890 and filled with shops selling imported goods. The area around Sensō-ji had by this time been designated a public park and was divided into seven sections; the sixth section, called Rok-ku, was Tōkyō's equivalent of 42nd Street and Times Square. The nation's first movie theater opened here in 1903—to be joined by dozens more, and these in turn were followed by music halls, cabarets, and revues. The first drinking establishment in Japan to call itself a "bar" was started in Asakusa in 1880; it still exists.

Most of this area was destroyed in 1945. As an entertainment district, it never really recovered, but Sensō-ji was rebuilt almost immediately. The people here would never dream of living without it—just as they would never dream of living anywhere else. This is the heart and soul of Shita-machi, where you can still hear the rich, breezy downtown Tōkyō accent of the 17th and 18th centuries. Where, if you sneeze in the middle of the night, your neighbor will demand to know the next morning why you aren't taking better care of yourself. Where a carpenter will refuse a well-paid job if he doesn't think the client has the mother wit to appreciate good work when he sees it. Where you can still go out for a good meal and not have to pay through the nose for a lot of uptown pretensions. Even today, the temple precinct embraces an area of narrow streets, arcades, restaurants, shops, stalls, playgrounds, and gardens. It is home to a population of artisans and small entrepreneurs, neighborhood children and their grandmothers, hipsters and hucksters and mendicant priests. In short, if you have any time at all to spend in Tōkyō, you really have to devote at least a day of it to Asakusa.

Numbers in the text correspond to numbers in the margin and on the Asakusa map.

A Good Walk

For more information on *depāto* and individual shops mentioned in this walk, *see* Shopping, *below*.

Start at Asakusa Station, at the end of the Ginza Line. This was in fact Tōkyō's first subway, opened from Asakusa to Ueno in 1927; it became known as the Ginza Line when it was later extended through Ginza to Shimbashi and Shibuya. Follow the signs, clearly marked in English, to Exit 1. When you come up to the street level, turn right and walk west along Asakusa-dōri. In a few steps you will come to **Kaminari-mon** ㊶, the main entrance to the grounds of Sensō-ji.

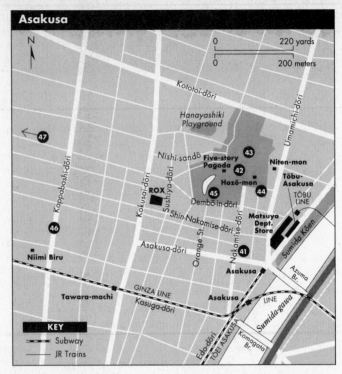

There are two other ways to get to Kaminari-mon. The "river bus" ferry from Hinode Pier stops in Asakusa at the south corner of the park called **Sumida Kōen.** Walk out to the three-way intersection, cross two sides of the triangle, and turn right. Kaminari-mon is in the middle of the second block. There is also a red double-decker bus that runs between Kaminari-mon and the Suzumoto Theater in Ueno. The service began in 1981, when the Merchants' Association in Asakusa borrowed a London double-decker for a month to move the overflow crowds they expected for a street fair. The idea proved popular enough to run a regular service—but there was an unexpected hitch: By law, a commercial bus could be no higher than 12½ ft, and the English double-decker was 28 inches over the limit. The solution was to order custom vehicles from a German company. Buses run every half hour weekdays (every 15–20 minutes weekends), 10–7 from Ueno and 10:25–7:25 from Asakusa. The fare is ¥250.

Take note of the **Asakusa Tourist Information Center** opposite Kaminari-mon. A volunteer staff with some English is on duty here 9–5 daily and will happily load you down with maps and brochures.

From Kaminari-mon, **Naka-mise-dōri**—a long, narrow avenue lined on both sides with small shops—leads to the courtyard of Sensō-ji. One shop worth stopping at is **Ichiban-ya,** about 100 yards down on the right, for its handmade, toasted *sembei* (rice crackers) and its seven-pepper spices in gourd-shape bottles of zelkova wood. Another shop, on the left, is **Hyōtan-ya,** which sells ivory carvings and utensils. At the end of Naka-mise-dōri, on the right, is **Sukeroku,** which specializes in traditional handmade dolls and models clothed in the costumes of the Edo period. Just beyond is a two-story gate called the **Hozō-mon.**

At this point, take an important detour. Left of the gate as you face the temple, in the far corner, is a modern two-story building that houses the Sensō-ji administrative offices: Walk in, go down the corridor on the right to the third door on the left, and ask for permission to see the **Garden of Dembō-in.** There is no charge. You simply enter your name and address in a register and receive a ticket. Hold on to the ticket to use it for Dembō-in later.

Return to the Hozō-mon and walk across the courtyard to **Sensō-ji Main Hall** ㊷. To the left of the Main Hall is the **Five-Story Pagoda.** To the right is **Asakusa Jinja** ㊸—a shrine to the Hikonuma brothers and their master, Naji no Nakatomo. Near the entrance to the shrine is the east gate to the temple grounds, **Niten-mon.**

From the Niten-mon, walk back in the direction of the Kaminari-mon to the southeast corner of the grounds. On a small plot of ground here stands the shrine to Kume no Heinai, a 17th-century outlaw who repented and became a priest of one of the subsidiary temples of Sensō-ji. Late in life he carved a stone statue of himself and buried it where many people would walk over it. In his will, he expressed the hope that his image would be trampled upon forever. Somehow, Heinai came to be worshiped as the patron god of lovers—as mystifying an apotheosis as you will ever find in Japanese religion.

Walk south again from Heinai's shrine along the narrow street that runs back to Asakusa-dōri, parallel to Naka-mise-dōri. On the left you pass a tiny hillock called **Benten-yama** and the **Toki-no-kane Belfry** ㊹. Opposite Benten-yama is a shop called **Naka-ya,** which sells all manner of regalia for Sensō-ji's annual Sanja Festival.

Next door is **Kuremutsu,** a good place to stop for a sake break. Next to Kuremutsu is **Hyaku-suke,** the last place in Tōkyō to carry government-approved skin cleanser made from powdered nightingale droppings. Ladies of the Edo period—especially the geisha—swore by the cleanser; they mixed the powder with water and patted it on gently as a boon to their complexion. There's only one source left in Japan for this powder—a fellow in the mountains of Aichi Prefecture who collects and dries the droppings from about 2,000 birds. (Nightingale ranching! Japan is a land of many vocations.) The range of products is quite intriguing. The shop is closed Tuesday.

Three doors up, on the same side of the street, is **Fuji-ya,** a shop that deals exclusively in printed cotton hand towels called *tenugui* (teh-*noo*-goo-ee). Owner Keiji Kawakami literally wrote the book on this subject. His *Tenugui fuzoku emaki* (roughly, *The Scroll Book of Hand Towel Customs and Usages*) is the definitive work on the hundreds of traditional towel motifs that have come down from the Edo period: geometric patterns, plants and animals, artifacts from folklore and everyday life, and scenes from Bunraku puppet theater, Kabuki, and festivals. Kawakami designed and dyed all of the tenugui himself. They unfold to about 3 ft, and many people buy them for framing. When Kawakami feels that he has made enough of one pattern, he destroys the stencil.

Turn right at the corner past Fuji-ya and walk west on Dembō-in-dōri until you cross Naka-mise-dōri. On the other side of the intersection, on the left, is **Yono-ya,** purveyor of pricey handmade boxwood combs. The residing master craftsman is Tasumi Minekawa, whose great-grandfather, he observes, was still making combs when he retired at 85. Yono-ya makes combs in all sizes, shapes, and serrations, which traditional Japanese coiffures and wigs demand. Some combs are carved with auspicious motifs, like peonies, hollyhocks, or cranes, and all are engraved with the family benchmark. The shop itself is postwar, but the family business goes back about 300 years.

Now it's time to cash in the ticket you've been carrying around. Walk west another 20 yards or so, and on the right you will see an old black wooden gate; this is the side entrance to **Dembō-in** ㊺, the living quarters of the Abbot of Sensō-ji. The only part of the grounds you can visit is the garden: Go through the small door in the gate, across the courtyard and through the door on the opposite side, and present your ticket to the caretaker in the house at the end of the alley. The entrance to the **garden** is down a short flight of stone steps to the left.

Turn right as you leave the Dembō-in and continue walking west on Dembō-in-dōri. You will pass a small Shintō shrine with a number of small statues of the bodhisattva Jizō; this is a shrine for prayers for the repose of the souls of *mizuko*—literally "water children"—those who were aborted or miscarried.

Farther on, in the row of knockdown clothing stalls along the right side of the street, is the booth of calligrapher Kōji Matsumaru, who makes *hyōsatsu*, the Japanese equivalent of doorplates. A hyōsatsu is a block of wood, preferably cypress, hung on a gatepost or an entranceway, with the family name on it in India ink. There is still enormous reverence in Japan for penmanship, and opinions are drawn about you from the way you write. The hyōsatsu is, after all, the first thing people will learn about a home. The characters on it must be felicitous and well formed, so one comes to Matsumaru. Famous in Asakusa for his fine hand, he also does lanterns, temple signboards, certificates, and other weighty documents. He will also render Western names in the *katakana* syllabic alphabet, which is reserved for foreign words, should you decide to take home a hyōsatsu of your own.

Opposite the row of clothing stalls, on the corner of Orange Street, is the redbrick **Asakusa Public Hall**; performances of Kabuki and traditional dance are sometimes held here, as well as exhibitions of life in Asakusa before World War II. Across the street is **Nakase,** one of the best of Asakusa's many fine tempura restaurants. Its interior is something of a haven, and the prices reflect this.

Now review your options. If you have the time and energy, you might want to explore the streets and covered arcades on the south and west sides of Dembō-in. Where Dembō-in-dōri meets Sushiya-dōri, the main avenue of the Rok-ku entertainment district, there is a small flea market. Turn right here, and you are in what remains—alas!—of the old movie-theater district. **Nishi-Sandō**—an arcade where you can find kimonos and yukata fabrics, traditional accessories, fans, and festival costumes at very reasonable prices—runs east of the movie theaters, between Rok-ku and Sensō-ji. If you turn to the left at the flea market, you soon come to the **ROX Building,** a misplaced attempt to endow Asakusa with a glitzy vertical mall. Just beyond it, you can turn left again and stroll along Shin-Naka-mise-dōri (New Street of Inside Shops). This arcade and the streets that cross it north–south are lined with stores selling clothing and accessories, purveyors of crackers, seaweed, tea, and restaurants and coffee shops. This is Asakusa's answer to the suburban shopping center.

When you have browsed to saturation, turn south, away from Dembō-in on any of these side streets, return to Asakusa-dōri, turn right, and walk to the end of the avenue. Cross Kokusai-dōri, turn left, and then right at the next major intersection on to Kasuga-dōri; on the corner is the entrance to Tawara-machi Station on the Ginza subway line. At the second traffic light, you will see the **Niimi Biru** (building) across the street, and atop the Niimi Biru is the guardian god of Kappa-bashi: an enormous chef's head in plastic, 30 ft high, beaming, mustached, and crowned, as every chef in Japan is crowned, with a tall white hat. Turn right, to explore the shops of **Kappa-bashi** ㊻, Tōkyō's whole-sale restaurant supply district.

At the second intersection, on the right, is the main showroom of the **Maizuru Company,** virtuosos in the art of counterfeit cuisine: the plastic models of food you see in the front windows of most popularly priced Japanese restaurants. In 1960 models by Maizuru were included in the "Japan Style" Exhibition at London's Victoria and Albert Museum. Here, you can buy individual pieces of plastic sushi or splurge on a whole Pacific lobster, perfect in coloration and detail down to the tiniest spines on its legs. A few doors down is **Biken Kōgei,** a good place to look for the folding red paper lanterns (*aka-chōchin*) that grace the front of inexpensive bars and restaurants.

Across the street from Maizuru is **Nishimura,** a shop specializing in *noren*—the short divided curtains that hang from bamboo rods over the doors of shops or restaurants to announce that they are open for business. The cotton, linen, or silk curtains are usually dyed to order with the name and logo of the shop or what it sells. Nishimura also carries ready-made noren with motifs of all sorts, from white-on-blue landscapes to geisha and sumō wrestlers in polychromatic splendor. Use your imagination. They make wonderful wall hangings and dividers.

In the next block is **Kondo Shōten,** which sells all sorts of bamboo trays, baskets, scoops, and containers. A block farther on, look for **Iida Shōten,** which stocks a good selection of embossed cast-iron kettles and casseroles, called *nambu* ware—craftwork certified by the Association for the Promotion of Traditional Craft Products.

On the far corner is the **Union Company,** which sells everything you need to run a coffee shop (or the make-believe one in your own kitchen): roasters, grinders, beans, flasks, and filters of every description. Coffee lovers pronounce the coffee shops of Japan among the best in the world; here's where the professionals come for their apparati.

The intersection here is about in the middle of Kappa-bashi. Turn left, and just past the next traffic light, on the right, you come to **Sōgen-ji** ㊼—better known as the Kappa Temple, with its shrine to the imaginary creature that gives this district its name.

From Sōgen-ji, retrace your steps to the intersection, as there is more of Kappa-bashi to the north. You can safely ignore it and continue east, straight past Union Company down the narrow side street. In the next block, on the left, look for **Tsubaya Hōchōten.** A *hōchō* is a knife. Tsubaya sells cutlery for professionals—knives of every length and weight and balance, for every imaginable use, from slicing sashimi to turning a cucumber into a paper-thin sheet to making decorative cuts in fruit.

Continue on this street east to Kokusai-dōri, and then turn right (south). As you walk you will see several shops selling *butsudan,* Buddhist household altars. The most elaborate of these, hand-carved in ebony and covered with gold leaf, are made in Toyama Prefecture and can cost as much as ¥1 million. No proper Japanese household is without a butsudan, even if it is somewhat more modest; it is the spiritual center of the family, where reverence for one's ancestors and continuity of the family traditions are expressed. In a few moments, you will be back at Tawara-machi Station—the end of the Asakusa walk.

TIMING

Unlike most of the areas to explore on foot in Tōkyō, Sensō-ji is admirably compact. You can easily see the temple and environs in a morning. The Dembō-in garden is worth half an hour. If you decide to include Kappa-bashi, allow yourself an hour more. Some of the shopping arcades in this area are covered, but Asakusa is essentially an outdoor experience. Be prepared for rain in June, heat and humidity in July and August.

Sights to See

THE SENSŌ-JI COMPLEX

Dedicated to the goddess Kannon, Sensō-ji is the heart and soul of Asakusa. Come for its local and historical importance, its garden, its 17th-century Shintō shrine, and the wild Sanja Matsuri in May. ⊠ 2-3-1 Asakusa, Taitō-ku, ☎ 03/3842–0181. ☜ Free. ☉ Temple grounds 6 AM–sundown. Subway: Ginza Line, Asakusa.

㊸ Asakusa Jinja. Several structures in the temple complex survived the bombings of 1945. The largest, to the right of the Main Hall, is a Shintō shrine to the putative founders of Sensō-ji. In Japan, Buddhism and Shintoism have enjoyed a comfortable coexistence since the former arrived from China in the 6th century. It's the rule, rather than the exception, to find a Shintō shrine on the same grounds as a Buddhist temple. The shrine, built in 1649, is also known as Sanja Sanma (Shrine of the Three Guardians). The Sanja Festival, held every year on the third weekend in May, is the biggest, loudest, wildest party in Tōkyō. Each of the neighborhoods under Sanja Sanma's protection has its own *mikoshi* (portable shrine), and on the second day of the festival, these palanquins are paraded through the streets of Asakusa to the shrine, bouncing and swaying on the shoulders of the participants all the way. Many of the "parishioners" take part naked to the waist, or with the sleeves of their tunics rolled up, to expose fantastic red and black tattoo patterns that sometimes cover their entire backs and shoulders. These are the tribal markings of the Japanese underworld.

Near the entrance to Asakusa Jinja is another survivor of World War II: the east gate to the temple grounds, **Niten-mon,** built in 1618 for a shrine to Ieyasu Tokugawa (the shrine itself no longer exists) and designated by the government as an Important Cultural Property.

★ ㊺ Dembō-in. Believed to have been made in the 17th century by Kōbori Enshū, the genius of Zen landscape design, the garden of Dembō-in is the best-kept secret in Asakusa. Anyone can see the front entrance to Dembō-in from Naka-mise-dōri—behind an iron fence in the last block of shops—but the thousands of Japanese visitors passing by seem to have no idea what it is. (And if they do, it somehow never occurs to them to visit it themselves.) The garden of Dembō-in is usually empty and always utterly serene, an island of privacy in a sea of pilgrims. As you walk along the path that circles the pond, a different vista presents itself at every turn. The only sounds are the cries of birds and the splashing of carp.

Spring, when wisteria is in bloom, is the ideal time to be here. In the best of all possible worlds, come on a Monday, when a tea ceremony is held in the pavilion at the far end of the pond. On Dembō-in-dōri, about 50 yards west of the intersection with Naka-mise-dōri, a sign in English indicates the entrance, through the side door of a large wooden gate. In order to see the abbot's garden, you need to get permission in the temple administration building, between the Hozō-mon and the Five-Story Pagoda, in the far corner. ☉ Daily 9–4; may be closed if abbot has guests. ☜ Free pass, available from Administration Office on temple grounds, required for entry to garden.

NEED A
BREAK?

The tatami-mat rooms in **Nakase,** *a fine tempura restaurant, look out on a perfect little interior garden—hung, in May, with great fragrant bunches of white wisteria. The pond is stocked with carp and goldfish; you can almost lean out from your room and trail your fingers in the water as you listen to the fountain. Nakase is expensive: Lunch at the tables inside is ¥2,800; more elaborate meals by the garden start at ¥7,000. It is across Orange Street from the redbrick Asakusa Public Hall. ⊠ 1-39-13 Asakusa, Taitō-ku, ☎ 03/3841–4015. No credit cards. Closed Tues.*

④ **Kaminari-mon** (Thunder God Gate). This is the proper Sensō-ji entrance, with its huge red paper lantern hanging in the center. The original gate was destroyed by fire in 1865. The replica that stands here now was built after World War II. Traditionally, two fearsome guardian gods are installed in the alcoves of Buddhist temple gates to ward off evil spirits. The Thunder God (*Kaminari-no-Kami*) of the Sensō-ji main gate is on the left. He shares his duties with the Wind God (*Kaze-no-Kami*) on the right. Few Japanese visitors neglect to stop at **Tokiwa-dō,** the shop on the west side of the gate, to buy some of Tōkyō's most famous souvenirs: *kaminari okoshi* (thunder crackers), made of rice, millet, sugar, and beans.

Kaminari-mon also marks the southern extent of **Naka-mise-dōri,** the Street of Inside Shops. The area from Kaminari-mon to the inner gate of the temple was once composed of stalls leased to the townspeople who cleaned and swept the temple grounds. The rows of redbrick buildings now belong to the municipal government, but the leases are, in effect, hereditary: Some of the shops have been in the same families since the Edo period. Shop names are mentioned in A Good Walk, *above.* (☞ Crafts and Gift Items *in* Shopping, *below.*)

④ **Sensō-ji Main Hall.** The **Five-story Pagoda** and the **Main Hall** of Sensō-ji are both faithful copies in concrete of originals that burned down in 1945. It took 13 years, when most of the people of Asakusa were still rebuilding their own bombed-out lives, to raise money for the restoration of their beloved Sensō-ji. To them—and especially to those involved in the world of entertainment—it is far more than a tourist attraction: Kabuki actors still come here before a new season of performances; sumō wrestlers come before a tournament to pay their respects; the large lanterns in the Main Hall were donated by the geisha associations of Asakusa and nearby Yanagi-bashi. Most Japanese stop at the huge bronze incense burner, in front of the Main Hall, to bathe their hands and faces in the smoke—it's a charm to ward off illnesses—before climbing the stairs to offer their prayers.

The Main Hall, about 115 ft long and 108 ft wide, is not an especially impressive piece of architecture. Unlike in many temples, however, part of the inside has a concrete floor, so you can come and go without removing your shoes. In this area hang the Sensō-ji's chief claims to artistic importance: a collection of votive paintings on wood, from the 18th and 19th centuries. Plaques of this kind, called *ema,* are still offered to the gods at shrines and temples, but they are commonly simpler and smaller. The worshiper buys a little tablet of wood with the picture already painted on one side and inscribes a prayer on the other. The temple owns more than 50 of these works, which were removed to safety in 1945 and so escaped the air raids. Only eight of them, depicting scenes from Japanese history and mythology, are on display. A catalog of the collection is on sale in the hall, but the text is in Japanese only.

Lighting is poor in the Main Hall, and the actual works are difficult to see. This is also true of the ceiling, done by two contemporary masters of Nihon-ga (traditional Japanese-style painting); the dragon is by Ryūshi Kawabata, and the motif of angels and lotus blossoms is by Inshō Dōmoto. One thing that visitors cannot see at all is the holy image of Kannon itself, which supposedly lies buried somewhere deep under the temple. Not even the priests of Sensō-ji have ever seen it, and in fact there is no conclusive evidence that it actually exists!

The **Hozō-mon,** the gate to the temple courtyard, serves as a repository for sutras (Buddhist texts) and other treasures of Sensō-ji. This gate, too, has its guardian gods; should either of them decide to leave his post for a stroll, an enormous pair of sandals is hanging on the back wall—the gift of a village famous for its straw weaving, in Yamagata Prefecture.

㊹ Toki-no-kane Shōrō (belfry). The tiny hillock Benten-yama, with its shrine to the goddess of good fortune, is the site for this 17th-century belfry. The bell here used to toll the hours for the people of the district, and it was said that you could hear it anywhere in a radius of some 4 mi. The bell still sounds at 6 AM every day, when the temple grounds open. It also rings on New Year's Eve—108 strokes in all, beginning just before midnight, to "ring out" the 108 sins and frailties of mankind and make a clean start for the coming year. Benten-yama and the belfry are at the beginning of the narrow street that parallels Naka-mise-dōri.

NEED A BREAK?   **Kuremutsu** is a tiny old teahouse now turned into a fairly expensive *nomiya*—literally, a "drinking place," the drink of choice in this case being sake. ✉ *2-2-13 Asakusa, Taito-ku,* ☎ *03/3842–0906.* ⊙ *Fri.–Wed. 4 pm–10 pm.*

ELSEWHERE IN ASAKUSA

★ **㊻ Kappa-bashi.** This area comprises nearly a kilometer (about ½ mi) of wholesale dealers—more than 200 of them—who sell everything the city's restaurant and bar trade could possibly need to do business, from paper supplies to steam tables, from signs to soup tureens. In their wildest dreams, the Japanese themselves would never have cast Kappa-bashi as a tourist attraction, but indeed it is.

For one thing, it is *the* place to buy plastic food. From the humblest noodle shop or sushi bar to neighborhood restaurants of middling price and pretension, it's customary in Japan to stock a window with models of what is to be had inside. The custom began, according to one version of the story, in the early days of the Meiji Restoration, when anatomical models made of wax first came to Japan as teaching aids in the new schools of Western medicine. A businessman from Nara decided that wax models would also make good point-of-purchase advertising for restaurants. He was right: The industry grew in a modest way at first, making models mostly of Japanese food, but in the boom years after 1960, restaurants began to serve all sorts of cookery ordinary people had never seen before, and the models offered much-needed reassurance: "So *that's* a cheeseburger. It doesn't look as bad as it sounds. Let's go in and try one." By the mid-1970s, the makers of plastic food were turning out creations of astonishing virtuosity and realism, and foreigners had discovered in them a form of pop art. ✉ *Nishi-Asakusa 1-chōme and 2-chōme, Taitō-ku.* ⊙ *Most shops daily 9–6. Subway: Ginza Line, Tawara-machi.*

㊼ Sōgen-ji. In the 19th century, so the story goes, there was a river in the present-day Kappa-bashi district, and a bridge. The surrounding area was poorly drained and was often flooded. A local shopkeeper began a project to improve the drainage, investing all his own money, but met with little success until a troupe of *kappa*—mischievous green water sprites—emerged from the river to help him. The local people still come to the shrine at Sōgen-ji to leave offerings of cucumber and sake—the kappa's favorite food and drink.

A more prosaic explanation for the name of the district points out that the lower-ranking retainers of the local lord used to earn money on the side by making straw raincoats, also called kappa, that they spread to dry on the bridge. To get here, walk north on Kappa-bashi-dōri from the Niimi Biru to the fifth intersection and turn left. ✉ *3-7-2 Matsugaya, Taitō-ku,* ☎ *03/3841–2035.* 🎟 *Free.* 🕐 *Temple grounds sunrise–sunset. Subway: Ginza Line, Tawara-machi.*

Tsukiji and Shimbashi

Tsukiji reminds us of the awesome disaster of the great fire of 1657. In the space of two days, it leveled almost 70% of Ieyasu Tokugawa's new capital and killed more than 100,000 people. Ieyasu was not a man to be discouraged by mere catastrophe, however; he took it as an opportunity to plan an even bigger and better city, one that would incorporate the marshes east of his castle. Tsukiji, in fact, means "reclaimed land," and a substantial block of land it was, laboriously drained and filled, from present-day Ginza to the bay.

The common people of the tenements and alleys, who had suffered most in the great fire, benefited not at all from this project; land was first allotted to feudal lords and to temples. After 1853, when Japan opened its doors to the outside world, Tsukiji became Tōkyō's first Foreign Settlement—the site of the American legation and an elegant two-story brick hotel, and home to a heroic group of missionaries, teachers, and doctors. Today, this area is best known for the largest fish market in Asia. This is where, if you are prepared to get up early enough, you should get your feet on the ground in the neighborhood.

Almost nothing remains in **Shimbashi** to recall its golden age—the period after the Meiji Restoration, when this was one of the most famous geisha districts of the new capital. Its reputation as a pleasure quarter is even older. In the Edo period, when there was a network of canals and waterways here, it was the height of luxury to charter a covered boat (called a *yakata-bune*) from one of the Shimbashi boathouses for a cruise on the river; a local restaurant would cater the excursion, and a local geisha house would provide the companionship. After 1868, the geisha moved indoors. There were many more of them, and the pleasure quarter became much larger and more sophisticated—a reputation it still enjoys among the older (and wealthier) generation of Japanese men.

There are perhaps 100 geisha still working in Shimbashi. They entertain at some 30 or 40 *ryōtei* (traditional restaurants) tucked away on the back streets of the district, but you are unlikely to encounter any exploring the area. From time to time, newspapers still delight in the account of some distinguished widower, a politician or captain of industry, who marries a Shimbashi geisha—in the vain expectation that he will be treated at home the way he was treated in the restaurant.

Numbers in the text correspond to numbers in the margin and on the Tsukiji and Shimbashi map.

A Good Walk

Take the Hibiya subway line to Tsukiji and exit by the stairs closest to the back of the train. You emerge on Shin-Ōhashi-dōri in front of the

Tsukiji Hongan-ji—a temple that looks like a transplant from India. You'll return to it later. Walk west on Shin-Ōhashi-dōri and cross Harumi-dōri, the broad avenue that runs northwest–southeast to the bay. Go over the bridge and take the first left. Walk to the end of the road and turn right. If you reach this point at precisely 5 AM, you will hear a signal for the start of Tōkyō's greatest ongoing open-air spectacle: the fish auction at the **Tōkyō Chūō Oroshiuri Ichiba** ㊽.

A word to the wise: These people are not running a tourist attraction. They're in the fish business, and this is their busiest time of day. The cheerful banter they use with each other can turn snappish if you get in their way. Also bear in mind that you are not allowed to take photographs while the auctions are under way (flashes are a distraction). The market is kept spotlessly clean, which means the water hoses are running all the time. Boots are helpful, but if you don't want to carry them, bring a pair of heavy-duty trash bags to slip over your shoes and secure them above your ankles with rubber bands.

By 9 AM the business of the Central Market is largely finished for the day, but there is still plenty to do and see. You'll have missed the auctions, but you can still explore the maze of alleys between the market and Harumi-dōri, where you'll come across the **Backstreet Shops of Tsukiji** ㊾. You'll find all kinds of eateries, as well as food and cookware stores. For a close-up shot of Japanese daily life, this is one of the best places in Tōkyō to visit.

Return to Shin-Ōhashi-dōri and walk back toward Hongan-ji. When you reach Harumi-dōri, you might want to make a detour to the **International Trade Center** ㊿ for one of its current exhibitions. If so, turn right here, cross two bridges, then take the second street to the right. From here it's a longish walk to the Trade Center.

If not, return to **Tsukiji Hongan-ji** (51), Tōkyō's main branch temple of Kyōto's Nishi Hongan-ji. Continue east on Shin-Ōhashi-dōri and turn right at the first corner. Walk south until you cross a bridge, and turn left on the other side. When you cross another bridge, turn right. In the traffic island at the next intersection are two stone memorials that mark the true importance of Tsukiji in the modern history of Japan.

The taller of the two is the **Monument to Ryōtaku Maeno and Gempaku Sugita.** With a group of colleagues, these two men translated the first work of European science into Japanese. Maeno and his collaborators were samurai and physicians. Maeno himself was in the service of the Lord Okudaira, whose mansion was one of the most prominent in Tsukiji. In 1770 Maeno acquired a book, a text in Dutch on human anatomy, in Nagasaki. It took his group four years to produce their translation. Remember that at this time Japan was still officially closed to the outside world, and the trickle of scientific knowledge accessible through the Dutch trading post at Nagasaki—the only authorized foreign settlement—was enormously frustrating to the eager young scholars who wanted to modernize their country. Also bear in mind that Maeno and his colleagues began with barely a few hundred words of Dutch among them and had no reference works or other resources on which to base their translation, except the diagrams in the book. It must have been an agonizing task, but the publication in 1774 of *Kaitai shinsho,* as it was called in Japanese, in a sense shaped the world we know today. From this time on, Japan would turn away from classical Chinese scholarship and begin to take its lessons in science and technology from the West.

The other stone memorial commemorates the founding of Keiō University by Yūkichi Fukuzawa (1835–1901), the most influential edu-

cator and social thinker of the Meiji period. Fukuzawa was the son of a low-ranking samurai in the same clan as Maeno. Sent by his lord to start a school of Western learning, he began teaching classes at the Matsu-daira residence in Tsukiji in 1858. Later the school was moved west to Mita, where the university is today. Engraved on the stone is Fukuzawa's famous statement: "Heaven created no man above another, nor below." Uttered when the feudal Tokugawa regime was still in power, this was an enormously daring thought. It took Japan almost a century to catch up with Fukuzawa's liberal and egalitarian vision.

Across the street to the left is **St. Luke's International Hospital,** founded in 1900 by Dr. Rudolf Teusler, an American medical missionary. In the several square blocks north of the hospital was the foreign settlement created after the signing of the U.S.-Japan Treaty of Commerce in 1858. Among the residents here in the latter part of the 19th century was a Scottish surgeon and missionary named Henry Faulds. Intrigued by the Japanese custom of putting their thumbprints on documents for authentication, he began the research that established for the first time that no two person's fingerprints are alike. In 1880 he wrote a paper for *Nature* magazine, suggesting that this fact might be of some use in criminal investigation.

Review your priorities. From here, you can retrace your steps to the subway, moving on to Higashi-Ginza and Shimbashi, or you can take a longish but rewarding detour to **Tsukuda-jima** ㊲. If you choose the latter, walk west from the monuments to the next corner, turn right, and walk north for two blocks. Cross the main intersection here, and turn right. The street rises to become the Tsukuda Ōhashi (bridge). Just before it crosses the water you'll find a flight of steps up to the pedestrian walkway that brings you to the island.

Tsukugen, a shop on the first street along the breakwater as you leave the bridge, is famous for its delicious *tsukudani*—whitebait boiled in soy sauce and salt—the island's most famous product. At the end of the breakwater, turn right. From here it's a short walk to the gate of the **Sumiyoshi Jinja** ⑤③, a shrine established by fishermen from Ōsaka when they first settled on the island in the 17th century.

If you've opted not to visit Tsukuda-jima, retrace your steps from St. Luke's to the Tsukiji subway station and walk west again on Shin-Ōhashi-dōri. Pass the turnoff to the Central Market on your left and the Asahi Newspapers Building on your right. The avenue curves and brings you to an elevated walkway. The entrance to the gardens of **Hama Rikyū Tei-en** ⑤④ is on the left.

On your way to Hama Rikyū Tei-en, as you walk west on Shin-Ōhashi-dōri, keep on the right side of the street. After you cross Harumi-dōri, take the first narrow street on the right, then the first left. Just off the corner is **Edo-Gin,** a venerable sushi bar that serves sizable portions of market-fresh sushi. Lunchtime set menus are quite a bargain.

SHIMBASHI

North of the entrance to Hama Rikyū is a major intersection, where Shin-Ōhashi-dōri crosses Shōwa-dōri. If you turned left on Shōwa-dōri, your route would take you past the huge JR Shiodome railroad yards—an "O" marker here and a section of the original tracks commemorate the starting point of Japan's first railway service, between Shimbashi and Yokohama, in 1872—and on to Shimbashi Eki.

But turn right instead onto Shōwa-dōri, away from Shimbashi Station. At the next major intersection, turn right again, and left at the third corner. Walk northeast in the direction of Higashi-Ginza Station. In the second block, on your right, is the **Shimbashi Enbujo** (☞ Dance *in the Arts, below*). On the left is the Nissan Motor Company headquarters.

A brisk minute's walk will bring you to the intersection of Harumi-dōri. Turn left, and on the next block, on the right, you will see the **Kabuki-za** ⑤⑤ (theater).

Just in front of the Kabuki-za is the Hibiya subway's Higashi-Ginza stop, where you can make your way back from whence you came.

TIMING

The Tsukiji walk offers few places to spend time *in*; backtracking and getting from point to point, however, can consume most of a morning—especially if you decide to devote an hour or so to Tsukuda-jima. Allow yourself an hour or more to explore the Central Market and the nearby shops; if fish in all its diversity holds a special fascination for you, take two or three. This part of the city can be brutally hot and muggy in August; during the O-bon holiday, in the middle of the month, Tsukiji is comparatively lifeless. Mid-April and early October are best for strolls in the Hama Rikyū garden.

Sights to See

★ ④⑨ **Backstreet Shops of Tsukiji.** Because of its proximity to the fish market, there are scores of fishmongers here—but also sushi bars, restaurants, and stores for pickles, tea, crackers, kitchen knives, baskets, and crockery. Markets like these are a vital counterpoint to the museums and monuments of conventional sightseeing. They bring you up close to the way people really live in the cities you visit. If you have time on your itinerary for just one market, this is the one to see. The area that these shops occupy is between the Tōkyō fish market and Harumi-dōri. ✉ *5-2-1 Tsukiji, Chūō-ku. Subway: Hibiya Line, Tsukuji.*

54 **Hama Rikyū Tei-en** (Detached Palace Garden). The land here was originally owned by the Owari branch of the Tokugawa family from Nagoya, and it extended to part of what is now the fish market. When one of the family became shōgun in 1709, his residence was turned into a shogunal palace—with pavilions, ornamental gardens, pine and cherry groves, and duck ponds. The garden became a public park in 1945, although a good portion of it is fenced off as a nature preserve. None of the original buildings survive, but on the island in the large pond is a reproduction of the pavilion where former U.S. president Ulysses S. Grant and Mrs. Grant had an audience with the emperor Meiji in 1879. The building can now be rented for parties. The path to the left as you enter the garden leads to the "river bus" ferry landing, from which you can leave this excursion and begin another: up the Sumida to Asakusa. ⊠ *Chūō-ku,* ☎ *03/3541–0200.* ▨ *¥300.* ☺ *Daily 9–4. Subway: Hibiya Line, Tsukiji.*

50 **International Trade Center.** The expositions presented here during the year—electronics and information systems, imported foods, toys, automobiles, recreation equipment—attract huge throngs. Check the publication *Tour Companion* to see if there's a show running that you might want to catch. ⊠ *5-3-53 Harumi, Chūō-ku,* ☎ *03/3533–5314. Subway: Hibiya Line, Tsukiji.*

★ **55** **Kabuki-za.** Soon after the Meiji Restoration and its enforced exile in Asakusa, Kabuki began to reestablish itself in this part of the city. The first Kabuki-za was built in 1889, with a European facade. Here, two of the hereditary theater families, Ichikawa and Onoe, developed a brilliant new repertoire that brought Kabuki into the modern era. In 1912 the Kabuki-za was taken over by the Shochiku theatrical management company, and in 1925 the old theater building was replaced. Designed by architect Shin'ichirō Okada, it was damaged during World War II but was restored soon thereafter. For information on performances, *see* the Arts, *below.* ⊠ *4-12-15 Ginza, Chūō-ku,* ☎ *03/3541–8597. Subway: Hibiya Line, Higashi-Ginza.*

53 **Sumiyoshi Jinja.** A few steps from the breakwater at the north end of ☞ Tsukuda-jima, this shrine dates from the island's earliest period, when Ōsaka fishermen settled here. The god enshrined here is the protector of those who make their livelihood from the sea. Once every three years (1996, 1999, etc.), the shrine celebrates its main festival. On the first weekend in August, the god is brought out for his procession in an unusual eight-sided palanquin, preceded by huge, golden lion heads carried high in the air, their mouths snapping in mock ferocity to drive any evil influences out of the path. As the palanquin passes, the people of the island douse it with water, recalling the custom, before the breakwater was built, of carrying it to the river for a high-spirited ducking.

If you have time, wander through the area bounded by the breakwater and the L-shape canal. It's ramshackle in places, even a little scruffy, but this is an authentic corner of Shita-machi that cannot last much longer. Having survived most of the natural disasters of the past three centuries, it faces a new threat—the huge development project on the north end of the island—which will eventually doom the village to modernity. ⊠ *1-1 Tsukuda, Chūō-ku,* ☎ *03/3531–3500.* ▨ *Free.* ☺ *Dawn-sunset. Subway: Yūraku-chō Line, Tsukishima.*

★ **48** **Tōkyō Chūō Oroshiuri Ichiba** (Central Wholesale Market). The city's fish market used to be farther uptown, in Nihombashi. It was moved to Tsukiji after the Great Kantō Earthquake of 1923, and it occupies the site of what was once Japan's first naval training academy. Today the market sprawls over some 54 acres of reclaimed land. Its warren of buildings houses about 1,200 wholesale shops, supplying 90% of the fish consumed in Tōkyō every day and employing some 15,000 people. One would expect to see docks here, and unending streams of fish spilling from the holds of ships, but, in fact, most of the seafood sold in Tsukiji comes in by truck, arriving through the night from fishing ports all over the country.

What makes Tsukiji a great show is the auction system. The catch—more than 100 varieties of fish in all, including whole frozen tuna, Styrofoam cases of shrimp and squid, and crates of crabs—is laid out in the long covered area between the river and the main building. Then the bidding begins. Only members of the wholesalers' association can take part. Wearing license numbers fastened to the front of their caps, they register their bids in a kind of sign language, shouting to draw the attention of the auctioneer and making furious combinations in the air with their fingers. The auctioneer keeps the action moving in a hoarse croak that sounds like no known language, and spot quotations change too fast for ordinary mortals to follow.

Different fish are auctioned off at different times and locations, and by 6:30 AM or so, this part of the day's business is over and the wholesalers fetch their purchases back into the market in barrows. Restaurant owners and retailers arrive about 7, making the rounds of favorite suppliers for their requirements. Chaos seems to reign, but everybody here knows everybody else, and they all have it down to a system. From the Hibiya subway's Tsujiki stop, walk west about 10 minutes on Shin-Ōhashi-dōri until you cross a bridge. Take the first left on the other side, walk to the end of the road, and turn right. ⊠ *5-2-1 Tsukiji, Chūō-ku,* ☎ *03/3542–1111.* 🎫 *Free.* ☉ *Business hrs 6–4; closed 2nd and 4th Wed. of month. Subway: Hibiya Line, Tsukuji.*

🟡 **Tsukiji Hongan-ji.** Disaster seemed to follow this temple since it was first located here in 1657: It was destroyed at least five times thereafter, and reconstruction in wood was finally abandoned after the Great Kantō Earthquake of 1923. The present stone building dates from 1935. It was designed by Chūta Ito, a pupil of Tatsuno Kingo, who built Tōkyō Station. Ito's other credits include the Meiji Jingū in Harajuku; he also lobbied for Japan's first law for the preservation of historic buildings. Ito traveled extensively in Asia. The evocations of classical Hindu architecture in the temple's domes and ornaments were his homage to India as the cradle of Buddhism. ⊠ *3-15-1 Tsukiji, Chūō-ku,* ☎ *03/3541–1131.* 🎫 *Free.* ☉ *Daily 6–4. Subway: Hibiya Line, Tsukiji.*

NEED A BREAK?   **Edo-Gin** is one of the area's older sushi bars, founded in 1924, and it is legendary for its portions—slices of raw fish that almost hide the balls of rice on which they sit. Dinner is pricey, but the set menu at lunch is a certifiable *bāgen* (bargain) at ¥1,000. Walk west on Shin-Ōhashi-dōri from its intersection with Harumi-dōri. Take the first right, then the first left, and look for Edo-Gin. ⊠ *4-5-1 Tsukiji, Chūō-ku,* ☎ *03/3543–4401. AE, MC, V. Closed Sun. Subway: Hibiya Line, Tsukiji.*

🟡 **Tsukuda-jima.** The island was reclaimed from mud flats at the mouth of the Sumida-gawa. The name dates to 1613, when the shogunate ordered a group of fishermen from the village of Tsukuda, now part of Ōsaka, to relocate here. Officially, they were brought here to provide the castle with whitebait; unofficially, their role was to keep watch and report on any suspicious maritime traffic in the bay. Over the years, more and more land has been reclaimed from the bay, more than doubling the size of the island and adding other areas to the south and west.

The part to explore is the original section: a few square blocks just west and north of the Tsukuda Ōhashi. This neighborhood—its maze of narrow alleys, its profusion of potted plants and bonsai, its old houses with tile roofs—could almost have come straight out of the Edo period. ✉ *1-1 Tsukuda, Chūō-ku. Subway: Yūraku-chō Line, Tsukishima.*

Nihombashi, Ginza, and Yūraku-chō

Tōkyō is a city of many centers. The municipal administrative center is in Shinjuku. The national government center is in Kasumigaseki. For almost 350 years, Japan was ruled from Edo Castle, and the great stone ramparts still define—for travelers, at least—the heart of the city. History, entertainment, fashion, traditional culture: Every tail we want to pin on the donkey goes in a different spot. Geographically speaking, however, there is one and only one center of Tōkyō: a tall, black iron pole on the north side of **Nihombashi** (Bridge of Japan)—and if the tail you were holding represented high finance, you would have to pin that one right here as well.

When Ieyasu Tokugawa had the first bridge constructed at **Nihombashi,** he designated it the starting point for the five great roads leading out of his city, the point from which all distances were to be measured. His decree is still in force: The black pole on the present bridge, erected in 1911, is the "Zero Kilometer" marker for all the national highways.

In the early days of the Tokugawa shogunate, Edo had no port. As the city grew, almost everything it needed was shipped from the western end of the country, which was economically more developed. Because the bay shore was marshy and full of tidal flats, ships would come only as far as Shinagawa, a few miles down the coast, and unload to smaller vessels. These in turn would take the cargo into the city through a network of canals to wharves and warehouses at Nihombashi. The bridge and the area south and east became a wholesale distribution center, not only for manufactured goods but also for foodstuffs. The city's first fish market, in fact, was established at Nihombashi in 1628 and remained here until the great earthquake of 1923.

All through the Edo period, this was part of Shita-machi (downtown). Except for a few blocks between Nihombashi and Kyō-bashi, where the city's deputy magistrates had their villas, it belonged to the common people—not all of whom lived elbow-to-elbow in poverty. There were fortunes to be made in the markets, and the early millionaires of Edo built their homes in the Nihombashi area. Some, like the legendary timber magnate Bunzaemon Kinokuniya, spent everything they made in the pleasure quarters of Yoshiwara and died penniless. Others founded the great trading houses of today—Mitsui, Mitsubishi, Sumitomo—that still have warehouses not far from Nihombashi.

It was appropriate, then, that when Japan's first corporations were created and the Meiji government developed a modern system of capital formation, the Tōkyō Stock Exchange (Shōken Torihikijo) go up on the west bank of the Nihombashi River. A stone's throw from the exchange now are the home offices of most of the country's major securities companies, which move billions of yen around the world electronically—a far cry from the early years of high finance, when they burned a length of rope on the floor of the exchange. Trading was over for the day when it had smoldered down to the end.

A little farther west, money—the problems of making it and moving it around—shaped the area in a somewhat different way. In the Edo period, there were three types of currency in circulation: gold, silver, and copper, each with its various denominations. Determined to unify the system, Ieyasu Tokugawa started minting his own silver coins in 1598, in his home province of Suruga, even before he became shōgun. In 1601 he established a gold mint; the building was only a few hundred yards from Nihombashi, on the site of what is now the Bank of Japan. In 1612 he relocated the Suruga plant on a patch of reclaimed land to the west of his castle. The area soon came to be known informally as the **Ginza** (Silver Mint).

The value of these various currencies fluctuated. There were profits to be made in the changing of money, and this business eventually came under the control of a few large merchant houses. One of the most successful of these merchants was a man named Takatoshi Mitsui, who had a dry-goods shop in Kyōto and opened a branch in Edo in 1673. The shop, called Echigo-ya, was just north of Nihombashi. By the end of the 17th century, it was the base of a commercial empire—in retailing, banking, and trading—known today as the Mitsui Group. Not far from the site of Echigo-ya stands its direct descendant: Mitsukoshi depāto.

Rui wa tomo wo yobu, so goes the Japanese expression: "Like calls to like." From Nihombashi through Ginza to Shimbashi is the domain of all the Noble Houses that trace their ancestry back to the dry-goods and kimono shops of the Edo period: Mitsukoshi, Takashimaya, Matsuzakaya, Matsuya. All are intensely proud of being at the top of the retail business, as purveyors of an astonishing range of goods and services. Together, they are but the latest expression of this area's abiding concern with money. Take some with you when you explore the neighborhoods: You might just find an opportunity to spend it.

The district called **Yūraku-chō** lies west of Ginza's Sukiya-bashi, stretching from Sotobori-dōri to Hibiya Kōen and the Outer Garden of the Imperial Palace. The name derives from one Urakusai Oda, younger brother of the warlord who had once been Ieyasu Tokugawa's commander. Urakusai, a Tea Master of some note—he was a student of Sen no Rikyū, who developed the tea ceremony—had a town house here, beneath the castle ramparts, on land reclaimed from the tidal flats of the bay. He soon left Edo for the more refined comforts of Kyōto, but his name stayed behind, becoming Yūraku-chō—the Pleasure (*yūraku*) Quarter (*chō*)—in the process. Sukiya-bashi was the name of the bridge near Urakusai's villa that led over the moat—long gone in the course of modernization—to the Silver Mint.

The "pleasures" associated with this district in the early postwar period stemmed from the fact that a number of the buildings here survived the air raids of 1945 and were requisitioned by the Allied forces. Yūraku-chō quickly became the haunt of the so-called *pan-pan* girls, who provided the GIs with female company. Because it was so close to the military Post Exchange in Ginza, the area under the railroad tracks became one of the city's largest black markets. Later, the black market gave way to clusters of cheap restaurants, most of them little more than counters and a few stools, serving yakitori and beer. Office workers on meager budgets, and journalists from the nearby *Mainichi, Asahi,* and *Yomiuri* newspaper headquarters, would gather here at night. Yūraku-chō-under-the-tracks was smoky, loud, and friendly, a kind of open-air substitute for the local taproom. Alas, the area has long since moved upscale, and no more than a handful of the yakitori stalls survive.

Numbers in the text correspond to numbers in the margin and on the Nihom-bashi, Ginza, and Yūraku-chō map.

A Good Walk
For more information on *depāto* and individual shops mentioned in this walk, *see* Shopping, *below.*

NIHOM-BASHI

Begin at Tōkyō Station. Take the Yaesu Central exit on the east side of the building, cross the broad avenue in front of you (Sotobori-dōri), and turn left. Walk north until you cross a bridge under the Shuto Expressway, and turn right at the second corner, at the **Bank of Japan** ㊻. From here, walk east two blocks to the main intersection at Chūō-dōri. On your left is the Mitsui Bank, on your right **Mitsukoshi** depāto. The small area around the store, formerly called Suruga-chō, is the birthplace of the Mitsui conglomerate.

Takatoshi Mitsui made his fortune by revolutionizing the retail system for kimono fabrics. The drapers of his day usually did business on account, taking payments semiannually. In his store (then called Echigo-ya), Mitsui started the practice of unit pricing, and his customers paid cash on the spot. As time went on, the store was always ready to adapt to changing needs and merchandising styles; these adjustments included garments made to order, home delivery, imported goods, and even—as the 20th century opened and Echigo-ya had grown, diversified, and changed its name to Mitsukoshi—the hiring of women to the sales force. The emergence of Mitsukoshi as Tōkyō's first depāto, also called *hyakkaten* (hundred-kinds-of-goods emporium), actually dates from 1908, with a three-story Western building modeled on Harrods of London. This was replaced in 1914 by a five-story structure that boasted Japan's first escalator. The present flagship store is vintage 1935.

Turn right on Chūō-dōri. As you walk south, you'll see on the left a shop founded in 1849, called **Yamamoto Noriten** (✉ 1-6-3 Nihombashi, Muro-machi, ☎ 03/3241–0261), which specializes in *nori*, the ubiquitous dried seaweed used to wrap everything from *maki* (rolls) and *onigiri* (rice balls), once the most famous product of Tōkyō Bay.

At the end of the next block is the **Nihom-bashi** ㊼, sadly stuck under the incessant rumbling of the expressway overhead. Before you cross the bridge, notice on your left the small statue of a sea princess seated by a pine tree: a monument to the fish market that stood here before the 1923 quake. To the right is the Zero Kilometer marker, from which all highway distances are measured. On the other side, also to the right, is a plaque depicting the old wooden bridge. In the Edo period, the south end of the bridge was set aside for posting public announcements—and for displaying the heads of criminals.

Turn left as soon as you cross the bridge, and walk past the Nomura Securities Building to where the expressway loops overhead and turns south. This area is called Kabuto-chō, after the small **Kabuto Jinja** ㊽ here on the left, under the loop. The shrine is named for the golden helmet of an 11th-century warrior. These days, Kabuto-chō invokes the prayers not of warriors but of stock brokers. With good reason: Just across the street from the shrine is the **Tōkyō Stock Exchange** ㊾.

At the main entrance to the Stock Exchange, turn right. Walk south two blocks to the intersection at Eitai-dōri and turn right again. The black building on the corner is the Yamatane Securities Building; on the eighth and ninth floors is the **Yamatane Museum of Art** ㊿. After stopping in the museum, continue west on Eitai-dōri, turn right onto Shōwa-dōri, and then left on the first small street behind the Bank of Hiroshima. Just off the next corner is a restaurant called Taimeiken. On the fifth floor of this building is the delightful little private **Kite Museum** ㉑—well worth the detour, for all ages.

Retrace your steps to Eitai-dōri, continue west to Chūō-dōri, and turn left. One block south, on the left, is the **Takashimaya** depāto; on the right is **Maruzen,** one of Japan's largest booksellers.

Nihom-bashi, Ginza, and Yūraku-chō

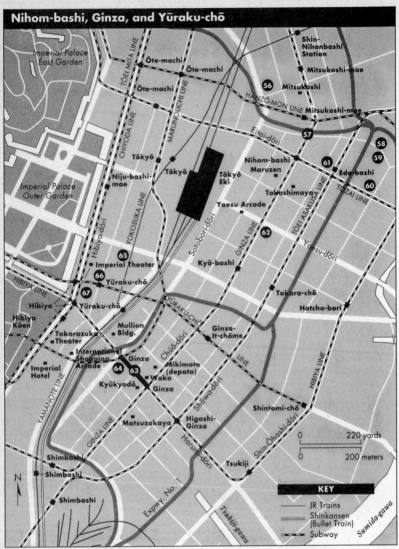

Imperial Palace East Garden

TŌEI MITA LINE

Ōte-machi

Ōte-machi

Ōte-machi

MARUNOUCHI LINE

CHIYODA LINE

Shin-Nihonbashi Station

Mitsukoshi-mae

56 Mitsukoshi

HANZŌ-MON LINE Mitsukoshi-mae

Eitai-dōri

57

58

59

Tōkyō

Tōkyō

Niju-bashi-mae

Tōkyō Eki

Nihom-bashi Maruzen

Takashimaya

61 Edo-bashi

TŌZAI LINE

60

Imperial Palace Outer Garden

Hibiya-dōri

YOKOSUKA LINE

Yaesu Arcade

GINZA LINE

TŌEI ASAKUSA LINE

62

Yaesu-dōri

65

Imperial Theater

66 Yūraku-chō

Sotobori-dōri

Kyō-bashi

HIBIYA LINE

67

Hibiya

Yūraku-chō

YŪRAKU-CHŌ

Takara-chō

Hatcho-bori

Hibiya Kōen

Mullion Bldg.

Chūō-dōri

Ginza-Itt-chōme

LINE

Takarazuka Theater

International Shopping Arcade

Ginza

64 63

Mikimoto (depato)

Wako

Shōwa-dōri

HIBIYA LINE

YAMANOTE LINE

Imperial Hotel

Kyūkyodō

Ginza

GINZA LINE

Matsuzakaya

Higashi-Ginza

Haruma-dōri

Shintomi-chō

Shin-Ōhashi-dōri

0   220 yards

0   200 meters

Shimbashi

Shimbashi

N

Shimbashi

Tsukiji

Expwy. No. 1

Tsukiji-gawa

Sumida-gawa

KEY

⎯⎯ JR Trains

⎯⎯ Shinkansen (Bullet Train)

⋯⋯ Subway

Nihom-bashi
Bank of Japan, **56**
Bridgestone Museum of Art, **62**
Kabuto Jinja, **58**
Kite Museum, **61**
Nihom-bashi, **57**
Tōkyō Stock Exchange, **59**
Yamatane Museum of Art, **60**

Ginza
Ginza, **63**
Sukiya-bashi, **64**

Yūraku-chō
Dai-ichi Mutual Life Insurance Company Building, **67**
Idemitsu Museum of Arts, **66**
Tōkyō International Forum, **65**

Look right at the next intersection; you'll see that you've come back almost to Tōkyō Eki. Below the avenue from here to the station runs the **Yaesu Underground Arcade,** with hundreds of shops and restaurants. The whole area here, west of Chūō-dōri, was named after Jan Joosten, a Dutch sailor who was shipwrecked on the coast of Kyūshū with William Adams—hero of James Michener's *Shogun*—in 1600. Like Adams, Joosten became an adviser to Ieyasu Tokugawa, took a Japanese wife, and was given a villa near the castle. "Yaesu" (originally Yayosu) was as close as the Japanese could come to the pronunciation of his name. Adams, an Englishman, lived out his life in Japan; Joosten drowned off the coast of Indonesia, in an attempt to return home.

On the southeast corner of the intersection is the **Bridgestone Museum of Art** ⑫, one of Japan's best private collections of early modern painting and sculpture, both Western and Japanese.

GINZA

Consider your feet. By now, they may be telling you that you would really rather not walk to the next point on this excursion. If so, get on the Ginza Line—there's a subway entrance right in front of the Bridgestone Museum—and ride one stop to **Ginza** ⑬. Take any exit directing you to the **4-chōme intersection** (yon-*chō*-me *kō*-sa-ten). When you come up to the street level, orient yourself by the Ginza branch of the **Mitsukoshi** depāto on the northeast corner and the round **Sanai Building** (⊠ 5-7-2 Ginza) on the southwest.

From Ginza 4-chōme, walk west on Harumi-dōri in the direction of the Imperial Palace. From Chūō-dōri to the intersection called **Sukiya-bashi** ⑭, named for a bridge that once stood here, your exploration should be free-form: The side streets and parallels north–south are ideal for wandering, particularly if you are interested in art galleries—of which there are 300 or more in this part of the Ginza.

YŪRAKU-CHŌ

From the Sukiya-bashi intersection, walk northwest on the right side of Harumi-dōri. Pass the curved facade of the **Mullion Building** depāto complex and cross the intersection. You'll go through a tunnel under the JR Yamanote Line tracks, then turn right and walk two blocks east, parallel to the tracks, until you get to the gleaming white expanse of the **Tōkyō International Forum** ⑮.

The plaza of the Tōkyō International Forum is that rarest of Tōkyō rarities—civilized open space: a long, tree-shaded central courtyard with comfortable benches to sit on and things to see. There is free-standing sculpture; there is triumphant architecture; there are people strolling— actually *strolling*—past in both directions. Need refreshment? **Cafe Wien,** next to the Plaza Information Center, has pastry and coffee.

From the southwest corner of the Forum, turn left and walk halfway down the block to the main entrance of the International Building. On the ninth floor you'll find the **Idemitsu Museum of Arts** ⑯. After a stop inside, continue west along the side of the International Building toward the Imperial Palace, to Hibiya-dōri.

Turn left, and less than a minute's walk along Hibiya-dōri will bring you to the **Dai-ichi Mutual Life Insurance Company Building** ⑰. Across the avenue is **Hibiya Kōen,** Japan's first Western-style public park, which dates from 1903. Its lawns and fountains make a pretty place for office workers from nearby buildings to have lunch on a warm spring afternoon, but it doesn't provide compelling reasons for you to make a detour. Press on, past the Hibiya Police Station, across the Harumi-dōri intersection, and at the second corner, just before you come to the **Imperial Hotel** (☞ Lodging, *below*), turn left.

At the end of the block, on the corner, you will see the **Takarazuka Theater** (☞ Modern Theater *in* the Arts, *below*), where all-female casts put on uproarious shows. Continue southeast, and in the next block, on both sides of the street (just under the railroad bridge), are entrances to the **International Shopping Arcade** (☞ Shopping, *below*), the last point of interest on this walk. Stores here sell kimono and happi coats, pearls and cloisonné, prints, cameras, and consumer electronics: one-stop shopping for presents and souvenirs.

Turn left down the narrow side street that runs along the side of the arcade to the Hankyū depāto—the horned monstrosity in the pocket park on the corner is by sculptor Taro Okamoto—and you will find yourself back on Harumi-dōri, just a few steps from the Sukiya-bashi crossing. From here, you can return to your hotel by subway, or a minute's walk will bring you to the JR Yūraku-chō Eki.

TIMING

There is something about this part of Tōkyō—the traffic, the numbers of people, the way it exhorts you to keep moving—that can make you feel you've covered a lot more ground than you really have. Take this walk in the morning; when you're done, you can better assess the energy you have left for the rest of the day. None of the stops along the way, with the possible exception of the Bridgestone and Idemitsu museums, should take you more than three-quarters of an hour. The time you spend shopping, of course, is up to you. In summer, make it a point to start early, even though many of the stores and attractions do not open until 10 or 11; by midday the heat and humidity can be brutal. On Sundays from noon and Saturdays from 3 PM, from Shimbashi all the way to Kyō-bashi, Chūō-dōri is closed to traffic until early evening, becoming a pedestrian mall with tables and chairs and sunshades out along the street. That's great if you plan only to shop, but some of the museums and other sights are closed Sunday—something to keep in mind if you want to see them.

Sights to See

56 Bank of Japan. The older part of the Bank of Japan is the work of Tatsuno Kingo, who also designed Tōkyō Eki. Completed in 1896, the bank is one of the very few surviving Meiji-era Western buildings in the city. ☒ *2-2-1 Nihombashi Hongoku-chō, Chūō-ku,* ☎ *03/3279–1111. Subway: Ginza and Hanzō-mon lines, Mitsukoshi-mae.*

62 Bridgestone Museum of Art. This is one of Japan's best private collections of French Impressionist art and sculpture and of post-Meiji Japanese painting in Western styles, by such artists as Shigeru Aoki and Tsuguji Fujita. The collection, assembled by Bridgestone Tire Company founder Shōjiro Ishibashi, also includes work by Rembrandt, Picasso, Utrillo, and Modigliani. The Bridgestone also puts on major exhibits from private collections and museums abroad. ☒ *1-10-1 Kyō-bashi, Chūō-ku,* ☎ *03/3563–0241.* ☜ *¥500.* ☉ *Tues.–Sun. 10–5:30. Subway: Ginza and Hanzō-mon lines, Mitsukoshi-mae.*

67 Dai-ichi Mutual Life Insurance Company Building. Built like a fortress, the edifice survived World War II virtually intact and was taken over by the Supreme Command of the Allied Powers. From his office here, General Douglas MacArthur directed the affairs of Japan from 1945 to 1951. The room is kept exactly as it was then; it can be visited by small groups, without appointment. ☒ *1-1-13 Yūraku-chō, Chiyoda-ku,* ☎ *03/3216–1211.* ☜ *Free.* ☉ *Mon.–Sat. 10–4. Subway: Hibiya stop.*

63 **Ginza.** Ieyasu's silver mint moved out of this area in 1800. The name *Ginza* remained, but only much later did it begin to acquire any cachet for wealth and style. The turning point was 1872, when a fire destroyed most of the old houses here. In the same year, the country's first railway line was completed, from nearby Shimbashi to Yokohama. This prompted the city to one of its periodic attempts at large-scale planning: The main street of Ginza, together with a grid of cross streets and parallels, was rebuilt as a Western *quartier*. It had two-story brick houses with balconies; it had the nation's first sidewalks and horse-drawn streetcars; and it had gas lights and, later, telephone poles. Before the turn of the century, Ginza had attracted the great mercantile establishments that still define its character. The **Wako** depāto, for example, on the northwest corner of the 4-chōme intersection, established itself here as Hattori, purveyors of clocks and watches. The clock on the present building was first installed in the Hattori clock tower, a Ginza landmark, in 1894.

Many of the shops nearby have lineages almost as old, or older. A few steps north of the intersection, on Chūō-dōri, **Mikimoto** (✉ 4-5-5 Ginza) sells the famous cultured pearls first developed by Kokichi Mikimoto in 1883. His first shop in Tōkyō dates from 1899. South of the intersection, next door to the Sanai Building, **Kyūkyodō** (✉ 5-7-4 Ginza) carries a great variety of handmade Japanese papers and related goods. Kyūkyodō has been in business since 1663, and on the Ginza since 1880. Across the street and one block south is the **Matsuzakaya** depāto, which began as a kimono shop in Nagoya in 1611. Exploring this area—there's even a name for browsing: *Gin-bura*, or "Ginza-wandering"—is best on Sundays, from noon to 6 or 7 (depending on the season), when Chūō-dōri is closed to traffic between Shimbashi and Kyō-bashi. *Subway: Ginza and Hibiya lines, Ginza.*

66 **Idemitsu Museum of Arts.** With its four spacious rooms, the Idemitsu is one of the largest and best designed private museums in Tōkyō. The strength of the collection is in its Tang and Song dynasty Chinese porcelain, and in Japanese ceramics—including works by Ninsei Nonomura and Kenzan Ōgata, and masterpieces of Old Seto, Oribe, Old Kutani, Karatsu, and Kakiemon ware. There are also outstanding examples of Zen painting and calligraphy, wood-block prints, and genre paintings of the Edo period. Of special interest to scholars is the resource collection of shards from virtually every pottery-making culture of the ancient world. ✉ *3-1-1 Maru-no-uchi, Chiyoda-ku,* ☎ *03/ 3213–9404.* ✎ *¥500.* ☉ *Tues.–Sun. 10–5. Subway: Yūraku-chō line, Yūraku-chō.*

58 **Kabuto Jinja.** This shrine, like the Nihombashi itself, is another bit of history lurking in the shadows of the expressway. Legend has it that a noble warrior of the 11th century, sent by the Imperial Court in Kyōto to subdue the barbarians of the north, stopped here and prayed for assistance. His expedition was successful, and on the way back he buried a *kabuto*, a golden helmet, on this spot as an offering of thanks. Few Japanese are aware of this legend, and the monument of choice in Kabuto-chō today is the ☞ Tōkyō Stock Exchange. ✉ *1-8 Kabuto-chō, Nihombashi, Chūō-ku. Subway: Tōei Asakusa Line, Edo-bashi; Ginza and Hanzō-mon lines, Mitsukoshi-mae.*

61 **Kite Museum.** Kite flying is an old tradition in Japan. The Motegi collection includes examples of every shape and variety, from all over the country, hand-painted in brilliant colors with figures of birds, geometric patterns, and motifs from Chinese and Japanese mythology. Call ahead, and the museum will arrange a kite-making workshop (in Japanese) for groups of children. ✉ *1-12-10 Nihombashi, Chūō-ku,* ☎ *03/*

3275–2704. ✆ ¥200. ⊙ *Mon.–Sat. 11–5. Subway: Tōei Asakusa Line, Edo-bashi.*

🟊 Nihom-bashi. Why, back in 1962, the expressway *had* to be routed directly over this lovely old landmark is one of the mysteries of Tōkyō and its city planning—or lack thereof. There were protests and petitions, but they had no effect. Planners argued the high cost of alternative locations; at that time Tōkyō had only two years left to prepare for the Olympics, and the traffic congestion was already out of hand. So the bridge, with its graceful double arch and ornate lamps, its bronze Chinese lions and unicorns, was doomed to bear the perpetual rumble of trucks overhead—its claims overruled by concrete ramps and pillars. *Subway: Tōzai and Ginza lines, Nihombashi; Ginza and Hanzō-mon lines, Mitsukoshi-mae.*

🟊 Sukiya-bashi. The side streets of the Sukiya-bashi area are full of art galleries, several hundred in fact. The galleries operate a bit differently here than they do in most of the world's art markets: A few, like the venerable **Nichidō** (✉ 7-4-12 Ginza), **Gekkōso** (✉ 6-3-17 Ginza), **Yoseidō** (✉ 5-5-15 Ginza), **Yayoi** (✉ 7-6-61 Ginza), and **Kabuto-ya** (✉ 8-8-7 Ginza), actually function as dealers, representing particular artists, as well as acquiring and selling art. The majority, however, are rental spaces. Artists or groups pay for the gallery by the week, publicize their show themselves, and in some cases even hang their own work. Not unreasonably, one suspects that a lot of these shows, even in so prestigious a venue as the Ginza, are "vanity" exhibitions by amateurs with money to spare—but that's not always the case. The rental spaces are also the only way for serious professionals, independent of the various art organizations that might otherwise sponsor their work, to get any critical attention; if they're lucky, they can at least recoup their expenses with an occasional sale. *Subway: Ginza, Hibiya, and Maru-no-uchi lines, Ginza.*

🟊 Tōkyō International Forum. The work of Uruguay-born American architect Raphael Vinoly, this is the first major convention and art center of its kind in Tōkyō. Vinoly's design was selected in a 1989 competition that drew nearly 400 entries from 50 countries. It is a postmodern masterpiece. Opened in January 1997, the forum is really two buildings. On the east side of the plaza is the Glass Hall, the main exhibition space—an atrium with a 180-ft ceiling, a magnificent curved wooden wall, and 34 upper-floor conference rooms. The west building has six halls for international conferences, exhibitions, receptions, and concert performances—the largest with seating for 5,012.

Tōkyō Multiscope, in the forum's Audio Visual Hall, has continuous screenings 11 AM–4 PM of well-made and informative short films on the city: its art and architecture, its history, the everyday life of the people who live here. State-of-the-art technology, including a "Video Wall" of 24 separate high-definition screens, makes this one of the best shows in town. ☏ *03/5221–9000.* ✆ *¥300.*

The **Cultural Information Lobby** (☏ 03/5221–9084) has the latest schedules of conventions and events in the forum itself; it also has an English-speaking staff and an excellent audiovisual library on tourist attractions, festivals, and events all over Japan—making this a worthwhile first stop when you come to town. Another useful resource is the information office of the **JNTO** (Japan National Tourist Organization; ☏ 03/3201–3331), at the north end of the lower concourse. ✉ *3-5-1 Maru-no-uchi, Chiyoda-ku,* ☏ *03/5221–9000. Subway: Yūraku-chō Line, Yūraku-chō.* ⊙ *Daily 10–8.*

NEED A
BREAK?

Amid all of Tōkyō's bustle and crush, you actually can catch your breath in the open space of the plaza of the Tōkyō International Forum. If you also feel like having coffee and a bite of pastry, stop in at **Café Wien,** next to the Plaza Information Center. ⊠ *3-5-1 Maru-no-uchi, Chiyoda-ku,* ☎ *03/3211–3111. Subway: Yūraku-chō Line, Yūraku-chō.*

59 **Tōkyō Stock Exchange.** From the Exchange's Exhibition Plaza and Gallery, you can watch the fast and furious action on the trading floor. A *Star Wars*–like robot demonstrates hand signals used on the floor at the touch of a button. The robot also lectures on the daily trading of securities at the Tōkyō Stock Exchange. An array of video exhibits introduces companies and offers worldwide stock news and information on trading terms. ⊠ *2-1 Nihombashi Kabuto-chō, Chūō-ku,* ☎ *03/3666–0141.* ⊡ *Free.* ☼ *Weekdays 9–4. Trading hrs weekdays 9– 11 and 12:30–3. Subway: Tōei Asakusa Line, Edo-bashi.*

60 **Yamatane Museum of Art.** The museum specializes in *nihon-ga*—traditional Japanese painting—from the Meiji period and later. It was designed with an interior garden by architect Yoshiro Taniguchi, who also did the **Tōkyō Kokuritsu Kindai Bijutsukan** in Take-bashi (☞ Imperial Palace, *above*). The museum's own private collection includes masterpieces by such painters as Taikan Yokoyama, Gyoshū Hayami, Kokei Kobayashi, and Gyokudō Kawai. The exhibitions, which sometimes include works borrowed from other collections, change every two months. The decor and display at the Yamatane make it an oasis of quiet and elegance in the world of high finance; the chance to buy the lavish catalog of the collection would be well worth the visit. ⊠ *7-12 Nihombashi, Kabuto-chō, Chūō-ku,* ☎ *03/3669–4056.* ⊡ *¥700.* ☼ *Tues.–Sun. 10–5. Subway: Tōei Asakusa Line, Edo-bashi.*

Akasaka

Modern-day Akasaka is just a 15-minute taxi ride west of the Imperial Palace, but little more than a hundred years ago, the gentle slopes of this area were still covered with tea bushes and *akane*—a plant that produced a red dye, and thus gave Akasaka (*aka* meaning red, *saka* meaning hill) its name. In 1936, with the construction of the granite ziggurat that houses the National Diet, the seat of the Japanese government moved to Nagata-chō, on the heights just to the north, and Akasaka blossomed in a different fashion. It became the favored haunt of politicians and their wealthy industrial backers: a quarter of discretely walled-off geisha houses and *ryōtei* (expensive traditional restaurants), where deals were cut that shaped the country's future.

After the Pacific War (the Japanese term for WWII), a number of countries—most importantly the United States—established embassies in the area. Deluxe hotels like the Okura and the Hilton (the latter now removed to Shinjuku) put even more of an international spin on Akasaka's upscale image. When TBS Television established its broadcast facilities and corporate headquarters here in 1960, the area grew downright glitzy. There were stars and celebrities to spot; there were foreigners to talk to in the bars; there were cabarets, and nightclubs— and, inevitably, mobsters. None of this deterred the ryōtei clientele. Akasaka remained the venue of choice for quiet backroom discussions of politics and high finance. Today, the few surviving ryōtei define the character of the area in one way, just as the new TBS Building—a postmodern confection of 1994, all flash and no fire—defines it in another. There's more to Akasaka than meets the eye, and less.

Numbers in the text correspond to numbers in the margin and on the Akasaka map.

A Good Walk

To begin this walk, take the Chiyoda subway line to Kokkai Gijidō-mae and follow signs to the **Capitol Tōkyū Hotel** exit. The rear entrance to the hotel will be directly across the street. To save yourself a climb up the hill and around the hotel, enter the building through this rear entrance and take the elevator to the main lobby. You may well stop here for breakfast; the dining room in the lobby overlooks an especially fine traditional Japanese pond and garden. Leave the hotel by the main entrance, and the **Hie Jinja** ⑱ and its large torii will be straight ahead of you.

Leave Hie Jinja by its east gate and walk down the hill to Akasaka's main street, Sotobori-dōri. On the opposite side, two smaller avenues run parallel to Sotobori-dōri: Ta-machi-dōri and Hitotsugi-dōri. On these two streets, and the narrow alleys between them, are the majority of Akasaka's small bars, restaurants, and cafés. The few remaining ryōtei and geisha houses are at the southern end of this area. Alas, none of these places look particularly intriguing from the outside. Interestingly enough, this part of town provides a clear-cut example of Japan's notorious outside-inside dichotomy. Call it a holdout of traditional Japanese social arrangements: Without an introduction from a known and trusted Japanese client, outside is as close as you are ever likely to get to one of these establishments.

Turn right on Sotobori-dōri and walk toward the Akasaka-mitsuke subway station. The five-way intersection at Aoyama-dōri is just beyond it. The Suntory Building and the **Suntory Museum** ⑲ stand across the intersection on the left, on the other side of the overpass.

Cross the street and the bridge over the moat on the far side of the Suntory Building, and walk to the **Hotel New Otani Tōkyō and Towers,** on the left. Billed as the largest hotel in Asia, the New Otani complex— 1,612 guest rooms, banquet halls, arcades, acres of bars and restaurants, tennis courts, and office towers—holds a certain futuristic fascination as a minicity. The main hotel building's lobby lounge makes for a civilized place for a respite, with a lovely Japanese garden to take in while you stop for a drink.

From the Suntory Building, turn west and walk uphill along Aoyama-dōri, which goes all the way through the area to Shibuya. Five minutes at a brisk pace will bring you to the walls of the **Geihinkan** ⑳, also known as Akasaka Detached Palace, on your right. A few minutes farther along, on the left, just before you reach the **Canadian Embassy,** you'll see the glass facade of the **Sōgetsu Kaikan** ㉑, headquarters of one of the more important modern schools of *ikebana,* flower arranging. Two blocks farther west, you come to the Aoyama Twin Tower Building and the Aoyama-1-chōme station on the Ginza and Hanzō-mon subway lines. From here you can ride one stop to Gaien-mae to get to the start of the next walk in Aoyama and Harajuku.

TIMING

Akasaka makes for a fairly easy walk. Even with a break and a stroll through the garden of the New Otani Hotel, it should take you no more than two hours. Weekdays are best, especially if you plan to have a lesson in flower arrangement at the Sōgetsu Kaikan—for which you should budget an hour more.

Sights to See

⑳ **Geihinkan** (Akasaka Detached Palace). Built in the Meiji period, this was the home of the crown prince, who later became the Taishō emperor. The Geihinkan has served since 1974 as an official state guest house for visiting foreign dignitaries. Inspired by the Louvre and the

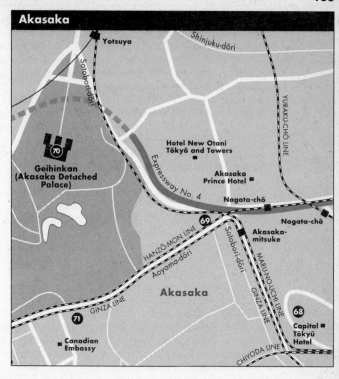

Palace of Versailles, it took some 45 years (1868–1912) to complete. The architecture and the grounds and gardens bear witness to the fierce determination of the Meiji government to imitate the achievements of the West. The interior, alas, is not open to the public. The Geihinkan is a five-minute walk west on Aoyama-dōri from the Akasaka-mitsuke intersection. ⊠ *2-1-1 Moto-Akasaka, Minato-ku,* ☎ *03/3478–1111.* ⊠ *Free tours of grounds can be arranged for groups of 20 or more by prior arrangement. Subway: Yūraku-chō and Maru-no-uchi lines, Akasaka-mitsuke.*

68 **Hie Jinja.** This shrine dates to the late 15th century and is dedicated principally to the Shintō deity Oyamakuni-no-kami. During the Edo period, the shrine became a favorite of the Tokugawa shogunate, who believed that Oyamakuni-no-kami took the city under his special protection. Several festivals take place here. By far the most important, held in alternate years, is the Sannō Matsuri (June 7–16), with processions of palanquins and attendants in historical costume that evoke the Tokugawa era—when the event was known as the Festival Without Equal. For the rest of the year, the shrine has a special appeal to those seeking protection against miscarriages; in the main courtyard note the statue of the female monkey holding her offspring. Worshipers also visit the shrine to protect themselves against traffic accidents; it is not unusual to see a Shintō priest blessing a new car. Notice the archway before the shrine, which is distinctive for its unusual triangular roof. Hie Jinja has been destroyed several times in fires. The present building was rebuilt in 1959, the torii in 1962. ⊠ *2-10-5 Nagata-chō, Chiyoda-ku.* ⊠ *Free.* ☉ *Sunrise–sunset. Subway: Yūraku-chō and Maru-no-uchi lines, Aksaka-mitsuke.*

NEED A
BREAK?

The Garden Lounge, in the main lobby of the **Hotel New Otani Tōkyō and Towers,** looks out on an immaculately sculpted 400-year-old Japanese garden, with red-lacquer bridges over ponds and waterfalls and winding paths: a perfect, if pricey, spot to unwind and have something to drink. ⊠ *4-1 Kioi-chō, Chiyoda-ku,* ☎ *03/3408–1126. Subway: Nagata-chō and Akasaka-mitsuke stops.*

㉛ Sōgetsu Kaikan. The "schools" of ikebana, like those of other traditional arts, from music and dance to calligraphy and tea ceremony, are highly stratified organizations. Students rise through levels of proficiency, paying handsomely for lessons and certifications as they go, until they are permitted to become teachers themselves. At the top of the hierarchy is the *iemoto,* the head of the school, a title usually held within a family for generations. The Sōgetsu School of flower arrangement is a relative newcomer to all this. It was founded by Sōfū Teshigahara in 1927, and, compared to the older schools, it espouses a style flamboyant, free-form, and even radical. Detractors call it overblown, but it draws students and admirers from the world over, and it has made itself wealthy in the process. The present iemoto is Hiroshi Teshigahara, who broke away from the family business earlier in life to be a film director. His *Woman in the Dunes* (1964) is among the classics of postwar Japanese cinema. The main hall of the Sōgetsu Kaikan is well worth a visit. It was created by the late Isamu Noguchi, one of the masters of modern sculpture. Lessons in flower arrangement are given in English on Mondays and Fridays, 10–noon. Sōgetsu Kaikan is a five-minute walk west on Aoyama-dōri from the Akasaka-mitsuke intersection. ⊠ *7-2-21 Akasaka, Minato-ku,* ☎ *03/3408–1126.* 🎫 *¥4,850 for 1st lesson, ¥3,800 thereafter. Reservations must be made a day in advance. Subway: Yūraku-chō and Maru-no-uchi lines, Akasaka-mitsuke.*

㉖ Suntory Museum. On the 11th floor of the Suntory Building, this museum houses a fine small collection of traditional paintings, prints, lacquerware, glassware, and costumes. It also holds special loan exhibitions throughout the year. For the size of the museum, the admission charge is high (and can be higher for special exhibits), but its displays are carefully selected and well displayed. ⊠ *1-2-3 Moto-Akasaka, Minato-ku,* ☎ *03/3470–1073.* 🎫 *¥500 (Sun. ¥300).* ☉ *Tues.–Thurs. and weekends 10–5, Fri. 10–7. Subway: Yūraku-chō and Maru-no-uchi lines, Akasaka-mitsuke.*

Aoyama, Harajuku, and Shibuya

Who would have known? As late as 1960, this was as unlikely a candidate as any area in Tōkyō to develop anything remotely chic. True, there was the Meiji Jingū, which gave the neighborhood a certain solemnity, and drew the occasional festival crowd. Between the Shrine and the Aoyama Cemetery to the east, however, the area was so unpromising that the municipal government designated a substantial chunk of it for low-cost public housing. Another chunk, called Washington Heights, was being used by U.S. Occupation forces—who spent their money elsewhere. The few young Japanese people in Harajuku and Aoyama were either hanging around Washington Heights to practice their English, or attending the Methodist-founded Aoyama Gakuin (university)—and seeking their leisure further south in Shibuya.

Then Tōkyō won its bid to host the 1964 Olympics, and Washington Heights was turned over to the city for the construction of the Olympic Village. Aoyama-dōri, the avenue through the center of the area was improved; under it ran the extension of the Ginza Line subway, and later the Hanzōmon Line. Public transportation is the chief ingredient in Tōkyō's commercial alchemy; suddenly, people could get to Aoyama and Harajuku easily, and they did—in larger and larger numbers, drawn by the Western-style fashion houses that now decided this was the place to be. Public housing residents started selling their apartments at premium prices, to hip young entrepreneurs who converted them to boutiques and design studios. By the 1980s the area was positively *smart*: If you were under 30 and had money in your pocket, this was your destination. A decade later, the area should still be high on your list of places to explore in Tōkyō.

On weekends, the heart of Harajuku belongs to high school and junior high school shoppers, who flock here with hoarded sums of pocket money and for whom last week was ancient history. Harajuku is where the market researchers come, pick 20 teenagers off the street at random, give them ¥2,000, and ask them to buy a tote bag. Whole industries convulse themselves to keep pace with those adolescent decisions. Stroll through Harajuku—with its outdoor cafés, its designer ice cream and Belgian waffle stands, its ever-changing profusion of mascots and logos—and you will find it impossible to believe that Japan is in fact the most rapidly aging society in the industrial world.

Shibuya is south and west of Harajuku and Aoyama. It might not be as hectic as Shinjuku, but it is no less major a city center for that. Two subway lines, three private railways, the JR Yamanote Line, and two bus terminals move about a million people a day through Shibuya. The hub's commercial character is shaped by the fierce battle for supremacy between the Seibu and Tōkyū depāto. As fast as one of them builds a new branch, vertical mall, or specialty store, its rival counters with another. And every new venture includes a trendy restaurant or a concert hall or a flashy gallery—something to draw a bigger share of Shibuya's predominantly younger crowd of students and office workers. The result: a consumer paradise, busy, noisy, confusing—and fun.

Numbers in the text correspond to numbers in the margin and on the Aoyama, Harajuku, and Shibuya map.

A Good Walk

For more information on *depāto* and individual shops mentioned in this walk, *see* Shopping, *below*.

AOYAMA

Begin outside of the Gaien-mae subway station on Aoyama-dōri. This is also the stop for the **Jingū Baseball Stadium** (⊠ 13 Kasumigaoka, Shinjuku-ku, ☎ 03/3404–8999), home field of the Yakult Swallows. You'll see it across the street from the Chichibu-no-miya Rugby and Football Ground. The stadium is actually within the **Meiji Jingū Outer Garden** ⑫. The **National Stadium** is on the other side of this park. It is Japan's largest stadium—the seat from which it hosted the 1964 Summer Olympics—with room for 75,000 people. East across the street from the National Stadium is the **Kaigakan:** The Meiji Memorial Picture Gallery, which, provided that you feel no great need to pay homage to images of Emperor Meiji, is hardly worth a detour.

From Gaien-mae, a five-minute walk southwest along the left side of Aoyama-dōri, toward Shibuya, will take you to the Aoyama san-chōme intersection and the **Zenkoku Dentoteki Kogeihin Sentā** ⑬, where you can see exhibits of and buy traditional Japanese crafts. From here, continue west some five blocks toward Shibuya, and turn left at the intersection where you see the Omotesandō subway station on the opposite side of the avenue. Hold tight to your credit cards here: This is the east end of Omotesandō, Tōkyō's premier fashion statement, lined on both sides with the boutiques of couturiers like Issey Miyake, Mis-

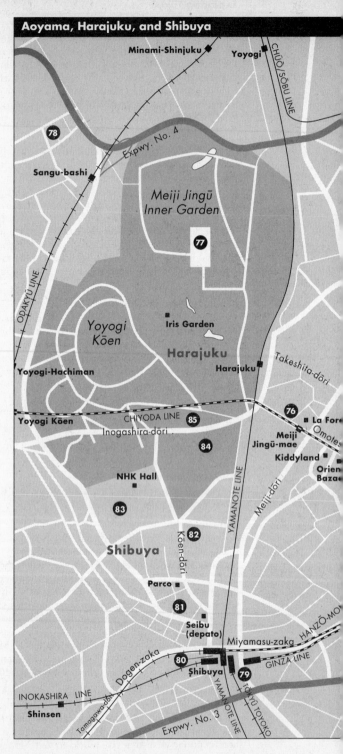

Aoyama, Harajuku, and Shibuya

Minami-Shinjuku
Yoyogi
CHŪŌ/SŌBU LINE
Expwy. No. 4
78
Sangu-bashi
Meiji Jingū
Inner Garden
77
ODAKYŪ LINE
Yoyogi
Kōen
Iris Garden
Harajuku
Takeshita-dōri
Yoyogi-Hachiman
Harajuku
76
CHIYODA LINE
85
La Fore
Yoyogi Kōen
Inogashira-dōri
Meiji
Jingū-mae
Omote
84
Kiddyland
Orien
Meiji-dōri
Baza
NHK Hall
YAMANOTE LINE
83
Shibuya
82
Kōen-dōri
Parco
81
Seibu
(depato)
Miyamasu-zaka
HANZŌ-MON
80
GINZA LINE
Dogen-zaka
79
Shibuya
TŌKYŪ TOYOKO
INOKASHIRA LINE
YAMANOTE LINE
Shinsen
Tamagawadōri
Expwy. No. 3

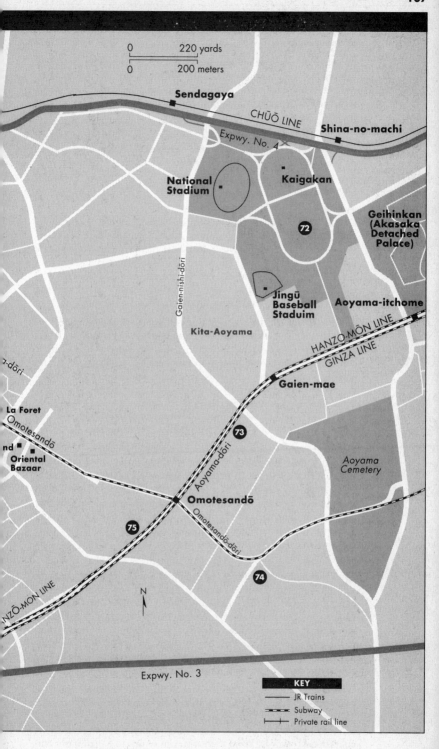

0 — 220 yards
0 — 200 meters

Sendagaya

CHŪO LINE

Expwy. No. 4

Shina-no-machi

National Stadium

Kaigakan

72

Geihinkan (Akasaka Detached Palace)

Gaien-nishi-dōri

Jingū Baseball Staduim

Aoyama-itchome

Kita-Aoyama

HANZO-MON LINE

GINZA LINE

Gaien-mae

-dōri

La Foret

Omotesandō

73

Aoyama-dōri

Aoyama Cemetery

nd

Oriental Bazaar

Omotesandō

75

Omotesandō-dōri

74

N

NZŌ-MON LINE

Expwy. No. 3

KEY
— JR Trains
-■-■- Subway
+++ Private rail line

soni, Calvin Klein, Gianfranco Ferre, and Comme des Garçons. At the end of the street, to the right, you'll see the walls of the **Nezu Institute of Fine Arts** ⑭.

As you walk toward the Nezu Institute, consider stopping for a treat at **Yoku Moku** on the right side of Omotesandō-dōri. The blue-tiled facade of its building marks an especially popular place with Aoyama's well-heeled shoppers, who stop in for cappuccino and pastries.

From the Nezu Institute of Fine Arts, retrace your steps to Aoyama-dōri. If you turned left here, you would come in due course (it's a longish walk) to Shibuya, by way of the **Aoyama Gakuin** (university) campus on the left and the kid's favorite **Kodomo-no-Kuni** ⑮. To make your way to Harajuku, continue straight across Aoyama-dōri northwest on Omotesandō.

HARAJUKU

On this side of Aoyama-dōri, Omotesandō becomes a broad divided boulevard, lined with ginko trees, sloping gently downhill—and downmarket—to the intersection of Meiji-dōri. True, there are a few conservative fashion houses on the west boulevard, like Mori Hanae and Ralph Lauren. But the pulse of Harajuku beats at the rate of the adolescents who turn the hard work of their weekdays into the hard work of weekend socializing, which often bears a striking resemblance to shopping.

On the left side of the boulevard as you approach the Meiji-dōri intersection is the **Oriental Bazaar,** a store especially popular with foreign visitors for its extensive stock of Japanese, Korean, and Chinese souvenirs at reasonable prices; browse here for scroll paintings and screens, kimono fabrics, antiques, ceramics, and lacquerware. A few doors down is **Kiddyland** (☎ 03/3409–3431), one of the city's largest toy stores. On the northwest corner of the intersection itself is **La Foret** (☎ 03/3475–0411). With some 110 boutiques on five floors, this was one of the earliest of Tōkyō's characteristic vertical malls.

Here you might want to make a brief detour, to the right on Meiji-dōri and left at the corner of the third narrow side street, called **Takeshita-dōri,** which rises to the JR Harajuku Station at the other end. This is where the youngest of Harajuku's consumers gather, from all over Tōkyō and the nearby prefectures, packing the street from side to side and end to end, filling the coffers of stores with names like Rap City and Octopus Army. If Japanese parents ever pause to wonder where their offspring might be on a Saturday afternoon, Takeshita-dōri is the likely answer.

After the detour to La Foret, turn right and walk uphill on the right side of Omotesandō to the first corner. Turn right again, and a few steps from the corner on this small street you'll find the **Ōta Kinen Bijutsukan** ⑯—an unlikely setting for an important collection of traditional wood-block prints. Retrace your steps, and continue on Omotesandō to the intersection at the top. Across the street to your right look for the JR Harajuku Station; straight ahead is the entrance to the **Meiji Jingū Inner Garden,** and the **Meiji Jingū** ⑰ itself.

When you have finished exploring the grounds of the shrine, you have two options. You can leave the Inner Garden on the northwest side, and walk west about five minutes from the Sangū-bashi Station on the private Odakyū railway line to the **Tōken Hakubutsukan** ⑱ to see its collection of swords. From there you can return to Sangū-bashi Station and take the train two stops north to Shinjuku, the next major exploring section. The other possibility is to return to Harajuku Station and take the JR Yamanote Line one stop south to **Shibuya.**

SHIBUYA

Begin your exploration of this area at the JR Shibuya station. With children in tow, you might want to take the east exit and walk across the bus terminal to the **Tōkyū Bunka Kaikan** (Culture Hall), which houses the **Gotō Planetarium** ⑦. Otherwise, use the **Statue of Hachiko** ⑧ as a starting point, in the plaza on the north side of the station. Cross the intersection and walk southwest on Dōgen-zaka. In a minute, the street will fork at a vertical mall called the **109 Fashion Community**; bear right on Bunka-mura-dōri, and walk about four blocks to where the street suddenly narrows. Ahead of you will be the main branch of the **Tōkyū** depāto chain; turn left in front of it, to the **Bunka-mura** ⑧ complex of theaters, exhibition halls, shops, and restaurants on the next corner. If you're feeling peckish, **Les Deux Magots** is a good neighborhood stop in the lower-level courtyard of Bunka-mura. It is a joint venture with the famous Paris brasserie of the same name.

Return to Bunka-mura-dōri and walk back toward Shibuya station on the left side of the street to the second corner. Turn left at the traffic light and walk northwest, crossing Sentā-gai, a street lined with fast food shops, down-market clothing stores, and game centers, to Inogashira-dōri. Ahead of you, across the street, will be the entrance to **Supein-dōri**—that's Spain-dōri to us English speakers—the heart of Shibuya's appeal to young consumers: a narrow, brick-paved passageway, climbing to a flight of steps at the other end, supposedly inspired by the Spanish Steps in Rome. Spain-dōri leads to Kōen-dōri, the smartest street in the neighborhood, by way of **Parco** (on the left), a vertical mall developed by the Seibu depāto conglomerate. The Parco Theater, on the top floor, has an interesting calendar of plays and art films. There are actually four Parco malls in the immediate area. Like Parco 1, Parco 2 specializes in fashion; Parco 3 carries mostly interior design merchandise and has a floor devoted to visiting cultural exhibitions; and Parco 4 focuses on younger styles and has a performance space called the Club Quattro on the fifth floor. Farther up Kōen-dōri, on the right, is the **Tobako to Shio Hakubutsukan** ⑧, an interesting paean of sorts to the uses of tobacco and salt.

Turn left at the top of Kōen-dōri, and you will see the **NHK Broadcasting Center** ⑧. The building next to it is the 4,000-seat **NHK Hall,** the pride of which is a 7,640-pipe organ, the foremost of its kind in the world (☞ Music *in* the Arts, *below*). At the north end of the NHK complex, across the street from auditorium, is the **National Yoyogi Sports Center** ⑧. From here, you can finish off Shibuya in either of two ways: Retrace your steps to the JR Shibuya Eki, or walk through **Yoyogi Kōen** ⑧ along the extension of Omotesandō to Harajuku and the JR station there.

TIMING

Aoyama and Harajuku together make a long walk, with considerable distances between the things you want to see. Ideally, you should devote an entire day to it, giving yourself plenty of time to browse in shops—especially the Traditional Craft Center. The Nezu Institute alone is worthy of an hour, the Meiji Shrine another. Don't be afraid to come on weekends; there are a lot more people on the streets, of course, but people-watching is a large part of the experience of Harajuku. Spring is the best time of year for the Meiji Inner Gardens; as with any other walk in Tōkyō, the June rainy season is horrendous, and the humid heat of midsummer can quickly drain your energy and add hours to the time you need for a comfortable walk.

Shibuya is fairly compact; you can easily cover it in about two hours. Unless you switch into shopping mode, no particular stop along the way should occupy you for more than half an hour; allow a full hour for the NHK Broadcasting Center, however, if you decide to take the guided tour. Spring is the best time of year for Yoyogi Park, and Sunday the best day. The area will be crowded, of course, but Sundays afford the best opportunity to delight—or despair—in Japan's younger generation on display.

Sights to See

⑧ Bunka-mura. This six-story theater and gallery complex is a venture of the next-door Tōkyū depāto and one of the liveliest venues in Tōkyō for music and art, hosting everything from science-fiction film festivals to opera, ballet to big bands. The design of the building would be impressive if there were any vantage point from which to see it whole. The museum on the lower-level Garden Floor often has well-planned, interesting exhibits on loan from major European museums. ⊠ 2-24-1 Dōgenzaka, Shibuya-ku, ☎ 03/3477–9111. ☞ Theater admission prices vary with events. ☉ Ticket counter in lobby open daily 10–7. Subway, JR, and private rail lines: Shibuya stop.

㊆ Gotō Planetarium. The planetarium has daily shows displaying the movements of the solar system, the constellations, and galaxies projected onto a dome 65 ft in diameter. Adjacent is a small museum of astronomy. A special Saturday show adds music to the stars. The narrative is only in Japanese. ⊠ Tōkyū Bunka Kaikan, 2-21-12 Shibuya, Shibuya-ku (opposite east exit of JR Shibuya station), ☎ 03/3407–7409. ☞ ¥900. ☉ Tues.–Sun. Shows run about 1 hr continuously from 11:20 AM (weekends from 10:30); the last show begins at 6 PM. No seating after show begins. Subway, JR, and private rail lines: Shibuya stop.

㊄ Kodomo-no-Kuni (National Children's Castle). Built in 1985, this complex includes a swimming pool, a gym, and an audiovisual library. The 1,200-seat theater presents a range of concerts, plays, and other performances regularly throughout the year, especially for kids. At the Omotesandō subway station on the Ginza, Hanzōmon, and Chiyoda lines, take the exit for Aoyama Gakuin and walk southwest on Aoyama-dōri about five minutes. Kodomo no Kuni is on the right side of the avenue. ⊠ 5-53-1 Jingū-mae, Shibuya-ku, ☎ 03/3797–5666. ☞ ¥500. ☉ Tues.–Fri. 12:30–5:30, weekends 10:30–5. Subway: Omotesandō stop.

NEED A BREAK? If you're hungry, **Les Deux Magots,** the Tōkyō sister of the famed Paris café, in the Bunka-mura complex, has a good selection of beers and wines, sandwiches, salads, and quiches, as well as the requisite tarts and coffee. There's a fine art bookstore next door, and the tables in the courtyard are perfect for people-watching. ⊠ Bunka-mura, basement, 2-24-1 Dōgenzaka, Shibuya-ku, ☎ 03/3477–9124. Subway, JR, and private rail lines: Shibuya stop.

㊇ Meiji Jingū. The Meiji shrine is dedicated to the spirits of the emperor Meiji, who died in 1912, and the empress Shōken. It was established by a resolution of the Imperial Diet, the year after the emperor's death, to commemorate his role in ending the long isolation of Japan under the Tokugawa shogunate and setting the country on the road to modernization. Completed in 1920 and virtually destroyed in an air raid in 1945, it was rebuilt in 1958 with funds raised in a nationwide public subscription.

The two torii at the entrance to the grounds of the jingū, made from 1,700-year-old cypress trees from Mt. Ari in Taiwan, tower 40 ft high; the crosspieces are 56 ft long. Torii are meant to symbolize the separation of the everyday secular world from the spiritual world of the Shintō shrine. Legend has it that the shape of the gate derives from the shape of a rooster's perch and that it was the rooster whose crowing awoke the sun goddess, who thus brought light to the world.

The buildings in the shrine complex—the main hall forms a quadrangle with the outlying structures—are made from Japanese cypress, and the curving green copper roofs seem to symbolize the eternal sweep of time. The surrounding gardens have some 100,000 flowering shrubs and trees, many of which were donated by private citizens. The annual festival at Meiji Jingū is held on November 3, the emperor's birthday, which is a national holiday. On the festival day and at New Year's, as many as a million people come to offer prayers and pay their respects. Even on a normal weekend, the shrine draws thousands of visitors, but this seldom disturbs its mood of quiet *gravitas*: The faster and more unpredictable the pace of modern life, the more respectable the Japanese seem to find the certainties of the Meiji era.

The **Jingū Nai-en** (Inner Garden), whose irises are in full bloom in the latter half of June, is on the left as you walk in from the main gates, before you reach the shrine. Beyond the shrine is the **Treasure House,** a repository for the personal effects and clothes of Emperor and Empress Meiji—perhaps of less interest to gai-jin than to the Japanese. ⊠ *1-1 Kamizono-chō, Yoyogi, Shibuya-ku,* ☎ *03/3379–5511.* 🖼 *Shrine free, Treasure House ¥500.* ☉ *Shrine daily sunrise–sunset; Inner Garden Mar. 1–Oct. 30, 8–5 (8–6 weekends); Treasure House daily 9–4 (closed 3rd Fri. of month). Subway: Chiyoda Line, Meiji-jingū-mae; JR Yamanote Line, Harajuku Eki.*

72 **Meiji Jingū Gai-en** (Outer Garden). This park is little more than the sum of its parts: The **Jingū Baseball Stadium** is the place to go for a Yakult Swallows game (the Japanese baseball season runs between April and October); the **National Stadium** was the main venue of the 1964 Summer Olympics and now hosts soccer matches, including a future World Cup; and the **Kaigakan** (Meiji Memorial Picture Gallery), which you needn't plan to see unless you are a particular fan of the emperor Meiji and don't want to miss some 80 otherwise undistinguished paintings depicting events in the emperor's life. ⊠ *Jingū Gai-en. Jingū Baseball Stadium: 13 Kasumigaoka, Shinjuku-ku,* ☎ *03/3404–8999; 10 Kasumigaoka, Shinjuku-ku,* ☎ *03/3403–1151; Kaigakan: 9 Kasumigaoka, Shinjuku-ku,* ☎ *03/3401–5179). Subway: Ginza and Hanzōmon lines, Gai-en-mae; JR Chūō Line, Shina-no-machi Eki.*

84 **National Yoyogi Sports Center.** The center consists of two paired structures created by Kenzō Tange for the 1964 Olympics. Tange's design, of flowing ferro-concrete shell structures and cable-and-steel suspension roofing, is a remarkably successful fusion of traditional and modern Japanese aesthetics. The stadium, which can accommodate 15,000 spectators for swimming and diving events, and the annex, which houses a basketball court with a seating capacity of 4,000, are open to visitors when there are no competitions. The bronze bust in the center of the complex is of Yoshitoshi Tokugawa, who became Japan's pioneer aviator in 1910 by staying aloft for four minutes and traveling 230 ft. ⊠ *2-1-1 Jinnan, Shibuya-ku,* ☎ *03/3468–1171.* 🖼 *Free.* ☉ *Daily 10–4. Subway: JR Yamanote Line, Harajuku Eki.*

★ **74** **Nezu Institute of Fine Arts.** This museum houses the private art collection of Meiji-period railroad magnate and politician Kaichirō Nezu. The permanent display in the main building (1955) and the annex (1990) includes superb examples of Japanese painting, calligraphy, and ceramics—some of which are registered as National Treasures—and Chinese bronzes, sculpture and lacquerware. The institute also has one of Tōkyō's finest, and most seldom visited, gardens: more than 5 acres of shade trees and flowering shrubs, ponds, and waterfalls, and seven tea pavilions. Walk southeast on Omotesandō-dōri from the intersection of Aoyama-dōri about 10 minutes, where the street curves away to the left. The Nezu Institute is opposite the intersection, behind a low sandstone-gray wall. ⊠ *6-5-1 Minami-Aoyama, Minato-ku,* ☎ *03/ 3400–2536.* 🎟 *¥1,000.* ☉ *Tues.–Sun. 9:30–4:30; closed day after national holidays. Subway: Ginza and Hanzō-mon lines, Omotesandō.*

⑧ NHK Broadcasting Center. The 23-story Japanese National Public Television facility was built as the Olympic Information Center in 1964. NHK (Nippon Hōsō Kyōkai) runs a "Studio Park" tour in the main building, during which you can see the latest developments in broadcast technology. Alas, there are no tours in English. The center is a 15-minute walk on Kōen-dōri from the JR Shibuya station. ⊠ *2-2-1 Jinnan, Shibuya-ku,* ☎ *03/3465–1111.* 🎟 *¥200.* ☉ *Daily 10–6; closed 2nd Mon. of month.*

★ ㊆ Ōta Kinen Bijutsukan (Ōta Memorial Museum of Art). The gift of former Tōhō Mutual Life Insurance chairman Seizō Ōta, this is probably the city's finest private collection of *ukiyo-e,* traditional Edo-period wood-block prints. The works on display are selected and changed periodically from the 12,000 prints in the collection, which includes some extremely rare work by artists such as Hiroshige, Sharaku, and Utamaro. From the JR Harajuku Eki, walk southwest downhill on Omotesandō-dōri and turn left on the narrow street before the intersection of Meiji-dōri. The museum is less than a minute's walk from the corner, on the left. ⊠ *1-10-10 Jingū-mae, Shibuya-ku,* ☎ *03/ 3403–0880.* 🎟 *¥500; ¥800 for special exhibitions.* ☉ *Tues.–Sun. 10:30–5; closed New Year's and from the 27th to the end of each month for new installations.*

⑧ Statue of Hachiko. The subject of at least one three-hanky motion picture, Hachiko is Japan's version of the archetypal faithful dog. The story dates to the 1920s. Hachiko's master, a professor at the University of Tōkyō, would take the dog with him every morning as far as Shibuya station on his way to work, and Hachiko would go back to the station every evening to greet him on his return. One day in 1925, the professor failed to appear; he had died that day of a stroke. Every evening for the next seven years, Hachiko would go to Shibuya and wait there hopefully until the last train had pulled out of the station. Then the dog died, too, and his story made the newspapers. A handsome bronze statute of Hachiko was installed in front of the station, funded by thousands of small donations from readers all over the country. The present version is a replica; the original was melted down for its metal in World War II—but it remains a familiar landmark where younger people, especially, arrange to meet. ⊠ *JR Shibuya Eki, west plaza.*

⑧ Tobako to Shio Hakubutsukan (Tobacco and Salt Museum). A museum that displays examples of every conceivable artifact associated with tobacco and salt since the days of the Maya might not seem, at first, to serve a compelling social need, but the existence of the T&S reflects one of the more interesting facts of Japanese political life. Tobacco and salt were both made government monopolies at the beginning of the century. Sales and distribution were eventually liberalized, but production remained under exclusive state control, through the Japan Tobacco and Salt Public Corporation, until 1985. The corporation was then privatized. Renamed Nihon Tabako Sangyō, Japan Tobacco, Inc., it continues to provide comfortable, well-paying second careers—called *amakudari*—for retired public officials. It remains Japan's exclusive producer of cigarettes, still holds a monopoly on the sale of salt, and dabbles in real estate, gardening supplies, and pharmaceuticals—ringing up sales of some $17 billion a year. Japan Tobacco, Inc., in short, has more money than it knows what to do with: Why not put up a museum? What makes it noteworthy is the special exhibit on the fourth floor, of *ukiyo-e* wood-block prints on the themes of smoking and traditional salt production. T&S is a 10-minute walk on Kōen-dōri from Shibuya Eki. ✉ *1-16-8 Jinnan, Shibuya-ku,* ☎ *03/3476–2041.* 🎫 *¥100.* ⏱ *Tues.–Sun. 10–6; closed 2nd Tues. of June and New Year's. Subway, JR, and private rail lines: Shibuya stop.*

78 Tōken Hakubutsukan (Japanese Sword Museum). In the late 16th century, before Japan closed its doors to the West, it is said that the Spanish tried to establish a trade here, in weapons of their famous Toledo steel. The Japanese were politely uninterested; they had already been making blades of incomparably better quality for more than 600 years. Early Japanese swordsmiths learned the art of refining steel from a pure iron sand called *tamahagane*, carefully controlling the carbon content by adding straw to the fire in the forge. The block of steel was repeatedly folded, hammered and cross-welded to an extraordinary strength, then "wrapped" around a core of softer steel for flexibility. At one time, there were some 200 schools of sword making in Japan; swords were prized not only for their effectiveness in battle but for the beauty of the blades and fittings, and as symbols of the higher spirituality of the warrior caste. There are few inheritors of this art today, and only a handful can devote themselves to it exclusively. The rest make cutlery and farming tools to supplement their incomes. The Japanese Sword Museum offers a unique opportunity to see the works of noted swordsmiths, ancient and modern—but don't expect any detailed explanations of them in English. ✉ *4-25-10, Yoyogi, Shibuya-ku,* ☎ *03/3379–1386.* 🎫 *¥525.* ⏱ *Tues.–Sun. 9–4. Odakyū private rail line, Sangū-bashi Eki.*

NEED A BREAK? How can you resist a café with a name like **Yoku Moku**? As you approach, you'll probably notice a steady stream of very smartly dressed young people on their way in and out. Tables alfresco in the tree-shaded courtyard continue to make Yoku Moku, which established itself as Japan's primo gourmet confectionery just after the Pacific War, an Aoyama favorite. Its blue-tiled front is on Omotesandō-dōri near the Nezu Institute. ✉ *5-3-3 Minami-Aoyama, Shibuya-ku,* ☎ *03/5485–3340. Subway: Omotesandō stop.*

85 Yoyogi Kōen. Once a parade ground for the Imperial Japanese Army, this area was known in the immediate postwar period—when it was appropriated by the Occupation for military housing—as Washington Heights. During the Tōkyō Games of 1964, it served as the site of the Olympic Village, and in 1967 it became a public park. On Sundays and holidays, the main thoroughfare that runs through it, along the side of the ☞ **National Yoyogi Sports Center**, is closed to traffic and becomes an open-air music festival. Aspiring rock bands arrive early to set up van-loads of amplifiers and equipment and play all day, just for the chance to practice with an audience—or perhaps to be discovered. Flocks of wanna-be Elvises gather here as well, groups of 10 or 20 in black leather jackets, sideburns, and pointy shoes, plant boom boxes in the center of the circle, and dance to the music of the '50s. Street vendors fill in the empty spaces with carts of soft drinks, hotdogs, and fried noodles. It's very loud, very crowded, and totally entertaining. Then at 5 the whistle blows, the crowds disperse, and the street returns to traffic as usual. ✉ *Jinnan 2-chōme. Subway: Chiyoda Line, Meiji Jingū-mae; JR Yamanote Line, Harajuku Eki.*

★ **73 Zenkoku Dentoteki Kogeihin Sentā** (Japan Traditional Crafts Center). Located on the second floor of the Plaza 246 Building, the center exhibits and sells a wide range of crafts from all over Japan, including lacquerware, ceramics, paper products, dolls, and metalwork. While some exhibits have English descriptions, others do not, but someone is usually available to answer a question if a particular item takes your fancy. The center's certification guarantees that you are seeing the best examples from the extensive variety of Japan's crafts traditions and techniques. Documentary films in a small audiovisual library provide interesting encounters with the masters of these traditions at work. From the Gaien-mae subway station, walk southwest toward Shibuya about five minutes, to the intersection of Gaien-nishi-dōri. ⊠ *3-1-1 Minami Aoyama, Minato-ku*, ☎ *03/3403–2460*. ⊞ *Free*. ⊘ *Fri.–Wed. 10–6. Subway: Ginza and Hanzōmon lines, Gaien-mae.*

Shinjuku

If you have a certain sort of love for big cities, you're bound to love Shinjuku. Come here, and for the first time Tōkyō begins to seem *real*. Shinjuku is where all the celebrated virtues of Japanese society—its safety and order, its grace and beauty, its cleanliness and civility—fray at the edges.

To be fair about all this, the area has been at the fringes of respectability for centuries. When Ieyasu, the first Tokugawa shōgun, made Edo his capital, Shinjuku was at the junction of two important arteries leading into the city from the west. It became a thriving post station, where travelers would rest and refresh themselves for the last leg of their journey; the appeal of this suburban pit stop was its "teahouses," where the waitresses dispensed a good bit more than sympathy with the tea.

When the Tokugawa dynasty collapsed in 1868, the 16-year-old emperor Meiji moved his capital to Edo, renaming it Tōkyō, and modern Shinjuku became the railhead connecting it to Japan's western provinces. As the haunt of artists, writers, and students, it remained on the fringes of respectability; in the 1930s Shinjuku was Tōkyō's bohemian quarter. The area was virtually leveled during the firebombings of 1945—a blank slate for developers to write on, as Tōkyō surged west after the war. By the 1970s, property values in Shinjuku were the nation's highest, outstripping even those of the Ginza. Two subway and seven railway lines converge here. Every day, more than 2 million commuters pass through Shinjuku Eki, making this the city's busiest and most heavily populated commercial center. The hub at Shinjuku Eki—a vast, interconnected complex of tracks and terminals, depāto and shops—divides that property into two distinctly different subcities, Higashi- (East-) Shinjuku and Nishi- (West-) Shinjuku.

Numbers in the text correspond to numbers in the margin and on the Shinjuku map.

A Good Walk

For more information on *depāto* and individual shops mentioned in this walk, *see* Shopping, *below*.

NISHI-SHINJUKU

After the Great Kantō Earthquake of 1923, Nishi-Shinjuku was virtually the only part of Tōkyō left standing; the whims of nature had given this one small area a gift of better bedrock. That priceless geological stability remained largely unexploited until the late 1960s, when technological advances in engineering gave architects the freedom to soar. Some 20 skyscrapers have been built here since then, including the new City Hall (officially the Metropolitan Government Office), and Nishi-Shinjuku has become Tōkyō's 21st-century administrative center.

JR trains and subways will leave you off below ground at Shinjuku Eki. You'll need to get up to the street level, in front of the **Odakyū** *depāto*, with **Keiō** depāto on your left, to avoid the passageway under the plaza. Walk across the plaza, through the bus terminal, or take the pedestrian bridge on the north side. Traffic in front of the station is rather confusing—what you're looking for is the wide divided avenue on the other side, called Chūō-dōri, or Yon-gō Gairo on some street markers, between the Fuji Bank on the left and the Dai-ichi Kangyō Bank on the right. Walk west on Chūō-dōri one block to the **Shinjuku Center Building,** cross at the traffic light, and turn right. In the next block is the tapering shape of the **Yasuda Fire and Marine Insurance Building,** the skyscraper closest to the station. The **Seiji Tōgō Museum** 86 is on the 42nd floor.

After a look at Tōgō's paintings, retrace your steps to Chūō-dōri, turn right, and walk west to where the avenue dead-ends at Kyū-gō Gairo, also called Higashi-dōri. You'll see the 52-story **Shinjuku Sumitomo Building,** ahead of you to the right, and to the left the unmistakable shape of City Hall—but you'll need to make a slight detour to reach it. Cross Kyū-gō Gairo, turn left, and walk south past the front of the **Keio Plaza Inter-Continental,** the first of the high-rise hotels to be built in the area, to the next corner.

Across the street you'll see the blue phallic shape of the sculpture in front of—tell it like it is!—the **Shinjuku Monolith Building.** Turn right and walk downhill. In the middle of this next block, on the left, is the **Shinjuku NS Building.** Visitors here, after they have gaped in appropriate awe at the 24-ft clock in the hollow-core lobby, head for the **O.A. Center** on the fifth floor, where some 20 computer companies display their latest wares. Opposite the NS Building, to the right, are the steps to the Citizens' Plaza of adored and reviled **Tōkyō City Hall** 87.

From City Hall, you have two options. You can turn east and walk back along any of the streets parallel to Chūō-dōri that return you to Shinjuku Eki. You may want to stop (especially if you haven't included Akihabara on your Tōkyō itinerary) at one of the giant discount electronics stores in the area—**Yodobashi** and **Doi** are a block from the eki—to get an eye- or bag-full of the latest gadgets that Japan is churning out.

Or, if you have energy to spare, leave the City Hall complex the way you came in, turn right, and walk west to Kōen-dōri, which runs along the east side of **Shinjuku Chūō Kōen,** where you might want to stroll for a break from Shinjuku's urban crush. Cross Kōen-dōri, turn left, and walk south about five minutes, past the end of the park and avoiding the expressway on-ramp, to the **Shinjuku Park Tower Building** 88 at the corner of the Kōshū Kaidō (highway). It's a worthy place to stop for lunch or, at the Park Hyatt, high tea high above the city.

From the intersection, turn right and walk about five minutes southwest on the Kōshū Kaidō to the **Tōkyō Opera City** 89. There's an entrance to the Hatsudai subway station on the west side of the courtyard. Stop in at the Tower Building and the architecture of the performance spaces of the **Shin Kokuritsu Gekijō** complex, and then ride the Keiō Shin-sen Line one stop back to Shinjuku Eki.

HIGASHI-SHINJUKU

The quarter east of Shinjuku Eki is Times Square writ large. By day, it is an astonishing concentration of retail stores, vertical malls, and discounters of every stripe and description. By night, it is an equally astonishing collection of bars and clubs, strip joints, hole-in-the-wall restaurants, pinball parlors and peep shows; just about anything that

Shinjuku

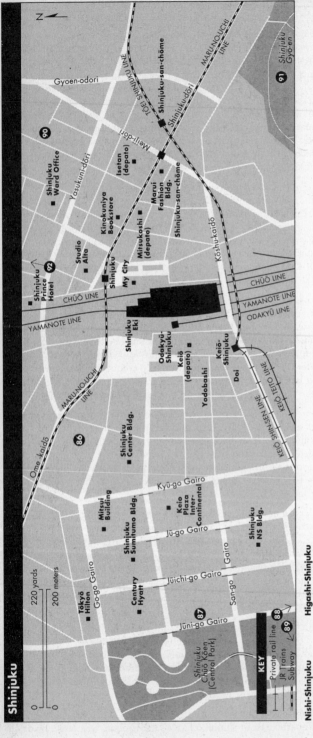

N

Gyoen-odori

MARUNOUCHI LINE

Shinjuku-san-chōme

Shinjuku-dōri

Shinjuku Gyō-en **91**

90

Meiji-dōri

Shinjuku Ward Office

Yasukuni-dōri

Isetan (depato)

Kinokuniya Bookstore

Marui Fashion Bldg.

Shinjuku-san-chōme

Studio Alta

Mitsukoshi (depato)

Kōshu-kaidō

92

Shinjuku Prince Hotel

My City

Shinjuku

CHŪŌ LINE

CHŪŌ LINE

YAMANOTE LINE

Shinjuku Eki

ODAKYŪ LINE

YAMANOTE LINE

Odakyū-Shinjuku

Keio (depato)

Keiō-Shinjuku

MARU-NO-UCHI LINE

Yodobashi

Doi

KEIŌ SHIN-SEN LINE

KEIŌ TEITO LINE

Ome-kaidō

86

Shinjuku Center Bldg.

Mitsui Building

Shinjuku Sumitomo Bldg.

Kyū-go Gairo

Keio Plaza Inter-Continental

Jū-go Gairo

Shinjuku NS Bldg.

Tōkyō Hilton

Go-go Gairo

Century Hyatt

Jūichi-go Gairo

San-go Gairo

Jūni-go Gairo

87

Shinjuku Chūō Kōen (Central Park)

88

89

220 yards

200 meters

0

0

KEY

Private rail line
JR Trains
Subway

Nishi-Shinjuku
Seiji Tōgō
Museum, **86**
Shinjuku Park
Tower Building, **88**
Tōkyō City Hall, **87**
Tōkyō Opera City, **89**

Higashi-Shinjuku
Hanazono Jinja, **90**
Kabuki-chō, **92**
Shinjuku Gyō-en, **91**

amuses, arouses, alters, or intoxicates is for sale in Higashi-Shinjuku, if you know where to look. Drunken fistfights are hardly unusual here; petty theft is not unknown. Not surprisingly, Higashi-Shinjuku has the city's largest—and busiest—police substation.

Looking out from the east exit of Shinjuku Eki, you can't miss the huge video screen that marks **Studio Alta,** underneath which lurks the largest subterranean plaza in Tōkyō, full of shops and restaurants. Studio Alta is on one end of shop-lined **Shinjuku-dōri,** which on Sundays, when the area is closed to traffic, becomes a sea of shoppers. As you amble southeast, **Kinokuniya Bookstore** looms up on your left; the sixth floor is devoted to foreign-language books, including some 40,000 titles in English. In the next block, on the same side of the street, is **Isetan** depāto, with a foreign customer-service counter on the fifth floor. **Mitsukoshi** depāto and the **Marui Fashion Building** are on the opposite end of Shinjuk-dōri.

At the Isetan corner, turn right on to Meiji-dōri and walk north. Cross Yasukuni-dōri, and another minute will bring you to **Hanazono Jinja** ⑨, a shrine in which to regather your wits, if you need to do so. From here, you can take two different directions—indeed, to two different worlds. You can retrace your steps to Isetan depāto and the Shinjuku-san-chōme subway station, and take the Maru-no-uchi Line one stop east to Shinjuku-Gyo-en-mae, a few steps from the north end of **Shinjuku Gyo-en** ⑨. Visit the gardens, and take the subway back to Shinjuku Eki. If you'd rather take a walk on the wild side of Shinjuku, turn back from Hanazono Jinja as far as Yasukuni-dōri and take a right. Two blocks further on is the south end of rough-and-tumble **Kabuki-chō** ⑨, and from here you can easily return to Shinjuku Eki on foot.

If you'd like to finish the day with a kaiseki or bentō box meal, head for Yaozen (☞ Dining, *below*), on the 14th floor of Takashimaya Times Square.

TIMING

Plan at least half a day for Shinjuku, if you want to see both the east and west sides. Subway rides can save you time and energy on the longer versions of these walks, but walking distances are still considerable. The Shinjuku Gyo-en is worth at least an hour, especially if you come in early April, in *sakura* (cherry blossom) time. City Hall can take longer than you expect; lines for the elevators to the observation decks are often excruciatingly long. Sunday, when shopping streets are closed to traffic, makes the best day to tramp around Higashi-Shinjuku; the rainy season in late June and the sweltering heat of August are best avoided.

Sights to See

⑨ **Hanazono Jinja.** Constructed in the early Edo period, Hanazono is not among Tōkyō's most imposing shrines, but it does have one of the longest histories. Chief among the deities enshrined here is Yamatotakeru-no-Mikoto, a legendary hero, supposedly a 4th-century imperial prince, whose exploits are recounted in the earliest Japanese mythologies. His fame rests on the conquest of aboriginal tribes, which he did at the bidding of the Yamato Court. When he died, legends say, his soul took the form of a swan and flew away. Hanazono Jinja is a tranquil oasis in Shinjuku, a welcome retreat from the madding crowd. Prayers offered here are believed to bring prosperity in business. The shrine is a five-minute walk north on Meiji-dōri from the Shinjuku-san-chōme Subway Station. ⊠ *5-17-3 Shinjuku, Shinjuku-ku,* ☎ *03/3200–3093.* ☜ *Free.* ☽ *Sunrise–sunset. Subway: Maru-no-uchi Line, Shinjuku-san-chōme.*

⓺ Kabuki-chō. In 1872 the Tokugawa-period formalities governing geisha entertainment were dissolved, and Kabuki-chō became Japan's largest center of prostitution. Later, when vice laws got stricter, prostitution just went a bit further underground, where it remains—deeply deplored and widely tolerated.

In an attempt to change the area's image after World War II, plans were made to replace Ginza's fire-gutted **Kabuki-za** with a new one in Shinjuku. The plans never came to fruition—the old theater was rebuilt. But the project gave the area its present name. Kabuki-chō's own theater is the 2,000-seat **Koma Gekijō** (⊠ 1-19-1 Kabuki-chō, Shinjuku-ku). The building, which also houses several discos and bars, serves as a central landmark for the quarter.

Kabuki-chō means unrefined nightlife at its best and raunchy seediness at its worst. Neon signs flash; street snakes proclaim the pleasures of the places you particularly want to shun. Even when a place looks respectable, ask prices first—drinks can cost ¥5,000 or more in hostess clubs—and avoid the cheap *nomiya* (bars) under the railway tracks. In Kabuki-chō 2-chōme, the area north and east of the Koma Gekijō— where many of the bars are decidedly gay—you might want to go with a knowledgeable guide. All that said, you needn't be intimidated by the area: It *can* be fun, and it remains one of the least expensive areas of Tōkyō for nightlife. *JR Shinjuku Eki.*

⓼ Seiji Tōgō Museum. The painter Seiji Tōgō (1897–1978) was a master of putting on canvas the grace and charm of young maidens. More than a hundred of his works are on display here, from the museum collection, at any given time. This is also the museum that bought van Gogh's *Sunflowers* for more than ¥5 billion. The gallery has an especially good view of the old part of Shinjuku. ⊠ *Yasuda Fire and Marine Insurance Bldg., 42nd floor, 1-26-1 Nishi-Shinjuku, Shinjuku-ku,* ☎ *03/3349–3081.* ☞ *¥500.* ☉ *Tues.–Sun. 9:30–4:30. Maru-no-uchi and Tōei Shinjuku subway lines; JR; Keiō Shin-sen and Teitō private rail lines: Shinjuku.*

★ ⓺ Shinjuku Gyo-en. Shinjuku Gyo-en Imperial Gardens were once the estate of the powerful Naitō family of feudal lords but became part of the imperial household after the Meiji Restoration. After World War II it was opened to the public as a national park, and it is, as a result, a perfect place for leisurely walks, with 150 acres of gardens, artificial hills, ponds and bridges, and thoughtfully placed stone lanterns. The paths wind their way through more than 3,000 different kinds of plants, shrubs, and trees and lead to Japanese-, French-, and English-style gardens, as well as a greenhouse filled with tropical plants. The best times to visit are April, when 1,900 trees of 65 different species flower, and the first two weeks of October, during the chrysanthemum exhibition. ⊠ *11 Naitō-chō, Shinjuku-ku,* ☎ *03/3350–0151.* ☞ *¥200.* ☉ *Tues.–Sun. 9.–4; open Mon. in Apr. cherry-blossom season. Subway: Maru-no-uchi Line, Shinjuku Gyo-en-mae.*

⓼ Shinjuku Park Tower Building. The Shinjuku Park Tower has in some ways the most arrogant, hard-edged design of any of the skyscrapers in Nishi-Shinjuku, but it does provide any number of opportunities to rest and take on fuel. You might have picked a day, for example, when there's a free chamber music concert in the atrium. Or you might have come for lunch at **Kushinobo** (☎ 03/5322–6400), on the lower level, for delicately deep-fried bamboo skewers of fish and vegetables. You might want simply to have a drink at the **Cafe Excelsior** (☎ 03/5322–6174). Or if you're here in the afternoon, indulge yourself and ride up to the sky-lit bamboo garden of the **Peak Lounge** on the 41st floor of the **Park Hyatt Hotel** (☎ 03/5322–1234) for high tea and a spectacular view of the city. ✉ *3-7-1 Nishi-Shinjuku, Shinjuku-ku. Subway: Shinjuku.*

★ **87 Tōkyō City Hall.** Work on architect Kenzō Tange's grandiose Metropolitan Government Office complex, which now dominates the western Shinjuku skyline, began in 1988 and was completed in 1991. Built at a cost of ¥157 billion, it was clearly meant to remind observers that Tōkyō's annual budget is bigger than that of the average developing country. The complex consists of a main office building, an annex, the Metropolitan Assembly building, and a huge central courtyard, often the venue of open-air concerts and exhibitions. The design has inspired a passionate controversy: Is the intricate lattice facade supposed to invoke a Gothic cathedral or a microchip? Tōkyōites either love it or hate it; it's been called everything from a "fitting tribute" to a "forbidding castle." The main building soars 48 stories, splitting on the 33rd floor into two towers. On a clear day, from the observation decks on the 45th floors of both towers, you can see all the way from Mt. Fuji to the Bōsō Peninsula in Chiba Prefecture. Several other skyscrapers in the area have free observation floors—among them the **Shinjuku Center Building**, the **Shinjuku Nomura Building**, and the **Shinjuku Sumitomo Building**—but City Hall is the best of the lot. ✉ *2-8-1 Nishi-Shinjuku, Shinjuku-ku,* ☎ *03/5321–1111.* ▣ *Free.* ☉ *Daily 9:30–5; in Aug., south deck 9:30–9; both decks closed Dec. 29–Jan. 3. Maruno-uchi and Tōei Shinjuku subway lines; JR; Keiō Shin-sen and Teitō private rail lines: Shinjuku.*

89 Tōkyō Opera City. This is certain to be the last major cultural project in Tōkyō for the foreseeable future. Unusually, it was a private venture by a consortium of major companies, not a public undertaking. The west side of the complex is the **Shin Kokuritsu Gekijō** (New National Theater), consisting of the 1,810-seat **Opera House**, the 1,038-seat **Playhouse**, and an *intime* performance space called the **Pit**, with seating for 468. The Opera House opened on October 10, 1997, with an all-Japanese cast performance of Dan Ikuma's *Takeru.* Architect Helmut Jacoby's design for this building, with its reflecting pools and galleries and granite slabs of wall, deserves real plaudits: The New National Theater is monumental and approachable at the same time.

The east side of the complex consists of a 55-story office tower—alas, an uninspired atrium-style slab, forgettable in almost every respect—flanked by a sunken garden and art museum on one side and a **concert hall** on the other. The concert hall is astonishing: The sheer cost of the wood alone, polished panels of it rising tier upon tier, is staggering to consider. The amount of research involved to perfect the acoustics in its daring vertical design is even harder to imagine. ✉ *3-20-2 Nishi-Shinjuku, Shinjuku-ku,* ☎ *03/5353–0704; 03/5353–0777 concert hall; 03/5351–3011 New National Theater. Keiō Shin-sen private rail line: Hatsudai Eki.*

AROUND TŌKYŌ

Try as we have to fit all of Tōkyō's interesting sights into neighborhoods and walking tours, the sheer size of the city and the diversity of its institutions defeat us. Plenty of worthy places—from Tōkyō Disneyland to sumō stables to the old Ōji district—fall outside of the city's neighborhood repertoire. Yet no guide to Tōkyō would be complete without them. The sights below are marked on the Tōkyō Overview map at the beginning of this chapter.

Amusement Centers

🖐 **Kōraku-en.** The Kōrakuen stop on the Maru-no-uchi subway line, about 10 minutes from Tōkyō Station, lets you out in front of the **Tōkyō Dome,** Japan's first air-supported indoor stadium, built in 1988 and home to the Tōkyō Giants baseball team. Just west of the Dome is a small park called **Koishikawa Kōraku-en,** and just west, across the Tōkyō Expressway, is the **Kōrakuen Amusement Park**—the chief attractions of which are a giant roller coaster and a "circus train" (a.k.a. roller coaster) that does a loop. ✉ *1-3-61 Kōraku, Bunkyō-ku,* ☎ *03/3811– 2111.* 🎫 *¥1,400.* ☉ *Weekdays 10–8, weekends 9:30–8.*

🖐 **Tōkyō Disneyland.** Since it opened in 1983, some 10 million people have been coming here every year. And at Tōkyō Disneyland Mickey-san and his coterie of Disney characters entertain just the way they do in the California and Florida Disney parks.

There are several types of admission tickets. You can purchase the entrance admission for ¥3,670, then buy individual event and activity tickets inside. If you plan to see most of the attractions, the Tōkyō Disneyland Passport at ¥5,200 is the most economical buy. You can buy tickets in advance in Tōkyō Eki, near the Yaesu North Exit—look for red-jacketed attendants standing outside the booth—or from any travel agent, such as the Japan Travel Bureau.

From Nihombashi, take the Tōzai Line subway to Urayasu and walk over to the Tōkyō Disneyland Bus Terminal for the 15-minute ride, which costs ¥230. ✉ *1-1 Maihama, Urayasu-shi,* ☎ *0473/54–0001.* ☉ *Daily 9–9; closed 6 days in Dec., 6 days in Jan., and 3 days in Feb.*

🖐 **Toshima-en.** This large, well-equipped amusement park in the northwestern part of Tōkyō has four roller coasters, a haunted house, and seven swimming pools. What makes it special, for us, is the authentic Coney Island carousel—left to rot in a New York warehouse when Coney Island closed down, discovered and rescued by a Japanese entrepreneur, and lovingly restored to the last gilded curlicue on the last prancing unicorn. Take the Maru-no-uchi Line subway from Tōkyō Station to Ikebukuro, and change to a special train that runs frequently on the private Seibu Ikebukuro line to Toshima-en; the fare is ¥1,000. ✉ *3-25-1 Koyama, Nerima-ku,* ☎ *03/3990–3131.* 🎫 *All-day pass ¥3,500.* ☉ *Daily 10–6.*

Zoo and Aquarium

🖐 **Shinagawa Suizokukan.** The best part of going to Tōkyō's small but well-stocked aquarium in southwestern Tōkyō is walking through an underwater glass tunnel while dozens of species of fish swim around and above you. Alas, there are no guidebooks or explanation panels in English. The aquarium grounds include a park with a saltwater pond and plenty of rocks for kids to climb on. Avoid Sundays, when crowds are impossible. Take the local Keihin-Kyūkō private rail line from Shinagawa to Ōmori-kaigan Eki on the Keihin-Kyūkō Line. Turn left as you exit the station and follow the ceramic fish on the sidewalk to the first traffic light; then turn right. ✉ *Katsushima 3-2-1, Shinagawa-ku,* ☎ *03/3762–3431.* 🎫 *¥900.* ☉ *Wed.–Mon. 10–5, dolphin shows 4 times daily, on varying schedule; closed Dec. 29–Jan. 1.*

🖐 **Tama Dōbutsu Kōen.** More a wildlife park than a zoo, this facility in western Tōkyō gives animals room to roam; moats typically separate them from us. You can ride through the Lions' Park in a minibus. To get here, take a Keiō Line train toward Takao from Shinjuku Eki and transfer at Takahata-Fudō Eki for the one-stop branch line that serves the park. ⊠ *7-1-1 Hodokubo, Hino-shi,* ☎ *0425/91–1611.* 🖭 *¥500.* 🕐 *Tues.–Sun. 9:30–5.*

Off the Beaten Path

Arakawa Line. Want to take a trip back in time? Get on the JR Ya-manote Line to Ōtsuka, cross the street in front of the station, and change to the Arakawa Line—Tōkyō's last surviving trolley. West, the line runs to Higashi-Ikebukuro, site of the Sunshine City skyscraper complex, billed as a "complete city within a city" and remarkable only as a major commercial flop, and Zōshigaya before turning south to the terminus at Waseda, not far from Waseda University.

East, however, the trolley takes you through the back gardens of old neighborhoods to Ōji—once the site of Japan's first Western-style paper mill, built in 1875 by the Ōji Paper Company, Ltd., the nation's oldest joint-stock company. The mill is long gone, but the memory lingers on at the **Ōji Paper Museum.** Some of the exhibits here show the pro-cess of milling paper from pulp. Others illustrate the astonishing va-riety of things that can be made from paper itself. To get to the museum, walk south from the trolley stop about 100 yards. The museum is be-tween the Arakawa tracks and those of the JR. ⊠ *1-1-8 Horifune, Kita-ku,* ☎ *03/3911–3545.* 🖭 *¥200.* 🕐 *Tues.–Sun. 9:30–4:30.*

Asakura Sculpture Gallery. Tourists have begun to "discover" the Nezu and Yanaka areas of Shita-machi (downtown)—much to the dismay of the handful of gai-jin who have lived for years in this charm-ing, inexpensive part of the city. To some, the appeal lies in its narrow streets, with their old shops and houses. Other people are drawn by the fact that many of the greatest figures in the world of modern Jap-anese culture lived and died in the area, including novelists Ōgai Mori, Sōseki Natsume, and Ryūnosuke Akutagawa; scholar Tenshin Okakura, who founded the Japan Art Institute; painter Taikan Yokoyama; and sculptors Kōun Takamura and Fumio Asakura. If there's one single at-traction here, it is probably Asakura's home and studio, converted into a gallery after his death in 1964.

Asakura's work was deeply influenced by Confucian thought, which he expressed symbolically by the arrangement of stones in the ex-traordinary little pond and rock garden in the central courtyard of the house. The studio is filled with Asakura's works, among them many of his most famous pieces. The tearoom on the opposite side of the court-yard is a haven of quietude from which to contemplate his garden.

From the south end of the JR Nippori Eki, walk west—Tennō-ji tem-ple will be on the left side of the street—until you reach a police box. Turn right, then right again at the end of the street; the museum is a three-story black building on the right, a few hundred yards down. ⊠ *7-18-10 Yanaka, Taitō-ku,* ☎ *03/3821–4549.* 🖭 *¥300.* 🕐 *Tues.– Thurs. and weekends 9:30–4:30.*

Asakusabashi and Ryōgoku. While tournaments and exhibitions are held in different parts of the country at different times, all stables in the Sumō Association—now some 30 in number—are in Tōkyō. Most of them are clustered on both sides of the Sumida River near the new **Kokugikan** (National Sumō Arena), with its distinctive green roof, in the areas called Asakusabashi and Ryōgoku. One of the easiest to find is the **Tatsunami Stable** (⊠ 3-26-2 Ryōgoku), only a few steps from the west end of the JR Sōbu Line Ryōgoku Station (turn left when you go through the turnstile and left again as you come out on the street; then walk along the station building to the second street on the right). Another, a few blocks farther south, where the Shuto Expressway passes overhead, is the **Izutsu Stable** (✉ 2-2-7 Ryōgoku). Wander this area when the wrestlers are in town (January, May, and September are best bets), and you are more than likely to see some of them on the streets, cleaving the air like leviathans in their wood clogs and kimonos. Come 7–11 AM, and you can peer through the doors and windows of the stable to watch them in practice sessions.

Sengaku-ji. One day in the year 1701, a young provincial baron named Asano Takumi-no-Kami, serving an official term of duty at the shōgun's court, attacked and seriously wounded a courtier named Yoshinaka Kira. Kira had demanded the usual tokens of esteem that someone in his high position would expect for his goodwill; Asano refused, and Kira had humiliated him in public to the point that he could no longer contain his rage.

Kira survived the attack. Asano, for daring to draw his sword in the confines of Edo Castle, was ordered to commit suicide. His family line was abolished and his fief confiscated. Headed by Kuranosuke Ōishi, the clan steward, 47 of Asano's loyal retainers vowed revenge. Kira was rich and well protected; Asano's retainers were *rōnin*—masterless samurai. It took them almost two years of plan making, subterfuge, and hardship, but on the night of December 14, 1702, they stormed Kira's villa in Edo, cut off his head, and brought it in triumph to Asano's tomb at Sengaku-ji, the family temple. Ōishi and his followers were sentenced to commit suicide—which they accepted as the reward, not the price, of their honorable vendetta—and were buried in the temple graveyard with their lord.

The event captured the imagination of the Japanese like nothing else in their history. Through the centuries it has become the national epic, the last word on the subject of loyalty and sacrifice, celebrated in every medium from Kabuki to film—Kenji Mizoguchi's *47 Loyal Rōnin*, for example. The temple still stands and the graves are still there, the air around them filled with the smoke from bundles of incense that visitors still lay reverently on the tombstones.

The story gets even better. There's a small museum on the temple grounds with a collection of weapons and other memorabilia of the event. One of these items dispels forever the myth of Japanese vagueness and indirection in the matter of contracts and formal documents. Kira's family, naturally, wanted to give him a proper burial, but the law insisted that this could not be done without his head. They asked for it back, and Ōishi—mirror of chivalry that he was—agreed. He entrusted it to the temple, and the priests wrote him a receipt, which survives even now in the corner of a dusty glass case. "Item," it begins, "One head."

Take the Tōei Asakusa subway line to Sengaku-ji, turn right as you exit, and walk up the hill. The temple is past the first traffic light, on the left. ✉ 2-11-1 Takanawa, Minato-ku, ☎ 03/3441–5560. ◫ Museum ¥200. ◷ Daily 9–4.

DINING

By Jared Lubarsky and Loren Edelson

At last count, there were more than 187,000 bars and restaurants in Tōkyō: Wining and dining is a major component in the local way of life. Japanese companies nationwide spend about ¥6.5 billion a day—that, at least, is what they report to the tax authorities—on business entertainment, and a good slice of that is spent in Tōkyō.

That gives you your first caveat: All that spending on company tabs tends to drive up the bill, and dining out can be unbelievably expensive. The other side of that coin, of course, is that Tōkyō's 187,000-odd choices also include a fair number of bargains—good cooking of all sorts that you can enjoy even on a budget. The options, in fact, go all the way down to street food and yakitori joints under railroad trestles, where the Japanese go when they have to spend their own money. Food and drink, incidentally, are safe wherever you go.

Tōkyō is not really an international city yet. In many ways, it is still stubbornly provincial. Whatever the rest of the world has pronounced good, however, eventually makes its way here—sometimes in astonishing variety. The Highlander Bar in the Hotel Okura, for example, stocks 224 different brands of Scotch whisky, 48 of them single malts. French, Italian, Chinese, Indian, Middle Eastern, Latin, East European: It's hard to think of a national cuisine of any prominence that goes unrepresented, as Japanese chefs by the thousand go abroad, learn their craft at great restaurants, and bring it home to this city.

Restaurants in Japan naturally expect most of their clients to be Japanese, and the Japanese are the world's champion modifiers. Only the most serious restaurateurs refrain from editing some of the authenticity out of foreign cuisines; in areas like Shibuya, Harajuku, and Shinjuku, all too many of the foreign restaurants cater to students and young office workers, who come for the *fun'iki* (atmosphere) but can't make much of an informed judgment about the food. Choose a French bistro or Italian trattoria carefully, and expect to pay dearly for the real thing. At the same time, you can count on the fact that Tōkyō's best is world-class.

Here are a few general hints and observations. Tōkyō's finest hotels also have some of the city's first-rate places to eat and drink. (Alas, this is not always the case elsewhere.) A good number of France's two- and three-star restaurants have established branches and joint ventures in Tōkyō, and they regularly send their chefs over to supervise. Some of them stay, find backers, and open restaurants of their own. The style almost everywhere is still "nouvelle cuisine": small portions, with picture-perfect garnishes and light sauces. More and more, you find interesting fusions of French and Japanese culinary traditions. Meals are served in poetically beautiful presentations, in bowls and dishes of different shapes and patterns. And fresh Japanese ingredients, like *shimeji* mushrooms and local wild vegetables, are often used.

Tōkyōites know and love French food. They have less of a chance, unfortunately, to experience the real range and virtuosity of Italian cuisine; only a small handful of the city's Italian restaurants would measure up to Italian standards. Indian food here, however, is consistently good and relatively inexpensive. And there have been solid attempts at transplanting California-style American cooking, as well. Chinese food is the most consistently modified; it can be quite appetizing, but for repertoire and richness of taste, it pales in comparison to Hong Kong fare. Significantly, Tōkyō has no Chinatown.

The quintessential Japanese restaurant is the *ryōtei,* something like a villa most often walled off from the bustle of the outside world and divided into a number of small, private dining rooms. These rooms are traditional in style, with tatami-mat floors, low tables, and a hanging scroll or a flower arrangement in the alcove. One or more of the staff is assigned to each room to serve the many dishes that compose the meal, pour your sake, and provide light conversation: "Waitress" is the wrong word; "attendant" is closer, but there really isn't a suitable term in English. Ryōtei is an adventure, an encounter with foods you've never seen before, and with a centuries-old graceful, almost ritualized style of service that is unique to Japan. Many parts of the city are proverbial for their ryōtei; the top houses tend to be in Akasaka, Tsukiji, Asakusa, and nearby Yanagi-bashi, and Shimbashi.

A few pointers are in order on the geography of food and drink. The farther "downtown" you go—into Shita-machi—the less likely you are to find the real thing in foreign cuisine. There is superb Japanese food all over the city, but aficionados of sushi swear (with excellent reason) by Tsukiji, where the central fish market supplies the neighborhood's restaurants with the freshest ingredients, which in turn serve the biggest portions and charge the most reasonable prices. Asakusa takes pride in its tempura restaurants, but tempura is reliable almost everywhere, especially at branches of the well-established, citywide chains. Every *depāto* and skyscraper office building in Tōkyō has at least one floor devoted to restaurants; none have any great distinction, but all are inexpensive and quite passable places to lunch.

Dining out in Tōkyō does not ordinarily demand a great deal in the way of formal attire. If it's a business meal, of course, and your hosts or guests are Japanese, a conservative approach is advisable: for men, a suit and tie; for women, a dress or suit in a basic color, stockings, and a minimum of jewelry. On your own, you'll find that only very few upscale Western venues (mainly the French and Continental restaurants in hotels) will even insist on ties for gentlemen; follow the unspoken dress codes you'd observe at home, and you're unlikely to go wrong. For Japanese-style dining on tatami floors, keep two things in mind: Wear shoes that are easy to slip on and off and presentable socks, and choose clothing you'll be comfortable in for a few hours with your legs gathered under you.

Price-category estimates for the restaurants below are based on the cost of an average meal (three courses, if Western style) per person, excluding drinks, taxes, and service charges; thus, a restaurant listed as $$ can easily slide up a category to $$$ when it comes time to pay the bill.

CATEGORY	COST*
$$$$	over ¥10,000
$$$	¥6,000–¥10,000
$$	¥3,000–¥6,000
$	under ¥3,000

per person, excluding drinks, service, and tax

Japanese

Akasaka-mitsuke

$　✕ **Sawanoi.** The homemade *udon* (thick wheat noodles) served at Sawanoi are perfect for a light meal or a midnight snack. The menu, available in English, lists a great range of noodle-seafood, -vegetable, or -meat combinations served as udon platters—served hot or cold seasonally—and rice dishes, which are generally side orders. *Inaka* (country-style) udon, topped with bonito and seaweed flakes and radish shavings, is "recommended for the ladies," and the raw egg dropped in cooks in the hot broth. For a heartier meal, chose the *tenkama* set, which consists of hot udon and tempura that you dip in a delicate soy-based sauce. Sawanoi is one of the last remaining neighborhood shops in this stylish business district, and its decor is a bit on the grungy side. Excellent food and friendly service more than make up for it. ⊠ *Shimpo Bldg., 1st floor, 3-7-13 Akasaka, Minato-ku,* ☎ *03/3582–2080. No credit cards. Subway: Ginza and Maru-no-uchi lines, Akasaka-mitsuke.*

Aoyama

$$ ✕ **Higo Batten.** This restaurant specializes in a style called *kushi-yaki,* which refers simply to a variety of ingredients—meat, fish, vegetables— cut into bits and grilled on bamboo skewers. There's nothing ceremonious or elegant about kushi-yaki; it resembles the more familiar yakitori, except that there is more variety to it. At Higo Batten you can feast on such dishes as shiitake mushrooms stuffed with minced chicken, scallops wrapped in bacon, and bonito, shrimp, and eggplant with ginger. The decor here is a postmodern-traditional cross, with wood beams painted black, paper lanterns, and sliding paper screens. There's tatami, table, and counter seating. This spot draws a young crowd, among them a lot of the fancy-free Westerners who like the scene in Aoyama—which probably accounts for the helpful English menu. ⌂ *AG Bldg., 1st floor, 3-18-17 Minami-Aoyama, Minato-ku,* ☎ *03/3423–4462. AE, V. Subway: Omotesandō stop.*

$ ✕ **Maisen.** You're likely to spend some time soaking in a Japanese bath-
★ house; eating in one is a different story. Maisen was converted from a former *sentō* (public bathhouse) in 1983, and you'll find the old high ceiling, characteristic of bathing rooms built during the first quarter of the century, as well as the original signs instructing bathers where to change intact. Large bouquets of seasonal flowers help transform the large, airy space into a pleasant dining room. Tonkatsu (deep-fried pork cutlets) is Maisen's chef d'oeuvre. Though it's more expensive than the regular tonkatsu roast, consider trying *kuroi buta no hire* (fillet of Chinese black pork), which is very juicy and tender. Spoon a generous serving of sauce, sweet, spicy, or extra thick for black pork, over the cutlets and the shredded cabbage that comes with the sets. Miso soup and rice are also included. Or consider salmon dishes, of which the most elegant is the *oyako* ("parent-child") set. This term usually refers to chicken mixed with soft-boiled egg, but this oyako consists of bite-size pieces of salmon with small salmon eggs. Many sets include a small dollop of fruity sherbet, but you can order this and other side dishes separately. There are no-smoking rooms upstairs. ⌂ *4-8-5 Jingu-mae, Shibuya-ku,* ☎ *03/3470–0071. No credit cards. Subway: Omote-sandō stop.*

Asakusa

$$ ✕ **Tatsumiya.** This is a *ryōtei* (traditional Japanese restaurant) with at least two delightfully untraditional features: It is neither inaccessible nor outrageously expensive. Most ryōtei tend to oppress the first-time visitor a little with the weight of their antiquity and the ceremonious formality of their service. Tatsumiya opened in 1980, and it takes a different attitude to the past: The rooms are almost cluttered—with antique chests, braziers, clocks, lanterns, bowls, utensils, and craftwork (some of which are for sale). The cuisine itself follows the *kaiseki* repertoire, derived from the tradition of the tea-ceremony meal. Seven courses are offered, including something raw, something boiled, something vinegared, something grilled. The atmosphere is relaxed and friendly, in the Shita-machi (downtown) style. You must arrive before 8:30 for dinner. ⌂ *1-33-5 Asakusa, Taitō-ku,* ☎ *03/3842–7373. Jacket and tie. No credit cards. Closed Mon. Subway: Ginza and Tōei Asakusa lines, Asakusa.*

Ginza

$$$–$$$$ ✕ **Rantsuki.** The increase in Japan's consumption of beef over the past century has much to do with the popular appeal of *shabu shabu* and *sukiyaki,* the house specialty here. Inside, four- (or more) person tables in semiprivate rooms are equipped with a tabletop stove. Only one dish can be cooked at your table, but this shouldn't stop you from trying both shabu shabu and sukiyaki. The former, named for the

Tōkyō Dining

N

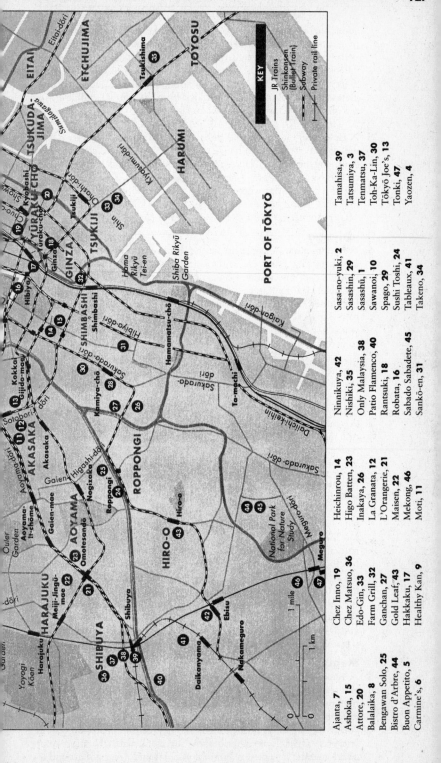

KEY

JR Trains
Shinkansen (Bullet Train)
Subway
Private rail line

PORT OF TŌKYŌ

Sasa-no-yuki, **2**
Sasashin, **29**
Sasashū, **1**
Sawanoi, **10**
Spago, **29**
Sushi Toshi, **24**
Sabado Sabadete, **45**
Sankō-en, **31**

Tamahisa, **39**
Tatsumiya, **3**
Tenmatsu, **37**
Toh-Ka-Lin, **30**
Tōkyō Joe's, **13**
Tonki, **47**
Yaozen, **4**

Ninnikuya, **42**
Nishiki, **35**
Only Malaysia, **38**
Patio Flamenco, **40**
Rantsuki, **18**
Robata, **16**

Heichinrou, **14**
Higo Batten, **23**
Inakaya, **26**
La Granata, **12**
L'Orangerie, **21**
Maisen, **22**
Mekong, **46**
Moti, **11**

Chez Inno, **19**
Chez Matsuo, **36**
Edo-Gin, **33**
Farm Grill, **32**
Ganchan, **27**
Gold Leaf, **43**
Hakkaku, **17**
Healthy Kan, **9**

Ajanta, **7**
Ashoka, **15**
Attore, **20**
Balalaika, **8**
Bengawan Solo, **25**
Bistro d'Arbre, **44**
Buon Appetito, **5**
Carmine's, **6**

swishing motion made while cooking the beef, is prepared in a light vegetable broth into which you submerge the beef briefly before dipping it in either a soy-based or a sesame dip. Sukiyaki is beef sautéed with vegetables in a sweet soy sauce, and you can dip the sizzling hot beef in raw egg if you choose. If that doesn't appeal, add the egg to the leftover broth along with rice or noodles to make a soup that completes the meal. Rantsuki is one block from the Ginza 4-chōme crossing on the side closest to the Wako clock. ⊠ *3-5-8 Ginza, Chūō-ku,* ☎ *03/3567–1021. AE, DC, MC, V. Subway: Ginza stop.*

$$ ✕ **Hakkaku.** On the second floor of the Yūraku Food Center building, crammed between other restaurants, this small bar is easy to recognize by the large red lantern hanging outside. At lunchtime, you can tuck into good tempura dishes for reasonable prices. There is table seating or a counter-bar where you'll be rubbing elbows with local businessmen. ⊠ *2-2 Nishi-Ginza, Chūō-ku,* ☎ *03/3561–0539. AE, DC, MC, V. Subway: Yūraku-chō Line, Yūraku-chō.*

Ichiyaga

$ ✕ **Healthy Kan.** Considering that Japan once espoused vegetarianism,
★ it is surprising that is one of the handful of restaurants in Tōkyō that specialize in this cuisine. Beloved by its regular Japanese and gai-jin clientele, Healthy Kan prepares an array of traditional vegetarian and fish dishes. The daily menu, listed on a white board, features a complete Japanese meal that includes *haigo* (brown rice) or *soba* (buckwheat noodles) served either hot or cold depending on the season. For something different, try the tempeh set. A classic Indonesian dish, Kan's tempeh—seasoned with either soy or miso—is dressed up to look Japanese. *Komatsuna* (mustard spinach), or a comparable leafy green vegetable such as spinach or chrysanthemum leaves, in addition to tasty *hijiki* (sea vegetable salad) and pickles are served on the side. Healthy Kan is a casual place; it's easy to linger over a glass of home-pureed vegetable juice or piece of homemade cake (desserts run out early, so call ahead to reserve something). The menu is written in English. ⊠ *Asahi Roku-ban-chō Mansion, 2nd floor, 6-4 Chiyoda-ku,* ☎ *03/ 3263–4023. No credit cards. Closed Sun. Subway: Ichigaya stop.*

Ikebukuro

$$$ ✕ **Sasashū.** Strictly speaking, Sasashū is not a restaurant but an iza-
★ kaya—a tavern that specializes in sake. We're including it here for two reasons. First, it stocks only the finest and rarest, the Latours and Mouton-Rothschilds, of sake: These are wines that take gold medals in the annual sake *concours* year after year. Second, the restaurant serves the best food of any izakaya in town—the Japanese wouldn't dream of drinking well without eating well. Sasashū is a rambling, two-story building in traditional style, with thick beams and step-up tatami floors. The specialty of the house is salmon steak, brushed with sake and soy sauce and broiled over a charcoal hibachi. ⊠ *2-2-6 Ikebukuro, Toshimaku,* ☎ *03/3971–6796. AE, DC, MC, V. Closed Sun. Subway: Yūrakuchō and Maru-no-uchi lines, Ikebukuro.*

Meguro

$ ✕ **Tonki.** Meguro, a neighborhood distinguished for almost nothing
★ else culinary, has the *ichiban-no* (number one) *tonkatsu ryōri* (deepfried pork cutlet cookery) in Tōkyō. It's a family joint, with Formicatop tables and a fellow who comes around to take your order while you're waiting the requisite 10 minutes in line. And people do wait in line, every night. Tonki is one of those successful places that never went conglomerate; it kept getting more popular and never got around to putting frills on what it does best: pork cutlets, soup, raw cabbage salad, rice, pickles, and tea. That's the standard course, and almost every-

body orders it, with good reason. ⊠ *1-1-2 Shimo-Meguro, Meguro-ku,* ☎ *03/3491–9928. DC, MC, V. Closed Tues. and every 3rd Mon. JR Yamanote Line, Meguro Eki.*

Nihombashi

$ ✕ **Sasashin.** No culinary tour of Japan would be complete without a visit to an izakaya, where the food is hearty and close to home cooking. Food at an izakaya, however, is meant—to most of the local clientele, at least—mainly as ballast for the earnest consumption of beer and sake. Arguably one of the two or three best izakaya in Tōkyō, Sasashin spurns the notion of decor: There's a counter laden with platters of the evening's fare, a clutter of rough wooden tables, and not much else. It's noisy, smoky, crowded—and absolutely authentic. Try the sashimi, the grilled fish, or the fried tofu; you really can't go wrong by just pointing your finger to anything on the counter that takes your fancy. ⊠ *20-3 Nihombashi, Ningyō-chō 2-chōme, Chūō-ku,* ☎ *03/3668–2456. Reservations not accepted. No credit cards. Closed Sun. Subway: Hanzō-mon Line, Suitengū-mae.*

Roppongi

$$$$ ✕ **Inakaya.** The style here is *robatayaki* (charcoal grill cookery), the ambience pure theater. The centerpiece is a large, U-shape counter. Inside, two cooks in traditional garb sit on cushions behind the grill, with a wonderful cornucopia of food spread out in front of them: fresh vegetables, seafood, skewers of beef and chicken. Point to what you want, or tell your waiter—they all speak a little English. The cook will bring it up out of the pit, prepare it, and hand it across on an 8-ft wooden paddle. Expect a half-hour wait any evening after 7. ⊠ *Reine Bldg., 1st floor, 5-3-4 Roppongi, Minato-ku (Subway: Roppongi),* ☎ *03/3408–5040. Reservations not accepted. AE, DC, MC, V. Closed New Year's Day. No lunch. Subway: Hibiya Line, Roppongi.*

$$$ ✕ **Sushi Toshi.** This contemporary and colorful sushi shop in Roppongi caters to an eclectic clientele, who are all on display thanks to the restaurant's U-shape counter. Don't expect intimacy here: The master often engages in conversation, invariably with some of the hostess-and-patron "couples" who come early in the evening. The sushi is also served in pairs: One order gives you two bite-size morsels of a superb array of the day's catch. In addition to *maguro* and *chutaro* (both tuna, the latter coming from the middle section of the fish), *kompachi* (a close relative of *hamachi,* yellow tail) and *tai* (sea bream) are spectacular, and the scallops still smack of sea salt. Or, if you don't see anything appealing in the glass case in front of you, ask one of the chefs to pull something from the tank. The usual pink pickled ginger, as well as *kamaboko* (white fish cakes) served on a *haran* (lily-flower) leaf, clears the palate between each "course." ⊠ *5-8-3 Nakano Bldg., 1st floor, Roppongi, Minato-ku,* ☎ *03/3423–0333. AE, DC, MC, V. Subway: Hibiya Line, Roppongi.*

$$ ✕ **Ganchan.** While the Japanese prefer their sushi bars to be immaculately clean and light, they expect yakitori joints to be smoky, noisy, and cluttered—like Ganchan. There's counter seating only, for about 15, and you have to squeeze to get to the chairs in back by the kitchen. The walls are festooned with festival masks, paper kites and lanterns, gimcracks of all sorts, handwritten menus, and greeting cards from celebrity patrons. Behind the counter, the cooks yell at each other, fan the grill, and serve up enormous schooners of beer. Try the *tsukune* (balls of minced chicken) and the fresh asparagus wrapped in bacon. ⊠ *6-8-23 Roppongi, Minato-ku,* ☎ *03/3478–0092. V. No lunch. Subway: Hibiya Line, Roppongi.*

Shibuya

$$$ ✕ **Tamahisa.** One of the hallmarks of Japanese cuisine is that one meal may consist of the same food served in myriad styles. So, for example, you can have a meal of tofu that is served *hiyako* (cold), *yudofu* (warm), *dengaku* (braised with miso), or as *shiro-ai* (sesame seed dip). Or you can have a meal that uses mainly beef or chicken. In Tamahisa, the entries are fish, fish, and fish. Unlike at most other Japanese-style restaurants, rice is not served. The menu changes daily depending on what's fresh from Tsukiji, Tōkyō's main fish market, which the chef visits every morning. Depending on the season when you dine here, raw oysters served with lemon wedges will be luscious, the array of tuna sashimi succulent, and the salt-grilled *kamasu* (barracuda) piquant. To complete the meal, order *shimeji no dobinmushi,* a delicate yet aromatic soup served in a small tea kettle. If you must have some greenery to go with your fish, *sora mame,* green peas that look like oversize gum balls, are nearly the only choice: Pop them open so as to just eat just the pea, not the pod. ✉ 2-30-4 *Dōgenzaka, Shibuya-ku,* ☎ 03/3461–4803. *No credit cards. No lunch. Subway/JR: Shibuya, Hachiko exit.*

$$–$$$ ✕ **Tenmatsu.** You don't really have to spend a lot of money to enjoy a first-rate tempura restaurant, and Tenmatsu proves the point. The best seats in the house, as in any *tempura-ya,* are at the immaculate wooden counter, where your tidbits of choice are taken straight from the oil and served up immediately. You also get to watch the chef in action. Tenmatsu's brand of good-natured professional hospitality just adds to your enjoyment of the meal. Here you can rely on a set menu or order à la carte from delicacies like lotus root, shrimp, *unagi* (eel), and *kisu* (a small white freshwater fish). Call ahead to reserve a seat at the counter. ✉ 1-6-1 *Dōgenzaka, Shibuya-ku,* ☎ 03/3462–2815. *DC, MC, V. Closed Mon. Subway/JR: Shibuya.*

Shinjuku

$$–$$$ ✕ **Yaozen.** After a hectic day shopping with the masses at Takashimaya Times Square, unwind on the 14th floor at Yaozen. Like all of the restaurants on this top floor, Yaozen has a magnificent view of the city, but none of the others have a 300-year history of serving the likes of Commodore Matthew Perry. The same type of elegant kaiseki banquets that Perry had are available for parties of three or more between set lunch and dinner hours (reserve in advance). The majority of the meals, however, are served by the kimono-clad waitresses as one course in bentō lunchboxes or on large trays, which preserve kaiseki's quest for an aesthetically pleasing and balanced food presentation. For a little taste of everything, try the two-tiered *okusama-gozen bentō* (Madame's lunchbox), which includes sashimi, simmered vegetables and grilled fish. Small desserts with *hōjicha* (parched twig tea) are popular during tea time, but with a full-course meal, it's easy to skip since so many of the foods—in traditional Japanese style—are prepared with sweet rice wine (*mirin*) and sugar. ✉ *Takashimaya Times Square, 5-24-2 Sendagaya, Shibuya-ku,* ☎ 03/5361–1872. *AE, DC, MC, V. Subway/JR: Shinjuku, south exit.*

$ ✕ **Buon Appetito.** Okonomi-yaki is ubiquitous carnival food in Japan. Literally translated as "fried fun," this meal-in-a-pancake uses cabbage, eggs, and flour as a base, with the option of adding in fillings that include beef, squid, octopus, shrimp, and/or pork. This low-culture food, which originated in western Japan, takes on high-style flair at Buon Appetito. In keeping with this modern decor, the third-floor restaurant has some classy okonomi-yaki indeed: the classic onion-and-beef combination, *modan-yaki* stuffed with soba noodles and vegetables or meat, and the "Italian pancake" topped with cheese, which is considered the "Japanese pizza." The pancakes will be partially cooked when they arrive at your table's individual grill; let them sit for a few minutes before spreading on the thick, sweet sauce and *ao-nori* (seaweed flakes) and *katsuobushi* (bonito fish flakes) that you'll find at your table. Slice them with the *ichimonji* (spatula) and distribute. Most salads— a seven-herb diced green salad, a basil and tomato, a cold vegetable vinaigrette, and a spicy carrot salad—are Western innovations that go well with the fried pancakes. Other side dishes, such as a scallops and broccoli stir-fry, help round out the meal. Dessert comes in the form of tiny scoops of citrus sherbet or green tea ice cream. ⊠ *Gorodo Biru, 3rd floor, 3-9-5 Shinjuku, Shinjuku-ku,* ☎ *03/3355–8545. No credit cards. Subway: Tōei Shinjuku and Maru-no-uchi lines, Shinjuku 3-chōme.*

Tsukishima

$ ✗ **Nishiki.** Any preconceived notion that you might have about Japanese food being pretty, neat, and healthy is tossed out the window at Nishiki, one of the dozens of *monjya-yaki* restaurants that line the streets of Tsukishima, a five-minute subway ride from Yūraku-chō. A close relative of the western Japanese pancake innovation *okonomi-yaki*, monjya-yaki, Tōkyō residents swear, is a cuisine that's genuinely Shitamachi—old Tōkyō downtown. Unlike okonomi-yaki, however, monjya-yaki uses no eggs and less flour; it goes heavy on the liquid instead. This makes frying the pancakes somewhat of a challenge, but that's half the fun. The menu lists more than 20 eclectic combinations, of which the most popular are sliced potatoes and mayonnaise, *tarako* (cod roe), and *mochi* (rice cakes), as well as the standard mix of beef, pork, shrimp, and squid seasoned in soy sauce. ⊠ *3-11-10 Tsukishima, Chūō-ku,* ☎ *03/3534–8697. No credit cards. Closed Tues. No lunch. Subway: Yūraku-chō Line, Tsukishima.*

Tsukiji

$$$ ✗ **Edo-Gin.** In an area that teems with sushi bars, Edo-Gin maintains its reputation as one of the best. Portions have shrunk a bit lately, but you would have to visit once every few years to notice. Edo-Gin still serves up generous slabs of fish that drape over the vinegared rice rather than perch demurely on top. The centerpiece of the main room is a huge tank, in which the day's ingredients swim about until they are required; it doesn't get any fresher than that! ⊠ *4-5-1 Tsukiji, Chūō-ku,* ☎ *03/3543–4401. Reservations not accepted. AE, MC, V. Closed Sun. Subway: Hibiya Line, Tsukiji.*

$$-$$$ ✗ **Takeno.** Just a stone's throw from the Tōkyō central fish market, Takeno is a rough-cut neighborhood restaurant that tends to fill up at noon with the market's wholesalers and auctioneers and office personnel from the nearby Dentsu ad agency and Asahi Shimbun (newspaper) company. There's nothing here but the freshest and the best—big portions of it, at very reasonable prices. Sushi, sashimi, and tempura are the staple fare; prices are not posted because they vary with the costs that morning in the market. ⊠ *6-21-2 Tsukiji, Chūō-ku,* ☎ *03/3541– 8698. Reservations not accepted. No credit cards. Subway: Hibiya Line, Tsukiji.*

Ueno

$$-$$$ ✗ **Sasa-no-yuki.** With its cross between the traditional shōjin ryōri (Bud-★ dhist vegetarian cuisine) and formal kaiseki dining, Sasa-no-yuki has been serving homemade silky, soft, and sensual tofu in an array of styles for the past 300 years. Thanks in large part to the scenic waterfall in the window garden and the artistic presentation of the dishes, the tatami-mat dining room is conducive to leisurely dining. In addition to a few non-tofu à la carte items, there are three all-tofu dinner/lunch sets, the most basic being a three-course meal including *ankake tofu*

(bean curd in a sweet soy sauce), *kake shōyu tofu* (tofu simmered with chicken and shiitake mushrooms), and *unsui* (a creamy tofu crepe filled with tiny morsels of sea scallops, shrimp, and minced red pepper). For the best sampling, choose the eight-course banquet. With this set, you'll have the heavenly pleasure of admiring the *yuba-kōya* tofu, a phallic arrangement of one bamboo shoot protruding from the *yuba*, soy-milk wrapped crepe. Star-crossed lovers will likely claim Tōkyō the capital of romance after this meal. ⊠ *2-15-10 Negishi, Taitō-ku,* ☎ *03/3873–1145, AE, DC, MC, V. JR Uguisudani Eki, north exit.*

Yūraku-chō

$$–$$$$ ✕ **Robata.** You might find this place a little daunting at first: It's old and funky, impossibly cramped, and always packed. But chef-owner Takao Inoue, who holds forth here with an inspired version of Japanese home cooking, is also a connoisseur of pottery; he serves his own work on pieces acquired at famous kilns all over the country. There's no menu; the best thing you can do is tell Inoue-san (who speaks some English) how hungry you are and how much you want to spend, and leave the rest to him. A meal at Robata—like the pottery—is simple to the eye but subtle and satisfying. ⊠ *3-8 Yūraku-chō 1-chōme, Chiyoda-ku,* ☎ *03/3591–1905. No credit cards. Closed Sun. Subway: Hibiya stop.*

Other Cuisines

Akasaka

$–$$ ✕ **Moti.** This is the second of three Motis, at last count; the original is in Akasaka-mitsuke, and the newest is in Roppongi. All serve the same good Indian cooking, but the Akasaka branch, right by the Chiyoda Line subway station, is the easiest to get into and the most comfortable. Vegetarian dishes here, including lentils, eggplant, and cauliflower, are very good; so is the chicken *masala* style, cooked in butter and spices. Moti has the inevitable Indian friezes, copper bowls, and white elephants, but the owners have not gone overboard on decor. The appeal here is food, as it should be. Cooks here are recruited from India by a family member who runs a restaurant in Delhi. ⊠ *Kimpa Bldg., 3rd floor, 2-14-31 Akasaka, Minato-ku,* ☎ *03/3584–6640. AE, DC, V. Subway: Chiyoda Line, Akasaka.*

$$–$$$ ✕ **La Granata.** Located on the basement level of the Tōkyō Broadcasting Systems building, La Granata and its companion restaurant Granata Moderna are both very popular with the media crowd upstairs. Deservedly so: They prepare some of the most accomplished, professional Italian food in town. La Granata is decked out trattoria style, with brickwork arches and red checkered tablecloths; Granata Moderna has the same menu but reaches for elegance with a polished rosewood bar, art deco mirrors, and stained glass. Specialties worth trying include spaghetti with garlic and red pepper and the batter-fried zucchini flowers filled with mozzarella and asparagus. ⊠ *TBS Kaikan, basement, 5-3-3 Akasaka, Minato-ku,* ☎ *03/3582–5891. AE, MC, V. Subway: Chiyoda Line, Akasaka.*

Akasaka-mitsuke

$$$$ ✕ **Tōkyō Joe's.** The very first foreign branch of famed Miami Joe's was in Ōsaka, a city where volume-for-value really counts in the reputation of a restaurant. The Tōkyō branch upholds its reputation the same way—by serving enormous quantities of stone crab, with melted butter and mustard mayonnaise. The turnover here is fierce; waiters in long red aprons scurry to keep up with it, but service is remarkably smooth. The crabs are flown in fresh from the Florida Keys, their one and only habitat. There are other choices on the menu, but it's madness to order anything else. Top it all off—if you have room—with Key lime pie. ✉ *Akasaka Eight-One Bldg. B1, 2-13-5 Nagata-chō, Chiyoda-ku,* ☎ *03/ 3508–0325. AE, DC, MC, V. Subway: Ginza and Maru-no-uchi lines, Akasaka-mitsuke.*

Azabu Jū-ban
KOREAN

$$–$$$ ✗ **Sankō-en.** With the embassy of the Republic of Korea a few blocks away, Sankō-en is in a neighborhood thick with barbecue joints; not much seems to distinguish one from another. About 15 years ago, however, Sankō-en suddenly caught on, and people started coming in droves. Not just neighborhood families showed up, but also customers who worked in the media industry. Sankō-en opened a branch, then moved the main operation across the street to new, two-story quarters. Korean barbecue is a smoky affair; you cook your own dinner— thin slices of beef and special cuts of meat—on a gas grill at your table. Sankō-en also makes a great salad to go with its brisket. ✉ *1-8-7 Azabu Jū-ban, Minato-ku,* ☎ *03/3585–6306. Reservations not accepted. AE, V. Closed Wed. Subway: Hibiya Line, Roppongi.*

Daikanyama
INTERNATIONAL

$$$ ✗ **Tableaux.** The mural in the bar depicts the fall of Pompeii, the ban- quettes in the restaurant are upholstered in red leather, and the walls are papered in antique gold. So with pony-tailed waiters gliding hither and yon, one suspects that somebody here really *believes* in Los An- geles. Tableaux may lay on more glitz than it really needs, but the ser- vice is cordial and professional and the food is superb. Try *bruschetta* (toasted bread with tomato, basil, and olive oil), fettuccine with smoked salmon and sun-dried tomatoes, or grilled pork chop stuffed with chutney, onion, and garlic. The lunch menu is—by Tōkyō standards— a bargain. Tableaux's bar is open until 3 AM. ✉ *Sunroser Daikanyama Bldg., basement, 11-6 Sarugaku-chō, Shibuya-ku,* ☎ *03/5489–2201. AE, DC, MC, V. Tōkyū Toyoko private rail line, Daikanyama Eki.*

Ebisu
INTERNATIONAL

$$ ✗ **Ninnikuya.** In Japanese, *ninniku* means "garlic"—an ingredient conspicuously absent from the traditional local cuisine and one that the Japanese were once supposed to dislike. Not so nowadays, if you can believe the crowds that cheerfully line up for hours to eat at this cluttered little place in the Ebisu section. Owner-chef Eiyuki Endo dis- covered his own passion for the savory bulb in Italy in 1976. Since then, he has traveled the world for interesting garlic dishes. Endo's family owns the building, so he can give free rein to his artistry without charging a lot. There is no decor to speak of, and you may well have to share a table. It's good fun. Ninnikuya is a little hard to find, but anybody you ask in the neighborhood can point the way. Try the lit- tleneck clams Italian-style with garlic rice, or the Peruvian garlic chicken. ✉ *1-26-12 Ebisu, Shibuya-ku,* ☎ *03/3446–5887. No reser- vations. No credit cards. Closed Sun. Subway: Hibiya Line, Ebisu.*

Ginza
AMERICAN

$–$$ ✗ **Farm Grill.** Tōkyō yuppies have finally become budget-conscious about
★ dining out, and restaurants like the Farm Grill have sprung up all over town, filling the new market niche with innovative California-style cui- sine in generous portions at truly reasonable prices. The Farm Grill is

odds-on the best of the lot, focusing on hearty salads and sandwiches, pasta and rotisserie entrées, and rich desserts. There are more than 90 entries on the wine list, a good percentage of them (gasp!) at ¥1,500 or less. The space is huge by any standard, with seating for 260 at wood-block pedestal tables with rattan chairs. Try Caesar salad, pasta Malibu (penne with chicken, mushrooms, bacon, mozzarella, and fresh herbs), or Farm Grill chili with garlic toast. The carrot cake is pretty good, the linzertorte to die for. ⊠ *Ginza Nine 3 Gokan, 2nd floor, 8-5 Ginza, Chūō-ku,* ☎ *03/5568–6156. AE, DC, MC, V. JR Yamanote Line and Ginza and Tōei Asakusa subway lines: Shimbashi.*

INDIAN

$–$$　✕ **Ashoka.** The owners of the Ashoka set out to take the high ground—to provide decor commensurate with a fashionable address. The room is hushed and spacious, incense perfumes the air, the lighting is recessed, and the carpets are thick. Floor-to-ceiling windows overlook Chūō-dōri, the main street of the Ginza. The waiters have spiffy uniforms. *Thali,* a selection of curries and other specialties of the house, is served up on a figured brass tray. *Khandari nan,* a flatbread with nuts and raisins, is excellent. So is chicken *tikka,* boneless chunks marinated and cooked in the tandoor (clay oven). All in all, this is a good show for the raj. ⊠ *Pearl Bldg., 2nd floor, 7-9-18 Ginza, Chūō-ku,* ☎ *03/3572–2377. AE, DC, MC, V. Subway: Ginza stop.*

Hiro-o

THAI

$$–$$$　✕ **Gold Leaf.** The hottest gastronomic fad in Tōkyō these days, liter-
★　　　　ally and figuratively, is "ethnic"; in effect, that's meant a welcome profusion of good new Thai restaurants—among which the Gold Leaf, as the name implies, is probably the most elegant. Gleaming hardwood floors, black-lacquered furniture, and fine linen complete the decor. The two chefs, trained in the cooking school of the famed Oriental Hotel in Bangkok, prepare a decidedly upscale version of this spicy yet subtle traditional cuisine. Try the prawn soup and the green curry with chicken. ⊠ *Taisei-Kōki Bldg., basement, 5-4-12 Hiro-o, Shibuya-ku,* ☎ *03/3447–1212. AE, DC, MC, V. No lunch Sun. Subway: Hibiya Line, Hiro-o.*

Ichiyaga

ITALIAN

$–$$　✕ **Carmine's.** Everybody pitched in, so the story goes, when Carmine Cozzolino opened this unpretentious little neighborhood restaurant in 1987: Friends designed the logo and the interior, painted the walls (black and white), and hung the graphics, swapping their labor for meals. They're good meals, too. For a real Italian gourmet five-course dinner, this could be the best deal in town. Specialties of the house include pasta twists with tomato and caper sauce, and veal scallopini à la Marsala. The tiramisu is a serious dessert. Carmine's is not easy to find, but it's well worth the effort. ⊠ *1-19 Saiku-chō, Shinjuku-ku,* ☎ *03/ 3260–5066. No credit cards. Closed Sun. Subway: Tōzai Line, Kagu-razaka.*

Jimbō-chō

RUSSIAN

$$$　✕ **Balalaika.** Until Russia devises some ingenious new take on its traditional cookery, this is the place to go when you are truly and seriously hungry. The Balalaika is by no means cheap, but it serves an excellent sort of ballast, if you have the room to stow it away. For example: *blinchiki* are small, sweet pancakes with garnishes of red and black caviar; *solyanka* is a savory broth with sausages and vegetables, which is just the thing to sop up with the Balalaika's excellent black-bread; and *walenicki* are crescent-shaped pastries filled with cheese and topped with sour cream. What atmosphere there is here is provided by the Balalaika Trio, which holds forth evenings from 6 PM. ⊠ *1-63 Kanda, Jimbō-chō, Chiyoda-ku,* ☎ *03/3291–8363. AE, DC, MC, V. No lunch Sun. Subway: Jimbō-chō stop.*

Kyō-bashi
FRENCH

$$$$ ✗ **Chez Inno.** Chef Noboru Inoue studied his craft at Maxim's in Paris and Les Frères Troisgros in Roanne; the result is brilliant, innovative French food. Try fresh lamb in wine sauce with truffles and *fines herbes,* or lobster with caviar. The main dining room, with seating for 28, has velvet banquettes, white stucco walls, and stained-glass windows. There is also a smaller room for private parties. Across the street is the elegant Seiyō Hotel—making this block the locus of the very utmost in Tōkyō upscale. ⊠ *3-2-11 Kyō-bashi,* ☎ *03/3274–2020. Reservations essential. Jacket and tie. AE, DC, V. Closed Sun. Subway: Ginza Line, Kyō-bashi.*

ITALIAN

$$–$$$$ ✗ **Attore.** The Italian restaurant of the elegant Hotel Seiyō Ginza (☞
★ Lodging, *below*), Attore is divided into two sections. The "casual" side, with seating for 60, has a bar counter, banquettes, and a see-through glass wall to the kitchen; its comfortable decor is achieved with track lighting, potted plants, marble floors, and Indian-looking print tablecloths. The "formal" side, with seating for 40, has mauve wall panels and carpets, armchairs, and soft recessed lighting. On either side of the room, you get what is hands-down the best Italian cuisine in Tōkyō. Chef Katsuyuki Muroi trained for six years in Tuscany and northern Italy and acquired a wonderful repertoire. Try pâté of pheasant and porcini mushrooms with white-truffle cheese sauce, or the walnut-smoked lamb chops with sun-dried tomatoes. ⊠ *1-11-2 Ginza, Chūō-ku,* ☎ *03/3535–1111. Jacket and tie. AE, DC, MC, V. Subway: Ginza stop.*

Meguro
INDOCHINESE

$ ✗ **Mekong.** The owner of Mekong fled Cambodia and came to Japan more than 20 years ago and went to work for a trading company. Later, with the help of some friends, he opened a hole-in-the-wall restaurant near Ebisu, with an eclectic menu of Cambodian, Thai, and Vietnamese cooking. Mekong prospered, and in 1987 it moved to larger quarters in Meguro—but it has remained very much a plastic tablecloth operation. The selections are few, and the service can be a little disorganized, but at these prices, nobody complains. A menu in English attests to Mekong's popularity with the local foreign community. Try the fried spring rolls and the beef with mustard-leaf pickles. ⊠ *Kōyō Bldg., 2nd floor, 2-16-4 Kamiosaki, Shinagawa-ku,* ☎ *03/3442–6664. MC, V. JR Yamanote Line, Meguro Eki.*

Niban-chō
INDIAN

$ ✗ **Ajanta.** The owner of Ajanta came to Tōkyō to study electrical engineering, and he opened a small coffee shop near the Indian embassy. That was about 40 years ago. He used to cook a little for his friends, and now the coffee shop is one of the oldest and best Indian restaurants in town. There's no decor to speak of. The emphasis instead is on the variety and intricacy of Indian cooking—and none of its dressier rivals can match Ajanta's menu for sheer depth. The curries are hot to begin with, but you can order them hotter. There's a small boutique in one corner, where saris and imported Indian foodstuffs are for sale.

Ajanta is open 24 hours. ✉ *3-11 Niban-chō, Chiyoda-ku,* ☎ *03/ 3264–6955. AE, DC, MC, V. Subway: Yūraku-chō Line, Kōji-machi.*

Omotesandō

FRENCH

$$–$$$$ ✕ **L'Orangerie.** This very fashion-minded restaurant is a joint venture of the original L'Orangerie in Paris and Mme. Mori's formidable empire in couture. Muted elegance marks the decor, with cream walls, deep brown carpets, and a few good paintings. Mirrors add depth to a room that actually seats only 40. The menu, an ambitious one to begin with, changes every two weeks; the salad of sautéed sweetbreads, when they have it, is excellent. The lunch ($$–$$$$) and dinner ($$$– $$$$) menus are nouvelle and very pricey. L'Orangerie is best approached on a Sunday between 11 and 2:30, for the buffet brunch, when for ¥3,500 you can graze through to what's arguably the best dessert tray in town. L'Orangerie is on the fifth floor of the Hanae Mori Building, just a minute's walk from the Omotesandō subway station on Aoyama-dōri. ✉ *Hanae Mori Bldg., 5th floor, 3-6-1 Kita–Aoyama, Minato-ku,* ☎ *03/3407–7461. Reservations essential. AE, DC, MC, V. No dinner Sun. Subway: Omotesandō stop.*

Roppongi

AMERICAN

$$$–$$$$ ✕ **Spago.** This was the first venture overseas by trendsetting Spago of Los Angeles, and owner-chef-celebrity Wolfgang Puck still comes periodically to Tōkyō to oversee the authenticity of his California cuisine. Will duck sausage pizza with Boursin cheese and pearl onions ever be as American as apple pie? Maybe. Meanwhile, Spago is a clean, well-lighted place, painted pink and white and adorned with potted palms. Service is smooth, and tables on the glassed-in veranda attract a fair sample of Tōkyō's gilded youth. ✉ *5-7-8 Roppongi, Minato-ku,* ☎ *03/3423–4025. AE, DC, MC, V. Closed Dec. 31 and Jan. 1. No lunch. Subway: Hibiya Line, Roppongi.*

INDONESIAN/MALAYSIAN

$$ ✕ **Bengawan Solo.** The Japanese, whose native aesthetic demands a separate dish and vessel for everything they eat, have to overcome a certain resistance to the idea of *rijsttafel*—a kind of Indonesian smorgasbord of curries, salad, and grilled tidbits that tends to get mixed up on a serving platter. Nevertheless, Bengawan Solo has maintained its popularity with Tōkyō residents for about 35 years—in fact this is one of the oldest and most durable restaurants in the city. The eight-course rijsttafel is spicy-hot and ample. If it doesn't quite stretch for two, order an extra Gado-Gado salad with peanut sauce. Bengawan Solo added a back room some years ago without appreciably reducing the amiable clutter of batik pictures, shadow puppets, carvings, and pennants that make up the decor. The parent organization, in Jakarta, supplies periodic infusions of new staff, as needed. The company also has a thriving import business in Indonesian foodstuffs. ✉ *7-18-13 Roppongi, Minato-ku,* ☎ *03/3408–5698. AE, DC, MC, V. Subway: Hibiya Line, Roppongi.*

Shibuya

INDONESIAN/MALAYSIAN

$–$$ ✕ **Only Malaysia.** Here's a restaurant with an official seal of approval: The Malaysian ambassador to Japan hires Only Malaysia to cater his parties. In fact, Haji Raman, who runs the kitchen, was the former ambassador's chef. This is a small place (seating for only 45) and not easy to book for dinner—especially on weekends. Try *ayam* (spicy chicken soup)or *rendang* (chicken or beef with coriander and chili peppers).

✉ *Ikushin Bldg., 3rd floor, 26-5 Udagawa-chō, Shibuya-ku,* ☎ *03/ 3496–1177. AE, MC, V. Subway/JR: Shibuya.*

SPANISH

$$$ ✗ **Patio Flamenco.** This restaurant rates less for its cuisine—good but not memorable—than for its dinner show. Owner Yoko Komatsubara, for many years Japan's leading professional flamenco dancer, travels regularly to Spain to find the talented singers, dancers, and guitarists who hold forth here nightly. A small room with seating for perhaps 30, the Patio Flamenco makes you feel as if you have the show to yourself. The specialty of the house is the paella Valenciana, with shrimp, squid, and mussels. Performances begin at 7, 8:30, and 9:45; expect a separate cover charge of ¥1,800 per person for the entertainment. ✉ *2-10-12 Dōgenzaka, Shibuya-ku,* ☎ *03/3496–2753. AE, DC, MC, V. No lunch. Subway/JR: Shibuya.*

Shiroganedai

FRENCH

$$–$$$ ✗ **Bistro d'Arbre.** This tiny restaurant (seating for only 12), on what has become one of the more fashionable avenues among Tōkyō's affluent young folks depends on word of mouth for its popularity. Chef Takahiro Taniguchi trained briefly in France but honed his skills mainly here on the job. His repertoire is not wide, but what he does he does beautifully. Especially good are smoked salmon crepes and fillet of beef in bordelaise sauce. After dinner, climb the narrow, wrought-iron spiral staircase to the lounge on the second floor—an amiable clutter of leather armchairs and footrests made of old wine kegs, stacks of cordwood, antique lamps, and threadbare carpets—and settle in front of the huge, country-French-style fireplace for coffee or a liqueur. There's nothing quite like this anywhere in town. ✉ *5-3-1 Shiroganedai, Minato-ku,* ☎ *03/3446–4855. AE, DC, MC, V. Closed Mon. No lunch Sun. Subway: Hibiya Line, Hiro-o.*

SPANISH

$$ ✗ **Sabado Sabadete.** Catalonia-born jewelry designer Mañuel Benito loves to cook. For a while, he indulged this passion by renting out a bar in Aoyama on Saturday nights and making an enormous paella for his friends; to keep them happy while they were waiting, he added a few tapas. Word got around: By 8 it was standing room only, and by 9 there wasn't room in the bar to lift a fork. Inspired by this success, Benito found a trendy location and opened his Sabado Sabadete full-time in 1991. The highlight of every evening is still the moment when the chef, in his bright-red Catalan cap, shouts out the Japanese equivalent of "Soup's on!" and dishes out his bubbling-hot paella. Don't miss the empanadas (three-cornered pastries stuffed with minced beef and vegetables) or the *escalivada* (a Spanish ratatouille with red peppers, onions, and eggplant). ✉ *Genteel Shiroganedai Bldg., 2nd floor, 5-3-2 Shiroganedai, Minato-ku,* ☎ *03/3445–9353. No credit cards. Closed Sun. No lunch. Subway: Hibiya Line, Hiro-o.*

Shōtō

FRENCH

$$$$ ✗ **Chez Matsuo.** Shōtō is the kind of area you don't expect Tōkyō to have—at least not so close to Shibuya Station. It's a neighborhood of stately homes with walls half a block long, a sort of sedate Beverly Hills. Chez Matsuo occupies the first floor of a lovely old two-story house in Western style. The two dining rooms look out on the garden, where you can dine by candlelight on summer evenings. Owner-chef Matsuo studied as a sommelier in London and perfected his culinary finesse in Paris. His food is nouvelle; the specialty of the house is supreme of duck.

✉ *1-23-15 Shōtō, Shibuya-ku,* ☎ *03/3465–0610. AE, DC, MC, V. Closed Mon. Subway/JR: Shibuya.*

Tora-no-mon

CHINESE

$$$–$$$$　✕ **Toh-Ka-Lin.** Year after year, the Hotel Okura is rated by business travelers as one of the three best hotels in the world. That judgment has relatively little to do with its architecture, which is rather understated. It has to do instead with its polish, its impeccable standards of service—and, to judge by Toh-Ka-Lin, the quality of its restaurants. The style of the cuisine here is eclectic; two stellar examples are the Peking duck and the sautéed quail wrapped in lettuce leaf. The restaurant also has one of the most extensive wine lists in town. ✉ *Hotel Okura, 2-10-4 Tora-no-mon, Minato-ku,* ☎ *03/3505–6068. AE, DC, MC, V. Subway: Hibiya Line, Kamiya-chō; Ginza Line, Tora-no-mon.*

Uchisaiwai-chō

CHINESE

$$$　✕ **Heichinrou.** This branch of one of the oldest and best restaurants in
★　Yokohama's Chinatown is on the top floor of a prestigious office building about five minutes' walk from the Imperial Hotel, and it commands a spectacular view of Hibiya Kōen and the Imperial Palace grounds. Much of the clientele comes from the law offices, securities firms, and foreign banks on the floors below. The decor is rich but subdued, lighting is soft, and table linens are impeccable. Heichinrou has a banquet room that can seat a hundred, and a "VIP Room" with separate telephone service for power lunches. The cuisine is first-rate Cantonese. Be sure to call to reserve a table by the window. ✉ *Fukoku Seimei Bldg., 28th floor, 2-2-2 Uchisaiwai-chō, Chiyoda-ku,* ☎ *03/3508–0555. Jacket and tie. AE, DC, MC, V. Closed Sun. Subway: Tōei Mita Line, Uchisaiwai-chō.*

LODGING

There are three things you can virtually take for granted when you look for a hotel in Tōkyō: cleanliness, safety, and service—impeccable almost anywhere you finally set down your bags. The factors that will probably determine your choice, then, are cost and location.

The relation between the two is not always what you'd expect. Real estate in Tōkyō is horrendously expensive; normally, the closer you get to the center of town, the more you ought to be paying for space. That's true enough for business property, but when it comes to hotels at the upper end of the market, the logic doesn't seem to apply: A night's lodging is not likely to cost you much less in Roppongi, Shinjuku, Ikebukuro, Meguro, or Asakusa than it would for a view of the Imperial Palace.

The reasons aren't complicated. A substantial number of Tōkyō's present hotels were built in the outlying subcenters during the "bubble" of the 1980s and early 1990s, when real estate speculation made prices outrageous everywhere. The bubble encouraged a "spare no expense" approach to hotel design: atriums, oceans of marble, interior decorators fetched in from London and New York. The cost of construction per square foot did not vary much from place to place, and that remains reflected in what you can anticipate paying for your room. Business travelers might have good reason to choose one location over another, but if you're in Tōkyō on holiday, that factor may be only marginally important. Nor should transportation be a concern: Wherever you're staying, Tōkyō's subway and train system—comfortable (except in rush hours), efficient, inexpensive, and safe—will get you back and forth.

Downmarket hotels, of course, offer less in the way of services and decor, but this affects the cost of accommodations—per square ft—less than you might imagine. Deluxe hotels make a substantial part of their profits from their banquet and dining facilities; they charge you more, but they can also give you more space. Further down the scale, you pay somewhat less, but the rooms are disproportionately smaller. Nay, they can be positively tiny.

Tōkyō accommodations can be divided into six categories: first-class (full-service) hotels, business hotels, *ryokan,* "capsule hotels, youth hostels, and "pink" hotels.

First-class (full-service) **hotels** are exactly what you would expect; most of them tend also to be priced in the $$$ and $$$$ categories. Virtually all have a range of Western and Japanese restaurants, room service, direct-dial telephones, minibars, *yukata* (cotton bedroom kimonos), concierge services, and porters. Most have business and fitness centers. A few also have swimming pools. At least 90% of the guest rooms are Western-style; the few Japanese rooms available (with tatami mats and futons) are more expensive.

Business hotels are meant primarily for travelers who need no more than a place to leave luggage, sleep, and change. Rooms are small; an individual guest will often take a double rather than suffer the claustrophobia of a single. Each room has a telephone, a small writing desk, a television (sometimes the pay-as-you-watch variety), slippers, a yukata, and a prefabricated plastic bathroom unit with tub, shower, and washbasin; the bathrooms are scrupulously clean, but if you're basketball-player size, you might have trouble coming to your full height inside. The hotel facilities are limited usually to one restaurant and a 24-hour receptionist, with no room service or porters. Business hotels are not listed below in a separate category, but entries in the $$ price category can be assumed to be of this type.

There are two kinds of **ryokan.** One is an expensive traditional inn, with impeccable personal service, where you are served dinner and breakfast in your room. The other is an inexpensive hostelry that offers rooms with tatami mats on the floors and futon beds; meals might be served in rooms, but more often they aren't. Tōkyō ryokan fall in the latter category. They are often family-run lodgings, where service is less a matter of professionalism than of good will. Many offer the choice of rooms with or without baths. Because they have few rooms and the owners are usually on hand to answer their guests' questions, these small, relatively inexpensive ryokan are very hospitable places to stay.

Capsule hotels are literally plastic cubicles stacked on top of each other. They are used by very junior business travelers or commuters who have missed their last train home. Guests crawl into their capsule, which has a small bed, an intercom, and a radio. Washing and toilet facilities are shared. (Very rarely, a capsule hotel will have a separate floor for women; otherwise, women are not admitted.) One such place is **Green Plaza Shinjuku** (✉ 1-29-2 Kabuki-chō, Shinjuku-ku, ☎ 03/3207–5411), two minutes from Shinjuku Eki. It is the largest of its kind, with 660 sleeping slots. Check-in starts at 3 PM; checkout in the morning is pandemonium. A night's stay in a capsule is ¥4,200.

Pink hotels are "love" hotels, where rooms are rented by the hour. After 11 PM or so, however, you can sometimes rent a room very inexpensively (about ¥4,000–¥5,000, depending on your negotiating skills) for the rest of the night. Be aware, though, that if you do not leave by the agreed-upon time in the morning, your extra time will be charged at the hourly rate! The rooms are clean, but what really makes this option worth trying is that the beds and baths are—by normal hotel standards—huge. Given their true purpose, you can also count on an array of toys and gadgets: Mirrors on the ceiling, saunas, theme decors, lights that dim or go on and off with the sound of your voice. Pink hotels are easily recognized by their garish facades and the hourly rates posted by the entrance; they are usually located near the entertainment quarters—in Shinjuku's Kabuki-chō, for example, and Roppongi—and along suburban highways.

Separate categories are provided in this section for (1) hotels near Narita Airport and (2) youth hostels and dormitory accommodations. All rooms at the hotels listed below have private baths, unless otherwise specified.

CATEGORY	COST*
$$$$	over ¥30,000
$$$	¥21,000–¥30,000
$$	¥10,000–¥21,000
$	under ¥10,000

All prices are for a double room, excluding service and tax.

Akasaka-mitsuke

$$$$ ⛅ **Akasaka Prince Hotel.** Architect Kenzō Tange designed this ultramodern, 40-story hotel, which opened in 1983; the simplicity of its half-moon shape may be considered either coldly sterile or classical. It's situated atop a small hill, and all guest rooms (the higher up, the better) have wide, sweeping views of Tōkyō. The decor of white and pastel grays in rooms accentuates the light from the wide windows that run the length of the room. The result is a feeling of spaciousness, though the rooms are no larger in size than those in other deluxe hotels. A welcome feature is the dressing mirror and sink in an alcove before the bathroom. The marble and off-white reception areas on the ground floor are pristine. The hotel's whole atmosphere is crisp but a little impersonal; it's ideal for the clusters of people at large weddings and convention parties (the Grand Ballroom can accommodate up to 2,500 guests). The Akasaka Prince has no fewer than 12 restaurants and bars, among them the Blue Gardenia on the 40th floor, which serves Continental food; the Top of the Akasaka, a bar that affords spectacular views of Tōkyō's skyline; and a French restaurant, Le Trianon. ⊠ *1-2 Kioi-chō, Chiyoda-ku, Tōkyō-to 102,* ☎ *03/3234–1111,* FAX *03/3205–1956. 761 rooms, most Western style. Restaurants, no-smoking rooms, massage, dry cleaning, travel services. AE, DC, MC, V. Subway: Ginza and Maru-no-uchi lines, Akasaka-mitsuke stop.*

$$$ ⛅ **Hotel New Otani Tōkyō and Towers.** The New Otani is virtually a town unto itself. When all rooms (almost 2,100) are occupied and all banquet facilities are in use, the traffic flow in and out of the restaurants, lounges, and shopping arcades is like rush hour at a busy railway station. The hotel's redeeming feature is its peaceful, 10-acre manicured garden. Among the many restaurants and bars are La Tour d'Argent, Japan's first Trader Vic's, and the revolving Sky Lounge. ⊠ *4-1 Kioi-chō, Chiyoda-ku, Tōkyō-to 102,* ☎ *03/3265–1111,* FAX *03/3221–2619. 2,051 rooms, 30 on 21st floor for women only. 37 restaurants and bars, no-smoking rooms, outdoor pool, spa, driving range, 2 tennis courts, shops, baby-sitting, chapel. AE, DC, MC, V. Subway: Ginza and Maru-no-uchi lines, Akasaka-mitsuke stop.*

Asakusa

$$$ ⊞ **Asakusa View Hotel.** If you want an elegant place to stay in the heart of Tōkyō's old Asakusa area—which was actually resurrected after the World War II fire bombings—then this hotel is the only choice. Off of the smart marble lobby there is a harpist in the tea lounge, and expensive boutiques line the second floor. The standard pastel guest rooms are similar to what you find in all modern Tōkyō hotels, but you also have access to communal *hinoki* (Japanese cypress) bathtubs that look onto a sixth-floor Japanese garden. There are Chinese, French, Italian, and Japanese restaurants, and a bar that will keep your personal bottle. ⊠ *3-17-1 Nishi-Asakusa, Taitō-ku, Tōkyō-to 111,* ☎ *03/3847–1111,* FAX *03/3845–0530. 350 rooms, mostly Western style. 4 restaurants, 2 bars, 2 coffee shops, no-smoking rooms, pool, health club, concierge floor. AE, DC, MC, V. Subway: Ginza Line, Tawara-machi stop.*

$ ⊞ **Kikuya Ryokan.** This small inn in the Asakusa district is a 10-minute walk from Sensō-ji temple. From Tawara-machi subway station, walk two blocks up Kokusai-dōri, take a left, and the ryokan is on the left-hand side just before Kappa-bashi-dōri. Be warned: The inn locks its doors at midnight, and everything here is midget-size. ⊠ *2-18-9 Nishi-Asakusa, Taitō-ku, Tōkyō-to 111,* ☎ *03/3841–6404. 8 tatami rooms, 4 with private bath. Air-conditioning. AE, MC, V. Subway: Ginza Line, Tawara-machi stop.*

Ebisu

$$ ⊞ **Westin Tōkyō.** In Yebisu Garden Place, one of the last grand, pharaonic development projects to go up in Tōkyō before the real estate bubble burst in 1994, the Westin provides easy access to a major department store (Mitsukoshi), the Tōkyō Metropolitan Museum of Photography, an elegant new concert hall, and the Taillevent-Robuchon restaurant ($$$$), this last housed in a full-scale reproduction of a Louis XV château. The decor of the hotel itself is updated art nouveau, with an excess of marble and bronze. Standard rooms are spacious, suites huge. ⊠ *1-4 Mita 1-chome, Meguro-ku, Tōkyō-to 155,* ☎ *03/5423–7000; 03/5424–1338 Taillevent-Robuchon restaurant;* FAX *03/5423–7600. 445 rooms. 5 restaurants, 2 bars, no-smoking rooms, health club, shops. AE, DC, MC, V. Subway (Hibiya Line)/JR eki: Ebisu.*

Hakozaki

$$$ ⊞ **Royal Park Hotel.** This hotel would recommend itself if only for the connecting passageway to the Tōkyō City Air Terminal, where you can complete all your check-in procedures before you climb on the bus for Narita Airport. There's no luxury—especially at the end of an intensive trip—like being able to pack, ring for the bellhop, and not have to touch your baggage again until it comes off the conveyor belt back home. Built in 1989, the 20-story Royal Park is well designed: The large, open lobby has perhaps a bit more marble than it needs, and the inevitable space-age chandelier, but this is offset by wood-paneled columns, brass trim, and lots of comfortable lounge space. Guest rooms, done in coordinated neutral grays and browns, are well proportioned; deluxe twins have handsome writing tables instead of built-in desktops. Ask for a room on one of the executive floors (16–18) with a northeast view of the Sumida-gawa. Another good option would be a room lower down (6th–8th floors) on the opposite side, overlooking the hotel's delightful fifth-floor Japanese garden. ⊠ *2-1-1 Nihombashi, Kakigara-chō, Chūō-ku, Tōkyō-to 103,* ☎ *03/3667–1111,* FAX *03/3665–7212. 441 rooms, 9 suites. 7 restaurants, 3 bars, coffee shop,*

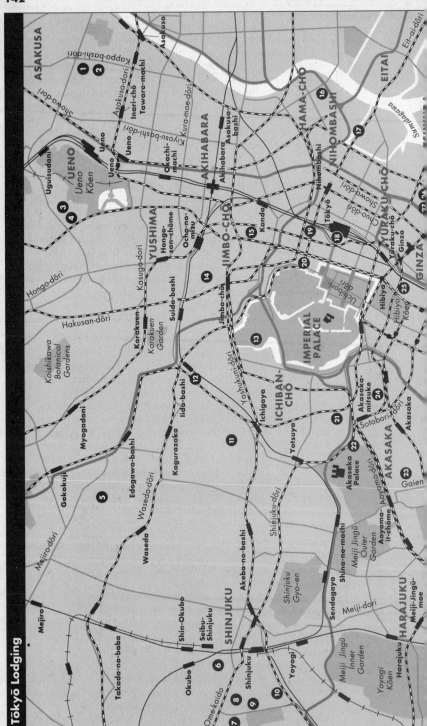

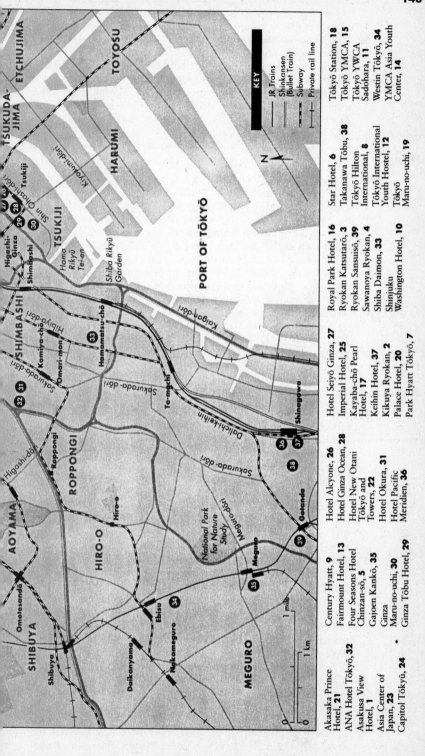

KEY

—— JR Trains
—— Shinkansen (Bullet Train)
════ Subway
—+—+— Private rail line

Tōkyō Station, 18
Tōkyō YMCA, 15
Tōkyō YWCA Sadohara, 11
Westin Tōkyō, 34
YMCA Asia Youth Center, 14

Star Hotel, 6
Takanawa Tōbu, 38
Tōkyō Hilton International, 8
Tōkyō International Youth Hostel, 12
Tōkyō Maru-no-uchi, 19

Royal Park Hotel, 16
Ryokan Katsutarō, 3
Ryokan Sansuisō, 39
Sawanoya Ryokan, 4
Shiba Daimon, 33
Shinjuku Washington Hotel, 10

Hotel Seiyō Ginza, 27
Imperial Hotel, 25
Kayaba-chō Pearl Hotel, 17
Keihin Hotel, 37
Kikuya Ryokan, 2
Palace Hotel, 20
Park Hyatt Tōkyō, 7

Hotel Alcyone, 26
Hotel Ginza Ocean, 28
Hotel New Otani Tōkyō and Towers, 22
Hotel Okura, 31
Hotel Pacific Meridien, 36

Century Hyatt, 9
Fairmount Hotel, 13
Four Seasons Hotel Chinzan-sō, 5
Gajoen Kankō, 35
Ginza Maru-no-uchi, 30
Ginza Tōbu Hotel, 29

Akasaka Prince Hotel, 21
ANA Hotel Tōkyō, 32
Asakusa View Hotel, 1
Asia Center of Japan, 23
Capitol Tōkyū, 24

no-smoking rooms, shops. AE, DC, MC, V. Subway: Hanzō-mon Line, Suitengū-mae stop.

$$ 🏨 **Kayaba-chō Pearl Hotel.** Rooms here are strictly utilitarian, but the price is low, unless you sleep late: The staff adds a ¥3,000–¥4,000 charge for late checkout (after 10 AM). The hotel is just across the bridge from Tōkyō City Air Terminal, a five-minute walk from Exit 3 or 4 of Kayaba-chō Station on the Hibiya or Tōzai Line. The restaurant is open from 7 AM to 10:30 PM. ✉ 1-2-5 Shinkawa, Chūō-ku, Tōkyō-to 104, ☎ 03/3553–2211, FAX 03/3555–1849. 262 rooms. Restaurant. AE, DC, MC, V. Subway: Kayaba-chō.

Hibiya

$$$$ 🏨 **Imperial Hotel.** The location of these prestigious quarters could not be better: in the heart of central Tōkyō, between the Imperial Palace and the Ginza district. The finest rooms, high up on the 30th floor in the New Tower, afford views of the palace grounds. The restaurants—there are 21 of them—include some of Tōkyō's best. The Old Imperial Bar is decorated with elements from the 1922 version of the hotel, which Frank Lloyd Wright designed. From its outset (the Imperial opened its doors in 1891), the hotel has been justly proud of its Western-style facilities and Japanese service. Now, with its new tower addition, the hotel is a vast complex, but it still retains its personalized service. Rooms range from standard twin size to suites that are larger than many homes. ✉ 1-1-1 Uchisaiwai-chō, Chiyoda-ku, Tōkyō-to 100, ☎ 03/3504–1111, FAX 03/3581–9146. 1,058 rooms. 21 restaurants, 5 bars, no-smoking rooms, indoor pool, massage, health club, shops. AE, DC, MC, V. Subway: Hibiya and Yūraku-chō.

Higashi-Ginza

$$$ 🏨 **Ginza Tōbu Hotel.** This hotel's relatively reasonable prices, friendly service, and comfortable rooms make it something of a bargain for the Ginza area. The more expensive concierge floors have much larger rooms, with extras such as terrycloth bathrobes and hair dryers, and breakfast, afternoon tea, and complimentary cocktails in the lounge are part of the package. Especially useful is the hotel's 24-hour coffee shop, and there are French and Japanese restaurants (the excellent Muraki among the latter) as well. ✉ 6-13-10 Ginza, Chūō-ku, Tōkyō-to 104, ☎ 03/3546–0111, FAX 03/3546–8990. 206 rooms, all Western style. 3 restaurants, coffee shop, 2 concierge floors. AE, DC, MC, V. Subway: Hibiya and Tōei Asakusa lines, Higashi-Ginza stop.

$$ 🏨 **Hotel Alcyone.** This hotel is not well known to Westerners, but the convenient location (near the Ginza), and the friendliness of the staff (some of whom speak a little English) make this place a real find. Formerly a ryokan, the Atamiso was transformed into a Western hotel in 1984 but has kept its Japanese tradition of hospitality and a number of Japanese-style rooms. For the size of the rooms, the hotel is an extremely good value. ✉ 4-14-3 Ginza, Chūō-ku, Tōkyō-to 104, ☎ 03/3541–3621, FAX 03/3541–3263. 74 rooms. Restaurant. AE, DC, MC, V. Subway: Hibiya and Tōei Asakusa lines, Higashi-Ginza stop.

$$ ★ 🏨 **Hotel Ginza Ocean.** This delightful small hotel is around the corner from the Kabuki-za in the Ginza area. Rooms are small but comfortable. Virtually no English is spoken here, but sign language serves to communicate basic needs. There's a fairly good Japanese restaurant, Matsuryū, on the premises. ✉ 7-18-15 Ginza, Chūō-ku, Tōkyō-to 104, ☎ 03/3545–1221, FAX 03/3545–1226. 32 Western-style rooms. Restaurant. AE, DC, V. Subway: Hibiya and Tōei Asakusa lines, Higashi-Ginza stop.

Higashi-Gotanda

$ ⊞ **Ryokan Sansuisō.** If you're traveling on a tight budget and want to immerse yourself in Japanese culture, consider this basic ryokan near the Tōei Asakusa Line's Gotanda stop. The proprietor will greet you with a warm smile and a bow and escort you to a small tatami room with a pay TV and a rather noisy heater/air conditioner mounted in the wall. Some rooms are stuffy (you can't open a window), and only two have private baths, but the Sansuisō is clean, easy to find, and only 20 minutes on the subway from Tōkyō Station and the Ginza. Although students and young travelers will be most comfortable here, the midnight curfew poses a problem for night owls. This hotel is a member of the Japanese Inn Group; the Japanese National Tourist Organization can help make reservations. ⊠ *2-9-5 Higashi-Gotanda, Shinagawa-ku, Tōkyō-to 141,* ☎ *03/3441–7475,* ⅁ *03/3449–1944. 2 rooms with bath, 7 rooms share bath. AE, V. Tōei Asakusa Line's Gotanda stop; JR Yamanote Line, Gotanda Eki.*

Kudan-Minami

$$$ ⊞ **Fairmount Hotel.** Nostalgia buffs will love the Fairmount; here's a ★   place in relentlessly high-tech Tōkyō with pull-chain ventilators, real tile in the bathrooms, and furniture (a little chipped) that Sears & Roebuck must have phased out of its catalog in 1955. The hotel has all that and exposed water pipes—left that way even after a major renovation, neatly wrapped and painted, of course, but exposed just the same. The hotel isn't seedy, mind you, just old (it was built in 1951) and a bit set in its ways. The best thing about the seven-story Fairmount is its frontage on the park that runs along the east side of the Imperial Palace grounds; rooms facing the park have a wonderful view of the moat and Chidorigafuchi pond, where Tōkyō couples take rented rowboats out on summer Sunday afternoons. ⊠ *2-1-17 Kudan-Minami, Chiyoda-ku, Tōkyō-to 102,* ☎ *03/3262–1151,* ⅁ *03/3264–2476. 205 rooms, 3 suites. Restaurant, bar. AE, DC, MC, V. Subway: Hanzō-mon and Tōzai lines, Kudanshita stop.*

Kyō-bashi

$$$$ ⊞ **Hotel Seiyō Ginza.** Location and personalized service are the two reasons to choose this exclusive hotel (double rooms start at ¥50,000). In hailing distance of the Ginza, it caters to celebrities and those who require a direct line in their rooms to a personal secretary who takes care of their every need. A staff of some 220 outnumber the guests by a considerable margin. Rooms and suites, it must be noted, are smaller than what most Westerners might expect for the price. There is are four restaurants, including the Attore for Italian food (☞ Dining, *above*) and the Pastorale for French-Continental. ⊠ *1-11-2 Ginza, Chūō-ku, Tōkyō-to 104,* ☎ *03/3535–1111,* ⅁ *03/3535–1110. 79 rooms. 4 restaurants, bar, lounge, patisserie, health club. AE, DC, MC, V. Subway: Ginza stop.*

Maru-no-uchi

$$$$ ⊞ **Palace Hotel.** The service here is extremely helpful and professional; ★   half the staff has been with the hotel for more than 10 years. The location is ideal: Only a moat separates the hotel from the outer gardens of the Imperial Palace; the Ginza and the financial districts of Maru-no-uchi are both a short taxi or subway ride away. The lobby spaces are rectangular and uninspiring; an air of calm conservatism bespeaks the Palace's half-century as an accommodation for the well-to-do and well connected. The guest rooms are spacious; those on the upper floors

facing the Imperial Palace are preferable. ⊠ *1-1-1 Maru-no-uchi, Chi-yoda-ku, Tōkyō-to 100,* ☎ *03/3211–5211,* FAX *03/3211–6987. 405 rooms. 7 restaurants, 2 bars, coffee shop, no-smoking rooms. AE, DC, MC, V. Subway: Tōkyō.*

$$$ 🏨 **Ginza Maru-no-uchi Hotel.** Since it opened in 1976, the Ginza Maru-no-uchi has been a popular choice for tour groups, both foreign and Japanese, for one reason: Given its location—a subway stop from the Ginza—the cost of accommodations here is very reasonable. Guest rooms are compact and clean, but there is nothing particularly remarkable about the decor or the service. ⊠ *4-1-12 Tsukiji, Chūō-ku, Tōkyō-to 104,* ☎ *03/3543–5431,* FAX *03/3543–6006. 114 rooms. Restaurant. AE, DC, MC, V. Subway: Hibiya and Tōei Asakusa lines, Higashi-Ginza stop.*

$$$ 🏨 **Tōkyō Maru-no-uchi Hotel.** In business since 1924, the Tōkyō Maru-no-uchi was last refurbished in 1987; the hotel has seen a lot of traffic since then, and the guest rooms tend to be a little drab, but they are—for Tōkyō—reasonably large, and the older furnishings have a bit of character. The Tōkyō Maru-no-uchi is very popular with Westerners, and the staff has come to anticipate their needs. The location is excellent: within two blocks of Tōkyō Eki, three blocks from the Imperial Palace, and two subway stops from Ginza. ⊠ *1-6-3 Maru-no-uchi, Chiyoda-ku, Tōkyō-to 104,* ☎ *03/3215–2151,* FAX *03/3215–8036. 210 rooms. Restaurant, bar, coffee shop, no-smoking rooms. AE, DC, MC, V. Subway: Maru-no-uchi line, Tōkyō stop; JR Tōkyō Eki.*

$$$ 🏨 **Tōkyō Station Hotel.** The Tōkyō Station building was the work of Kingo Tatsuno, one of Japan's first modern architects. Completed in 1914, it was saved in 1990 from the wrecker's ball by a determined historical preservation movement—one of the few times, in this part of the city, that cultural values triumphed over commerce. The original charming facade remains—so far—untouched. The hotel is on the west side of the station building, on the second and third floors; the windows along the corridor look out over the station rotunda. The hotel's frosted glass and flocked wallpaper, its heavy red drapes, and its varnished wooden staircases have seen better days, but Western travelers will appreciate the wide corridors and high ceilings. If you're moving on from Tōkyō by train to another part of the country, the location is ideal. ⊠ *1-9-1 Maru-no-uchi, Chiyodu-ku, Tōkyō-to 100,* ☎ *03/3231–2511,* FAX *03/3231–3513. 170 rooms, 56 with bath. AE, DC, MC, V. Subway/JR eki: Tōkyō Eki.*

Meguro

$$ 🏨 **Gajoen Kankō Hotel.** Away from the noise and bustle of Tōkyō traffic, this hotel offers good value in a residential area. The Gajoen Kankō is full of old prints, scrolls, and rococo Asian decor. Facilities in the modern annex, built for the banquet and wedding business, are perhaps more comfortable but lack the character of those in the original prewar structure. ⊠ *1-8-1 Shimo-Meguro, Meguro-ku, Tōkyō-to 153,* ☎ *03/3491–0111,* FAX *03/3495–2450. 108 rooms. 2 restaurants. AE, DC, MC, V. JR Yamanote Line, Meuro Eki.*

Nagata-chō

$$$$ 🏨 **Capitol Tōkyū Hotel.** The Tōkyū Hotel chain's flagship operation, the Capitol is only 31 years old, but it feels a bit like a grand hotel of a bygone era and commands a loyal repeat clientele among foreign business travelers. It is also relatively small by Tōkyō standards, and with two full-time staff to every guest, service is excellent. Guest rooms are furnished in dark wood, but *shoji* (sliding paper screens) on the windows provide a feeling of soft warmth and light. Ask for one of the

rooms that overlook the adjacent Hie Jinja. Two of the hotel's dining rooms, the Origami breakfast café and the Tea Lounge, also have views of the shrine. To the left of the lobby is a small garden with a pond. ⊠ *2-10-3 Nagata-chō, Chiyoda-ku, Tōkyō-to 100,* ☎ *03/3581–4511,* FAX *03/3581–5822. 459 rooms. 5 restaurants, bar, coffee shop, no-smoking rooms, outdoor pool, steam room, massage, shops. AE, DC. Subway: Chiyoda and Maru-no-uchi lines, Kokkai Gijidō-mae stop.*

Nishi-Shinjuku

$$$$ 🏨 **Century Hyatt Hotel.** This Hyatt has the trademark atrium-style lobby: seven stories high, with open-glass elevators soaring upward and three huge chandeliers suspended from above. Single rooms tend to be small and lack good views from their windows; larger rooms are designed to create the impression of a separate sitting area. The Hyatt emphasizes its cuisine (there are 12 restaurants and bars), with special week-long gourmet "fairs" supervised by visiting international chefs. ⊠ *2-7-2 Nishi-Shinjuku, Shinjuku-ku, Tōkyō-to 160,* ☎ *03/3349–0111,* FAX *03/3344–5575. 774 rooms, including a few luxurious Japanese-style rooms and 1- and 2- bedroom Western-style suites. 6 restaurants, 2 bars, coffee shop, no-smoking rooms, indoor pool, 2 concierge floors. AE, DC, MC, V. Subway/JR eki: Shinjuku.*

$$$$ 🏨 **Park Hyatt Tōkyō.** An elevator whisks you to the 41st floor, where the hotel begins with an atrium lounge enclosed on three sides by floor-to-ceiling plate-glass windows. The panorama of Shinjuku spreads out before you; the tops of neighboring skyscrapers add to the three-dimensional spectacle. At the check-in desks, registration forms are put before you already filled with the details and simply awaiting your signature. Service is so efficient and personal, the staff seem to know your name before you introduce yourself. The mood of the hotel is contemporary and understated. Guest rooms, from the 42nd to the 50th floor, are large by any standard. King-size beds have Egyptian cotton sheets and down-feather duvets; other appointments include pale olive-green carpets and black lacquer cabinets. Even bathrooms have views, with tubs situated by windows. Between the 45th and 47th floors there is a well-equipped health facility staffed with trainers. The Park Hyatt's restaurants include the Girandole (Continental cuisine), the Peak Lounge, and (on the 52nd floor) the very popular New York Grill, with an open kitchen that specializes in steaks and seafood. ⊠ *3-7-1-2 Nishi-Shinjuku, Shinjuku-ku, Tōkyō-to 163,* ☎ *03/5322–1234,* FAX *03/5322–1288. 178 rooms. 4 restaurants, bar, no-smoking rooms, indoor pool, massage, sauna, steam room, aerobics, health club, video games. AE, MC, V. Subway/JR eki: Shinjuku.*

$$$$ 🏨 **Tōkyō Hilton International.** A short walk from the megalithic new Tōkyō City Hall, the Hilton is a particular favorite of Western business travelers. When it opened in 1984, it was the largest Hilton in Asia but opted away from the prevailing atrium style in favor of more guest rooms and banquet facilities; as a result, the lobby is on a comfortable, human scale. The bar-lounge in the reception area is highlighted by a copper-clad spiral staircase to the mezzanine floor above. Shoji screens instead of curtains bathe the guest rooms in soft, relaxing light. The Imari Room, with its displays of museum-quality traditional pottery, is one of Tōkyō's more elegant places to dine. ⊠ *6-6-2 Nishi-Shinjuku, Shinjuku-ku, Tōkyō-to 160,* ☎ *03/3344–5111,* FAX *03/3342–6094. 807 rooms. Restaurants, no-smoking rooms, indoor and outdoor pools, sauna, 2 tennis courts, shops, dance club, cabaret. AE, DC, MC, V. Subway/JR eki: Shinjuku.*

$$ 🏨 **Shinjuku Washington Hotel.** This is truly a business hotel, where service is computerized as much as possible. The third-floor lobby has an automated check-in and checkout system; you are assigned a room and provided with a plastic card that opens the door and the minibar. The clerk at the counter will explain the process, but after that you are on your own. ✉ *3-2-9 Nishi-Shinjuku, Shinjuku-ku, Tōkyō-to 160,* ☎ *03/3343–3111,* FAX *03/3342–2575. 1,650 rooms. Minibar, refrigerators, no-smoking rooms. AE, DC, MC, V. Subway/JR eki: Shinjuku.*

$$ 🏨 **Star Hotel.** This small, friendly hotel has rates more reasonable
★ than most others in the area. The staff speaks only Japanese but is sympathetic to sign language. The rooms are clean, though not spacious. A small, pleasant restaurant serves Japanese and Western food. Don't expect a doorman or a porter to help with your bags, but the size of the Star at least allows the people at the front desk to remember your name without the help of a computer. ✉ *7-10-5 Nishi-Shinjuku, Shinjuku-ku, Tōkyō-to 160,* ☎ *03/3361–1111,* FAX *03/3369–4216. 80 Western-style rooms. Restaurant, no-smoking rooms. AE, DC, MC, V. Subway/JR eki: Shinjuku.*

Roppongi

$ 🏨 **Asia Center of Japan.** Established mainly for Asian students and other Asian visitors on limited budgets, these accommodations have become generally popular with foreign travelers for their easy access (a 15-minute walk) to the nightlife of Roppongi. Rooms are small, minimally furnished, and not too well soundproofed—but they are clean and comfortable: You get good value for what you pay. To get here, walk toward Roppongi from the Akasaka Post Office and take the first side street on the left. ✉ *2-10-32 Akasaka, Minato-ku, Tōkyō-to 107,* ☎ *03/3402–6111,* FAX *03/3402–0738. 172 Western-style rooms, some with private bath. Bar, cafeteria. No credit cards. Subway: Ginza and Hanzō-mon lines, Aoyama-it-chōme stop.*

Sekiguchi

$$$$ 🏨 **Four Seasons Hotel Chinzan-sō.** Where else will you have a chance
★ to sleep in a million-dollar room? That's about what it cost, on the average, to build and furnish each of the accommodations in this elegant hotel, which opened in 1992. The interiors were designed by Frank Nicholson, Inc., the firm responsible for the Chicago Ritz-Carlton; most of the furnishings are American, complemented by Japanese accessories: ceramic lamps, gold-framed prints, tea sets, and so on. Rooms are large by any standard; Conservatory Suites have their own private garden patios. The Italian marble floor in the lobby is accented with huge woolen area rugs woven in Ireland. Once the estate of an imperial prince, Chinzan-sō rejoices in one of the most beautiful settings in Tōkyō; in summer, the gardens are famous for their fireflies. The hotel's complimentary shuttle-bus service to the Waseda subway station (Tōzai Line) and limousine service to Tōkyō Eki make it easy to get downtown. ✉ *2-10-8 Sekiguchi, Bunkyō-ku, Tōkyō-to 112,* ☎ *03/3943–2222 or 800/332–3442,* FAX *03/3943–2300. 284 rooms, 2 Japanese-style suites. 3 restaurants, bar, coffee shop, lounge, no-smoking rooms, indoor pool, barbershop, beauty salon, hot tub, Japanese baths, massage, exercise room, shops, chapels. AE, DC, MC, V. Subway: Tōzai Line, Waseda stop.*

Shiba Kōen

$$ 🏨 **Shiba Daimon Hotel.** A minute's walk from Zōjō-ji, this moderately priced hotel is popular with Japanese travelers. The decor is unremarkable, but the rooms are reasonably spacious for the price. The staff is a bit ill at ease with guests who cannot speak Japanese, but no less

willing to help. A good restaurant on the ground floor serves break-fast and then Chinese fare in the evening. ✉ *2-3-6 Shiba-kōen, Mi-nato-ku, Tōkyō-to 105,* ☎ *03/3431–3716,* 𝐅𝐀𝐗 *03/3434–5177. 96 rooms. Restaurant, no-smoking rooms. AE, DC, MC, V. Subway: Tōei Asakusa Line, Daimon stop.*

Shinagawa

$$$ ⛨ **Hotel Pacific Meridien.** Just across the street from the JR Shinagawa Eki, the Pacific Meridien is on grounds that were once part of an im-perial family estate. The hotel markets itself to convention groups and business travelers. The decor is pastel and lilac all the way to the Sky Lounge on the 30th floor, which overlooks Tōkyō Bay. The entire back wall of the coffee lounge on the ground floor is glass, the better to con-template a tranquil Japanese garden, sculpted with rocks and water-falls. The Pacific Meridien has nine restaurants and bars, and a good bookstore with English-language books. ✉ *3-13-3 Takanawa, Mi-nato-ku, Tōkyō-to 108,* ☎ *03/3445–6711,* 𝐅𝐀𝐗 *03/3445–5137. 954 rooms. 5 restaurants, 3 bars, coffee shop, no-smoking rooms, outdoor pool, shops, free parking. AE, DC, MC, V. Subway (Tōei Asakusa Line)/JR eki: Shinagawa.*

$$$ ⛨ **Takanawa Tōbu Hotel.** A five-minute walk from Shinagawa Eki, the Takanawa Tōbu offers good value for the price. Rooms are on the small side, and there is no proper sitting area in the lobby, but the hotel atones for these shortcomings with a friendly staff (which speaks a bit of En-glish) and a cozy bar. There's also a small Western restaurant, the Boulogne. ✉ *4-7-6 Takanawa, Minato-ku, Tōkyō-to 108,* ☎ *03/ 3447–0111,* 𝐅𝐀𝐗 *03/3447–0117. 190 rooms. Restaurant, bar. AE, DC, MC, V. Subway (Tōei Asakusa Line)/JR eki: Shinagawa.*

$$ ⛨ **Keihin Hotel.** Directly across the street from Shinagawa Eki, the Kei-hin is best described as a business hotel. The building is small, as are the rooms, but the staff is personable and the manager speaks English enthusiastically and enjoys having Westerners stay. For a modest hotel, the Keihin is a good value, given its convenient location. ✉ *4-10-20 Takanawa, Minato-ku, Tōkyō-to 108,* ☎ *03/3449–5711,* 𝐅𝐀𝐗 *03/3441–7230. 52 Western-style rooms. Restaurant. AE, DC, MC, V. Subway (Tōei Asakusa Line)/JR eki: Shinagawa.*

Tora-no-mon

$$$$ ⛨ **ANA Hotel Tōkyō.** A short walk from the U.S. Embassy, the ANA Hotel arrived on the Tōkyō scene in 1986. It typifies the ziggurat-atrium style that seems to have been a requirement for hotel architecture at the time. The reception floor, with its two-story fountain, is clad in enough marble to have depleted an Italian quarry. Guest rooms are airy and spacious; the concierge floor (35th floor) has a separate breakfast room and a private cocktail lounge if you stay there. In general, the interior designers have made skillful use of artwork and furnishings to take some of the chill off the ANA's relentless modernism. There are Chinese, French, and Japanese restaurants and three bars; the As-tral Lounge on the top (37th) floor affords a superb view of the city. ✉ *1-12-33 Akasaka, Minato-ku, Tōkyō-to 107,* ☎ *03/3505–1111,* 𝐅𝐀𝐗 *03/3505–1155. 900 rooms. 3 restaurants, 3 bars, no-smoking rooms, exercise room, outdoor pool, beauty salon, men's sauna, shops, travel services. AE, DC, MC, V. Subway: Hibiya Line, Kamiya-chō; Ginza Line, Tora-no-mon.*

$$$$ ⛨ **Hotel Okura.** Year after year, a poll of business travelers ranks the
★ Okura, for its exemplary service, among the best two or three hotels in Asia. It is the kind of place you can come back to five years later, and—even if you're not staying—the duty manager will remember your

name. The Okura opened just before the 1964 Olympics, and, understated in its sophistication, human in scale, it remains a favorite of diplomatic visitors as well. The spacious guest rooms are tastefully furnished; amenities include remote-control draperies, hair dryers, and terrycloth bathrobes. The odd-numbered rooms, 871–889 inclusive, look onto a small Japanese landscaped garden. The Okura Art Museum, on the hotel grounds, has a fine collection of antique porcelain, mother-of-pearl, and ceramics; a tea ceremony is held there every day 11 am–noon and 1–5 PM (no charge for guests of the hotel). The main building is preferable to the South Wing—which you reach by an underground shopping arcade—and the Japanese-style rooms are superb. ⊠ *2-10-4 Tora-no-mon, Minato-ku, Tōkyō-to 105,* ☎ *03/3582–0111,* 🆅🅰🆇 *03/3582–3707. 789 rooms, 83 suites, 11 Japanese-style rooms. 7 restaurants, 3 bars, 2 coffee shops, no-smoking rooms, indoor and outdoor pools, massage, steam room, exercise room. AE, DC, MC, V. Subway: Hibiya Line, Kamiya-chō; Ginza Line, Tora-no-mon.*

Ueno

$　🏨 **Ryokan Katsutarō.** This small, simple, economical hotel is a five-minute walk from the entrance to Ueno Park and a 10-minute walk from the Tōkyō National Museum. The quietest rooms are in the back, away from the main street. To get here, leave the Nezu subway station by the Ike Nōata exit, cross the road, take the street running northeast, and turn right at the "T" intersection; Ryokan Katsutarō is 25 yards along Dōbutsuen-Uramon-dōri, on the left-hand side. ⊠ *4-16-8 Ike Nōata, Taitō-ku, Tōkyō-to 110,* ☎ *03/3821–9808,* 🆅🅰🆇 *03/3891–4789. 7 rooms, 4 with private bath. Breakfast room. AE, DC, MC, V. Subway: Chiyoda Line, Nezu stop.*

Yanaka

$　🏨 **Sawanoya Ryokan.** Sawanoya is in a quiet area northwest of Ueno
★　Kōen. The residential neighborhood and the hospitality of the ryokan make you feel at home in this traditional part of Tōkyō. The family that operates this little inn truly welcomes you—helping plan trips and arrange future accommodations. Two rooms have private baths (at a ¥600 premium), while the rest share Japanese-style common baths. No dinner is offered, but breakfast (Continental or Japanese) is available at an extra charge. Sawanoya has become very popular with low-budget travelers; make a reservation by fax well before you arrive. To get here from the Nezu subway station, walk 300 yards north along Shinobazu-dōri, and take the street on the right; the Sawanoya is 180 yards on the right. ⊠ *2-3-11 Yanaka, Taitō-ku, Tōkyō-to 110,* ☎ *03/3822–2251,* 🆅🅰🆇 *03/3822–2252. 12 rooms. Breakfast room. AE, MC, V. Subway: Chiyoda Line, Nezu stop.*

Hostels and Dormitory Accommodations

$$　🏨 **Tōkyō YMCA.** Rooms come with and without bath. Both men and women can stay at the hostel, which is a three-minute walk from Awaji-chō Station on the Maru-no-uchi Line or seven minutes from Kanda Station on the Ginza Line. ⊠ *7 Kanda-Mitoshiro-chō, Chiyoda-ku, Tōkyō-to 101,* ☎ *03/3293–1919,* 🆅🅰🆇 *03/3293–1926. 40 rooms. No credit cards.*

$$　🏨 **Tōkyō YWCA Sadohara.** Rooms are available here with baths, as are rooms for married couples. The hostel is a three-minute walk from Ichigaya Station on the Tōei Shinjuku Line and the JR Chūō Line. ⊠ *3-1-1 Ichigaya Sadohara-chō, Shinjuku-ku, Tōkyō-to 162,* ☎ *03/3268–7313,* 🆅🅰🆇 *03/3268–4452. 16 rooms. No credit cards*

$ 🏨 **Tōkyō International Youth Hostel.** In typical hostel style, you are required off the premises between 10 AM and 3 PM. The hostel is very close to JR Iidabashi Eki on the Tōzai and Yūraku-chō lines. ⊠ *Central Plaza Bldg., 18th floor, 1-1 Kagura-kashi, Shinjuku-ku, Tōkyō-to 162,* ☎ *03/3235–1107. 138 bunk beds. No credit cards*

$ 🏨 **YMCA Asia Youth Center.** Both men and women can stay here; all rooms have private baths. The hostel is an eight-minute walk from Suidō-bashi Eki on the JR Mita Line. ⊠ *2-5-5 Saragaku-chō, Chiyoda-ku, Tōkyō-to 101,* ☎ *03/3233–0611,* 𝖥𝖠𝖷 *03/3233–0633. 55 rooms. No credit cards.*

Near Narita Airport

$$$ 🏨 **ANA Hotel Narita.** Opened in 1990, this hotel—like many others in the ANA chain—aspires to architecture in the grand style; expect the cost of brass and marble to show up on your bill. The amenities measure up, and the proximity to the airport (about 15 minutes by shuttle bus) makes this a good choice if you are in transit. ⊠ *68 Hori-no-uchi, Narita-shi, Chiba-ken 286,* ☎ *0476/33–1311,* 𝖥𝖠𝖷 *0476/33–0244. 422 rooms. 5 restaurants, bar, coffee shop, no-smoking rooms, pool, shops. AE, DC, MC, V.*

$$ 🏨 **Holiday Inn Tōbu Narita.** A 10-minute ride by shuttle bus from the airport, this hotel has Western-style accommodations with the standard—if unremarkable—range of amenities. You can also rent one of its soundproof rooms for daytime-only use (¥19,000 for two beds). ⊠ *320-1 Tokkō, Narita-shi, Chiba-ken 286,* ☎ *0476/32–1234,* 𝖥𝖠𝖷 *0476/ 32–0617. 500 rooms. 4 restaurants, bar, coffee shop, no-smoking rooms, pool, barbershop, beauty salon, massage, steam room. AE, DC, MC, V.*

$$ 🏨 **Narita Airport Rest House.** A basic business hotel without much in the way of frills, the Rest House offers the closest accommodations to the airport itself, less than five minutes away by shuttle bus. You can also rent one of its soundproof rooms for daytime-only use from 8 AM to 6 PM (a double runs ¥12,000). ⊠ *New Tōkyō International Airport, Narita-shi, Chiba-ken 286,* ☎ *0476/32–1212,* 𝖥𝖠𝖷 *0476/32–1209. 210 rooms. Restaurant, no-smoking rooms. AE, DC, MC, V.*

$$ 🏨 **Narita Winds Hotel.** A regular shuttle bus (at Terminal 1, Bus Stop 14; Terminal 2, Bus Stop 31) makes the 10-minute trip to this modern, efficient, all-purpose hotel, which has five restaurants, banquet rooms, and meeting facilities. All rooms are soundproof. ⊠ *560 Tokkō, Narita-shi, Chiba-ken 286,* ☎ *0476/33–1111,* 𝖥𝖠𝖷 *0476/33–1108. 321 rooms. 5 restaurants, no-smoking rooms, pool, sauna, 2 tennis courts, shops, meeting rooms. AE, DC, MC, V.*

$$ 🏨 **Radisson Hotel Narita Airport.** On 72 spacious acres of land, this modern hotel feels somewhat like a resort—and has Narita's largest outdoor pool. A shuttle bus runs between the Radisson and the airport every 20 minutes or so (between 1 and 10 PM from Terminal 1, between 12:50 and 9:50 PM from Terminal 2); the trip takes about 15 minutes. ⊠ *650-35 Nanaei, Tomisato-machi, Inaba-gun, Chiba-ken 288,* ☎ *0476/93–1234,* 𝖥𝖠𝖷 *0476/93–4834. 500 rooms. Restaurants, no-smoking rooms, pool, 2 tennis courts, jogging, shop. AE, DC, MC, V.*

$ 🏨 **Narita View Hotel.** Boxy and uninspired, the Narita View offers no view of anything in particular but can be reached by shuttle bus from the airport in about 15 minutes. Short on charm, it tends to rely on promotional discount "campaigns" to draw a clientele. You can also rent rooms for daytime-only use from 7 AM to 9 PM at 50% of the normal rate. ⊠ *700 Kosuge, Narita-shi, Chiba-ken 286,* ☎ *0476/32–1111,* 𝖥𝖠𝖷 *0476/32–1078. 504 rooms. 4 restaurants, coffee shop, no-smoking rooms, beauty salon, massage. AE, DC, MC, V.*

THE ARTS

Few cities have as much to offer as Tōkyō does in the performing arts. It has Japan's own great stage traditions: Kabuki, Nō, Bunraku puppet drama, music, and dance. It has an astonishing variety of music, classical and popular; Tōkyō is a proving ground for local talent and a magnet for orchestras and concert soloists from all over the world. The Rolling Stones, Jean Pierre Rampal, the Berlin Philharmonic, Oscar Peterson: Whenever you visit, the headliners will be here. It has modern theater—in somewhat limited choices, to be sure, unless you can follow dialogue in Japanese; but Western repertory companies can always find receptive audiences here for plays in English. In recent years musicals have found enormous popularity here; it doesn't take long for a hit show in New York or London to open in Tōkyō.

Film, too, presents a much broader range of possibilities than it used to. The major commercial distributors bring in the movies they expect will draw the biggest receipts—horror films and Oscar nominees—but there are now dozens of small theaters in Tōkyō catering to more sophisticated audiences. Japan has yet to develop any serious strength of its own in opera or ballet, but for that reason touring companies like the Metropolitan and the Bolshoi, Sadler's Wells, and the Bayerische Staatsoper find Tōkyō a very compelling venue—as well they might, when ¥30,000 seats are sold out even before the box office opens.

Information and Tickets

The best comprehensive guide in English to performance schedules in Tōkyō is the "Cityscope" insert in the monthly *Tōkyō Journal* magazine. You can probably pick up the *Journal* at one of the newsstands at Narita Airport on your way into the city; if not, it's on sale in the bookstores at major international hotels. In addition to reviewing and recommending films, plays, and concerts, "Cityscope" also covers museums and art galleries, television, festivals, and special events. Another source, rather less complete, is the *Tour Companion*, a tabloid visitor's guide published every two weeks that is available free of charge at hotels and at Japan National Tourist Organization offices. For a weekly update, the Monday edition of the English-language *Mainichi Daily News* also runs information on performances.

If your hotel cannot help you with bookings, two of the city's major ticket agencies have numbers to call for assistance in English: **Ticket Pia** (☎ 03/5237–9999) and **Ticket Saison** (☎ 03/3250–9999). A third possibility is the **Playguide Agency,** which has outlets in most of the *depāto* and in other locations all over the city; you can stop in at the main office (✉ Playguide Bldg., 2-6-4 Ginza, Chūō-ku, ☎ 03/3561–8821) and ask for the nearest counter. Note that agencies normally do not have tickets for same-day performances but only for advanced booking.

Traditional Theater

Kabuki

Certainly the best place to see Kabuki is at the **Kabuki-za** (✉ 4-12-15 Ginza, Chūō-ku, ☎ 03/5565–6000; call by 6 PM the day preceding performance for reservations; subway: Hibiya and Tōei Asakusa lines, Higashi-Ginza), built especially for this purpose in 1925, with its *hanamichi* (runway) passing diagonally through the audience to the revolving stage. Built originally in 1925, the Kabuki-za was destroyed in an air raid in 1945 and rebuilt in the identical style in 1951. The facade of the building recalls the castle architecture of the 16th century; the lanterns and banners and huge theater posters outside identify it unmistakably. Matinees usually begin at 11 AM and end at 3:30 PM; evening performances, at 4:30 pm, end around 9 PM. Reserved seats are expensive and hard to come by on short notice; for a mere ¥600 to ¥1,000, however, you can buy an unreserved ticket that allows you to see one act of a play from the topmost gallery. The gallery is cleared after each act, but there's nothing to prevent you from buying another ticket: The price is low for an hour or so of this fascinating spectacle. Bring binoculars—the gallery is very far from the stage. You might also want to rent an earphone set (¥650) to follow the play in English, but this is really more of an intrusion than a help—and you can't use the set in the topmost galleries.

Two other venues in Tōkyō specialize in traditional theater and offer Kabuki at various times during the year. The **Shimbashi Enbujō**, which dates from 1925 (⊠ 6-18-2 Ginza, Chūō-ku, ☎ 03/5565–6000; subway: Hibiya and Tōei Asakusa lines, Higashi-Ginza), was built originally for the geisha of the Shimbashi quarter to present their spring and autumn performances of traditional music and dance. It's a bigger house than the Kabuki-za, and it still presents a lot of traditional dance as well as conventional drama (in Japanese). Reserved seats commonly run ¥3,000–¥13,500; and there is no gallery. The **National Theater of Japan** (⊠ 4-1 Hayabusa-chō, Chiyoda-ku, ☎ 03/3265–7411; subway: Hanzō-mon Line, Hanzō-mon), mentioned under the Imperial Palace in our Exploring section, hosts Kabuki companies based elsewhere; it also has a training program for young people who may not have one of the hereditary family connections but want to break into this closely guarded profession. Debut performances, called *kao-mise*, are worth watching to catch the stars of the next generation. Reserved seats are usually ¥1,400–¥8,200.

Nō

Somewhat like Kabuki, Nō is divided into a number of schools, the traditions of which developed as the exclusive property of hereditary families. It is occasionally performed in public halls, like the **National Nō Theater** (⊠ 4-18-1 Sendagaya, Shibuya-ku, ☎ 03/3423–1331; subway: JR Chūō Line) but primarily in the theaters of these schools—which also teach their dance and recitation styles to amateurs. The most important of these are the **Kanze Nō-gakudō** (⊠ 1-16-4 Shōtō, Shibuya-ku, ☎ 03/3469–5241; subway: Ginza and Hanzō-mon lines, Shibuya); the **Hosho Nō-gakudō** (⊠ 1-5-9 Hongo, Bunkyō-ku, ☎ 03/3811–4843; subway/JR eki: Suidō-bashi); and the **Umewaka Nō-gakuin** (⊠ 2-6-14 Higashi-Nakano, Nakano-ku, ☎ 03/3363–7748; subway: Maruno-uchi Line, Nakano-Saka-ue). The very best way to see Nō, however, is in the open air, at torchlight performances called Takigi Nō, held in the courtyards of temples. The setting and the aesthetics of the drama combine to produce an eerie theatrical experience. These performances are given at various times during the year. Consult the "Cityscope" or Tour Companion listings. Tickets are normally available only through the temples; they sell out very quickly.

Bunraku

The spiritual center of Bunraku today is Ōsaka, rather than Tōkyō, but there are a number of performances in the small hall of the National Theater (☞ *above*). In recent years, it has come into vogue with younger audiences, and Bunraku troupes will occasionally perform in trendier locations. Consult the "Cityscope" listings, or check with one of the English-speaking ticket agencies.

Modern Theater

The *Shingeki* (Modern Theater) movement began in Japan at about the turn of the last century. The first problem its earnest young actors and directors encountered was the fact that they had no native reper- toire. The "conservative" faction at first tended to approach the prob- lem with translations of Shakespeare, the "radicals" with Ibsen, Gorky, and Shaw. It wasn't until around 1915 that Japanese playwrights began writing for the Shingeki stage. Japan of the 1930s and 1940s, in any case, was none too hospitable an environment for modern drama; the movement did not develop any real vitality until after World War II.

The watershed years came around 1965, when experimental theater companies—unable to find commercial space—began taking their work to young audiences in various unusual ways: street plays and "hap- penings"; dramatic readings in underground malls and rented lofts; tents put up on vacant lots for unannounced performances (miraculously filled to capacity by word of mouth) and taken down the next day. It was in this period that surrealist playwright Kōbō Abe found his stride and director Tadashi Suzuki developed the unique system of training that now draws aspiring actors from all over the world to his "theater community" in the mountains of Toyama Prefecture. Japanese drama today is a lively art indeed; theaters small and large, in unexpected pock- ets all over Tōkyō, attest to its vitality.

The great majority of these performances, however, are in Japanese, for Japanese audiences. You're unlikely to find one with program notes in English to help you follow it. Unless it's a play you already know well, and you're curious to see how it translates (*Fiddler on the Roof,* for ex- ample, has been running in Japanese for more than 20 years), you might do well to think of some other way to spend your evenings out.

There is one exception: the **Takarazuka**—the wonderfully goofy all- female review. The troupe was founded in the Ōsaka suburb of Takarazuka in 1913 and has been going strong ever since; today it has not one but five companies, one of them with a permanent home in Tōkyō, right across the street from the Imperial Hotel (✉ 1-1-3 Yūraku- chō, Chiyoda-ku, ☎ 03/3591–1711; subway: Hibiya stop). A Takarazuka chorine never gives her parents a moment's anxiety about her chosen career, because this is show business with a difference—a life chaste and chaperoned, where the yearning admirers waiting with roses by the stage door are mostly teenage girls. Everybody sings; everybody dances; the sets are breathtaking; the costumes are swell. Where else but at the Takarazuka could you see anything from *The Rose of Versailles* to *Gone With the Wind,* sung in Japanese, with a young woman in a mustache and a frock coat playing Rhett Butler?

Music

Traditional Japanese music (koto, shamisen, et cetera) is hard to come by in Tōkyō; check newspaper listings for concerts and school recitals. The availability of all other kinds of music, on the other hand, keeps getting better and better. Every year, a host of new promoters and book- ing agencies get into the act; major corporations, eager to polish their images as cultural institutions, are building concert halls and unusual performance spaces all over the city, adding to what was already an excellent roster of public auditoriums. It would be impossible to list them all; here are a few of the most important:

The biggest acts from abroad in **rock** and **popular music** tend to ap- pear at the 56,000-seat **Tōkyō Dome** sports arena, which opened in 1988 on the site of the old Kōrakuen Stadium (✉ 1-3-61 Kōraku, Bunkyō-ku, ☎ 03/3811–2111; subway: Maru-no-uchi and Namboku lines, Kōraku-en), and at **Nakano Sun Plaza** (✉ 4-1-1 Nakano, Nakano-ku, ☎ 03/3388–1151; subway: Tōzai Line, Nakano). For **Western classical music,** including **opera,** the major venues are NHK Hall (✉ 2-2-1 Jinnan, Shibuya-ku, ☎ 03/3465–1111; subway: Ginza and Hanzō-mon lines, Shibuya), home base for the Japan Broadcasting Corporation's NHK Symphony Orchestra; **Tōkyō Metropolitan Festival Hall** (Tōkyō Bunka Kaikan; ✉ 5-45 Ueno Kōen, Taitō-ku, ☎ 03/3828–2111; nearest JR/subway station: Ueno), which we've mentioned under Ueno in the Exploring section, *above*; the **New National Theatre** and **Tōkyō Opera City Concert Hall** (✉ 3-20-2 Nishi-Shin-juku, Shinjuku-ku, ☎ 03/5353–0704, 03/5353–0777 for Concert Hall information, 03/5351–3011 for the New National Theatre; subway: Keiō Shin-sen private rail line, Hatsudai Eki), discussed in the Shinjuku Exploring section, *above*; and **Suntory Hall,** in the Ark Hills complex (✉ 1-13-1 Akasaka, Minato-ku, ☎ 03/3505–1001; subway: Chiyoda and Maru-no-uchi lines, Kokkai Gijidō-mae). To these should be added three fine places designed especially for **chamber music: Iino Hall** (✉ 2-1-1 Uchisaiwai-chō, Chiyoda-ku, ☎ 03/3506–3251; subway: Ginza Line, Tora-no-mon), **Ishi-bashi Memorial Hall** (✉ 4-24-12 Higashi Ueno, Taitō-ku, ☎ 03/3843–3043; subway/JR eki: Ueno), and **Casals Hall** (✉ 1-6 Kanda Surugadai, Chiyoda-ku, ☎ 03/3294–1229; subway: Maru-no-uchi Line, Ocha-no-mizu), designed by architect Arata Isozaki, who also did, among other things, the Museum of Contemporary Art in Los Angeles.

Dance

Traditional Japanese dance, like flower arranging and the tea ceremony, is divided into dozens of styles, ancient of lineage and fiercely proud of their differences from each other. In fact, only the aficionado can really tell them apart. They survive not so much as performing arts but as schools, offering dance as a cultured accomplishment to interested amateurs. At least once a year, teachers and their students in each of these schools will hold a recital, so that on any given evening there's very likely to be one somewhere in Tōkyō. Truly professional performances are given, as we've mentioned, at the **National Theater** (Kokuritsu Gekijō) and the **Shimbashi Enbujō** (☞ Traditional Theater, *above*); the most important of the classical schools, however, developed as an aspect of Kabuki, and if you attend a play at the **Kabuki-za** (☞ Traditional Theater, *above*) you are almost guaranteed to see a representative example.

Ballet began to attract a Japanese following in 1920, when Anna Pavlova danced *The Dying Swan* at the old Imperial Theater. The well-known companies that come to Tōkyō from abroad perform to full houses, usually at the **Tōkyō Metropolitan Festival Hall** in Ueno (☞ Music, *above*). There are now about 15 professional Japanese ballet companies, several of which have toured abroad, but this has yet to become an art form on which Japan has had much of an impact.

Modern dance is a different story—a story that begins with a visit in 1955 by the Martha Graham Dance Company. The decade that followed was one of great turmoil in Japan; it was a period of dissatisfaction—political, intellectual, artistic—with old forms and conventions. The work of pioneers like Graham inspired a great number of talented dancers and choreographers to explore new avenues of self-expression. One of the fruits of that exploration was **Butō,** a movement that was at once uniquely Japanese and a major contribution to the world of modern dance.

The father of Butō was the dancer Tatsumi Hijikata (1928–86). The watershed work was his *Revolt of the Flesh*, which premiered in 1968.

Others soon followed: Kazuo Ono, Min Tanaka, Akaji Marō and the Dai Rakuda Kan troupe, Ushio Amagatsu and the Sankai Juku. To most Japanese, their work was inexplicably grotesque. Dancers performed with shaved heads, dressed in rags or with naked bodies painted completely white, their movements agonized and contorted. The images were dark and demonic, violent and explicitly sexual. Butō was an exploration of the unconscious: Its gods were the gods of the Japanese village and the gods of prehistory; its literary inspirations came from Mishima, Genet, Artaud. Like many other modern Japanese artists, the Butō dancers and choreographers were largely ignored by the mainstream until they began to appear abroad—to thunderous critical acclaim. Now they are equally honored at home. Butō does not lend itself to conventional spaces (a few years ago, for example, the Dai Rakuda Kan premiered one of its new works in a limestone cave in Gunma Prefecture), but if there's a performance in Tōkyō, "Cityscope" will have the schedule. Don't miss it.

Film

One of the positive things about the business of foreign film distribution in Japan is that it is extremely profitable—so much so that the distributors can afford to add Japanese subtitles rather than dub their offerings, the way it's done so often elsewhere. The original soundtrack, of course, may not be all that helpful to you if the film is Polish or Italian, but the vast majority of first-run foreign films here are made in the United States. There are, however, other disincentives: Choices are limited, good films take so long to open in Tōkyō that you've probably seen them all already at home, and tickets are expensive—around ¥1,700 for general admission, and ¥2,200–¥2,500 for a reserved seat, called a *shitei-seki*.

The native Japanese film industry has been in a slump for more than 20 years, and it shows no signs of recovery. It yields, at best, one or two films a year worth seeing, and these are invariably by independent producers or directors. A very small number of theaters will offer one showing a week, with English subtitles, of films that seem to have some international appeal; "Cityscope" will have the listings.

First-run theaters that have new releases, both Japanese and foreign, are clustered for the most part in three areas: Shinjuku, Shibuya, and Yūraku-chō-Hibiya-Ginza. The most astonishing thing about them is how early they shut down; in most cases, the last showing of the evening starts at around 7. This is not the case, however, with the best news on the Tōkyō film scene: the growing number of small theaters that take a special interest in classics, revivals, and serious imports. Many of them are in the "vertical boutique" buildings that represent the latest Japanese thinking in urban architecture and upscale marketing; somewhere on the premises will also be a chrome-and-marble coffee shop, a fashionable little bar, or even a decent restaurant. Most of them have a midnight show—at least on the weekends. One such is the **Cine Vivant** (⊠ Wave Building, 6-2-27 Roppongi, Minato-ku, ☎ 03/3403–6061; subway: Hibiya Line, Roppongi); another is the **Cine Saison Shibuya** (⊠ Prime Building, 2-29-5 Dōgenzaka, Shibuya-ku, ☎ 03/3770–1721; JR Yamanote Line, Shibuya Eki); still others are the **Haiyū-za Cinema Ten** (⊠ 4-9-2 Roppongi, Minato-ku, ☎ 03/3401–4073; subway: Hibiya Line, Roppongi), and the **Hibiya Chanter Cinema** (⊠ 1-2-2 Yūraku-chō, Chiyoda-ku, ☎ 03/3591–1511; JR Yamanote Line, Yūraku-chō Eki). **Bunka-mura,** the showcase complex next door to the Tōkyū depāto in Shibuya (⊠ 2-24-1 Dōgenzaka,☎ 03/3477–9111; subway/JR eki: Shibuya), has two movie theaters, a concert hall, and a performance space; it is the principal venue for many of Tōkyō's film festivals.

NIGHTLIFE

Tōkyō has more sheer diversity of nightlife than any other Japanese city. That diversity can be daunting—if not downright hazardous. Few bars and clubs have printed price lists; fewer still have lists in English. That drink you've just ordered could set you back a reasonable ¥1,000; you might, on the other hand, have wandered unknowingly into a place that charges you ¥15,000 up front for a whole bottle—and slaps a ¥20,000 cover charge on top. If the bar has hostesses, it is often unclear what the companionship of one will cost you, or whether she is there just for conversation. There is, of course, a certain amount of safe ground: Hotel lounges, jazz clubs, bars and cabarets where foreigners come out to play—and the unspoken rules of nightlife are pretty much the way they are anywhere else. But wandering off the beaten path in Tōkyō can be like shopping for a yacht: If you have to ask how much it costs, you probably can't afford it anyhow.

There are five major districts in Tōkyō that have an extensive nightlife and have places that make foreigners welcome. The *kinds* of entertainment will not vary much from one to another; the tone and style— and the price ranges—will.

Akasaka nightlife concentrates mainly on two streets, Ta-machi-dōri and Hitotsugi-dōri, and the small alleys connecting them. The area has several cabarets and nightclubs, and a wide range of wine bars, coffee shops, late-night restaurants, pubs and "snacks"—counter bars that will serve (and charge you for) small portions of food with your drinks, whether you order them or not. Akasaka is sophisticated and upscale, not quite as expensive as Ginza and not as trendy as Roppongi. Being fairly compact, it makes a convenient venue for testing the waters of Japanese nightlife.

Ginza is probably the city's most well-known entertainment district, and one of the most—if not *the* most—expensive in the world. It does have affordable restaurants and pubs, but its reputation rests on the exclusive hostess clubs where only the highest of high rollers on corporate expense accounts can take their clients. In recent years, a lot of corporations have been taking a harder look at those accounts, and Ginza as a nightlife destination has suffered in the process.

Roppongi is where Westerners out for the evening will probably feel most comfortable; it often seems that you're as likely to hear English, French, or Spanish on the street as Japanese. The prices are more reasonable here than in Ginza, or even in Akasaka. Not long ago, Roppongi had a nearly exclusive reputation as Disco City; some of that action has fled elsewhere, but when the 20-something gets out of the office and changes to her vinyl miniskirt and stiletto heels, this is still where she probably heads first. Akasaka and Ginza virtually close down by midnight, but some of the Roppongi bars stay open until the subways start running in the morning, so if you have the stamina, this is the place to prowl on an all-nighter.

Shibuya, less expensive than Roppongi and not as raunchy as Shinjuku, attracts mainly students and young professionals to its many *nomiya* (inexpensive bars). There's something a bit provincial about it, in that respect, and there are few places where you can count on communicating in English, but if you know a little Japanese, this is a pleasant and inexpensive area for an evening out.

Shinjuku's Kabuki-chō is the city's wildest nightlife venue. The options range from the marginally respectable down through the merely sleazy to where you can almost hear the viruses mutating. Bars (straight, gay, cross-dress, S&M), nightclubs, cabarets, discos, hole-in-the-wall pubs, love-by-the-hour hotels: Kabuki-chō has it all. Just stay clear of places with English-speaking touts out front and you'll be fine. If you're a woman unescorted, however, you probably want to stay out of Kabuki-chō after 9 PM; by then there are bound to be a few men drunk enough to make nuisances of themselves.

Bars

Ari's Lamplight. An intimate, comfortable place popular with foreign businesspeople and journalists, Ari's serves some of the best hamburgers in town. A "traditional classic" atmosphere is maintained, there's live music on Thursday nights, and the old standards on the piano tend to discourage the black vinyl crowd. ⊠ *Odakyū Bldg., 7-8-1 Minami-Aoyama, Minato-ku,* ☎ *03/3499–1573. Drinks start at ¥800.* ☾ *Mon.–Sat. 6 PM–2 AM. Subway/JR: Shibuya.*

Charleston. This has been for years the schmoozing and hunting bar for Tōkyō's single (or *soi-disant* single) foreign community, and the young Japanese who want to meet them. It's noisy and packed until the wee small hours. ⊠ *3-8-11 Roppongi, Minato-ku,* ☎ *03/3402–0372. Drinks are ¥800 and up.* ☾ *Nightly 6 PM–5 AM. Subway: Hibiya Line, Roppongi.*

Den. Launched by the mammoth beer and whiskey maker Suntory, Den is partly an exercise in corporate-image making. Meant to express the company's ecoconsciousness and its roots in traditional Japanese culture, the motif here is confected of stones, trees, and articles of folkcraft. Den draws a fashionable crowd from the TV production, PR, and design companies thick in this part of town. ⊠ *DST Bldg., 1st floor, 4-2-3 Akasaka, Minato-ku,* ☎ *03/3584–1899. Drinks start at ¥800.* ☾ *Weekdays 6 PM–2 AM, Sat. 6–11. Subway: Chiyoda Line, Akasaka.*

Garbus Cine Café. Young sophisticates, especially those with latent screen ambitions, come to this smart café for exotic coffees and oddly colored cocktails. The large plate-glass windows of the café overlook a small square, where palms of famous movie actors are imprinted in stone. The square also flickers with a digital clock flashing the time from under a water fountain. ⊠ *Hibiya Chanter, 1st floor, 1-2-2 Yūraku-chō, Chiyoda-ku,* ☎ *03/3501–3185. Coffees start at ¥600.* ☾ *Daily 10–11. Subway: Hibiya stop.*

Highlander. The Highlander Bar in the Hotel Okura purports to stock 224 different brands of Scotch whisky, 48 of them single malts. This is a smart place to meet business acquaintances or to have a civilized drink. ⊠ *Hotel Okura, 2-10-4 Tora-no-mon, Minato-ku,* ☎ *03/3505–6077. Drinks start at ¥1,100.* ☾ *Mon.–Sat. 11:30 AM–1 AM, Sun. 11:30 AM–midnight. Subway: Ginza Line, Tora-no-mon.*

The Old Imperial Bar. Comfortable and sedate, this is the pride of the Imperial Hotel, decorated with elements saved from Frank Lloyd Wright's earlier version of the building—alas, long since torn down. ⊠ *Imperial Hotel, 1-1-1 Uchisaiwai-chō, Chiyoda-ku,* ☎ *03/3504–1111. Drinks start at ¥1,000.* ☾ *Daily 11:30 AM–midnight. Subway: Hibiya stop.*

Stonefield's. A small bar that really wanted to be born a Nashville saloon, Stonefield's surrounds you with down-home hospitality and takes pride in its collection of country-and-western tapes. Now and again, it'll book a live band; drop by on one of those evenings and discover how surprisingly good Japanese pickers 'n fiddlers can be. ⊠ *Sunlight Akasaka Bldg., 4th floor, 3-21-4 Akasaka, Minato-ku,* ☎ *03/*

3583–5690. Drinks start at ¥500; a bottle of bourbon is ¥7,000. ⊙
Mon.–Sat. 7 PM–midnight. Subway: Ginza and Maru-no-uchi lines,
Akasaka-mitsuke.

Wine Bar. Racks and casks and dimly lit corners: The atmosphere at
this European-style bistro appeals to Japanese and gai-jin. This is a good
place to take a date before moving on to the Roppongi discos. ⊠ *3-
21-3 Akasaka, Minato-ku,* ☎ *3586–7186. Drinks start at ¥380.* ⊙
*Daily 5–11:30 PM. Subway: Ginza and Maru-no-uchi lines, Akasaka-
mitsuke.*

Yūraku Food Center. Inside this building and one floor up is a collection of small, popular-priced bars and restaurants where people who
work in the area go after hours. One such is the **Americana** (☎ 03/
3564–1971), where drinks start at ¥800. Farther along the hallway is
the **Ginza Swing** (☎ 03/3563–3757), which has live bands playing swing
jazz. The cover varies but is usually ¥2,800; drinks start at ¥700. The
Yūraku Food Center is one building east of the Kōtsū Kaikan Building (where the Japan National Tourist Organization has its offices);
you can recognize the latter by the circular sky lounge on the roof. ⊠
2-2 Nishi-Ginza, Chūō-ku. Subway/JR: Yūraku-chō.

Beer Halls

Kirin City. There's somewhat less glass-thumping and mock-Oktober-
fest good cheer here than at other brewery-sponsored beer halls, but
the menu (grilled chicken, fried potatoes, onion rings—stuff to wash
down with a brew) is just as good. The clientele tends to be groups of
white-collar youngsters from area offices, unwinding after work.
Bunshōdo Bldg., 2nd floor, 3-4-12 Ginza, Chūō-ku, ☎ *03/3562–
2593. Beer is ¥460.* ⊙ *Daily 11–11. Subway: Ginza stop.*

Levante Beer Hall. This is a favorite for Japanese men to stop in and
have some drinks and down a half dozen raw oysters. Over the years,
this old-fashioned beer hall has become a landmark, an anachronism
in an area known for its marble and flashing lights. Levante is in the
Ginza district, behind the Imperial Hotel and opposite the Tōkyū
Kōtsū Kaikan store. ⊠ *2-8-7 Yūraku-chō, Chiyoda-ku,* ☎ *03/3201–
2661. Beer starts at ¥560.* ⊙ *Mon.–Sat. 11:30 AM–10 PM. Subway:
Hibiya stop.*

Sapporo Lion. For a casual evening of beer and ballast—anything from
yakitori to spaghetti—the Sapporo Lion is a popular and inexpensive
choice. The entrance is off Chūō-dōri, near the Matsuzakaya depāto.
⊠ *6-10-12 Ginza, Chūō-ku,* ☎ *03/3571–2590. Beer starts at ¥590.*
⊙ *Daily 11:30 AM–11 PM. Subway: Ginza stop.*

What the Dickens. Sixteenth-century English-style pubs have been the
big trend in Tōkyō in the past few years, and this is the king of them
all, particularly for the gai-jin crowd. In a former Aum Shinri Kyō headquarters in Ebisu (the cult held responsible for the gas bomb in the Tōkyō
subway), it is nearly always packed. There are live stage acts and poetry readings (first Sunday of the month), and live music starts nightly
at 8:30. ⊠ *1-13-3 Ebisu-Nishi, Shibuya-ku, Roob 6 Bldg., 4th floor,*
☎ *03/3780–2099.* ⊙ *Sun. 3 PM–midnight, Tues.–Wed. 5 PM–1 AM,
Thurs.–Sat. 5 PM–2 AM. Subway: Hibiya Line, Ebisu.*

Discos

The disco scene is alive in Tōkyō, but less well than it was before the
uptown crowd started to feel the pinch in its discretionary income. Discos have always been ephemeral ventures, anyhow. They disappear fairly
regularly, to open again with new identities, stranger names, and newer
gimmicks. The money behind them is usually the same. Even those we've

listed here come with no guarantee that they'll be around when you arrive, but it can't hurt to investigate. Where else can you work out, survey the vinyl miniskirt brigades, and get a drink at 3 AM?

Cave. Disregard the Roppongi scene and let loose in youthful and less raunchy Shibuya at the Cave. The DJs are great, the space is small—which makes even a quiet night look hopping—and Shibuya is a much nicer place to face in the morning sunlight than Roppongi. The Cave is across from Bunkamura, at the end of Center-gai and all the izakaya. ⊠ *34-6 Udagawa-chō, Shibuya-ku,* ☎ *03/3780–0715.* ☜ *¥3,000.* ☉ *Nightly 9 PM–5:30 AM. Subway: Ginza Line, Shibuya.*

Club 99 Gaspanic. Part of the long-running Gaspanic family of clubs and bars in Roppongi, Club 99 is a good example of what the typical nightclub in Japan will provide: ever-changing music to appeal to all sorts of tastes and long hours that'll make you forget about the last train/first train dilemma. Next to Deja vu, this club is a must-see for anyone new to the Tōkyō scene. ⊠ *3-15-24 Roppongi, Minato-ku,* ☎ *03/3470–7190.* ☜ *1-drink minimum.* ☉ *Thurs.–Sat. 6 PM to 9 AM. Subway: Hibiya Line, Roppongi.*

Geoid/Flower. Geoid's way-after-hours (it opens at 5 AM) techno beats keep after-Roppongi-party clubbers going until it closes at 1 PM—the next day. It is on Telebi Asahi-dōri, halfway between Roppongi and Hiro-o. ⊠ *Togensha Visiting Bldg., basement, 3-5-5 Nishi-Azabu, Minato-ku,* ☎ *03/3479–8161.* ☜ *¥2500 (varies per event).* ☉ *Sat. 5 AM–1 PM. Subway: Hibiya Line, Roppongi.*

Maniac Love. Known by Tōkyōites for its consistently excellent techno, garage, and ambient music, Maniac Love proves that Japanese DJs have technique to support their style. It helps that they tend to become experts in their genres by collecting even the most obscure tracks. Just off Kotto-dōri, its nearest subway stop is Omotesandō. ⊠ *5-10-6 Minami-Aoyama,* ☎ *03/3406–1166.* ☜ *¥2,500.* ☉ *Nightly until 5 AM; Sat. until 10 AM; closed Wed. Subway: Ginza and Hanzōmon lines, Omotesandō.*

Milk. In the basement beneath What the Dickens pub (☞ Beer Halls, *above*), this place is a milk bar à la *Clockwork Orange*. With tables shaped like nude women and obscene inflatable goodies, this club caters to young Tōkyōites who yearn for digital sounds, techno, or even hard rock in an erotic atmosphere. Milk hosts hip live acts (John Cale did a "secret concert" here) and avant-garde events. DJs and the types of music change daily. ⊠ *1-13-3 Ebisu-Nishi, Roob 6 Bldg., basement and 2nd-level basement, Shibuya-ku,* ☎ *03/5458–2826.* ☜ *¥3,500, with 2 drinks.* ☉ *Nightly 8 PM–4 AM.*

328 (San-ni-pa). One of the most lasting discos from the early '90s, 328 hosts all genres of music. Across the street from Hobson's Ice Cream and next to the police box at the Nishi-Azabu intersection, 328 is often crowded due to its reputation as a consistently good time. It is rumored that Ryuichi Sakamoto and famous fashion designers sometimes stop by. ⊠ *3-24-20 Nishi-Azabu, basement, Minato-ku,* ☎ *03/3401–4968.* ☜ *¥2,500, with 2 drinks.* ☉ *Nightly 8 PM–5 AM. Subway: Hibiya Line, Roppongi, then a 10-min walk; from Shibuya, take a Roppongi-bound bus.*

Live Music

Blue Note Tōkyō. Young entrepreneur Tōsuke Itō acquired the Tōkyō franchise for this famed New York nightspot in 1988 and set about making it the premier jazz club in town. ⊠ *5-13-3 Minami-Aoyama, Minato-ku,* ☎ *03/3407–5781.* ☜ *Cover charge varies from ¥8,000 for relative unknowns to as high as ¥17,000 for superstars.* ☉ *2 sets a night, at 7 and 9:30. AE, DC, V. Subway: Omotesandō stop.*

Body and Soul. Owner Kyoko Seki has been a jazz fan and an impresario for nearly 20 years. There's nothing fancy about this place—just good, serious jazz, some of it played by musicians who come in after hours, when they've finished gigs elsewhere, just to jam. ⊠ *Senme Bldg., 1st floor, 3-12-3 Kita-Aoyama, Minato-ku,* ☎ *03/5466–3525.* 🍴 *Cover charge ¥3,000–¥3,500, drinks from ¥700.* ⊘ *Mon.–Sat. 7 PM–midnight. AE, MC, V. Subway: Hibiya Line, Roppongi.*

Club Quattro. More of a concert hall than a club, the Quattro does one show nightly, with a heavy accent on "ethnic" music—especially Latin and African—by both Japanese and foreign groups. Audiences tend to be young and enthusiastic. ⊠ *Parco IV Bldg., 32-13 Utagawa-chō, Shibuya-ku,* ☎ *03/3477–8750.* 🍴 *Cover charge ¥2,500–¥7,000.* ⊘ *Shows usually start at 7 PM. Subway/JR eki: Shibuya.*

Nightclubs and Cabarets

Cordon Bleu. A full-course meal, seating for about 150 that feels more intimate than its size suggests, Muhammad Ali's name in the guest book—this dinner theater has two shows nightly (7:30 and 10) with singers and topless dancers. Reservations are advised. ⊠ *6-6-4 Akasaka, Minato-ku,* ☎ *03/3582–7800.* 🍴 *¥8,000–10,000 for dinner, plus ¥4,000 cover charge for show.* ⊘ *Mon.–Sat. 7–11:30 PM. Subway: Chiyoda Line, Akasaka.*

Showboat. This small, cheerful club and its international cabaret acts are downstairs at the Hilton. The cover charge is reasonable, by Tōkyō standards, so Showboat tends to draw both from the hotel and from outside. There are two shows nightly, at 7:30 and 10. ⊠ *Tōkyō Hilton Hotel, 6-6-2 Nishi-Shinjuku, Shinjuku-ku,* ☎ *03/3344–0510.* 🍴 *Cover charge ¥2,000 for 7:30 show, ¥3,000 for 10 show. Drinks start at ¥1,000.* ⊘ *Mon.–Sat. 6 PM–midnight. Subway/JR eki: Shinjuku.*

Skyline Lounges

Pole Star Lounge. For a view of old and new Shinjuku flickering beneath you, this lounge bar on the penthouse floor of the Keiō Plaza is hard to beat. ⊠ *Keiō Plaza Inter-Continental, 2-2-1 Nishi-Shinjuku, Shinjuku-ku,* ☎ *03/3344–0111. Drinks start at ¥1,450.* ⊘ *Weekdays 5–11:30 PM, weekends 4–11:30 PM. Subway/JR eki: Shinjuku.*

Top of the Akasaka. On the 40th floor of the Akasaka Prince Hotel, you can enjoy some of the finest views of Tōkyō. If you can time your visit for dusk, the price of one drink gets you two views—the daylight sprawl of buildings and the twinkling lights of evening. ⊠ *Akasaka Prince, 1-2 Kioi-chō, Chiyoda-ku,* ☎ *03/3234–1111. Drinks start at ¥1,100.* 🍴 *Table charge ¥800 per person.* ⊘ *Weekdays 1 PM–2 AM, weekends 5 PM–midnight. Subway: Ginza and Hanzō-mon lines, Akasaka-mitsuke.*

SHOPPING

Horror stories abound about prices in Japan—and some of them are true. Yes, a cup of coffee can cost $10, if you pick the wrong coffee shop. A gift-wrapped melon from a department-store gourmet counter can cost $100. And a taxi ride from the airport to central Tōkyō does cost about $200. Take heart: The dollar has risen quite a bit against the yen over the past few years, shopping here isn't always impossibly expensive, and you can still find bargains. If you're looking for gifts and souvenirs you will still be able to find them, with a little ingenuity and effort.

Some items are better bought at home: Why go all the way to Tōkyō to buy European designer clothing? Concentrate on Japanese goods that are hard to get elsewhere, especially traditional handicrafts and fabrics. Such things can be found in areas easy to reach by public transportation. Also, try to avoid taxis: Traffic and Tōkyō's labyrinthine maze of streets make this sort of travel time-consuming and very expensive. Instead, use the city's convenient subways and trains. If time is limited, stick to hotel arcades and department stores, or make one meaningful trip to a market area that interests you. With a schedule that lets you indulge your sense of adventure, Tōkyō can be a fascinating place to explore.

Remember that in some smaller stores and markets prices might be listed with *kanji* (Japanese pictographs derived from Chinese written characters) instead of Arabic numbers. In such cases, just ask, "How much?" It's a phrase that all Japanese will recognize, because it is the name of a popular TV game show in Japan, and the clerk will either tell you, write the price for you, or display it on a calculator.

Salespeople are invariably helpful and polite. In the larger stores, they greet you with a bow when you arrive—and many of them speak at least enough English to help you find what you're looking for. There is a saying in Japan: *o-kyaku-sama wa kami-sama,* "the customer is a god"—and since the competition for your business is fierce, people do take it to heart.

Japan has an across-the-board 5% value added tax (VAT), imposed on luxury goods as well as on restaurant and hotel bills. This tax can be avoided at some duty-free shops in the city (don't forget to bring your passport). It is also waived in the duty-free shops at the international airports, but because these places tend to have higher profit margins, your tax savings there are likely to be offset by the higher markups.

Stores in Tōkyō generally open at 10 or 11 AM and close at 7 or 8 PM.

For further descriptions of shopping areas, *see* Exploring, *above.*

Shopping Districts

Ginza

Ginza was the first entertainment and shopping district in Tōkyō, dating back to the Edo period (1603–1868). Tōkyō's first department store, Mitsukoshi, was founded in this area, which once consisted of long, willow-lined avenues. The willows have long since gone, and the streets are now lined with department stores and boutiques. The exclusive stores in this area feature quality and selective merchandise at higher prices. Here it is not unusual to see a well-turned-out Japanese woman in a kimono on a shopping spree, accompanied by her daughter, who is exquisitely dressed in a Chanel suit. *Subway: Maru-no-uchi, Ginza, and Hibiya lines, Ginza stop; Yūraku-chō Line, Ginza 1chōme stop. JR Yamanote Line, Yūraku-chō Eki.*

Shibuya

This area is primarily an entertainment district filled with movie theaters, restaurants, and bars that are mostly geared toward teenagers and young adults. The shopping also caters to these groups, with many reasonably priced smaller shops and a few department stores that are casual yet chic. *Subway: Ginza Line, Hanzōmon stop. JR Yamanote Line, Harajuku Eki.*

Shinjuku

This area is not without its honky-tonk and sleaze, but it also has some of the city's most fashionable department stores. Shinjuku's mer-

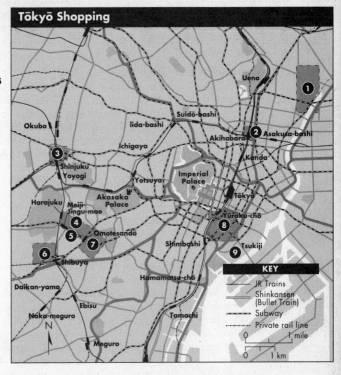

Tōkyō Shopping

chandise reflects the crowds—young, stylish, and hip. In the station area, you will also find a number of discount electronics and home appliance outlets. *Subway: Maru-no-uchi and Tōei Shinjuku lines, Shinjuku stop. JR Yamanote Line, Shinjuku Eki.*

Harajuku

The average shopper in Harajuku is under 20; a substantial percentage are under 16. This shopping and residential area extends southeast from Harajuku station along both sides of Omotesandō and Meiji-dōri; the shops that target the youngest consumers concentrate especially on the narrow street called Takeshita-dōri. A wild sense of fashion prevails here, from the '50s greaser look to punk and postmodern. Most stores focus on moderately priced clothing and accessories, with a lot of kitsch mixed in, but there are also a number of upscale fashion houses in the area. *Subway: Meiji Jingū-mae (Chiyoda Line, Meiji Jingū-mae stop. JR Yamanote Line, Harajuku Eki.*

Omotesandō

Known as the Champs-Elysées of Tōkyō, this long, wide avenue, which runs from Aoyama-dōri to Meiji Jingū, is lined with cafés and designer boutiques. There are also a number of antiques and print shops here, as well as one of the best toy shops in Tōkyō—Kiddyland (☞ Aoyama and Harajuku's Good Walk, *above*). Closed to traffic on Sundays, Omotesandō is perfect for browsing, window shopping, and lingering over a café au lait before strolling to your next activity. *Subway: Chiyoda and Hanzōmon lines, Omotesandō stop.*

Aoyama

Shopping in Aoyama is aesthetically pleasing, and it can empty your wallet in no time: This is where many of the leading Japanese and Western designers have their cash-cow boutiques. European and American imports will be high, but Japanese designer clothes are usually 30%–

40% lower than they are elsewhere. Aoyama tends to be a showcase, not merely of couture but of the latest concepts in commercial architecture and interior design. *Subway: Chiyoda and Hanzōmon lines, Omotesandō stop.*

Akihabara and Jimbō-chō

For the ultimate one-stop display of photographic and electronic gadgetry, Akihabara is high-tech heaven, block after block of multistory buildings filled with everything that beeps, buzzes, computes, or responds to digital suggestions. Portable tape and CD players, for example, were showcased here long before they made it across the ocean. The best deals in Japan can be found in Akihabara, but prices are generally comparable to those in American discount stores. West of Akihabara, the bookstores of Jimbō-chō make up Tōkyō's book district. You'll find pretty much whatever you're looking for, in Japanese books, from dictionaries to art books to rare books and prints. *Subway: Hibiya Line, Akihabara and Jimbō-chō stops. JR Yamanote Line, Akihabara Eki.*

Asakusa

While sightseeing in this area, take the time to stroll through its arcades. Many of the goods here are the kind of souvenirs you would expect to find in any tourist trap, but if you look a little harder, you will find shops that have tortoiseshell accessories, beautiful wooden combs, delicate fans, and other items of fine traditional craftsmanship. Venture on to some of the back streets, where small shops have been making these things for generations (☞ Miscellaneous *under* Books, Crafts, and Gift Items, *below*). There are also the cookware shops of Kappa-bashi-dōri, with everything from sushi knives to plastic lobster. *Subway: Tōei Asakusa Line, Asakusa stop; Ginza Line, Asakusa and Tawara-machi stops.*

Tsukiji

Best known for its daily fish-market auctions, Tsukiji also has a warren of streets that carry useful, everyday Japanese items that serve as a lens onto the lives of the Japanese. This is a fascinating area to poke around after seeing the fish auction and before stopping in the neighborhood for a fresh-as-it-can-be sushi lunch.

Books, Crafts, and Gift Items

Books

Bookstores of Jimbō-chō. If you love books, put the shops on the quarter-mile strip of Yasukuni-dōri high on your Tōkyō itinerary. The Japanese print aesthetic and concern with paper and production quality put Japanese books in a category of their own. If you don't read Japanese, art books, coffee-table books, and old prints make a trip here worthwhile. *Subway: Chiyoda, Tōei Mita, and Hanzō-mon lines, Jimbō-chō.*

ENGLISH-LANGUAGE BOOKSTORES

Most top hotels have a bookstore with a modest selection of English-language books. For a wide selection of English and other non-Japanese-language books, **Kinokuniya Bookstore** (⌧ 3-17-7 Shinjuku, Shinjuku-ku, ☎ 03/3354–0131) has some 40,000 books and magazine titles. It is closed the third Wednesday of each month, except April and December. Kinokuniya also has a branch store in the Tōkyū Plaza Building (⌧ 1-2-2 Dōgenzaka, Shibuya-ku, ☎ 03/3463–3241) across from the Shibuya Station. The **Jena Bookstore** (⌧ 5-6-1 Ginza, Chūō-ku, ☎ 03/3571–2980) carries a wide range of books as well and is near the Ginza and Maru-no-uchi subway line exits in Ginza. **Maruzen**

(✉ 2-3-10 Nihombashi, Chūō-ku, ☎ 03/3272–7211), one of Japan's largest booksellers, prospers in large part on its imports—which are sold at grossly inflated rates of exchange. On the second floor, you can find books in Western languages on any subject from Romanesque art to embryology. There's an extensive collection here of books about Japan, and also a small crafts center. The store is on Chūō-dōri south of the Tōzai and Ginza lines' Nihombashi stops. **Yaesu Book Center** (✉ 2-5-1 Yaesu, Chūō-ku, ☎ 03/3281–1811) is near Tōkyō Eki and the Imperial Palace.

Ceramics

Granted, pottery and fine ceramics can fill up and weigh down your luggage, but the shops will pack wares safely for travel—and they do make wonderful gifts. The Japanese have been making extraordinary pottery for more than 2,000 years, but the art began to flourish especially in the 16th century, with the popularity and demand for tea ceremony utensils. Feudal lords competed for possession of the finest pieces, and distinctive styles of pottery developed in regions all over the country. Some of the more prominent styles are those of Arita in Kyūshū, with painted patterns of flowers and birds; Mashiko, in Tochigi Prefecture, with its rough textures and simple, warm colors; rugged Hagi ware from the eponymous Western Honshū city; and Kasama, in Ibaraki Prefecture, with glazes made from ash and ground rocks. Tōkyō's specialty shops and department stores carry fairly complete selections of these and other wares.

Tachikichi. Pottery from different localities around the country is sold here. ✉ *5-5-8 Ginza, Chūō-ku,* ☎ *03/3571–2924.* ⊙ *Mon.–Sat. 11–6:30. Subway: Hibiya and Tōei-Asakusa lines, Higashi-Ginza stop.*

Kisso. This store has an excellent variety of ceramics in modern design, using traditional glazes, as well as a restaurant and a gift shop. ✉ *Axis Bldg., basement, 5-17-1 Roppongi, Minato-ku,* ☎ *03/3582–4191.* ⊙ *Mon.–Sat. 11:30–2 and 5:30–10. Subway: Hibiya Line, Roppongi stop.*

Dolls

Many types of traditional dolls are available in Japan, each with its own charm. **Kokeshi** dolls are long, cylindrical, painted, and made of wood, with no arms or legs. Fine examples of Japanese folk art, they date from the Edo period (1603–1868). **Daruma** are papier-mâché dolls with rounded bottoms and faces that are often painted with amusing expressions. They are constructed so that no matter how you push them, they roll and remain upright. Legend has it that they are modeled after a Buddhist priest who remained seated in the lotus position for so long that his arms and legs atrophied. **Hakata** dolls, made in Kyūshū's Hakata City, are ceramic figurines in traditional costume, such as geisha, samurai, or festival dancers.

Kyūgetsu. In business for more than a century, Kyūgetsu offers every kind of doll imaginable. ✉ *1-20-4 Yanagibashi, Taitō-ku,* ☎ *03/3861–5511.* ⊙ *Weekdays 9:15–6, weekends 9:15–5. Subway: Tōei-Asakusa Line, Asakusa-bashi.*

Sukeroku. Come to this shop for traditional handmade Edokko dolls and models, clothed in the costumes of the Edo period. ✉ *2-3-1 Asakusa, Taitō-ku,* ☎ *03/8844–0577. Subway: Ginza Line, Asakusa stop.*

Electronics

The area around Akihabara Station has more than 200 stores with discount prices on stereos, refrigerators, CD players, and anything else that can be plugged in. The larger of these have sections or floors (or even whole annexes) of goods made for export. These products come with instructions in most major languages, and if you have a tourist visa in your passport, you can purchase them duty free. Two such stores are **Yamagiwa** (⊠ 4-1-1 Soto Kanda, Chiyoda-ku; ☎ 03/3253–2111; JR Akihabara Eki), open daily 10–7:30, and **Minami** (4-3-3 Soto Kanda, Chiyoda-ku, ☎ 03/3255–3730; JR Akihabara Eki), open weekdays 10:30–7, weekends 10–7.

Consider Shinjuku as well. Two mammoth discount camera stores, **Yodobashi** (⊠ 1-11-1 Nishi-Shinjuku, Shinjuku-ku) and **Doi** (⊠ 1-18-27 Nishi-Shinjuku, Shinjuku-ku), are within a block of the Shinjuku Eki, and they carry an astounding array of consumer electronics.

Folk Crafts

Japanese folk crafts, called *mingei*—among them bamboo vases and baskets, fabrics, paper boxes, dolls, and toys—achieve a unique beauty in their simple and sturdy designs. Be aware, however, that simple does not mean cheap. Long hours of loving hand labor go into these objects. And every year, there are fewer and fewer craftspeople left, producing their work in smaller and smaller quantities. Include these items in your budget ahead of time: The best of it—worth every cent—can be fairly expensive.

Bingo-ya. A complete selection of crafts from all over Japan can be found here. ⊠ *10-6 Wakamatsu-chō, Shinjuku,* ☎ *03/3202–8778.* ☉ *Tues.– Sun. 10–7. Subway: Maru-no-uchi Line, Waseda stop.*

Japan Traditional Craft Center. This gallery is a good place to learn about the range and variety of Japanese folk crafts nationwide, from the works themselves on sale and from the center's library of documentary films on video. ⊠ *Plaza 246, 2nd floor, 3-1-1 Minami-Aoyama, Minato-ku,* ☎ *03/3403–2460.* ☉ *Fri.–Wed. 10–6. Subway: Ginza and Hanzō-mon lines, Gaien-mae stop.*

Oriental Bazaar. Here are three floors of just about everything you might want in a traditional Japanese (or Chinese or Korean) handicraft souvenir, from painted screens to pottery to antique chests, at fairly reasonable prices. Kimonos are one flight down. ⊠ *5-9-13 Jingū-mae, Shibuya-ku,* ☎ *03/3400–3933.* ☉ *Fri.–Wed. 9:30–6:30. Subway: Chiyoda Line, Meiji Jingū-mae.*

Foodstuffs and Wares

This hybrid category includes everything from crackers and pickled foods to standard restaurant supply items like cast-iron kettles, paper lanterns, and essential food-kitsch like plastic sushi sets. Unless otherwise noted, shops below are centered either on Asakusa's Kappa-bashi-dōri (subway: Ginza Line, Tawara-machi stop) or around the Tsukiji fish market (subway: Hibiya Line, Tsukiji stop).

The Backstreet Shops of Tsukiji. In Tsukiji, between the Central Wholesale Market and Harumi-dōri, among the many fishmongers you'll also find stores where you can buy pickles, tea, crackers, kitchen knives, baskets, and crockery. For a picture of real Japanese life, it is not to be missed. ⊠ *5-2-1 Tsukiji, Chūō-ku.*

Biken Kōgei. If you want to take home an *aka-chōchin* (a folding red paper lantern) like the ones that hang in inexpensive bar and restaurant fronts, look no further. ⊠ *1-5-16 Nishi-Asakusa, Taitō-ku,* ☎ *03/ 3842–1646.* ☉ *Mon.–Sat. 9–6, Sun. 11–4.*

Iida Shōten. Solid, traditional *nambu* ware, such as embossed cast-iron kettles and casseroles, is Iida Shōten's specialty. ⊠ *2-21-6 Nishi-*

Asakusa, Taitō-ku, ☎ *03/3842–3757.* ⊙ *Mon.–Sat. 9–5:30, Sun. 10–5.*

Kondo Shōten. Your kitchen wouldn't quite be complete without a bamboo tray, basket, scoop, or container of some sort. If you are of that mind, stop in at Kondo Shōten. ⊠ *3-1-13 Matsugaya, Taitō-ku,* ☎ *03/ 3841–3372.* ⊙ *Weekdays and Sun. 9–5:30, Sat. 9–5.*

Maizuru Company. This is the sine qua non of counterfeit cuisine: all of that plastic food you'll see in restaurant fronts nationwide. Stop in to pick up plastic sushi or udon or unagi—you'll never (or always) go hungry. ⊠ *1-5-17 Nishi-Asakusa, Taitō-ku,* ☎ *03/3843–1686.* ⊙ *Daily 9–6.*

Nishimura. This shop specializes in *noren*—the curtains that shops and restaurants hang to announce that they are open. Typical fabric is cotton, linen, or silk, which is most often dyed to order for individual shops. The store also sells premade noren of an entertaining variety for your decorating pleasure. ⊠ *1-10-10 Matsugaya, Taitō-ku,* ☎ *03/3844–9954.* ⊙ *Mon.–Sat. 9–5.*

Tokiwa-dō. Come here to buy some of Tōkyō's most famous souvenirs: *kaminari okoshi* (thunder crackers), made of rice, millet, sugar, and beans. The shop is on the west side of Asakusa's Thunder God Gate, the Kaminari-mon entrance to Sensō-ji. ⊠ *1-3 Asakusa, Taitō-ku, Subway: Ginza Line, Asakusa stop.*

Tsubaya Hōchōten. Tsubaya sells professional-quality cutlery for professionals. Its remarkable array of *hōchō* (knives) is designed for every imaginable use, as the art of food presentation in Japan requires a great variety of cutting implements. The best of these carry the Traditional Craft Association seal: hand-forged tools of tempered blue steel, set in handles banded with deer horn to keep the wood from splitting. ⊠ *3-7-2 Nishi-Asakusa, Taitō-ku,* ☎ *03/3845–2005.* ⊙ *Mon.–Sat. 9–6, Sun. 9–5.*

Union Company. Coffee paraphernaliacs, beware: Roasters, grinders, beans, flasks, and filters of every shape and description will make your eyes bulge in anticipation of the caffeine ritual. Japanese *kōhi* (coffee) wares are ingenious and remarkable. ⊠ *2-22-6 Nishi-Asakusa, Taitō-ku,* ☎ *03/3842–4041.* ⊙ *Mon.–Sat. 9–6, Sun. 10–5.*

Yamamoto Nori-ten. The Japanese are resourceful in their uses of products from the sea. *Nori,* the paper-thin dried seaweed used to wrap *maki* sushi and *onigiri* (rice balls), is the specialty here. A tip if you plan to bring some home with you: Buy unroasted nori and toast it yourself at home; the flavor of the nori will be far better than that of the pre-roasted sheets. ⊠ *1-6-3 Nihombashi Muro-machi, Chūō-ku, no phone. Subway: Hanzō-mon and Ginza lines, Mitsukoshi-mae.*

Kimono

Unless they work in traditional Japanese restaurants, Japanese women now wear kimono mainly on special occasions, such as weddings or graduations, and like tuxedos in the United States, they are often rented instead of purchased. Kimono are extremely expensive and difficult to maintain. A wedding kimono, for example, can cost as much as ¥1 million.

Most visitors, naturally unwilling to pay this much for a garment that they probably want to use as a bathrobe or a conversation piece, settle for a secondhand or antique silk kimono. These vary in price and quality. You can pay as little as ¥1,000 in a flea market, but to find one in decent condition, you should expect to pay about ¥10,000. Cotton summer kimono called *yukata*, however, with attractive geometric blue-and-white designs, can be bought brand-new for about ¥8,000.

Hayashi. This store specializes in ready-made kimonos, sashes, and dyed yukata. ⊠ *1-7-23 Uchisaiwai-chō, Chiyoda-ku*, ☎ *03/3501–4014.* ☉ *Mon.–Sat. 10–7, Sun. 10–6. Subway: Hibiya stop.*

Lacquerware

For its history, diversity, and fine workmanship, lacquerware rivals ceramics as the traditional Japanese craft nonpareil. One warning: Lacquerware thrives on humidity. Cheaper pieces usually have plastic rather than wood underneath. Because these won't shrink and crack in dry climates, they make safer—and no less attractive—buys.

Inachu. Specializing in lacquerware from the town of Wajima, a famous crafts center on the Noto Peninsula (☞ Chapter 6), this is one of the most elegant (and expensive) crafts shops in Tōkyō. ⊠ *1-5-2 Akasaka, Minato-ku*, ☎ *03/3582–4451.* ☉ *Mon.–Sat. 10–6. Subway: Chiyoda and Maru-no-uchi lines, Kokkai Gijidō-mae stop.*

Miscellaneous

Handmade combs, towels, and cosmetics are other uniquely Japanese treasures to consider picking up while in Tōkyō.

Fuji-ya. Master textile creator Keiji Kawakama's cotton *tenugui* (teh-*noo*-goo-ee) hand towels are collectors items, often as not framed instead of used as towels. Kawakama is also an expert on the history of tenugui of his Edo-period craft. The shop is near the corner of Dembō-in-dōri on Naka-mise-dōri. ⊠ *2-2-15 Asakusa, Taitō-ku*, ☎ *03/3841–2283. Subway: Ginza Line, Asakusa stop.*

Hyaku-suke. This 100-year-old-plus cosmetics shop sells little of the nightingale powder these days that ladies used in the Edo period, but its theatrical makeup for Kabuki actors, geisha, and traditional weddings—as well as interesting things to fetch home like seaweed shampoo and camellia oil, handmade wool cosmetic brushes, bound with cherry wood—make it a worthy addition to your Asakusa shopping itinerary. ⊠ *2-2-14 Asakusa, Taitō-ku*, ☎ *03/3841–7058.* ☉ *Wed.–Mon. 11–5. Subway: Ginza Line, Asakusa stop.*

Jusan-ya. A shop selling handmade boxwood combs, this business was started in 1736 by a samurai who couldn't support himself in the martial arts. It has been in the same family ever since. Jusan-ya is on Shinobazu-dōri a few doors west of its intersection with Chūō-dōri in Ueno. ⊠ *2-12-21 Ueno, Taitō-ku*, ☎ *03/3831–3238. Subway: Ginza Line, Ueno-hirokō-ji; JR Ueno Eki.*

Naka-ya. If you want to equip yourself for Sensō-ji's annual Sanja Festival in May in Asakusa, this is the place to come. Best buys here are *sashiko hanten*, which are thick, woven firemen's jackets, and *happi* coats, cotton tunics printed in bright colors with Japanese characters or *ukiyo-e* wood-block pictures, which are available in children's sizes. ⊠ *2-2-12 Asakusa, Taitō-ku*, ☎ *03/3841–7877. Subway: Ginza Line, Asakusa stop.*

Yono-ya. Traditional Japanese coiffures and wigs are very complicated, and they require a variety of tools to shape them properly. Tasumi Minekawa is the current master at Yono-ya—the family line goes back 300 years—who deftly crafts and decorates a stunning array of very fine boxwood combs. ⊠ *1-37-10 Asakusa, Taitō-ku*, ☎ *03/3844–1755. Subway: Ginza Line, Asakusa stop.*

Paper

What packs light and flat in your suitcase, won't break, doesn't cost much, and makes a great gift? The answer is traditional handmade *washi*, which the Japanese make in thousands of colors, textures, and designs, and fashion into an astonishing array of useful and decorative objects.

Kyūkyodō. Kyūkyodō has been in business since 1663—on the Ginza since 1880—selling its wonderful variety of handmade Japanese papers, paper products, incense, brushes, and other materials for calligraphy. ⊠ *5-7-4 Ginza, Chūo-ku,* ☎ *03/3571–4429. Subway: Ginza and Hibiya lines, Ginza.*

Ōzu Gallery. In business since the 17th century, this shop has one of the largest washi (paper) showrooms in the city and its own gallery of antique papers. ⊠ *2-6-3 Nihombashi-Honchō, Chūo-ku,* ☎ *03/3663–8788.* ⊙ *Mon.–Sat. 10–6. Subway: Mitsukoshi-mae, Ginza Line.*

Yūshima no Kobayashi. Here you can also tour a papermaking workshop and learn the art of *origami*, paper folding. ⊠ *1-7-14 Yūshima, Bunkyō-ku,* ☎ *03/3811–4025.* ⊙ *Mon.–Sat. 9–5. Subway: Chiyoda Line, Yūshima stop.*

Pearls

Japan remains one of the best places in the world to buy cultured pearls. They will not be inexpensive, but pearls of the same quality cost considerably more elsewhere. It is best to go to a reputable dealer where you know that quality will be high and you will not be misled.

Mikimoto. Kokichi Mikimoto created his technique for cultured pearls in 1893. Since then, the name Mikimoto has become associated with the best quality in the industry. Prices are high, but design and workmanship are uniformly first-rate. ⊠ *4-5-5 Ginza, Chūo-ku,* ☎ *03/3535–4611.* ⊙ *Thurs.–Tues. 10:30–6:30. Subway: Ginza stop.*

Tasaki Pearl Gallery. Tasaki offers pearls at slightly lower prices than does Mikimoto. The store has several showrooms and offers tours that demonstrate the technique of culturing pearls and explain how to maintain and care for them. ⊠ *1-3-3 Akasaka, Minato-ku,* ☎ *03/5561–8881.* ⊙ *Daily 9–6:30. Subway: Chiyoda and Maru-no-uchi lines, Kokkai Gijidō-mae.*

Toys

Hakuhinkan (Toy Park). This is reputedly the largest toy shop in Japan. It's on Chūo-dōri, the main axis of the Ginza shopping area. ⊠ *8-8-11 Ginza, Chūo-ku,* ☎ *03/3571–8008.* ⊙ *Daily 11–8. Subway: Ginza and Tōei Asakusa lines, Shimbashi stop.*

Arcades and Shopping Centers

If you do not have the time or energy to dash about Tōkyō in search of the perfect gifts, there are arcades and shopping centers that carry a wide selection of merchandise. Most of these are used to dealing with gai-jin.

Axis. On the first floor of this Gaien-higashi-dōri complex in Roppongi, **Living Motif** is a home-furnishings shop with high-tech foreign and Japanese goods of exquisite design. **Nuno,** on the basement floor, is a fabric shop that sells traditional Japanese materials with modern touches. The fabrics are all creations of Junichi Arai, who once designed fabrics for such famous Japanese designers as Rei Kawakubo of Comme des Garçons and Issey Miyake. Be sure to look at the restaurant **Kisso,** which sells, along with lacquered chopsticks and fine baskets, an extraordinary selection of unique, modern handmade ceramics in contemporary designs, shapes, and colors. *5-17-1 Roppongi, Minato-ku Subway: Hibiya Line, Roppongi stop.*

International Shopping Arcade. This collection of shops in Hibiya has a range of goods—including cameras, electronics, pearls, and kimono—and a sales staff with excellent English. The arcade is conveniently located near the Imperial Hotel, and the shops are all tax-free. ✉ *1-7-3 Uchisaiwai-chō, Chiyoda-ku. Subway: Hibiya stop.*

Nishi-Sandō. This Asakusa arcade has kimonos and yukata fabrics, traditional accessories, fans, and festival costumes at very reasonable prices. It runs east of the area's movie theaters, between Rok-ku and the Sensō-ji complex. ✉ *Asakusa 2-chōme, Taitō-ku. Subway: Ginza Line, Asakusa stop.*

Boutiques

Japanese boutiques pay as much attention to interior design and lighting as they do to the clothing they sell; like anywhere else, it's the image that moves the merchandise. Although many Japanese designers are represented in the major upscale department stores, you will probably enjoy your shopping more in the elegant boutiques of Aoyama and Omotesandō—most of which are conveniently within walking distance of one another.

Comme Des Garçons. This is one of the earliest and still most popular "minimalist" design houses, where you can get almost any kind of $70 tank top you want, as long as it's black. ✉ *5-11-5 Minami-Aoyama, Minato-ku,* ☎ *03/3407–2480.* ☉ *Daily 11–8. Subway: Omotesandō stop.*

From 1st Building. This building houses the boutiques of several of Japan's leading designers, including **Issey Miyake** and **Alpha Cubic,** as well as several smart restaurants. "Produced" by Yasuhiro Hamano, whose atelier designs many of Tōkyō's trendiest commercial spaces, From 1st is one of the earliest and best examples of the city's chic vertical malls. ✉ *5-3-10 Minami-Aoyama, Minato-ku. Subway: Omotesandō stop.*

Hanae Mori Building. This glass-mirrored structure, designed by Kenzō Tange, houses the designs of the doyenne of Japanese fashion, Mori Hanae, whose clothing has a classic look with a European influence. The café on the first floor is a good vantage point for people-watching, Harajuku's favorite sport. ✉ *3-6-1 Kita-Aoyama, Minato-ku,* ☎ *03/3406–1021.* ☉ *Daily 10:30–7. Subway: Omotesandō stop.*

Koshino Junko. Come here for sophisticated clothing and accessories with a European accent. ✉ *6-5-36 Minami-Aoyama, Minato-ku,* ☎ *03/3406–7370.* ☉ *Tues.–Sun. 10–7. Subway: Omotesandō stop.*

Depāto

Today, most Japanese department stores are part of conglomerates that own railways, real estate, and even baseball teams. These stores often include travel agencies, theaters, and art galleries. You can easily spend an afternoon or an entire day without having to leave the premises. There are reasonably priced restaurants on the upper or basement floor, with coffee shops strategically located in between.

Major department stores accept credit cards and provide shipping services. Some staff will speak English. If you are having communication difficulties, someone will eventually come to the rescue. On the first floor you will invariably find a general information booth with useful maps of the store in English.

A visit to a Japanese department store is not merely a shopping excursion—it's a lesson in Japanese culture. Arrive just before opening hours, and you will witness a ceremony with all of the pomp of the changing of the guard at Buckingham Palace. Promptly on the hour, two immaculately groomed young women will face the customers from inside, bow ceremoniously, and open the doors. As you walk through the store, you will find that everyone is standing at attention, in postures of nearly reverent welcome. Notice the uniform angle of incline: Many stores have training sessions to teach their new employees the precise and proper degree at which to bend from the waist.

For yet another lesson, head for the foodstuffs and gourmet specialty departments on the basement floor. No Japanese housewife in her right mind would shop here regularly for her groceries. A brief exploration, however, will give you a pretty good picture of what she might select for a special occasion—and the astonishing price she's prepared to pay for it. Many stalls have small samples out on the counter, and nobody will raise a fuss if you help yourself, even if you make no purchase.

Most major department stores close one or two days a month, different stores on different days of the week—but normally on Tuesdays or Wednesdays. These schedules vary considerably; in holiday gift-giving seasons, for example, they may be open every day. In the listings below, we've simply indicated (in parentheses) the day on which you *might* find the store closed. To be on the safe side, call ahead.

Ginza/Nihombashi

Matsuya. The slightly frazzled presentation here is a welcome change from the generally refined and immaculately ordered shopping in the Ginza/Nihombashi area. The merchandise at Matsuya is meant for a younger crowd, and shoppers with the patience to comb through the hordes of goods will be rewarded with many finds, particularly in women's clothing. ⊠ *3-6-1 Ginza, Chūō-ku,* ☎ *03/3567–1211.* ☽ *Sun., Mon., Wed. 10:30–7:30, Thurs.–Sat. 10:30–8. Subway: Ginza stop.*

Matsuzakaya. The Matsuzakaya conglomerate was founded in Nagoya and still commands the loyalties of shoppers with origins in western Japan. Style-conscious Tōkyōites tend to find the sense of fashion here a bit countrified. ⊠ *6-10-1 Ginza, Chūō-ku,* ☎ *03/3572–1111.* ☽ *Mon., Tues., and Thurs.–Sat. 10:30–7:30, Sun. 10:30–7. Subway: Ginza stop.*

Mitsukoshi. Founded in 1673 as a dry-goods store, Mitsukoshi later played one of the leading roles in introducing Western merchandise to Japan. It has retained its image of quality and excellence, with a particularly strong representation of Western fashion designers, such as Chanel, Lanvin, and Givenchy. Mitsukoshi also has a fine selection of traditional Japanese goods. ⊠ *1-41 Nihombashi Muro-machi, Chūō-ku (subway: Mitsukoshi-mae),* ☎ *03/3241–3311.* ☽ *Tues.–Sun. 10–7:30.* ⊠ *4-6-16 Ginza, Chūō-ku (subway: Ginza),* ☎ *03/3562–1111.* ☽ *Tues.–Sun. 10–7:30.*

Takashimaya. The kimono department here, one of the best in Tōkyō, draws its share of brides-to-be to shop for their weddings. In addition to a complete selection of traditional crafts, antiques, and curios, Takashimaya sells very fine Japanese and Western designer goods, and so has a broad, sophisticated appeal. ⊠ *2-4-1 Nihombashi, Chūō-ku,* ☎ *03/3211–4111.* ☽ *Mon., Tues., Thurs., Fri. 10–7, weekends 10–6:30). Subway: Ginza stop.*

Wako. Deftly avoiding the classification of a mere department store by confining itself to a limited selections of goods at the top end of the market, Wako is particularly known for its glassware, jewelry, and accessories. It is also known for its lovely saleswomen, who, interestingly enough, tend to marry well-to-do customers. ⊠ *4-5-11 Ginza, Chūō-ku,* ☎ *03/3562–2111.* ⊙ *Mon.–Sat. 10:30–6. Subway: Ginza stop.*

Shibuya

Parco. Owned by Seibu (☞ *below*), Parco is actually not one store but four, all located near one another. Parco Part 1, Part 2, Part 3, and Part 4, as they are called, are in fact vertical malls filled with small retail stores and boutiques. Parts 1 and 4 cater to a very young crowd, Part 2 houses mainly designer fashions, and Part 3 sells a mixture of men's and women's fashions and household goods. ⊠ *15-1 Udagawa-chō, Shibuya-ku,* ☎ *03/3464–5111.* ⊙ *Daily 10–8:30. Subway: Ginza and Hanzō-mon lines, Shibuya stop.*

Seibu. The mammoth main branch of this department store—where even many Japanese customers get lost—is in Ikebukuro. The Shibuya branch, which still carries an impressive array of merchandise, is smaller and more manageable. Seibu is the flagship operation of a conglomerate that owns a railway line and a baseball team, the Seibu Lions. When the Lions win the pennant, prepare to go shopping: All of the Seibu stores have major sales the following day. This store has an excellent selection of household goods, from furniture to china and lacquerware. ⊠ *21-1 Udagawa-chō, Shibuya-ku,* ☎ *03/3462–0111.* ⊙ *Mon., Tues., Thurs., weekends 10–8, Fri. 10–9. Subway: Ginza and Hanzō-mon lines, Shibuya stop.*

Tōkyū. A standard department store, Tōkyū offers a good selection of imported clothing, accessories, and home furnishings. ⊠ *2-24-1 Dōgen-zaka, Shibuya-ku,* ☎ *03/3477–3111.* ⊙ *Wed.–Mon. 10–8. Subway: Ginza and Hanzō-mon lines, Shibuya stop.*

Tōkyū Hands. Known commonly as just "Hands," this do-it-yourself and hobby store carries an excellent selection of carpentry tools, sewing accessories, kitchen goods, plants, and other related merchandise. The toy department is unbearably cute, and the stationery department has a comprehensive selection of Japanese papers. ⊠ *12-18 Udagawa-chō, Shibuya-ku,* ☎ *03/5489–5111.* ⊙ *Tues.–Sun. 10–8. Subway: Ginza and Hanzō-mon lines, Shibuya stop.*

Shinjuku

Isetan. Often called the Bloomingdale's of Japan—a description that doesn't quite do this store justice—Isetan has become a nearly universal favorite, with one of the most complete selections of Japanese designers in one place. If you're looking for distinctive looks without paying designer prices, the store carries a wide range of knockoff brands. But expect to look long and hard for something that fits; these clothes are made specifically for the Japanese market. Ceramics, stationery, and furniture here are generally of high quality and interesting design; the folk-crafts department carries a small but good selection of fans, table mats, and other gifts. ⊠ *3-14-1 Shinjuku, Shinjuku-ku,* ☎ *03/3352–1111.* ⊙ *Thurs.–Tues. 10–7:30. Subway: Shinjuku.*

Keiō. This no-nonsense department store has a standard but complete selection of merchandise. A me-too operation, it seems somehow to have avoided creating an image uniquely its own. ⊠ *1-1-4 Nishi-Shinjuku, Shinjuku-ku,* ☎ *03/3342–2111.* ⊙ *Fri.–Wed. 10–7. Subway: Shinjuku.*

Marui. Marui is not so much a department store as a group of specialty stores that focus on young fashions and household effects. Wildly successful for its easy credit policies, Marui is where you go when you've just landed your first job, moved into your first apartment, and need to outfit yourself presentably on the cheap. Twice a year, in February and July, prices are slashed dramatically in major clearance sales; if you are in the neighborhood, you will know exactly when the sales are taking place: The lines will extend into the street and around the block. (Let it not be said that Japanese men do not care about fashion. The most enthusiastic customers line up from 6 AM for the men's sales.) ⊠ *3-30-16 Shinjuku, Shinjuku-ku,* ☎ *03/3354–0101.* ⊙ *Thurs.–Tues. 11–8. Subway: Shinjuku.*

Odakyu. Slightly snazzier than neighboring Keiō (☞ *above*), Odakyu is a very family-oriented store, particularly good for children's clothing. Across the street from the main building is Odakyu Halc, with a varied selection of home furnishings and interior goods on its upper floors. ⊠ *1-1-3 Nishi-Shinjuku, Shinjuku-ku,* ☎ *03/3342–1111.* ⊙ *Wed.–Mon. 10–7:30. Subway: Shinjuku.*

TŌKYŌ A TO Z

Arriving and Departing

By Bus
Most bus arrivals and departures are at Tōkyō Eki or Shinjuku Bus Station.

By Plane
Tōkyō has two airports, Narita and Haneda. **Narita Kūkō** is 80 km (50 mi) northeast of Tōkyō and serves all international flights, except those operated by (Taiwan's) China Airways, which uses Haneda Kūkō. Narita added a new terminal building in 1992, which has somewhat eased the burden on it, but it can still be bottlenecked. In both wings, money exchange counters are located in the wall between the customs inspection area and the arrival lobby. In the shopping-restaurant area between the two wings is the Japan National Tourist Organization's Tourist Information Center, where you can get free maps, brochures, and other information. Directly across from the customs area exits at both terminals are the ticket counters for Airport Limousine Buses to Tōkyō (☞ By Bus, *above*).

Haneda Kūkō, 16 km (10 mi) southwest of Tōkyō, serves all domestic flights. At Haneda, Japan Airlines (JAL), All Nippon Airways (ANA), and Japan Air System have extensive domestic flight networks. For information on arrival and departure times, call the individual airlines.

See Air Travel *in* the Gold Guide for more information on Tōkyō's airports.

BETWEEN NARITA AIRPORT AND CENTER CITY

By Bus. Two services, the **Airport Limousine Bus** and the **Airport Express Bus,** run from Narita to major hotels in the $$$$ category (☞ Lodging, *above*) in the city's different areas, and to the JR Tōkyō and Shinjuku stations; the fare is ¥2,700–¥3,050, depending on your destination. Even if you are not staying at one of the route's drop-off points, you can take the bus as far as the one closest to your hotel and then use a taxi for the remaining distance. Keep in mind that these buses only run every hour, and they do not run after 11 PM. The trip is scheduled for 70–90 minutes but can take two hours in heavy traffic. Ticket counters are in the arrival lobbies, directly across from the customs area exit. Buses leave from platforms just outside terminal exits, exactly on schedule; the departure time is on the ticket.

A bus to the Tōkyō City Air Terminal (TCAT) leaves approximately every 10–15 minutes from 6:45 AM to 11 PM; the fare is ¥2,900, and you can buy tickets at the hotel bus ticket counter. TCAT is in Nihombashi in north-central Tōkyō, a bit far from most destinations, but from here you can connect directly with the Suitengū station on the Hanzōmon subway line, then to anywhere in the subway network. A taxi from TCAT to most of the major hotels will cost about ¥3,000.

By Taxi. Taxis are rarely used between Narita Airport and central Tōkyō—at ¥20,000 or more depending on traffic, and where you're going, the cost is prohibitive. Station-wagon taxis do exist, and the meter rates are the same as for the standard sedans, but they are not always available. Limousines are also very expensive; from Narita Airport to the Imperial Hotel downtown, for example, will set you back about ¥35,000.

By Train. Trains run every 30–40 minutes between Narita Airport Train Station and the Keisei-Ueno Station on the privately owned Keisei Line. The Keisei Skyliner takes 57 minutes and costs ¥1,920. The first Skyliner leaves at 9:20 AM, the last at 9:58 PM. It only makes sense to take the Keisei, however, if your final destination is in the Ueno area; otherwise, you must change to the Tōkyō subway system or the Japan Railways loop line at Ueno (the station is adjacent to the Keisei-Ueno Station) or take a cab to your hotel.

Japan Railways (JR East Infoline ☎ 03/3423–0111) has greatly improved its airport service with trains that stop at both terminals. The fastest and most comfortable is the **Narita Limited Express** (N'EX), which makes 23 runs a day in each direction. Trains from the airport go directly to the central Tōkyō Eki in just under an hour, then continue to Yokohama and Ōfuna. Daily departures begin at 7:40 AM; the last train is at 9:42 PM. The one-way fare is ¥2,940 (¥4,980 for the first-class "Green Car" and ¥5,380 per person for a private compartment that seats four). All seats are reserved, and you'll need to reserve one for yourself in advance, as this train fills quickly. The less elegant **kaisoku** (rapid train) on JR's Narita Line also runs from the airport to Tōkyō Station, by way of Chiba; there are 16 departures daily, starting at 7 AM. The fare to Tōkyō is ¥1,280 (¥930 more for the Green Car); the ride takes 1 hour and 27 minutes.

BETWEEN HANEDA AIRPORT AND CENTER CITY

By Monorail. The monorail from Haneda Airport to Hamamatsu-chō Station in Tōkyō is the fastest and cheapest way into town; the journey takes about 17 minutes and trains run approximately every 5 minutes; the fare is ¥470. From Hamamatsu-chō Station, change to a JR train or take a taxi to your destination.

By Taxi. A taxi to the center of Tōkyō takes about 40 minutes; the fare is approximately ¥6,000.

By Train

The **JR Shinkansen** (bullet train) and **JR express trains** on the **Tōkaidō Line** (to Nagoya, Kyōto, Kōbe, Ōsaka, Hiroshima, and the island of Kyūshū) use **Tōkyō Eki** in central Tōkyō. The JR Shinkansen and express trains on the **Tōhoku Line** (to Sendai and Morioka) use **Ueno Eki,** just north of Tōkyō Eki. JR Shinkansen and express trains on the **Jōetsu Line** (to Niigata) also use Ueno Eki. JR express trains to the **Japan Alps** (Matsumoto) use **Shinjuku Eki.** A new bullet train now runs from Tōkyō Station to Nagano. Named the *Hokuriku* Shinkansen, it uses the Jōetsu Shinkansen tracks to Takasaki, where it branches off for Nagano.

If you buy a Japan Rail Pass for further travel throughout the country you can use it on all JR trains except the *Nozomi* Shinkansen out of Tōkyō on the Tōkaidō Line. *See* Train Travel *in* the Gold Guide for information on Japanese rail networks and obtaining JR Passes.

Getting Around

Daunting in its sheer size, Tōkyō is, in fact, an extremely easy city to negotiate. If you have any anxieties about getting from place to place, remind yourself first that a transportation system obliged to cope with 4 or 5 million commuters a day simply *has* to be efficient, extensive, and reasonably easy to understand. Remind yourself also that virtually any place you're likely to go as a visitor is within a 15-minute walk of a train or subway station—and that station stops are always marked in English. Of course, exceptions to the rule exist; the system has its flaws. In the outline here you'll find a few things to avoid, and also a few pointers that will save you time—and money—as you go.

By Bus

Because Tōkyō has no rational order—no grid—bus routes are impossibly complicated. The Tōkyō Municipal Government operates some of the lines; private companies run the rest. There is no telephone number even a native Japanese can call for help. And buses all have tiny seats and low ceilings. With one exception, the red double-decker in Asakusa (☞ Asakusa *in* Exploring Tōkyō, *above*), forget about taking buses.

By Ferry

The best ride in Tōkyō, hands down, is the *suijō basu* (river bus), operated by the Tōkyō Cruise Ship Company from **Hinode Pier** (✉ 2-7-104 Kaigan, Minato-ku, ☎ 03/3457–7830), from the mouth of the Sumida-gawa upstream to Asakusa. The glassed-in double-decker boats depart roughly every 30 minutes, 10:30 AM–3 PM daily (extended weekday service to 4:45 PM July–Aug.). The trip takes 35 minutes and costs ¥800. The pier is a seven-minute walk from the Hamamatsu-chō Station on the JR Yamanote Line.

The Sumida-gawa was once Tōkyō's lifeline, a busy highway for travelers and freight alike. The ferry service dates back to 1885. Some people still take it to work, but today most passengers are Japanese tourists. On its way to Asakusa, the boat passes under 11 bridges, and though all are of modern construction, they are deemed worthy of lengthy comment by the guided tour (a recording on the boat's loudspeaker). There are far more interesting things to see: **Tsukiji Market,** the largest wholesale fish and produce market in the world (☞ Tsukiji *in* Exploring Tōkyō, *above*); the vast reclamation/construction projects meant to sate the city's insatiable need for high-tech office space; the old lumberyards and warehouses upstream; and the **Kokugikan** (☞ Off the Beaten Path, *above*), with its distinctive green roof, which is the new arena and headquarters of sumō wrestling.

Another place to catch the ferry is at the **Hama Rikyū Tei-en** (Detached Palace Garden), a 15-minute walk from Ginza. Once part of the imperial estates, the gardens are open to the public for a separate ¥200 entrance fee. The ferry landing is inside, a short walk to the left as you enter the main gate. Boats depart at 45-minute intervals every weekday 10:15–4:05; the fare to Asakusa is ¥660; from Asakusa to Hama Rikyū, for some unfathomable reason, the fare is ¥620.

By Hired Car

You can hire large and comfortable cars (the Japanese call them *haiya*) for about ¥6,000 per hour for a midsize car, up to ¥18,000 per hour for a Cadillac limousine. Call **Hinomaru** (☎ 03/3505–0707). The Imperial, Okura, and Palace hotels also have limousine services.

By Rental Car

Congestion, lack of road signs in English, and the difficulty of parking make driving in Tōkyō impractical. That said, should you wish to rent a car, contact **Nippon Interrent** (⊠ 2-1 Yaesu, Chūō-ku, ☎ 03/3271–6643) or **Toyota Rent-a-Car** (⊠ 2-3-18 Kudan Minami, Chiyoda-ku, ☎ 03/3263–6321), national car-rental companies with offices all around Tōkyō and Japan. The cost is approximately ¥15,000 per day. An international driving license is required.

By Subway

Tōkyō is served by 12 subway lines (a 13th is under construction), seven of them operated by the Rapid Transportation Authority (Eidan) and five by the Tōkyō Municipal Authority (Tōei). Maps, bilingual signs at entrances, and even the trains are color-coded for easy identification. Subway trains run roughly every five minutes from about 5 AM to midnight; except during rush hours, the intervals are slightly longer on the newer Tōei lines.

The network of interconnections (subway-to-subway and train-to-subway) is particularly good. One transfer—two at most—will take you in less than an hour to any part of the city you're likely to visit. At some stations—such as Ōte-machi, Ginza, and Iidabashi—long underground passageways connect the various lines, and it does take time to get from one to another. Directions, however, are clearly marked. Less helpful is the system of signs that tell you which of the 15 or 20 exits (exits are often numbered and alphabetized) from a large station will take you aboveground closest to your destination; only a few stations have such signs in English. Try asking the agent when you turn in your ticket; he may understand enough of your question to come back with the exit number and letter (such as A3 or B12), which is all you need.

Subway fares begin at ¥160. Tōei trains are generally a bit more expensive than Eidan trains, but both are competitive with the JR. From Ueno across town to Shibuya on the old Ginza Line (orange), for example, is ¥190; the ride on the JR Yamanote Line will cost you the same. The Eidan (but *not* the Tōei) has inaugurated an electronic card of its own, called Metrocard. The denominations are ¥1,000, ¥3,000, and ¥5,000. Automatic card dispensers are installed at some subway stations.

By Taxi

In spite of the introduction of ¥340 initial-fare cabs, Tōkyō taxi fares remain among the highest in the world. Most meters start running at ¥660 and tick away at the rate of ¥80 every 280 meters (about ⅕ mi). Keep in mind that the ¥340 taxis (which are a very small percentage of those on the street) are only cheaper for trips of 1 km (.6 mi) or less; at 2 km (1¼ mi) the fare catches up with the ¥660 cabs. The ¥340 taxis have a sticker on the left-rear window.

There are also smaller cabs, called *kogata*, which charge ¥640 and then ¥80 per 299 meters (⅕ mi). If your cab is caught in traffic—hardly an uncommon event—the meter registers another ¥90 for every 2¼ minutes of immobility. Between 11 PM and 5 AM, a 30% surcharge is added to the fare.

You do get very good value for the money, though. Taxis are invariably clean and comfortable. The doors open automatically for you when you get in and out. The driver takes you where you want to go by the shortest route he knows, and he does not expect a tip. Tōkyō cabbies are not, in general, a sociable species (you wouldn't be either if you had to drive for 10–12 hours a day in Tōkyō traffic), but you can always count on a minimum standard of courtesy. And if you forget something in the cab—a camera, a purse—your chances of getting it back are almost 100%.

Hailing a taxi during the day is seldom a problem. You would have to be in a very remote part of town to wait more than five minutes for one to pass by. In the Ginza, drivers are allowed to stop for passengers only in designated areas. Elsewhere, you need only step off the curb and raise your arm. If the cab already has a fare, there will be a green light on the dashboard, visible through the windshield; if not, the light will be red.

Night changes the rules a bit, when everyone's been out drinking and wants a ride home. Don't be astonished if a cab with a red light doesn't stop for you: The driver may have had a radio call, or he may be heading for an area where he can pick up a long, profitable fare to the suburbs. (Or he may simply not feel like coping with a passenger in a foreign language. Refusing a fare is against the law—but it's done all the time.) Between 11 PM and 2 AM on Friday and Saturday nights, you have to be very lucky to get a cab in any of the major entertainment districts; in Ginza, it is almost impossible.

By Train

Japan Railways (JR) trains are color-coded, making it easy to identify the different lines. The **Yamanote Line** (green or silver with green stripes) makes a 35-km (22-mi) loop around the central wards of the city in about an hour. The 29 stops include the major hub stations of Tōkyō, Yūraku-chō, Shimbashi, Shinagawa, Shibuya, Shinjuku, and Ueno.

The **Chūō Line** (orange) runs east to west through the loop from Tōkyō to the distant suburb of Takao. During the day, however, these are limited express trains that don't stop at most of the stations inside the loop. For local cross-town service, which also extends west to neighboring Chiba Prefecture, you have to take the **Sōbu Line** (yellow).

The **Keihin Tōhoku Line** (blue) goes north to Ōmiya in Saitama Prefecture and south to Ōfuna in Kanagawa, running parallel to the Yamanote Line between Tabata and Shinagawa. Where they share the loop, the two lines usually use the same platform—Yamanote trains on one side, and Keihin Tōhoku trains headed in the same direction on the other. This requires a little care. Suppose, for example, you want to take the loop line from Yūraku-chō around to Shibuya, and you board a blue train instead of a green one; four stops later, where the lines branch, you'll find yourself on an unexpected trip to Yokohama.

JR Yamanote Line fares start at ¥130; you can get anywhere on the loop for ¥250 or less. Most stations have a chart in English somewhere above the row of ticket vending machines, so you can check the fare to your destination. If not, you can simply buy the cheapest ticket and pay the difference at the other end. In any case, hold on to your ticket: You'll have to turn it in at the exit. Tickets are valid only on the day you buy them, but if you plan to use JR a lot, you can save time and trouble with an Orange Card, available at any station office. The card is electronically coded; at vending machines with orange panels, you insert the card, punch the cost of the ticket, and that amount is automatically deducted. Orange Cards come in ¥1,000 and ¥3,000 denominations.

Shinjuku, Harajuku, and Shibuya are notorious for the long lines that form at ticket dispensers. If you're using a card, make sure you've lined up at a machine with an orange panel; if you're paying cash and have no change, make sure you've lined up at a machine that will change a ¥1,000 note—not all of them do.

Yamanote and Sōbu Line trains begin running about 4:30 AM and stop around 12:30 at night. The last departures are indicated at each station—but only in Japanese. Bear in mind that 7–9:30 AM and 5–7 PM trains are packed to bursting with commuters; avoid the trains at these times, if possible. During these hours, smoking is not allowed in JR stations or on platforms.

Maps

Excellent maps of the subway system, with major JR lines included as well, are available at any station office, free of charge. You'll find the same map in the monthly *Tour Companion* magazine. Hotel kiosks and English-language bookstores stock a wide variety of pocket maps, some of which have suggested walking tours that also mark the locations of JR and subway stations along the way. A bit bulkier to carry around, but by far the best and most detailed resource, is *Tōkyō: A Bilingual Atlas* (Kodansha International, ¥1,850; $14.95 in the United States), which contains subway and rail-system guides and area maps. Because all notations are in both English and Japanese, you can always get help on the street, even from people who do not speak your language, just by pointing at your destination.

Tōkyō Addresses

The standard postal system the Japanese themselves use to indicate addresses in Tōkyō begins with the ward—designated by the suffix -*ku* (as in Minato-ku)—followed by the name of the district within the ward, such as Roppongi or Nishi-Azabu. The district is usually divided into numbered subsections, sometimes designated by the suffix -*chōme*; the subsections can be further divided into units of one or more blocks, each with its own building numbers. Apartment blocks will often have a final set of digits on the address to specify an apartment number. Thus, *Taitō-ku 1-4-301 Asakusa 3-chōme* will be recognizable to the mail carrier as "Apartment No. 301 in Bldg. 4 on the first block of Asakusa subsection No. 3 in Taitō Ward"—but don't count on the driver of a taxi you hail on the other side of the city having the faintest idea how to find it. And don't count on the blocks or the building numbers appearing in any rational geographic order, either. The whole system is impossibly complicated, even for the Japanese. People usually direct each other to some landmark or prominent building in a given neighborhood and muddle on from there. Bear in mind that addresses written in Japanese appear in reverse order, that is, with the postal code, prefecture, and ward first and the name of the person or establishment last; however, Japanese addresses written in English follow Western order, with the name first and the ward, prefecture, and postal code last.

The system that we use throughout this guide follows the Western order: ✉ *1-4-301 Asakusa, 3-chōme, Taitō-ku.*

Contacts and Resources

Currency Exchange and Banks

Most hotels will change both traveler's checks and notes into yen. However, their rates are always lower than at banks. Because Japan is so safe and virtually free from street crime, one may consider exchanging large sums of money into yen at banks at any time. Most of the larger banks have a foreign exchange counter. Banking hours are week-days 9–3.

Major banks can transfer funds to and from overseas. Two banks that may be familiar to you are **Bank of America** (⊠ Arc Mori Bldg., 1-12-32 Akasaka, Minato-ku, ☎ 03/3587–3111) and **Citibank** (⊠ 1-1-3 Ōte-machi, Chiyoda-ku, ☎ 0120–322–522 toll-free). **American Express** has a banking office in its headquarters in the American Express Tower (⊠ 4-30-16 Ogikubo, Suginami-ku, ☎ 03/3220–6000) and at its branch in the Yūraku-chō Denki Building (1-7-1 Yūraku-chō, Chiyoda-ku, ☎ 03/3214–0280).

Directory Assistance

For Tōkyō telephone numbers, dial 104; for elsewhere in Japan, dial 105.

Doctors and Dentists

DOCTORS

International Catholic Hospital (Seibō Byōin). ⊠ 2-5-1 Naka Ochiai, Shinjuku-ku, ☎ 03/3951–1111. ☉ Appointments Mon.–Sat. 8–11 AM; outpatient services closed 3rd Sat. of month.

International Clinic. ⊠ 1-5-9 Azabu-dai, Roppongi, Minato-ku, ☎ 03/3582–2646 or 03/3583–7831. Accepts emergencies. ☉ Appointments weekdays 9–noon and 2:30–5, Sat. 9–noon.

St. Luke's International Hospital. A member of the American Hospital Association. ⊠ 10-1 Akashi-chō, Chūō-ku, ☎ 03/3541–5151. Accepts emergencies. ☉ Appointments Mon.–Sat. 8:30–11 AM.

Tōkyō Medical and Surgical Clinic. ⊠ 32 Mori Bldg., 3-4-30 Shiba Kōen, Minato-ku, ☎ 03/3436–3028. ☉ Appointments weekdays 9 AM–4:45 PM, Sat. 9 AM–1 PM.

DENTISTS

Yamauchi Dental Clinic. A member of the American Dental Association. ⊠ Shiroganedai Gloria Heights, 1st floor, 3-16-10 Shiroganedai, Minato-ku, ☎ 03/3441–6377. ☉ Weekdays 9–1 and 3–6, Sat. 9–noon.

Embassies and Consulates

U.S. Embassy and Consulate. ⊠ 1-10-5 Akasaka, Minato-ku, ☎ 03/3224–5000. ☉ Consulate weekdays 8:30–12:30 and 2–5:30.

Australian Embassy. ⊠ 2-1-14 Mita, Minato-ku, ☎ 03/5232–4111. ☉ Weekdays 9–noon and 1:30–5.

British Embassy and Consulate. ⊠ 1 Ichiban-chō, Chiyoda-ku, ☎ 03/3265–6340. ☉ Consulate Sun.–Fri. 9–noon and 2–5:30.

Canadian Embassy. ⊠ 7-3-38 Akasaka, Minato-ku, ☎ 03/3408–2101. ☉ Weekdays 9–12:30 and 1:30–5:30.

New Zealand Embassy. ⊠ 20-40 Kamiyama-chō, Shibuya-ku, ☎ 03/3467–2271. ☉ Weekdays 9–12:30 and 1:30–5:30.

Emergencies

Ambulance and **Fire**, ☎ 119. **Police**, ☎ 110. **Tōkyō English Life Line** (TELL; ☎ 03/5481–4347) is a telephone service available 9 AM–4 PM and 9–11 PM for anyone in distress who cannot communicate in Japanese. The service will relay your emergency to the appropriate Japanese authorities and/or will serve as a counselor. Assistance in English is available 24 hours a day on the toll-free **Japan Helpline** (☎ 0120/461–997).

Guided Tours

EXCURSIONS

To Nikkō, **Sunrise Tours** (☎ 03/5620–9500) runs one-day tours (¥14,500–¥20,000 depending on whether you return by bus or Shinkansen Bullet Train; lunch included) and two-day tours (¥24,000–¥30,000, one lunch and overnight accommodation included). **Tōbu**

Travel (☎ 03/3278–1251, a division of Tōbu Railways) has full-day trips to Nikkō (with pickup and return to major hotels), including an English-speaking guide, reserved train travel, lunch, and entrance fee; the fare is ¥20,000. **Sunrise Tours** (☎ 03/5620–9500), **Japan Amenity Travel** (☎ 03/3542–7200), and the **Japan Gray Line** (☎ 03/3433–5745) have Mt. Fuji and Hakone tours, with return either by bus or train; one-day trips cost ¥14,000–¥17,500 (lunch included), and two-day tours cost ¥28,500 (meals and accommodation included). Some of these tours include a quick visit to Kamakura. There are also excursions to Kyōto via Shinkansen that cost from ¥44,200 to ¥69,400.

NIGHTLIFE TOURS

Sunrise Tours (☎ 03/5620–9500) offers night tours (6–11 PM) of Tōkyō, which, depending on the one selected, include Kabuki drama at the Kabuki-za, a geisha show at Matsubaya, or a cabaret-floor show at the Shōgun in Roppongi. Prices are ¥10,950–¥13,480, depending on which portions of the tour you include. **The Japan Gray Line** (☎ 03/3433–5745) has similar programs.

ORIENTATION TOURS

Sunrise Tours (☎ 03/5620–9500) and the **Japan Gray Line** (☎ 03/3433–5745) run a number of bus excursions around Tōkyō with English-speaking guides. The tours vary with the current demands of the market. Most include the Tōkyō Tower Observatory, the Imperial East Garden, a demonstration of flower arrangement at the Tasaki Pearl Gallery, and/or a Sumida-gawa cruise to Sensō-ji in Asakusa. These are for the most part four-hour morning or afternoon tours; a full-day tour (seven hours) combines most of what is covered in half-day excursions with a tea ceremony at Happō-en (garden) and lunch at the traditional Chinzan-sō restaurant. Costs range from ¥4,500 to ¥11,850. Tours are conducted in large, air-conditioned buses that set out from Hamamatsu-chō Bus Terminal, but there is also free pickup and return from major hotels. (If you travel independently and use the subway, we estimate that you could manage the same full-day itinerary for under ¥3,000, including lunch.)

PERSONAL GUIDES

The **Japan Guide Association** (☎ 03/3213–2706) will introduce you to English-speaking guides. You will need to negotiate your own itinerary and price with the guide. Assume that the fee will be ¥20,000–¥30,000 for a full eight-hour day.

SPECIAL-INTEREST TOURS

Sunrise Tours (☎ 03/5620–9500) has a free-schedule trip to Tōkyō Disneyland—but this operates only on weekends and works in only one direction: Buses pick you up at major hotels but leave you to manage your own way back to Tōkyō at the end of the day. The cost for the trip is ¥8,850.

Late-Night Pharmacies

No drugstores in Tōkyō are open 24 hours a day, but grocery stores carry basics such as aspirin. The **American Pharmacy** (⊠ Hibiya Park Building, 1-8-1 Yūraku-chō, Chiyoda-ku, ☎ 03/3271–4034) and **Hill Pharmacy** (⊠ 4-1-6 Roppongi, Minato-ku, ☎ 03/3583–5044) both stock American products. The American Pharmacy is conveniently near the Tourist Information Center (☞ *below*) and is open Monday–Saturday 9–7 and Sunday 11–7; Hill Pharmacy is open Monday–Saturday 8–7.

Nagai Yakkyoku (⊠ 1-8-10 Azabu Jū-ban, Minato-ku, ☎ 03/3583–3889) will mix a Chinese and/or Japanese herbal medicine for you after a consultation. A little English is spoken.

Lost and Found

The **Central Lost and Found Office** of the Metropolitan Police (✉ 1-9-11, Kōraku, Bunkyō-ku, ☎ 03/3814–4151) is open on weekdays 8:30–5:15 and Saturday 8:30–12:30. It's closed Sunday, the second and fourth Saturday of every month, and holidays. If you leave something on a JR train, report it to the lost-and-found office at any station. You can also call either of the two central **JR Lost Property Offices,** at Tōkyō Eki (☎ 03/3231–1880) or Ueno Eki (☎ 03/3841–8069).

If you leave something on a subway car, contact the **Teitō Rapid Transit Authority** (TRTA) at its Ueno Lost Properties Office (☎ 03/3834–5577).

If you leave something in a taxi, contact the **Tōkyō Taxi Kindaika Center** (✉ 7-3-3 Minami-Suna, Koto-ku, ☎ 03/3648–0300). Only Japanese is spoken here.

Post and Telegraph Offices

Most hotels have stamps and will mail your letters and postcards; they will also give you directions to the nearest post office. The main **International Post Office** is on the Imperial Palace side of JR Tōkyō Eki (✉ 2-3-3 Ōte-machi, Chiyoda-ku, ☎ 03/3241–4891). For cables, contact the **KDD International Telegraph Office** (✉ 2-3-2 Nishi-Shinjuku, Shinjuku-ku, ☎ 03/3344–5151).

Travel Agencies

Japan Travel Bureau (✉ 1-13-1 Nihombashi, Chūō-ku, ☎ 03/3276–7777) has the most extensive network of agencies throughout Tōkyō and Japan. The organization arranges tours conducted in English in and around Tōkyō. It will also set up reservations for trips throughout Japan, if you wish.

Other travel agencies include **American Express International** (✉ Yūraku-chō Denki Bldg., 1-7-1 Yūraku-chō, Chiyoda-ku, ☎ 03/3214–0280) and **Japan Amenity Travel** (✉ 2-3-5 Yūraku-chō, Chiyoda-ku, ☎ 03/3542–7545).

Visitor Information

The **Tourist Information Center** (TIC) in the Tōkyō International Forum, at the north end of the lower concourse, is an extremely useful source of free maps and brochures. The center also advises on trip planning in Japan. Make a point of dropping by early in your stay in Tōkyō. ✉ 3-5-1 Maru-no-uchi, Chiyoda-ku, ☎ 03/3201–3331. ⊙ Weekdays 9–5, Sat. 9–noon. Subway: Yūraku-chō Line, Yūraku-chō.

Asakusa Tourist Information Center, opposite Kaminari-mon, has some English-speaking staff and plenty of maps and brochures to take away with you. ✉ 2-18-9 Kaminari-mon, Taitō-ku, ☎ 03/3842–5566. ⊙ Daily 9–5. Subway: Ginza Line, Asakusa.

CURRENT EVENTS/EXHIBITIONS

A taped recording in English (☎ 03/3201–3331) gives information on current events in Tōkyō and vicinity. The **Tour Companion,** a free weekly newspaper available at hotels, provides some information on events, exhibitions, festivals, plays, etc. The **Tōkyō Journal,** however, has a more comprehensive monthly listing of what's happening in Tōkyō. It also lists services and stores that may be of special interest to foreigners (¥600). The **Japan Times,** the country's daily English-language newspaper, is good for national and international news coverage, as well as for entertainment reviews and listings.

GENERAL INFORMATION

NTT (Japanese Telephone Corporation, ☎ 03/5295–0101) will help find information (in English), such as telephone numbers, museum openings, and various other facts that it has in its databases.

TRAVEL INFORMATION

Information in English on all domestic travel, buses, and trains can be acquired by phoning the TIC (☎ 03/3502–1461). You may also call **Japan Railways** (☎ 03/3423–0111) or the toll-free **Japan Travel Phone** (☎ 0120/222–800 for eastern Japan; 0120/444–800 for western Japan) for information in English.

4 Side Trips from Tōkyō

Most people are drawn to Nikkō first by Tōshō-gū, the astonishing shrine to the first Tokugawa shōgun Ieyasu. Kamakura, the 13th-century capital of Japan, has a great legacy of historical and cultural sights. And no matter how many pictures of Fuji-san (Mt. Fuji) you've seen, the genuine majesty of this dormant volcano will fill you with awe. Yokohama, which demographers would now include in the Greater Tōkyō conurbation, is a port city with an international character all its own.

By Jared
Lubarsky

NIKKŌ—which means "sunlight"—is the site not simply of the Tokugawa shrine but also of a national park, Nikkō Kokuritsu Kōen, on the heights above it. The centerpiece of the park is Chūzenji-ko, a deep lake some 21 km (13 mi) around, and the 318-ft Kegon-no-taki, Japan's most famous waterfalls. "Think nothing splendid," asserts an old Japanese proverb, "until you have seen Nikkō." Whoever said it first might well have been thinking more of the park than of the shrine below.

One caveat: The term "national park" does not quite mean what it does elsewhere in the world. In Japan, pristine grandeur is hard to come by; there is *nowhere* in this country where intrepid hikers can go to contemplate the beauties of nature for very long in solitude. If a thing's worth seeing, it's worth exploiting: a world view that tends to fill the national parks with bus caravans, ropeways and gondolas, "prospect points" with coin-fed telescopes, signs that tell you where you may and may not walk, fried noodle joints and vending machines, and shacks full of kitschy souvenirs. That's true of Nikkō, and it's true as well of Fuji-Hakone-Izu National Park, southwest of Tōkyō, another of Japan's most popular resort areas.

The park's chief attraction is, of course, Fuji-san—spellbinding in its perfect symmetry, immortalized by centuries of poets and artists. South of Fuji-san, the Izu Peninsula projects out into the Pacific, with Suruga Bay to the west and Sagami Bay to the east. The beaches and rugged shoreline of Izu, its forests and highland meadows, and its numerous hot-springs inns and resorts (*izu* means "spring") make the region a favorite destination for the Japanese, especially honeymooners.

Kamakura and Yokohama, both close enough to Tōkyō to provide ideal day trips, could not make for more contrasting experiences. Kamakura is an ancient city—the birthplace, one could argue, of the samurai way of life. Its place in Japanese history begins late in the 12th century, when Minamoto no Yoritomo became the country's first shōgun and chose this site, with its rugged hills and narrow passes, as the seat of his military government. The warrior elite of the Kamakura period took much of their ideology—and their aesthetics—from Zen Buddhism, endowing splendid temples that still exist today. A walking tour of Kamakura's Zen temples and Shintō shrines is a must for anyone with a day to spend out of Tōkyō. Yokohama, too, can lay claim to an important place in Japanese history: In 1869, after centuries of isolation, this city became the first important port for trade with the West and the site of the first major foreign settlement. Twice destroyed, the city retains very few remnants of that history, but it remains Japan's largest port and has an international character that rivals—if not surpasses—that of Tōkyō. Its waterfront park, and its ambitious Minato Mirai bayside development project, draw visitors from all over the world.

Side Trips Glossary. Key Japanese words and suffixes for this chapter include *bijutsukan* (art museum), *-chō* (street or block), *chūō* (central, as in Central Street), *daimyō* (feudal lord), *-den* (hall), *-dō* (temple or hall), *dōri* (avenue), *eki* (train station), *gai-jin* (foreigner), *-gawa* (river), *-gū* (Shintō temple), *-gun* (district), *-in* (Buddhist temple), *-ji* (temple), *jinja* (Shintō shrine), *kita* (north), *-ko* (lake), *kōen* ("ko-en," park), *-ku* (section or ward), *machi* (town), *michi* (street), *-mon* (gate), *onsen* (hot springs), *sakura* (cherry blossoms), *-san* (mountain, as in Fuji-san, Mt. Fuji), *-shima* (island), *Shinkansen* (bullet train, literally "new trunk line"), *shōgun* (commander in chief), *torii* ("to-ree-ee," gate), and *yama* (mountain).

Pleasures and Pastimes

Dining

Nikkō has no shortage of popular restaurants catering to its tourist trade, and we've listed several in that section of this chapter; there is, alas, nothing special to distinguish one from another. Because they tend to have display cases outside with price-tagged plastic models of the food they serve, at least you know what you're getting into. Noodle shops are always safe for lunch: *soba* (buckwheat noodle) and *udon* (thick, wheat noodle) dishes are inexpensive, filling, and tasty. In recent years Nikkō has also come into its share of Western-style fast-food restaurants.

Three things about Kamakura make it a fairly good place to look for a restaurant. It is on the ocean (properly speaking, on Sagami Bay), which means that seafood is good nearly everywhere. Kamakura is a major tourist stop, and it has long been a prestigious place to live, a favorite with Japan's worldly and well-to-do, and with the more successful of her writers, artists, and intellectuals. On a day-trip from Tōkyō, feel confident picking a place for lunch almost at random; we've chosen a few of the best, below.

Yokohama, as befits a city of more than 3 million people, lacks for very little in the way of food, from humble quick-fix lunch counters to elegant dining rooms, and almost every imaginable cuisine. Your best bet is Chinatown—Japan's largest Chinese community—with well over 100 restaurants, representing every regional style. If you have a fancy for Greek food, or Italian, or Indian instead, this international port is still guaranteed to provide an eminently satisfying meal.

CATEGORY	COST*
$$$$	over ¥8,000
$$$	¥5,000–¥8,000
$$	¥2,000–¥5,000
$	under ¥2,000

per person, excluding drinks, service, and tax

Lodging

Yokohama and Kamakura are mostly treated as day-trips, and as it is unlikely that you will stay at either, we do not list accommodations for them. Nikkō is something of a toss-up: You can easily see Tōshō-gū and be back in Tōkyō by evening. But when the weather turns glorious in spring or autumn, why not spend some time in the national park, staying overnight at Chūzen-ji, and return to the city the next day. Fuji-san and Hakone, on the other hand—and more especially the Izu Peninsula—are pure resort destinations. Staying overnight is an intrinsic part of the experience, and it makes little sense to go without hotel reservations confirmed in advance.

In both Nikkō and the Fuji-Hakone-Izu area, you will find modern, Western-style hotels that operate in a fairly standard, international style. More common, however, are the Japanese-style *kankō* (literally "sight-seeing") hotels and the traditional *ryokan* (inns). Both types quote prices on a per-person basis with two meals, breakfast and dinner. Remember to stipulate whether you want a Japanese or Western breakfast. If you do not want dinner at your hotel, it is usually possible to renegotiate the price, but the management will not be happy about it; the two meals are a fixture of their business. The typical ryokan, in fact, takes great pride in its cuisine, and very often with good reason; the evening meal is an elaborate affair of 10 or a dozen different dishes, based on the fresh produce and specialties of the region, served to you—nay, *orchestrated*—in your room on a wonderful variety of trays and tableware designed to celebrate the season. The undisputed pleasure of either of these destinations is to return to your hotel at the end of a hard day of sightseeing, soak for an hour in a hot bath, put on the hotel's *nemaki* (sleeping gown), and sit down to your own private dinner party.

There's little point to staying at a kankō hotel, on the other hand, beyond being able to say you've had the experience and survived with your good humor intact. Like everywhere else in Japan, these places do most of their business with tour groups—big, boisterous groups that tend to drink a lot and tamely submit to rigid routines of service. At 7 or 7:30 AM, someone will knock on your door, demanding to remove the bedding; by 8:30, in most cases, breakfast is no longer available. An English-speaking clerk is a phenomenal rarity. The turnover of guests is ruthless at kankō hotels, and the cost is way out of proportion to the service they provide.

Categories below reflect the cost of a double room with private bath and no meals, exclusive of service and tax. However, the rate quoted when you make reservations will probably include breakfast and dinner, unless you specify otherwise. Be aware also that hotels may add a surcharge to the basic rate at various times: weekends, nights before local festivals, July–August, October—in other words, whenever you are likely to want a room. In peak season, July 15–August 31, prices can increase by 40%. Call ahead, or check with your travel agent for the prevailing rate at the time.

CATEGORY	COST*
$$$$	over ¥25,000
$$$	¥17,000–¥25,000
$$	¥10,000–¥17,000
$	under ¥10,000

All prices are for a double room, excluding service and tax.

Onsen

Japan's biggest natural headache—the slip and slide of vast tectonic plates deep below the archipelago that spawn volcanoes and make earthquakes an everyday fact of life—provides one of Japan's greatest delights as well: thermal baths. Wherever there are volcanic mountains—Japan is mostly volcanic mountains—you can usually count on drilling or tapping into springs of hot water, rich in all sorts of restorative minerals. Any place where this happens is called, generically, an *onsen*; any place where lots of spas have tapped these sources, to cash in on the Japanese passion for total immersion, is an *onsen chiiki* (hot-springs resort area). The Izu Peninsula is particularly rich in onsen. It has, in fact, one-fifth of the 2,300-odd officially recognized hot springs in Japan.

The spas in famous areas like Shuzenji or Yugashima take many forms. The ne plus ultra is that small, secluded Japanese inn, up in the mountains, where you sleep on futons on tatami floors, in a setting of almost poetic traditional furnishings and design. Such an inn will have its own *rotemburo*, an open-air mineral-spring pool, in a screened-off nook with a panoramic view, for the exclusive use of its guests. These inns must be booked at least six months in advance. More typical is the large resort hotel, geared mainly to groups, with one or more large indoor mineral baths of its own. Where whole towns and villages have developed to exploit a local supply of hot water, there will be several of these large hotels, an assortment of smaller inns, and probably a few modest public bathhouses, with no accommodations, where you just pay an entrance fee for a soak of whatever length you wish.

As with any Japanese bath, you soap up and rinse off *before* you get in an onsen's tub. The atmosphere at these resorts is quite informal— spending hours up to your neck in hot water makes for mellow dispositions. No one dresses up. Feel free to walk about in your hotel and on the street in your *yukata* (cotton bathrobe). The only thing to keep in mind is that hotels and bathhouses almost never have full-size bath towels. You must bring your own if you don't want to make do with the skimpy ones (cloths the size of hand towels) provided.

NIKKŌ

At Nikkō there is a monument to a warlord so splendid and powerful that he became a god. In the year 1600, Ieyasu Tokugawa won a battle at a place called Seki-ga-hara, in the mountains of south-central Japan, that left him the undisputed ruler of the archipelago. He died in 1616, but the Tokugawa shogunate would last another 252 years, holding in its sway a peaceful, prosperous, and united country.

A fit resting place would have to be made for the founder of such a dynasty. Ieyasu (ee-eh-*ya*-su) had provided for one in his will: a mausoleum at Nikkō, in a forest of tall cedars, where a religious center had been founded more than eight centuries earlier. The year after his death, in accordance with Buddhist custom, he was given a *kaimyō*— an honorific name to bear in the afterlife. Thenceforth, he was Tōshō-Daigongen: the Great Incarnation Who Illuminates the East. The Imperial Court at Kyōto declared him a god, and his remains were taken in a procession of great pomp and ceremony to be enshrined at Nikkō.

The dynasty he left behind was enormously rich. Ieyasu's personal fief, on the Kantō Plain, was worth 2.5 million *koku* of rice; one koku, in monetary terms, was equivalent to the cost of keeping one retainer in the necessities of life for a year. The shogunate itself, however, was still an uncertainty. It had only recently taken control after more than a century of civil war. The founder's tomb had a political purpose: It was meant to inspire awe and to make manifest the wealth and power of the Tokugawas. It was Ieyasu's legacy, a statement of his family's right to rule.

Tōshō-gū was built by his grandson, the third shōgun, Iemitsu. It was Iemitsu who established the policy of national isolation, which closed the doors of Japan to the outside world for more than 200 years. The mausoleum and shrine required the labor of 15,000 people for two years (1634–36); craftsmen and artists of the first rank were assembled from all over the country. Every surface was carved and painted and lacquered in the most intricate detail imaginable. Tōshō-gū shimmers in the reflections from 2,489,000 sheets of gold leaf. Roof beams and rafter ends with dragon heads, lions, and elephants in bas-relief; friezes of phoenixes, wild ducks, and monkeys; inlaid pillars and red-lacquer corridors—Tōshō-gū is everything a 17th-century warlord would consider gorgeous, and the inspiration is very Chinese.

Foreign visitors have differed about the effect Iemitsu achieved. Victorian-era traveler Isabella Bird, who came to Nikkō in 1878, was unrestrained in her enthusiasm: "To pass from court to court," she writes in her *Unbeaten Tracks in Japan,* "is to pass from splendour to splendour; one is almost glad to feel that this is the last, and that the strain on one's capacity for admiration is nearly over." Fosco Mariani, a more recent visitor, felt somewhat different: "You are taken aback," he observes in his *Meeting with Japan* (1959). "You ask yourself whether it is a joke, or a nightmare, or a huge wedding cake, a masterpiece of sugar icing made for some extravagant prince with a perverse, rococo taste, who wished to alarm and entertain his guests." Clearly, it is impossible to feel indifferent about Tōshō-gū; perhaps, in the end, that is all Ieyasu could ever really have expected.

Exploring Nikkō

Numbers in the margin correspond to points of interest on the Nikkō Area map.

Tōshō-gū Area

The town of Nikkō is essentially one long avenue—Sugi Namiki (Cryptomeria Avenue)—extending for about a mile from the railway stations to Tōshō-gū. The street is lined with tourist inns and shops, and if you have time, you might want to make this a leisurely stroll. The antiques shops along the way may turn up interesting—but expensive—pieces like armor fittings, hibachi, pottery, or dolls, and the souvenir shops will have ample selections of local wood carvings. Or save yourself the hike up through town by taking the bus from either railway station (¥190) to Shinkyō.

For admission to Tōshō-gū and surrounding sites, you can purchase a multiple-entry ticket (¥900) for Rinnō-ji (temple), the Daiyū-in (mausoleum of the third shōgun, Iemitsu Tokugawa), Tōshō-gū, and Futarasan Jinja (shrine). Separate fees are charged for admission to other areas. The ticket window is at the top of the stone stairway leading from the ☞ **Monument to Masatane Matsudaira** in the corner of the car park.

① Built in 1636 for shōguns and imperial messengers on their visits to the shrine, the red-lacquered, wooden **Shinkyō** (Sacred Bridge) is still used for ceremonial occasions. The original structure was destroyed in a flood; the present one dates from 1907. Once, ordinary mortals were not permitted on the bridge. Now you can pay ¥300 for the privilege of walking over it. Shinkyō is on the rise to the left, opposite the entrance to the Tōshō-gū, where the road curves and crosses the Daiya-

② gawa. Take note of the **Kanaya Hotel,** a Nikkō landmark that has been in the same family for 100 years. The main building is a delightful, rambling Victorian that has hosted royalty and other important personages—as the guest book attests—from all over the world. The entrance to the hotel is just below the Shinkyō, at the top of the hill on the left.

There is a **Monument to Masatane Matsudaira,** opposite the Shinkyō, at the main entrance to the precincts of Tōshō-gū. Matsudaira was one of the two feudal lords charged with the actual construction of the shrine. Matsudaira's great contribution was the planting of the wonderful cryptomeria trees (Japanese cedars) around the shrine and along all the approaches to it. The project took more than 20 years, from 1628 to 1651; the result was some 64 km (40 mi) of cedar-lined avenues. Fire and attrition have taken their toll, but some 13,000 of these trees still stand—a setting of solemn majesty the buildings alone could never have achieved. From the monument, take either the ramp or the stone stairway to the grounds of the shrine itself.

★ ③ Rinnō-ji belongs to the Tendai sect of Buddhism, the head temple of which is Enryaku-ji, on Mt. Hiei near Kyōto. Behind the Hon-dō—the abbot's quarters—is an especially fine little Japanese garden, made in 1815, and a museum, which has a good collection of lacquerware, paintings, and Buddhist sculpture.

The main hall of the temple, called the **Sambutsu-dō,** is the largest single building at Tōshō-gū; it enshrines an image of Amida Nyorai, the Buddha of the Western Paradise, flanked on the right by a Senju (Thousand-Armed) Kannon, the goddess of mercy, and on the left by a Bato-Kannon, regarded as the protector of animals. These three images are

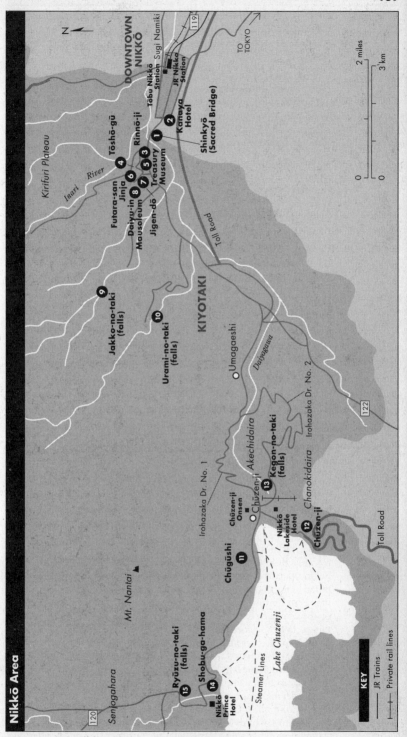

Nikkō Area

N

DOWNTOWN NIKKŌ

Sugi Namiki

Tōbu Nikkō Station

JR Nikkō Station

TO TOKYO

119

Kanaya Hotel

Shinkyō (Sacred Bridge)

Rinnō-ji

Tōshō-gū

1

2

3

5

4

6

7

8

Futara-san Jinja

Daiyu-in Mausoleum

Jigen-dō

Treasury Museum

Kirifuri Plateau

Inari River

Toll Road

9

10

Jakko-no-taki (falls)

Urami-no-taki (falls)

KIYOTAKI

Umagaeshi

Daiyagawa

122

Irohazaka Dr. No. 1

Irohazaka Dr. No. 2

Akechidaira

Kegon-no-taki (falls)

Chanokidaira

13

Chūzen-ji Onsen

Chūzen-ji

Nikkō Lakeside Hotel

12

Chūzen-ji

Toll Road

Mt. Nantai

11

Chūgūshi

Ryūzu-no-taki (falls)

Shobu-ga-hama

14

15

Nikkō Prince Hotel

Senjogahara

120

Lake Chuzenji

Steamer Lines

KEY

—— JR Trains

+—+ Private rail lines

2 miles

3 km

0
0

lacquered in gold and date from the early part of the 17th century. The original Sambutsu-dō is said to have been built in 848 by the priest Ennin (794–864), also known as Jikaku-Daishi; the present building dates from 1648.

Opposite, on the north side of the compound, is the **Gohōten-dō**, a hall that enshrines three of the Seven Gods of Good Fortune. These three are Buddhist deities derived from Chinese folk mythology: Daikoku and Bishamon, who bring wealth and good harvests, and Benten, patroness of music and the arts. The grounds of Rinnō-ji are to the left of the ticket area. ▨ *Museum and gardens ¥300.* ⊘ *Daily 8–5 (enter by 4).*

★ ❹ From the west gate of Rinnō-ji a cedar-lined avenue leads uphill to the stone torii of **Tōshō-gū.** On the left as you approach is the **five-story pagoda** of the shrine—a reconstruction dating from 1818. The first story is decorated with the 12 signs of the zodiac; the black-lacquer doors above each sign bear the three hollyhock leaves of the Tokugawa family crest.

From the torii, a flight of stone steps brings you to the front gate of the shrine—the Omote-mon, also called the Nio-mon (Gate of the Deva Kings), with its fearsome pair of red-painted guardian gods. From here the path turns to the left; in the first group of buildings you reach on the left, the **stable** is decorated with carved panels of pine trees and monkeys. The second panel from the left is the famous group of three monkeys—"Hear no evil, see no evil, speak no evil"—that has become something of a symbol for Nikkō, reproduced endlessly on plaques, bags, and souvenirs of every sort. The stable houses a white horse; this animal, either real or represented in a painting or carving, is traditionally found in Shintō shrines. A few steps farther, where the path turns to the right, is a granite font where visitors purify themselves by washing their hands and rinsing their mouths before entering the shrine. Behind the font is the Kyōzō (Sutra Library), a repository for some 7,000 Buddhist scriptures, kept in a huge revolving bookcase nearly 20 ft high. Unfortunately, the Kyōzō is not open to the public.

As you pass under the second (bronze) torii and up the steps, you see on the right a belfry and a tall bronze candelabrum; on the left is a drum tower and a bronze revolving lantern. The two works in bronze were presented to the shrine by the Dutch government in the mid-17th century. Under the policy of national seclusion, only the Dutch retained trading privileges with Japan, and even they were confined to the tiny artificial island of Dejima, in the port of Nagasaki; they regularly sent tokens of their esteem to the shogunate to keep their precarious monopoly. Behind the drum tower is the **Yakushi-dō**, which enshrines a manifestation of the Buddha as Yakushi Nyorai, the healer of illnesses. The original 17th-century building was famous for a huge India-ink painting on the ceiling of the nave, *The Roaring Dragon*, so named for the rumbling echoes it seemed to emit when visitors clapped their hands beneath it. The painting was by Yasunobu Kanō (1613–85), from a family of artists that dominated the profession for 400 years. The Kanō School was founded in the late 15th century and patronized by successive military governments until the fall of the Tokugawa shogunate in 1868. The leadership was hereditary; the artists who trained in the Kanō ateliers specialized in Chinese-style ink paintings, landscapes, and decorative figures of birds and animals—typically for screens and the paneled sliding doors that stand as the interior "walls" of Japanese villas and temples. The Yakushi-dō was destroyed by fire in 1961, then rebuilt; the dragon on the ceiling now is by Nampu Katayama (1887–1980).

At the top of the steps is the **Yomei-mon** (Gate of Sunlight). The centerpiece of the shrine, it is designated a National Treasure. It is also called the Higurashi-mon (Twilight Gate), implying that one could spend all day until sunset looking at its richness of detail. Rich the gate certainly is; dazzling white, two stories (36 ft) high, it has 12 columns, beams, and roof brackets carved with dragons, lions, clouds, peonies, Chinese sages, and demigods, painted in vivid hues of red, blue, green, and gold. On one of the central columns, there are two carved tigers; the natural grain of the wood is used to bring out its "fur." To the right and left of the Yomei-mon as you enter, there are galleries running east and west for some 700 ft, their paneled fences also carved and painted with a profusion of motifs from nature: pine and plum branches, pheasants, cranes, and wild ducks.

Inside the gate to the left is the **Mikoshigura,** a storeroom for the portable shrines that appear in the annual Tōshō-gū Festival on May 17–18. The paintings on the ceiling, of *tennin* (Buddhist angels) playing harps, are by Ryōkaku Kanō. To the right is the **Kagura-den,** a hall where ceremonial dances are performed to honor the gods. Directly ahead, across the courtyard, is the **Kara-mon** (Chinese Gate), the official entrance to the inner shrine—also a National Treasure, and, like the Yomei-mon, carved and painted in elaborate detail with dragons and other auspicious figures. Extending right and left from the gate is a wall, which encloses the **Hon-den** (Main Hall) of the shrine.

The entrance is to the right. Here you remove your shoes (lockers are provided) and pass into the outer part of the hall, called the **Hai-den** (Oratory), with its lacquered pillars, carved friezes, and coffered ceilings painted with dragons. Over the lintels are paintings of the 36 great poets of the Heian period, by Mitsuoki Tosa (1617–91), with their poems in the calligraphy of Emperor Go-Mizuno-o. The Hai-den is divided into three chambers: At the back of the central chamber is the Sacred Mirror, believed to represent the spirit of the deity enshrined; the room on the right was reserved for visiting shōgun and members of the three principal branches of the Tokugawa family; and the room on the left was for the chief abbot of Rinnō-ji—who was always a prince of the imperial line.

Beyond the Hai-den is a passage called the **Ishi-no-Ma** (Stone Room). This connects in turn with the sanctum, which is divided into three parts: the Hai-den (Sanctuary), the Nai-jin (Inner Chamber), and the Nai-Nai-jin (Innermost Chamber). No visitors come this far. Here, in the very heart of Tōshō-gū, is the gold-lacquer shrine where the spirit (but not the body) of Ieyasu resides—along with two other deities, whom the Tokugawas later decided were fit companions. One was Hideyoshi Toyotomi, Ieyasu's mentor and liege lord in the long wars of unification at the end of the 16th century; the other was Minamoto no Yoritomo, brilliant military tactician and founder of the earlier (12th-century) Kamakura shogunate. (Ieyasu, born Takechiyo Matsudaira, son of a lesser baron in what is today Aichi Prefecture, claimed Yoritomo for an ancestor.)

From the courtyard between the Kara-mon and Yomei-mon gates, a long passage painted in red cinnabar leads away to the left, and then left again into an open corridor. Just above the gateway there is another famous symbol of Tōshō-gū, the **Sleeping Cat**—a small panel said to have been carved by Hidari Jingoro (Jingoro the Left-handed), a late-16th-century master carpenter and sculptor credited with important contributions to numerous Tokugawa-period temples, shrines, and palaces. A separate admission charge (¥500) is levied to go beyond this point to the **Sakashita-mon** (Gate at the Foot of the Hill) and to the flight of 200 stone steps, up through the cryptomeria trees to **Ieyasu's Tomb.** The climb is worth making, if only for the view of the Yomei-mon and Kara-mon from above—the tomb itself is unimpressive. ✉ *¥900 multiple-entry ticket includes all shrine precincts.* ☉ *Apr.–Oct., daily 8–5; Nov.–Mar., daily 8–4.*

⑤ An unhurried visit to the precincts of Tōshō-gū should definitely include the **Treasury Museum,** which houses a collection of antiquities from its various shrines and temples. From the west gate of Rinnō-ji, turn left off of the cedar-lined avenue to Tōshō-gū, before you reach the pagoda. A minute's walk will bring you to the museum, on the left. ✉ *¥500.* ☉ *Daily Apr.–Oct., 8:30–4:30, Nov.–Mar., 8:30–4.*

★ ⑥ The holy ground at Nikkō is far older than the Tokugawa dynasty, in whose honor it was improved upon. To the gods enshrined at **Futara-san Jinja,** Ieyasu Tokugawa must seem but a callow newcomer. Founded in the 8th century, Futara-san is sacred to the Shintō deities Okuninushi-no-Mikoto (god of the rice fields, bestower of prosperity), his consort Tagorihime-no-Mikoto, and their son Ajisukitaka-hikone-no-Mikoto. The shrine is actually in three parts: the Hon-sha (main shrine) at Tōshō-gū; the Chū-gushi (middle shrine) on Chūzenji-ko; and the Okumiya (inner shrine) on top of Mt. Nantai.

The bronze torii at the entrance to the shrine leads to the **Kara-mon** (Chinese Gate) and the **Hon-den** (sanctum)—the present version of which dates from 1619. To the left, in the corner of the enclosure, is an antique bronze lantern, some 7 ft high, under a canopy. Legend has it that the lantern would assume the shape of a goblin at night; the deep nicks in the bronze were inflicted by swordsmen of the Edo period— on guard duty, perhaps, startled into action by a flickering shape in the dark. This proves, if not the existence of goblins, the incredible cutting power of the Japanese blade, a peerlessly forged weapon. To get to Futara-san, take the avenue to the left as you're standing before the stone torii at Tōshō-gū, and follow it to the end. ✉ *Free.* ☉ *Daily Apr.– Nov., 8–5; Dec.–Mar., 9–4.*

★ ⑦ Tenkai (1536–1643), the first abbot of Rinnō-ji, has his own place of honor at Tōshō-gū: the **Jigen-dō.** A path south of the entrance to ☞ Futara-san Jinja runs between the Jōgyō-do and Hokke-dō—which are popularly called the **Futatsu-dō** (Twin Halls) of Rinnō-ji. Take this to the Jigen-dō compound: The Hall itself is at the north end of the compound, to the right. At the west end is the **Go-oden,** a shrine to Prince Kitashirakawa (1847–95), last of the imperial princes to serve as abbot. Behind it are his tomb and the tombs of his 13 predecessors. ✉ *Free.* ☉ *Daily Apr.–Nov., 8–5; Dec.–Mar., 9–4.*

★ ⑧ The second of the grandiose Tokugawa monuments at Nikkō is the **Daiyu-in Mausoleum,** resting place of the third shōgun, Iemitsu (1603– 51)—who imposed a policy of national isolation on Japan that was to last more than 200 years. Iemitsu, one suspects, had it in mind to upstage his illustrious grandfather; he marked the approach to his own tomb with no fewer than six different decorative gates. The first is another Nio-mon—a Gate of the Deva Kings—like the one at Tōshō-gū. The dragon painted on the ceiling is by Yasunobu Kanō (1613–85). A flight of stone steps leads from here to the second gate, the Niten-mon, a two-story structure protected front and back by carved and painted images of guardian gods. Beyond it, climb two more flights of steps to the middle courtyard. There is a bell tower on the right and a drum tower on the left, and directly ahead is the third gate, the remarkable **Yasha-mon,** so named for the figures of *yasha* (she-demons) in the four niches. This structure is also called the Botan-mon (Peony Gate) for the carvings that decorate it.

On the other side of the courtyard is the Kara-mon (Chinese Gate), gilded and elaborately carved; beyond it is the Hai-den, the shrine's oratory. The Hai-den, too, is richly carved and decorated, with the ceiling covered with dragons; the Chinese lions on the panels at the rear are by two distinguished painters of the Kanō school. Behind the Hai-den is the Ai-no-ma (anteroom, or connecting chamber). From here you can see the **Hon-den** (sanctum). Designated a National Treasure, it houses a gilded and lacquered Buddhist altar some 9 ft high, decorated with paintings of animals, birds, and flowers, in which resides the object of all this veneration: a seated wooden figure of Iemitsu.

To the left of the Kara-mon, at the far west end of the wall, on the right, is the fifth gate: the Koka-mon, built in the style of the late Ming Dynasty in China. From here, another flight of stone steps leads to a small, white-painted oratory. There is one last climb, to the sixth and last gate—the bronze Inuki-mon—and Iemitsu's tomb. 🎫 *Included in the ¥900 multiple-entry ticket to Tōshō-gū.* ⊙ *Apr.–Oct., daily 8–5; Nov.–Mar., daily 8–4.*

If you take the avenue called Nishisan-dō from Futara-san Jinja south, you will soon come to an exit from the Tōshō-gū area on the main road. At this point, you may have given Nikkō all the time you had to spare. If so, turn left, and a short walk will bring you back to the Shinkyō (Sacred Bridge). If not, turn right, and in a minute or so you will come to the Nishisan-dō bus stop, where you can take the local bus to Chūzenji-ko.

To Chūzenji-ko (Lake Chūzen-ji)
Falling water is one of the special charms of the Nikkō National Park area; visitors going by bus or car from Tōshō-gū to Chūzen-ji often stop off en route to see the **Jakko-no-taki** (falls), which descend in a series of seven terraced stages, forming a sheet of water about 100 ft high. About 1 km (½ mi) from the shrine precincts, at the Tamozawa bus stop, a narrow road to the right leads to an uphill walk of some 3 km (2 mi) to the falls. At the Arasawa bus stop, a turn to the right off the Chūzen-ji road leads to the **Urami-no-taki** (falls). "The water," wrote the great 17th-century poet Bashō, "seemed to take a flying leap and drop a hundred feet from the top of a cave into a green pool surrounded by a thousand rocks. One was supposed to inch one's way into the cave and enjoy the falls from behind." It's a steep climb to the cave; the falls and the gorge are striking, but only if you have good hiking shoes and a willingness to get wet should you try this particular view.

The real climb to Chūzenji-ko begins at **Uma-gaeshi** (literally, "Horse Return"). Here, in the old days, the road became too rough for horse riding, and riders had to alight and proceed on foot. The lake is 4,165 ft above sea level. From Uma-gaeshi, the bus climbs a one-way toll road up the pass; the old road has been widened and is used for the traffic coming down. The two roads are full of steep hairpin turns, and on a clear day the view up and down the valley is magnificent—especially from the halfway point at **Akechi-daira** (plain), from which you can see the summit of **Mt. Nantai,** reaching 8,149 ft. Hiking season is from May through mid-October; if you push it, you can make the ascent in about four hours. Uma-gaeshi is about 10 km (6 mi) from Tōbu Eki in Nikkō, or 8 km (5 mi) from Tōshō-gū.

The bus trip from Nikkō to the national park area ends at Chūzen-ji village, named after the temple established here in 784. The temple was renamed **Chūgūshi** in the 19th century and incorporated into Futara-san Jinja. The **Hōmotsu-den** (Treasure House) has an interesting historical collection, including swords, lacquerware, and medieval shrine palanquins. Chūgūshi lies just outside the village, on the road along the north side of the lake. 🖼 *Treasure House ¥300.* 🕓 *Apr.–Oct., daily 8–5; Nov.–Mar., daily 9–4.*

⑫ The present-day **Chūzen-ji** (Tashiki Kannon) is a sub-temple of Rinnō-ji, at Tōshō-gū. The principal object of worship here is a 17-ft statue of Kannon, the goddess of mercy, said to have been carved more than 1,000 years ago by the priest Shōdō from the living trunk of a single Judas tree. You reach Chūzen-ji by turning left (south) as you leave the village of Chūzen-ji and walking about 1½ km (1 mi) along the eastern shore of the lake. 🖼 *¥300.* 🕓 *Apr.–Oct., daily 8–5; Mar. and Nov., daily 8–4; Dec.–Feb., daily 8:30–3:30.*

Formerly in front of the temple was **Uta-ga-hama** (Singing Beach), so named because an angel was said to have descended from heaven here to sing and dance for Shōdō; unfortunately, the "beach" is now a parking lot and a pier.

Just by the bus stop at Chūzen-ji village is a gondola (¥820 round-trip) to **Chanoki-daira** (plain). About 1,000 ft above the lake, it commands a wonderful view of the surrounding area. A few minutes' walk from the gondola terminus is a small **Botanical Garden.**

★ ⑬ What draws the crowds of Japanese visitors to Chūzen-ji, more than anything else, is **Kegon-no-taki,** the country's most famous waterfall. Fed by the eastward flow of the lake, the falls drop 318 ft into a rugged gorge; an elevator (¥530) takes you to an observation platform at the bottom. The volume of water over the falls is carefully regulated, but it is especially impressive after a summer rain or a typhoon. In the winter, the falls do not freeze completely but form a beautiful cascade of icicles. The elevator is just a few minutes' walk from the bus stop, at the east end of the village.

⑭ If you have budgeted an extra day for Nikkō, you might want to consider a walk around the lake. A paved road along the north shore extends for about 8 km (5 mi), one-third of the whole distance, as far as **Shobu-ga-hama** (beach); a "nature trail" parallels the road, but it's not very attractive, especially in summer, when there are hordes of visitors. It is better to come this far by boat or bus. From here the road branches off to the north for Senjo-ga-hara (plain) and Yu-no-ko (lake). Just above ⑮ the Nikkō Prince Hotel at Shobu-ga-hama are the **Ryūzu-no-taki** (Dragon's Head Falls). To the left is a steep footpath that continues around the lake to Senju-ga-hama and thence to a campsite at Asegata. The path is well marked but can get rough in places. From Asegata, it's less than an hour's walk back to Chūzen-ji village.

Dining

For a meal in upscale surroundings, try the dining room at one of the hotels listed below. Lunch will cost about ¥3,500 per person. Lunch at the Kanaya, with its air of old-fashioned gentility, is especially pleasant; the boathouse at the hotel's branch hotel on the shore of Chūzenji-ko often has fresh trout from the lake.

Dining in Nikkō, as in virtually all resort areas in Japan, is informal. Even in hotel restaurants, in winter, men might feel more comfortable in jackets but will not need neckties; for women, wearing pants is perfectly acceptable.

Lodging

Nikkō

$$$$ 🏨 **Nikkō Kanaya Hotel.** A little worn around the edges after a cen-
★   tury of operation, the Kanaya still has the best location in town—just
across the street from the Tōshō-gū shrine precincts. The hotel is very
touristy; daytime visitors, especially Westerners, come to browse
through the old building and its gift shops. The staff is very helpful
and is better at giving information on the area than the city information office. Rooms vary a great deal, as do their prices—up to ¥25,000
per person on holiday weekends. The more expensive are all spacious
and comfortable, with wonderful high ceilings; in the annex you fall
asleep to the sound of the Daiya-gawa murmuring below by the Sacred Bridge. Horseback riding and golf are available nearby. ⊠ *1300
Kami Hatsuishi-chō, Nikkō, Tochigi-ken 321,* ☎ *0288/54–0001; 03/
3271–5215 for Tōkyō office. 77 rooms, 62 with bath. Restaurant, pool.
AE, DC, MC, V.*

$–$$ 🏨 **Pension Turtle.** This member of the Japanese Inn Group offers
friendly, modest, and cost-conscious accommodations with or without private bath. Keep in mind that rates go up about 10% in high
season, from July 25 to September l. To get to the Pension Turtle, take
the bus bound for Chūzen-ji from either railway station and get off at
the Sōgō Kaikan-mae bus stop. The inn is two minutes from the bus
stop and within walking distance of Tōshō-gū. ⊠ *2-16 Takumi-chō,
Nikkō, Tochigi-ken 321,* ☎ *0288/53–3168. 7 Western-style rooms, 5
Japanese-style rooms. Restaurant. AE, MC, V.*

Chūzen-ji

$$$$ 🏨 **Chūzen-ji Kanaya.** On the road from the village to Shobu-ga-hama,
this branch of the Nikkō Kanaya has its own boathouse and restaurant on the lake. The atmosphere here is something like that of a private club. ⊠ *2482 Chū-gūshi, Nikkō, Tochigi-ken 321,* ☎ *0288/
51–0001. 60 rooms. Restaurant, waterskiing, boating, fishing. AE, DC,
MC, V.*

$$–$$$ 🏨 **Nikkō Lakeside Hotel.** In the village of Chūzen-ji at the foot of the
lake, the Nikkō Lakeside has no particular character, but the views are
good and the transportation connections (to buses and excursion
boats) are ideal. Prices vary considerably from weekday to weekend
and season to season. Check ahead. ⊠ *2482 Chū-gūshi, Nikkō, Tochigi-
ken 321,* ☎ *0288/55–0321. 100 rooms with bath. Restaurant, tennis, bicycles, boating, fishing. AE, DC, MC, V.*

Shobu-ga-hama

$$$–$$$$ 🏨 **Nikkō Prince Hotel.** This luxury hotel is within walking distance of
the Ryū-no-taki (falls). The Prince chain is one of Japan's largest and
most successful leisure conglomerates, with hotels in most major cities
and resorts. Minor differences in architecture aside, they are all pretty
much the same experience: modern creature comforts and professional
service. ⊠ *Shobu-ga-hama, Chū-gūshi, Nikkō, Tochigi-ken 321,* ☎ *0288/
55–0661. 60 twin rooms with bath. Restaurant, pool, 2 tennis courts,
water sports. AE, DC, MC, V.*

Nikkō A to Z

Arriving and Departing

BY CAR

It's possible, but unwise, to go by car from Tōkyō to Nikkō. The trip
will take at least three hours; merely getting from central Tōkyō to the
toll-road system can be a nightmare. Coming back, especially on a Sat-
urday or Sunday evening, is even worse. If you absolutely *must* drive,
take the Tōkyō Expressway 5 (Ikebukuro Line) north to the Tōkyō

Gaikandō, go east on this ring road to the Kawaguchi interchange, and pick up the Tōhoku Expressway northbound. Take the Tōhoku to Utsunomiya, and change again at Exit 10 (marked in English) for the Nikkō–Utsunomiya Toll Road, which brings you from there into Nikkō.

BY TRAIN

Far easier and more comfortable are the Limited Express trains of the Tōbu Railway, with two direct connections every morning, starting at 7:30 AM (additional trains on weekends, holidays, and in high season) from the Tōbu Asakusa Eki, a minute's walk from the last stop on the Ginza subway line in Tōkyō. The one-way fare is ¥2,750. All seats are reserved. Bookings are not accepted over the phone; consult your hotel or a travel agent. From Asakusa to the Tōbu Nikkō Eki is about two hours, which is quicker than the JR trains. If you are making a day trip, the last return trains are at 4:25 (direct express) and 7:41 PM (with a transfer at Shimo–Imaichi).

If you have a JR Pass, we suggest you use JR service, which connects Tōkyō and Nikkō, from Ueno Eki. Take the Tōhoku Line limited express to Utsunomiya (about 1½ hours) and transfer to the train for JR Nikkō Eki (45 mins). The earliest departure from Ueno is at 5:09 AM; the last connection back leaves Nikkō at 8:24 PM and brings you into Ueno at 10:45. More expensive but faster is the *Yamabiko* train on the north extension of the Shinkansen. The first one leaves Tōkyō Eki at 6:00 AM (or Ueno at 6:06 AM) and takes about 45 minutes to Utsunomiya; change there to the train to Nikkō Eki. To return, take the 9:43 PM train from Nikkō to Utsunomiya and catch the last *Yamabiko* back at 10:37, arriving in Tōkyō at 11:27.

Getting Around

In Nikkō itself, you won't need much in the way of transportation but your own two feet; nothing is terribly far from anything else. Local buses leave the railway station for Lake Chūzen-ji, stopping just above the entrance to Tōshō-gū, approximately every 30 minutes from 6:20 AM. The fare to Chūzen-ji is ¥1,100; the ride takes about 50 minutes. The last return bus from the lake leaves at 7:39 PM. Cabs are readily available; the one-way fare from the Tōbu Nikkō Eki to Chūzen-ji is about ¥6,000.

Guided Tours

From Tōkyō, **Japan Amenity Travel** (☎ 03/3542–7545) operates a one-day motor-coach tour to Nikkō, daily March 20–November 30. The tour includes Tōshō-gū and Chūzenji-ko. Pickup from major hotels begins at 8 AM; the cost is ¥14,500, lunch included.

KAMAKURA

Updated by
Jared Lubarsky

Kamakura, about 40 km (25 mi) southwest of Tōkyō, is an object lesson in what happens when you set the fox to guard the henhouse.

For the aristocrats of Heian-period (794–1185) Japan, life was defined by the Imperial Court in Kyōto. Who in his right mind would venture elsewhere? In Kyōto there was grace, and beauty, and poignant affairs of the heart; everything beyond was howling wilderness. Unfortunately, it was the howling wilderness that had all the estates: the large grants of land called *shōen*, without which there would be no income to pay for all that grace and beauty. Somebody had to go *out there*, to govern the provinces and collect the rents, to keep the restive local families in line, and to subdue the barbarians at the fringes of the empire. Over time, a number of noble families began to produce not only good poets and courtiers but good administrators. To the later dismay of their fellow aristocrats, some of them—with their various clan connections, vassals, and commanders in the field—also turned out to be extremely good fighters.

By the 12th century, two clans—the Taira (*ta*-ee-ra) and the Minamoto, themselves both offshoots of the imperial line—had come to dominate the affairs of the Heian Court and were at each other's throats in a struggle for supremacy. In 1160 the Taira won a major battle that should have secured their absolute control over Japan—and in the process made one serious mistake. They killed the Minamoto leader Yoshitomo but spared his 13-year-old son, Yoritomo and sent him into exile. Yoritomo bided his time, gathered support against the Taira, and planned his revenge. In 1180 he launched a rebellion and chose Kamakura—a superb natural fortress, surrounded on three sides by hills and guarded on the fourth by the sea—as his base of operations.

The rivalry between the two clans became an all-out war; by 1185, Yoritomo and his half-brother, Yoshitsune, had destroyed the Taira utterly, and the Minamoto were masters of all Japan. In 1192 Yoritomo forced the Imperial Court to name him shōgun; he was now de facto and de jure the military head of state. The emperor was left as a figurehead in Kyōto; the little fishing village of Kamakura became—and for 141 years remained—the seat of Japan's first shogunal government.

Yoritomo kept his antagonists at bay during his lifetime, but his heirs were less than successful. His two sons were assassinated; both died childless, and the Minamoto line came to an end. Power passed to Yoritomo's wife, Masako, and her family, the Hōjō—who remained in control, often as regents for figurehead shōguns, for the next hundred years. The decline of the Kamakura shogunate began with the two 13th-century invasions of Japan (1274 and 1281) by the Mongol armies of China's Yuan dynasty. On both occasions, typhoons—the original *kamikaze* (divine wind)—destroyed the Mongol fleets, but Kamakura was still obliged to reward the various clans it had rallied to the defense of the realm. A number of these clans were unhappy with their portions; they resented as well the virtual monopoly of the Hōjō family itself on high positions in the government. The end came suddenly, in 1333, when two important Hōjō vassals, Ashikaga Takauji and Nitta Yoshisada, who had been sent into battle against the emperor Go-Daigo, switched sides. The Hōjō regent committed suicide, and the locus of power returned to Kyōto.

Kamakura reverted to being a sleepy backwater on the edge of the sea. It remained relatively isolated until the Yokosuka railway line was built in 1889, and not until after World War II did the town begin to develop as a residential area for the well-to-do. Nothing *secular* survives, from the days of the Minamoto and Hōjō; very little was there to begin with. What the Kamakura shogunate thought about castles and palaces might best be appreciated by its other name for itself: the *bakufu*—literally, the "tent government." As a *religious* center, however, the town presents us with an extraordinary legacy. The bakufu endowed shrines and temples by the score in Kamakura, especially temples of the Rinzai sect of Zen Buddhism. The austerity of Zen, its directness and self-discipline, had a powerful appeal for a warrior class that in some ways imagined itself on perpetual bivouac. Most of those temples and shrines are in settings of remarkable beauty; many are designated National Treasures. If you can afford the time for only one day-trip from Tōkyō, you should probably spend it here.

Exploring Kamakura

Numbers in the margin correspond to points of interest on the Kamakura map.

There are three principal areas in Kamakura, and you can easily get from one to another by train. From Tōkyō, come first to Kita-Kamakura for most of the important Zen temples, including Engaku-ji and Kenchō-ji. The second area is downtown Kamakura, with its shops and museums, and the venerated shrine Tsuru-ga-oka Hachiman-gū. The third is Hase, to the southwest, a 10-minute train ride from Kamakura on the Enoden Line. Hase's main attractions are the great bronze figure of the Amida Buddha at Kōtoku-in, and the Kannon Hall of Hase-dera. There is a lot here to see, and even to hit just the highlights will take you most of a busy day. You may need to edit your choices—especially if you want to leave yourself enough time for the Enoshima resort area, described at the end of this section.

Kita-Kamakura (North Kamakura)

Hierarchies were important to the Kamakura shogunate. In the 14th century, it established a ranking system called *Go-zan* (literally, "Five Mountains") for the Zen Buddhist monasteries under its official sponsorship. **Engaku-ji,** founded in 1282, was ranked second—one of the select few temples where prayers were to be offered regularly for the prosperity of the well-being of the government. The temple complex once contained as many as 50 buildings. Often damaged in fires and earthquakes, it has been completely restored.

Engaku-ji belongs to the Rinzai sect of Zen Buddhism. Introduced into Japan from China at the beginning of the Kamakura period (1192–1333), the ideas of Zen were quickly embraced by the emerging warrior class. The samurai especially admired the Rinzai sect, with its emphasis on the ascetic life as a path to self-transcendence, and the monks of Engaku-ji played an important role as advisers to the shogunate in matters spiritual, artistic, and political. The majestic old cedars of the temple complex bespeak an age when this was both a haven of quietude and a pillar of the state.

Among the National Treasures here is the **Shari-den** (Hall of the Holy Relics of Buddha). Built in 1282, it has survived the many fires at Engaku-ji over the past seven centuries and is the only building to have kept its original form. Alas, you won't be able to go any farther than the main gate. The other National Treasure at Engaku-ji is the great **belfry** on the hilltop. The bell—Kamakura's most famous—was cast in 1301, and it stands 8 ft tall. It is rung only on rare occasions, such as New Year's Eve. The two buildings open to the public at Engaku-ji are the **Butsunichi-an,** which has a long ceremonial hall where you can enjoy the Japanese tea ceremony, and the **Obai-in.** The latter is the mausoleum of the last three regents of the Kamakura shogunate: Hōjō Tokimune—who led the defense of Japan against the Mongol invasions—his son Sadatoki, and his grandson Takatoki. Off to the side of the mausoleum is a quiet garden with apricot trees, which bloom in February. When you leave Kita-Kamakura Eki, keep the train tracks on your right and walk five minutes to the south. Engaku-ji will be on your left. ⊠ *409 Yama-no-uchi,* ☎ *0469/22–0478.* ☜ *¥200.* ☉ *Nov.–Feb., daily 8–4; Mar.–Sept., daily 8–5:30; Oct., daily 8–4:30.*

★ ⓱ **Tōkei-ji** is another Zen temple of the Rinzai sect—one with special significance for the study of feminism in medieval Japan. More popularly known as the Enkiri-dera, or "Divorce Temple," it was founded in 1285 by the widow of the Hōjō regent Tokimune as a refuge for the victims of unhappy marriages. Under the shogunate, a husband of the warrior

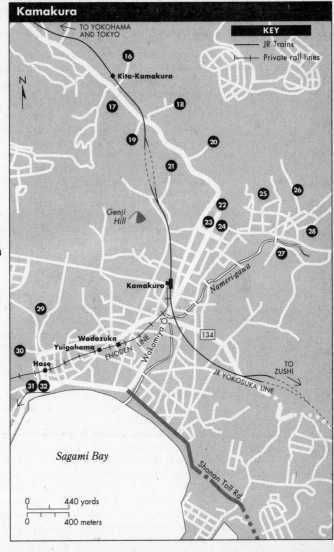

class could obtain a divorce simply by sending his wife back to her family. Not so for the wife; no matter what cruel and unusual treatment her husband meted out, she was stuck with him. If she ran away, however, and managed to reach Tōkei-ji without being caught, she could receive sanctuary at the temple and remain there as a nun. After three years (later reduced to two), she was officially declared divorced. The temple survived as a convent through the Meiji Restoration of 1868. The last abbess died in 1902; her headstone is in the cemetery behind the temple, beneath the plum trees that blossom in February. Tōkei-ji was later reestablished as a monastery.

The **Hōmotsukan** (Treasure House) has a number of Kamakura-period wooden Buddhas, ink paintings, scrolls, and works of calligraphy on display, some of which have been designated by the government as Important Cultural Objects. The library, called the Matsu-ga-oka Bunko, was established in memory of the great Zen scholar D.T. Suzuki (1870–1966). From Kita-Kamakura Eki, follow the directions for Engaku-ji;

Tōkei-ji is a 10-minute walk farther south, on the other side of the railway tracks. ⊠ *1367 Yama-no-uchi,* ☎ *0467/22–1663.* ⌸ *¥50 (an additional ¥300 for the Treasure House).* ⊘ *Tues.–Sun. 10–3.*

If your time on this trip is limited, return from Tōkei-ji to Kita-Kamakura Eki and take the train one stop to Kamakura. If not, follow the main road all the way to Tsuru-ga-oka Hachiman-gū and visit four additional temples en route.

★ ⑱ In June, when the hydrangeas are in bloom, **Meigetsu-in** becomes one of the most popular places in Kamakura. The gardens become a sea of color—pink, white, and blue—and visitors can number in the thousands. From Tōkeiji, cross back over the railway tracks and return to the main road. Meigestsu-in is a hundred yards or so farther south, on a narrow side street to the left. ⊠ *189 Yama-no-uchi,* ☎ *0467/24–3437.* ⌸ *¥300.* ⊘ *Daily 8–4:30, hydrangea season 8–5.*

⑲ In the "Five Mountains" hierarchy established by the Kamakura shogunate, **Jōchi-ji** was ranked fourth. The buildings now in the temple complex are replacements (about 50 years old) of the originals, which were destroyed by fire. The garden here is especially fine; take note of the figures of the Seven Gods of Good Fortune in the north corner—a curious group of Indian, Chinese, and Japanese deities, believed to bring wealth and long life and widely revered in the 15th to 17th centuries. Jōchi-ji is on the same side of the railway tracks as Tōkei-ji, a few minutes' walk farther south. Turn right off the main road and cross over a small bridge; the temple is at the top of a flight of moss-covered steps. ⊠ *1402 Yama-no-uchi,* ☎ *0467/22–3943.* ⌸ *¥150.* ⊘ *July–May, daily 9–4:30; June, daily 8:30–4:30.*

★ ⑳ Founded in 1249, **Kenchō-ji** was the foremost of Kamakura's five great Zen temples. It was modeled on one of the great Chinese monasteries of the time and built for a distinguished Zen master who had just arrived in Japan from China. Over the centuries, fires and other disasters have taken their toll on Kenchō-ji, and while many of the buildings have been authentically reconstructed, the temple complex today is half its original size. Near the **San-mon** (main gate) is a **bronze bell** cast in 1255; it is the temple's most important treasure. The San-mon and the **Hattō** (Lecture Hall) are the only two structures to have survived the devastating Great Kantō Earthquake of 1923. Like Engaku-ji, Kenchō-ji is a functioning temple of the Rinzai sect, where novices are trained and lay people can come to take part in Zen meditation. The entrance to Kenchō-ji is about halfway along the main road from Kita-Kamakura Eki to Tsuru-ga-oka Hachiman-gū, on the right. ⊠ *8 Yama-no-uchi,* ☎ *0467/22–0981.* ⌸ *¥300.* ⊘ *Daily 8:30–4:30.*

★ ㉑ In the feudal period, Japan acquired from China a belief in *Enma,* the Lord of Hell, who, with his court attendants, judges the souls of the departed and determines their destination in the afterlife. Kamakura's **Ennō-ji** (temple), otherwise undistinguished, houses some remarkable statues of these judges—as grim and merciless a court as you're ever likely to confront. To see them is enough to make you put you on your best behavior, at least for the rest of your excursion. ⊠ *1543 Yama-no-uchi,* ☎ *0467/25–1095.* ⌸ *¥200.* ⊘ *Daily 9–4.*

A few minutes' walk along the main road, south from Ennō-ji, will bring you to Tsuru-ga-oka Hachiman-gū. For the benefit of those who took the train from Kita-Kamakura to Kamakura, however, we begin the next section of this excursion from the station.

Kamakura

When the first Kamakura shōgun, Minamoto no Yoritomo, learned that he was about to have an heir, he had the tutelary shrine of his family moved to Kamakura from nearby Yui-ga-hama and ordered a stately avenue to be built through the center of his capital from the shrine to the sea. Along this avenue would travel the procession that brought his son—if there was a son—to be presented to the gods. Yoritomo's consort did indeed bear him a son, Yoriie (yo-*ree*-ee-eh), in 1182; Yoriie was indeed brought in great pomp to the shrine, and consecrated to his place in the shogunal succession. Alas, the blessing of the gods did Yoriie little good. He was barely 18 when Yoritomo died, and the regency established by his mother's family, the Hōjō, kept him virtually powerless until 1203, when he was banished and eventually assassinated. The Minamoto were never to hold power again, but Yoriie's memory lives on in the street—Wakamiya Oji, "The Avenue of the Young Prince"—that his father built for him.

THE TSURU-GA-OKA HACHIMAN-GŪ COMPLEX

★ ㉒ The Minamoto shrine, **Tsuru-ga-oka Hachiman-gū,** is dedicated to the legendary emperor Ōjin, his wife, and his mother, from whom Minamoto no Yoritomo claimed descent. At the entrance, a small, steeply arched vermilion bridge—the **Drum Bridge**—crosses a stream between two lotus ponds. The ponds were made to Yoritomo's specifications. His wife, Masako, suggested placing islands in each. In the larger **Genji Pond,** to the right, filled with white lotus flowers, she placed three islands. Genji was another name for the Minamoto clan, and three is an auspicious number. In the smaller **Heike Pond,** to the left, she put four islands. Heike (*heh*-ee-keh) was another name for the rival Taira clan, which the Minamoto had destroyed, and four—homophonous in Japanese with the word for "death"—is very unlucky indeed.

On the far side of the Drum Bridge is the **Mai-den.** This hall is the setting for a story of the Minamoto celebrated in Noh and Kabuki theater; it bears telling here. Though Yoritomo was the tactical genius behind the downfall of the Taira and the establishment of the Kamakura shogunate, it was his dashing half-brother, Yoshitsune, who actually defeated the Taira in battle. In so doing, he won the admiration of many, and Yoritomo came to believe that he had ambitions of his own. Despite Yoshitsune's declaration of allegiance, Yoritomo had him exiled and sent assassins to have him killed. Yoshitsune spent his life fleeing from one place to another until, at the age of 30, betrayed in his last refuge, he took his own life.

Earlier in his exile, Yoshitsune's lover, the dancer Shizuka Gozen, had been captured and brought to Kamakura. Yoritomo and his wife, Masako, commanded Shizuka to dance at the family shrine, as a kind of penance. Instead, she danced to the joy of her love for Yoshitsune and her concern for his fate. Yoritomo was furious, and only Masako's influence kept him from ordering her death. When he discovered, however, that Shizuka was carrying Yoshitsune's child, he ordered that, if the child was a boy, he was to be killed. A boy was born. Some versions of the legend have it that the child was slain; others say that he was placed in a cradle, like Moses, and cast adrift in the reeds. This heart-rending drama is enacted once a year during the Spring Festival (early or mid-April, when the cherry trees bloom) on the stage at the Mai-den.

Beyond the Mai-den, a flight of steps leads to the shrine's Hon-dō (Main Hall). To the left of these steps is a ginko tree that—according to legend—was witness to a murder that ended the Minamoto line in 1219. From behind this tree, a priest named Kugyō leapt out and beheaded his uncle, the 26-year-old Sanetomo, Yoritomo's second son and the last Minamoto shōgun. The priest was quickly apprehended, but Sanetomo's head was never found. Like all other Shintō shrines, the Hongū is unadorned; the building itself, an 1828 reconstruction, is not particularly noteworthy.

To reach Tsuru-ga-oka Hachiman-gū from the east side of Kamakura Eki, cross the plaza, turn left, and walk north along Wakamiya Oji. Straight ahead is the first of three arches leading to the shrine, and the shrine itself is at the far end of the street. ⊠ *2-131 Yuki-no-shita,* ☎ *0467/22–0315.* ☑ *Free.* ☉ *Daily 8:30–6.*

㉓ Within the shrine precincts are two museums. The **Kamakura Shiritsu Kindai Bijutsukan** (Municipal Museum of Modern Art), near Heike Pond, has a collection of Japanese oil paintings and watercolors, wood-block prints, and sculpture. ☎ *0467/22–5000.* ☑ *¥720–¥1,000, depending on the exhibition.* ☉ *Tues.–Sun. 9:30–4:30; closed the day after national holidays.*

㉔ The **Kokuhōkan** (Treasure Museum) has a fine collection of objects pertaining to the Kamakura period and a display of Edo-period *ukiyo-e* prints. ☎ *0467/22–0753.* ☑ *¥100.* ☉ *Tues.–Sun. 9–4.*

OTHER KAMAKURA SIGHTS

The man who put Kamakura on the map, so to speak, chose not to leave it when he died: It is only a short walk from ☞ **Tsuru-ga-oka**
㉕ **Hachiman-gū** to **Yoritomo's Tomb.** If you've already been to Nikkō and seen how a later dynasty of shōguns sought to glorify their own memories, you will be surprised at the plainness of this monument, but the route of your excursion takes you this way anyhow, and you may as well stop and pay your respects. Cross the Drum Bridge at Tsuru-ga-oka Hachiman-gū and turn right. Leave the grounds of the shrine, and walk east along the broad street that forms the T-intersection at the end of Wakamiya Oji. A 10-minute walk will bring you to a narrow street on the left that leads uphill to the tomb, about 100 yards off the street to the west. ☑ *Free.* ☉ *Daily 9–4:30.*

㉖ **Kamakura-gū** is a Shintō shrine built after the Meiji Restoration of 1868 and dedicated to Prince Morinaga (1308–36), third son of the emperor Go-Daigo. When Go-Daigo overthrew the Kamakura shogunate and restored Japan to direct imperial rule, Morinaga—who had been in the priesthood—was appointed supreme commander of his father's forces. The prince lived in turbulent times and died young: When the Ashikaga clan in turn overthrew Go-Daigo's government, Morinaga was taken into exile, held prisoner in a cave behind the present site of Kamakura-gū, and eventually beheaded. To reach the shrine, retrace your steps from Yoritomo's Tomb and turn left; Kamakura-gū is a few steps farther north on the right. ⊠ *154 Nikaidō, Kamakura,* ☎ *0467/22–0318.* ☑ *¥300.* ☉ *Daily 9:30–4:30.*

If you still have time and energy, two temples in this area are worth brief
㉗ visits. *Gai-jin* tend, alas, to overlook **Hōkoku-ji,** a lovely little Zen temple of the Rinzai sect that was built in 1334. Over the years, it had fallen into disrepair and neglect, until an enterprising priest took over, cleaned up the gardens, and began promoting the temple for meditation sessions and calligraphy exhibitions and tea ceremony. Behind the main hall is a thick grove of bamboo, and a small tea pavilion—a restful oasis and a fine place to go for *matcha* (tea ceremony green tea). Hōkoku-ji is about 2 km (1 mi) east on the main road that begins at the intersection in front of the Drum Bridge at ☞ **Tsuru-ga-oka Hachiman-gū,** on the right. ⊠ *2 Jōmyō-ji,* ☎ *0467/22–0762.* ☑ *¥200, tea ceremony ¥500.* ☉ *Daily 9–4.*

㉘ Jōmyō-ji, founded in 1188, is the only one of the "Five Mountains" Zen monasteries in this part of Kamakura. It lacks the grandeur and scale of Engaku-ji and Kenchō-ji—naturally enough, as it was ranked behind them, in fifth place—but it still merits the status of an Important Cultural Property. To reach it from Hōkoku-ji, cross the main street that brought you the mile or so from ☞ **Tsuru-ga-oka Hachiman-gū,** and take the first narrow street north. Jōmyō-ji is about 100 yards from the corner, on the right. ✉ *3 Jōmyō-ji,* ☎ *0467/22–2818.* ✇ *¥100.* 🕐 *Daily 9–4.*

A bus from Kamakura Eki (sign No. 5) traces the route you've taken, with stops at most of the access roads to the temples and shrines. We recommend walking out as far as Hōkoku-ji and taking the bus back; it's easier to recognize the end of the line than any of the stops in between. You can also go by taxi to Hōkoku-ji—any cab driver knows the way—and walk this last leg in reverse. In any event, downtown Kamakura is a good place to stop for lunch and shop. Restaurants and shops selling local crafts objects, especially the carved and lacquered woodwork called Kamakura-bori, abound on Wakamiya Oji and the street parallel to it, Komachi-dōri.

Hase

★ **㉙** The single biggest attraction in Hase (*ha*-seh) is the Kōtoku-in's **Daibutsu** (Great Buddha)—sharing the honors with Fuji-san, perhaps, as the quintessential picture-postcard image of Japan. The statue of the compassionate Amida Buddha sits cross-legged in the temple courtyard, the drapery of his robes flowing in lines reminiscent of ancient Greece, his expression profoundly serene. The 37-ft bronze figure was cast in 1292, three centuries before Europeans reached Japan; the concept of the classical Greek lines in the Buddha's robe must have come over the Silk Route through China during the time of Alexander the Great. The casting was probably first conceived in 1180, by Minamoto no Yoritomo, who wanted a statue to rival the enormous Daibutsu in Nara. Until 1495, the Amida Buddha was housed in a wooden temple, which was washed away in a great tidal wave. Since then, the loving Buddha has stood exposed, facing the cold winters and hot summers for the last five centuries.

It may seem sacrilegious to some actually to walk inside the Great Buddha, but for ¥20, you can enter the figure from a doorway in the right side and explore (until 4 PM) his stomach. To reach Kōtoku-in and the Daibutsu, take the Enoden Line train from the west side of the JR Kamakura Eki three stops to Hase. To the left of the exit is the main street that heads north to the Daibutsu, about a 10-minute walk. ✉ *4-2-28 Hase,* ☎ *0467/22–0703.* ✇ *¥200.* 🕐 *Apr.–Sept., daily 7–6; Oct.–Mar., daily 7–5:30.*

★ **㉚** The other major sight in Hase is **Hase-dera**—one of the most beautiful, and saddest, temples in Japan. Flanking the steep flight of stone steps that lead to the temple grounds are hundreds of small stone images of the bodhisattva Jizō, one of the "saints" in the Buddhist pantheon who have deferred their own ascendance into Buddha-hood to guide the souls of others to salvation. Jizō is the savior of children—particularly the souls of the stillborn, aborted, and miscarried; the mothers of these children dress the statues of Jizō in bright red bibs and leave them small offerings of food, strangely touching acts of prayer and penitence.

The **Kannon Hall** at Hase-dera enshrines the largest carved wood statue in Japan: the votive figure of Jūichimen Kannon, the Eleven-Headed Goddess of Mercy. Standing 30 ft tall, the goddess bears a crown of 10 smaller heads, symbolizing her ability to search out in all directions for those in need of her compassion. No one knows for certain when the figure was carved. According to the temple records, a monk named Shōnin carved two images of the Jūichimen Kannon from a huge laurel tree in 721. One was consecrated to the Hase-dera in present-day Nara Prefecture; the other was thrown into the sea, to go wherever the sea decided that there were souls in need, and that image washed up on shore near Kamakura. Much later, in 1342, Ashikaga Takauji—the first of the 15 Ashikaga shōguns who followed the Kamakura era—had the statue covered with gold leaf.

The **Amida Hall,** the other major building of Hase-dera, enshrines the image of a seated Amida Buddha, who presides over the Western Paradise of the Pure Land. Minamoto no Yoritomo ordered the creation of this statue when he reached the age of 42; popular Japanese belief, adopted from China, holds that a man's 42nd year is particularly unlucky. Yoritomo's act of piety earned him another 10 years; he was 52 when he was thrown by a horse and died of his injuries. The Buddha is popularly known as the *yakuyoke* (good-luck) Amida, and many visitors—especially students facing graduation and entrance exams—make a point of coming here to offer prayers. To the left of the Amida Hall is a small restaurant where you can buy good-luck candy and admire the view of Kamakura Beach and Sagami Bay; Hase-dera is the only Kamakura temple facing the sea. From Hase Eki, head north on the main street to the left of the station exit. About a quarter of the way out to Kōtoku-in's Daibutsu, look for directions to Hase-dera on a side street to the left. ⊠ *3-11-2 Hase,* ☎ *0467/22–6300.* ☞ *¥300, including admission to the Hōmotsukan.* ⊙ *Mar.–Nov., daily 8–5; Dec.–Feb., daily 8–4:30.*

Dining

$$$–$$$$ ✕ **Kaseiro.** In an old Japanese house on the street that leads toward the Daibutsu at Kōtoku-in, this establishment offers the best Chinese food in the city. The dining-room windows look onto a small, restful garden. ⊠ *3-1-14 Hase, Kamakura,* ☎ *0467/22–0280. AE, DC, MC, V.*

$$–$$$ ✕ **Hachinoki Honten.** Traditional *shōjin ryōri* (the vegetarian cuisine of Zen monasteries) is served here in an old Japanese house adjacent to Kenchō-ji. There is some table service, but most of the seating is in tatami rooms, with beautiful antique wood furnishings. Allow plenty of time; this is not a meal to be hurried through. Meals are served 11–4 Tuesday–Friday, 11–6 weekends. ⊠ *7 Yama-no-uchi, Kamakura,* ☎ *0467/22–8719. DC, MC, V.*

$$ ✕ **Tori-ichi.** This elegant restaurant serves traditional Japanese fare
★ called *kaiseki.* In an old country-style building, waitresses in kimono serve sumptuous multicourse meals, including one or more subtle-tasting soups, sushi, tempura, grilled fish, and other delicacies. ⊠ *7-13 Onari-machi, Kamakura,* ☎ *0467/22–1818. No credit cards. Closed Tues.*

$ ✕ **Kado Restaurant.** This is a small noodle shop on the right side of the main road leading into town from Tokei-ji. The owners don't speak English and the menu is in Japanese, but the large portions of noodles with vegetables, meat, and/or fish will supply the energy you'll need to finish getting around Kamakura. ⊠ *Kamakura-Kaido, no phone. Reservations not accepted. No credit cards.*

Ryūko-ji and Enoshima

The Kamakura story would not be complete without the tale of **Nichiren** (1222–82), the monk who founded the only native Japanese sect of Buddhism. Nichiren's rejection of both Zen and Jōdo ("Pure Land") teachings brought him into conflict with the Kamakura shogunate, and the Hōjō regents sent him into exile on the Izu Peninsula in 1621. Later allowed to return, he continued to preach his own interpretation of the Lotus Sutra—and to assert the "blasphemy" of other Buddhist sects, a stance that finally persuaded the Hōjō regency, in 1271, to condemn him to death. Execution was to take place on a hill to the south of Hase. As the executioner swung his sword, legend has it that a lightning bolt struck the blade and snapped it in two. Taken aback, the executioner sat down to collect his wits, and a messenger was sent back to Kamakura to report the event. On his way, he met another messenger, who was carrying a writ from the Hōjō regents commuting Nichiren's sentence to exile on the island of Sado-ga-shima.

Followers of Nichiren built a temple in 1337 to mark his miraculous deliverance from the headman, on the hill where he was to be executed. ❸ The temple is **Ryūkō-ji.** While there are other Nichiren temples closer to Kamakura—Myōhon-ji and Ankokuron-ji, for example—Ryūkō-ji not only has the typical Nichiren-style main hall with gold tassels hanging from its roof but also a beautiful pagoda, built in 1904. To reach it, take the Enoden Line west from Hase to Enoshima—a short, scenic ride that cuts through the hills surrounding Kamakura to the shore. From Enoshima Eki, walk about 100 yards east, keeping the train tracks on your right, and you'll come to the temple. ⊠ *3-13-37 Katase, Fujisawa,* ☎ *0466/25–7357.* 🎫 *Free.* ☉ *Daily 10–4.*

The Sagami Bay shore in this area, incidentally, has some of the closest beaches to Tōkyō, and in the hot, humid summer months it seems that all of the city's teeming millions pour onto these beaches in search of a vacant patch of rather dirty gray sand. Pass up this mob scene and ❸ press on instead to **Enoshima** (island). The island is only 4 km (2½ mi) around, with a hill in the middle. Partway up the hill is a shrine where the local fishermen used to pray for a bountiful catch—before it became a tourist attraction. Once upon a time it was quite a hike up to the shrine; now there is a series of escalators, flanked by the inevitable array of stalls selling souvenirs and snacks. The island has a number of cafés and restaurants; on clear days, some of them have spectacular views of Fuji-san and the Izu Peninsula. To reach the causeway from Enoshima Eki to the island, walk south from the station for about 3 km (2 mi), keeping the Katase-gawa (river) on your right.

To return to Tōkyō from Enoshima, take a train to Shinjuku on the Odakyū Line. From the island, walk back across the causeway and take the second bridge over the Katase-gawa. Within five minutes you'll come to Katase-Enoshima Eki. There are 14 afternoon trains, two each hour on express schedules, between 2:20 and 8:20 (more in summer). The express takes about 70 minutes to make the trip and costs ¥1,220. Or you can retrace your steps to Kamakura and take the JR Yokosuka Line to Tōkyō Eki.

Kamakura A to Z

Arriving and Departing

Traveling by train is by far the best way to get to Kamakura. Trains run from Tōkyō Eki (and Shimbashi Eki) every 10–15 minutes during the day. The trip takes 56 minutes to Kita-Kamakura (*kita* meaning north), which is where the section above begins, and one hour to Kamakura. Take the JR Yokosuka Line from Track 1 downstairs in Tōkyō Eki. (Track 1 upstairs is on a different line and does not go to Kamakura.) The cost is ¥760 to Kita-Kamakura, ¥880 to Kamakura (or use your JR Pass).

Guided Tours

Unfortunately, no bus company in Kamakura offers a guided tour in English. You can, however, take one of the Japanese tours, which depart from Kamakura Eki eight times daily, starting at 9:40 AM. Purchase tickets at the bus office to the right of the station. There are two itineraries, one lasting two hours, 10 minutes (¥2,500), the other about 2½ hours (¥3,300). The last tours leave at 1:40 PM. Take Michael Cooper's book *Exploring Kamakura: A Guide for the Curious Traveler* with you, and you'll have more information at your fingertips than any of your fellow passengers.

On Saturday and Sunday, the Kanagawa Student Guide Federation has a free guide service. Students show you the city in exchange for the chance to practice their English. Arrangements need to be made in advance through the Japan National Tourist Office in Tōkyō (☎ 03/3201–3331). Be at Kamakura station by 10 AM.

Tours from Tōkyō depart every day, often combined with trips to Hakone (☞ Fuji-Hakone-Izu National Park, *below*). You can book through, and arrange to be picked up at, any of the major hotels. Before you do, however, be certain that the tour covers everything in Kamakura that you want to see; many include little more than a passing view of the Daibutsu (Great Buddha) in Hase. Given how easy it is to get around—most of the sights are within walking distance of each other; others are short bus or train rides apart—you're better off seeing Kamakura on your own.

YOKOHAMA

Updated by
Jared Lubarsky

In 1639 the Tokugawa shogunate adopted a policy of national seclusion that closed Japan to virtually all contact with the outside world—a policy that remained in force for more than 200 years. Then, in 1853, a flotilla of American ships under Commodore Matthew Perry sailed into the bay of Tōkyō (then Edo) and forced the reluctant shogunate to abandon its isolation. Three years later, New York businessman Townsend Harris became America's first diplomatic representative to Japan. Once the commercial treaty with the United States was signed, Harris lost no time in setting up his residence in Hangaku-ji (temple) in Kanagawa, now a part of Yokohama. Kanagawa, however, was one of the 53 relay stations on the Tōkaidō, the highway from Edo to the Imperial Court in Kyōto, and the presence of foreigners—perceived as unclean barbarians—offended the Japanese elite. Die-hard elements of the warrior class, moreover, wanted Japan to remain in isolation and were willing to give their lives to rid the country of intruders. Unable to protect them in Kanagawa, the shogunate required Harris and his fellow foreigners, diplomatic and commercial, to establish themselves instead in a special settlement in nearby Yokohama.

At the time, Yokohama was a small fishing village on mud flats, 20 km (12½ mi) southwest of Tōkyō. The foreign diplomats and traders were confined here to a guarded compound—placed, in effect, in isolation. Not for long, however. Within 30 years, the seven centuries of shogunal rule would come to an end, and Japan would begin to modernize. Western ideas were welcomed, as well as Western goods. In 1869 Yokohama was designated an international port, and as the port grew, so did the international community.

The English enjoyed a special cachet in the new Japan. Was not Britain, too, a small island nation? And did it not do great things in the wide world? These were people to learn from, and to trade with, and the Japanese welcomed them in considerable numbers. You can still watch the occasional game of cricket at the Yokohama Country and Athletic Club—no longer an exclusively British institution. Americans came, too, and so did the French and Germans. In 1872 Japan's first railway was built, linking Yokohama and Tōkyō. By the early 1900s, the city had one of the world's busiest ports.

Then Yokohama came tumbling down. On September 1, 1923, the Great Kantō Earthquake devastated the city. The ensuing fires destroyed some 60,000 homes and took more than 20,000 lives. During the six years it took to rebuild, many foreign businesses took up quarters elsewhere, primarily in Kōbe and Ōsaka, and did not return.

Over the next 20 years Yokohama continued to grow, as an industrial center—until May 29, 1945, when in a span of four hours, 700 American B-29 bombers leveled nearly half of the city. After the war, Yokohama rose once more from the debris, and, boosted by Japan's postwar economic miracle, extended its urban sprawl north to Tōkyō and south to Kamakura.

The development of air travel, and the competition from other ports, has changed the city's role in Japan's economy. The great liners that once docked at Yokohama's piers are now but a memory, kept alive by a museum ship and the occasional visit of a luxury vessel on a Pacific cruise. The only regularly scheduled passenger services are Russian and Chinese. Modern Yokohama thrives instead in its industrial, commercial, and service sectors—and a large percentage of its people commute to work in Tōkyō. Is Yokohama worth a visit?—not, certainly, at the expense of Nikkō or Kamakura, and not if you are looking for history in the physical fabric of the city. Most of Yokohama's late-19th- and early 20th-century buildings are long gone. In some odd, undefinable way, however, Yokohama is a more *cosmopolitan* city than Tōkyō. The waterfront is fun, and city planners have made an exceptional success of their port redevelopment project. The museums are excellent. And if you spend time enough here, Yokohama can still invoke for you the days when, for intrepid Western travelers, Japan was a new frontier.

Exploring Yokohama

Numbers in the margin correspond to points of interest on the Yokohama map.

Large as Yokohama is, the central area is very negotiable. As with any other port city, much of what it has to offer centers on the waterfront—in this case, the "Bund," on the west side of Tōkyō Bay. The downtown area is called Kannai (literally, "within the checkpoint"); this is where the international community was originally confined by the shogunate. Though the center of interest has expanded to include the waterfront and Ishikawa-chō to the south, Kannai remains the heart of town.

Think of that heart as two adjacent areas. One is the old district of Kannai, bounded by Basha-michi on the northwest and Nippon-ōdori on the southeast, the Keihin Tōhoku Line tracks on the southwest, and the waterfront on the northeast. This area contains the business offices of modern Yokohama. The other area extends southeast from Nippon-ōdori to the Moto-machi shopping street and the International Cemetery, bordered by Yamashita Kōen (Ya-*ma*-sh-ta *Ko*-en) and the waterfront to the northeast; in the center is Chinatown, with Ishikawa-chō Eki to the southwest. This is the most interesting part of town if you have a short time here.

Whether you are coming from Tōkyō, Nagoya, or Kamakura, make **Ishikawa-chō Eki** your starting point. Take the south exit from the station and head in the direction of the waterfront. Within a block of

33 Ishikawa-chō Eki is the beginning of **Moto-machi,** the street that follows the course of the Nakamura-gawa to the harbor. This is where the Japanese set up shop 100 years ago to serve the strange foreigners living in Kannai. The street is now lined with smart boutiques and jewelry stores that cater to fashionable young Japanese consumers.

34 The **International Cemetery,** a Yokohama landmark and a reminder of the port city's heritage, was established in 1854 when an American sailor chose this spot for his final resting place. Since then the burial ground has been restricted to non-Japanese. About 4,000 graves are on this hillside, and the inscriptions on the crosses and headstones attest to some 40 different nationalities who lived and died in Yokohama. The museum is at the far west end of Moto-machi, on a small hill to the

35 right. The **Yamate Shiryōkan,** an archival collection of materials from the city's 19th-century European enclave, is likely more interesting to the Japanese than it is to gai-jin. The Shiryōkan is behind the International Cemetery. ⊠ *247 Yamate, Naka-ku,* ☎ *045/622–1188.* 🖂 *¥200.* ☉ *Daily 11–4; closed Dec. 30–Jan. 1.*

Once the barracks of the British forces in Yokohama, the hilltop

36 **Minato-no-Mieru-Oka Kōen** (Harbor View Park) affords fine views of the harbor. The view at night, when the harbor and the gardens of Yamashita Kōen are floodlit, is a treat. The park is 100 yards east of Yamate Shiryōkan, or just up from the east end of the Nakamura-gawa.

37 **Yamashita Kōen,** an oasis of green along the waterfront, is perhaps the only positive legacy of the Great Kantō Earthquake of 1923. The debris of the warehouses and other buildings that once stood here was swept away, and the area was made into a 17-acre park. The fountain, representing the "Guardian of the Water," was presented to Yokohama by San Diego, California, one of its sister cities.

38 The **Yokohama Doll Museum** houses a collection of some 4,000 dolls from all over the world. In Japanese tradition, dolls are less to play with than to display—either in religious folk customs or as the embodiment of some spiritual quality. Japanese visitors to this museum never seem to outgrow their affection for the Western dolls on display here, to which they tend to assign the role of timeless "ambassadors of good will" from other cultures. The museum is worth a quick visit, with or without a child in tow. It's just off the corner of Moto-machi and the Yamashita Park promenade, to the left. ⊠ *18 Yamashita-chō, Naka-ku,* ☎ *045/671–9361.* 🖂 *¥300.* ☉ *Sept.–June, Tues.–Sun. 10–5; July–Aug., Tues.–Sun. 10–6:30; closed the day after national holidays, Dec. 29–Jan. 1.*

One of the least successful buildings in Yokohama, architecturally, is

39 the 348-ft decagonal **Marine Tower.** The tower has a navigational beacon at the 338-ft level and purports to be the tallest lighthouse in the world. At the 328-ft level, an observation gallery provides 360-degree views of the harbor and the city; on clear days in autumn or winter, you can often see Fuji-san in the distance. To get here, turn left at the northeast end of Moto-machi and walk along the Yamashita Park promenade to the middle of the second block. ⊠ *15 Yamashita-chō, Naka-ku,* ☎ *045/641–7838.* 🖂 *¥700.* ☉ *Jan.–Feb., daily 10–7; Mar.–Dec., daily 10–9 (or later).*

40 Moored on the waterfront halfway down Yamashita park is the ***Hikawamaru,*** which for 30 years shuttled passengers between Yokohama and Seattle, Washington, making a total of 238 trips. The ship evokes, perhaps, the time when Yokohama was a great port of call for the transpa-

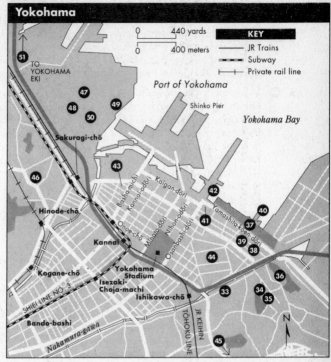

Yokohama

cific liners, but you can safely skip the tour below deck. The *Hikawa-maru* has a restaurant, and in summer there is a beer garden on the upper deck.

41 The **Silk Museum** pays tribute to the period at the turn of the last century when Japan's exports of silk were all shipped out of Yokohama. The museum has an extensive collection of silk fabrics, and an informative exhibit on the silk-making process. People on staff are very happy to answer questions. In the same building, on the first floor, are the main offices of the Yokohama International Tourist Association and the Kanagawa Prefecture Tourist Information Service. The museum is at the northwestern end of the Yamashita Park promenade, on the second floor of the Silk Center Building. ⊠ *1 Yamashita-chō, Naka-ku,* ☎ *045/641–0841.* ☞ *¥300.* ⊙ *Tues.–Sun. 9–4:30; closed the day after national holidays, Dec. 29–Jan. 1.*

42 The **Yokohama Archives of History,** housed in what was once the British Consulate, has some 140,000 items recording the history of Yokohama since the opening of the port to international trade. Across the street is the monument to the U.S.-Japanese Friendship Treaty. Walk west from the Silk Building, at the end of Yamashita Kōen promenade, to the corner of Nihon-ōdori; the Archives are on the left. ⊠ *3 Nihon-ōdori, Naka-ku,* ☎ *045/201–2100.* ☞ *¥200.* ⊙ *Tues.–Sun. 9:30–4:30; closed the day after national holidays, Dec. 29–Jan. 1.*

Basha-michi (literally, "Horse-Carriage Street") runs northeast between Kannai Eki and Shinko Pier. The street was so named in the 19th century, when it was widened to accommodate the horse-drawn carriages of the city's European residents; now this redbrick road has become a nostalgic symbol of that international past, with "antique" telephone booths and imitation gas lamps. The **Kanagawa Prefectural Museum,**

43 built in 1904, is one of the few buildings in Yokohama to have survived both the Great Kantō Earthquake and World War II. Alas, the exhibits—archaeological artifacts and the natural history of the region—have only marginal interest. The museum is about a 10-minute walk from Kannai Eki, roughly midway along Basha-michi, on the left. ⊠ *5-60 Minami Naka-dōri, Naka-ku,* ☎ *045/201–0926.* 🎫 *¥300.* ☉ *Tues.–Sun. 9–5; closed last Tues. of month, the day after national holidays.*

★ ㊹ Yokohama's **Chinatown** (Chūka-gai) is the largest settlement of Chinese in Japan. Its small alleys are full of shops selling foodstuffs, herbal medicines, cookware, toys and ornaments, and clothing and accessories: If China exports it, you'll find it here. Wonderful exotic aromas waft from the shops selling spices. Even better aromas drift from the restaurants: This is the best place for lunch in Yokohama. Chinatown is a 10-minute walk southeast of Kannai Eki. When you get to Yokohama Stadium, turn left and cut through the municipal park to the top of Nihon-ōdori. Then take a right, and you'll enter Chinatown through the North Gate, which leads to the vermilion, 50-ft-high Hairō-mon.

Around Yokohama

★ ㊺ **Sankei-en** was once the estate and gardens of Hara Tomitaro, one of Yokohama's wealthiest men, who made his money as a silk merchant before becoming a patron of the arts. On the extensive grounds of the estate he created a kind of open-air museum of traditional Japanese architecture, some of which was brought here from Kamakura and the western part of the country. Especially noteworthy is Rinshunkaku, a villa built for the Tokugawa clan in 1649. There is also a tea pavilion, Chōshūkaku, built by the third Tokugawa shōgun, Iemitsu. Other noteworthy buildings include a small temple transported from Kyōto's famed Daitoku-ji, and a farmhouse from the Gifu district in the Japan Alps (around Takayama). The garden was opened to the public in 1906.

Walking through Sankei-en is a special delight in spring, when the flowering trees are at their best: plum blossoms in February and cherry blossoms in early April. In June come the irises, followed by the water lilies. With the coming of autumn, the trees come back into their own with their tinted golden leaves. To reach Sankei-en, take the JR Keihin Tōhoku Line to Negishi Eki, and a local bus from there for the 10-minute trip to the garden. ⊠ *293 Honmoku San-no-tani, Naka-ku,* ☎ *045/621–0635.* 🎫 *Inner and outer gardens ¥700.* ☉ *Inner garden daily 9–4, outer garden daily 9–4:30; both gardens closed Dec. 29–31.*

㊻ **Iseyama Kodai Jingū,** a branch of the nation's revered Grand Shrines of Ise, is the most important Shintō shrine in Yokohama—but probably worth a visit only if you have seen most of everything else in town. The shrine is a 10-minute walk west of Sakuragi-chō Eki. ⊠ *64 Miyazaki-chō, Nishi-ku,* ☎ *045/241–1122.* 🎫 *Free.* ☉ *Daily dawn–dusk.*

㊼ If you want to see Yokohama urban development in its flat-out "Tōkyō? Where's that?" mode, **Minato Mirai 21** is a must. The aim of this project, launched in the mid-1980s, was to turn some three-quarters of a square mile of waterfront, lying east of the JR Negishi Line railroad tracks between Yokohama and Sakuragi-chō stations, into a model "city of the future." As a hotel, business, international exhibition, and conference center, it is a smashing success. Minato Mirai 21 is also the site

㊽ of the **Yokohama Bijutsukan** (Yokohama Museum of Art), designed by Kenzō Tange. Its collection includes works by Western and Japanese artists, including Cézanne, Picasso, Braque, Klee, Kandinsky, Kishida Ryūsei, and Yokoyama Taikan. ⊠ *3-4-1 Minato Mirai, Nishi-ku,* ☎ *045/221–0300.* 🎫 *¥500.* ☉ *Mon.–Wed. and Fri.–Sun. 10–6; closed the day after national holidays. Subway: Sakuragi-chō.*

49 Nippon-maru Memorial Park is Yokohama's tribute to *Nippon-maru*, a full-rigged three-masted ship popularly called the "Swan of the Pacific." Built in 1930, now retired from service as a training vessel and occasional participant in Tall Ships festivals, it is open for guided tours. The ship is in Minato Mirai. ✉ *2-1-1 Minato Mirai, Nishi-ku,* ☎ *045/221–0280.* ✇ *¥600.* ☉ *Sept.–June, Tues.–Sun. 10–5; July–Aug., daily 10–6:30. JR eki: Sakuragi-chō.*

50 Japan's tallest building, too, is in Minato Mirai: the 70-story **Landmark Tower.** Its observation deck has a spectacular view of the city, especially at night. On the first level is the Mitsubishi Heavy Industry Corporation's **Minato Mirai Museum,** with rocket engines, power plants, a submarine, various gadgets, and displays that simulate piloting helicopters—great fun for kids. ✉ *3-3-1 Minato Mirai, Nishi-ku,* ☎ *045/224–9031.* ✇ *¥500.* ☉ *Mon.–Wed. and Fri.–Sun. 10–5:30. Subway: Sakuragi-chō.*

OFF THE BEATEN PATH

SŌJI-JI – In Yokohama's Tsurumi Ward, Sōji-ji is one of the two major centers of the Sōtō Sect of Zen Buddhism, founded in 1321. The center was moved here from Ishikawa on the Noto Peninsula (on the Sea of Japan, north of Kanazawa), after a fire in the 19th century. There is also a Sōji-ji monastic complex at Eihei-ji in Fukui Prefecture. The Yokohama Sōji-ji is one of the largest and busiest Buddhist institutions in Japan, with more than 200 monks and novices in residence. The 14th-century patron of Sōji-ji was the emperor Go-Daigo, who overthrew the Kamakura shogunate; the emperor is buried here, although his mausoleum is off-limits to visitors. You can see, however, the **Buddha Hall,** the **Main Hall,** and the **Treasure House.** To get to Sōji-ji, take the JR Keihin Tōhoku Line two stops from Sakuragi-chō to Tsurumi. From the station, walk five minutes south (back toward Yokohama), passing Tsurumi University on your right. You'll soon reach the stone lanterns that mark the entrance to the temple complex. ✉ *2-1-1 Tsurumi, Tsurumi-ku,* ☎ *045/581–6021.* ✇ *¥300.* ☉ *Sōji-ji Center daily dawn–dusk, Treasure House daily 10–4:30.*

Dining

$$$$ ✗ **Rinka-en.** If you visit Sankei-en, you might want to have lunch at this traditional country restaurant that serves *kaiseki*-style (traditional Japanese) cuisine. The owner, by the way, is the granddaughter of Hara Tomitaro, who donated the gardens to the city. ✉ *Honmoku Sanno-tani, Naka-ku,* ☎ *045/621–0318. Jacket and tie. No credit cards. Closed Wed. and Aug.*

$$$$ ✗ **Scandia.** Known for its smorgasbord, Scandia is near the Silk Center and the business district. It is popular for business lunches as well as for dinner and stays open later than many other restaurants. ✉ *1-1 Kaigandōri, Naka-ku,* ☎ *045/201–2262. No credit cards. No lunch Sun.*

$$$–$$$$ ✗ **Miroir.** One of the most elegant venues in town, Miroir is on the sec-
★ ond floor of a seven-story banquet facility called Excellent Coast, between the Moto-machi and Chinatown districts. The facade of the building evokes the Paris Opera House; the restaurant itself is a bit more casual and understated than its surroundings. The classic French food is superb, and service is exceptional. ✉ *105 Yamashita-chō, Naka-ku,* ☎ *045/211–2252. Jacket and tie. AE, DC, MC, V. Closed Mon.*

$$$ ✗ **Aichiya.** This seafood restaurant purports to have the only chef in
★ Yokohama licensed to prepare *fugu* (blowfish)—a delicacy that must be treated with expert care, to remove the organs containing a deadly toxin. Fugu is served only in winter. The crabs here are also a treat. ✉ *7-156-1 Sezaki-chō, Naka-ku,* ☎ *045/251–4163. Jacket and tie. No credit cards. Closed Mon.*

$$$ ✕ **Kaseiro.** A smart Chinese restaurant with red carpets and gold-toned walls, Kaseiro serves Beijing cuisine and is the best of its kind in the city. ✉ *164 Yamashita-chō, Naka-ku,* ☎ *045/681–2918. Jacket and tie. AE, DC, V.*

$$$ ✕ **Seryna.** This establishment is famous for its ishiyaki steak, which is grilled on a hot stone, as well as for its shabu-shabu. Keep in mind that Sernya closes at 8:30 pm. ✉ *Shin-Kannai Bldg. B-1, Sumiyoshi-chō, Naka-ku,* ☎ *045/681-2727. AE, DC, MC, V.*

$$–$$$ ✕ **Chongking.** This is the city's best restaurant for Szechuan cooking. Food is what really matters here; don't expect much in the way of decor. ✉ *164 Yamashita-chō, Naka-ku,* ☎ *045/641–8288. AE, DC, MC, V.*

$$ ✕ **Rome Station.** Located between Chinatown and Yamashita Kōen, Rome Station is a popular venue for Italian food. The spaghetti *vongole* is particularly good. ✉ *26 Yamashita-chō, Naka-ku,* ☎ *045/ 681–1818. No credit cards.*

$$ ✕ **Saronikos.** The Akebono-chō district of Yokohama, east of Chinatown, has long been home to a small cluster of Greek restaurants; sailors off the Greek ships in port still drift over this way to bring gifts of feta cheese, spices, and *sirtaki* music tapes to friends and relatives of the owners. Saronikos is among the best of these restaurants, not the least because it invests more effort in the food than in tarted-up reproductions of the Parthenon and other pretensions to decor. Try eggplant with garlic, Greek salad—and, of course, moussaka. ✉ *3-30 Akebono-chō, Naka-ku,* ☎ *045/251–8980. No credit cards. Closed 1st and 3rd Mon. of month.*

Yokohama A to Z

Arriving and Departing

BY PLANE

Between the Airport and Center City. From Narita Airport, a direct limousine-bus service departs once or twice an hour between 6:45 AM and 10:20 PM for Yokohama City Air Terminal (YCAT). The fare is ¥3,300. YCAT is a five-minute taxi ride from Yokohama Eki. JR Narita Express trains going on from Tōkyō to Yokohama leave the airport every hour from 7 AM to 9:42 PM. The fare is ¥4,100 (or ¥4,900 for the first-class "Green Car" coaches). Or you can take the limousine-bus service from Narita to Tōkyō Eki and continue on to Yokohama by train. Either way, the journey will take more than two hours—closer to three, if traffic is heavy.

BY TRAIN

From Tōkyō. JR trains from Tōkyō Eki leave approximately every 10 minutes, depending on the time of day. Take the Yokosuka, the Tōkaidō, or Keihin Tōhoku Line to Yokohama Eki. (The Yokosuka and Tōkaidō lines take 30 minutes, and the Keihin Tōhoku Line takes 40 minutes) From there, the Keihin Tōhoku Line (Platform 3) goes on to Kannai and Ishikawa-chō , Yokohama's business and downtown areas. If you are going directly to downtown Yokohama from Tōkyō, the blue commuter trains of the Keihin Tōhoku Line are best. From Shibuya Eki in Tōkyō, the Tokyū Toyoko Line, which is private, connects directly with Yokohama Eki and, hence, is an alternative if you leave from the western part of Tōkyō.

From Nagoya and Points South. The Hikari and Kodama Shinkansen stop at Shin-Yokohama Eki, 8 km (5 mi) from the city center. Take the local train from there for the seven-minute ride into town.

Getting Around

BY BUS

There *are* buses, of course, but even locals will be hard put to tell you which ones go where: By and large, forget taking buses in Yokohama.

BY SUBWAY

One line connects Shin-Yokohama, Yokohama, and Totsuka. The basic fare is ¥180.

BY TAXI

There are taxi stands at all the train stations, and you can always flag a cab on the street. Vacant taxis show a red light in the windshield. The basic fare is ¥680 for the first 2 km (1 mi), then ¥90 for every additional 350 meters (⅒ mi). Traffic is heavy in downtown Yokohama, however, and you will often find it faster to walk.

BY TRAIN

Yokohama Eki is the hub that links all the train lines and connects them with the city's subway and bus services. Kannai and Ishikawa-chō are the two downtown stations, both on the Keihin Tōhoku Line. Trains leave Yokohama Eki every two to five minutes from Platform 3. From Kannai or Ishikawa-chō, most of Yokohama's points of interest are within easy walking distance; the one notable exception is Sankei-en (☞ Exploring, *below*), for which you need a train and bus connection.

Contacts and Resources

DOCTORS

Washinzaka Hospital (⊠ 169 Yamate-chō, Naka-ku, ☎ 045/623–7688).

EMERGENCIES

Ambulance or **Fire,** ☎ 119. **Police,** ☎ 110. The **Yokohama Police station** (☎ 045/623–0110) has a Foreign Assistance Department.

ENGLISH-LANGUAGE BOOKSTORES

Maruzen (⊠ 2-34 Benten-dōri, Naka-ku, ☎ 045/212–2031) has a good selection of popular paperbacks and books on Japan in English.

GUIDED TOURS

The **Teiki Yuran Bus** is a seven-hour sightseeing bus tour that covers the major sights and includes lunch at a Chinese restaurant in Chinatown. The tour is in Japanese only, though pamphlets written in English are available at most sightseeing stops. Buy tickets (¥6,670) at the bus offices at Yokohama Eki (east side) and at Kannai Eki; the tour departs daily at 10 AM from Bus Stop 14 on the east side of Yokohama Eki.

The sightseeing boat *Marine Shuttle* (☎ 045/651–2697) makes 40-, 60-, and 90-minute tours of the harbor and bay for ¥900, ¥1,400, and ¥2,000, respectively. Boarding is at the pier at Yamashita Kōen. Boats depart roughly every hour between 10:20 AM and 6:30 PM. Another boat, the *Marine Rouge,* runs 90-minute tours departing at 11 AM, 1:30 PM, and 4 PM, and a special two-hour evening tour at 7 PM (¥2,500).

HOME-VISIT SYSTEM

The Yokohama International Tourist Association arranges visits to the homes of English-speaking Japanese families. These usually last a few hours and are designed to give gai-jin a glimpse into the Japanese way of life. To arrange a visit or to find out more information, call the Yokohama International Tourist Association (☎ 045/641–5824).

VISITOR INFORMATION

The **Yokohama Tourist Office** (☎ 045/441–7300) is in the central passageway of Yokohama Eki. It is open daily 10–6; closed December 28–January 3. A similar office with the same closing times is located at

Shin-Yokohama Eki (☎ 045/473–2895). The head office of the **Yokohama International Tourist Association** (☎ 045/641–5824), open Monday–Saturday 9–5, is in the Sangyō Bōeki Center Building (⊠ 2 Yamashita-chō, Naka-ku).

FUJI-HAKONE-IZU NATIONAL PARK

Updated by
Jared Lubarsky

Fuji-Hakone-Izu National Park, southwest of Tōkyō between Suruga and Sagami bays, is one of Japan's most popular resort areas. The region's main attraction of course, is Fuji-san, a dormant volcano—it last erupted in 1707—rising to a height of 12,388 ft. The mountain is truly beautiful, utterly captivating in the ways it can change in different light and from different perspectives. Its symmetry and majesty have been immortalized by poets and artists for centuries. Keep in mind that during spring and summer, Fuji-san often hides behind a blanket of clouds, to the disappointment of the crowds of tourists who travel to Hakone or the Fuji Five Lakes to see it.

Apart from Fuji-san itself, each of the three areas of the park—the Izu Peninsula, the town of Hakone, and the Five Lakes—has its own special appeal. Izu has a dramatic rugged coastline, beaches, and onsen. Hakone has mountains, volcanic landscapes, and lake cruises. The Five Lakes form a recreational area with some of the best views of Fuji-san. And in each of these areas there are monuments to Japan's past.

Though it is possible to make a grand tour of all three areas at one time, most people make each of them a separate excursion from Tōkyō. If you are interested in climbing Fuji-san, a popular activity in July and August, *see* the Fuji-san section, *below.* Because these are tourist attractions where people are accustomed to foreign visitors, there is always someone to help out in English if you want to explore off the beaten track.

Izu Peninsula

Numbers in the margin correspond to points of interest on the Fuji-Hakone-Izu National Park map.

Atami

51   *48 mins southwest of Tōkyō by Kodama Shinkansen.*

The gateway to the Izu Peninsula is **Atami.** Most Japanese honeymooners make it no farther into the peninsula, so Atami itself has a fair number of hotels and traditional inns. When you arrive, collect a map from the Atami Tourist Information Office (☎ 0557/85–2222) at the train station.

★   The major sight in Atami is the **MOA Art Museum,** which houses the private collection of the messianic religious leader Okada Mokichi. Okada (1882–1955), who founded a movement called the Sekai Kyūsei Kyō ("Religion for the Salvation of the World"), also acquired more than 3,000 works of art, dating from the Asuka period (6th and 7th centuries) to the present day, including a most notable exhibit of *ukiyo-e* (Edo-era woodblock prints) and ceramics. Located on a hill above the station and set in a garden full of old plum trees and azaleas, the museum also offers a sweeping view over Atami and the bay. ⊠ 26-2 Momoyama, Atami, ☎ 0557/84–2511. ≦ ¥1,600. ⊙ Fri.–Wed. 9:30–6.

Barely worth the 15-minute walk from Atami Eki is the **Oya Geyser,** which used to gush on schedule once every 24 hours but stopped after the Great Kantō Earthquake. Not happy with this, the local chamber of commerce rigged a pump to raise the geyser for four out of every five minutes and gives it top billing in its tourist brochures.

Fuji-Hakone-Izu National Park

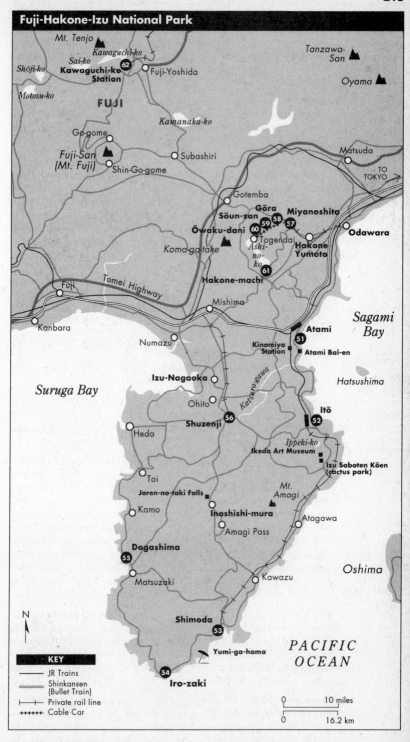

Mt. Tenjo
Kawaguchi-ko
Sai-ko
Shōji-ko
Kawaguchi-ko Station 62 Fuji-Yoshida
Motosu-ko
FUJI
Kamanaka-ko

Tanzawa-San
Oyama

Go-gome
Fuji-San (Mt. Fuji)
Shin-Go-gome Subashiri

Matsuda
TO TOKYO

Gotemba
Gōra **Miyanoshita**
Sōun-zan 59 58 57
Ōwaku-dani 60 Togendai **Odawara**
Ashi-no-ko **Hakone Yumoto**
Koma-ga-take

Tomei Highway
Fuji
Hakone-machi 61

Mishima

Kanbara
Numazu

Sagami Bay

Atami 51
Kinomiya Station **Atami Bai-en**

Hatsushima

Suruga Bay

Izu-Nagaoka
Ohito
Shuzenji 56
Heda

Katsura-gawa

Itō 52
Ippeki-ko
Ikeda Art Museum
Izu Saboten Kōen (cactus park)

Toi
Joren-no-taki Falls
Kamo

Mt. Amagi

Inoshishi-mura
Amagi Pass

Atagawa

Oshima

Dogashima 55
Matsuzaki

Kawazu

N

Shimoda 53

KEY
— JR Trains
═ Shinkansen (Bullet Train)
┠ Private rail line
++++ Cable Car

PACIFIC OCEAN

Yumi-ga-hama
54 **Iro-zaki**

0 ——— 10 miles
0 ——— 16.2 km

The time to visit **Atami Bai-en** (plum garden) is in late January or early February, when the 850 trees in the garden come into bloom. If you do visit, also stop by the small shrine in the shadow of an enormous old camphor tree: The tree has been designated a national monument. Atami Bai-en is 15 minutes by bus from Atami, or an 8-minute walk from Kinomiya Eki, the next stop south of Atami served by local trains.

Another excursion from Atami, but only if you have the time and the inclination for a beach picnic, is to take the 40-minute high-speed ferry from the pier over to **Hatsu-shima.** You can easily walk around the island, which is only 4 km (2½ mi) in circumference, in less than two hours.

LODGING

$$$$ ⚏ **Taikansō Ryokan.** A Japanese inn of the old style with beautiful fur-
★   nishings and individualized service, this villa was once owned by the Japanese artist Yokoyama Taikan. Views of the sea must have been his inspiration. Breakfast and dinner are served in your room. The inn is a 10-minute walk from Atami Eki. ⊠ *7-1 Hayashi-ga-oka-chō, Atami, Shizuoka-ken 413,* ☎ *0557/81–8137. 44 rooms. AE, DC, V.*

$$$ ⚏ **New Fujiya Hotel.** A modern resort hotel and a useful base for sightseeing, the New Fujiya is inland (five minutes by taxi from Atami Eki). Only the top rooms have a view of the sea. Service is impersonal but professional, and a foreign visitor is no cause for consternation. ⊠ *1-16 Ginza-chō, Atami, Shizuoka-ken 413,* ☎ *0557/81–0111. 158 Western-style rooms, 158 Japanese-style rooms. 5 restaurants, indoor pool, hot springs, sauna. AE, DC, MC, V.*

Itō

❺❷ *25 mins south of Atami by JR local; 1 hr and 40 mins southwest of Tōkyō via Atami by Kodama Shinkansen, then JR local.*

Sixteen kilometers (10 miles) south of Atami, Itō is a hot-springs re-sort that traces its history of associations with the West to 1604, when William Adams (1564–1620), the Englishman whose adventures served as the basis for James Clavell's novel *Shōgun,* came ashore.

Four years earlier, Adams beached his disabled Dutch vessel, *De Liefde,* on the shores of Kyūshū and became the first Englishman to set foot on Japan. The authorities, believing that he and his men were Portuguese pirates, put Adams in prison, but he was eventually befriended by the shōgun Ieyasu Tokugawa, who brought him to Edo (present-day Tōkyō) and granted him an estate. Ieyasu appointed Adams his adviser on foreign affairs. The English castaway taught mathematics, geogra-phy, gunnery, and navigation to shogunal officials and in 1604 was or-dered to build an 80-ton Western-style ship. Pleased with this venture, Ieyasu ordered the construction of a larger ocean-going vessel. These two ships were built at Itō, and Adams lived there from 1605 to 1610.

This history was largely forgotten until British Commonwealth occu-pation forces began coming to Itō for rest and recuperation after World War II. Adams's memory was revived, and since then, the Anjin Fes-tival (the Japanese gave Adams the name *anjin*—which means "pilot") has been held in his honor every August. A monument to the Englishman stands at the mouth of the river.

One reason the British forces chose Itō is that there are some 800 ther-mal springs in the area. These springs—and the beautiful, rocky, in-dented coastline nearby—remain the resort's major attractions. Some 150 hotels and inns serve the area. In addition to the hot springs, the Itō area has a number of other attractions.

Izu Saboten Kōen (Izu Cactus Park) consists of a series of pyramidal greenhouses set up at the base of Mt. Omuro that contain 5,000 kinds of cacti from around the world. The park is 20 minutes south of Itō Eki by bus. ✉ *1317-13 Futo, Itō,* ☎ *0557/51–1111.* 🎫 *¥1,800.* ⊙ *Daily 8:40–4:30; closed Dec. 26–28.*

The **Ikeda Kinen Bijutsukan** (Memorial Art Museum), at Lake Ippeki, has a collection of works by Picasso, Dalí, Chagall, and Matisse and a number of wood-block prints. The museum is a 15-minute walk from the Cactus Park (☞ *above*). ✉ *614 Sekiba, Itō,* ☎ *0557/45–2211.* 🎫 *¥900.* ⊙ *July–Aug., daily 10–5; Sept.–June, daily 10–4:30.*

Ōmura-san Kōen (Mt. Ōmura Park) has, on its east side, 3,000 cherry trees of 35 different varieties that bloom at various times throughout the year. The park is about 20 minutes south of Itō Eki by bus. 🎫 *Free.* ⊙ *Daily dawn–dusk.*

$$$$ ★ 🏠 **Ryokan Nagoya.** This small, very charming inn is furnished simply and elegantly with antiques. The staff does not speak English, but smiles and a few words in Japanese seem to go a long way. Breakfast and dinner are served in your room. ✉ *1-1-18 Sakura-ga-oka, Itō, Shizuoka-ken 413,* ☎ *0557/37–4316. 14 rooms. No credit cards.*

Shimoda and Irō-zaki (Irō Point)
1 hr south of Itō by Izu Railways.

South of Itō, the coastal scenery is more of the same—each sweep around a headland gives another picturesque sight of a rocky, indented shoreline. There are several spa towns en route to Shimoda. Higashi-Izu (East Izu) has a number of hot-springs resorts, of which **Atagawa** is the most fashionable. Farther south is **Kawazu,** a place of relative quiet and solitude, with pools in the forested mountainside and waterfalls plunging through lush greenery. For history, however, none of these resort towns

❸ have the distinction of **Shimoda.**

Shimoda's encounter with the West began when Commodore Matthew Perry, bearing a commission from the United States government to open—by force, if necessary—diplomatic relations with Japan, anchored his fleet of black ships off the coast here in 1854. To commemorate the event, the Kurofune Matsuri (Black Ship Festival) is held annually May 16–18. It was here, too, that the first American Consulate was located, in 1856. The first American consul was New York businessman Townsend Harris—who soon after his arrival seems to have asked the Japanese authorities to provide him with a female servant. The Japanese sent him a young girl named Saitō Kichi; one version of the ensuing sad story has it that she was ordered to leave her lover, Tsurumatsu, to serve as Harris's unofficial consort. In any case, the arrangement brought her only a new name—Tōjin ("The Foreigner's") Okichi—and a tragic end. Harris soon sent her away, compounding poor Okichi's shame and ridicule. She tried and failed to rejoin her lover, moved to Yokohama, and later returned to Shimoda to open a restaurant—which went bankrupt. Okichi took to drink and drowned herself in 1890.

Hōfuku-ji was Okichi's family temple. The museum-annex displays a life-size image of her, and just behind the temple is her grave—where incense is still kept burning in her memory. The grave of her lover, Tsurumatsu, is at Tōden-ji, a temple about midway between Hōfuku-ji and Shimoda Eki. ✉ *18-26 1-chōme, Shimoda,* ☎ *0558/22–0960.* 🎫 *¥300.* ⊙ *Daily 8–5.*

The major sight on a Shimoda walk is **Ryosen-ji,** the temple where the negotiations took place that led to the United States–Japan Treaty of Amity and Commerce of 1858. The temple's **Treasure Hall** also contains personal articles that belonged to Tōjin Okichi. ⌧ *12-12 1-chōme, Shimoda,* ☎ *0558/22–2805.* 🎫 *Treasure Hall ¥500.* ⊙ *Daily 8:30–5.*

Slightly farther down the road is a **Monument to Perry and Harris,** built to celebrate the establishment of U.S.–Japanese relations. Still farther along, overlooking Shimoda Harbor, is another monument to Perry. The last sight in Shimoda is **Sushikane,** said to be the restaurant run by Tōjin Okichi in the last years of her life. On display here, too, are some of Okichi's belongings.

The **Shimoda Tourist Office** (☎ 0558/22–1531), in front of the station, has the easiest of the local English itineraries to follow. The 2½-km (1½-mi) tour covers most of the major sights, and all of those concerning Okichi. The tourist office will also find local accommodations for you, on request.

54 The southernmost point of the Izu Peninsula is **Irō-zaki** (Irō Point), reached either by bus or sightseeing boat from Shimoda. If you visit in January, you are in for a special treat: The cape is covered in a blanket of daffodils. Your best plan, in any case, is to take the boat one way and the bus the other; both take about 40 minutes. The bus from Shimoda Eki stops at **Yumi-ga-hama,** one of the prettiest sandy beaches on the whole peninsula, then continues to Irō-zaki, the last stop on the route. From the bus stop there is a walk that takes you past the **Irō-zaki Jungle Park** (⌧ 546-1 Irō-zaki, Minami-Izu, ☎ 0558/65–0050) with its 3,000 different varieties of colorful tropical plants. Beyond the park there you can walk to a lighthouse at the edge of the cliff. The park is open daily 9–5 (¥900).

Shimoda is the end of the line for east Izu coast trains, and most visitors take the 2-hour, 45-minute express train from here back to Tōkyō.

LODGING

$$$$ 🏨 **Shimoda Prince Hotel.** This modern, V-shape resort hotel faces the Pacific, steps away from a white-sand beach. The decor is more functional than aesthetic, but the panoramic view of the Pacific from the picture windows in the dining room makes this one of the best hotels in town. The Prince is just out of Shimoda, 10 minutes by taxi from the station. Among numerous facilities, the Prince has a Continental-style main dining room, a Japanese restaurant, and a terrace lounge. ⌧ *1547-1 Shira-hama, Shimoda, Shizuoka-ken 415,* ☎ *05582/2–7575. 70 Western-style rooms, 6 Japanese-style rooms. 2 restaurants, bar, outdoor pool, sauna, 3 tennis courts, nightclub. AE, DC, MC, V.*

$$$$ 🏨 **Shimoda Tokyū Hotel.** Perched just above the bay, the Shimoda Tokyū has impressive views of the Pacific from one side (where rooms cost about 10% more) and mountains from the other. The lobby areas lack character and warmth, but that is typical of Japanese resort hotels. The hotel's dining options include a Western-style dining room, a Japanese restaurant, a sushi bar, and a summer garden restaurant. Prices run significantly higher in midsummer. ⌧ *5-12-1 Shimoda, Shimoda, Shizuoka-ken 415,* ☎ *05582/2–2411. 100 Western-style rooms, 8 Japanese-style rooms. 4 restaurants, pool, hot springs, shops. AE, DC, MC, V.*

Dogashima

55 *1 hr northwest of Shimoda by bus.*

If the trip to Shimoda and Irō-zaki isn't adventurous enough, take a bus (¥1,360) from Shimoda around the Izu Peninsula to the seaside town of Dogashima, on the west coast—famous for its coastal rock formations, eroded by the sea into fantastic shapes. A sightseeing boat from Dogashima pier makes 20-minute runs to see the rocks (¥850).

In the typical Japanese excess of kindness, a recorded loudspeaker tour—which you can safely ignore—names every rock you pass on the trip. The Dogashima tourist office (☎ 05585/2–1268) is near the pier, in the small building behind the bus station.

LODGING

$$$$ 🏨 **Ginsuisō.** This is the smartest luxury resort on Izu's west coast. Service is first class, despite its popularity with tour groups. The location along the top of the cliff, with every room overlooking the sea, is superb. ✉ *2977-1 Nishina, Nishi-Izu-chō, Dogashima, Shizuoka-ken 415,* ☎ *0558/52–1211. 90 Japanese-style rooms. Restaurant, pool, shops, nightclub. AE, DC, MC, V.*

Shuzenji Onsen

56 *2 hrs north of Shimoda by bus, 32 mins south of Mishima by Izu-Hakone Railways.*

From Dogashima, another bus travels up the coast as far as Heda and then turns inland to Shuzenji, a hot-springs resort in the center of the peninsula. Shuzenji is a lavish spa town along the valley of the Katsuragawa. It enjoys a certain historical notoriety as the place where the second Kamakura shōgun, Minamoto no Yoriie, was assassinated early in the 13th century. Don't judge the town by the area around the station; most of the hotels and hot springs are a mile to the west.

From Shimoda, a bus runs to Shuzenji through the Amagi Mountains (one departure daily at 10:45 AM, ¥2,180). Leaving Shuzenji, take the private Izu-Hakone line through the mountains and change in Mishima to a Kodama Shinkansen for Tōkyō or Kyōto. If you're heading north instead to Ashi-no-ko (Lake Ashi) and Fuji-san, frequent buses (¥980) make the 40-minute trip from Mishima Eki to Hakone-machi.

Around Shuzenji

If you've planned a longer visit to Izu, consider spending a night at **Inoshishi-mura,** en route by bus between Shimoda and Shuzenji. The scenery in this part of the peninsula is dramatic, and the specialty of the house at the local inns is roast mountain boar. In the morning, a pleasant 15-minute walk from town brings you to **Joren-no-taki,** where you can gaze at the waterfall before rejoining the bus.

About 24 km (15 mi) northwest of Shuzenji, **Izu-Nagaoka** has several deluxe ryokan.

LODGING

$$$$ 🏨 **Ryokan Sanyōsō.** The former villa of the Iwasaki family, founders
★   of the Mitsubishi conglomerate, the Sanyōsō is furnished with museum-quality antiques; this is as luxurious and beautiful a place to stay as you will find on the Izu Peninsula. The best rooms—which are quite expensive—have traditional baths made of fragrant cypress wood that look out on exquisite little private gardens. Breakfast and dinner, served in your room, are included in the rate. The Sanyōsō is a five-minute taxi ride from Izu-Nagaoka Eki. ✉ *270 Doma-no-ue, Izu-Nagaoka, Shizuoka-ken,* ☎ *05594/8–0123. 21 rooms. Restaurant. AE, DC, MC, V.*

$$$ 🏨 **Matsushiro-kan.** This small inn, five minutes by bus or taxi from
★   Izu-Nagaoka Eki, is nothing fancy; it's a family operation, and the owners make you feel like a guest in their home. Some English is spoken. Japanese meals are served in a common dining room. Room-only reservations (no meals) are accepted only on weekdays. ✉ *55 Kona, Izu-Nagaoka, Shizuoka-ken,* ☎ *05594/8–0072. 16 rooms. Restaurant. AE, V.*

Arriving and Departing

BY CAR

From Tōkyō, take the Tōmei expressway as far as Ōi-matsuda (about 84 km [52 mi]); then pick up Routes 255 and 135 to Atami (approximately 28 km [17 mi]). From Atami you'll drive another 55 km (34 mi) or so down the east coast of the Izu Peninsula to Shimoda. It takes some effort—but exploring the peninsula *is* a lot easier by car than by public transportation. The best solution is to call either the Nissan or Toyota rental agency in Tōkyō and book a car to be picked up at the Shimoda branch, and go to Shimoda by train. From Shimoda, you can drive back up the coast to Kawazu (35 mins), on to Yūgashima (1 hr), and then to Shuzenji (30 mins).

BY TRAIN AND BUS

To Atami, Itō and Shimoda. The Kodama Shinkansen from Tōkyō to Atami (48 mins) costs ¥4,080, or use a JR Pass. The JR local to Itō (25 mins) costs ¥1,460. Itō (and Atami) is also served by the JR Odoriko Super Express (not a Shinkansen train). The Tōkyō–Itō run (1 hr, 52 mins) costs ¥4,090, or use a JR Pass. Privately owned Izu Railways makes the Itō–Shimoda run (1 hr, ¥1,570), on which JR Passes are not valid.

To continue around the Izu Peninsula from Shimoda or up through its center you must use buses, which run frequently during the day. Whatever your destination, always check the time of the last departure to make sure that you are not left stranded.

To Shuzenji via Mishima. The Izu-Hakone Railway Line runs from Tōkyō to Shuzenji via Mishima (2 hrs, 20 mins; ¥4,590) and is the cheapest option if you don't have a JR Pass. With a JR Pass, a Shinkansen–Izu Line combination will save about 45 minutes and will be the cheapest option. The Tōkyō–Mishima Shinkansen leg (62 mins) costs ¥4,400; the Mishima–Shuzenji Izu Line leg (32 mins) costs ¥500.

Hakone

The national park and resort area of Hakone is a popular day trip from Tōkyō and a good place for a close-up view of Fuji-san. A word of caution, though, before you dash off to see Fuji-san: The mountain is often swathed in clouds, especially in summer. And on summer weekends, it often seems that all of Tōkyō has come out to Hakone with you. Expect long lines at cable cars, and traffic jams everywhere.

You can cover the best of Hakone in a one-day trip out of Tōkyō, but if you want to try the curative powers of the thermal waters or do some hiking, then stay overnight. The two areas we recommend are around the old hot-springs resort of Miyanoshita, and the western side of Mt. Koma-ga-take. The route may sound complex, but in fact this is one excursion from Tōkyō so well defined that you really can't get lost—no more so, at least, than any of the thousands of Japanese tourists ahead of and behind you.

The first leg of the journey is from Odawara or Hakone-Yumoto, by train and cable car through the mountains to Togendai, on the north shore of Ashi-no-ko (Lake Ashi). The scenery en route is spectacular, but if you have problems with vertigo you might be better off on the bus. The long way around, from Odawara to Togendai, takes about an hour—in heavy traffic, an hour and a half. The trip over the mountains will take about two hours.

Credit the difference to the Hakone Tōzan Tetsudō Line—possibly the slowest train you'll ever ride. It takes 50 minutes to travel the 16 km

(10 mi) from Odawara to Gōra (35 mins from Hakone-Yumoto), using three switchbacks to inch its way up the side of the mountain. The steeper it gets, the grander the view.

Trains do not stop at any station en route for any length of time, but they do run frequently enough to allow you to disembark, visit a sight, ㊼ and catch another train. The first stop to make is **Miyanoshita,** a small but very pleasant and popular resort. Especially charming is the 19th-century Western-style **Fujiya Hotel** (☞ Lodging, *below*). Even if you're not staying there, drop in for a morning coffee on the first floor overlooking the garden and, on the way out, take a peek at the vintage collection of old books and magazines in the library.

★ Past Miyanoshita, by all means get off the train to visit the **Hakone Chōkoku-no-mori Bijutsukan** (Open-Air Museum). Established in 1969, the museum has a really astonishing collection of 19th- and 20th-century Western and Japanese sculpture, most of it on display in a spacious, handsome garden. There are works here by Rodin, Moore, Arp, Calder, Giacometti, Takeshi Shimizu, and Kōtarō Takamura. One section of the garden is devoted to Emilio Greco. Inside are works by Picasso, Léger, and Manzo, among others. Chōkoku-no-mori is within a minute's walk of Miyanoshita Eki; directions are posted in English. ✉ *1121 Mi-no-taira,* ☎ *0460/2–1161.* 🎫 *¥1,500.* ⊙ *Mar.–Oct., daily 9–5 (July 19–Sept. 23, daily 9–9); Nov.–Feb., daily 9–4.*

㊽ The final stop on the line is **Gōra,** a small town at the lower end of the Sōun-zan cable car and a jumping-off point for hiking and exploring. Ignore the little restaurants and souvenir stands here: Get off the train as quickly as you can and make a dash for the cable car at the other end of the station. If you let the rest of the passengers get there before you, and perhaps a tour bus or two, you may stand 45 minutes in line.

㊾ The cable car up to **Sōun-zan** departs every 20 minutes and takes 9 minutes (¥400; free with the Hakone Free Pass, ☞ Getting Around, *below*) to the top. There are four stops en route, and you can get off and reboard the cable car if you've paid the full fare. At **Kōen-kami,** the second stop, you'll find the **Hakone Bijutsukan** (Art Museum), sister institution to the MOA Museum of Art in Atami (☞ Atami, *above*). Opened in 1952, the museum consists of two buildings set in a garden, and it houses a modest collection of porcelain and ceramics from China, Korea, and Japan. ✉ *1300 Gōra,* ☎ *0460/2–2623.* 🎫 *¥900.* ⊙ *Fri.–Wed. 9–4.*

At Sōun-zan, a gondola begins its 28-minute descent to **Togendai.** The gondola is in the same building as the cable car terminus. With your ¥1,330 ticket or your Hakone Free Pass, stand in line to get a boarding pass, which determines when you can line up for a car. Gondolas seat about eight adults and depart every minute.

Less than 10 minutes out of Sōun-zan, the gondola swings up over a ★ ridge and crosses the **Ōwaku-dani** (valley). The landscape below is blasted and desolate, sulfurous billows of steam escaping through holes from some inferno deep in the earth. Why this fascinates the Japanese—who need no reminders that they live on a chain of volcanic islands—is any-㊿ body's guess. At the top of the ridge above the valley, **Ōwaku-dani** is one of the two stations where you can leave the gondola. From the station, a ¾-km (½-mi) walking course wanders among the sulphur pits in the valley. Local entrepreneurs make a passable living boiling eggs in these holes and selling them to tourists at exorbitant prices. Just below the station is a restaurant, where the food is truly terrible—but on a clear day the view of Fuji-san is perfect. Next to the station is the Ōwaku-dani Shizen Hakubutsukan (Ōwaku-dani National Science Museum), an uninspired collection of exhibits on the ecosystems and volcanic history of the area, none of which have explanations in English (¥400, open daily 9–4:30). Remember, if you get off the gondola here, you—and others in the same situation—will have to wait for someone to make space on a later gondola before you can continue down to Togendai and Ashi-no-ko (but again, the gondolas come by every minute).

From Ōwaku-dani the descent to Togendai on the shore of **Ashi-no-ko** takes 25 minutes. There is no reason to linger at Togendai; it is only a terminus for buses to Hakone-Yumoto and Odawara, and to the resort villages in the northern part of Hakone. Head straight for the pier, a few minutes' walk down the hill, where boats set out on the lake for Hakone-machi. The ride is free with your Hakone Free Pass. Without the pass, buy a ticket (¥970) at the office in the terminal. A few ships of conventional design ply the lake; the rest are astonishingly corny Disney knock-offs. One, for example, is rigged like a 17th-century warship. There are departures every 30 minutes, and the cruise to Hakone-machi takes about 30 minutes. With still water and good weather, you will get a breathtaking reflection of the mountains in the waters of the lake as you go.

61 ★ The main attraction in **Hakone-machi** is the **Hakone Sekisho** (Hakone Barrier). In days gone by, the town of Hakone was on the Tōkaidō, the main highway between the Imperial Court in Kyōto and the shogunate in Edo (present-day Tōkyō). The road was the only feasible passage through this rugged, mountainous country. Travelers could scarcely avoid passing through Hakone—which made it an ideal place for a checkpoint to control traffic. The Tokugawa shogunate built the barrier here in 1618; its most important function was to monitor the *daimyō* (feudal lords) and their retainers passing through—to keep track, above all, of weapons coming into Edo—and womenfolk coming out.

When Ieyasu Tokugawa came to power, Japan had been through nearly 100 years of bloody struggle among rival coalitions of daimyō, betraying and assassinating each other at every opportunity. Ieyasu emerged supreme from all this, mainly because some of his opponents had switched sides at the last moment, in the Battle of Sekigahara in 1600. The shōgun was justifiably paranoid about his "loyal" barons—especially those in the outlying domains, and he required the daimyō to live in Edo for periods of time every two years. It was an inspired policy. The rotation system turned the daimyō into absentee landlords, which undercut their bases of power. They had to travel both ways in processions of great pomp and ceremony and maintain homes in the capital befitting their rank—expenses that kept them perennially strapped for cash. When they did return to their own lands, they had to leave their wives behind in Edo, hostages to their good behavior. A noble lady coming through the Hakone Sekisho without an official pass, in short, was a prima fac*ie* case of treason.

The checkpoint served the Tokugawa dynasty well for 250 years. It was demolished only when the shogunate fell, in the Meiji Restoration of 1868. An exact replica, with an exhibition hall of period costumes and weapons, was built as a tourist attraction in 1965. The restored Hakone Sekisho is a few minutes' walk from the pier, along the lakeshore in the direction of Moto-Hakone. ✉ *Ichiban-chō, Hakone-machi,* ☎ *0460/3–6635.* 🎟 *¥200.* ☾ *Daily 9–4:30.*

From Hakone-machi, buses run every 15–30 minutes to the Odakyū private line's Hakone-Yumoto Eki (40 mins, ¥930), and Odawara Eki (1 hr, ¥1,160), where you can take either the Odakyū *Romance Car* back to Shinjuku Eki or a JR Shinkansen to Tōkyō Eki. The buses are covered by the Hakone Free Pass.

Lodging

LAKE ASHI

$$$$ ★ ⊞ **Hakone Prince Hotel.** This resort complex at Hakone-en draws both tour groups and individual travelers. It's also a popular venue for business conferences. The location is superb, with the lake in front and the mountains of Koma-ga-take behind. The Hakone Prince has two Japanese-style annexes; the exclusive Ryū-gū-den, which overlooks the lake and has its own thermal bath, is absolutely superb. Several restaurants are on site: a formal Western dining room, a steak and seafood restaurant, a Chinese, a couple of Japanese, and a coffeehouse. ⊠ *144 Moto-Hakone, Hakone-machi, Ashigarashimo-gun, Kanagawa-ken 250,* ☏ *0460/3–7111. 96 rooms in main building, 12 in chalet, 77 in lakeside lodge, 73 total in 2 annexes. 2 restaurants, bar, lounge, 2 pools, 7 tennis courts, shops. AE, MC, V.*

MIYANOSHITA

$$$$ ★ ⊞ **Fujiya Hotel.** This Western-style hotel is showing signs of age (it was built in 1878, but with modern additions), but that somehow adds to its charm. The library, with its stacks of old books, would make a character out of Dickens feel positively at home. In the gardens behind the hotel is an old imperial villa, which serves as a dining room. The Fujiya combines the best of traditional Western decor with the exceptional service and hospitality of a fine Japanese inn. There are both Western and Japanese restaurants. ⊠ *359 Miyanoshita, Hakone-machi, Kangawa-ken 250,* ☏ *0460/2–2211. 149 Western-style rooms. 3 restaurants, 2 pools, hot springs, golf. AE, DC, MC, V.*

$$$$ ⊞ **Hotel Kowakien.** This hotel attracts busloads of tourists. It's far from ideal, but the rooms are fairly large, and you can usually get a reservation on short notice. (The hotel also owns the adjacent Hakone Kowakien, which is equally large and uninspiring but has Japanese-style rooms.) There are both Western and Japanese restaurants on site. ⊠ *1297 Nino-taira, Hakone-machi, Kanagawa-ken 250,* ☏ *0460/2–4111. 256 Western-style rooms, 9 Japanese-style rooms. 6 restaurants, 2 pools, hot springs, sauna, 2 tennis courts, exercise room. AE, DC, MC, V.*

$$$$ ★ ⊞ **Ryokan Naraya.** The same family has owned this inn for generations and perfected the art of exquisite formal hospitality. The Naraya has an annex, but the main building has the authentic understated elegance of the traditional ryokan style. Room rates include breakfast and dinner, which are served in your room. ⊠ *162 Miyanoshita, Hakone-machi, Kanagawa-ken 250,* ☏ *0460/2–2411. 19 rooms, 18 with bath. AE, DC, MC, V.*

SENGOKU

$$$ ⊞ **Fuji-Hakone Guest House.** A small, family-run Japanese inn, this guest house has simple tatami rooms with the bare essentials. The owners, Mr. and Mrs. Takahashi, speak English and are a great help in planning trips off the beaten path. The inn is between Odawara Eki and Togendai; take a bus from the station (Lane 4), get off at the Senkyōro-mae stop, and walk one block. The family also operates the nearby Moto-Hakone Guest House (⊠ 103 Moto-Hakone, ☏ 0460/3–7880), which has five Japanese-style rooms that share a typical Japanese-style bath. ⊠ *912 Sengoku-hara, Hakone, Kanagawa-ken 250,* ☏ *0460/4–6577. 12 rooms. Hot springs. AE, MC, V.*

Arriving and Departing

BY TRAIN

Commuter trains on the privately owned Odakyū Line leave Shinjuku Eki in Tōkyō for Odawara every 6–12 minutes. Odakyū also has an upscale train called the *Romance Car,* with comfortable seats and big observation windows, which goes one stop beyond Odawara to Hakone-

Yumoto. Reservations are required for the *Romance Car*; buy tickets (¥1,820) at any Odakyū railway station or Odakyū Travel Service agency. Beyond Hakone-Yumoto, travel is on the privately owned Hakone Tōzan Tetsudō Line, or by bus.

If you have a JR Pass, it is cheaper to take a *Kodama* Shinkansen from Tōkyō Eki to Odawara. (The faster *Hikari* does not stop at Odawara.) Then change to the Odakyū private line in Odawara.

The cheapest way to get to and around Hakone is with a **Hakone Free Pass.** Sold by the Odakyū Railways, this coupon ticket (¥5,510 from Shinjuku, with a surcharge of ¥1,100 for the Romance Car) allows you to use any mode of transportation in the Hakone area, including the Hakone Tōzan Railway, the Hakone Tōzan Bus, the Hakone Ropeway, the Hakone Cruise Boat, and the Sōun-zan Cable Car. If you have a JR Pass, buy the Hakone Free Pass for travel within the Hakone region only (¥4,500), and take the JR Kodama Shinkansen as far as Odawara. The coupon is valid for four days and covers all transportation covered in the Hakone section above—except a detour up the east side of Lake Ashi to the Prince Hotel.

Getting Around

Hakone has a fairly complete network of trains, buses, cable cars, and excursion boats—and getting around on them is half the fun. Because traffic on the narrow mountain roads can back up for hours, renting a car is inadvisable.

Guided Tours

Sunrise Tours, a division of the **Japan Travel Bureau** (☎ 03/5620–9500), runs a tour to Hakone, crossing Lake Ashi on the cruise boat and traveling the gondola over Ōwaku-dani (¥17,500 includes lunch and return to Tōkyō by Shinkansen). Sunrise tours depart daily (Mar. 14–Dec. 19) from Tōkyō's Hamamatsu-chō Bus Terminal; there are also pickups at some major hotels.

Fuji Go-ko (Fuji Five Lakes)

Hakone is the southeast of Fuji-san. Fuji Go-ko is to the north—affording the best view of the mountain and the best base for a climb to the summit. With its various outdoor activities, from skating and fishing in winter to boating and hiking in summer, this is a popular resort area for families and business conferences.

The five lakes are, from the east, Yamanaka-ko, Kawaguchi-ko, Sai-ko, Shōji-ko, and Motosu-ko. Kawaguchi and Yamanaka are the largest and most developed as resort areas, Kawaguchi being more or less the centerpiece of the group. You can visit this area on a day trip from Tōkyō, but unless you want to spend most of it on buses and trains, plan on staying overnight.

62 From **Kawaguchi-ko station,** it's a 5- to 10-minute walk to the lakeshore. Kawaguchi is the most developed of the five lakes, ringed with weekend retreats and vacation lodges—many of them maintained by companies and universities for their employees. If you turn right and walk along the shore, another five minutes will bring you to the gondola for a quick ride up to **Mt. Tenjo** (3,622 ft). At the top there is an observatory, from which the whole of Lake Kawaguchi is before you, and beyond the lake is a classic view of Fuji-san. Back down the gondola and across the road is the pier from which excursion boats leave on 30-minute tours of the lake. The promise, not always fulfilled, is to have two views of Fuji-san: one of the thing itself, and the other inverted in its reflection on the water.

One of the little oddities at Lake Kawaguchi is the **Fuji Hakubutsukan** (Fuji Museum). Don't be diverted by the conventional exhibits on the first floor, of local geology and history; head straight upstairs (you must be 18 or over) and browse in the museum's astonishing collection of—well, for want of a euphemism—phalluses. Mainly wood and stone, carved in every shape and size, these figures played a role in certain local fertility festivals; one suspects that they were not unknown in Japanese homes as well. The museum is on the north shore of the lake, next to the Fuji Lake Hotel. ✉ *3964 Funatsu, Mizuminako, Kawaguchi-ko-machi,* ☎ *0555/73–2266.* 🎟 *¥200; 2nd floor ¥200.* ⊙ *Wed.–Mon. 9–4.*

The largest of the recreational facilities at Lake Kawaguchi is the **Fuji-kyū Highland.** Not particularly worth a visit unless you have children in tow, it does have an impressive assortment of rides, roller-coasters, and other amusements. The park stays open all year and in the winter has superb skating, with Fuji-san for a backdrop. Fuji-kyū Highland is about 15 minutes' walk east from Kawaguchi-ko station. ☎ *0555/23–2111.* 🎟 *¥1,000 admission or ¥4,200 for a full-day pass.* ⊙ *Daily 9–5.*

Buses from Kawaguchi-ko station go to all the other lakes. The farthest west is **Motosu-ko,** the deepest and clearest of the Fuji Go-ko, which takes about 50 minutes. Many people consider **Shōji-ko,** the smallest of the lakes, to be the prettiest—not least because it still has relatively little vacation-house development. The **Shōji Trail** leads from the Shōji-ko to Fuji-san through Aoki-ga-hara ("Sea of Trees"), a forest with an underlying magnetic lava field that makes compasses go haywire. Any number of people go into Aoki-ga-hara every year and never come out, some of them on purpose—the forest seems to hold a morbid fascination for the Japanese, as a place to commit suicide and disappear. If you're planning to climb Fuji-san from Motosu-ko, go with a guide.

Between Shōji-ko and Kawaguchi-ko is **Sai-ko.** The third largest lake of the five, it is only moderately developed. From the western shore there is an especially good view of Fuji-san. Near Sai-ko, there are two natural caves, an ice cave and a wind cave. You can take a bus or walk to them. The largest of the Go-ko is **Yamanaka-ko,** 35 minutes by bus to the southeast of Kawaguchi. Yamanaka-ko is the closest lake to the popular trail up Fuji-san that starts at Go-gōme (☞ The Climb, *below*), and many climbers use this resort area as a base.

Lodging

KAWAGUCHI-KO

$$$$ 🏨 **Fuji View Hotel.** Conveniently located on Lake Kawaguchi, the Fuji View is a little threadbare but comfortable. The terrace lounge offers fine views of the lake and of Fuji-san beyond. The staff speak English and are helpful in planning excursions. Rates are significantly higher on weekends and in August. There is a Western restaurant on site, and the hotel can arrange golf, boating, and tennis. ✉ *511 Katsuyama-mura, Minami Tsuru-gun, Yamanashi-ken 401,* ☎ *05558/3–2211. 40 Western-style rooms, 30 Japanese-style. Restaurant. AE, DC, MC, V.*

YAMANAKA-KO

$$$$ 🏨 **Hotel Mount Fuji.** The best resort hotel on Lake Yamanaka, the Mount Fuji offers all the facilities for a recreational holiday, and its guest rooms are larger than those at the other hotels on the lake. The lounges are spacious, and they have fine views of the lake and mountain. Rates are about 20% higher on weekends. ✉ *Yamanaka, Yamanaka-ko-mura, Yamanashi-ken 401,* ☎ *0555/62–2111. 88 Western-style rooms, 4 Japanese-style rooms. 2 restaurants, pool, tennis court, ice-skating. AE, DC, MC, V.*

$$–$$$ ▯ **New Yamanaka-ko Hotel.** Though the rooms are slightly smaller than those at Hotel Mount Fuji (☞ *above*), the New Yamanaka-ko has its own thermal bath, especially pleasant for soaking after summer hiking or winter skating. Rates go up dramatically on weekends and in August. ⊠ *Yamanaka, Yamanaka-ko-mura, Yamanashi-ken 401,* ☎ *05556/2–2311. 63 rooms, mostly Western style. 2 restaurants, 2 tennis courts. AE, DC, V.*

Arriving and Departing

BY BUS

Direct bus service runs twice daily from Shinjuku to Kawaguchi-ko at 7:30 AM and 6 PM (¥1,700). For a different route back to Tōkyō, you may want to consider taking the two-hour bus ride from Kawaguchi-ko to Mishima (¥2,280). Three or four buses a day make the trip, skirting the western lakes and circling Fuji-san before descending to Mishima. At Mishima, transfer to the JR Shinkansen Line for Tōkyō or Kyōto. A shorter bus ride (70 mins, ¥1,370), goes from Kawaguchi-ko to Gotemba with a transfer to the JR local line.

If you want to go to Hakone rather than Tōkyō from Fuji Go-ko, take the bus from Kawaguchi-ko first to Gotemba, then change to another bus to Sengoku. From Sengoku, there are frequent buses to Hakone-Yumoto, Togendai, and elsewhere in the Hakone region. If you want to go to the Izu Peninsula, take the bus to Mishima and, from there, go by train either to Shuzenji or Atami.

BY TRAIN

The transportation hub, as well as one of the major resort areas in the Fuji Go-ko area, is Kawaguchi-ko. Getting there from Tōkyō requires a change of trains at Ōtsuki. The JR Chūō Line *Kaiji* and *Azusa* express trains leave Shinjuku Eki for Ōtsuki on the half hour throughout the morning (less frequently in the afternoon) and take approximately one hour. At Ōtsuki, change to the private Fuji-Kyūkō Line for Kawaguchi-ko, which takes another 50 minutes. The total traveling time is about two hours, and you can use your JR Pass as far as Ōtsuki; otherwise, the fare would be ¥1,260. The Ōtsuki–Kawaguchi-ko leg costs ¥990.

There are about seven trains a day (more in the summer) from Shinjuku that make convenient connections at Ōtsuki. There are also one or two trains on Sundays and national holidays (Mar.–Nov.) that operate directly between Shinjuku and Kawaguchi-ko station. On weekends (Mar.–June 28), an express train departs from Shinjuku early in the morning and arrives at Kawaguchi-ko about 1½ hours later; the train back leaves Kawaguchi-ko in the late afternoon and arrives at Shinjuku in the early evening. Check the express timetables before you go—and be aware that only the first three cars of the train go all the way to the lake.

Getting Around

Buses leave from Kawaguchi-ko station to all parts of the area and to all five lakes. On a day trip, you will probably only have the time to visit Kawaguchi-ko—and maybe Yamanaka-ko, if you don't take a break.

Fuji-san (Mt. Fuji)

★   There are six possible routes to the summit of **Fuji-san,** but only two are recommended: from Go-gōme (fifth station) on the north side, and from Shin-Go-gōme (new fifth station) on the south. From Go-gōme you have a five-hour climb to the summit—the shortest way up—and a three-hour descent. From Shin-Go-gōme the ascent is slightly longer and stonier, but the way down, via the **sunabashiri** (☞ *below*) is faster.

The Climb

The ultimate experience of climbing Fuji-san is to reach the summit just before dawn, and greet the extraordinary sunrise. *Go-raikō* ("The Honorable Coming of the Light" [here "go" means "honorable"]), as the sunrise is called, has a mystical quality, because the reflection shimmers across the sky just before the sun itself appears over the horizon. Mind you, there is no guarantee of seeing it: Fuji-san is often clouded in, even in the early morning.

The climb is taxing, but not as hard as you might think scaling Japan's highest mountain would be. That said, the air *is* thin, and it *is* humiliating to struggle for the oxygen to take another step while some 83-year-old Japanese grandmother blithely leaves you in her dust. (It happens: Japanese grannies are made of sterner stuff than me and thee.) Have no fear of losing the trail on either of the two main routes. Just follow the crowd—some 196,000 people make the climb during the official season, July 1–August 31. In all, there are 10 stations to the top; you start at the fifth. There are stalls selling food and drinks along the way, at exorbitant prices; consider bringing your own.

Also, along the route are huts where, dormitory-style, you can catch some sleep. A popular one is at the Hachi-gōme (eighth station), from which it is about a 90-minute climb to the top. The mountain huts (about ¥6,000 with two meals, ¥4,000 without food; Saturday surcharge: ¥1,000) are open from the end of April to Nov. 23—and should be avoided at all costs. The food is vile. There is no fresh water. The bedding is used by so many people, and so seldom properly aired, you'd feel better sleeping on fish skins. Sensible folk leave Go-gōme at midnight with good flashlights, climb through the night, and get the summit just before dawn. Camping on the mountain is prohibited.

Be prepared for fickle weather around and atop the mountain. Summer days can be unbearably hot and muggy; and the nights can be a shocking contrast of freezing cold (bring numerous warm layers and be prepared to put them all on). Wear strong hiking shoes. The sun really burns at high altitudes, so wear protective clothing and a hat; gloves are a good idea. Use a backpack: It keeps your hands free, and serves a useful function on the way down. Instead of returning to Go-gōme, descend to Shin-Go-gōme on the volcanic sand slide called the *sunaba-shiri*. Sit down on your pack, push off, and away you go.

Arriving and Departing

Buses (¥1,700) take about one hour from Kawaguchi-ko station to Go-gōme; there are only three buses a day until the climbing season (July–Aug.) opens, when there are 15 departures or more, depending on the demand. There are also daily buses direct to the Kawaguchi-ko Go-gōme from Tōkyō, July through August, leaving Hamamatsu-chō Eki at 8:15 AM, and Shinjuku Eki at 7:45 AM, 8:45 AM, and 7:30 PM. The last bus allows sufficient time for the tireless to make it to the summit before sunrise. The journey takes about three hours from Hamamatsu-chō (¥2,800), and 2 hours, 30 minutes from Shinjuku (¥2,600). Reservations are required; you can book through the Fuji Kyūkō Railway (☎ 03/3376–1118), the Japan Travel Bureau (☎ 03/3284–7605), or other major travel agents.

To return: A bus makes the 70-minute trip from Shin-Go-gōme to Gotemba (¥1,500). From Gotemba take the JR Tōkaidō and Gotemba lines to Tōkyō Eki, or the JR Line to Matsuda and change to the Odakyū Line for Shinjuku (¥1,120).

5 Nagoya, Ise-Shima, and the Kii Peninsula

Nagoya is Japan's fourth largest city, an industrial metropolis whose appeal is, admittedly, limited. Prospects change dramatically as you head south of the city to Ise-Shima National Park and the highly venerated Grand Shrines of Ise. Circling the Kii Peninsula will take you past magnificent marine scenery, coastal fishing villages and resorts, and Yoshino-san, with perhaps the finest springtime display of sakura in Japan. Then, inland, the mountaintop monastery of Kōya-san looms almost as large as myth with its 123 temples.

By Nigel Fisher

GAZING OUT THE WINDOW of the Shinkansen as you speed from Tōkyō to Nagoya, you will pass the continuous strip of factories and concrete office blocks of the modern *Tōkaidō*—the industrialized makeover of the famous road that connected Edo and Kyōto. Before Meiji, it was one of five post roads that the shogunate maintained. Now the industrial belt stretches all the way to Hiroshima. For some, it represents Japan's "economic miracle."

The sight of this industrial sprawl is likely to make you want to stay on the train in the vain hope of reaching the greenery of postcard Japan. All the more reason to disembark: Kyōto, Japan's capital for more than 10 centuries, is along this route, and lush countryside and small towns still rich in traditional culture lie just north and south of the corridor.

Use industrial Nagoya to escape the Tōkaidō's industry—north to locales that are windows onto traditional Japan and south to Ise-shima and the Kii Peninsula, where you will find two of Japan's famous temple complexes, at Ise and Kōya-san, and natural beauty unspoiled by the economic miracle.

Nagoya, Ise-Shima, and the Kii Peninsula Glossary

Key Japanese words and suffixes for this chapter include the following: -*bashi* (bridge), -*chō* (street or block), -*chōme* (street), -*dōri* (street or avenue), *eki* (train station), *gai-jin* (foreigner), -*gawa* (river), *hama* (beach), -*in* (Buddhist temple), -*ji* (Buddhist temple), *jinja* (Shinto shrine), *jingū* (Shinto temple), -*jō* (castle), -*ken* (prefecture), -*ku* (section or ward), -*mon* (gate), *onsen* (hot springs), *sakura* (cherry blossoms), -*san* (mountain, as in Kōya-san, Mt. Kōya), -*shima* or -*jima* (island), *Shinkansen* (bullet train, literally "new trunk line"), *taisha* (shrine), *torii* (*to*-ree-ee, gate), and *yama* (mountain).

Pleasures and Pastimes

Castles

Plenty of feudal castles stand in Japan, but most of them are ferro-cement replicas—Nagoya has one of these. In Inuyama, north of Nagoya, the original still bears witness to the past. Its special delight is not its warlike stance but the fairy-tale quality of its perch atop a bluff over the Kiso-gawa.

Dining

Nagoya is known for only a few special dishes: *kishimen*, white, flat noodles of the *udon* variety, with a velvety smoothness; *misonikomi udon*, a thick noodle boiled with chicken and Welsh onion; *moriguchizuke* (Japanese pickle), made from a special radish, pickled either with or without sweet sake; and *uiro*, a sweet cake made of rice powder and sugar, most often eaten during the tea ceremony. The most highly prized food product is the *Nagoya-tori*, a type of chicken similar to the famous French *poulet Bresse*. These chickens are given special feed that is said to improve the texture and taste of their white meat.

Other than these items, Nagoya's cuisine is mostly Kyōto-style (☞ Pleasures and Pastimes *in* Chapter 7), but you can find every type of Japanese and international food in this cosmopolitan city. For Western fare, the best choices are the French restaurants at the Nagoya Castle Hotel, the Nagoya Kanko Hotel, and the International Hotel Nagoya. The one good Western eatery outside of hotels is the Okura Restaurant.

On the Ise Peninsula, lobster is especially fine. On the Kii Peninsula, farmers raise cattle for Matsuzaka beef—the town of Matsuzaka is 90 minutes by train from Nagoya. However, the best beef is typically shipped to Tōkyō, Kyōto, and Ōsaka.

CATEGORY	COST*
$$$$	over ¥6,000
$$$	¥4,000–¥6,000
$$	¥2,000–¥4,000
$	under ¥2,000

per person, excluding drinks, service, and tax

Lodging

Nagoya has a range of lodging—from clean, efficient business hotels to large luxury hotels with additional amenities—in three major areas: the district around JR Nagoya Eki, downtown, and the Nagoya-jō area. Though ryokan are listed below, international-style hotels are often more convenient if you want flexible dining hours.

For a short course on accommodations in Japan, *see* Lodging *in* the Gold Guide.

CATEGORY	COST*
$$$$	over ¥20,000
$$$	¥15,000–¥20,000
$$	¥10,000–¥15,000
$	under ¥10,000

All prices are for a double room, excluding service and tax.

Outdoor Activities and Sports

Beyond Nagoya there are several tempting outdoor diversions. In Gifu, look for *u-kai*, cormorant fishing. The birds do all the work while you party. For something more serene, not far from Gifu is rafting on the Kiso-gawa along a stretch that the Japanese call Nihon Rhine. More rafting, through deep gorges with placid water, is popular on the Kii Peninsula at Doro-kyō. For swimming, sandy beaches are limited—the best is at Shiro-hama, but the Kii Peninsula's coast is littered with beautiful bays and rocky coves.

Shopping

People in and around Nagoya produce several unique crafts. In Gifu you'll find paper lanterns and umbrellas. In Seki the traditional skill in forging samurai swords is still practiced. Nagoya has the world's largest producer of porcelain. Toba, on the Shima Peninsula, is where Kokichi Mikimoto perfected the technique for harvesting pearl-bearing oysters. None of these items is easy on the pocket. If they exceed your budget consider a visit to observe the creation of these items.

Temples

There is no shortage of religious architecture on the Shima and Kii peninsulas, but two Buddhist temple complexes, Kōya-san and Yoshino-san, are exceptional. Kōya-san, founded in 816, is the most famous of the two. If you would like to get a true taste of the place, spend a night at one of its temples.

South of Nagoya are the Grand Shrines of Ise. In fact, the architecture is so simple and what you can see is so minimal that you might wonder what all the fuss is about. To the Japanese, however, the shrines, rebuilt every 20 years for the last 1,500 years, are among the most sacred. The inner shrine is the home to Amaterasu, the Sun Goddess and highest deity in the Shinto pantheon.

On the lighter side, there are two delightful shrines north of Nagoya, Oagata Jinja and Tagata Jinja. The former is a female shrine that assists women with their hopes of fertility. The latter is a male shrine with a collection of penises that makes every Japanese man squirm with envy.

Exploring Nagoya, Ise-Shima, and the Kii Peninsula

Nagoya, Japan's fourth largest city, has only a couple of major national treasures. The two most important are Nagoya-jō and Atsuta Jingū. The city is not among Japan's most attractive, but it is a convenient point from which to set out into the countryside. After seeing the major sights of Nagoya—or skipping them—the first excursion we recommend takes you north of the city to see fertility shrines, cormorant fishing, and lantern and sword making, among other things. Heading south from Nagoya, the second and longer excursion covers the Grand Shrines of Ise, the Shima Peninsula and its pearl industry, and proceeds to the Kii Peninsula, including Kōya-san and Yoshino-san. The logical place to finish the second trip is Nara, which is covered in Chapter 8.

Numbers in the text correspond to numbers in the margin and on the Nagoya and the South Gifu-ken, Ise, and the Kii Peninsula maps.

Great Itineraries

You can see Nagoya's sights in a day, allowing another day for a trip north of the city, two if you watch cormorant fishing at Gifu or Inuyama. If you plan to cover all of the Shima and Kii peninsulas, you would want to take four days or more, but you can be selective. The Grand Shrines at Ise and either Toba or Kashikojima, for example, could be a one-night, two-day trip. Similarly, you could manage Kōya-san and/or Yoshino-san in two days. If you prefer the outdoors to temples, a complete loop of the Kii Peninsula from Nagoya to Ōsaka or Kyōto takes six hours by train. So plan one night at Shingū in order to raft through Doro-kyō (gorge), then another night in Shiro-hama for a swim in the Pacific and a walk on the coastal cliffs for a delightful three-day, two-night trip.

IF YOU HAVE 3 DAYS

With such limited time, head straight from ⬚ **Nagoya** to ⬚ **Inuyama**, perhaps visiting **Oagata Jinja** and **Tagata Jinja** on the water. In Inuyama, see the castle and in the evening enjoy u-kai. If you don't return to Nagoya for a night's sleep, plan to get a very early start the next day for the most mystical place in the region, the 9th-century Buddhist complex of temples at Kōya-san—via Ōsaka, the quickest way. From there you could press on to Yoshino-san, or linger and just go straight to Nara.

IF YOU HAVE 5 DAYS

Start your trip with a full day and night in ⬚ **Nagoya** covering the castle, the **Tokugawa Bijutsukan, Atsuta Jingū,** and **Noritoke China Factory** to see the making of porcelain. On the next day, go up to ⬚ **Gifu** to visit the umbrella- and lantern-making shops. Include **Seki** on your tour if sword-making demonstrations are occurring that day—usually the first Sunday of the month. The next stop is ⬚ **Inuyama** with its original castle. Enjoy a ceremonial tea at the **Jo-an Teahouse.** If you are here during u-kai, be sure to take in the spectacle. On the next day return to Nagoya to change trains for ⬚ **Ise** and a visit to venerated **Ise Jingū,** one of Japan's three most important Shintō shrines. For the night continue out onto the peninsula to ⬚ **Toba,** home of Mikimoto pearls, or the fishing town of ⬚ **Kashikojima.** On the fourth day backtrack north to Taki to pick up the train to ⬚ **Shingū,** where you can spend the night after taking a river trip through the steep-cliffed **Doro-kyō.** On day six, take a four-hour bus ride north to ⬚ **Yoshino-san** first thing in the morning. This is a particularly worthy inclusion at cherry-blossom time. You'll need all of the afternoon and a little time the next morning both to breathe in the atmosphere and to visit the temples. On day seven, take a train to Hashimoto and on to ⊞ **Kōya-san** and plan to spend the night at a Buddhist temple. From Kōya-san, it is easy to reach Kyōto, Nara, and Ōsaka (Chapters 7, 8, and 9, respectively).

IF YOU HAVE 9 DAYS

Keep to the seven-day itinerary as far as ⊞ **Shingū**. Then, instead of taking the bus to Yoshino-san, continue along the coast of the Kii Peninsula to spend the night, even two if you wish to rest up, at the spa and beach resort of ⊞ **Shira-hama**. From there, via **Wakayama**, go to ⊞ **Kōya-san** for a full 24 hours in and around the monasteries. Then go to ⊞ **Yoshino-san** for the next night before exiting the region by taking the train to Nara.

When to Tour Nagoya, Ise-Shima, and the Kii Peninsula

Springtime throughout Japan is the most popular season for travel, especially so when cherry trees bloom around early to mid-April. The weather can be sunny and warm but nowhere near as hot as it can get in late July and August. Autumn is another popular season, especially on the Kii Peninsula, where the Pacific Ocean stays warm and the trees take on their golden colors. One caveat: If you want to watch cormorant fishing in Gifu or Inuyama, the season runs from June through September.

NAGOYA

By Shinkansen, 2 hrs west of Tōkyō, 40 mins east of Kyōto.

Nagoya today gives little indication of its role during the Tokugawa period (1603–1868), when the city was an important stop between Kyōto and Edo (Tōkyō) on the Tōkaidō post road. In 1612 Ieyasu Tokugawa established Nagoya town by permitting his ninth son to build a castle. In the shadow of this magnificent castle, industry and merchant houses sprang up, as did pleasure quarters for samurai. A town was born—an important one considering its location on the way to the seat of the shogunate in Edo. As a result it quickly grew in strategic importance. Supported by taxing the rich harvests of the vast surrounding Nobi plain, the Tokugawa family used the castle as its power center for the next 250 years. By the early 1800s, Nagoya's population had grown to around 100,000. Although it was smaller than Edo, where the million-plus population surpassed even Paris, Nagoya had become as large as the more established cities of Kanazawa and Sendai.

With the Meiji Restoration in 1868, when Japan began trade with the West in earnest and embraced Western ideas and technology, Nagoya developed as a port city. Once its harbor was open to international shipping in 1907, Nagoya's industrial growth accelerated. By the 1930s it was supporting Japanese expansionism in China with munitions and aircraft. That particular choice of industry caused Nagoya's ruin. For that very reason American bombers virtually flattened the city during World War II. Very little was left standing by the time the Japanese surrendered unconditionally, on August 14, 1945.

Nagoya came back as an industrial metropolis. Except for the fact that every building is of recent vintage, there is no evidence of its war-blitzed past. Now the fourth largest city in Japan, Nagoya bustles with 2.2 million people living in its 126½-square-mi area. Industry is booming with shipbuilding, food processing, and the manufacture of textiles, ceramics, machine tools, automobiles, railway rolling stock, even aircraft. Nagoya has become prosperous, a comfortable cosmopolitan city for its 36,000 foreign residents, but with only a few sights to interest travelers.

In rebuilding Nagoya, urban planners laid down a grid system, with wide avenues intersecting at right angles. Hisaya-odōri, a broad avenue with a park in its 328-ft-wide median, bisects the city. Nagoya's symbol of modernity is at its center, an imposing 590-ft-high television tower. As much of an eyesore as it is, it is also useful for getting your bearings. Nagoya-jō is north of the tower, Atsuta Jingū is to the south, Kenchū-ji temple is to the east, and the JR eki is to the west. The downtown commercial area is centered on the Sakae subway station, and a secondary commercial area has developed next to the JR eki.

Sights to See

❽ Atsuta Jingū. If Nagoya-jō is the number one attraction in Nagoya, Atsuta Jingū is number two. For 1,700 years, a shrine has been at the site of Atsuta Jingū. The current one is, like Nagoya-jō, a concrete replica of the one destroyed in World War II. That diminishes neither its importance nor the reverence in which it is held by the Japanese. Atsuta Jingū remains one of the three most important shrines in the country and has the distinction of serving as the repository of one of the emperor's three imperial regalia, the Kusanagi-no-Tsurugi (Grass Mowing Sword). The shrine is located on thickly wooded grounds, with a 15th-century bridge, Nijūgo-chō-bashi. The shrine is an oasis of tradition in the midst of bustling, modern industrialism. When you witness Shinto priests blessing newborn children held in the arms of their kimono-clad mothers, you will easily recognize the reverence Atsuta Jingū is still accorded. Some 60 traditional festivals, albeit many small ones, are held here each year—check with the tourist office so that you may schedule your trip to the shrine to coincide with an old Japanese event.

To get to the shrine from downtown, take the Meijo subway line south to Jingū-nishi Station. Take a right as you leave the station and walk down the main avenue. ☒ ¥300. ⊙ *Daily 9–4:30; closed last Wed. and Thurs. of month.*

❻ Go-hyaku Rakan (Hall of the 500 Disciples) **and Nittai-ji.** In the first of these two Buddha sites, each statue of Buddha's 500 disciples carved in wood appears in a slightly different pose from the others. Nittai-ji was given to Japan by the king of Siam in 1904. Supposedly, its function is to serve as a repository for Buddha's ashes, but all you can see is a magnificent gilded Buddha. Of these two sites, the former is the more impressive. Take Bus 8 from the JR Nagoya Eki and alight one stop after the Shindeki stop. Or take the Sakura-dori subway line from the JR station to Kuruma-michi Station and walk north and east for 15 minutes. ☒ *Free.* ⊙ *Daily 9–7.*

❶ JR Nagoya Eki. A Visitor's Information Office is in the middle of the station's central mall—look for a large red question mark. Even if the tourist section, with its English-speaking attendant, is closed, you can collect an English-language map from the other officials behind the counter. In Japanese or sign language, they can also give directions and obtain hotel reservations for you.

Four subway lines run under the city's main avenues; the Sakura-dōri and Higashiyama lines have stops under the JR eki. The minimum subway fare is ¥200, and the system is easy to manage, as all subway signs are written in both Japanese and English.

❼ Kenchū-ji. This temple is famous for its original 1651 two-story gate and for its survival of the bombings of World War II—few buildings in town managed that. From the JR eki take the Sakura-dori subway to Kuruma-michi Station, then walk three blocks north and turn left. After about 400 yards the temple will be on the right. ☒ *Free.* ⊙ *Daily 9–4:30.*

234

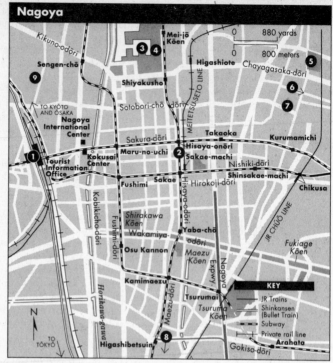

③ Nagoya-jō. The castle was originally built in 1612, severely damaged in 1945, and rebuilt with ferro-concrete in 1959. It is famous for its impressive size and the pair of golden dolphins, male and female, mounted on the roof of the *donjon* (principal keep). The donjon and the dolphins are replicas, but they are faithful to their originals. In contrast to the castle's exterior, however, the interior makes no attempt to replicate the original residential quarters of the Tokugawa family. Instead, you'll find a museum containing artifacts—toys, armor, swords, and so forth—from the original castle. Completely incongruous to this re-created 17th-century castle is an elevator that takes you between floors, without which you might miss the castle's fourth floor and its collection of paper dolls representing the people who take part in the city's Chrysanthemum Exhibition, held in October.

To get to the castle, take the Higashiyama subway line, located in front of the railway station, to the center of town (walking this takes about 15 minutes). Get off at Sakae, the second stop, where you can either change for the Meijo subway line and ride one stop to Shiyakusho Station or exit in the middle of downtown Nagoya and walk up Hisaya-odōri. On foot, you'll pass the 590-ft-tall TV tower, then the Prefectural Government Office and Shiyakusho subway station, after which you catch your first glimpse of Nagoya-jō. You can also take Bus 8 directly to Nagoya-jō from the JR eki. 🚌 *Castle and gardens ¥500.* ⊙ *Daily 9:30–4:30; closed Dec. 29–Jan. 1.*

Nagoya-kō (port). From Nagoya-kō, Japan's third largest port after Kōbe and Tōkyō, Toyota, whose factories are in Nagoya's suburbs, ships its automobiles around the world. The port is a little farther south than Atsuta Jingū.

④ Ninomaru Tei-en. The refined simplicity of these gardens makes them a place to restore one's inner harmony, which Nagoya's traffic does its best to undermine. However, during the October festival, the display of chrysanthemum bushes can be disconcerting. Each bush is shaped so that its flowers form faces and hands. Then, the bush is dressed in costumes and arranged to represent a legend or historic event. The effect is extremely surrealistic, resembling a fantasy filled with flower children. Ninomaru Tei-en is east of Nagoya-jō within the castle complex. ▨ *Castle and gardens ¥500.* ✆ *Daily 9:30–4:30; closed Dec. 29–Jan. 1.*

❾ **Noritake China Factory.** Noritake is the world's largest manufacturer of porcelain. You can take a free, one-hour tour of the factory with an English-speaking guide and see a short film. The company shop is in front of the north gate to the factory, but you might find that there are wider selections of porcelain in Nagoya's downtown shops. The factory is a 15-minute walk north of JR Nagoya Eki, or five minutes from the Kamajima subway station, one stop north of Nagoya Station on the Higashiyama Line. ☎ *052/561–7114 factory, 052/572–5072 shop.* ✆ *Factory weekdays 10–4, 1-hr tours at 10 and 1 (reservations required); shop Tues.–Sun. 9–5, closed 2nd Sun. of month.*

Sakae. This is Nagoya's shopping and entertainment center, with hundreds of bars and small restaurants. Many of the restaurants display their dishes with prices in the windows, so you can decide what you want and how much it will cost before you enter. And because Nagoya strives to be an international city, as a *gai-jin* you will usually be welcomed without the fluster of embarrassment that might greet you in less cosmopolitan areas. To get to Sakae, take the Higashiyama subway line to the Sakae-machi stop.

★ ❺ **Tokugawa Bijutsukan** (art museum). Some 7,000 historical treasures are stored in the Tokugawa Bijutsukan, but only a fraction of the collection is displayed at any one time. All that you can be sure of seeing are ancient armor, swords, paintings, and assorted artifacts from the Tokugawa family. For many, the main reason for visiting the museum is the various picture scrolls, including one illustrating *The Tale of Genji.* If you would like to see the scrolls, ask someone at your hotel to telephone the museum to make sure they are on display.

Take the JR Chūō or Meitetsu Seto train lines to Ozone Eki. Or take Bus 8 from the JR station or Nagoya-jō to the Shindeki bus stop, then walk five minutes to the north. Because the museum is on a back street, you may need to ask directions. ☎ *052/935–6262.* ▨ *¥1,000.* ✆ *Tues.–Sun. 10–4:30; closed mid-Dec.–Jan. 4.*

❷ **TV Tower.** The Nagoya tourist brochure will suggest taking the elevator up the tower 330 ft to its observation platform for the view. Certainly, if there is no smog, haze, or clouds, you will get a wide panorama that reaches the Japan Alps to the north and Ise Bay to the south. However, what you mostly see is the city, and, if you have seen urban sprawl before, the view will simply add to that tiresome list. ▨ *¥700.* ✆ *Daily 10–9 (10–6 in winter).*

Dining and Lodging

$$$$ **✕ Koraku.** One of the most exclusive restaurants in Nagoya, Koraku
★ is nationally known for its chicken dishes. The traditional setting in an old samurai mansion is refined, as is formal service by women dressed in beautiful kimonos. You are likely to feel here that you are stepping back into Japan's more noble past. When you make a reservation, it is preferable to have an introduction from a local Japanese person. ▨ *3-3 Chikara-machi, Higashi-ku,* ☎ *052/931–3472. Reservations essential. Jacket and tie. AE. No lunch.*

$$$ ✕ **Kamone.** The innovative Japanese menu here adds Chinese and/or French touches to the dishes, and, as if to enhance the foreign culinary influences on the Japanese dishes, the decor is more Western than Japanese—window drapes instead of *shōji* screens, for example. Since the restaurant is on the 15th floor of the Meiji Seimei Building, try to reserve a table with a view. ✉ *1-1 Shin-Sakae-machi, Naka-ku (across from Sakae-chō subway station exit),* ☎ *052/951–7787. Jacket and tie. DC, MC, V. Closed Mon.*

$$$ ✕ **Okura Restaurant.** The Okura has the best French cuisine in Nagoya
★ outside of the hotels. This is the place where Western businessmen often entertain their Japanese partners. Recommended dishes include veal slices with mushrooms in madeira sauce as well as steamed salmon. Another good choice is Matsuzaka beef, a Nagoya specialty, served with béarnaise sauce. ✉ *Tōkyō Kaijo Bldg., 23rd floor, Naka-ku,* ☎ *052/ 201–3201. Reservations essential. Jacket and tie. AE, DC, V.*

$$$ ✕ **Tori-kyū.** This traditionally decorated restaurant in a Meiji-period building specializes in chicken dishes—raw, grilled, in a casserole, or as a very formal meal. The restaurant is next to a river, and in the old days, patrons used to arrive by boat. ✉ *1-15 Naiya-chō, Nakamura-ku,* ☎ *052/541–1888. Jacket and tie. AE. Closed Sun.*

$$$ ✕ **Yaegaki.** This is the best tempura restaurant in town, and the fish
★ and vegetables are cooked in front of you. One of the few wood structures in a sea of concrete, Yaegaki has its own small garden. An English-language menu is available. ✉ *3-7 Nishiki, Naka-ku,* ☎ *052/ 951–3250. Jacket and tie. AE, V. Closed Sun.*

$$ ✕ **Kani Doraku.** The specialty here is crab, either boiled or steamed, elegantly served by kimono-fitted waitresses. To find the restaurant, opposite the Nagoya Tokyu Hotel's entrance, look for its small sign of a crab. ✉ *4-chōme, Sakae, Naka-ku,* ☎ *052/242–1234. Jacket and tie. AE, V.*

$$ ✕ **Kisoji.** Not far from the International Hotel Nagoya, Kisoji has a reasonably priced (¥4,000) *shabu-shabu* beef dinner, but if you take the shabu-shabu special with tempura and sashimi, the price increases dramatically. The decor is rustic, but the waitresses, in kimono, give it a smart touch of tradition. ✉ *Nishiki 3-chōme, Naka-ku,* ☎ *052/ 951–3755. V.*

$$ ✕ **Usquebaugh.** This bar-restaurant with polished wood decor takes its name from the Gaelic word for "water of life"—whiskey. Nautical paintings and gear hang on the walls, and there are some impressive glass-enclosed wine racks. Modern *kaiseki* cuisine is served at reasonable prices; you can also have a light meal at the bar. The restaurant is on Hirokuji-dōri, one block east of the Rich Hotel. ✉ *2-4-1 Sakae, Naka-ku,* ☎ *052/201–5811. Reservations not accepted. Jacket and tie. AE, DC, MC, V.*

$ ✕ **Yamamotoya.** For Nagoya's local dish, misonikomi, you can't beat this no-frills eatery, which serves a steaming bowl of udon for ¥1,500. The superb misonikomi is especially welcome in colder months. Yamamotoya is a block east of the Rich Hotel. ✉ *2-4-5 Sakae, Naka-ku,* ☎ *052/471–5547. Reservations not accepted. No credit cards.*

$$$$ ▥ **Century Hyatt.** The distinct advantage of the newest (1993) and smallest of the city's leading hotels is its personal service. Stay here a day and the staff, most of whom speak some English, will know you. Besides this boutique-hotel approach, another advantage is the location, a five-minute walk from the JR Nagoya Eki. Unlike at most other Hyatts, which have a Regency floor, free coffee is served here all day in the ground-floor lounge. In the evening, you can gather with other guests in the restaurant-bar called the Whizz, a comfortable, wood-paneled room that serves a variety of Asian and other fare—from cheese spring

rolls to pizza to such main dishes as Thai-style chicken with shallots and leeks, and *tataki* (lightly blanched bonito). A formal dining room prepares Continental fare and has a lounge for afternoon tea. Rooms are pleasantly decorated with dark wood furniture. Space is at a premium, and an extra ¥3,000 for deluxe rooms buys a much-appreciated extra 10 square ft. Bathrooms are cozy but have all modern necessities. ✉ 2-43-6 Meiki, Nakamura-ku, Nagoya, Aichi-ken 450, ☎ 052/541–1234; 800/233–1234 for U.S. reservations; 0171/580–8197 for U.K. reservations; FAX 052/569–1717. 115 rooms. 2 restaurants, bar, lobby lounge. AE, DC, MC, V.

$$$$ 🏨 **Nagoya Hilton.** Rooms on the upper floors of this late-'80s skyscraper ★ have a panoramic view of the city. Light pastel furnishings and *shōji* window screens add to the bright, airy feel of the rooms. And in this land of narrow beds and small rooms, king-size American beds are pure pleasure. Single travelers do especially well because the hotel has none of the closet-size rooms found in most Japanese hotels. The staff is attentive and enthusiastic, and the location is central: two things that make this Nagoya's leading hotel. ✉ 1-3-3 Sakae, Naka-ku, Nagoya, Aichi-ken 460, ☎ 052/212–1111, FAX 052/212–1225. 427 rooms, 26 suites. 3 restaurants, coffee shop, indoor pool, massage, sauna, tennis court, health club, shops, concierge floors. AE, DC, MC, V.

$$$–$$$$ 🏨 **Nagoya Castle Hotel.** Its location next to Nagoya-jō makes this the sightseer's choice in Nagoya. A room with a view onto the castle shows Nagoya at its best—especially at night, when the castle is floodlit. Bedrooms are spacious, pleasantly furnished, and hung with oil paintings. Even the lobby is attractively and hospitably decorated, with plenty of wood paneling. The establishment is efficiently run, with a range of restaurants and bars; at the Rosen Bar, Western and Japanese businessmen meet for a drink after work. The hotel has an hourly shuttle that runs to the JR Eki. ✉ 3-19 Hinokuchi-chō, Nishi-ku, Nagoya, Aichi-ken 451, ☎ 052/521–2121, FAX 052/531–3313. 269 rooms, 5 suites. 5 restaurants, indoor pool, beauty salon, health club, shops. AE, DC, MC, V.

$$$ 🏨 **International Hotel Nagoya.** With the best location in the city, the International Hotel has been a longtime favorite with business travelers. It is not the newest accommodation in town, but it maintains a high standard. The lobby resembles that of a European hotel, with gold and dark brown tones and antique furnishings. Some of the rooms are small for the price, but they are comfortably appointed. ✉ 3-23-3 Nishiki, Naka-ku, Nagoya, Aichi-ken 460, ☎ 052/961–3111, FAX 052/962–5937. 265 Western-style rooms. 3 restaurants, bar. AE, DC, MC, V.

$$$ 🏨 **Ryokan Suiho-en.** A large concrete city, Nagoya is not the ideal setting for old-style ryokan, but this one, in the thick of downtown chaos, is the most traditional, luxurious, and expensive of its kind in Nagoya. The tatami rooms are furnished with good reproductions of traditional furniture. Meals can be served in your room. ✉ 1-19-20 Sakae, Naka-ku, Nagoya, Aichi-ken 460, ☎ FAX 052/241–3521. 25 rooms, most with bath. AE.

$$ 🏨 **Castle Plaza Hotel.** A five-minute walk from the main railway station, the Castle Plaza is an efficient, top-notch businessperson's hotel, with more amenities than most. The few Japanese-style rooms available are larger than the others, and there are Japanese and Western restaurants on site. ✉ 4-3-25 Meieki, Nakamura-ku, Nagoya, Aichi-ken 450, ☎ 052/582–2121, FAX 052/582–8666. 258 Western-style rooms, 4 Japanese-style rooms. 2 restaurants, indoor pool, sauna, exercise room. AE, V.

$–$$ 🏨 **Fitness Hotel 330.** This new business hotel is considerably smarter than neighboring business-category hotels. Rooms, albeit typically small, are done in gay, cheerful fabrics, and there's the ubiquitous wooden cabinet to serve as desk- and tabletop for the TV. The fitness center is indeed high-tech, and a friendly, intimate café and bar area is on the ground level next to the lobby. The welcoming staff are good with gesturing, if whatever Japanese you have fails you. The hotel is a five-minute walk from the JR Nagoya Eki. ✉ *1-2-7 Sakae, Nakamura-ku, Nagoya, Aichi-ken 450,* ☎ *052/562–0330,* FAX *052/562–0331. 120 Western rooms. Restaurant, bar, café, health club. AE, DC, MC, V.*

$ 🏨 **Oyone Ryokan.** In a small wood building, Oyone is a friendly B&B-like inn. Its rooms are small, sparsely furnished, and air-conditioned. There is a traditional Japanese-style shared bath. ✉ *2-2-12 Aoi, Higashi-ku, Nagoya, Aichi-ken 460,* ☎ *052/936–8788,* FAX *052/936–8883. 18 rooms. AE, MC, V.*

$ 🏨 **Ryokan Meiryu.** Economy is the biggest draw to this four-story concrete building and its two-story annex. There is no particular charm here, just small tatami rooms with a table and a futon and a traditional Japanese shared bath. Meals (optional) are served in a small dining room. About half of the rooms have air-conditioning. The ryokan is a three-minute walk from Kamimaezu Eki, Exit 3. ✉ *2-24-21 Kami mae zu, Naka-ku, Nagoya, Aichi-ken 460,* ☎ *052/331–8686,* FAX *052/321–6119. 23 rooms. AE, V.*

SOUTH GIFU-KEN

No more than an hour north of Nagoya by train, in the southern part of Gifu Prefecture that precedes the Hida Mountains' ascent to the Japan Alps, you'll find echoes of old Japan in the area's umbrella, lantern, and sword makers; in its cormorant fishing; in the country's oldest castle, Inuyama-jō; and in two fascinating shrines, Oagata Jinja for women and Tagata Jinja for men.

Gifu

🔟 *30 mins northwest of Nagoya on the JR Tōkaidō Line.*

Bombing during World War II destroyed the attractiveness of Gifu, but the city still has its appeal. Gifu is famous for paper lantern and umbrella making, for cormorant fishing, and for its bathhouses, which have been described as "sex spas." The last may not interest you, but they do seem to raise the local hotel prices. Gifu is also a major clothing manufacturer, and you'll see some 2,000 wholesale shops crammed on a couple of city blocks as you leave the station. A city tourist office (☎ 0582/62–4415) is located at the train station.

Umbrellas are made by certain families in small shops. Though these umbrellas are available in Gifu's downtown stores, there are one or two umbrella-making shops a 15-minute walk to the southeast of the JR eki. If you speak a little Japanese, the shop owner may invite you back to watch the process. The easiest store to visit is **Sakaida's** (☎ 0582/63–0111).

Lantern making is easier to observe. The major factory, **Ozeki** (☎ 0582/63–0111), welcomes visitors. To reach Ozeki, take the tram toward downtown Gifu and disembark at the Daigaku Byōin-mae stop, the fifth from Gifu Station. It's at the junction of the main road, which leads to the Kinkazan Tunnel. The factory is up this road on the left. Inside, you will be led through the process of winding bamboo or wire around several pieces of wood to make the lantern shape. The tour then progresses to where the paper is pasted onto the bamboo. Once the paste has dried, the pieces of wood that have given the lantern its shape are removed from one end of the lantern. The actual design on the lantern may either be stenciled on the paper at the beginning of the process or painted on by hand after the lantern has been made. To arrange to see the lantern-making process, consult the information desk at your hotel.

South Gifu-ken, Ise-Shima, and the Kii Peninsula

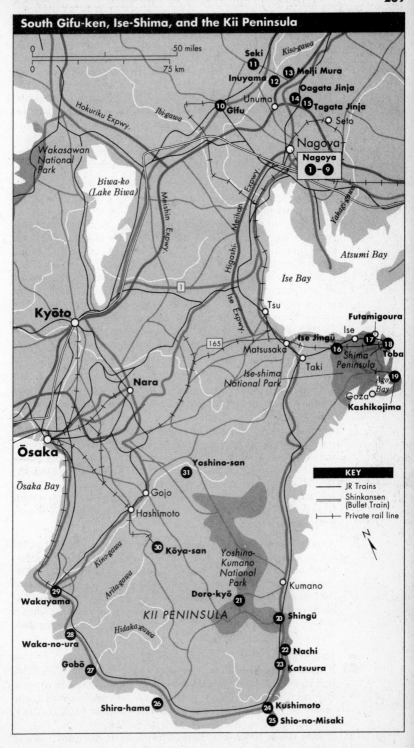

Seki ⑪

Kiso-gawa

Inuyama ⑫ ⑬ Meiji Mura

Ōagata Jinja

Unuma ⑭ ⑮ Tagata Jinja

⑩ Gifu

Seto

0 — 50 miles

0 — 75 km

Hokuriku Expwy.

Ibi-gawa

Nagoya

Nagoya ①–⑨

Wakasawan National Park

Biwa-ko (Lake Biwa)

Meishin Expwy.

Higashi-Meihan Expwy.

Meihan Expwy.

Yahagi-gawa

Atsumi Bay

Ise Bay

1

Kyōto

Ise Expwy.

Tsu

Futamigoura

Ise ⑰

165

Matsusaka

Ise Jingū ⑯ Shima Peninsula ⑱ Toba

Nara

Taki

Ise-shima National Park

Ago Bay ⑲

Goza

Kashikojima

Ōsaka

Ōsaka Bay

Yoshino-san

㉛

Gojo

Hashimoto

Kino-gawa

Arita-gawa

㉚ Kōya-san

Yoshino-Kumano National Park

Kumano

KII PENINSULA

Doro-kyō ㉑

⑳ Shingū

㉙ Wakayama

Hidaka-gawa

㉒ Nachi

㉓ Katsuura

㉘ Waka-no-ura

Gobō ㉗

Shira-hama ㉖

㉔ Kushimoto

㉕ Shio-no-Misaki

KEY

— JR Trains

══ Shinkansen (Bullet Train)

├──┤ Private rail line

N

U-kai (cormorant fishing) is the major summer evening event. It is an organized opportunity to party while watching a centuries-old way of catching fish. Fishermen, dressed in the traditional costume of reed skirts, glide down the river in their boats. Suspended in front of each boat is a wood brazier burning bright to attract *ayu* (river smelt or sweet fish) to the surface. *U* (cormorants), several to a boat, are slipped overboard on leashes to snap up the fish. Because of a small ring around each of the birds' necks, the fish never quite reach the cormorants' stomachs. Instead, their long necks expand to hold five wiggling fish. When a bird can't take in another fish, the fisherman hauls the bird back to the boat, where it is made to regurgitate its neckful. The actual fishing takes less than a half hour, but the partying lasts much longer.

Approximately 130 boats, carrying 10 to 30 spectators each, heave-to in the Nagara-gawa about two hours before the fishing commences. This is party time, given to eating and drinking. A separate boat full of singing and dancing maidens dressed as geisha drifts through the spectator boats. Other boats ply the river, selling food and drink. Because the ayu are attracted by the light from a boat's wood-burning braziers, no fishing occurs when the river is muddy from heavy rains or on nights when there is a full moon. Tickets for the spectator boats are sold in most of Gifu's hotels and also at the main ticket office downstream from the Nagara-bashi. ☎ *0582/62–0104 for advance reservations through the Gifu City Spectators Office; 0582/62–4415 for advance reservations through the Gifu City Tourist Agency at the station. ✉ About ¥3,100 (more in July and Aug., less in June and Sept.) without food or drink, ¥3,500 with food and drink. ⊙ Ticket office opens at 6 PM.*

Architectural sights in Gifu are worth visiting only if you have the spare time to wander around waiting for u-kai. An unusual statue of Buddha (45 ft tall), with a 6-ft-long ear as a symbol of omnipotent wisdom, is housed in an orange and white building, **Sho-ji.** This building is easy to recognize from the street as you ride the bus from the train station into downtown Gifu and toward the river. It is about a five-minute walk from its entrance to the cable car that takes you to Kinka-san (Mt. Gold). The statue, one of the three largest Buddhas in Japan, was completed in 1832 after 38 years of pasting together 2,000 pounds of paper *sutra* (prayers). This was then coated with clay and stucco before being lacquered and gilded.

A major Gifu landmark is **Gifu-jō,** which houses a museum and stands before Kinka-san. The castle is relatively new (1951), having replaced a 16th-century structure that was destroyed by an earthquake in 1891. You can either climb up the mountainside or take the aerial gondola—the Japanese call it a ropeway, another term oddly borrowed from English—but the castle looks its best at night from down below, when it is illuminated. ✉ *¥400. ⊙ Spring and fall, daily 9–6; summer, daily 9–7; winter, daily 9–4:30.*

Lodging

$$$　🏯 **Ryokan Sugiyama.** Close to the Nagara River, Sugiyama is Gifu City's best Japanese inn. The presence of the river adds to the mood of peace and quiet. Very good food, including ayu, is usually served in the rooms. ✉ *73-1 Nagara, Gifu-shi, Gifu-ken 502,* ☎ *0582/31–0161,* FAX *0582/33–5250. 49 Japanese-style rooms. AE.*

$$　🏯 **Gifu Grand Hotel.** This large resort hotel is efficiently run and slightly impersonal, but it is popular with the Japanese, who come for its thermal baths. ✉ *648 Nagara, Gifu-shi, Gifu-ken 502,* ☎ *0582/33–1111,* FAX *0582/33–1122. 147 rooms, half Western-style. 2 restaurants, pool, hot springs, sauna. AE, V.*

Seki

⑪ *20 mins north of Gifu by tram, car, or JR.*

Seki is one of the most famous traditional centers of sword production and is a must to visit if you can time your trip to coincide with a (free) demonstration. This show will help you understand the artistry and mystique of traditional Japanese swords, which can cost up to ¥6 million. Demonstrations are held at the Sangyo Shinko (Industry Promotion) Center. ☎ *05752/2–3131 Sangyo Shinko Center.* ☺ *Demonstrations 5 times on 1st Sun. of month, 2nd Sun. in Oct., and Jan. 2.*

Inuyama

⑫ *30 mins northwest of Gifu by Meitetsu Line, 40 mins north of Nagoya by Meitetsu Line.*

★ Inuyama is known for having Japan's oldest existing castle, **Inuyama-jō,** built in 1440 and perched on a cliff commanding the Kisogawa below. It is not a grand structure, but it is a welcome change to see the real thing instead of another concrete replica. And rather than having a heavy, foreboding image, Inuyama-jō has fairy-tale qualities that make it even more appealing. The top floor of this quaint four-story castle is a lookout room with a great view of the river. ☒ *¥300.* ☺ *Daily 9–5; closed Dec. 29–Jan. 1.*

The pretty stretch of the **Kiso-gawa** that flows beneath the cliff-top Inuyama-jō has been dubbed the Nihon Rhine—the Japanese Rhine. A large rock rises dramatically out of the water here. A pleasant way to see the river is on a completely tame raft. To take this hour-long, 13-km (8-mi) river trip (¥3,400), take the train on the Meitetsu Hirome Line from Inuyama to Nihon-Rhine-Imawatari. Once there, check out several companies before selecting the type of boat you prefer. One well-established company is Nippon Rhine Kanko (☎ 0574/26–2231).

Inuyama is another cormorant-fishing town, and, as in Gifu, tickets are available from the major hotels. Because there is little difference between cormorant fishing in Gifu and Inuyama, make your decision between the two based on where you'll be at nightfall, bearing in mind that Inuyama is the more attractive town. Ticket prices for the spectator boats in Inuyama are the same as in Gifu (☞ *above*). Trips also run from Nagoya to watch cormorant fishing; the cost, which includes round-trip transportation, is ¥7,680 (☎ 052/541–4036 Nagoya Yuran Bus).

In Uraku-en, the garden of the Meitetsu Inuyama Hotel, the **Jo-an Teahouse** is a registered National Treasure. The building was constructed by Grand Master Urakusai Oda in 1618 and moved to its present site only recently. You can also hire the teahouse for your own private ceremony at ¥20,000. It is less than ¼ mi from the castle. ☒ *Teahouse and gardens ¥800; tea additional ¥500.* ☺ *Daily 9–5.*

Lodging

$$ 🏨 **Mietetsu Inuyama Hotel.** This resort hotel's location on the Kiso River makes it a good base for shooting the rapids. Guest rooms are on the small side, but the lobby is large, with a sitting area where guests mingle and chat. Most of the rooms are Western-style, but there are some Japanese-style rooms in the annex. ✉ *107 Kita-Koken, Inuyama, Aichi-ken 484,* ☎ *0568/61–2211,* 🖷 *0568/67–5750. 99 rooms. 2 restaurants, pool. AE, V.*

Getting Around

If you are headed to Inuyama from Seki, take the JR Line. From Gifu, you can take the JR Line, but the privately operated Meitetsu Line is more convenient. If you want to use your JR Pass, take the JR train to Unuma and change to the Meitetsu Line for a three-minute ride to Inuyama.

Meiji Mura

⑬ *By bus, 20 mins southeast of Inuyama Eki; 1 hr north from Nagoya's Meitetsu Bus Center.*

More than 50 buildings from the Meiji Restoration (1868–1912) have been transplanted to this open-air village museum, Meiji Mura. Emperor Meiji, who regained his imperial power from the Tokugawa Shōgun, opened the doors of Japan to the West and began Japan's rapid transformation into a modern economy. This transformation is illustrated by Meiji Mura's exhibits. Traditional buildings, such as a kabuki theater and a bathhouse, exist alongside Christian places of worship and Western-style mansions. Generally speaking, the 19th-century buildings and Western architecture make this park more appealing to the Japanese than to Westerners. One exception might be the old Imperial Hotel lobby, which was designed by Frank Lloyd Wright. ☎ *0568/67–0314.* 💴 *¥1,550.* ☉ *Mar.–Oct., daily 10–5; Nov.–Feb., daily 10–4.*

Oagata and Tagata Jinja

5 mins south of Meiji Mura, 25 mins from Inuyama, 30 mins north of Nagoya on the Meitetsu Line.

These fertility shrines, two of the country's most accessible, are fascinating in their own way—you sure won't see anything like them in the ⑭ Christian West. **Oagata Jinja** is the female shrine, designed for women who are about to marry and wives who want children. Most of the objects in the shrine are symbols to that end, such as a cleft rock resembling female genitalia.

⑮ Within walking distance of Oagata Jinja is **Tagata Jinja,** the male shrine. Its bewildering collection of phalluses, left as offerings by thankful mothers, range in size from a few inches to 6 ft. The big event at Tagata Jinja is on March 15, when a splendid festival is held; sake flows liberally from morning to night. The festival's focal point is a 9-ft phallus, carried by a woman who is accompanied by a Shinto priest with an elongated nose and by several other women carrying more modest-size male accoutrements. The procession, which starts from a minor shrine on the other side of town, makes frequent stops to imbibe from sake casks set up at the side of the road. The participants become progressively drunker; when they finally reach Tagata Jinja in the late afternoon, the entire village is seeing double.

If you have to wait for a train in Takata Jinja to get back to Nagoya or Inuyama, drop into **Terukumni** (☎ 0508/77–9647), a small *nomiya* (informal bar) located on the main street not far from the station. There is sushi if you are hungry, or just beer.

Getting Around

To get to these shrines, take the private Meitetsu Line. Oagata Jinja is the first stop after Meiji Mura-guchi Eki, Tagata is the second. The two shrines are 25 and 28 minutes, respectively, southwest of Inuyama. From Nagoya, take the Meitetsu Line about half an hour north from Kamiji-ba Eki, which you can reach on the Mie-jō subway line.

ISE-SHIMA NATIONAL PARK AND THE KII PENINSULA

Hanging like a fin underneath central Honshū, the Ise-Shima and Kii peninsulas provide a scenic and sacred counterweight to Japan's over-built industrial corridor. Ise-Shima National Park—which holds the supremely venerated shrines of Ise Jingū—extends from the city of Ise to Toba, the center of the pearl industry, and south to Kashikojima, with its indented coastline studded with pine-clad islands. Dipping south along the coast, the Kii Peninsula has magnificent marine scenery, coastal fishing villages and resorts, and the remarkable temple-mountain, Kōya-san. And the nearby Yoshino-Kumano National Park has pristine gorges, holy mountains, and another large, ancient Buddhist community at Yoshino-san, with its gorgeous hillside sakura flowering in early April.

Ise

🔟 *80 mins south of Nagoya by Kintetsu Limited Express (longer by JR local), 2 hrs east of Kyōto by JR Kyūko Express, 1 hr and 40 mins east of Nara by JR, 2 hrs east of Ōsaka by private Kintetsu Line.*

The journey out of Nagoya takes you through depressing industrial suburbs, but don't despair. Thirty minutes before Ise, the polluting factories end and the farmlands begin. Ise is a small town whose major business comes from the pilgrims who pay respects to its *Ge-kū* and *Nai-kū,* its Outer and Inner shrines. From either the Kintetsu Eki or the JR Eki it is only a 10-minute walk through town to the Outer Shrine. A frequent shuttle bus makes the 6-km (4-mi) trip between Ge-kū and Nai-kū; a bus also goes directly from the Inner Shrine to Ise Eki. The most crowded times to visit Ise Jingū are during the Grand Festival, held October 15–17 every year, when thousands come to see the pageantry, and on New Year's Eve and Day, when Shinto believers pray for a good new year.

★ The **Ise Jingū** (Grand Shrines of Ise) are the most famed attractions to visit outside of Nagoya. Astounding as it may be, all of the temple complex buildings, in accordance with Shinto tradition, are rebuilt every 20 years. To begin a new generational cycle, exact replicas of the previous halls are erected with new wood, using the same centuries-old method, on adjacent sites. Then the old buildings are dismantled. The main halls you see now—the 61st set—were completed in 1993 at a cost estimated to be more than ¥4.5 billion.

Both Grand Shrines possess a natural harmony that the more contrived buildings in later Japanese architecture do not. The Inner Shrine's architecture is simple. If you did not know its origin, you would almost think it classically modern. The use of unpainted cypress causes Nai-kū to blend into the ancient forest that circles it and covers the grounds of the 63-acre park. As with Ge-kū, you can see very little of it through the wooden fences surrounding the shrine. But even though the major sightseeing has certain limits, the reward is in feeling the sanctity surrounding Nai-kū and Ge-kū. This phenomenon is quintessentially Japanese—where the inner experience has higher value than the material encounter—in a way that Westerners can only begin to understand. That said, keep in mind that you will see other structures in the temple complexes built in the very same style as Ge-kū and Nai-kū, as well as plenty of torii. Entry to the grounds of both shrines, which are open sunrise to sunset, is free.

Deep in a park full of ancient cryptomeria (Japanese cedar), **Ge-kū,** which dates from AD 478, is dedicated to Toyouke Ō-kami, goddess of grain and agriculture. Its buildings are simple, predating the surge of Chinese influence that swept through the country in the 6th century. Its plain design makes it seem part of the magnificent grounds. It is made from unpainted *hinoki* (cypress), with a fine, closely shaven thatched roof. Again, you can see very little of the exterior of Ge-kū—its roof and glimpses of its walls—and none of its interior. Four fences surround the shrine, and only the imperial family and its envoys may enter.

The same is true for the even more venerated **Nai-kū,** southwest of Ge-kū. Don't let that deter you, however, as there are numerous other buildings around the mound on which the Inner Shrine stands. Nai-kū is where the Yata-no-Kagami (Sacred Mirror) is kept, one of the three sacred treasures of the imperial regalia. The shrine also houses the spirit of the sun goddess Amaterasu, the highest deity in the Shinto pantheon—*Nihon* (*nee*-hone), the Japanese word for Japan, means "the origin of the sun." Amaterasu was born of the left eye of Izanagi, who, according to Japanese mythology, was the first god to inhabit Earth. Amaterasu was the great-great-grandmother of the first mortal emperor of Japan, Jimmu. Seventy generations later, Hirohito, who led Japan through World War II and into prosperous peacetime, became the 123rd divine emperor. Hirohito, however, renounced his divine relationship at the insistence of the U.S. occupation forces.

In their massive travel compendium, *Japan Inside Out,* Jay and Sumi Gluck describe in truncated prose past experiences at the curtained gate that blocks one final view at Nai-kū: "We have been lucky every visit: wind has risen to raise curtain and allow us impressive view head on." Their 10-page description of Ise Jingū includes a fascinating account of the 59th *Sengu-no-gi,* the rite honoring the rebuilding of the temples in 1953, at which they were the first Westerners ever to see an Ise consecration.

Dining and Lodging

$$$ ✕ **Restaurant Wadakin.** If you are a lover of beef and want to make a
★ gustatory pilgrimage—to Matsuzaka, a train stop west of Ise—this restaurant claims to be the originator of Matsuzaka beef. And the cattle it serves has been raised with loving care on its farm. Sukiyaki or the chef's steak dinner will satisfy both your taste buds and any craving for red meat. ⊠ *1878 Naka-machi, Matsuzaka 515, Mie-ken,* ☎ *0598/21–3291. Jacket and tie. No credit cards. Closed 4th Tues. of month.*

$ ⌂ **Hoshide Ryokan.** A small Japanese inn in a traditional-style wood building a short walk from the Ge-kū and the Kintetsu Eki, Hoshide Ryokan is bare and simple, with a shared Japanese bath, but it has clean tatami rooms and congenial hosts. The food served follows a macrobiotic diet, though instant coffee is available at breakfast. ⊠ *2-15-2 Kawasaki, Ise, Mie-ken 516,* ☎ *0596/28–2377,* ℻ *059/627–2830. 13 rooms with shared bath. Laundry service. AE, MC, V.*

Getting Around

You can travel to the shrines from Nagoya by JR, but the trip requires a train change, usually at Taki, and each train is a local. The fastest and most direct route is on the privately owned Kintetsu Line's Limited Express (¥2,320). Even if you have a JR Rail Pass, the time saved on the Kintetsu may be worth the extra cost. Ise has two stations five minutes apart, Ise-shi and Uji-Yamada, the main station.

Futamigoura

⑰   *25 mins east of Ise by JR.*

One route between Ise and Toba follows the shoreline on the JR train (which in turn follows the coast road, should you be traveling by car). Somewhat closer to Toba than Ise is a romantic spot where Japanese come to contemplate eternal love. Two rocks, one said to be male and the other female, rise out of the water. Because they are of the opposite sex, the Japanese "married" them, linking the two together with a straw rope (replaced every January 5 as part of a cheerful festival). These rocks, known as the **Meoto-Iwa** (wedded rocks), represent Izanagi and Izanami, Japan's Adam and Eve.

Lodging

$$$ 🏨 **Ryokan Futamikan.** This traditional Japanese inn is on the coast near
★   the wedded rocks of Ise Peninsula, about 10 km (6 mi) north of Toba. It is an extremely quiet place, where guests spend much of their time in their rooms, which overlook a small garden. The ryokan is a three-minute taxi ride from Futamigoura Eki. ⊠ *569-1 Futami-machi, Mie-ken 519,* ☎ *05964/3–2003. 43 rooms. AE.*

Toba

⑱   *40 mins east of Ise by JR train or bus.*

Toba's world fame spread because it is where the cultivation of pearls was perfected. Before Kokichi Mikimoto (d. 1954) completed his technique for harvesting pearl-bearing oysters at the turn of the century, pearls were a rare freak of nature. *Ama* (female divers)—women were believed to have bigger lungs—could dive all day long, but even after bringing up a thousand oysters, they might not find one with a valuable pearl. Thanks to Mikimoto, the odds have changed, slightly. For even after the considerable effort of injecting an irritating substance—muscarine, as it happens, from Iowa—into two-year-old oysters, only one in two bears pearls, and no more than 5% are of gem quality. On top of that, because the two-year-old oyster takes three more years to secrete layer after layer of nacre over this irritating implant to form the pearl, these gems remain expensive.

Before pearl-oyster farming, women dove for pearls with more frequency than now. Such a hit-or-miss operation can no longer support them in the face of the larger quantities (and cheaper prices) possible through Mikimoto's research and farming. However, on the outlying islands, women do still dive for abalone, octopus, and edible seaweed.

On Pearl Island, 500 yards from Toba Eki, **Mikimoto's Museum** gives a fascinating, if long-winded, account of pearl cultivation. The tours are conducted in Japanese, but the guides usually speak some English, and the accompanying film has an English voice-over. A demonstration is also given by female pearl divers. 🎫 *¥850.* ⊙ *Daily 8:30–5 (9–4 in winter).*

Toba is a resort town with resort hotels and resort activities. An **aquarium** displays native and exotic marine life, such as rare Alaskan sea otters and Baikal seals (¥2,000; open daily 8–5). The ship **Brazil Maru,** which transported many Japanese rice farmers to Brazil, is now a floating entertainment center with restaurants and souvenir shops (¥1,100; open aily 8:30–4:30). **Cruise boats** make 50-minute tours of Toba Bay (¥1,460), and ferries go to the outer islands.

Because Toba is popular among vacationing Japanese, the town has a couple of worthwhile hotels. Staying in Kashikojima, 40 minutes away by rail, is arguably more interesting.

Lodging

$$ 🏨 **Toba International Hotel.** Toba's chief resort hotel sits up on a bluff overlooking the town and bay. Take a room facing the sea, and be sure to get up for the marvelous sunrises. Rooms are mostly Western-style, but there are some Japanese-style rooms in the annex. ✉ *1-23-1 Toba, Mie-ken 517*, ☎ *0599/25−3121*, 🖷 *0599/25−3139. 147 rooms. Pool, boating, fishing. AE, DC, V.*

Getting Around

You can take one of two routes from Ise to Toba, the resort town made famous by Mikimoto pearls—a 45-minute bus ride from near Nai-kū for ¥980, or the possibly more memorable JR train, for ¥610, with a stop at Futamigoura (☞ *above*). Buses run every hour, the last one at 3:56 PM. The bus goes along the Ise-Shima Skyline Drive, which has fine mountainous and wooded scenery.

Kashikojima

★ ⑲   *From Toba, 50 mins south by bus; from Nagoya, 2 hrs south by train on the Kintetsu Line.*

The jagged coastline at Ago Bay presents a dramatic final view of the Ise Peninsula, and one approach to Kashikojima—now the real pearl center—is very scenic: out to the tip of the headland to Goza, through the fishing village of Goza itself, then into the bay on a ferry, past hundreds of rafts from which pearl-bearing oysters are suspended, to Kashikojima.

Be sure to visit **Daio,** the fishing village tucked behind a promontory. Standing above the village is a grand lighthouse, open daily 9–5 for an entrance fee of ¥80. To reach this towering structure, walk up the narrow street lined with fish stalls at the back of the harbor. From this lighthouse, you can see Anori, the oldest (1870) stone lighthouse in Japan, 11 km (7 mi) east. Between the two lighthouses on the curving bay are small fishing villages, coffee shops, and restaurants. And there are three **golf courses** here. The Hamajima Country Club (✉ Hamajima 517, ☎ 05995/2−1141) has especially fine views of Ago Bay, dotted with numerous small islands and oyster beds. Greens fees run ¥8,750 weekdays, ¥18,000 weekends; a caddy costs ¥3,750.

Lodging

Kashikojima has a few reasonable hotels. The most sophisticated is the Shima Kanko Hotel. Consider, however, one of the smaller guest houses, such as the Asanaro, where you will have the opportunity to meet the local community.

$$–$$$ 🏨 **Shima Kanko Hotel.** This large and established resort hotel has
★   grand views over Ago Bay, especially at sunset. Certainly for its location, it's a choice hotel. Staff members are friendly and efficient, speak some English, and are willing to advise you in your touring and make arrangements for golf, fishing, and boating. The hotel's smart French restaurant serves the best Western cuisine on the Shima Peninsula, creatively using the delicious local lobster to its best advantage. Guest rooms are spacious and well furnished, though in a rather dreary pale yellow-beige color. All rooms have views of the bay. A shuttle will pick you up from Kashikojima Eki if you come by train. ✉ *731 Shimmei Ago-chō, Shima-gun, Mie-ken 517*, ☎ *05994/3−1211*, 🖷 *05994/3−3538. 147 Western-style rooms, 51 Japanese-style rooms. 2 restaurants, pool, beauty salon, shops. AE, DC, V.*

$ ⊞ **Asanaro Minshuku.** Owner Yuzo Matsumura is boisterously friendly.
★   In broken English, he will welcome you with enthusiastic abandon. The inn is in a small fishing village facing the Pacific between Daio and Anori lighthouses. Rooms are large and spotless and come with air-conditioning and heating. Bathrooms, also spotless, are just down the hall. Breakfast and dinner are included in the rates and served in your room. Dinner is absolutely superb—fresh broiled lobsters, sashimi, fried oysters, fish cooked in soy sauce or grilled, and fresh fruit. Matsumura-san will insist you use his bicycles to explore and will take you in his car to all the places you missed. He also owns an *izakaya* (tavern), similarly called Asanaro (☎ 05994/3–4197) in Ugata, where he will no doubt take you after dinner. And if you phone on arrival from Ugata Eki, he will pick you up. ⊠ *3578 Ko-oka Ago-chō, Shima-gun, Mie-ken 517,* ☎ *05994/5–3963,* ᄩ *05994/5–3393. 8 rooms. No credit cards.*

$ ⊞ **Ryokan Ishiyama-so.** On tiny Yokoyama-jima, in Ago Bay, this
★   small concrete inn is just a two-minute ferry ride from Kashikojima. Phone ahead, and your hosts will meet you at the quay. The inn is nothing fancy, but it has warmth and hospitality. The meals are good, too, but don't let the hosts try pleasing you with Western-style food—local dishes are much better. ⊠ *Yokoyama-jima, Kashikojima, Ago-chō, Shima-gun, Mie-ken 517,* ☎ *05995/2–1527,* ᄩ *059/952–1240. 12 Japanese-style rooms, 3 with private bath. AE, MC, V.*

Getting Around

The Kintetsu Line continues from Toba to Kashikojima (about ¥900) on an inland route. There are also two buses a day at 9:40 and 2:25 (¥1,400). To take a coastal route, get off the train at Ugata and take a bus to Nakiri; then change buses for one to Goza, from which frequent ferries go to Kashikojima. A trip directly to Kashikojima from Nagoya on the Kintetsu rail line costs ¥3,300.

It is possible to follow the coast from Kashikojima to the Kii Peninsula, but there is no train and in many places the road cuts inland, making the journey long and tedious. From Kashikojima or Toba you are better off taking the Kintetsu Line back to Ise to change to the JR Sangu Line and travel to Taki, where you can change to another JR train to go south to the Kii Peninsula. If you prefer to skip the peninsula, take the Kintetsu Line directly to Nagoya, or to Matsuzaka to connect to Nara and Kyōto.

THE KII PENINSULA

If you plan to take a train down the Kii coast, take your nap at the beginning of the train ride, for about a half hour south of Taki the scenery becomes more and more picturesque as the train follows the shoreline.

The first major town is **Kumano,** not a particularly attractive place but one that hikers use as a gateway to the Yoshino-Kumano National Park— one of the few north–south roads bisecting the Kii Peninsula begins in town and continues inland to Nara by way of Yoshino-san.

Shingū

㉔   *2 hrs south of Taki by JR Limited Express, 2 hrs southwest of Kashiko-jima by the Kintetsu and JR lines, 3½ hrs south of Nagoya by JR.*

Shingū is home to one of the Kii Peninsula's three main shrines, Ku-mano-Hayatama Taisha. Though it is a bright and cheerful place, the shrine isn't reason enough to miss your train, unless you happen to be here on October 15 for its festival. The other two main shrines are at

Hongu, near Doro-hatchō, and at Nachi, the next stop around the Kii Peninsula. By far the best reason for getting off the train in Shingū is an inland excursion to Doro-kyō (☞ *below*).

Dining and Lodging

$ ✕ **Dai Kichi.** This easy-to-find *yakitori-ya* (Japanese grill) across the plaza from the train station has the traditional red lantern hanging outside and a crimson frieze above its doorway. Inside, it is tiny, with just a few tables and a counter with stools. This informal ambience usually means you'll be chatting with fellow diners after the first sip of sake. The place serves typical grilled meats, with each selection running about ¥400. ⊠ *JR Eki Plaza*, ☏ *0735/22–6577. No credit cards.*

$–$$ ⊞ **Shingū-Yui Hotel.** Should you find yourself in town for the night, this modern business hotel is your best choice. A spacious lobby area, friendly staff, and clean, reasonably sized rooms are what you'll find, along with a small restaurant that you might safely limit to breakfast. Situated next to the post office, it is a five-minute walk from the train station. ⊠ *Shingū 6696-10, Shingū-shi, Wakayama-ken 647,* ☏ *0735/ 22–6611,* ℻ *0735/22–4777. 52 rooms. Restaurant. MC, V.*

Doro-kyō

㉑   *40 mins north of Shingū by JR bus.*

As you travel up the Kumano River from Shingū, the walls of the steep-sided Doro-kyō (Doro Gorge) begin to rise around you out of the emerald green water. From late May to early June, with azaleas and rhododendrons lining the banks, the valley is a beautiful and gentle introduction to the gorge that lies farther upstream, which is perhaps Japan's finest. Sheer 150-ft cliffs tower above the Kumano-gawa, which alternates between gushing rapids and calm waters.

The best way to take in this marvel is on a four-hour trip (¥5,100) upriver on a flat-bottom, air-propeller–driven boat. Outside seats on the boats are the preferred ones. Usually these have odd numbers from 3 to 23 and even numbers from 26 through 48. You can book a trip that includes bus and boat from the tourist information office in the JR Shingū Eki plaza or, if you have a JR Pass, save ¥1,120 by taking a 40-minute bus ride from Shingū Eki to Shiko, the embarkation point for the boats going up river.

The boat trip doesn't venture much farther than Doro-hatchō before returning to Shiko. You can, however, hire other long, fiberglass boats (two-hour round-trip, ¥3,280) to explore the two other gorges and rapids that extend for several miles upstream.

From Doro-hatchō (or Shiko), you can take a bus back to Shingū. If you do not want to continue around the Kii Peninsula, an alternative is to backtrack by bus as far as Shiko and pick up the Shingū-Nara bus. The bus travels seven hours from Shingū (six from Shiko) through the heart of Yoshino-Kumano National Park to Nara, stopping at Gojo, from which you can make your way to Kōya-san and Yoshino-san.

Nachi

㉒   *10 mins south of Shingū by JR.*

A 20-minute bus ride from the Nachi train station will bring you to **Nachi-no-taki**, the highest waterfall in Japan, with a drop of 430 ft. At the bus stop near the falls, you'll see a torii at the top of several stone steps that lead down to a paved clearing near the foot of the falls.

For a view from the top, climb up the path from the bus stop to **Nachi Taisha,** one of the three great shrines of the Kii area. Reputed to be 1,400 years old, it is perched just above the waterfall. Next to the shrine is the 1587 Buddhist temple Seiganto-ji, which is the starting point for a 33-temple Kannon pilgrimage through western Honshū.

Katsuura

㉓ *5 mins south of Nachi by JR, 4 hrs south of Nagoya or Ōsaka by JR.*

On a pleasant bay surrounding pine-covered islands, Katsuura Bay takes after one of the big three tourist sights for the Japanese, Matsu-shima Bay near Sendai (☞ Chapter 14). Sightseeing boats that cruise Katsuura Bay (¥1,690) promote it as Kii-no-Matsu-shima (literally "The Matsu-shima of Kii"). If you have seen or plan to see Matsu-shima, then you needn't consider taking the Katsuura cruise.

Kushimoto

㉔ *30 mins south of Katsuura by JR.*

A notable and odd formation of 30 large rocks, spaced evenly as they file out into the sea, follows a line from Kushimoto toward Ō-shima, an island a mile offshore. They resemble what their name, Hashi-kui-iwa (Rock Pillars), suggests, though the more imaginative have seen them as a procession of hooded monks trying to reach Ō-shima. Interestingly enough, it was here that the first American set foot on Japanese soil some 100 years before Commander Perry did, if only to refuel and replenish his ship's water supply.

Kushimoto is a resort town, about 50 km (30 mi) down the coast from Katsuura at the bottom of the Kii Peninsula. With direct flights to Nagoya and Ōsaka, it has become popular with those cities' vacationers.

Shio-no-Misaki

㉕ *5 mins south of Kushimoto by bus.*

A couple of miles from Kushimoto, Shio-no-misaki is Honshū's southernmost point. It is marked by a white lighthouse, constructed by an Englishman in 1873, high above its rocky cliffs. Adjacent to the lighthouse is park land, delightful for picnics and wind-filled walks along the cliff paths. If you're feeling adventurous, clamber down the rocks to the beach below. Swimming here is ill advised.

Shira-hama

㉖ *From Kushimoto, 40 mins west by JR train. From Ōsaka, 3 hrs south by JR train.*

Rounding the peninsula, 54 km (34 mi) northeast of Kushimoto, Shira-hama is considered by the Japanese to be one of the three best hot-spring resorts in the country. (The other two are Beppu on Kyūshū and Atami on the Izu Peninsula. We would add Noboribetsu Onsen in Hokkaidō to these.) Unfortunately, the Japanese have a penchant for building mammoth, drab hotels around their spa waters—which in turn provide an excuse for building other atrocities in the name of tourism, such as monkey parks—and this town fits that mold. But it does have some attractive qualities, particularly craggy headlands and coves. One cove with caves, Sandanbeki, used to be the lair of pirates during the Heian era (794–1185). It now exhibits the type of boats manned by the sea-faring lawless entrepreneurs (¥1,000). It is open daily 10–5:30. Another popular spot is the Sandanbeki cliffs, where, all too frequently, alas, souls beyond hope leap onto the rocks 150 ft below. A sign atop the cliffs encourages would-be jumpers to call a suicide hot line before making their final step, but, cruelly perhaps, there is no phone nearby.

The resort has one of the peninsula's few sandy beaches, **Shira-hama.** The open-air **Saki-no-yu Onsen** is nearby in a hollow among the wave-beaten rocks facing the Pacific. It is said that Emperors Saimei (594–661) and Mommu (683–707) bathed here. ☞ *Free.* ☉ *Daily during daylight hrs; closed 4th Wed. of month.*

Another outside thermal spring, **Sogen-no-yu,** is set delightfully in a peaceful garden. Its tacky aspects aside, a climate that allows beach days in the winter does give Shira-hama appeal as a base to explore the area. It is open daily 6 AM–7 PM, and admission is ¥500. The town itself is a 17-minute bus ride from the train station.

Lodging

$$$ ☷ **Seamone.** This shoreline hotel is the kind that the Japanese like—a cavernous lobby lounge with huge floor-to-ceiling windows facing the bay. Rooms are large and restful, and they have magnificent views of the coast. Western-style rooms are slightly smaller and less expensive than the Japanese-style rooms. Meals are prepared with attention to detail and presentation, and, unless you have a suite, are served in the main dining hall. ✉ *1821 Shira-hama-chō, Nishimuro-gun, Wakayama-ken 049,* ☎ *0739/43–1100,* FAX *0739/43–1110. 140 rooms. Restaurant, pool. AE, V.*

$$ ☷ **Tenzanankaku.** Facing the sea, a Japanese room here—for example
★ Room 501—has marvelous views of Shira-hama to the right and the small fishing harbor to the left. The tatami rooms are spacious: A small window balcony with a Western table and chairs adds dimension to the room. Though every room has a private bath, the place to relax and soak is at the mineral baths on the seventh floor. Dinner is served in a huge hall at banquet tables. The set meal comprises a dozen small dishes, each a delicacy, many of which are from the sea. A live show, often a takeoff of Japanese theater, is performed after dinner. ✉ *1863 Shira-hama-chō, Nishimuro-gun, Wakayama-ken 049,* ☎ *0739/42–2500,* FAX *0739/42–3220. 70 rooms. Restaurant, video games. AE, V.*

Gobō

㉗ *40 mins north of Shira-hama by JR.*

Between Shira-hama and Waka-no-ura is the famous **Dōjō-ji** in Gobō. According to legend, Kiyohime, a farmer's daughter, became enamored of a young priest, Anchin, who often passed by her house. One day she blurted out her feelings to him. He, in turn, promised to return that night to see her. However, during the course of the day, the priest had second thoughts and returned to Dōjō-ji. Spurned, Kiyohime became enraged. She turned herself into a dragon and set out in pursuit of Anchin, who, scared out of his wits, hid under the temple bell that had not yet been suspended. Kiyohime sensed his presence and wrapped her dragon body around the bell. Her fiery breath heated the bell until it became red-hot. The next morning, only the charred remains of Anchin's body were found under the bell.

If you plan to stop at the temple, get off the train at Dōjō-ji Eki, one stop south of Gobō Eki.

Waka-no-ura

㉘ *By JR: 40 mins north of Gobō, 1 hr southwest of Shin-Ōsaka, 90 mins south of Kyōto.*

This major resort—which makes the rather ambitious claim of having the most beautiful coastal scenery in Japan—is in fact not quite as good as Shira-hama for an overnight stay. Waka-no-ura is popular with Ōsaka residents who live only an hour away.

㉙ The main resort area of Waka-no-ura is on the southern boundary of **Wakayama,** the largest town on the peninsula. From Wakayama-kō (port), ferries depart for Tokushima on the island of Shikoku (☞ Chapter 12). As a city, Wakayama has little of historic interest—the castle, originally built in 1585 by Hideyoshi Toyotomi, is a postwar reconstruction.

A new minicity, Wakayama Marina City, built on a man-made island, has developed a theme park called **Porto Europa.** Here the buildings have been given the look of a Mediterranean port town with modern technological amusements that include an underwater safari, a water ride that climaxes in a 72-ft drop, and a high-tech maze that you have to walk and shoot your way through. You don't even have to leave the indoors to enjoy the sea. Just put on a headset and head to VR, a virtual-reality interactive game where you find treasure and adventure under a digital ocean. It's open daily 9–9; admission is ¥1,900. If this is not your bailiwick, use Wakayama to replenish your supply of yen, film for the camera, and other needs, then turn inland to the revered Kōya-san and Yoshino-san.

KŌYA-SAN AND YOSHINO-SAN

Kōya-san

㉚ *2 hrs west of Wakayama by JR, 90 mins west of Ōsaka on the Kōya-san Line of the Nankai Dentetsu Electric Railway.*

Every year about a million visitors pass through Kōya-san's **Dai-mon,** a huge wooden-gate structure typical of many entrances to Japanese temples. In this case, they are stepping into a great complex of 120 temples, monasteries, schools, and graves on a mesa in the mountains. This is the seat of the Shingon sect of Buddhism, founded by Kōbō Daishi in 816.

If your time is limited, head for **Okuno-in Cemetery** first. From the Okuno-in-mae *noriba* (bus stop)—where you can pick up a wide, well-worn path that provides a shortcut to the cemetery's Lantern Hall—you can take the long route out. Many of your fellow visitors will be Japanese who are making pilgrimages to the mausoleum of Kōbō Daishi or paying their respects to their ancestors buried here. Dressed in white and carrying wooden staffs, the pilgrims often travel in groups. Make sure you arrive very early in the morning, before the groups take over.

Entering this cemetery is like stepping into Alice's Wonderland. Magnificent 300-year-old cedar trees reach skyward, some of their dark, textured trunks forming columns 12 ft around. This old-growth forest is a rarity in most places, including Japan. Among the trees are buried some of the country's most illustrious families, their graves marked by moss-covered pagodas and red- and white-robed Buddhas carved from black stone. You will feel small here, but contemplative; the holiness of Kōya-san is strong.

The path from Okuno-in-mae leads into the main avenue of mausoleums, a cobblestone lane that ends at the **Lantern Hall,** named after its 11,000 lanterns. Two fires burn in this hall: One has been alight since 1016, the other since 1088. Behind the hall is the mausoleum of Kōbō Daishi (774–835). ⊘ *Lantern Hall Apr.–Oct., daily 8–5; Nov.–Mar., daily 8:30–4:30.*

You may be tempted to spend the day wandering through the cemetery, but be careful—it is easy to get lost if you stray from the main avenue. Some people prefer to visit the cemetery at dusk, when the cobbled lane is lit by lanterns, creating an eerie mood. In any case, exit Okuno-in by way of the 2½-km (1½-mi) main avenue, lined with tombs, monuments, and statues. More than 100,000 historical figures are honored here. The lane exits the cemetery at Ichi-no-hashi-guchi; follow the main street straight ahead to return to the center of town (a 20-minute walk) or wait for the bus that is headed for Kongōbu-ji.

On the southwestern side of Kōya-san, **Kongōbu-ji** (Temple of the Diamond Seat) is the chief temple of Shingon Buddhism, a sect that is closest to Tibetan Buddhism. Kongōbu-ji was built in 1592 as the family temple of Hideyoshi Toyotomi. It was rebuilt in 1861 and is now the main temple of the Kōya-san community. ☞ ¥500. ⊘ *Daily 8–5 (8–4:30 in winter).*

Danjogaran is a complex consisting of many halls as well as the **Kompon Dai-tō** (Great Central Pagoda). This red pagoda, with its interior of brilliantly colored beams, contains five sacred images of Buddha. Built in 1937, the two-story structure stands out in part because of its unusual style but also because of its rich vermilion color. It's worth taking a look inside. From Kongōbu-ji, walk down the temple's main stairs and take the road to the right of the parking lot in front of you; in less than five minutes you will reach Danjogaran. ☞ *Each building* ¥100. ⊘ *Apr.–Oct., daily 8–5; Nov.–Mar., daily 8:30–4:30.*

The exhibits at **Reihōkan** (Treasure Hall), with its 5,000 art treasures, are continually changing. At any given time, some of the 180 pieces that have been designated national treasures will be on display. The most notable of these are *Shaka-nehan-zō*—the scroll of Reclining Image of Sakyamuni Buddha on His Last Day—and the exotic *Hachi-dai-doji-zō*—images of the Eight Guardian Deities. The hall is south of Danjōgaran across a small path. ☞ ¥500. ⊘ *Daily 9–5 (9–4 in winter).*

Dining and Lodging

Kōya-san has no hotels, per se. Fifty-three of the temples offer Japanese-style accommodations—tatami floors, futon mattresses, and traditional Japanese shared baths—and only a handful accept foreign guests. The two meals served are *shōjin ryōri*, vegetarian cuisine that uses locally made tofu, which is the same as what the priests eat. The price is either side of ¥10,000 per person, including the meals. These prices are higher than those at other temples in Japan. This may be because this is the only Buddhist sect in which wealth is necessary for advancement in the religious hierarchy. If possible, make reservations in advance through **Kōya-san Kanko Kyokai** (✉ Kōya-san, Kōya-machi, Itsu-gun, Wakayama-ken, ☎ 07365/6–2616). You can also reserve through the Nankai Railway Company office in Ōsaka and the Japan Travel Bureau in most Japanese cities. One especially lovely temple that is open to foreigners is **Rengejo-in** (☎ 0736/56–2231). Both the head priest and his mother speak English. Be sure to ask where the morning service takes place and rise before 6 to see and hear it. Another option is **Shinnō-in** (☎ 076/56–2227).

Getting Around

Depending on where you are coming from, there are many ways to approach Kōya-san. The penultimate leg of the trip is a cable car from the private Nankai Rail Line's Gokuraku-bashi Eki. The cable car will deposit you at Kōya-san station, at the top of 3,000-ft Kōya-san, where you can pick up a map. You will need to take a bus to the main attractions, which are about 2½ km (1½ mi) from the station and about 5½ km (3½ mi) from each other, on opposite sides of town.

Two buses leave the station every 20 or 30 minutes, when the cable car arrives. One goes to Okuno-in Cemetery, on the east end of the main road, and the other goes to the Dai-mon to the west. Both go first to the center of town to a "T" junction, where the tourist office is located (⊠ 600 Kōya-san, Kōya-chō, Ito-gun, Wakayama-ken, ☎ 07365/6–2616). The bus fare is ¥300 to the tourist office. En route from the station, you will pass the mausoleums of the first and second Tokugawa shoguns. You may want to walk back and visit these two gilded structures later; they're open daily 9–5.

If you have a JR Pass, take the JR Wakayama line to Hashimoto and change to the Nankai Line for the final 19 km (12 mi) to Gokuraku-bashi Eki, from which the cable car runs to the top of Kōya-san. (If you have cut across the Yoshino-Kumano National Park by bus from Shingū or Hongu on Route 168, instead of circling the Kii Peninsula, get off the bus at Gojo and backtrack one station on the JR Line to Hashimoto; then take the Nankai Line.)

You can also take the private Nankai Line to reach Kōya-san from Ōsaka's Nankai Namba Eki, from which a train departs for Kōya-san every 30 minutes. (To reach Namba Eki from Shin-Ōsaka Shinkansen Eki, use the Mido-suji subway line.) The Ōsaka–Kōya-san journey takes 90 minutes, including the five-minute cable-car ride up to Kōya-san Eki, and costs around ¥2,200 (try to reserve a seat if you're traveling on a weekend).

Yoshino-san

㉛ *3½ hrs east of Kōya-san by cable car, Nankai, JR, and Kintetsu lines; 1 hr south of Nara by JR and private Kintetsu Rail Line.*

Though the community of temples at Yoshino-san is less impressive than that of Kōya-san, Yoshino-san is one of the most beautiful places in Japan to visit during cherry-blossom season. The Sakura Festival, which attracts thousands of visitors each year, is April 11–12. Because the 100,000 trees in four groves are staggered on the mountainside, peak blossom time climbs the slope as the weather warms the trees from bottom to top. As a result you're virtually guaranteed to see perfect sakura sometime within a two-week period in mid-April. When you look upon this vision of color, thank En-no-Ozunu, the 7th-century Buddhist priest who planted the trees and put a curse on anyone who tampered with them.

In the middle of the cherry groves is **Kimpusen-ji**, the main temple of the area. Make a point of seeing the main hall, Zaō-dō, which not only is the second largest wooden structure in Japan but also has two superb sculptures of Deva kings at the main gate. The other important temple is **Nyoirin-ji**, founded in the 10th century and located just south of Kimpusen-ji. Here the last remaining 143 warriors prayed before going into their final battle for the imperial cause in the 14th century. Behind the temple is the mausoleum of Emperor Go-daigo (1288–1339), who brought down the Kamakura Shogunate. 🎫 ¥350. ⊙ *Daily 9–5.*

Built into the surrounding mountains, Yoshino is a quaint town where the shops—and there are many to serve the thousands of visitors—are on the third floor of the house, the first and second floors being below the road. All around Yoshino there are superb mountain vistas and isolated temples. For pilgrims, Sanjo-san is considered the holiest mountain, with two temples at the summit, one of which is dedicated to En-no-Ozunu, the cherry-tree priest. Lodgings are available at both temples May 8–September 27. The **tourist office** (Yoshinoyama, Yoshino-machi, Yoshino-gun, Nara-ken, ☎ 07463/2–3014) can arrange accommodations at local minshuku.

Getting Around

From Nara, take JR to Yoshino-guchi or the Kintetsu Line to Kashihara Jingū-mae Eki and connect with a Kintetsu Line train for Yoshino. From Kōya-san, return to JR Hashimoto Eki; take a train one hour southeast to Yoshino-guchi and then change for the Kintetsu Line to Yoshino. From Ōsaka, take a two-hour ride on the Kintetsu Line from Abeno-bashi Eki.

NAGOYA, ISE-SHIMA, AND THE KII PENINSULA A TO Z

Arriving and Departing

By Bus

Buses connect Nagoya with Tōkyō and Kyōto. The bus fare is half that of the Shinkansen trains, but the journey by bus takes three times longer.

By Car

The journey on the expressway to Nagoya from Tōkyō takes about five hours; from Kyōto, allow two hours.

By Plane

There are direct overseas flights to Nagoya on **Japan Airlines** (JAL) from Honolulu, Hong Kong, and Seoul. The major airlines that have routes to Japan have offices in downtown Nagoya. For domestic travel, Japan Airlines, **All Nippon Airways** (ANA), and **Japan Air System** have flights between Nagoya and most major Japanese cities.

BETWEEN THE AIRPORT AND CENTER CITY
The **Meitetsu Airport** bus makes the 50-minute run from the airport to the Meitetsu Bus Center, near Nagoya Eki, for ¥690.

By Train

Frequent bullet trains run between Tōkyō and Nagoya (1 hr, 52 mins on the fast *Hikari* Shinkansen; 2½ hrs on the slower *Kodama* Shinkansen; JR Passes are not accepted on the ultra-fast *Nozomi*); Nagoya and Kyōto (43 mins); and Nagoya and Shin-Ōsaka (1 hr). You can also take the less expensive Limited Express trains. Limited Express trains proceed from Nagoya into and across the Japan Alps—to Takayama and Toyama, and to Matsumoto and Nagano.

Getting Around

By Bus

Buses crisscross Nagoya, running either north–south or east–west. The basic fare is ¥200.

By Subway

Several main subway lines run under Nagoya's major avenues. The Higashiyama Line runs from the north down to the JR Nogoya Eki and then due east, cutting through the city center at Sakae. The Meijō Line runs north–south, passing through the city center at downtown Sakae. The Tsurumai Line also runs north–south through the city, then turns from the JR eki to Sakae to cross the city center. A fourth subway line, the Sakura-dōri, cuts through the city center from the JR eki, paralleling the east–west section of the Higashiyama Line. The basic fare, good for three stops, is ¥200. A one-day pass, good for Nagoya's buses and subways, is ¥820.

By Taxi
Metered taxis are plentiful, initial fares are ¥620.

Contacts and Resources

Emergencies
Police, ☎ 110. **Ambulance,** ☎ 119. **National Nagoya Hospital,** ☎ 0521/951–1111. **Kokusai Central Clinic,** ✉ Nagoya International Center Bldg., ☎ 0521/201–5311.

English-Language Bookstore
Maruzen (✉ 3-23-3 Nishiki, Naka-ku, Nagoya ☎ 0521/261–2251) has a broad selection of English-language books downtown, behind the International Hotel Nagoya.

Guided Tours
The **Nagoya Yuran Bus Company** (☎ 052/561–4036) runs five different bus tours of the city. The three-hour "panoramic course" tour (¥2,610) includes Nagoya-jō and Atsuta Jingū and has scheduled morning and afternoon departures. A full-day tour (¥6,270) will take you out of Nagoya to visit Meiji Mura and Tagata Jinja. These tours have only a Japanese-speaking guide.

You can arrange a full-day tour to Ise and the Mikimoto Pearl Island at Toba from Kyōto or Ōsaka (¥24,800) through **Sunrise Tours** (☎ 075/361–7241).

Travel Agencies
Japan Travel Bureau (☎ 0521/563–1501) has several locations, including the JR Nagoya Eki and in the Matsuzakaya Department Store downtown. The major domestic airlines (JAL, ☎ 052/563–4141; JAS, ☎ 052/201–8111; and ANA, ☎ 052/962–6211) have offices in Nagoya, as do major international carriers.

JAPAN TRAVEL-PHONE
This toll-free service will answer travel-related questions and help with communication, daily 9–5. Dial 0120/444–800 for information on western Japan.

Visitor Information
Nagoya International Center (✉ Nagoya Kokusai Center Bldg., 3rd floor, 1-47 Nakono 1-chōme, Nakamura-ku, Nagoya, ☎ 052/581–5679) is quite possibly the best-equipped information center in Japan for assisting gai-jin. Not only is there an information desk to answer your questions, but there are also audiovisual presentations and an extensive library of English-language newspapers (both Japanese and foreign), magazines, and books. The center also provides an English-language telephone hot line service (☎ 052/581–0100) from 9 to 8:30. The **City Tourist Information Office** (✉ 1-4 Meieki 1-chōme, Nakamura-ku, Nagoya, ☎ 052/541–4301) will give you city maps and make hotel reservations. There is another branch of the tourist office in the center of the JR Nagoya Eki (☎ 052/541–4301), open 9–5 daily.

6 The Japan Alps and the North Chūbu Coast

Soaring mountain peaks, slices of traditional Japan, delightful natural color from spring's flowering trees and summer's alpine wildflowers to the kaleidoscopic hues of autumn, and superb hiking and skiing make this central alpine block one of the finest districts in the country. West along the Nihon-kai, Kanazawa is as enjoyable a city as you'll find in Japan, and the Chūbu region's coastal scenery on islands and peninsulas perfectly balances a turn through the mountains.

By Nigel Fisher

EIGHTY PERCENT OF JAPAN is mountainous—compliments of the cataclysmic forces of Pacific Rim plate tectonics. As an apt expression of respect for this natural power, the Japanese for centuries looked at their mountains as sacred precincts where spirits dwelled and gods alit from the heavens and kept their distance. Inhibitions gone, the Japanese now take full advantage of this alpine splendor, and hiking and skiing are popular national pastimes.

Considering Japan's centuries of isolation from the West, it's no surprise that it took a European—a Briton, the Reverend Walter Weston—until the end of the 19th century to popularize the term Japan Alps, which his countryman William Gowland first used a few years earlier to describe the north–south mountain ranges of central Honshū's Chūbu region. Through his writings and his mountain man's derring-do, Reverend Weston helped to change Japanese attitudes about these ranges from reverence and superstition to physical appreciation. Another Englishman, Archdeacon A. C. Shaw, who served as his church's prelate in Tōkyō, gave prestige to the mountains by building his summer villa on the lower slopes of Mt. Asama to escape the muggy summers of the capital. Since then, over the course of the past hundred years, the Japan Alps have been "discovered" by the Japanese, not only for their grandeur but also for the rural traditional culture, architecture, and folk crafts that have been bulldozed away elsewhere by the industrial progress that has swept the coastal plains. The relatively small city of Takayama is particularly famous for having held on to local traditions.

The northern slopes of the Japan Alps—those facing the Nihon-kai—have the deepest snowfalls. This no doubt was the draw for the XVIII Winter Olympics, which Nagano and the surrounding mountain towns hosted in 1988. As melting snow turns rivers into spring torrents, fruit trees blossom. By summer, alpine wildflowers burst out, and temperatures are warm and crisp compared with the heavy humidity of lowland Chūbu and much of the rest of Japan. Autumn foliage blankets the hills in yet another spectacle of color. When winter returns, fishermen begin plucking the sweetest shrimps from the icy waters of the Nihon-kai.

The name "Japan Alps" applies to the mountains within the Chūbu region, which is bracketed by Niigata in the north, Tōkyō to the east, Kyōto in the south, and Fukui to the west. After taking in the mountains, this chapter continues west to the pleasant coastal city of Kanazawa, then turns north along the Nihon-kai to the Noto Hantō before finishing at Sado-ga-shima, Japan's fifth largest island, slightly north of Niigata.

Japan Alps and North Chūbu Coast Glossary

Key Japanese words and suffixes for this chapter include *-bashi* (bridge), *-chō* (street or block), *-chōme* (street), *chūō* (central, as in JR Central Line), *daimyō* (feudal lord), *dōri* (avenue), *eki* (train station), *gai-jin* (foreigner), *-gawa* (river), *hama* (beach), *hantō* (peninsula), *jinja* (Shintō shrine), *-jō* (castle), *-ken* (prefecture), *kōen* ("ko-en," park), *kōgen* (plateau), *-ku* (section or ward), *kūkō* (airport), *machi* (town), *matsuri* (festival), *-mon* (gate), *Nihon-kai* (Japan Sea), *ōhashi* (large bridge), *onsen* (hot springs), *sake* (rice wine), *sakura* (cherry blossoms), *-san* (mountain, as in Asama-san, Mt. Asama), *-shima* or *jima* (island), *Shinkansen* (bullet train, literally "new trunk line"), *tōge* (pass), *torii* ("*to*-ree-ee," gate), and *yama* (mountain).

Pleasures and Pastimes

Architecture
The Chūbu mountains have served as a barrier to invasion from homogenizing influences of the country's power centers. In the Japan Alps you'll find distinctive local architecture, such as the preserved post villages of Tsumago and Magome, which have been bypassed by modern highways and high-speed trains. In Takayama, the traditional wooden teahouses, dye houses, and sake breweries with latticed windows and doors still stand. Ogimachi's *gasshō-zukuri* farmhouses have at their center a chimney-less open fire pit, vented by a hole in the thatched roof. Matsumoto has one of the few original castles remaining from the days of feudal Japan. All of this constitutes the greatest diversity of traditional building styles that you'll find in the country.

Dining
Virtually all regions in Japan have their own cookery, not to mention local culinary pride. Nowhere in Japan is this more pronounced than in the microregions within the Japan Alps and on the Nihon-kai coast. In the area called Hokuriku, which consists of the Ishikawa, Fukui, and Toyama prefectures, fish from the cold, salty waters of the Nihon-kai is superb.

Toyama has *beni-zuwaigani,* a long-legged red crab that is a special delicacy during November through March. *Ama-ebi,* a sweet prawn that, when eaten raw with *wasabi* (Japanese horseradish), literally melts in the mouth, is available from Toyama Bay. Another local treat is *masuzushi,* salmon trout pressed onto shallow, round cakes of vinegared rice.

In **Ishikawa,** which includes Kanazawa and the Noto Hantō, the cuisine is called *Kaga,* in which the harvest from the sea is prepared with Kyōto-style elegance. *Tai* (sea bream), cooked in a style called *karamushi,* is certainly one dish to try. And *Kaga-ryōri* is a kind of cooking in which the mountain vegetables of mushrooms and ferns are used. Fish and shellfish are frequently included in regional dishes. Miso soup, for example, often contains tiny clams still in their shells; sweet crab legs are a mouthwatering delicacy.

In **Fukui,** the *echizen-gani* (crabs) are 28 inches long on the average. These crabs are pure heaven after they're boiled with a little salt and dipped in rice vinegar. *Wakasa-karei* is a fresh sole that is dried briefly before being lightly grilled. In both Fukui and Ishikawa, there is *echizen-soba,* buckwheat noodles, handmade and served with mountain vegetables. Echizen-soba is also served with dips of sesame oil and bean paste, a reflection of the Buddhist vegetarian tradition.

In **Niigata Prefecture,** try *noppei,* a hot or cold soup with *sato-imo* (a kind of sweet potato) as its base, and mushrooms, salmon, and other local ingredients. It goes with hot rice and grilled fish. *Wappameshi* is a hot dish of steamed rice garnished with local ingredients. In autumn, try *kiku-no-ohitashi,* a side dish of chrysanthemum petals marinated in vinegar. Like other prefectures on the Nihon-kai coast, Niigata has outstanding fish in winter—yellowtail, flatfish, sole, oysters, abalone, and shrimp. A local specialty is *namban ebi,* raw shrimp dipped in soy sauce and wasabi. It's butter-tender and especially sweet on Sado-shima. Also on Sado-shima, take advantage of the excellent *wakame* (seaweed) dishes and *sazae-no-tsuboyaki* (wreath shellfish) broiled in their shells with a soy or miso sauce.

In the landlocked **Hida Prefecture** around Takayama, cooks look to the mountains and rivers for produce. The typical cuisine of the district is called *sansai,* in which mountain vegetables such as edible ferns and wild plants are cooked with the rich local miso. *Sansai ryōri* includes fresh river fish, such as *ayu,* which are grilled with salt or soy sauce. The local specialty is *hoba-miso,* where miso, mixed with vegetables, is roasted on a magnolia leaf. Other local foods are *mitarashi-dango,* grilled rice balls flavored with soy sauce, and *shio-sembei,* salty rice crackers.

Nagano Prefecture is famous for its handmade *soba* (buckwheat noodles); more esoteric dishes in the area include raw horse meat and sweet-boiled baby bees. Matsumoto is known for its wasabi and its *sakura-nabe,* horsemeat cooked and served in an earthenware pot.

CATEGORY	COST*
$$$$	over ¥6,000
$$$	¥4,000–¥6,000
$$	¥2,000–¥4,000
$	under ¥2,000

per person, excluding drinks, service, and tax

Festivals

If not the most famous festivals in Japan, Takayama's springtime Sanno Matsuri and the autumn Yahata Matsuri are serious competitors for that distinction. These matsuri picked up steam more than two centuries ago in an attempt to appease the gods and prevent the spread of the plague. Because the festivals seemed to work, they have continued and grown to become spectacular events during which mammoth floats make their way through town.

Hiking

The Japan Alps have myriad mountain peaks. None of them are tremendously high—the tallest tops out at 10,450 ft—but the sheer number of them over 8,000 ft makes for splendid scenery and fantastic hiking. These alpine lands are wondrous in spring and summer when flowers burst into life as the snow retreats back up the peaks. Kamikochi, for good reason, is where many hikers come—trails and lodges line the wooded banks of the Azusa-gawa. Farther north, paths top the Tateyama range. Some trails are tough; some can be taken leisurely. Choose your pleasure or punishment accordingly.

Hot Springs

There are thermal springs throughout Japan, but there is a special quality to those in the mountains, especially those in the open air. Nothing compares to soaking in healing mineral waters that are steaming away in brisk mountain air while snow-capped peaks crowd your vision.

Lodging

Accommodations cross the spectrum, from Japanese-style inns to large, characterless, modern resort hotels that have the facilities of international hotels. All of the large city and resort hotels serve Western and Japanese food. In summer, hotel reservations are advised.

We have not listed youth hostels, which are in all the major areas. You can easily obtain their names by requesting the Japan National Tourist Organization's free booklet *Youth Hostels in Japan.*

For a short course on accommodations in Japan, *see* Lodging *in the* Gold Guide.

CATEGORY	COST*
$$$$	over ¥20,000
$$$	¥15,000–¥20,000
$$	¥10,000–¥15,000
$	under ¥10,000

All prices are for a double room, excluding service and tax.

Skiing

With some 20 resorts of international quality, the Alps are one of Japan's three major winter playgrounds. That has only been enhanced by the presence of the XVIII Olympic Winter Games in 1988. Ski areas are within easy reach of Tōkyō—less than four hours—which makes them convenient but also very crowded on weekends. If you haven't skied in Japan, don't miss the unique pleasure of skiing during the day and soaking in a steaming onsen at night. Some are outdoors, surrounded with snow.

Exploring the Japan Alps and the Chūbu North Coast

The Japan Alps is not a defined political region. It is a name that has come to be accepted for the mountains in Chūbu, the Middle District. Chūbu encompasses nine prefectures in the center of Honshū, three of which—Gifu-ken, Nagano-ken, and Yamanashi-ken—make up the Central Highlands proper. In this chapter, we have extended the Japan Alps to include neighboring coastal areas: Kanazawa, Fukui, and the Noto Hantō to the northwest and Niigata and Sado-ga-shima to the northeast. Getting around the Alps is somewhat determined by the valleys and river gorges that run north and south. East–west routes through the mountains are nearly nonexistent, except between Matsumoto and Takayama in summer.

Numbers in the text correspond to numbers in the margin and on the Japan Alps, Takayama, and Kanazawa maps.

Great Itineraries

You can approach the Alps by several routes, either from the Nihonkai or the Pacific side of Japan. Our approach from Tōkyō enters the eastern edge of the Alps at Karuizawa. From there we stay up in the mountains and work over to Nagano, then west to Matsumoto. The old post towns Tsumago and Magome are next; they were once on the route between Kyōto and Tōkyō during the Edo period (1603–1868). Heading back north, Takayama is one of Japan's most attractive and preserved towns.

Kanazawa is likewise a remarkably pleasant city, and the nearby Noto Peninsula has its share of scenic coastline. You may want to end your journey here and take the train from Kanazawa to Kyōto. Or, continue north along the Sea of Japan to Niigata for the short ferry ride to the lonely isle of Sado-ga-Shima.

To cover and enjoy everything in this chapter would take a couple of weeks, or 10 days if you did not go up to Niigata and Sado-ga-Shima. The best idea, however, is to pick two or three areas to focus on and avoid spending all of your time making train connections.

IF YOU HAVE 2 DAYS

With such limited time, pick one town to visit. ⚏ **Takayama** ⑨–⑲, perhaps the most attractive of the Alps towns, is ideal. It has enough to hold your attention for a couple of days, and you can get there in just over two hours from Nagoya. ⚏ **Matsumoto** ⑥, with direct trains to Tōkyō and to Nagoya, would be another good place to get a taste of the Alps.

IF YOU HAVE 4 DAYS

⚏ **Takayama** ⑨–⑲ should take two of these days. For the other two, consider spending one of them in either of the traditional post villages **Tsumago** or **Magome** in the ⚏ **Kiso Valley** ⑦, then the last night in ⚏ **Matsumoto** ⑥. As you leave Matsumoto, head back to Tōkyō via Nagano and spend a couple of hours visiting **Zenkō-ji** temple before catching the new Shinkansen into Ueno Eki in the city.

IF YOU HAVE 7 DAYS

From Tōkyō, take a Shinkansen to ⊞ **Nagano** ⑤, then spend the night in ⊞ **Matsumoto** ⑥. Head the next day for the interesting old post towns of the ⊞ **Kiso Valley** ⑦. On the third day travel through the mountains to ⊞ **Kamikochi** ⑧, spending the night there. Take the fourth and fifth nights in ⊞ **Takayama** ⑨–⑲. On the sixth day, perhaps in the afternoon, head out of the mountains to ⊞ **Kanazawa** ㉑–㉜ and spend all of the next day there. From Kanazawa there are express trains that go directly south to Nagoya, Kyōto, and Ōsaka. If you would like to get out onto **Sado-ga-Shima** ㊻–㊽, consider simplifying your trip overall: Start in Takayama, then pop over the mountains through the old farm town of ⊞ **Ogimachi** ⑳ to Kanazawa, and then follow the coast to **Niigata** ㊺ for the crossing to the island.

TIMING

Snow covers the Alps from November through March—later on the high mountain slopes—and the route between Matsumoto and Takayama via Kamikochi is closed from November to April. So unless you are a skier, spring, summer, and fall are the best times to visit the area. With Japanese and gai-jin tourists escaping the heat of the coastal cities, summer is the most crowded. Be aware that the spring Sanno Matsuri and the autumn Yahata Matsuri in Takayama are extremely popular, and local hotels fill up months in advance.

THE JAPAN ALPS

Karuizawa

❶ *80 mins by Shinkansen and JR local from Tōkyō's Ueno Eki.*

Fashionable Karuizawa's popularity began when Archdeacon A. C. Shaw, an English prelate, built his summer villa here in 1886. Other gai-jin living in Tōkyō soon followed his example, and the town is still popular among affluent Tōkyōites, who in summer transfer their urban lifestyle to this small town 3,000 ft above sea level. The whole support culture decamps to Karuizawa, too—branches of more than 500 trendy boutiques open their doors here to sell the same goods as their main stores back in Tōkyō, and the town becomes a little Ginza. Shopping isn't the reason to come, however: better to get in on archery, skating, tennis, hiking, and horseback riding, all of which you can arrange through your hotel. The winter pace, always genteel, slows down, and appropriately the only event of the XVIII Winter Olympic Games to be held in Karuizawa was curling.

Nature nonetheless prevails over Karuizawa. **Mt. Asama,** an active, triple-cratered volcano, soars 8,399 ft above town to the northwest. Occasionally, Asama-san makes grumbling sounds, possibly threatening to erupt, which causes the authorities to take prudent action in prohibiting climbing up to the volcano's crater. In such a case, you'll have to be satisfied with a panoramic view of Asama-san and its neighbor, **Mt. Myogi,** as well as the whole **Yatsugatake Mountain Range,** from the observation platform at **Usui Pass.** The view justifies the 90-minute uphill walk from Nite (*nee*-teh) Bridge at the end of Karuizawa Ginza, the shop-strewn street.

Outside Karuizawa are the **Shiraito Falls,** only about 10 ft high but 220 ft across. In autumn, crimson maples frame the scene and the sun glints in the streaks of white water that tumble over the rocks. You can either take a bus straight to the falls or walk from Mine-no-chaya. They are a direct 30-minute ride from Karuizawa Eki. To make the trip on foot, take a 25-minute bus ride to Mine-no-chaya (mountain-top tea-

0   50 miles
0   75 km

KEY
— JR Trains
═ Shinkansen (Bullet Train)
┼┼ Private rail line
🚢 Ferry

NIHON-KAI
(Sea of Japan)

Cape Rokkō

Sosogi 39 **Suzu** 40 Tako-jima
Wajima 38
Noto
Monzen 37 *Hantō*
Anamizu
Noto Ogi

Noto-jima
41 **Wakura Onsen**
Nanao

36 **Hakui**
Kurobe
Takaoka
42
Un
Or
43 44
Toyama
Tonami   Airport   Keyakidaira
8

Airport

Kanazawa
21 32
see detail
map

Chubu-
Sangaku
Nat'l Park

Awara Onsen
35

Ogimachi 20
Mt.Yari
Mt. Hotaka
41
Mt. Yake
Ka
8

Mt.
Haku
Miboro-ko

Fukui
33
Takayama
9 19
see detail
map

Eihei-ji
34
Ono

Katsuyama
Mt. Haku
Nat'l Park

Mt. Norikura
Shimas

Izumi
Mt. Ontake

8

Hida-gawa
Gero

27
TO
KYOTO

TO
NAGOYA

Kiso
Valley 7

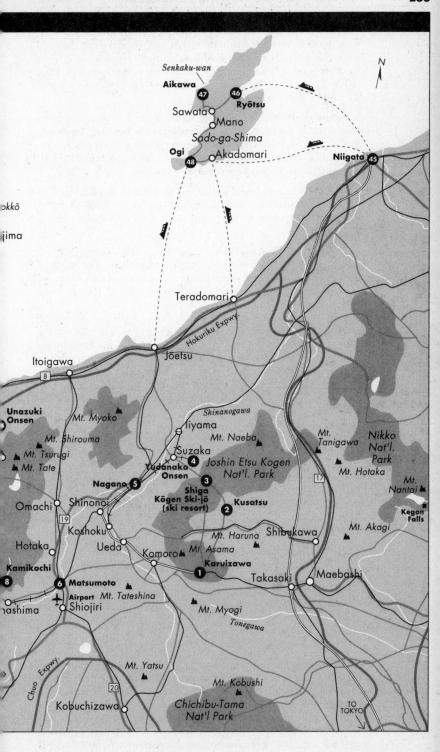

Senkaku-wan

Aikawa ⓐ47 ⓐ46 Ryōtsu

Sawata Mano

Sado-ga-Shima

Ogi ⓐ48 Akadomari

Niigata ⓐ45

okkō

jima

Teradomari

Hokuriku Expwy.

Itoigawa Jōetsu

8

Unazuki Onsen

Mt. Myoko Shinanogawa

Mt. Shirouma Iiyama Mt. Naeba Mt. Tanigawa Nikko Nat'l. Park

Mt. Tsurugi Suzaka ⓐ4

Mt. Tate Yudanaka Onsen Joshin Etsu Kogen Nat'l. Park Mt. Hotaka

Mt. Nantai

Nagano ⓐ5 ⓐ3

Kōgen Ski-jō (ski resort) Kusatsu ⓐ2 17 Kegon Falls

Omachi Shinonoi Shiga

Koshoku Mt. Haruna Shibukawa Mt. Akagi

Hotaka Ueda Komoro Mt Asama

Kamikochi ⓐ1 Karuizawa

⓼8 ⓐ6 Matsumoto Takasaki Maebashi

ashima Airport Mt. Tateshina

Shiojiri Mt. Myogi

Tonegawa

Mt. Yatsu

Chuo Expwy.

20 Mt. Kobushi

Kobuchizawa Chichibu-Tama Nat'l Park TO TOKYO

N

house), and then hike for an hour down through the forests of birch and larch to the falls. You can then return to Karuizawa by bus or continue the walk, via more falls at **Ryugaeshi**, and return through the small spa village of **Kose Onsen** to the **Mikasa Hotel**, the oldest wooden Western-style hotel in Japan. From the Mikasa it is a 30-minute walk back to Karuizawa. The total course from Mine-no-chaya to town is about 11 km (7 mi) and takes 4½ hours.

Yachō-no-mori (Wild Bird Forest), where about 120 species of birds have taken up residence, is also a short distance by bus from Karuizawa and close to **Hoshino Onsen,** another spa. There are two observation huts, from which you can look more closely at the birds' habitat, along a 2½-km (1½-mi) forest course.

The best way to get around Karuizawa proper is by **bicycle,** plenty of which are available for hire (about ¥800 an hour, ¥2,000 a day) at Karuizawa Eki, about 1½ km (1 mi) south of the downtown area.

Lodging

$$$$ 🏨 **Hotel Kayu Kajima-no-Mori.** An exclusive resort, this hotel is tastefully furnished with Japanese handicrafts and antiques. The buildings are surrounded by forest, which heightens the mood of tranquillity. ⊠ *Hanareyama, Karuizawa-machi, Nagano-ken 389,* ☎ ℻ *0267/42–3535. 50 rooms. Restaurant, 2 tennis courts. AE, DC, V.*

$$$–$$$$ 🏨 **Karuizawa Prince Hotel.** Though the Prince is a large resort hotel, ★ it is quiet and relaxing. Because of its popularity, you need to reserve well in advance for a room in summer. In winter, the neighboring mountain serves as a modest ski slope for the hotel. There are a Western- and a Japanese-style restaurant in the hotel. ⊠ *Karuizawa, Karuizawa-machi, Kitasaku-gun, Nagano-ken 389,* ☎ *0267/42–8111,* ℻ *0267/42–7139. 240 rooms, mostly Western style. 2 restaurants, pool, horseback riding. AE, MC, V.*

$ 🏨 **Pensione Grasshopper.** This guest house has friendly hospitality, Western beds (great views of Asama-san from Room 208), and a mix of Japanese and Western fare. The owner, Mrs. Kayo Iwasaki, speaks English. The house is in the suburbs, but the management will transport you to and from the station. There is a standard, Japanese-style shared bath. ⊠ *5410 Karyada, Karuizawa, Kitasaku-gun, Nagano-ken 389-01,* ☎ *0267/46–1333. 10 rooms. Dining room. MC, V.*

Karuizawa to Nagano

The same JR train that brought you from Takasaki climbs steeply from Karuizawa through the mountains to a plateau (*kōgen*) before making a quick descent into Nagano. This is the easiest route to take. An alternative is through the mountains by road, by bus, or car, via ➋ **Kusatsu,** one of Japan's best-known onsen resorts. More than 130 ryokan cluster around the *yuba* (hot-spring field) that supplies the gushing, boiling, sulfur-laden water. **Netsunoyu,** open 7 AM–10 PM, is the main public bath; its water is unbearably hot, even for some Japanese.

The Shiga-Kusatsu-kōgen Highway (a toll road, closed in winter) continues from Kusatsu across the Kusatsu Tōge, climbing at times as high ➌ as 6,550 ft, to Yudanaka, the base from which skiers set out to the **Shiga Kōgen Ski-jō** (Shiga Heights Ski Resort). This is Nagano's largest ski area, with 22 slopes and a combination of 81 lifts, gondolas, and ropeways. Shiga Kōgen was the venue for the XVIII Winter Olympics' alpine skiing and snowboarding giant slalom courses. Some 20 km (12 ➍ mi) northwest of Shiga Highlands is **Yudanaka Onsen,** a resort made famous by photographs of snow-covered Macaque monkeys sitting on rocks in open-air thermal pools to keep warm. A bus runs to Yudanaka from Shiga Kōgen. From town, both the road and train line (the private Nagano Dentetsu Railway) descend for the 30-minute, 24-km (15-mi) run to Nagano.

Lodging

$$ 🏨 **Hotel Shiga Heights.** This large modern structure caters to skiers in the winter and tennis players and hikers in the summer. Its best feature is a thermal bath, which is always a good way to end a day's activities. Rooms are uniform and uninteresting, but efficient. Single rooms are typically small. The bus from Yudanaka Eki takes 20 minutes to get to the hotel. ✉ *Shimo-Takai-gun 381,* ☎ *0269/34–2111,* FAX *0269/34–2827. 142 Western-style rooms, 8 Japanese-style rooms. 2 restaurants, hot springs, 4 tennis courts. AE, MC, V.*

$$ 🏨 **Uotoshi Ryokan.** This small Japanese inn has only eight tatami rooms, which share a delightful *hinoki* (cypress) bathtub filled with hot thermal spring waters to ease your weary muscles. Japanese dinners are a particular delight: a treat of mountain vegetables and fresh seafood from the Nihon-kai. The owners can arrange for you to try Japanese archery (*kyūdō*). The inn is a seven-minute walk from Yudanaka Eki. The owners will also collect you, for a fee, from the JR Nagano Eki. ✉ *2563 Sano, Yama-no-uchi-machi, Shimo-Takai-gun, Nagano-ken 381-04,* ☎ *0269/33–1215,* FAX *0269/33–0074. 8 Japanese-style rooms. Restaurant. AE, V.*

Nagano

⑤ *90 mins by Shinkansen northwest of Tōkyō's Ueno Eki, 40 mins northwest of Karuizawa by JR, 3 hrs northeast of Nagoya by JR Limited Express.*

In 1998 Nagano City (population 300,000) hosted the XVIII Winter Olympics, from February 7 to 22. And the construction and preparations for the event were completed in the nick of time. This included laying tracks for the Shinkansen to run between Nagano and Tōkyō's Ueno Eki, making Nagano as closely connected to the capital as it is to its surrounding mountains. While most of the Olympic ceremonies and stadium events took place in the vicinity of Nagano City, many of the venues for the alpine competitions are as much as 2½ hours' travel out of town.

Nagano City has little to hold your attention beyond its alpine setting and an interesting temple, **Zenkō-ji.** Behind the temple is an amusement park for small kids, and at Mt. Jizuki there is a zoo, but, aside from that, Nagano remains a pilgrims' town and a gateway into the surrounding mountains. However, should you find yourself staying overnight in Nagano, there is an ancient traditional ryokan, Hotel Fujiya (☞ Lodging, *below*), just before the pedestrian avenue to Zenkō-ji. The ryokan's pride is its daimyō suite; for ¥30,000 per person, you can enjoy the suite's several rooms decorated with ancient scrolls and look into a garden that is magnetic in its contrasting complexity and simplicity.

Nagano Prefecture, of which Nagano is the capital, is famous in Japan for its delicious *soba* (buckwheat noodles), which you can see being made in the window at a couple of the restaurants. This sight may be enough to tempt you to fortify yourself before you start up the two flights of steps on your way through the magnificent roofed gate into Zenkō-ji.

★ **Zenkō-ji** draws thousands of pilgrims each year. Founded in the 7th century by Yoshimitsu Honda, the temple is unique to Japan for two reasons: It belongs to no particular Buddhist sect, and it has never closed its doors to women. Its most venerated statue, a bronze dating from 552, is displayed only once every seven years—the next time will be in 1999.

In the courtyard before the Main Hall are six magnificent Buddhas that represent various aspects of life. To the left and right are several small shrines; in the center of the courtyard, pilgrims deposit smoldering sticks of incense into a giant brass burner. The temple has burned to the ground many times; each time it has been resurrected with donations from all over Japan. The most recent version was finished in 1707, and the present Main Hall is the largest thatched-roof building in Japan. The fishnets covering the inside of the roof dissuade pigeons from resting and dropping "good fortune" on the pilgrims' heads or on the scribe who sits on the temple floor writing short inscriptions in the small books that pilgrims carry.

The essential goal of pilgrims is a lock on the wall of a tunnel under the Inner Sanctuary. You'll notice the entrance to the right of the altar. Pilgrims walk through the pitch-dark tunnel to touch the lock, a specific stone in the wall known as the "Key to Paradise," to gain assurance of an easy path to salvation.

You can pick up a free map at the City Tourist Office (☎ 0262/26–5626) inside the new JR eki before hopping on one of the frequent buses that make the 10-minute journey through the center of Nagano to the temple. After getting off at the temple bus stop, walk down the 200-yard pedestrian avenue lined with food and souvenir shops, and smaller temples. ⊙ *Inner Sanctuary daily 5:30 AM–4:30 PM.*

Lodging

$$–$$$$
★
🏨 **Hotel Fujiya.** The antique Fujiya appears the same today as it did 300 years ago. The age-darkened wood and creaking floors are a link to the days when feudal lords stayed here while making pilgrimages to Zenkō-ji. Tatami guest rooms vary from small (¥15,000 per person, including meals) to the royal suite (¥30,000 per person, including meals), which has three rooms with sliding doors onto an old, slightly overgrown garden. The furnishings are priceless antiques and scrolls. The hotel also has a deep, indulgent Japanese bath. Fujiya is not smart or sophisticated but wonderfully old-fashioned. No English is spoken, but the management loves its inn and will respect gai-jin who show their appreciation. ⊠ *Central Ave., Nagano-shi, Nagano-ken 380,* ☎ *0262/32–1241,* FAX *0262/32–1243. 30 rooms. AE.*

$$
🏨 **Nagano Royal Hotel.** Across from the JR Nagano Eki, this new hotel sparkles with crisp efficiency. Enter the marble lobby at street level and take the escalator up to the first-floor reception area and tea lounge. On the 10th floor, the Sky Bar offers seats with a view out to the city below. You'll find a similar view in the Lambert restaurant, which serves French fare. A Japanese restaurant is on the second floor. A coffee table and two easy chairs are squeezed into the compact, neat guest rooms. ⊠ *1-28-3 Minami-Chitose, Nagano-shi, Nagano-ken 380,* ☎ *0262/28–2222,* FAX *0262/28–2244. 114 rooms. 2 restaurants, bar, coffee shop. AE, DC, MC, V.*

Matsumoto

❻ *1 hr by JR Shinonoi Line from Nagano, 2 hrs and 40 mins by JR Chūō Line from Tōkyō Shinjuku Eki, 2¼ hrs by JR Chūō Line from Nagoya.*

On its alpine plateau, Matsumoto is surrounded by the high peaks of the mountain ranges. The town has one of Japan's finest castles, set in spacious grounds planted with cherry trees. You'll also find crafts and *ukiyo-e* (wood-block painting) museums, and outside of town a wasabi farm. If you walk to the castle from the JR eki, you'll pass through the old section of Matsumoto on the way, with its many stone *kura* (warehouses), which are typical of the early Meiji period. They are unusual in their use of irregular stones held in place by mortar.

★ Known as **Karasu-jō** (Crow Castle) for its atypical black protective walls, Matsumoto's castle was built in 1504, during the turbulence of civil wars. The surrounding moats and walls remain, and the imposing five-tier, six-story *donjon* (inner tower) is the oldest surviving keep in Japan. And it is quite simply a handsome castle. While it is an exercise in agility to climb and walk through all six stories, the effort adds to the feeling of what life as a samurai was like during feudal Japan. The views from the sixth story are inspiring, with a broad panorama of the surrounding alpine peaks. Karasu-jō is a very popular attraction; be there when it opens to avoid the overwhelming crowds. You will have to wear the slippers provided while walking through the castle.

In front of Karasu-jō is the **Nihon Minzoku Shiryōkan** (Japan Folklore Museum; ☎ 026/32–2902), whose 70,000 artifacts display the folklore, history, and everyday life of pre-daimyō days and of the Edo period (1603–1868). In January, an ice-sculpture exhibition is held in the park before the museum, about a 20-minute walk to the north and east from the train station (pick up a map from the tiny tourist office on the right-hand side, as you exit, of the JR eki). ⌨ *Castle and museum ¥500.* ◷ *Daily 8:30–4:30; closed Dec. 29–Jan. 3.*

Matsumoto Mingeikan (Folkcraft Museum) displays some 600 local domestic wood, bamboo, and glass utensils. The Mingeikan is across town from the castle, east of the JR eki. To get here, take a taxi or a 15-minute bus ride to the Shimoganai Mingeikan-guchi bus stop. ⌨ *¥300.* ◷ *Tues.– Sun. 9–5; closed Dec. 29–Jan. 3.*

★The **Nihon Ukiyo-e Hakubutsukan** (Japan Ukiyo-e Museum) is dedicated to the lively, colorful, and widely popular *ukiyo-e* wood-block prints of artists from the middle and late Edo period, such as the well-known Hiroshige, Hokusai, and Sharaku. The museum's collection of 100,000 prints, which it rotates monthly, contains some of Japan's finest prints and is the largest of its kind in the world. The **Shiho Butsukan** (Japan Judicature Museum; ☎ 026/47–4515, ¥750), next to the Ukiyo-e Hakubutsukan, is the oldest extant Japanese palatial court building.

These museums are west of the JR eki. Unfortunately, it is too far to walk, and there is no bus, so you must invest in a ¥1,250 taxi ride. You can also take the Kamikochi train on the private Matsumoto Dentetsu Line from Matsumoto Eki four stops to Oniwa Eki, from which it is a 10-minute walk to the museum. *Ukiyo-e Hakubutsukan:* ☎ 026/ 47–4440. ⌨ *¥900.* ◷ *Tues.–Sun. 10–4:30.*

Also outside of Matsumoto, **Hakubutsukan Rokuzan** (art museum) displays the work of Rokuzan Ogiwara, a master sculptor often referred to as the Rodin of the Orient, who died at the age of 32. Aside from the appeal of Rokuzan's works, the gallery is in a beautiful verdant setting against a backdrop of the Northern Alps. The museum is in Hotaka, one stop north of Matsumoto Eki on the JR Oito Line. From Hotaka Eki it is a 10-minute walk. ☎ 026/82–2094. ⌨ *¥500.* ◷ *Apr.–Oct., Tues.–Sun. 9–5; Nov.–Mar., Tues.–Sun. 9–4; closed days following national holidays.*

Near Hotaka, one stop down the Oito Line from Matsumoto, the **Gohoden Wasabi-en** is the largest *wasabi* (Japanese horseradish) farm in the country. To reach it you must rent a bike or take a 40-minute walk along a path from the train station. (The station attendant will give you directions.) Wasabi is cultivated in the clean water beds built in a shallow, curving valley. Surrounded by rows of acacia and poplar trees on the embankments, the fields of fresh, green wasabi leaves bloom with white flowers in late spring. Be sure to try some of the farm's unique foods, which range from wasabi cheese and chocolate to green wasabi ice cream.

Dining and Lodging

$$ ✕ **Kura.** For an informal evening dining on feathery tempura or sushi
★ from the Sea of Japan, Kura is well priced. In an old moated house—the moat smells a bit—in the center of town, husband and wife run the cashier's desk while the two waitresses bring trays of food from the kitchen to a high-ceilinged, tavernlike dining room. There are tables and counter service and *shabu-shabu* if you feel like grilling your food at your table. ⊠ *Ko Kudesai (behind Parco department store),* ☎ *0263/33–6444. Reservations not accepted. No credit cards.*

$ ✕ **Hachimen.** Named after a local resistance hero from the time of the shogunate, this bar is full of youthful spirit. You'll sit on stools at three counter areas, eating, talking, and drinking. Most of the Japanese food is grilled, but noodles and a hotpot are available as well. It is in the central shopping area, down a small alley that has a Mister Donut on the corner. ⊠ *Ise-machi-dōri,* ☎ *0263/35–3832. Reservations not accepted. No credit cards.*

$$$ ▥ **Hotel Buena Vista.** One of Matsumoto's newest and most expensive hotels, the Buena Vista has a large, spartan marble lobby; a coffee lounge; and Chinese, sushi, kaiseki, and teppanyaki restaurants as well as a French restaurant with a sky lounge bar. The rooms are decorated in pastels. Singles snugly fit a small double bed; standard double and twin-bed rooms have enough space for a table and easy chairs. Corner rooms are the choice at ¥20,000. ⊠ *1-2-1 Hon-jō, Matsumoto, Nagano-ken 390,* ☎ *0263/37–0111,* FAX *0263/37–0666. 127 Western-style rooms. 5 restaurants, coffee shop, dance club, parking. AE, DC, MC, V.*

$$–$$$ ▥ **Matsumoto Tōkyū.** The location of this hotel across from the JR eki makes it a good choice as a functional base in Matsumoto. The rooms are not much larger than those of a typical business hotel, so you may want to upgrade yours. But beware—while the small doubles fall in the $$ price range, the deluxe twin-bed rooms with a separate mirror and sink outside the bathroom climb to the $$$ category. There are Japanese and Western restaurants on the premises. ⊠ *1-2-37 Fukashi, Matsumoto, Nagano-ken 390,* ☎ *0263/36–0109,* FAX *0263/36–0883. 99 Western-style rooms. 2 restaurants. AE, V.*

$–$$ ▥ **Hotel New Station.** As at all other business-class hotels, the single rooms here are tiny, but the furniture that can fit into the rooms is worn wood rather than plastic. The hotel offers good value and has at least some character. The smallest singles are ¥5,000; the deluxe twin for ¥12,000 is actually a full-size room. The staff is friendly and cheerful. The location is a minute from the station in the direction of the castle and close to many restaurants, but you should be sure to have one meal in the hotel. In the rock pool just inside the door are *iwana,* a freshwater fish special to the region with a taste akin to that of smoked salmon, which quickly become sashimi or are grilled or boiled in sake. (If this hotel is fully booked, the Mount Hotel is an adequate, slightly more expensive hotel at the back of the JR eki, ☎ *0263/35–6480.)* ⊠ *1-1-11 Chūō, Matsumoto, Nagano-ken 390,* ☎ *0263/35–3850,* FAX *02361/ 83–6301. 103 rooms. Restaurant, conference rooms. AE, V.*

$ ▥ **Enjō Bekkan.** This small, concrete inn is just outside Matsumoto in Utsukushigahara Onsen. The tatami rooms don't have much space after your futon is laid out, but the inn is neat and clean. Some English is spoken. Only half the rooms have a private bath, but no matter—the village is a hot-spring resort, and you can take to the thermal waters 24 hours a day. Utsukushigahara bus terminal is a 20-minute ride from JR Matsumoto Eki. ✉ *110 Utsukushigahara Onsen, Satoyam-abe-ku, Matsumoto, Nagano-ken 390-02,* ☎ *0263/33–7233,* FAX *0263/36–2084. 19 rooms, 11 with bath. Dining room. AE, MC, V.*

En Route   Decisions, decisions: There are a number directions you can choose after Matsumoto. Pop over the hills to Takayama, possibly stopping in Kamikochi on the way. Or if you're keen on getting to Kyōto and the cities of Kansai, exit through the Kiso Valley to Nagoya.

Kiso Valley

★ ❼   *1 hr south of Matsumoto by JR Chūō Line (2 hrs north of Nagoya), then 10 mins by bus to Tsumago.*

The Kiso Valley is halfway between Matsumoto and Nagoya. Called Kisoji by the Japanese, the deep river valley is surrounded by the Central Alps to the east and the Northern Alps to the west. It was through this valley that the old Nakasendo (highway) connected Kyōto and Edo (present-day Tōkyō) between 1603 and 1867. For 250 years, daimyō and their retinue used the highway on their annual trip to Edo to pay their respects to the shogunate. The Kisoji was the most arduous part of their journey. The valley's thick forests and steep slopes required three days to traverse. You can make the same trip now in a few hours.

With the building of the Tōkaidō from Kyōto to Edo along the Pacific coast, and the post-shogunate construction of the Chūō train line from Nagoya to Niigata bypassing the towns on the Nakasendo, the 11 old post villages where travelers had stopped to refresh themselves became deserted backwaters, sometimes referred to as Minami-Kiso (south Kiso). Two of the villages, **Tsumago** and **Magome**, are easy to reach. Both have retained much of their old character. Indeed, more than in most other places in Japan, walking along the main street of Tsumago is like stepping back in time to the shōgun era—except for the unavoidable souvenir shops. If you have time, it's a pleasant three-hour walk along the old post trail between Tsumago and Magome. Be sure to go from Tsumago to Magome, as walking in the other direction is almost completely uphill.

Both towns are served by buses from Nagiso and Nakatsukawa stations, so you can bus to one village and return from the other. There are ryokan and minshuku throughout the valley should you wish to stay overnight, and both Tsumago and Magome have tourist information offices that will help find accommodations and provide free maps.

To go directly to Takayama from Kisoji, take the 50-minute bus ride from Magone to Gero; then transfer to a JR train for the 45-minute run to Takayama. Buses leave three times daily (7:21 AM and 12:05 PM with a change at Sakashita, or a direct bus at 4 PM); the fare is ¥2,300.

Lodging

If you do decide to stay in the area, reserve a room in advance, especially on weekends. The **Magome Tourist Information Office** (☎ 0264/59–2336) and the **Tsumago Tourist Information Office** (☎ 0264/57–3123) can make reservations for you. Telephone between 9 and 5. Magome's office is closed Sunday December–March; Tsumago's office closes January 1–3.

$$ 🏠 **Matsushiro Ryokan.** For surroundings and service that match Tsumago's traditional atmosphere, check in at Matsushiro Ryokan, which has been operating as a guest house for 140 years. Ten large tatami

rooms share a single bath and four old-time pit toilets that are immaculately clean. Dinner is a delicious feast served in your room (¥9,000–¥12,000 per night per person). The Japanese breakfast is also satisfying. No one speaks English here; a Japanese speaker or the tourist office will need to make your reservation. ✉ *Tsumago, Nagiso-machi, Kiso-gun, Nagano-ken 399,* ☎ *0264/57–3022. 10 rooms with shared bath. No credit cards.*

$ 🏠 **Onyado Daikichi.** At this particularly good minshuku (¥6,500 per person), all six tatami rooms face the valley. The traditional wood bath is shared, and the dinners, making good use of the local exotic specialties (horse sashimi, fried grasshoppers, and mountain vegetables), are excellent. With her limited English, lady of the house Nobaka-san makes gai-jin feel very welcome. ✉ *Tsumago, Minami Kiso-machi, Kiso-gun, Nagano-ken 399-54,* ☎ *0264/57–2595,* ☎ *0274/57–2209. 6 rooms with shared bath. No credit cards.*

Getting Around

The central valley town of Nagiso is one hour by JR Chūō Line south of Matsumoto; two hours north of Nagoya. Tsumago is then a 10-minute bus ride (¥240) from JR Nagiso Eki. Buses from JR Nagiso Eki leave every hour. From Tsumago you can take either the footpath to Magome or another bus. A bus travels from Magome to Nakatsugawa, closer to Nagoya on the JR Chūō line.

Kamikochi

❽ *2 hrs west of Matsumoto by train (private Dentetsu Line) and bus, 2 hrs east of Takayama by bus.*

The route from Matsumoto to Takayama—straight over the mountains through Chūbu-Sangaku National Park via Kamikochi—is one of the most scenic routes through the Japan Alps: don't miss it. Even consider spending the night at Kamikochi to enjoy the scenery fully. You will have to make a bus–train connection en route, but it is straightforward and poses no problems—unless you want to take it in winter: snow closes the road November through April.

Just before you reach Kamikochi, the valley opens onto a plain with a backdrop of mountains. **Mt. Oku-Hotaka** is the highest, at 10,466 ft. **Mt. Mae-Hotaka,** 10,138 ft tall, is on the left. To the right is **Mt. Nishi-Hotaka,** 9,544 ft. Through the narrow basin flow the icy waters of the Azusa-gawa, from the small **Taisho-ike** (pond) at the entrance to the basin. You'll find lodges and inns here, and the bus terminal is a few hundred yards beyond.

There are all levels of hiking and climbing trails in and around Kamikochi. One easy three-hour walk follows the river past the rock sculpture of the Reverend Walter Weston, the Briton who was the first to explore and climb these mountains, to Kappa-bashi, a small suspension bridge over crystal-clear Azusa-gawa. Continuing on the south side of the river, the trail cuts through the pasture to rejoin the river at Myoshin-bashi. The small Hotaka Shrine is on the other side at the edge of the pond, Myoshin-ike, where another bridge leads to the trail on the opposite side of the river back to Kappa-bashi.

Lodging

Hotels and ryokan in Kamikochi close mid-November–late April.

$$$–$$$$ 🏠 **Imperial Hotel.** Refurbishment of this 1933 hotel, which resembles
★   an alpine lodge with high ceilings, wood paneling, and verandas, has made it the most desirable place to stay in the Japan Alps between Matsumoto and Takayama—reserve a room well in advance. Open April

through November 4, it is owned by Tōkyō's Imperial Hotel, with many of the staff borrowed from that establishment for the summer to bring service to an international level. You'll see the hotel right near the bus terminal. There are Western and Japanese restaurants on the premises. ✉ *Kamikochi, Azumi-mura, Minami-Azumi-gun, Nagano-ken 390,* ☎ *0263/95–2006 (03-3504-1111 Nov. 4–Mar.); 212/692–9001 in the U.S.; 0171/355–1775 in the U.K.;* 🖷 *0263/95–2412. 75 rooms. 3 restaurants. AE, V.*

$$ 🏯 **Gosenjuku Ryokan.** This standard Japanese inn is reasonably priced and located just beyond the bus terminal en route to Kappa-bashi. ✉ *4468 Kamikochi, Azumi-mura, Minami-Azumi-gun, Nagano-ken 390,* ☎ *0263/95–2131. 31 Japanese-style rooms. AE, V.*

Getting Around

To get to Kamikochi from Matsumoto, first take the Matsumoto Electric Railway from Matsumoto Eki to Shin-Shimashima; this leg, which costs ¥670, takes 30 minutes. (Do not make the mistake of getting off the train at Shimojima, three stops before Shin-Shimashima.) Once off the train, cross the road at Shin-Shimashima Eki for the bus to Naka-no-yu and Kamikochi. The total bus journey takes about 80 minutes, with a fare of ¥2,500. The most scenic part is the 20 minutes from Naka-no-yu to Kamikochi, and you'll quickly understand why the road is closed by winter snows.

From Kamikochi, buses costing ¥1,550 (six a day, only between early May and early November) take 75 minutes to **Hirayu Onsen,** where you must change to another bus (operates all year) for the 70-minute ride to Takayama (¥1,500; total transportation cost from Matsumoto: ¥5,720).

Takayama

2 hrs and 10 mins north of Nagoya by JR Limited Express, 4 hrs from Matsumoto by JR via Nagoya.

Takayama is one of the most attractive towns in the Japan Alps, but gai-jin often leave it out of their Japan itineraries—mistakenly, you might say. In the heart of the Hida Mountains, this tranquil town has held on to its old-fashioned charm, which no doubt is why so many artists have made their homes here. The delight of Takayama is that the entire town is something of a museum piece—it's a perfect place to indulge those fantasies of old Japan that industrial overdevelopment elsewhere in the country doesn't accommodate. There is also a "Folk Village" less than 3 km (2 mi) away. It is a museum, of course, though it's so well done that it looks like a working village you would expect to find in feudal Japan.

Takayama is the site of the hugely popular springtime Sannō Matsuri (April 14–15) and the smaller autumn Yahata Matsuri (October 9–10). Spectators come in the hundreds of thousands from around Japan for the parades of floats at these festivals, nearly overwhelming Takayama's population of 68,000. Hotels are booked solid—if you plan to visit in festival time, make a reservation months in advance.

The city is laid out in a grid pattern. It's compact and easy to explore on foot or by bicycle (there's a rental shop south of the station building; bikes cost ¥300 per hour), or if you feel like using someone else's muscles, on a 15-minute ricksha tour of the old town (¥3,000 for two). You'll find the rickshas based in San-machi-suji. If you just want to pose in one for a photograph, be ready to hand over ¥500.

Make a point of collecting maps and information from the tourist office in front of the JR eki. It's open April–October, daily 8:30–6:30, and November–March, daily 1:30–5. Also, throughout Takayama you can get help at businesses that are designated as Travel Information Desks (look for the "?" sign in the window). In most cases, the person at the cash register in these establishments will speak English or will find someone else who does to assist you.

From the JR eki, walk (or ride) east on Hirokoji-dōri for a few blocks, and you'll come to the old section of town, with its small shops, houses, and tearooms. Before the bridge, which crosses the small Miya-gawa, go right, pass another bridge, and the **Takayama Jinya** will be on your right. Though perhaps not worth the admission charge to enter, this imposing structure was the manor house of the governor, with samurai barracks and a garden behind the house. In front of Takayama Jinya, from 7 AM to noon each morning, the **Jinya-mae Asa-ichi** (morning market) sells vegetables, fruits, and local handcrafts. ☎ 0577/32–1395. ⌨ *Jinya ¥400.* ⏱ *Daily 8:45–4:30.*

🔟 **Shōren-ji.** The Main Hall of this temple was built in 1504 and was moved here in 1961 from its original site in Shirakawa-gō before the area was flooded by the Miboro Dam. Now, in the temple's new position on the hill looking down on Takayama, the sweep of its curved roof, its superb drum tower, and the surrounding gardens give an earthy tranquillity that symbolizes the atmosphere of all of Takayama. Shōren-ji is in Shiroyama Kōen, across the Miya-gawa from Takayama Jinya and the market area, and up the hill. A small street leads into the park. ☎ 0577/ 32–2052. ⌨ *¥200.* ⏱ *Daily 8–4:30 (Shiroyama Kōen is always open).*

⓫ The **Kyōdo Gangukan** (Folk Toy Museum) is filled with more than 2,000 folk toys from all over Japan, some of them more than 300 years old. The museum is at the corner of San-machi-dōri and Ichino-machi-dōri. ☎ 0577/32–1183. ⌨ *¥250.* ⏱ *Tues.–Sun. 8:30–5; closed Dec. 29–31.*

Takayama-shi Kyōdokan (city museum) exhibits various antiques, traditional crafts, and folklore materials of the local Hida people. The museum is opposite ☞ Kyōdo Gangukan at the corner of San-machi-dōri and Ichi-no-machi-dōri. ☎ 0577/32–1205. ⌨ *¥300.* ⏱ *Tues.–Sun. 8:30–5; closed Dec. 29–31.*

⓬ **Tenshō-ji,** which is both a temple and a youth hostel, is a magnificent building, though the rooms are sure to be bitterly cold in the winter.

⓭ The temple is at the east end of San-machi-dōri. The **Hida Minzoku Kōkokan** (archaeology museum) resides in an old house that once belonged to a physician who served the local daimyō. The unique structure of the mansion—with its hanging ceilings, secret windows, and hidden passages—hints of espionage, which was so prevalent in the Edo period. Now the house displays wall hangings, weaving machines, and sundry other items, both archaeological and folkloric, collected from the Hida region. The museum is near the corner of San-no-machi-dori on San-machi-dōri. ☎ 0577/32–1980. ⌨ *¥350.* ⏱ *Mar.– Nov., daily 7–7; Dec.–Feb., daily 8–5.*

⓮ The **San-machi-suji** section includes Ichi-no-machi, Ni-no-machi, and San-no-machi streets, which all parallel Miya-gawa. This was the merchant area in feudal times—merchants were the lowest class then, in part because they handled the money. Most of the old teahouses, inns, dye houses, and sake breweries with latticed windows and doors are preserved in their original state, making San-machi-suji a rare vestige of old Japan before the Meiji Restoration. Down along the river in the San-machi-suji section is the **Miya-gawa Asa-ichi** (morning market), where flowers and vegetables are sold until noon each day. It is gen-

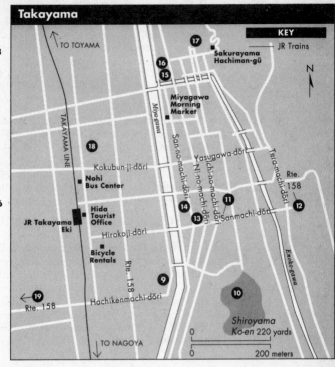

erally speaking less interesting than the asa-ichi in front of **Takayama Jinya.**

★ ⓯ Kusakabe was a wealthy merchant family in the days of Edo. The **Kusakabe Mingeikan** (folk-craft museum) is in the old family house of the 1880s. The interior, with heavy beams of polished wood that emphasize the refined taste of that period, is fascinating, and it acts as an appropriate setting for a display of Hida folk crafts. The Mingeikan is north of a small tributary of the Miya-gawa and on the west side of Ni-no-machi-dōri. ☎ 0577/32–0072. ☞ ¥500. ⊗ Mar.–Nov., daily 9–5; Dec.–Feb., Sat.–Thurs. 9–4:30; closed Dec. 27–Jan. 4.

⓰ The **Yoshijima-ke** is another elegant merchant house. It was rebuilt in 1908, but it retains the distinctive characteristics of the Hida architectural style. Yoshijima-ke is north of the Miya-gawa tributary next to ☞ **Kusakabe Mingeikan** on Ni-no-machi-dōri. ☎ 0577/32–0038. ☞ ¥500. ⊗ Mar.–Nov., daily 9–5; Dec.–Feb., Wed.–Mon. 9–4:30; closed Dec. 28–Jan. 1.

★ ⓱ The **Takayama Yatai Kaikan** displays four of the 11 Takayama *yatai* (festival floats), which are used in Takayama's famous Sanno and Yahata matsuri. These floats have many figurines representing people in the parade, as well as elaborately carved wooden lion heads used for dances in the parade. The hall is in the northeast corner of town, a couple of blocks north of the Enako-gawa. ☎ 0577/32–5100. ☞ ¥800. ⊗ Mar.–Nov., daily 8:30–5; Dec.–Feb., daily 9–4:30.

More than two centuries ago, when the country was ravaged by the plague, building yatai and parading them through the streets was a way of appeasing the gods. Because these actions seemed to work in Takayama, they continued building bigger and more elaborate yatai as preventive medicine. The yatai are gigantic (the cost to build one today would exceed ¥1.5 million ($12,000), and the embellishments of wood-carved panels and tapestries are works of art. Technical wizardry is also involved. Each yatai has puppets, controlled by rods and wires, that perform amazing feats, including gymnastics that you would expect only Olympian athletes to perform. The yatai are taken out both day and night at the spring and autumn festivals. Evening processions find hundreds of lanterns on the floats.

🟤 **Kokubun-ji** is the oldest temple in the city. Founded in 1588, it preserves many objects of art, including the precious sword used by the Heike clan. In the Main Hall (built in 1615) there is a seated figure of Yakushinyorai (Healing Buddha), and before the three-story pagoda is a statue of Kannon. The ginkgo tree standing beside the pagoda is said to be more than 1,200 years old. Kokubun-ji is north of the JR eki off the main modern shopping street, Kokubun-ji-dōri. ☎ *0577/ 32–1395.* ☞ *Main Hall ¥300.* ⊗ *Daily 9–4; closed Dec. 31–Jan. 1.*

🟤 Set against a mountain backdrop, **Hida Minzoku Mura** (Hida Folk Village) is a collection of traditional farmhouses moved to a park from several areas within the Hida region. Because the traditional Hida farmhouse is held together by ropes rather than nails, the dismantling and reassembling of the buildings posed few problems. Many of them have high-pitched thatched roofs, called *gasshō-zukuri* ("hands in prayer"); others are shingle-roofed. Twelve of the buildings are "private houses" that display such folk materials as tableware and spinning and weaving tools. Another five houses are folk-craft workshops, with demonstrations of *ichii ittobori* (wood carving), Hidanuri (Hida lacquering), and other traditional arts of the region.

To get to Hida Minzoku Mura, either walk the 20 minutes or take the bus at platform No. 2 from the bus terminal in a bay on the left side (same side as the tourist information booth) of the JR eki. If you walk, go south from the JR Takayama Eki and take a right over the first bridge onto Route 158. Continue walking straight for 20 minutes to the village. ☎ *0577/33–4714.* ☞ *¥700.* ⊗ *Apr.–Oct., daily 8:30–5; Nov.– Mar., daily 8:30–4:30; closed Dec. 30–Jan. 2.*

Dining and Lodging

The **Hida Tourist Information Office** (☎ 0577/32–5328) in front of the train station can help you find accommodations, both in town and in the surrounding mountains. This is one of the most helpful information offices in Japan.

$$$ ✕ **Suzaki.** This is Takayama's number one restaurant for *kaiseki* cui-
★ sine served traditionally by kimono-clad waitresses. Make a point of trying a meal prepared with wild plants from the Hida mountains and salted river fish. Each dish is exquisitely presented on beautiful ceramic ware. ⊠ *4-14 Shinmei,* ☎ *0577/32–0023. Jacket and tie. AE, V.*

$$–$$$ ✕ **Kakushō.** The most established restaurant for Takayama's well-
★ known *shōjin-ryōri,* a vegetarian meal that consists of various mountain vegetables, Kakushō is on the far side of Miya-gawa from the railway station and near Tenshō-ji. There is no sign outside in English; look for a small building with a courtyard patio diagonally across from a parking lot. Meals here are both nourishing and tasty—often a local bean paste is used in the cooking to add extra flavor. If the freshwater fish *ayu* is on the menu, be sure to try it. Owner Sumitake-san will happily help you with the menu; her English is delightful. ⊠ *2 Baba-chō-dōri,* ☎ *0577/32–0174. Jacket and tie. AE, V.*

$$ ✕ **Susuya.** This delightful, small Japanese restaurant is in a traditional Hida-style house across Kokobunji-dōri from the Sogo Palace hotel (☞

below). Owned by the same family for generations, the intimate, timbered restaurant specializes in *sansai-ryōri*, with mountain plants and freshly caught river fish, such as ayu, grilled with soy sauce. It's superb. ⊠ *24 Hanakawa,* ☎ *0577/32–2484. AE, V.*

$$$$ 🏯 **Ryokan Kinkikan.** This splendid traditional Japanese inn is
★ Takayama's top place to stay. It is also rather small, and reservations are essential. Antique Hida furniture is used throughout. The ryokan is in the center of town, left off Kokobunji-dōri, two blocks from the river. ⊠ *48 Asahi-chō, Takayama, Gifu-ken 506,* ☎ *0577/32–3131,* FAX *0577/31–3130. 9 Japanese-style rooms. AE.*

$$$ 🏯 **Ryokan Hishuya.** For the genuine atmosphere of a Japanese inn, which
★ properly includes kaiseki-style meals and refined furnishings, stay at this ryokan. Quiet and contemplative, it is apart from Takayama, close to Hida Minzoku Mura. ⊠ *2581 Kami-Okamoto-chō, Takayama, Gifu-ken 506,* ☎ *0577/33–4001,* FAX *0577/34–5065. 16 Japanese-style rooms. AE, MC.*

$$–$$$ 🏯 **Hida Plaza Hotel.** This is the best international-style hotel in town.
★ In the older structure, the traditional Hida ambience is present, particularly in the old, exposed beams and wide-plank floors of the Japanese restaurant. Although its newer, modern wing is not exactly attractive, its rooms are larger. In terms of value, all the rooms are a cut above those of most other Japanese hotels. The Hida Plaza is a three-minute walk from the train station and a 10-minute walk from downtown. ⊠ *2-60 Hanaoka-chō, Takayama, Gifu-ken 506,* ☎ *0577/33–4600,* FAX *0577/33–4602. 152 Western-style rooms. 2 restaurants, coffee shop, indoor pool, mineral baths, sauna, health club, dance club, shops. AE, DC, MC, V.*

$$ 🏯 **Honjin Hiranoya.** There are two parts to this hotel, Honkan (old) Hiranoya and Shinkan (new) Hiranoya, in two buildings on the same street, across from one another. Though both have the same name and ownership, they were built three centuries apart. Years ago the old structure was a samurai house; now it is a friendly ryokan with lots of aged charm, though it is short on elegance. Rooms vary from Western-style to tatami-style. The Shinkan Hiranoya has modern tatami rooms and a superb multiperson bath on the seventh floor overlooking the Hida Mountains. Meals are included. ⊠ *1-chōme, Hon-machi, Takayama, Gifu-ken 506,* ☎ *0577/34–1234,* FAX *0577/34–7721. 19 rooms in the old building, 27 rooms in the new. Restaurant. AE, DC, MC, V.*

$$ 🏯 **Sogo Palace.** Conveniently in the center of Takayama, this is a fairly modern Japanese inn. It may not have the charm of the older, traditional inns, but it caters to and understands international travelers' needs. Service is extremely friendly and helpful, which adds to the pleasure of this hotel. ⊠ *54 Suehiro-chō, Takayama, Gifu-ken 506,* ☎ *0577/33–5000. 20 Japanese-style rooms, 7 Western-style rooms. V.*

$–$$ 🏯 **Yamaku.** This inn offers one of the best values in town. Though listed
★ as a minshuku, Yanaku is more like a small, privately run Japanese-style hotel. The building is old, and cozy nooks in the lobby with chairs and coffee tables serve as small lounges. The tatami guest rooms are typically small, but ample closets help add space. Room 33 is the quietest. Japanese-style shared baths are large and are given the kind of social importance found in an onsen—in the men's bath, a water wheel slowly turns to hypnotize you as you soak. Dinner hours are more flexible than those at the typical minshuku: The food is good, though not extraordinary. The inn is on the other side of town from the JR Takayama Eki (a 20-minute walk). ⊠ *58 Tenshoji-machi, Takayama, Gifu-ken 506,* ☎ *0577/32–3756,* FAX *0577/35–2350. 22 rooms. Dining room, shop. No credit cards.*

$ ☷ **Minshuku Sosuke.** Although this concrete building is a private home, it feels more like a boardinghouse for travelers, both Japanese and Western. Mama-san rules with a firm hand and speaks essential English, but don't expect her or her husband to go out of the way to be helpful. Rooms are small, either four tatami or six tatami mats, and have electric (rather than kerosene) heaters. The shared baths and toilets are kept spotless. The food here is average and the beer expensive, but because meals are taken at long tables (tatami seating), you have the opportunity to meet other guests. Although this minshuku is 15 minutes from the town's center, the room rate makes it a good value. To get here, turn right from the JR Takayama Eki, then right at the first bridge, and walk seven minutes. The minshuku is opposite the huge, unsightly Green Hotel. ⊠ *1-64 Okamoto-chō, Takayama, Gifu-ken 506,* ☎ *0577/32–0818,* ℻ *0577/33–5570. 14 rooms. Dining room. No credit cards.*

En Route From Takayama there are frequent trains out of the mountains to Toyama and on to Kanazawa (another absolute must to visit) and the Noto Peninsula, but before heading for the coast consider taking a side trip to Ogi-machi, a traditional town in Shirakawa-gō Valley.

Ogimachi

➁⓪ *2½ hrs northwest of Takayama by bus.*

Surrounded by mountains and dotted with terraced rice fields and gardens, Ogimachi is one of the most beautiful old-style towns in Japan. The majority of the residents in this quiet little village still live in gasshō-zukuri–style farmhouses, many of which serve as minshuku. Locals still cook inside their houses over a central *irori,* an open hearth. You sit around the fire as its smoke rises through the open room to escape out of the thatched roof. Among local specialties are mountain vegetables cooked in dark miso over a small burner. You can make reservations through the Ogimachi tourist office (☎ 0576/96–1751). It's best to ask a Japanese-speaking person to do this for you before you arrive, but do stop at the office in the square at the center of town for a map. Most buildings here look pretty much the same, and none of the minshukus have signs, so get someone to circle the location of your minshuku on your map. Once you've checked in, go out and stroll, and make sure you have a camera. Find your way to the hill that looks out over the town. In the evening, try to locate the local bar, which again looks like all the other structures from the outside; the noise of people partying will give it away.

Opposite Ogimachi, on the banks of the Shō-gawa, is **Shirakawa Gasshō Mura,** a restored village where you can learn how the farmers in this part of Chūbu used to live. The gasshō-zukuri–style houses here were actually transplanted from four villages that fell prey to progress— the building of the Miboro Dam upriver in 1972. There are demonstrations of local crafts making in some of the 25 buildings. ☷ ¥600. ☉ *Apr.–Nov., daily 8:30–5; Dec.–Mar., daily 9–4.*

From Ogimachi and Shirakawa-gō, instead of returning to Takayama you may want to take a bus that leaves Ogimachi for Kanazawa. The trip takes just under three hours (departs Ogimachi 2:40 PM; arrives Kanazawa 5:27 PM). On the way you'll see more of the Hida Mountains than you can from the JR train out of Takayama, which passes through tunnels and narrow valleys.

Getting Around

From Takayama, take the Nohi bus to Makido for 95 minutes (¥2,100), then the JR bus another hour to Ogimachi (¥1,270). There are only six buses per day (four December–March) from Takayama; plan your schedule with the help of the tourist office at the JR Takayama Eki before you leave.

KANAZAWA AND THE NORTH CHŪBU COAST

Culturally rich Kanazawa is one of Japan's most enjoyable cities. North of it, the Note Hantō curls into the sea—its rugged outer coast and quieter inner shore set off a hilly, rural interior patched with rice paddies. Farther up the coast, the industrial capital of the Chūbu region's northernmost prefecture is Niigata. Use the city's ferry terminal to catch a boat for Sado-ga-Shima, the island once used to banish emperors and monks whose ideas threatened the political orders of their times.

Kanazawa

2¼ hrs north of Kyōto (via Maibara) by JR Limited Express trains; 2½ hrs northeast of Takayama by JR Limited Express, changing trains at Toyama; 4 hrs southwest of Niigata by JR Limited Express.

Many sizable Japanese cities have been ravished by the bombs that fell during World War II and the bulldozers of Japan's modernity; Kanazawa is an exception. Quite a few of its old neighborhoods have remained intact for the past two or three centuries. Interestingly enough, despite being on the Nihon-kai coast, separated by mountain ranges from the rest of Japan—this is in fact the reason why—Kanazawans are more cosmopolitan and friendly than Japanese even in Kyōto.

During the Tokugawa period, the fertile Kaga region around Kanazawa was dominated by the Maeda daimyō. Their wealth was tremendous, based on the 1-million-*koku* (the Edo-Period measure of how much rice would feed one person in a year) rice harvests of the region. With this wealth came power and distrust. They distrusted the daimyō in Edo, and the daimyō distrusted them. The manifestation of this distrust was a mighty castle that had not only the protection of high walls and moats but also the intentionally winding, narrow town streets around the castle, which made attacks more difficult. Two other security measures were taken. A Buddhist temple complex was set up on the road to Edo as a delaying tactic—Myōryū-ji, otherwise known as Ninja-dera—which supplied an underground escape route from the castle. Then, at two other approaches to the city, entertainment quarters were established so that invaders might be distracted from fighting by amorous pursuits.

These security measures appear to have been successful. Kanazawa maintained its independence and prospered for three centuries. Moreover, throughout its dynasty, the Maeda clan encouraged education and cultural pursuits. It seems fitting, therefore, that the castle grounds are now the site of Kanazawa University.

Because Kanazawa was a fortress town centered on its castle, the **㉑ Kanazawa-jō** precinct is the best point to start taking in Kanazawa and its past. The castle itself has fallen victim to seven fires in all, and only the **Ishikawa-mon** (gate) remains intact; it was rebuilt in 1788. Note the gate's lead tiles: The daimyō never knew when they might be under siege and require more munitions, which could be made from the tiles. To reach the castle from the train station, take any bus (¥200) from Gate 11 at the bus terminal outside the JR eki.

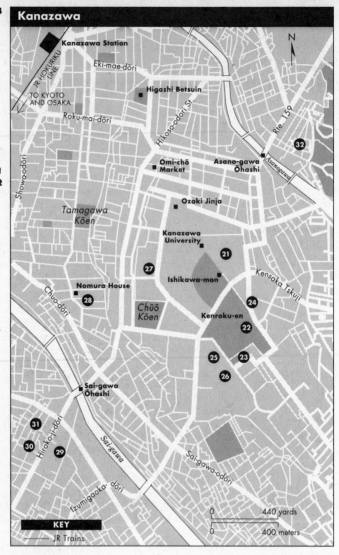

★ **22** The best-known tourist attraction in Kanazawa is **Kenroku-en,** a garden across from Kanazawa-jō's Ishikawa-mon. For many Japanese, Kenroku-en is one of the three finest landscaped gardens in the country. (The other two are Mito's Kairaku-en and Okayama's Koraku-en.) Kenroku-en began as the outer garden of Kanazawa-jō in 1676 under the fifth daimyō. Two hundred years and eight generations of daimyō later, Kenroku-en reached its final form. It received its name—which means Garden of Six Qualities (*roku* meaning six)—because it possessed the six superior qualities required for the perfect garden: extensiveness, factitiousness, antiquity, abundant water, wide prospect, and quiet seclusion. Today, the last quality seems in question. The gardens are near bedlam in Golden Week (beginning April 29), with Japanese tourists being told the names of the trees through their group leader's megaphone. Either arrive at the garden first thing in the morning or risk missing its intended solemnity. ☎ 0762/21–5850. ☜ ¥300. ⏲ *Mar. 16–Oct. 15, daily 6:30–6; Oct. 16–Mar. 15, daily 8–4:30.*

㉓ In the southeast of Kenroku-en is **Seisonkaku,** a two-story villa built in 1863 by one of the Maeda lords for his mother's retirement. Its elegant rooms now house the family heirlooms and a collection of art objects that have been handed down through the generations of the Maeda clan. ☎ *0762/21–0580.* ▨ *¥500.* ◷ *Thurs.–Tues. 8:30–4.*

★ ㉔ A much quieter garden, one generally preferred for tranquillity, is **Gyokusen-en.** Its owner, a wealthy merchant, sought calm and contemplative peace rather than accolades for his green thumb. And its intimacy results from both its smaller number of visitors and the subtle arrangement of moss, maple trees, and small stepping-stones by the pond, which are markedly different from the bold strokes of Kenroku-en. The garden is northeast of Kenroku-en before the **Kanko Bussankan,** a building that demonstrates Yuzen dyeing, pottery, and lacquerware production. ☎ *0762/21–0181.* ▨ *¥500.* ◷ *Mid-Mar.– mid-Dec., daily 9–4.*

㉕ The **Ishikawa Kenritsu Bijutsukan** (Ishikawa Prefectural Art Museum) displays the country's best permanent collection of Kutani porcelain, dyed fabrics, old Japanese paintings, and various other art objects. It is on the northeast side of Kenroku-en. ☎ *0762/31–7180.* ▨ *¥350.* ◷ *Daily 9–5.*

㉖ A narrow path at the back of the **Ishikawa Kenritsu Bijutsukan** leads to the **Hanrō Honda Zōhinkan** (Honda Museum). The Honda family members were the key political advisers to the Maeda daimyō, and the museum contains 700 art objects, armor, and household utensils used by the Hondas during their tenure. Don't miss the uniforms of the family's personal firefighters and the trousseau of the Maeda brides marrying into the Honda family. ☎ *0762/61–0500.* ▨ *¥500.* ◷ *Daily 9–5; closed Thurs. Nov.–Feb. and Dec. 29–Jan. 2.*

㉗ Built in 1599, **Oyama Jinja** is dedicated to Lord Toshiie Maeda, the founder of the Maeda clan. The shrine is noted for its three-story gate, Shim-mon, designed in 1875 with the assistance of two Dutch instructors. At the top of the gate's squared arch is a stained-glass window that originally beamed a light to guide ships in from the Sea of Japan to Kanaiwa port, 6 km (4 mi) to the northwest. If you are coming to the shrine from the JR eki, take Bus 30 or 31 from Gate 8. ▨ *Free.*

㉘ A few blocks southwest of Oyama Jinja is the **Naga-machi Samurai District,** where the Maeda clan's samurai lived. Narrow, crooked streets are lined with tiled-roof earthen walls designed to protect the quarters from curious eyes. One of the houses has been carefully restored and turned into a museum, **Buke Yashiki.** Another old house is now the **Saihitsuan Yuzen Silk Center,** which demonstrates the art of painting intricate designs on Yuzen silk, used for kimonos. ☎ *0762/64–2811.* ▨ *¥500.* ◷ *Fri.–Wed. 9–noon and 1–4:30; closed Dec. 28–Jan. 4.*

NEED A BREAK? While in Naga-machi Samurai District, you can take green tea and *okashi,* Japanese cookies, at **Nikore.** Mrs. Mori and her son converted a samurai house in order to serve tea on a veranda facing a small garden. To find Nikore, walk straight ahead from Saihitsuan Yuzen Silk Center and cross the street. It's on your right, marked by three Japanese *kanji* characters in yellow. ☎ *0762/61–0056.* ◷ *Daily 10–5.*

In the Naga-machi Samurai District, **Nomura House** was rebuilt at the turn of the last century by an industrialist after most of the samurai houses were demolished early in the Meiji Restoration. Nomura furnished it in that period's traditional style. Visit the Jōdan-no-ma drawing room made of cypress, with elaborate designs in rosewood and ebony,

Each of the sliding *shōji* (paper) doors has a great landscape drawn by Sasaki Senkai of the Kano school. A small garden with a winding stream and a bridge made of cherry granite faces the living room. ☎ *0762/21–3553.* ◻ *¥500.* ⊙ *Daily 10–5.*

★ ㉙ On the south side of the Sai-gawa, a five-minute walk after crossing Sai-gawa Ōhashi, **Myōryū-ji** is a temple famous for its complicated structure. Its popular name, **Ninja-dera**—Temple of the Ninja, ninja being those martial artists in black who are expert in the art of concealment—tells all. The innocent-looking temple is a complex of labyrinthine corridors, trapdoors, hidden chambers, secret tunnels, and 29 staircases to 22 of its 23 rooms. This seems to suggest an exaggerated case of paranoia, but it was designed to hold off would-be invaders until the daimyō could make good his escape. In high season, lines form a tour in Japanese. Reservations are essential, though late in the afternoon you might be able to slip in with a small group.

The small housed *jizo* figure—a representation of bodhisattva, an altruist Buddhist deity—in the temple grounds is not on the tour, but he does have a story to tell. His facial features are almost rubbed away. In days before penicillin, syphilitics would rub the little jizo's nose in the hope that their disease would go away. Today Japanese come to scrub him ritually with a nail brush and take photographs of themselves with the little figure. Why the little jizo is here at the temple is a mystery, but its presence may be related to the belief that the daimyō used the secret passages of Ninja-dera as a way of reaching the ☞ **Western Pleasure Quarter** undetected. There's no fee to rub the jizo, although donations are accepted. ☎ *0762/41–0888.* ◻ *¥700.* ⊙ *Mar.–Nov., daily 9–4:30; Dec.–Feb., daily 9–4.*

㉚ At the **Kosen Kutani Kiln,** you can watch the entire process of making local Kutani pottery. It is one street west and one block south of Myōryū-ji. ◻ *Free.* ⊙ *Daily 8:30–noon and 1–5; closed Sun. afternoon.*

㉛ In **Nishi-no-Kuruwa,** the Western Pleasure Quarter, the geishas are no longer walled in, but the checkpoint that kept the ladies from escaping has been preserved. Without question the area lacks the bustle of intrigue that it had 200 years ago. But in the maze of narrow, crooked streets, you might just see a geisha or two. They are said to be younger and more beautiful in this quarter than those in Higashi-no-Kuruwa (Eastern Pleasure Quarter). From the JR station take Bus 30, 31, or 32 from Gate 8.

㉜ **Higashi-no-Kuruwa,** the Eastern Pleasure Quarter, in the northeast part of town over Asano-gawa, Kanazawa's other river, was set aside as a high-class area of entertainment. Now, the pleasures of visiting here are the old buildings with wood-slat facades in the narrow, winding streets. Most of the old geisha houses have been turned into tearooms or minshuku, but occasionally you see a scurrying geisha traveling to her appointment. One elegant former geisha house, **Shimake,** is open to the public: a chance to see the inside, its relaxing garden, and the trappings, at least, of a way of life that gai-jin are rarely privileged actually to experience. ☎ *0762/52–5675.* ◻ *¥200.* ⊙ *Tues.–Sun. 9–5.*

The easiest way to reach the Eastern Pleasure Quarter is to take the JR bus from JR Kanazawa Eki using a JR Pass (¥160 without the pass). The bus stops at Hachira-chō, just before the Asano-gawa Ōhashi. Cross the bridge and walk east and north into the quarter.

OFF THE
BEATEN PATH   **Omi-chō Market** is a tangle of shops that make for an interesting diversion amid the stuff of everyday Japanese life. If you have a JR Pass, take

In case you want to see the world.

At American Express, we're here to make your journey a smooth one. So we have over 1,700 travel service locations in over 120 countries ready to help. What else would you expect from the world's largest travel agency?

do more ®

Travel

In case you want to be welcomed there.

We're here to see that you're always welcomed at establishments everywhere. That's why millions of people carry the American Express® Card – for peace of mind, confidence, and security, around the world or just around the corner.

do more ®

Cards

In case you're running low.

We're here to help with more than 118,000 Express Cash locations around the world. In order to enroll, just call American Express before you start your vacation.

do more

Express Cash

And just in case.

We're here with American Express® Travelers Cheques and Cheques *for Two.*® They're the safest way to carry money on your vacation and the surest way to get a refund, practically anywhere, anytime.
Another way we help you...

do more ®

Travelers Cheques

the JR bus from the station or Hachira-chō at the east end of its route, by Asano Ōhashi.

Kanazawa is a city full of surprises, such as a small temple that does an amazing business reading *sutra* (Buddhist precepts) and dispensing curative herbs. If you plan to stay for more than a day, look for a copy of Ruth Stevens's detailed English-language guide, **Kanazawa,** written with a love for the city. It will lead you to all the discoveries Ms. Stevens has made during her many years of living here. You'll find the book in English-language bookstores in Tōkyō, and sometimes it is available in the lobby bookstand of the Holiday Inn Hotel across from the JR Kanazawa Eki and at the Kanazawa Information Office at the station.

Dining and Lodging

$$$$ ✕ **Goriya.** The specialty here is river fish, including the tiny *gori.* One of Kanazawa's oldest restaurants—more than 200 years old—Goriya is justly famous, with its lovely garden on the banks of the Asano-gawa. The dining areas consist of several small rooms, and the setting is unusual, even if the cooking may not be Kanazawa's finest. Prices at lunch are considerably more modest (around ¥7,000) than at dinner. ✉ *60 Tokiwa-chō,* ☎ *0762/52–5596. Jacket and tie. AE, MC, V.*

$$$$ ✕ **Tsubajin.** One of Kanazawa's best restaurants for Kaga cooking, Tsu-
★ bajin is actually part of a small, traditional, and expensive ryokan. Try the crab, and also the house specialty, a chicken stew called *jibuni.* Be forewarned that dinner for one will exceed ¥20,000. Lunch is less elaborate and less expensive than dinner. ✉ *5-1-8 Tera-machi,* ☎ *0762/ 41–2181. Reservations essential. AE.*

$$$ ✕ **Kincharyō.** This restaurant, associated with the famous Ryokan
★ Kincharyō, is in the Tōkyū Hotel and is now its showpiece. The private dining room's Go-tenyo ceiling is an impressive piece of delicate craftsmanship. Equally compelling is the lacquered, curved countertop of the sushi bar. The main dining room's decor is less noteworthy, but the chef's culinary skill is superb. The menu here features seasonal specialties. In the spring, for example, your seven or eight dishes may include *hotaru-ika* (baby squid that by law may be taken from Toyama Bay only in spring) and *I-doko* (baby octopus) no larger than a thumbnail. ✉ *Kanazawa Tokyu Hotel, 3rd floor, 1-1 Korimbo, 2-chōme,* ☎ *0762/31–2411. Jacket and tie. AE, DC, MC, V.*

$$ ✕ **Miyoshian.** Excellent *bento* (box lunches), at approximately ¥2,000
★ apiece, and fish and vegetable dinners have been served here for about 100 years in the renowned Kenroku-en garden. ✉ *11 Kenroku-chō,* ☎ *0762/21–0127. Jacket and tie at dinner. AE, MC, V. Closed Tues.*

$$ ✕ **Sennin.** For a restaurant near the station, the Sennin is a lively, friendly *izakaya* (tavern) with counter service or tatami-mat seating (you sit on the floor with a well for your feet). It is a more affordable option for getting a taste of Kaga cooking, from succulent sweet shrimp to *kani* (crab) and vegetables served in steaming broth. The restaurant is beyond the right side of the Miyako Hotel in the basement of the Live One building—look for a plaque above the stairs reading "Kirin"— the actual name of the restaurant is written in *kanji.* ✉ *2-13-4 Kata-machi,* ☎ *0762/21–1700. Reservations not accepted. No credit cards.*

$$$$ ⌂ **Ryokan Asadaya.** This small luxury ryokan is designed in a grand
★ style that combines the trappings of modernity with classical simplicity. Antique furnishings and carefully positioned scrolls and paintings establish a pleasing harmony. There is no ferro-concrete or plastic here. Enjoy superb regional cuisine in your room or in the restaurant. ✉ *23 Jukken-machi, Kanazawa, Ishikawa-ken 920,* ☎ *0762/32–2228,* FAX *0762/52–4444. 5 rooms. Restaurant. AE.*

$$$$ 🏯 **Ryokan Kincharyō.** This small, picture-postcard Japanese inn with
★ six small houses on an incline overlooks the Sai-gawa. Prime minis-
ters and princes have slept here, and you will need references in order
to reserve a room. The Kaga-style preparations of regional fresh fish
and vegetables are superb. ✉ 1 Tera-machi, Kanazawa, Ishikawa-ken
920, ☎ 0762/43–2121. AE.

$$$–$$$$ 🏨 **ANA Kanazawa.** This member of the ANA chain has established
itself as the most ostentatious and expensive hotel in the proximity of
JR Kanazawa Eki. The building has a moon-shape tower, an expan-
sive lobby with a waterfall and pond, and more than its share of mar-
ble glitter. Guest rooms are remarkably soothing. Soft beige wallpaper,
fabrics, and furnishings give a restful ambience, and the L-shape plan
is a pleasant change from the usual boxiness of most Japanese hotel
rooms. The staff, most of whom speak English, go out of their way to
help foreign guests. Of the several restaurants, the penthouse Teppan-
yaki offers succulent grills with a panoramic view of the city, while Unkai
serves kaiseki dinners with excellent sashimi and a view of a minia-
ture version of Kanazawa's renowned Kenroku-en. The hotel is within
a block of the JR eki, 10 minutes by taxi from Kanazawa's center. ✉
16-3 Showa-chō, Kanazawa, Ishikawa-ken 920, ☎ 0762/24–6111, 🖷
0762/24–6100. 255 rooms. 5 restaurants, coffee shop, exercise room,
shops, parking. AE, DC, MC, V.

$$$ 🏨 **Holiday Inn Kanazawa.** Standing in the shadow of the ANA hotel
on the other side of the station plaza, this modern redbrick facility lacks
the character of the city, as do most of the other contemporary hotels.
On the other hand, it has a fresh, smart lobby with a bookstand, and
guest rooms have good-size American beds—a rare find, especially in
single rooms. As an added benefit, coffee refills are free in the coffee
lounge, instead of the usual ¥400-plus per cup. Much of the staff
speaks some English. ✉ 1-10 Horikawa-chō, Kanazawa, Ishikawa-ken
920, ☎ 0762/23–1111, 🖷 0762/23–1110. 169 Western-style rooms.
2 restaurants, coffee shop, lounge, shops. AE, DC, MC, V.

$$$ 🏨 **Kanazawa New Grand Hotel.** English is spoken at this large, es-
★ tablished, international hotel in the center of the city. Service is excel-
lent, and its location across from the Oyama Shrine is another plus.
Watching the sunset is especially pleasant from the hotel's sky lounge
or from the adjacent Sky Restaurant Roi, which serves French nou-
velle cuisine, some of the best of its kind in Kanazawa. Guest rooms
are done in soft colors and are reasonably spacious. ✉ 1-50 Takaoka-
machi, Kanazawa, Ishikawa-ken 920, ☎ 0762/33–1311, 🖷 0762/
33–1591. 109 rooms, mostly Western style. 3 restaurants, coffee shop,
lounge, shops. AE, DC, MC, V.

$$$ 🏨 **Kanazawa Tōkyū Hotel.** In the heart of town, this modern hotel has
a spacious lobby on the second floor and a pleasant coffee shop. Guest
rooms are standard and efficient, with pale cream walls. Kincharyō is
a superb Japanese restaurant here; the Schloss Restaurant on the 16th
floor (oddly enough) serves French cuisine and has a skyline view. ✉
1-1 Korimbo 2-chōme, Kanazawa, Ishikawa-ken 920, ☎ 0762/31–2411,
🖷 0762/63–0154. 120 rooms. 3 restaurants, coffee shop, shops, meeting rooms. AE, DC, MC, V.

$$$ 🏯 **Ryokan Miyabo.** Once the teahouse of Kanazawa's first mayor,
this traditional inn is peaceful, authentic, and charming, though it
could use some sprucing up. Guest rooms open onto beautiful gardens,
and some of the cheerful tatami rooms have little sitting areas that also
overlook the gardens. ✉ 3 Shimo-Kakinokibatake, Kanazawa, Ishikawa-
ken 920, ☎ 0762/31–4228, 🖷 0762/32–0608. 39 Japanese-style
rooms. AE, V.

$ 🏨 **Kanazawa Station Hotel.** Rooms here are not as coffin-like as they often are at inexpensive business hotels; hence, we rate it Kanazawa's best in this category. A three-minute walk from the station and across from the Holiday Inn, it is also convenient to the bus stop to downtown. There is a small, comfortable lounge for tea, coffee, and drinks; a Japanese restaurant; and a room for breakfast. ✉ *18-8 Horikawa-chō, Kanazawa, Ishikawa-ken 920,* ☎ *0762/23–2600,* 🗎 *0762/23–2607. 62 rooms. Restaurant, coffee shop. AE, DC, MC, V.*

$ 🏨 **Minshuku Toyo.** This very small, private house is just across the wooden pedestrian bridge, Ume-no-hashi, in the Eastern Pleasure Quarter. Rooms are small, but the price is only ¥3,800 for a single and ¥4,800 for a double, and you are not required to take meals at the inn. There is a common Japanese shared bath. Next door is a small restaurant and an excellent traditional Japanese restaurant, the Seifuso, is across the street, but a kaiseki dinner there will exceed ¥10,000 per person. To get here, take the JR bus from the station to Higashi-hashi (bridge). ✉ *1-18-19, Higashiyama, Kanazawa, Ishikawa-ken 920,* ☎ *0762/52–9020. 5 rooms. No credit cards.*

$ 🏨 **Yogetsu.** This small minshuku is in a 100-year-old geisha house in the Eastern Pleasure Quarter. With aged wood and beams, it's a delightful home. The guest rooms are small, but owner Temeko Ishitata is a welcoming hostess and offers rooms without meals (¥4,500), with breakfast (¥5,000), and with breakfast and dinner (¥6,000). The bath is of the shared Japanese style. ✉ *1-13-22 Higashiyama, Kanazawa, Ishikawa-ken 920,* ☎ *0762/52–0497. 5 rooms. Dining room. No credit cards.*

Getting Around

You might want to purchase, for ¥900, an intracity "Free Pass" from the Hokutetsu Bus Ticket Office, in front of the JR eki. The pass permits unlimited day travel on the city's buses. If you have time to kill at the JR Kanazawa Eki before catching a train, the new station complex has arcades with numerous restaurants and shops.

To go directly downtown from the JR station, or to Oyama Jinja or the New Grand or Tōkyū hotel, take Bus 30, 31, or 32 from Gate 8, or Bus 20, 21, 22, or 41 from Gate 9.

Visitor Information

Adjacent to the JR reserved seat ticketing office is the **Kanazawa Information Office** (☎ 0762/32–6200), whose volunteer staff is extremely helpful and will assist in finding accommodations. It is open daily 9–5.

Fukui

㉝ *1 hr southwest of Kanazawa by JR Limited Express, 2 hrs north of Nagoya by JR Limited Express.*

㉞ Fukui is not especially interesting in itself, but **Eihei-ji,** 19 km (12 mi) southeast of the town, is one of the two main temples of the Soto sect of Zen Buddhism (the other is now in Yokohama). Founded in 1244, the complex of 70 temple buildings sits on a hillside surrounded by trees, some of which are as old as the original structures. The temple is still very active, and there are 200 novitiates in training at any given time. Visitors are welcome, and an English-language pamphlet—once you have had a long-winded introductory lesson to the Soto sect—given at the gate points out the key buildings. Gai-jin are also welcome to stay at the temple; make arrangements by writing in advance. If you decide to spend the night, arrive by 4 PM, prepare to rise at 3 AM, and check out at 8 AM.

The easiest way to get to Eihei-ji from Fukui is by train. If you do not want to return to Fukui and reboard the train for Kyōto and Ōsaka, take a bus to the JR line, then ride up to Ono and two beautiful gorges, Kuzuryu and Managawa. ⌨ ¥300. ☉ *Daily 5–5. Reservations:* ⌨ *Eihei-ji Kokusaibu (International Dept.),* ⌨ *Eiheiji-chō, Yoshida-gun, Fukui 920,* ☎ *0776/63–3102. ¥7,000 per night, including 2 meals.*

There are several hotels in Fukui, but consider spending the night at
35 Awara Onsen, just northwest of Fukui. The area is close to the rocky shore of the Sea of Japan and off the beaten track for foreigners. It is, however, a popular resort for Japanese families. There are attractive and expensive ryokan as well as less-expensive minshuku (one of which is listed below). From Fukui, take a JR local train to Awara Onsen, and then get on a bus from Gate 2 to Awara-chō Onsen; the fare is ¥270.

Lodging

$ ☷ Hotel Akebono Bekkan. This small, two-story wooden building is a simple and convenient Japanese inn if you choose to stay in Fukui. The owners can arrange training sessions in Zen meditation and classes in pottery and papermaking. All of the small tatami rooms share a communal bath. Both Japanese and Western breakfasts are served, but only Japanese food is available at dinner. The inn, a member of the Welcome Inn group, is next to Sakura Bridge, 10 minutes by foot from the JR Fukui Eki. ⌨ *3-9-26 Chūō, Fukui-shi, Fukui-ken 910,* ☎ *0776/22–0506,* ℻ *0776/22–8023. 10 Japanese-style rooms. Restaurant. AE, V.*

$ ☷ Minshuku Kimuraya. This quiet minshuku in the center of the spa town is a welcome alternative to staying in a plain hotel in Fukui. A few words of Japanese help here, but the family that runs the place will do its best to understand your sign language. Rooms are large— 8 or 10 tatami mats—and heated by kerosene stoves. A table with a blanket heater is the sole furnishing. The home-style Japanese fare served for breakfast and dinner is average. Awara-chō Onsen is close to the Nihon-kai coast west of Fukui. From the JR Awara Onsen Eki, take a bus from Gate 2 to the Awarayu-no-machi stop in town. The minshuku is a five-minute walk from the bus stop. ⌨ *Awara-chō Onsen 910-41,* ☎ *0776/77–2229. 10 rooms. No credit cards.*

Noto Hantō (Noto Peninsula)

Wajima, on the north coast of Noto Hantō, is 2¼ hrs northeast of Kanazawa by JR Limited Express.

The Noto Peninsula is rolling countryside with paddies, divided by steep hills, and a coastline that is mild and peaceful. On the eastern, *uchi* (inner) shore, there are plenty of indentations and sea-bathing opportunities, while the western, *soto* (outer) coast is rugged and rock-strewn. It's best to work your way around the peninsula by car or, because it is relatively flat, by bicycle. You can also explore by combining train and bus, and daylong bus tours of the area set out from Kanazawa (☞ Guided Tours, *below*).

Northerly Wajima is the terminal point for train travel on the peninsula. But the line turns inland after Hakui and misses some of the peninsula's best sights. Hence the best plan is to take the 40-minute train
36 ride from Kanazawa as far as **Hakui.** Chiri-hama, a 20-minute walk from the station or a bus ride right out onto the sand, is a good stretch of beach for taking in the summer sun and for swimming. It is one of the noted scenic spots along the Noto coast. The Japanese like this area because they can drive their cars along the sand and bring *bento* picnic lunches.

A few miles north by bus from Hakui (buses leave outside the train station) is the 17th-century **Myōjō-ji,** a five-story pagoda that stands out from the surrounding plain. It was originally built in the 13th century, though the present structure dates from the 1600s.

Instead of following the inland bus route north from Hakui to Monzen, take the longer (70-min) bus ride that runs to Monzen along the coast. This way you'll take in the 13-km (8-mi) stretch known as Noto-Kongo, noted for fantastic formations of eroded rock. **Monzen** is where the Zen temple Sōji-ji stands. Sōji-ji was once the headquarters of the Soto sect, but a fire destroyed most of the buildings in 1818 and the sect moved its headquarters to Yokohama.

The next stop on the bus, only 16 km (10 mi) up the road from Monzen, is **Wajima,** a fishing town that is known not for its fish but for its lacquerware. Every shop in town seems to sell this craft, but before you buy, visit the **Wajima Shikki Kaikan** (Lacquerware Hall). It's easy to find; ask the ticket-booth conductor at the bus station for directions. Here the painstaking process of lacquerware production is shown: It involves about 18 different steps, from wood preparation to the application of numerous layers of lacquer, with careful polishing in between each coat. 🎫 *¥300.* 🕒 *Daily 8:30–5:30.*

Once you are familiar with the lacquerware phenomenon, walk to the *asa-ichi* (morning market), held every day between 8 and 11:30 except the 10th and 25th of each month. Here, among the fruit, vegetables, and seafood, local crafts and lacquerware are sold to tourists. There is also a *yū-ichi* (evening market), a smaller version of the asa-ichi, which starts around 3:30 PM. Stop in at Wajima's tourist office at the station for maps of the area (☎ 0768/22–1503); it is open daily 10–6.

From Wajima, a bus travels 20 minutes northeast to **Sosogi,** a small village, passing terraced rice fields that descend from the hills to the edge of the sea. At Sosogi the road forks inland. Soon after the fork (five minutes) are two traditional farm manor houses. The **Shimo-Tokikuni House** is more than 300 years old and is furnished with antiques. Rent a tape recorder at the entrance for an English explanation of each room. Close by is **Kami-Tokikuni House,** which took 28 years to rebuild in the last century and remains in near-perfect condition. Each room has a special purpose, and by following the English leaflet, you'll get a short course on the strictness of the social hierarchy of medieval Japan. Both houses charge a small admission fee. 🕒 *Daily 9–4:30.*

The same hourly bus service that runs between Wajima and Sosogi goes on to **Suzu** on the *uchi* coast. And you can continue around the northern tip of the Noto Peninsula by bus—from Sosogi to **Cape Rokkō** and down to the northern terminus of the Noto Railway Line at Takojima. But because the views and scenery don't quite justify the infrequency of the service on this leg of the peninsula, it is better to take the inland route from Sosogi to Suzu.

From Suzu, take the train line south to Tsukumowan Ogi Eki. **Tsuku-mowan** means "a bay with 99 indentations." To appreciate this part of the rocky coastline, take a ride on one of the glass-bottom boats that circle the bay. Farther south of Tsukumowan (60 min by train from Suzu), **Wakura Onsen** is a smart resort town with many hotels and ryokan. Emperor Hirohito came here in 1983, and his trip gave the spa prestige throughout Japan. But even in the Tokugawa period, the waters of Wakura were in demand. Large casks of thermal water were sent to Edo and other major cities because of the water's supposed curative powers. Many of the ryokan here are along the beach, so while taking the waters, you get the pleasure of marvelous views of the island's crowded bay. Wakura Onsen is especially popular among Japanese families, who take their children across the bridge to Noto-jima (Noto Island), where there is an elaborate marine park. Wakura Onsen is a direct one-hour train ride from Kanazawa, but there is good scenery on the bus ride south and east along the coastal road (Route 160) to the city of Takaoka.

42 **Takaoka,** the southern gateway to the Noto Peninsula, is not worth lingering in, though it does claim to have Japan's third largest **Daibutsu** (Great Buddha), after those at Kamakura and Nara (☞ Chapters 4 and 8). It is made of bronze and stands 53 ft high. Also in Takaoka, a 10-minute walk from the station, is **Zuiryu-ji,** a delightful Zen temple of the Soto sect that doubles as the local youth hostel. However, the city is mostly known for its crafts traditions of copper, lacquerware, and ironware, especially its cast-iron bells.

Lodging

There are accommodations along the Sosogi coast. Wakura Onsen is the most popular base from which the Japanese explore the Noto Peninsula.

$$ 🏨 **Wakura Park Hotel.** Facing the bay, this small hotel has an extremely hospitable owner who speaks English well and is enthusiastic about hosting gai-jin. Good Japanese meals are served in the dining room, and there is a small bar–coffee shop for refreshments. While every room, in both Western and Japanese styles, has a private bathroom, a public bath is the place to relax after a day's exploring. ✉ *6-6-5 Wakura-machi, Nanao-shi, Ishikawa-ken 926. 36 Western-style rooms, 15 Japanese-style. Bar, dining room. MC, DC.*

Toyama

43 *30 mins southeast of Takaoka by JR local; 1 hr east of Kanazawa by JR Limited Express; 3 and 4 hrs north of Kyōto and Nagoya, respectively, by JR.*

Busy, industrial Toyama has as its redeeming virtue the Toyama-jōshi (castle park), a spread of greenery with a reconstructed version of the original (1532) castle. Forty minutes northeast of Toyama, one stop **44** after Kurobe on the Toyama Chiho Tetsudō Line, **Unazuki Onsen** sits at the mouth of a mountain valley. A tram-like train—the Kurobe Kyōkoku Railway, which operates May through mid-November—runs through this picturesque valley past gushing springs and plunging waterfalls and through the Kurobe Gorge to Keyakidaira 19 km (12 mi) up the line; the fare is ¥1,350.

Niigata

45 *2 hrs northwest of Tōkyō's Ueno Eki by Jōetsu Shinkansen.*

The coast between Kurobe and Niigata is flat and not so interesting. Two towns along the way, Jōetsu and Teradomari, are useful as ferry ports for Ogi and Akadomari, respectively, on Sado-ga-Shima. Niigata is likewise most useful as the major port from which to board the ferry to Sado. As Japan's major port and industrial city on the Nihon-kai coast, it is a good place for replenishing supplies and changing money— the city otherwise has limited appeal. The tourist information office (☎ 025/241–7914) to the left of the station can help you find a hotel and supply city maps and ferry schedules for Sado-ga-Shima.

Dining and Lodging

$–$$ ✕ **Ishihawa.** Two blocks from the JR eki (on the left just before the second traffic light as you head downtown), Ishihawa is run by a charming woman, who will guide you through the menu in her best English. You can settle for tempura or try the more interesting local dishes, such as *wappaneshi* (steamed rice with fish and vegetables), or fresh fish caught in the Nihon-kai. Seating is either at the counter or in a raised alcove on tatami matting. Ishihawa is one flight down from the street—look for the signs for a barber shop, which is also in the building's basement. ⊠ *4-19 Kawabata-chō, basement,* ☎ *0252/45–2602. Reservations not accepted. DC, V.*

$$$$ 🏠 **Onaya Ryokan.** This is a classic ryokan—the most fashionable in
★ the city. It is a joy to stay in, with excellent food and service. Rooms look over a tranquil Japanese garden. All have private toilets, but the Japanese bath is separate and prepared for guests individually. No English is spoken, and you should know at least a few words of Japanese. ⊠ *981 Fura-machi-dōri, Niigata City, Niigata-ken 951,* ☎ *0252/29–2951,* ℻ *025/229–3199. 24 Japanese-style rooms. AE.*

$$–$$$ 🏠 **Okura Hotel Niigata.** A modern, sparkling hotel on the Shinano-gawa, across the bridge from the station, the Okura is one of Niigata's international hotels. Service is first-class, and rooms are tastefully decorated, with rich-colored bedspreads contrasting with the pastel walls. If you plan to read or work at the hotel, the Okura is one of few places that have ample lighting in their rooms. Rooms overlooking Shinano-gawa have the best views. The formal French restaurant in the penthouse looks down on the city lights and over the Nihon-kai to Sado-ga-Shima. The Japanese restaurant has superb kaiseki dinners; the Chinese restaurant is nothing special. Breakfast and lighter meals are served in the Grill Room. (If you cannot get reservations here, the next choice is the Hotel Niigata, ☎ 0252/45–3331, a 15-minute walk from the station.) ⊠ *6-53 Kawabata-chō, Niigata City, Niigata-ken 951,* ☎ *0252/24–6111,* ℻ *025/225–7060. 300 rooms, mostly Western style. 3 restaurants, shops, business services. AE, DC, MC, V.*

$$ 🏠 **Niigata Toei Hotel.** For an inexpensive business hotel conveniently located a block and a half from the station, this ranks the best. The ninth floor has two restaurants and a bar for evening entertainment. ⊠ *1-6, 2 Benten, Niigata 950,* ☎ *025/244–7101,* ℻ *025/241–8485. 90 rooms. 2 restaurants, bar, conference rooms. AE, D, MC, V.*

Sado-ga-Shima (Sado Island)

2 hrs by hydrofoil from Niigata or Jōetsu.

Sado has always been a melancholy island. Its role in history has been as a place where antigovernment intellectuals, such as the Buddhist monk Nichiren, were banished to endure the harshest exile. Then, when gold was discovered during the Edo period (1603–1868), the homeless, especially those from Edo, were sent to Sado to work as forced laborers in the mines. This heritage of hardship has left behind a tradition of soulful ballads and folk dances. Even the bamboo grown on the island is said to be the best for making *takohachi,* the plaintive flutes that accompany the ballads.

May through September is the best time to visit Sado. At other times weather can prevent sea and air crossings, and in January and February Sado is bitterly cold. Though the island is Japan's fifth largest, it is comparatively small (331 square mi). Two parallel mountain chains, running along the north and south coasts, are split by an extensive plain containing small rice farms and the island's principal cities. Despite the fact that more than a million tourists visit the island each year (more than 10 times the number of island inhabitants), the pace of life is slow, even preindustrial. That is Sado's appeal.

46 Sado's usual port of entry is **Ryōtsu,** the island's largest township. The center of town is the strip of land that runs between Lake Kamo and the Nihon-kai, with most of the hotels and ryokan on the shore of the lake. Lake Kamo is actually connected to the sea by a small inlet running through the middle of town. Ryōtsu's Ebisu quarter has the island's concentration of restaurants and bars. Every evening (8:30–9:30) from April to early November, the Ryōtsu Kaikan here stages a performance of *Okesa*, melancholic folk dances and songs performed by women, and the *Ondeko*, a lion dance to drum beats. Tickets cost ¥600, with a ¥100 discount if you buy a ticket at any ryokan in town. Similar performances during the summer season are given elsewhere on Sado: the Sado Kaikan in Aikawa; the Niigata Kotsu, second floor, in Ogi; and the Sado Chūō Kaikan in Sawata.

The simplest way to begin exploring Sado is to take the bus from Ryōtsu **47** west to **Aikawa.** This was once a small town of 10,000 people. When, in 1601, gold was discovered, the rush was on. The population swelled to 100,000 until the ore was exhausted. Now it is back to 10,000 inhabitants, and tourists coming to see the old gold mine are a major source of the town's income.

Though some 10,000 tons of silver and gold ore are still mined annually, Aikawa's **Sodayu-ku** (mine) is more of a tourist attraction than anything else. There are about 250 mi of underground tunnels, some running as deep as 1,969 ft beneath sea level; some of this extensive digging is open to the public. Instead of the slave labor that was used throughout the Edo period, there are now robots serving the mine. These robots are, in fact, quite lifelike, and they demonstrate the appalling conditions that were endured by the miners. Sound effects of shovels and pick axes add to the sobering reality. The mine is a tough 40-minute uphill walk or a five-minute taxi ride (about ¥900) from the bus terminal. The walk back from Sado Kinzan is easier. The mine (¥700) is open daily 8–5:30 (until sunset in autumn and winter).

★ The North of Aikawa is **Senkaku-wan** (Senkaku Bay), the most dramatic stretch of coastline and a must-see on Sado-ga-Shima. From a boat you can look back at the fantastic, sea-eroded rock formations and cliffs that rise 60 ft out of the water. You will get off the boat at Senkaku-wan Yu-en, a park where you can picnic, stroll, and gaze upon the varied rock formations offshore. From the park, you can return by bus to Aikawa. To reach the bay, take a 15-minute bus from Aikawa to Tassha for the 40-minute sightseeing cruise. *One-way cruise-boat runs Apr.–Oct.* ✆ *¥750, including the park.*

The most scenic drive on Sado is the **Osado Skyline.** No public buses follow this route. You must take either a tour bus from Ryōtsu or a taxi from Aikawa across the skyline drive to Chikuse (¥3,950), where you connect with a public bus either to Ryōtsu or back to Aikawa.

To reach the southwestern tip of Sado, first make your way on a bus to Sawata from Aikawa or Ryōtsu, and then transfer to the bus for Ogi. En route you may want to stop at the town of **Mano,** where the emperor Juntoku (1197–1242) is buried. The mausoleum (Mano Goryō) and the museum that exhibits some of the emperor's personal effects are in **Toki-no-Sato** (park), a half-hour walk from the center of town. There is a sadness to this mausoleum built for a man who at 24 was exiled on Sado for life by the Kamakura shogunate for his unsuccessful attempt to regain power. Admission to the mausoleum and museum is ¥500; it is open daily Apr.–mid-Nov.

At Mano, incidentally, the *tsuburo-sashi* dance is given nightly at the Sado New Hotel. The unique dance is performed by a man holding a *tsuburo* (phallic symbol) with the goddesses Shagri and Zeni Daiko.

48 The trip from Sawata to **Ogi** takes 50 minutes, the highlight of it being the beautiful *Benten-iwa* (rock formations), just past Tazawaki. Be sure to take a window seat on the right-hand side of the bus. You can use Ogi as a port for returning to Honshū by the ferry (2½ hrs to Jōetsu) or on the jetfoil (1 hr). Other than that, Ogi's chief attraction is the *taraibune,* round, tublike boats used in the past for fishing. You can rent them now (¥450 for a 30-minute paddle) and with a single oar wend your way around the harbor. You'll also find them at Shukunegi, a more attractive town on the Sawasaki coast, where the water is dotted with rocky islets and the shore is covered with rock lilies in summer. Shukunegi has become a sleepy backwater since it stopped building small wood ships to ply the waters between Sado and Honshū, and it has retained its traditional atmosphere and buildings. You can reach Shukunegi from Ogi by a sightseeing boat or by bus. Both take about 20 minutes, so consider using the boat at least one way for the view of the cliffs that were created by an earthquake 250 years ago.

If you prefer to return to Honshū at Niigata rather than Jōetsu and don't feel like going back to Ryōtsu, take the bus along the coast from Ogi to Akadomari and catch the ferry for Niigata from there.

Lodging
You can make hotel reservations at the information counters of Sado Kisen ship company at Niigata Port or Ryōtsu Port.

$$$ ▦ **Sado Royal Hotel Mancho.** This is the best hotel on Sado's west coast. It caters mostly to Japanese tourists, but the staff makes the few Westerners who come by feel welcome, even if they don't speak English. There is a Japanese restaurant at which a few Western dishes are offered. ⊠ *58 Shimoto, Aikawa, Sado-ga-shima, Niigata-ken 952,* ☏ *0259/74–3221.* FAX *0259/74–3222. 87 rooms. Restaurant. DC, V.*

$ ▦ **Sado Seaside Hotel.** Twenty minutes by foot from Ryōtsu Port, this
★ is more a friendly inn than a hotel. If you telephone before you catch the ferry from Niigata, the owner will meet you at the dock. He'll be carrying a green Seaside Hotel flag. ⊠ *80 Sumiyoshi, Ryōtsu City, Sado-ga-shima, Niigata-ken 952,* ☏ *0259/27–7211. 7 Japanese-style rooms with shared Japanese-style bath, 5 with private bath. Dining room, laundry service. AE, V.*

Getting Around
BY BUS
Frequent bus service is available between major towns, making travel around-island simple. For example, buses leave Ryōtsu every 30 minutes for Aikawa. The trip takes about 90 minutes and costs ¥630.

May through November, there are also four- and eight-hour tours of the island that depart from both Ryōtsu and Ogi. However, these buses seem to have a magnetic attraction to souvenir shops. The best combination is to use the tour bus for the mountain skyline drive (¥3,720) or the two-day Skyline and Historic Site combined tour (¥5,210), then rent a bike to explore on your own. You can make reservations directly with the Niigata Kōtsū Regular Sightseeing Bus Center (☏ 0259/52–3200).

BY FERRY

There are two main ferry routes, each with both a regular ferry and a hydrofoil service. The bus from bay No. 6 at the terminal in front of the JR Niigata Eki takes 15 minutes (¥160) to reach the dock for the Sado Kisen ferries (☎ 025/245–1234) sailing to Ryōtsu on Sado. The same company has ferries going to Ogi, leaving from Jōetsu (☎ 0225/43–3791), south of Niigata.

From Niigata to Ryōtsu the ferry crossing takes 2½ hours, with six or seven crossings a day; the fare is ¥1,780 for ordinary second class, ¥2,600 for a seat reservation, ¥3,560 for first class, and ¥5,340 for special class. The hydrofoil takes one hour, with 7 to 10 crossings in the summer, two in the winter, and anywhere between three and eight at other seasons depending on the weather. In February, the hydrofoil service is down to one crossing per day, for ¥5,460 one-way, ¥10,590 round-trip. Between Ogi and Jōetsu the hydrofoil cost is the same as the Niigata–Ryōtsu crossing, while the regular ferry is ¥1,960 for ordinary second class, ¥2,780 for a seat reservation, ¥3,930 for first class, and ¥5,890 for special class. The ferry terminal is a ¥150 bus ride or ¥900 taxi ride from the JR Jōetsu Eki.

There are also three ferries a day from Niigata to Akadomari in summer, one in winter. The route takes two hours and costs ¥1,550. Depending on the season, one to three ferries sail between Teradomari (between Niigata and Jōetsu) and Akadomari, taking two hours. The fare is ¥1,220 for second class and ¥2,450 for first class.

JAPAN ALPS A TO Z

Arriving and Departing

By Plane

Kanazawa. The flight from Tōkyō's Haneda Kūkō to Komatsu Kūkō takes 1 hour on Japan Airlines (JAL) or All Nippon Airlines (ANA); allow 55 minutes for the bus transfer to downtown Kanazawa.

Matsumoto. Japan Air System (JAS) offers daily flights to and from Fukuoka, Ōsaka, and Sapporo.

Sado-ga-Shima. Small planes take 25 minutes from Niigata; there are six flights a day in summer and three in winter (☎ 025/275–4352); the fare is ¥7,360.

Toyama. ANA has five flights daily between Tōkyō and Toyama.

By Train

Tōkyō–Nagano Shinkansen service has effectively shortened the distance to the Alps from the east. From Kyōto and Nagoya to the south, the Alps are still three and more hours distant. Unless you are coming from Niigata, you will need to approach Takayoma and Kanazawa from the south (connections through Maibara are the speediest).

Getting Around

Roads and railways through the Japan Alps follow the valleys. This greatly lengthens trips *around* mountains—as in the four-hour Matsumoto–Takayama ride via Nagoya. All major stations have someone who speaks sufficient English to plan your schedule. Each major town described in the following excursion section has a tourist office at the railway station that will supply free maps and, if necessary, find you accommodations. Remember that the last train or bus in the evening can be quite early.

Rental cars are available at the major stations, but it is best to reserve the car before you leave Tōkyō, Nagoya, or Kyōto. The Nippon-Hertz company has the greatest number of locations in this region.

In winter certain roads through the central Japan Alps are closed. In particular, the direct route between Matsumoto and Takayama via Kamikochi is closed between November and April.

Contacts and Resources

Emergencies
Police, ☎ 110. **Ambulance,** ☎ 119.

Guided Tours
The **Japan Travel Bureau** has offices at every JR eki in each major city and town and can assist in local tours, hotel reservations, and travel ticketing. Though you should not assume that any English will be spoken, you can usually find someone whose knowledge is sufficient for your basic needs. Most of the travel through this region is very straightforward, using public transport. In the two places where public transportation is infrequent—the Noto Peninsula and Sado-ga-Shima—local tours are available, and the guides speak only Japanese.

NOTO PENINSULA
The **Hokuriku-Tetsudō Co.** (☎ 0762/37–8111) has a 6½-hour tour that covers much of the peninsula for ¥6,200, with a Japanese-speaking guide. It operates year-round and departs from Kanazawa Eki.

SADO-GA-SHIMA (SADO ISLAND)
A tour of Sado-ga-Shima is useful only because it covers Skyline Drive, which public buses do not travel. The price for this tour, which departs from Ryōtsu, May–November, is ¥3,750. Contact the **Niigata Kotsu Information Center** at the Ryōtsu Bus Terminal (☎ 0259/27–3141).

REGIONAL TOUR
The **Japan Travel Bureau** operates a five-day tour from Tōkyō that departs every Tuesday, April 1–October 26. The tour goes via Lake Shirakaba to Matsumoto (overnight), to Tsumago and Takayama (overnight), to Kanazawa (overnight), to Awara Onsen (overnight), and ends in Kyōto; The fare is ¥150,000, including four breakfasts and two dinners.

Visitor Information
JR Travel Information Centers and **Japan Travel Bureaus** have offices at all the train stations at the major cities and towns.

JAPAN TRAVEL-PHONE
The nationwide service for English-language assistance or travel information is available 9–5 daily. Dial toll-free 0120/444–800 for information on western Japan. When using a yellow, blue, or green public phone (do not use the red phones), insert a ¥10 coin, which will be returned.

KANAZAWA
The **Kanazawa Tourist Information Service** is inside the JR eki (☎ 0762/31–6311).

KARUIZAWA
The **Karuizawa Eki Tourist Office** is at the JR eki (☎ 0267/42–2491).

KISO VALLEY
The **Magome Tourist Information Office** (☎ 0264/59–2336) is open daily 8:30–5, closed Sunday December–March. The **Tsumago Tourist**

Information Office (☎ 0264/57–3123) is open daily 9–5, closed January 1–3. Both offices will make reservations at local inns for you.

MATSUMOTO

The **Matsumoto City Tourist Information Office** is on the street level to the right as you exit the JR eki (☎ 0263/32–2814).

NIIGATA

The **Niigata City Tourist Information Center** is in front of the JR eki (☎ 0252/41–7914).

TAKAYAMA

The **Hida Tourist Information Office,** in front of the JR eki (☎ 0577/32–5328), is open daily April–October 8:30–6:30, November–March 8:30–5.

7 Kyōto

Kyōto is a cross-section of 11 centuries of Japan's history—including the present. Its hundreds of temples and shrines and its gardens have tremendous allure, for gai-jin and for Japanese. Add to that traditional shopping districts and intriguing local foods and you come up with some of the best reasons to travel to Japan.

KYŌTO'S HISTORY is full of contradictions: famine and prosperity, war and peace, calamity and tranquillity. Although the city was Japan's capital for more than 10 centuries, the real center of political power was often elsewhere, be it Kamakura (1192–1333) or Edo (1603–1868). Such was Kyōto's decline in the 17th and 18th centuries that, when the power of the government was returned from the shōguns to the emperor, he moved his capital and imperial court to Edo, renaming it Tōkyō. Though that move may have pained Kyōto residents, it actually saved the city from destruction. While most major cities in Japan were bombed flat in World War II, Kyōto survived. And where old quarters of Tōkyō have been replaced with characterless modern buildings—a fate that Kyōto has shared in part—much of the city's wooden architecture of the past still stands.

By Nigel Fisher

Until 710, Japan's capital was moved to a new location with the succession of each new emperor. When it was decided that the expense of this continuous movement had become overly bloated with the size of the court and the number of administrators, Nara was chosen as the permanent capital. But its life as the capital lasted 74 years. During that time, Buddhists rallied for, and achieved, tremendous political power. In an effort to thwart them, Emperor Kammu moved the capital in 784 to Nagaoka, leaving the Buddhists behind in their elaborate temples. Within 10 years, Kammu decided that Kyōto (then called Uda) was better suited for his capital. Poets were asked to compose verse about Uda, and invariably they included the phrase Heian-kyō, meaning "Capital of Peace," which no doubt reflected the hope and desire of the time.

For 1,074 years, Kyōto remained the capital, though at times only in name. From 794 to the end of the 12th century, the city flourished under imperial rule. It might be said that this was the time when Japan's culture started to become independent of Chinese influences and began to develop its unique characteristics. Unfortunately, the use of wood for construction, coupled with Japan's two primordial enemies, fire and earthquakes, has destroyed all the buildings from this era, except Byōdō-in in Uji. The short life span of a building in the 11th century is exemplified by the Imperial Palace, which burned down 14 times in a 122-year period. As if natural disasters were not enough, imperial power waned in the 12th century. There followed a period of shogunal rule, but each shōgun's reign was tenuous. By the 15th century, civil wars tore the country apart. Many of Kyōto's buildings were destroyed or looted.

The Ōnin Civil War (1467–77) was a particularly devastating period for Kyōto. Two feudal lords, Yamana and Hosokawa, disputed who should succeed the reigning shōgun. Yamana camped in the western part of the city with 90,000 troops, and Hosokawa settled in the eastern part with 100,000 troops. Central Kyōto was the battlefield.

Not until the end of the 16th century, when Japan was brought together by the might of Nobunaga Oda and Hideyoshi Toyotomi, did Japan settle down. This period was soon followed by the usurpation of power by Ieyasu Tokugawa, founder of the Tokugawa shogunate, which lasted for the next 264 years. Tokugawa moved the political center of the country to Edo, current-day Tōkyō. Kyōto did remain the imperial capital—the emperor being little more than a figurehead—and the first three Tokugawa shōguns paid homage to it by restoring old temples and building new villas. In the first half of the 17th century, this was yet another show of Tokugawa power. Much of what you see in Kyōto dates from this period.

Steeped in history and tradition, Kyōto has in many ways been the cradle of Japanese culture, especially with its courtly aesthetic pastimes, such as moon-viewing parties, and tea ceremonies. A stroll through Kyōto today is a walk through 11 centuries of Japanese history. The city has been swept into the modern industrialized world with the rest of Japan—plate-glass windows, held in place by girders and ferroconcrete, dominate central Kyōto. Elderly women, however, continue to wear kimono as they make their way slowly along the canal walkways. Geisha still entertain, albeit at prices out of reach for most of us. Sixteen hundred temples and several hundred shrines surround central Kyōto. There's rather a lot to see, to say the least. With this in mind, don't run yourself ragged. Balance a morning at temples and museums with an afternoon in traditional shops, and a morning at the market with the rest of the day in Arishiyama or at one of the imperial villas.

Kyōto Glossary

Key Japanese words and suffixes for this chapter include *bijutsukan* (art museum), *-chō* (street or block), *-chōme* (street), *chūō* (central, as in Central Street), *daimyō* (feudal lord), *-den* (hall), *-dō* (temple or shrine), *dōri* (avenue), *eki* (train station), *gai-jin* (foreigner), *-gawa* or *kawa* (river), *-gū* (Shintō shrine), *higashi* (east), *ike* (ee-keh, pond), *-in* (Buddhist temple), *izakaya* (tavern), *-ji* (temple), *jinja* (Shintō shrine), *jingū* (Shintō shrine), *-jō* (castle), *kado* (street corner), *kita* (north), *kōen* (park), *-ku* (section or ward), *kūkō* (airport), *machi* (town), *matsuri* (festival), *michi* (street), *minami* (south), *-mon* (gate), *sakura* (cherry blossoms), *-shi* (city or municipality), *Shinkansen* (bullet train, literally "new trunk line"), *taisha* (Shintō shrine), *torii* ("*to*-ree-ee," gate), *yama* (mountain), and *-zan* (mountain, as in Hiei-zan, Mt. Hiei).

Pleasures and Pastimes

Although Tōkyō has been the imperial capital since 1868, Kyōto—which wore the crown for the 10 centuries before—is still the classic Japanese city. The traditional arts, crafts, customs, language, and literature were all born, raised, and refined here. Kyōto has the matchless villas, the incomparable gardens, the magnificent temples and shrines—2,000 of them. And it is to Kyōto that you travel for the most artful Japanese cuisine.

Architecture

No other city in Japan has such a glorious array of religious architecture. Over its 1,200 year history it has accumulated more than 1,600 Buddhist temples (30 of which are the headquarters for major sects spread throughout Japan), 200 Shinto shrines, and three imperial palaces. All of these vying for your attention can be a bit daunting, but there are easy standouts where you can get the best of Japan's harmonious, graceful architectural styles without having to dash here and there with a checklist.

Crafts

Temples, shrines, gardens, and the quintessential elements of Japanese culture are all part of Kyōto's appeal, but you can't take them home with you. You can, however, pack up a few *omiyage* (mementos)—tangible gifts for which this city is famous. The ancient craftsmen of Kyōto served the imperial court for more than 1,000 years, and the prefix *kyō-* before a craft is synonymous with fine craftsmanship. The wares that you will find in Kyōto are, for their superb artistry and refinement, among the world's finest.

Kyō-ningyō are the exquisite display dolls that have been made in Kyōto since the 9th century. Constructed of wood coated with white shell paste

Kyōto *(Boxes Refer to Detail Maps)*

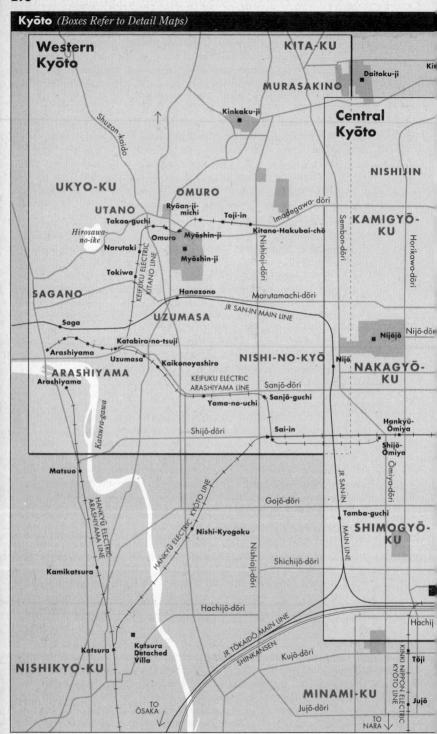

Western Kyōto

KITA-KU

Daitoku-ji

Kit

MURASAKINO

Central Kyōto

Kinkaku-ji

NISHIJIN

UKYO-KU

OMURO

Ryōan-ji-michi

KAMIGYŌ-KU

UTANO

Takao-guchi

Toji-in

Kitano-Hakubai-chō

Imadegawa-dōri

Sembon-dōri

Horikawa-dōri

Hirosawa-no-ike

Omuro

Myōshin-ji

Narutaki

Myōshin-ji

Shijōji-dōri

Tokiwa

SAGANO

Hanazono

Marutamachi-dōri

Saga

JR SAN-IN MAIN LINE

UZUMASA

Nijōjō

Nijō-dō

Arashiyama

Katabira-no-tsuji

Uzumasa

Kaikonoyashiro

NISHI-NO-KYŌ

Nijō

NAKAGYŌ-KU

ARASHIYAMA

Arashiyama

KEIFUKU ELECTRIC ARASHIYAMA LINE

Sanjō-dōri

Sanjō-guchi

Yama-no-uchi

Hankyū-Ōmiya

Shijō-dōri

Sai-in

Shijō-Ōmiya

Matsuo

Ōmiya-dōri

JR SAN-IN MAIN LINE

Gojō-dōri

HANKYŪ ELECTRIC KYŌTO LINE

Tamba-guchi

HANKYŪ ELECTRIC ARASHIYAMA LINE

Nishi-Kyogoku

SHIMOGYŌ-KU

Kamikatsura

Nishioji-dōri

Shichijō-dōri

Hachijō-dōri

Hachij

NISHIKYO-KU

Katsura

Katsura Detached Villa

JR TŌKAIDŌ MAIN LINE

SHINKANSEN

Kujō-dōri

KINKI NIPPON ELECTRIC KYŌTO LINE

Tōji

TO ŌSAKA

MINAMI-KU

Jujō-dōri

Jujō

TO NARA

Shuzan-kaido

Keifuku Electric Kitano Line

Katsura-gawa

- ■ Botanical Garden
- ■ Kamigamo Jinja
  Kita-ōji-dōri

SHIMOGAMO

Kamo-gawa

Kita-ōji

Kurama-guchi

TAKANO

Takanogawa

EIZAN ELECT. KURAMA LINE

EIZAN ELECT. EIZAN LINE

Ichij-ōji

Chayama

KITA-SHIRAKAWA

Mt. Uryu ▲

KEY

JR Trains
Shinkansen (Bullet Train)
Subway
Private rail line

0 _____ 1 mile
0 _____ 1 km

N

Eastern Kyōto

Mototanaka

SAKYO-KU

Ginkaku-ji

SUBWAY

Imadegawa

Karasuma-dōri

Kawara-machi-dōri

Demachi-Yanagi

Imadegawa- dōri

Demachi-Yanagi Keihan

Kyōto Imperial Palace

Shirakawa-dōri

Shishig atani-dōri

Nyoigatake ▲

Maruta-machi

Maruta-machi

Maruta-machi-dōri

Higashiōji-dōri

■ Heian Jingū

OKAZAKI

Oike

Oike-dōri

Kawara-machi

Higashiyama-Sanjō

Sanjō-dōri

KEIHAN ELECTRIC KEISHIN LINE

Keage

Keihan-Sanjō

Keishin-Sanjo

AWATAGUCHI

Shijō-dōri

Karasuma Shijō

Kawara-machi

Shijō Keihan

GION

Kujō-yama

Gojō-dōri

Gojō

Gojō

Kiyomizu-dera

Hino-oka

TO TOKYO

YAMASHINA-KU

Misasagi

HIGASHIYAMA-KU

Mt. Kiyomizu ▲

Mt. Kazan ▲

Yamashina

Keihan-Yamashina

Shinomiya

Shichijō

JR TŌKAIDŌ MAIN LINE

Mt. Rokujō ▲

KANSAI REGION

Kyōto Station

jō-dōri

SHINKANSEN

JR NARA LINE

Kujō-dōri

Tōfukuji

KEIHAN ELECTRIC MAIN LINE

Jūjō-dōri

Tobakaido

Kyōto

Lake Biwa

Kōbe

Osaka Bay

Ōsaka

Nara

Yoshino-san ▲

Kōya-san ▲

and clothed in elaborate, miniature patterned silk brocades, Kyōto dolls are considered the finest in Japan. Kyōto is also known for fine ceramic dolls and Kyō-gangu, its local varieties of folk toys.

Kyō-sensu are embellished folding fans used as accoutrements in Nō theater, tea ceremonies, and Japanese dance. They also have a practical use—to ward off heat. Unlike other Japanese crafts, which have their origin in Tang Dynasty China, the folding fan originated in Kyōto.

Kyō-shikki refers to Kyōto lacquerware, which also has its roots in the 9th century. The making of lacquerware, adopted from the Chinese, is a delicate process requiring patience and skill, not only in the application of numerous coats of lacquer. Finished lacquerware products range from furniture to spoons and bowls, which are carved from cypress, cedar, or horse-chestnut wood. These pieces have a brilliant luster; some designs are decorated with gold leaf and inlaid mother-of-pearl.

Kyō-yaki is the general term used for ceramics made in local kilns; the most popular ware is from Kyōto's Kiyomizu district. Often colorfully hand-painted in blue, red, and green on white, these elegantly shaped teacups, bowls, and vases are thrown on potters' wheels located in the Kiyomizu district and in Kiyomizu-danchi in Yamashina. Streets leading up to Kiyomizu-dera—Chawan-zaka, Sannen-zaka, and Ninnen-zaka—are sprinkled with kyō-yaki shops.

Kyō-yuzen is a paste-resist silk-dyeing technique developed by 17th-century dyer Yuzen Miyazaki. Fantastic designs are created on plain white silk pieces through the process of either *tegaki yuzen* (hand-painting) or *kata yuzen* (stenciling).

Nishijin-ori is the weaving of silk. Nishijin refers to a Kyōto district producing the best of silk textiles in all of Japan, and it is used to make kimono. Walk along the narrow backstreets of Nishijin and hear the persistently rhythmic sound of looms.

Dining

"Paris East" is a difficult epithet to live up to, but in many ways the elegant sister cities do seem to be of the same flesh and blood—not least in that both serve up their nation's haute cuisine. The presence of the imperial court was the original inspiration for Kyōto's exclusive *yusoku ryōri*. Once presented on lacquered pedestals to the emperor himself, it is now offered at but one restaurant in the city, Mankamero.

The experience not to miss in Kyōto is *kaiseki ryōri,* the elegant full-course meal that was originally intended to be served with the tea ceremony. All the senses are engaged in this culinary event: the scent and flavor of the freshest ingredients at the peak of season; the visual delight of a continuous procession of porcelain dishes and lacquered bowls, each a different shape and size, gracefully adorned with an appropriately shaped morsel of fish or vegetable; the textures of foods unknown and exotic, presented in sequence to prevent boredom; the sound of water in a stone basin outside in the garden; and, finally, that other necessity—the atmosphere of the room itself, complete with a hanging scroll displayed in the alcove and a flower arrangement, both to evoke the season and to accent the restrained appointments of the tatami room. Kaiseki ryōri is often costly yet always unforgettable.

For an initiation or a reasonably priced sample, the *kaiseki bentō* (box lunch) served by many *ryōtei* (high-class Japanese restaurants) is a good place to start. Box lunches are so popular in Kyōto that the restaurants that serve them compete to make their bentō unique, exquisite, and delicious.

Because it is a two-day journey from the sea, Kyōto is historically more famous for ingenious ways of serving preserved fish—dried, salted, or pickled—than for its raw fish dishes, though with modern transportation there are now good sushi shops in town. Compared with the style of cooking elsewhere in Japan, *Kyōto-ryōri* (Kyōto cuisine) is lighter and more delicate. The natural flavor of ingredients is stressed over the enhancement of heavy sauces and broths. *Tsukemono* (pickled vegetables) and *wagashi* (traditional sweets) are two other local specialties; they make excellent souvenirs. Food shops are often kept just as they were a century ago—well worth the trip if only to browse.

Kyōto is also the home of *shōjin ryōri*, the Zen vegetarian-style cooking, best sampled on the grounds of one of the city's Zen temples. Local delicacies like *fu* (glutinous wheat cakes) and *yuba* (soy milk skimmings) have found their way into the mainstream of Kyōto ryōri but were originally devised as ways of providing protein in the traditional Buddhist diet.

Famed throughout Japan for the best in traditional Japanese cuisine, Kyōto was slower to pick up the fine French, American, Indian, and Chinese restaurants that it now has. Try them if you need a break from Japanese fare.

Gardens

Simplicity and symbolism are the perfected goals of Kyōto's temple gardens. The tea garden at Kinkaku-ji, with stepping stones paving the way through manicured grounds, sets the spirit at rest. The timeless arrangement of the dry-garden sand and rocks at Ryōan-ji is an eternal questing for completeness. The tree-shrouded gardens at Jakkō-in feed melancholy.

Lodging

Considering the huge numbers of people who visit Kyōto, the city has a surprising dearth of good hotels. Apart from pricey ryokan, the hotels do not compare with their counterparts in Ōsaka or Tōkyō. So don't expect too much and you won't be disappointed. As for the superexpensive ryokans, $500 to $600 per night will bring genteel attention, an elegant dinner, and the classical harmony of the tatami rooms. No other Japanese city can compete with this Kyōto style and grace, but it is not always given to foreigners. Remember that it helps to have a Japanese person make a reservation for you at a ryokan, unless you can speak Japanese yourself. The idea is to let the ryokan know that you understand the customs of staying at traditional inns.

Matsuri (Festivals)

Kyōto's festival calendar includes five spectacular events: the Aoi (hollyhock), Gion (geisha), Jidai (costume), and the Daimon-ji and Kurama fire matsuri, held between May and October. *See* Festivals and National Holidays *in* Chapter 1.

Museums

Kyōto and Tōkyō are rivals for the role as the nation's leading repository of culture. Certainly Kyōto wins hands down for its treasures from traditional and courtly Japan. You won't get this feeling from walking the busy, congested streets of modern downtown, but a step into any of the nine major museums will sweep you back in a virtual time machine to the days of refinement and efforts toward artistic perfection.

Shopping

Perhaps even more than Tōkyō, Kyōto is the Japanese city in which to shop both for yourself and for gifts to take home. As Japan's self-proclaimed cultural capital, Kyōto has no shortage of art and antiques shops. Folk crafts from surrounding regions are brought into town for shops to sell. Second-hand kimono can be a steal at $50 after image-conscious Japanese discard them for new ones priced in the thousands of dollars. Ceramics and woven bamboo make great gifts and souvenirs, and if you are looking for interesting odds and ends, there are always the monthly flea markets.

Exploring Kyōto

Most of Kyōto's interesting sights are north of Kyōto Eki. Think of this northern sector as three rectangular areas abutting each other.

The middle rectangle fronts the exit of Kyōto Eki. This is **central Kyōto.** Here are the hotels, the business district, the Ponto-chō geisha district, and the Kiya-machi entertainment district. Central Kyōto also contains one of the oldest city temples, Tōji, the rebuilt Imperial Palace, and Nijō-jō, the onetime Kyōto abode of the Tokugawa shōguns. **Eastern Kyōto,** Higashiyama, is chock-a-block with temples and shrines, among them Ginkaku-ji (Temple of the Silver Pavilion), Heian Jingū, and Kiyomizu-dera. Gion—a traditional shopping neighborhood by day and a geisha entertainment district by night—is also here. You could easily fill two days visiting eastern Kyōto. **Western Kyōto** includes the temples Ryōan-ji and Kinkaku-ji (Temple of the Golden Pavilion), and Katsura Rikyū (Detached Villa) a bit south.

You could skim over these three areas, so crowded with historical attractions, in three days. However, two other areas have major sights to lure you. West of the western district is **Arashiyama,** with its temple, Tenryū-ji. And north of central Kyōto are **Hiei-zan** and the suburb of **Ōhara,** where the poignant story of Kenreimon-in takes place at Jakkō-in.

Kyōto's sights do spread over a wide area, but many of the them are clustered together, and you can walk from one to another. Where the sights are not near each other, you can use Kyōto's buses, which run on a grid pattern that is easy to follow. Pick up route maps at the JNTO (Japan National Tourist Organization) office. The following exploring sections keep to the divisions described above so as to allow walking from one sight to another. However, notwithstanding traffic, and armed with a bus map, you could cross and recross Kyōto without too much difficulty, stringing together sights of your own choosing.

Admission to Kyōto sights adds up. Over the course of three days, charges of ¥400 to ¥500 at each sight can easily come to $100 per person.

Great Itineraries

IF YOU HAVE 1 DAY

Heaven forfend if you have such limited time. Should it be so, start with Ginkaku-ji for the simplicity of its exterior shape and its gardens. Walk a little way down the Path of Philosophy before taking a taxi to Kiyomizu-dera, a vast wooden temple built on the side of a hill. Walk through Maruyama Kōen to Chion-in, taking special notice of the awesome San-mon at its entrance. From here take a taxi to the Kyōto Craft Center to browse through the traditional and regional crafts. You may also want to take a break for lunch here. Another taxi ride will take you to central Kyōto and Nijō-jō, a grandiose statement of Tokugawa military might. Now make tracks for western Kyōto, where you should have time for abbreviated visits to Kinkaku-ji, built in 1393, and Ryōan-ji for its soul-searching *kare sansui* (dry) garden. You can travel between the two on Bus 12. Or, you could head from lunch to Nishiki-Kōji market before heading out to Kinkaku-ji. Because you're here so briefly, don't miss an all-out kaiseki dinner to end the day magically.

IF YOU HAVE 3 DAYS

Give your first day to visiting the attractions in eastern Kyōto described above, but after Ginkaku-ji and the Path of Philosophy slip in Nanzen-ji, the Heian Jingū, and Sanjūsangen-dō before going onto visit Kiyo-mizu-dera. On your second day, spend the morning in central Kyōto at the Imperial Palace and Nijō-jō. In the afternoon cover western Kyōto to include Kinkaku-ji, Ryōan-ji, Ninna-ji, and Myōshin-ji. The morning of day three, take the Hankyū Railway Line from Kyōto's Hankyū Kawara-machi Eki to Katsura Eki and walk 10 minutes to get to Katsura Rikyū (having obtained your permit to do so the morning before). Then return to Kyōto and head to northern Kyōto and Hiei-zan to spend a calm afternoon wandering through the temple complex and appreciate the views of Kyōto below. Or get in a little shopping so as not to miss local foods and crafts to stuff into your suitcase.

IF YOU HAVE 5 DAYS

Concentrate on eastern Kyōto for your first day. Then take on the Imperial Palace and Nijō-jō in central Kyōto the next morning and western Kyōto in the afternoon. On day three, visit the Katsura Rikyū in the morning and the sights in Arashiyama in the afternoon. When you come back into central Kyōto try to visit Higashi-Hongan-ji. On day four, leave early for northern Kyōto to visit the temples in Ōhara—Sanzan-in, Jikko-in, and Jakkō-in. By lunchtime, be up at Hiei-zan to spend the afternoon on top of the world exploring the temple complexes. On the fifth day head for the Kyōto Craft Center, traditional shops, and the Nishiki-kōji market for finding a few treasures to bring home.

When to Tour Kyōto

Cherry-blossom time in Spring is remarkable. And except for in the depths of winter, Kyōto's climate is mild enough to make sightseeing pleasant for 10 months of the year. In the high season, May through October, the large numbers of visitors to the city can make accommodations scarce and you must apply in advance to visit those attractions that require permits, such as the Katsura and the Shūgaku-in Imperial Villas. You can also expect lines for admission tickets to the Imperial Palace.

Religious buildings are mostly open seven days a week, but many museums close Mondays. If you are lucky enough to be in Kyōto for the Jidai Festival, held on October 22, which celebrates the founding of Kyōto, be sure to head for the Heian Jingū for the procession of 2,000-odd people attired in costumes from every period of Kyōto history.

EXPLORING EASTERN KYŌTO

Start your Kyōto odyssey in Higashiyama (literally, "Eastern Mountain"). If you have time to visit only one district, this is the one. There is more to see here than you could cover comfortably in one day, so pick and choose from the following itinerary according to your interests.

Numbers in the text correspond to numbers in the margin and on the Eastern Kyōto map.

A Good Walk

Ginkaku-ji ① is one of Kyōto's most famous sights, a wonderful villa turned temple. To get here, take Bus 5 from Kyōto Eki to Ginkaku-ji-michi bus stop. Walk on the street along the canal, going east. Just after the street crosses a north–south canal, you'll see **Hakusha Son-sō Garden,** a small villa with an impeccable garden, and then Ginkaku-ji. You'll want to spend a good half hour here soaking up the atmosphere. When you can tear yourself away from Ginkaku-ji, retrace your steps on the entrance road until you reach, on your left, the **Path of Philosophy** ②, which follows alongside the canal and is reminiscent of former aristocratic days. At the fourth bridge as you walk south—it is larger than the first three—off the path, cross the canal and take the road east to the modest **Hōnen-in** ③, with its thatched roof and quiet, comforting park. After Hōnen-in, return to the Path of Philosophy and continue south. In 15 minutes or so you'll reach on your left the temple **Eikan-dō** ④, known for its un-usual image of the Amida Buddha. If you cross the street from Eikan-dō and continue south, you'll see on the right the **Nomura Bijutsukan** ⑤, a museum with a private collection of Japanese art.

If the day is close to an end, walk from the Nomura Bijutsukan to the Heian Shrine and the Kyōto Handicraft Center on Maruta-machi-dōri behind it. If not, continue this tour, which returns shortly to the Heian Shrine.

Next, walk south from the Nomura Art Museum and follow the main path. On your left will be **Nanzen-ji** ⑥, headquarters of the Rinzai sect of Zen Buddhism, with its classic triple gate, San-mon. See also **Nanzen-in,** a smaller temple within Nanzen-ji. Outside the main gate of Nanzen-ji but still part of the complex, take the side street to the left and you will come to **Konchi-in** ⑦, with its pair of excellent gardens, classics of their kind. At the intersection at the foot of the road to Nanzen-ji, you'll see the expansive grounds of the **Kyōto International Community House** ⑧ across the street to the left. Walk back to the main road to Nanzen-ji and turn left. Cross at the traffic light to **Murin-an Garden** ⑨, whose entrance is on a side road half a block east. The Meiji-period garden is of interest for its incorporation of new ideas into Japanese garden design. Walk back north toward the canal and turn left. If you were to cross the canal at the first right, you would be at the **Dobutsu-en** ⑩, Kyōto's zoo. There is no pressing reason to visit it, unless you have children in tow. If you skip the zoo, continue to the next right and cross the bridge over the canal. You'll see an immense vermilion torii that acts as a distant entry for the Heian Shrine. There are two museums flanking the other side of the torii, the **Kyōto-shi Bijutsukan** ⑪ on your right, and the **Kindai Bijutsukan** ⑫ on your left. Close by is the **Dentō Sangyō Kaikan** ⑬, which exhibits traditional Kyōto crafts.

If the urge comes on to do some shopping, cross Maruta-machi-dōri and turn left, and you'll come to the **Kyōto Handicraft Center** ⑮. At the crossroads of Maruta-machi-dōri and Higashi-ōji-dōri, west of the Handicraft Center, is the Kumano Jinja-mae bus stop. If you've had enough sightseeing for one day, take Bus 202 or 206 five stops south on Higashioji-dōri to the Gion bus stop; here, some of the city's best restaurants and bars are at your disposal. If you are going to continue sightseeing, stay on Bus 202 for five more stops (Higashiyama-Shichijō) to explore the southern part of Higashiyama, starting with **Sanjūsan-gen-dō** ⑯. If you have taken Bus 206, stay on it for one more stop (it makes a right turn onto Shichijō-dōri and heads for the station) and get off at the Sanjūsangen-dō-mae bus stop. To start exploring here, take Bus 206 or 208 from Kyōto Eki to the Sanjūsangen-dō-mae stop.

From the Sanjūsangen-dō-mae stop, the temple is to the south just be-yond the Kyōto Park Hotel. If you get off of Bus 202 at the Hi-gashiyama-Shichijō stop, walk down Shichijō-dōri and take the first major street to the left. If you plan to see Chishaku-in, go there first. It will allow you to avoid doubling back.

From Sanjūsangen-dō, retrace your steps back to Shichijō-dōri and take a right. **Chishaku-in** ⑰, famous for its paintings, will be facing you on the other side of Higashioji-dōri. Back across Higashioji-dōri is the pres-tigious **Kokuritsu Hakubutsukan** ⑱. Just north, less than a five-minute

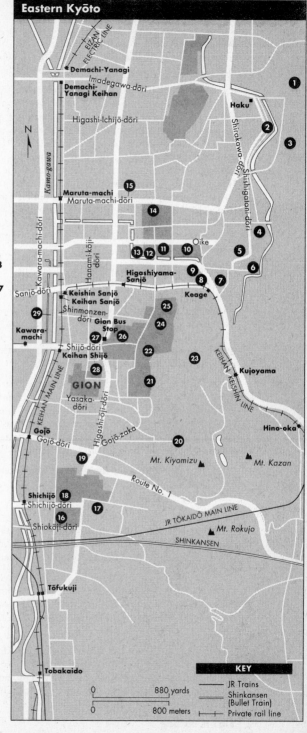

walk along Higashi-ōji-dori of the hakubutsukan, is the **Kawai Kanjiro Kinenkan** ⑲ museum, with the works of renowned potter Kanjiro Kawai. The next place to visit is a very special temple, **Kiyomizudera** ⑳. To get there from the museum, cross the major avenue Gojō-dōri and walk up Higashi-ōji-dori. The street to the right, Gojō-zaka, leads into Kiyomizu-zaka, which you'll take to the temple.

If you take a right halfway down the road leading from Kiyomizu-dera, you can walk along the Sannen-zaka and Ninen-zaka (slopes). Take a left after Ninen-zaka and then an immediate right, and continue walking north. After another five minutes you will see, on the right, **Kōdai-ji** ㉑, a sedate nunnery founded in the early 17th century with contemplative gardens and decorated ceilings inside the temple. Keep heading north: By doing a right–left zigzag at the Maruyama Music Hall, you'll get to **Maruyama Kōen** ㉒. The road to the right (east) leads up the mountainside to **Choraku-ji** ㉓, a temple famous today for the stone lanterns that lead to it. Proceed north through Maruyama Kōen and you'll find **Chion-in** ㉔, headquarters of the Jōdo sect of Buddhism. More paintings by the Kanō school are on view at **Shōren-in** ㉕, a five-minute walk north of Chion-in.

Should you have missed visiting the Heian Shrine, the National Museum of Modern Art, and the Municipal Museum of Art described in the first part of this tour, note that these are just 10 minutes north of Shōren-in on foot, on the other side of Sanjō-dōri. If you turn right (east) from Shōren-in on Sanjō-dōri, you'll eventually reach the Miyako Hotel; left (west) on Sanjō-dōri leads across Higashi-ōji-dōri to the downtown area and the covered mall. If you turn left on Higashioji-dōri, you will reach Shijō-dōri and the **Gion** district.

At the Gion bus stop, Shijō-dōri goes off to the west. Before going down this street, consider taking a short walk east (back into Maruyama Kōen) to **Yasaka Jinja** ㉖, a shrine that is said to bring good health and wealth. Walk back from Yasaka Jinja, cross Higashioji-dōri, and you are in Gion, on Shijō-dōri. On the right-hand corner is the **Kyōto Craft Center** ㉗, with fine contemporary and traditional crafts.

Parallel to Shijō-dōri and to the north is **Shinmonzen-dōri**, a great place to go for a little shopping and browsing. Shijō-dōri itself has interesting, less-expensive items.

Off Shijō-dōri, halfway between Higashioji-dōri and the Kamo-gawa, is Hanami-kōji-dōri. The section of this street that runs south of Shijō-dōri (on the right, if you are walking back from the river) will bring you into the heart of the **Gion** district, where the top geisha live and work.

If you continue west on Shijō-dōri you'll cross over the Kamo-gawa. Pontochō-dōri is on the right. Like Gion, this area is known for its nightlife and geisha entertainment. At the north end of Pontochō-dōri, the **Pontochō Kaburenjō Theater** ㉙ puts on geisha song-and-dance performances.

TIMING

This route is extensive and it would, if you dutifully covered everything along it, take at least two days. You do need to be selective, especially because you might want to spend 40 minutes or more at such places as Ginkaku-ji, Sanjūsangen-dō, the Kokuritsu Hakubutsukan, and Kiyomizu-dera.

Sights to See

★ ㉔ **Chion-in.** The entrance to the temple is through the 79-ft, two-story Sanmon. In many people's minds, this is the most daunting temple gate in all of Japan, and it leads to one of Japan's largest temples, the very headquarters of the Jōdo sect of Buddhism, the second largest Buddhist sect in Japan. All of this distinction owes itself to the fact that this is the site on which Hōnen, the founder of the Jōdo sect, chose to take his leave of this world by fasting to death in 1212. Chion-in was built in 1234. Because of fires and earthquakes, the oldest standing buildings are the Hon-dō (Main Hall, 1633) and the Daihōjō (Abbots' Quarters, 1639). The temple's belfry houses the largest bell in Japan, which was cast in 1633 and requires 17 monks to ring. The corridor behind the Main Hall, which leads to the Assembly Hall, is called *uguisu-bari* (nightingale floor). It was constructed to "sing" at every footstep to warn the monks of intruders. Walk underneath the corridor to examine the way the boards and nails are placed to create this inventive burglar alarm. From Kyōto Eki, take Bus 206 to the Gion stop. The temple is north of Maruyama Kōen. ⊠ *400 Hayashi-shita-chō 3-chōme, Yamato-ōji, Higashi-Hairu, Shimbashi-dōri, Higashiyama-ku.* ☜ *¥400.* ⊘ *Daily 9–4:30 (9–4 in winter); not all buildings open to public.*

⑰ Chishaku-in. The major reason for visiting this temple is for its famous paintings, which were executed by Tōhaku Hasegawa and his son Kyūzo—known as the Hasegawa school, rivals of the Kanō school (☞ Nanzen-ji, *below*)—and are some of the best examples of Momoyama art. These paintings were originally created for the sliding screens at Shōun-in, a temple built in 1591 on the same site but no longer in existence. Shōun-in was commissioned by Hideyoshi Toyotomi. When his concubine, Yodogimi, bore him an heir in 1589, Hideyoshi named his son Tsurumatsu (Crane-pine), two symbols of longevity. Ironically, the child died when he was two, and Shōun-in was built for Tsurumatsu's enshrinement. The Hasegawas were then commissioned to make the paintings. Saved from the fires that destroyed Shōun-in, the paintings are now on display in the Exhibition Hall of Chishaku-in. These paintings, rich in detail and using strong colors on a gold ground, splendidly display the seasons by using the symbols of cherry, maple, pine, and plum trees and autumn grasses.

You may also want to take a few moments in the pond-viewing garden. It has only a vestige of its former glory, but from the temple's veranda, you'll have a pleasing view of the pond and garden. From Kyōto Eki take Bus 206 or 208 to the Higashiyama-Shichijō stop. Chishaku-in is on the east side of Higashi-ōji-dōri. ☜ *¥350.* ⊘ *Daily 9–4:30.*

㉓ Choraku-ji. Mostly it is the procession of stone lanterns along the path that gives this temple a modest fame. Although it's a pleasant temple, it may not be worth the hard climb up the mountainside. Choraku-ji is east of Maruyama Kōen.

⑬ Dentō Sangyō Kaikan (Kyōto Museum of Traditional Industry). Housed here is a wide array of traditional Kyōto crafts. There are craft-making demonstrations that are both educational and useful. Should you wish to collect a few items, there is a shop on the premises. In the basement is a model interior of a traditional town house. From the Dobutsuen-mae bus stop, head down the street that leads to the Heian Shrine. The museum is inside the torii on your left after the Kindai Bijutsukan. ⊠ *9-2 Seishōji-chō, Okazaki, Sakyō-ku,* ☎ *075/761–3421.* ☜ *Free.* ⊘ *Tues.–Sun. 9–5 (enter by 4:30).*

☾ ⑩ Dobutsu-en (Kyōto Zoo). The prime reason to stop at the zoo is to entertain your children, if you have any in tow. The zoo has a Children's Corner, where your youngsters can feed the farm animals. It is across from the Dobutsu-en-mae bus stop. ⊠ *Hoshōji-chō, Okazaki, Sakyō-ku,* ☎ *075/771–0210.* ☜ *¥400.* ⊘ *Tues.–Sun. 9–5 (winter 9–4:30); when Mon. is national holiday, zoo stays open Mon. and closes the following day.*

❹ **Eikan-dō.** Eikan-dō is the temple's popular name. Officially it is Zen-rin-ji, founded in 856 by Priest Shinsho, but it honors the memory of an 11th-century priest, Priest Eikan. He was a man of the people, and he would lead them in a dance in celebration of Amida Buddha. On one such occasion, the Amida statue came to life and stepped down from his pedestal to join the dancers. Taken aback, Eikan slowed his dancing feet. Amida looked back over his shoulder to reprimand Eikan for slowing his pace. This is the legend that explains why the unusual statue in the Amida-dō has its face turned to the side, as if glancing backward. A climb to the top of the pagoda offers superb views of the grounds below and Kyōto beyond. In autumn, the color of the maple leaves makes the grounds especially magnificent. The buildings here are 16th-century reconstructions made after the originals were destroyed in the Ōnin Civil War (1467–77). Eikan-dō is a 15-minute walk south of the fourth bridge on the Path of Philosophy on the left side of the path. 🎫 ¥400. ⊙ Daily 9–5 (enter by 4:30).

★ ❶ **Ginkaku-ji.** Ginkaku-ji means "Temple of the Silver Pavilion," but the temple is not silver. It was only intended to be. Shōgun Yoshimasa Ashikaga (1435–90) had this villa built for his retirement. He started building it as early as the 1460s, but it was not until 1474 that, disillusioned with politics, he gave his full attention to the construction of his villa and to the arts of romance, moon-gazing, and the tea ceremony, which he helped develop into a high art. Though he never had time to complete the coating of the pavilion with silver foil, he constructed a dozen or so buildings. Many of them were designed for cultural pursuits, such as incense and tea ceremonies. On his death, the villa was converted into a Buddhist temple, as was often the custom during the feudal era. However, with the decline of the Ashikaga family, Ginkaku-ji fell into decline, and many buildings were destroyed.

What we see today are the two remaining original buildings, **Tōgu-dō** (East Request Hall) and Ginkaku-ji itself. The four other structures on the grounds were built in the 17th and 19th centuries. The front room of Tōgu-dō is where Yoshimasa is thought to have lived, and the statue of the priest is probably of Yoshimasa himself. The back room, called Dojin-sai (Comradely Abstinence), became the prototype for traditional tea-ceremony rooms.

Ginkaku-ji is a simple and unadorned two-story building. On the upper floor it contains a gilt image of Kannon (Goddess of Mercy) said to have been carved by Unkei, a famous Kamakura-period sculptor; it is not ordinarily open to public view. Mostly it is the exterior shape of the structure that is so appealing and restful, as it combines Chinese elements with the developing Japanese Muro-machi (1333–1568) ar-
★ chitecture. Ginkaku-ji overlooks the complex **gardens** attributed to artist and architect Soami. They are in two sections and serve to contrast with each other in order to establish a balance. Adjacent to the pavilion is a pond garden, with a composition of rocks and plants designed to offer different perspectives from each viewpoint. The other garden has two sculpted mounds of sand, the higher one symbolizing, perhaps, Mt. Fuji. The garden sparkles in the moonlight and has been aptly named "Sea of Silver Sand." The composition of the approach to the garden is also quite remarkable.

To reach Ginkaku-ji, take Bus 5 from Kyōto Eki to Ginkaku-ji-michi bus stop. Walk on the street along the canal, going east. Cross a north–south canal and Hakusha Son-sō Garden on your right; then continue straight and Ginkaku-ji will be in front of you. ✉ Ginkaku-ji-machi, Sakyō-ku. 🎫 ¥400. ⊙ Mar. 15–Nov., daily 8:30–5; Dec.–Mar. 14, daily 9–4:30.

★ **Gion** (ghee-*own*). Arguably Kyōto's most interesting neighborhood, this is the legendary haunt of geisha. In the evening, amid the glow of tea-house and restaurant lanterns, you can see them scurrying about, white faced, on the way to their appointments. In their wake their *maiko* follow—the young apprentice geisha whom you can identify by the longer sleeves of their kimono. On an exotic level equal to the world of temples and gardens, Gion is the place for gai-jin to fantasize about Japan's fabled floating world.

The heart of the district is on Hanami-kōji-dōri. Heading north, it intersects with Shinmonzen-dōri, which is famous for its antiques shops and art galleries. Here you'll find collectors' items—at collectors' prices—which make for interesting browsing, if not buying. The shops on **Shijō-dōri**, which parallels Shinmonzen-dōri to the south, carry slightly more affordable items, from hand-crafted hair ornaments to incense to parasols—all articles that are part of the geisha world.

★ ㉘ **Gion Kaburenjō Theater.** Because Westerners have little opportunity to enjoy a geisha's performance in a private party setting—which would require a proper recommendation of, and probably the presence of, a geisha's respected client—a popular entertainment during the month of April is the Miyako Odori (cherry blossom dance). Miyako Odori features musical presentations by geisha, who are dressed in their elaborate traditional kimono and makeup. Next door to the theater is **Gion Corner,** where demonstrations of traditional performing arts are held nightly from March through November (☞ Nightlife and the Arts, *below*). ⊠ *Gion Hanamikōji, Higashiyama-ku,* ☎ *075/561–1115.*

Hakusha Son-sō Garden. The modest villa of the late painter Hashimoto Kansetsu has an exquisite stone garden and teahouse open to the public. To get here, take Bus 5 from Kyōto Eki to the Ginkaku-ji-michi stop. Walk east on the street along the canal. Just after the street crosses another canal flowing north–south, Hakusha Son-sō will be on the right. 🎫 *¥700; with tea and sweets, an extra ¥800.* ⊙ *Daily 10–5 (enter by 4:30).*

⑭ **Heian Jingū.** One of Kyōto's newest historical sites, Heian Jingū was built in 1895 to mark the 1,100th anniversary of the founding of Kyōto. The shrine is dedicated to two emperors: Kammu (737–806), who founded the city in 794, and Kōmei (1831–66), the last emperor to live out his reign in Kyōto. The new buildings are for the most part replicas of the old Imperial Palace, at two-thirds the original size. In fact, because the original palace (rebuilt many times) was finally destroyed in 1227, and only scattered pieces of information are available relating to its construction, Heian Jingū should be taken as a Meiji interpretation of the old palace. Still, the dignity and the relative spacing of the **East Hon-den** and **West Hon-den** (the main halls), and the **Daigoku-den** (Great Hall of State), in which the Heian emperor would issue decrees, conjure up an image of the magnificence that the Heian court must have had.

During **New Year,** the imposing gravel forecourt leading to Daigoku-den is trampled by kimono-clad and gray-suited Japanese who come to pay homage. One superb time to visit is in the spring, in sakura time. The gardens are also a modern interpretation of a Heian garden, but they follow the Heian aesthetic of focusing on a large pond whose shores are gracefully linked by the arched Taibei-kaku Chinese-style bridge. An even better time to see the shrine is during the Jidai Festival, held on October 22, which celebrates the founding of Kyōto. The pageant, featuring a procession of 2,000 people attired in costumes from every period of Kyōto history, winds its way from the original site of the Imperial Palace and ends at the Heian Shrine.

Another choice time to come to the shrine is on June 1–2 for **Takigi Nō performances,** so named because they are held at night, in open air, lit by *takigi* (burning firewood). Performances take place on a stage built before the shrine's Daigoku-den.

From the Dobutsuen-mae bus stop, follow the street between the Municipal Art Museum and the National Museum of Modern Art directly to the shrine. ✉ *Okazakinishi Tennō-chō, Sakyō-ku.* 💴 *Garden ¥600.* 🕐 *Mar. 15–Aug., daily 8:30–5:30; Sept.–Oct. and Mar.–Mar. 14, daily 8:30–5; Nov.–Feb., 8:30–4:30.* 💴 *Takigi Nō ¥3,000 at the gate, ¥2,000 in advance. Call the Tourist Information Center for advance tickets:* ☎ *075/371–5649.*

❸ **Hōnen-in.** The walk through the trees leading to the temple is mercifully quiet and comforting, but not many people come to this humble, thatched-roof structure. The temple was built in 1680, on a site that in the 13th century simply consisted of an open-air Amida Buddha statue. Hōnen-in honors Priest Hōnen (1133–1212), who brought Buddhism down from its lofty peak to the common folk by making the radical claim that all were equal in the eyes of Buddha. Hōnen focused on faith in the Amida Nyorai; he believed that *nembutsu*—"Namu Amida Butsu," the invocation of Amida Buddha—which he is said to have repeated up to 60,000 times a day, and reliance on Amida, the All-Merciful, were the path to salvation. Because his ideas threatened other sects, especially the Tendai sect, Hōnen's teachings of Jōdo-shu, "the Pure Land Sect," were accused of advocating that the masses seduce the ladies of noble classes. At the insistence of the established Buddhist powers, Emperor Gotoba had several of Hōnen's followers executed and Hōnen sent into exile. Eventually, in 1211, Hōnen was pardoned and permitted to return to Kyōto, where a year later, at Chion-in, he fasted to death at the age of 79. From the Path of Philosophy, cross the fourth bridge as you're walking south (it is larger than the first three), and take the road east. 💴 *Free.* 🕐 *Daily 7–4.*

⓳ **Kawai Kanjiro Kinenkan** (memorial house). Now a museum, this was the home and studio of one of Japan's most renowned potters. The house was designed by Kanjiro Kawai, who took for his inspiration a traditional rural Japanese cottage. He was one of the leaders of the Mingei (Folk Art) Movement, which sought to promote a revival of interest in traditional folk arts during the 1920s and '30s, when all things Western were in vogue in Japan. On display are some of the artist's personal memorabilia and, of more interest, some of his exquisite works. An admirer of Western, Chinese, and Korean ceramic techniques, Kawai won many awards, including the Grand Prix at the 1937 Paris World Exposition. From Kyōto Eki take Bus 206 or 208 to the Sanjūsan-gen-dō-mae stop, and then walk east to the end of Shichijō-dōri. The house is a five-minute walk north along Higashi-ōji-dōri. ✉ *Gojō-zaka, Higashiyama-ku,* ☎ *075/561–3585.* 💴 *¥700.* 🕐 *Tues.–Sun. 10–5; closed Aug. 10–20 and Dec. 24–Jan. 7; when Mon. is national holiday, museum stays open Mon. and closes the following day.*

⓬ **Kindai Bijutsukan** (National Museum of Modern Art). The museum is known for its collection of 20th-century Japanese paintings and its ceramic treasures by Kanjiro Kawai, Rosanji Kitaoji, Shoji Hamada, and others. Established in 1903, it reopened in 1986 in a new building designed by Fumihiko Maki, one of the top contemporary architects in Japan. From the Dobutsuen-mae bus stop, walk down the street that leads to the Heian Shrine. The museum is on the left inside the torii. ✉ *Enshōji-chō, Okazaki, Sakyō-ku,* ☎ *075/761–4111.* 💴 *¥400 (more for special exhibitions).* 🕐 *Tues.–Sun. 9:30–5.*

★ ⓴ **Kiyomizu-dera.** Kiyomizu-dera is one of the most visited temples in Kyōto and is closely associated with the city's skyline. In the past, people would come here to escape the open political intrigue of Kyōto and to scheme in secrecy. Visually, Kiyomizu-dera is unique because it is built on a steep hillside. Part of its Main Hall is held up by 139 giant pillars. It is one of the few temples where you can walk around the veranda without removing your shoes.

The temple's location is marvelous—one reason for coming here is the view. From the wooden veranda there are fine views of the city and a breathtaking look at the valley below. "Have you the courage to jump from the veranda of Kiyomizu?" is a saying asked when someone sets out on a daring new venture.

Interestingly enough, Kiyomizu-dera does not belong to one of the local Kyōto Buddhist sects but rather to the Hossō sect that developed in Nara. The temple is dedicated to the popular 11-faced Kannon (Goddess of Mercy), who can bring about easy childbirth. Over time, Kiyomizu-dera has become "everyone's temple." You'll see evidence of this throughout the grounds, from the little Jizō Bosatsu statues (representing the god of travel and children) stacked in rows to the many *koma-inu* (mythical guard dogs) marking the pathways, which have been given by the temple's grateful patrons. The original Kiyomizu-dera was built here in 798, four years after Kyōto was founded. The current structure is a 1633 reconstruction.

Kiyomizu-zaka, the street that leads to the temple, is lined with shops selling souvenirs, religious articles, and ceramics. There are also tea shops where you can sample *yatsuhashi*, doughy, triangular sweets filled with cinnamon-flavored bean paste—a Kyōto specialty. Because of the immense popularity of the temple above it on the hill, this narrow slope is often crowded with sightseers and bus tour groups, but the magnificent temple is worth the struggle. From Kyōto Eki, take Bus 206 to the Kiyomizu-michi stop. From Kawai Kanjiro Kinenkan, cross the major avenue, Gojō-dōri, and walk up Higashi-ōji-dōri. The street to the right, Gojō-zaka, leads into Kiyomizu-zaka, which you'll take to the temple. ✉ *Kiyomizu 1-chōme, Higashiyama-ku.* 🎫 *¥300.* 🕐 *Daily 8–6.*

㉑ **Kōdai-ji.** This quiet nunnery was established in the early 17th century and only recently opened to the public. This temple was built as a memorial to Hideyoshi Toyotomi by his wife Kita-no-Mandokoro, who lived out her remaining days in the nunnery there. Kōdai-ji has gardens designed by Kobori Enshū, and the Kaisan-dō (Founder's Hall) has ceilings decorated in raised lacquer and paintings by artists of the Tosa school. The teahouse above on the hill, designed by tea master Sen-no-Rikyū, has a unique umbrella-shape bamboo ceiling and a thatched roof. From Kyōto Eki use Bus 206 to Higashiyama bus stop. 🎫 *¥500.* 🕐 *Daily 9–4:30 (9–4 in winter).*

⑱ **Kokuritsu Hakubutsukan** (Kyōto National Museum). This prestigious museum, with a collection of more than 8,000 works of art, is housed in two buildings. Exhibitions change regularly, but you can count on an excellent display of paintings, sculpture, textiles, calligraphy, ceramics, lacquerware, metalwork, and archaeological artifacts from its permanent collection. From Kyōto Eki take Bus 206 or 208 to the Sanjūsan-gen-dō-mae stop. The museum is across Higashi-ōji-dōri from Chisaku-in. ✉ *Yamato-ōji-dōri, Higashiyama-ku,* ☎ *075/541–1151.* 🎫 *¥400 (more for special exhibitions).* 🕐 *Tues.–Sun. 9–4:30.*

❼ **Konchi-in.** Though not on the same grounds as Nanzen-ji, this temple is in fact part of the Nanzen-ji complex. Its pair of gardens, designed by the famous tea master and landscape designer Enshū Kobori in 1632, is especially worth a visit. One has a pond in the shape of the Chinese character *kokoro* (heart). The other is a dry garden with a "sea of sand" and a backdrop of greenery borrowed from the mountains behind. The two rock groupings in front of a plant-filled mound are in the crane-and-tortoise style. Since ancient times these creatures have been associated with longevity, beauty, and eternal youth. In the feudal eras, the symbolism of the crane and the tortoise became very popular with the samurai class, whose profession often left them with only the hope of immortality. To get here, leave Nanzen-ji and take the side street to the left. ⊠ *86 Fukuchi-chō, Nanzen-ji, Sakyō-ku.* 💴 ¥400. ⊙ *Daily 8:30–5 (8:30–4:30 in winter).*

㉗ Kyōto Craft Center. This collection of stores is where Kyōto residents shop for fine contemporary and traditional crafts—ceramics, lacquerware, prints, and textiles. You can also find moderately priced souvenirs, such as dolls, coasters, bookmarks, and paper products. From Kyōto Eki take Bus 206 to the Gion stop. The center is on the corner of Shijō-dōri and Higashi-ōji-dōri. ⊠ *Higashi-Kitagawa, Hanami-kōji, Gion-Shijō-dōri, Higashiyama-ku,* 🕾 *075/561–9660.* ⊙ *Thurs.–Tues. 10–6.*

⑮ Kyōto Handicraft Center. Seven floors of everything Japanese, from dolls to cassette recorders, is on sale. The center caters to tourists with its English-speaking staff. It's a good place to browse, even if you end up deciding that prices are too high. From the Gion bus stop take Bus 202 or 206 five stops north on Higashi-ōji-dōri to Kumano Jinja-mae bus stop. From Kyōto Eki, use Bus 206; the center is across Maruta-machi-dōri from the Heian Jingū. (☞ Shopping, *below.*) ⊠ *Kumano Jinja Higashi, Sakyō-ku,* 🕾 *075/761–5080.* ⊙ *Daily 9:30–6 (9:30–5:30 in winter); closed Dec. 31–Jan. 3.*

❽ Kyōto International Community House. On expansive grounds, the center offers library and information facilities and rental halls for public performances. The bulletin board by the entryway is full of tips on housing opportunities, study, and events in Kyōto. The KICH also offers weekly lessons in tea ceremony, koto, calligraphy, and Japanese language at reasonable prices. The book *Easy Living in Kyōto* (available free) gives helpful information for a lengthy stay. The Community House is just off the intersection at the foot of the road to Nanzen-ji. ⊠ *2-1 Awata-guchi, Torii-chō, Sakyō-ku,* 🕾 *075/752–3010.* 💴 *Free.* ⊙ *Tues.–Sun. 9–9;. when Mon. is national holiday, Community House stays open Mon. and closes the following day.*

⑪ Kyōto-shi Bijutsukan (City Art Museum). This space serves mostly as a gallery for traveling shows and local art society exhibits. It owns a collection of Japanese paintings of the Kyōto school, a selection of which goes on display once a year. From the Dobutsu-en-mae bus stop, walk down the street that leads to the Heian Jingū. The museum is on the right inside the torii. ⊠ *Enshōji-chō, Okazaki, Sakyō-ku,* 🕾 *075/771–4107.* 💴 *Depends on exhibition, but usually around ¥800.* ⊙ *Tues.–Sun. 9–5 (enter by 4:30).*

㉒ Maruyama Kōen. This small park, home to the Maruyama Music Hall, is a place to rest weary feet, and there are usually a few wandering vendors around to supply refreshment. From Kyōto Eki take Bus 206 to the Higashiyama stop; the park is north of Kōdai-ji.

❾ Murin-an Garden. The property was once part of Nanzen-ji, but it was sold to Prince Yamagata, a former prime minister and advocate of the reforms that followed the Meiji Restoration. Unlike more traditional Japanese gardens, which adopt a more restrained and contained sense of harmony, Murin-an allows more freedom of movement. This is right in step with the Westernizing that the Meiji Restoration brought upon Japan. The garden is south of the Dobutsuen-mae bus stop. Enter from the side road on the other side of a canal. ☞ ¥300. ☉ *Daily 9–4:30; closed Dec. 29–Jan. 3.*

❻ Nanzen-ji. Like ☞ **Ginkaku-ji,** this former aristocratic retirement villa was turned into a temple on the death of its owner, Emperor Kameyama (1249–1305). The later Ōnin Civil War demolished the buildings, but some were resurrected during the 16th century, and Nanzen-ji has become one of Kyōto's most important temples, in part because it is the headquarters of the Rinzai sect of Zen Buddhism. You enter the temple through the 1628 **San-mon** (Triple Gate). This is the classic "gateless" gate of Zen Buddhism that symbolizes entrance into the most sacred part of the temple precincts. From the top floor of the gate there is a view of Kyōto spread out below. Whether or not you ascend the steep steps, give a moment to the statue of Goemon Ishikawa, a Robin Hood–style outlaw of Japan who hid in this gate until his eventual capture.

On through the gate is **Hōjō** (Abbot's Quarters), a National Treasure. Inside, the chambers are divided by screens with impressive 16th-century paintings. These wall panels of the *Twenty-four Paragons of Filial Piety and Hermits* are by Eitoku Kanō (1543–90) of the Kanō school—in effect the Kanō family, because the school consists of eight generations, Eitoku being from the fifth, of one bloodline. The Zen-style garden attached to the Hōjō has stones amid the sculpted trees and sand. This garden has been assigned several names; the one that stands out is "Leaping Tiger Garden."

Within Nanzen-ji's 27, pine-tree-covered acres are several other temples, known more for their gardens than for their buildings. One worth visiting if you have time is **Nanzen-in,** once the temporary abode of the Kameyama (1249–1305), who founded the temple. Nanzen-in holds a mausoleum and has a garden that dates to the 14th century; a small creek passes through it. Not long open to the public, Nanzen-in is not as famous as other temples, making it a peaceful place to visit. South from the Nomura Art Museum, follow the main path. The temple complex will be on your left. ☞ ¥350. ☉ *Nov.–Mar., daily 8:30–4:30; Apr.–Oct., daily 8:20–5.*

❺ Nomura Bijutsukan. Instead of bequeathing their villas to Buddhist sects, the modern wealthy Japanese tend to donate their art collections to museums. Such is the case here. Founder of the Daiwa Bank and a host of other companies, Tokushichi Nomura gave his collection of scrolls, paintings, tea ceremony utensils, ceramics, and other art objects to establish his namesake museum. The museum is south of Eikan-dō on the west side of the street. ✉ *61 Shimogawara-chō, Nanzen-ji, Sakyō-ku,* ☎ *075/751–0374.* ☞ ¥600. ☉ *Late Mar.–mid-June and mid-Sept.–early Dec., Tues.–Sun. 10–4:30 (enter by 4); when national holiday on Mon., museum is open and will close the following day.*

❷ Path of Philosophy. This walkway along the canal, known in Japanese as "Tetsugaku-no-michi," is lined with cherry trees, which are spectacular when in bloom. It has traditionally been a place for contemplative strolls since a famous scholar, Ikutaro Nishida, took his constitutional here. Now professors and students have to push their way through tourists who take the same stroll and whose interest lies mainly with the path's specialty shops. Along the Path are several coffee shops and small restaurants. **Omen** (☞ Dining, *below*), one block west of the Path of Philosophy, is an inexpensive, popular restaurant, known for its homemade white noodles. If you are desperate for Western food, you can try **Bobby Soxer** for pizza.

From Kyōto Eki take Bus 5 to Ginkaku-ji-michi bus stop. Walk east on the street that follows the canal. Just after the street crosses a north–south canal, the Path begins on your right.

㉙ **Ponto-chō Kaburenjō** (theater). Like Gion, Ponto-chō is known for its nightlife and geisha entertainment. At the north end of Pontochō-dōri, the Ponto-chō Kaburenjō presents geisha song-and-dance performances in the spring (May 1–24) and autumn (Oct. 15–Nov. 7). The theater is on the west side of the Kamo-gawa between Sanjō and Shijō streets. ✉ *Ponto-chō, Sanjō-sagaru, Nakagyo-ku,* ☎ *075/221–2025.*

★ ⑯ **Sanjūsangen-dō.** Everyone knows this temple as Sanjūsangen-dō even though it's officially called Rengeō-in. Sanjūsan means 33, which is the number of spaces between the 35 pillars that lead down the narrow, 394-ft-long hall of the temple. Enthroned in the middle of the hall is the 6-ft-tall, 1,000-handed Kannon—a National Treasure—carved by Tankei, a sculptor of the Kamakura period (1192–1333). Surrounding the statue are 1,000 smaller statues of Kannon, and in the corridor behind are 28 guardian deities who are protectors of the Buddhist universe. Notice the frivolous-faced Garuda, a bird that feeds on dragons. If you are wondering about the 33 spaces mentioned earlier, Kannon can assume 33 different shapes on her missions of mercy. Because there are 1,001 statues of Kannon in the hall, 33,033 shapes are possible. People come to the hall to see if they can find the likeness of a loved one (a deceased relative) among the 1,001 statues.

From Kyōto Eki take Bus 206 or 208 to the Sanjūsangen-dō-mae stop. The temple will be to the south, just beyond the Kyōto Park Hotel. ✉ *657 Sanjūsangen-dō Mawari-chō, Higashiyama-ku.* 🎫 *¥500.* ☉ *Daily 8–5 (9–4 in winter).*

Sannen-zaka and Ninen-zaka (Sannen and Ninen slopes). These two lovely winding streets are fine examples of old Kyōto, with their cobbled paths and delightful wooden buildings. This area is one of four historic preservation districts in Kyōto, and the shops along the way sell local crafts and wares such as *Kiyomizu-yaki* (Kiyomizu-style pottery), Kyōto dolls, bamboo basketry, rice crackers, and antiques. From Kiyomizu-dera turn right halfway down the Kiyomizu-zaka.

㉕ **Shōren-in.** More paintings by the Kanō school are on view at this temple, a five-minute walk north of Chion-in. Though the temple's present building dates only from 1895, the sliding screens of the Main Hall have the works of Motonobu Kanō, second-generation Kanō, and Mitsunobu Kanō of the sixth generation. The gardens of this temple are pleasant—with an immense camphor tree at the entrance gate and azaleas surrounding a balanced grouping of rocks and plants. It was no doubt more grandiose when Soami designed it in the 16th century, but with the addition of paths through the garden, it's a pleasant place to stroll. Another garden on the east side of the temple is sometimes attributed, probably incorrectly, to Kobori Enshū. Occasionally, koto concerts are held in the evening in the Soami garden. (Check with a Japan Travel Bureau office for concert schedules.) From Kyōto Eki, take Bus 206 to the Higashiyama-Sanjō stop. 🎫 *¥400.* ☉ *Daily 9–5; closed 1 day in Oct. or Nov. for a special Buddhist ceremony (no specific date is set).*

㉖ **Yasaka Jinja.** Your business and health problems might come to a resolution at this Shinto shrine—leave a message for the God of Prosperity and Good Health, to whom Yasaka Jinja is dedicated. Because it is close to the shopping districts, worshipers drop by for quick salvation. Especially at New Year, Kyōto residents flock here to ask for good fortune in the coming year. From Kyōto Eki use Bus 206 to the Gion bus

Pick up
the phone.

Pick up
the miles.

MCI Calling Card

415 555 1234 2244
J.D. SMITH

WorldPhone

Use your MCI Card® to make an international call from virtually anywhere in the world and earn frequent flyer miles on one of seven major airlines.

Enroll in an MCI Airline Partner Program today. In the U.S., call **1-800-FLY-FREE.** Overseas, call MCI collect at **1-916-567-5151.**

1. To use your MCI Card, just dial the WorldPhone access number of the country you're calling from.
   (For a complete listing of codes, visit www.mci.com.)
2. Dial or give the operator your MCI Card number.
3. Dial or give the number you're calling.

# Bahrain	800-002	# Kuwait	800-MCI (800-624)
# Brunei	800-011	Lebanon ÷	600-MCI (600-624)
# China ❖	108-12	# Macao	0800-131
For a Mandarin-speaking		# Malaysia (CC) ♦	800-0012
operator	108-17	# Philippines (CC) ♦	
# Cyprus ♦	080-90000	To call using PLDT ■	105-14
# Egypt ♦	355-5770	To call using PHILCOM ■	1026-14
(Outside of Cairo, dial 02 first)		Philippines IIIC via PLDT	
# Federated States of Micronesia	624	in Tagalog ■	105-15
# Fiji	004-890-1002	Philippines IIIC via PHILCOM	
# Guam (CC)	950-1022	in Tagalog ■	1026-12
# Hong Kong (CC)	800-1121	# Qatar ★	0800-012-77
# India (CC) ❖	000-127	# Saipan (CC) ÷	950-1022
# Indonesia (CC) ♦	001-801-11	# Saudi Arabia (CC)	1-800-11
Iran ÷	(Special Phones Only)	# Singapore	8000-112-112
# Israel (CC)	177-150-2727	# Sri Lanka	440-100
# Japan (CC) ♦		(Outside of Colombo, dial 01 first)	
To call using KDD ■	0039-121▶	# Syria	0800
To call using IDC ■	0066-55-121	# Taiwan (CC) ♦	0080-13-4567
To call using ITJ ■	0044-11-121	# Thailand ★	001-999-1-2001
# Jordan	18-800-001	# United Arab Emirates ♦	800-111
# Korea (CC)		Vietnam ●	1201-1022
To call using KT ■	009-14	Yemen	008-00-102
To call using DACOM ■	00309-12		
Phone Booths ÷	Red Button 03, then press ★		
Military Bases	550-2255		

Is this a great time, or what? :-)

Urban
planning.

stop; the shrine is just off Higashi-ōji-dōri. ⊠ *625 Gion-gawa, Kita-gawa, Higashiyama-ku.* ⌦ *Free.* ⊙ *24 hrs.*

EXPLORING WESTERN KYŌTO

Our exploration of western Kyōto begins with the major northern sights, Kitano Tenman-gū first of all. If you are short on time, start instead at Daitoku-ji. Southwest of this group of shrines and temples, Arashiyama is a delightful hillside area along and above the banks of the Oi-gawa.

As in eastern Kyōto, the city's western precincts are filled with remarkable religious architecture, in particular the eye-popping golden Kinkaku-ji and Kitano Tenman-gū, with its monthly flea market.

Numbers in the text correspond to numbers in the margin and on the Western Kyōto and Arashiyama map.

A Good Tour

Start with the Shinto **Kitano Tenman-gū** ㉚. Its flea market is held on the 25th of each month. About a five-minute walk north of Kitano is **Hirano Jinja** ㉛, another shrine with wonderful cherry trees in its garden. Now head for **Daitoku-ji** ㉜, a large 24-temple complex of the Rinzai sect of Zen Buddhism known for its architectural magnificence. From Hirano Jinja head east to the bus stop on Sembon-dōri. Climb on Bus 206 and take it north for about 10 minutes. Be sure to see the subtemple, **Daisen-in** ㉝, well known for its landscape paintings and for its *kare-sansui* (dry-style) garden. Other subtemples to visit if you have time are **Kōtō-in** and **Ryogen-in**. To get to the next stop, **Kinkaku-ji** ㉞, hop on Bus 12 west on Kita-ōji-dōri for a 10-minute ride to the Kinkaku-ji-mae stop. In contrast to Ginkaku-ji, which never got its silver-leaf covering, this temple *has* been coated with gold leaf. It is the impressive former retirement home of 14th-century Shōgun Yoshimitsu Ashikaga.

From Kinkaku-ji, walk back to the Kinkaku-ji-mae bus stop and take Bus 12 or 59 south for 10 minutes to the Ritsumeikan-Daigaku-mae stop. The nearby **Dōmoto Bijutsukan** ㉟ (art museum) exhibits paintings and sculpture by the 20th-century abstract artist Inshō Dōmoto. When you leave the museum, either get on Bus 12 or 59, or walk for about 10 minutes south; **Ryōan-ji** ㊱ will be on your right. Take all of the time you need here to be swept up by the temple's contemplative Zen garden.

From Ryōan-ji, it is about 1½ km (1 mi) farther south on Bus 26 to Myōshin-ji. En route you'll pass **Ninna-ji** ㊲ on the right, a temple that was once the palace of Emperor Omuro. From Ninna-ji, take the street veering to the left (southwest); within ¾ km (½ mi) you'll reach **Myōshin-ji** ㊳. Another option from Ryōan-ji is to take Bus 12 or 59 three stops south to Ninna-ji and then change to Bus 8 or 10. Here you will see Japan's oldest bell. The other (sub-) temple to visit here is **Taizō-in,** which contains the painting *Four Sages of Mt. Shang,* by Sanraku Kanō. Leave the temple complex by the south side and you can pick up Bus 61 or 62; both go southwest to **Uzumasa Eiga Mura** ㊴, Japan's equivalent of Hollywood's Universal Studios. If you have no interest in stopping off here—a visit will take at least two or three hours—continue on the bus to **Kōryū-ji** ㊵, a short walk south of Uzumasa Eiga Mura. Kōryū-ji is one of Kyōto's oldest temples, with many famous works of art, including the Miroku Bosatsu.

Because you are so close to the Arashiyama district, take the Keifuku Electric Railway Arashiyama Line west to Tenryū-ji Eki and the bamboo forests just to the north, which make a pleasant end to the day. You may get the chance to watch some cormorant fishing on the Oi-

Western Kyōto and Arashiyama

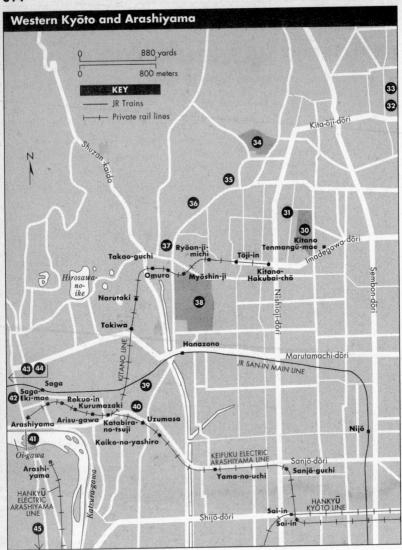

0 ──── 880 yards
0 ──── 800 meters

KEY
── JR Trains
╫─╫ Private rail lines

Shuzan-kaido

Kita-ōji-dōri

N

33

32

34

35

36

31

30

Kitano
Tenmangū-mae

Imadegawa-dōri

37 Ryōan-ji-
michi

Tōji-in

Takao-guchi

Omuro

Myōshin-ji

Kitano-
Hakubai-chō

Sembon-dōri

Hirosawa-
no-ike

Narutaki

38

Nishiōji-dōri

Tokiwa

Hanazono

Marutamachi-dōri

JR SAN-IN MAIN LINE

43 44

Saga

KITANO LINE

39

42 Saga-
Eki-mae

Rokuo-in

Kurumazaki

40

Uzumasa

Nijō

Arashiyama

Arisu-gawa

Katabira-
no-tsuji

41

Kaiko-no-yashiro

Oi-gawa

KEIFUKU ELECTRIC
ARASHIYAMA LINE

Yama-no-uchi

Sanjō-dōri

Sanjō-guchi

Arashi-
yama

HANKYŪ
ELECTRIC
ARASHIYAMA
LINE

Katsura-gawa

Shijō-dōri

Sai-in

HANKYŪ
KYŌTO LINE

Sai-in

45

gawa. If you decide to postpone Arashiyama until tomorrow, come back out here on the JR San-in Line from Kyōto Eki and get off at Saga Eki; or use the Keifuku Electric Railway to Arashiyama Eki.

If you would rather head back into central Kyōto, it is easy to do so from Kōryū-ji. Either take the bus (60–64) back past the Movie Village to JR Hanazono Eki, where the JR San-in Line will take you into Kyōto Eki, or take the privately owned Keifuku Electric Railway Arashiyama Line east to its last stop at Shijō-Ōmiya. This stop is on Shijō-dōri, from which Bus 201 or 203 can take you to Gion; or take Bus 26 to Kyōto Eki.

TIMING

If you are quick, you can cover all of these sights in a day. It would be better, while you're in western Kyōto, to skip a few sights so that you can make your way to Arashiyama in the afternoon.

Sights to See

㉟ Dōmoto Bijutsukan (Dōmoto Inshō Art Museum). The painting and sculpture exhibited here is by Inshō Dōmoto, the 20th-century abstract artist. From the Kinkaku-ji-mae bus stop, take Bus 12 or 59 south for 10 minutes to the Ritsumeikan-Daigaku-mae stop. ☒ *Kami-Yanagi-chō, Hirano, Kita-ku,* ☎ *075/463–1348.* ☜ *¥500.* ☉ *Tues.–Sun. 10–5; closed Dec. 28–Jan. 4.*

㉛ Hirano Jinja. This complex of four shrine buildings dates from the 17th century, but its ancestry is ancient. The shrine was brought from Nagaoka—Japan's capital between Nara and Kyōto—as one of many shrines used to protect the budding new Heian-kyō, as Kyōto was then called, during its formative years. The buildings are less remarkable than the gardens, with their 80 varieties of cherry trees. Take either Bus 50 or 52 from downtown Kyōto or Kyōto Eki. The ride takes a little more than half an hour. The shrine is about a 10-minute walk north of Kitano Tenmangū-mae bus stop. ☒ *Miyamoto-chō 1, Hirano, Kita-ku.* ☜ *Free.* ☉ *Daily 6 AM–5 PM.*

★ **㉞ Kinkaku-ji** (Temple of the Golden Pavilion). For a retirement home, Kinkaku-ji is pretty magnificent. Shōgun Yoshimitsu Ashikaga (1358–1409) had it constructed in 1393 for the time when he quit politics—the following year, in fact—to manage the affairs of state through the new shōgun, his 10-year-old son. On Yoshimitsu's death, his son followed his father's wishes and converted the villa into a temple named Rokuōn-ji. The structure is positioned, following the Shinden style of the Heian period, at the edge of the lake. The three-story pavilion is supported on pillars, extends over the pond, and is reflected in the calm waters. It is a beautiful sight, designed to suggest an existence somewhere between heaven and earth. The pavilion was the shōgun's political statement of his prestige and power. To underscore that statement, he had the ceiling of the third floor of the pavilion covered in gold leaf. Hence, not only the harmony and balance of the pavilion and its reflection, but also the richness of color shimmering in the light and in the water, make Kinkaku-ji one of Kyōto's most powerful visions.

In 1950 a student-monk with metaphysical aspirations torched Kinkaku-ji—he burned it to the ground. (Yukio Mishima's *Temple of the Golden Pavilion* is a fictional attempt to get into the mind of the student.) Kinkaku-ji was rebuilt in 1955 following the original design, except that all three stories were covered with gold leaf (after the shōgun's original intention) instead of only the third-floor ceiling.

Marveling at this pavilion, you might find it difficult to imagine the era in which Shōgun Yoshimitsu Ashikaga lived out his golden years. The country was in turmoil, and Kyōto residents suffered severe famines and plagues—local death tolls sometimes reached 1,000 souls a day. The temple is a short walk from the Kinkaku-ji-mae bus stop. From Daisen-in, the ride on Bus 12 is about 10 minutes. ✉ *1 Kinkaku-ji-chō, Kita-ku.* 🚊 *¥400.* ☉ *Apr.–Sept., daily 9–5:30; Oct.–Mar., daily 9–5.*

30 Kitano Tenman-gū. This shrine was originally dedicated to Tenjin, the god of thunder. Then, around 942, Michizane Sugawara was enshrined here. In his day, Michizane (*mee-chee-za-neh*) was a noted poet and politician—until Emperor Go-daigo ascended to the throne. Michizane was accused of treason and sent to exile on Kyūshū, where he died. For decades thereafter, Kyōto suffered inexplicable calamities. The answer came in a dream: Michizane's spirit would not rest until he had been pardoned. Because the dream identified Michizane with the god of thunder, Kitano Tenman-gū was dedicated to him. On top of that, Michizane's rank as minister of the right was posthumously restored. When that was not enough, he was promoted to the higher position of minister of the left, and later to prime minister.

Kitano Tenman-gū was also the place where Hideyoshi Toyotomi held an elaborate tea party, inviting the whole of Kyōto to join him—creating a major opportunity for the local aristocracy to show off their finest tea bowls and related paraphernalia. Apart from unifying the warring clans of Japan and attempting to conquer Korea, Toyotomi is remembered in Kyōto as the man responsible for restoring many of the city's temples and shrines during the late 16th century. The shrine's present structure dates from 1607. A large **flea market** is held on the grounds on the 25th of each month. There are food stalls and an array of antiques, old kimono, and other collectibles. Take either Bus 50 or 52 from downtown Kyōto or Kyōto Eki. The rides take a little more than a half hour. ✉ *Bakuro-chō, Kamigyō-ku. Shrine:* 🚊 *Free;* ☉ *Daily 5:30 AM–6 PM. Plum garden:* ☉ *Feb. and Mar., daily 10–4;* 🚊 *¥400 (includes green tea).*

37 Ninna-ji. The original temple here was once the palace of Emperor Omuro, who started the building's construction in 896. Needless to say, nothing of that remains. The complex of buildings that stands today was rebuilt in the 17th century. There is an attractive five-story pagoda (1637), and the Hon-dō (Main Hall), which was moved from the Imperial Palace, is also worth noting as a National Treasure. Its focus of worship is the Amida Buddha. Take either Bus 26 or 59 to the Omuro-Ninnai-ji stop. 🚊 *¥350.* ☉ *Daily 9–5.*

★ **36 Ryōan-ji.** The garden at Ryōan-ji, rather than the temple, attracts people from all over the world. Knowing that the temple belongs to the Rinzai sect of Zen Buddhism will help you appreciate the austere aesthetics of the garden. It is a *kare sansui,* a dry garden: just 15 rocks arranged in three groupings of seven, five, and three in gravel. From the temple's veranda, the proper viewing place, only 14 rocks can be seen at one time. Move slightly and another rock appears and one of the original 14 disappears. In the Buddhist world, the number 15 denotes completeness. You must have a total view of the garden to make it a whole and meaningful experience—and yet, in the conditions of this world, that is not possible.

If possible, visit Ryōan-ji in the morning before the crowds arrive and disturb the garden's contemplative quality. If you do need a moment or two to yourself, there is a small restaurant on the temple grounds near an ancient pond, where you can find solace with an expensive beer if need be. From a southbound 12 or 59 bus, the temple will be on your right. ✉ *13 Goryoshita-machi, Ryōan-ji, Ukyō-ku.* 🚊 *¥400.* ☉ *Mar.–Nov., daily 8–5; Dec.–Feb., daily 8:30–4:30.*

㊴ Uzumasa Eiga Mura. This is Japan's equivalent of Hollywood. And had Kyōto been severely damaged in World War II, this would have been the place to see old Japan. Traditional country villages, ancient temples, and old-fashioned houses make up the stage sets, and if you are lucky, a couple of actors dressed as samurai will be snarling at each other, ready to draw their swords. It is a fine place to bring children. For adults, whether it is worth the time touring the facilities and visiting the museum depends on your interest in Japanese movies and your willingness to give Eiga Mura (literally, "movie village") the two or three hours it takes to visit it. The village is on the 61, 62, and 63 bus routes. ✉ *10 Higashi-Hachigaoka-chō, Uzumasa,* ☎ *075/881-7716.* ☞ *¥2,000.* ⊙ *Daily 9–5 (9:30–4 in winter); closed Dec. 21–Jan. 1.*

DAITOKU-JI

㉜ Daitoku-ji. The name of this sizable temple of the Rinzai sect of Zen Buddhism refers to a complex of 24 temples in all, several of which are open to the public. The original temple was founded in 1319 by Priest Daito Kokushi (1282–1337), but fires during the Ōnin Civil War destroyed it in 1468. Most of the buildings you see today were built under the patronage of Hideyoshi Toyotomi. However, it is thought that Priest Ikkyū oversaw its development. Ikkyū, known for his rather startling juxtapositions of the sacred and the profane—he was both a poet and a priest—is reported to have said, "Brothels are more suitable settings for meditation than temples."

The layout of the temple is straightforward. Running from north to south are the Chokushi-mon (Gate of Imperial Messengers), the San-mon (Triple Gate), the Butsu-den (Buddha Hall), the Hattō (Lecture Hall), and the Hōjō (Abbot's Quarters). The 23 subtemples are on the west side of these main buildings and were donated mainly by the wealthy vassals of Toyotomi.

The **Chokushi-mon** originally served as the south gate of Kyōto's Imperial Palace when it was constructed in 1590. Then, Empress Meisho in the mid-17th century bequeathed it to Daitoku-ji. It is appreciated today for its curved-gable style, typical of the Momoyama period. The San-mon is noteworthy for the addition of its third story, designed by tea master Sen-no-Rikyū (1521–91), who is, by the way, buried in the temple grounds. Three subtemples in the complex are noteworthy: **Daisen-in, Kōtō-in,** and **Ryogen-in** (☞ *below*).

There are several ways to get to the temple from downtown Kyōto. Take the subway north from Kyōto Eki to Kitano-ji Eki-mae Eki, from which any bus going west along Kitaōji-dōri will take you to the Daitoku-ji-mae stop. You can also take Bus 12 north up Horikawa-dōri and disembark soon after the bus makes a left on Kita-ōji-dōri. From western Kyōto, Bus 204, which runs up Nishi-ōji-dōri, and Bus 206, which runs up Sembon-dōri, will also take you to the temple. ✉ *Daitoku-ji-chō, Murasakino, Kita-ku.* ☞ *Admission to different temples varies; the average is ¥500.* ⊙ *Temple hrs vary between 9 and 4.*

㉝ Daisen-in. Of all the subtemples at Daitoku-ji, Daisen-in is perhaps the best known—in part for its excellent landscape paintings by the renowned Soami (1465–1523), as well as its *karesansui* garden, which some attribute to Soami and others to Kogaku Soko (1465–1548). In the garden, the sand and stone represent the eternal aspects of nature, while the streams suggest the course of life. The single rock, once owned by Shōgun Yoshimasa Ashikaga, may be seen as a ship. Be aware that Daisen-in has its share of commercial accretions on site. *See* Daitoku-ji, *above,* for directions to Daisen-in. ☞ *¥400.* ⊙ *Daily 9–5 (9–4:30 in winter).*

Kōtō-in. This Daitoku-ji subtemple is famous for its long, maple-tree-lined approach and the single stone lantern that is central to the main garden. *See* Daitoku-ji, *above,* for directions to Kōtō-in. ⚏ *¥350.* ☉ *Daily 9–4:30 (enter by 4).*

Ryogen-in. This is another of the 24 subtemples in the Daitoku-ji complex. It is not as popular as some of the others that are open to the public, and it is often quiet and peaceful. Ryogen-in has five small gardens of moss and stone, one of which, on the north side, is the oldest in Daitoku-ji. *See* Daitoku-ji, *above,* for directions to Ryogen-in. ⚏ *¥350.* ☉ *Daily 9–4:30 (enter by 4).*

KŌRYŪ-JI

40 **Kōryū-ji.** One of Kyōto's oldest temples, Kōryū-ji was founded in 622 by Kawakatsu Hata in memory of Prince Shōtoku (572–621). Shōtoku, known for issuing the Seventeen-Article Constitution, was the first powerful advocate of Buddhism after it was introduced to Japan in 552. In the Hattō (Lecture Hall) of the main temple stand three statues, each a National Treasure. The center of worship is the seated figure of Buddha, flanked by the figures of the Thousand-Handed Kannon and Fukukenjaku-Kannon. In the Taishi-dō (Rear Hall), there is a wood statue of Prince Shōtoku, which is thought to have been carved by him personally. Another statue of Shōtoku in this hall was probably made when he was 16 years old.

The numerous works of art in Kōryū-ji's Reihō-den (Treasure House) include many National Treasures. The most famous of all is the **Miroku Bosatsu,** Japan's number one National Treasure. This image of Buddha is the epitome of serenity, and of all the Buddhas that you see in Kyōto, this is likely to be the one that will most captivate you. No one knows when it was made, but it is thought to be from the 6th or 7th century, carved, perhaps, by Shōtoku himself.

From Kyōto Eki, take the JR San-in Line to Hanazono Eki, and then board Bus 61. From Shijō-Ōmiya Eki in central Kyōto, take the Keifuku Electric Arashiyama Line to Uzumasa Eki. From central or western Kyōto, take Bus 61, 62, or 63 to the Uzumasa-Kōryūji-mae stop. ✉ *Hachigaoka-chō, Uzumasa, Ukyō-ku.* ⚏ *¥500.* ☉ *Mar.–Nov., daily 9–5; Dec.–Feb., daily 9–4:30.*

MYŌSHIN-JI

38 **Myōshin-ji.** Japan's oldest bell—cast in 698—hangs in the belfry near the South Gate of this 14th-century temple. When Emperor Hanazono died, his villa was converted into a temple; the work required so many laborers that a complex of buildings was built to house them. In all, there are some 40 structures here, though only four are open to the public. Beware of the dragon on the ceiling of Myōshin-ji's Hattō (Lecture Hall). Known as the "Dragon Glaring in Eight Directions," it looks at you wherever you stand. A sub-temple at Myōshin-ji to seek out is ☞ Taizō-in. Buses 61, 62, and 63 all stop at the Myōshin-ji-mae stop. ⚏ *¥400.* ☉ *Daily 9–4.*

Taizō-in. Within the Myōshin-ji complex, the temple Taizō-in has a famous painting by Sanraku Kanō called *Four Sages of Mt. Shang,* recalling the four wise men who lived in isolation on a mountain to avoid the reign of destruction. The garden of Taizō-in is gentle and quiet—a good place to rest. The temple structure, originally built in 1404, suffered like the rest of the Myōshin-ji complex in the Ōnin Civil War (1467–77) and had to be rebuilt. *See* Myōshin-ji, *above,* for directions to Taizō-in. ⚏ *¥400.* ☉ *Daily 9–5.*

Arashiyama and Katsura Rikyū (Detached Villa)

The pleasure of Arashiyama, the westernmost part of Kyōto, is the same as it has been for centuries. The gentle foothills of the mountains, covered with cherry and maple trees, are splendid, but it is the bamboo forests that really create the atmosphere of untroubled peace. It is no wonder that the aristocracy of feudal Japan came here to leave behind the famine, riots, and political intrigue that plagued Kyōto with the decline of the Ashikaga shogunate a millennium ago.

A Good Tour

The easiest ways to get to Arashiyama are by the JR San-in Line from Kyōto Eki to Saga Eki, or the Keifuku Electric Railway to Arashiyama Eki. South of Arashiyama Eki (Saga Eki is just north of Arashiyama Eki), the Oi-gawa flows under the **Togetsu-kyō Bridge** ㊶, where you can watch *ukai* (cormorant fishing) July and August evenings. The first temple to visit is **Tenryū-ji** ㊷—walk north from Arashiyama Eki or west from JR Saga Eki. Tenryū-ji is noted for a huge "Cloud Dragon" painted on the ceiling, and its garden for an arrangement of vertical stones in the large pond. One of the best ways to enjoy some contemplative peace is to walk the estate grounds of one of Japan's new elite—Denjiro Ōkōchi, a renowned silent-movie actor of samurai films. To reach Ōkōchi's villa, either walk through the temple garden or leave Tenryū-ji and walk north on a narrow street through a **bamboo forest** ㊸, one of the best you'll see around Kyōto. The **Ōkōchi Sansō** ㊹ will soon be in front of you, with its superb location. The final sight is the Imperial villa, **Katsura Rikyū** ㊺, which reaches to the heights of cultivated Shoin architecture and garden design. It is south of Arashiyama on the Hankyū Arashiyama Line; the station is south of the Togetsu-kyō Bridge. Take the train to Katsura Eki. You will need to make reservations for one of the scheduled guided tours of Katsura. To return to central Kyōto, take the Hankyū Kyōto Line from Katsura Eki to one of the central Kyōto Hankyū stations: Hankyū-Ōmiya, Karasuma, or Kawara-machi.

TIMING

You can see most of Arashiyama in a relaxed morning or afternoon, with the jaunt south to Katsura before or afterward.

Sights to See

㊸ **Bamboo forest.** Dense bamboo forests provide a feeling of composure and tranquility unlike the wooded tracts of the Western world. Nowadays they are few and far between. This one, which can be found on the way to Ōkōchi Sansō from Tenryū-ji, is a delight.

★ ㊺ **Katsura Rikyū** (Katsura Detached Villa). Built in the 17th century for Prince Toshihito, brother of Emperor Go-yōzei, Katsura is beautifully set in southwestern Kyōto on the banks of the Katsura-gawa, with peaceful views of Arashiyama and the Kameyama Hills. Perhaps more than anywhere else in the area, the setting is the most perfect example of Japanese integration of nature and architecture. The villa is fairly remote from other historical sites—allow several hours here.

Katsura's faultless craftsmanship is evident in its meticulous structural details. And though the various parts of the villa were built over several decades, beginning in 1620—by then the prince's garden was mostly finished—the overall architectural effect is remarkably unified. The main building includes the Nakasho-in, with three apartments containing nature paintings by the Kanō family, and the Hall for Imperial Visits, with decorations made from different kinds of rare wood, including sandalwood and ebony.

The garden is a study in the placement of plantings and stones and the progressive unfolding of views that the Japanese have so artfully mastered in garden design. Alongside a central pond, there are several rustic teahouses. The names of these teahouses—such as the **Geppa-rō**, Tower of Moonlit Waves, or the **Manji-tei**, Hut of Smiling Thoughts, or the important **Shōkin-tei**, Pine Zithern Pavilion—conjure up the physical control and delicate aesthetics of the tea ceremony. Look also for the **Shōka-tei** teahouse at the top of the garden.

Katsura requires special permission for a visit. To obtain this permission, applications must be made by mail or in person, preferably a day in advance. Indicate which of the tour times listed below you prefer. Application forms are available at JNTO (Japan National Tourist Organization) offices around the world. If you mail an application, enclose a self-addressed envelope with an international postage coupon. Send the application to the Imperial Household Agency (Kyōto Gyoennai, Kamigyō-ku, Kyōto, ☎ 075/211–1215). To apply in person (the Imperial Household Agency, at the Imperial Palace, is open weekdays 8:45–noon and 1–4), take the subway in the direction of Kitayama. Stay in the last car of the subway train; get off at the fifth stop, Imadegawa Station, and use the No. 6 exit. Walk a short distance south on Karasuma-dōri and go through the Inui Go-mon into the Imperial Palace. You will need your passport to pick up a permit, and you must be at least 20 years of age. The time of your tour will be stated, and you must not be late. The tour is in Japanese only, although a videotape introducing various aspects of the garden in English is shown in the waiting room before each tour begins.

To reach the villa, take the Hankyū Railway Line from one of the Hankyū Kyōto Line stations to Katsura Eki; then walk 10 minutes to the villa or take a taxi for a ¥530 fare. ✉ *Katsura Shimizu-chō, Ukyō-ku,* ☎ *075/381–2029.* 🎫 *Free.* ☉ *Tours at 10, 11, 2, and 3; closed Sat. (except in May, Oct., and Nov.), Sun., national holidays, Dec. 25–Jan. 25, and when special ceremonies are held (call the Imperial Household Agency to check).*

㊹ Ōkōchi Sansō. Walk the estate grounds of Ōkōchi's Mountain Villa to breathe in some contemplative peace—Denjiro Ōkōchi, a renowned silent-movie actor of samurai films and of one of Japan's new elite, chose for his home this location because of superb views of Arashiyama and Kyōto. Admission to the villa includes tea and cake to enjoy while you absorb nature's pleasures. ✉ *8 Tabuchiyama-chō, Ogurayama, Saga, Ukyō-ku,* ☎ *075/872–2233.* 🎫 *¥800.* ☉ *Daily 9–5.*

㊷ Tenryū-ji. For good reason is this known as the Temple of the Heavenly Dragon: Emperor Go-daigo, who had successfully brought an end to the Kamakura shogunate, was unable to hold on to his power. He was forced from his throne by Takauji Ashikaga. After Go-daigo died, Takauji had twinges of conscience. That is when Priest Musō Sōseki had a dream in which a golden dragon rose from the nearby Oi-gawa. He told the shōgun about his dream and interpreted it to mean the spirit of Go-daigo was not at peace. Worried that this was an ill omen, Takauji built Tenryū-ji in 1339 on the same spot where Go-daigo had his favorite villa. Apparently that appeased the spirit of the late emperor. In the Hattō (Lecture Hall), where today's monks meditate, a huge "Cloud Dragon" is painted on the ceiling. Now for the bad news. The temple was often ravaged by fire, and the current buildings are as recent as 1900; the painting of the dragon was rendered by 20th-century artist Shōnen Suzuki.

The **garden** of Tenryū-ji, however, dates from the 14th century and is one of the most notable in Kyōto. It is famed for the arrangement of vertical stones in its large pond and for its role as one of the first gardens to use "borrowed scenery," incorporating the mountains in the distance into the design of the garden. Take the JR San-in Line from Kyōto Eki to Saga Eki or the Keifuku Electric Railway to Arashiyama Eki. From Saga Eki, walk west; from Arashiyama Eki, walk north. ⊠ *68 Susuki-no-bamba-chō, Saga-Tenryū-ji, Ukyō-ku.* ☎ *Garden ¥500 (an additional ¥100 required to enter the temple building).* ⊘ *Apr.–Oct., daily 8:30–5:30; Nov.–Mar., daily 8:30–5.*

④① **Togetsu-kyō Bridge.** Spanning the Oi-gawa, the bridge is a popular spot from which you can watch ukai during the evening in July and August. Fishermen use cormorants to scoop up small sweet fish, which are attracted to the light from the flaming torches that the fishermen hang over their boats. The cormorants would swallow the fish for themselves, of course, but small rings around their necks prevent this. After about five fish, the cormorant has more than his gullet can hold. Then the fisherman pulls the bird back on a string, makes the bird regurgitate his catch, and sends him back for more. The best way to watch this spectacle is to join one of the charter passenger boats. Make a reservation using the number below, or call the Japan Travel Bureau (☎ 075/361–7241) or use your hotel information desk. Take the JR San-in Line from Kyōto Eki to Saga Eki or the Keifuku Electric Railway to Arashiyama Eki. The bridge is south of both stations. ☎ ¥1,960. *Reservations: Arashiyama Tsusen, 14-4 Nakaoshita-chō, Arashiyama, Nishikyō-ku,* ☎ *075/861–0223 or 075/861–0302.*

EXPLORING CENTRAL AND SOUTHERN KYŌTO

Our exploration of central Kyōto comes after eastern and western Kyōto because the sights here are likely to be convenient to your hotel, and you are likely to see each individually rather than combining them into a single itinerary. Treat sights south of Kyōto Eki the same way, choosing the most interesting for a morning or afternoon venture. The two major sights in central Kyōto are Nijō-jō and the Kyōto Gosho, the castle and the Imperial Palace. The latter requires permission, and you must join a guided tour. The most interesting southern Kyōto sights are Tōfuku-ji and Byōdō-in and the tea-producing Uji-shi.

Numbers in the text correspond to numbers in the margin and on the Central Kyōto map.

A Good Tour

The easiest ways to reach **Kyōto Gosho** ④⑥, the Imperial Palace, are to take the subway to Imadegawa or to take a bus to the Karasuma-Imadegawa stop. You will join the tour of the palace at the Seisho-mon entrance. If you go to Kyōto Gosho, **Nijō-jō** ④⑦ is easily combined on the same trip. The castle is a crass military intruder on imperial Kyōto's landscape. It was the Kyōto residence of the Tokugawa shogunate. Allow a couple of hours to see it all.

For an excursion into the culture of the tea ceremony, make your way west to the **Raku Bijutsukan** ④⑧, a museum that displays the Raku family's tea bowls. For another change of pace, visit the Nishijin silk-weaving district south from the Raku Museum on Horikawa-dōri at the corner of Imadegawa-dōri. At the **Nishijin Orimono** ④⑨ here, you can watch demonstrations. Buses 9, 12, 50, and 52 run up and down Horikawa-dōri past these two sights.

From the museum, the textile center, or Nijō-jō, take Bus 9 south on Horikawa-dōri. Disembark at the Kyōto Tōkyū Hotel. Across from

Fūzoku Hakubutsukan
(Kyōto Costume
Museum), **50**

Higashi-Hongan-ji, **52**

Kyōto Gosho
(Imperial Palace), **46**

Nijō-jō, **47**

Nishi-Hongan-ji, **51**

Nishijin Orimono
(Textile Center), **49**

Raku Bijutsukan, **48**

Tō-ji, **53**

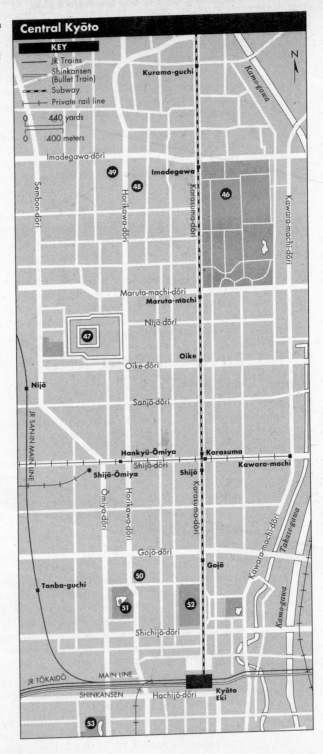

Central Kyōto

KEY
— JR Trains
Shinkansen
(Bullet Train)
Subway
Private rail line

0 — 440 yards
0 — 400 meters

Kurama-guchi

Kamo-gawa

Imadegawa-dōri

49 **48**

Imadegawa

46

Horikawa-dōri

Sembon-dōri

Karasuma-dōri

Kawara-machi-dōri

Maruta-machi-dōri
Maruta-machi

Nijō-dōri

47

Oike
Oike-dōri

Nijō

Sanjō-dōri

JR SAN-IN MAIN LINE

Hankyū-Ōmiya **Karasuma**
Shijō-dōri **Kawara-machi**
Shijō-Ōmiya **Shijō**

Ōmiya-dōri

Horikawa-dōri

Karasuma-dōri

Gojō-dōri

Kawara-machi-dōri

Takase-gawa

Gojō

50

Tanba-guchi

51 **52**

Kamo-gawa

Shichijō-dōri

JR TŌKAIDŌ   MAIN LINE

SHINKANSEN   Hachijō-dōri   **Kyōto
Eki**

53

N

the hotel, on the fifth floor of the Izutsu Building at the intersection of Horikawa and Shin-Hanaya-chō, is the **Fūzoku Hakubutsukan** ⑤⓪, which has clothes that were worn from the pre-Nara era, before 710, to the Meiji period, post-1868. The most famous temples in the area are **Nishi-Hongan-ji** ⑤① and **Higashi-Hongan-ji** ⑤②. Higashi-Hongan-ji is the largest wood structure in Japan. Nishi-Hongan-ji has interesting art objects, but the temple proper requires special permission to enter.

From Nishi-Hongan-ji, it is a 10-minute walk southeast to Kyōto Eki. If you have time, visit ⑤③, **Tō-ji** one of Kyōto's oldest temples, southwest of the station. It holds a flea market on the 21st of each month. The best way here is to leave Nishi-Hongan-ji by the west exit and take Bus 207 south on Ōmiya-dōri. Get off at the Tō-ji-Higashimon-mae bus stop, and Tō-ji will be across the street.

Points of interest south of Kyōto Eki require individual trips, returning each time to Kyōto Eki. **Byōdō-in,** a former 10th-century residence turned temple, is in Uji, a famous tea-producing area where you can taste the finest green tea. **Daigo-ji,** in the Yamashina suburb southeast of Kyōto, is a charming 9th-century temple with a five-story pagoda. To get to Daigo-ji, take the 40-minute Kyōto City Bus Higashi 9, or the Keihan Bus 12 from Keihan Sanjō, and get off at the Daigo-Samboin stop. **Tōfuku-ji** is a Zen temple of the Rinzai sect that ranks as one of the most important Zen temples in Kyōto. It is on the Bus 208 route from Kyōto Eki; or it is a 15-minute walk from Tōfuku-ji Eki on the JR Nara Line or the Keihan Main Line. You may want to combine a visit here with the **Fushimi-Inari Taisha,** farther south. This shrine is one of Kyōto's oldest and most revered, dedicated to the goddesses of agriculture and prosperity. Fushimi-Inari Taisha is a three-minute walk from the JR Nara Line's Inari Eki.

TIMING

The temples and shrines in southern Kyōto are a distance from each other and so traveling time can eat into your day. On the other hand, central Kyōto's sights are fairly close to each other and quickly accessible by bus or taxi. A morning would be mostly taken up with the Imperial Palace and Nijō-jō (remember that the Imperial Palace is closed Saturday afternoon and Sunday and also all day on the second and fourth Saturday of the month).

Sights to See

★ **Byōdō-in.** South of Kyōto in Uji-shi, this temple was originally the villa of a 10th-century member of the influential Fujiwara family. The Amida-dō, also called the Phoenix Hall, was built in the 11th century by the Fujiwaras and is still considered one of Japan's most beautiful religious buildings—something of an architectural folly—where heaven is brought close to earth. There is also a magnificent statue of a seated Buddha by one of Japan's most famous 11th-century sculptors, Jōchō. Uji itself is a famous tea-producing district, and the slope up to the temple is lined with shops where you can sample the finest green tea and pick up a small package to take home. Take the JR train to Uji Eki; from there, the temple is a 12-minute walk. ✉ Ujirenge, Uji-shi, ☎ 0774/21–2861. ☑ ¥400. ☉ Mar.–Nov., daily 8:30–5; Dec.–Feb., daily 9–4.

Daigo-ji. This temple was founded in 874. Over the succeeding centuries, other buildings were added and its gardens expanded. Its five-story pagoda, which dates from 951, is reputed to be the oldest existing structure in Kyōto. By the late 16th century, the temple had begun to decline in importance and showed signs of neglect. Then Hideyoshi Toyotomi paid a visit one April, when the temple's famous cherry trees were in blossom. Hideyoshi ordered the temple restored. Be sure also to see the paintings by the Kanō school in the smaller **Sambo-in.** To reach Daigo-ji in the southeast suburb of Yamashina, take City Bus Higashi 9 or the Keihan Bus 12 from Keihan Sanjō, and disembark at the Daigo-Sambo-in stop. The ride takes about 40 minutes. ⊠ *22 Higashi Uji-chō, Fushimi-ku.* ☎ *¥700.* ⊙ *Daily 9–5 (9–4 in winter).*

Fushimi-Inari Taisha. One of Kyōto's oldest and most revered shrines, the Fushimi-Inari is dedicated to the goddesses of agriculture (rice and rice wine) and prosperity. It also serves as the headquarters for all the 40,000 shrines representing Inari. The shrine is noted for its bronze foxes and for some 10,000 small torii, donated by the thankful, which stretch up the hill behind the structure. Take the JR Nara Line to Inari Eki, from which it is a three-minute walk to the shrine. From Tōfuku-ji, join the JR train at Tōfuku-ji Eki and go one stop south, toward Nara. ⊠ *68 Fukakusa Yabu-no-uchi-chō, Fushimi-ku.* ☎ *Free.* ⊙ *Daily sunrise–sunset.*

★ ⑤⓪ **Fūzoku Hakubutsukan** (Kyōto Costume Museum). It is well worth a stop here to marvel at the range of fashion that starts in the pre-Nara era and works up through the historical eras to the Meiji period. It is one of the best of its kind and, in its own way, gives an account of the history of Japan. Exhibitions change twice a year, with each exhibition highlighting a specific period in Japanese history. From the Raku Museum, the Nishijin Textile Center, or Nijō-jō, take Bus 9 south on Horikawa-dōri. Disembark at the Kyōto Tōkyū Hotel. The museum is across from the Tōkyū Hotel on the fifth floor of the Izutsu Building at the intersection of Horikawa and Shin-Hanaya-chō. ⊠ *Izutsu Bldg., Shimogyō-ku,* ☎ *075/361–8388.* ☎ *¥400.* ⊙ *Mon.–Sat. 9–5; closed June 1–19 and Dec. 16–Jan. 6.*

⑤② **Higashi-Hongan-ji.** Until the early 17th century Higashi-Hongan-ji and ☞ Nishi-Hongan-ji were one temple. Then Ieyasu Tokugawa took advantage of a rift among the Jōdo Shinshu sect of Buddhism and, to diminish its power, split them apart into two different factions. The original faction has the west temple, Nishi-Hongan-ji, and the latter faction the eastern temple, Higashi-Hongan-ji.

The rebuilt (1895) structure of Higashi-Hongan-ji is the second-largest wooden structure in Japan, after Nara's Daibutsu-den. The **Daishi-dō** is a double-roofed structure that is admirable for its curving, swooping lines. Inside are portraits of all the head abbots of the Jōdo Shinshu sect, but, unfortunately, it contains fewer historical objects of interest than does its rival, Nishi-Hongan-ji. From Kyōto Eki, walk 500 yards northwest; from the costume museum walk south on Horikawa-dōri and you will come to Nishi-Hongan-ji first. ⊠ *Shichijō-agaru, Karasuma-dōri, Shimogyō-ku.* ☎ *Free.* ⊙ *Daily 9–4.*

④⑥ **Kyōto Gosho** (Imperial Palace). The present palace is a third-generation construction. The original, built for Emperor Kammu to the west of the present site, burned down in 1788. A new palace, modeled after the original, then went up on the present site, but it, too, ended in flames. The present structure was completed in 1855, which gave it time to house only two emperors, including the young emperor Meiji before he moved his Imperial Household to Tōkyō. On the 30-minute tour, you will only have a chance for a brief glimpse of the Shishin-den— the hall where the inauguration of emperors and other important imperial ceremonies take place—and a visit to the gardens. Though a trip to the Imperial Palace is on most people's agenda and though it fills a fair amount of space in downtown Kyōto, it holds somewhat less interest than do some of the older historic buildings in the city. The palace is near the Imadegawa subway and Karasuma-Imadegawa bus stops. Guided tours start at the Seisho-mon entrance.

To visit the Imperial Palace, arrive before 9:40 AM for the 50-min, 10 AM guided tour in English. Present yourself, along with your passport, at the office of the Kunaichō (Imperial Household Agency) in the palace grounds. For the 2 PM guided tour in English, arrive by 1:40 PM. ⊠ *Kunaichō, Kyōto Gyoen-nai, Kamigyō-ku,* ☎ *075/211–1211.* 🎫 *Free.* ⊙ *Office weekdays 8:45–noon and 1–4, Sat. 8:45–noon (Sat. afternoon tours only on 1st and 3rd Sat. of month); no tours Sun.*

★ ➍➐ **Nijō-jō.** Nijō-jō was the local Kyōto address for the Tokugawa shogunate. Dominating central Kyōto, it is an intrusion, both politically and artistically. The man who built the castle in 1603, Ieyasu Tokugawa, did so to emphasize that political power had been completely removed from the emperor and that he alone determined the destiny of Japan. As if to emphasize that statement, he built and decorated his castle with such ostentation as to make the populace cower with his wealth and power. This kind of display was antithetical to the refined restraint of Kyōto's aristocracy.

Ieyasu Tokugawa had risen to power through skillful politics and treachery. His military might was unassailable, and that is probably why his Kyōto castle had relatively modest exterior defenses. However, as he well knew, defense against treachery is never certain. The interior of the castle was built with that in mind. Each building had concealed rooms where bodyguards could maintain a watchful eye for potential assassins, and the corridors had built-in "nightingale" floors, so no one could walk in the building without making noise. Rooms were locked only from the inside, thus no one from the outer rooms could gain access to the inner rooms without admittance. The outer rooms were kept for visitors of low rank and were adorned with garish paintings that would impress them. The inner rooms were for the important lords, whom the shōgun would impress with the refined, tasteful paintings of the Kanō school.

The opulence and grandeur of the castle were, in many ways, a snub to the emperor. They relegated the emperor and his palace to insignificance, and the Tokugawa family even appointed a governor to manage the emperor and the imperial family. The Tokugawa shōguns were rarely in Kyōto. Ieyasu stayed in the castle three times, the second shōgun twice, including the time in 1626 when the emperor Gomizuno-o was granted an audience. After that, for the next 224 years, no Tokugawa shōgun came to Kyōto. The castle started to fall into disrepair and neglect. Only when the Tokugawa shogunate was under pressure from a failing economy, and international pressure developed to open Japan to trade, did the 14th shōgun, Iemochi Tokugawa (1846–66), come to Kyōto to confer with the emperor. The emperor told the shōgun to rid Japan of foreigners, but Iemochi did not have the strength. As the shōgun's power continued to wane, the 15th and last shōgun, Keiki Tokugawa (1837–1913), spent most of his time in Nijō-jō. Here he resigned, and the imperial decree was issued that abolished the shogunate after 264 years of rule.

After the Meiji Restoration in 1868, Nijō-jō became the Kyōto Prefectural Office until 1884; during that time, it suffered from acts of vandalism. Since 1939, the castle has belonged to the city of Kyōto, and considerable restoration work has taken place.

You enter the castle through the impressive **Kara-mon** (Chinese Gate). Notice that you must turn right and left at sharp angles to make this entrance—a common attribute of Japanese castles, designed to slow the advance of any attacker. From the Kara-mon, the carriageway leads to the **Ni-no-maru Palace** (Second Inner Palace), the five buildings of which are divided into many chambers. The outer buildings were for visits by men of lowly rank, the inner ones for higher ranks. The most notable room, the Ōhiroma (Great Hall), is easy to recognize. In the room, figures in costume reconstruct the occasion when Keiki Tokugawa returned the power of government to the emperor. This spacious hall was where, in the early 17th century, the shōgun would sit on a raised throne to greet important visitors seated below him. The sliding screens of this room have magnificent paintings of forest scenes.

As impressive as the Ni-no-maru Palace is the garden created by landscape designer Kobori Enshū shortly before Emperor Gomizuno-o's visit in 1626. Notice the crane and tortoise islands flanking the center island (the land of paradise). The symbolic meaning is clear: strength and longevity. The garden was originally designed with no deciduous trees, for the shōgun did not wish to be reminded of the transitory nature of life by autumn's falling leaves.

The other major building on the grounds is the **Hon-maru Palace**, but, because it is a replacement for the original that burned down in the 18th century, Hon-maru holds less interest than Ni-no-maru. The castle is on the 9, 12, 50, and 52 bus lines; get off at Nijō-jō-mae. ✉ *Horikawa Nishi-Iru, Nijō-dōri, Nakagyō-ku,* ☎ *075/841–0096.* 🎫 *¥500.* ⊙ *Daily 8:45–5 (enter by 4); closed Dec. 26–Jan. 4.*

❺❶ Nishi-Hongan-ji. You might consider applying for permission to visit this temple, as it has so many marvelous artifacts from the 16th century. These were confiscated from Hideyoshi Toyotomi's Jurakudai Palace in Kyōto and from Fushimi-jō by Ieyasu Tokugawa, who had the buildings dismantled in an attempt to erase the memory of his predecessor.

Hideyoshi Toyotomi was quite a man. Though most of the initial work in unifying Japan was accomplished by the warrior Nobunaga Oda (he was ambushed a year after defeating the monks on Hiei-zan), it was Hideyoshi who completed the job. Not only did he stop civil strife, but he also restored the arts. For a brief period (1582–98), Japan entered one of the most colorful periods of its history. How Hideyoshi achieved his feats is not exactly known. One legend relates that he was the son of the emperor's concubine. She had been much admired by a man to whom the emperor owed a favor, so the emperor gave the concubine to him. Unknown to either of the men, she was soon with child, namely, Hideyoshi. In fact, Hideyoshi was brought up as a farmer's son. His nickname was Saru-san (Mr. Monkey), because he was small and ugly. Whatever his origins (he changed his names frequently), he brought peace to Japan after decades of civil war.

Because much of what was dear to Hideyoshi Toyotomi was destroyed by the Tokugawas, it is only at Nishi-Hongan-ji that you can see the artistic works closely associated with his personal life, including the great **Kara-mon** (Chinese Gate) and the **Daisho-in,** both brought from Fushimi-jō, and the **Nō stage** from Jurakudai Palace.

Nishi-Hongan-ji is on Horikawa-dōri, a couple of blocks north of Shichijō-dōri. Visits to some of the buildings are permitted four times a day on application from the temple office. Prior to leaving home, write to the temple (enclosing a self-addressed envelope with an international postage coupon) at Shichijō-agaru, Horikawa-dōri, Shimogyō-ku. Give your name, the number of people in your party, and the day and time you would like to visit. You can also phone for an appointment after you arrive in Kyōto. ☎ *075/371–5181; because you'll probably experience language problems, ask your hotel to make the arrangements for you. Tours of Daisho-in (in Japanese) are given occasionally throughout the year. Call for information. Reservations essential. Shichijō-agaru, Horikawa-dōri, Shimogyō-ku.* ✉ *Free.* ⊙ *Mar.–Apr. and Sept.–Oct., daily 5:30 AM–5:30 PM; May–June and July–Aug., daily 5:30 AM–6 PM; Nov.–Dec. and Jan.–Feb., daily 6 AM–5 PM.*

49 **Nishijin Orimono** (Textile Center). The Nishijin district still hangs on to the artistic thread of traditional Japanese silk weaving. At Nishijin Orimono demonstrations are given of age-old weaving techniques, and fashion shows and special exhibitions are presented. On the mezzanine, you can buy kimono and gift items, such as *happi* (workmen's) coats and silk purses. The center is on the 9 and 12 bus routes, south of the ☞ **Raku Museum**, at the corner of Horikawa-dōri and Imadegawa-dōri. ✉ *Horikawa-dōri, Imadegawa-Minami-Iru, Kamigyō-ku,* ☎ *075/451–9231.* ✉ *Free.* ⊙ *Daily 9–5.*

48 **Raku Bijutsukan.** Any top collector of tea-ceremony artifacts is likely to have a Raku bowl in his or her collection. Here you'll find tea bowls made by members of the Raku family, whose roots can be traced back to the 16th century. As a potter's term in the West, *raku* refers to a low-temperature firing technique, but the word originated with this family, who made exquisite tea bowls for use in the shōgun's tea ceremonies. The museum is on Horikawa-dōri, two blocks south of Imadegawa-dōri; it is on the 9 and 12 bus routes. ✉ *Aburakōji, Nakadachuri-agaru, Kamigyō-ku,* ☎ *075/414–0304.* ✉ *¥800 (additional charge for special exhibitions).* ⊙ *Tues.–Sun. 10–4; closed Aug. 14–17 and Dec. 27–Jan. 5.*

Tōfuku-ji. In all, two dozen subtemples and the main temple compose the complex of this Rinzai sect Zen temple, which ranks as one of the most important in Kyōto, along with the Myōshin-ji and Daitoku-ji. Southeast of Kyōto Eki, Tōfuku-ji was established in 1236. Autumn is an especially fine time for visiting, when the burnished colors of the maple trees add to the pleasure of the gardens. There are at least three ways to get to Tōfuku-ji: Bus 208 from Kyōto Eki; a JR train on the Nara Line to Tōfuku-ji Eki; or a Keihan Line train to Tōfuku-ji Eki. From the trains, it is a 15-minute walk to the temple. Consider combining a visit here with one to ☞ **Fushimi-Inari Taisha** farther south. ✉ *Hon-machi 15-chōme, Higashiyama-ku.* ✉ *¥300.* ⊙ *Daily 9–4.*

53 **Tō-ji.** Established by imperial edict in 796 and called Kyō-ō-gokoku-ji, Tō-ji was built to guard the city. It was one of the two temples that Emperor Kammu permitted to be built in the city. He had enough of the powerful Buddhists during his days in Nara. The temple was later given to Priest Kūkai (Kōbō Daishi), who began the Shingon sect of Buddhism. Tō-ji became one of Kyōto's most important temples.

Fires and battles during the 16th century destroyed the temple buildings, but many were rebuilt, including the Kon-dō (Main Hall) in 1603. The Kō-dō (Lecture Hall), on the other hand, has managed to survive the ravages of war since it was built in 1491. Inside this hall are 15 original statues of Buddhist gods that were carved in the 8th and 9th centuries. Perhaps Tōji's most eye-catching building is the 180-ft, five-story pagoda, reconstructed in 1695.

An interesting time to visit the temple is on the 21st of each month, when a flea market, known locally as Kōbō-san, is held. Antique kimono, fans, and other memorabilia can sometimes be found at bargain prices, if you know your way around the savvy dealers. Many elderly people flock to the temple on this day to pray to Kōbō Daishi, the temple's founder, and to shop. From Kyōto Eki take the Kinki Nippon Electric Train one stop to Tō-ji Eki or foot the 10-minute walk west from the central exit of JR Kyōto Eki. The 207 bus also runs past Tō-ji: either south from Gion then west, or west from Karasuma-dōri along Shijō-dōri then south. Get off at the Tō-ji-Higashimon-mae stop. ⊠ *1 Kujō-chō, Minami-ku.* 🚏 *Main buildings* ¥500. ☺ *Daily 9–4:30.*

EXPLORING NORTHERN KYŌTO

Hiei-zan and Ōhara are the focal points in the northern suburbs of Kyōto. Ōhara was for several centuries a sleepy Kyōto backwater surrounded by mountains. Although it is now catching up with the times, it still has a feeling of old Japan, with several temples that deserve visiting. Hiei-zan is a fount of Kyōto history. On its flanks Saichō founded Enryaku-ji and with it the vital Tendai sect of Buddhism. It is an essential Kyōto site, and walking on forested slopes among its 70-odd temples is one reason to make the trek to Hiei-zan.

A Good Tour

To get to Ōhara, take private Kyōto Line Bus 17 or 18 from Kyōto Eki and get out at the Ōhara bus stop. This is about a 90-minute ride; it costs ¥480. From the bus station, walk northeast for about seven minutes along the signposted road to **Sanzen-in,** a small Tendai-sect temple on delightful grounds with a remarkable carved Amida Buddha. Two hundred yards from Sanzen-in is the quiet **Jikkō-in,** where you can drink traditional *matcha* (powdered tea ceremony tea). On the ★ other side of Ōhara and the Takano-gawa is **Jakkō-in,** a romantic temple full of pathos and a sanctuary for nuns. To get here, return to the Ōhara bus stop and walk 20 minutes north up the road.

The next stop is **Hiei-zan.** Take the Kyōto Line bus (16, 17, or 18) down the main highway, Route 367, to the Yase Yuenchi bus stop, next to Yase Yuen Eki. You'll see the entrance to the cable car on your left. It departs every 30 minutes, and you can transfer to the ropeway at Hiei for the remaining distance to the top. At the summit is an observatory with panoramic views of the mountains and of Biwa-ko (Lake Biwa). From the observatory, a serpentine mountain path leads to **Enryaku-ji,** which remains an important center of Buddhism. Before day's end, return from Hiei-zan by taking the Eizan Railway from Yase Yuen Eki to Shūgaku-in Eki and making a 15-minute walk to the **Shūgaku-in Imperial Villa,** which consists of a complex of three palaces. The return to downtown Kyōto takes an hour on Bus 5 to Kyōto Eki, or 20 minutes by Keifuku Eizan train to Demachi-Yanagi Eki, just north of Imadegawa-dōri.

One final sight, closer to central Kyōto, is **Kamigamo Jinja,** built by the legendary warrior Kamo. It is near the end of the Bus 9 route north from Kyōto Eki by the Kamigamo-Misonobashi stop.

TIMING

It's best to make this a day trip to allow for unhurried exploring in Ōhara and on Hiei-zan. If you are short of time, you could cover the sights in about four hours.

Sights to See

Hiei-zan and Enryaku-ji. From the observatory at the top of Hiei-zan, a serpentine mountain path leads to Enryaku-ji, which remains a vital center of Buddhism. At one time it consisted of 3,000 buildings and had its own standing army. That was its downfall. Enryaku-ji really began in 788. Emperor Kammu, the founding father of Kyōto, requested Priest Saichō (767–822) to establish a temple on Hiei-zan to protect the area (including Nagaoka, which was the current capital) from the evil spirits. Demons and evil spirits were thought to come from the northeast, and Hiei-zan was a natural barrier between the fledgling city and the northeastern Kin-mon (Devil's Gate), where devils would pass. The temple's monks were to serve as lookouts and, through their faith, keep evil at bay.

The temple grew, and, because neither women nor police were allowed on its mountaintop sanctuary, criminals also flocked here, ostensibly to seek salvation. By the 11th century, the temple had formed its own army to secure order on its estate. In time, this army grew and became stronger than that of most other feudal lords, and the power of Enryaku-ji came to threaten Kyōto. No imperial army could manage a war without the support of Enryaku-ji, and when there was no war, Enryaku-ji's armies would burn and slaughter monks of rival Buddhist sects. Not until the 16th century was there a force strong enough to sustain an assault on the temple. With accusations that the monks had concubines and never read the sutras, Nobunaga Oda (1534–82), the general who unified Japan by ending the Ōnin Civil Wars (1467–77), attacked the monastery in 1571 to rid it of its evil. In the battle, monks were killed, and most of the buildings were destroyed. Structures standing today were built in the 17th century.

Enryaku-ji is divided into three precincts: the Eastern Precinct, where the main building in the complex, the **Kompon Chū-dō**, stands; the Western Precinct, with the oldest building, the **Shaka-dō**; and the Yokawa district, a few miles north. The Kompon Chū-dō dates from 1642, and its dark, cavernous interior quickly conveys the sense of mysticism for which the esoteric Tendai sect is known. Giant pillars and a coffered ceiling shelter the central altar, which is surrounded by religious images and sacred objects. The ornate lanterns that hang before the altar are said to have been lit by Saichō himself and have remained so throughout the centuries.

The Western precinct is where Saichō founded his temple and where he is buried. An incense burner wafts smoke before his tomb, which lies in a small hollow. The peaceful atmosphere of the cedar trees surrounding the main structures—Jōdo-in, Ninai-dō, and Shaka-dō—offers an imitation of the essence of the life of a Tendai Buddhist monk, who has devoted his life to the esoteric. Enryaku-ji is still an important training ground for Buddhism, on a par with the temples at Kōya-san (☞ Chapter 5). The value of coming here is Enryaku-ji's overall aura of spiritual profundity rather than its particular buildings. It is experiential, and, though the temple complex is only a twentieth of its original size, the magnitude of the place and the commitment to esoterica pursued here are awesome.

Take Kyōto Line Bus 16, 17, or 18 up the main highway, Route 367, to the Yase Yuenchi bus stop, next to Yase Yuen Eki. You'll see the entrance to the cable car on your left. It departs every 30 minutes, and you can transfer to the ropeway at Hiei for the remaining ride to the summit, where there is an observatory with panoramic views of the mountains and of Biwa-ko. *Hiei-zan ropeway:* ☎ *¥500 mid-Mar.–Nov., ¥300 Dec.–mid-Mar.* ☉ *Apr.–Sept., daily 9–6; Oct.–Mar., daily 9–5 (mid-July–late Aug., observatory stays open until 9). Enryaku-ji:* ✉ *4220 Sakamoto-hon-machi, Ōtsu-shi.* ☎ *¥400.* ☉ *Mar.–Nov., daily 8:30–4:30; Dec.–Feb., daily 9–4.*

★ **Jakkō-in.** In April 1185, the Taira clan met its end in a naval battle against the Minamoto clan. For two years, Yoshitsune Minamoto had been gaining the upper hand in the battles. In this one, the Minamotos slaughtered the Tairas, making the Seto Nai-kai (Inland Sea) run red with Taira blood. Recognizing that all was lost, the Taira women drowned themselves, taking with them the young infant Emperor An-toku. His mother, Kenreimonin, too, leapt into the sea, but Minamoto soldiers snagged her hair with a grappling hook and hauled her back on board their ship. She was the sole surviving member of the Taira clan, and at 29, she was a beautiful woman.

Taken back to Kyōto, Kenreimonin shaved her head and became a nun. First, she had a small hut at Choraku-ji (☞ Exploring Eastern Kyōto, *above*), and when that collapsed in an earthquake, she was accepted at Jakkō-in. She was given a 10-ft-square cell made of brushwood and thatch and was left with images of her drowning son and her massacred relatives. Here she lived in solitude and sadness until, 27 years later, death erased her memories and with her the Taira. Her mausoleum is in the temple grounds.

When Kenreimonin came to Jakkō-in, it was far removed from Kyōto. Now Kyōto's sprawl reaches this far out, but the temple, hidden in trees, is still a place of solitude and a sanctuary for nuns. It is easy to relive the experience eight centuries ago, when Kenreimonin walked up the tree-shrouded path to the temple with the autumn drizzle falling and reflecting her tears. From Kyōto Eki take Kyōto Line Bus 17 or 18 for a 90-minute ride and get out at the Ōhara bus stop; the fare is ¥480. Walk 20 minutes or so along the road leading to the northwest. ☜ *¥500.* ⊙ *Daily 9–5 (10–4:30 in winter).*

★ **Jikkō-in.** At this small, little-frequented temple you can sit, relax, and have a taste of the powdered *matcha* of the tea ceremony. To enter, ring the gong on the outside of the gate, and then wander through the carefully cultivated garden. Take Kyōto Line Bus 17 or 18 for 90 minutes from Kyōto Eki; the fare is ¥480. From the Ōhara bus stop, walk northeast for about seven minutes along the signposted road. Jikkō-in is 200 yards from ☞ **Sanzen-in.** ☜ *¥500.* ⊙ *Daily 9–5.*

Kamigamo Jinja. Along with its sister shrine, Shimogamo Jinja (farther south on the Kamo-gawa), Kamigamo was built by the warrior Kamo. Such is Kamo's fame that even the river that flows by the shrine and through the center of Kyōto bears his name. Kamigamo has always been associated with Wakeikazuchi, a god of thunder, rain, and fertility. Now the shrine is famous for its Aoi (hollyhock) Festival, which started in the 6th century when people thought that the Kamigamo deities were angry at being neglected. Now held every May 15, the festival consists of 500 people wearing Heian-period costumes riding on horseback or in ox-drawn carriages from the Imperial Palace to Shimogamo and then to Kamigamo. To get to the shrine, take Bus 9 north from Kyōto Eki or from a stop on Horikawa-dōri. Or take the subway north to Kitayama Station, from which the shrine is 20 minutes on foot northwest. ✉ *339 Motoyama, Fushimi-ku.* ☜ *Free.* ⊙ *Daily 9–4:30.*

Miho Museum. Built in and around a mountaintop and thoughtfully landscaped—its wooded setting in the hills of Shigariki north of Kyōto is part of the experience of a visit here—the new, I. M. Pei–designed Miho Musem is home of the remarkable Shumei Family Collection of traditional Japanese art and Asian and Western antiquities. An Egyptian falcon-headed deity, a Roman fresco, a Chinese tea bowl, and a Japanese Bosatsu (Buddha) are among the superb pieces here. A restaurant on site serves bentō with organic ingredients, and a tearoom serves Japanese and Western beverages and desserts. From Kyōto Eki take the JR Tōkaidō Line (¥230) to Ishiyama Eki (15 mins); from there the bus to the museum will take 50 minutes. You must arrive by 4 PM to be admitted; call ahead for hours on public holidays. ✉ *300 Momodani, Shigariki,* ☎ *0748/82–3411.* ☜ *¥1,000.* ⊙ *Mar. 15–June 10 and Sept.–Dec. 15, Tues.–Sun. 10–5.*

Sanzen-in. This small temple of the Tendai sect was founded by a renowned priest, Dengyo-Daishi (767–822). The Main Hall was built by Priest Eshin (942–1017), who probably carved the temple's Amida Buddha—though some say it was carved 100 years after Eshin's death. Flanked by the two disciples, Daiseishi and Kannon, the statue is a remarkable piece of work, because rather than representing the bountiful Amida, it displays much more the omnipotence of Amida. Although Eshin was not a master sculptor, this statue possibly reflects Eshin's belief that, contrary to the prevailing belief of the Heian aristocracy that salvation could be achieved through one's own actions, salvation could be achieved only through Amida's limitless mercy. The statue is in the Hon-dō (Main Hall), itself an ancient building from the 12th century. Unusual for a Buddhist temple, it faces east, not south. Note its ceiling. The painting depicts the descent of Amida, accompanied by 25 bodhisattvas, to welcome the believer.

Not only is the temple worth visiting, but the grounds are also delightful. Full of maple trees, the gardens are serene in any season. During autumn, the colors are magnificent, and the approach to the temple up a gentle slope enhances the anticipation for the burned gold trees guarding the old, weathered temple. Snow cover in winter is also magical. Take Kyōto Line Bus 17 or 18 90 minutes north from Kyōto Eki; the fare is ¥470. From the Ōhara bus station, walk northeast for about seven minutes along the signposted road. ⊠ *Raigōin-chō, Ōhara, Sakyō-ku.* ⊑ *¥500.* ⏱ *Daily 8:30–5 (8:30–4 in winter).*

Shūgaku-in Imperial Villa. This villa complex consists of three palaces. The Upper and Lower Villas were built in the 17th century by the Tokugawa family to entertain the emperor. The Middle Villa was added later as a palace home for Princess Ake, daughter of the emperor. When she decided that a nun's life was her calling, the villa was transformed into a temple. The most pleasant aspects of a visit here are the grounds and the panoramic views from the Upper Villa.

Special permission is required to visit the villa; follow the same instructions to obtain it as for Katsura Detached Villa (☞ Exploring Western Kyōto, *above*). From Hiei-zan, take the Eizan Railway from Yase Yuen Eki to Shūgaku-in Eki. The villa is a 15-minute walk from there. From downtown Kyōto, the trip takes an hour on Bus 5 from Kyōto Eki. Or take the 20-minute ride north on a Keifuku Eizan Line train from the Demachi-Yanagi terminus, which is just northeast of the intersection of Imadegawa-dōri and the Kamo-gawa. ⊠ *Shūgaku-in Muro-machi, Sakyō-ku.* ⊑ *Free. Tours (in Japanese only) at 9, 10, 11, 1:30, and 3; closed Sat. (except in May, Oct., and Nov.), Sun., national holidays, and Dec. 25–Jan. 5.*

DINING

Many of Kyōto's finest traditional restaurants have done business in the old style for generations and do not believe in modern nuisances like credit cards. Though a number of places are changing their ways, it's wise to check in advance. Also, people generally dine early in Kyōto, between 7 and 8 PM, so most restaurants apart from hotel restaurants and drinking places close relatively early. In some cases this means 7 PM, though most are open until 9.

The average Japanese businessman wears a suit and tie to dinner—anywhere. Young people tend to dress more informally. If you think that you'll feel uncomfortable without a jacket, take one along to wear. Many Kyōto restaurants do have someone who speaks English if it turns out that you need assistance making reservations.

Apart from the restaurants listed below, Kyōto does have its share of the sort of budget quasi-Western–style chain restaurants found all over Japan, serving things like sandwiches and salads, gratins, curried rice, and spaghetti. These are easy to locate along Kawara-machi-dōri downtown, and they usually come complete with plastic models in the window to which you can point if other methods of communication fail.

CATEGORY	COST*
$$$$	over ¥15,000
$$$	¥7,000–¥15,000
$$	¥3,000–¥7,000
$	under ¥3,000

per person, excluding drinks, service, and tax

Eastern Kyōto

Japanese

$$$$ ✕ **Ashiya Steak House.** A short walk from the Gion district, famous for its teahouses and geisha, Ashiya Steak House is the best place in Kyōto to enjoy "a good steak . . . a real martini . . . and the essence of traditional Japan," in the words of 30-year-resident and owner Bob Strickland and his wife, Tokiko. While you are seated at a *kotatsu* (recessed hearth), your *teppanyaki* dinner of the finest Ōmi beefsteak, grilled and sliced in style, will be prepared as you watch. Cocktails, domestic and imported wines, and beer are available, as well as the best Japanese sake. You can take cocktails in the art gallery upstairs, which has a display of traditional and contemporary arts and crafts. You're sure to be impressed by the service and the $160 price tag for a 12-ounce steak. ✉ 172-13 4-chōme, Kiyomizu, Higashiyama-ku, ☎ 075/541–7961. *Reservations essential. AE, DC, V. Closed Mon.*

$$$ ✕ **Yagembori.** North of Shijō-dōri in the heart of Kyōto's still-thriv-
★ ing geisha district, this restaurant is in a teahouse just a few steps down a cobbled path from the romantic Shirakawa, a small tributary of the Kamo-gawa, in Gion. The *o-makase* full-course meal is an elegant sampler of Kyōto's finest kaiseki cuisine, with local delicacies beautifully presented on fine handmade ceramics. The *shabu-shabu* (thinly sliced beef, dipped briefly into hot stock) and *suppon* (turtle dishes) are excellent. Don't miss the *hoba miso*—bean paste with *kinoko* mushrooms and green onions, which are wrapped in a giant oak leaf and grilled at your table over a charcoal hibachi—on the à la carte menu. ✉ Sueyoshi-chō, Kiridoshi-kado, Gion, Higashiyama-ku, ☎ 075/551–3331. *AE, DC, V.*

$$ ✕ **Rokusei Nishimise.** Few restaurants in Kyōto have matched Rokusei Nishimise's magical combination of traditional cuisine served in a contemporary setting. Polished marble floors and manicured interior-garden niches offset the popular *te-oke bentō* lunch, a collage of flavors and colors presented in a handmade cypress-wood bucket–serving tray for ¥3,000. With a history as caterers of formal kaiseki cuisine that began in 1899, Rokusei also offers a different exquisite full-course meal each month at ¥10,000—expensive, you may say, but in the world of Kyōto's haute cuisine, this is reasonable. A three-minute walk west of the turn-of-the-century gardens of Heian Shrine, the restaurant itself overlooks a tree-lined canal and is famous for its colorful azaleas in May. ✉ 71 Nishitennō-chō, Okazaki, Sakyō-ku, ☎ 075/751–6171. *AE, DC, V. Closed Mon.*

$–$$ ✕ **Kappa Nawate.** Lively—noisy to some ears—and fun, Kappa Nawate has all the boisterous local atmosphere, grilled goodies, and *nama* (draft) beer a dozen people crammed around a counter could ever hope for. The head cook vacillates between edgy and jovial—he has fish to grill and little patience with indecision. The English menu helps, but the choices are next to limitless: *oden* (vegetables and other foods simmered in broth), *yakitori* (grilled skewers of chicken), sashimi, you name it. A favorite after-work watering hole in the middle of Gion, Kappa stays open later than most other such grills in Kyōto. ⊠ *Sueyoshi-chō, Higashi-Kita Kado, Nawate-dōri, Shōji 2-sujime-agaru, Higashiyama-ku,* ☎ *075/531–4048. Reservations not accepted. No credit cards. Closed 1st, 2nd, and 3rd Mon. of month.*

$ ✕ **Nishimura.** You do the cooking at this casual eatery, where the specialty is *okonomiyaki,* a kind of Japanese frittata made with a batter of egg and flour mixed with vegetables and your choice of meat or seafood. It's all smothered with green onions and ginger and topped with a special sauce, and then you grill it at your table. Nishimura is a stone's throw from Kyōto University, down a path beside the Asahi Shimbun Building, and is surrounded with shrubbery. The food is good, the garden view is wonderful, and the prices are very reasonable. ⊠ *Hyakumamben Kosaten-agaru, Nishi-Iru, Sakyō-ku,* ☎ *075/ 721–5880. Reservations not accepted. No credit cards. Closed Fri.*

$ ✕ **Omen.** Just south of Ginkaku-ji, this is one of the best places to stop
★ for an inexpensive home-style lunch before proceeding down the old canal—the walkway beneath the cherry trees known as the Path of Philosophy—on the way to Nanzen-ji. Omen is not only the name of the shop but also the name of the house specialty: thick white noodles brought to your table in a basket with a bowl of hot broth and a platter of seven different vegetables. The noodles are added to the broth a little at a time, along with the vegetables: spinach, cabbage, green onions, mushrooms, burdock, eggplant, radishes, and others, depending on the season. Sprinkle the top with roasted sesame seeds and you have a dish so popular that you can expect a few minutes' wait before you're seated. Like the food, the restaurant itself is country-style, with a choice of counter stools, tables and chairs, or tatami-mat seating. The waiters dress in *happi* (workmen's) coats and headbands; the atmosphere is lively and comfortable. ⊠ *74 Ishi-bashi-chō, Jōdo-ji, Sakyō-ku,* ☎ *075/771–8994. Reservations not accepted on weekends. No credit cards. Closed Thurs.*

$ ✕ **Rakushō.** Along the path between Maruyama Kōen and Kiyomizu-
★ dera, this tea shop in a former villa is a pleasant place to stop for morning coffee or afternoon tea. A table beside the sliding glass doors looks out on an elaborately landscaped garden that features a pond in which the owner's colorful array of prize-winning *koi* (carp), hoping it's feeding time again, lurks just beneath the surface. Flowering plum trees, azaleas, irises, camellias, and maple trees take turns coloring the four seasons while you sip your bowl of frothy *matcha* (tea-ceremony tea) or freshly brewed coffee. The tea shop is minutes on foot from Sannen-zaka, one of Kyōto's historic preservation districts—a cobblestone path lined with shops on the way to Kiyomizu-dera. Rakusho closes at 6 PM. ⊠ *Kōdai-ji Kitamon-mae-dōri, Washio-chō, Higashiyama-ku,* ☎ *075/561–6892. Reservations not accepted. No credit cards. Closed 4 times a month (call ahead).*

American

$ ✕ **Time Paradox.** The Japanese owner-chef here learned most of his tricks in California. The tantalizing menu includes homemade gratins; thick-crust pizza; spinach omelets; scallops in garlic and wine sauce; bread sticks baked fresh while you wait; and crispy spinach, bacon, and avocado salads. Beer and wine are also served. Located a few blocks south of Kyōto University (just north of Heian Shrine), it is a popular student haunt, heavy on the foreign element. ⊠ *Yoshida-hon-dōri, Maruta-machi-agaru, Sakyō-ku,* ☎ *075/751–6903. MC, V. Closed Thurs.*

334

Kyōto Dining

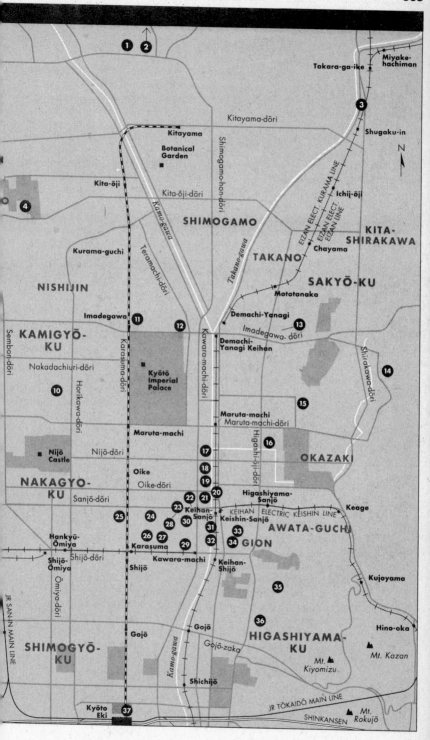

Takara-ga-ike
Miyake-hachiman
Shugaku-in
Kitayama-dōri
Kitayama
Botanical Garden
Shimogamo-hon-dōri
EIZAN ELECT. KURAMA LINE
Ichij-ōji
KITA-SHIRAKAWA
Kita-ōji
Kita-ōji-dōri
Kamo-gawa
SHIMOGAMO
EIZAN ELECT. EIZAN LINE
Chayama
Kurama-guchi
Teramachi-dōri
Takano-gawa
TAKANO
SAKYŌ-KU
NISHIJIN
Mototanaka
Imadegawa
Demachi-Yanagi
Imadegawa-dōri
KAMIGYŌ-KU
Sembon-dōri
Nakadachiuri-dōri
Horikawa-dōri
Karasuma-dōri
Kawara-machi-dōri
Kyōtō Imperial Palace
Demachi-Yanagi Keihan
Shirakawa-dōri
Maruta-machi
Maruta-machi
Maruta-machi-dōri
Nijō-dōri
Nijō Castle
NAKAGYŌ-KU
Higashi-ōji-dōri
OKAZAKI
Oike
Oike-dōri
Sanjō-dōri
Higashiyama-Sanjō
KEIHAN
Keihan-Sanjō
Keishin-Sanjō
ELECTRIC KEISHIN LINE
Keage
Keishin-Sanjō
AWATA-GUCHI
Hankyū-Ōmiya
Karasuma
Kawara-machi
GION
Shijō-Ōmiya
Shijō-dōri
Ōmiya-dōri
Shijō
Keihan-Shijō
Kujoyama
JR SANIN MAIN LINE
Gojō
Gojō
Gojō-zaka
Hino-oka
SHIMOGYŌ-KU
HIGASHIYAMA-KU
Mt. Kiyomizu
Mt. Kazan
Shichijō
Kyōto Eki
JR TOKAIDŌ MAIN LINE
SHINKANSEN
Mt. Rokujō

N

Western Kyōto

Japanese

$$$$ ✕ **Kitcho.** What Maxim's is to Paris, Kitcho is to Kyōto—classic cuisine, unparalleled traditional atmosphere, exclusive elegance. Lunch here starts at ¥45,000, dinner at ¥50,000, making this perhaps the world's most expensive restaurant. Although the original restaurant is in Ōsaka, the Kyōto branch has the advantage of a stunning location beside the Oi-gawa River, nestled at the foothills of Arashiyama. Here you can experience the full sensory delight of formal kaiseki cuisine. Only the finest ingredients are used, prepared by master chefs and served in exquisite antique porcelain ware on priceless lacquered trays—all in an elegant private room sparsely decorated with a hanging scroll painted by a famous master, whose message sets the seasonal theme for the evening. The ability to identify the vessels used, an appreciation of the literary allusions made in the combination of objects and foods served, and knowledge of the arts of Japan all add depth to the experience. Expect to spend a minimum of two hours here. Kitcho closes for dinner at 7 PM. ⊠ *58 Susuki-no-bamba-chō, Tenryū-ji, Saga, Ukyō-ku,* ☎ *075/881–1101. Reservations essential. Jacket and tie. AE. Closed 1st and 3rd Wed. of month.*

$$
★ ✕ **Nishiki.** Tucked inside a rustic bamboo fence, Nishiki sits on an island in the middle of the Oi-gawa (the local name for the Katsura-gawa as it courses through Arashiyama), surrounded by the densely forested Arashiyama mountains. The *oshukuzen-bentō* lunch is the best sampler of formal, Kyōto-style kaiseki cuisine available at the reasonable price of ¥3,800. Unlike most other bentō lunches, it is served in seven courses and is so beautifully presented in a tiered lacquer box, with meticulous attention to the finest foods in season, that it rivals other meals at three times the price. A summer lunch might include a course of *kamo-nasu*, the prized Kyōto eggplant, served *dengaku*-style, smothered in sweet miso sauce in a silver serving dish the shape of an eggplant. The top layer of the lacquered box might be covered with a miniature bamboo trellis in which are nestled tiny porcelain cups the shape of morning glories, a favorite summer flower in Kyōto, each one filled with a different appetizer—a touch of sea urchin or a few sprigs of spinach in sesame sauce. Nishiki is close to Togetsu-kyō Bridge. Call for reservations, or expect a 30-minute wait. The last dinner order is at 7 PM. ⊠ *Nakanoshima Kōen-guchi, Arashiyama, Ukyō-ku,* ☎ *075/ 871–8888. DC, MC, V. Closed Tues.*

$$
★ ✕ **Sagano.** Amid Arashiyama's lush, green bamboo forests, this quiet retreat serves one of the finest *yudōfu* meals—cubes of bean curd simmered in a broth at your table—in Kyōto. The full course includes such local delicacies as tempura and *aburage* (deep-fried tofu) with black sesame seeds and a gingko-nut center garnished with a sprig of *kinome* leaves from the Japanese pepper tree. Take a seat at the sunken counter, and waitresses in kimono will prepare the meal in front of you—with a backdrop of antique wood-block prints on folding screens, surrounded by walls lined with delicately hand-painted antique porcelain bowls—or walk out through the garden to private, Japanese-style rooms in the back. If weather permits, dine on low tables in the courtyard garden beneath the towering bamboo. Reservations are a good idea year-round, particularly during the busy fall foliage season when the maple trees of Arashiyama are stunning. Sagano closes at 8 PM. ⊠ *45 Susuki-no-bamba-chō, Saga, Tenryū-ji, Ukyō-ku,* ☎ *075/861– 0277. No credit cards.*

Spanish

$$ ✕ **Bodegon.** A white-walled, tile-floored, wrought-iron and blown-glass Spanish restaurant in Arashiyama is about as rare (and welcome) as decent paella in a neighborhood famous for its tofu. Bodegon sits unobtrusively along the main street that runs through the center of this scenic district, combining Spanish wine and Kyōto hospitality. A wildly popular tourist area in daylight, Arashiyama rolls up its sidewalks after dark, so Bodegon is a good place to escape the crowds downtown in the evening after other places close. ✉ *1 Susuki-no-bamba-chō, Tenryū-ji, Saga,* ☎ *075/872–9652. MC, V. Closed Thurs.*

Central Kyōto

Japanese

$$$$ ✕ **Daimonji-ya.** One of Kyōto's many famous *ryōri-ryokan* (restaurant-inns), Daimonjiya is noted for its superb formal kaiseki cuisine. Located on the Sanjō Arcade in the downtown shopping district, its inconspicuous traditional entrance is easy to miss among the boutiques and record shops that now line the street. A narrow stone path leads down a bamboo-fence corridor to the doorway of this classic 80-year-old inn, a popular haunt of literary men such as the late Eiji Yoshikawa, author of *Musashi*. The evening kaiseki meal is exquisitely presented; the *kaiseki bentō* offered at lunchtime is one of Kyōto's finest and is moderately priced. The last dinner seating is at 7 PM. ✉ *19 Ishibashi-chō, Sanjō Tera-machi Higashi-Iru, Nakagyō-ku,* ☎ *075/221–0603. Dinner reservations essential. Jacket and tie. AE, DC, V.*

$$–$$$ ✕ **Ebisugawa-tei.** Annexed to the Fujita Hotel, this is the Meiji-period villa of former industrialist Baron Fujita. It contains two excellent steak restaurants, both serving the celebrated, beer-fed, massaged Ōmi beef. The Ōmi is the more expensive and formal of the two, serving slightly higher-quality beef (men should wear jacket and tie). The **Chidori** is a bit less formal but also serves superb beef and has a better view of the garden. Stop in at the bar in the basement of the Fujita Hotel for a drink beside the beautiful duck pond and waterfall. ✉ *Fujita Hotel, Nijō-dōri, Kiya-machi Kado, Nakagyō-ku,* ☎ *075/222–1511. AE, DC, MC, V.*

$$–$$$ ✕ **Mankamero.** Established in 1716, Mankamero is the only restaurant in Kyōto that offers formal *yusoku ryōri,* the type of cuisine once served to members of the imperial court. The preparation of foods is carried out by a specially appointed imperial chef, using unique utensils made only for the preparation of this type of cuisine. Dressed in ceremonial robes, the chef "dismembers" the fish and elaborately arranges its sections to have them brought to you on pedestal trays. Prices are also quite elaborate—up to ¥30,000 per person for the full yusoku ryōri repertoire—though in recent years an incomparable *take-kago bentō* lunch (served in a bamboo basket) has been within reach of wealthy commoners at ¥6,000. Mankamero is on the west side of Inokuma-dōri north of Demizu-dōri. It closes at 8 PM. ✉ *Inokuma-dōri, Demizu-agaru, Kamigyō-ku,* ☎ *075/441–5020. Reservations essential. Jacket and tie. AE, DC, MC, V. No credit cards for take-kago bentō at lunch. Closed once a month.*

$$–$$$ ✕ **Mishima-tei.** This is really the one choice for sukiyaki in Kyōto. In the heart of the downtown shopping district, it is also one of the best restaurants in the area. Kyōto housewives line up out front to pay premium prices for Mishima-tei's famous high-quality beef, sold by the 100-gram over the counter at the meat shop downstairs. Mishima-tei was established in 1904, and climbing the staircase of this three-story, traditional wood-frame restaurant with its turn-of-the-century atmosphere is like journeying into the past. Down the long, dark corridors, with polished wood floors, kimono-clad maidens bustle about with trays

of beef and refills of sake to dozens of private tatami-mat rooms. Ask for a room that faces the central courtyard garden for the best view, and enjoy your meal in privacy. Plan on dining by 7 PM or so, as the service—and the preparation of your food—can be rushed toward the end of the evening. ⊠ *Tera-machi, Sanjō-sagaru, Higashi-Iru, Nakagyō-ku,* ☎ *075/221–0003. AE, DC, MC, V. Closed Wed.*

$$–$$$ ✕ **Yoshikawa.** This quiet, traditional inn with its beautiful landscaped gardens is within walking distance of the downtown shopping area. The specialty of the house is tempura, either a full-course kaiseki dinner served in a tatami room or a lunch at the counter in its cozy "tempura corner," where the chef fries each vegetable and shrimp in front of you while you wait. Tempura should be light and crisp—best right from the pot—and for this Yoshikawa is famous. English is spoken. Yoshikawa closes at 8:30 PM. ⊠ *Tomino-kōji, Oike-sagaru, Nakagyō-ku,* ☎ *075/221–5544 or 075/221–0052. Jacket and tie at dinner. AE, DC, MC, V. Closed Sun.*

$$ ✕ **Agatha.** This restaurant offers a "mystery" twist on the Japanese *robatayaki* (charcoal grill). The decor is period Agatha Christie—'40s book covers and movie posters, polished marble walls, potted palms, decent jazz, black-and-white checkerboard floors, and counter or table seating. Watch the chef grill interesting variations of traditional Japanese delicacies, such as white, long-stem *enoki* mushrooms wrapped in strips of thinly sliced beef, scallops in bacon, or pork in *shiso* (a mint-like leaf). Both the A-course and the B-course combine these treats with unadorned standards such as *tebasaki* (grilled chicken wings). Salad and appetizers are included, and a wide selection of drinks are available—everything from sake to a gin fizz. Popular with the *juppie* (Japanese yuppie) crowd, this restaurant has two other branches in Kyōto, and one each in Ōsaka, Tōkyō, and . . . Boston. ⊠ *Yurika Bldg., 2nd floor, Kiya-machi-dōri, Sanjō-agaru, Nakagyō-ku,* ☎ *075/223–2379. AE, DC, MC, V. No lunch.*

$$ ✕ **Ōiwa.** At the head of the Takase-gawa (canal), south of the Fujita Hotel, Ōiwa serves *kushikatsu*, skewered meats and vegetables battered, deep-fried, and then dipped in a variety of sauces. The building itself is actually a *kura* (treasure house) that belongs to a kimono merchant family, and it is one of the first to have been turned into a restaurant in Kyōto, where restorations of this type are still a relatively new idea. The Japanese chef was trained in one of the finest French restaurants in Tōkyō, and his version of kushikatsu (usually considered a working man's snack with beer) has an unpretentious elegance. Order by the skewer or ask for the *o-makase* set course. Ōiwa is a fine place to spend a relaxing evening. ⊠ *Kiya-machi-dōri, Nijō-sagaru, Nakagyō-ku,* ☎ *075/231–7667. No credit cards. Closed Wed.*

$–$$ ✕ **Daikokuya.** If you're shopping downtown and want a quick meal, stop in at Daikokuya for a *soba* (buckwheat noodle) dish or *domburi*, a bowl of rice with your choice of toppings. The *oyako domburi*, rice with egg and chicken, is the best choice (*oyako* means "parent and child"). Both tatami and table-and-chair seating are available. The buckwheat for the soba is ground in-house on an antique stone mill powered by a wooden water wheel. Fresh noodles are also served with exceedingly delicate tempura. You can recognize Daikokuya by its red lantern and water mill. ⊠ *281 Minami-kurumaya-chō, Takoyakushi, Kiya-machi Nishi-Iru, Nakagyō-ku,* ☎ *075/221–2818. Reservations not accepted. No credit cards. Closed Tues.*

$–$$ ✕ **Yamatomi.** The geisha district that runs along the west bank of the Kamo-gawa is known as Ponto-chō. Many of the places along the narrow street are teahouses, and you must be formally introduced by a regular patron to enter. There are a few reasonably priced restaurants in Ponto-chō, and Yamatomi is among the best. The specialty of the house is *teppan-age,* a tempura-style meal of battered vegetables, seafood, and meat that you cook in a small iron kettle at your table. In winter, the favorite is *oden,* a combination of vegetables and local specialties simmered in copper vats behind the counter. But it's really the hot, humid summers that make Kyōto-ites flock to Yamatomi. In summer, the restaurants and teahouses along Ponto-chō set up verandas over the riverbank so patrons can enjoy meals and the cool river breeze under the stars. You might see geisha entertaining guests on the veranda of the teahouse next door—paying 10 times the price you'll pay at Yamatomi. ⊠ *Ponto-chō, Shijō-agaru, Nakagyō-ku,* ☎ 075/221–3268. *Reservations not accepted. No credit cards. Closed Tues.*

$ ✕ **Fujiya.** Under Kyōto Eki, the Porta shopping arcade has a mall called Restaurant Alley, where a dozen or more restaurants serve a range of Japanese food at reasonable prices. While none of them warrant a special visit, if you are waiting for a train and need sustenance, come here and take your pick. Fujiya has noodle and rice dishes with different toppings. ⊠ *Kyōto Eki, Chika 1-kai,* ☎ 075/343–2641. *Reservations not accepted. No credit cards.*

$ ✕ **Suzu.** Don't trek across town just for a meal here, but if you find yourself in Ponto-chō and are staggered by the prices at most restaurants, this little place will come as a relief. A cheerful crowd crams in either at the counter or at one of the closely packed tables, and you are sure to start up one or more conversations. The food is a Japanese rendition of American-style snacks, from pizza with bacon to batter-fried shrimp and vegetables; prices average around ¥650 a dish. ⊠ *Ponto-chō, Shijō-agaru, Nakagyō-ku,* ☎ 075/252–1760. *Reservations not accepted. No credit cards.*

$ ✕ **Tagoto.** One of the best noodle shops in which to stop for lunch in the downtown area, Tagoto is on the north side of the covered Sanjō Arcade, half a block west of Kawara-machi-dōri. Tagoto has been serving soup with homemade *soba* for more than a hundred years in the same location on a shopping street that is now almost completely modernized. Tagoto, too, has remodeled, and the result is a pleasant surprise—modern, yet in traditional Japanese style: natural woods; *shōji* paper windows; tatami mats; and an interior garden integrated with slate floors, tables and chairs; and the comfort of air-conditioning. Tagoto serves both thin soba and thick white *udon* noodle dishes with a variety of ingredients, such as shrimp tempura, hot or cold to suit the season. ⊠ *Sanjō-dōri, Tera-machi Higashi-Iru, Nakagyō-ku,* ☎ 075/ 221–3030. *Reservations not accepted. No credit cards. Closed Tues.*

Coffee Shops

$ ✕ **Inoda.** Hidden down a side street in the center of town, this 100-year-old establishment is one of Kyōto's oldest and best-loved *kissaten* (coffee shops). The turn-of-the-century, Western-style brick buildings along Sanjō-dōri nearby are part of a historic preservation district, and Inoda's original old shop blends well with its surroundings. Floor-to-ceiling glass windows overlook an interior garden; a spacious room seats nearly 100 people. And the coffee is excellent: for breakfast, toast and coffee; for lunch, sandwiches and coffee; for a break from sightseeing, coffee and coffee. It even has some stained-glass windows and a pair of witty parrots. Inoda closes at 6 PM. ⊠ *Sakai-machi-dōri, Sanjō-sagaru, Nakagyō-ku,* ☎ 075/221–0505. *Reservations not accepted. No credit cards.*

French

$$–$$$ ✕ **Ogawa.** Down a narrow passageway across from the Takase-gawa, ★ this is the place to taste the best in Kyōto-style nouvelle cuisine. Finding a seat at the counter of this intimate French restaurant is like getting tickets for opening night at the opera—one you've never seen. With particularly Japanese sensitivity to the best ingredients only in the

peak of the season, proprietor Ogawa promises never to bore by serving the same meal twice. *Ayu* (a popular local river fish) is offered in summer (or perhaps abalone), salmon in fall, crab in winter, shrimp in spring. Ogawa prepares marvelous sauces, puddings—even fresh papaya sherbet and mango mousse with mint sauce. The full-course meal at lunch and dinner is spectacular, but some prefer to order hors d'oeuvres with wine over which to languish ecstatically for hours. Counter seating is available for only 16. ⊠ *Kiya-machi Oike-agaru Higashi-Iru, Nakagyō-ku,* ☎ *075/256–2203. Reservations essential. Jacket and tie. AE, DC, MC, V. Closed Tues.*

$$ ✕ **Natsuka.** This fine French restaurant overlooks the Kamo-gawa. The
★ Japanese couple who manage the place lived and learned their trade in Paris for several years. Natsuka has the most reasonably priced French lunch menu in town; there is a ¥1,750 fixed menu. The dessert tray here is sumptuous, with a choice of two freshly baked delights from about eight possibilities. The last order must go in by 9 (at 8 on Sunday). ⊠ *Ponto-chō, Shijō-agaru, Higashi-gawa, Nakagyō-ku,* ☎ *075/255–2105. MC. Closed Wed.*

Indian

$ ✕ **Ashoka.** Unlike cosmopolitan Tōkyō, Kyōto, with all its fine Japanese restaurants, suffers from a serious lack of international options—particularly when it comes to cuisine. That was true until the owners of Ashoka brought their tandoori chicken (and their wonderful Indian chefs) to town: This chicken dish is the closest you'll get to downright spiciness in the capital of the culinary dainty. Ashoka's atmosphere is evoked by red carpets, carved screens, brass lanterns, and tuxedoed waiters, though you'll find other diners in everything from denim to silk. The dazzling *Thali* course dinner serves half a dozen curries in small bowls on a brass tray with rice and tandoori—order this only if you're very hungry. Ashoka closes at 9 PM. ⊠ *Kikusui Bldg., 3rd floor, Tera-machi-dōri, Shijō-agaru, Nakagyō-ku,* ☎ *075/241–1318. AE, DC, MC, V. Closed 2nd Tues. of month.*

Italian

$–$$ ✕ **divo-diva.** In the relatively short time divo-diva has been in business,
★ it has become one of the most popular restaurants in Kyōto. You'll dine here on authentic Italian food prepared by chefs trained in Italy but using a Japanese flair for color and design. The long, narrow room has a counter, three small tables, and one long table for parties and large groups; tasteful lighting sets off the contemporary decor. The wine list is interesting (and not prohibitively expensive), the pasta and breads homemade. ⊠ *Nishiki-kōji, Takakura-Nishi-Iru, Nakagyō-ku,* ☎ *075/256–1326. AE, DC, MC, V. Closed Wed. and 2nd and 3rd Tues. of month.*

Mixed Menu

$ ✕ **Tinguely.** Located in the same basement as a Chinese restaurant, Mr. Chow's Tinguely overlooks a mini-terrace and has a black interior. This dining spot may be described as ethnic (the menu covers a lot of bases), East and West (eclectic), not the place you'd think the local banking district would frequent (but it does), and kinetic (the flashing, jangling work of artist Jean Tinguely hangs from every rafter). It's a "mysterious space for city adults" in the evening, as the restaurant's funny-English slogan suggests. ⊠ *Basement of the Karasuma Plaza 21, Karasuma-dōri, Rokkaku-sagaru, Nakagyō-ku,* ☎ *075/255–6810. No credit cards. Closed Sun.*

Northern Kyōto

To get to these northern Kyōto restaurants, take the Eizan Electric Railway on the Kurama Line to Shūgaku-in Eki; then proceed by taxi.

Japanese

$$ ✕ **Heihachi-Jaya.** A bit off the beaten path in the northeastern corner
★ of Kyōto, along the old road to the Sea of Japan, this roadside inn has
offered comfort to many a weary traveler in its 400-year history. Hei-
hachi-Jaya hugs the levee of the Takano-gawa and is surrounded by
maple trees in a quiet garden with a stream. Apart from the excellent
mugitoro bentō lunch that includes, among other dishes, grated moun-
tain potato salad served with barley rice, and the full-course kaiseki
dinner, what makes this restaurant special is its clay sauna, the *kama-
buro,* a mound-shaped clay steam bath heated from beneath the floor
by a pinewood fire. Have a bath and sauna, change into a cotton ki-
mono if you wish, and retire to the dining room (or to a private room)
for a *very* relaxing meal—an experience not to be missed. Heihachi-
Jaya closes at 9 PM. ✉ *8-1 Kawagishi-chō, Yamabana, Sakyō-ku,* ☎
075/781–5008. AE, DC, MC, V. Closed Wed.

$$ ✕ **Izusen.** In the garden of Daiji-in, a subtemple of Daitoku-ji (a
revered center of Zen Buddhism in Japan), this restaurant specializes
in *shojin ryōri,* vegetarian Zen cuisine. Lunches are presented in sets
of red-lacquer bowls of diminishing sizes, each one fitting inside the
next when the meal is completed. Two Kyōto specialties, *fu* (glutinous
wheat cake) and *yuba* (curd from steamed soy milk), are served in a
multitude of inventive forms—in soups and sauces that prove vege-
tarianism to be as exciting a culinary experience as any meat dishes
can hope to be. Meals are served in tatami-mat rooms, Japanese-style,
and in warm weather on low tables outside beneath the trees in the
temple garden. Reservations are recommended in spring and fall;
Izusen closes at 5 PM. ✉ *4 Daitoku-ji-chō, Murasakino, Kita-ku,* ☎
075/491–6665. No credit cards. Closed Thurs.

$–$$ ✕ **Sagenta.** Discovering the town of Kibune is one of the best parts of
★ summer in Kyōto. A short bump-and-rumble train ride into the mountains north of Kyōto on the nostalgic little Keifuku train lets you off
on a mountain path that leads farther up into the forest beside a cool
stream. (Take the Eizan Electric Railway on the Kurama Line to Ki-
buneguchi Eki and then transfer to the Keifuku train to Kibune. Allow
a good 45 minutes from central Kyōto.) The path is lined on both sides
with restaurants that place tables near the stream in summer, when you
can dine beneath a canopy of trees, with the water flowing at your feet.
Most of the river restaurants are excellent, some quite expensive.
Sagenta is the last restaurant, at the very top of the slope, serving kaiseki
lunches year-round, as well as one-pot *nabe* (stew) dishes in fall and
winter. It is reasonably priced, particularly for its popular summertime
specialty, *nagashi-somen,* chilled noodles that flow down a bamboo
spout from the kitchen to a boat-shaped trough; you catch the noodles from the trough as they float past, dip them in a sauce, and eat
them with mushrooms, seasonal green vegetables, and shrimp. Reservations are advised in summer. ✉ *76 Kibune-chō, Kurama, Sakyō-ku,*
☎ *075/741–2244. AE, DC, MC, V. Closed periodically in winter.*

$ ✕ **Azekura.** On the northern outskirts of Kyōto, not far from Kami-
★ gamo Shrine, Azekura serves home-style buckwheat noodles under the
giant wooden beams of a 300-year-old sake warehouse. Originally built
in Nara, the warehouse was moved here more than 20 years ago by
kimono merchant Mikio Ichida, who also maintains a textile exhibition hall, a small museum, and a weavers' workshop within the walls
of this former samurai estate. Have lunch on low stools around a
small charcoal brazier or on tatami next to a window overlooking the
garden and waterwheel outside. The soba noodles at Azekura have a
heartier country flavor than you'll find in most of the other noodle shops
in town. This is a perfect place to stop while exploring the *shake-machi*
district around the shrine, an area in which shrine priests and farmers

have lived for more than 10 centuries. Azekura closes at 5 PM. ⊠ *30 Okamoto-chō, Kamigamo, Kita-ku,* ☎ *075/701–0161. Reservations not accepted. No credit cards. Closed Mon.*

American

$ ✕ **Knuckle's.** In search of a taste of the Big Apple in the Ancient Cap-
★   ital of Japan? What could be better after a visit to Daitoku-ji, a cen-
ter of Zen Buddhism, than a Reuben sandwich, some nachos, and a margarita, or the house specialty, Knuckle Sandwich (with homemade Italian sausage), washed down with a cold Corona beer? And don't forget the fresh-baked blueberry cheesecake for dessert. Knuckle's has good espresso and a comfortable atmosphere—the Big Apple without the bite. ⊠ *Kitaoji-dōri, Sembon Higashi-Iru, Kita-ku,* ☎ *075/441–5849. Reservations not accepted. No credit cards. Closed Mon.*

Coffee Shops

$ ✕ **Honyaradō.** Kyōto has always been a university town, and Doshisha
★   Daigaku on the north side of the old Imperial Palace is one of the old-
est and most respected schools in the city. Honyaradō is a "home-away-from-dormitory" for many of its students. During the student movement of the '60s and '70s, Kyōto had its share of "incidents." What's left of the spirit of the peace movement—the environmentalists, the poets, and the musicians of that era—eat their lunches at Honyaradō. The notices on the bulletin are of a less incendiary nature these days (rooms for rent, poetry readings, used stereos for sale), but the sandwiches are still on homemade wheat bread, the stew is still good, and the company is still real. Take along a good book (this guide, perhaps?), order lunch, and relax. ⊠ *Imadegawa-dōri, Tera-machi Nishi-Iru, Kamigyō-ku,* ☎ *075/222–1574. Reservations not accepted. No credit cards. Closed 1st Wed. of month.*

$ ✕ **Papa Jon's.** Just north of Doshisha Daigaku, this American-owned café serves a light quiche lunch and the finest home-style cakes and espresso in town. Owner-chef Charles Roche hangs the work of local artists on the walls of his elegant little shop. This, with the antique European decor and sunlit coziness, provides a welcome place to rest after a visit to the nearby Imperial Palace. ⊠ *642-2 Shōkoku-ji Monzen, Karasuma Kamidachiuri Higashi-Iru, Kamigyō-ku,* ☎ *075/415–2655. Reservations not accepted. No credit cards. Closed Mon.*

LODGING

Kyōto is a tourist city, and its hotel rooms are often designed merely as places to rest at night. Most rooms are small by international standards, but they are adequate for relaxing after a busy day of sightseeing. As it is throughout Japan, service in this city is impeccable; the information desks are well stocked with maps and pamphlets about the sights. Assistant managers, concierges, and guest-relations managers are always available in the lobby to respond to your needs, although English may or may not be spoken.

Each room in expensively ($$$) and moderately ($$) priced lodgings comes with a hot-water thermos and tea bags or instant coffee. Stocked refrigerators, television with English-language CNN, and radio are standard, as are *yukata* (cotton kimono), intended for in-room use.

Kyōto has Western- and Japanese-style accommodations, including traditional ryokan. If you choose a ryokan, be sure to read the section on lodging in the Gold Guide, at the front of this book. Some ryokan have shared toilets and baths, so ask about these if you don't like to share facilities.

Most accommodations in the $$$$, $$$, and $$ categories have representation abroad, and the nearest Japan National Tourist Organization (JNTO) office will have information on booking. If there is no representation, bookings must be made by writing directly to the establishment. Book at least a month in advance, or as early as three months ahead, if you are traveling during peak spring and autumn seasons or around important Japanese holidays and festivals. Keep in mind the following festival dates when making reservations: May 15, July 16–17, August 16, and October 22. Rooms will be scarce at these times.

CATEGORY	COST*
$$$$	over ¥30,000
$$$	¥20,000–¥30,000
$$	¥8,000–¥20,000
$	under ¥8,000

All prices are for a double room, excluding service and tax.

Central Kyōto

$$$$ ⊞ **Hiiragiya.** Hiiragiya is on par with the Tawaraya (☞ *below*) as the preferred ryokan among dignitaries and celebrities. The inn was founded in 1818 to accommodate provincial lords and their parties who were visiting the capital. The founder himself was a metalsmith whose artful sword guards were commissioned by powerful samurai. Elegance combined with strength is the pervasive style here, and the ryokan echoes with memories of its samurai visitors of the 19th century. Charlie Chaplin and Yukio Mishima have been among its noted past fans. As the motto of the inn implies: "A guest arrives . . . back home to comfort." Some baths have stained-glass windows. The least expensive rooms are in the newer annex. ⊠ *Fuyacho-Oike-kado, Nakagyō-ku, Kyōto-shi 604,* ☎ *075/221–1136,* ℻ *075/221–1139. 33 rooms, 28 with bath. AE, DC, MC, V.*

$$$$ ⊞ **Tawaraya.** The most famous of Kyōto's inns, this is the abode of
★ kings and queens, princes and princesses, and presidents and dictators when they visit Kyōto. Tawaraya was founded more than 300 years ago and is currently run by the 11th generation of the Okazaki family. For all its subdued beauty and sense of tradition, the inn does have modern comforts such as heat and air-conditioning, but they hardly detract from the venerable atmosphere of yesteryear. The rooms' superb antiques come from the Okazaki family collection. The service and food here might be disappointing, however, if you have not been recommended to the ryokan by a respected Japanese. You are given the option of staying on a European Plan basis and, if you wish, of ordering a selection of dinners from ¥12,000 to ¥60,000, the former option being rather meager. ⊠ *Fuyacho-Aneyakōji-agaru, Nakagyō-ku, Kyōto-shi 604,* ☎ *075/211–5566,* ℻ *075/211–2204. 18 rooms. AE, DC, V.*

$$$ ⊞ **ANA Hotel Kyōto.** The best thing about this hotel is its location, directly across from Nijō-jō. If your room faces the castle rather than another high-rise, you can be assured that you are indeed in Kyōto. Now for the less-good news: Off the long, narrow, rather depressing corridors are long, narrow guest rooms that could use refurbishing—especially considering the rates charged. There are French, Chinese, and Japanese restaurants on site. ⊠ *Nijō-jō-mae, Horikawa-dōri, Nakagyō-ku, Kyōto-shi 604,* ☎ *075/231–1155,* ℻ *075/231–5333. 303 rooms. 7 restaurants, 3 bars, indoor pool, health club, shops. AE, DC, MC, V.*

$$$ ⊞ **Daimonjiya.** Just off the busy shopping area of Sanjō-dōri, this tiny inn is as famous for its guest rooms as for the food served (in the guest rooms). Each room, with fine wood interiors, overlooks a small garden. Kaiseki is the specialty of the house; the chef was trained at the

ANA Hotel Kyōto, **5**
Daimonjiya, **16**
Hiiragiya, **7**
Hiraiwa, **20**
Hirota Guest
House, **6**
Holiday Inn Kyōto, **2**
Hotel Fujita Kyōto, **9**
Iwanami, **15**
Kyōto Brighton
Hotel, **4**
Kyōto Gion Hotel, **17**
Kyōto Grand Hotel, **22**
Kyōto Tōkyū Hotel, **21**
Kyōto Traveler's Inn, **11**
Miyako Hotel, **13**
Myōken-ji, **3**
New Miyako Hotel, **23**
Pension
Higashiyama, **14**
Ryokan Yuhara, **18**
Seikōrō, **19**
Takaraga-ike Prince
Hotel, **1**
Tawaraya, **8**
Three Sisters Inn
Annex, **10**
Yachiyo, **12**

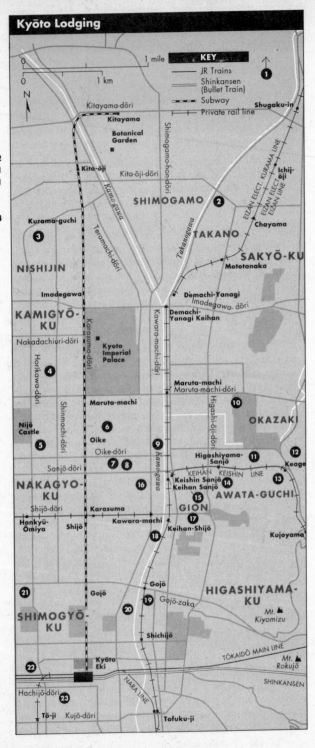

Kyōto Lodging

best Kyōto culinary establishment. You do not need to be a guest to use one of the rooms for a meal, but then you would be missing out on the quintessential ryokan experience. A branch of the restaurant Daimonjiya is located in the Tōkyō Hilton International Hotel. ✉ *Nishi-Iru, Kawara-machi-Sanjō, Nakagyō-ku, Kyōto-shi 604,* ☎ *075/221–0603. 7 rooms. AE, DC.*

$$$ 🏨 **Hotel Fujita Kyōto.** This pleasant hotel is situated along the famed
★ Kamo-gawa, not far from the nightlife center of Gion. In the light of a full moon, the waterfall in its garden sparkles while waterfowl play. The lobby is narrow and long, with comfortable gray armchairs playing nicely against deep red carpeting. The Fujita has Japanese and Scandinavian decor throughout, and 18 rooms have Japanese-style furnishings. The two main restaurants are a kaiseki dining room and a steak house with counter and table service. ✉ *Nishizume, Nijō-Ōhashi, Kamo-gawa, Nakagyō-ku, Kyōto-shi 604,* ☎ *075/222–1511,* FAX *075/256–4561. 177 Western-style rooms, 18 Japanese-style rooms. 4 restaurants, 2 bars, beauty salon, shops. AE, DC, MC, V.*

$$$ 🏨 **Kyōto Brighton Hotel.** Opened in 1987, the Brighton is still unques-
★ tionably the city's best hotel in this price range (and the most expensive). Its simple, clean design gives it an airy and spacious quality lacking in most other Kyōto hotels. Hallways circle a central atrium, and plants hang from the banisters of every floor. Glass elevators carry you up into the atrium to your room. Large by Japanese standards, rooms have separate seating areas with a couch and TV. No need to worry about city noise: The Brighton is on a quiet side street close to the Imperial Palace, although not within walking distance of most of Kyōto's main attractions. ✉ *Nakadachiuri, Shin-machi-dōri, Kamigyō-ku, Kyōto-shi 602,* ☎ *075/441–4411; 800/223–6800 in the U.S.; 0800/181–123 in the U.K.;* FAX *075/431–2360. 181 rooms, 2 suites. 5 restaurants, 2 bars, outdoor pool, beauty salon, shops. AE, DC, MC, V.*

$$$ 🏨 **Kyōto Grand Hotel.** The Grand's lobby can sometimes be crowded because the hotel is popular with tour groups. The green concrete building, which is on the drab side, has a circular attachment on the roof—a revolving restaurant. Terrycloth bathrobes, CNN TV, and remote-control toilet gadgetry are all part of the hotel's effort to keep up-to-date. If your room faces the street, make sure to draw the curtains or slide the shōji screens before undressing, because office buildings are right across the way. The Grand is famous for its cheerful and friendly staff. A free bus continuously shuttles guests to and from the Shinkansen central exit of Kyōto Eki. The Grand's neighbors include the temples Nishi-Hongan-ji and Tō-ji (☞ Exploring Central and Southern Kyōto, *above*). ✉ *Shiokōji-Horikawa, Shimogyō-ku, Kyōto-shi 600,* ☎ *075/341–2311,* FAX *075/341–3073. 554 rooms. 4 restaurants, bar, indoor pool, barbershop, beauty salon, sauna, shops, travel services. AE, DC, MC, V.*

$$$ 🏨 **Kyōto Tōkyū Hotel.** This seven-story hotel is part of Japan's largest hotel chain. The pillared main entrance, the entrance hall, and the lobby are expansive, and the courtyard, with its reflecting pool and waterfall, creates a dramatic atmosphere. The well-appointed rooms, predominantly decorated in off-white tones, are comfortable and spacious. ✉ *580 Kakimoto-chō, Gojō-sagaru, Horikawa-dōri, Shimogyō-ku, Kyōto-shi 600,* ☎ *075/341–2411,* FAX *075/341–2488. 437 rooms. 3 restaurants, 2 bars, pool, beauty salon, shops, travel services. AE, DC, MC, V.*

$$ 🏨 **New Miyako Hotel.** This large hotel in front of Kyōto Eki is under the same management as the Miyako Hotel (☞ *below*); it is used widely by groups and tours. The 10-story white edifice has two protruding wings with landscaping and street lamps reminiscent of a hotel in the United States. Its location makes it attractive if you are planning train trips from the city. ✉ *17 Nishi-Kujōin-chō, Minami-ku, Kyōto-*

shi 601, ☎ *075/661–7111,* ✆ *075/661–7135. 71 Western-style rooms, 4 Japanese-style rooms. 3 restaurants, bar, tea shop, barbershop, shops. AE, DC, MC, V.*

$ 🏨 **Hiraiwa.** Imagine the ambience of a friendly, Western-style youth hostel with tatami-mat rooms, and you have the Hiraiwa ryokan, a member of the hospitable and economical Japanese Inn Group. To be a member, inns must have English-speaking staff and offer clean, comfortable accommodations. Hiraiwa is the most popular of these inns in Kyōto; it's a great place to meet fellow travelers from around the world. Rules and regulations during your stay are posted on the walls. Guests are welcome to eat with the family owners around the dining table in the small kitchen. The inn has shared toilets and showers. ✉ *314 Hayao-chō, Kaminoguchi-agaru, Ninomiya-chō-dōri, Shimogyō-ku, Kyōto-shi 600,* ☎ *075/351–6748. 21 rooms. AE, MC, V.*

$ 🏨 **Hirota Guest House.** This hidden treasure of an inn, south of the Im-
★ perial Palace, is run by a professional English-speaking guide. A long passageway behind the family's accounting office leads to a lush garden that surrounds a beautifully restored sake storehouse. The Japanese-style rooms have a great view of the secluded, quiet garden. Reserve well in advance. ✉ *665 Nijō-dōri, Tominokōji Nishi-Iru, Nakagyō-ku, Kyōto-shi 604,* ☎ *075/221–2474. 3 rooms, 1 with bath and kitchen. No credit cards.*

$ 🏨 **Myōken-ji.** This temple lodging is an alternative that gives you a first-hand look at the activities of monks. Be ready to share a room with several fellow travelers. If you are modest, write ahead for a private room. The reasonable room rate includes breakfast. ✉ *Teranouchi, Higashi-Iru, Horikawa-dōri, Kamigyō-ku, Kyōto-shi 602,* ☎ *075/414–0808. 12 rooms. No credit cards.*

Eastern Kyōto

$$$ 🏨 **Miyako Hotel.** The Miyako, the grand dame of Kyōto's Western-style hotels, has been around for more than a century. The hotel spreads across the hills of Kyōto, near the temples and shrines of the eastern district. Be sure to request a room with a view of the surrounding hills. Japanese-style rooms in two annexes have the feeling of a traditional ryokan. ✉ *Sanjō-Keage, Higashiyama-ku, Kyōto-shi 605,* ☎ *075/771–7111,* ✆ *075/751–2490. 320 rooms, 20 Japanese-style. 5 restaurants, 2 bars, coffee shop, outdoor pool, shops, meeting rooms. AE, DC, MC, V.*

$$$ 🏨 **Seikōrō.** This lovely inn is just a stone's throw away from busy Gojō
★ Station, a convenience that makes it popular among gai-jin and Japanese. Established in 1831, the ryokan is managed by a native resident who is fluent in English. Among the interesting decor are Western antiques that mysteriously blend in quite well with the otherwise traditional Japanese setting. When you return to Seikōrō after a day of sightseeing, you get the distinct feeling that you are returning to your Japanese home. ✉ *Toiya-machi-dōri, Gojō-sagaru, Higashiyama-ku, Kyōto-shi 605,* ☎ *075/561–0771,* ✆ *075/541–5481. 23 rooms with bath. AE, DC, MC, V.*

$$$ 🏨 **Yachiyo.** The special entrance to Yachiyo has low-hanging tiled eaves
★ and woodwork surrounded by carefully shaped bushes, pine trees, and rocks. The sidewalk from the gate to the ryokan curves snakelike into the doorway. Yachiyo is less expensive than its brethren in the deluxe category but nevertheless provides fine, attentive care. You can reduce the cost of staying at this ryokan by choosing not to dine here. Perhaps the biggest draw of Yachiyo is its proximity to Nanzen-ji, one of the most appealing temples in Kyōto (☞ Exploring Eastern Kyōto, *above*). ✉ *34 Nanzen-ji-fukuchi-chō, Sakyō-ku, Kyōto-shi 606,* ☎ *075/771–4148,* ✆ *075/771–4140. 25 rooms, 20 with bath. AE, DC, MC, V.*

$$ ⚟ **Holiday Inn Kyōto.** This member of the American chain has the best sports facilities of any Kyōto hotel, including a bowling alley and ice-skating rink. The hotel is in a residential area with small, modern houses, occasionally interrupted by large, traditional Japanese estates. To compensate for its location away from most of the action, a shuttle bus makes the 30-minute run to and from Kyōto Eki every 90 minutes. The hotel is a 15-minute taxi ride from Kyōto's downtown area. ✉ *36 Nishihiraki-chō, Takano, Sakyō-ku, Kyōto-shi 606,* ☎ *075/721–3131,* FAX *075/781–6178. 270 rooms. 3 restaurants, 2 bars, coffee shop, indoor pool, outdoor pool, exercise room, sauna, driving range, tennis court, bowling, ice-skating, shops. AE, DC, MC, V.*

$$ ⚟ **Iwanami.** Amid the antiques shops of Shinmonzen-dōri is this priceless little inn, whose loyal clientele, including many gai-jin, would like to keep its existence a secret. Iwanami has gained such a reputation, in fact, that you should reserve a room months in advance. When booking, be sure to ask for a room with a view of the garden or canal. ✉ *Higashi-ōji, Nishi-Iru, Shinmonzen-dōri, Higashiyama-ku, Kyōto-shi 605,* ☎ *075/561–7135. 7 rooms. No credit cards.*

$$ ⚟ **Kyōto Gion Hotel.** This modest, clean hotel is in the heart of the Gion geisha district—just west of Yasaka Jinja, across from the Kyōto Craft Center, a 5-minute walk from downtown, and a 10-minute bus ride from Kyōto Eki. ✉ *555 Gion-machi, Minami-machi, Higashiyama-ku, Kyōto-shi 605,* ☎ *075/551–2111,* FAX *075/551–2200. 130 rooms. Bar, beer garden, coffee shop. AE, DC, MC, V.*

$$ ⚟ **Three Sisters Inn Annex** (Rakutō-sōso Bekkan). A traditional inn popular with gai-jin for decades, the annex—which is nicer than the main branch—sits on the northeast edge of Heian Jingū, down a trellised path that hides it from the street. This is a quiet and friendly place, and a good introduction to inn customs because the management is accustomed to foreign guests. On the down side, the rooms could use refurbishment, and the doors close at 11:30 PM sharp. ✉ *Heian Jingū, Higashi-Kita-Kado, Sakyō-ku, Kyōto-shi 606,* ☎ *075/761–6333,* FAX *075/761–6335. 12 rooms. AE, DC.*

$ ⚟ **Kyōto Traveler's Inn.** This no-frills modern inn is located in the perfect spot for sightseeing, with Heian Jingū, Nanzen-ji, and the museums in Okazaki Park just minutes away on foot. Its 40 Western-style and 38 Japanese-style rooms are plain and small but clean and practical, all with private bath and toilet. Ask for a room with a view (most don't have one). Because of its location, size, and price, it is used for group travel as well as for individuals. Head for the coffee shop on the first floor to look out over the river and plot your course for the day. In contrast to some of Kyōto's other budget inns, this one imposes no curfew. ✉ *Heian Jingū Torii-mae, Okazaki, Sakyō-ku, Kyōto-shi 606,* ☎ *075/771–0225. 40 Western-style rooms, 38 Japanese-style rooms. Coffee shop, meeting rooms. AE, MC, V.*

$ ⚟ **Pension Higashiyama.** A 10-minute walk from downtown and the major temples along the eastern foothills, this relatively new, small pension overlooks the lovely Shira-kawa canal south of Sanjō-dōri. The pension has created a friendly atmosphere for families on a budget and is accustomed to gai-jin. ✉ *474-23 Umemiya-chō, Shirakawa-suji, Sanjō-sagaru, Higashiyama-ku, Kyōto-shi 605,* ☎ *075/882–1181. 15 rooms, some with toilet; all share bath. Dining room. AE.*

$ ⚟ **Ryokan Yuhara.** A 15-minute walk from the old quarters of Gion and Ponto-chō, Yuhara is popular among repeat visitors wishing to save a few yen while exploring Kyōto. The friendliness of the staff more than compensates for the spartan amenities. Especially rewarding is a springtime stay, when the cherry trees are in full bloom along the Takase-gawa, which the inn overlooks. ✉ *188 Kagiya-chō, Shomen-agaru,*

Kiya-machi-dōri, Higashiyama-ku, Kyōto-shi 600, ☎ 075/371–9583. 8 rooms. No credit cards.

Northern Kyōto

$$$$ ☐ **Takaraga-ike Prince Hotel.** Kyōto's only deluxe hotel is on the northern outskirts of the city, across from the International Conference Hall and Takaraga-ike (pond). Although useful if you are attending an event at the conference hall, the hotel is a good 30 minutes from the city center and not convenient for sightseeing. Nevertheless, its unusual doughnut-shape design provides each room with a view of the surrounding mountains and forests. Corridors along the inside overlook an inner garden. Finer touches include huge floral arrangements in the lobby, impressive chandeliers all around the building, and original Miró prints, which hang in every suite. The spacious rooms have beds that are probably the largest you'll find in Japan. All rooms are tastefully decorated in colors that complement the greenery of the outside views. This is one of the only hotels in Kyōto with their own authentic teahouse; this one overlooks the pond. Demonstrations of tea ceremony can be arranged upon request. ✉ *Takaraga-ike, Sakyō-ku, Kyōto-shi 606, ☎ 075/712–1111, FAX 075/712–7677. 322 rooms. 6 restaurants, 4 bars, tea shop, shop. AE, DC, MC, V.*

NIGHTLIFE AND THE ARTS

The Arts

Kyōto is quickly following Tōkyō and Ōsaka on domestic and international performing artist's circuits. Kyōto has hosted the likes of Bruce Springsteen, but it is famous for traditional arts—dance and Kabuki and Nō theater. All dialogue at theaters is in Japanese, of course.

Information on performances is available from a number of sources, the most convenient being your hotel concierge or guest-relations manager. He or she may even have a few tickets on hand, so don't hesitate to ask.

Kyōto has a 24-hour weekly recording of festivals, sporting events, and performances. Call 075/361–2911 for a recording in English. Another source is **JNTO's Tourist Information Center (TIC)**, directly across from Kyōto Eki. It is strongly suggested that you stop by the TIC if you are interested in Kyōto's arts scene. The monthly *Kyōto Visitor's Guide* devotes a few pages to "This Month's Theater." If you don't have time to go to TIC, call 075/371–5649 for an English-speaking information officer.

See also Chapter 2 for descriptions of Japanese performing arts.

Gion Corner

If there is one performance to see, it is the quick but comprehensive overview of Kyōto's performing arts at Gion Corner. The one-hour show has court music and dance, ancient comic plays, Kyōto-style dance performed by *maiko*—apprentice geisha—and puppet drama. Segments are also offered on tea ceremony, flower arrangement, and koto music.

★ For tickets, contact your hotel concierge or call **Gion Corner** (✉ Yasaka Hall, 1st floor, Gion, ☎ 075/561–1119). The show is quite a bargain at ¥2,500. Two performances nightly are given at 7:40 and 8:40 March 1–November 29. No performances are offered August 16 and December–February.

Before attending a show, walk around Gion and Ponto-chō. You are likely to see beautifully dressed geisha and maiko making their way to work. It is permissible to take their picture—"*Sasshin o totte mō ii desu ka?*" is the polite way to ask—but as they have strict appointments, don't delay them.

Seasonal Dances

★ If you are in Kyōto in April, be sure to take in the **Miyako Odori;** or, in May and October, the **Kamo-gawa Odori.** These geisha and apprentice dances—singing is also involved—pay tribute to the seasonal splendor of spring and fall. The stage setting is spectacular.

Performances are held at the **Gion Kaburenjō Theater** (⊠ Gion Hanamikōji, Higashiyama-ku, ☎ 075/561–1115), where tickets cost ¥1,650, ¥3,300, and ¥3,800, and the **Ponto-chō Kaburenjō Theater** (⊠ Ponto-chō, Sanjō-sagaru, Nakagyō-ku, ☎ 075/221–2025); where tickets range from ¥1,650 to ¥3,800.

Kabuki

Kabuki has found quite a following in the United States due to recent tours by Japan's Kabuki troupes in Washington, D.C., New York, and a few other cities. Kabuki is faster paced than Nō, but a single performance can easily take half a day. Devoted followers pack bentō and sit patiently through the entire performance, mesmerized by each movement of the performers.

For a first-timer, however, the music and seemingly bizarre intonations of Kabuki might be a bit of an overload. Unless you are captured by the Kabuki spirit, don't spend more than an hour or two at Kyōto's famed **Minami-za** (⊠ Shijō Kamo-gawa, Higashiyama-ku, ☎ 075/561–1155), the oldest theater in Japan. Beautifully renovated, it hosts a variety of performances year-round. Top Kabuki stars from around the country make guest appearances during the annual, monthlong **Kaomise** (Face Showing) Kabuki festival in December. Again, go to the Tourist Information Center for information. Tickets range from ¥2,000 to ¥9,000.

Nō

Nō is another form of traditional theater, more ritualistic and sophisticated than Kabuki. Some understanding of the plot of each play is necessary to enjoy a performance, which is generally slow moving and solemnly chanted. Major Nō theaters often provide synopses of the plays in English. The masks used by the main actors are carved to express a whole range of emotions, though the mask itself may appear expressionless until the actor "brings it to life." Particularly memorable are
★ the outdoor performances of Nō, especially **Takigi Nō,** held outdoors by firelight on the nights of June 1–2 in the precincts of the Heian Shrine.

Performances are given year-round at **Kanze Kaikan Nō Theater** (⊠ 44 Enshōji-chō, Okazaki, Sakyō-ku, ☎ 075/771–6114) and **Kongo Nō Theater** (⊠ Muro-machi, Shijō-agaru, Nakagyō-ku, ☎ 075/221–3049). Prices vary per performance and range from ¥4,000 to ¥6,000.

Nightlife

Kyōto's nightlife is more sedate than Ōsaka's, but the areas around the old geisha quarters downtown are still thriving with nightclubs and bars. The Kiya-machi area along the small canal near Ponto-chō is as close to a consolidated nightlife area as you'll get in Kyōto. It is full of small watering holes with red lanterns (indicating inexpensive places) or small neon signs in front. It is also fun to walk around the Gion and Ponto-chō areas to try to catch a glimpse of a geisha or apprentice geisha coming or going to or from work.

One of three Kansai-area **Pig & Whistle** pubs (⊠ Across from the Keihan Sanjō Eki, Shobi Bldg., ☎ 075/761–6022) is a popular hangout, and every weekend the Kyōto branch bulges at the seams. For jazz, blues, and soul, **Live Spot Rag** (⊠ Kyōto Empire Bldg., 5th floor, Kiya-machi, ☎ 075/241–0446), north of Sanjō-dōri, has a reasonable cover charge of about ¥1,200 for its live sessions between 7 and 11 PM. Though only open on Saturday nights from 8:30 to 11:00, **Kenny's** (⊠ Northwest corner of Shimei-dōri and Karasuma-dōri, ☎ 075/415–1171) is a well-known country-and-western bar with live performances by one of Japan's C&W legends. Kenny has even played the Grand Old Opry in Nashville. A good stop for late-night food is **Ninniku-ya** (⊠ Gion Theater, 4th floor, Higashi-ōji dōri, near Yasuka Shrine, ☎ 075/533–4192)—literally, "Garlic House"—which is open until midnight Sunday–Friday and until 3 AM weekends. Food is reasonably priced and very garlicky, and the atmosphere is very cosmopolitan.

One of the best clubs in Kansai is Kyōto's **Metro** (⊠ Ebisu Bldg., 2nd floor, Shimotsutsumi-chō 82, Maruta-machi Sagaru, Kawabata-dōri, Sakyō-ku, ☎ 075/752–4765), which has an extremely wide range of regular events, from salsa to reggae, as well as frequent guest appearances by famous DJs from both Tōkyō and abroad. The club is small but has a good atmosphere, and it is usually packed—even on weekday nights.

SHOPPING

Most shops slide open their doors at 10. Most shopkeepers partake of the morning ritual of sweeping and watering the entrance to welcome the morning's first customers. Shops lock up at 6 or 7 in the evening. Usually, once a week shops remain closed. As Sunday is a big shopping day for the Japanese, most stores remain open.

The traditional greeting of a shopkeeper to a customer is *o-ideyasu* ("honored to have you here" in *Kyōto-ben*, Kyōto dialect), voiced in a lilting Kyōto dialect with the required bowing of the head. When a customer makes a purchase, the shopkeeper will respond with *o-okini* ("thank you" in Kyōto-ben), a smile, and a bow. Take notice of the careful effort and adroitness with which purchases are wrapped; it is an art in itself. Also, you'll still hear the clicking of an abacus, rather than the crunching of a cash register, in many Kyōto shops. American Express, MasterCard, Visa, and traveler's checks are widely accepted.

If you plan to make shopping one of your prime pursuits in Kyōto, look for a copy of Diane Durston's thorough *Old Kyōto: A Guide to Traditional Shops, Restaurants, and Inns.*

Crafts Centers

For a description of Kyōto crafts, *see* Pleasures and Pastimes, *above.*

The **Kyōto Craft Center** on Shijō-dōri in Gion has two floors of contemporary and traditional crafts for sale in a modern setting. More than 100 crafts studios are represented, giving a diversity to the products for sale. ⊠ *Shijō-dōri, Gion-machi, Higashiyama-ku,* ☎ *075/561–9660.* ☉ *Thurs.–Tues. 10–6.*

The **Kyōto Handicraft Center** is a seven-story shopping emporium offering everything from tape decks and pearl necklaces to porcelains and lacquerware designed to appeal to tourists. It's a good place to compare prices and grab last-minute souvenirs. ⊠ *Kumano Jinja Higashi, Sakyō-ku,* ☎ *075/761–5080.* ☉ *Daily, Feb.–Dec. 9:30–6; Jan. 9:30–5:30; closed Dec. 31–Jan. 3.*

Shopping Districts

Compared with sprawling Tōkyō, Kyōto is compact and relatively easy to navigate. Major shops line both sides of **Shijō-dōri,** which runs east–west, and **Kawara-machi-dōri,** which runs north–south. Concentrate on Shijō-dōri between Yasaka Jinja and Karasuma Station as well as Kawara-machi-dōri between Sanjō-dōri and Shijō-dōri.

Whereas the shopping districts above are traditional in atmosphere, Kyōto's latest shopping "district" is the modern underground arcade, **Porta,** at Kyōto Eki. You'll find more than 200 shops and restaurants in this sprawling, subterranean arcade.

Roads leading to Kiyomizu-dera are steep inclines, yet you'll hardly notice the steepness for all of the alluring shops that line the way to the temple. Be sure to peek in for unique gifts. Food shops offer sample morsels, and tea shops serve complimentary cups of tea.

Shin-Kyōgoku, a covered arcade running parallel to Kawara-machi-dōri, is another general-purpose shopping area with many souvenir shops.

Gift Ideas

Art and Antiques

Shinmonzen-dōri holds the key to shopping for art and antiques in Kyōto. It is an unpretentious little street of two-story wood buildings that is lined with telephone and electricity poles between Higashi-ōji-dōri and Hanamikōji-dōri, just north of Gion. What gives the street away as a treasure trove are the large credit-card signs jutting out from the shops. There are no fewer than 17 shops specializing in scrolls, *netsuke* (small carved figures to attach to Japanese clothing), lacquerware, bronze, wood-block prints, paintings, and antiques. Shop with confidence, because shopkeepers are trustworthy and goods are authentic. Pick up a copy of the pamphlet *Shinmonzen Street Shopping Guide* from your hotel or from the Tourist Information Center.

Nawate-dōri, between Shijō-dōri and Sanjō-dōri, is noted for fine antique textiles, ceramics, and paintings.

Tera-machi-dōri, between Oike-dōri and Maruta-machi, is known for antiques of all kinds and tea-ceremony utensils.

Bamboo

The Japanese hope for their sons and daughters to be as strong and flexible as bamboo. Around many Japanese houses are small bamboo groves, for the deep-rooted plant has the ability to withstand earthquakes. On the other hand, bamboo is so flexible that it bends into innumerable shapes. The entire city of Kyōto is surrounded by bamboo groves. The wood is carefully cut and dried for several months before being stripped and woven into baskets and vases.

Kagoshin is a historic shop that has made bamboo baskets since 1862. Only the best varieties of bamboo are used in this fiercely proud little shop. ⊠ *Ōhashi-higashi, Sanjō-dōri, Higashiyama-ku,* ☎ *075/771–0209.* ☼ *Mon.–Sat. 9–6.*

Ceramics

Tachikichi, on Shijō-dōri west of Kawara-machi, has four floors of contemporary and traditional wares and the best reputation in town. ⊠ *Shijō-Tominokōji, Nakagyō-ku,* ☎ *075/211–3143.* ☼ *Thurs.–Tues. 10–7.*

Asahi-do, in the heart of the pottery district near Kiyomizu-dera, specializes in Kyōto-style hand-painted porcelain and a variety of other ceramics. ⊠ *1-280 Kiyomizu, Higashiyama-ku,* ☎ *075/531–2181.* ☺ *Mon.–Sat. 8:30–6, Sun. 9–6.*

Dolls

Ningyō were first used in Japan in the purification rites associated with the Doll Festival, an annual family-oriented event on March 3. Kyōto *ningyō* are made with fine detail and embellishment.

Nakanishi Toku Shōten has old museum-quality dolls. The owner, Mr. Nakanishi, turned his extensive doll collection into the shop two decades ago and has since been educating customers with his vast knowledge of the doll trade. ⊠ *359 Moto-chō, Yamato-ōji Higashi-Iru, Furumonzen-dōri, Higashiyama-ku,* ☎ *075/561–7309.* ☺ *Daily 10–5.*

Folk Crafts

Yamato Mingei-ten, next to Maruzen Book Store downtown, has the best selection of Japanese folk crafts, including ceramics, metal work, paper, lacquerware, and textiles. ⊠ *Kawara-machi, Takoyakushi-agaru, Nakagyō-ku,* ☎ *075/221–2641.* ☺ *Wed.–Mon. 10–8:30.*

At **Ryushido** you can stock up on calligraphy and *sumi* supplies, including writing brushes, ink sticks, ink stones, Japanese paper, paperweights, and water stoppers. ⊠ *Nijō-agaru, Tera-machi-dōri (north of Nijō), Kamigyō-ku,* ☎ *075/252–4120.* ☺ *Daily 10–7.*

Kuraya Hashimoto has one of the best collections of antique and newly forged swords, as well as reproductions. ⊠ *Nishihorikawa-dōri, Oike-agaru (southeast corner of Nijō-jō), Nakagyō-ku,* ☎ *075/821–2791.* ☺ *Thurs.–Tues. 10–6.*

Kimono and Accessories

Shimmering new silk kimono can cost well over ¥1,000,000—they are art objects, as well as couture—while equally stunning old silk kimono can cost less than ¥3,000. You can find used kimono at two local end-of-the-month markets (☞ *Flea Markets, below*). Shop accordingly.

The **Nishijin Orimono** (Textile Center), in central Kyōto, will provide an orientation on silk-weaving techniques. ⊠ *Horikawa-dōri, Imadegawa-Minami-Iru, Kamigyō-ku,* ☎ *075/451–9231.* 🎟 *Free.* ☺ *Daily 9–5.*

Two blocks east of the textile center on Imadegawa-dōri and a block south is **Aizen Kobo,** which specializes in the finest handwoven indigo-dyed textiles. The shop is in a traditional weaving family's home, and the friendly owners will show you a wide variety of dyed and woven goods, including garments designed by Hisako Utsuki, the owner's wife. ⊠ *Ōmiya Nishi-Iru, Nakasuji-dōri, Kamigyō-ku,* ☎ *075/441–0355.* ☺ *Daily 9–5:30.*

Umbrellas are used to protect kimono from the scorching sun or pelting rain. Head for **Kasagen** to purchase authentic oiled paper umbrellas. The shop has been in existence since 1861, and its umbrellas are guaranteed to last years. ⊠ *284 Gion-machi, Kita-gawa, Higashiyama-ku,* ☎ *075/561–2832.* ☺ *Daily 9:30–9.*

Authentic silk kimono are very heavy; this factor may dissuade some of you from making that special purchase. If smaller objects are your fancy, try a fan or comb. The most famous fan shop in all of Kyōto is **Miyawaki Baisen-an,** in business since 1823. It delights customers not only with its fine collection of lacquered, scented, painted, and paper fans but also with the Old World atmosphere that emanates from the building that houses the shop. ⊠ *Tominokōji Nishi-Iru, Rokkaku-dōri, Nakagyō-ku,* ☎ *075/221–0181.* ☺ *Daily 9–5.*

If you are looking for kimono accessories like *obi* (sashes), handbags, and *furoshiki* (the cloth used to wrap gifts), **Takumi** is the place to go. ⊠ *Sanjō-sagaru, Kawara-machi-dōri, Nakagyō-ku,* ☎ *075/221–2278.* ⊙ *Daily 10:30–9.*

Depāto

Kyōto *depāto* (department stores) are small by comparison with their mammoth counterparts in Tōkyō and Ōsaka. One looks just like the other, as they have similar floor plans. Scarves, shoes, jewelry, and handbags can be always found on the ground floor. The basement floor is devoted to foodstuffs, and the top floor is reserved for pets and pet-care goods, gardening, and restaurants.

Daimaru, on the main Shijō-dōri shopping avenue, is the most conveniently located of these one-stop shopping emporiums. ⊠ *Shijō-Karasuma, Shimogyō-ku,* ☎ *075/211–8111.* ⊙ *Thurs.–Tues. 10–7.*

Hankyū, directly across from Takashimaya on Kawara-machi-dōri, has two restaurant floors. Window displays show the type of food served, and prices are clearly marked. ⊠ *Shijō-Kawara-machi, Shimogyō-ku,* ☎ *075/223–2288.* ⊙ *Fri.–Wed. 10–7.*

Kintetsu is on Karasuma-dōri, the main avenue leading north from Kyōto Eki. ⊠ *Karasuma-dōri, Shimogyō-ku,* ☎ *075/361–1111.* ⊙ *Fri.–Wed. 10–7.*

Takashimaya, on Kawara-machi-dōri, has a well-trained English-speaking staff at its information desk, as well as a convenient money-exchange counter on its premises. ⊠ *Shijō-Kawara-machi, Shimogyō-ku,* ☎ *075/221–8811.* ⊙ *Thurs.–Tues. 10–7.*

Food and Flea Markets

Kyōto has a wonderful food market, **Nishiki-kōji,** which branches off from the Shin-Kyōgoku covered arcade across from Daimaru department store in central Kyōto. Look for delicious grilled fish dipped in soy for a tasty snack. Try to avoid the market in late afternoon, when housewives come to do their daily shopping. The market is long and narrow; in a sizable crowd, there is always the possibility of being pushed into the display of fresh fish.

Two renowned **flea markets** take place monthly in Kyōto. Reserve the 21st of the month for the famous **Tō-ji market** (☞ Central Kyōto, *above*) and the 25th of the month for the **Kitano Tenman-gū market** (☞ Western Kyōto, *above*). Both are open from dawn to dusk. Among the old kimono, antiques, and bric-a-brac may be an unusual souvenir.

Unusual Shopping

Shops dedicated to incense, wood tubs and casks, Buddhist objects, and chopsticks indeed offer unusual experiences. But the prized souvenir of a visit to Kyōto should be the **shuinshu,** a booklet usually no larger than 4 by 6 inches. It is most often covered with brocade, and the blank sheets of heavyweight paper inside continuously fold out. You can find them at stationery stores or at temples for as little as ¥1,000 and use them as "passports" to collect ink stamps from places you visit while in Japan. Stamps and stamp pads are ubiquitous in Japan—at sights, train stations, and some restaurants. Most ink stamping will be done for free; at temples ask a monk to write calligraphy over the stamp for a small fee.

KYŌTO A TO Z

Arriving and Departing

By Plane

The closest international airport to Kyōto is **Kansai International Airport** (KIX), near Ōsaka. KIX does have domestic flights, particularly to major cities, but the majority of internal air traffic still uses Ōsaka's **Itami Airport.** Flight time between Tōkyō and Ōsaka is about 70 minutes.

BETWEEN THE AIRPORTS AND CENTER CITY

From KIX: To Kyōto Eki, take the JR Haruka Limited Express, which departs every 30 minutes to make the 75-minute run at ¥3,340; or use a JR Pass. **From Itami:** Buses depart for Kyōto approximately every 20 minutes, 7:45 AM–9:30 PM, stopping at nine hotels and Kyōto Eki. The trip takes 55 to 90 minutes and costs ¥890 or ¥950, depending on the Kyōto destination.

Taxis cost more than ¥10,000 from KIX and Itami to Kyōto.

By Train

JR Shinkansen. Frequent daily Shinkansen run between Tōkyō and Kyōto (2 hours, 40 minutes). The one-way fare, including charges for a reserved seat, is ¥12,970. Service between Ōsaka and Kyōto (30 minutes) costs ¥530, one-way. From the Shin-Ōsaka Eki, you can take the Shinkansen and be in Kyōto in 15 minutes; tickets cost ¥2,250. You may use a Japan Rail Pass on Hikari and Kodama Shinkansen.

Private Lines. The Keihan and the Hankyū trains (40 minutes each), are less expensive than the JR, unless you have a JR Pass. The one-way Ōsaka–Kyōto fare is ¥360 on the Keihan and ¥350 on the Hankyū line.

Getting Around

By Bicycle

For the most part Kyōto is flat, making getting around by bicycle easy and very convenient. Rental Cycle Yasumoto Kawabata has bikes at ¥200 per hour or ¥1,000 per day (⊠ 243 Sanjūsangen-dō, Higashiyama-ku, ☎ 075/751–0595).

By Bus

A network of bus routes covers the entire city. Most city buses run 7 AM–9 PM daily, but a few start as early as 5:30 AM and run until 11 PM. The main bus terminals are Kyōto Eki, Keihan Sanjō Eki, Karasuma-Kitao-ji, and at the Shijō-dōri–Karasuma-dōri intersection. Many city buses do not have signs in English, so you will need to know the bus number. Because you will probably ride the bus at least once in Kyōto, try to pick up a bus map early in your stay from the Tourist Information Center (☎ 075/371–5649) at the Kyōto Tower Building, across from the JR Kyōto Eki.

At each bus stop, a guidepost indicates the stop name, the bus route, and the bus-route number. Because the information at most guideposts is only in Japanese (except for the route number, which is given as an Arabic numeral), you are advised to ask your hotel clerk beforehand to write down your destination in Japanese, along with the route number, to show to the bus driver and fellow passengers; this will allow the driver and others to help you if you get lost. You might also ask your hotel clerk beforehand how many stops your ride will take.

Within the city, the standard fare is ¥220, which you pay before leaving the bus; outside the city limits, the fare varies according to distance. Special one-day passes are valid for unlimited rides on the subway, city buses, and the private Kyōto Line buses, with restrictions on some routes. The passes, which cost ¥1,250, are sold at travel agencies, main bus terminals, and information centers in Kyōto Eki.

You can use a JR Pass on the local bus that travels between Kyōto Eki and Takao (in northwestern Kyōto), passing close to Nijō Eki.

By Taxi

Taxis are readily available in Kyōto. Fares for smaller-size cabs start at ¥590 for the first 2 km (1 mi), with a cost of ¥90 for each additional ⅓ mi.

By Train

Kyōto has a 13-station **subway** line that runs between Takeda Station in the south and Kitayama Station in the north. The entire run takes 20 minutes. Purchase tickets at the station's automatic vending machines before boarding. Fares increase with distance traveled and begin at ¥180. Service runs 5:30 AM–11:30 PM. In Kyōto, the **Keihan Line** from Ōsaka is now partly underground (from Shichijō Eki to Demachi-Yanagi Eki) and extends all the way up the east bank of the Kamo-gawa to Imadegawa-dōri. At Imadegawa-dōri a passage connects the Keihan Line with the **Eizan Railway**'s Demachi-Yanagi Eki. The Eizan has two lines, the Kurama Line, running north to Kurama, and the Eizan Line, running northeast to Yase. The **Hankyū Line**, which runs to the Katsura Rikyū, connects with the subway at Karasuma Eki. From Shijō-Ōmiya Eki, the **Keifuku Arashiyama Line** runs to western Kyōto. **JR** also runs to western Kyōto on the San-in Main Line.

Contacts and Resources

Consulates

The nearest U.S., Canadian, and British consulates are in Ōsaka (☞ Ōsaka A to Z *in* Chapter 9).

Doctors and Dentists

Daiichi Sekijuji (Red Cross Hospital). ⊠ *Higashiyama Hon-machi, Higashiyama-ku,* ☎ 075/561–1121.

Daini Sekijuji Byoin (2nd Red Cross Hospital). ⊠ *Kamanza-dōri, Maruta-machi-agaru, Kamigyō-ku,* ☎ 075/231–5171.

Japan Baptist Hospital. ⊠ *Kita-Shirakawa, Yamanomoto-chō, Sakyō-ku,* ☎ 075/781–5191.

Sakabe Clinic has 24-hour emergency facilities. ⊠ *435 Yamamoto-chō, Gokō-machi, Nijō Sagaru, Nakagyō-ku,* ☎ 075/231–1624.

Emergencies

Police, ☎ 110. **Ambulance,** ☎ 119.

English-Language Bookstores

Maruzen Kyōto (⊠ 296 Kawara-machi-dōri, Nakagyō-ku, ☎ 075/241–2169) has the city's broadest selection of books. **Izumiya Book Center** (⊠ Avanti Bldg., 6th floor, Minami-ku, ☎ 075/671–8987) has a large corner of its store devoted to English-language books and is across from Kyōto Eki, Shinkansen side. **Kyōto Shoin** (⊠ Kawara-machi, 3rd floor, north of Shijō, Nakagyō-ku, ☎ 075/221–1062) has a useful array of books on Japan and a limited selection of fiction.

Guided Tours

EXCURSIONS

Full- and half-day tours to Nara are offered by Sunrise Tours (☎ 075/341–1413), a subsidiary of **Japan Travel Bureau** (☎ 075/361–7241). Other tour companies include **Fujita Travel Service** (☎ 075/222–0121) and **Kintetsu Gray Line Tours** (☎ 075/691–0903). An afternoon tour to Nara costs about ¥6,500. Morning and afternoon trips to Ōsaka, for ¥7,900 and ¥5,000, respectively, are not worth the cost, especially if you have a JR Pass. **Sunrise Tours** organizes excursions down an 15-km (8-mi) stretch (about 90 minutes) of the Hozu Rapids in flat-bottom boats, from Kameoka to Arashiyama, for ¥9,800.

ORIENTATION TOURS

Half-day morning and afternoon deluxe motor-coach tours featuring different city highlights are offered daily by the Japan Travel Bureau's **Sunrise Tours** (⊠ Kyōto Eki-mae, ☎ 075/341–1413). Tours are also given daily March–November by **Kintetsu Gray Line Tours** (⊠ New Miyako Hotel, Minami-ku, ☎ 075/691–0903) and **Japan Amenity Travel** (⊠ International Hotel Kyōto lobby, ☎ 075/222–0121; ⊠ Kyōto Grand Hotel lobby, ☎ 075/343–2304). Pickup service is provided at major hotels. A ¥5,200 morning tour commonly covers Nijō-jō, Kinkaku-ji, Kyōto Imperial Palace, Higashi-Hongan-ji, and the Kyōto Handicraft Center. A ¥5,200 afternoon tour includes the Heian Shrine, Sanjūsangen-dō, and Kiyomizu Temple. A ¥11,000 full-day tour covers all the above sights and includes lunch.

PERSONAL GUIDES

Contact **Japan Amenity Travel** (☎ 075/222–0121), **Joe Okada Travel Service** (☎ 075/241–3716), or **Inter Kyōto** (☎ 075/256–3685). **Volunteer guides** are available free of charge through the Tourist Information Center (TIC), but arrangements must be made by visiting the TIC in person one day in advance (☞ Visitor Information, *below*).

SPECIAL-INTEREST TOURS

Joe Okada Travel Service (⊠ Masugata Bldg., 3rd floor, Tera-machi-agaru Imadegawa, Kamigyō-ku, ☎ 075/241–3716) conducts special tours of Kyōto and arranges home visits for individuals and groups. Call Joe and he will tailor your tour to fit your interests and budget. Private tours are more expensive, so it's best to get together a group. Home visits are also arranged by the **Tourist Section, Department of Cultural Affairs and Tourism** (⊠ Kyōto City Government, Kyōto Kaikan, Okazaki, Sakyō-ku, ☎ 075/752–0215).

WALKING TOURS

Personable Kyōto-ite **Johnnie Hajime Hirooka** has walking tours of Kyōto, in English, that leave from Kyōto Eki at 10:30 AM Monday–Thursday, early March through late-November, rain or shine. Itineraries vary—often taking people to sights they might not otherwise see—and walks last three hours and cost ¥2,000 per person, ¥3,000 per couple. The **Japan National Tourist Organization** JNTO) publishes suggested walking routes, which offer maps and brief descriptions for five tours (ranging in length from about 40 minutes to 80 minutes). The walking-tour brochures are available from the JNTO's Tourist Information Center office at the Kyōto Tower Building in front of Kyōto Eki (☎ 075/371–5649).

Travel Agencies

Japan Travel Bureau (⊠ Kyōto Eki-mae, Shiokōji Karasuma Higashi-Iru, Shimogyō-ku, ☎ 075/361–7241).

Japan Amenity Travel (⊠ International Hotel Kyōto lobby, ☎ 075/222–0121).

Kintetsu Gray Line Tours Reservation Center (⊠ New Miyako Hotel, Minami-ku, ☎ 075/691–0903).

Joe Okada Travel Service (⊠ Masugata Bldg., Tera-machi-agaru Imadegawa, Kamigyō-ku, ☎ 075/241–3716).

Visitor Information

The Japan National Tourist Organization's (JNTO) **Tourist Information Center** (TIC) is in the Kyōto Tower Building, in front of the JR
Kyōto Eki (take the Karasuma exit, on the side opposite the Shinkansen
tracks). ✉ *Karasuma-dōri Higashi-Shiokōji-chō, Shimogyō-ku,* ☎
075/371–5649. ⊙ *Weekdays 9–5, Sat. 9–noon.*

The JNTO Teletourist Service (☎ 075/361–2911) offers taped information
on events in and around the city.

The **Kyōto City Government** operates a tourist information office. ✉
Kyōto Kaikan, Okazaki, Sakyō-ku, ☎ *075/752–0215.* ⊙ *Weekdays
8:30–5, Sat. 8:30–noon; closed 2nd and 4th Sat. of month.*

The Japan Travel Phone, a nationwide telephone information system
in English for visitors, is available 9–5 daily, year-round. It is run out
of the same office as the TIC (☞ *above*). In Kyōto, a three-minute call
(☎ 075/371–5649) costs ¥10.

8 Nara

Nara's parks and ancient temples and traditional shops and restaurants make it one of Japan's quintessential old cities. It might not have the volume of sacred sights that Kyōto has—or all of its concrete and steel—but Nara's shrines and parks are among the country's finest. The fact that it exists in the midst of Japan's overbuilt industrial corridor makes Nara's restful quality that much more precious.

THE ANCIENT CITY OF NARA was founded in 710 by Emperor Kammu—thus predating Kyōto—and it was the first Japanese capital to remain in one place over

By Nigel Fisher a long period of time. Until then, capitals had been established in new locations with each successive ruler. The founding of Nara, then known as Heijō-Kyō, occurred during a period when Japan's politics, arts, architecture, and religion were being heavily influenced by China. The Japanese also began using and adapting *kanji,* Chinese characters, in their writing system at this time.

Introduced from China in the 6th century, Buddhism flourished in Nara and enjoyed the official favor of the rulers and aristocracy, even as it coexisted with the indigenous Shinto religion. Many of Nara's Buddhist temples and monasteries were built by emperors and noble families, while other temples were transferred to Nara from former capitals. At its peak during the 8th century, Nara was said to have had as many as 50 pagodas. Emperor Shōmu built Tōdai-ji, a grand temple complex that was to serve as a central monastery for other Buddhist monasteries constructed in each province of Japan. Tōdai-ji's construction began in 745 and was completed in 752. Established not only for spiritual purposes, Tōdai-ji also served as a symbol of a united Japan. Emperor Shōmu, who saw much to emulate in Chinese culture, astutely realized that religion could play a strong role in consolidating Japan.

In 784, the capital of Japan was transferred to Kyōto, and Nara lost its status as a city of political consequence. As a result, the many buildings of Nara, including Tōdai-ji, remained essentially untouched by the ravages of war. Kōfuku-ji recalls the power of the Fujiwara clan in the 7th century. Its close connection with Kasuga Taisha, the Fujiwara family shrine, demonstrates the peaceful coexistence of Buddhism and Shintoism. Both Tōdai-ji and Tōshōdai-ji show how pervasively and consistently Buddhism has influenced the Japanese way of life.

Nara Glossary

Key Japanese words and suffixes in this chapter include *-bashi* (bridge), *-chō* (street or block), *-den* (hall), *dōri* (avenue), *eki* (train station), *gaijin* (foreigner), *ike* ("*ee*-keh," pond), *izakaya* (pub), *-ji* (temple), *-jō* (castle), *-ken* (prefecture), *kōen* ("*kō*-en," park), *-mon* (gate), *sakura* (cherry blossoms), and *torii* ("*to*-ree-ee," gate).

Pleasures and Pastimes

Architecture

Many of Nara's temples and shrines are among the oldest wooden structures in the world—unlike the replicas found elsewhere in Japan. Crafted in the period when Buddhism was first imported to Japan, they have a purity of intention that reflects the spirit of newly born imperial and religious institutions.

Dining

The foods of Nara resemble those of its neighbor, Kyōto. The specialty of this region is *kaiseki,* carefully prepared and aesthetically pleasing 7- to 12-course meals. One local dish is *cha-gayu,* rice porridge flavored with green tea and served with vegetables in season. Nara claims the lowest rate of stomach cancer in Japan, and local wisdom attributes this to the healthfulness of cha-gayu. Even Western doctors have acknowledged its benefits. An unforgettable gourmet experience is your first bite of *narazuke,* tangy vegetables pickled in sake, often served as a side dish with traditional meals in Nara.

Most day-trippers to Nara do not plan to dine in town, but an elegant Japanese meal in a traditional Nara restaurant is a fine way to conclude a day of temple viewing. If you do not have time for dinner, at least try a leisurely lunch.

A few words of advice: Many Nara restaurants are small and have limited menus with set courses and no à la carte dishes, so it is a good idea to make reservations in advance. Restaurants tend to close early in Nara; plan accordingly. Because some places do not have English-speaking staff or menus in English, ask someone from your hotel to help make your arrangements. This may seem like a lot of trouble for the sake of eating, but the quiet atmosphere and the hospitality of local residents make Nara a memorable place to enjoy a traditional meal.

The best area for finding small restaurants and *izakaya* is in the maze of streets that make up Nara-machi. Unless you know a few words of Japanese, you may need to point to an appetizing dish that another diner is enjoying. That is okay, but remember that each time you point, it might add ¥500–¥800 to your bill. Expect to pay about ¥750 for a large bottle of beer.

CATEGORY	COST*
$$$$	over ¥7,000
$$$	¥5,000–¥7,000
$$	¥3,500–¥5,000
$	under ¥3,500

per person, excluding drinks, service, and tax

Lodging

Nara has fine accommodations in every style and price range, and because most people think of the city as a day-trip destination, the streets are deserted at night. If you stay over, you'll have a chance to stroll undisturbed beside the ponds and in temple grounds.

CATEGORY	COST*
$$$$	over ¥30,000
$$$	¥20,000–¥30,000
$$	¥10,000–¥20,000
$	under ¥10,000

All prices are for a double room, excluding tax and service.

Shopping

The hidden treasures of Nara-machi's narrow back streets, just south of Sarusawa-ike, are among Nara's delights. Alongside merchants' houses and traditional restaurants, old wooden shops sell the crafts for which Nara is famous: *fude* ("*foo*-deh," handmade brushes) and *sumi* (ink sticks) for calligraphy and ink painting, Nara dolls carved in wood, and Nara *sarashi-jofu*—fine, handwoven, sun-bleached linen.

EXPLORING NARA

At its founding in the 8th century, Nara was planned as a rectangular city with checkerboard streets based on the model of the Chinese city of Ch'ang-an. The city has maintained this highly organized pattern, and it is therefore extremely easy to navigate. Central Nara sights are within walking distance of picturesque Nara Kōen. Other major temples, such as Hōryū-ji, Yakushi-ji, and Tōshōdai-ji, are in western Nara on one bus route.

Great Itineraries

In spite of the numbers of people who try to take Nara by storm in one day, you simply cannot do justice to all of its temples and shrines on a day trip. Two days is the proper allowance—one for central Nara and the second for western Nara. Should you have just a day, start with the sights around Nara Kōen, such as Tōdai-ji and its Daibutsuden, Kōfuku-ji with its five-story pagoda, and Kasuga Taisha, and leave the afternoon to see western Nara's Hōryū-ji, the oldest remaining temple complex in all of Japan, and possibly Yakushi-ji or Tōshōdai-ji.

When to Tour Nara

As with most of Japan, spring, especially in sakura time, is ideal. In winter, cold, gray skies can dampen one's spirits. Summer is invariably hot and humid. Autumn, like spring, has the best temperature for walking from sight to sight gazing at fall foliage color.

Numbers in the text correspond to numbers in the margin and on the Central Nara and Western Nara maps.

Central Nara

Much of what you will come to Nara to see will be in the central part of the city, such as the temples and Great Buddha in Nara Kōen and the back streets of Nara-machi.

A Good Walk

Begin exploring Nara at the resplendent **Tōdai-ji** ①, in Nara Kōen. To get there, board Bus 2 from the front of either the JR or Kintetsu eki; get off at the Daibutsu-den stop. Cross the street and you will be at the path that leads to the Tōdai-ji complex. You can also walk from Kintetsu Nara Eki to Tōdai-ji in about 15 minutes. From the east end of the station walk east on Noborioji-dōri, the avenue that runs parallel to the station. In Nara Kōen, turn left onto the pedestrians-only street that leads to Tōdai-ji. It is lined with souvenir stalls and small restaurants. You can walk from the JR eki, but the route is longer and passes through the less attractive modern sections of town.

As you walk along the path leading to the temple complex, you will pass through the impressive dark wood front gate known as **Nandai-mon** ②, which is supported by 18 large wood pillars.

Continue straight on the path to the main buildings of the Tōdai-ji temple compound. The entrance of the Daibutsu-den is in front of you, but before entering this hall, first go to the small temple on the left, **Kaidan-in** ③, guarded by four ferocious-looking statues. From Kaidan-in, return to the entrance of the **Daibutsu-den** ④, purportedly the largest wooden structure in the world. The **Daibutsu,** Nara's famous statue of Buddha, is inside.

As you exit the Daibutsu-den, turn left and walk up a winding path. Turn right, ascend the stone staircase, and then veer left on the slope lined with stone lanterns. On your left, on top of the slope, you will come to the **Ni-gatsu-dō** ⑤, which has fine views of Nara Kōen. Return along the same incline that led to Ni-gatsu-dō and turn left. The wood structure on your left is **San-gatsu-dō** ⑥, the oldest building in the Tōdai-ji compound. The entrance is on the right side as you face the building.

From the entrance of San-gatsu-dō, walk straight ahead, following the signs in English for Mt. Wakakusa. You will be leaving the temple grounds and walking along a street. On the left is the base of **Mt. Wakakusa** ⑦. Because there are few areas to eat in Nara Kōen, this street near Mt. Wakakusa is a good place to take a nutritional break.

If you continue past all of the restaurants and shops, at the end of the street you will see stone steps. Descend these and cross a small bridge over a stream; then walk along the path that leads into shady and peace-

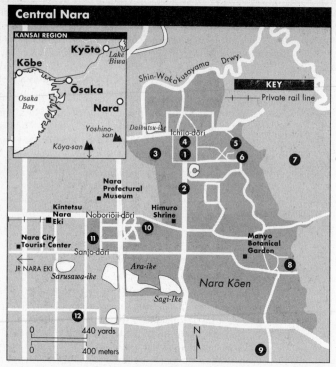

ful woods. At its end, turn left up the staircase, and you will be in front of **Kasuga Taisha** ⑧. This shrine used to be rebuilt according to Shinto custom every 20 years, but the current Kasuga has not been rebuilt for more than a century. After you pass through the torii, the first wooden structure you'll see is the Hai-den (Offering Hall), and to its left is the Naorai-den (Entertainment Hall). In back of the latter are the four Hon-den (Main Shrines).

Leaving Kasuga-Taisha, walk south down the path lined with stone lanterns past the Kasuga-Wakamiya Shrine. Continue on this wooded path until you reach a paved road. Cross the road and take the first right onto a residential street with many traditional Japanese houses. Take the first left and follow it south about 100 yards, until it curves to the right and leads to the entrance of **Shin-Yakushi-ji** ⑨, founded in 747. Of the many original buildings that once stood here, only the Main Hall remains.

Leaving Shin-Yakushi-ji, retrace your steps to the residential street you walked down earlier. Turn left on this street and walk to the major intersection at the end of it. Across the street you will see a bus stop, where you can board Bus 1 back to the Daibutsu-den stop. Or, take time out to see **Nara Kokuritsu Bijutsukan** ⑩, which specializes in Buddhist art. Leaving the west exit of the east wing of the museum, walk west for about five minutes and you will find yourself at the **Kōfuku-ji** ⑪ complex, which used to contain 175 buildings. Now fewer than a dozen remain. The most eye-catching structure is the Five-Story Pagoda, the second-tallest pagoda in all Japan. The adjacent Three-Story Pagoda is equally appealing. If you are feeling peckish, there are good restaurants within minutes of the Kōfuku-ji Pagoda (☞ Dining, *below*).

Before continuing to western Nara and Hōryū-ji, take some time out from temple-viewing to walk through **Nara-machi** ⑫, just south of Saru-sawa-ike. This old section of Nara has retained many of its traditional houses and shops selling arts and crafts. Maps to the area are available from the city's tourist information centers and the Shiryokan: A signboard map on the southwest edge of Sarusawa-ike shows the way to all the important shops, museums, and galleries.

TIMING

You could literally see all of the sights on the walk in a day, but there is no need to see every last one: pick six or seven religious sights, have lunch on Mt. Wakakusa, then go to a musuem and shop in Nara-machi in the afternoon.

Sights to See

TŌDAI-JI TEMPLE COMPLEX

The temple complex of Tōdai-ji was conceived by Emperor Shōmu as as the seat of authority for all of Buddhist Japan. The power of Tōdai-ji is in its many structures, among which the ☞ **Daibutsu-den** is the most grand, with its huge beams that seem to converge somewhere in infinity just beyond the mind's eye.

★ ❹ **Daibutsu-den** (Hall of the Great Buddha). This elegant and austere white building, its wood beams darkened from age, is an impressive sight. A pair of gilt ornaments decorate the roof ridge. These are called *kutsu-gata* (shoe-shaped) because they resemble footwear, and in ancient times they were believed to ward off fire. Unfortunately, they didn't prevent the original building from getting scorched. The current Daibutsu-den was restored in 1709 at two-thirds its original scale. At 157 ft tall (about 15 stories) and 187 ft long, it is still held to be the largest wooden structure in the world.

Inside Daibutsu-den is the **Daibutsu,** a 53-ft bronze statue of Buddha that is perhaps the most famous sight in Nara. The Daibutsu was originally commissioned by Emperor Shōmu in 743. After numerous unsuccessful castings, this figure was finally made in 749. A statue of this scale had never before been built in Japan, and it was hoped that it would serve as a symbol to unite the country. Daibutsu was dedicated in 752 in a grand ceremony attended by then-retired Emperor Shōmu, the imperial court members, and 10,000 priests and nuns.

Behind the Daibutsu to the right, you'll see a large wooden pillar with a hole at its base. You will also observe many Japanese tourists attempting to crawl through the opening, which is barely large enough for a petite adult. Local superstition has it that those who pass through the opening will eventually go to paradise. Children in particular love easing through and watching adults suffer the indignity of barely squeezing through the opening. In the back of the Daibutsu, to the left, is a model of the original Tōdai-ji. ☜ ¥400. ☉ *Daily, Jan.–Feb. 8–4:30; Mar. 8–5; Apr.–Sept. 7:30–5:30; Oct. 7:30–5; Nov.–Dec. 8–4:30.*

❸ **Kaidan-in.** Inside the small Kaidan-in temple are clay statues of the Four Heavenly Guardians. The images are depicted in full armor, wielding weapons and displaying fierce expressions. *Kaidan* is a Buddhist word for the terrace on which priests are ordained; the Chinese Buddhist priest Ganjin (688–763) ordained many Japanese Buddhist priests here. The original temple was destroyed repeatedly by fire, and the current structure was built in 1731. Kaidan-in is in northwestern Nara Kōen, west of Daibutsu-den. ☜ ¥400. ☉ *Daily 8–5 (8–4:30 in winter).*

❷ **Nandai-mon** (Great Southern Gate). The impressive Tōdai-ji gate is supported by 18 large wooden pillars, each 62 ft high and 39 inches in diameter. The original was destroyed in a typhoon in 962 and rebuilt in 1199. Two outer niches on either side of the gate contain wooden figures of Deva kings, who guard the great Buddha within. They are the work of master sculptor Unkei, of the Kamakura period (1185–1335). In the inner niches are a pair of stone *koma-inu* (Korean dogs); these creatures are mythical guardians placed beside the gates to ward off evil. Nandai-mon stands over the path leading to the Tōdai-ji compound.

⑤ Ni-gatsu-dō (Second Month Temple). Named for the religious rite that used to be performed here each February, Ni-gatsu-dō was founded in 752. It houses some important images that are, alas, not on display to the public. Nonetheless, its hilltop location and veranda afford a breathtaking view of Nara Kōen. ⊠ *Free.* ⊙ *Daily 8–5:30.*

⑥ San-gatsu-dō (Third Month Temple). A March rite is the reason for San-gatsu-dō's name. Founded in 733, this temple is the oldest original building in the Tōdai-ji compound. As you enter, to your left are some benches covered with tatami mats, where you can sit and contemplate the 1,200-year-old National Treasures that crowd the small room. The principal image is the dry lacquer statue of Fukukenjaku Kannon, the Goddess of Mercy, whose diadem is encrusted with thousands of pearls and gemstones. The two clay statues on either side of her, the Gakko (Moonlight) and the Nikko (Sunlight) bodhisattvas, are considered fine examples of the Nara (or Tenpyo) period, the height of classic Japanese sculpture. ⊠ *¥400.* ⊙ *Daily 7:30–5:30 (8–4:30 in winter).*

★ ① Tōdai-ji. It's hard to say which is the most magnificent Buddhist temple in Nara, but resplendent Tōdai-ji in Nara Kōen is certainly a contender. It was completed in 752, and even though the imperial household later moved out of Nara, Tōdai-ji remained the symbol of Buddhist authority. An earthquake damaged it in 855, and in 1180 the temple was burned to the ground. Its reconconstruction met a similar fate during the 16th-century civil wars. A hundred years later only the central buildings were rebuilt; these are what we see today.

To reach the Tōdai-ji compound, board Bus 2, which departs from the front of the JR eki and Kintetsu eki, and get off at the Daibutsu-den stop. Cross the street and you will be at the path that leads to the complex. You can also walk from Kintetsu Nara Eki to Tōdai-ji in about 15 minutes. Exit the east end of the station and walk east along Noborioji-dōri into Nara Kōen. At the next large intersection turn left onto the pedestrians-only street, lined with souvenir stalls and small restaurants, that leads to Tōdai-ji. The walk from the JR eki takes about 20 minutes on Sanjo-dōri. Once in Nara Kōen, take the same pedestrians-only street to Tōdai-ji.

ELSEWHERE IN NARA KŌEN

★ Nara Kōen. It is a singular pleasure to wander around this lush green park dotted with ponds as you stroll from temple to temple. Nara Kōen is inhabited by some thousand tame, if at times aggressive, deer, which roam freely around the various temples and shrines. They are considered to be divine messengers and are particularly friendly when you feed them deer crackers, which you can buy at stalls in the park.

★ ⑧ Kasuga Taisha. Kasuga is famous for the more than 2,000 stone lanterns that line the major pathways that lead to it, all of which are lit three times a year on special festival days (Feb. 2, Aug. 14–15). Kasuga was founded in 768 as a tutelary shrine for the Fujiwaras, a prominent feudal family. For centuries, according to Shinto custom, the shrine was reconstructed every 20 years on its original design, as is the case with the famous Ise Jingū in Mie Prefecture. The reason that many Shinto shrines are rebuilt is not only to renew the materials but also to purify the site. It is said that Kasuga Taisha has been rebuilt more than 50 times, the last time in 1893. After you pass through the torii, the first wooden structure you'll see is the **Hai-den** (Offering Hall), and to its left is the

Naorai-den (Entertainment Hall). In back of the latter are the four **Honden** (Main Shrines). They are National Treasures, all built in the same Kasuga style and painted vermilion and green—a striking contrast to the dark wooden exterior of most Nara temples. The sacred deer of this shrine are protected, and they roam freely about the grounds.

Taking Sanjo-dōri, Nara's main street, walk east. You will find the shrine just after the Manyo Botanical Garden at the western end of Nara Kōen. ✉ *Kasuga Shrine Museum ¥400, shrine's outer courtyard free, inner precincts with 4 Hon-den structures and gardens ¥500.* ⊙ *Museum daily 9–4; inner precincts Apr.–Oct., daily 8:30–5; Nov.–Mar., daily 9–4:30.*

⑪ **Kōfuku-ji** (Happiness Producing Temple). This temple was originally founded in 669 in Kyōto by the Fujiwara family. After Nara became the capital, Kōfuku-ji was transferred to its current location in 710. At its peak in the 8th century, it was a powerful temple that had 175 buildings, of which fewer than a dozen remain. The history of Kōfuku-ji reflects the intense relationship between Buddhism and Shintoism in Japan. In 937, a Kōfuku-ji monk had a dream in which the Shinto deity, Kasuga, appeared in the form of a Buddha, asking to become a protector of the temple. In 947, a number of Kōfuku-ji monks held a Buddhist ceremony at the Shinto Kasuga Taisha to mark the merging of the Buddhist temple with the Shinto shrine.

Although you can enter many buildings in this temple complex, perhaps the most interesting is the **Kokuhōkan** (National Treasure House). This unattractive, modern concrete building holds a fabulous collection of National Treasure sculpture and other works of art from the Nara period.

Kōfuku-ji also contains two magnificent pagodas. The **Five-Story Pagoda,** at 164 ft, is the second tallest in all Japan. The original pagoda in this spot was built in 730 by Empress Komyo. It and several succeeding pagodas were destroyed by fire, but the current 1426 pagoda is an exact replica of the original. The **Three-Story Pagoda** was built in 1114 and is renowned for its graceful lines and fine proportions.

Kōfuku-ji is a five-minute walk west of Nara Kokuritsu Hakubutsukan in the central part of Nara Kōen, and it is an easy 15-min walk from the JR eki or Kintetsu eki. ✉ *¥500.* ⊙ *Daily 9–5 (enter by 4:30).*

⑩ **Nara Kokuritsu Bijutsukan** (Nara National Art Museum). The East Wing, built in 1973, has many examples of calligraphy, paintings, and sculpture. The West Wing, built in 1895, features objects of archaeological interest. Each fall during the driest days of November, when the Shosoin Repository, located behind Tōdai-ji, opens its doors to air its magnificent collection, some of its ancient treasures are displayed at the National Art Museum. ✉ *10-6 Noborioji-chō,* ☎ *0742/22–7771.* ✉ *¥400.* ⊙ *Tues.–Sun. 9–4:30 (enter by 4).*

OTHER CENTRAL NARA SIGHTS

⑦ **Mt. Wakakusa.** Each January 15, 15 priests set Mt. Wakakusa's dry grass afire, and the blazes that engulf the hill create a grand spectacle. The rest of the year, the street at the base of Mt. Wakakusa is a good place to have a cup of coffee, a snack, or even lunch when you are visiting the sights of Nara Kōen. Most of the restaurants along here are similar, but a few have better *ryōri* (cooking) than others. **Shiroganeya** (☎ 0742/22–2607) has noodles for ¥650–¥750 and lunches for ¥1,000–¥2,500. **Asahiken** (☎ 0742/22–2384) has a tasty tempura lunch for ¥1,500 and eel for ¥1,200. In both places, you pay when served.

From San-gatsu-dō in Tōdai-ji compound, walk south following the signs in English for Mt. Wakakusa.

⑫ **Nara-machi.** This neighborhood is a maze of narrow residential streets lined with traditional houses and old shops, many of which deal in Nara's renowned arts and crafts. On foot or by bicycle, Nara-machi can offer a change of pace from ordinary sightseeing, and local residents are friendly and eager to help.

Look for **"Yu" Nakagawa** (☎ 0742/22–1322), which specializes in hand-woven, sun-bleached linen textiles, a Nara specialty known as sarashi-jofu. For 400 years, **Kobaien** (☎ 0742/23–2965) has made fine Nara ink sticks for calligraphy and ink painting. From October to April, make an appointment at the shop to watch the making of the ink sticks. Gango-ji lies at the heart of Nara-machi, and near it the little town museum known as Nara-machi Shiryōkan (Historical Library). Visit the Silk Road folk-craft shop **Kikuoka** (☎ 0742/26–3889) near Nara-machi Shiryōkan.

Nara-machi is just south of Sarusawa-ike. Maps to the area are available at the city's tourist information centers and the Shiryōkan: A sign-board map on the southwest edge of Sarusawa-ike shows the way to all the important shops, museums, and galleries. Coming from JR eki, walk up to the top of the main street and turn right.

⑨ **Shin-Yakushi-ji.** This temple was founded in 747 by Empress Komyo (701–760) as a prayer requesting the recovery of her sick husband, Emperor Shōmu. Most of the temple buildings were destroyed over the years; only the Main Hall, which houses many fine objects of the Nara period, still exists. In the center of the hall is a wood statue of Yakushi Nyorai, the Physician of the Soul. Surrounding this statue are 12 clay images of the Twelve Divine Generals who protected Yakushi. Eleven of these figures are originals. The generals stand in threatening poses, bearing spears, swords, and other weapons, and display terrifying expressions. ▨ ¥500. ☉ *Daily 8:30–sunset.*

Western Nara

There are four major temples on the western outskirts of Nara, Hōryū-ji being the most famous. If you have just one day in Nara, be sure to see Hōryū-ji. If you are in Nara for two days, you may want to spend the second day in western Nara.

A Good Tour

It is easy to get to the four major temples on the outskirts of Nara from JR Nara Eki or Kintetsu Nara Eki. Take Bus 52: It stops at Tōshōdai-ji, Yakushi-ji, Hōryū-ji, and Chūgū-ji, returning along the same route. The ride to Hōryū-ji, the farthest temple, takes about 50 minutes and costs ¥680. You can also take the JR train on the Kansai Main Line to Hōryū-ji Eki, from which the temple is a short shuttle-bus ride or a 15-min walk. **Hōryū-ji** ⑬ is the most remarkable temple in western Nara, and its compound contains buildings that are among the oldest wooden structures in the world. After passing through two gates, the second of which has stood since 607, you enter the western precincts of the temple. The first building on your right is the Kon-dō. On its left is an ancient five-story pagoda, behind which you'll find the Daikō-dō. From there, walk back past the second gate; then turn left and walk past the pond on your right. You will come to two concrete buildings, Daihōzō-den. After seeing the exhibits of Daihōzō-den, turn left from its exit, walk a short distance until the path ends, and turn left again. You will be at the Tōdai-mon, which leads to the eastern precincts of the temple compound. The octagonal building is the evocative Yume-dono (Hall of Dreams).

An exit from the rear of the eastern precinct of Hōryū-ji leads along carefully raked pebbles to the quiet nunnery of **Chūgū-ji** ⑭ home to a

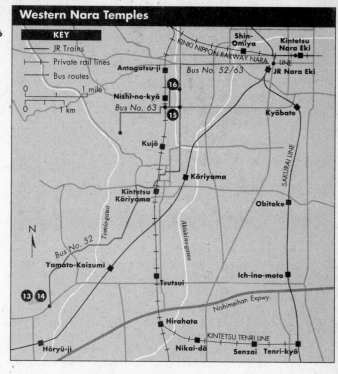

Western Nara Temples

KEY

— JR Trains
— Private rail lines
— Bus routes

0 ——— 1 mile
0 ——— 1 km

N

Shin-Omiya
Kintetsu Nara Eki
KINKI NIPPON RAILWAY NARA LINE
JR Nara Eki
Amagatsu-ji
Bus No. 52/63
Nishi-no-kyō
Bus No. 63
Kyōbate
Kujō
SAKURAI LINE
Kōriyama
Kintetsu Kōriyama
Obitoke
Bus No. 52
Yamato-Koizumi
Akishinogawa
Tomiogawa
Ich-ino-moto
Tsutsui
Nishimeihan Expwy.
Hirahata
KINTETSU TENRI LINE
Hōryū-ji
Nikai-dō
Senzai
Tenri-kyō

graceful statue of Buddha that dates from the Asuka period (552–645). If you are pushed for time, you might want to skip this temple.

Get back on Bus 52 in the direction from which you came and get off at the Yakushi-ji-mae stop. **Yakushi-ji** ⑮ was founded in 680 and moved to its current location in 718. As you enter the temple grounds, on your right you will see the East Tower, a pagoda that dates to 1285. The West Tower, to your left, was built in 1981. The new vermilion building in the center is Yakushi-ji's Kon-dō.

From the rear gate of Yakushi-ji it is a 10-minute walk to the 8th-century temple **Tōshōdai-ji** ⑯ down the "Path of History," lined with clay-wall houses, gardens, small shops selling antiques, crafts, and narazuke, and restaurants. In order to enter the temple compound, you pass through the **Nandai-mon.** The first building, an excellent example of Nara architecture, is the Kon-dō. In back of the Kon-dō is Tōshōdai-ji's Daikō-dō, once an assembly hall of the Nara Imperial Court.

When you leave Tōshōdai-ji, you can take Bus 63 back to Kintetsu Nara Eki or JR Nara Eki; pick it up right in front of the temple.

TIMING

You can take in one or two temples in an afternoon—Hōryū-ji should be one of them—but a day's exploration of western Nara's sights is the proper allowance for some of Japan's finest religious architecture.

Sights to See

⑭ **Chūgū-ji.** Chūgū-ji was originally the home of Prince Shōtoku's mother. After she passed away, it became a temple dedicated to her memory. This quiet nunnery houses a graceful wooden image of the Miroku Bodhisattva, the Buddha of the Future. The statue dates from the Asuka period (552–645), and its gentle countenance has made it famous as an ageless view of hope for the future. Also of interest is the oldest example of embroidery in Japan, which also dates from the Asuka period. The framed cloth depicts Tenjukoku (Land of Heavenly Longevity). In front of the temple is a small, carefully tended pond with a rock garden emerging from just below the surface.

From the JR or Kintetsu eki, take Bus 52, which covers the temples in the Western district. From Hōryū-ji, the path at the rear of the temple's eastern precinct takes you to Chūgū-ji. 🎫 ¥400. 🕐 *Daily 9–4:30 (9–4 in winter).*

★ ⓭ **Hōryū-ji.** This is the most captivating of the temples in western Nara. Hōryū-ji was founded in 607 by Prince Shōtoku (573–621), and its original wooden buildings are among the most ancient in the world. The first gate you pass through at Hōryū-ji is the **Nandai-mon,** which needed to be rebuilt in 1438. The second is the **Chū-mon** (Middle Gate), which is remarkably the 607 original—1,400 years old. Unlike most other Japanese gates, which are supported by two pillars at the ends, this gate is supported by central pillars. Note the unusual shape of the pillars, which are entastic (curved outward in the center), an architectural technique used in ancient Greece that traveled as far as Japan. Entastic pillars in Japan exist only in the 7th-century structures of Nara.

As you pass through the gate, you enter the western precincts of the temple. The first building you see on your right is the **Kon-dō** (Main Hall). On its left is a five-story pagoda both ancient and new. The entire pagoda was disassembled in World War II, after which it was reconstructed in its original form, using the same materials that were first used to build it in 607. Behind the pagoda is the **Daiko-dō** (Lecture Hall), which was destroyed by fire and rebuilt in 990. Inside the hall is an image of Yakushi Nyorai (Physician of the Soul).

From the Daikō-dō, walk back past the Kon-dō and Chū-mon; then turn left and walk past the pond on your right. You will come to two concrete buildings known as the **Daihōzō-den** (Great Treasure Hall), which display statues, sculptures, ancient Buddhist religious articles, and brocades. Of particular interest is a miniature shrine that belonged to Lady Tachibana, mother of Empress Komyo. The shrine is a little over 9 ft tall; the Buddha image inside is about 20 inches tall.

Tōdai-mon (Great East Gate) opens onto the eastern part of Hōryū-ji's grounds. The octagonal **Yumedono** (Hall of Dreams) was so named because Prince Shōtoku used to meditate in it.

Bus 52 to Hōryū-ji is a 50-min ride from the JR Nara Eki and Kintetsu Nara Eki; it costs ¥680. The Hōryūji-mae bus stop is in front of the temple. Or take a JR Kansai Main Line train to Hōryū-ji Eki; the temple is then a short shuttle ride or a 15-minute walk. 🎫 ¥1,000. 🕐 *Daily 8–5 (8–4:30 in winter); enter 1 hr before closing.*

⓰ **Tōshōdai-ji.** The entrance to this temple is brazenly called the "Path of History," since in Nara's imperial days dignitaries and priests trod this path, now lined with clay-walled houses, gardens, and small shops selling antiques, crafts, and narazuke, a popular local specialty. There are also several good restaurants here (☞ *Van Kio in Dining, below*). Tōshōdai-ji was founded in 751 by Ganjin, a Chinese priest who traveled to Japan at the invitation of Emperor Shōmu. At that time, Japanese priests had never received formal instruction from a Buddhist priest. The invitation was extended by two Japanese priests who had traveled to China in search of a Buddhist willing to undertake the arduous and perilous journey to Japan.

On Ganjin's first journey, some of his disciples betrayed him. His second journey resulted in a shipwreck. During the third trip, his ship was blown off course, and on his fourth trip, he was refused permission to leave China by government officials. Before his next attempt, he contracted an eye disease that left him blind. Nevertheless, he persevered in his goal of reaching Japan and finally arrived in 750. Ganjin shared his knowledge of Buddhism with his adopted country and served as a teacher to many Japanese priests as well as Emperor Shōmu. He is also remembered for bringing the first sugar to Japan. In the back of the temple grounds, the **Miei-dō** contains a lacquer statue of Ganjin that dates from 763. The image goes on public display only once a year, on June 6, to commemorate the birthday of the illustrious priest.

The temple's entrance, the **Nandai-mon** (Great South Gate), is supported by entastic pillars like those in the Chū-mon of Hōryū-ji. Beyond Nandai-mon, the **Kon-dō** (Main Hall) is a superb piece of Nara architecture. Inside the hall is a lacquer statue of Vairocana Buddha, the same incarnation of Buddha that is enshrined at Tōdai-ji. The halo surrounding this figure originally was covered with 1,000 Buddhas—only 864 remain. In back of the Kon-dō is the **Daikō-dō** (Lecture Hall), formerly an assembly hall of the Nara Imperial Court that was moved to its current location when Tōshōdai-ji was founded. Because all the other buildings of the Nara imperial court have been destroyed, the Diako-dō is the only remaining example of Nara palace architecture.

Tōshōdai-ji is a 10-minute walk from the rear gate of ☞ **Yakushi-ji** along the "Path of History." From central Nara or Hōryū-ji take Bus 52. There is a stop in front of Tōshōdai-ji. ✉ *¥500.* ⊙ *Daily 8:30–5.*

★ ⓕ **Yakushi-ji.** Officially named one of the Seven Great Temples of Nara, Yakushi-ji was founded in 680 and moved to its current location in 718. Yakushi-ji's **East Pagoda** dates from 1285. The tower has an interesting asymmetrical shape, so startling that it inspired American scholar Ernest Fenollosa (1853–1908) to remark that it was as beautiful as "frozen music." Although it appears to have six stories, in fact it has only three—three roofs with smaller ones attached underneath. The **West Tower** was built in 1981. The central **Kon-dō** (Main Hall) was rebuilt in 1976 and is painted a garish vermilion. These newer buildings are not nearly as attractive as the older structures, and they look out of place in the otherwise appealing temple complex.

From central Nara take Bus 52 to Yakushi-ji; from Hōryū-ji or Chūgū-ji, take Bus 52 back toward Nara. In either case, get off at the Yakushi-ji-mae stop. ✉ *¥500.* ⊙ *Daily 8:30–5.*

DINING

$$$$ ✗ **Onjaku.** Not far from Nara Kōen, this restaurant offers exquisitely
★ presented kaiseki meals in a serene Japanese-style room with gentle lighting. The exterior, with its faded wood walls, is in keeping with the architectural style of Nara. The menu consists only of kaiseki meals of varying prices. ✉ *1043 Kita-Tenma-chō,* ☎ *0742/26–4762. Reservations essential. No credit cards. Closed Tues.*

$$$$ ✗ **Tsukihitei.** A quiet restaurant set in the hills behind Kasuga Taisha, Tsukihitei serves kaiseki feasts. The walk up the shaded, wooded path leading to the restaurant sets the mood for this classic Japanese dining. When you make your reservation, ask for a kaiseki set meal. As you dine on delicate morsels of fish, vegetables, and rice and sip on sweet plum wine, you can gaze out on the forests surrounding the restaurant. ✉ *158 Kasugano-chō,* ☎ *0742/26–2021. Reservations essential. Jacket and tie. DC, V.*

\$\$\$ ✕ **Bekkan Kikusuiro.** If you want to try kaiseki but do not want a formal and complicated meal, Bekkan Kikusuiro serves what it calls "mini kaiseki," an abridged version with fewer courses. Unlike standard kaiseki, where each course is served separately, your whole meal will be served on one tray. You can sit either at a table, which is less expensive, or in a Japanese-style room with a tatami mat. ⊠ *1130 Takahata-chō,* ☎ *0742/23–2001. No credit cards. Closed Dec. 31.*

\$\$ ✕ **Tempura Asuka.** Directly south of Sarusawa-ike in Nara-machi, Asuka serves full-course tempura meals and reasonably priced *bento* or tempura-soba noodle lunches. Sit at the counter, reserve a tatami room, or enjoy a table overlooking the garden. ⊠ *11 Chonanin-chō,* ☎ *0742/26–4308. Reservations not accepted. MC, V. Closed Tues.*

\$\$ ✕ **Uma no Me.** Kaiseki is not the only Japanese food available in
★   Nara. Uma no Me prides itself on home cooking—roast fish, tofu, and other home-style Japanese dishes. The atmosphere is friendly and informal, with dark wood walls and attractive pottery. This restaurant is a few minutes' walk from Nara Kōen. ⊠ *1158 Takahata-chō,* ☎ *0742/23–7784. Reservations essential. No credit cards. Closed Thurs.*

\$\$ ✕ **Van Kio.** The deer of Nara are sacred but still available for a price: Located outside the south gate of Yakushi-ji, this traditional restaurant is famous for its hot stone steam cookery, which includes costly Nara venison. Sushi and vegetarian dishes are also available. The resident landscape gardener, Kawatake-san, sells a selection of stone lanterns, basins, and other garden ornaments, as well as a variety of Nara antiques on the premises. ⊠ *410 Rokujo-chō,* ☎ *0742/33–8942. AE, MC, V. Closed Mon.*

\$\$ ✕ **Yanagi-cha-ya.** Yanagi-cha-ya specializes in excellent bento meals,
★   served in basic black-lacquer boxes. The food is Nara style: elegantly simple, with sashimi, stewed vegetables, and tofu. There are two branches of this revered old teahouse: the elder Yanagi-cha-ya is on the north bank and overlooks Sarusawa-ike. The younger sister is just east of Kōfuku-ji. *Elder:* ⊠ *49 Noborioji-chō,* ☎ *0742/22–7460; closed Wed. Younger:* ⊠ *48 Teraoji-chō,* ☎ *0742/22–7560; closed Mon. Reservations essential. No credit cards.*

\$ ✕ **Ginsho.** Across from the Nara Shiryōkan (Historical Library) on a tiny side street in Nara-machi, this soba noodle shop has a strikingly contemporary Japanese-style interior in a traditional building that blends in with the old neighborhood around it. Great *ten-zaru* soba (cold noodles and tempura) or tempura soba (hot tempura noodle soup) makes a fabulous lunch stop. ⊠ *18 Nishishinya-chō,* ☎ *0742/23–1355. Reservations not accepted. No credit cards. Closed Mon.*

\$ ✕ **Harishin.** Old, unassuming, and small, this lunch place is easy to miss in the maze of Nara-machi. You can find it by looking for its red *noren* (short curtain hanging in the doorway) decorated with a crest of crossed arrows. Open for lunch only, Harishin serves a Katsumichi bento that comes in a double-layer lacquer box and often includes almond fried chicken, shrimp, seasonal pilaf, vegetables, soup, fruit, and an aperitif of homemade strawberry wine. It's an excellent bargain. ⊠ *15 Chushinya-chō,* ☎ *0742/22–2669. Reservations not accepted. No credit cards. Closed Mon.*

\$ ✕ **To-no-chaya.** One distinctive Nara meal is cha-gayu. To-no-chaya offers a light meal of this special dish, combined with some sashimi and vegetables, plus a few sweetened rice cakes for dessert. From the restaurant you can see the Five-Story Pagoda of Kōfuku-ji. Appropriately, the name of this restaurant means the "tearoom of the pagoda." Bento-box meals are served between 11:30 and 4. ⊠ *47 Noborioji-chō,* ☎ *0742/22–4348. Reservations essential for cha-gayu kaiseki. No credit cards. Closed Wed.*

LODGING

$$$ 🏠 **Edo-San.** A night in this *ryokan* will envelop you in Japanese tra-
★ dition. Accommodations consist of small, private cottages—old-fash-
ioned Japanese structures with thatched roofs, all surrounded by trees,
flowers, and greenery. Deer from Nara Kōen occasionally wander
onto the grounds of the inn. The excellent food, served in your private
cottage, is included in the cost of your stay and consists of a variety
of seafood dishes. ☒ *1167 Takahata-chō, Nara-shi, Nara-ken 630,* ☎
0742/26–2662, 🆇 *0742/26–2663. 11 rooms. AE, DC, V.*

$$$ 🏠 **Hotel Fujita Nara.** This hotel, on the main street running from JR
Nara Eki to Nara Kōen, has attractive, simply decorated rooms. The
Japanese restaurant serves excellent food, and succulent Kōbe steaks
are available in the steak house. ☒ *47-1 Shimo Sanjo-chō, Nara-shi,
Nara-ken 630,* ☎ *0742/23–8111,* 🆇 *0742/22–0255. 118 rooms. 2
restaurants, coffee shop. AE, DC, MC, V.*

$$$ 🏠 **Kankaso.** Elegance reigns at this ryokan, right in the heart of Nara
★ Kōen. Rooms have all been exquisitely decorated with Japanese scrolls,
pottery, and other artwork. Great care is taken with the flower ar-
rangements set in the alcove of each room. The communal baths look
out on a lovely garden. ☒ *10 Kasugano-chō, Nara-shi, Nara-ken 630,*
☎ *0742/26–1128,* 🆇 *0742/26–1301. 10 rooms. V.*

$$$ 🏠 **Nara Garden Hotel.** This small hotel on a hillside above Tōdai-ji is
within walking distance of all the sights in central Nara. Rooms here
are furnished in light woods with green carpeting and floral bed-
spreads and curtains. Each has a view of the hillside cherry trees. The
restaurant serves excellent Japanese and French food. ☒ *Wakakusa,
Sanroku-chō, Nara-shi, Nara-ken 630,* ☎ *0742/27–0555,* 🆇 *0742/
27–0203. 21 rooms. Restaurant, coffee shop. AE, DC, MC, V.*

$$$ 🏠 **Nara Hotel.** Set in the southern perimeter of Nara Kōen, this es-
★ tablishment is itself a site of historical interest. Built in the Meiji pe-
riod (1868–1912), the architecturally delightful Nara Hotel has a
graceful Japanese tiled roof and a magnificent lobby with high wooden
ceilings. No wonder the emperor and his family stay here when visit-
ing Nara. Although most rooms have a good view of the surrounding
temples, those in the new wing are not as interesting as the turn-of-
the-century–style rooms in the old wing. Dining in a superb, old-fash-
ioned Edwardian-style room is a special occasion—mostly Japanese fare,
but a few Western choices as well. ☒ *1096 Takabatake-chō, Nara-shi,
Nara-ken 630,* ☎ *0742/26–3300,* 🆇 *0742/23–5252. 132 rooms.
Restaurant, tearoom. AE, DC, MC, V.*

$$ 🏠 **Hotel Sun Route Nara.** With clean and comfortable rooms, this
hotel is a cut above business hotels, with a friendly bar and a bit of
sparkle in its lounge. Being on the edge of Nara-machi makes it a short
walk to discover your favorite *izakaya.* ☒ *1110 Takabatake Bodai-
chō, Nara-shi, Nara-ken 630,* ☎ *0742/22–5151,* 🆇 *0742/27–3759.
95 rooms. Restaurant, coffee shop. AE, DC, MC, V.*

$$ 🏠 **Japan Pension (Nara Club).** With only traces of Japanese influence,
this family-run pension resembles a small European hotel. Some of its
modest-size rooms have skylights, and all are decorated in delicate pink
printed fabrics with simple, dark wooden furniture. Each room has a
private bath and toilet. The restaurant's dining room overlooks a small
garden; Western food is served. You can book a room here with or with-
out meals. ☒ *21 Gomon-chō, Nara-shi, Nara-ken 630,* ☎ *0742/22–
3450,* 🆇 *0742/22–3490. 10 rooms. Restaurant. AE, V.*

$$ 🏠 **Kotton Hyaku-pasento.** The name of this pleasant little hotel is a
play on words written with Chinese characters that mean 100% Old
Capital (rather than 100% Cotton). Popular with young Japanese, it
is on a side street near Sarusawa-ike, a short walk south of Nara Kōen.

✉ *1122-21 Bodaiji-chō, Nara-shi, Nara-ken 630,* ☎ *0742/22–7117,* FAX *0742/26–2771. 14 rooms. No credit cards.*

$$ 🏨 **People's Inn Hanakomichi.** This attractive, slightly overpriced establishment is near Kintetsu Nara Eki; it is also close to shops and within walking distance of Nara Kōen. A drawback to its central locale—its finest feature—is the street noise, especially annoying in summer, when you need to keep your bedroom window open for fresh air. The first and second floors have boutiques, a gallery, and a café. ✉ *23 Konishi-chō, Nara-shi, Nara-ken 630,* ☎ *0742/26–2646,* FAX *0742/26–2771. 20 Western-style rooms, 8 Japanese-style rooms. AE, DC, MC, V.*

$ 🏨 **Matsumae Ryokan.** There are several small ryokans in the Nara-machi district—the quaint area of Nara that consists of a maze of streets just southeast of Nara Kōen, a 10-min walk from JR Nara Eki. This one is typical—with small, clean tatami rooms and a public bath—but the owners here are happy to muddle through a mix of Japanese and English to assist gai-jin. You can make reservations from the Nara City Tourist Center (☞ Contacts and Resources *in Nara A to Z, below*). ✉ *28-1 Higashi-Terabayashi-chō, Nara-machi, Nara-shi, Nara-ken 630,* ☎ *0742/22–3686,* FAX *0742/26–3927. 12 Japanese-style rooms with shared bath. No credit cards.*

$ 🏨 **Nara-machi Seikanso.** This family-run inn has a relaxed atmosphere. Most rooms in the wooden structure overlook a central garden. It's a 15-minute walk from Kintetsu Nara Eki and a 25-minute walk from JR Nara Eki to the inn; most of the walk is under arcades. This place is extremely popular with gai-jin, so try to reserve a room in advance. ✉ *29 Higashikitsuji-chō, Nara-shi, Nara-ken 630,* ☎ *0742/22–2670,* FAX *0742/22–2670. 13 rooms with shared bath. AE, MC, V.*

$ 🏨 **Ryokan Hakuhoh.** This member of the low-priced Japanese Inn Group chain has the advantage of being in the center of town, one traffic light up the main street (Sanjo-dōri) from the JR eki on the right-hand side. It's a three-story concrete building with no particular charm. However, set back from the road, it is quiet and the tatami rooms (ignore the scuff marks on the walls) are clean. There are also two very small Western-style rooms, neither of which has a bath (half of the Japanese-style rooms do). No food is served, but there are many restaurants along the street. The owners don't speak English but cheerfully communicate in sign language. ✉ *4-1 Kamisanjo-chō, Nara-shi, Nara-ken 630,* ☎ *0742/26–7891. 21 rooms, 10 with bath. AE, V.*

NARA A TO Z

Arriving and Departing

By Plane

The nearest airports are in Ōsaka. International and a few domestic flights use **Kansai International Airport** (KIX); most domestic flights use **Itami Airport.** A JR Rapid Train from Nara to KIX takes 85 minutes and costs ¥1,630.

By Train

From Kyōto, the Kintetsu Railway's Limited Express trains (¥980) leave every half hour for the 33-minute trip to Nara. Three JR trains from Kyōto run to Nara every hour. The express takes 45 minutes (¥680), while the two locals take 70 minutes (¥680).

From Ōsaka's Kintetsu Nanba Eki, Nara is a 30-min ride on Kinki Nippon Railway's Limited Express. Trains leave every hour, and the fare is ¥920. The Ordinary Express to Nara takes 40 minutes, leaves every 20 minutes, and costs ¥480. The JR Yamato-ji Line train to Nara takes

50 minutes. It leaves every 20 minutes and costs ¥760 or is free with the JR Rail Pass.

From Kōbe, take the JR Tōkaidō Line rapid train from San-no-miya Eki to Ōsaka and transfer to one of the trains described above.

Getting Around

By Bicycle

Because Nara is a small city with relatively flat roads, it is a good place for cycling. You can rent a bicycle from **Kintetsu Sunflower** (☎ 0742/24–3528) on Konishi-dōri near Kintetsu Nara Eki; the cost is ¥800 for four hours, ¥1,150 for eight hours. Ask the Nara City Tourist Information Office on the first floor of this eki for further information or directions. Some hotels also rent bicycles.

By Bus

The most economical way to explore Nara is by bus. Two local routes circle the main sites (Tōdai-ji, Kasuga Taisha, and Shin-Yakushi-ji) in the central and eastern parts of the city: Bus 1 runs counterclockwise and Bus 2 runs clockwise. This urban loop line costs ¥180 for a ride of any distance. Both stop at JR Nara Eki and Kintetsu Nara Eki. Bus 52 west to Hōryū-ji (with stops at Tōshōdai-ji and Yakushi-ji) takes about 50 minutes and costs ¥680; you can catch it in front of either eki. Pick up a bus map at the Nara City Tourist Center (☞ *below*).

By Taxi

The rate is ¥600 for the first 1½ km (1 mi) and ¥90 for each additional 400 yards. From Kintetsu Nara Eki to Kasuga Taisha by taxi runs about ¥900 one-way; to Hōryū-ji, about ¥5,000 one-way.

By Train

Because Nara's principal sights are concentrated in one area in the western part of the city, you will do much of your sightseeing on foot. The JR Kansai Main Line and the Kintetsu Railway's Nara Line slice through the city and bring you close to major sights. Rates depend upon the distance you travel. The ride from downtown to Hōryū-ji costs about ¥300.

Contacts and Resources

Consulates

The nearest U.S., U.K., and Canadian consulates are in Ōsaka (☞ Chapter 9).

Emergencies

Police, ☎ 110. **Ambulance,** ☎ 119. **Nara Police Station,** ☎ 0742/35–1110. **Nara National Hospital,** ☎ 0742/24–1251.

Guided Tours

ORIENTATION TOURS

Tours of Nara in English must be arranged in advance through the Kyōto or Ōsaka office of the **Kintetsu Gray Line Bus Company.** You can also make arrangements at the travel office in the basement of the New Miyako Hotel in Kyōto (☎ 075/691–0903) or by calling 06/313–6868 in Ōsaka. The fare for the afternoon tour is ¥7,200. If you can get yourself to Nara without assistance, then an afternoon tour is only ¥4,500 with Sunrise Tours (☎ 075/341–1413.)

PERSONAL GUIDES

The **Student Guide Service** (✉ Sarusawa Tourist Information Center, 4 Nobori Oji-chō, north side of Sarusawa-ike, ☎ 0742/26–4753) and the **YMCA Guide Service** (✉ Kasuga Taisha, ☎ 0742/44–2207) are available for free at JR Nara Eki information center and Kintetsu Nara Eki. Because these services use volunteer guides, it is best to call in advance to determine availability. Guides' English can be extremely limited; many take the job to practice their English and meet foreigners.

WALKING TOURS

The **Japan National Tourist Organization** (JNTO) publishes the leaflet "Walking Tour Courses in Nara," which gives brief descriptions of highlights along the way. One two-hour tour includes Nara Kōen and several nearby temples and shrines; other tours start with a bus ride from the center of the city. There is no JNTO office in Nara; *see* the Gold Guide for addresses in Japan and the United States.

Visitor Information

Nara City Tourist Information Office (☎ 0742/24–4858) is on the first floor of Kintetsu Nara Eki and is open daily 9–5.

A **City Information Window** (☎ 0742/22–9821), open daily 9–5, can be found at JR Nara Eki—and it is always extremely helpful.

Nara City Tourist Center (⊠ 23-4 Kami-Sanjo-chō, Nara-shi, ☎ 0742/22–3900) is open daily 9–9, but the English-language staff is on duty only until 5. This center, a 10-minute walk from both Kintetsu Nara Eki and JR Nara Eki, has free maps, information on sightseeing in English, local crafts, a souvenir corner, and a lounge where you can rest and plan your day.

JAPAN TRAVEL PHONE

A nationwide service for English-language assistance or travel information is available seven days a week, 9–5, at ☎ 0120/444–800. When using a yellow, blue, or green public phone (do not use red phones), insert a ¥10 coin, which will be returned.

9 Ōsaka

Japan's "Second City" in terms of industry, commerce, and technology— after Tōkyō, naturally—Ōsaka is known for its bunraku puppet theater, its superb restaurants, and its dynamic spirit. It is not a window to Japan's past—go to Kyōto and Nara for that— but a storefront display of what moves the country today.

Ō

By Nigel Fisher

SAKA BEGAN EXPANDING as a trading center at the end of the 16th century. But until the Meiji Restoration (1868), the merchant class was at the bottom of the social hierarchy, even though plenty of merchants were among the richest people in Japan. Denied the usual aristocratic cultural pursuits, merchants sought and developed their pleasures in the theater and in dining. Indeed, it is often said that many a successful Ōsaka businessman has eventually gone bankrupt by spending so much on eating.

In the 4th and 5th centuries, the Ōsaka-Nara region was the center of the developing Japanese (Yamato) nation. It was through Ōsaka that knowledge and culture from mainland Asia filtered into the fledgling Japanese society. During the 5th and 6th centuries, several emperors maintained an imperial court in Ōsaka, but the city lost its political importance after a permanent capital was set up in Nara in 694.

For the next several hundred years, Ōsaka, then known as Naniwa, was just another backwater port on the Seto Nai-kai (Inland Sea). Then, at the end of the 16th century, Hideyoshi Toyotomi (1536–98), a great warrior and statesman, had one of Japan's most majestic castles built in Ōsaka as part of his successful unification of Japan. The castle took three years to build and was completed in 1586. Hideyoshi encouraged merchants from around the country to set up their businesses in the city, which soon prospered.

After Hideyoshi died, Ieyasu Tokugawa usurped power from the Toyotomi clan in 1603. However, the Toyotomi clan still maintained Ōsaka as its base. In 1614, Ieyasu sent his troops from Kyōto to Ōsaka to oppose rebellious movements in support of the Toyotomis. Ieyasu's army defeated the Toyotomi clan and its followers and destroyed the castle in 1615. Even though the Tokugawa Shogunate eventually rebuilt the castle, Ōsaka once again found itself at a distance from Japan's political scene. Ōsaka's merchants, left to themselves far from the shōgun's administrative center in Edo (Tōkyō), continued to prosper, and they sent products from the hinterland through the city to Kyōto and Edo. During this time of economic growth, some of Japan's business dynasties were founded, whose names we still hear of today—Sumitomo, Marubeni, Sanwa, and Daiwa. Their growing wealth gave them the means to pursue pleasure, and, by the end of the 17th century (the Genroku Era), Ōsaka's residents were giving patronage to such literary giants as the dramatist Chikamatsu (1653–1724), often referred to as the Shakespeare of Japan, and the novelist Saikaku Ihara (1642–1693). Chikamatsu's genius as a playwright elevated Bunraku to a dignified dramatic art. Also at this time, Ōsaka merchants' patronage of Kabuki helped that dramatic form in the city.

With the opening of Japan to Western commerce in 1853 and the end of the Tokugawa Shogunate in 1868, Ōsaka stepped into the forefront of Japan's commerce. At first Yokohama was the major port for Japan's foreign trade, but when the Great Kantō earthquake leveled that city in 1923, foreigners looked to Kōbe and Ōsaka as alternative gateways for their import and export business. Ōsaka's merchant heritage placed the city in a good position for industrial growth—iron, steel, fabrics, ships, heavy and light machinery, and chemicals all became part of its output. As a result the region accounts for 25% of Japan's industrial product and 40% of the nation's exports. Since the building of its new harbor facilities, Ōsaka has become a major port in its own right, and it relies less on the facilities in Kōbe.

Ōsaka is still a merchant city, with many streets devoted to wholesale business activity. For example, medical and pharmaceutical companies congregate in Dosho-machi, and fireworks and toys are found in Matcha-machi-suji, which is also famous for shopping. Head to Umeda, Shin-Sai-bashi, or Nanba for the greatest concentration of department stores, movie theaters, and restaurants.

Anyone over 50 in Japan remembers Ōsaka as an exotic maze of criss-crossing waterways that provided transportation for the booming merchant trade. All but a few of the canals and nearly all traditional wooden buildings were destroyed by the bombings of World War II. Architecturally, the city is leaping toward the next century with buildings like the Imperial Hotel on the banks of the Yodo-gawa and the dazzling Twin 21 Towers. At the moment, the city is working hard to restore some of the beauty that was lost, with a movement for the greening of Ōsaka running strong.

Ōsaka Glossary

Key Japanese words for this chapter include -*bashi* (bridge), *bijutsu-kan* (art museum), -*chō* (street or block), -*chōme* (street), *Chūō-ku* (Central District), *dōri* (avenue), *eki* (train station), *gai-jin* (foreigner), -*gawa* (river), -*jō* (castle), *Kita-ku* (North District), *kōen* ("ko-en," park), -*ku* (district or ward), *matsuri* (festival), *Minami-ku* (South District), *ōhashi* (large bridge), *onsen* (hot springs), -*shi* (city or municipality), -*shima* (island), *Shinkansen* (bullet train, literally "new trunk line"), *shōgun* (general or commander-in-chief), -*suji* (street), *taisha* (shrine), and *torii* ("to-ree-ee," gate).

Pleasures and Pastimes

Dining

Not only are Osakans passionate about food, they also insist on eating well. They expect the restaurants they frequent to use the freshest ingredients available—a reasonable conceit that developed over centuries of reliance on nearby Seto Nai-kai, which allowed all classes easy access to fresh seafood. Osakans continue to have discriminating palates and demand their money's worth. Prices in Osaka, both for food and lodging, are generally better value for money than in Kyoto.

Ōsaka cuisine is flavored with a soy sauce that is lighter in color, milder in flavor, and saltier than the soy used in Tōkyō. One local delicacy is *okonomiyaki*, pancakes filled with cabbage, mountain yam, pork, shrimp, and other ingredients then grilled.

Ōsaka-zushi (Ōsaka-style sushi), made in wooden molds, has a distinctive square shape. Another type is wrapped around an omelet and filled with pickles and other delights. *Unagi* (eel) prepared in several different styles remains a popular local dish; grilled unagi is often eaten in summer for quick energy. *Fugu* (blowfish) served boiled or raw is a delicacy that is less expensive in Ōsaka than in other Japanese cities.

Another Ōsaka invention is *takoyaki*, griddle-cooked dumplings with bits of octopus, green onions, and ginger smothered in a delicious sauce. Sold by street vendors in Dōtonbori, these tasty snacks and their lively makers also appear at every festival and street market in Kansai.

CATEGORY	COST*
$$$$	over ¥6,000
$$$	¥4,000–¥6,000
$$	¥2,500–¥4,000
$	under ¥2,500

*per person, excluding drinks, service, and tax

Lodging

Ōsaka is known more as a business than as a tourist destination. The city has modern accommodations for almost every taste, from first-class hotels to more modest business hotels, which unfortunately aren't very distinctive. And guest quarters aren't exactly stylish. Japanese hotel designers are often concerned with efficiency rather than elegance. However, you should appreciate the individual attention of solicitous staff at most hotels. Because Ōsaka hotels offer much the same both in decor and room size within a given price range, choose accommodations in terms of location rather than amenities.

A hotel room in Ōsaka does cost less than one of comparative size in Tōkyō. And Ōsaka has more hotels to choose from than Kyōto, which is especially important to keep in mind during peak tourist seasons.

CATEGORY	COST*
$$$$	over ¥20,000
$$$	¥15,000–¥20,000
$$	¥10,000–¥15,000
$	under ¥10,000

*All prices are for a double room, excluding service and tax.

Performing Arts

Ōsaka is home of the National Bunraku Theater. This puppet drama began during the Heian period (794–1192), and in the late 17th and early 18th centuries the genius of playwright Chikamatsu distilled Bunraku as an art form. A typical play deals with themes of tragic love or stories based on historical events. The story is chanted in song by a *joruri*, who is accompanied by ballad music played on a three-stringed *shamisen*. Although you may not understand the words, the tone of the music will set an appropriate mood of pathos.

Also, perhaps out of rivalry with Tōkyō, the city has built a grander and more resplendent Kabuki theater, the Shin-Kabuki-za, which puts on Kabuki, modern plays, and variety shows. For a fuller description of Bunraku and Kabuki, *see* Chapter 2.

Shopping

Ōsaka's role as a transportation hub for more than 1,500 years has paved the way for its significant stock of today's latest fashions and electronics.

Sumō

Ōsaka is one of Japan's centers for Sumō wrestling, in which athletes weighing from 90 to 160 kg (198 to 352 lbs) battle to throw an opponent to the floor or out of the ring. See Chapter 2 for a further description of Sumō. Bouts in Ōsaka are held from the second through the fourth Sunday in March.

Exploring Ōsaka

Although Ōsaka may not have many sites of historical interest, it is a good starting point for trips to Nara, Kyōto, Kōya-san (Mt. Koya), and Kōbe. And it has very good Japanese food. As the old saying goes, *Ōsaka wa kuida-ore*—Ōsaka people squander their money on food. The city's nightlife is also legendary. Be sure to stroll through Dōtonbori district, beside Dōtonbori-gawa, which has more nightclubs and bars per square foot than any other part of town.

Numbers in the text correspond to numbers in the margin and on the Ōsaka map.

Great Itineraries

Ōsaka is known for its dynamism, and you can enjoy the fruits of this energy in a couple of days. If you stay longer, use Ōsaka as a base to explore the surrounding Kansai region. Kyōto (☞ Chapter 7), Nara (☞ Chapter 8), and Kōbe (☞ Chapter 10) are but 30 minutes away by train. Ōsaka is also the most convenient jumping-off point for a trip to the mountainside monasteries of Kōya-san (☞ Chapter 6), two hours away on the Nankai private rail line.

IF YOU HAVE 1 DAY

Twenty-four hours in Ōsaka will give you a chance to catch many of the city's major sights. Ōsaka-jō should be first on your list. Then head south to Tennō-ji Kōen, a park that contains the Shiritsu Bijutsukan and its collection of classical Japanese art. Shitennō-ji, or Tennō-ji, is the oldest Buddhist temple in Japan. In the afternoon head to Den Den Town to browse through the gadget stores or to Europe Mura and America Mura for fashion. At the end of the day, Dōtonbori-dōri is the place to go for dinner and nightlife.

IF YOU HAVE 2 DAYS

With two full days in Ōsaka, you can cover all of the city's major sights. To the above day-in-town suggestions, add Sumiyoshi Taisha, one of the three most famous shrines in Japan, Senri Expo Park and its museums, Shiritsu Tōyō Jiki Bijutsukan in Naka-no-shima Kōen, and the shops on Midō-suji. Instead of heading to Dōtonbori-dōri after dark, go to central Ōsaka and, if you plan ahead and buy tickets, attend a performance at the National Bunraku Theater.

When to Tour Ōsaka

The crisp air of spring and fall are the best seasons—Ōsaka can become quite hot and humid in the summer, and winter is cold and wet. Most museums are closed Monday. One notable exception is Senri Expo Park, which closes Wednesday instead.

EXPLORING ŌSAKA

Ōsaka is divided into 26 wards, and, though the official city population is only 2.6 million, if one were to include the suburbs, this number would be around 6 million. Central Ōsaka is predominantly a business district, but there is also shopping and entertainment. The JR Kanjo (Loop) Line circles the city center. The primary Ōsaka Eki is at the north end of this loop. In front of Ōsaka Eki, to the east of Hankyū Umeda Eki is the center of Kita-ku. While ultramodern skyscrapers soar above the streets, Umeda Chika Center is an underground maze of malls, crowded with dozens of restaurants, shops that sell the latest fashions, and department stores that offer every modern gadget. Kita-ku is one of Ōsaka's two major shopping areas.

If you continue south, you come to two rivers, Dojima-gawa and Tosabori-gawa, with the island Naka-no-shima separating them. Here is Ōsaka's oldest park, which is home to many of the city's cultural and administrative institutions, including the Bank of Japan and the Museum of Oriental Ceramics.

South of these rivers and Naka-no-shima are the Minami and Shin-Sai-bashi districts. They are close together and are surrounded by the JR Kanjo Line. Shin-Sai-bashi is Ōsaka's expensive shopping street. Nearby America Mura, with American-style boutiques, and Europe Mura, with Continental shops, appeal to young Ōsaka trendsetters. Minami-ku has a wonderful assortment of bars and restaurants, especially on Dōtonbori-dōri. The National Bunraku Theater is also close by, a few blocks to the southeast, near the Nippon-bashi subway station.

You are likely to arrive in town at Shin-Ōsaka Eki, terminal for the Shinkansen Super Express trains. Located 3 km (2 mi) north of Ōsaka Eki, the main railway station, amid some of the city's most modern architecture, Shin-Ōsaka is close to Senri Expo Park. From Shin-Ōsaka Eki, take either the Midō-suji subway line to Umeda or, if you have a Japan Rail Pass, the JR Kōbe Line to Ōsaka Eki. The Umeda Subway station and Ōsaka Eki are right next to each other, on the edge of central Ōsaka.

A Good Tour

Start your exploration of Ōsaka with the city's major landmark, **Ōsaka-jō** ①, the castle that Hideyoshi Toyotomi had 100,000 men build in the late 16th century. It is easily reached by taking the JR Kanko (Loop) Line from JR Ōsaka Eki to Ōsaka-jō Kōen Eki, from which it is a 10-minute walk uphill through the park. If you have time and the interest, stop in at the **Ōsaka City Museum** ② on the castle grounds.

Leave the castle and, facing north, walk down the hill past Ōsaka-jō Hall, which is used for sports competitions and concerts, and cross the overpass near the Aqua Liner waterbus pier. On the other side of Hirano-gawa is the New Otani Hotel and, just behind it, the **Twin 21 Towers** ③ of Ōsaka Business Park. Panasonic Square, on the second floor of the National Tower Building, displays the Matsushita Electric Group's high-tech developments.

Next, stop in to see the ceramic exhibits of **Shiritsu Tōyō Jiki Bijutsukan** ④ on Naka-no-shima. The art museum is in the island's Naka-no-shima Kōen, the city's oldest park, which opened in 1891 on the eastern end of the island. To get to it from Ōsaka Business Park, take the JR train from Katamichi Eki to the Kyō-bashi stop and transfer to the Keihan Line, which you take to the Yodoya-bashi stop. The museum is a five-minute walk away. Ōsaka University and Ōsaka Festival Hall, which is considered the city's best concert hall, are also on the island.

Take the Midō-suji subway line from Yodoya-bashi to Shin-Sai-bashi Station. When you emerge you'll be on **Midō-suji** ⑤. Shin-Sai-bashi and Ebisu-bashi, which run parallel to Midō-suji, are two of Ōsaka's best shopping and entertainment streets. West of Midō-suji, **America Mura** ⑥ is a group of streets with trendy American clothing stores. East of Midō-suji, **Europe Mura** ⑦ is chockablock with fashionable European boutiques.

Walk south on Midō-suji and cross Dōtonbori-gawa to **Dōtonbori-dōri** ⑧, a broad cross street that runs alongside the canal. The street and the area around it are filled with restaurants and nightclubs.

Two blocks south of Dōtonbori-dōri is **Niji-no-machi** ⑨, an underground shopping mall that extends six blocks east to west. About two blocks from Niji-no-machi is **Nan Nan Town,** another underground mall, which runs eight blocks south from the southern end of Midō-suji. At the far southern end of Midō-suji are the Kabuki-za and the Takashimaya department store. East of the southern terminus of Nankai Nanba Eki is **Den Den Town** ⑩, the place to go for discounted electronics and appliances. About a block south of the eki is Ōsaka Stadium, where local baseball teams square off.

From Nanba Station (the subway station, not Nankai Nanba Eki), take the Sennichi-mae subway line one stop east to the Nippon-bashi Station and the **National Bunraku Theater** ⑪. Take Exit 7, and you will

America Mura, **6**
Den Den Town, **10**
Dōtonbori-dōri, **8**
Europe Mura, **7**
Keitaku-en, **15**
Midō-suji, **5**
National Bunraku Theater, **11**
Niji-no-machi (Rainbow Town), **9**
Ōsaka City Museum, **2**
Ōsaka-jō, **1**
Shiritsu Bijutsukan (Municipal Museum of Fine Arts), **14**
Shiritsu Tōyō Jiki Bijutsukan (Museum of Oriental Ceramics), **4**
Shitennō-ji, **12**
Sumiyoshi Taisha, **16**
Tennō-ji Kōen, **13**
Twin 21 Towers, **3**

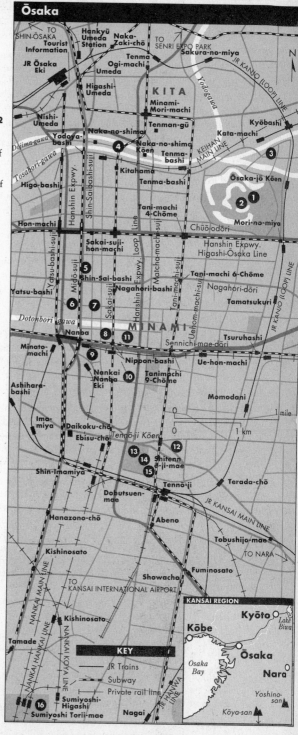

be right outside the theater. Osakans have helped make Bunraku a sophisticated art form. Try to attend an afternoon performance, which begins at 4 PM.

Now head for **Tennō-ji Kōen** ⑬ and its peaceful ponds and gardens. In the park, consider visiting the **Shiritsu Bijutsukan** ⑭, with its ancient and modern art and ancient pottery and artifacts. Rest awhile in the adjacent **Keitaku-en** ⑮, a calming garden with cherry trees and azaleas around a pond. Then head for **Shitennō-ji** ⑫, usually referred to as Tennō-ji. Founded in 593, though resurrected many a time, it claims to be the oldest Buddhist temple in Japan. To get here straight from Ōsaka-jō, take the JR Kanjo Line from Ōsaka-jō Kōen Eki or Kyobashi Eki going south. If you exit at Tennō-ji Eki, you'll see the street going north up to Shitennō-ji; Tennō-ji Kōen will be on the left.

To supplement or substitute sights on the tour above, keep in mind the following. At the southern reaches of Ōsaka is one of the three most famous shrines in Japan, **Sumiyoshi Taisha** ⑯. In the city's northern quarters you'll find **Senri Expo Park** and its four museums. Two are particularly worth your time: **Nihon Mingei-kan** for its outstanding traditional regional handicrafts and **Kokuritsu Minzokugaku Hakubutsukan** for its exhibits on comparative cultures of the world.

Sights to See

North of Chūō-dōri

Mino Park. Osakans come here in autumn to admire the dazzling fall foliage, especially the maple trees, whose leaves turn to brilliant crimson. The path along the river leads to the Mino Waterfall. Monkeys reside in a protected habitat. ⊠ *30 mins from Hankyū Umeda Station on Mino subway line, north of Mino Station.* ⊡ *Free.*

❷ **Ōsaka City Museum.** This storehouse of municipal memorabilia stands on Ōsaka-jō's grounds. Books, photographs, and other records of the city's history are on display. ⊠ *1-1 Ōsaka-jō, Chūō-ku,* ☎ *06/941–7177.* ⊡ *Permanent collection ¥400 (special exhibits vary).* ⊙ *Daily 9:15–4:45 (enter by 4:15); closed 2nd and 4th Mon. of month.*

★ ❶ **Ōsaka-jō.** Ōsaka's castle is without doubt its most famous sight. Ōsaka-jō was one of Hideyoshi Toyotomi's finest buildings. The first stones were laid in 1583, and for the next three years as many as 100,000 workmen labored to build a majestic and impregnable castle. Note the thickness and the height of the walls. In order to demonstrate their loyalty to Hideyoshi, the feudal lords from the provinces were requested to contribute immense granite rocks. The largest piece of stone is said to have been donated by Hideyoshi's general, Kiyomasa Katō (1562–1611), who had it brought from Shodo-shima off of Shikoku (☞ Chapter 12). Known as Higo-Ishi, the rock measured a gigantic 19 ft high and 47 ft wide.

Hideyoshi was showing off with this castle. He had united Japan after a period of devastating civil wars, and he wanted to secure his western flanks. He also wanted to establish Ōsaka as a merchant town that could distribute the produce from the surrounding wealthy territories. The castle was intended to demonstrate Hideyoshi's power and commitment to Ōsaka in order to attract merchants from all over Japan.

Hideyoshi's plan succeeded, but within two years of his death in 1598, Ieyasu Tokugawa, an executor of Hideyoshi's will, took power and got rid of the guardians of Hideyoshi's son. However, it was not until 1614 that Ieyasu sent his armies to defeat the Toyotomi family and their allies. In 1615, the castle was destroyed.

Over a 10-year period, the Tokugawa Shogunate rebuilt the castle, according to original plans, and this version stood from 1629 until 1868, when the Tokugawa Shogunate's power reached its end. Rather than let the castle fall into the hands of the forces of the Meiji Restoration, the Tokugawa troops burned it. In 1931, the present five-story (eight stories inside) donjon was built in ferro-concrete for the prestige of the city. An exact replica of the original, though marginally smaller in scale, it stands 189 ft high and has 46-ft-high stone walls. At night, when illuminated, it becomes a brilliant backdrop to the city.

Inside the castle, there is a museum with artifacts of the Toyotomi family and historical objects relating to Ōsaka prior to the Tokugawa Shogunate. Unless you are a Hideyoshi fan, these exhibits are of marginal interest. The castle's magnificent exterior and the impressive view from the eighth floor of the donjon are the reasons to see Ōsaka-jō. If you plan ahead and get lucky, you might catch the cherry blossoms and **Nishi-no-maru Tei-en** (garden) at its best.

If you have a JR Pass, the best access to Ōsaka-jō is to take the JR Kanjo Line from Ōsaka Eki to Ōsaka-jō Kōen-mae Eki. From there it's about a 10-minute walk up the hill to the castle. Alternatively, take the Tani-machi subway line from Higashi-Umeda Station (just southeast of Ōsaka Eki) to Tani-machi 4-Chome Station. From there it is a 15-minute walk up the hill to Ōsaka-jō. ⊠ *1-1 Ōsaka-jō, Chūo-ku,* ☎ *06/941–3044.* 🎟 *¥500 (Nishi-no-maru Tei-en additional ¥200).* ⊙ *Daily 9–5 (enter by 4:30); July 15–Aug., 9–8:30 (enter by 8); closed Dec. 28–Jan. 1.*

❹ **Shiritsu Tōyō Jiki Bijutsukan** (Museum of Oriental Ceramics). Set in Naka-no-shima Kōen, the island's park, this world-class museum houses some thousand pieces of Chinese and Korean ceramics. The artworks come from the priceless Ataka Collection, which belonged to a wealthy Japanese industrialist and were donated to the museum by the giant Sumitomo Group conglomerate. The ceramic collection, rated as one of the finest in the world, includes 14 works that have been designated National Treasures or Important Cultural Properties.

Take the Sakai-suji subway line to Kitahama and walk north across the Tosabori-gawa to the museum. ⊠ *1-1 Naka-no-shima, Kita-ku,* ☎ *06/223–0055.* 🎟 *¥500 (special exhibitions vary).* ⊙ *Tues.–Sun. 9:30– 5 (enter by 4:30); closed Tues. if Mon. is national holiday.*

Tenmangu Shrine. This 10th-century shrine is the main site of the annual **Tenjin Matsuri,** held July 24–25, one of the three largest and most enthusiastically celebrated festivals in Japan. During Tenjin Matsuri, dozens of floats are paraded through the streets, and more than 100 vessels, lighted by lanterns, sail along the canals amid a dazzling display of fireworks. A renowned scholar of the 9th century, Michizane Sugawara, is enshrined at Tenmangu; he is now considered the God of Academics. Tenmangu is a short walk from Minami-Mori-machi Station on the Tani-machi-suji subway line. ⊠ *2-1-8 Tenjin-bashi, Kita-ku,* ☎ *06/353–0025.* 🎟 *Free.* ⊙ *Apr.–Sept., daily 5:30 AM–sunset; Oct.–Mar., daily 6 AM–sunset.*

❸ **Twin 21 Towers.** The two mighty skyscrapers in Ōsaka Business Park are a symbol of Japan's rush into the 21st century. **Panasonic Square,** on the second floor of one of the Twin 21 structures, the National Tower Building, displays the Matsushita Electric Group's high-tech developments and presents a hands-on experience of the electronic age in the **Futuristic Electro-Fun Zone.** Both fun and educational, the exhibits are divided into four zones: Knowing, Learning, Experiencing, and Creating with Electronics. On any given day, you'll see crowds of Japanese schoolchildren absorbed in testing the TV telephone that allows them to see the person they're talking to on a monitor screen, or donning Superman costumes to star in and direct their own mini-TV shows. Other displays allow you to check your golf, baseball, or tennis skills on a video camera at the Swing Check Corner; have your portrait drawn by a robot; and test what you've learned with a computerized question-and-answer session. Moderately priced food shops serve sushi and other light fare, and there is a souvenir shop.

From Ōsaka-jō, walk north down the hill past Ōsaka-jō Hall (a center used for sports and concerts) and cross the overpass near the Aqua Liner (water bus) pier. On the other side of Hirano-gawa is the New Otani Hotel and, just behind it, the Twin 21 Towers of Ōsaka Business Park. From Ōsaka Eki, take the JR Kanko Line to Kyo-bashi Eki, cross the bridge, and walk west for five minutes along Neya-gawa. ⊠ *Twin 21, National Tower Bldg., 2nd floor, 1-61 Shiromi 2-chōme, Chūō-ku,* ☎ *06/949–2122.* ⊒ *¥500.* ☼ *Daily 10–6 (enter by 5:30).*

Zohei (Mint Museum). This money museum displays about 16,000 examples of Japanese and foreign currencies. It also exhibits Olympic medals, prehistoric currency, and ancient Japanese gold coins. Near the museum is the Mint Garden, part of which is open to the public for a short period during the cherry-blossom season (usually April). At that time you can stroll on a path shaded by blossoms along the Yodo-gawa. The museum is a 15-minute walk east of Minami-Mori-machi or Tenma-bashi station on the Tani-machi subway line. ⊠ *1-1-79 Tenma, Kita-ku,* ☎ *06/351–8509.* ⊒ *Free.* ☼ *Mon.–Sat. 9–4 (enter by 3:30); closed 2nd and 4th Sat. of month.*

SENRI EXPO PARK

Kokuritsu Minzokugaku Hakubutsukan (National Museum of Ethnology). This modern black-and-silver building has a variety of regional exhibits on world cultures. Automatic audiovisual equipment, called Videotheque, provides close-up views of the customs of the peoples of the world. An English pamphlet that comes with your admission ticket illuminates these fascinating displays. The museum is on the right side of the main road that runs north–south through Senri Park. ⊠ *Senri Expo Park, Senri, Suitashi,* ☎ *06/876–2151.* ⊒ *¥400.* ☼ *Thurs.–Tues. 10–5 (enter by 4:30); closed Dec. 28–Jan. 4.*

Nihon Mingei-kan (Japan Folk Art Museum). This mingei-kan contains outstanding examples of traditional regional handicrafts. On view are ceramics, textiles, wooden crafts, bamboo ware, and other items offering one of the best displays for you to familiarize yourself with Japanese folk art. ⊠ *10-5 Banpaku Kōen, Senri, Suitashi,* ☎ *06/877–1971.* ⊒ *¥400 (special exhibitions vary).* ☼ *Thurs.–Tues. 10–5 (enter by 4:30).*

Senri Expo Park. On the former site of Expo '70, this 647-acre park contains the ☞ **Kokuritsu Minzokugaku Hakubutsukan** and ☞ **Nihon Mingei-kan,** two other smaller museums, an amusement park called Expo Land, sports facilities, a Japanese garden with two teahouses, and other gardens.

To reach the park, take the Midō-suji subway line to Senri-Chūō Station (30 minutes from Umeda); then take the Expo Land bus to Nihon Teien-mae Station (30 minutes) or monorail to Banpaku Kōen-mae (20 minutes). ⊠ *Senri Expo Park, Senri, Suitashi,* ☎ *06/877–0560 for Expo Land.* ⊒ *Natural garden ¥150, Japanese garden ¥300, Expo Land ¥1,200; other facilities within park impose additional entrance fees, which vary.* ☼ *Thurs.–Tues. 9–5; closed Dec. 28–Jan. 1; Expo Land closed Wed.*

South of Chūō-dōri

❻ America Mura (American Village). On this group of streets clotted with stores full of youthful American clothing, bright neon signs with the Japanese version of American names hang over shop doors as the sound of trendy music booms from inside. The stores carry an assortment of U.S.–made jeans and sportswear and are tended by punkishly coifed Japanese youth. ⊠ *On west side of Midō-suji, 6 blocks south of Midō-suji subway line's Shin-Sai-bashi Station.*

❿ Den Den Town. Nearly 300 specialty shops in this gadget gulch flaunt the latest electronic wonders from games, calculators, and computers to toasters and tape players at discounted prices. ⊠ *2 blocks east of southern terminus of Nanba Station.*

★ ❽ Dōtonbori-dōri. The good life of Dōtonbori's restaurants and bars lures flocks of Ōsakans here to forget their daily toils. The street—a virtual feast for neonophiles—runs alongside Dōtonbori-gawa, and it is *the* place to stroll in the evening for a glimpse of Ōsaka nightlife. Look for the giant, undulating Kani Dōraku crab sign, a local landmark. ⊠ *From Umeda, take Midō-suji subway line to Nanba and walk north 2 blocks up Midō-suji; or walk south from Europe Mura 5 blocks on Midō-suji and cross Dōtonbori-gawa.*

❼ Europe Mura (European Village). The heart and soul of Europe Mura is Ōsaka's attempt at a display of cosmopolitanism and high fashion—designer boutiques with clothing from Paris, London, and Milan that attract well-to-do Ōsakans. Here, too, are Parco, Sogo, and Daimaru department stores, some of Japan's top chains. The cobblestone sidewalks in the area attempt to re-create the feeling of a Continental city. ⊠ *East side of Midō-suji, 6 blocks south of Midō-suji subway line's Shin-Sai-bashi Station.*

Fujii-dera. An 8th-century, 1,000-handed seated statue of Kannon, the Goddess of Mercy, is the main object of worship at this temple. The statue is a National Treasure, the oldest Buddhist sculpture of its kind. Take the Midō-suji subway line to Tennō-ji Station; then transfer to the Kintetsu Minami–Ōsaka Line and take it to Fujii-dera Station. The temple is a few minutes' walk away. ⊠ *1-16-21 Fujii-dera, Fujii-dera-shi,* ☎ *0729/38–0005. Statue on view the 18th of each month, 9–5.*

Hattori Ryokuchi Park. This recreational park has facilities for horseback riding and tennis, a youth hostel, and a museum of old farmhouses (museum entry ¥410). No reservation is necessary for tennis (¥610–¥710) during the week; for weekend play you may need to reserve a week in advance. Take the Midō-suji subway line from Umeda to Esaka Station, then the Kita-Ōsaka Kyuko Line to Ryokuchi Kōen Station. The park is a 10-minute walk away. ☉ *Apr.–Oct., daily 9:30–5 (enter by 4:30); Nov.–Mar., daily 9:30–4 (enter by 3:30).*

❺ Keitaku-en. This small garden, originally constructed in 1908 and offering an example of the Japanese circular garden, was given to the city by the late Baron Sumitomo. Its cherry trees and azaleas surrounding a pond are lovely to behold when in bloom. The garden offers a welcome respite from the rest of the city. Keitaku-en is adjacent to ☞ **Shiritsu Bijutsukan** in ☞ **Tennō-ji Kōen.** ⊡ *¥150.* ☉ *Tues.–Sun. 9:30–4:30 (enter by 4).*

❺ Midō-suji. This is one of Ōsaka's major boulevards, with the Midō-suji subway running underneath it. Shin-Sai-bashi and Ebisu-bashi parallel Midō-suji and are two of Ōsaka's best shopping and entertainment streets. The Shin-Sai-bashi stop on the Midō-suji subway line is on the western edge of the city's shopping districts.

Nan Nan Town. Ōsaka's shops and restaurants are as much below ground as they are above. Nan Nan Town is yet another underground mall that has a varied selection of clothes, appliances, and unpretentious restaurants. It runs eight blocks south from the southern end of Midō-suji. ⊠ *2 blocks southeast of Nanba Station, and about 2 blocks from Niji-no-machi.*

★ ⑪ **National Bunraku Theater.** Osakans have helped make Bunraku a sophisticated art form—don't miss it. Bunraku puppets are about two-thirds human size. Three puppeteers move the puppets, and they are completely visible to the audience. These master puppeteers not only skillfully manipulate the puppets' arms and legs but also roll the eyes and move the lips so that the puppets express fear, joy, and sadness.

To reach the theater from Nanba subway station, take the Sennichi-mae subway line one stop east to the Nippon-bashi Station. Take Exit 7, and you will be right outside the theater. ⊠ *12-10 Nippon-bashi 1-chōme, Chūō-ku,* ☎ *06/212–2531; 06/212–122 for reservations.* ⊠ *¥4,400 and ¥5,600. Performances scheduled 6 times a year (Jan., Mar., Apr., June, July, Aug., Nov.); each run starts on the 3rd of the month and lasts about 3 wks.*

⑨ **Niji-no-machi** (Rainbow Town). This underground shopping mall, which extends six blocks east to west, offers a good selection of clothes, appliances, and unpretentious restaurants. It is two blocks south of Dōtonbori-dōri.

Nintoku Mausoleum. The 4th-century mausoleum of Emperor Nintoku is in Sakai City, southeast of Ōsaka. The mausoleum was built on an even larger scale than that of the pyramids of Egypt—archaeologists calculate that the central mound of this site is 1.3 million square ft. Its construction took more than 20 years and required a total work force of about 800,000 laborers. Surrounding the emperor's burial place are three moats and pine, cedar, and cypress trees. You can walk around the outer moat to get an idea of the size of the mausoleum and the grounds. However, entry into the mausoleum is not allowed. From Tennō-ji Eki, take the JR Hanwa Line to Mozu Eki (a half-hour ride). From there, the mausoleum is a five-minute walk away. ⊠ *7 Daisen-chō, Sakai-shi,* ☎ *0722/41–0002.*

⑭ **Shiritsu Bijutsukan** (Municipal Museum of Fine Arts). In ☞ **Tennō-ji Kōen** southwest of ☞ **Shitennō-ji** itself, this museum is best known for its collection of 12th- to 14th-century classical art. An exception to this are the special exhibitions that show the works of an Edo-period artist, Ogata Korin. Some modern art is also included in its permanent collection (but the Japanese pieces are more exceptional), as well as a collection of Chinese paintings and archaeological artifacts. Take the JR Kanko Line or the Midō-suji subway line to Tennō-ji Eki; or the Tani-machi-suji subway to Shitennō-ji-mae. ⊠ *1-82 Chausuyama-chō, Tennō-ji-ku,* ☎ *06/771–4874.* ⊠ *Permanent collection ¥300 (special exhibitions vary).* ☉ *Tues.–Sun. 9:30–5 (enter by 4:30).*

⑫ **Shitennō-ji.** Tennō-ji, as it is popularly known, is one of the most important historical sights in Ōsaka. Architecturally, the temple has suffered: Fire has destroyed it many times. Maintaining the original design and adhering to the traditional mathematical alignment, the last reconstruction of the Kondō (Main Hall), Kodo Taishi-den, and the five-story pagoda was in 1965. What has managed to survive is the stone torii that was built in 1294 and stands at the main entrance. One does not often see a torii at a Buddhist temple.

Shitennō-ji claims to be the oldest Buddhist temple in Japan. Outdating Hōryū-ji in Nara (607), it was founded by Prince Shōtoku in 593. Umayado no Mikoto (573–621), who is posthumously known as Prince Shōtoku, or Shōtoku Taishi, is seen as one of early Japan's most enlightened rulers for his furthering of Buddhism and his political acumen. He was made regent over his aunt, Suiko, and set about instituting reforms and establishing Buddhism as the state religion. Buddhism had been introduced to Japan from China and Korea in the early 500s, but it had been seen as a threat to the aristocracy, who claimed prestige and power based upon their godlike ancestry. Prince Shōtoku recognized both the power of Buddhism and its potential as a tool for the state. His swords and a copy of his Hokkekyo Lotus Sutra, made during the Heian period (897–1192), were stored at Shitennō-ji, though today they are kept in the National Museum of Tōkyō. On the 21st of every month, the temple has a flea market that sells antiques and baubles; don't miss it if you're in town at the time.

Three other sights near Shitennō-ji are worth seeing as well: ☞ **Shiritsu Bijutsukan** and two parks, ☞ **Tennō-ji Kōen** and ☞ **Keitaku-en.**

Three train lines will take you near Shitennō-ji. The Tani-machi-suji subway line's Shitennō-ji-mae Station is closest both to the temple and the temple park. The JR Kanjo Line's Tennō-ji Eki is several blocks south of the temple. The Mido-suji subway line also has a Tennō-ji stop, which is next to the JR eki. Or, you can transfer from the Sakai-suji subway line to the Mido-suji line at Dobutsuen-mae stop, then continue to the Tennō-ji stop. ⊠ *1-11-18 Shitennō-ji, Tennō-ji-ku,* ☎ *06/771–0066.* ☜ *¥200.* ☉ *Apr.–Sept., daily 8:30–4:30; Oct.–Mar., daily 8:30–4.*

❶❻ **Sumiyoshi Taisha** (Grand Shrine). Most of the Shinto shrines in Japan today were built after the 8th century and were heavily influenced by Buddhist architecture. The three shrines that were built prior to the arrival of Buddhism in Japan are the great Ise Jingū (☞ Chapter 6), Izumo Taisha near Matsue (☞ Chapter 11), and Sumiyoshi Taisha.

Sumiyoshi Taisha is dedicated to the goddess of sea voyages, Sumiyoshi, and, according to legend, was founded by Empress Jingu in 211 to express her gratitude for her safe return from a voyage to Korea. In those days, the shrine faced the sea rather than the urban sprawl that now surrounds it. On the shrine's grounds are many stone lanterns donated by sailors and shipowners as dedications to Sumiyoshi and other Shinto deities that guard the voyages of seafarers. Note the arched bridge, said to have been given by Yodogimi, the consort of Hideyoshi Toyotomi, who bore him a son. Of the three ancient shrines (Ise Jingū, Izumo Taisha, and Sumiyoshi Taisha), only Sumiyoshi has a Japanese cypress structure that is painted vermilion; the other two have a natural wood finish. According to Shinto custom, shrines were torn down and rebuilt at set intervals to the exact specifications of the original. Sumiyoshi, which, incidentally, is also the name given to the style of architecture of this shrine, was last replaced in 1810.

Sumiyoshi Matsuri, one of the city's largest and liveliest festivals, is held from July 30 to August 1. A crowd of rowdy young men carries a 2-ton portable shrine from Sumiyoshi Taisha to Yamato-gawa and back; this event is followed by an all-night street bazaar. To reach Sumiyoshi Taisha, take the 20-minute ride south on the Nankai Main Line from Nankai Nanba Eki to Sumiyoshi Kōen Eki. ⊠ *2-9-89 Sumiyoshi, Sumiyoshi-ku,* ☎ *06/672–0753.* ☜ *Free.* ☉ *Apr.–Oct., daily 6–5; Nov.–Mar., daily 6:30–5.*

⑬ Tennō-ji Kōen. This park not only has the **Shiritsu Bijutsukan** and the garden of **Keitaku-en,** it also contains the **Tennō-ji Shokubutsu-en** (Botanical Gardens), and the **Municipal Zoological Gardens,** one of the largest in Japan, with some 22,000 caged animals. You might also notice in Tennō-ji Kōen **Chausuyama Kofun,** a prehistoric burial mound that was the site of Ieyasu Tokugawa's camp during the siege of Ōsaka-jō in 1614–1615. Take the JR Kanko Line from Ōsaka Eki to Tennō-ji Eki. The park is on the left side of the road going north to Shitennō-ji. ⊠ 6-74 Chausuyama-chō, Tennō-ji-ku, ☎ 06/771–8401. ⊡ ¥500. ✆ Tues.–Sun. 9:30–4:30 (enter by 4); closed Dec. 29–Jan. 1.

DINING

Surrounding Ōsaka Umeda Station there are a number of "gourmet palaces" with several floors of restaurants of every type imaginable. Exploring them can be fun. Head for restaurants in the Hankyū Grand Building, the Hankyū Sanban-gai (in the basement below Hankyū Eki), and Acty Ōsaka (in front of JR Ōsaka Eki). Most large department stores also house scores of good restaurants, notably the Daimaru department store in front of JR Ōsaka Eki.

Ōsaka's shopping arcades and underground shopping areas abound in affordable restaurants and coffee shops, but when in doubt, head to Dōtonbori and Soemon-chō, two areas along Dōtonbori-gawa that specialize in restaurants, nightclubs, and bars. Kita-Shinchi is the city's most exclusive dining quarter; the area is similar to Tōkyō's Ginza district. Just about every type of cuisine is available in Ōsaka, so choose your restaurant on the basis of what you feel like eating and at what cost.

Japanese

$$$$ ✕ Benkay. If you appreciate Japanese-style red snapper, which is served with stewed plums, Benkay is the place to go. Sea urchin, squid, and prawns are staples on the menu here; tempura and sushi are popular as well. The restaurant uses the traditional Japanese decor of blond wood paneling, and there's a sushi bar on one side. ⊠ Hotel Nikkō Ōsaka, 1-3-3 Nishi-Shin-Sai-bashi, Chūō-ku, ☎ 06/244–1111. Jacket and tie. AE, DC, MC, V.

$$ ✕ Fuguhisa. This no-nonsense little restaurant specializes in fugu ryori, the blowfish delicacy for which Ōsaka is famous. Extremely expensive almost everywhere else, Chef Kato's tessa (raw blowfish) and techiri (one-pot blowfish stew) are the most reasonable and delicious around. What the place lacks in glamour it makes up for in good, down-to-earth Ōsaka-style food. It's across from the west exit of Tsuruhashi Eki on the JR Kanjo Line. ⊠ 3-14-24 Higashi-Ōhashi, Higashi-Nari-ku, ☎ 06/972–5029. No credit cards. Closed Mon.

$$ ✕ Kani Dōraku. The most famous restaurant on Dōtonbori-dōri, Kani Dōraku is noted for its fine crab dishes at reasonable prices. The giant mechanical crab above the door is a local landmark. As you sit at tables or on tatami mats overlooking Dōtonbori Canal, the ultramodern Kirin Plaza Building glitters across the water. For lunch, a crab dish will run around ¥4,000, while dinner will be above ¥6,000. Other, less expensive dishes include delicious nabe (one-pot stews). There is an English-language menu. ⊠ 1-6-18 Dōtonbori, Chūō-ku, ☎ 06/211–8975. Reservations essential weekends. AE, DC, MC, V.

$$ ✕ Kanki. Akachōchin, or red lanterns, are the symbol of inexpensive eating in Japan, but the wonderful combination of Western and Japanese dishes offered at this friendly place makes it different from most other nomiya, as these inexpensive drinking places are called. Order Kyō-no osusume, the daily special. You might end up with Florentine-style scallops. Table seating is available on the second and third floors.

1-3-11 Shibata-chō, Kita-ku (on northeast end of Hankyū Umeda Eki), ☎ *06/374−0057. No credit cards. Closed Sun.*

$$ ✕ **Mimiu.** *Udon-suki* was born here. The thick, white noodle stew simmered in a pot over a burner at your table—with Chinese cabbage, clams, eel, yams, shiitake mushrooms, *mitsuba* greens, and other seasonal ingredients—is an old favorite in Ōsaka, particularly when served in this traditional restaurant. *6-18 Hirano-machi 4-chōme, Chūō-ku (near Hon-machi Station on Chūō-dōri subway line),* ☎ *06/231−5770. Reservations not accepted. V. Closed Sun.*

$$ ✕ **Tako-ume.** Take a rest from the glitter of Dōtonbori nightlife at this
★ 200-year-old traditional dining spot, which specializes in *oden,* a mixture of vegetables, fish cakes, hard-boiled eggs, and fried tofu, cooked in a broth they say has been simmering here in the same pot for the past 30 years (just add liquid . . .). Sake is poured from pewter jugs that were handmade in Ōsaka. A hot Chinese mustard dip is mixed with sweet miso—a house recipe. This is one of Ōsaka's most famous establishments. *1-1-8 Dōtonbori, Chūō-ku,* ☎ *06/211−0321. Reservations essential weekends. No credit cards. Closed Wed.*

$–$$ ✕ **Kushitaru.** Specializing in dinners served up piping hot on skewers,
★ Kushitaru is another Ōsaka favorite. Your possible selections include *tsukune* (chicken meatballs), celery with sea eel, quail egg with half beak, Chinese mushrooms, pineapple with sliced pork, and oysters with bacon. Of two dining rooms, the one upstairs is a throwback to the 1970s, with period furniture and music. Kushitaru is behind the Hotel Nikkō. *Sander Bldg., 13-5 Nishi-Shin-Sai-bashi 1-chōme, Unagidani, Chūō-ku,* ☎ *06/281−0365. AE, DC, MC, V.*

French/Continental

$$$$ ✕ **Chambord.** Named for the castle in France's Loire Valley, the Cham-
★ bord restaurant is French in every way, from the crystal chandeliers to the chef's innovative cuisine. Specialties served by tuxedoed waiters include tenderloin with chestnuts and mushrooms, boiled lobster with tomato and cream sauce, and roast lamb with green peppers. From its perch on the 29th floor of the Royal Hotel, the restaurant has a panoramic view of Ōsaka's lights and river activities. *Royal Hotel, 5-3 Naka-no-shima, Kita-ku,* ☎ *06/448−1121. Reservations essential. Jacket and tie. AE, DC, MC, V.*

$$$$ ✕ **Le Rendezvous.** Atop the Plaza Hotel, Le Rendezvous offers guests not only an elegant meal but also expansive views of the city. A regal French restaurant with lovely wood paneling and formal place settings, it features nouvelle French cuisine and a fine wine selection. Chef Paul Bocuse, who advises the kitchen here, has an established reputation in Japan and elsewhere for presenting eye-pleasing gourmet dishes ranging from beef cuts to choice salmon. *2-2-49 Oyodo-minami, Oyodo-ku,* ☎ *06/453−1111. Jacket and tie. AE, DC, MC, V. No lunch.*

$$$$ ✕ **Les Célébrités.** On the menu at Les Célébrités are French items identified by their association with such painters as Cézanne, Degas, Renoir, and Toulouse-Lautrec—such dishes as terrine of eel and spinach, *dodine* of stuffed wild duck with foie gras, chilled consommé flavored with tomato, and tenderloin steak with morels. Two intimate dining rooms (only 33 seats total) are decorated in lavender and pink with fresh flowers and beautiful chandeliers. You can also come here for breakfast. Les Célébrités is in the Hotel Nikkō along with the excellent Benkay (☞ *above*). *Hotel Nikkō Ōsaka, 1-3-3 Nishi-Shin-Sai-bashi, Chūō-ku,* ☎ *06/244−1111. Jacket and tie. AE, DC, MC, V.*

$$$$ ✕ **Rose Room.** Yet another elegant hotel restaurant, this one is dressed
★ up in green marble and has color-coordinated furnishings. The Rose Room features a formal atmosphere, enhanced by candlelit tables, fresh flowers, and a mirrored ceiling. This intimate establishment seats

only 59 guests and serves Continental cuisine. Fish and beef dishes are the specialties, which include grilled sea bass with onion-flavored vinegar, steamed turbot with ravioli, grilled sirloin steak, and Châteaubriand. ⊠ *ANA Sheraton Hotel Ōsaka, 1-3-1 Dojimahama, Kita-ku,* ☎ *06/347–1112. Reservations essential. Jacket and tie. AE, DC, MC, V.*

$$$$ ✕ **The Seasons.** This grand, elegant dining room in the Hilton Inter-
★   national is in the bustling restaurant and retail sector around Ōsaka Eki. You'll recognize a number of items on the Continental menu from home: Maine lobster, the local favorite Kōbe beef, and superb wines. Specialties include duckling terrine with goose liver, sliced beef in red wine sauce, and fillet of beef with goose liver in a puff pastry. The quick, lower-priced lunch menu is ideal for a sampling of what the Hilton chef has to offer; at night, a pianist entertains. ⊠ *Ōsaka Hilton International, 8-8 Umeda 1-chōme, Kita-ku,* ☎ *06/347–7111. Jacket required. AE, DC, MC, V.*

Steak Restaurants

$$$$ ✕ **Ron.** For all of its claims of having the best steak in the world, Ron does indeed do a bustling business on its three floors. On the menu you'll find fried prawns, fried vegetables, boiled rice, tossed salad, and, of course, prime Kōbe-beef steak. The setting is casual and homey, with only 13 tables in the entire restaurant. Your beef and other delectables will be prepared on the iron grill table around which you sit—the preparation is half the experience. A five-minute walk from Ōsaka Eki, Ron is housed in a five-story brick building. ⊠ *1-10-2 Sonezakishinchi, Kita-ku,* ☎ *06/344–6664. AE, DC, MC, V. No lunch Sun.*

$$$–$$$$ ✕ **Kōbe Misono.** This dining spot is a branch of a restaurant in Kōbe, and the chefs have managed to transfer the successful Kōbe-beef recipe to Ōsaka. Amid dozens of other less distinguished restaurants, Kōbe Misono stands out for its attentive service and casual ambience. Besides the Kōbe-beef dinners with all the fixings, other dishes include a chef salad, scallops, and fried vegetables. One family or couple is seated at each iron grill table; there are only six tables, which seat a maximum of 43 persons. ⊠ *Near Ōsaka Eki, Star Bldg., 3rd floor, 11-19 Sonezakishinchi, Kita-ku,* ☎ *06/341–4471. AE, DC, MC, V.*

$$$–$$$$ ✕ **Ōsaka Joe's.** First came Miami Joe's, then Tokyo Joe's; now here is the third version of that formidable institution for stone crabs. The obvious specials are the crabs (with melted butter and mustard mayonnaise) flown in from Florida and, for dessert, Key lime pie. Also on the menu are baked prawns, T-bone steak, and lamb chops. The setting is casual and American, and even the music is from the States. A cozy, rustic bar at the entry seats eight; the two dining rooms seat a total of 99. Lunch is served until 3 PM and is relatively inexpensive at about ¥1,500. Dinner can be considerably higher—around ¥6,000 for crab claws. This is one good opportunity to make the comparison between American crab meat and the *kani* (crab) found in Japanese waters. Ex-pats are the regular clientele. ⊠ *IM Excellence Bldg., 2nd floor, 1-11-20 Sonezakishinchi, Kita-ku,* ☎ *06/344–0124. AE, DC, MC, V.*

Seafood

$–$$ ✕ **Little Carnival.** You'll find Little Carnival tucked away on the lower
★   level of the Umeda Center Building, where singing waiters serve up lobster, salmon, crab, and raw fish. The restaurant's library theme, multiwood paneling, and dining areas on different levels create a casual, friendly atmosphere. Little Carnival also has a large buffet and salad bar, and from 6 to 10 in the evening, a pianist accompanies the singing servers. This place is very popular with young people. ⊠ *Umeda Center Bldg., basement, 2-4-12 Nakazaki-Nishi, Kita-ku,* ☎ *06/373–9828. Reservations not accepted. AE, DC, MC, V.*

Mexican

$$ ✕ **La Bamba.** The owner-chef learned his craft in Mexico and learned
★ it so well that success has caused him to relocate for larger space in
Umeda and to open a branch in Dōtonbori-Minami (☎ 06/213–
9612). And you'll find the same superior quality of the tacos, guacamole,
burritos, quesadillas, and magnificent pitchers of margaritas in both
locales. Decor is typically "Mexican"—sombreros and posters—which
can for a time release you from the land of raw fish and chopsticks.
✉ *Shiko Crown Bldg., 10-7 Doyama-chō, Kita-ku,* ☎ *06/367–0192.
No credit cards. Closed Mon.*

Vegetarian

$ ✕ **Country Life.** With Japan's healthy economy, no longer is brown rice
seen as the food of those who can afford little more. Country Life, with
its Early American decor, has inexpensive yet gourmet vegetarian
meals. Food (no meat, fish, eggs, or milk) is served buffet-style—all
you can eat, and all delicious. The restaurant is across Tosabori-gawa
and southeast of the Museum of Oriental Ceramics (☞ *above*). ✉ *3-
11 Kyō-bashi, Chūō-ku,* ☎ *06/943–9597. Reservations not accepted.
No credit cards. Closed Sat.*

Nightspots with Food

$$ ✕ **Kirin City.** This beer hall is on the second floor of the fantastic Kirin
Plaza Building designed by Shin Takamatsu, one of Japan's most con-
troversial new architects. This hyper-techno postmodern extravaganza
presides over the old Naru-bashi on Dōtonbori Canal. Stop here for
a cold draft beer and a bite to eat in the Shin-Sai-bashi district. The
menu's fried chicken, "city potatoes" (french fries), and chorizo are
among other gai-jin delights. ✉ *Kirin Plaza Bldg., 2nd floor, 7-2 Soemon-chō, Chūō-ku,* ☎ *06/212–6572. Reservations not accepted. V.*

$–$$ ✕ **Yasubei.** This small *izakaya* (pub) has a fun atmosphere and good
food. Sit at the counter, where you can watch the chefs at work, or at
a table and select from an extensive menu that includes grilled fish, hi-
bachi-grilled chicken, and scallops wrapped in bacon. ✉ *Dai-ichi-
dōri, 2nd level basement, 1-3 Umeda, Kita-ku (close to Umeda Station),*
☎ *06/344–4545. Reservations not accepted. No credit cards.*

$ ✕ **Karma.** A reasonably priced night spot and gathering place, Karma
has a full-service bar, snacks and complete menus, audiovisual entertainment, and Friday- and Saturday-night dancing to tunes spun by local
DJs. The cover charge is ¥1,500; drinks average ¥800, and a BLT on
a bagel costs ¥800. Karma is across Route 2 from the Ōsaka Dai-ichi
Biru. ✉ *Eiraku Biru, Sonezaki Shinchi, Chūō-ku,* ☎ *06/344–6181.
Reservations not accepted. No credit cards.*

$ ✕ **Pig & Whistle.** Both branches of this place (one in Umeda and one
in Shin-Sai-bashi) have a publike atmosphere with a standup bar and
tables, a variety of imported beers, a dart board, and an informal ambience conducive to conversation. ✉ *IS Bldg., 2nd floor, 1-32 Shin-
Sai-bashi-suji 2-chōme, Chūō-ku,* ☎ *06/213–6911;* ✉ *B1 Ohatsutenjin
Biru, 2-5 Sonezaki, Kita-ku,* ☎ *06/361–3198. Reservations not accepted.
No credit cards. No lunch.*

LODGING

$$$$ 🏨 **ANA Sheraton Hotel Ōsaka.** One of only a half-dozen Ōsaka hotels
to classify as deluxe, the ANA Sheraton overlooks the city's picturesque
Naka-no-shima. A handsome 24-story white-tile structure, it has some
unusual architectural features, including a six-story rock sculpture behind its main stairway and great fluted columns in the lobby. There is
also an enclosed courtyard with trees. Guest rooms are done in pastel
shades and have travertine-marble baths. Each room is furnished with

twin or double beds; some have extra sofa beds. The hotel's restaurants include the elegant Rose Room (☞ Dining, *above*). ⊠ *1-3-1 Dojima-hama, Kita-ku, Ōsaka 530*, ☎ *06/347–1112; 800/262–4683 for U.S reservations; 0171/995–8211 for U.K. reservations;* ℻ *06/347–9208. 500 rooms. 5 restaurants, coffee shop, indoor pool, sauna, health club, business services, parking (fee). AE, DC, MC, V.*

$$$$ ★   🏨 **Hotel New Otani Ōsaka.** Popular with Japanese and Westerners, the New Otani offers such amenities as indoor and outdoor pools, tennis courts, superior rooms, and a sparkling marble atrium lobby. The rooms, large by Japanese standards, afford handsome views of Ōsaka-jō and the Neya-gawa. Room decor is modern, with twin or double beds, light color schemes, dining tables, lined draperies, and excellent bathrooms. A large number of bars and restaurants provides enough diversity to suit almost any taste. Indeed, the New Otani is like a minicity within the Ōsaka Business Park. As a result, its drawback is that you need to take the Aqua Liner water bus, which stops in front of the hotel, whenever you need to go to midtown Ōsaka. The hotel is next to Ōsaka-jō Kōen on the JR Kanjo Line. ⊠ *4-1 Shiromi 1-chōme, Chūō-ku, Ōsaka 540*, ☎ *06/941–1111,* ℻ *06/941–9769. 559 rooms. 18 restaurants and bars, health club. AE, DC, MC, V.*

$$$$ 🏨 **Hotel Nikkō Ōsaka.** An impressive and rather striking white tower in the colorful Shin-Sai-bashi Station area, the Nikkō Ōsaka is within easy reach of Ōsaka's nightlife. The hotel's atmosphere is lively, even exciting: As you enter, you'll probably be greeted by a doorman in top hat and tails. Some rooms offer contemporary furnishings with Japanese touches and traditional light decor. Higher-priced rooms have expensive furniture, thick carpets, and bedside controls. Tiled baths on executive floors are particularly well appointed. The bars and restaurants (☞ Benkay *and* Les Célébrités *in* Dining, *above*) are varied, and service here is an art. ⊠ *1-3-3 Nishi-Shin-Sai-bashi, Chūō-ku, Ōsaka 542*, ☎ *06/244–1111,* ℻ *06/245–2432. 640 rooms. 3 restaurants, 3 bars, coffee shop, shops. AE, DC, MC, V.*

$$$$ 🏨 **Hyatt Regency Ōsaka.** In the city's newest development area, Nanko Cosmosquare, this Hyatt, which opened in 1994, bills itself as a city resort hotel. The good 40 minutes by shuttle bus or subway from Ōsaka Eki makes it an unlikely choice for sightseeing. For business travelers, though, with nearby meetings and Kansai International Airport a 45-minute bus ride away, this Hyatt does have Ōsaka's best in modern comfort. Guest rooms are spacious even by American standards, especially deluxe doubles. Choose one on an upper floor for sweeping views of Ōsaka Bay. Modern conveniences are everywhere. The marble bathrooms have a separate shower stall, and bath towels are very generous. For entertainment and dining there are 15 restaurants and bars ranging from haute Cantonese (with Shanghainese appetizers) at Ten Kuh on the 28th floor to a basement complex of small bistro-style eating shops that includes pâtisseries, snack bars, Italian and Japanese restaurants, and a bar with live music. Across the street at the Asia and Pacific Trade Center is a host of other restaurants, most with a Japanese emphasis. ⊠ *1-13 Nanko-Kita, Suminoe-ku, Ōsaka 559*, ☎ *06/612–1234; 800/233–1234 for U.S. reservations; 0171/580–8197 for U.K. reservations;* ℻ *06/614–7800. 500 rooms. 15 restaurants and bars, health club, pool. AE, DC, MC, V.*

$$$$ 🏨 **Nankai South Tower Hotel.** One of the best features of this three-year-old hotel is its location, right inside Nankai Nanba Eki, where you can connect with a number of rail lines, including the Nankai train to Kansai International Airport. This modern tower has 36 floors, but because public spaces are on the lower levels, all of the guest rooms have views of the city. Rooms are decorated in three color schemes—light shades of blue, brown, and purple—with low-pile rugs, electronically controlled curtains, and brass fixtures. Suites have kitchenettes and Jacuzzis as well as showers and two toilets. Bathrobes are supplied on executive floors. This is a bright, Western-style hotel, akin to what you'd expect in a Hilton: first-rate comfort but little character. Some will find this a welcome escape from the noise of the city and the challenge of traveling in a foreign land. Be sure to have a drink in the Sky Lounge. ⊠ *1-60 Nanba 5-chōme, Chūō-ku, Ōsaka 542,* ☎ *06/646–1111,* FAX *06/648–0331. 548 rooms, including 11 Western suites and 2 Japanese suites. 12 restaurants, indoor pool, hot tubs, sauna, massage, health club, Christian and Shinto chapels.*

$$$$
★ 🏨 **Ōsaka Hilton International.** Glitz and glitter draw both tourists and expense accounters to the Hilton International, Ōsaka's most convenient hotel. Across from Ōsaka Eki in the heart of Ōsaka's business district, it is a typical Western-style hotel, replete with marble and brass. The high-ceiling lobby is dramatic, and the hotel's arcade contains several designer boutiques. Standard rooms come with almost all of the extras, and three executive floors offer the convenience of a lounge for complimentary Continental breakfasts and evening cocktails. One of the restaurants is the Seasons (☞ Dining, *above*). ⊠ *8-8 Umeda 1-chōme, Kita-ku, Ōsaka 530,* ☎ *06/347–7111,* FAX *06/347–7001. 526 rooms. 11 restaurants, café, coffee shop, indoor pool, massage, sauna, tennis, health club, shops, business services. AE, DC, MC, V.*

$$$$ 🏨 **Royal Hotel.** With a host of restaurants (☞ Chambord *in* Dining, *above*) and bars from the basement to the top floor of its tower, the Royal is a self-contained city—which it needs to be, as there is nothing of interest in easy walking distance. The lobby is the perfect spot for people-watching, with crowds going in and out of the hotel's many lounges. Standard rooms, either with twin beds or a queen-size bed, are reasonably spacious and have a coffee table, two chairs, and big picture windows (views improve with the higher floors). Taking a room in the VIP tower will give you access to the swimming club's two sun-roofed pools. A shuttle runs from the hotel to the Grand Hotel (nearby) and to the Yodoya-bashi subway station. ⊠ *5-3-68 Naka-no-shima, Kita-ku, Ōsaka 530,* ☎ *06/448–1121,* FAX *06/448–4414. 1,167 rooms. 15 restaurants, 2 indoor pools, massage, sauna, steam room, health club. AE, DC, MC, V.*

$$$–$$$$ 🏨 **Hotel Ōsaka Grand.** A sister to the Royal Hotel, the Grand is a lively first-class commercial hotel with free shuttle service every few minutes to the Royal and to Yodoya-bashi Subway Station. Everything is neat and clean; the staff is large and hardworking. Housekeeping is very good, and the rooms are bigger than average for Japan. The decor is somewhat dated but in good repair. ⊠ *2-3-18 Naka-no-shima, Kita-ku, Ōsaka 530,* ☎ *06/202–1212,* FAX *06/227–5054. 350 rooms. 2 restaurants, shops. AE, DC, MC, V.*

$$$–$$$$ 🏨 **Miyako Hotel Ōsaka.** A 21-story high rise, the Miyako is filled with expansive public rooms—like the two-story lobby, which is decorated with marble columns and attractive pastel color schemes. The rooms are also modern and inviting, with such extras as dining tables. Executive rooms occupy two floors and have plusher appointments. The Miyako is near the Ue-hon-machi subway station, and trains for Kyōto on the Kintetsu Line leave from an adjacent building. The National Bunraku Theater is also fairly close. ⊠ *6-1-55 Ue-hon-machi, Tennō-ji-ku, Ōsaka 543,* ☎ *06/773–1111,* FAX *06/773–3322. 608 rooms. Restaurants, bars, coffee shop, grill, lounge, indoor pool, health club, racquetball, shops. AE, DC, MC, V.*

$$–$$$ 🏨 **Hotel Do Sports Plaza.** Situated in the heart of Ōsaka's colorful nightlife district, the Do Sports Plaza earned its reputation by catering to sports enthusiasts and athletic teams. Most of the rooms are small but fairly bright singles; doubles are not much larger. Fitness activities are the main attraction here. The hotel adjoins a members-only sports club that is open to hotel guests for an additional ¥2,500 per person. ⊠ 3-3-17 Minami-Senba, Chūō-ku, Ōsaka 542, ☎ 06/245–3311, FAX 06/245–5803. 208 rooms. Restaurant, coffee shop, pub, indoor pool, sauna, health club. AE, DC, MC, V.

$$–$$$ 🏨 **Hotel Hanshin.** Popular mostly with Japanese businessmen, the 15-story Hotel Hanshin does manage to attract a few travelers. Furnishings are mostly Scandinavian; the tile baths are so small you might call them claustrophobic. Waterbeds are available. Moderately priced rooms are between the 10th and 15th floors. The hotel is near the underground shopping center at Umeda and Ōsaka Eki. ⊠ 2-3-30 Umeda, Kita-ku, Ōsaka 530, ☎ 06/344–1661, FAX 06/344–9860. 243 rooms. Restaurant, 2 bars, coffee shop, sauna, shops. AE, DC, MC, V.

$$–$$$ 🏨 **International Hotel Ōsaka.** Popular mostly with Japanese, this massive L-shape hotel may be a bit hard to reach in traffic, but it's a reliable choice. The best rooms are in an annex; if you're on a budget, ask for a room in the back. The International's lobby and public areas are often busy with groups coming or going, and the overall appearance is reserved and uninspiring. ⊠ 2-3-3 Hon-machi-bashi, Chūō-ku, Ōsaka 540, ☎ 06/941–2661, FAX 06/941–5362. 393 rooms. 5 restaurants, coffee shop, lobby lounge. AE, DC, MC, V.

$$–$$$ 🏨 **New Hankyū Hotel and New Hankyū Annex.** This busy hotel complex is in the popular area around Ōsaka Eki, with its restaurants and shopping. The 17-story Annex, a block from the main hotel, houses the newest, largest, and best rooms; it also offers a café, three other eateries, and an indoor pool. The single rooms in the main hotel, however, are about as roomy as telephone booths. Guests are permitted the use of facilities in both buildings. ⊠ 1-1-35 Shibata, Kita-ku, Ōsaka 530, ☎ 06/372–5101, FAX 06/374–6885. 1,249 rooms. 7 restaurants, 3 bars, indoor pool, health club. AE, DC, MC, V.

$$–$$$ 🏨 **Ōsaka Airport Hotel.** This place is for those with an early flight out of Ōsaka's Itami Airport: It's right inside the airport terminal building. These are not the most luxurious rooms for the price, but the location saves time and trouble for the busy. ⊠ Ōsaka Airport Bldg., 3rd floor, Tōyō-naka, Ōsaka-ku, ☎ 06/855–4621, FAX 06/855–4620. 105 rooms. 2 restaurants, 2 bars, shops. AE, DC, MC, V.

$$–$$$ 🏨 **Ōsaka Dai Ichi Hotel.** As Japan's first cylinder-shape skyscraper, known as the Maru-Biru (Round Building), the Dai Ichi is easy to locate amid the Ōsaka cityscape. Now somewhat overshadowed by the Hilton, it still receives many groups. The rooms are wedge-shape, and half are small singles that are usually taken on weekdays by Japanese businessmen. The hotel has a coffee shop, which is open around the clock, and an underground shopping arcade. The Dai Ichi is conveniently located across from Ōsaka Eki. ⊠ 1-9-20 Umeda, Kita-ku, Ōsaka 530, ☎ 06/341–4411, FAX 06/341–4930. 478 rooms. 3 restaurants, bar, shops. AE, DC, MC, V.

$$ 🏨 **Hotel Echo Ōsaka.** This hotel is recommended for those seeking good, moderately priced accommodations. Though near the JR eki, the Echo Ōsaka is far from other major parts of the city. The 83 plain rooms have air-conditioning and routine furnishings, including double or twin beds, uncoordinated carpeting, and small baths. The hotel is neat and clean, if nothing more, and has an accommodating young staff. ⊠ 1-4-7 Abeno-suji, Abeno-ku, Ōsaka 545 (near Tennō-ji Eki), ☎ 06/633–1141, FAX 06/633–3849. 84 rooms. 2 restaurants, bar, coffee shop. AE, DC, MC, V.

$$ 🏨 **Ōsaka Castle Hotel.** This square mid-rise building is unexceptional and receives its name for its location near Ōsaka-jō, not for any majestic manner. It has a rooftop beer garden in summer and a subway stop in the basement. Rooms are small and not very bright; the furni-

ture is uninspired. Some rooms in front have good views, but all have the standard dwarf-size baths found in business hotels. ✉ *2-35-7 Kyō-bashi, Chūō-ku, Ōsaka 540 (at Tenma-bashi Station on Tani-machi Line),* ☎ *06/942–2401,* FAX *06/946–9043. 120 rooms. 3 restaurants, beer garden, café, shops. AE, DC, MC, V.*

$$ 🏨 **Ōsaka International Community Center Hotel.** The city community center has a hotel with pleasant, well-furnished rooms at reasonable rates. The center hosts lectures and cultural events and offers simultaneous interpreting services. ✉ *8-2-6 Kamimoto-chō, Tennō-ji-ku, Ōsaka 543,* ☎ *06/773–8181,* FAX *06/772–7600. 50 rooms. Restaurant, bar, café, library, conference rooms. AE, DC, MC, V.*

$$ 🏨 **Umeshin East Hotel.** In the antiques shop and art gallery neighborhood near the U.S. consulate, this small brick hotel has an attractive modern design, with a lush green interior garden café, a restaurant, and a bar in its tiled lobby. Rooms are small but comfortably furnished. ✉ *4-11-5 Nishi-Tenma, Kita-ku (10-min walk from Midō-suji subway line and Umeda Station),* ☎ *06/364–1151,* FAX *06/364–1150. 144 rooms. AE, DC, MC, V.*

$ 🏨 **Ebisu-so Royan.** This, Ōsaka's only member of the inexpensive Japanese Inn Group, is a partly wooden structure with 15 Japanese-style rooms. It's a very basic, no-frills operation, with traditional shared baths and no restaurant, though there are plenty nearby. Close to the electrical appliance and computer center of Den Den Town and the National Theater, Ebisu-so Royan is a five-minute walk from the Ebisu-chō Station on the Sakai-suji-sen subway line. ✉ *1-7-33 Nippon-bashi-nishi, Naniwa-ku, Ōsaka 556,* ☎ *06/643–4861. 15 rooms with shared bath. AE, MC, V.*

NIGHTLIFE AND THE ARTS

The Arts

National Bunraku Theater. Ōsaka is famous for its Bunraku (puppet form of drama). Bunraku performances are scheduled six times a year (Jan., Mar., Apr., June, July, Aug., Nov.), and each runs for about three weeks. The Ōsaka tourist offices will have the current schedule, which is also printed in the quarterly tourist booklet, *Meet Ōsaka.* Tickets are ¥4,400 and ¥5,600; performances usually begin at 11 AM and 4 PM. From Nanba subway station, take the Sennichi-mae subway line one stop east to the Nippon-bashi Station. Take Exit 7, and you will be right outside the theater. ✉ *12-10 Nippon-bashi 1-chōme, Chūō-ku, Ōsaka,* ☎ *06/212–2531 or* ☎ *06/212–122 for reservations.*

Shin-Kabuki-za Theater. Ōsaka has built a grander and more resplendent Kabuki theater than its counterpart in Tōkyō. The Shin-Kabuki-za has performances of Kabuki, modern plays, and variety shows. ✉ *Southern end of Midō-suji and 1 block east of Nanba Station.*

Nightlife

Ōsaka has as diverse a nighttime scene as Japan's capital, Tōkyō. There are two main areas: Kita—North, the area surrounding JR Umeda Eki—and Minami—South, between the Shin-sai-bashi and Nanba districts. Many Japanese refer to Minami as being "for kids," but there are still a great number of good restaurants and drinking spots for more seasoned bon vivants.

The mainstay of foreign bars in Kansai is the **Pig & Whistle** minichain of English pub-style places. Established in the early 1980s, there are now three in the area—two in Ōsaka (Kita: ✉ Ohatsutenjin Bldg., basement, 2–5 Sonezaki, Kita-ku, ☎ 06/361–3198; Minami: IS Bldg., 2nd floor, 2-chōme Shinsaibashi-suji, Chūo-ku, ☎ 06/213–6911). Guinness and fish and chips are available, as well as bottled beers and a good selection of spirits. These places get very busy on weekends. **Canopy** (✉ IM Excellence Bldg., 1st floor, 1-11-20 Sonezaki-Shinchi, Kita-ku, ☎ 06/341–0339) is frequented by foreigners and Japanese; it's open until 5 AM. Portions are healthy, the happy hour is generous, and there is a terrace for open-air dining in summer. **Club Karma** (Kasai Bldg., 1st floor, 1-5-18 Sonezaki-shinchi, Kita-ku, ☎ 06/344–6181) is a trendy place where style gurus and businessmen coexist in harmony. It is more expensive, but people-watching is great. Club Karma hosts all-night techno rave parties weekends (cover about ¥2,500).

In Minami there is a **Hard Rock Cafe** (✉ Ōsaka Stadium, 2-8-110 Nanba-naka, Naniwa-ku, ☎ 06/646–1470). **Two good Irish pubs** are Murphy's (✉ Lead Plaza Bldg., 6th floor, Higashi-Shinsai-bashi, Chūo-ku, ☎ 06/282–0677) and The Dubliners' Ōsaka (✉ Itoyama Bldg. basement, Soemon-chō-dōri, ☎ 06/212–7030). Murphy's is the more intimate of the two; Dubliners' is the more authentic. **Club Quattro** (✉ Shin-sai-bashi Parco Bldg., 8th floor, ☎ 06/281–8181) features up and coming Japanese rock bands as well as popular British and (more expensive) American bands almost every night. The sound system is excellent.

Ōsaka's hip young things hang out in **America Mura,** where there are innumerable bars and clubs. **Balabushka** (✉ Nippo Mittera Kaikan, 4th floor, 9-5 2-chōme Nishi-Shinsai-bashi, ☎ 06/211–5369) has happy hours, pool, and darts, and plenty of places to sit even when it's busy. **The Cellar** (✉ Dai-3-Hirata Bldg., basement, 2-17-13 Nishi-Shinsaibashi, Chūo-ku, ☎ 06/212–6437) is smaller than Balabushka and has live music three times a week.

Tramps (✉ Wataya Carrot Bldg., 3rd floor, 2-3-28 Higashi-noda-chō, Miyako-jima-ku, ☎ 06/356–0797) is the best place in the Kyō-bashi area. It has live music Fridays and Saturdays, many world beers, reasonable food, and darts.

OUTDOOR ACTIVITIES AND SPORTS

Ōsaka Stadium. For a taste of Japanese *besuboru* (baseball), this is where local teams square off. ✉ *About a block south of Nankai Nanba Eki.*

From the second Sunday through the fourth Sunday in March, one of Japan's six **sumō** tournaments is held in the Ōsaka Furitsu Taiikukaikan (Ōsaka Prefectural Gymnasium; ✉ 3-4-36 Nanba Naka, Naniwa-ku, Ōsaka, ☎ 06/631–0120). Most seats, known as *masu-seki,* are pre-booked before the tournament begins, but standing room is usually available for ¥1,000. The ticket office opens at 9 AM. The stadium is a 10-minute walk from Nanba Station.

SHOPPING

Ōsaka has two main shopping areas: One is centered on Nanba Station in Minami-ku, the other on Ōsaka and Umeda stations in Kita-ku. Minami is the older of the two, and its merchandise is a mixture of traditional and modern goods.

Northeast of Nanba Station are the **Ebisu-bashi** shopping area and the **Niji-no-machi** underground shopping mall. To the southeast are **Nanba City** and **Nan Nan Town** underground malls. Farther east of Nanba Station, but still within walking distance, is **Den Den Town** (☞ Electronics, *below*).

Near Ōsaka and Umeda stations, which connect with underground concourses, are the **Umeda Chika Center** and the **Hankyū Sanban-gai** and **Hankyū Higashi-dōri** malls. This complex of stores is the largest underground shopping area in all of Japan, perhaps even the world, complete with man-made streams and its own version of Rome's Trevi Fountain.

Over Ōsaka Eki is the **Acty Ōsaka Building,** a 27-story shopping and office building. To the west of this complex, near Nishi-Umeda Station on the Yotsu-bashi subway line, are the **Dojima** and **Naka-no-shima** underground malls.

Shin-Sai-bashi-suji is Ōsaka's most elegant shopping arcade. It is paved with marble and covered, and it is near Shin-Sai-bashi Station on the Midō-suji Line, halfway between the Minami and Kita districts. To the east of the arcade is yet another shopping arcade, **Europe Mura,** with trendy, European-influenced clothing. Across Midō-suji to the west is **America Mura,** with clothing styles inspired by U.S. designers for both young and old.

Specialized wholesale areas can be found throughout the city. A few retail shops are in these areas, so it is worth a visit. **Dobuike** is the wholesale area for clothing and accessories (located near Hon-machi Station on the Chūō, Tani-machi, and Yotsu-bashi subway lines, or Sakai-suji-hon-machi Station on the Sakai-suji subway line). **Matcha-machi-suji** is famous for its rows of toy and doll shops.

Department Stores

All major Japanese department stores are represented in Ōsaka. Many of them, such as Hankyū, Hanshin, and Kintetsu, are headquartered here. All are open 10–7, except for Matsuzakaya, which closes at 6:30 (its food hall is open until 7). The following are some of Ōsaka's leading department stores: **Hankyū** (⊠ 8-7 Kakuta-chō, Kita-ku, ☎ 06/361–1381), closed Thursday; **Hanshin** (⊠ 1-13-13 Umeda, Kita-ku, ☎ 06/345–1201), closed Wednesday; **Matsuzakaya** (⊠ 1-1 Tenmabashi Kyo-machi, Chūō-ku, ☎ 06/943–1111), closed Wednesday; **Mitsukoshi** (⊠ 7-5 Korai-bashi 1-chōme, Chūō-ku, ☎ 06/203–1331), closed Tuesday; **Daimaru** (⊠ 1-7-1 Shin-Sai-bashi-suji, Chūō-ku, ☎ 06/343–1231), closed Wednesday; **Sogo** (⊠ 1-8-3 Shin-Sai-bashi-suji, Chūō-ku, ☎ 06/281–3111), closed Tuesday; **Takashimaya** (⊠ 5-1-5 Nanba, Chūō-ku, ☎ 06/631–1101), closed Wednesday; **Kintetsu** (⊠ 1-1-43 Abeno-suji, Abeno-ku, ☎ 06/624–1111; ⊠ 6-1-55 Ue-hon-machi, Tennō-ji-ku, ☎ 06/775–1111), closed Thursday.

Gifts

At one time famous for its traditional crafts, particularly its ornately carved *karaki-sashimono* furniture, its fine Naniwa Suzuki pewter ware, and its Sakai *uchihamono* cutlery, Ōsaka lost much of its traditional industry during World War II. The simplest way to find a wide selection of Ōsaka crafts is to visit one of the major department stores, many of which carry a selection of locally made wares.

For folk crafts from all over the country, including ceramics, basketry, paper goods, folk toys, and textiles, visit the **Nihon Kogeikan Mingei Fukyubu** (Japan Folkcraft Collection), near the Umeshin East Hotel in the popular gallery district, within walking distance of the U.S. Consulate. ⊠ *4-7-15 Nishi-Tenma, Kita-ku,* ☎ *06/362–9501.* ☉ *Mon.– Sat. 10–6; closed 2nd Sat. of month.*

Electronics

Den Den Town has about 300 retail shops that specialize in electronic products (Den Den is a take-off on the word *denki,* which means electricity) as well as stores for cameras and watches. The area is near Ebisu-chō Station on the Sakai-suji Subway Line (Exit 1 or 2), and Nippon-bashi Station on the Sakai-suji and Sennichi-mae subway lines (Exit 5 or 10). Shops are open 10–7 daily. Take your passport, and make your purchases in stores with signs that say "Tax Free." (Note: Because Japan discounts goods sold to America, prices without the tax are still considerably higher than they are for the same goods purchased in the U.S.)

ŌSAKA A TO Z

Arriving and Departing

By Plane

All international flights arrive at **Kansai International Airport** (KIX). There are also connecting domestic flights to major Japanese cities. The airport, built on reclaimed land in Ōsaka Bay, is laid out vertically. The first floor is for international arrivals; the second floor is for domestic departures and arrivals; the third floor has shops and restaurants; and the fourth floor is for international departures. A small Tourist Information Center (☏ 0724/56–6025) on the first floor of the passenger terminal building is open 9–5. Major carriers are **British Airways** (☏ 0120/122881), **Canadian Airlines** (☏ 06/346–5591), **Japan Airlines** (☏ 0120/255–931 international, 0120/255–971 domestic), and **Northwest Airlines** (☏ 06/228–0747).

The majority of domestic flights use Ōsaka's old airport, **Itami Airport,** about 30 minutes from Ōsaka. Flights from Tōkyō, which operate frequently throughout the day, take 70 minutes. Japan Airlines (JAL), All Nippon Airways (ANA), and Japan Air System (JAS) have domestic flights to major cities.

BETWEEN THE AIRPORT AND CENTER CITY

KIX is designed to serve the entire Kansai region, not just Ōsaka. There are four main access routes from Ōsaka: **From Shin-Ōsaka,** take the JR Kansai Airport Express "Haruka" for the 45-minute run (¥2,930); **from Tennō-ji Eki,** the same JR train will get you to the airport in 29 minutes (¥2,250); from **JR Kyo-bashi Eki,** take the Kansai Airport Rapid trains for a 70-minute run (¥1,140); finally, from **Nankai Nanba Eki,** take the Nankai Rapid Limited Express (private line) for a 29-minute trip (¥1,370).

An **airport bus limousine** runs a service between KIX and many of Ōsaka's downtown hotels. The trip takes about 80 minutes (¥1,800).

Airport buses from Itami Airport operate at intervals of 15 minutes to one hour, 6 AM–9 PM, and take passengers to seven locations in Ōsaka: Shin-Ōsaka Eki, Umeda, Nanba (near the Nikko and Holiday Inn hotels), Ue-hon-machi, Abeno, Sakai-higashi, and Ōsaka Business Park (near the New Otani Hotel). Buses take 25–50 minutes, depending on destination, and cost ¥340–¥680. Schedules, with exact times and fares, are available at the information counter at the airport.

Taxis to the city from Kansai International Airport are prohibitively expensive; between Itami Airport and hotels in central Ōsaka, taxis cost approximately ¥7,500 and take about 40 minutes.

By Train

Hikari Shinkansen from Tōkyō to Shin-Ōsaka Eki take just under three hours and cost ¥13,750 for reserved seats, ¥12,980 for nonreserved. You can use a JR Pass for the *Hikari,* but not for the faster *Nozomi* Shinkansen, which cost ¥14,720. Shin-Ōsaka Eki, on the north side of Shin-Yodo-gawa, is linked to the city center by the JR Kōbe Line and the Midō-suji subway line. The ride, which takes 6–20 minutes, depending on your midcity destination, costs ¥180–¥230. Train schedule and fare information can be obtained at the Travel Service Center in the Shin-Ōsaka Eki. A taxi from Shin-Ōsaka Eki to central Ōsaka costs ¥1,500–¥2,700.

Getting Around

By Bus

Economical one-day transportation passes (☞ By Subway, *below*) for Ōsaka are valid on bus lines as well as subway routes, and the service operates throughout the day and evening, but bus travel is a challenge best left to local residents or those fluent in Japanese.

By Subway

Ōsaka's fast, efficient subway system offers the most convenient means of exploring the city—complicated bus routes display no signs in English, and taxis, while plentiful, are costly. The six subway lines converge at Ōsaka Eki in Umeda, where they are linked underground. The main line is the Midō-suji, which runs between Shin-Ōsaka and Umeda in six minutes, Shin-Ōsaka and Shin-Sai-bashi in 12 minutes, Shin-Ōsaka and Nanba in 14 minutes, and Shin-Ōsaka and Tennō-ji in 20 minutes.

Subways run from early morning until nearly midnight at intervals of three to five minutes. Fares begin at ¥180 and are determined by the distance traveled. You can purchase a one-day pass (¥850) for unlimited municipal transportation on subways, the New Tram (a new train line that runs to the docks area), and city buses, at the commuter ticket windows in major subway stations, and at the Japan Travel Bureau office in Ōsaka Eki. A subway network map of Ōsaka is available from the Japan National Tourist Organization (☞ Visitor Information *in* the Gold Guide), the city tourist offices and most hotels, and at the Japan Travel Bureau office in Ōsaka Eki.

Adding to the efficiency of the subway system is the JR Kanjo (Loop) Line, which circles the city above ground and intersects all subway lines. Fares range from ¥180 to ¥420, or you can use your JR Pass.

By Taxi

You'll have no problem hailing taxis on the street or at specified taxi stands. (A red light in the lower left corner of the windshield indicates availability.) The problem is moving in Ōsaka's heavy traffic. Fares are metered at ¥640 for the first 2 km (1¼ mi), plus ¥80 for each additional 500 yards. It is not customary to tip the driver.

Contacts and Resources

Business Assistance

Contact **Information Service System Co., Ltd.** (✉ Hotel Nikko Ōsaka, 1-3-5 Nishi-Shin-Sai-bashi, Chūō-ku, ☎ 06/245–4015) for business-related assistance, including quick-print business cards and interpreting.

Consulates

U.S. (✉ 2-11-5 Nishi-Tenma, Kita-ku, ☎ 06/315–5900).

Canadian (✉ 2-2-3 Nishi-Shin-Sai-bashi, Chūō-ku, ☎ 06/212–4910).

U.K. (✉ Seiko Ōsaka Bldg., 19th floor, 35-1 Bakuro-machi, Chūō-ku, ☎ 06/281–1616).

Doctors and Hospitals

Tane General Hospital (⊠ 1-2-31 Sakai-gawa, Nishi-ku, ☎ 06/581–1071); **Sumitomo Hospital** (⊠ 2-2 Naka-no-shima 5-chōme, Kita-ku, ☎ 06/443–1261); **Yodo-gawa Christian Hospital** (⊠ 9-26 Awaji 2-chōme, Higashi Yodo-gawa-ku, ☎ 06/322–2250); **Ōsaka University Hospital** (⊠ 1-50 Fuku-shima 1-chōme, Fuku-shima, ☎ 06/451–0051), accepts emergency patients by ambulance only.

For medical advice, call the **International Medical Information Center** (☎ 06/213–2393) or the International Medical Center Kansai (☎ 06/636–2333).

Emergencies

Police, ☎ 110. **Ambulance,** ☎ 119. **Metropolitan Police Office Service,** ☎ 06/943–1234.

English-Language Bookstore

Kinokuniya Book Store Co., Ltd. (⊠ Hankyū Sanban-gai 1-1-3, Shibata, Kita-ku, ☎ 06/372–5821) is open daily 10–9, except for the third Wednesday of the month. It is across the street from the Midō-suji entrance of Ōsaka Eki in the Hankyū Eki building complex.

Guided Tours

EXCURSIONS

Japan Travel Bureau (☎ 06/343–0617) runs afternoon tours daily to Kyōto and Nara. Pickup is available at several hotels. **Japan Amenity Travel** (☎ 075/222–0121) has two full-day tours: one to Kyōto only (¥12,000) and one to Kyōto and Nara (¥13,500). They depart from the Ōsaka Hilton International and include train fare to Kyōto.

ORIENTATION TOURS

The **Municipal Bus System** (☎ 06/311–2995) has regular sightseeing tours of the city conducted in Japanese on its double-deck "Rainbow" bus. Five tour routes start at the Umeda Sightseeing Information Center. They vary in length from three to four hours and cost from ¥2,810 to ¥4,230.

The **Aqua Liner** (☎ 06/942–5511) runs a 60-minute tour (¥1,800) through Ōsaka's waterways, departing every hour 10–4 April through September; there are also evening tours from 6 to 7 PM on Friday, Saturday, Sunday, and national holidays from three piers at Ōsaka-jō, Tenma-bashi, and Yodoya-bashi. This is the only tour of Ōsaka conducted in both Japanese and English.

SPECIAL-INTEREST TOURS

Japan's **Home Visit System,** which enables foreign visitors to meet local people in their homes for a few hours and learn more about the Japanese lifestyle, is available in Ōsaka. Apply in advance through the **Ōsaka Tourist Information Center** (☎ 06/305–3311) at JR Shin-Ōsaka Eki, at the **Ōsaka Tourist Association** (☎ 06/208–8955) at the Sumitomo Seimei Yodoya-bashi Building, or at the **Ōsaka City Tourist Information Office** (☎ 06/345–2189) at the JR Ōsaka Eki.

Telephone Assistance

Directory assistance in English, ☎ 06/313–1010.

Travel Agencies

Japan Travel Bureau (⊠ Foreign Tourist Division, Sakai-suji-hon-machi Center Bldg., 7th floor, 2-1-6 Hon-machi, Chūō-ku, ☎ 06/271–6195); **Hankyū Express International** (⊠ 8-47 Kakuta-chō, Kita-ku, ☎ 06/373–5471); **Tokyu Tourist Corp.** (⊠ Kansai Foreign Tourist Center, Wakasugi Ōsaka Eki-mae Bldg. 10th floor, 2-3-13, Sonezaki-shinchi, Kita-ku, ☎ 06/344–5488).

Visitor Information

Ōsaka Tourist Information Center (☎ 06/305–3311), open daily 8–8 and closed December 29–January 3, is on the east side of the main exit of the JR Shin-Ōsaka Eki; there is another location at the Midō-suji gate of JR Ōsaka Eki (☎ 06/345–2189), open daily 8–8, closed December 31–January 4.

The **Information Center** in Ōsaka-jō (☎ 06/941–0546) is open daily 9–5.

Tourist Information Service, Ōsaka Prefectural Government (☎ 06/941–9200), open Monday–Saturday 9–5, is in the lobby of the International Hotel (✉ 58 Hashizume-chō, Uchi-hon-machi, Chūō-ku), a five-minute walk from Sakai-suji-hon-machi subway station.

JAPAN TRAVEL PHONE

Japan Travel Phone (☎ 0120/444–800), open daily 9–5, provides free information in English.

10 Kōbe

Kōbe is unique in Japan for its blending of European and Japanese influences both in its architecture and in the attitudes of its inhabitants. For these reasons, Kōbe is often the choice of residence for many Westerners, who would rather avoid the bustle and crowding of more expensive Ōsaka.

KŌBE HAS BEEN a prominent harbor city throughout Japanese history. In the 12th century, the Taira
family moved the capital from Kyōto to Fukuhara,
the western part of modern Kōbe, with the hope of increasing Japan's
international trade. Fukuhara remained the capital for a mere six
months, but its port, known as Hyōgo, continued to flourish. Japan
actually didn't open its ports to Western trade until 1868, after a long
period of isolationism. At the time, in order to prevent foreigners from
using the profitable and active port of Hyōgo, the more remote port
of Kōbe was opened to international trade. Within a few years, Kōbe,
which is slightly northeast of Hyōgo, eclipsed it in importance as a
port.

By Nigel Fisher

Now a major industrial city, Kōbe has an active port that serves as many
as 10,000 ships a year. A century of exposure to international cultures
has left its mark on Kōbe, a sophisticated and cosmopolitan city. Of
its population of 2 million, some 70,000 residents are gai-jin. Most are
Chinese or Korean, but a noticeable European contingent also lives and
works in Kōbe. Over the years, foreign merchants and traders have settled in the hills above the port area. Many Western-style houses built
in the late 19th century are still inhabited by Kōbe's large foreign population, while others have been open to the public as buildings of historical interest. Many sailors passing through Kōbe, attracted by the
charm of this city, have settled here. So don't expect to find exotic or
traditional Japan in modern Kōbe. Come here instead to relax in a cosmopolitan setting with excellent places to shop and a variety of international cuisines to sample.

Though the damage wreaked by the Great Hanshin earthquake in
January 1995 was indeed tremendous—approximately 5,000 people
were killed and some 100,000 buildings destroyed—the process of recovery has been speedy, especially in the city proper. The only cultural
attractions completely wiped out were the wonderful 19th-century
sake breweries that had been converted into museums. Only in Kōbe's
suburban shoreline sprawl will you still find ruined buildings.

Kōbe Glossary

Key Japanese words and suffixes in this chapter include -*chō* (street or
block), -*chōme* (street), *chūō* (central, as in *Chūō-ku*, central district),
-*dōri* (street or avenue), *eki* (train station), *gai-jin* (foreigner), *ijinkan*
(Western-style house), *kōen* ("*ko*-en," park), -*ku* (section or ward), *onsen*
(hot springs), *Seto Nai-kai* (Inland Sea), -*shi* (city or municipality),
Shinkansen (bullet train, literally "new trunk line"), and *torii* ("*to*-ree-
ee," gate).

Pleasures and Pastimes

Dining

Think Kōbe, think beef. Kōbe beef is considered a delicacy all over
Japan—and the world. Tender, tasty, and extremely expensive, it is a
must for beef lovers. Raised in the nearby Tajima area of Hyōgo Prefecture, Kōbe cows are fed beer and are massaged to improve the quality of their meat and give it its marbled (with fat) texture.

There are many international cuisines available in Kōbe. Some sailors
stay on in the city and open restaurants that become popular with the
large foreign community and with resident and visiting Japanese. The
quality and authenticity of these places are unsurpassed.

CATEGORY	COST*
$$$$	over ¥10,000
$$$	¥6,000–¥10,000
$$	¥3,500–¥6,000
$	under ¥3,500

*per person, excluding drinks, service, and tax

Lodging

Kōbe has a wide range of hotels varying in price and quality. Because it is a heavily industrialized city, Kōbe caters to a lot of business travelers. As a result, the business hotels are conveniently located. Most are quite comfortable.

CATEGORY	COST*
$$$$	over ¥20,000
$$$	¥15,000–¥20,000
$$	¥10,000–¥15,000
$	under ¥10,000

*All prices are for a double room, excluding tax and service.

EXPLORING KŌBE

Downtown Kōbe, where most businesses are located, is near the harbor area. The rest of Kōbe is built on slopes that extend as far as the base of Mt. Rokko—this hill-and-harbor combination brings San Francisco to some people's minds. In the middle of the harbor is the manmade Port Island, which has conference centers, an amusement park, and the Portopia Hotel. The island is linked with the downtown area by a fully computerized monorail that is without a human conductor. The major nightlife area, Ikuta (a subsection of the Kitano area), is just north of San-no-miya Eki.

Numbers in the text correspond to numbers in the margin and on the Kōbe map.

Great Itineraries

If you are interested in seeing the indigenous culture of Japan—as opposed to the expatriate culture of Kōbe—this city needn't be high on your list. It does make for a good break from a standard Japan itinerary, though, and a stroll around its hillside precinct punctuated by a café stop and a great dinner would be time well spent. A short day is usually enough as an excursion from Ōsaka or Kyōto. You could even stop off here for a few hours on your way down the San-yō coast (which is covered in Chapter 11). You could spend a second day here if you make a couple of side trips to Mt. Rokko and Arima Onsen.

TIMING

Except for the cold days of winter, Kōbe enjoys a mild climate tempered by the Seto Nai-kai. Spring, especially at cherry blossom time, and autumn are the optimal times to visit Kobe, as well as most of Japan. In mid summer it can become quite humid; in winter it is wet, chilly, and damp, though the Inland Sea keeps it from becoming very cold.

A Good Tour

A good place to start your visit to Kōbe is the **Kōbe Shiritsu Hakubu-tsukan** ①, a museum where you can take in the history of this international port town, including memorabilia from the heyday of the old foreign settlement. To get to the museum, walk south down Flower Road from San-no-miya Eki, past the Flower Clock and City Hall to Higashi-Yuenchi Kōen. Walk through the park to the Kōbe Minato Post Office, across the street on the west side. Walk east on the road in front of the post office toward the Oriental Hotel. Turn left at the corner in front of the hotel and you'll find the City Museum in the old Bank of Tōkyō building, at the end of the block.

Return to San-no-miya Eki, browsing through **Nankin-machi** ② and the Moto-machi and San-no-miya shopping arcades if time permits. Then, down by the water, stop into Meriken Kōen and the **Kōbe Kokusai Kaiyo Hakubutsukan** ③, with its exhibits of ships and things nautical. Once back at San-no-miya Eki, begin your tour of the northern district by crossing the street that runs along the tracks and turning left at the first main intersection. Here you'll see the orange torii of **Ikuta Jinja** ④, a temple founded by Empress Jingu in the 3rd century. The road that runs up the right side of the shrine leads up the slope to Naka-yamate-dōri. Cross the avenue and continue up the slope. Turn right at the corner of Yamamoto-dōri, a road lined with high-fashion boutiques and restaurants. Turn left at Kitano-zaka, which leads to **Kitano,** an area where Western traders and businessmen have lived since the late 19th century. Many of the older ijinkan have been turned into museums. Continue up the slope from Nakayamate-dōri. At the first intersection after Yamamoto-dōri (nicknamed Ijinkan-dōri), just past Rin's Gallery, which is filled with boutiques of Japan's top designers, turn right and walk east to visit the 1907 **Eiko-kukan** ⑤.

Three of the ijinkan in Kitano-ku area are publicly owned and free of charge. **Rhein-no-Yakata** ⑥, opposite Eiko-kukan, has a German-style coffee shop inside. Near Kitano Tenman Jinja at the top of the hill is the **Kazami-dōri-no-Yakata** ⑦, made famous on a national TV series some years ago. Continue back down the slope via Kitano-zaka toward San-no-miya Eki and turn right on Yamamoto-dōri. One ijinkan house not to miss is the **Choueke Yashiki** ⑧, built in 1889 and filled to the rafters with turn-of-the-century memorabilia from East and West.

Return to San-no-miya Eki and walk to the **Portliner** ⑨ platform, which will take you to the consumerist diversions on **Port Island** ⑩.

Sights to See

DOWNTOWN KŌBE AND PORT ISLAND

④ **Ikuta Jinja.** Entrance to this Shinto shrine is through an impressive orange torii, which was rebuilt after the 1995 earthquake. According to legend, the shrine was founded by Empress Jingū in the 3rd century. Hence it is one of the oldest in Japan. The shrine is about 450 yards west of San-no-miya Eki.

③ **Kōbe Kokusai Kaiyo Hakubutsukan** (Kōbe Maritime Museum). To the right of Meriken Kōen on Port Island stands the Port Tower, Kōbe's Eiffel Tower. From the revolving restaurant at its top, you can look out on a magnificent view of the harbor and the prowlike roof of the Hakubutsukan. This museum is worth a visit. All types of vessels, from ancient designs to modern hydrofoils, are displayed in model form. The *Oshoro Maru* model is one to look for—it was one of Japan's earliest sailing ships, and it is adorned with pearls, rubies, gold, and silver. On the first floor is a model of HMS *Rodney,* the British flagship that led a 12-ship flotilla into Kōbe harbor on January 1, 1868—the date that marked the official opening of Japan after 250 years of isolationism. In contrast to all of this backward looking, there is a Submarine Travel 2090 exhibit, where an audiovisual puts you in the center of a biosphere on the sea floor. ⊠ *Meriken Kōen,* ☎ *078/242–2333.* ☞ *¥500.* ◷ *Tues.– Sun. 10–5.*

★ ① **Kōbe Shiritsu Hakubutsukan** (Kōbe City Museum). This is the place to look into the past life of this international port town. Alongside earlier artifacts, the museum has an interesting collection of memorabilia from the heyday of the old foreign settlement, including a scale model

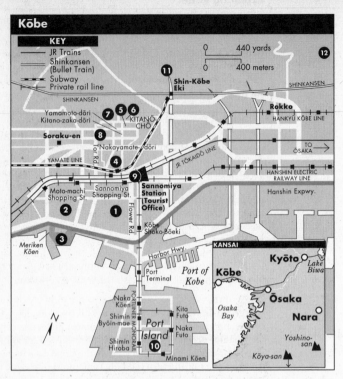

of the foreign concession. Three entire rooms from a turn-of-the-century Western house are on display. You'll also discover selections from the museum's famous *namban* collection of prints, screens, and paintings by Japanese artists of the late 16th to 17th century that depict foreigners in Japanese settings from that period. The 1995 earthquake caused severe damage to the museum, especially to the ground floor. From San-no-miya Eki, walk south on Flower Road to Higashi-Yuenchi Kōen. Walk through the park to the Kōbe Minato Post Office, across the street on the west side. Walk east on the road in front of the post office toward the Oriental Hotel. Turn left at the corner in front of the hotel and you'll find the City Museum in the old Bank of Tōkyō building, at the end of the block. ⊠ 24 Kyo-machi, Chūō-ku, ☎ 078/391–0035. ☞ ¥200 (more for special exhibitions). ♥ Tues.–Sun. 10–5.

② **Nankin-machi** (Chinatown). This area centered on Daimaru depāto (department store) has recently become a hot exotic destination for Japanese who come here to buy souvenirs and try the many Chinese restaurants. To find Chinatown from Moto-machi Eki, walk on the port side and enter the ethnic enclose through the large, fake marble gate.

⑩ **Port Island.** The degree to which Kōbe has been internationalized is reflected in the Japanese name for this piece of landfill: Pōto Airando, a wholesale borrowing from English pronounced Japanese-style to sound like Port Island. The Portliner monorail's Shimin Hiroba Station is right in the heart of the island's futuristic complex, with parks, hotels, restaurants, and fashion boutiques to explore.

⑨ **Portliner.** This digitally driven monorail leaves every six minutes from San-no-miya Eki downtown on its loop to and around Port Island, with eight stops along the way. The ride affords a close-up view of Kōbe Harbor. ☞ ¥520 round-trip.

KITANO-CHŌ

★ In the area known as **Kitano** wealthy foreigners in the late 19th century set up their residences, bringing to Japan Western-style domestic architecture, referred to in Kōbe as ijinkan. The district is extremely popular with young Japanese tourists, who enjoy the rare opportunity of seeing old-fashioned Western houses, which are rare in Japan. The curious mêlée of Japanese and Western Victorian and Gothic architecture makes for an interesting walk in the hills of this neighborhood. Many of the residences are still inhabited by Westerners, but more than a dozen 19th-century ijinkan in Kitano-chō are open to the public. Seeing all of them can get repetitious; we recommend the following.

To reach the Kitano area to see the ijinkan, take a 15-minute walk north along Kitano-zaka-dōri from San-no-miya Eki or a 10-minute walk west along Kitano-dōri from Shin-Kōbe Eki. Yamamoto-dōri (nicknamed Ijinkan-dōri) is Kitano's main street, and the ijinkan are on the small side streets ascending the hill.

❽ Choueke Yashiki (Choueke Mansion). Built in 1889—and pronounced "chew-eh-keh"—this is the only house open to the public that is still inhabited. It is filled to the rafters with turn-of-the-century memorabilia from East and West. Mrs. Choueke is on hand to show you her treasures, which include a large number of *nanban* wood-block prints, and to share her vast knowledge of Kōbe. Her ijinkan is not to be missed. ⊠ *Yamamoto-dōri (street also known as Ijinkan-dōri), Chūō-ku,* ☎ *078/221–3209.* ⊞ *¥500.* ⊙ *Wed.–Mon. 9–5.*

❺ Eiko-kukan (English House). This typical old-fashioned Western house was constructed in 1907 by an English architect—then inhabited by another Englishman, named Baker—and continued as a private residence until 1979. ⊠ *2-3-16 Kitano-dōri, Chūō-ku,* ☎ *078/241–2338.* ⊞ *¥700.* ⊙ *Weekdays 9–5, weekends 9–5:15.*

❼ Kazami-dōri-no-Yakata (Weathercock House). It is the most elaborate of Kōbe's ijinkan, listed as an Important Cultural Property. Kazami-dōri-no-Yakata is near Kitano Tenman Jinja at the top of the hill. ⊠ *Kazami-dōri, Chūō-ku,* ☎ *078/243–3223.* ⊞ *Free.* ⊙ *Wed.–Mon. 9–5.*

❻ Rhein-no-Yakata (Rhine House). Opposite Eiko-kukan, Rhein-no-Yakata has a pleasant German-style coffee shop inside. ⊠ *Kitano-dōri, Chūō-ku,* ☎ *078/222–3403.* ⊞ *Free.* ⊙ *Fri.–Wed. 10–5.*

AROUND KŌBE

⓫ Nunobiki Falls. A quiet side trip from the city is the 20-minute walk up the hill behind Shin-Kōbe Eki to Nunobiki Falls, whose beauty has been referred to in Japanese literature since the 10th century. It is actually a series of four cascades of varying heights, together described as one of the three greatest falls in Japan.

⓬ Rokko-san and Arima Onsen. The highest peak of the Rokko Mountains, which form a backdrop to Kōbe, is Mt. Rokko. A cable car climbs **Rokko-san,** and some of the most exciting views are en route, so have your camera ready. Once at the top in the cool mountain air—a delight in summer—you get a staggering view of the city and the Seto Nai-kai. On the mountain are various recreational areas, including the oldest golf course in Japan, designed in 1903 by Englishman Arthur H. Gloom, a merchant who resided in Kōbe, and the summer houses of some of Kōbe's wealthier residents.

Even before Nara became the capital in the 7th century, **Arima Onsen** had established itself as a place to take the thermal waters. Its fame reached a high point when Hideyoshi Toyotomi took the waters here in the late 16th century. Arima is on the north slope of Rokko-san and is a maze of tiny streets still lined with traditional houses. Some 30 ryokan have established themselves here using the thermal waters' reputed curative powers to attract guests. As the water gushes up freely from springs, some ryokan charge an outrageous sum, as much as ¥10,000, to use their baths. So, to hell with them! Go instead to the public bath, **Arima Onsen Kaikan,** in the center of the village and near the bus terminal. Here ¥410 will gain you entrance and a soak in the steaming hot waters. ⊙ *Daily 8 AM–10 PM; closed 1st and 3rd Tues. of month.*

To get to Rokko-san, take the Hankyū Kōbe Line from JR San-no-miya Eki to Rokko Eki (¥160). A cable car travels up the mountain to Rokko-sanjo Station (¥560). From there, take either a taxi or a bus to Rokko Cable-shita Station. The cable car continues after Rokko-sanjo Station to pass over the mountain's crest at Country Station before traversing a beautiful valley to Arima Onsen. Because the cost of the rather uninspiring ride between Rokko-sanjo Station and Country Station is ¥2,500, you might want to take a local bus between the two stations, then get back on the cable car for the final trip (¥250), which is well worthwhile, to Arima Onsen. You can either return to Kōbe by the cable car or go directly back on the Kōbe Dentetsu (electric railway, ¥620), which uses Shinkaichi Eki, two stops west of Kōbe's Moto-machi Eki.

DINING

North of San-no-miya Eki in the Kitano area—from the corner of Hanta-dōri and Yamamoto-dōri, also known as Ijinkan-dōri—there are at least a dozen good Italian, German, French, Swiss, Middle Eastern, Thai, American, and, of course, Japanese restaurants. Port Island has also taken on a reputation for its variety—look in the vicinity of the Portopia Hotel.

Kōbe Beef

$$$$ ✕ **Aragawa.** Japan's first steak house is famed for its superb hand-fed
★ Kōbe beef. The wood-paneled, chandeliered dining room has an old-country atmosphere. Aragawa serves melt-in-your-mouth *sumiyaki* (charcoal-broiled) steak that is worth its weight in yen. An evening here is the ultimate splurge, but this is considered *the* place for Kōbe beef—as well it should be, at ¥20,000. ⊠ *2-15-18 Nakayamate-dōri, Chūō-ku,* ☏ *078/221–8547. Jacket and tie. AE, DC, MC, V.*

$$$ ✕ **Highway.** This small, exclusive restaurant has a reputation for serving fine Kōbe beef. The quality of the meat is extraordinary. ⊠ *13-7 Shimoyamate-dōri 2-chōme, Chūō-ku,* ☏ *078/331–7622. No credit cards. Closed Mon.*

$$ ✕ **A-1.** For affordable Kōbe beef in the neighborhood north of Hankyū San-no-miya Eki, come to A-1. The *teppan*-style steak is served on a hot grill with a special spice-and-wine marinade that is as memorable as the garlic-and-crisp-fried potatoes. Right across from the Washington Hotel, A-1 has a relaxed and friendly atmosphere. ⊠ *Amashi Bldg., 2nd floor, 2-2-9 Shimoyamate-dōri, Chūō-ku,* ☏ *078/331–8676. No credit cards. Closed Tues.*

$$ ✕ **Wakkoku.** If you want to try world-famous Kōbe beef without spending a bundle, come to this smart but plain restaurant on the third floor of the shopping plaza adjacent to the Oriental Hotel, across from Shin-Kōbe Eki. Don't be distracted by the other restaurants on this floor—Wakkoku is the best choice. Lunchtime prices are lower than dinner—count on ¥3,000 for Kōbe beef. ⊠ *Shin-Kōbe Oriental Park Ave., Shin-Kōbe,* ☏ *078/262–2838. AE, DC, V.*

International

$$$ ✕ **Totenkaku.** This establishment has been famous among Kōbe residents since 1945 for its Peking duck, flown in fresh from China. The building itself is worth the splurge—built at the turn of the century, it is one of Kōbe's ijinkan, the F. Bishop House. You can keep the price down by ordering one of the Chinese noodle specialties to fill you up. ✉ *3-14-18 Yamamoto-dōri, Chūō-ku,* ☎ *078/231–1351. DC, V.*

$$ ✕ **Gaylord.** A few minutes' walk from San-no-miya Eki, this Indian restaurant with flashy decor is a favorite with Kōbe's resident gai-jin. Curries are on the mild side but are very tasty. ✉ *Meiji Seimei Bldg., basement, 8-3-7 Isogami-dōri, Chūō-ku,* ☎ *078/251–4359. AE, DC, MC, V.*

$$ ✕ **King's Arms.** Famous for its excellent platter of roast beef and its traditional British atmosphere, the old King's Arms pub has become a Kōbe landmark. A portrait of Sir Winston Churchill still presides over the old wooden bar that some 40 years ago was the exclusive territory of some of Kōbe's thirstiest Englishmen. The clientele has increased in number and kind, but the flavor of the legendary roast beef, the finest Scotch whiskey, and the seriousness of the annual dart tournament haven't changed. ✉ *4-2-15 Isobe-dōri, Chūō-ku,* ☎ *078/221–3774. AE, DC, MC, V.*

$$ ✕ **Marrakech.** Elmaleh Simon, a former Moroccan sailor turned chef, and his wife serve excellent Middle Eastern food. In this cozy little basement dining spot, it is easy to forget that you are in Japan. The couscous and kabobs are particularly delicious, and portions are generous. ✉ *Maison de Yamate, basement, 1-20-15 Nakayamate-dōri, Chūō-ku, Kōbe-shi,* ☎ *078/241–3440. AE, V. Closed Mon.*

$$ ✕ **Rote Rose.** A block east of the Kōbe Club on the west end of Kitano, this restaurant is owned by a wine importer and is most famous for its wine list, with more than 180 fine German wines. To sample them, order the six-glass flight. Although Rote (German for red) Rose has long been known as a family-style German pub, it now serves a range of European dishes, including French sausage and *tournedos aux champignons* (filet mignon with mushrooms). ✉ *9-14 4-chōme, Kitano-chō, Chūō-ku,* ☎ *078/222–3200. AE, V. Closed Wed.*

$$ ✕ **Salaam.** A light and airy restaurant with potted palms and white
★ walls, Salaam credits itself with being the first Middle Eastern restaurant in Japan. It has a very complete menu with a variety of pickles, desserts, and main courses, such as kabobs, grilled seafood, and lamb. Special dinners come with a little of everything. Finish off your meal with refreshing hot mint tea and a piece of baklava. ✉ *Ijin Plaza Bldg., 2nd floor, 12-21 Yamamoto-dōri 2-chōme, Chūō-ku,* ☎ *078/ 222–1780. AE, V. No lunch weekdays.*

$ ✕ **Attic.** Several years ago, former U.S. baseball player Marty Kuehnert opened this little haven for ballpark refugees and beer lovers of all sorts. Along with the Budweiser, Marty brought to Kōbe his American take on eating—complete with pizza, fried chicken, roast beef, jukeboxes, and peanut shells. ✉ *Ijinkan Club Bldg., 3rd floor, 4-1-12 Kitano-chō, Chūō-ku,* ☎ *078/222–1586 or 078/222–5368. AE, DC, MC, V. Closed Tues.*

$ ✕ **Raja.** A former chef of Gaylord (☞ *above*) opened this small, unas-
★ suming place near Moto-machi Eki. Raja serves home-style Indian food, with spicy, tasty curries and excellent saffron rice. ✉ *Sanonatsu Bldg., basement, Sakae-machi 2-chōme, Chūō-ku,* ☎ *078/332–5253. AE, D, V.*

$ ✕ **Wang Thai.** This is one of the few Thai restaurants in the area; it
★ features a menu with spicy Thai and slightly less hot Chinese dishes. ✉ *President Arcade, 2nd floor, 14-22 Yamamoto-dōri 2-chōme, Chūō-ku,* ☎ *078/222–2507. No credit cards. Closed Wed.*

LODGING

$$$$ 🏨 **Hotel Okura Kōbe.** This 35-story hotel on the wharf in Meriken Park
★   is Kōbe's finest. Beautifully furnished, the Okura Kōbe lives up to the
Okura chain's worldwide reputation for excellence. Room interiors were
done by David Hicks, who has designed interiors for the royal family.
The hotel has a well-equipped health club with pool and gym, stunning views of the bay from the Emerald Restaurant, and a hotel shuttle bus to San-no-miya Eki. ✉ *Meriken Kōen, 2-1 Hatoba-chō, Chūō-ku,
Kōbe-shi, Hyōgo-ken 650,* ☎ *078/333–0111,* 📠 *078/333–6673. 472
rooms. 5 restaurants, 2 bars, coffee shop, health club. AE, DC, MC,
V.*

$$$$ 🏨 **Kōbe Portopia Hotel.** Situated on Port Island, the Portopia is a dazzling modern hotel with every facility imaginable. Spacious rooms
look over the port, and the restaurants and lounges on the top floors
have panoramic views of Rokko-san and Ōsaka Bay. Because of its location, the hotel can only be reached by the Portliner monorail or by
taxi. This inconvenience is counterbalanced by the fact that everything
from food—Chinese, Japanese, and French—to clothing is available
inside the hotel. ✉ *6-10-1 Minatojima Naka-machi, Chūō-ku, Kōbe-
shi, Hyōgo-ken 650,* ☎ *078/302–0111,* 📠 *078/302–6877. 761 rooms.
3 restaurants, coffee shops, indoor and outdoor pools, beauty salon,
sauna, tennis courts, exercise room, shops. AE, DC, MC, V.*

$$$$ 🏨 **Shin-Kōbe Oriental Hotel.** The tallest building in Kōbe, this luxury
★   hotel faces JR Shin-Kōbe Eki, where the Shinkansen arrives, three
minutes from downtown by subway. Guest rooms, with marble-tiled
bathrooms, are neatly decorated in pastel fabrics and furnished with
a desk, a coffee table, and two reading chairs. Corner rooms on higher
floors have superb views over Kōbe. Beneath the hotel there are five
floors of shops and French, Chinese, Japanese, steak, and sushi restaurants. ✉ *Kitano-chō 1-chōme, Chūō-ku, Kōbe-shi, Hyōgo-ken 650,*
☎ *078/291–1121,* 📠 *078/291–1154. 600 rooms. 5 restaurants, indoor pool, beauty salon, sauna, exercise room, shops. AE, DC, MC,
V.*

$$$ 🏨 **Hotel Monterey.** Not far from San-no-miya Eki, this little hotel
takes you off the busy streets and into old Italy, with its marvelous
Mediterranean-style courtyard fountains and European furnishings.
Modeled after a monastery in Florence, the Monterey has modern fea-
tures that most hotels in Japan lack, such as a fitness room, Jacuzzi,
and pool (available at a slight additional charge). Twin rooms are
standard size; duplex (maisonette) rooms come with a carpeted bed-
room upstairs and a small lounge area with a tiled floor. Both the Ital-
ian and Japanese restaurants on the premises are charming. ✉ *2-11-13
Shimoyamate-dōri, Chūō-ku, Kōbe-shi, Hyōgo-ken 650,* ☎ *078/392–
7111,* 📠 *078/322–2899. 164 rooms. Restaurants, bar, pool, exercise
room. AE, DC, MC, V.*

$$$ 🏨 **San-no-miya Terminal Hotel.** In the terminal building above the JR
San-no-miya Eki, this hotel is extremely convenient, particularly for
anyone who has to catch an early train. The rooms are large for this
price range and are clean and pleasant. The slight damage incurred during the 1995 earthquake has been fully repaired. ✉ *8 Kumoi-dōri, Chūō-
ku, Kōbe-shi, Hyōgo-ken 650,* ☎ *078/291–0001,* 📠 *078/291–0020.
190 rooms. 3 restaurants. AE, DC, MC, V.*

$$ 🏨 **Arcons.** You'll need a taxi to get here from San-no-miya Eki, be-
cause it's up on the hill in Kitano-chō, in the heart of the ijinkan dis-
trict. Many of the immaculate rooms at this little white hotel have a
view out over the city to the sea. There's patio dining at the first-floor
café when the weather is good. Renovations made as a consequence
of the 1995 earthquake have smartened up the hotel. ✉ *3-7-1 Kitano-*

chō, Chūō-ku, Kōbe-shi, Hyōgo-ken 650, ☎ *078/231–1538. 22 rooms. Café. AE, DC, V.*

$$ 🔁 **Kōbe Gajoen Hotel.** This delightful hotel is a change from the modern, impersonal hotels that flourish in Japan. Although it is distinctly Japanese, with delicate Japanese cuisine served in a dining room paneled with decorated screens and a staff that bows to guests, the hotel has European furnishings, reminders of the time when Kōbe was a major port for Western traders. Close to downtown, it is a couple of minutes' walk from the west exit of the Hanaku-mae Eki on the Hankyū Line. ✉ *8-4-23 Shimoyamate-dōri, Chūō-ku, Kōbe-shi, Hyōgo-ken 650,* ☎ *078/341–0301. 52 rooms. Restaurant. AE, DC, MC, V.*

$ 🔁 **Union Hotel.** The most attractive feature of this business hotel, a short walk from San-no-miya Eki, is its low rates. A 24-hour convenience store is right next door, which comes in handy for midnight snacks. ✉ *1-9 Nunobiki-chō 2-chōme, Chūō-ku, Kōbe-shi, Hyōgo-ken 650,* ☎ *078/242–3000,* ⅢⅩ *078/242–0220. 167 rooms. Restaurant. AE, DC, MC, V.*

NIGHTLIFE

Though in some ways it is still Japan's most cosmopolitan city, Kōbe doesn't have as diverse a nighttime scene as Ōsaka does. However, Kōbe has an advantage in its compactness—virtually all of the best places are within walking distance of each other. Probably the best, and certainly the most authentic, Western bar in the whole of Kansai is the **Dubliners Irish Pub** (✉ 47 Akashi-chō, Chūō-ku, ☎ 078/334–3614), a true "local" for many gai-jin residents without being a foreigners-only hangout. It has good food and drink, a friendly staff, and a relaxed atmosphere. St. Patrick's Night here is not to be missed. A good British-style pub is the **King's Arms** (✉ Flower Rd. opposite City Hall, ☎ 078/221–3774). It's a little off the beaten path but has a long history and good, if expensive, food. The very stylish **Polo Dog** bars (✉ K Bldg., 2nd floor, 1-3-21 Sannomiya-chō, Chūō-ku, ☎ 078/331–3944; ✉ Akematsu Bldg., 1st floor, 1-14-2 Moto-machi-chō, Chūō-ku, ☎ 078-321–3396) serve reasonable meals and are tastefully arrayed with '50s and '60s Americana. Out on Rokko Island, the Kōbe Bay Sheraton has its **Arena** sports bar (✉ Kōbe Bay Sheraton Hotel, Rokko Island, ☎ 078/857–7040) with a big-screen TV and a selection of world beers.

SHOPPING

Kōbe is a shopper's paradise. Unlike in Tōkyō, Ōsaka, and other places in Japan where individual shops are scattered all over the city, most of the shopping districts in Kōbe are in clusters, so you can visit numerous shops with great ease.

Kōbe's historic shopping area is known as **Moto-machi,** which extends for 2 km (1 mi) between JR Moto-machi Eki and Daimaru Department Store. Most of the district is under a covered arcade, which allows for inclement weather forays. You can purchase nearly anything in Moto-machi, ranging from antiques to cameras to electronics. A favorite stop for many travelers is **Maruzen** bookstore (✉ 1-4-12 Moto-machi-dōri, Chūō-ku, ☎ 078/391–6003) at the entrance on the Moto-machi Eki side of the arcade, which has an excellent selection of books in English. Two small shops at the opposite end of the arcade sell traditional Japanese goods. **Sakae-ya** (✉ 8-5 Moto-machi-dōri 5-chōme, Chūō-ku, ☎ 078/341–1307) specializes in traditional Japanese dolls. **Naniwa-ya** (✉ 3-8 Moto-machi-dōri 4-chōme, Chūō-ku, ☎ 078/341–6367) has an excellent selection of Japanese lacquerware at reasonable prices.

Also try **Harishin** (✉ 3-10-3 Moto-machi-dōri, Chūō-ku, ☎ 078/331–2516), on the west end of the arcade, for antiques.

Nearly connected to the Moto-machi arcade, extending from the Sogo department store to the Moto-machi area for 1 km (½ mi), is **Sannomi-ya Center Gai** arcade. This mall has fewer shops and more restaurants than the neighboring Moto-machi. Because it is right next to San-no-miya Eki, this is a good place for a quick bite to eat.

The famous pearl company **Tasaki Shinju** (✉ Tasaki Bldg., 6-3-2 Minatojima Naka-machi, Chūō-ku, ☎ 078/302–3321), in Center Plaza across from San-no-miya Eki, has a museum and demonstration hall along with its retail pearl shop.

The new **Santica Town** underground shopping mall, which runs for several blocks beneath Flower Road south from San-no-miya Eki, has 120 shops and 30 restaurants. It's closed the third Wednesday of the month.

Kōbe's trendy crowd tends to shop in the exclusive shops lining **Tor Road,** which stretches north–south on a slope lined with trees. Fashionable boutiques featuring Japanese designers and imported goods alternate with chic cafés and restaurants.

KŌBE A TO Z

Arriving and Departing

By Plane
Kansai International Airport (KIX; ☞ Ōsaka A to Z *in* Chapter 9) handles the region's international flights as well as some domestic flights to Japan's larger cities. Most domestic flights still fly out of **Ōsaka's Itami Airport,** approximately 40 minutes away.

BETWEEN THE AIRPORTS AND CENTER CITY

From KIX, take the JR Kansai Airport Express "Haruka" to Shin-Ōsaka and change to the JR Tōkaidō Line for Kōbe's JR San-no-miya Eki, 70 minutes away (¥1,800). You can also ride a boat from the airport ferry terminal to Kōbe City Air Terminal (K-CAT), which takes 30 minutes (¥2,200).

From Itami Airport, a bus to San-no-miya Eki leaves from the domestic terminal's main entrance and from a stop between the domestic and international terminals approximately every 20 minutes, 7 AM–10 PM. The trip takes about 40 minutes (¥940).

Excellent public transport makes using **taxis** impractical.

By Train
Hikari Shinkansen run between Tōkyō and Shin-Kōbe Eki in about 3½ hours. If you don't have a JR Pass, the fare is ¥14,000. The trip between Ōsaka Eki and Kōbe's San-no-miya Eki takes 30 minutes on the JR Tōkaidō Line Rapid Train, which leaves at 15-minute intervals throughout the day; without a JR Pass the fare is ¥390. The Hankyū and Hanshin private lines run between Ōsaka and Kōbe for ¥280.

Getting Around

By Bus
City **bus** service is frequent and efficient, though it might be somewhat confusing to first-timers. At each stop, you will find a pole that displays a route chart of official stops. Enter at the rear or center of the bus; pay your fare as you leave at the front with exact change. The fare is ¥200, regardless of the distance. A special **city loop bus** that looks like a trol-

ley and has a wood interior with brass fittings stops at 15 major sights on its 12½-km (7½-mi), 80-minute run between Nakatottei Pier and Shin-Kōbe. The buses operate at 16- to 20-minute intervals and cost ¥250 per ride or ¥650 for a day pass, which you can purchase on the bus. ("Loop Bus" signs in English indicate stops along the route.) Service runs 9:30–4:25 weekdays, 9:30–5:25 weekends and holidays.

By Portliner

The Portliner is a computerized monorail that services Port Island. Its central station is connected to the JR San-no-miya Eki; the ride from the station to Port Island takes about 10 minutes and costs ¥520 round-trip.

By Taxi

Taxis are plentiful; hail them on the street or at taxi stands. Fares start at ¥620 for the first 2 km (1¼ mi) and go up ¥90 for each additional 380 meters (approximately ¼ mi).

By Train

Within Kōbe, **Japan Railways** and the **Hankyū** and **Hanshin** lines run parallel from east to west and are easy to negotiate. San-no-miya and Moto-machi are the principal downtown stations. Purchase tickets from a vending machine; you will surrender them upon leaving the train. Fares depend upon your destination.

The city's **subway** system runs from Shin-Kōbe Eki west to the outskirts of town. Fares start at ¥180 and are determined by destination. The San-no-miya–Shin-Kōbe trip costs ¥200.

Contacts and Resources

Consulates

The closest U.S., U.K., and Canadian consulates are in Ōsaka (☞ Chapter 9).

Doctors

Kōbe Adventist Hospital (⊠ 4-1 Arinodai 8-chōme, Kita-ku, ☎ 078/981–0161); **Kōbe Kaisei Hospital** (⊠ 3-11-15 Shinohara-Kita-machi, Nada-ku, ☎ 078/871–5201).

Emergencies

Police, ☎ 110. **Ambulance,** ☎ 119.

English-Language Bookstores

Bunyodo (⊠ Kōbe Kokusai Kaikan, 1st floor, 1-6 Goko-dōri 8-chōme, Chūō-ku, ☎ 078/221–0557); **Maruzen** (⊠ 1-4-12 Moto-machi-dōri, Chūō-ku, ☎ 078/391–6003).

Guided Tours

Between March 21 and November 30, the City Transport Bureau has several half-day tours of major attractions in and around the city. The tours are conducted in Japanese, but they do provide an overview of Kōbe. Buses depart from the south side of the Kōbe Kotsu Center Building, near San-no-miya Eki. Information and tickets, which cost ¥2,500–¥3,000, can be obtained at the **Shinai Teiki Kanko Annaisho** (Sightseeing Bus Tour Information Office) on the second floor of the Kōbe Kotsu Center Building (☎ 078/391–4755).

Authorized **taxi services** also run tours (¥4,200 per hour) that cover 11 different routes and last two to five hours. Reserve at the Kōbe Tourist Information Center (☎ 078/271–2401).

Pharmacies

Daimaru Department Store (⊠ 40 Akashi-chō, Chūō-ku, ☎ 078/331–8121) has a pharmacy three minutes on foot from JR Moto-machi Eki.

Travel Agencies

Japan Travel Bureau (✉ JR San-no-miya Eki, ☎ 078/231–4118).

Visitor Information

The **Kōbe Information Center** (☎ 078/322–0220), on the west side of the JR San-no-miya Eki, is open daily 9–5:30. Here you can pick up a free detailed map of the city in English. The Tourist Information Center has branches at the JR Kōbe Station (☎ 078/341–5277) and Shin-Kōbe Station (☎ 078/241–9550), both open daily 10–6.

JAPAN TRAVEL PHONE

The **Japan Travel Phone** (☎ 0120/444–800), open daily 9–5, provides free information in English on Kōbe and other points in western Japan.

11 Western Honshū

The two coasts of Western Honshū make for very different experiences of Japan. The industrial San-yō strip on the Inland Sea does have its attractive cities, most notably Kurashiki, as well as Hiroshima, and the nearby Miyajima, a small island whose vermilion torii (Shintō gate) rises famously out of the water. The more remote northern San-in region has a slower pace, and the mountainside town of Tsuwano, coastal Matsue, and coastal points in between make great escapes from the overdevelopment of the modern world.

By Nigel Fisher
and David
Miles

WESTERN HONSHŪ IS SPLIT through the center by mountains that run east to west. Two distinct regions fall away alongside this mountain range. The south side faces the Seto Nai-kai and is referred to as the San-yō region (Mountains in the Sun). The north side of Western Honshū, which faces the Nihon-kai, is called San-in (In the Shadow of the Mountains). From these descriptive names you might think that San-yō is the more attractive of the two, but the southern coast—the route that the JR Shinkansen (bullet train) travels between Ōsaka and Hakata on Kyūshū—is heavily industrialized and visually, if not environmentally, polluted. Many of the culturally important sights are found in the midst of Japanese urban sprawl.

The San-in coast, on the other hand, has so far escaped the onslaught of overdevelopment and retains its more traditional Japanese identity. This is partially due to the fact that Izumo Taisha holds significance as a "birthplace of the gods"—which includes the origins of the Japanese imperial lineage—and partially due to the traditional customs that remain a part of many people's lives. Charming fishing villages and rocky bays dot the entire coastline, and visual variety is a matter of course. Beaches, rice paddies, *onsen* (hot springs), dunes, and remote mountain temples are part of a Japan remarkably less crowded than the rest of Honshū.

Western Honshū Glossary

Key Japanese words and suffixes for this chapter include the following: -*bashi* (bridge), *bijutsukan* (art museum), -*chō* (street or block), *chūō* (central, as in Central Street), *daimyō* (feudal lord), *dōri* (street or avenue), *donjon* (castle stronghold), *eki* (train station), *gai-jin* (foreigner), -*gawa* or *kawa* (river), -*gū* (Shintō temple), *hantō* (peninsula), -*in* (Buddhist temple), *jinja* (Shintō shrine), -*jō* (castle), -*ken* (prefecture), *kōen* (park), -*ku* (section or ward), *kūkō* (airport), *machi* (town), *Nihon-kai* (Japan Sea), *onsen* (hot springs), *rōmaji* (Japanese words rendered in roman letters), *sake* (rice wine), -*shima* or *jima* (island), *Shinkansen* (bullet train, literally "new trunk line"), *taisha* (Shintō shrine), *torii* (*to-ree-ee*, gate), and *yama* (mountain).

Pleasures and Pastimes

Culture

Cultural activities and events are very alive in Western Honshū. The pottery towns of Imbe/Bizen and Hagi hold annual pottery festivals, which are educational and make for good shopping. Kurashiki always has events of either artistic or musical merit, and Hiroshima's international flavor adds another element to its year-round events. As for cultural artifacts, Izumo's importance among Japanese shrines is matched by its serene beauty.

Dining

When touring this region, we strongly recommend that you eat out at local Japanese restaurants. Regional specialties from the Sea of Japan and the Inland Sea are the reason. Oysters in Hiroshima, *fugu* (blowfish) in Shimonoseki, and crab and seaweed on the San-in coast are superb. And Matsue's position, with both fresh- and saltwater fish all around, provides a great variety of fish.

Most reasonably priced establishments will have a visual display of the menu in the window. On this basis, you can decide what you want before you enter. If you cannot order in Japanese and no English is spoken, after you secure a table, lead the waiter to the window display and point. Unless an establishment is a ryōtei (the finest traditional Japanese restaurant), reservations are usually not required.

CATEGORY	COST*
$$$$	over ¥6,000
$$$	¥4,000–¥6,000
$$	¥2,000–¥4,000
$	under ¥2,000

per person, excluding drinks, service, and tax

Lodging

Accommodations cover a broad spectrum, from pensions and minshuku to large, modern resort hotels that have little character but have all the facilities of an international hotel. Large city and resort hotels have Western as well as Japanese restaurants. In summer, hotel reservations are highly advised.

For a short course on accommodations in Japan, *see* Lodging *in* the Gold Guide.

CATEGORY	COST*
$$$$	over ¥20,000
$$$	¥15,000–¥20,000
$$	¥10,000–¥15,000
$	under ¥10,000

All prices are for a double room, excluding service and tax.

Outdoor Activities and Sports

Western Japan might not have as much volcanic spectacle as the rest of Japan, but the scenic qualities of the Seto Nai-kai and the San-in seascapes are considerable. The San-in coast is perfect for bicycling—the topography changes frequently enough to sustain interest, and the air is clear and cool. The area east of Tottori, particularly the fishing villages directly west of Ama-no-hashidate, has plenty of natural beauty to hold your interest. Matsue is known for its water sports, Mt. Daisen is a good climb, and the Oki Islands are great for hiking and camping.

Exploring Western Honshū

This chapter sketches an itinerary from Ōsaka down the San-yō coast, stopping at Himeji, Okayama, Kurashiki, Hiroshima, and Miyajima before reaching Honshū's westernmost point, Shimonoseki. Then we return to Kyōto by way of the San-in coast. The scenic and cultural highlights of the San-in are in and around Hagi, Tsuwano, Matsue, Tottori Dunes, and Ama-no-hashidate, but if you're feeling more adventurous, there are smaller towns like Kundani, Kinosaki, and Misasa Onsen where you can drink in the slower pace of the San-in as well.

Numbers in the text correspond to numbers in the margin and on the Western Honshū and Hiroshima maps.

Great Itineraries

The trick with Western Honshū is not trying to cover too much ground in the time that you have. The Shinkansen makes getting around the San-yō easy, but the San-in's towns and sights are stretched out along a coast not well served by trains—look at train schedules before you leave home to plan connecting times, which can be long in the San-in. Unless you allot seven days to Western Honshū on the whole, stick to the San-yō or the San-in—going back and forth by train would eat up too much time.

IF YOU HAVE 2 DAYS

Two San-yō options are to spend a day in ☷ **Hiroshima** ④–⑭ and another in ☷ **Miyajima** ⑮; or pass the first day in the old town in ☷ **Kurashiki** ③ and then go to Hiroshima for the second. Both plans will give you a taste of both old and new Japan. If you're feeling a bit adventurous, or if you've seen the San-yō coast already, select a tight area on the quieter San-in coast for a couple of days. For a bit of relaxation, head to **Ama-no-hashidate** ㉔, then move on to ☷ **Kinosaki** ㉓ or ☷ **Kasumi** ㉒ for the night, and spend some time resting in a nearby onsen's radium waters.

IF YOU HAVE 4 DAYS

Four days start to open up your options nicely in Western Honshū, giving enough extra time for train connections and still allowing you to see areas in more depth—but stick to either the San-yō or the Sani-in coast. You could cover much of the San-yō coast in four days, thanks to the Shinkansen. Stop in **Himeji** ① on the way down the coast to see its remarkable castle. Spend the rest of the day in ☷ **Kurashiki** ③; then on the following day, turn back toward ☷ **Okayama** ② and the pottery town of **Bizen** for a side trip. ☷ **Hiroshima** ④–⑭ needs at least a full day. And you could see ☷ **Miyajima** ⑮ the fourth day either ferrying out from Hiroshima or staying on the island overnight. Up on the San-in coast, extending the two-day itinerary of **Ama-no-hashidate** ㉔ to ☷ **Tottori** ㉑ or **Mt. Daisen** would prove to you that there are some parts of Japan packed with things to see and do but not with crowds. Then finish off with the cultural-historical pursuits in ☷ **Matsue** ⑱ and **Izumo** ⑲. To take on the western end of the coast, split your days between any three of the following four—☷ **Hagi** ⑯, ☷ **Tsuwano** ⑰, **Matsue**, and **Izumo**. You'll see part of the region's charm on slow, one-car trains with hunchbacked elderly locals sharing the ride between rice paddies.

IF YOU HAVE 7 DAYS

You could assemble an abbreviated grand tour of both the San-yō and San-in in seven days, using all types of trains. Start in ☷ **Hiroshima** ④–⑭ or ☷ **Miyajima** ⑮, moving on to ☷ **Hagi** ⑯ or **Tsuwano** ⑰. Then head back east through the San-in to ☷ **Matsue** ⑱ and **Izumo** ⑲. Wrap up the trip in one of two ways: Choose sights of interest between Yonago and **Ama-no-hashidate** ㉔, which might include the small fishing village of ☷ **Kundani**; or take a train south from Matsue to ☷ **Kurashiki** ③ for a last taste of old Japan. On the way back to Ōsaka or Kyōto, you could stop in the pottery town of Bizen or in **Himeji** ① for a look at its castle. On such a trip, you would want to vary your overnights: two nights in one place, one in the next, et cetera, to keep from tiring yourself out.

TIMING

The San-in coast has a beautiful spring—cooler, crisper, and longer than much of Japan before the breezy summer begins. Though muggy like much of Japan in mid- to late summer, the wind off the Nihon-kai does cool the coast, and it makes Lake Shinji near Matsue an ideal windsurfing spot. Autumn colors are beautiful, then the coast gets covered in snow for a slightly longer winter than the San-yō region gets. Precisely because of the heavy snowfall, the San-in coast is a popular onsen area in winter for many San-yō-ites—it *is* one of the best times to visit the region.

THE SAN-YŌ REGION

Though the San-yō region faces the Seto Nai-kai, you'll only catch glimpses of the Inland Sea from the train en route from Ōsaka to Shimonoseki. Most of the coastal plain is heavily industrialized all the way

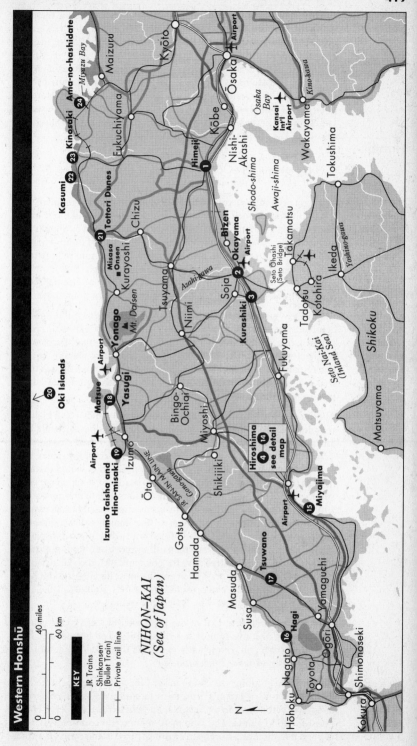

Western Honshū

KEY
—— JR Trains
══ Shinkansen
  (Bullet Train)
+−+ Private rail line

40 miles
60 km

NIHON-KAI
(Sea of Japan)

Oki Islands

Ama-no-hashidate
Maizuru
Miyazu Bay
Kinosaki 24
Kasumi 23
Tottori Dunes 22
21
Fukuchiyama
Kyōto
Osaka
Airport
Kōbe
Himeji 1
Nishi-Akashi
Osaka Bay
Kansai Int'l Airport
Wakayama
Kino-kawa

Chizu
Misasa Onsen
Kurayoshi
Tsuyama
Asahi-kawa
Bizen
Okayama 2
Airport
Sōja
Kurashiki 3
Fukuyama
Shodo-shima
Awaji-shima
Takamatsu
Seto Ohashi (Seto Bridge)
Tadotsu
Kotohira
Ikeda
Yoshino-gawa
Tokushima

Matsue
Airport
Yasugi
Yonago
Mt. Daisen
Niimi

Oki Islands 20

Matsue 18
Bingo-Ochiai
Miyoshi
Shikijiki
Hiroshima 4 — 14
see detail map

Seto Nai-Kai
(Inland Sea)
Shikoku
Matsuyama

Izumo
Airport
Izumo Taisha and Hino-misaki
Ōta
JR SAN-IN MAIN LINE
Gō-no-kawa
Gotsu
Hamada
Masuda
Susa
Hagi 16
Nagato
Toyota
Hōhoku
Kokura
Shimonoseki
Ogōri
Yamaguchi
Tsuwano 17
Airport
Miyajima 15

N

to Hiroshima. From there to the outskirts of Shimonoseki, the post-war grayness diminishes and open country begins. If you're keen on absorbing some of the serenity of the Seto Nai-kai, there are day cruises from Hiroshima, and you can travel the length of the sea on ferries that ply the waters between Ōsaka and Beppu, on Kyūshū. Miyajima, near Hiroshima, is one of the most beautiful, albeit tourist-filled, of the sea's islands, and it makes a great day trip. If you are interested in ferrying from Himeji or Okayama out to Shodo-shima, the second largest island in the Seto Nai-kai, turn to the next chapter, Shikoku.

Himeji

❶ *42 mins west of Shin-Ōsaka, 1 hr west of Kyōto, 3 hrs and 52 mins west of Tōkyō by Shinkansen.*

The sight of Himeji's castle commands attention from the moment your train pulls into Himeji Eki. Himeji-jō is the grandest and most attractive of Japan's 12 surviving feudal castles. Also known as Shirasagi-jō (White Egret Castle), it stands on a 150-ft-high bluff dominating the city. Himeji was severely damaged in World War II, and the town has little of interest in itself. The castle miraculously escaped the air attacks, and, because of the frequent train service, it is easy to disembark one train, visit the castle, and reboard another train two hours later.

★ The present structure of **Himeji-jō** took eight years to build and was completed in 1609. Ieyasu Tokugawa, the great shōgun who unified feudal Japan, had given his son-in-law the surrounding province as a reward for his victory at the Battle of Sekigahara. This magnificent castle was built to isolate the Ōsaka *daimyō* (lord) from his friends in the western provinces. It served both as a military stronghold and an expression of Tokugawa power.

The five-story, six-floor main donjon (stronghold) stands 102 ft high and is built into a 50-ft-high stone foundation. Surrounding this main donjon are three lesser ones; all four are connected by covered passageways. This area was the central compound of the castle complex. There were also other compounds to the south and west. Enemies would therefore have to scale the bluff, cross three moats, breach the outer compounds, and then be raked by fire from the four donjons. Its military function as a tool controlling the Hyōgo Province was unimpeachable; likewise its aesthetic appeal. Note the qualities of the donjon's dormerlike windows, cusped gables, and walls finished with white plaster, displaying both stark power and elegance that still inspire awe. From a distance, this white vision does indeed have the grace and steadiness of an egret—hence the castle's nickname, White Egret. Japanese filmmaker Akira Kurosawa used Himeji-jō's exterior and the castle's grounds in his 1985 movie *Ran*; interior shots were filmed in a studio set.

From the central north exit of the JR Himeji Eki, the castle is a 15-minute walk or a five-minute bus ride (¥160). The bus departs from the station plaza, on your left as you exit. ☎ 0792/85–1146. 🎫 ¥500. ☉ *Daily 9–5 (grounds open until 6).*

En Route The next stop along the Shinkansen Line is Okayama, noted for Kōraku-en, one of Japan's three most famous gardens. If you are interested in getting out on the Seto Nai-kai, five ferries a day leave Himeji Port for Shodo-shima. The 1-hour, 40-minute trip costs ¥1,170. Keep in mind that there are shorter sea crossings to the island from Okayama.

Arriving and Departing

Himeji is served by Shinkansen, with trains arriving and departing every 15 minutes during the day. The Shinkansen to Okayama, the next destination to the west on this itinerary, arrives and departs every hour during the day. There is a Tourist Information Office (☎ 0792/85–3792) to the right of the station's north exit.

Okayama

❷ *30 mins west of Himeji and 1 hr west of Ōsaka by Shinkansen.*

Okayama has become quite cosmopolitan these days, attracting students from overseas. It is also the best departure point for Shodo-shima (☞ Chapter 12) for anyone coming from Ōsaka or Hiroshima. Twenty-three ferries a day make the 40-minute run from Okayama Port to the island. To make the 45-minute trip to Okayama Port from the JR Okayama Eki, take Bus 12.

The three most famous gardens in Japan are Kenroku-en in Kanazawa, Kairaku-en in Mito, and **Kōraku-en** in Okayama. Kōraku-en is a stroller's garden, with rustic tea arbors, extensive lawns, ponds, and artificial hills that were laid out three centuries ago on the banks of the Asahi-gawa. The maple, apricot, and cherry trees give the 28 acres a seasonal contrast. The garden's emphasis is on the classic harmony of its elements, and as such it is not astounding in its beauty—and can thus get quite crowded. The garden's strong point is its wide expanse of lawns, a rare commodity in Japan but less of a novelty to Westerners. What is attractive, though, is Kōraku-en's setting along the banks of the Asahi-gawa, against the backdrop of Okayama Castle, which seems to float above the garden. Bus 20 (¥160) from Platform 2 in front of the JR eki goes directly to Kōraku-en. ☎ 086/272–1148. ➹ ¥350. ☼ Apr.–Sept., daily 7:30–6; Oct.–Mar., daily 8–5.

Four-story **Okayama-jō** is painted black and known as U-jō (Crow Castle). Okayama's castle was first built in 1573, but, except for the turrets, it fell victim to the bombs of World War II. A ferro-concrete replica was constructed in 1966 and now houses objects of the region's history, including the requisite collection of armor and swords. There is also, as behooves its modern construction, an elevator to take you between floors. It takes less than five minutes to walk from the south exit of Kōraku-en to the castle. ☎ 086/225–2096. ➹ ¥300. ☼ Daily 9–5.

You will recognize the **Orient Bijutsukan** (Museum of Near Eastern Art) by its Parthenon-like temple front. If you have the time, you may want to go inside to see the 2,000 items of Asian art on display. It was one of the first museums in Japan to devote its collection to Asian art and has special exhibits showing how Middle Eastern art reached Japan via the Silk Route. To reach the bijutsukan from in front of the JR eki, take the streetcar (¥140) bound for Higashiyama directly north for 10 minutes. The museum is across Asahi-gawa from Kōraku-en (about a 10-minute walk). ☎ 086/232–3636. ➹ ¥300. ☼ Daily 9–5.

Should you need a map or information on the city, there is a **Tourist Information Office** (☎ 086/222–2912), open daily 9–6, in the JR eki.

Getting Around

Because you will need to change from the Shinkansen to a local train at Okayama in order to travel to Kurashiki, the next destination on our itinerary, it is convenient to stop and visit the gardens as well as Okayama Castle, which you can compare with Himeji-jō. If the castle and garden here are not of great interest, skip Okayama and go directly to Kurashiki.

Kurashiki

★ ❸   *1½ hrs west of Ōsaka by Shinkansen.*

Kurashiki is a great town to take that fantasy trip into old Japan. In feudal times, merchants shipped rice and cotton from its port to Ōsaka. No longer a granary or textile town, Kurashiki has become a living museum of the past, surviving on the income produced by some 4 million visitors a year. Miraculously, Kurashiki escaped war damage and the wrecker's ball that has so often preceded Japan's industrial growth.

Though you can tour Kurashiki in half a day, the ideal way to enjoy this traditional town is to arrive late on a Monday afternoon—most museums are closed Mondays, which means that there are fewer visitors in town—and stay the night in a ryokan. Tuesday morning head for the museums.

Amid the industrialized San-yō coastal plains, Kurashiki is an oasis of traditional Japanese culture. The curving tiled roofs of the houses, the swaying willows lining the canal, and the stone half-circle bridges from which to watch the white swans float by can transport you back in time. The real pleasure of Kurashiki is not the museums but the ambience of the old town. Even the tourist hordes don't destroy it. Try to rise early in the morning to stroll through the old neighborhood and catch the pink glow of the early morning light dancing off the buildings, the waterways crossed by arched bridges, and the willows lining the streets.

The major museum is the **Ōhara Bijutsukan** (art museum), in the old town. Magosaburo Ōhara built this Greek pantheon–type building to house a collection of art that includes works by El Greco, Corot, Manet, Monet, Rodin, Gauguin, Picasso, Toulouse-Lautrec, and many other Western artists. To counter this preponderance of Western art, an additional wing was constructed in 1961 for modern Japanese paintings and, more recently, tapestries, wood-block prints, pottery, and antiques. ☎ *086/422–0005.* ☞ *¥1,000.* ⊙ *Tues.–Sun. (and Mon. public holidays) 9–4:30; closed Dec. 28–Jan. 1.*

The **Kurashiki Ninagawa Bijutsukan** has more Western art, particularly Greek and Roman sculpture. Somehow, many of these works seem to appeal to the Japanese impression of Western neoclassical sculpture, as only endearing cupids and innocent maidens can. This museum and the Mingeikan and the Nihon Kyōdo Ganjukan are clustered together on the north bank of the Kurashiki River, close to the tourist office and two minutes from Ōhara Bijutsukan. ☞ *¥800.* ⊙ *Daily 9–5.*

In four converted granaries, which still have their Edo-period white walls and black-tile roofs, the **Kurashiki Mingeikan** (Kurashiki Folkcraft Museum) houses some 4,000 folk-craft objects, including ceramics, rugs, wooden carvings, and bamboo wares from all over the world. This museum can be disappointing to some—displays are dusty and not very well lit, and the descriptions of objects are in Japanese. At the same time, the experience of taking off your shoes and walking in slippers on the wooden floors provides an appropriate context for this art. The Mingeikan is around the corner from ☞ **Ninagawa Bijutsukan** next to the tourist office. ☞ *¥700.* ⊙ *Tues.–Sun. (and Mon. public holidays) 9–5 (9–4:15 Dec.–Feb.); front desk closes 15 mins before closing; closed Dec. 29–Jan. 1.*

The **Nihon Kyōdo Gangukan** (Japan Rural Toy Museum) is one of the two top toy museums in Japan, and if you can find a Japanese person to show you around and explain the tales behind the toys, it is that much more interesting. It exhibits some 5,000 toys from all regions of the country and has one room devoted to foreign toys. The toy museum and the ☞ **Mingeikan** and the ☞ **Ninagawa Bijutsukan** are clustered together on the north bank of the Kurashiki River. ☎ 086/ 422–8050. ⊠ ¥500. ☉ Daily 8:30–5; closed Jan. 1.

Ivy Square is an ivy-covered complex that used to be a weaving mill. With artful renovation, it now contains the aptly named Ivy Hotel, several boutiques, a restaurant, and, in the central courtyard, a summer beer garden. The courtyard and beer garden are popular rendezvous points in the early evening, when locals and tourists gather for refreshment. Be sure to browse through the shop that sells Japanese textiles, pottery, and other crafts, keeping in mind that you'll find better deals if you have time to stroll through the side streets. Ivy Square is across the bridge from the short street of museums and up the ivy-lined alleyway.

Three museums can be found in the **Ivy Square** complex, though only one is of any real interest: **Kurabo Memorial Hall** retells the history of spinning and textiles, an industry that, along with the shipping of rice and cotton, was a major source of income for Kurashiki. In many ways it is a museum of Japan's industrial revolution, and it includes a video of the factory workshop floor, the dormitory that housed its unmarried female employees. The other two museums are the **Torajiro Kajima Memorial Museum**, which has Western and Asian art, and the **Ivy Gakkan**, an educational museum using reproductions to explain Western art to the Japanese. ⊠ ¥350 for Kurabo, ¥600 for all 3 museums. ☉ Tues.–Sun. 9–5.

Kanryu-ji and **Achi Shrine**, neighbors on the top of the sole hill in Old Kurashiki, provide an excellent view of the town, particularly when the trees are not fully leaved. It is a pleasant, easy climb and a must-see if you have time. You can see the hill and the temple straight ahead when you exit the Ōhara museum. ⊠ Free. ☉ Daily 9–5.

Dining and Lodging

$$ ✕ **Kiyutei.** For the best grilled steak in town, come to this attractive restaurant, where chefs work over the fires grilling your steak to order. The entrance to the restaurant is through a courtyard just across from the entrance to the Ōhara Museum. ⊠ 1-2-25 Chūō, ☎ 086/422–5140. DC, MC, V. Closed Mon.

$$ ✕ **Hamayoshi.** Only three tables and a counter bar make up this personable restaurant specializing in fish from the Inland Sea. Sushi is just one option; another is mamakari, a kind of sashimi sliced from a live (very ugly) fish. A less adventurous dish is lightly grilled fish fillet. Another delicacy is shako, chilled boiled prawns. No English is spoken, but the owner will help you order and instruct you on how to enjoy the chefs' delicacies. Hamayoshi is on the main street leading from the station just before the Kurashiki Kokusai Hotel. ⊠ Achi 2-19-30, ☎ 086/421–3430. No credit cards.

$$$ ✕⊡ **Ryokan Kurashiki.** Close to the Ōhara Museum, with the Kurashiki-
★ gawa flowing gently before it, this elegant ryokan maintains its serenity, no matter how many visitors are walking the streets in town. The cuisine is famous for its regional dishes, making the most of the oysters in the winter, fish straight from the Seto Nai-kai in spring and autumn, and freshwater fish in summer. There is a wonderful inner garden on which to gaze while sipping green tea in the afternoon. Here is Japanese hospitality at its best. If you are not staying here, you can still experience the ryokan by having lunch (¥10,000 per person) or dinner (¥14,000 per person). ⊠ 4-1 Hon-machi, Kurashiki, Okayama-ken 710, ☎ 086/422–0730, ℻ 086/422–0990. 19 rooms, 5 with private bath. Restaurant. AE, DC, MC, V.

$$–$$$ ✗🍴 **Kurashiki Kokusai Hotel.** Owned by Japan Airlines, this is the best Western-style hotel in town. The lobby has a black tile floor and dramatic Japanese wood-block prints. The older part of the hotel was redecorated in summer of 1997, but ask for a room in the newer annex at the back of the building overlooking a garden. The location of the Kokusai is ideal—a 10-minute walk on the main road leading from the station and just around the corner from the old town and the Ōhara Museum. The Alicante Western and Japanese restaurant serves fresh seafood from the Seto Nai-kai with an interesting melange of Mediterranean and Japanese ingredients; the wine list is international and reasonable. ✉ 1-1-44 Chūō, Kurashiki, Okayama-ken 710, ☎ 086/422–5141, FAX 086/422–5192. 106 rooms, 4 Japanese style. Restaurant, bar, beauty salon, parking. AE, DC, MC, V.

$$$ 🍴 **Tsurugata Ryokan.** In the atmosphere of the Edo period, this de-
★ lightful ryokan is made up of a merchant's mansion and a converted rice and sugar storehouse. The window bars, the roof ends and outer wall tiles, and the brass plates at the intersections of the beams prove the authenticity of this nearly 300-year-old structure. Rooms are on the cozy side, but the pine bathtubs and the location—it's directly across the bridge from the Ōhara Museum—create a feeling that you are experiencing life in another era. The suite overlooking the garden is especially fine. Since the ryokan is managed by the Kurashiki Kokusai Hotel, questions in English can be directed toward the hotel staff, as more of them tend to speak some English. ⊘ 1-3-15 Chūō, Kurashiki, Okayama-ken 710, ☎ 086/424–1635, FAX 086/424–1650. 10 rooms. AE, DC, MC, V.

$$ 🍴 **Hotel Kurashiki.** Just above the station, this is an efficient business hotel that is useful if you have an early morning train to catch. It is a little dreary, but at least the bathrooms are custom-made, not the usual plastic cubicles. Certainly, this Japan Railways hotel is better than the adjacent Kurashiki Terminal hotel, where rooms are downright shabby. ✉ 1-1-1 Achi, Kurashiki, Okayama-ken 710, ☎ 086/426–6111, FAX 068/426–6163. 133 Western-style rooms. Restaurant. AE, DC, MC, V.

$ 🍴 **Kamoi.** This hostelry is the best bargain in Kurashiki. The rooms are simple—tatami style. The food is good, as it should be; the owner is also the owner and chef of Kamoi Restaurant, across from the Ōhara Museum. A visual display in the window shows what is offered, and the walls are decorated with artifacts such as cast-iron kettles and ancient rifles. A Japanese breakfast, or a Western one if you prefer, and dinner are available. An eight-minute walk from the Ōhara Museum, this minshuku is close to Tsurugatayama Park and Achi Jinja. ✉ 6-21 Hon-machi, Kurashiki, Okayama-ken 710, ☎ 086/422–4898, FAX 086/427–7615. 17 Japanese-style rooms with shared bath. No credit cards. Closed Mon.

En Route The next stop down the San-yō Line is Hiroshima, a city destroyed in the deepest sense and energetically rebuilt—a world away from Kurashiki. The ride from Kurashiki is only an hour if you take the local JR train to Shin-Kurashiki (two stops) and transfer to the Shinkansen rather than doubling back to Okayama to catch the fast train.

Hiroshima

2 hrs west of Ōsaka by Shinkansen.

Hiroshima will forever be etched in the collective conscience as the first city to suffer atomic destruction. No visitor can fail to be acutely aware of the event, which took place at 8:15 AM, August 6, 1945. On that morning, three B-29s flew toward Hiroshima. Two planes were decoys, but one flew directly over the city and cut loose a single 4-ton bomb, code-named "Little Boy." The bomb exploded at 1,900 ft above the Industrial Promotion Hall, in the center of the city. Two hundred thousand people died, including 10,000 Korean prisoners forced to serve the Japanese empire as slave laborers. The only bomb to fall on Hiroshima during World War II, it wiped out half the city.

Only one obvious reminder remains from the havoc and death wrought by the atomic bomb. Miraculously, the Industrial Promotion Hall did not completely collapse; its charred structure remains untouched since that fated morning. It has been renamed the A-Bomb Dome and stands surrounded by the rebuilt city of ferro-concrete buildings.

Heiwa Kinen Kōen (Peace Memorial Park)

The Heiwa Kinen Kōen contains the key sights to visit in Hiroshima. Entirely rebuilt after World War II, Hiroshima is a modern city. The atomic bomb is its living history. The monuments and the museum in the park are dedicated to "No More Hiroshimas." The park sits in the top of the triangle formed by two of Hiroshima's rivers, the Ota-gawa and Motoyasu-gawa. Take Streetcar 2 or 6 to the Gembaku-Dōmu-mae stop, and then cross the river to the park.

★ ❹ Your first sight will be the **Gembaku Dōmu** (A-Bomb Dome)—a powerful and poignant symbol. The old Industrial Promotion Hall, with its half-shattered structure, stands in sharp contrast to the vitality and wealth of the new Hiroshima. The A-Bomb Dome is the only structural ruin of the war left erect in Hiroshima and, for that, its impact is even stronger.

❺ The **Heiwa Kinen Shiryōkan** (Peace Memorial Museum) is as disturbing as it is educational. Through exhibits of models, charred fragments of clothing, melted tiles, and photographs of devastation and contorted bodies, the story of havoc and agonizing death unfolds. Nothing can capture the reality of 7,000°C (12,632°F), the surface heat of the atomic fireball, but the remains of the melted statue of Buddha or the imprinted human shadow on granite steps is enough to unnerve us about the human potential for destruction. Most exhibits have brief explanations in English. However, more detailed information is given on tape cassettes, which you can rent for ¥150. ☎ 082/241–4004. ¥50. ☉ May–Nov., daily 9–5:30; Dec.–Apr., daily 9–4:30; closed Dec. 29–Jan. 2.

❻ The **Peace Memorial Hall** shows documentary films on the effects of the atomic explosion given in English—times are posted at the museum's entrance. It is on the east side of the Peace Museum (the International Conference Center is on the west side).

❼ The **Memorial Cenotaph,** designed by Japanese architect Kenzō Tange, resembles the primitive A-frame houses of Japan's earliest inhabitants. Buried inside the vaults of the cenotaph is a chest containing the names of those who died in the holocaust. On the exterior of the cenotaph is the inscription (in Japanese), "Repose ye in Peace, for the error shall not be repeated." The cenotaph is in front of the museum on its north side.

★ ❽ The **Peace Flame** burns behind the **Memorial Cenotaph.** The flame will be extinguished only when all atomic weapons in the world are banished. In the meantime, every August 6, there is a solemn commemoration in which the citizens of Hiroshima float paper lanterns on the city's rivers for the repose of the souls of the atomic-bomb victims.

❾ Pause before the **Statue for the A-Bomb Children** before you leave the park. The figure is of a young girl who died of leukemia caused by the atomic radiation. Her will to live was strong. She believed that if she could fold 1,000 paper cranes—cranes being a symbol of good for-

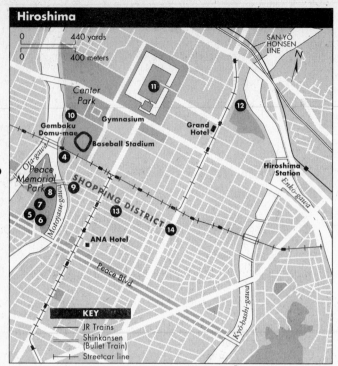

tune and long life—her illness would be cured. She died after making her 954th crane.

Getting Around. From the Gembaku-Dōmu-mae streetcar stop, walk onto Aichi Bridge, the double bridge that crosses the rivers Ota-gawa (also called Hon-kawa) and Motoyasu-gawa. In the middle of the bridge is the entrance to the Peace Memorial Park. The Peace Memorial Museum is at the far end of the park. En route are statues and monuments, but, because you'll probably be returning through the park, head straight for the museum, about a 10-minute walk from the bridge. If you are interested in picking up more information on the city, there is an information center in the rest house on the left-hand side of the park near another bridge crossing Motoyasu-gawa. A less dramatic approach from Hiroshima Eki is to take the Hiroshima Bus Company's red-and-white Bus 24 to Kōkaido-mae, which is only a two-minute walk from the museum, or to take Streetcar 1 to Chūden-mae for a five-minute walk to the museum.

Elsewhere in Hiroshima

⑩ The **Kodomo Bunka Kagakukan** (Hiroshima Science and Cultural Center for Children) is a wonderfully laid out hands-on museum. The joy and enthusiasm of the youngsters here dispel some of the depression that the Peace Memorial Park is bound to cause. To get here, cross the Aichi Bridge at the park's northern entrance and walk yards north and east, keeping the river on your left and the baseball stadium where the Hiroshima Carps play on your right. There is a planetarium next door. ▨ *Center free, planetarium ¥410.* ☺ *Tues.–Sun. 9–5; closed days following public holidays.*

⑪ The resurrected **Hiroshima-jō** (Broad Island Castle), gave the city of Hiroshima its name when Terumoto Mori built it in 1589. A Japanese

Army headquarters in World War II, it was (intentionally) destroyed by the bomb. In 1958 the five-story donjon was rebuilt to its original specifications. Its interior has been used as a local museum, but since 1989 it has served as Hiroshima's historical museum, with exhibits from Japan's feudal period. It is a 10-minute walk farther north of the A-Bomb Dome. ✉ *Castle grounds free, museum ¥300.* ⊙ *Apr.–Sept., daily 9–5:30; Oct.–Mar., daily 9–4:30.*

⑫ The garden **Shukkei-en** was laid out in 1630 by Lord Nagakira Asano in a design resembling that of a famed scenic lake in Hangzhou, China. The beauty of the garden stems from the streams and islets winding their way between the sculpted pine trees. Small bridges cross the streams, which are filled with exotic-colored carp, so praised for their long lives. They make a fitting end for a visit to Hiroshima, even as a complement to the garden's current generation of young plants and new construction—all the ancient plantings and structures, of course, were destroyed by the bomb. Shukkei-en is east of the castle on the banks of the Kyō-bashi-gawa. Return to the JR eki on Streetcar 9; at the end of the line transfer to Streetcar 1, 2, 5, or 6. ✉ *¥250.* ⊙ *Apr.– Sept., daily 9–5:30; Oct.–Mar., daily 9–4:30.*

⑬ Around **Hon-dōri,** Hiroshima's central district, you'll find major department stores and masses of smaller shops. The major stores—Fukuya (closed Wed.), Tenmaya (closed Tues.), Mitsukoshi (closed Mon.), and Sogo (closed Tues.)—are open from 10 to 7:30 (Mitsukoshi closes at 7). Restaurants abound, and oysters are the specialty of the region, best washed down with sake, of which Hiroshima produces some of Japan's finest. There is, of course, a range of modern hotels from which to choose (☞ Dining and Lodging, *below*), in the city center to the east of the Peace Memorial Park and around the JR eki.

⑭ **Shintenchi** is an entertainment district east of the Hon-dōri shopping district. If you like cities and want an urban base to explore the Seto Nai-kai, this side of Hiroshima, with its international and Japanese urban pleasures, competes only with Fukuoka in Kyūshū for Western Japan's hottest nightlife.

Dining and Lodging

$$$ ✗ **Mitakiso Ryokan.** For a kaiseki lunch or an elaborate kaiseki dinner
★ in a private tatami room, Mitakiso Ryokan is superb. One of the most respected ryokan in Hiroshima, it makes an excellent place to entertain Japanese guests. And you needn't stay at the ryokan in order to enjoy its cuisine. If you do stay, it is worth going all out and choosing a room with sliding doors onto the private garden. ✉ *1-7 Mitaki-machi, Nishi-ku,* ☎ *082/237–1402. Reservations essential. AE, MC, V.*

$$ ✗ **Kanawa Restaurant.** Hiroshima is known for its oysters, especially
★ in winter when they are fresh and sweet. Kanawa, on a barge moored on the Motoyasu River, near the Peace Memorial Park, is Hiroshima's most famous oyster restaurant. Dining is on tatami matting, with river views. Only oysters are served here, in at least 10 different ways. ✉ *Moored on the river at Heiwa Bridge, Naka-ku,* ☎ *082/241–7416. Jacket and tie. AE, DC, MC, V. Closed 1st and 3rd Sun. Oct.–Mar.; closed each Sun. and Wed. Apr.–Sept.*

$$ ✗ **Suishin Restaurant.** Famous for its sashimi and sushi, this restaurant offers the freshest fish from the Seto Nai-kai—globefish, oysters, and eel, to name but a few. Order à la carte or from a set selection. If you do not like raw fish, try rockfish grilled with soy sauce. Suishin now has an English-language menu. Ambience is plain and simple; there's a counter bar and four tables. ✉ *6-7 Tate-machi, Naka-ku,* ☎ *082/ 247–4411. AE, DC, MC, V. Closed Wed.*

$$ ✕ **Ten Ko.** The specialty in this small restaurant is seafood tempura. Part of the secret to good tempura is the continual changing of the oil (after every fourth or fifth order) so that a delicate crispness can be achieved. This shop changes the oil frequently (probably selling the old oil to the lesser tempura shops in the city). Other dishes are on the menu, but come for the tempura. ✉ *Naka-machi 5-1, 2nd floor, Naka-ku,* ☎ *082/242–3933. AE, DC, MC, V.*

$ ✕ **Okonomi Mura.** In this modern, three-story building there are two dozen small shops serving *okonomi-yaki,* sometimes called Japanese pizza but more like a Japanese frittata. ("Mura" means village.) A bed of noodles is topped with heaps of onions and green and red peppers, as well as your choice of shrimp, pork, mussels, or chicken. Different areas in Japan have their own style of creating okonomi-yaki; in Hiroshima, the ingredients are layered rather than mixed, as in Ōsaka. Seating in these shops is either at a wide counter in front of a grill or at tables with their own grills. The chef-waiter prepares the ingredients and starts the grilling; you complete the task. Choosing one shop over the other is a dilemma, only partially solved by looking at the displays. Consider trying Chii-Chau, which is owned by the man who conceived the idea of creating a mall of okonomi-yaki shops. The complex is close to the Hon-dōri shopping area, just west of Chūō-dōri. ✉ *Okonomi Mura Bldg., 8-15 Shōwa-machi, Naka-ku,* ☎ *082/241–8758. No credit cards.*

$$$ ★ **ANA Hotel Hiroshima.** In the business district on Peace Boulevard, the hotel is within walking distance of the Peace Museum. With glittering chandeliers, the pink-carpeted lobby looks onto a small garden with a waterfall. The tea lounge facing the garden is an excellent place to be after visiting Peace Memorial Park. The furnishings of the guest rooms are uninspired, but the rooms have all the extras of a first-class hotel, including English-speaking channels on the television. The Unkai restaurant on the fifth floor has not only good Japanese food but also a view onto a Japanese garden of dwarf trees, rocks, and a pond of colorful carp. ✉ *7-20 Naka-machi, Naka-ku, Hiroshima 730,* ☎ *082/241–1111,* FAX *082/241–9123. 427 Western-style rooms, 4 Japanese-style rooms. 3 restaurants, beer garden in summer, indoor pool, health club, sauna, shops. AE, DC, MC, V.*

$$$ **Hiroshima Prince.** This hotel, built in 1994, is a sparkling triangular complex down by Hiroshima Port. Its advantages are its newness and its views of the Seto Nai-kai. Its disadvantage is its location, a 15-minute taxi ride from downtown and the Peace Park. Because of its isolation, the Prince bills itself as a resort hotel, with a swimming pool, a gallery of shops, an amusement hall, bowling alleys, an indoor snowboarding arena, and a marina. The mammoth scale is echoed in the hotel's expansive marble lobby with a fountain and pool the size of a small lake. Add to this the lobby's circular staircase and you have the paradigm of new Japan's love affair with expansive spaces for glamour's sake. The hotel has several restaurants: the Boston Steak House, a Chinese restaurant, the Hago-romo Japanese restaurant, and a coffee shop. The best spot is the bar and lounge at the top of the building, the 23rd floor, with its unique view of the Seto Nai-kai. Ask for a suite, as they are quite reasonable under their family plan, and the bathtub juts right against a large window for an equally spectacular view. ✉ *23-1 Moto-ujina-machi, Minami-ku, Hiroshima 734,* ☎ *082/256–1111,* FAX *082/256–1134. 550 rooms. 4 restaurants, bar, lobby lounge, outdoor pool, shops. AE, DC, MC, V.*

$$–$$$ **Hiroshima Terminal Hotel.** This is the smartest and largest hotel near the station (located at the back, not the front). An expansive vaulted marble lobby greets you as you enter. The guest rooms, spacious by

Japanese standards, are awash in pink tones and have strictly functional furniture. The staff is briskly efficient, and many employees speak English. On the penthouse (21st) floor, the Japanese, Chinese, and French restaurants offer panoramic vistas, and there are cafés and a coffee shop on the second floor. Downtown Hiroshima and the Peace Park are only 10 minutes away by streetcar. ⊠ *1-5 Matsubara-chō, Minami-ku, Hiroshima 732,* ☎ *082/262–1111,* FAX *082/262–4050. 437 rooms, mostly Western style. 4 restaurants, 2 bars, coffee shop, business services, travel services. AE, DC, MC, V.*

$ 🏨 **Kenmin Bunka Center.** For a no-nonsense place to stay close to the Peace Memorial Park, this accommodation is the best value in Hiroshima. It is strictly a business hotel, with small rooms and tiny bathrooms, but the decor is cheerful and refreshing, and the bathtubs are deep enough for a good soak. The Kenmin Bunka Center has neither lobby space nor lounges, but it does have an inexpensive coffee shop with Japanese and Western fare. Check-in is at 4 PM, and advance reservations are recommended. ⊠ *1-5-3 Ote-machi-ku, Hiroshima 730,* ☎ *082/245–2322,* FAX *082/245–2315. 50 rooms. Coffee shop. No credit cards.*

$ 🏨 **Mikawa Ryokan.** This simple wooden ryokan offers the basics—tatami rooms, coin-operated television, air-conditioning, but no rooms with private baths. There are too many guests for the limited toilet facilities—indeed, they can get rather grubby. However, the inn has a good location seven minutes on foot south of the JR eki; turn right on the street before Aori-dōri. Advance reservations are advised. ⊠ *9-6 Kyobashi-chō, Minami-ku, Hiroshima 730,* ☎ *082/261–2719,* FAX *082/263–2706. 13 rooms. AE, V.*

Getting Around

By Ferry. Hiroshima is also a ferry hub. There are eight boats daily to Miyajima (¥1,460 round-trip). Two important connections are to and from Matsuyama on Shikoku—14 hydrofoil ferries a day take one hour (¥5,800) and 12 regular ferries a day take three hours (¥4,340 first class, ¥2,170 second class)—and to and from Beppu on Kyūshū—one departs Hiroshima at 9:30 PM to arrive at Beppu at 6 AM, another departs Beppu at 2 PM to arrive at Hiroshima at 7 PM (¥4,000 to ¥16,000). ⊠ *Seto Nai-kai Kisen Co., 12-23, Ujinakaigan 1-chōme, Minami-ku, Hiroshima City,* ☎ *082/253–1212,* FAX *082/505–0134.*

By Plane. Seven daily flights run between Hiroshima and Tōkyō's Haneda Kūkō, and there are flights to Kagoshima, on Kyūshū, and Sapporo, on Hokkaidō.

By Streetcar. The streetcar (tram) is the easiest form of transport in Hiroshima. Enter the tram from its middle door and take a ticket. Pay the driver at the front door when you leave. All fares within the city limits are ¥130. A one-day pass is ¥600, available for purchase at the platform outside the JR Hiroshima Eki. There are seven streetcar lines; four of them either depart from Hiroshima Eki or make it their terminus. Stops are announced by a tape recording, and each stop has a sign in *rōmaji* posted on the platform. Buses also ply Hiroshima's streets; the basic fare is ¥180.

By Taxi. Taxis are available throughout the city. The initial fare for small taxis is ¥570 (¥620 for larger taxis) for the first 1½ km (1 mi), then ¥70 for every 335 yards. There are also sightseeing taxis; for a two-hour tour, the charge is approximately ¥8,400 (Kojin taxi; ☎ 082/283–2311). Because these taxi drivers are not guides, you should rent a taped recording describing key sights in English. These special taxis depart from a special depot in front of Hiroshima Eki at the Shinkansen entrance. If you want to arrange for one of them ahead of time, telephone the **Hiroshima Station Tourist Information Center** (☎ 082/261–1877).

By Train. Hiroshima is Western Honshū's major city, and it is a major terminal for the JR Shinkansen trains; several Shinkansen end their runs at Hiroshima rather than continuing to Hakata on Kyūshū. During the day, Shinkansen arrive and depart for Okayama, Ōsaka, Kyōto, and Tōkyō approximately every 30 minutes and about every hour for Hakata. From Tōkyō, train time is 4 hours, 37 minutes, and unless you have a Japan Rail Pass, the fare is ¥18,050. Hiroshima Eki also serves as the hub for JR express and local trains traveling along the San-yō Line. There are also two trains a day that link Hiroshima to Matsue on the northern shore (the Nihon-kai coast) of Western Honshū.

Guided Tours

Hiroshima International Relations has recently established a **Home Visit Program.** To make arrangements, go the day before you wish to visit a Japanese home to the International Center on the ground floor of the International Conference Center in Peace Memorial Park (⊠ 1-5 Nakajima-chō, Naka-ku, Hiroshima 730, ☎ 082/247-8007, 𝔽𝔸𝕏 082/247-2464). An inexpensive gift such as flowers or homemade treats from your home country are not at all required, but would ensure a successful beginning for your visit.

A number of sightseeing tours are available, including tours of Hiroshima and cruises on the Seto Nai-kai, in particular to Miyajima, the island with the famous sea-bound torii. A 4-hour, 40-minute tour (Japanese-speaking guide only) to Hiroshima's major sights costs ¥3,510 . An eight-hour tour of both the city and Miyajima costs ¥9,470. These tours are operated by the **Hiroshima Bus Company** (☎ 082/243-7207, 𝔽𝔸𝕏 082/243-0272) and depart from in front of Hiroshima Eki's Shinkansen entrance.

The **Seto Nai-kai Kisen Company** (☎ 082/255-1212, 𝔽𝔸𝕏 082/505-0134) operates several cruises on the Seto Nai-kai. Its cruise boat, the *Southern Cross,* operates a 7¼-hour trip (9:30-4:45) daily, March-November, which takes in Etajima, Ondo-no-Seto, Kure (*koo*-reh) Bay, and Ōmishima (¥4,500-¥6,500 includes lunch and soft drinks). There are also a variety of river cruises, one of which includes dinner (¥6,000-10,000).

Visitor Information

There are two **Tourist Information offices** at JR Hiroshima Eki: one at the south exit (☎ 082/261-1877), the exit for downtown, and one at the north exit (☎ 082/263-6822), the exit for the Shinkansen. Both provide free maps and brochures as well as help in securing accommodations. There is also the main office, **Hiroshima City Tourist Information,** in the Peace Memorial Park (☎ 082/247-6738).

Miyajima

★ ⑮ *30 mins southwest of Hiroshima by ferry.*

Miyajima is one of the delights of the San-yō coast—a pleasant counterpoint to Hiroshima's solemn aspects. It is one of what the Japanese call their "Big Three Scenic Attractions"; Matsushima in Tōhoku is another, Ama-no-hashidate on the San-in coast is the third. This small island just off the coast in the Seto Nai-kai is the site of the famous Itsukushima Jinja, a shrine built on wooden supports that extend the buildings into the sea. Itsukushima Jinja's much-photographed vermilion torii is as quintessentially Japanese as landmarks get. As evocative as it is from land, it was meant to be approached from the water as a gate marking the boundaries of the temple precincts.

The island is only 30 km (19 mi) in circumference, but its center peaks at Mt. Misen's 1,740-ft forested slopes. As much as the mountain and the surrounding Seto Nai-kai are scenic, the village *is* touristy. Still, Miyajima, with history and tradition everywhere, is delightful either for a day trip or for an overnight stay.

You will note that there are no cemeteries on Miyajima—neither is anyone allowed to die or be born here. All of the island is sacred, and when either time comes, concerned parties must be taken over to the mainland.

Miyajima has become a vacation spot for Japanese families, hence the numerous hotels and ryokan in and around the village. One of these ryokan is worth remembering. It is the famous **Iwaso Ryokan,** which has hosted pilgrims and vacationers for 130 years. Even if you are not staying in town overnight, Iwaso is a great place to go for lunch (☞ Dining and Lodging, *below*). Also, be aware that the most exciting—and the most congested—time to visit Miyajima is in June (by the lunar calendar) for the annual **Kangen-sai Festival,** when three stately barges bearing a portable shrine, priests, and musicians cross the bay, flanked by a squadron of festooned boats.

When you arrive in Miyajima, follow the coast to the right (west) from the pier. This leads to the village, which is crowded with restaurants, hotels, and souvenir shops. At the far end of the village is the park, which leads past the torii and on to Itsukushima Jinja. Expect to be greeted by deer as you walk through the park. The deer are protected, and they take full advantage of their status, demanding edibles and nudging you if you're not forthcoming.

★ The **torii,** 500 ft from the shore at an entrance to the cove where the shrine stands, rises 53 ft out of the water, making it one of the tallest torii in Japan. Built in 1875, it has become a symbol not only of Miyajima but also of Japan. Especially as the sun sets over the Seto Nai-kai, the vermilion structure and its reflection in the rippling water make an unforgettable sight. Past the torii stands the shrine. Poets write of how the shrine's building seems to float on the water, and poetic license allows them to omit the fact that it "floats" only at high tide. Photographers, take note: At other times, the shrine stands on wooden stilts above less photogenic mud flats.

Itsukushima Jinja was founded in 593 and dedicated to the three daughters of Susano-o-no-Mikoto, the Shintō god of the moon and the oceans. The structure has had to be continually repaired and rebuilt, and the present structure is thought to be a 16th-century copy of the 12th-century buildings. Most of the shrine is closed to the public, but you can walk around its deck, which gives some idea of the size of the building complex, as well as gorgeous views of the torii. ▧ ¥300 *(combined ticket with Treasure House ¥500).* ⊘ *Mar.–Oct., daily 6:30 AM–6 PM; Nov.–Feb., daily 6:30–5:30.*

The **Hōmotsukan** (Treasure House) is a must-see. Because every victor of battles that took place on the Seto Nai-kai saw fit to offer his gratitude to the gods by giving gifts to Itsukushima Jinja, the Hōmotsukan is rich with art objects, 246 of which have been designated as either National Treasures or Important Cultural Properties. It's across from the shrine's exit. ▧ ¥300 *(combined ticket with Itsukushima Jinja ¥500).* ⊘ *Daily 8:30–5.*

Senjōkaku (Hall of One Thousand Mats), dedicated by Hideyoshi Toyotomi in 1587, has rice scoops attached to the walls, symbols of the soldiers who died fighting for Japan's expansionism. The **Gojū-no-**

to (Five-Story Pagoda) dates from 1407. Both are on top of a small hill overlooking the shrine. If you climb up the steps to these two buildings for a closer look, a small street on the other side (away from the shrine) serves as a shortcut back to the village.

Though many people spend only a half day on the island, if you have more time to enjoy its beauty, take a stroll through **Momijidani Kōen,** inland from the shrine. Here in the park is the start of the mile-long gondola that takes you virtually to the summit of **Mt. Misen.** The top is just a short hike past the gondola's terminus, and the views of the Seto Nai-kai and Hiroshima beyond are splendid. Consider walking back down to the park. ⛟ *¥900 one-way, ¥1,500 round-trip. Entrance to park free.*

Dining and Lodging

$$$$ ✕⛨ **Iwaso Ryokan.** For tradition and elegance, this is the Japanese inn
★   at which to dine and overnight on the island. Older rooms have character, those in the newer wing less so. Two cottages on the grounds have Japanese suites that are superbly decorated with antiques. Prices vary according to the size of your room, its view, and the kaiseki dinner that you select. Be sure, when you make reservations in advance, to specify what you want and fix the price. Breakfast, Western style if you ask, and dinner are usually included. ✉ *345 Miyajima-chō, Hiroshima-ken 739-05,* ☎ *0829/44–2233,* ⛛ *0829/44–2230. 45 rooms. Restaurant. AE, DC, V.*

$$$ ⛨ **Jyukeiso Ryokan.** For a more modest place to stay, this family ryokan (the owner speaks English) makes a pleasant home. It is to the east of the ferry pier, away from the town and shrine, which might be a bit inconvenient. Check to be sure that breakfast (Western-style available) and dinner are included. ✉ *Miyajima-chō, Hiroshima-ken 739,* ☎ *0829/44–0300,* ⛛ *0829/44–0388. 13 rooms with bath. Restaurant. AE, DC, MC, V.*

Arriving and Departing

The easiest, least expensive way to Miyajima is to take the commuter train on the JR San-yō Line from Hiroshima Eki to Miyajima-guchi Eki. From Miyajima-guchi Eki, it is a three-minute walk to the pier from which ferries make the trip to Miyajima. The train takes about 25 minutes and departs from Hiroshima every 15–20 minutes. The first train leaves Hiroshima at 5:55 AM; the last ferry returns from Miyajima at 10:05 PM. There are two boats, one of which belongs to JR— your Japan Rail Pass is valid on this boat only. The one-way cost for the train and ferry, without a JR Pass, is ¥560. There are also eight direct ferries (¥1,440) daily from Hiroshima Ujina Port that make the 22-minute trip. Allow a minimum of three hours for the major sights of Miyajima.

En Route   From Hiroshima the Shinkansen continues to Shimonoseki, 1 hour west, before crossing to Kyūshū and terminating in Hakata. Instead of crossing over to Kyūshū with the Shinkansen, consider turning north at Ogōri to take in the quieter reaches of Western Honshū's San-in coast.

THE SAN-IN REGION

Where the coastline that faces the Seto Nai-kai receives the direct light of the sun, San-in has a misty, eerie light that diffuses to cause an ever-changing mood of flirting shadows. San-in means "In the Shadow of the Mountains," and the area has also been in the shadow of Japan's economic miracle. The presence of the mountains makes transport expensive between the north and south coasts and has staved off the onrush of sprawling factories and the modern urbanization that have destroyed so much of the San-yō coast. The influx of tourists, both Japanese and foreign, has also been smaller. San-in is off the beaten track, which only adds to its appeal.

San-in moves at a slower pace. Trains and buses are less frequent. There is an austerity in the architecture, the crafts, and in the attitudes of the people—a reflection of the cold winters and the isolation from mainstream Japan. An example of their art may help illustrate this: To the people of the San-in, a chipped tea bowl has more aesthetic appeal than the perfected symmetry used by Kyōto's craftspeople. San-in potters will create an imperfection in a bowl, then artfully glaze the piece. The imagination must then make the leap to what ultimate perfection could be. This is San-in—inspiring, restrained, forever conceiving perfection but never harnessing it.

San-in officially stretches from Shimonoseki all the way to Kyōto. Its special atmosphere actually ends on the Nihon-kai coast at Maizuru, just inside the border of Kyōto Prefecture.

The JR San-in Main Line from Shimonoseki to Kyōto is the second longest in Japan, at 680 km (422 mi). It has the most stations of any line, which means plenty of stops and longer traveling times. Only two Limited Express trains a day cover the Shimonoseki–Kyōto route in either direction. Local trains run more frequently between major cities on the San-in coast.

Shimonoseki

Try not to find yourself stranded in Shimonoseki overnight—it is little more than an industrial port town from which ferries leave for ports on Kyūshū, the Seto Nai-kai, and Pusan, across the Nihon-kai in Korea. Even as you leave the city on the train, the first hour en route to Hagi shows landscape heavily built up with factories. Gradually the scenery becomes more natural, and views of the coastline start setting the tone of San-in and its first major city, Hagi.

Unless you do not mind waiting around train stations or being stranded overnight, research schedules for your route in advance. Trains run so infrequently east out of Shimonoseki that you will need to plan your time to fit their schedule, unlike in many other regions in Japan, where the next train is never too far off. Only a few trains set out each day from Shimonoseki to Hagi, so either plan ahead for those trains or cross to the San-in farther east in Western Honshū at Ogōri, Hiroshima, Okayama, or Himeji.

Hagi

★ ⑯ *3hrs north of Ogōri by JR train, 1½ hrs by JR bus; 2½ hrs north of Ogōri by JR Yamaguchi Line only; 2 hrs northeast of Shimonoseki by JR Limited Express.*

Although its castle was dismantled in 1874 as a relic of feudalism, Hagi retains the atmosphere of a traditional castle town. The city is rich with history, a history that is closely linked to the Mōri family. Even though they had opposed the Tokugawa shogunate and were defeated by Ieyasu Tokugawa in 1600 at the Battle of Sekigahara, the Mōri were able to keep their fiefdom for 13 generations. The Tokugawa shogunate had tried to isolate the Mōri as much as possible, but in so doing, the Mōri, who had never forgotten their defeat, became the forerunners of the movement to restore power to the emperor. It was the army from Hagi and the surrounding Nagato Province that, on the second attempt, captured

Kyōto and turned the tide against the shogunate. Hagi's fame lies not simply in defeating the shogunate but also in supplying the intellectual framework for the new Japan, even to the extent that Japan's first prime minister, Hirobumi Ito (1841–1909), was born and educated in Hagi.

Hagi has another claim to fame: Hagi-yaki, a pottery that has been cherished for 375 years for its soft colors and its milky, translucent glazes. Mind you, the tradition of Hagi-yaki has less than noble beginnings. Returning from Japan's aborted attempt to invade Korea in the late 16th century, a Mōri general brought home two Korean potters as "souvenirs." With techniques that were probably used during the Silla Kingdom, these Korean brothers, Sukkweng Yi and Kyung Yi, created Hagi-yaki for their masters. Hagi-yaki has since become second to Raku-yaki as the most praised pottery in Japan. Alas, the two most famous kilns, Rikei's Saka Kiln and Miwa Kiln, do not accept visitors, but several others do, including Shizuki Kiln, conveniently located on the way to the castle grounds.

Surrounded by mountains on three sides and by the Nihon-kai on the fourth, Hagi is set in the "V" formed by two rivers, Matsumoto-gawa on the east side and the Hashimoto-gawa on the west. The major train station is Higashi-Hagi (not Hagi), on the east side of town.

Central Hagi

The second-floor **Ishii Chawan Museum** has a small collection of rare antique tea bowls produced in Hagi, including some by Ri Sampei, whose creations first captured the attention of the Japanese. Also in this prized collection are Korean tea bowls made during the Koryo Dynasty (916–1392). For aficionados this museum is a pleasure, but if you are short on time you may want to skip it in order to look around ☞ **Kumaya Art Museum**. From Higashi-Hagi Eki, cross the bridge over the Matsumoto-gawa and, bearing right, continue on the street until you reach the Hagi Grand Hotel. Turn left here, walk seven blocks, then turn right. Walk straight for at least ten minutes until you reach a curve. Take the first right after the curve; the museum is up on the left. *¥500.* ☺ *Daily 9–11:30 and 1–5.*

Tamachi Mall is the busiest street in Hagi, with some 130 shops offering the latest fashions from Tōkyō and the more interesting local products from Yamaguchi Prefecture. You might want to come here to purchase Hagi-yaki after touring the sights and the kilns where the pottery is made. Two stores worth noting are **Harada Chojuan** and **Miwa Seigado**. The latter is at the top end of Tamachi, past the San Marco restaurant. Another gallery and store is **Saito-an**, in which both the masters and "unknown" potters display their works for sale. Prices range from ¥500 for a small sake cup to ¥250,000 for a tea bowl by such living master potters as Miwa Kyusetsu. Tamachi Mall is six blocks southwest from the Hagi Grand Hotel, across the Matsumoto-gawa from Higashi-Hagi Eki.

The **Tera-machi** section of town has numerous temples crying out for someone to pay heed to them—locals just take them for granted. Each one of these temples has something of interest; all have a tranquillity rarely transgressed by tourists. There are about 10 from which to choose and explore, from the old wooden temple of **Hōfukuji**, with its bibbed statues of Jizo, guardian deity of children, to **Kaichoji**, with its two-story gate and veranda around the Main Hall's second floor. From the top of Tamachi Mall, a right turn toward Hagi Bay will take you to the Tera-machi area.

The **Kumaya Art Museum** was once the home of a wealthy merchant, and the warehouse has been made into a museum, which houses art objects and antiques. Of special note are the scrolls, paintings, a screen of the Kano school, and a collection of ceramics, which includes some of the first Hagi-yaki produced. Instead of walking all the way to Hagi Bay, take a left after Kaicho-ji, and the museum will be on the left at the large metal gate. ☎ 0838/22–7547. 💳 ¥500. ☉ *Daily 9–5; closed Jan. 1.*

The **Kikuya-ke Jūtaku** (Kikuya House) was once the home of the chief merchant family to the Mōri clan. Though the Kikuya were only merchants, they held a special relationship with the Mōri. In fact, after the Mōri defeat at Sekigahara, the Kikuya family sent their daimyō money to return to Hagi. As a result of this rapport, the Kikuya house has more extravagance than merchants were normally allowed to display. *Keyaki* (Japanese zelkova wood) was, for example, forbidden to merchants, yet notice its extensive use here. This is not a typical Edo-period family home—it indicates the good life of the few. To get here from the Kumaya Art Museum, take the next left (south and away from the sea); it is not far after the turn. ☎ 0838/25–8282. 💳 ¥500. ☉ *Daily 9–5; closed Dec. 31.*

Shizuki Kōen, Hagi-yaki, and Hagi-jō (castle)

Shizuki Kōen, washed on three sides by the sea, surrounds 475-ft Shizuki-yama at the western end of Hagi. The park contains the ruins of Hagi-jō and Hana-no-e Teahouse. 💳 ¥210 *(covers entrance to Shizuki Kōen and Hagi-jō grounds).*

There are several **pottery kilns** in the vicinity of the park. At **Shizuki Kiln,** near the park, stop in and browse through its Hagi-yaki and, if the wallet can bear it, purchase some of the magnificent work. Most of the time, you will be welcome to enter the adjoining building where the kilns are fired. On the way to the castle you will pass **Shogetsu Kiln** and **Hagi-jō Kiln,** both of which offer the opportunity for browsing, watching the potters at work, and, of course, purchasing Hagi ware.

At the next major intersection after Shizuki Kiln, take a left and walk or bicycle along the street between the **Toida Masuda House Walls.** These are the longest mud walls of the Horiuchi samurai section of town, and, for a moment, they will thrust you back into feudal times. Follow the walls around and head west to the grand wooden **Fukuhara Gate.** A right turn here leads directly to **Tenju-in,** a memorial to Terumoto Mōri, who founded the clan that ruled in the area for 13 generations.

Mōri House is a 170- by 17-ft-wide building that was once home to the samurai foot soldiers. To find it, turn left from the Tenju-in Mōri memorial and head toward the park grounds. It is on the left, past the Shizuki Youth Hostel. ☉ *Apr.–Oct., daily 8–6:30; Nov.–Feb., daily 8:30–4:30; Mar., daily 8:30–6.*

Hagi-jō itself is no more. Its demise was unusual. Neither warfare nor fire destroyed it. Instead, the castle was dismantled as a gesture of support for the Meiji Restoration. Many of the Meiji instigators were from Western Honshū and Kyūshū, and such acts of support for the return of power to the emperor were abundant in these areas.

In fact, the Mōri family had moved from the castle in 1863 to create a new home and provincial capital at landlocked Yamaguchi. All that remains of the castle are its high walls and wide moats. But the real pleasure of Shizuki Kōen is its space and setting. Inside the actual castle grounds is **Shizukiyama Jinja,** built as recently as 1879; the wood used has weathered to give the shrine a comfortable, reassuring presence. From the top of the castle walls, there is a panoramic view of Hagi, the bay, and the surrounding mountains inland.

★ The **Hana-no-e Teahouse** is set in delightful gardens and exudes peace and tranquillity. The attendants will make the classic, slightly bitter-tasting tea-ceremony *matcha* for you while you drink in the quiet of the gardens. *¥450 tea.*

The best view of the area is from **Shizuki-yama,** which rises up behind the castle. It takes about 20 minutes to hike the path to the top. On one side of Mt. Shizuki there is an amusement park, which is part of a resort hotel that attracts Japanese families but needn't detain you, unless you'd like to take the monorail that climbs Shizuki-yama. *Amusement park ¥1,000.* ☉ *9ᴀᴍ–10:30 ᴘᴍ.*

Hagi Shiryōkan is the local history museum. You will find it on the way back down Mt. Shizuki. If your time is limited, forgo a visit to the museum and head for ☞ Daishō-in, the interesting southern Hagi temple, instead. *Shiryōkan:* ☜ *¥350.* ☉ *Apr.–Oct., daily 9–5; Nov.– Mar., daily 9–4:30.*

Outer Precincts Shrines and Temples

Daishō-in is the counterpart to the more frequented ☞ Tōkō-ji. Screened by the surrounding mountains, Daishō-in is the final resting place for half of the Mōri family: The first two Mōri generations are buried here; the third rests at Tōkō-ji. Thereafter, even-numbered generations of the Mōri generations are buried at Daishō-in, odd-numbered generations at Tōkō-ji. What is unusual about both funerary temples are the lanterns and the placement of the daimyō's wife next to her husband's tomb. Such a close affiliation, or even recognition of the wife, in death was not the custom in feudal Japan. The lanterns tell another story.

When Hidehari Mōri, the first Mōri daimyō to be buried at Daishō-in, died, seven of his principal retainers followed him in death, dutifully committing ritual suicide. Extending this custom further, one of the daimyō's retainers also killed himself. The eight graves are lined up in a row of descending rank. The Tokugawa shogunate realized that this custom could decimate the aristocracy and decreed that such ritual suicide upon the death of one's lord was illegal. Future generations of retainers gave up their suicidal rights and, instead, donated lanterns. The path leading to the main hall of Daishō-in is lined with 603 lanterns. The temple is a special place to visit at any time, but in May the grounds burst into a purple haze of wisteria blossoms. Another special time to visit is from August 13 to 15, when all the lanterns are lit for Obon, the Buddhist festival of the dead.

Daishō-in is in the southern outskirts of Hagi, five minutes west of the JR Hagi Eki. You can take a train from Higashi-Hagi Eki to Hagi Eki or take a bus south to Hagi-eki-mae bus stop. From Shizuki Kōen, Daishō-in is about 20 minutes by bicycle. If you have a bike, cross over the canal that marks the boundary of Shizuki Kōen and follow it south to the Tokiwa-bashi. Once over the Hashimoto-gawa, take the main road that follows the river upstream. Daishō-in is on the right, on the other side of the JR San-in Main Line tracks. ☜ *¥200.* ☉ *Daily 8:30–5.*

Tōkō-ji contains the other cemetery of the Mōri family. Directly east of Matsumoto-bashi, the temple was founded by the Zen priest Domio in 1691 under the auspices of Yoshinari Mōri, the third lord of Hagi. It is here that he (and every succeeding odd-numbered generation of the Mōri family) is buried. You enter the temple grounds through the three-story San-mon (gate) to reach the Main Hall, which contains rather garish images of Buddha. Behind this building are the monuments of the Mōri lords and their wives. Needless to say, it is easy to point to the husbands' graves; they are the grandest of all. Amid pine trees, ranks of 500 stone lanterns lead the way on small, moss-covered lanes to the daimyōs' monuments. The retainers of the Mōri daimyō donated these lanterns upon the deaths of their lords. On August 15, during the Obon festival, all of the lanterns are lit—an impressive sight, indeed.

If you are coming from Daishō-in on foot, take the train from Hagi Eki to Higashi-Hagi Eki, then walk south to Matsumoto-bashi and turn left to cross the river. If you have a bicycle, return to Hashimoto-gawa, follow it upstream to Hashimoto Bridge, then head into central Hagi. At the Bōchō Bus Center, turn right and cross Matsumoto-bashi over the river. ☎ *0838/22–4643.* ☎ *¥200.* ☉ *Daily 8:30–5.*

The **Monument to Shōin Yoshida** (1830–59) commemorates an important era in Japanese history. Yoshida was a revolutionary. With the coming of Commodore Matthew Perry's Black Ships in 1853, Shōin recognized the need for Japan to step out of feudalism and accept certain Western practices. In his quest to understand the West, he attempted to slip aboard an American ship. He was caught by the shogunate, imprisoned, and later sent home to Hagi to be kept under house arrest. During his arrest, he started expounding a liberal philosophy that suggested both adapting to Western practices and introducing democratic elements into government. In the eyes of the shogunate, these preachings were outright sedition. At age 29, Shōin was executed. His execution inflamed and united the antishogunate elements of Hagi and the Namoto Province (now Yamaguchi Prefecture). The monument is within walking distance of Tōkō-ji.

Shōin Jinja, with the Shōka Sonjuku, was the private school that Shōin founded to teach his students his revolutionary philosophy. At the shrine's exit there is a museum that recounts Shōin's life depicted in three-dimensional scenes with model figures. There are, however, no English explanations of their meaning. Come down the hill from Yoshida's monument, and take a left turn. You will pass the house of one of Shōin's students, Hirobumi Ito, the first prime minister of Japan. The shrine is across the street from the **Ito House.** From Shōin Jinja you can cross the Matsumoto-bashi and go straight to Ta-machi Mall and the center of Hagi. ☞ *Shrine-school ¥550.* ☉ *Daily 8:30–5.*

Dining and Lodging

$$ ✕ **Higaku-Mangoku.** One of the delights of traveling along the San-in coast is enjoying the seafood. For each season the cold waters of the Nihon-kai produce some of the sweetest delicacies, and there is no finer place in Hagi than this to try them. Most of the fish is served as sashimi, but a few items are lightly grilled, and the crabs are boiled. ✉ *Shimo Goken-machi,* ☎ *0838/22–2136. No credit cards.*

$$ ✕ **Nakon-mu.** This is one of Hagi's better reasonably priced restaurants. The set menu (¥2,500) might include sashimi, baked fish, fish grilled in soy sauce, mountain vegetables, miso soup, and steamed rice. Nakon-mu has tatami and Western seating but no English menu (select your food from the window display). ✉ *Furu-Hagi-chō,* ☎ *0838/ 22–6619. Reservations not accepted. No credit cards.*

$ ✕ **Fujita-ya.** This is a casual restaurant, full of color, where locals de-
★ light in handmade *soba* (buckwheat noodles) and hot tempura served on handmade Japanese cypress trays. ✉ *Kumagai-chō,* ☎ *0838/22–ₓ 1086. No credit cards. Closed 2nd and 4th Wed. of month.*

$$$$ ☵ **Hokumon Yashiki.** This elegant ryokan with luxurious rooms overlooks a garden. The gracious and refined service makes you feel pampered in a style to which the ancient Mōri clan were surely accustomed. Japanese meals are served in your room. The inn is in the samurai section, near the castle grounds. ✉ *210 Horiuchi, Hagi, Yamaguchi-ken*

758, ☎ *0838/22–7521,* FAX *0838/22–7521. 42 Japanese-style rooms, 5 Western-style rooms. No credit cards.*

$$–$$$ 🏨 **Hagi Grand Hotel.** Convenience to the JR Higashi-Hagi Eki makes this the number one choice for an international-style hotel in Hagi. The staff here is helpful, and guest rooms, half of which are Western style, are relatively spacious. There are Japanese- and Western-style restaurants on site. ✉ *25 Furu-Hagi-chō, Hagi, Yamaguchi-ken 758,* ☎ *0838/25–1211,* FAX *0838/25–4422. 190 rooms. 2 restaurants, shops, travel services. AE, DC, MC, V.*

$$ 🏨 **Hotel Royal.** In the Rainbow Building above JR Higashi-Hagi Eki, this business hotel is friendly and efficient. Guest rooms are on the small size, but they are clean and comfortable. Business travelers and tourists stay here, and the front desk can arrange bicycle rentals for you. ✉ *3000-5 Chinto, Hagi, Yamaguchi-ken 758,* ☎ *0838/25–9595,* FAX *0838/25–8434. 51 Japanese-style rooms, 4 Western-style rooms. AE, DC, MC, V.*

$–$$ 🏨 **Hifumi Ryokan.** Although the carpets in the ground-floor lounge and along the corridors aren't exactly pristine, the tatami rooms here are clean and well kept. Many have a private bath and a separate alcove with two easy chairs and a table. Ask for a quiet room; those facing the main street suffer from traffic noise. The food, served in your room, is above average but not as interesting as it should be with the Nihon-kai so close. The common bath is small and can be congested just before dinner, so time yourself accordingly. Just across the bridge from the JR Higashi-Hagi Eki, on your right, Hifumi is 1½ km (1 mi) from the center of Hagi. Bicycles can be rented nearby. ✉ *13 Hijiwara, Hagi, Yamaguchi-ken 758,* ☎ *0838/22–0123,* FAX *0838/25–3593. 25 Japanese-style rooms, 10 with bath. No credit cards.*

$–$$ 🏨 **Minshuku Susa.** Instead of staying in Hagi, consider taking one of
★ this minshuku's huge rooms—at least 10-tatami in size, with an alcove for a coffee table and two chairs. The best rooms look onto the harbor of this picturesque fishing village between Hagi and Masuda on the Nihon-kai. The shared bathroom is splendid, with an iron Goemon tub (Goemon Ishikawa, a Japanese version of Robin Hood, was boiled alive). Traditional service includes such niceties as an orange in the bath to scent the water. No English is spoken, but the staff's friendliness overcomes any language barrier. Dinner served in a tatami-floor dining room is an occasion to try the region's seafood delicacies. ✉ *Irie, Susa-chō, Abu-gun, Yamaguchi-ken, 690,* ☎ *08387/6–2408. 6 rooms, 2 with private toilet. Dining room. No credit cards.*

$ 🏨 **Fujita Ryokan.** This two-story concrete building is Hagi's best choice for inexpensive accommodations. The tatami rooms are standard but better kept than at the nearby Higashi-Hagi Minshuku, and the common bath is clean. There is a small lounge for relaxing. Ask for a room facing the river and with luck you'll see fishermen at work when you wake up. The owners do like their guests to take two meals (Japanese breakfast and dinner) here, but if you would prefer to dine elsewhere, you might be able to arrange to do so. Fujita is across the river from downtown Hagi, a five-minute walk from JR Higashi-Hagi Eki. ✉ *Shinkawa Nishi-ku, Hagi, Yamaguchi-ken 758,* ☎ *0838/22–0603,* FAX *0838/26–1240. 13 Japanese-style rooms. V.*

Getting Around

The most convenient way to get to Hagi is by crossing the mountains from the San-yō town of Ogōri, at which the Hiroshima–Hakata Shinkansen stops. From Ogōri, you can take a train to Tsuwano, then continue to Hagi by bus. You can also travel directly to Hagi from Ogōri by JR bus, which is the quicker way. Without a JR Pass, the one-way bus fare is about ¥2,000 (☎ 0838/22–3816 for bus center). Remember, the bus is covered by the JR Pass, even if some JR-seat reservation clerks seem to think otherwise.

The ideal way to explore Hagi is by bicycle, and there are many outlets where you can rent a bike for approximately ¥1,000 per day. Try the shop across from the Rainbow Building, left of the station plaza. Alternatively, you can hire a "sightseeing taxi" (¥4,300 per hour); it takes about three hours to complete a hurried city tour.

The **Bōchō Bus Company's** four-hour sightseeing bus tour (Japanese-speaking guides only) departs from the Bōchō Bus Station on the eastern edge of the central city. The ¥2,810 fare, plus ¥1,200 for lunch, varies with the departure time; the 8:35 AM tour from Higashi-Hagi is the best deal.

Visitor Information

For local information at the station try **Hagi Ryokan Kyōdō-kumiai** (☎ 0838/22–7599, FAX 0838/24–2202). Its main business is booking accommodations, but its English-speaking owner, Mr. Oki, serves as a helpful adviser to tourists and dispenses official guide maps. The agency is in the Rainbow Building to the left of the station, in the first office on the left side of the shopping arcade. The **City Tourist Office** is downtown (☎ 0838/25–3131 or 0838/25–1750).

En Route   The next San-in stop is Tsuwano, nestled inland in the mountains. En route between Hagi and Masuda is the small fishing village of **Susa**, on an attractive bay. Few foreigners ever come here, and it has one of Japan's best minshuku (☞ Lodging, *above*).

Tsuwano

★ ⓱   *1 hr northeast of Ogōri by JR Yamaguchi Line. Ogōri is 1 hr west of Hiroshima by Shinkansen.*

The castle town of Tsuwano is much smaller than Hagi. Because of that, it has a more intimate atmosphere, and you can quickly come to feel part of the town and its 700-year history. Like other treasured Old Japan towns, Tsuwano is occasionally referred to as a "little Kyōto"— for its genteel qualities and for the river that flows through town. But Tsuwano's uniqueness needs no comparison to Kyōto. This mountain town is small and compact, often shrouded in mists drifting through the valley that give it a surreal effect.

Except for its stone walls, nothing is left of the mountaintop castle. Tsuwano's other attraction, the multicolored carp that fill the waters of the Tsuwano-gawa and the water-filled ditches, is still much in evidence. Indeed, the carp outnumber Tsuwano's residents by 10 to 1. Carp were originally introduced into the river and sewers as a ready source of food should the town ever be under siege. There was no siege, and because carp live about 60 years, they have had a rather privileged existence. Life is still good for them. If you make your way from the JR eki to Tono-machi (a 5-minute walk), you can feed these exotic-colored fish, swimming in the ditches along the street, with "carp snacks" bought at the coffee shop across from the Catholic church. If you're so inclined, you might like to dine on carp at the Yuki Restaurant on Hōnchō-dōri, close to the post office.

The **Catholic church,** built in 1931, is a reminder of the time when Christianity was outlawed in Japan. In 1865, in an effort to disperse Christian strongholds and cause them extreme hardship—with the hope that they would recant their faith—the Tokugawa shogunate transported 153 Christians from Nagasaki to Tsuwano. By the time the Meiji government lifted the ban on Christianity, 53 Christians remained in Tsuwano. Thirty-six had been martyred; the rest had either recanted or died of natural causes. It's worth stopping at the church: Where else but Japan can you find a Catholic church whose floors are covered with tatami?

The **Shiryōkan** was originally a feudal school where the sons of samurai would train in the arts of manhood. Today, in its fencing hall, there is a folk-craft museum. It is a few steps past the Catholic church on the left side of Tono-machi-dōri. ☎ 08567/2–1000. ✉ ¥200. ☉ Daily 8:30–5.

The **Kyōdōkan** is a museum with a collection of exhibits that recount regional history. At the top of Tono-machi-dōri, the road crosses the Tsuwano-gawa. You will find it just on the other side of the Ōhashi (bridge). ✉ ¥450. ☉ Daily 8:30–5; closed Dec. 29–Jan. 3.

The **Taikodani Inari Jinja** is one of the five most important Inari shrines in Japan. The approach resembles a tunnel, because you pass under numerous red torii—1,174 of them—to reach the shrine high on the cliffside. Or you can opt out of the ascent on a bus that takes another road. **Yasaka Jinja** is another shrine on site where, every July 20, 24, and 27, the festival of the Heron Dance Festival is held.

To get to **Tsuwano-jō,** you can either hike a hard 20 minutes up to the site from **Taikodani Inari Jinja** or take the road down the other side of the shrine to the chairlift, which takes five minutes to reach the base of the castle grounds. To ascend the summit from the top of the chairlift requires a further eight-minute walk. Whichever way you make it to the top, it is worth every effort. The view from the place where this mountaintop castle once stood sweeps over the tiled-roof town of Tsuwano and the valley below. What a marvelous castle it must have been! The original edifice was built in the 13th century over the course of 30 years. Its demise took a lot less time. Like Hagi-jō, this castle was dismantled during the Meiji Restoration as a sign of good faith. You can walk back down from the castle grounds to the main street or use the chairlift (¥450). Because the views from the chairlift are so superb, you might prefer the latter.

The **Old House of Ōgai Mori** is a brief and worthwhile visit. Ōgai Mori (1862–1922) was one of the prominent literary figures in the Meiji Restoration. He spent only his first 11 years in Tsuwano (he went to the Yōrōkan school), but his hometown never forgot him, nor he his hometown. His success as a doctor led him to travel overseas, and in so doing, he tried to reconcile the differences between Western and Japanese cultures. His tomb is at **Yōmei-ji** (¥300), open daily 8:30–5, a temple east of the JR Tsuwano Eki. To get to the house from the bottom of the chairlift, turn left and then right to cross over the Tsuwano-gawa. Immediately on crossing the river, take the right-hand street and follow it around to the left. From the center of town, take a bus west to Kyūkyo-mae stop, from which the house is a short walk.

Sekishūkan displays *washi,* Japanese handmade paper. There are demonstrations of papermaking, as well as a display of Iwami-style paper. On the second floor there are displays of washi made from other regions of Japan. If you have not seen the process of creating handmade paper or wish to compare different regional types, this is a good museum to visit. It is next door to the Mori House (☞ *above*). ✉ Free. ☉ Daily 8:30–5.

The **Tsuwano Photo Gallery** displays the photographs of contemporary Japanese photographers, which might provide a welcome respite from old Japan. It's across the parking lot from the Tourist Information Office, in front of the train station. ☎ 08567/2–3171. ¥200. ☉ Daily 9–5.

St. Maria's Church was built in 1951 to commemorate the Christian martyrs, whose plight is portrayed in the stained-glass windows. The Pass of the Virgin (in Japanese, *otome-tōge*) is the site of the grave-yard where 36 martyrs have their crosses. The church is five minutes east of the JR eki, up the hill through the Pass of the Virgin.

A surprising local find is Tsuwano's **Katsushika Hokusai Museum,** just a block from the train station. Katsushika Hokusai (1760–1849) was the famous *ukiyo-e* ("floating world") painter from the end of the Toku-gawa era who influenced future generations of painters both in Japan and overseas. This museum exhibits his wood-block prints, illustrated books, and paintings. ☎ 08567/2–1850. ⊠ ¥450. ☉ *Daily 9:30–5.*

A recent addition to Tsuwano's attractions is a **geyser,** which erupts 175 ft into the air every 5 to 10 minutes. It is across from Washibara Hachiman-gū. ☎ 08567/468–7883.

Dining and Lodging

$$ ✕ **Yūki.** This restaurant is famous for its carp dishes (such as carp sashimi and carp miso soup) and mountain vegetables. The decor includes tra-ditional beams and a stream running through the center of the dining room. There are sunken pits for your feet under the tables. ⊠ *Hon-chō-dōri,* ☎ 08567/2–0162. *No credit cards. Closed Thurs.*

$ ✕ **Hibaya.** A pub could get no tinier than this. There are only six stools at the counter, and Mama-san behind has barely enough room to turn. Somehow, though, she is able to make up *yaki-soba* (noodles fried Chi-nese style), fried dumplings, hotpots, and horse-meat sashimi for her clients and keep the beer and sake flowing. Although she speaks no more than 20 words of English, she'll make you feel welcome, and what may have begun as a quick drink will end up as a full evening of food and amiable company. ⊠ *Higashi-dōri,* ☎ 08567/2–2288. *Reserva-tions not accepted. No credit cards.*

$$ 🏨 **Sunroute Tsuwano.** This is the only place in town that has Western-style accommodations. Rooms, as in other Sunroute hotels, are compact: The mass-produced furniture is crammed in. Bathrooms are plastic mod-ules with tiny bathtubs. Still, all is clean, and the staff, though unable to speak English, is friendly. There is a restaurant and bar, but it is better to eat in and then drink in town. The down side is that the hotel is a stiff 10-minute walk from town and the station. ⊠ *Terada, Tsuwano-chō, Kanoashi-gun, Yamaguchi-ken 699,* ☎ 0856/72–3232, ℻ 08567/2–2805. *50 Western-style rooms. Restaurant, bar. AE, MC, V.*

$$ 🏨 **Tsuwano Onsen Kanko Hotel.** This pleasant establishment is the most centrally located hotel in town, with fair-size guest rooms and friendly staff. The furnishings have become worn and drab, however, and the Japanese restaurant is only passable. Western-style breakfast is avail-able on request. ⊠ *Ushiroda, Tsuwano-machi, Kanoashi-gun, Yama-guchi-ken 699-56,* ☎ 08567/2–0333, ℻ 08567/2–1543. *19 rooms, 31 with bath. Restaurant. AE, V.*

$ 🏨 **Wakasagi-no-Yado.** Despite the limited English of the family who
★ runs this small minshuku, the staff is eager to help overseas tourists and will meet you at Tsuwano Eki, an eight-minute walk away. Typi-cal of minshuku, there is a common bath. Japanese and Western break-fast is served. ⊠ *Mori, Tsuwano-chō, Kanoashi-gun, Yamaguchi-ken 699-56,* ☎ 08567/2–1146. *8 rooms. No credit cards.*

Getting Around

Taking JR trains from Hagi to Tsuwano is problematic: Service is lim-ited and train-changing in Masuda involves long layovers. It is best to take a bus from Hagi's Bōchō Bus Center directly to Tsuwano, a trip that takes two hours (¥2,000). This is not covered by the JR Pass, but because travel time is a good hour less than by JR, it may be worth the expense.

In Tsuwano, all sights are within easy walking distance. You could also rent a bicycle. Four rental shops are located around the station plaza (¥800 for three hours, ¥1,050 for a full day). Taxis cost ¥10,400 for two hours and ¥15,600 for three hours; it takes about two to three hours to visit the sights.

Visitor Information

There is a **Tourist Information Office** (☎ 08567/2–1144), open daily 9–5, at the railway station that has free brochures and will help in securing accommodations.

En Route   The next stop east along the San-in coast is Matsue. However, you may want to break off of the trip an hour before Matsue and visit Izumo Taisha, the second most visited shrine in Japan after the Grand Shrines at Ise. If so, leave the train at Izumo and take the JR Taisha Line to the shrine.

Matsue and Izumo Taisha

Of all the towns and cities in the San-in district, **Matsue** is the one best known as a summer vacation spot. Like the rest of San-in, though, Matsue sees few gai-jin, yet it is rich in beauty and heritage. Only scattered archaeological remains exist from the days when the people of "The Eightfold-Towering-Thunderhead Land of Izumo" lived here in the 2nd and 3rd centuries, and only ruins have been left behind of Matsue's early days, when the town became the capital of the Izumo in the 8th century. Many of the shrines still standing do originate from that time, and the more recent past is also visible. Matsue is the only town along the San-in coast with part of its castle intact. In fact, Matsue's castle is one of the dozen castles in Japan that are originals and not ferroconcrete replicas.

Matsue's location, inland from the Nihon-kai at the conjunction of two small lagoons, is unique. Known as the City of Water, Matsue lies at a point where the lagoon Naka-umi, to the east, connects with Lake Shinji, to the west. This makes Matsue a culinary haven, with not only fresh fish taken from the cold waters of the Nihon-kai but also the seven delicacies—eel, shrimp, shellfish, carp, sea bass, pond smelt, and whitebait—from Lake Shinji. The narrow isthmus between Naka-umi and Lake Shinji divides the city. Most of Matsue's points of interest lie on the northern side of the isthmus; the JR eki, the bus terminal, and the majority of the population are on the south side.

No matter how many shrines you visit in Japan, **Izumo Taisha** never fails to impress. Once a shrine on pilings that may have been as tall as 330 ft, this Taisha still humbles with its large torii at the entrance and the serene walk through towering pines to the shrine grounds. Since Izumo Taisha was one of three kingdoms that united to form the core of the emperor's legendary lineage, it only stands to reason that marriages are especially blessed when performed here.

Matsue

⓲ *3½ hrs northeast of Tsuwano by JR Limited Express, 5 hrs northeast of Hiroshima by JR Geibi and Kitsugi lines (1 train daily departs Hiroshima at 8:45 AM), 2 hrs and 25 mins northwest of Okayama by JR Yakumo Limited Express (13 daily).*

★   The place to start is **Matsue-jō** and its environs, diagonally across town from the JR eki. Made entirely out of pine, Matsue-jō was built in 1611, and with a partial reconstruction in 1642, it was never ransacked or burned during the Tokugawa shogunate. Amazingly, soon after the Meiji Restoration, the castle was put on the auction block. Sentimental locals, whose ancestors had been living under its shadow for 345 years, pooled their resources and purchased the castle for posterity.

Yoshiharu Horio built the castle for protection. The donjon is, incidentally, the tallest (98 ft) left in Japan. Camouflaged among the surrounding trees, Matsue-jō seems to move with the shadows of San-in's opaque light. Note the overhanging eaves above the top floor, designed to cut down glare that might have prevented the spotting of an attacking force. The castle is a fabulously preserved structure, with six interior levels belied by a facade that suggests only five. The lower floors exhibit a collection of samurai swords and armor. The climb to the uppermost floor is worth it—the view encompasses the city, Lake Shinji, and the distant mountains.

Take the bus (¥200) to Ken-chō-mae from either stop No. 1 or stop No. 2, both in front of the JR eki. (The same buses continue on to Matsue Onsen, should you want to go there first to check into a hotel.) It is about a 10-minute ride to the castle, and the Ken-chō-mae stop is near the Prefectural Government Office. When you leave the bus, walk a little farther to the north; the castle, in Jōzen Kōen, is on the left. ☎ 0852/21–4030. 🎟 ¥500. ⊙ Daily 8:30–6.

The **Matsue Kyōdokan** (Matsue Cultural Museum) displays art, folk craft, and implements, including such items as *bentō* (lunch boxes) and hairpins, used during the first three imperial eras after the fall of the Tokugawa shogunate. The Kyōdokan is in a Western-style building on the first tier of your climb toward the castle. ☎ 0852/22–3958. 🎟 ¥200. ⊙ Daily 8:30–5.

Lord Fumai Matsudaira of the Matsue clan built the **Meimei-an Teahouse** in 1779, and it is one of the best-preserved teahouses of the period. You must walk up a long flight of stairs to this thatched-roof teahouse, but your effort will be rewarded by both a fine view of Matsue-jō and, if you so desire, tea. To get here, leave Jōzen Kōen at its east exit and follow the moat going north; at the top of the park a road leads to the right. The teahouse is a little way up this road, no more than a five-minute walk. 🎟 ¥200, ¥350 green tea. ⊙ Daily 9–5.

Buke Yashiki is a samurai house built in 1730. It is the first of four historical sights that stand next door to each other. Samurai at this time lived fairly well, depending on their rank. This house belonged to the Shiomi family, a chief retainer to the daimyō, and you'll notice the separate servant quarters, a shed for the palanquin, and slats in the walls to allow cooling breezes to flow through the rooms. These four sights are right on the main road at the base of the side street on which ☞ **Meimei-an Teahouse** is located (keep the castle moat on your left). ☎ 0852/22–2243. 🎟 ¥250. ⊙ Apr.–Sept., daily 9–6; Oct.–Mar., daily 8:30–5.

The **Tanabe Art Museum** is dedicated mainly to objects of the tea ceremony and beautiful contemporary ceramics from the region. It is next to ☞ Buke Yashiki. ☎ 0852/26–2211. 🎟 ¥500 (varies with exhibition). ⊙ Tues.–Sun. 9–4:30; closed Dec. 29–Jan. 1.

The **Koizumi Yakumo Kyūkyo** (Lafcadio Hearn Residence), next to the ☞ Tanabe Art Museum, has remained unchanged since Koizumi left Matsue in 1891. Koizumi (1850–1904) was born of an Irish father and a Greek mother and was christened Lafcadio Hearn. He spent his early years in Greece, which he left to study in Britain before traveling to the United States, where he became a journalist. In 1890 he traveled to Japan and soon became a teacher in Matsue. During his tenure he met a samurai's daughter, who nursed him when he fell sick. Recovered, he married her and later became a Japanese citizen, taking the name Koizumi Yakumo. He spent only 15 months in Matsue, but it was here that he became enthralled with Japan, and in his writings—*Japan: An Interpretation* and *In Ghostly Japan*, among others—he helped introduce Japan to the West. He died at the age of 54 while working as a professor at Waseda University in Tōkyō. ☎ 0852/23–0714. ☒ ¥200. ⊘ *Daily 9–4:30.*

The **Koizumi Yakumo Kinenkan** (Lafcadio Hearn Memorial Hall), contains a good collection of Koizumi's manuscripts and other items, including his desk, that reflect his life in Japan. If at all possible, read his essay "In a Japanese Garden," contained in the volume *Glimpses of Unfamiliar Japan*, in which he writes his impressions of Matsue. You will surely be asked by every local resident whether you are familiar with his work. It is adjacent to Koizumi Yakumo's former home. Two minutes from the Memorial Hall is the Hearn Kyūkyo bus stop, where you can catch a bus back to Matsue's center and the JR eki. ☎ 0852/21–2147. ☒ ¥250. ⊘ *Daily 8:30–5.*

The main shopping street, Kyōmise Shopping Arcade, is just before the bridge to the JR eki. However, you may prefer to shop for crafts at the **Matsue Meisan Center** (open daily 9–6), next to the smartest hotel in town, the Ichibata (☞ *Dining and Lodging, below*). (You can also shop on the north shore of Lake Shinji in the area known as Matsue Onsen.) At the center, products from all over Shimane Prefecture are on display and for sale, and on its fourth floor, performances of folk dances are given four times a day. The Tourist Information Office at the JR eki has the current schedule. ☒ *Performances ¥500 (buy tickets at tourist office).*

Should dusk soon be falling, position yourself to see the sun set over **Lake Shinji.** You can watch from the Matsue Meisan Center or from Shinjiko Ōhashi, the first bridge over to the south side of Matsue (the same side as the JR eki).

Izumo Taisha and Hino-misaki (Cape Hino)

⑲ *1 hr west of Matsue by Ichibata Dentetsu (electric railway).*

Izumo Taisha claims the oldest site for a shrine in Japan, though the contemporary structure was built in 1874. After you enter through the giant torii, there is a 15-minute walk along a pine-shaded path. At the end of the path stands the impressive Main Hall, shielded by a double fence so that—like the Ise Jingū—one can only catch glimpses of the architectural style, which is representative of Japan's oldest shrine construction. The taisha is dedicated to a male god, Ō-Kuni-Nushi, known as the creator of the land. Over time, his role has broadened to include managing fruitful relationships such as marriage and, even more recently, corporate mergers.

Notice the very steep, gabled roof of compressed bark descending from the ridge line, which runs from front to back rather than from side to side. Notice, too, that the ornately carved beams at the roof peak have their ends beveled perpendicular to the ground, an indication that the shrine is dedicated to a male god. Shrines dedicated to female gods have their crossed beams beveled parallel to the ground.

On either side of the compound there are two rectangular buildings that are said to be the home of the Shintō gods, who meet annually at the shrine in October (the lunar month, which often falls in our November). That is why in the rest of Japan, the lunar October is referred to as Kanna-zuki (Month Without Gods), while in Izumo, October is called Kamiari-zuki (Month with Gods). This is where Japan was born, where her mythology was founded, and where the invading and successful Yamato and Izumo peoples accommodated each other's gods during the 2nd and 3rd centuries.

If you would like to go out to **Hino-misaki**, exit the temple grounds to the west and take an hourly bus from the Ichibata Bus Terminal for the 25-minute ride (¥1,150). The seascape contains more of the beauty you see all along the San-in coast when traveling between Hagi and Matsue. The lighthouse on the cape is open to the public, and you can climb the 127 ft to the top (remove your shoes first). Built in 1903, **Hino-misaki Lighthouse** is Japan's tallest, and it beams its light 21 nautical mi out to sea. For your climb, you will receive a certificate of ascent. ☜ ¥150. ⊘ Apr.–Sept., daily 8:30–4; Oct.–Mar., daily 9–4.

Hino-misaki Jinja is a Kasuga shrine dedicated to the goddess Amiterasu Ōmikami. This means that it is brightly painted in orange and white, typical of the Kasuga style. The most well-known shrine of this style is in Nara, but be sure to take 20 minutes out of your schedule to walk out on the road you came in on to see this shrine—the majestic cliffs and aquamarine bays somehow demand such colorful images. ☜ Free. ⊘ Daily 9–5.

Dining and Lodging

$$ ✕ **Ginsen Restaurant.** Ginsen is popular with locals for its fresh seafood casseroles. The season determines what these are, and with Lake Shinji on hand, the fish is superb and the prices are reasonable. The restaurant is across from the Green Hotel a few blocks west of the north exit of the JR Matsue Eki. ⊠ Asahi-machi, Matsue, ☎ 0852/21–2381. No credit cards.

$-$$ ✕ **Kawabata Sushi.** Take sweet, succulent fish from the Nihon-kai, com-
★ bine them with top-rate sushi chefs, and you have Kawabata. No English is spoken, but the chefs will make you feel comfortable, and you can point to the fish that take your fancy. The long counter bar is a good place to sit and watch the action, but there are also tables with tatami seating. This sushi bar has more atmosphere than many, with Japanese drums hanging from the walls. The restaurant is upstairs from a spacious entrance hall—models of the dishes are displayed in a window downstairs—three short blocks from the Matsue Washington Hotel. Walk left from the hotel's entrance to where the street becomes a pedestrian-only mall and then take a right. The restaurant is at the next corner on your right. ⊠ Off Kyōmise Arcade, Matsue, ☎ 0852/21–0689. Reservations not accepted. No credit cards.

$ ✕ **Daikichi.** For having fun and socializing with locals, this yakitori bar with counter service offers a delightful evening's entertainment, good grilled chicken, and flowing sake. The owner, Toshiyuki Hidaka, speaks great English and is wonderfully friendly to foreigners. Two doors from Ginsen restaurant, it's easily recognized by its red lanterns outside. ⊠ Asahi-machi, Matsue, ☎ 0852/31–8308. No credit cards. No lunch.

$$$ ✕🏠 **Minami-kan.** This is Matsue's most elegant and prestigious ryokan,
★ tastefully furnished and known for its refined service. It also has the best restaurant in Matsue for kaiseki haute cuisine and tai-meshi (sea bream with rice). Even if you do not stay here, make reservations for dinner. ⊠ Ōhashi, Matsue, Shimane-ken 690, ☎ 0852/21–5131, FAX 0852/26–0351. 9 rooms. Restaurant. DC, MC, V.

$$–$$$ 🏠 **Hotel Ichibata.** In the spa section of town, next to Lake Shinji, the Ichibata appeals if you're on a restful vacation and want to enjoy the thermal waters—or a busy trip and need relief. For a long time, the hotel has been the leading place to stay in central San-in. Guest

rooms facing the lake are the nicest, and the most expensive. All Japanese-style rooms face the lake; not so those in Western-style. Still, if you do not mind the 20-minute walk from the station or downtown (or a ¥ 1,000 taxi ride), the Ichibata is Matsue's first choice. Beware of its vermilion lounge on the penthouse floor, however, for even if the view of the sunsets over Lake Shinji is spectacular, you may be charged $40 for two small glasses of beer. ⊠ *30 Chidōri-chō, Matsue, Shimane-ken 690,* ☎ *0852/22–0188,* ℻ *0852/22–0230. 148 rooms, half Western style. 2 restaurants, beer garden, hot springs. AE, DC, MC, V.*

$$ 🏨 **Matsue Washington Hotel.** The rooms here are modern but very small; take a more expensive room if you don't want to trip over your suitcase. The coffee shop on the ground floor serves both as a lounge and a place for light meals. There is also a formal restaurant serving *shabu-shabu* and other Japanese meals. The big advantage of this business hotel is its location in the old downtown section of Matsue, where restaurants abound. There's a pedestrian mall lined with shops nearby, the castle is a 10-minute walk away, and the lake is even closer. ⊠ *Higashi Hon-machi 2-22, Matsue, Shimane-ken,* ☎ *0852/22–4111,* ℻ *0852/ 22–4120. 158 rooms. 2 restaurants, coffee shop. AE, DC, MC, V.*

Less expensive (about ¥4,200) accommodations close to the JR eki are the business hotels—the 🏨 **Green Hotel** (☎ 0852/27–3000) and the 🏨 **Business Yamamoto** (☎ 0852/21–6121)—or two small, 10-room lodging houses, the 🏨 **Business Ishida** (☎ 0852/25–0452) and the popular 🏨 **Ryokan Terazuya** (☎ 0852/21–3480), both of which have only Japanese-style rooms.

Getting Around

Matsue. An added delight of Matsue is that, even though its population is 140,000, most of its sights are within walking distance of each other. Where they are not, Matsue has a comprehensive bus system. If you would like to have some local company on your tour of Matsue, the city has a Goodwill Guide Program, in which English-speaking volunteers show you around the city or escort you to Izumo Taisha. There is no charge for this, though you should pay your guide's expenses, including lunch. To arrange for a Goodwill Guide, contact the **Matsue Tourist Information Office,** Asahi-machi, Matsue (☎ 0852/27–2598), a day in advance. The office is in the JR Matsue Eki and is open daily 9:30–6. You can also use this office to collect free maps and brochures.

Izumo. To go from Matsue Onsen to Taisha, the location of Izumo Taisha, takes only one hour on the Ichibata Dentetsu (electric railway, ¥790). You will need to change trains at Kawato Eki for the final leg to Izumo Taisha-mae Eki. The shrine is a five-minute walk from there.

You can also get there by taking the JR train from Matsue Eki back to Izumo, then transferring to the JR Taisha Line and taking that to Taisha Eki, where you can either take a 5-minute bus ride to Taisha-mae Eki or walk directly to the shrine in about 20 minutes. The only advantages of using the JR trains are the savings of using a JR Rail Pass (if you have one) and arriving at the ornate, palace-style JR Taisha Eki—it is quite an oddity.

En Route You might consider making a couple of stops on the way from Izumo or Matsue to Tottori. The town of **Yasugi** is best known for the **Adachi Museum of Art,** which exhibits the works of both past and contemporary Japanese artists and has an inspiring series of gardens. ⊠ *320 Furukawa-chō, Yasugi, Shimane-ken,* ☎ *0854/28–7111.* 🎫 *¥2,200, ½ price if you show your passport.* ☺ *Mon.–Sun. 9–4:30.*

Mount Daisen, popular with hikers, is a volcanic cone that locals liken to Mt. Fuji. In autumn the beauty of the region is particularly worth a detour. On the slopes above the town of Daisen there is an ancient Tendai sect temple, **Daisen-ji.** A few sub-temples have lodgings, such as Dōmyō-in (☎ 0859/52–2038) and Renjō-in (☎ 0859/52–2506)— novelist Shiga Naoya stayed at the latter and used the setting for the ending of his *A Dark Night's Passing.* These cost about ¥6,300 per person with two meals. There are also several overpriced minshuku, such as the well-worn and dormitory-like Hakuun-so (✉ 25 Daisen, Daisen-chō, Saihaku-gun, Tottori-ken, ☎ 0859/52–2331), which costs around ¥8,000 per person, including two meals. Buses leave the non-descript town of Yonago every hour for the 50-minute ride to **Daisen** (¥730).

Farther up the coast toward Tottori, **Misasa Onsen** is a revered 1,000-year-old hot-spring resort claiming the hottest, highest radium waters in the country. The closest train station is Kurayoshi, from which a 25-minute bus ride takes you to the town of Misasa Onsen.

Oki Islands

 1 hr northeast of Matsue by bus via Shichirui (¥1,100) and ferry (¥2,530).

The history of the Oki Islands as a place of exile for dethroned Emperors and fallen nobility somehow continues to reside in the islands' stark, harsh landscape, and their odd attractions. One noteworthy local activity is the bloodless bullfighting, in which two bulls pair off against each other in a ring. You can also find this bullfighting on Shikoku and Okinawa, but it is said to have originated here out of the exiles' boredom. There are four principle islands—more than a hundred others are little more than boulders peaking out above the waves. Chiburi Island is considered to have the most striking natural beauty, while the red cliffs of Nishi-no-shima and the temples on Naka-no-shima are interesting enough. (Nishi-no-shima is the least appealing, despite its cliff-side views.) The most complete island, Dogo, is also the largest: Its beaches, cliffs, flora, and temples are as scenic as those on the other islands, and they are all part of a great, parklike setting. The pleasure of a trip to the Oki Islands is in the sum of its parts: coastal rock formations, a little fishing, the sumōlike phenomenon of the bull v. bull fights, and just getting away from the bustle of the mainland.

Dining and Lodging

Dogo's town of Saigo-chō is full of what the Japanese call "snacks," rather than full-service restaurants, so it is best to stay at either a ryokan or a hotel where meals are included. The only city with mainland-style Western or Japanese hotels is Saigo, on Dogo Island. There are also ryokan and minshuku; camping is available as well if you feel like roughing it. Two worthy Dogo hotels are **Island Hotel Shimaji** (✉ Minato-machi, Saigo-chō, Oki-gun, Shimane-ken 685, ☎ 08512/2–1569; 38 rooms; Restaurant; AE, V), which serves beautiful meals full of freshly caught fish, and the recently built **Oki Viewport Hotel** directly across from the ferry (✉ Naka-machi, Saigo-chō, Oki-gun, Shimane-ken 685, ☎ 08512/2–7007, ℻ 08512/2-7020; 160 rooms; 2 restaurants; AE, DC, MC, V).

Arriving and Departing

Oki Line (☎ 08512/2–1122) boats leave from Sakai-Minato for the islands. Because it is very expensive to bring a car over on the ferry, either rent a car in Saigo, or on Dogo use the bus system to get around the island. Travel between the islands is nearly as expensive as traveling back to the mainland, so plan ahead which islands you'll visit.

Visitor Information

Tourist Association (☎ 08512/2–1577, FAX 08512/2–1406) is particularly helpful with September bull tournament details, which change annually.

Tottori Dunes

㉑ *2 hrs west of Matsue by JR San-in Main Line, 4½ hrs north of Ōsaka by Bantan and San-in Main lines.*

The reason for stepping off the train at Tottori is to visit the *sakyū* (dunes). A unique feature of the San-in coast, the dunes stretch along the shore for 16 km (10 mi) and are 2 km (1¼ mi) wide. Some of the crests rise up to 300 ft, and they are always in motion. Ceaselessly, the sands shift and the shadows change. Each dune has wavy rivulets that seem to flow in the wind. The Tottori Dunes are an unexpected phenomenon, and therein lies their interest for the Japanese, though world travelers are likely to be disappointed. The dunes have appealed to the Japanese for making humans seem so temporal and insignificant. Literary figures would come to be mesmerized by the continually changing patterns of the dunes and the isolation they offered—Kobo Abe's haunting *Woman in the Dunes* is set here.

Now tourists come in droves during the summertime. You can have your picture taken with a camel, and there is a "kiddieland" (¥280) that appeals to Japanese families. You'll have to walk farther to escape the crowds and find your solitude. Better yet, rent a bicycle from the Cycling Terminal at Kodomo-no-kuni, near the entrance to the dunes, and work your way east to the Uradome (oo-ra-*do*-meh) Seashore. At the pier near the Iwamoto-bashi, you can board the San-in Matsushima Yuran sightseeing boat for a 50-minute trip (¥1,000) along the coast to see the twisted pines and eroded rocks of the many islands that stand offshore (☎ 0857/73–1212).

To get to the dunes, take Bus 20, 24, 25, or 26 from Gate 3 at the bus terminal in front of the JR eki for the 20-minute ride (¥330) north. You will be dropped off at the top of the dunes, and the only way down is the chair lift (¥200, round-trip). Though Tottori is the prefectural capital, it has only marginal points of interest. Rather than stay in Tottori, continue on the JR San-in Main Line up the coast to either Kasumi or Kinosaki. The **City Tourist Information Office** (☎ 0857/ 22–3318) is at the station.

Lodging

$$–$$$ 🏨 **New Otani.** This multistory red-concrete building across from the JR eki is the most modern hotel in town. The staff is helpful, and the guest rooms are compact and smartly decorated. Rooms on the higher floors afford a view of Tottori, although one can argue that it isn't much of an improvement over the brick wall you see from the rooms on the east side of the building. ✉ *2-153 Ima-machi, Tottori-shi, Tottori-ken 650,* ☎ *0857/23–1111,* FAX *0857/23–0979. 136 rooms. 2 restaurants. AE, DC, MC, V.*

Kasumi to Kinosaki

70 mins west of Tottori by JR.

㉒ The train along the coast east of Tottori parallels the shoreline, providing glimpses of the beautiful seascapes. One sleepy fishing village, **Kasumi,** east of Kasumi Bay, is particularly appealing. If you stay in town overnight (☞ *below*), be sure to get up early, around 6 AM, to go down to the quay to watch the offloading of the night's catch and visit the fish market. Boats go out in the late evening and trawl during the night with a string of lights running fore and aft to attract the fish. They return to harbor at about 4 AM, but the market action doesn't begin until after the sun has come up.

To the left of Kasumi Harbor is a small headland, **Okami Kōen,** a park that used to be popular for lovers' suicides—a classic way for the Japanese to give honor and dignity to a fatefully degraded, true love—because of its high cliffs and the waves crashing on the rocks below. (An apt place to end a searing passion indeed.) The shrine on the same hillside is a hidden visual treasure, as sometimes you may find cranes perched in the trees around it. Various sightseeing boats leave from the quay, which is straight ahead when you leave the park. ☉ *Free. Daily 9–5.*

Be sure to visit **Daijō-ji,** directly inland from the JR Kasumi Eki. This temple's history began in 746, but it didn't become well known until the 18th century, when Ōkyo Maruyama, a leading artist of the time, came from Kyōto on a field trip with his students. Apparently Maruyama felt inspired, and he assigned his students to paint various themes in several rooms of the temple. Some of these themes took a long time to paint, especially the Gilded Peacock; the field trip lasted eight years. 🖃 *¥500.* ☉ *Daily 8:30–4:30.*

Kundani is an even more picturesque village. This small town of 300 people and two bars is a quiet haven on a horseshoe-shape bay. There is nothing to do here but relax. You can stay at a very hospitable minshuku (☞ *below*). Kundani is two stations farther down the track on the local train from Kasumi (get off at Satsu Eki).

㉓ Stop in **Kinosaki** as an alternative to spending the night at Kasumi or Kundani. There are a couple of small temples in town, **Onsen-ji** and **Gokuraku-ji,** but the real reason for staying here is the thermal baths. Virtually every inn and hotel has its own springs, but, even better, join in the traditional custom of visiting the seven public baths. Don't bother dressing up: It is perfectly correct simply to wear your yukata and join the procession from one bath to another. Each of these public baths charges about ¥300 and closes at 10:30 PM (Mandata-yu closes at 11:00) . Before taking the baths, you may want to visit the **Mugisen Folk-craft Shop,** at the top of the village's main street, to look at the wickerwork baskets and cases for which the area is known.

Dining and Lodging

KASUMI

$–$$ ✕ **Hyōtan.** You'll probably encounter someone here who knows ten words of English, which, combined with your ten words of Japanese, will be enough for an evening of conviviality. Hyōtan is small, with counter seating for about ten people and space on tatami matting for only a small group. Tatsumi Nishimoto, his wife, and his mother work behind the counter fulfilling requests for beer, sake, sashimi, and grilled fish. Some sashimi is likely to be presented with your drink order, so you may want to order the *hata-hata,* a small fish that is dusted with salt and grilled—an order is usually three fish that taste like they were caught moments ago. ⊠ *340-1 Nonokaichi, Kasumi-chō,* ☏ *0796/36–4047. Reservations not accepted. No lunch. No credit cards.*

$$ 🏠 **Marusei Ryokan.** This small, quiet inn is in a two-story concrete building between the JR eki and the harbor. The tatami rooms are quite spacious, made larger by the minimal furnishings. Bathrooms are cramped, but the narrow tubs are deep. Meals are served in your room on request, but unless *kani-suki* (succulent crab casserole) is being offered you may want to venture out to the small pub named Hyōtan (☞ *above*). ✉ *Kasumi-chō, Kinosaki-gun, Hyōgo-ken, 669,* ☏ *0796/36–0028,* FAX *0796/36–2018. 11 rooms, 4 with bath. AE, V.*

KUNDANI

$ 🏠 **Minshuku Genroku Bekkan.** This private guest house is a true find.
★ The eight tatami guest rooms are spacious and freshly decorated, though none has a private bath. Breakfast and excellent Japanese dinner are served. The husband speaks English—his wife tries—and he will likely invite you to the local bar after dinner. The house is in the center of the quiet fishing village, two streets from the sea. The closest JR eki is Satsu; call on arrival and the owners will meet you at the station. ✉ *Kundani Kasumi, Kinosaki-gun, Hyōgo-ken,* ☏ *0796/38– 0018. 8 rooms. No credit cards.*

KINOSAKI

$$$ 🏠 **Mikiya Ryokan.** This three-story wood inn is delightfully old-
★ fashioned, with creaking timbers and spacious tatami rooms. It has its own thermal baths, which look out onto the garden. ✉ *Kinosaki-gun, Hyōgo-ken,* ☏ *0796/32–2031. 20 rooms. Hot springs. AE, DC, V.*

Ama-no-hashidate

㉔ *45 mins east of Kinosaki by JR, 1 hr and 55 mins north of Kyōto by the Tokkyu Line.*

Ama-no-hashidate, one of the "Big Three" Japanese scenic wonders, is the next and final major stop on the San-in coast. Most Westerners are slightly disappointed by it, and younger Japanese are, too. However, in the past, Japanese literati have waxed poetic about Ama-no-hashidate, so you may want to hop off the train at Ama-no-hashidate Eki, rent a bicycle from one of the stores in front of the station, and go and see what all the fuss is about.

Ama-no-hashidate is a 3-km-long (2-mi-long) sandbar that stretches across **Miyazu Bay.** Its width varies from 100 to 350 yards, and it is lined with those contorted pine trees that so stir the Japanese imagination. For the best vantage point, take the cable car (¥640) from the northwest side of the **Kasamatsu Kōen.** When you have finally reached the top of Kasamatsu Kōen, don't be surprised to see masses of people standing on stone benches with heads between their legs. This is the "proper" viewing stance to see Ama-no-hashidate (Bridge of Heaven), as the sandbar becomes a bridge in the sky. It is even more amusing to watch people taking photographs. To get to this phenomenon, take the 15-minute bus ride from Ama-no-hashidate Eki to Ichinomiya, or take the ferry boat from Ama-no-hashidate Pier. There are also bicycles for rent at the stores in front of the JR eki.

The San-in coast continues north as far as Maizuru, and though this tour ends at JR Ama-no-hashidate Eki, there are other sights to see. If you want to see more of traditional Japan, continue to leisurely explore the areas covered above, and you'll invariably chance upon secrets of your own.

WESTERN HONSHŪ A TO Z

Arriving and Departing

By Plane

Hiroshima is the major airport for this region, with seven daily flights to Tōkyō's Haneda Kūkō (1 hr, 15 mins) as well as direct daily flights to the city of Kagoshima (1 hr, 10 mins) on Kyūshū, and Sapporo (1 hr, 55 mins) on Hokkaidō. There are also airports at Hiroshima, Izumo, Tottori, and Yonago that have daily flights to Tōkyō.

By Train

By far the easiest way to travel to Western Honshū and along its southern shore is by Shinkansen from Tōkyō, Kyōto, and Ōsaka. Major Shinkansen stops are Himeji, Okayama, and Hiroshima. It takes approximately 4 hours, 54 minutes on the Shinkansen to travel to Hiroshima from Tōkyō, 1 hour, 39 minutes from Ōsaka (times vary depending on which stops trains make). To cover the length of the San-yō coast from Ōsaka to Shimonoseki (the last city on Honshū before Kyūshū) takes 3 hours, 10 minutes.

JR express trains runs along the San-yō and San-in coasts, making a more or less elliptical loop beginning and ending in Kyōto. Crossing from one coast to the other in Western Honshū requires traveling through the mountains (slower going), but there are several train lines that link the cities on the northern Nihon-kai coast to Okayama, Hiroshima, and Ogōri. These are discussed above in the San-in section.

Getting Around

Except for the 22-minute crossing to Miyajima from the environs of Hiroshima, traveling through **San-yō** means hopping on and off JR's Shinkansen and local commuter and express trains on the main trunk railway line that follows the southern shore of Western Honshū between Ōsaka and Shimonoseki. Local buses or streetcars are the way to get around major cities. Renting a car to drive the stretch doesn't pay off: Roads are congested in urban areas, tolls are costly, and travel by train is usually faster and less expensive.

Routes cross the mountains to cities on the Seto Nai-kai at several points along the **San-in** coast. The major connecting routes are Himeji–Kasumi, Okayama–Tottori, Hiroshima–Izumo, Ogōri–Tsuwano, and Ogōri–Hagi.

JR and Bōchō bus lines also run over the mountains. It is important to reserve seats for these buses at JR station seat reservation counters. Despite what some JR booking offices say, the JR bus *is* covered by the JR Pass.

Contacts and Resources

Emergencies
Police, ☎ 110. **Ambulance,** ☎ 119.

Visitor Information
Most major towns or sightseeing destinations have tourist information centers that offer free maps and brochures. They will also help in securing accommodations. The following telephone numbers are for the tourist information centers located at the major tourist destinations in Western Honshū:

Hagi City Information Office, ☎ 0838/25–3131. **Hagi City Tourist Association** at Emukai, ☎ 0838/25–1750. **Himeji Tourist Information Office,** ☎ 0792/85–3792. **Hiroshima City Tourist Office,** ☎ 082/247–6738. **Hiroshima Prefectural Tourist Office,** ☎ 082/228–9907. **Hiroshima Tourist Information Office,** ☎ 082/249–9329. **Kurashiki Tourist Information Office,** ☎ 086/422–0542. **Matsue Tourist Information Office,** ☎ 0852/21–4034 or 0852/27–2598. **Matsue Tourism Association,** ☎ 0852/27–5843. **Miyajima Tourist Association,** ☎ 08294/4–2011. **Okayama Prefectural Tourist Office,** ☎ 086/224–2111. **Okayama**

Tourist Information Office, ☎ 086/222–2912. **Okayama Tourist Association,** ☎ 086/256–2000. **Tsuwano Tourist Association Information Office,** ☎ 08567/2–1144.

The **Japan Travel Bureau** (JTB) has offices at every JR eki in each of the major cities and can assist in local tours, hotel reservations, and ticketing. Except for JTB's Hiroshima office (☎ 082/261–4131), one should not assume that any English will be spoken beyond the essentials.

JAPAN TRAVEL PHONE

The nationwide service for English-language assistance or travel information is available seven days a week, 9–5. Dial toll-free 0120/444–800 for information on western Japan. When using a yellow, blue, or green public phone (do not use the red phones), insert a ¥10 coin, which will be returned.

12 Shikoku

The smallest of Japan's four main islands, Shikoku rests neatly beneath western Honshū, a comfortable distance away across the famed Seto Nai-kai (Inland Sea). Rugged east–west mountain ranges halve Shikoku, where you will be treated more as a welcome foreign emissary than as an income-bearing tourist. Perhaps that reflects on the Japanese who still make pilgrimages to the island's 88 sacred temples, as they have done for centuries.

By Nigel Fisher
and Simon
Richmond

FOR QUITE SOME TIME, Japanese and foreigners have left Shikoku off their itineraries. This is due in part to the fact that, until rather recently, the ferry ride across the Seto Nai-kai discouraged most people. But with the 1989 opening of the Seto Ōhashi (bridge)—the 12-km-long (7½-mi-long) series of six bridge spans that connect Shikoku to Honshū in great leaps from island to island, arching high above the ships that pass in the sea beneath—the island is becoming more popular. Many come to see the engineering marvel itself. Driving across it, you can get off on the various islands, with their lookout areas and souvenir shops. Otherwise the train from Okayama will whisk you across the Inland Sea in 15 minutes, before turning east to Takamatsu and Tokushima, west to Matsuyama, or south to Kōchi. These four cities are the capitals of the four prefectures—Kagawa, Tokushima, Kōchi, and Ehime—which explains the island's name: *shi* (four) *koku* (countries).

The rugged heart of Shikoku consists of mountain ranges that run east to west, dividing the island into two. The northern half, which faces the Seto Nai-kai, has a dry climate, with only modest autumn rains during typhoon season. The southern half, which faces the Pacific, is more likely to have ocean storms sweep in, bringing rain throughout the year. With its shores washed by the warm waters of the Kuroshio (Black Current), it has a warmer climate and especially mild winters. The mountain ranges of the interior are formidable, achieving heights up to 6,400 ft, and are cut by wondrous gorges and valleys. Nestled in these valleys are small farming villages that have remained almost unchanged since the Edo period (1603–1868).

Despite the fact that Shikoku has been part of Japan's political and cultural development since the Heian period (794–1192), the island has a certain independence from mainstream Japan. Some factories litter the northern coast, but, to a great extent, Shikoku has been spared the ugliness of Japan's industrialization. The island is still considered by many Japanese as a rural backwater where pilgrims follow the route of the 88 sacred temples.

The Buddhist saint Kōbō Daishi was born on Shikoku in 774, and it was he who founded the Shingon sect of Buddhism that became popular in the shōgun eras. (During the Tokugawa Shogunate, travel was restricted, except for pilgrimages.) Pilgrims visit the 88 temples to honor the priest, and by doing so, they can be released from having to go through the cycle of rebirth. Many Japanese wait until they retire to make this pilgrimage, in part because the time is right and in part because it takes two months on foot—the traditional way to visit all the temples. Most pilgrims now scoot around by bus in 13 days.

The success of the Seto Ōhashi has encouraged a spate of bridge building, further breaking down Shikoku's isolation. The opening in early 1998 of the Akashi Kaikyo Ōhashi, the longest single-span suspension bridge in the world, joins Shikoku to Honshū via Awaji-shima, an island to the west of Tokushima. An even more ambitious set of 10 bridges, set for completion in 1999, will leapfrog across seven islands and will carry the Nishiseto Express roadway from Onomichi in Hiroshima Prefecture to Imabari, on Shikoku's northwest coast. This will undoubtedly bring changes to the coastal cities and tempt more people to come to the balmy southern shores, but it is unlikely to harm the island's rural charm or its hospitality.

Shikoku Glossary

Key Japanese words and suffixes in this chapter include -*bashi* (bridge), *bijutsukan* (art museum), -*chō* (street or block), *chūō* (central, as in Central Street), *dōri* (avenue), *eki* (train station), *gai-jin* (foreigner), *hama* (beach), *hōmotsukan* (treasure house), -*jō* (castle), -*ken* (prefecture), *kōen* ("ko-en," park), *ōhashi* (large bridge), *onsen* (hot springs), *Seto Nai-kai* (Inland Sea), -*shima* (island), *Shinkansen* (bullet train, literally "new trunk line"), and *shōgun* (commander-in-chief).

Pleasures and Pastimes

Dining

The delight of Shikoku is the number of small Japanese restaurants that serve the freshest fish, either caught in the Inland Sea or in the Pacific. You will know that the seafood is fresh because it is often killed in front of you—or because it arrives, still wriggling, on the plate. Takamatsu and Kōchi are the best places to eat seafood, especially so Kōchi, which specializes in *Tosa ryōri* (Tosa is the old name for Kōchi, and ryōri means cooking)—fresh fish dishes, such as *tataki*: tender bonito steaks seared lightly over a fire of pine needles and served with garlic-flavored soy sauce. In Matsuyama the local specialty is *ikezukuri*, a live fish with its meat cut into strips. In Tokushima try *kaizoku ryōri* (Pirate's Cuisine), in which you grill seafood on your own earthenware brazier.

Noodle restaurants abound, too: In Takamatsu you should try *sanuki udon* (a thick noodle), while in Matsuyama go for thin *somen* noodles, which traditionally come in five different colors. The main cities each have lively entertainment districts where you will have no problem finding a range of other cuisines, if Japanese food does not appeal. Also consider ordering what the chef recommends. That dish is always the best. Just mention that you wish to keep the price within certain limits. Outside the main cities, make sure you eat earlier in the evening: Few places remain open after 8:30.

CATEGORY	COST*
$$$$	over ¥6,000
$$$	¥4,000–¥6,000
$$	¥2,000–¥4,000
$	under ¥2,000

*per person, excluding drinks, service, and tax

Local Traditions

Being something of a backwater has allowed Shikoku to preserve more of its traditional arts and culture than other parts of Japan have. You can learn about pottery and indigo dying near Matsuyama and Tokushima and even try your hand at *washi* papermaking close to Kōchi and Tokushima. The performing arts are represented by *ningyō joruri* puppet shows in Tokushima and kabuki at Uchiko and Kotohira, which has the oldest kabuki stage in Japan. In country towns like Kotohira, Uwajima, and Uchiko, narrow streets and well-preserved old wooden houses are a delight. And there are late-summer dance festivals in Kōchi, Naruto, Takamatsu, and the most famous of all—perhaps in all of Japan—Tokushima's Awa Odori.

Lodging

Accommodations on Shikoku range from pensions and minshuku to large, modern resort hotels that have little character but all the facilities of an international hotel. Large city and resort hotels serve Western and Japanese food. During summer and major Japanese holiday periods, such as Golden Week in late spring, reservations are essential.

For a short course on accommodations in Japan, *see* Loding *in* the Gold Guide.

CATEGORY	COST*
$$$$	over ¥20,000
$$$	¥15,000–¥20,000
$$	¥10,000–¥15,000
$	under ¥10,000

All prices are for a double room, excluding service and tax.

Outdoor Activities

The dramatic interior of Shikoku, especially around Ōboke-kyō (gorge) and Iya-dani (Iya Valley), is great for hiking and cycling. On the southern coast of the island, the rocky capes at Ashizuri and Muroto, lapped by the unimpeded Pacific Ocean, are favored by Japan's surfing fraternity. Takamatsu, with its excellent Ritsuren Kōen, one of the best traditional gardens in Japan, and Matsuyama, with Dogo Onsen—a great hot spring resort—are particularly worth visiting.

Exploring Shikoku

With more than just a couple of days, you can take in the island's mountainous interior, the sun-kissed city of Kōchi with its castle and rugged coastline, and Uwajima, another castle town with interesting shrines. Two weeks would easily allow you to add Shikoku's other major sights, including Tokushima as a base from which you can practice traditional handicrafts, and a trip out to Shōdo-shima, the second largest island in the Seto Nai-kai.

Numbers in the text correspond to numbers in the margin and on the Shikoku map.

Great Itineraries

IF YOU HAVE 2 DAYS

Spend a day in ⊡ **Takamatsu** ① strolling around **Ritsurin Kōen** and then go on to **Kotohira** ④ and its much revered **Kotohira-gū** (shrine). From here the obvious choice is to travel west along the north coast to ⊡ **Matsuyama** ⑭ for its castle and justly famous **Dogo Onsen.** From Matsuyama, you can take a hydrofoil to Hiroshima. Alternatives include a visit to **Yashima** ② for **Shikoku Mura,** a collection of traditional Edoperiod houses, and the highland plateau, which provides a stunning view of the Seto Nai-kai; a trip out to **Naruto** ⑥ to see the whirlpools; or a trip to ⊡ **Tokushima** ⑤ to take part in making traditional crafts.

IF YOU HAVE 4 DAYS

In addition, or as an alternative, to the sights around ⊡ **Takamatsu** ①, take a day trip to **Shōdo-shima** ③, a rural island in the Inland Sea. A more adventurous option is to head for the mountainous interior after checking out **Kotohira** ④ and stop off at **Ōboke** ⑦, where you can inspect the gorge from a boat. If you start off early enough you should be able to make ⊡ **Kōchi** ⑧ for the night. Spend the third day at Kōchi's castle and nearby Katsura-hama (beach) before heading across to ⊡ **Matsuyama** ⑭.

IF YOU HAVE 7 DAYS

It is possible to see all of Shikoku's major sights in a week by spending two nights in ⊡ **Takamatsu** ①, a night each in ⊡ **Kōchi** ⑧ and ⊡ **Uwajima** ⑪, for its castle and sex shrine, and the final two nights in ⊡ **Matsuyama** ⑭. Alternatively you could use Matsuyama as a base for forays out to Uwajima and the well-preserved country towns of **Unomachi** ⑫ and **Uchiko** ⑬. Or you could strike out from Kōchi for either of the rugged capes, **Ashizuri** ⑩ or **Muroto** ⑨. Completing the 1,000-

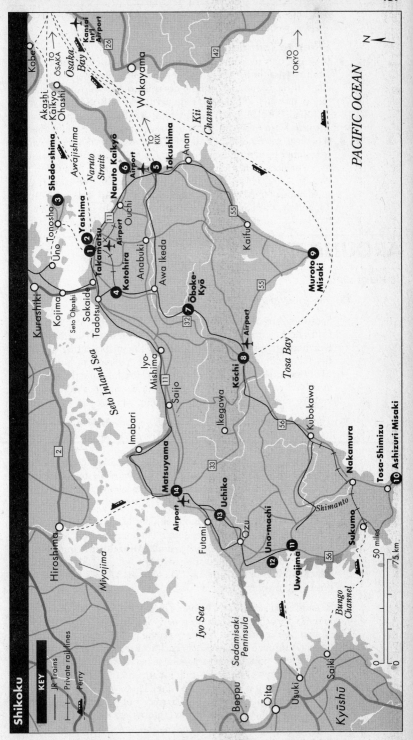

Shikoku

KEY
— JR Trains
— Private railways
— Ferry

Kobe
Akashi Kaikyo Ohashi
Osaka Bay
TO OSAKA
TO OSAKA
Kansai Int'l Airport
26
42
Wakayama
TO TOKYO
PACIFIC OCEAN
N

Shōdo-shima
Tonosho
Uno
3
Awajishima
Naruto Straits
Naruto Kaikyō
6
Airport
5
Tokushima
Anan
Kii Channel
TO KIX

1 2 Yashima
Takamatsu
Airport
Ouchi
4 Kotohira
Anabuki
Awa Ikeda
7 Oboke-Kyō
55
55
9 Muroto Misaki

Kurashiki
Kojima
Seto Ohashi
Sakaide
Tadotsu
Seto Inland Sea
Iyo-Mishima
Saijo
11
32
Airport
8 Kōchi
Tosa Bay
Kaifu

Imabari
Ikegawa
56
Kubokawa

2
33
Matsuyama
14
Airport
13 Uchiko
Ōzu
Uno-machi
Shimanto
Nakamura
Tosa-Shimizu
10 Ashizuri Misaki

Hiroshima
Miyajima
Iyo Sea
Futami
12
11 Uwajima
56
Sukumo
56
50 miles
75 km

Sadamisaki Peninsula
Bungo Channel

Beppu
Ōita
Usuki
Saiki
Kyūshū

0

plus-km (620-plus-mi), 88-temple pilgrimage on foot is the biggest challenge. It would take at least six weeks.

When to Tour Shikoku

In winter, only the snow-bound valleys and hills of the interior are difficult to pass. In February, crimson camellias bloom along the south coast of the island, particularly at Ashizuri Misaki. April is the only month in which kabuki plays are performed in Kotohira at Kompira O-Shibai, the oldest such theater in Japan. June is the time to head for Ritsurin Kōen to see its ponds filled with purple and white irises, although at any time of the year there are flashes of color in the garden. In summer, head for the cool of the mountains or stay by the coast and its sea breezes. Dance festivals run in late summer, the Awa Odori from August 12 to 15. The bullfights in Uwajima are held on January 2, the third Sunday in March, the second Sunday in April, July 24, August 14, and the third Sunday in November. Plan to be in Kōchi on a Sunday for its colorful market's antiques and farm produce.

AROUND THE ISLAND

Takamatsu

❶ *1 hr from Okayama by JR.*

Sprawling, prosperous Takamatsu is most people's first stop on Shikoku. Come here to stroll in the gardens of Ritsurin Kōen—the city's major landmark after wholesale destruction of Takamatsu during World War II—and to admire the Seto Nai-kai panorama from Yashima plateau. Many ferries still call at Takamatsu from Honshū—and the central port area is currently being redeveloped—but because of the Seto Ōhashi, you are most likely to come by train, bus, or car.

★   The number one attraction in Takamatsu is **Ritsurin Kōen,** once the summer retreat of the Matsudaira clan. The gardens—for there are actually two: the northern Hokutei and the southern Nantei—were completed in the late 17th century after 100 years of careful planning, landscaping, and cultivation. The Hokutei is more modern and has wide expanses of lawns. The more appealing Nantei follows a classical Japanese design. Ritsurin Kōen is open daily 7–5; admission is ¥350.

Within the **Hokutei** is an **exhibition hall** that displays and sells local products from Kagawa Prefecture, including wood carvings, masks, kites, and umbrellas. The nearby **Sanuki Mingei-kan** (Sanuki Folk Art Museum) has more interesting displays of local handicrafts and folkcrafts. It is open Thursday–Tuesday 8:45–4:30 and Wednesday until 4; admission is free.

Ritsurin's real gem is in the **Nantei.** The garden's six ponds and 13 scenic mounds are arranged to frame a new view or angle to hold the focus of attention at virtually every step on the intersecting paths. You cannot hurry through Ritsurin Kōen: Each rock, each tree shape, each pond rippling with multicolored carp—and in turn the reflections of the water and the shadows of the trees—calls for attention. The teahouse, Kikugetsutei, looks as if it is floating on water. Here, you may enjoy a cup of green tea and muse on the serene harmony of the occasion, just as the lords of Matsudaira did in previous centuries. ☒ *¥510 for sencha green-leaf tea or ¥710 for macha powdered green tea; combination tickets for gardens and tea ¥830 (sencha) and ¥1,030 (macha).*

To reach Ritsurin Kōen, which is at the far end of Chūō-dōri, take a 10-minute ride (¥220) on any bus that leaves from in front of the Grand Hotel, stop No. 2. (The bus makes a short detour from the main avenue to include a bus depot on its route. Don't disembark from the bus until it rejoins the main avenue—Chūō-dōri—and travels two more stops.) Or take the JR train toward Tokushima and disembark five minutes later at the second stop, Ritsurin Kōen Kita Guchi.

Tamamo-jō, built in 1588, was once the home of the Matsudaira clan, who ruled Takamatsu during the Edo period. All that is left of the castle in Tamano Kōen are a few turrets and the inner section of its three-ring moat, but the surrounding park, with the Seto Nai-kai in the background, makes it a pleasant place to relax while waiting for a train or ferry. The park's entrance is beside the Chikko terminus for the Kotoden tram network at the top of Chūō-dōri, where you will also find the JR eki and the main ferry pier. ☞ ¥150. ☉ *Daily 9–5.*

The department stores, shops, and restaurants of the city's **covered shopping arcades** are 300 yards down Chūō-dōri from the JR eki on the left-hand side. The east–west Hyōgo-machi arcade is intersected by the Marugama-machi arcade running north–south (parallel to Chūō-dōri). The small streets off the arcades are crowded with bars, cabarets, and smaller restaurants. **Takamatsu-shi Bijutsukan** (City Museum of Art) on Bijutsukan-dōri is in the shopping area. It has a small permanent collection of local *Sanuki* lacquerware and Japanese contemporary art, but visiting exhibitions are likely to be of most interest. ☞ ¥200. ☉ *Tues.–Sun. 9–5.*

The **Takamatsu Information Office** (☎ 0878/51–2009) is just outside the JR eki. The maps and brochures are limited to Kagawa Prefecture, of which Takamatsu is the capital. If you need information on the entire island, make sure that you visit the Tourist Information Center in Tōkyō or Kyōto before you set out for Shikoku. A bus tour (Japanese-speaking guide only) departs at 8:45 AM from Takamatsu-Chikko Bus Station (near the JR eki) and covers Ritsurin Kōen, Kotohira, and other sights. The tour takes about eight hours, 45 minutes.

Dining and Lodging

$$–$$$ ✕ **Tenkatsu.** You will find this classy restaurant, which serves all manner of fish dishes from succulent sushi to steaming *nabe* stews, at the far west end of the Hyōgo-machi arcade. Elegant, kimono-clad waitresses pad silently between tatami-mat booths and a jet-black counter bar that surrounds a central, sunken pool where the fish and seafood swim until their number is up. ✉ *Nishizumi Hiroba, Hyōgo-machi,* ☎ *0878/21–5380. AE, DC, MC, V.*

$$ ✕ **Kamaizumi.** The sound of plucked koto strings sets the tone for this intimate sanuki udon noodle restaurant. The set meals (you can choose from a picture menu) come with a wooden brazier to keep the udon and *dashi* fish stock warm while you decide how much of the spring onions, freshly ground ginger, seaweed flakes, tiny bird's eggs, and sesame seeds to add to the noodle broth. Top it off with a flask of sake. Look for a huge red paper lantern hanging outside the entrance. In the afternoon, one of the chefs makes noodles inside the front window. ✉ *Ferry-dōri,* ☎ *0878/21–6688. AE, MC, V.*

$ ✕ **Ikkaku.** The unfinished concrete of this ultramodern single-story chicken and beer restaurant close to Kotoden Yashima Eki might make it look like a night club, but once you sit down in its stylish, brightly lit interior, the reason for the lines of people waiting for a table becomes clear. The food—spicy barbecued chicken, served on silver platters with an accompaniment of raw cabbage leaves—is delicious. There are side dishes available, and it would be a sin not to have a glass of the restaurant's own brewed beers with your meal. ✉ *Yashima Naka-machi,* ☎ *0878/44–3711. No credit cards.*

$ ✕ **Macou's Bagel Café.** Authentic bagels—made on the premises—and a fantastic range of freshly ground coffees are the order of the day at this sleek venture, worth considering for breakfast or a snack. You can either sip a Seattle-style cappuccino and munch on a bagel with cream cheese and lox in the bright interior or take away for a picnic lunch. Macou's is a two-minute walk west of Chūō-dōri, along Route 11. ⊠ *1-9-11 Ban-chō,* ☎ *0878/22–3558. No credit cards. No lunch.*

$$–$$$ ✕🏯 **Kawaroku Ryokan.** The original Kawaroku was bombed out in
★ World War II. This replacement—the best traditional Japanese hotel in the center of town—is unappealing from the outside but pleasantly furnished on the inside. The rooms have a light, refreshing decor, and all have private bath. The restaurant serves French food, but Japanese food can be served in your room. ⊠ *1-2 Hyakken-chō, Takamatsu, Kagawa-ken 760,* ☎ *0878/21–5666,* 🗏 *0878/21–7301. 70 rooms, 21 Western style. Restaurant. AE, V.*

$$–$$$ ✕🏯 **Takamatsu Grand Hotel.** The lobby here is on the third floor (there are nine independently owned restaurants on the second floor), and the main Yashima restaurant is on the seventh floor. Tamamo Kōen, within which are the remains of Tamamo-jō, is behind the hotel, so the views on that side of the building are quite splendid. Some of the guest rooms could use refurbishing, but they are all clean. Right on the city's main avenue, Chūō-dōri, the Grand is within a five-minute walk of the JR eki. ⊠ *1-5-10 Kotobuki-chō, Takamatsu, Kagawa-ken 760,* ☎ *0878/51–5757,* 🗏 *0878/21–9422. 136 Western-style rooms. 2 restaurants. AE, DC, MC, V.*

$$$ 🏯 **Tokiwa Honkan.** This small ryokan runs a close second behind the Kawaroku as the best Japanese-style place to stay. Close to Kotoden Kawara-machi Eki and Takamatsu's lively nightlife, Tokiwa Honkan has spacious and well-furnished, if slightly gloomy, tatami-mat rooms. Its highlights are a compact traditional garden, complete with miniature red bridge and bonsai trees, and a spectacularly over-the-top gold-and-lacquer dining hall—worth a look, even if you don't stay here. ⊠ *1-8-2 Tokiwa-chō, Takamatsu, Kagawa-ken 760,* ☎ *0878/61–5577,* 🗏 *0878/61–5584. 18 rooms. DC, MC, V.*

Yashima

❷ *20 mins by JR or Kotoden tram from Takamatsu.*

Once an island, Yashima is now connected to Shikoku by a narrow strip of land. Its tabletop plateau, standing nearly 1,000 ft above Seto Nai-kai, is an easy half-day trip from Takamatsu. This was the battle site where the Minamoto clan defeated the Taira family in 1185, allowing Yoritomo Minamoto to establish Japan's first shogunate in Kamakura, southwest of what is now Tōkyō.

★ Easily the most interesting sight in the area is **Shikoku Mura,** an open-air museum village. Similar to Hida Village near Takayama, Shikoku Mura has 21 houses that have been relocated from around Shikoku to represent what rural life was like during the Edo period and earlier, 200–300 years ago. The village may be artificial, but in this age, in which ferroconcrete has replaced so much of old Japan, Shikoku Mura provides an opportunity to see traditional thatched-roof farmhouses, a papermaking workshop, a ceremonial teahouse, a rural kabuki stage, and other buildings used in earlier times. 🎫 ¥800. ⏲ *Apr.–Oct., daily 8:30–5; Nov.–Mar., daily 8:30–4:30.*

The major reason for ascending **Yashima Plateau** is the expansive vista over the Seto Nai-kai and Shōdo-shima. There is also Yashima-ji, originally constructed in 754 and 84th of the 88 temples in the sacred pilgrimage. The temple's Hōmotsukan contains some interesting screens and pottery and a mixed bag of relics of the battle between the Minamoto and Taira clans; admission costs ¥500, and the museum is open daily 9–5. A five-minute walk west of Shikoku Mura's entrance is a cable car that takes five minutes to climb to the top of the plateau; it costs ¥700 one-way, ¥1,300 round-trip.

Arriving and Departing. Local JR trains from Takamatsu Eki run at least every hour to Yashima Eki, from which it is a 10-minute walk north to Shikoku Mura. You can also take the **Kotoden tram** from the Chikko terminal (across from the JR eki). These run 10 times a day; the tourist office can supply a schedule. Kotoden Yashima Eki is only a couple minutes' walk from both Shikoku Mura (to the east) and the Yashima cable car station (directly north).

Shōdo-shima

★ ❸ *35 mins north of Takamatsu by hydrofoil, 1 hr by ferry.*

For something of a rural escape, take a ferry out to Shōdo-shima, the second-largest island in the Seto Nai-kai. Craggy Shōdo's mountains are spectacular, and its seacoasts equally so for the contrast of their ruggedness and sandy beaches. The island is also the site of quarries from which the stone used to build the original Ōsaka-jō was cut. Inland, the 3½- by 2½-mi **Kankakei Gorge** is hemmed in by a wall of mountainous peaks with weather-eroded rocks. The thick maple and pine forest lining the gorge is splashed with color in autumn; in spring, the profusion of azaleas makes for an equally colorful spectacle. There are excellent walks among the rocks and streams. If you'd rather not hike, you can gain the summit on an aerial tramway that travels frighteningly close to the cliffs' walls. Kankakei is an hour by bus from the principle town of Tonosho, to which you will want to return for lodging or the ferry back to Shikoku; the bus fare is ¥610.

Also on Shōdo: At **Kujuku-en** (15 minutes by bus from Tonosho), 3,000 peacocks roam the grounds. The **Choshikei Gorge** (25 minutes by bus from Tonosho) extends along the upper stream of the Dempo River. Seven hundred wild monkeys cavort at **monkey park.**

At mealtime, try **Shimamusume** (☎ 0879/62–1666), which serves thin somen noodles and is close to Tonosho port. Another option in Tonosho town is **Nangoku** (☎ 0879/62–2021), which specializes in fish *robatayaki* (barbecue). **Minshuku** are a reasonable way to stay on the island and will allow you to get closer to Shōdo-shimans. Try Chushichi (☎ 0879/62–3679), with 10 rooms, or Maruse (☎ 0879/62–2385), with 6 rooms, both in Tonosho.

Arriving and Departing
To get to Tonosho, the island's largest port and town, from Takamatsu pier, there are two options: a ferry (¥500) and a hydrofoil (¥1,000). There is also a hydrofoil to Shōdo-shima (40 minutes, ¥1,600) from Okayama Port (take Bus 12 from JR Okayama Eki to Okayama Port) and a regular ferry from Himeji Port (1 hour, 40 minutes; ¥1,300).

Getting Around
Sightseeing buses depart from Tonosho to all island sights; public buses cover the island efficiently and thoroughly. You can also rent motorized bicycles for ¥3,000 a day, including insurance, from Ryobi Rent-a-Bike (☎ 0879/62–6578) near Tonosho's pier, open 8:30–5.

Kotohira

★ ❹ *55 mins by JR or Kotoden tram from Takamatsu.*

The reason for visiting Kotohira is to climb the 785 steps to its shrine, **Kotohira-gū.** Fondly known as Kompira-san, the shrine may be quite as important as the Grand Shrines at Ise or Izumo Taisha near Matsue, but it is one of Japan's oldest and most stately. It is also one of the most popular: Four million pay their respects each year.

Founded in the 11th century and built on the slopes of Mt. Zozu, Kotohira-gū is dedicated to Omono-nushi-no-Mikoto (also called Kompira), the guardian god of the sea and patron of seafarers. Traditionally, fishermen and sailors would come to visit the shrine and solicit godly help for their safe passage at sea. However, their monopoly on seeking the aid of Kompira has ended as his role has expanded to include all travelers, including tourists—though it is uncertain whether messages written in English will be understood.

To reach the main gate of the shrine, you have to mount 365 granite steps. On either side of the steps are souvenir and refreshment stands, but don't dawdle. There are yet 420 steps to the main shrine. Beyond the main gate, the souvenir stands are replaced by stone lanterns, and the climb becomes a solemn, spiritual exercise. Just before the second torii is the shrine's **Hōmotsukan,** with a rather dry display of sculpture, scrolls, and, despite their potentially interesting Buddhist origins, Nō masks. It is open daily 9–4; the entrance fee is ¥200.

The next important building, on your right, is the 1659 **Shoin** (formerly a reception hall), its interior covered in delicate screen paintings by the famous 18th-century landscape artist Okyo Maruyama (1733–95). Maruyama came from a family of farmers and, not surprisingly, looked to the beauty of nature for his paintings. Such was his talent that a new style of painting—the Maruyama school—a sort of return to nature, developed. Entrance to the Shoin is ¥200; it is open daily 9–4.

Onward and forever upward, you'll see the intricate carvings of animals on the facade of **Asahi-no-Yashiro,** and, at the next landing, you'll finally be at the main shrine, a complex of buildings that were rebuilt 100 years ago. Aside from the sense of accomplishment in making the climb, the views over Takamatsu and the Seto Nai-kai to the north and the mountain ranges of Shikoku to the south justify the effort, even more perhaps than a visit to the shrine itself—that is, unless you ask Kompira for good fortune. And after climbing 785 steps you might just want to.

Allow a total of an hour and a half from the time you start your ascent up the granite stairs until you return. Just as the feudal lords once did, you may hire a palanquin to porter you up and down; the fee is ¥5,000 one-way, ¥6,500 round-trip. Riding in a palanquin has a certain appeal, and it most certainly saves the calf muscles, but the motion and narrow confines are not exactly comfortable.

It is worth making the time to visit **Kanamaru-za,** the oldest kabuki theater in Japan. The theater is exceptionally large and was moved from the overcrowded center of Kotohira and restored in 1975. Kabuki plays are now performed only in April, but throughout the year the theater is open for viewing. Because it was built in 1835, one of the interesting aspects is how the theater managed its special effects without electricity. Eight men in harness, for example, rotate the stage. Within the revolving stage are two trap lifts. The larger one is used for quick changes in stage props, the smaller one for lifting actors up to floor level.

Equally fascinating are the sets of sliding *shōji* (screens) used to adjust the amount of daylight filtering onto the stage. The theater is in Kotohira Kōen, a 10-minute walk from Kotohira Eki near the first flight of steps leading to Kotohira-gū. ✉ *¥500.* ☺ *Wed.–Mon. 9–4.*

Arriving and Departing. From **JR Kotohira Eki** it is an eight-minute walk to the steps that ascend to Kotohira-gū. There is an open cloakroom to the left of the JR eki (¥200) which is open daily 6:30–9, but if you are visiting only for the day, travel lightly—even small packs become very heavy while you are mounting the 785 stairs to the shrine. The **Kotoden tram** runs every half hour between Kawara-machi Eki in Takamatsu and Kotoden Eki in Kotohira.

From Kotohira Eki, **trains** continue south to Kōchi, the principal city of Shikoku's southern coast. If you aren't heading south to the coast, you can return to the north coast of Shikoku and travel west to Matsuyama, or change at Awa Ikeda for the branch line east to Tokushima.

Tokushima

❺ *1 hr, 10 mins by JR from Takamatsu and Awa Ikeda.*

If you decide to visit Tokushima, you can count yourself among few gai-jin who do. Between August 12 and the 15th, you will witness one
★ of the liveliest, most humor-filled festivals in Japan. The **Awa Odori** (dance) is an occasion for the Japanese to let all their reserves fall away and act out their fantasies. Prizes are even given to the "Biggest Fool" in the parades, and gai-jin are welcome to compete for these awards. If you decide to visit at this time, make sure you reserve accommodations well in advance, since more than a million people pack the city during the four-day festival.

At other times of the year, come to Tokushima for the opportunity to watch and participate in local traditional **Japanese crafts,** such as papermaking, indigo dying, and making pots. Although the city is quite modern, its small scale and well-designed riverside walkways make it a pleasant place to spend a day.

The best use of limited time in Tokushima is to head directly to **ASTY Tokushima,** a state-of-the-art tourist facility. As well as a conference hall and restaurants, there is a large shopping area where you can make washi paper, practice indigo dying, and watch many other local crafts being made, including ningyō jorui (*neen*-gyo jo-*roo*-ee) puppets. The major reason for coming to ASTY, though, is the **Tokushima Taikenkan.** This high-tech exhibition covers the highlights of the prefecture. As well as simulated bus, bike, and windsurfing rides, there is a 360-degree cinema in which you will find yourself at the center of the Awa Odori festival. After, you can practice the dance routines and play the instruments, all with the assistance of immaculately dressed young ladies. In addition, there is a ningyō jorui section, with puppets and daily shows. ASTY Tokushima is a 15-minute bus ride from Tokushima Eki. ✉ *¥900.* ☺ *Daily 9–5.*

Tokushima Chūō Kōen is a pretty park, five minutes' walk east of the JR eki. The first lord of Tokushima, Hachisuka Iemasa, built his fortress here in 1586, and his family lived in it for the next 280 years. In 1896 the castle was destroyed; all that remains of it are a few stone walls, moats, and a beautiful formal garden that has been designated a national scenic spot. The adjacent **Tokushima-jō Hakubutsukan** (museum), built in 1992, is not out of place amid these refined surroundings. Its displays relate to the Hachisuka clan and give a good idea of what the castle looked like. *Museum:* ✉ *¥300.* ☺ *Tues.–Sun. 9:30–5.*

❻ At each ebb and flow of the tide in the **Naruto Kaikyō** (straights), the currents rush through this narrow passage to form hundreds of foaming whirlpools of various sizes—some giant. You'll see the Awa-no-Naruto whirlpools at their fiercest one hour on either side of the tidal change, below the beginning of the long Naruto Ōhashi (suspension bridge), which crosses the straits to Awaji-shima. To get here, take yellow Bus 1 from JR Tokushima Eki plaza to Seto Inland Sea National Park, of which the Naruto whirlpools are a part. From the station it's a 15-minute walk to the bridge. The bus fare is ¥690.

The town of **Otani,** on the way back to Tokushima from Naruto on the JR Naruto branch line, is the home of *Otani-yaki*, a distinctive local pottery that has a heavy texture and is traditionally crafted into enormous standing pots. There are several places in town where you can make your own cups or plates, such as **Yano Toen** (☎ 0886/89–0023) and **Harumoto Togyo Kaikan** (☎ 0886/89–0048), if you make an appointment first. To make a simple cup costs around ¥3,000, and the finished result is mailed to your home after firing.

Natural indigo dyeing in Tokushima dates back at least 400 years and was the source of much of the area's wealth. The best place to learn about it is at the informative **Aizomi Ai-no-Yakata** (historical museum), where minidioramas show the coloring process and examples of blue patterned cloth. You can wander around the old buildings of the complex and try your hand at dyeing. A handkerchief costs ¥500, a T-shirt ¥2,800. The museum is 20 minutes by bus from JR Tokushima Eki (get off at Higashi Nakatomi). ☞ *¥300.* ☉ *Daily 9–5.*

At the **Awa Washi Dentō Sangyō Kaikan** (Hall of Awa Japanese Handmade Paper), west of Tokushima, you might be able to meet "Prefectural Intangible Cultural Asset" Fujimori Minoru—a genial, gray-haired expert in the art of papermaking. The hall holds exhibitions, a shop where it sell its multicolored products, and a huge work space in which you can try your hand at making washi postcards. Take the JR Tokushima main line to Yamakawa Eki; the hall is then a 15-minute walk south. ☎ *0883/42–6120.* ☞ *¥300.* ☉ *Tues.–Sun. 9–5.*

Dining and Lodging

$$$ ✕🏨 **Kappo Hotel Isaku.** At the foot of Mt. Bizan, just to the left of the atmospheric Zuigan-ji (temple), this is one of the most traditional ryokans in Tokushima. The tatami-mat rooms are of a good standard, and some open onto a delightful ornamental garden. Meals start at ¥3,000 for a beautifully presented bentō box and ¥5,000 for the "course" menu, including fresh seafood, tempura, and other delights. You can also eat in Isaku's restaurant if you are not a ryokan guest. ✉ *1 Iga-chō, Tokushima, Tokushima-ken 770,* ☎ *0886/22–1392,* 🆖 *0886/23–8764. 24 rooms, AE, DC, MC, V.*

$$ ✕🏨 **Four Season.** The dagger-sharp triangular window design of this small business hotel, a minute's walk west of the JR eki, first catches your eye. Inside, rooms are functional and comfortable, and the management is friendly. It's owned by the same family that runs the larger, similarly stylish Grand Palace hotel nearby. The son, who is the chef in the attached café, speaks fluent English and serves up his own special variation on curry rice. ✉ *1-54 Terashima Honchō-Nishi, Tokushima, Tokushima-ken 770,* ☎ *0886/22–2203,* 🆖 *0886/56–3132. 20 Western-style rooms. Restaurant. AE, MC, V.*

Getting Around

Trains arrive at Tokushima Eki from Takamatsu and Kōchi via the Dosan and Tokushima lines. City and prefectural **buses** depart from outside Clement Plaza. For the **airport,** take the bus from platform 2. Tokushima is also connected by **ferry** to Kansai International Airport, Kōbe, Ōsaka, and Tōkyō.

Visitor Information

For brochures and other information, **Tokushima Prefecture International Exchange Association** (⌧ TOPIA, Clement Plaza, 6th floor, ☎ 0886/56–3303) is just outside the exit of Tokushima Eki and is open daily 10–6.

Ōboke-kyō (Oboke Gorge)

❼ On the way south to Kōchi, you won't regret exploring the area around **Ōboke-kyō.** The road and rail lines south from Awa Ikeda follow the valleys, cut deep by swift-flowing rivers. The earth is red and rich, the foliage lush and verdant. It is an area of scenic beauty that lends itself to exploration by car, though once you are off the main roads, a little knowledge of Japanese will help your navigation. You can also take a boat trip down the river from near Ōboke Eki. In the heart of the mountains there are hot springs and the **Kazura-bashi,** a 50-yard-long bridge made of vines and bamboo that spans the Iyadani-kei Gorge. For ¥410 you can walk across; it's safe enough, since the bridge is remade every three years and is strung through with steel cables.

To get here, take the branch rail line that runs from Tokushima to Kōchi or the main line that runs from Okayama on Honshū to Kōchi via Kotohira. The jumping-off point is Awa Ikeda, an unremarkable town at the head of the spectacular gorge. Very infrequent buses run from Awa Ikeda and Ōboke to Kazura-bashi. For details, check with the Tourist Section of Awa Ikeda's town hall (☎ 0883/72–1111), or at the information booth (Japanese only) beside Awa Ikeda JR eki.

Kōchi

❽ *2 hrs by JR from Kotohira.*

On the balmy southern coast of Shikoku, Kōchi is a relaxed city with a cosmopolitan atmosphere, enhanced by its trundling trams and the swaying palms that line the streets. The prefecture is reputed to be one of the poorest in Japan, with residents relying on fishing and agriculture for their living. However, perhaps because of its warm climate, the people of Kōchi are full of humor. Even their local folk songs poke fun at life, for example "On Harimaya-bashi, people saw a Buddhist priest buy a hairpin. . . ." Priests in those days were forbidden to love women, and they shaved their heads—some naughty business must have been afoot.

★ The city's major sight is **Kōchi-jō.** The castle dominates the town and is the only one in Japan to have kept both its *donjon* (stronghold) and its daimyō's residence intact. The donjon—its stone foundation seemingly merging into the cliff face against which Kōchi-jō is built—admittedly was rebuilt in 1753, but it faithfully reflects the original (1601–03). The donjon has the old style of watchtower design, and, by climbing up to its top floor, you can appreciate its purpose—the view is splendid. The daimyō's residence, **Kaitokukan,** is southwest of the donjon. Its formal main room is laid out in Shoin style, which is known for its decorative alcove, staggered shelves, decorative doors, tatami-covered floors, and shōji screens reinforced with wooden lattices. ⌂ ¥350. ◷ *Daily 9–5 (enter before 4:30).*

Kōchi's **Bijutsukan** is also worth a visit. The main collection in this spacious two-story facility, set in landscaped grounds, includes modern Japanese and Western art, with one room dedicated to works by Marc

Chagall. Take any tram from Harimaya-bashi bound for Kenritsu Bijutsukan-dōri, a 15-minute ride. ☜ *¥300.* ◷ *Tues.–Sun. 9–5.*

Except for these places, Kōchi is not architecturally inspired, but it is friendly and fun-loving. People congregate every evening in the compact downtown area. Several streets downtown are closed to traffic to form shopping arcades. Should you be in Kōchi on a Sunday morning, go to the **Nichi yō-ichi** (Sunday open-air market), which runs for 1 km (½ mi) along Otetsuji-dōri, from the main gate of Kōchi-jō. Farmers have been bringing their produce to sell at some 650 stalls for 300 years. At the market, you might get to see the incredibly long-tailed (more than 20 ft) *Onagadori* roosters for which Kōchi is known.

In summer, Kochi-ites flock to **Katsura-hama,** 13 km (8 mi) southeast of town. The beach consists of gravelly white sand, but the swimming is good, and there are scenic rock formations offshore. On the headland above the beach is the architecturally dazzling **Sakamoto Ryoma Kinenkan** (memorial museum), built in memory of local hero Ryoma, a progressive samurai who helped bring about the Meiji Restoration of the 19th century. It is open daily 9–5; entry costs ¥350. Also at Katsura-hama is the **Tosa Token** (fighting dog) **Centre** (☎ 0888/42–3315), where canine victors are paraded around the ring dressed in sumō wrestlers' aprons and given the same ranking titles as their human counterparts. The center's entrance fee is ¥1,500.

If you prefer to spend an afternoon amid lawns and greenery by an old temple, take a bus to Mt. Godai and **Godai-san Kōen.** First visit **Chikurin-ji,** a temple with an impressive five-story pagoda that is in fact a fairly uncommon sight in Japan. This one stands up to those of Kyōto; the people from Kōchi say it's more magnificent. The temple belongs to the Shingon sect of Buddhism and, founded in 724, is the 31st temple in Shikoku's sequence of 88 sacred temples. Down from the temple is the **Makino Shokubutsuen** (botanical garden), built to honor the botanist Dr. Tomitaro Makino (1862–1957). The greenhouse has a collection of more than 1,000 plants, and the gardens were designed to have something in bloom in all seasons. ☜ *¥350.* ◷ *Daily 9–5.*

The bus to Godai-san Kōen departs from the Toden stop, next to Seibu department store on Harimaya-bashi. The ride costs ¥300 and takes 20 minutes.

Kōchi's helpful **Tourist Information Office** (☎ 0888/82–1634), with an English-speaking assistant, is to the left of Kōchi Eki's exit.

Dining and Lodging

$$–$$$ ✕ **Tosahan.** This outlet of a famous local chain of restaurants that serves Tosa ryōri is easy to find at the start of the Obiya-machi shopping arcade, close by Harimaya-bashi. The restaurant is decorated in farmhouse style with dark wooden beams and red paper lanterns. A picture menu and plastic food displays in the window help you select a meal. Seafood *nabe* (stews), cooked at the table, and tataki are particularly good bets. ✉ *1-2-2 Obiya-machi Arcade,* ☎ *0888/21–0002. AE, DC, MC, V.*

$ ✕ **Hakōbe.** It isn't much to look at, but this *okonomi-yaki* restaurant on the Obiya-machi shopping arcade is reputed to be the best in town. Its batter-mix omelettes, and, if you would like, *yaki-soba* (fried noodles), come in various combinations for you to cook yourself at hot plates in the middle of your table—good, cheap fun. ✉ *Obiya-machi Arcade, no phone. No credit cards.*

$ ✕ **Jacaranda.** There's barely room to swing your chopsticks in this ★ stylishly designed second-floor restaurant on one of Kōchi's trendiest shopping streets. But the couple of young women who run this lunch-only operation are right on top of their cooking. The menu roams around

Southeast Asia for inspiration, cobbling together Thai, Nepalese, Indonesian, and local dishes, all presented with a Japanese attention to detail. This eatery is not to be missed. ⊠ *Taniguchi Bldg., 2nd floor, 1-2-23 Hon-machi,* ☎ *0888/25–4807. Closed Sun.*

$$$ ✕▥ **Hotel Shin-Hankyu.** Right in the center of town, within sight of
★ Kōchi-jō, the Shin-Hankyu is indisputably the best hotel in Kōchi. The ground floor has a modern, open-plan lobby, with a lounge away from the reception area and a small cake-and-tea shop to the side. On the second floor are several excellent restaurants that serve Japanese, Chinese, and French fare. Spacious guest rooms, most of which are Western style, are pleasantly decorated with light pastel furnishings, and the staff is extremely helpful to foreign guests. ⊠ *4-2-50 Hon-machi, Kōchi-shi, Kōchi-ken 780,* ☎ *0888/73–1111,* ℻ *0888/73–1145. 201 rooms. 4 restaurants, health club. AE, DC, MC, V.*

$$$$ ▥ **Joseikan.** This is Kōchi's most elegant Japanese-style hotel, which has hosted the emperor on his visits to Kōchi. The rather monumental exterior masks a more restrained, airy lobby and a small central garden. Tatami-mat bedroom suites are immaculate, and there's a communal sauna and bath on the eighth floor with a spectacular night view of Kōchi-jō. There is also a restaurant and a coffee lounge. The ryokan is close to the castle, two stops west of Harimaya-bashi by tram. ⊠ *2-5-34 Kami-machi, Kōchi-shi, Kōchi-ken 780,* ☎ *0888/75–0111,* ℻ *0888/24–0557. 50 rooms. Restaurant. AE, DC, MC, V.*

$$ ▥ **Ikawa Ryokan.** English is not spoken here, but the genteel hospitality and sophistication of this inn make a stay relaxing and comfortable. Elegant simplicity, which extends into the traditional Japanese garden, achieves harmony. Even the few Western guest rooms are simply adorned. A kaiseki-style dinner is served in your room and uses produce of the sea to full advantage. Ikawa is five minutes by taxi from Kōchi Eki. ⊠ *5-1 Niyudai-machi, Kōchi-shi, Kōchi-ken 780,* ☎ *0888/ 22–1317,* ℻ *0888/24–7401. 20 rooms. V.*

$$ ▥ **Washington Hotel.** Something of a Kōchi landmark, this is part of the nationwide chain of business hotels and has a prime position on the same street leading to Kōchi-jō, on which the Sunday market is held. It is convenient to the JR eki, too, being a 15-minute walk away. There is a small restaurant, and rooms are a good size for this kind of lodging. ⊠ *1-8-25 Otesuji, Kōchi-shi, Kōchi-ken 780,* ☎ *0888/23–6111,* ℻ *0888/25–2737. 62 rooms. Restaurant. AE, V.*

Getting Around

Kōchi Eki is a 10-minute walk from the city center at Harimaya-bashi. The tram system, which starts directly opposite the eki, costs a flat ¥180 to go anywhere within the city center. A taxi ride from Kōchi Eki to downtown is about ¥550. There are also buses.

Half- and full-day **sightseeing tours** (☎ 0888/82–3561) of Kōchi and environs leave from the JR bus terminal at Kōchi Eki at 8:30 AM and 1:50 PM. Full-day sightseeing tours (☎ 0880/35–3856) travel down to Cape Ashizuri from Nakamura Eki; these are not available throughout the whole year, so be sure to call ahead.

If you want direct **Matsuyama–Kōchi** transportation, take the three-hour JR bus from Kōchi Eki (there is no direct train). The fare is covered by the JR Pass. For the **Kōchi–Uwajima** train trip, you will need to change at Kubokawa, where you must pick up a branch line.

Side Trips from Kōchi

❾ **Muroto Misaki** (Cape Muroto). The road east (there's no train line) follows a rugged shoreline cut by frequent inlets and indentations. Most of the coast consists of a series of 100- to 300-ft terraces. Continuous wave action, generated by the *Kuroshio* (Black Current, literally "black salt"), has shaped these terraces. The result is a surreal coastline of rocks, surf, and steep precipices. It is about a 2½-hour drive along the coast road out to the cape, a popular sightseeing and surfing spot, where the sea crashes against the cliffs and there are black-sand beaches.

❿ **Ashizuri Misaki** (Cape Ashizuri). Part of Ashizuri National Park at the southwestern tip of Shikoku, this is wonderfully wild country, with a sky-line-drive road running down the cape's middle. At its tip is a lighthouse and Kongōfuku-ji, 38th of Shikoku's 88 sacred temples. Its origins go back 1,100 years, although what you see was rebuilt 300 years ago. By train, take JR from Kōchi Eki southeast to Nakamura, keeping in mind that the Kubokawa–Nakamura leg is on the private Kuroshio Tetsudō Line (¥210, not covered by the JR Pass). At Nakamura Eki, continue by bus to Ashizuri Misaki—you might have to change buses at Tosa Shimizu. Sightseeing buses (☎ 0880/35–3856) also travel from JR Kōchi Eki to Ashizuri Misaki. None of these buses take JR Passes.

There is also the **John Mung House,** which has a small museum on the extraordinary life of Nakahama Manjiro. In 1841 the 14-year-old Manjiro, who hailed from Ashizuri, was shipwrecked on a remote Pacific island. He was eventually rescued by an American whaling ship. John Whitfield, the ship's captain, took a shine to Manjiro and nick-named him John Mung. The boy adapted quickly, sticking with the whaling crew for years and eventually settling in Bedford, Massachusetts, where the captain educated him. Mung's fluency in English assigned him a pivotal role in negotiating the opening of Japan to the world after Commodore Perry's Black Ships arrived in 1853. ✉ *Ashizuri Misaki, Tosa Shimizu-shi,* ☎ *0880/8–1136.* 💴 *¥200.* 🕐 *Sept.–July, daily 8:30–5; Aug., daily 8–6.*

Returning from Ashizuri Misaki, you can follow the coastline west to **Sukumo,** or go back to Nakamura to take a bus there (1 hr; ¥1,100). Change buses to continue north to Uwajima, the terminal for JR rail lines running between Matsuyama and Kōchi. Four ferries a day (¥1,650) sail from Sukumo for Saiki, on Kyūshū (☞ Chapter 13).

Uwajima

⓫ *3½ hrs by JR from Kōchi.*

This agreeable, peaceful town is famous for its bull vs. bull fights and a shrine dedicated to sex. Like Kōchi (☞ *above*), Uwajima contains one of Japan's 12 extant feudal castles. **Uwajima-jō** is a compact, friendly castle, free of the usual defensive structures, such as a stone drop. The first castle was torn down and replaced with this updated version in 1665, suggesting that by the end of the 17th century, war—at least the kind fought around castles—was a thing of the past. The castle and park are a 10 minutes' walk south of Uwajima Eki. 💴 *¥200.* 🕐 *Daily 9–5.*

For a shrine dedicated to fertility, the small, shady **Taga-jinja** strikes, at first glance, a modest pose. It's only on closer inspection that you notice the distinctly phallic nature of the statues and stones, and of course the giant, penis-shaped tree trunk beside the main shrine. There are many, many more like artifacts in the three-story museum, where every available inch of space is used to display some kind of sexual object. One marvels at the dedication of the priest who spent a lifetime collecting this stuff, but the overall effect is more clinical than titillating. The shrine is 10 minutes on foot northwest of Uwajima Eki, beside the Suka-gawa (Suka River). 💴 *¥800.* 🕐 *Daily 8–5.*

Most people come to Uwajima for the **tōgyū,** in which two bulls lock horns and, like sumō wrestlers, try to push each other out of the ring. Though there are very similar bouts in the Oki islands, Uwajima claims that these bullfights are a unique tradition dating back 400 years—an obvious tourism ploy. There are six tournaments a year: January 2, the third Sunday in March, the second Sunday in April, July 24, August 14, and the third Sunday in November. The Tōgyū-jō (stadium) is at the foot of Mt. Tenman, a 30-minute walk from Uwajima Eki.

Uwajima's **Warei-Taisai Matsuri** is celebrated every July 23–24 with a parade of *mikoshi* (portable shrines), decorated fishing boats, and two giant *uni-oshi* (demon bulls). The climax is a battle in the local river between the teams carrying the bulls.

The **Tourist Information Centre** is opposite Uwajima Eki. ☎ *0895/22–3934.* ◷ *Daily 9–5.*

Dining and Lodging

$$ ✕ **Kadoya.** This bustling two-story restaurant specializes in crab and *tai-meshi,* flaked sea bream on top of rice, and its set menus, which include tempura and noodle dishes, are a good value. For quieter dining, you can choose a private tatami-mat booth. Kadoya is on the main street near Uwajima Eki. ⊠ *8-1 Nishiki-machi,* ☎ *0895/22–1543. DC, MC, V.*

$$$$ ✕▥ **Tensha-en Hotel.** Staying at this delightful, small ryokan beside the former private gardens of the Date (*da*-teh) clan will certainly make a visit to Uwajima more pleasant. You will be waited on in a suite of traditional Japanese-style rooms overlooking Tensha-en Kōen. You can also possibly dine here if you are not staying; set courses start at ¥3,500 per person. ⊠ *1-3 Tensha-en Kōen, Uwajima, Ehime-ken, Shikoku 399,* ☎ *0895/22–4700,* ℻ *0895/22–5794. 10 rooms. AE, V.*

Getting Around

JR trains connect Uwajima with Kōchi and Matsuyama. **Ferries** depart from Uwajima for Usuki, two JR train stops from Beppu on Kyūshū, and cost about ¥2,200.

Uno-machi and Uchiko

⑫ *Uno-machi is 17 mins and Uchiko is 1 hr north of Uwajima by JR. Uchiko is 30 mins south of Matsuyama by JR.*

★ Uno-machi is a charming town with a well-preserved strip of old Japanese houses. It also contains the **Museum of Ehime History and Culture.** This huge new facility, perched on a hill overlooking the town, provides a wonderful overview of Ehime Prefecture's history from prehistoric times to current lifestyles. Whole buildings, including a shrine and thatched-roof house, have been reconstructed inside the museum, which is made up of four linked exhibition areas that use state-of-the-art technology. The highlight is being able to see close-up the fabulous portable shrines and decorations used in local festivals, such as Uwajima's Warei-Taisai Matsuri (☞ *above*). ▧ *¥500.* ◷ *Tues.–Sun. 9–5.*

⑬ **Uchiko** prospered during the Edo era from the development of its *Moku-ro* wax industry, and it, too, has preserved some of its architectural heritage. **Yokaichi,** a 650-yard stretch of old wooden and white-and-cream plaster buildings, is a highlight. Some of the houses are now gift shops and teahouses, others have been preserved as they once were. The impressive **Kami-Haga Residence,** built in 1894 by a family of rich wax merchants, houses the **Japan Wax Museum,** the best place to learn about the industry. Yokaichi is a 1½-km (¾-mi) walk from Uchiko Eki. ▧ *¥400.* ◷ *Daily 9–4:30.*

On the way to Yokaichi you will pass **Uchiko-za,** an attractive, restored kabuki theater originally built in 1916. ☜ *¥300.* ⏱ *Tues.–Sun. 9–4:30.*

Matsuyama

⑭ *1½ hrs north of Uwajima and 3 hrs west of Takamatsu by JR; 1 hr south of Hiroshima by fast boat, 3 hrs by ferry.*

Shikoku's largest city, Matsuyama bristles with industry: from chemicals to wood pulp and textiles to porcelain. Most of its appeal is in its famous literary associations, its castle, and the spas of Dogo Onsen.

Matsuyama-jō—the third such feudal castle in Shikoku to have survived intact, though barely—is on top of Katsuyama Hill, right in the center of the city. Construction began in 1602; then the original five-story donjon burned down in 1784, to be rebuilt in 1820 with a complex of a major three-story donjon and three lesser donjons. The lesser ones succumbed to fire in this century, but all have been reconstructed. Unlike other postwar reconstructions, these smaller donjons were rebuilt with original materials, not ferroconcrete. The main donjon now serves as a museum for feudal armor and swords owned by the Matsudaira clan, the daimyō family that lorded over Matsuyama and Takamatsu throughout the Edo period. ☜ *¥350.* ⏱ *Daily 9–5.*

There are several walking routes to Matsuyama-jō, the most pleasant passing the **Ninomaru Shiseki Teien,** an agreeable park on the west side of the hill, which covers the grounds of the former outworks of the castle. The park and grounds are open Tuesday–Sunday 9–4:30, with a fee of ¥100. If you're not feeling so plucky, you can take a cable car or chairlift up to the castle from Okaido, the shopping street on the east side of the hill; the fare is ¥210 one-way, ¥400 round-trip.

★ Rather than staying downtown in Matsuyama, consider spending the night at **Dogo Onsen.** With a history that is said to stretch back for more than two millennia, Dogo Onsen is one of Japan's oldest hot-spring spas. It hasn't outlived its popularity, either. There are more than 60 ryokan and hotels, old and new. Most of them now have their own thermal waters, but at the turn of the last century, one went to public bathhouses. The grandest of them all was, and still is **Dogo Onsen Honkan,** the municipal bathhouse.

Bathing is a social pastime, and to stay in the area and not socialize at the municipal bathhouse is to miss the delight of this spa town. The grand, three-story, castlelike wooden building was built in 1894, and with its sliding panels, tatami floors, and shōji screens, it looks like an old-fashioned pleasure palace. It is, in many ways. Two thousand bathers or more come each day for a healthy scrub and soak. Many pay extra to lounge around after their bath, drinking tea in the communal lounge or private rooms. Even if you decide not to pay for a private room, make sure you visit the third floor to see the **Botchan Room,** named after the comic novel by local writer Natsume Sōseki.

There are different price levels of enjoyment. A basic bath is ¥280; a bath, rented *yukata* (cotton robe), tea and snack, and access to the communal tatami lounge is ¥620; access to a smaller lounge and bath area away from hoi polloi is ¥980; and a private tatami room is ¥1,240. A separate wing was built in 1899 for imperial soaking. It is no longer used, but for ¥210 you can follow a guide through this royal bathhouse daily from 6:30 AM to 9 PM. The baths are open 6:30 AM–11 PM.

Dogo Onsen is 18 minutes away from Matsuyama on Tram 5, which you can take from Matsuyama Eki or catch downtown at the stop in front of the ANA Hotel (Trams 3, 5, and 6).

Matsuyama has eight of Shikoku's 88 sacred temples. The best known is **Ishite-ji,** 20 minutes on foot east of Dogo Onsen Honkan. The Kamakura-style temple has its origins early in the 14th century, and its simple three-story pagoda is a pleasant contrast to the public bathhouse. Note the two Deva king statues at the gate. One has an open mouth, representing life; the other's closed mouth represents death. Praying at Ishite-ji is said to cure one's aching legs and crippled feet—the elderly hang up their sandals here as a hope offering.

Downtown Matsuyama revolves around the **Okaido covered shopping arcade,** at the foot of the castle grounds, and is best reached by taking Tram 5 (fare ¥170) from the plaza in front of Matsuyama Eki.

The **City Tourist Information Office** (☎ 0899/31–3914) in Matsuyama Eki provides maps and brochures Monday–Saturday, 8:30–5. **Ehime Prefectural International Centre** (EPIC, ☎ 089/943–6688), on the south side of Katsuyama Hill below the castle, has information in English on the rest of the prefecture and on the city's efforts to encourage haiku poetry—Matsuyama was the home of Masaoka Shiki, one of Japan's most famous haiku poets.

Dining and Lodging

$$$ ✕ **Kaiseki Club Kawasemi.** At this modern interpreter of traditional *kaiseki ryōri,* you can sit at tables or on tatami mats in private booths and savor delicate morsels of marinated seafood, or slivers of poached fish and vegetables artfully arranged in a mound, surrounded by a savory coulis. The slightly gloomy interior is decorated in minimalist black and grays, with seasonal flower arrangements adding splashes of color. The restaurant is on the second floor, two streets east of Okaido—look for a purple sign with "Club" in English. ✉ *2-5-18 Niban-chō,* ☎ *089/933–9697. No credit cards.*

$$–$$$ ✕ **à table.** If you are in the mood for delicious French country cooking by a French chef, set out for the heart of town to this slightly offbeat place. Dark wood beams line the ceiling, some tinsel and risqué photographs serve as decoration, and you sit either at long wooden bench tables or around the kitchen, watching the burly chef hard at work with his assistant. Lunchtime set menus from only ¥850 are a bargain, and they can tempt you to return for more expensive dinner courses. There is a good selection of wines and teas. ✉ *5-2-6 Chifunemachi,* ☎ *089/947–8001. No credit cards.*

$$ ✕ **Dan Dan Jaya.** A large *izakaya* (pub) with counter seating encircles the cooking area, and there are small, semi-enclosed areas with tatami seating to the sides. The menu has helpful pictures, and there are dozens of hearty country dishes that range in price from ¥500 to ¥1,000. Dan Dan Jaya is handily located near the Okaido shopping arcade. ✉ *3-7-1 Niban-chō,* ☎ *089/945–7101. AE, DC, MC, V.*

$$ ✕ **Nikitatsu-an.** This innovative, modern-and-traditionally designed Japanese restaurant is attached to a beer and sake brewery. Dishes include grilled fish, marinated beef strips, and specially prepared rice. Delicate Japanese presentation of the food and a more Western use of pungent spices come together in interesting combinations of crunchy, soft, and silky textures. Try the brewery's light Botchan ale and heavier brown Madonna ale. ✉ *3-1-8 Dogo Shita-machi,* ☎ *089/924–6617. No credit cards.*

$$$ ✕🏨 **ANA Hotel Matsuyama.** The best international hotel downtown, the ANA is five minutes on foot from the cable car to Matsuyama-jō, and Tram 5 out to Dogo Onsen stops right out front. Guest rooms are well maintained, reasonably spacious, and fully equipped, with everything from bathrobes to hair dryers. Ask for a room on the 11th or

12th floor that overlooks the Bansuiso Mansion, an imitation French château (housing the missable Prefectural Museum Annex), which is floodlit at night. The hotel has shopping arcades, several restaurants, and a rooftop beer garden. ⊠ *3-2-1 Ichiban-chō, Matsuyama, Ehime-ken 790,* ☎ *089/933–5511,* FAX *089/921–6053. 334 rooms. 4 restaurants, beer garden. AE, DC, V.*

$$ ✕🏨 **Hotel Patio Dogo.** Many of the spacious, well-furnished rooms in this Western-style hotel overlook the Dogo Onsen Honkan, which is right outside the lobby door. The hotel has business facilities and is small enough for the friendly staff to take an interest in you—something that doesn't always happen at the larger hotels in Dogo, geared up for the package-tour trade. There's also a good-value sushi restaurant on the ground floor. ⊠ *Honkanmae, Dogo Onsen, Matsuyama, Ehime-ken 790,* ☎ *089/941–4128,* FAX *089/941–4129. 101 rooms. Restaurant. AE, DC, MC, V.*

$$$$ 🏨 **Funaya Ryokan.** The best Japanese inn in Dogo Onsen, this is where the imperial family stays when it comes to take the waters. The ryokan has a long history, but the present building was built in 1963, and there are some Western-style rooms. The finest rooms look out on the garden. Breakfast and dinner are included in the tariff. ⊠ *1-33 Godo Yumo-machi, Matsuyama, Ehime-ken 790,* ☎ *089/947–0278,* FAX *089/ 943–2139. 43 rooms, some with private bath. AE, V.*

$$ 🏨 **Hotel Sunroute.** This business hotel has no particular charm, but its rooms are not too small, and it is just a five-minute walk from Matsuyama Eki. The best part of the hotel is its rooftop beer garden (open summer only), from which you can catch a glimpse of the castle. ⊠ *Miyata-chō, Matsuyama, Ehime-ken 790,* ☎ *089/933–2811,* FAX *089/ 933–2763. 110 rooms. AE, V.*

Getting Around

There is frequent **JR train service** between Matsuyama and Takamatsu, as well as hourly **high-speed boat service** (1 hr, ¥5,700) and **ferry service** (three hours; ¥4,260 for first class, ¥2,130 for second class) between Matsuyama and Hiroshima.

SHIKOKU A TO Z

Arriving and Departing

By Plane

Takamatsu is served by seven daily flights from Tōkyō and by 10 daily flights from Ōsaka; **Tokushima** by five daily from Tōkyō and 10 from Ōsaka; **Kōchi** by five daily from Tōkyō and 23 from Ōsaka; and **Matsuyama** by six daily from Tōkyō and six from Ōsaka.

By Ship

Another way to Takamatsu is the **Kansai Kisen** (steamship), which takes five hours, 30 minutes from Ōsaka's Bentenfuto (pier), and four hours, 30 minutes from Kōbe's Naka-Tottei Pier. The boat leaves Ōsaka at 8:30 AM and 2:20 PM, and Kōbe at 9:50 AM and 3:40 PM. It arrives at Takamatsu at 2 PM and 8:10 PM. The cost is ¥2,500 and up from Ōsaka, slightly less from Kōbe.

There are **ferry connections** between Tokushima and Kansai International Airport, which take 1 hour, 20 minutes and cost ¥4,000. Tokushima is also linked to Kōbe and Ōsaka Tempozan—both journeys take around 1 hour, 50 minutes and cost ¥4,530. Passenger ships travel to Kōchi from Ōsaka (depart at 9:20 PM and arrive in Kōchi at 6:40 AM, returning to Ōsaka with departures at 9:20 PM and arriving in Ōsaka at 7 AM). There is also a ship to Kōchi from Tōkyō that departs at 7:40 PM, stops in Katsuura, Wakayama Prefecture, at 8:50 AM, and arrives in Kōchi at 5 AM.

By Train

To get to Shikoku, take the JR Hikari Shinkansen to Okayama (four hours from Tōkyō; one hour from Ōsaka), then transfer to the JR Limited Express for either Takamatsu (one hour) or Matsuyama or Kōchi (three hours).

You can also get to Matsuyama by taking the JR Shinkansen to Hiroshima (five hours, 10 minutes from Tōkyō; two hours, 20 minutes from Kyōto). From Hiroshima's Ujina Port, the ferry takes three hours to cross to Matsuyama; the high-speed boat takes one hour.

Getting Around

By Car

Because traffic is light, the scenery marvelous, and the distances relatively short, Shikoku is one region in Japan where renting a car makes sense. (Remember that an international driving driver's license is required.) **Budget Rent-a-Car** has rental offices in Matsuyama, Takamatsu, and Kōchi, as do other car-rental agencies.

By Train and Bus

All major towns on Shikoku are connected either by JR express and local trains or by bus. Because of the lower population density on Shikoku, transportation is not so frequent as on the southern coast of Honshū. So before you step off a train or bus, find out how long it will be before the next one departs for your next destination.

The main routes are from Takamatsu to Matsuyama by train (two hours, 45 minutes); from Takamatsu to Kōchi by train (three hours), from Takamatsu to Tokushima (90 minutes); from Matsuyama to Kōchi by JR bus (approximately three hours, 15 minutes); from Matsuyama to Uwajima by train (two hours); and from Kōchi to Nakamura by train (two hours).

Contacts and Resources

Emergencies

Police, ☎ 110. **Ambulance,** ☎ 119.

Guided Tours

No guided tours covering the island of Shikoku are conducted in English, though the **Japan Travel Bureau (JTB)** will make individual travel arrangements. JTB has branches in each of the prefectural capitals and can assist in local tours, hotel reservations, and ticketing onward travel. Local city tours, conducted in Japanese, cover the surrounding areas of each of the four major cities in Shikoku. You can arrange these through your hotel.

Visitor Information

Major tourist information centers are located at each of Shikoku's main cities: **Takamatsu** (☎ 0878/51–2009), **Kōchi** (☎ 0888/82–1634), **Matsuyama** (☎ 089/931–3914), and **Tokushima** (☎ 0886/56–3303).

JAPAN TRAVEL PHONE

A nationwide service for English-language assistance or travel information is available seven days a week, 9–5. Throughout Shikoku, dial toll-free 0120/444–800 or 0088/224–800 for information on western Japan. When using a yellow, blue, or green public phone (do not use red phones), insert a ¥10 coin, which will be returned.

13 Kyūshū

The relatively quiet island of Kyūshū, which hangs like a tail off the south end of Honshū, has a mild climate, lush green countryside, hot springs, and eerie volcanic formations. Its cities are mostly free of skyscrapers and filled with sights of historical and cultural significance.

JAPANESE CIVILIZATION as we know it was born in Kyūshū. Because of its geographic proximity to Korea and China, from the 4th century on Kyūshū was the first area of Japan to be culturally influenced by its more sophisticated neighbors. Through the gateway of Kyūshū, Japan was first introduced to Buddhism, the Chinese writing system, pottery techniques, and other aspects of Chinese and Korean culture. Legend has it that the grandson of Amaterasu Ōmikami, the sun goddess, first ruled Japan from Kyūshū. Another tale relates that Jimmu Tenno, Japan's first emperor, traveled from Kyūshū to Honshū, consolidated Japan, and established the imperial line that exists to this day.

By Kiko Itasaka

Updated by
David Miles

Not all outside influence, however, was welcome. In 1274 Kublai Khan led a fleet of Mongol warriors in an unsuccessful attempt to invade Japan. The Japanese, in preparation for further attacks, built a stone wall along the coast of Kyūshū. Remnants of it still stand outside Fukuoka. When the Mongols returned in 1281 with a force 100,000 strong, they were repelled by the stone wall and by the fierce fighting of the Kyūshū natives; the fighters were aided by a huge storm, known as *kamikaze* (divine wind), which blew the Mongol fleet out to sea. (This term is likely more familiar in its World War II form, describing suicide pilots.)

In the mid-16th century, Kyūshū was once again the first point of contact with the outside world, when Portuguese ships first landed on the shores of Japan. The arrival of these ships signaled Japan's initial introduction to the West and its medicine, firearms, and Christianity. The Portuguese were followed by the Dutch and the Spanish. The Tokugawa shogunate was not entirely pleased with the intrusion of the Westerners and feared political interference. In 1635 the shogunate established a closed-door policy that permitted *gai-jin* to land only on a small island, Dejima, in the harbor of Nagasaki. As a result, until 1859, when Japan opened its doors to the West, the small port town of Nagasaki became the most important center for both trade and Western learning for Kyūshū and the entire nation. The historical influence of Europe is still apparent in Nagasaki, with its 19th-century Western-style buildings and the lasting presence of Christianity.

Kyūshū Glossary

Key Japanese words and suffixes for this chapter include *-chō* (street or block), *-chōme* (street), *chūō* (central, as in Central Street), *daimyō* (feudal lord), *dōri* (avenue), *eki* (train station), *gai-jin* (foreigner), *-gun* (county or district), *-gawa* (river), *hama* (beach), *ike* ("ee-keh," pond), *-in* (Buddhist temple), *izakaya* (pub), *-ji* (Buddhist temple), *-jō* (castle), *-ken* (prefecture), *kōen* ("ko-en," park), *-ku* (section or ward), *kūkō* (airport), *onsen* (hot springs), *sake* (rice wine), *sakura* (cherry blossoms), *-san* (mountain, as in Aso-san, Mt. Aso), *-shi* (city or municipality), *-shima* (island), *Shinkansen* (bullet train, literally "new trunk line"), and *yama* (mountain).

Pleasures and Pastimes

Arts and Culture

Because Kyūshū was the threshold of artistic influences arriving from the wider world, the history of Japanese porcelain—of craftsmanship "borrowed" from Korea—begins here. And the pottery towns of Arita, Karatsu, and Ōkawachi-yama in Imari are interesting windows on the arts, trade, and foreign relations in Edo-era Japan. In 1616, after waging war on Korea, the Japanese brought the artisan Ri Sampei to

Kyūshū in order to produce ceramic objects for the shogun. The kilns that sprung up to support him continue to produce exquisite pieces of art for the emperor and other dignitaries.

Fukuoka is known for its *kyōgen*—traditional Japanese drama unique for its sing-song dialogue—and its contemporary pan-Asian commerce. Nagasaki's internationalism is based upon the open port's history of Buddhism, Christianity, and Dutch Studies (Ran-gaku).

Dining

Until the 20th century, Kyūshū was the most international part of Japan. Certain Kyūshū dishes, not surprisingly, show the influence of China and Europe. Tempura, for example, is often thought of as a standard Japanese dish. In fact, it was introduced by Europeans to Kyūshū in the 17th century. Particularly in Nagasaki, the influence of foreign cuisines is still apparent. Beppu is famous for its seafood. Because it is primarily a resort town, most people tend to remain in their hotels or inns for meals, and thus many of the hotels have fresh, locally caught fish. One particularly popular local dish is *fugu* (blowfish).

Fukuoka, Kyūshū's largest city, has excellent Japanese and Western restaurants. Many of the best Western restaurants are in hotels. One well-known dish is Hakata ramen, noodles with a strongly flavored pork-base soup with negi (scallions) and strips of roast pork. It is also known for its ikesu restaurants, places that have a fish tank from which you can select your entrée, guaranteeing its freshness.

The challenging regional specialty of Kumamoto is horse meat, which is served roasted, fried, or raw. An easier delicacy is *dengaku,* tofu or fish covered with a strong bean paste and grilled. In contrast to the delicate taste of Kyōto cuisine, dengaku is a good example of Kyūshū's stronger flavors.

One type of cooking is available only in Nagasaki, *shippoku*—a variety of dishes that, when combined, make a full meal. Dinners center on a fish-soup base with European flavorings, to which many foods are added, including rice cakes, a variety of vegetables, and stewed chunks of pork cubes prepared Chinese-style, marinated in ginger and soy sauce. Shippoku usually is served as one large communal dish, which is very unlike the typical preparations of individual portions in Japan. Another distinctive Nagasaki dish is *champon,* heavy Chinese-style noodles in a soup. Not surprisingly, Nagasaki also has some of the best Western restaurants in Kyūshū.

CATEGORY	COST*
$$$$	over ¥9,000
$$$	¥6,000–¥9,000
$$	¥3,000–¥6,000
$	under ¥3,000

per person, excluding drinks, service, and tax

Lodging

Accommodations in Kyūshū are plentiful, and because the number of visitors is not overabundant, it is almost always possible to get reservations. Fukuoka has major hotels with excellent facilities. Nagasaki has grand old hotels and ryokan that, like the city itself, seem to be frozen in the 19th century. If you are looking for a more active vacation, spend a few days in the Mt. Aso region at a pension: something like a bed-and-breakfast where supper is served as well. Pensions near Aso are set in the mountains and are located near trails for hiking.

For a short course on accommodations in Japan, *see* Lodging *in* the Gold Guide.

CATEGORY	COST*
$$$$	over ¥20,000
$$$	¥15,000–¥20,000
$$	¥10,000–¥15,000
$	under ¥10,000

All prices are for a double room, excluding service and tax.

Outdoor Activities

Kyūshū is one of the best parts of Japan in which to enjoy the outdoors. There is plenty of natural drama—outside of Kokura and Fukuoka—from mountains and volcanoes to islands and seascapes that all afford great hiking and cycling. Water sports are plentiful, and there tend to be fewer people than on crowded Honshū. The islands west of Fukuoka and Nagasaki are good for a bit of adventure, likewise those south of Kagoshima. Kagoshima has hot springs that make it ever so easy to relax after a long trip, as does Mt. Aso, and the landscapes between Aso and Beppu are particularly beautiful.

Exploring Kyūshū

One approach to Kyūshū is to circle the island, which will bring you past rich green rice fields, mountains, and the ocean. The starting point of most visits is Fukuoka, where there is a major airport and a JR Shinkansen train station. Of course, you can take in the island's sights in any order; here, we circle through Fukuoka to Nagasaki on the west coast, then go east to Kumamoto and Mt. Aso, and conclude at the Seto Nai-kai (Inland Sea) hot-spring resort of Beppu, from which you can return to Fukuoka.

Numbers in the text correspond to numbers in the margin and on the Kyūshū and Nagasaki maps.

Great Itineraries

The three things Kyūshū is most noted for are its history, its food, and its natural beauty. And you can cover the island's must-sees in a brief tour from Nagasaki to Beppu via Mt. Aso, with pauses for local wonders and delicacies. Ferries run frequently between peninsulas, but the Tsubame express trains will be your principle mode of transport if you're planning a rapid tour of Kyūshū.

IF YOU HAVE 2 DAYS

In two days you can easily get a sense of Kyūshū's relaxed, international atmosphere and still have a chance to see some gorgeous countryside. Spend one day en route from ⊞ **Fukuoka** ① to ⊞ **Nagasaki** ④–⑫, as there are pottery towns in misty valleys and rich green mountains on the way to the culinary treats of Nagasaki. The new **Atomic Bomb Museum** in Nagasaki is the one must-see if time is limited. If possible, a jaunt from Nagasaki to **Kujukushima** would allow a quick look at more of Kyūshū's natural drama without having to spend most of the day on the train.

IF YOU HAVE 4 DAYS

You really needn't spend much time in ⊞ **Fukuoka** ①—set right off for the cultural and athletic opportunities that are in easy reach of the city or en route to Nagasaki. Spend the first day in Arita or Karatsu, ending up in ⊞ **Takeo Onsen** ③ for the night. ⊞ **Nagasaki** ④–⑫, the hilly, cosmopolitan setting for *Madame Butterfly* and the atomic bomb site, is entirely unique. No other port city in Japan has its history while solemnly instructing the world of the horrors of nuclear war. From Nagasaki, head for the garden and castle of ⊞ **Kumamoto** ⑬, or go straight to ⊞ **Mt. Aso** ⑮ for a day amid its geological wonders or a two-day stint of intense hiking. Travel distances are not terribly far—except for the four-

Kyūshū

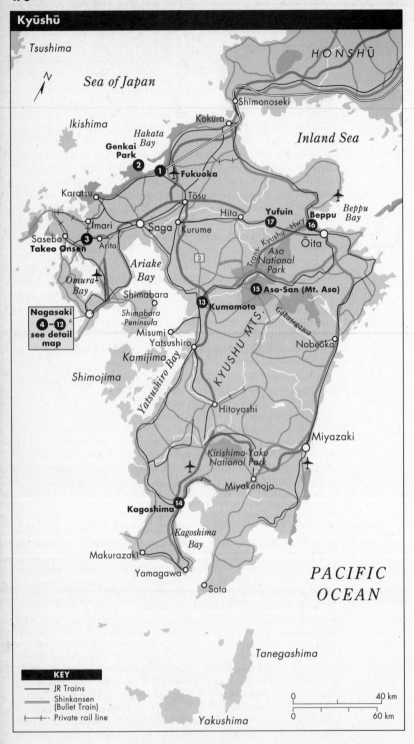

Tsushima

Sea of Japan

HONSHŪ

Shimonoseki

Ikishima

Kokura

Hakata Bay

Genkai Park

2

1 ✈ **Fukuoka**

Inland Sea

Karatsu

Tōsu

⚓ Imari

Saga

Hita

Yufuin

17

Beppu

16

Beppu Bay

Sasebo

3

Arita

Kurume

Ōita

Takeo Onsen

Omura Bay ✈

Ariake Bay

3

Trans-Kyushu Hwy

Aso National Park

Nagasaki

4–**12**

see detail map

Shimabara

Shimabara Peninsula

13 **Kumamoto**

15 **Aso-San (Mt. Aso)**

Misumi

Yatsushiro

Gokasegawa

Nobeoka

Kamijima

Yatsushiro Bay

KYUSHU MTS.

Shimojima

Hitoyoshi

Miyazaki

Kirishima-Yaku National Park

✈

Miyakonojo

Kagoshima

14

Kagoshima Bay

Makurazaki

Yamagawa

Sata

PACIFIC OCEAN

Tanegashima

Yakushima

KEY

— JR Trains

═ Shinkansen (Bullet Train)

—┼— Private rail line

| 0 | | 40 km |

| 0 | | 60 km |

hour Nagasaki–Kumamoto leg—but changing trains and getting between places will always take more time than expected.

IF YOU HAVE 7 DAYS

You can cover all of Kyūshū's major points in seven days without running yourself ragged. Start in ⊞ **Fukuoka** ① to get a taste of the island's main metropolis; then head to ⊞ **Nagasaki** for a day and a half for easygoing exploring. Many people feel that Beppu is a bit overrated, so head instead to **Unzen** and **Shimabara** and then take the one-hour ferry to ⊞ **Kumamoto** ⑬. As you drop south on Kyūshū, **Kagoshima** ⑭ scores points for its unique twist on "Japanese-ness," particularly since Sakura-jima, the local active volcano, is often spewing smoke. Nearby **Ibusuki** city is worth the hour-long train ride from Kagoshima solely for a soak in the therapeutic hot-sand baths. Though the countryside north of **Miyazaki** is gorgeous and the beaches pristine, accommodations are slim until you get to ⊞ **Beppu** ⑯. Nearby ⊞ **Yufuin** ⑰ is actually more appealing than Beppu, which makes it the better place to spend the night in the area. After a night in Yufuin, stop at ⊞ **Mt. Aso** ⑮ on the way back to Fukuoka for a dramatic, Beethoven-esque Kyūshū finale.

When to Tour Kyūshū

Kyūshū is at its most beautiful in early spring when the greenery is richest—and because the island is nearly tropical, temperatures will be plenty warm. April can be magical; late May to June tends to be wet. Summer is usually hot and sticky, more so than the rest of Japan. Autumn colors are rich and luxurious, particularly in the north, and they arrive in mid- to late October. Winter sees little snow, except in mountainous central Kyūshū, and the island's weather is milder than is most of Honshū's. Look for the migration of cranes from Siberia, which adds drama to Kyūshū's winter landscape.

FUKUOKA

❶ *1½ hrs west of Tōkyō by plane, 5–7½ hrs west of Tōkyō by Shinkansen, 2½–4½ hrs west of Ōsaka by Shinkansen (both depending on which train you take).*

Fukuoka is the most logical starting point for travel around Kyūshū. It is the commercial, political, and cultural center of the island and its largest city. With 1.2 million inhabitants, it is the eighth largest city in Japan. Virtually flattened by bombing in World War II, it was rebuilt on a grid plan. It is obviously small and provincial in comparison to Tōkyō, but there is a dynamic quality to Fukuoka, whose city council is determined to position the city as Japan's gateway to Asia.

You'll find most activities and entertainment around the two city centers, Hakata Eki and the downtown Tenjin district—use the subway (¥180) to travel between them. The city is divided in two parts by the Naka-gawa. All areas west of the river are known as Fukuoka; everything east of it is known as Hakata. Fukuoka was originally a castle town founded at the end of the 16th century, and Hakata was the place for commerce. In 1889 the two districts were officially merged as Fukuoka, but the historical names are still used. Nakasu—the largest nightlife district in western Japan, with 3,000 bars, restaurants, and street vendors—is along the Naka-gawa and Hakata-gawa.

Exploring Fukuoka

Shōfuku-ji is a good place to start a tour of Fukuoka. The temple was founded in 1195 by Eisai (1141–1215) upon his return to Kyūshū after years of study in China. He was one of the first Japanese priests to introduce Zen Buddhism to Japan—the claim is often made that this is the site of Japan's first Zen temple. Eisai is also said to have brought the first tea seeds from China to Japan. Note the Korean-style bronze bell in the belfry, designated an Important Cultural Property by the Japanese government. The temple is a 15-minute walk from Hakata Eki, or a 5-minute Nishitetsu bus ride from the adjacent Hakata Kōtsū Bus Center to the Okunodo stop. ☞ *Free.* ◷ *Daily 9–5.*

Dedicated to the guardian gods of seafarers, **Sumiyoshi Jinja** is the oldest Shintō shrine in Kyūshū, founded in 1623. An annual festival is held here October 12–14, complete with sumō wrestling. The temple sits atop a hill with a lovely view of both the Naka-gawa and the city, and the grounds are dotted with camphor and cedar trees. From Hakata Eki take a bus from the adjacent Hakata Kōtsū Bus Center to Sumiyoshi Station. ☞ *Free.* ◷ *Daily 9–4.*

Ōhori Kōen is a spacious park built around a lake that was once part of a moat surrounding Fukuoka-jō. Bridges connect three small islands in the center of the lake. In early April, the northern part of the park is graced with the blossoms of **2,600** sakura. On weekends you will see many Fukuoka residents taking advantage of this oasis in the middle of an otherwise bustling, efficient, industrial city. Bring a picnic and enjoy a leisurely walk, or boat and fish on the lake. Take the subway from Hakata Eki to Ōhori Kōen Station, about a 20-minute ride.

If you tire of lakeside idylls, take a look at the ruins of **Fukuoka-jō** on the outskirts of Ōhori Kōen. The castle was originally built in 1607. Little remains here—only a turret, gates, and a small portion of the castle itself—but the hillside grounds afford a panoramic view of the city.

Dining and Lodging

$$$$ ✕ **Ikesu Kawataro.** A large tank full of fish—potential dinner—sits in the middle of this large establishment, which has counter seating, Japanese-style rooms with tatami mats, and regular tables. If you don't mind sitting on the floor for the duration of the meal, the tatami section is the most pleasant, because the other areas of the restaurant tend to be noisy. Try any of the remarkably fresh sashimi dishes. If you order certain kinds of fish and shrimp, they will still be wriggling on your plate when served. ✉ *1-6-6 Nakasu, Hakata-ku,* ☎ *092/271–2133. AE, DC, MC, V.*

$$ ✕ **Inankuru.** This cozy restaurant in the heart of Tenjin specializes in *okonomi-yaki,* a Japanese-style frittata made with egg, bean sprouts, and fillings of your choice. This is a very foreigner-friendly food, which you ought to try in Japan at least once. Run by four young and cheerful ladies, Inankuru is famous for its mashed-potato okonomi-yaki and is convenient to the nightlife of Fukuoka. ✉ *Dai-ni Kōtsū Bldg., 1st floor, 3-14-2 Tenjin, Chūō-ku,* ☎ *092/752–0120. No credit cards.*

$ ✕ **Deko.** A cheerful izakaya three minutes on foot from the Hotel New
★ Otani (☞ *below*), this is a delightful place to while away an evening over good food. Seating is Japanese-style at the counter and at shared tables, at which there are wells for your legs. Western-style seating in the back is outside the fraternity of communal dining. Deko has no English menu, but the staff will do their best to make suggestions. Usually the special of the day is a good choice; it might be an egg roll stuffed with spinach for ¥750. Mackerel lightly grilled in soy sauce and salt is superb. From the New Otani go diagonally across the intersection, pass the pachinko parlor on the left-hand side of the street, and you'll come to a tall, new building outside of which there is a large sign that

reads LHASA; Deko is down one flight of stairs. ⊠ *1-24-22 Jonansen-dōri, basement, Chūō-ku,* ☎ *092/526–7070. No credit cards.*

$ ✗ **Ichiki.** If you are interested in checking out Japanese nightlife but are not sure where to go, try this bar-restaurant and see how numerous Japanese spend their recreational evenings. The atmosphere is relaxed and friendly, and as the evening wears on, it is more likely than not that one of your Japanese neighbors will attempt to make your acquaintance. Try *kushiyaki,* a sort of Japanese shish kabob with fish, meat, and vegetables, fried on a hot, flat grill and served on a wood skewer. This isn't a place where you just sit down and order your meal. Plan to settle in for a while, have a few beers, and order a few small dishes at a time. The price range for each dish is ¥300–¥1,000. ⊠ *1-2-10 Maizara, Chūō-ku,* ☎ *092/751–5591. No credit cards.*

$$$$ ⌘ **Hotel Il Palazzo.** Fukuoka's most chic lodging is a boutique hotel created by art director Shigeru Uchida and architect Aldo Rossi. It's a showpiece of contemporary design that the American Institute of Architects awarded. The interior is classically simple yet dramatic. The glow of muted lights in the Italian restaurant reflects off the walls, and the ceiling lights sparkle as if they were stars. The Western-style guest rooms have simple furnishings; rich, deep-pile carpets; and soft colors. The nine Japanese rooms are traditional except for half partitions that give a feeling of increased space. ⊠ *3-13-1 Haruyo-shi, Chūō-ku, Fukuoka, Fukuoka-ken 810,* ☎ *092/716–3333,* ℻ *092/724–3330. 62 rooms, mostly Western style. Restaurant, 3 bars, café, nightclub. AE, DC, MC, V.*

$$$$ ⌘ **Hotel New Otani Hakata.** This New Otani member is typical of modern Japanese comfort—smart, characterless, and efficient, with sparkling surrounds. Within those parameters, this top Fukuoka hotel is a quick taxi ride from the station. The rooms, decorated in muted tones, are spacious and have a writing table and easy chair. This is one of the few hotels in all of Kyūshū where you can expect most of the staff to speak English. The large lobby reception area has a coffee lounge and adjoins a complex of boutiques whose merchandise is the height of fashion and price. ⊠ *1-1-2 Watanabe-dōri, Chūō-ku, Fukuoka, Fukuoka-ken 810,* ☎ *092/714–1111,* ℻ *092/715–5658. 407 rooms. 3 restaurants, bar, tearoom, barbershop, beauty salon, massage, shops, baby-sitting, travel services. AE, DC, MC, V.*

$$$ ⌘ **Hyatt.** There are two Hyatts Fukuoka, the Hyatt Regency, near the station, and the Grand Hyatt in Canal City, a new American-style shopping mall between Tenjin and Ōhori Kōen. The Hyatt Regency, eight minutes from Hakata Eki (Shinkansen side), focuses on business travelers looking for polite, efficient service with comfortable, if innocuously furnished, guest rooms filled with plastic-veneer furniture. The rooms are pleasantly spacious, and the futon-style coverlets for the bedding are welcome, but water pressure is low in the showers. Guests on the Regency Floor (the sixth) are served good complimentary breakfasts, afternoon tea, and evening cocktails. On the ground floor off the atrium lobby are several outlets. Le Café offers light snacks with a Spanish flavor; the Boston bar is for cocktails; and the Bansai restaurant serves Japanese fare. The newer Grand Hyatt, somewhat inconveniently located, seems positioned only for conventions or shopoholics, and the staff's attitude won't be attracting many guests. ⊠ *Regency: 2-14-1 Hakata Eki-higashi, Hakata-ku, Fukuoka, Fukuoka-ken 812,* ☎ *092/412–1234; 800/233–1234 for U.S. reservations; 0345/581–666 or 0171/580–8197 for U.K. reservations;* ℻ *092/414–2490; 248 rooms; 2 restaurants, bar, conference rooms. ⊠ Grand Hyatt: 1-2-82 Sumiyo-shi,* ☎ *092/282–1234,* ℻ *092/282-2817; 3 restaurants, 2 bars, pool, health club; AE, D, MC, V.*

$$$　　🅷 **Fukuoka Yama-no-ue Hotel.** The name of this hotel means "on a mountain," and it is on a hill above Fukuoka with excellent views of the ocean on one side and the city on the other. The service is quietly polite and extremely helpful. Rooms are on the small side but not uncomfortably so. The hotel is a little out of the way—10 minutes from Hakata Eki by taxi or bus (catch Nishitetsu Buses 56–58)—but the spectacular views make the travel time worthwhile. ✉ *1-1-33 Terakuni, Chūo-ku, Fukuoka, Fukuoka-ken 810,* 🕾 *092/771–2131,* ☎ *092/771–8888. 55 rooms. 2 restaurants, tennis courts, public bath. AE, DC, MC, V.*

$$　　🅲 **Clio Court Hotel.** This hotel is the best value in Fukuoka. Across the
★　　street from Hakata Station (Shinkansen side), it has remarkably attractive rooms furnished with great care in a variety of styles, such as Art Deco and early American. Request your decor of preference when you make a reservation. Rooms in the front—1202 and 1203—are particularly good choices. One whole floor contains tea-ceremony rooms modeled on designs by Kamiya Sotan and Hosokawa-Sansai, both disciples of the founder of the tea ceremony, Sen-no-Rikyū. Another tea-ceremony room is designed with benches and tables for gai-jin. One floor higher is the hotel's revolving restaurant, which serves grilled steak and seafood cooked Western-style; in 60 minutes, you will take one full turn around Fukuoka. ✉ *5-3 Hakata Eki Chūo-gai, Hakata-ku, Fukuoka, Fukuoka-ken 812,* 🕾 *092/472–1111,* ☎ *092/474–3222. 194 rooms. 2 restaurants, bar, café, 5 tearooms (their usage free for guests upon request at check-in). AE, DC, MC, V.*

$–$$　 🅢 **Sun Life Hotels.** Across the station plaza from the Shinkansen exit there are actually three Sun Life hotels within 100 yards of each other. All three are business hotels: no romance, just convenient and reasonable. Rooms at Sun Life 1 are not as new and spacious as at Sun Life 2 and 3. In addition, Sun Life 2 and 3 have Japanese restaurants that are open all day. ✉ *Hakata-ku, Fukuoka, Fukuoka-ken 812 (across from JR Hakata Eki's Shinkansen side),* 🕾 *092/473–7112,* ☎ *092/471–5075. 256 Western-style rooms. 2 restaurants, coffee shop. AE, MC, V.*

Shopping

Fukuoka is famous for two local products—***Hakata ningyō*** (dolls) and ***Hakata obi*** (kimono sashes).

Hakata ningyō are popular throughout Japan. They are made with fired clay and are hand-painted with bright colors and distinctive expressions. The dolls are mostly ornamental, representing children, women, samurai, and geisha.

Hakata obi are made of an interesting local silk that has a rougher texture than most Japanese silk, which is usually perfectly even and smooth. For local young girls, the purchase of their first Hakata obi is an initiation into adulthood. Other products, such as bags and purses, are also made of this Hakata silk.

The main area for shopping is the downtown **district of Tenjin,** which you can reach by subway from Hakata Eki (third stop). Many boutiques, department stores, and restaurants are along Tenjin Nishi-dōri. Underground at Tenjin subway station is an arcade of small shops and restaurants with high fashion and affordable merchandise from clothes to souvenirs.

Iwataya Department Store (✉ *2-11-1 Tenjin, Chūo-ku,* 🕾 *092/721–1111*) carries the most complete selection of merchandise in the area, including Hakata ningyō, Hakata silk, and an excellent china department that sells Kyūshū's distinctive pottery. The store is in the center of the Tenjin shopping area.

Hakusen (✉ Tenjin 2-chōme, Shirai, Chūō-ku, ☎ 092/712–8900), also in the Tenjin shopping district, is a specialty shop with an extensive selection of Hakata dolls.

Hakata Ori Kaikan (✉ 1-14-12 Hakata Eki-minami, Hakata-ku, ☎ 092/472–0761) specializes in Hakata silk and is the best place to get obi and bags.

Fukuoka A to Z

Arriving and Departing

BY FERRY

Ferries run between the Hakata Pier Ferry Terminal at Fukuoka and Yosu and Pusan, both in Korea. There is also hydrofoil service to Pusan.

BY PLANE

Fukuoka has Kyūshū's only international airport. Japan Airlines (JAL), All Nippon Airways (ANA), and Japan Air System (JAS) have 1½-hour flights between Haneda-kūkō in Tōkyō and Fukuoka-kūkō. There are 10 daily flights. JAL also flies once daily (1 hr, 45 mins) between Narita International Airport and Fukuoka-kūkō. JAL and ANA also offer a total of eight direct flights between Ōsaka and Fukuoka (1 hr, 45 mins), making it convenient to begin or end a Japan trip in Kyūshū. Northwest Airlines has direct flights from Hawaii.

Between the Airport and Center City. Fukuoka Airport is very near the center of the city. A subway line (fare is ¥220) links the airport with the JR Hakata Eki.

BY TRAIN

JR *Hikari* Shinkansen trains travel between Tōkyō and Hakata Eki in Fukuoka (6 hrs, 26 mins, to 7 hrs, 24 mins). The superfast *Nozomi* Shinkansen takes only 5 hours, but it is not included in the JR Pass. There are 15 daily runs. Shinkansen trains travel between Ōsaka and Hakata Station and also between Hiroshima and Hakata. Regular JR express trains travel these routes but take twice as long.

Getting Around

The easiest way to get around Fukuoka is by bus or by one of the two subway lines (¥180 minimum). The city's two major transportation centers are around Hakata Eki and in the downtown area known as Tenjin, the terminal station for both of the subway lines. Buses leave from the Kōtsū Bus Center just across the street from Hakata Eki, and from the Fukuoka Bus Center at Tenjin.

Contacts and Resources

CONSULATE

U.S. Consulate. ✉ *5-26 Ōhori 2-chōme, Chūō-ku, Fukuoka,* ☎ *092/751–9331.*

GUIDED TOURS

Sightseeing buses leave from the **Tenjin Bus Center** (☎ 092/771–2961), the **Nishitetsu Bus Center** (☎ 092/734–2727), and the **Kōtsū Bus Center** (☎ 092/431–1171). Very few tours are held in English, so it is better to have your hotel call for further information or to ask at the tourist information office. A three-hour tour costs approximately ¥1,950.

TRAVEL AGENCIES

Japan Travel Bureau. ✉ *Yamato Seimei Kaikan Bldg., 1-14-4 Tenjin, Chūō-ku, Fukuoka,* ☎ *092/731–5221.*

VISITOR INFORMATION

The Fukuoka City Tourist Information Office (☎ 092/431–3003) is in Hakata Station. Some of the office staff speak English, and excellent maps of the city and neighboring areas are available. The office is open daily 9–7. If you plan on staying in Fukuoka for more than a day or two, you might want to contact the **Fukuoka International Association** (✉ Rainbow Plaza, IMS, 8th floor, 1-7-11 Tenjin, Chūō-ku, Fukuoka 810, ☎ 092/733–2220, 🅵🅰🆇 092/733–2215), which serves as an information resource and center for networking.

Pick up a copy of *Metro,* a monthly publication in English that details various activities in the city.

SIDE TRIPS FROM FUKUOKA

Genkai Park

➋ *2 hrs and 10 mins west of Fukuoka by bus.*

Genkai Park, which extends from Hakata Bay along the coasts of Fukuoka and Saga prefectures, has long beaches with white sands and eerie Japanese black pines. The waters of Hakata Bay facing the Genkai Sea (Genkai-nada) are surprisingly clean and relatively uncrowded. You can combine a swim in the bay with a visit to the *boheki,* the ruins of stone walls (next to a beach) that were built in the 13th century to stave off the invasions of the Mongols. From Hakata Kōtsū Center, take the Nishitetsu bus to Karatsu-Oteguchi (90 mins, ¥1,050), then transfer to the Showa bus for Yobiko (40 mins, ¥700).

Takeo Onsen and Arita

➌ *2 hrs southwest of Fukuoka by JR, 1 hr and 35 mins north of Nagasaki by JR.*

Consider a stop in Takeo Onsen, a small town known for its hot springs, as an alternative to a direct two-hour JR train ride to Nagasaki. Surrounded by mountains, the spa became famous when, approximately 1,700 years ago according to legend, Empress Jingū stopped in Takeo Onsen to recover from childbirth on her way home from invading Korea. Since that time, the Japanese have been coming here to take its waters.

The town's other claim to fame is its pottery—the work of Korean potters whom Hideyoshi Toyotomi's armies imported to Kyūshū 400 years ago. The pottery is noted for its simple designs and subdued natural colors. Takeo Onsen is also home to three lofty camphor trees, all of them more than 3,000 years old and designated as National Natural Monuments. Takeo Onsen may not be postcard-perfect, but it does have an intimate atmosphere not found in big-city Japan. This makes it an intriguing and convenient overnight alternative to Fukuoka or Nagasaki. All of the ryokan and *izakaya* (casual drinking and eating establishments) are within walking distance of the station.

Dining and Lodging

$ ✕ **Muraichi-ban.** This cheerful izakaya is for the young or young-at-heart. Locals meet here to while away the evening eating an array of foods from sashimi to grilled fish, yaki-tori (soy-roasted chicken) to omelettes. The centerpiece of the restaurant is a large, square kitchen where cooks energetically fillet fish, stir-fry noodles, and generally put on a show for whoever's at the counter. If you don't want these distractions, there are booths around the edge of the dining room. Bric-a-brac hang from the wood-beamed ceilings, and posters on the walls give a light ambience to this local joint. ✉ *Takeo-ku, Owada Takeo, Fukuoka-ken,* ☎ *0954/23–4995. No credit cards.*

$$ 🏨 **Kyōto-ya.** There are some 20 ryokan in Takeo Onsen. Kyōto-ya, a comfortable choice in the middle price range, genuinely welcomes gai-jin guests. Tatami guest rooms are reasonably spacious and include a separate alcove with a table and two chairs by a window. If you reserve Room 405, you'll have a view of the hotel's open-air thermal pools. These, with their forced air jets to create a whirlpool effect, are wonderfully massaging. Those with tender skin will be pleased to know that the thermal waters here are not as hot as in other onsen. Meals are brought to your room, though you can opt to pay for just the room and eat at one of the local restaurants. ✉ *Takeo-ku 843,* ☎ *0954/23–2171,* 𝔽𝔸𝕏 *0954/23–2176. 34 rooms, most with private bath. Thermal baths, shop. MC, V.*

$$ 🏨 **Takeo Century Hotel.** A welcome oasis in the center of beautiful pottery towns, the Takeo Century has all the Western amenities with a traditional Japanese public bath. Rooms in back of the hotel overlook a traditional Japanese garden and the swimming pool. The staff is extremely helpful, and the hotel is in a perfect location to enjoy puttering around the towns of Arita and Imari, not to mention Takeo Onsen. It is a 15-minute walk to the station, but well worth the trip. ✉ *4053-13 Takeo, Takeo City, Saga-ken 843,* ☎ *0954/22–2200,* 𝔽𝔸𝕏 *0954/22–2888. 150 rooms. 4 restaurants, bar, café, pool, 4 tennis courts, shops. AE, D, MC, V.*

En Route **Arita** is a small village with one main street that is entirely lined with pottery shops, each with its own kilns and run by the same family for generations. Prices depend on quality, but you can get a beautiful handmade teacup for around ¥2,000 or a set of five cups and a teapot for ¥10,000. Once a year, at the end of April or early May (contact the Arita town office: ☎ 0955/43–2101, 𝔽𝔸𝕏 0955/43–2107), there is a large pottery fair, when everything in all the shops goes on sale. At these times, many of the ceramic pieces are priced as low as ¥500. Arita is about 20 minutes by local train from Takeo Onsen.

Continuing east, the train will take you to the Huis Ten Bosch and **Holland Village** (☞ Off the Beaten Path *in* Nagasaki, *below*). From Huis Ten Bosch, it is a 90-minute run down to Nagasaki.

NAGASAKI

2 hrs southwest of Fukuoka by JR, 1 hr and 35 mins south of Takeo Onsen by JR.

Nagasaki, a quiet city of hills with a peaceful harbor, is often called the San Francisco of Japan. The harbor, now serenely dotted with a few fishing boats, was once the most important trading port in the country. In 1639, when Japan decided to close its ports to all gai-jin, it appointed the small island of Dejima in Nagasaki Harbor as the one place where gai-jin were allowed to land. The only Japanese allowed to have contact with the gai-jin were merchants and prostitutes. The Tokugawa shogunate established this isolationist policy to prevent Western powers from having political influence in Japan. With Nagasaki as the focal point, however, knowledge of the West, particularly in fields such as medicine and weaponry, began to spread throughout Japan. Japan reopened its doors to the West in 1859, thus ending Nagasaki's heyday as the sole international port. Many of the original buildings and churches from the 19th century still stand as testaments to this unique period in Japanese history.

After more than two centuries of prominence, Nagasaki became a relatively obscure Japanese city until the atomic bomb was dropped on it in 1945. Although the bomb destroyed one-third of the city, enough remained standing so that, to this day, Nagasaki has an atmosphere that mixes both Eastern and Western traditions from the last century.

Exploring Nagasaki

Nagasaki is a beautiful harbor city that is small enough to cover on foot if you have the energy to face some of the steep inclines, which veer and meander, drawing comparison to the hills of San Francisco. Most interesting sights and restaurant and shopping areas are south of Nagasaki Eki. The Peace Park, the memorial and ruins left in memory of the victims of the second atomic bomb in 1945, and Nishi-zaka are to the north.

When you get to Nagasaki, pick up a copy of *Harbor Light,* a monthly publication in English that provides detailed information on activities throughout the city.

★ ❹ **Glover Gardens,** which affords panoramic views of Nagasaki and the harbor, is a good place to get your feet on the ground in Nagasaki. The gardens contain Western-style houses that were built in the late 19th century. The principle one is Glover Mansion (1863), former home of Thomas Glover, a British merchant who married a Japanese woman and settled in Nagasaki. Glover introduced the first steam locomotive and established the first mint in Japan. The house remains as it was in Glover's time, and his furniture and possessions are on display. The story for Puccini's opera *Madame Butterfly* is said to have been set here. Escalators going up the slopes toward the Glover Mansion seem out of place, but they can be a welcome way to ascend the hill and take in Nagasaki harbor below. The gardens are distinctly Western in design, providing a sense of what Glover's little colonial sanctuary was like when Japan opened up to the West.

To get to the Glover Gardens, board Streetcar 1 from the JR eki to the downtown stop Tsuki-machi and transfer (don't forget to collect a transfer ticket) to Streetcar 5. Get off at the Ōura-Tenshudo-shita stop (the second-to-last stop on the line). Take the side street to the right, cross the bridge over the small canal, and then take the second street on your left up the hill. Tōkyū Hotel, a place to keep in mind for afternoon tea, will be on your left, an array of souvenir shops to the right. ☞ **Ōura Catholic Church** will be facing you as you turn one corner on the hill. ☎ *0958/27–6111.* 🎟 *¥600.* ⊙ *Mar.–Nov., daily 8–6; Dec.– Feb., daily 8:30–5.*

❺ **Jurokuban-kan** was built in 1860 as accommodations for the American consular staff. The mansion is now a museum that displays Dutch and Portuguese objects related to the history of early trade between these countries and Japan. It is just outside the exit of the Glover Gardens, before the street filled with shops. ☎ *0958/27–6811.* 🎟 *¥400.* ⊙ *Mar.–Nov., daily 8:30–5:30; Dec.–Feb., daily 8:30–5.*

❻ **Ōura Tenshu-dō** (Catholic Church) is the oldest Gothic-style building in Japan. The church was constructed in 1865 by a French missionary and was dedicated to the memory of the 26 Christians who were crucified in 1597 after Christianity was outlawed. The church has beautiful stained-glass windows. The church is past the base of ☞ **Glover Gardens,** a few minutes on foot. Look for the stairs to the church on your right. 🎟 *¥250.* ⊙ *Dec.–Feb., daily 8:30–5; Mar.–Nov., daily 8–6.*

❼ The **Tojinkan** (Chinese Mansion) was built in 1893 by the Chinese residents of Nagasaki. The hall now houses treasures on loan from the

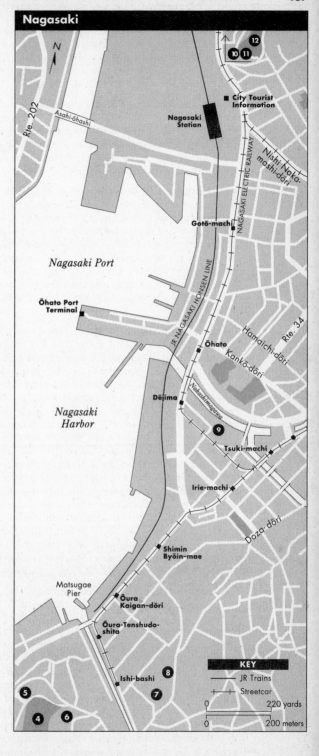

Nagasaki

N

Rte. 202

Asahi-ōhashi

Nagasaki Station

City Tourist Information

Nishi Neko-mashi-dōri

NAGASAKI ELECTRIC RAILWAY

Gotō-machi

Nagasaki Port

JR NAGASAKI HONSEN LINE

Ōhato Port Terminal

Ōhato

Kankō-dōri

Hamaichi-dōri

Rte. 34

Dejima

Nakashimagawa

9

Nagasaki Harbor

Tsuki-machi

Irie-machi

Doza-dōri

Shimin Byōin-mae

Matsugae Pier

Ōura Kaigan-dōri

Ōura-Tenshudo-shita

Ishi-bashi

8

7

5

4   **6**

KEY

—— JR Trains

�┼╼ Streetcar

0   220 yards

0   200 meters

Palace Museum, Beijing, which are rotated every two years. Many descriptions are in English, and though the collection is small, it is a worthwhile introduction to the Chinese feeling that pervades Nagasaki. Walk southeast from the Ishi-bashi streetcar stop, take the first left turn toward Oranda-zaka, then take the first right and walk straight ahead to the Chinese wall in front of you. 🕮 ¥525. ⊘ Daily 8:30–5.

❽ **Oranda-zaka** (Holland Slope) is a cobblestone incline with 19th-century wood houses built by Dutch residents. Though you can't get in to see the interiors of these 19th-century buildings, the quaint old facades may give the impression that you are not in Japan at all. To get there, follow the street on the southeast side of the Tojinkan; after about 100 yards, the pleasant walk begins on your left.

❾ The original site of **Dejima** suggests Nagasaki's rich, international trading past. It was the man-made island where the Dutch were allowed to land in the years when Japan maintained its isolationist policy. It is no longer an island, because the area has been land-filled, but there is a miniature reconstruction of the entire village and community of Dejima, as part of the **Nagasaki City Dejima Museum,** which is to be completed in September of 1998. Until then, the old **Dejima Historical Museum** will remain open; its hours are Tuesday–Sunday 9–5. Dejima village will be visible from the Dejima and Tsuki-machi streetcar stops.

If you were to see all of Nagasaki's picturesque sights, the city might seem like a quaint port town that time and progress have somehow passed by. But it is important to remember that Nagasaki suffered the devastation of an atomic bomb. So that the memory of this tragedy

❿ endures, **Heiwa Kōen** (Peace Park) was built at the exact site of the epicenter of the August 9, 1945, atomic blast. In a blinding flash, 2.59 square mi were obliterated and 74,884 people were killed, with another 74,909 injured out of an estimated population of 204,000. Compared to present-day atomic weaponry, it was only a small bomb that destroyed Nagasaki. At one end of the park, a black pillar grimly marks the exact center of the blast. At the other end is a graceless 32-ft statue of a male figure with one arm pointing horizontally (symbolizing world peace), the other pointing toward the sky (indicating the harm of nuclear power). Despite the park's small size—only a fraction of Hiroshima's Heiwa Kōen—an appropriately somber gloom pervades this memorial. Every year on August 9 there is an anti-nuclear-war demonstration here. To get to the park, take Streetcar 1 to the Matsuya-machi stop. From the JR eki, take either Streetcar 1 or 3 to the Matsuya-machi stop, about a 10-minute ride. 🕮 Free. ⊘ Daily 9–6.

⓫ The **Gembaku Shiryōkan** (Nagasaki Atomic Bomb Museum) is the ultimate in museum technology, with interactive TV displays, video testimonies, and hands-on exhibits. The architecture literally steers you spiraling downward into the displays of photos and objects demonstrating the devastation caused by the atomic bomb. The museum is far more grim and informative than the Peace Park itself. Walking through the hall is a sobering experience. Note the section given to the foreign victims of the bomb dropped by the American B-29 *Bockscar,* which tells of the 500 Allied POWs interned in the middle of a factory site that was decimated, although 200 of them had died of disease, malnutrition, and torture before the bomb was dropped. The interactive displays are the latest in museum visuals, and the testimonies of Japan's neglect of Korean bomb survivors are particularly educational. To get to the museum, take Streetcar 1 to the Hamaguchi stop, then follow the road in front of you up the slope to the modern building built into the hill next to the tall red Nagasaki Municipal Museum, which you can see from the streetcar stop. ✉ *7-8 Hirano-machi,* ☎ *0958/44–1231,* FAX *0958/46–5170.* 🎫 *¥200. Earphones ¥150.* ⊙ *Daily 8:30—5:30; Closed Dec. 29–31.*

⑫ Nishi-zaka (West Slope), a short walk from Nagasaki Eki, is the site of 16th-century Christian martyrdom. At the time, Christian missionaries successfully converted many Japanese to Christianity. Because Japanese leaders feared the potential influence of Christianity, they banned its practice in 1587. Ten years later, 20 Japanese and six Europeans were crucified on this hill for refusing to renounce their religious beliefs. A monument was built in 1962 dedicated to the memory of the 26 martyrs, and a small museum documents the history of Christianity in Japan. To get there, exit the front of the JR eki, turn left, and walk along the road next to the train tracks for a few minutes. Turn right on the first major road and you will be at Nishi-zaka. 🎫 *¥250.* ⊙ *Daily 9–5; Closed Dec. 31–Jan. 2.*

OFF THE BEATEN PATH

NAGASAKI HOLLAND VILLAGE HUIS TEN BOSCH – Believe it or not, these 375 acres of Netherlandia, which cost $1.75 billion to build, make up Japan's largest theme park. The attractions are modeled after 17th-century Holland, with replicas of a Dutch village and the Cathedral of Horn (Dom Horn). Though there are scheduled activities such as horse parades, many of the Japanese tourists spend their time choosing among the many restaurants available and shopping at the numerous souvenir outlets. With an admission cost of ¥3,900 and additional fees for specific attractions, it can become an expensive day's outing and one that Westerners might find only marginally interesting. The complex includes the 330-room Hotel Europa. It is an hour-long bus ride (¥1,300) north of Nagasaki, near Sasebo. You can also take the JR train from Nagasaki (or Takeo Onsen), which takes 90 minutes to reach the Huis Ten Bosch station. ✉ *1-1 Huis Ten Bosch-machi, Sasebo,* ☎ *0956/27–0001,* FAX *0956/27–0912.* ⊙ *Daily 9 AM–11 PM.*

Dining and Lodging

$$$$ ✕ **Harbin.** It isn't difficult to imagine the residents of the 19th-century Western-style houses of Nagasaki eating at this dark, romantic, Continental enclave. Sauces are a bit heavy, and the food is slightly overcooked—perhaps the chef is trying to re-create authentically the dishes as they would be served in Europe. ✉ *2-27 Kozen-machi,* ☎ *0958/ 22–7443. AE, DC, MC, V.*

$$$$ ✕ **Kagetsu.** This quiet, hilltop restaurant is Nagasaki's most prestigious. Dishes are served in the kaiseki manner, but the menu combines Japanese and Chinese cuisine. The building that houses Kagetsu was visited long ago by the Meiji Restoration leader, Ryoma Sakamoto. According to local legend, Sakamoto, while involved in a fight, slashed his sword into a wood pillar and left a gash that is still visible in the restaurant today. ✉ *2-1 Maruyama-chō,* ☎ *0958/22–0191. DC, V.*

$$$ ✕ **Fukiro.** Some of the best shippoku in Nagasaki is served in this roomy Japanese restaurant with tatami mats and shoji screens. Shippoku combines tasty morsels of Chinese and Japanese food, all presented in an aesthetically pleasing way. To get to Fukiro, you must first walk up a steep set of stone steps. The restaurant is an old Japanese-style building, with a tiled roof and long wooden beams. ✉ *146 Kami-nishiyama-machi,* ☎ *0958/22–0253. DC.*

$–$$ ✕ **Shikai-rō.** This large restaurant—1,500 can be seated in its variety ★ of garishly decorated rooms—is the birthplace of the well-known Nagasaki champon noodles. Champon is the house specialty, but there is an extensive menu to look at as well. Seafood dishes are particularly good, and beef with bamboo shoots is recommended. There is excellent Chinese fare from the Fukien region—a surprise, because most Chinese food in Japan is rather bland. Service is somewhat brusque by Japanese standards. ⊠ *4-5 Matsugae-machi,* ☎ *0958/822–1296. DC.*

$ ✕ **Hamakatsu.** Fans of Japanese *tonkatsu* (fried pork cutlets) will enjoy the Nagasaki version, which uses ground pork mixed with scallions. Hamakatsu specializes in this local treat. Other dishes are available, but most people stick to tonkatsu, especially because it is one of the lower-priced dishes on the menu. ⊠ *1-14 Kajiya-machi,* ☎ *0958/ 27–5783. No credit cards.*

$ ✕ **Kosanko.** Within Nagasaki's compact Chinatown district are a dozen or so Chinese restaurants. Most famous among them is Kosanko. Dining is on the second floor, though you'll probably have to wait in the ground-floor lobby for a table. Dishes cost approximately ¥800–¥1,000 each and run the gamut from champon noodles to egg rolls and sweet-and-sour pork. Even though its reputation is grander than its cooking, Kosanko is a fun, lively restaurant, especially enjoyable if you are with a group. ⊠ *12-2 Sakura-machi,* ☎ *0958/21–3735. No credit cards.*

$$$$ 🏨 **Hotel New Nagasaki.** Losing its preeminence to the Prince Hotel
★   (☞ *below*), this hotel still has the advantage of being just a two-minute walk from Nagasaki Station. The standard twin guest rooms, the largest in the city, have enough space for a couple of easy chairs and a table. The lobby lounge is sparklingly fresh, and the French restaurant, Hydrangea, has the airy, light ambience of a conservatory. On the 13th floor are a Chinese restaurant and the Moonlight Lounge for evening drinks; the Steak House serves beef from Gotō Island. Many staff members are fluent in English. ⊠ *14-5 Daikoku-machi, Nagasaki, Nagasaki-ken 850,* ☎ *0958/26-8000,* 🅵🅰🆇 *0958/26–6162. 140 Western-style rooms. 5 restaurants, indoor pool, exercise room, sauna, shops. AE, DC, MC, V.*

$$$$ 🏨 **Nagasaki Prince Hotel.** This is the city's newest, grandest, and most expensive hotel. Despite its monolithic exterior, the inside is the closest imitation of a fine European hotel in Kyūshū. The long, rectangular lobby shimmers with glass, marble, and ponds, but the warm red carpet softens the glare. Sharply dressed staff in suits or uniforms hurry to cater to your every need; concierges are particularly attentive. Guest rooms are decorated in the ubiquitous pastels and have natural-color processed wood furniture. Each room has bedside panels and is equipped with the amenities of a first-class hotel. Restaurants run the gamut from the New York Steak and Seafood dining room to a Japanese sushi bar. Note: The Prince is a 10-minute walk from Nagasaki Station in the opposite direction from downtown, though the streetcar passes by the front entrance and taxis are plentiful. ⊠ *2-26 Takara-machi, Nagasaki-chō, Nagasaki, Nagasaki-ken 850,* ☎ *0958/21–1111,* 🅵🅰🆇 *0958/ 23–4309. 183 rooms. 5 restaurants, room service, beauty salon, parking. AE, DC, MC, V.*

$$$$ 🏨 **Sakamoto-ya.** This ryokan, started in 1895, seems to have changed
★   very little from its founding days. Cedar baths are offered, and the wood building is a testament to the beauty and simplicity of Japanese architecture. The restaurant specializes in shippoku, and the cost per night includes breakfast and dinner. The inn is very small and has extremely personalized service. The cost of the rooms varies depending on size and location. ⊠ *2-13 Kanaya-machi, Nagasaki, Nagasaki-ken 850,* ☎ *0958/26–8211,* 🅵🅰🆇 *0958/25–5944. 15 rooms. AE, DC.*

$$$ 🏨 **Nagasaki Grand Hotel.** This hotel is small and quiet, with a dignified atmosphere. Rooms are compact but pleasantly decorated. Best of all is the outdoor beer garden; there are Japanese and Western

restaurants as well. ✉ *5-3 Manzai-machi, Nagasaki, Nagasaki-ken 850,* ☎ *0958/23–1234,* FAX *0958/22–1793. 142 Western-style rooms, 8 Japanese-style rooms. 2 restaurants. AE, DC, MC, V.*

$$ 🏨 **Yataro.** On top of a mountain, about 20 minutes by taxi from the center of Nagasaki, this ryokan and its hotel annex have excellent views of Nagasaki. Meals are plentiful and presented with great care. The view from the shared bath is particularly good. You'll probably enjoy staying in the ryokan, where meals are served in your room, more than the hotel annex. Request a room with a view when you make your reservation. The hotel is less expensive than the inn. ✉ *2-1 Kazagoshiramachi, Nagasaki, Nagasaki-ken 850,* ☎ *0958/22–8166,* FAX *0958/ 28–1122. 56 ryokan rooms, 133 hotel rooms. Restaurant. AE, DC, MC, V.*

$ 🏨 **Ajisai Inn One.** Rooms are small but clean at this small establishment near the station, opposite the Hotel New Nagasaki (☞ *above*). The staff members are friendly and speak a few words of English. ✉ *11-4 Daikoku, Nagasaki, Nagasaki-ken 850,* ☎ *0958/27–3110,* FAX *0958/27–3109. 42 rooms. AE, DC, MC, V.*

Shopping

In **Hamano-machi** you can find traditional crafts, antiques, and restaurants. Not far from Dejïma, Hamano-machi is the major shopping district in downtown Nagasaki. Keep in mind that it is illegal to bring tortoiseshell products into the United States.

Gift Ideas

Castella cake. Based on a Dutch cake, this dessert resembles a pound cake with a moist top. It has long been the most commonly known Nagasaki product and was popular here when baked goods were still unknown in the rest of Japan. **Fukusaya** is a bakery that has been in business since the beginning of the Meiji period (1868–1912). When you say "castella," most people think of this famous shop and its distinctive yellow packaging of the cake. Tōkyōites would never return from a trip to Nagasaki without their Fukusaya castella. ✉ *3-1 Funadaiku-machi,* ☎ *0958/21–2938.* ☉ *Daily 8:30–8; closed 2nd Thurs. of month.*

Glass Road 1571. This shop is noted for its Nagasaki glassware, an art that was introduced by the Dutch during the Tokugawa period. It is near the Ōura Catholic Church, and its objects range from ¥200 to ¥100,000. ✉ *2-11 Minami-yamate-machi,* ☎ *0958/22–1571,* FAX *0958/28–6009.* ☉ *Daily 9–5:30.*

Nagasaki A to Z

Arriving and Departing

BY BUS

The Kyūshū Kyūkō Bus Company runs between Fukuoka and Nagasaki (3 hrs, 20 mins); the bus leaves from the Fukuoka Bus Center in the Tenjin downtown district. A bus service also runs between Nagasaki and Kumamoto (4 hrs; ☞ *Kumamoto, below*).

BY PLANE

Ōmura Kūkō (airport) is approximately one hour by bus or car from Nagasaki. ANA and JAS have five direct flights daily from Haneda Kūkō in Tōkyō to Ōmura Kūkō (1 hr, 40 mins). From Ōsaka the flights are 1 hour and 10 minutes.

Between the Airport and Center City. A regular shuttle bus travels between Ōmura Kūkō and Nagasaki Station in 55 minutes. The cost is ¥1,150.

Take the JR Nagasaki Line Limited Express train from Fukuoka (approximately 2 hrs). To get to Kumamoto from Nagasaki by train, take the Kamone Line from Nagasaki to Tosu Station (2 hrs). From Tosu, board the Kagoshima Main Line and get off at Kumamoto (1 hr).

Getting Around
BY BUS

Bus routes exist in Nagasaki, but they are complicated and not very convenient.

BY STREETCAR

Streetcars are the most convenient way of getting around Nagasaki. Although slow, they appropriately reflect the relaxed atmosphere of Nagasaki and evoke earlier days. Streetcars stop at most major sights, and many stops have signs in English. You can purchase a one-day pass (¥500) for unlimited streetcar travel at the City Tourist Information Center or at major hotels. Otherwise, you pay ¥100 as you get off the streetcar. If you wish to transfer from one streetcar to another, take a *norikae kippu* (transfer ticket) from the driver of the first streetcar as you alight and drop ¥120 in the fare box.

Contacts and Resources
GUIDED TOURS

By Boat. A 50-minute port cruise of Nagasaki Harbor (¥900) departs at 11:40 and 3:15. Take a streetcar to Ōhato Station, and then go to Pier No. 1.

By Ricksha. Rickshas, once ubiquitous, are now a rare sight in Japan. Prices vary according to the course you take, but the minimum is ¥2,000 per person. Ask your hotel or the tourist information office to call in Japanese to arrange a tour (☎ 0958/24–4367).

City Tours. Japan Travel Bureau (☎ 0958/24–3200) offers a few city tours with English-speaking guides. A three-hour tour of the city's major sights costs ¥2,950.

VISITOR INFORMATION

City Tourist Information Center (✉ 1-88 Onoue-chō, ☎ 0958/23–3631), open Monday–Saturday 9–6, is on the left-hand corner (as you leave the station) of the station plaza. There is no sign written in English, so it takes perseverance to find, but the office is useful for maps and directions.

The Nagasaki Prefecture Tourist Office (✉ Nagasaki Kōtsū Sangyo Bldg., 2nd floor, 3-1 Daikoku-machi, ☎ 0958/23–4041) is across the street from the JR *eki* one floor above street level in a department store. To reach it from the station, use the pedestrian bridge. The staff is not very helpful, but maps and bus schedules to various areas within the prefecture are available. It's open weekdays 9–5:30, Saturday 9–12:45.

KUMAMOTO

⑬ *1 hr east of Nagasaki by ferry, 1½ hrs south of Fukuoka by JR Limited Express.*

Kumamoto was one of Japan's major centers of power in the years of the Tokugawa shogunate (1603–1868). The city's primary historical sights—the castle and the gardens of Suizen-ji Kōen—date from this period and are among the most famous in Japan. Kumamoto may no longer be a major political center, but, with its broad and lush tree-lined avenues, it is an extremely attractive city. Despite having no real political importance since the Meiji Restoration, the city is currently enjoying a commercial boom.

Exploring Kumamoto

Unlike in many other Japanese cities, there is very little activity around the JR eki in Kumamoto. Instead, shops, restaurants, and hotels are clustered downtown under the shadow of the castle. The heart of the town is a broad shopping arcade; small streets branch off of it. The area comes alive at night with neon lights advertising restaurants and bars.

Kumamoto-jō is in the heart of Kumamoto. The castle was first built in 1607 under the auspices of Kiyomasa Katō, the area's daimyō. It is especially famous for its unique, massive concave defensive walls, known as *mushagaeshi,* which made it exceedingly difficult for attackers to scale. It is often referred to as Ginko-jō, after a giant ginko tree that was supposedly planted by Lord Katō. Much of the original castle was destroyed in 1877, after it lay under siege for 57 continuous days by an army from Kagoshima led by Takamori Saigō. It was rebuilt in 1960.

Often, reconstructed buildings are of little interest, but this concrete replica manages to evoke the magnificence of the original. By walking around the expansive grounds, you can get a true sense of the grandeur of feudal Japan. Few castles in Japan today, reconstructed or not, have as many as Kumamoto-jō's 49 turrets, 18 turret gates, and 29 castle gates. Inside, there is a museum full of samurai armor and palanquins, in case you are interested in feudal history. As you look at the displays, you cannot help but imagine samurai in full regalia, fiercely protecting their lord. From the top floor there is an excellent view of Kumamoto. If time permits further exploration of the grounds, go to the lovely Higo Gardens, a peaceful place to conclude your visit. To get to the castle, board Streetcar 2, get off at the Kumamoto-jō-mae stop, and walk up a tree-lined slope toward the castle. 🖼 *Grounds ¥200, castle ¥300.* ☉ *Apr.–Sept., daily 8:30–5:30; Nov.–Mar., daily 8:30–4:30.*

In spring and fall, the **Kumamoto Kenritsu Bijutsukan** (Prefectural Art Museum) exhibits the famous Hosokawa collection of antiques from the Tokugawa era. Be sure to see the full-scale models of the burial chambers with Kumamoto's design of painted geometrical shapes. The bijutsukan is west of Kumamoto-jō (☞ *above*) in a modern redbrick building. 🖼 *¥210.* ☉ *Tues.–Sun. 9:30–4:30.*

Suizen-ji Kōen, a 300-year-old garden that is a classic of Japanese garden design, was originally created in 1632 by the Hosokawa clan as part of the grounds of their villa. Although the park is often crowded with tour groups and lacks a certain serenity, there are still elements of beauty where artistry characteristically fuses with nature. A part of the garden with ponds and small artificial mounds re-creates the 53 stations of the Tōkaidō—the old post road between Edo and Kyōto—and its prominent features, such as Biwa-ko (Lake Biwa) and Fuji-san. To get to Suizen-ji Kōen, take Streetcar 2 or 3 east from the castle to the Suizen-ji Kōen-mae stop. 🖼 *¥400.* ☉ *Daily 7:30–6.*

NEED A BREAK? | In Suizen-ji Kōen, stop at the small, **old-fashioned teahouse** by the garden's pond. Here, for ¥500, you can sip green tea as you sit on tatami mats and appreciate the exquisite view. It's open daily 9-5.

Honmyō-ji is a Nichiren temple—Nichiren being a type of Buddhism with its own architectural style—that daimyō Kiyomasa Katō built. And

Katō is buried here, in the tomb at the top of a flight of stairs, so that his spirit may look across at eye level to the donjon of his castle, Kumamoto-jō. The temple's museum contains Katō's personal effects, including the helmet that he wore while campaigning in Korea for his master, Hideyoshi Toyotomi. It is on the hill to the west of town. Take a streetcar from JR Kumamoto Eki or Bus 12 from the Kōtsū Center. ▨ *Museum ¥300.* ☉ *Tues.–Sun. 9–5.*

Dining and Lodging

$$$$ ✕ **Loire.** If you are tired of Japanese food and want a good French meal, try this elegant, spacious restaurant on the 11th floor of the Kumamoto Castle Hotel (☞ Lodging, *below*) with an excellent view of the castle. The set-course meals, which feature fish or meat dishes, change monthly. Some months, special all-you-can-eat buffets are available. Desserts are delicious and varied. If you do not feel like paying so much for the view, come for the more reasonably priced lunches. ▨ *4-2 Joto-machi,* ☎ *096/326–3311. AE, DC, MC, V.*

$$$–$$$$ ✕ **Togasaku Honten.** Formal Japanese cuisine is at its best in this restau-
★ rant, which serves a set menu. The dinners, served at low, Japanese-style tables, consist of several small courses of fish, meat, tofu, and vegetables, which add up to a very filling meal. Prices are high, but your yen are well spent on meals that are not only tasty but also presented with exquisite beauty. Togasaku Honten overlooks a peaceful garden, and the staff are formal and polite without being stiff. Ask for a table with a view when you make reservations. ▨ *1-15-3 Hamazuno,* ☎ *096/353–4171. Reservations essential. AE, DC, MC, V.*

$$–$$$ ✕ **Togasaku Honten.** A branch of Togasaku Honten (☞ *above*) with good food at slightly lower prices is located in nearby Suizen-ji Kōen. This restaurant is more informal and has Western-style tables. ▨ *Togasaku Suizen-ji Kōen, Tsuchiyama Bldg., 2nd floor, 3-4 Suizen-ji Kōen,* ☎ *096/385–5151. AE, DC, MC, V.*

$$ ✕ **Mutsugoro.** This casual dining spot, with pale paper-and-wood walls, is in the basement of the Green Hotel. Curious, adventurous eaters will note that this restaurant serves horse meat in 40 different ways, including raw horse-meat sashimi and fried horse meat. If you go and decide that these specialties are not to your taste, you can choose from a variety of seafood dishes. As is the case with many informal Japanese restaurants, you order many small dishes. Each costs between ¥800 and ¥1,000; for a full meal, you will probably want four or five dishes. ▨ *12-11 Hanabata-chō,* ☎ *096/356–6256. No credit cards. No lunch.*

$$ ✕ **Senri.** Couple a visit to beautiful Suizen-ji Kōen with lunch or dinner at Senri, situated right in the gardens. You will find a variety of dishes, including seafood, eel, and horse-meat sashimi. Although Western-style tables and chairs are available, the tatami rooms and low tables are more appropriate to the ambience of the gardens. Even if you do not choose to have a meal here, you can come for a light snack or an appetizer. ▨ *7-17 Suizen-ji,* ☎ *096/384–1824. No credit cards.*

$$ ▦ **Fujie.** On the main street leading directly away from the station, this is a smart business hotel with Western single rooms and attractive Japanese double rooms. The lobby lounge faces a Japanese garden, and the restaurant serves well-presented Japanese food. Service is personable and friendly, though the English language is not the staff's strong point. ▨ *2-2 Kasuga, Kumamoto, Kumamoto-ken 860,* ☎ *096/353–1101,* ℻ *096/322–2671. 47 rooms. AE, DC, MC, V.*

$$ ▦ **Kumamoto Castle Hotel.** This hotel is conveniently situated near Kumamoto-jō and the downtown district. Request a room with a view of the castle, if possible. The rooms here are quiet, a cut above those of business hotels. But not many of the staff speak English. ⊠ *4-2 Joto-machi, Kumamoto, Kumamoto-ken 860,* ☎ *096/326–3311,* FAX *096/326–3324. 185 rooms. 3 restaurants, coffee shop. AE, DC, MC, V.*

$$ 🏨 **New Sky Hotel.** Managed by the ANA group, the New Sky is in many ways the best lodging in Kumamoto. In addition to having several good restaurants, the hotel maintains a relationship with a health club down the street so that guests can use the pool for ¥700, or all facilities for ¥2,100. The rooms are small, bright, and cheerful. ⊠ *2 Amidaji-chō, Kumamoto, Kumamoto-ken 860,* ☎ *096/354–2111,* FAX *096/354–8973. 342 rooms. 3 restaurants, barbershop, beauty salon. AE, DC, MC, V.*

$ 🏨 **Kumamoto Station Hotel.** A three-minute walk from the station, this hotel is strictly utilitarian and only marginally less expensive than the others listed here. ⊠ *1-3-6 Kumamoto, Kumamoto-ken 860,* ☎ *096/325–2001,* FAX *096/354—2900. 75 rooms. Restaurant. No credit cards.*

$ 🏨 **Minshuku-ryokan Kajita.** This two-story, Japanese wooden house has been made into a friendly inn (part of the Japanese Inn Group). The small public room has some Western trappings, but the tatami rooms, also small, are typically Japanese—with a shared bath. Breakfast (¥700) and dinner (¥2,000) are offered. To reach the inn, take a city bus from the JR Kumamoto Eki to Shin-machi bus stop, and then cross the street and walk two minutes up the side street. ⊠ *1-2-7 Shin-machi, Kumamoto, Kumamoto-ken 860,* ☎ *096/353–1546. 10 Japanese-style rooms with shared bath. AE.*

Shopping

One of Kumamoto's most famous products is *higo zogan,* a form of metalwork consisting of black steel inlaid with silver and gold that create a delicate yet striking pattern. Originally an ornamentation technique for the samurai swords, scabbards, and gun stocks of the Hosokawa clan, it is now used mostly in jewelry and other accessories. (The more higo zogan is worn, the glossier it becomes.) Another popular local product is the *Yamaga doro,* lanterns of gold paper. On August 16, as part of the annual Bon festival, young women carry these gold lanterns through the streets of Kumamoto.

One of the best places for higo zogan, Yamaga doro, and other local crafts is **Dentō Kogei-kan** (Kumamoto Traditional Crafts Center, ⊠ 3-35 Chiba-jō, ☎ 096/324–4930), a combination gallery and shop that displays crafts from all over Kumamoto Prefecture. It is next to the Kumamoto Castle Hotel and is open Tuesday–Sunday 9–5. **Shimatori Shopping Arcade,** near Kumamoto-jō, is a good place to find everything from toothpaste to local crafts. The **Tsuruya Department Store** (⊠ Tetori-hon-chō-dōri, ☎ 094/356–2111) is a good source for Yamaga doro as well as a host of other items.

Kumamoto A to Z

Arriving and Departing

BY BUS
The bus from Nagasaki Bus Terminal takes four hours to get to Kumamoto. It goes as far as Shimabara, after which you ferry across Ariake Bay to Misumi, then take the bus directly to Kumamoto Kōtsū Center. This trip takes you through some of Kyūshū's most beautiful scenery and costs ¥3,600, including the ferry.

BY PLANE
Five daily flights on ANA and JAS connect Tōkyō's Haneda Kūkō with Kumamoto Kūkō (1 hr, 45 mins). ANA has four hour-long flights daily from Ōsaka Kūkō.

Between the Airport and Center City. A bus regularly makes the 55-minute run from the airport to JR Kumamoto Eki (¥670 one-way).

BY TRAIN

JR's Limited Express from Hakata stops in Kumamoto (1½ hrs) en route to Kagoshima. From Nagasaki, take JR to Shimabara, board a one-hour ferry across Ariake Bay to Misumi, and then take another train to Kumamoto. JR Pass holders can save the ferry fare by taking the train to Tosu and changing to the train to Kumamoto (3 hrs total).

Getting Around

BY BUS

The main bus terminal is the Kōtsū Center, a few minutes' walk from Kumamoto-jō. Although the buses travel all over the city, the routes are more complicated than those of the streetcars.

BY STREETCAR

The easiest way to get around Kumamoto is by the two streetcar lines that connect the major areas of the city. When you board the streetcar, take a ticket. When you get off, you will pay a fare based on the distance you traveled. A fare chart is posted at the front to the left of the driver. Your ticket will bear the number of the zone in which you boarded the bus; on the chart, the fare will flash for each numbered zone. From the (JR) Kumamoto Eki-mae streetcar stop, it is a 10-minute ride downtown (¥150). One-day travel passes good for use on streetcars and municipal buses are available for ¥500 from the Kumamoto Station Travel Information Bureau (☎ 096/352–3743).

Contacts and Resources

VISITOR INFORMATION

City Information Office (⊠ 3-15-1 Kasuga, ☎ 096/352–3743), open daily 9–5, is inside the JR Kumamoto Eki complex to the left as you exit the platforms.

KAGOSHIMA

❶❹ *3 hrs south of Kumamoto by JR.*

If you have time, consider going to the modern city of Kagoshima south of Kumamoto. The scenic train ride to Nishi-Kagoshima passes mountains on the left and the sea on the right. The downtown area is five minutes on foot from JR Nishi-Kagoshima Eki, and there is a tourist information office to the left as you leave the station.

Though Kagoshima proper has few sightseeing attractions, there are other reasons to take the trip south—the surrounding countryside is gorgeous, and a day's jaunt to the volcano Sakurajima or the hot sands of Ibusuki could turn out to be a unique experience. Kagoshima's mild climate gives the city a tropical feeling, and getting around is easy and inexpensive. Two streetcar lines cover the city, and ¥160 takes you any distance. There is a ¥600 one-day pass for unlimited rides.

Kagoshima serves as a jumping-off point to the surrounding country and Okinawa islands, or as a stopover on the train ride to Kyūshū's east coast. In the downtown entertainment district you'll find the moderately priced **Edokko Sushi** (⊠ Bunka St., 4-1 Sannichi-chō, ☎ 099/225–1890), an excellent sushi bar with counter seating and two tables with tatami seating, and a very hospitable owner. Take the first right off Yubudo (the wide shopping-arcade street); Edokko is the last restaurant on the left. The **Park Hotel** (⊠ 15-24 Chūō-machi, Kagoshima, Kagoshima-ken 890, ☎ 099/251–1100), two minutes from Nishi-Kagoshima Station, has reasonable rates, clean rooms, a pleasant coffee lounge, a Japanese restaurant, and helpful staff. There is also the more expensive (¥14,000 for a twin) and slightly smarter **Kagoshima Tōkyū Inn** (⊠ 5-1 Chūō-chōme, Kagoshimam, Kagoshima-ken 890, ☎ 0992/56–0109, ℻ 099/253–3692), with 190 rooms.

ASO-SAN (MT. ASO)

★ ⑮ *1 hr east of Kumamoto by JR, then 40 mins by bus; 3½ hrs northeast of Kagoshima by JR.*

The road to Mt. Aso passes through the splendor of rural Kyūshū. As you look upon farmers bent over rice fields, bamboo groves, and other idyllic sights, you will get a sense of the relationship that people of this region have with nature. That serene image quickly fades when you arrive at the Mt. Aso volcano, where the bare force of Pacific Rim geology smokes and rumbles.

Mt. Aso is in fact a series of five volcanic peaks, one of which, Nakadake, is still active. The five peaks, along with lakes and fields at its base, form a beautiful national park. You can take in Mt. Aso either on a day trip from Kumamoto or on a stop on the way from Kumamoto to Beppu. If you want to spend more time in the park, you can stay in one of the many mountain pensions on the south side of Mt. Aso (☞ Dining and Lodging, *below*).

Exploring Aso-San

The one active volcano, **Nakadake,** is a fine reason to come to Mt. Aso National Park. From the inside of Nakadake's largest crater, which is 1,968 ft across and 525 ft deep, you hear the rumblings of the volcano and see billowing smoke. Sometimes the volcano is deemed dangerous, and you can't view it up close—so be sure to check at Kumamoto or Beppu before you make this excursion. After viewing the volcano you can descend via the ropeway or walk along a path that leads you back to the ropeway station. If you are up for a hike of several hours, you can skip the ropeway altogether and follow the path up to Nakadake. Because most people choose not to take this arduous route, the paths are delightfully uncrowded, and the views of the live crater and the gorge are awesome.

Lodging

$$$$ ⛩ **Aso Prince Hotel.** This Prince is a stunning hotel tucked away at the base of Nakadake, with half of its 180 rooms overlooking two uncrowded golf courses designed by Arnold Palmer. The public bath is tapped from a mineral source, and a stay here will take you to heights of luxury. ⊠ *Komezuka-onsen, Akamizu, Aso-machi, Aso-gun, Kumamoto 869,* ☎ *0967/35–2111,* ℻ *0967/35–1124. Restaurant, bar, massage, 2 golf courses, 3 tennis courts, shops. AE, DC, MC, V.*

$$ ⛩ **Pension Cream House.** The rooms at this pension are on the small side, but they are pleasant. If you are traveling with friends, the owners do not object to squeezing a group of people into one room, lowering the costs per head accordingly. ⊠ *Takamori-machi, Ozu, Takamori, Kumamoto-ken 3096,* ☎ *0967/62–3090. 8 rooms. AE, DC, V.*

Arriving and Departing

BY BUS

Sanko Buses leaving from the Kumamoto Kōtsū bus terminal go directly to the Aso Nishi ropeway station (1½ hrs).

The JR Hōhi Line runs between Kumamoto Eki and Aso Eki. From Aso Eki to Beppu there are three JR express trains daily. From the JR Aso Eki, you must board a bus (40 mins, ¥610) to get to the Aso Nishi ropeway station. The ropeway leads you to the top of the crater in four minutes and costs ¥410 one-way. It is better to begin your trip well before noon, because the last buses for the ropeway station leave mid-afternoon.

BEPPU AND YUFUIN

Beppu is one of the most popular—read crowded and overdeveloped—resorts in all of Japan. After all your travels, an enjoyable way to rest your weary body is to soak in an *onsen* (hot spring), and Beppu is the place—or at least a place—for hot springs. It provides more than 3,000 sources of hot water not only to the hotels and inns but also to private homes. Its location—the sea in the foreground and mountains to its rear—and the variety of hot mineral springs make it a favorite vacation spot for the Japanese. As a result, Beppu is a garish town with neon lights, amusement parks, pachinko halls by the dozen, and souvenir shops. Many tourists come here and do not leave their hotel or inn to see any of the local sights. The leisurely pace of this resort is indicated by the many Japanese tourists walking around the streets in their *yukata* (cotton kimonos), casually strolling and looking as though they have not a care in the world.

In contrast to all of Beppu's affronts, nearby Yufuin allows a quieter, more tasteful getaway. Yufuin sits on a plateau an hour's bus ride inland from Beppu. The air here—Yufuin is 1,400 ft above sea level—is intoxicatingly fresh, and the pace slow and leisurely.

Beppu

16 *2½ hrs northeast of Mt. Aso by JR, 5 hrs and 50 mins northeast of Kagoshima by JR.*

Beppu is a resort area where the main attractions are the hot springs. If you do decide to look around, here are a few sights to see.

★ If you grow tired of inactivity, visit the **Eight Hells,** the Kannawa section of Beppu, with eight distinctive hot springs. Take Bus 2, 7, 15, 16, 17, 41, or 43 from the stop across from the JR eki for the 30-minute trip (¥330) to Kamenoi Bus Station. One of the springs, **Chi-no-ike Jigoku** (Blood Pond Hell), is a boiling spring with red gurgling water, the vapors of which are purported to have curative powers for skin diseases. **Umi Jigoku** (Sea Hell) has not only water the color of the ocean but also tropical plants. **Oniyama Jigoku** (Devil Mountain Hell) is a place where crocodiles are bred. An entertaining aspect of the Eight Hells is the many vendors nearby who try to sell their wares, such as eggs placed in baskets and boiled in the water. Although it is fascinating to see just how *hot* hot springs can be, keep in mind that this very popular attraction is crowded year-round. Each hot spring charges ¥400 admission; a combined ticket for ¥2,000 will admit you to all except Jigoku Meguri.

Take a bath at **Hyotan Onsen,** one of the more interesting thermal baths, after your tour of the springs. The pool is outdoors, with waterfalls, hot stones, and sand. It is across the road from Kamenoi Bus Station. ¥700. ☉ *Daily 8 AM–9 PM.*

Every good Japanese tourist trap needs a monkey park, and **Takasakiyama Monkey Park** is home to 1,900 of them. These once-wild monkeys were a problem for local farmers, but now they are domesticated. The monkeys are divided into three groups, each carefully guarding its territory. Observation of the hierarchy within each group is fascinating for adults and endlessly diverting for children. To get here, take a 10-minute bus ride from Kitahama Bus Station. ☎ 0975/32-5010. ✉ ¥500. ⊙ Daily 8–5. Feeding times 8:30, noon, 3, and 5.

All hotels and inns in Beppu have baths. If you want to spend a day in a veritable amusement park of hot springs, the **Suginoi Palace,** part of Suginoi Hotel (☞ Dining and Lodging, below), is quite a spectacle. The indoor complex has a variety of hot springs that include a sand bath and a saltwater bath. There is also live cabaret in the evening as well as a vast souvenir-shopping complex, with electronic games—quite ghastly, but a place to visit once. ⊠ Kankai-ji Onsen, ☎ 0977/24-1141. ✉ ¥2,000. ⊙ Daily 9 AM–11 PM.

The **Beppu Ropeway** (¥1,400), open daily 9–5, up Mount Tsunumi will take you to good views of the city and bay and to the **Marine Palace Aquarium** (¥1,050), open daily 8:30–5. The appeal here seems to be greater for Japanese vacationers than for gai-jin. After riding Bus 2 or any buses 32 through 38 from Beppu Station, the ropeway is 10 minutes to the top.

The small **Take-no Museum** (☎ 0977/25–7776) in the center of town exhibits Beppu's celebrated bamboo-work crafts. You can purchase bamboo objects in Kishima, the adjoining shop. The museum is open daily from 8:30 until 6, and admission is ¥310.

Dining and Lodging

$$–$$$ ✕ **Fugumatsu.** This small, popular restaurant, with a simple, Japanese-style interior, has counters, tables, and private rooms. Its specialty is a local favorite, fugu, the potentially poisonous blowfish that restaurants must be licensed to serve. In summer Fugumatsu serves a type of karei (flatfish) that can be caught only in Beppu Bay. Courses start at ¥7,000. Upon request you can have less- or more-expensive food; the restaurant will adjust to your budget. It is one block north of the Tokiwa department store and one block from the bay. ⊠ 3-6-14 Kitahama, ☎ 0977/21–1717. No credit cards.

$ ✕ **Jin.** For an inexpensive evening of beer, sake, and izakaya cuisine that includes yakitori (skewered chicken) and grilled seafood, Jin is popular with Japanese and foreign visitors. You'll sit either at wooden tables and chairs or at the bar looking over displays of fish resting on crushed ice and waiting to be chosen for a meal. The mood is jovial, and you are sure to start up a conversation with your neighbors. Jin is easy to find: Walk from JR Beppu Eki on the right side of Eki-mae-dōri and toward the bay; it is just before the "T" junction and across from Tokiwa department store. ⊠ 1-15-7 Eki-mae-dōri, ☎ 0977/21–1768. No credit cards.

$$$$ ▥ **Suginoi Hotel.** More than just a hotel, this is a miniresort—the most popular place in Beppu. Once you arrive and check in, you may not feel any need to go anywhere else. Suginoi sits on a hill with a panoramic view of the city and the ocean. Connected to the hotel is the Suginoi Palace, with its two large hot springs, aptly named the "Dream Public Bath" and the "Flower Public Bath." Once you've washed and rinsed off, you proceed into a room full of plants and trees. You can soak in a standard hot spring, bury yourself in warm sand, or, if you get bored with hot water, move to a sauna. Breakfast and dinner are included in the price of accommodations, and there are both Western- and Japanese-style buffets. Guests tend to wander around the hotel and attend meals in their yukata. The rooms—rather austere in decor—are a wel-

come break from the opulence of the rest of the hotel. If you are looking for a quiet, refined stay, this is not the right choice. It feels a little
bit like a Japanese Las Vegas—particularly with the glitzy nightly
cabaret, which is free for hotel guests. ⊠ *Kankai-ji Onsen, Beppu, Ōita-
ken 874,* ☎ *0977/24–1141,* 𝔽𝔸𝕏 *0977/21–0010. 494 Japanese-style
rooms, 80 Western-style rooms. 3 restaurants, 3 bars, pool, beauty salon,
driving range, bowling, shops, playground. AE, DC, MC, V.*

$$$ 🏨 **Beppu Kankaiso.** This ryokan used to be a hotel with many Japa-
nese-style rooms. It now serves two meals, which are included in the
price of accommodations. Rooms are large and clean, and Japanese
rooms can sleep as many as five. Although the baths here are nothing
special, the ryokan is close enough to the Suginoi Hotel (☞ *above*) that
it is easy to pay the daily admission of around ¥2,000 and take ad-
vantage of its facilities. The food in the Japanese restaurant Orion is
excellent. ⊠ *Kankai-ji Onsen, Beppu, Ōita-ken 874,* ☎ *0977/23–1221,*
𝔽𝔸𝕏 *0977/21–6285. 43 Japanese-style rooms, 8 Western-style rooms.
Restaurant. AE, DC, V.*

$ 🏨 **Minshuku Kokage.** If you cannot get a room at Sakaeya (☞ *below*),
the Tourist Information Center at Beppu Station has a listing of sev-
eral other inexpensive minshuku. This is one. Just two minutes on foot
from the station in the direction of the bay, the very reasonable three-
story concrete inn has functional rooms, most of which have private
baths. Japanese breakfast (¥825) and dinner (¥1,860) are available. ⊠
8-9 Eki-mae-chō, Beppu, Ōita-ken 874, ☎ *0977/23–1753,* 𝔽𝔸𝕏 *0977/
23–3895. 16 rooms, 11 with bath. AE, MC, V.*

$ 🏨 **Sakaeya.** Many minshuku are drab concrete buildings that are dif-
★ ferent from youth hostels only in that they have private rooms. This
one is a rare gem in a beautiful old wooden building with surprisingly
low rates, which include meals. Meals consist of straightforward Jap-
anese food with fish and rice, but they are prepared in the oven in the
backyard, which is heated from the hot springs. Only one public bath
is available, but as you relax in it with your fellow guests, you have a
sense that this is how the Japanese have been enjoying the wonders of
hot springs for centuries. This minshuku is small and gaining popu-
larity quickly, so reserve ahead. To reach the inn, take Bus 16, 17, 24,
or 25 from Beppu Station (a 30-minute ride). ⊠ *Idonikumi, Ida, Kan-
nawa, Beppu, Ōita-ken 874,* ☎ *0977/66–6234. 10 rooms. No credit
cards.*

Yufuin

★ ⑰ *20 mins west of Ōita by JR, 2 hrs southeast of Fukuoka by JR.*

Yufuin has become the artsy alternative to Beppu, with clusters of gal-
leries showing and selling crafts. One popular grouping is Kusonomori,
but beware of the prices both for admission (ranging from ¥250 to ¥600)
and of the items for sale. Yufuin also has a film and music festival Au-
gust 20–24 and outdoor summer concerts. There are a few historic mon-
uments in Yufuin—Rokushogu, Bussan-ji, Kozen-ji—but it's the
Yunotsubo public onsen alongside the lake that is the most evocative
of traditional Japan.

Quaint **Yunohira Onsen,** with cobblestone streets, traditional inns,
and a history of 270 years of people coming to take its waters, is even
farther off the beaten track. For those who find Yufuin too commer-
cial—and its popularity is increasing—Yunohira Onsen might provide
you that hidden inn away from the crowds. At least three buses a day
make the 36-minute trip from Yufuin to Yunohira Onsen.

Lodging

$–$$ 🛏 **Pension Momotaro.** The owners of this modern pension go out of their way to make you feel at home—they'll even take you to the station when you depart. For dinner you can choose from the regional specialty *gi-tori* (wild chicken), pork, *ayu* (sweet river fish), and shiitake cooked in a pot at the table, or the standard meal, which might be grilled beef over a charcoal brazier and mountain vegetables. Momotaro has three thermal baths, one of which is a *rotemburo* (open-air bath) where you can soak in 60° C water and view the inspiring mountains. There are both Western- and Japanese-style rooms in the main building and Japanese-style rooms in four A-frame chalets. ✉ *Yufuin, Ōita-gun, Oita-ken 879,* ☎ *0977/85–2187,* 𝔽𝔸𝕏 *0977/85–4002. 6 Western-style rooms, 3 Japanese-style rooms, 4 chalets. Dining room, hot springs. No credit cards.*

Beppu and Yufuin A to Z

Arriving and Departing

BY BUS

Buses travel between Kumamoto and Beppu (3½ hrs) and between Mt. Aso and Beppu on the Trans-Kyūshū Highway (3 hrs). The Kyūshū Kokusai Kanko Bus Company's sightseeing buses run regularly between Beppu and Kumamoto, stopping at Mt. Aso.

BY FERRY

Three ferries (two of which call on Shikoku cities: Matsuyama and Imabari or Takamatsu and Sakaide; ☞ Chapter 9) and Kōbe (☞ Chapter 10) on the Kansai Kisen Line (☎ 0977/22–1311 in Beppu; 03/274–4271 in Tōkyō; 06/572–5181 in Ōsaka). These overnight ferries leave in the early evening. The direct ferry for Ōsaka leaves Beppu at 5:20 PM and arrives at 7:10 AM (fare: ¥5,870 second-class). Reservations are necessary for first class (fare: from ¥7,030 to ¥56,360 for a deluxe room). A ferry to Hiroshima (☎ 0977/21–2364) leaves Beppu at 2 PM and arrives at Hiroshima at 7 PM; in reverse, Hiroshima at 9:30 PM and into Beppu at 6 AM (fare: ¥3,600–¥5,550).

BY PLANE

The closest airport to Beppu is Ōita Kūkō, which is served by ANA and JAS domestic flights from Tōkyō's Haneda Kūkō (1 hr, 30 mins) and from Ōsaka Kūkō (1 hr).

Between the Airport and Center City. Buses leave regularly from the airport for Beppu City. The one-hour trip costs ¥1,450 and terminates at Kitahama bus stop on the bay side of Beppu's main street.

BY TRAIN

The Hōhi Main Line travels between Kumamoto and Beppu (3⅓ hrs), stopping at Mt. Aso. The Nichirin Limited Express runs more than 10 times daily (2½ hrs) between Beppu and Hakata Eki in Fukuoka.

Getting Around

BY BUS

Regular buses travel to most places of interest in Beppu. The main terminal, Kitahama Bus Station, is just down the road from the JR Beppu Eki. The minipass for one day's travel within the city limits is a good buy at ¥900. Because the cost of travel between the station and the hot springs with single tickets adds up to a small fortune (¥400 entrance to one "hell"), it makes sense to purchase the "minipass plus 8 hells" for ¥1,800 from the Foreign Tourist Information Service (☞ Visitor Information, *below*).

Because most sights in Beppu are relatively close to one another but too far to walk, this is one of the few places in Japan where it may be worthwhile simply to hop in a taxi. Fares range from ¥1,000 to ¥3,000. Hiring a taxi for two hours to visit the major thermal pools would run approximately ¥8,320.

Contacts and Resources

GUIDED TOURS
A regular sightseeing bus service, which leaves from Kitahama Bus Station just east of JR Beppu Eki, covers most of the major sights in the area. The tour lasts about 2½ hours. Although there is no English-speaking guide available, most of the sights are self-explanatory.

VISITOR INFORMATION
A helpful **tourist office** (☎ 0977/84–3111) at Yufuin Eki, open daily 9–5, will supply a map and make hotel reservations for you. Because Yufuin is spread out, you may want to rent a bicycle to get around; rentals go for ¥300 per hour.

Beppu City Information Office (✉ 12-13 Eki-mae-chō, ☎ 0977/24–2838) in Beppu Eki has, as long as you persevere in asking for them, several useful maps and brochures in English; it's open daily 9–5. **Foreign Tourist Information Service** (✉ Furosen, 2nd floor, 7-16 Chūō-machi, Beppu City, Ōita-gun 874, ☎ 0977/23–1119, FAX 0977/21–6220) is four minutes from the station—use the map posted on the City Information Booth in the JR eki. This office, open Monday–Saturday 10–4, has an enthusiastic and helpful volunteer staff.

14 Tōhoku

Tōhoku is, undeservedly, one of Japan's least-visited areas. Almost a world apart from the Japan of the Tōkyō–Ōsaka corridor, Tōhoku is one of the best places to take in rural Japan, high-country plateaus and volcanic lakes, and mountainside temples. Summer here is refreshingly cool, and the sensational August festivals held in the cities of Akita, Aomori, Hirosaki, and Sendai offer a convenient excuse for a trip to the north.

By James M.
Vardaman Jr.

T IS A SHAME that so few foreign travelers venture farther above Tōkyō than Nikkō, because Tōhoku, the name given to the six prefectures of northern Honshū, has an appealing combination of country charm, coastal and mountain scenery, old villages, and revered temples. For a long time the area was known as Michinoku—the "end of the road" or "backcountry"—and it retains the spirit of Bashō's poetic travel journal, *Narrow Road to the Interior*. Many Japanese still hold that image of remote rusticity, the result being that Tōhoku is one of the least-visited areas in modern Japan.

In a nation where politeness is paramount, the people in Tōhoku are friendlier than their more urbanized fellow citizens. With the exception of Sendai, Tōhoku's cities are small, and the fast pace of city life is foreign to their residents. Bullet train lines extend only halfway into the region, and most of the people of Tōhoku live their lives with less of the postmodern intensity than is the norm in the southern two-thirds of Honshū.

Tōhoku's six largest cities are prefectural capitals, and they have the amenities of any international community. With the exception of Sendai, these cities don't have numerous sights to explore. In hopes of attracting tourists, they have been building modern complexes that serve as giant souvenir shops, museums, and information centers rolled into one, but these aren't what you would come halfway around the world to see.

The consequence of this is that many of the traditional ways and folk arts have been maintained here, as well as an independence of spirit, much like you find in Hokkaidō, farther north. In the Tōno valley people still live in the traditional northern Japan *magariya* (houses), and the old people still know the stories of mystical creatures and how place-names came into being. Kakunodate preserves the architecture of the *bushi* residences, and its people continue to make traditional folkcrafts from cherry wood and bark.

Ruggedness is a feature of the people and of the landscape, be it Cape Tappi's windblown slopes or Mt. Zaō's huddled "ice monster" trees, which get covered with air-born crystals. In the midst of the mountains there is also the verdant calm of Lake Towada and the gurgling Oirase Gorge, where gentleness has replaced the violence of volcanic eruptions.

Tōhoku Glossary

Key Japanese words and suffixes for this chapter include: *-bashi* (bridge), *bijutsukan* (art museum), *-chō* (street or block), *-chōme* (street), *chūō* (central, as in Central Street), *-den* (hall), *-dera* (Buddhist temple), *dōri* (avenue), *eki* (train station), *gai-jin* (foreigner), *-gawa* or *kawa* (river), *hama* (beach), *-in* (Buddhist temple), *izakaya* (pub), *-ji* (Buddhist temple), *jinja* (Shintō shrine), *-jō* (castle), *-ken* (prefecture), *kita* (north), *-ko* (lake, as in Tazawa-ko, Lake Tazawa), *kōen* ("ko-en," park), *Kōgen* (plateau), *-ku* (section or ward), *minami* (south), *-mon* (gate), *Nihon-kai* (Japan Sea), *ōhashi* (large bridge), *onsen* (hot springs), *sake* ("sa-keh," rice wine), *-san* (mountain, as in Haguro-san, Mt. Haguro), *-shi* (city or municipality), *-shima* (island), *Shinkansen* (bullet train, literally "new trunk line"), and *yama* (mountain).

Pleasures and Pastimes

Dining

Tōhoku is famous for its clean water and its rice, and these two ingredients are made into delicious *sake* throughout the region. *Sansai*, wild vegetables, and mushrooms appear in an amazing variety of dishes as do river fish (mostly carp and sweet fish). Along the coast you will find squid that is so fresh that it is translucent, along with delicious *uni*, sea urchin, which will convert even the squeamish.

In Sendai, look for Sendai *miso*, a red version of fermented soybeans, in soups, and grilled *gyūtan*, beef tongue, which is worth standing in line for with locals. Akita's *kiritampo* is made from boiled rice that is pounded into cakes and molded on sticks and is simmered in broth with chicken and vegetables. Aomori and Iwate's apples often appear in the form of desserts and juice.

CATEGORY	COST*
$$$$	over ¥6,000
$$$	¥4,000–¥6,000
$$	¥2,000–¥4,000
$	under ¥2,000

*per person, excluding drinks, service, and tax

Lodging

Tōhoku has a broad spectrum of accommodations, from inns and minshuku to large, modern resort hotels. Because the region has only recently opened itself up to tourists, many accommodations are of recent vintage and have little local character. That means that hotels are often utilitarian and functional. Higher prices tend to mean larger lobby areas and guest rooms. Price categories below reflect the cost of a double room with private bath but *no* meals. All large city and resort hotels serve Western and Japanese food. In summer, hotel reservations are advised. For a short course on accommodations in Japan, *see* Lodging *in* the Gold Guide.

CATEGORY	COST*
$$$$	over ¥20,000
$$$	¥15,000–¥20,000
$$	¥10,000–¥15,000
$	under ¥10,000

*All prices are for a double room, excluding service and tax.

Mountains, Lakes, and Onsen

In a country that is split by mountains top to bottom, Tōhoku, because of its relative emptiness, is one of the best places in Japan to take in its rugged landscapes. Deep, volcanic lakes and a slew of hot-spring resorts are a classic Japanese escape.

Rural Japan

The Japanese themselves, not unlike the rest of the modernized world, have turned their backs on their rural areas. If seeing traditional farmhouses and agricultural areas has some appeal, look to the Tōno Basin near Morioka for, among other things, traditional L-shaped *magariya* homesteads.

Exploring Tōhoku

The mountains that rise on the spine of Honshū continue through Tōhoku. Most of the island's trains and highways run north–south on either side of the mountains. Hence, when traveling the major roads or railway trunk lines, you tend to miss some of the grandest mountain scenery. This chapter, laid out as an itinerary up the Pacific side of Tōhoku's spine and down the Nihon-kai side, takes in the best of Tōhoku using the JR trains as much as is possible, but it covers more remote areas as well. If you want to continue north to Hokkaidō from Aomori, consider returning from Hokkaidō down the west coast of Tōhoku.

Keep in mind that Shinkansen lines end in the central city of Morioka and on the Nihon-kai coast at Niigata. Travel slows beyond those points—which is part of what Tōhoku is all about.

Numbers in the text correspond to numbers in the margin and on the Tōhoku map.

Great Itineraries

IF YOU HAVE 3 DAYS

In 🔲 **Sendai** ⑤, start at **Aoba-jō** (castle), then walk down to the **Sendai-shi Hakubutsukan** for a visual and historical overview of the city. From there stroll along the Hirose-gawa to **Zuihō-den,** the extravagant mausoleums of the *Date* (*da*-teh) leaders. Then spend the afternoon at **Yamadera** ⑧, climbing to the top of the mountainside temple for spectacular views of the town and the Yamagata Basin, returning to Sendai or spending the night at 🔲 **Sakunami Onsen.** The next day, travel to 🔲 **Matsu-shima** ⑦, relaxing on the ferry that travels through the islets of the bay to Matsu-shima itself. Spend the night in Matsu-shima or return to Sendai. On the third day, take the train north for a day outdoors in one of two areas. Around **Hiraizumi,** see **Gembikei Gorge** ⑫ then continue to **Takkoku-no-Iwaya** and **Mōtsu-ji.** From there, wander along the fields to **Chūson-ji** and **Konjiki-dō.** If you pick 🔲 **Tōno** ⑭ instead, get an early start in order to have a full afternoon to cover the distances around town. See **Kappa-buchi,** a small riverside pool of lore, and the **Denshō-en** folk museum for a look at local farm life. On foot or bicycle, this will take the afternoon. If you go by taxi, also go up the mountainside to see the **Go-hyaku Rakan** carved on moss-covered boulders.

IF YOU HAVE 5 DAYS

One five-day approach to Tōhoku would offer two days for 🔲 **Sendai** ⑤, another day for an excursion to the temple of **Yamadera** ⑧ or the gorges and temples around **Hiraizumi** ⑬, then the final two days for the rural splendor of 🔲 **Tōno** ⑭. You would also begin to have the option of heading farther north: two days in 🔲 **Sendai** ⑤ and either **Yamadera** ⑧ or 🔲 **Matsu-shima** ⑦; a third day in **Hiraizumi** ⑬, ending for the night in 🔲 **Morioka** ⑮; then the last two days taking in the scenery at 🔲 **Towada-ko** ㉒ from sightseeing boats or on a hike along **Oirase** (o-*ee*-ra-seh) cascade on the east side of the lake. Spend the night at the lakeside resort of 🔲 **Yasumi-ya** ㉓, taking a morning hike before moving on.

IF YOU HAVE 7 DAYS

With a week to take in Tōhoku's natural beauty, start in 🔲 **Sendai** ⑤, then take a second day jaunt west for a climb up **Yamadera** ⑧ and a relaxing bath in the open-air hot springs at 🔲 **Sakunami Onsen.** From there, return to Sendai Eki and transfer to the train out to **Hon-Shiogama** ⑥ and the ferry to 🔲 **Matsu-shima** ⑦; spend the night there or return to Sendai. On the third day head north, either to **Hiraizumi** ⑬ or **Tōno** ⑭ for a day of strolling between sights. On day four, take it easy in 🔲 **Morioka** ⑮, and enjoy some of the best Tōhoku cooking at dinner. On the fifth day, head by bus to 🔲 **Towada-ko** ㉒ and take on the 9-km (5½-mi) trail that parallels the **Oirase** cascades before spending the night at 🔲 **Yasumi-ya** ㉓. From there, take the bus to 🔲 **Hirosaki** ㉔ for a look at the castle town and the Neputa museum on day six. On the seventh day, begin heading south, with seaside stops either at **Oga Peninsula** ㉘, 🔲 **Akita** ㉗, or an inland excursion to 🔲 **Kakunodate** ⑳ for a look at a small castle town with surviving buildings from the Tokugawa era.

When to Tour Tōhoku

If your timing is perfect, you can see all of the big summer Tōhoku festivals, commencing in Aomori's Nebuta Festival (Aug. 3–7), Hirosaki's

Tōhoku

KEY

— JR Trains
═ Shinkansen (Bullet Train)
┤├ Private rail line
- - - Ferry Line

0   50 miles
0   75 km

Fukushima

Tsugaru Straits

TO HAKODATE

Cape Tappi

Minmaya

Tsugaru Peninsula

Mt. Osorezan

Mutsu

Mutsu Bay

Shimokita Peninsula

25 Aomori

26 Sukayu Onsen

Misawa

Mt. Iwaki

24 Hirosaki

Hachinohe

22 Towada-ko

23 Yasumi-ya

Nenokuchi

4

Kuji

Ōdate

7

Towada-minami

Noshiro

Yoneshiro-gawa

Goshogake Onsen

Hachimantai

4

Tamagawa Onsen

Tosichi Onsen

Ōbuke

Oga Peninsula

Oga Onsen **28**

Oga

Towada-Hachimantai National Park

19

21 Higashi-Hachimantai

Komaga-take

Tarō

27

Akita

Nyūtō Onsen

17

18

15

Morioka

Jōdō-ga-hama

Miyako

Tazawa-ko

16

Shiwa

Sea of Japan

20

Kakunodate

Omagari

■ Take

Hanamaki

14 Tōno

Kamaishi

Ōmono-gawa

398

Hiraizumi

Geibikei Gorge

13

Gembikei Gorge

12

11

13

Ichi-no-seki

Tsuruoka

29

Mogami-gawa

30

Haguro-san

Atsumi Onsen

31

Nobiru

Yamadera

7 Matsu-shima

8

6 Hon-Shiogama

9 Yamagata

5 Sendai

10 Mt. Zaō

4

Niigata

Yonezawa

Abukuma

PACIFIC OCEAN

49

Kitakata

Hibara-ko

Fukushima

3

Agano-gawa

1 Bandai Kōgen

4

Aizu-Wakamatsu

2

Inawashiro-ko

TO TŌKYŌ

Koriyama

6

N

Neputa (Aug. 1–7), Akita's Kantō (Aug. 5–7), and Sendai's Tanabata (Aug. 6–8). The festivals are very popular and very crowded, but you'll see all of Tōhoku's energy released in colorful parades of lanterns and floats and wild dancing. Reserve for hotels and trains well ahead.

Tōhoku's climate is similar to New England's. Winters are cold, and in the mountains snow blocks off some of the minor roads. At the same time, snow rarely falls in Sendai and Matsu-shima and along the Pacific coast, and temperatures rarely dip below freezing. Spring and autumn are the most colorful seasons. Summer is refreshingly cool and as a result attracts Japanese tourists escaping the heat and humidity of Tōkyō and points south.

SOUTH TŌHOKU

Fukushima Prefecture is tamer both in scenery and in attitude than the rest of Tōhoku. Nonetheless, there are lakes, hot springs, and traces of traditional Japanese life that are worth seeing.

Bandai Kōgen (Bandai Plateau)

❶ *30 mins northwest of JR Inawashiro Eki by bus.*

Fukushima was the first region in northern Honshū to become a popular resort area for Japanese families, especially around the tableland known as Bandai Kōgen. The volcano Bandai-san erupted in 1888 and in 15 short minutes wiped out more than 40 small villages, killing 477 people and resculpting the landscape. The eruption dammed several streams to form hundreds of lakes, the largest of which is Hibara-ko, with its crooked shoreline and numerous islets. Bandai Kōgen is also the name for the tourist center at Hibara-ko, where Japanese vacationers disperse to their campgrounds, bungalows, or modern ryokan.

★ Though the Bandai Kōgen area is somewhat spoiled by hordes of tourists, a particularly pleasant walk, the Goshiki-numa Trail, meanders past the dozen or more tiny lakes (ponds, really) that are collectively called **Goshiki-numa** (Five-Color Lakes), because each throws off a different color. The trail begins across from the Bandai Kōgen bus station and runs in the opposite direction from Lake Hibara; the round-trip takes two hours. There are other lake and mountain trails in the area as well.

❷ Japan's third largest lake is **Inawashiro-ko,** and the town of Inawashiro is on its northern shore. Unlike Tōhoku's other large lakes, Towada-ko and Tazawa-ko, Inawashiro-ko is not a caldera lake but instead is formed by streams. Hence, its flat surrounding shore is not particularly spectacular, though the scenery is pretty enough as far as Japanese beaches go. The Japanese like the lake for the gaudy, swan-shape sightseeing cruise boats that circle on the water. Of more cultural interest (10 minutes by bus from Inawashiro Station) is **Hideo Noguchi's birthplace** and a memorial museum in honor of his extraordinary life and his research of yellow fever, which eventually killed him in Africa in 1928. The bus between Bandai Kōgen and Aizu-Wakamatsu stops at Inawashiro.

Lodging

$$$$ 🏨 **Ura-Bandai Royal Hotel.** A comfortable resort hotel with a magnificent setting, the Royal also has seven restaurants for every taste, including traditional Japanese, robatayaki, sushi, and French. Rooms come with two meals, served in the main dining room, or you can pay for a room alone and choose where you will eat. In the back garden behind the hotel there is a path leading around a small lake, and the west entrance of the Goshiki-numa trail is nearby. If you are just visiting the hotel for the day, try its blueberry rare cheesecake in the coffee shop. ⊠ *1093 Hibara Kengamine, Kita-Shiobara Mura, Yama-gun, Fukushima-ken 969,* ☎ *0241/32–3111,* ℻ *0241/32–3130. 227 Japanese- and Western-style rooms. 5 restaurants. AE, D, MC, V.*

$$$ 🏨 **Pension Heidi.** The ever-accommodating manager of this pension deserves an award. Rooms are simple but comfortable, and the location (within walking distance of the Kengamine Intersection at Ura-Bandai) is certainly convenient, but what wins return visits is the food—very few pensions in Japan offer this level of cuisine in an area so delightful for hiking. Alternating between French one night and Chinese the next, it is served at just the right moment. You will be happy to stay more than one night here in between hikes and tours on the lake. ⊠ *1093 Ura-Bandai Kengamine, Kita-Shiobara Mura, Yama-gun, Fukushima-ken 969,* ☎ *0241/32–2008,* ℻ *0241/32–3456. 10 rooms, 2 with private bath. AE, D, MC, V.*

Kitakata

★ ❸ *45 mins west of Bandai Kōgen by bus (summer only); 1 hr, 50 mins northwest of Kōriyama by JR.*

Mud-wall *kura* (storehouses) are to be seen all over Japan, but for some reason Kitakata has more than 2,600 of them. Kura are not only simple places to store rice, miso, soy sauce, sake, fertilizer, and charcoal, however—they are also status symbols of the local merchants. The kura fascination spread in the past so that shops, homes, and inns were built in this architectural style as each citizen tried to outdo his neighbor. One can quickly use up a couple of rolls of film taking photographs of the many different kura—some are of black-and-white plaster, some simply of mud, some with bricks, and some with thatched roofs; still others have tiles.

Aside from Kitakata's major architectural attraction—**Kai Honke Kura Zashiki,** an elaborate mansion that took seven years to build (¥200; open mid-March–early December, daily 9–5), and the **Aizu Lacquer Museum** (¥300; open daily 9–5)—your final goal should be the **Yamatogawa Sake Brewery** (☎ 0241/22–2233), across the center of town from the Lacquer Museum. The brewery consists of seven kura, one of which serves as a small museum to display old methods of sake production. The other buildings are still used for making sake. After a dutiful tour, you are offered the pleasurable reward of tasting different types of sake. 🎫 *Free.* ⊙ *Daily 9–4:30; closed Dec. 31–Jan. 5.*

If you are short on time, the area northeast of the station has a selection of storehouses, including **Kai Shōten,** a black kura storefront of an old miso and soy-sauce factory. Incidentally, Kitakata is also famous for its variety of delicious **ramen noodles;** several tourism-conscious entrepreneurs have combined the two attractions by converting storehouses into ramen shops. The town also has a **kura-shaped carriage,** towed by a brawny carthorse, in which you can ride if the spirit of Japanese kitsch moves you.

The **tourist office** (☎ 0241/32–0688) at the local JR eki has a kura walking-tour map for the city. It is open Monday–Saturday 9:30–5:30, Sunday 10–5. There is JR service to Kitakata from Koriyama.

Aizu-Wakamatsu

❹ *20 mins by JR south of Kitakata, 70 mins west of Kōriyama.*

As the locus of a tragic, if partly misconceived, event in the course of the Meiji overthrow of Japan's feudal shogunate in the mid-1800s, Aizu-

Wakamatsu has a couple of relevant sights. That said, the compelling story of the Byakkotai far outshines the town itself.

Byakkotai Monument. Every Japanese knows this story, so it bears telling: Twenty young warriors, known as Byakkotai (White Tigers), had been fighting pro-Restoration forces outside the city, when they were sent back to Tsuruga-jō (☞ *below*) to aid in its defense. The boys arrived on a nearby hillside, Iimori-yama. Then, to their horror, they saw smoke rise from the castle and mistakenly believed the castle to be over-run by the enemy. As good samurai, all 20 boys began a mass suicide ritual. One boy was saved before he bled to death. For a samurai, this was a curse. He spent the rest of his life with a livid scar and the shame of having failed to live up to the samurai code. Ironically, the castle had not at that point fallen into enemy hands and the fighting con-tinued for another month—indeed, had they lived, the Byakkotai might have helped to turn the battle in their side's favor. On the hill next to their graves there is now a monument to the 19 who died. The small memorial museum and a strange hexagonal Buddhist temple, Sazaedō, are reached by a 10-minute bus ride from the station. You may want to visit Iimori-yama September 22–24, when a special festival is held in memory of the Boshin civil war and the Byakkotai. ☜ *¥400.* ○ *Apr.–Nov., daily 8–5; Dec.–Mar., daily 8:30–4; closed 1st Mon.–Thurs. of July and 1st Tues.–Thurs. of Dec.*

Tsuruga-jō was the most powerful stronghold of the northeast during the shōgun period. The Aizu clan was closely linked to the ruling fam-ily in Edo and remained classically loyal until the end. When the im-perial forces of the Meiji Restoration pressed home their successful attack in 1868, that loyalty caused the castle, which had stood for five cen-turies, to be partly burned down, along with most of the city's build-ings. The new government destroyed the castle completely in 1874. The five-story castle was rebuilt in 1965 as a museum and is said to look like its original, but without the presence it must have had in 1868, when 19 Byakkotai (☞ *above*) committed ritual suicide. From the JR eki plaza, take a bus from Gate 14 or 15, but check with the infor-mation booth first. The bus loops around the city past the castle and the Byakkotai monument. ☜ *¥400.* ○ *Daily 8:30–5 (enter by 4:30).*

★ **Aizu Buke Yashiki** (Aizu Samurai Residence). To the east of the castle is an excellent reproduction of a wealthy samurai's manor house. The 38-room house gives an idea of how well one could live during the shogun period. A museum on the grounds displays Aizu craft, culture, and his-tory, and there are several other old or reconstructed buildings in ad-dition to the manor house. To get here take the Higashiyama bus from the JR eki. ☜ *¥800.* ○ *Apr.–Nov., daily 8:30–5; Dec.–Mar., daily 9–4:30.*

Train and bus routes south from Aizu-Wakamatsu go to Nikkō. Trav-eling east by train to Kōriyama puts you back on the Tōhoku Shinkansen for Sendai to the north and Tōkyō to the south. The train going west leads you to Niigata and the Nihon-kai. The JR information and reser-vation office at the station distributes a free English-language map and leaflets about the area. The city **tourist office** is in the center of town (☎ 0242/32–0688).

Higashiyama Onsen

30 mins from Aizu-Wakamatsu by bus.

Higashiyama Onsen, a spa town with several modern ryokan, is an al-ternative overnight spot to Aizu-Wakamatsu, especially if you enjoy hot mineral baths. The village is in a gorge, and the bus route terminates at the bottom end of the village. Most ryokan will send a car to collect you so that you don't have to hike up the narrow village street. The village's scenic location and its shamble of older houses deserve better than the new and monstrous-looking ryokan that have supplanted most of the old. Nevertheless, Higashiyama is a spa town and a pleasant alternative to staying in Aizu-Wakamatsu.

The tourist information booth at Higashiyama bus stop will telephone a ryokan for you, if you give the attendant the ¥10 for the pay phone. To get to Higashiyama, take the bus from Platform 4 at the JR Aizu-Wakamatsu Eki for the 20-minute ride, which costs ¥310.

Lodging

$$$ ⬚ **Mukaitaki Ryokan.** This is the one ryokan in Higashiyama Onsen that retains a traditional ambience, thanks to its plank floors, shoji screens, and screen prints. English is spoken, and rooms can be reserved until 9:30 PM, though the place is open 24 hours a day. The inn serves Japanese food only. ✉ *200 Kawamukō, Yumoto, Higashiyama-machi, Fukushima-ken 965,* ☎ *0242/27–7501. 25 Japanese-style rooms. Mineral baths. AE, DC, MC, V.*

$$ ⬚ **Hotel Kōyō.** Although the Kōyō is in the upper part of Higashiyama Onsen, the buildings across the street block its view of the gorge. A modest hotel with large (10 tatami-mat) Japanese-style rooms, each equipped with a computerized dice game to keep you entertained, it could use some sprucing up, but the room rate is low. The owner also has a fish market, so the meals, served in your room and included in the price, are prepared with good, fresh seafood. Meat can be provided if requested in advance. Two staff members speak some English. A driver will pick you up at the bus stop. ✉ *Higashiyama Onsen, Fukushima-ken 965,* ☎ *0242/26–9000 or 0120/26–4504 toll-free,* ℻ *0242/26–9166. 18 Japanese-style rooms. Snack, bar, mineral baths. AE, V.*

Getting Around South Tōhoku

The easiest way in and out of Tōhoku is the Tōhoku Shinkansen route. A detour west will take you to Kōriyama to Ura-Bandai and farther to Kitakata and Aizu-Wakamatsu. What you will lose in backtracking to Kōriyama you will make up in reduced travel time and more interesting sights.

From Kōriyama, Inawashiro-ko is reached by local train on the Banetsusai Line (30 minutes). Buses connect from the JR Inawashiro Eki and the Noguchi Hideo Kinenkan to the lake area's main Bandai-Kōgen stop in 30 minutes. From the city of Fukushima buses depart from near the Shinkansen Eki daily between April 22 and November 5 and travel Bandai-Azuma Skyline Drive, offering splendid views of mountains by climbing up through Jōdōdaira Pass at 5,214 ft. The whole mountain resort is, in fact, crisscrossed by five scenic toll roads. All sightseeing buses as well as local Inawashiro buses arrive at Bandai Kōgen bus stop.

SENDAI

❺ *By Shinkansen, 40 mins north of Kōriyama, 2 hrs north of Tōkyō.*

With a population of nearly 900,000, Sendai is the largest city between Tōkyō and Sapporo, the northern island of Hokkaidō's major city. Because American firebombs left virtually nothing unscorched by the end of World War II, it is a very modern city. The buildings that replaced the old ones are not particularly attractive, but Sendai is an open city with a generous planting of trees that justifies its nickname *mori-no-miyako*, "the city of trees." With eight colleges and universities, including the prestigious Tōhoku University, the city has intentionally developed an international outlook and appeal. This has attracted many foreigners to take up residency. Sendai's old customs and modern attitudes make it a comfortable southern base from which to explore Tōhoku.

Sendai is easy to navigate, and even the major streets have signs in *romaji* (Japanese words rendered in roman letters). Downtown Sendai is compact, with modern hotels, department stores with fashionable international clothing, numerous Japanese and Western restaurants, and hundreds of small specialty shops. Three broad avenues, Aoba-dōri, Hirose-dōri, and Jōzen-ji-dōri, and the Chūō-dōri shopping arcade head out from the station area toward Sendai Castle and cut through the heart of downtown, where they are bisected by the wide shopping arcade of Ichiban-chō. Between these two malls and extending farther east are narrow streets, packing in the 3,000 to 4,000 bars, tea shops, and restaurants that make up Sendai's entertainment area.

While it is easy to get your bearings in Sendai, public transport is not so convenient. Most awkwardly, the subway runs north–south only, and its stations are far from most interesting sights. A new east–west subway line is being planned, which may improve the situation. Fortunately, the center of the city is within easy walking distance from the train station, and all hotels are between the center and the station. City buses will work for sightseeing, but it's advisable to consult the bus and subway information office, near the subway station in front of the JR *eki*, beforehand. Here you can pick up English-language brochures that tell you about bus departure points, stops, and fares necessary for getting to each of the major sights. Otherwise, taxis are a convenient way of covering the (generally) short distances between the sights.

Sendai, unlike other urban centers in Tōhoku, has a larger number of sights worth visiting, and you can easily spend a day looking around. Sendai's history focuses almost entirely on a fantastic historic figure, Date (*da*-teh) Masamune (1567–1636). Affectionately called the "one-eyed dragon" for his valor in battle and the loss of an eye from smallpox when he was a child, Date Masamune established a dynasty that maintained its position as one of the three most powerful *daimyō* (feudal lord) families during the shogun period. In addition to his military skills and progressive administration—he constructed a canal linking two rivers, thus improving the transport of rice—he was also an artist and a scholar who did not close his eye to new ideas.

Sights to See

Aoba-jō. To get an overview of the city and save yourself an uphill hike, take a bus to the top of Aoba-yama. There never was a traditional military stronghold here, but the grand residence that once stood here was the Date clan's residence for 266 years. Because it sat 433 ft above the city on Aobayama and was protected by the Tatsunokuchi Gorge to the south, even without a traditional castle the site was considered impregnable when the first structure went up 1602. The castle was destroyed during the Meiji Restoration. The outer gates did manage to survive another 70 years, until firebombs destroyed them in 1945. The rather grandiose, heavy, and cumbersome **Gokoku Shrine** is the main feature of the area where the castle stood. Near the observation terrace is a mounted statue of the city's founder, Date Masamune, who looks out over the city with his one good eye. On a clear day you can see the Pacific Ocean on the horizon to the right. From here you can plan your route down the hill, across the river, and along the river to **Zuihō-den** (☞ *below*), the Date family mausoleum, a 30-minute walk. As you walk down from the castle site toward the bridge, you will pass

Aoba-yama Kōen, where you will find ☞ **Sendai International Center** farther toward the Hirose-gawa on the left. To get to Aoba-jō, take the bus from Stand 9 outside the JR eki for the 15-minute ride to the Aoba-jōshi-mae stop.

Ōsaki Hachiman Jinja. This shrine is the main historic building in Sendai to have survived the war. It was actually built in Yonezawa, in 1527, and was later moved to Toda-gun. Date Masamune liked it and, in 1607, had it moved from its second site to be rebuilt in Sendai. Its free-flowing architectural form has a naturalness similar to the architectural style in Nikkō, and its rich, black-lacquered main building more than justifies its designation as a National Treasure. In the northwest section of the city, by taxi it is about 10 minutes from downtown or Aoba-yama and 15 minutes from the **Zuihō-den** (☞ *below*) area. You can also take Bus 15 from the JR Sendai Eki for ¥220. ✉ *Free.* ☉ *Daily sunrise–sunset.*

★ **Rinnō-ji.** Of the several gardens in the neighborhood, the Zen-type garden of this temple is the most peaceful. A small stream leads the eye to the lotus-filled pond, the garden's focal point. Waving, undulating hummocks covered with clusters of bamboo flow around the pool, creating a balance with it. In June the garden is a blaze of color, with irises everywhere, but there are so many visitors that much of the tranquillity is often lost. The temple is a 20-minute walk from Ōsaki Hachiman Jinja northwest of the city center. Use Bus 24 if you are going directly there from the JR Sendai Eki. ✉ *¥300.* ☉ *Daily 8–5.*

Sendai International Center. Across the street from the Sendai-shi Hakubutsukan, this has more English information than the downtown office, which makes it a good stop before you cross the Hirose-gawa on your way to **Zuihō-den** (☞ *below*).

Sendai-shi Hakubutsukan (Sendai Municipal Museum). At the foot of the hill beneath Aoba-jō, the Sendai-shi Hakubutsukan has a nicely presented history of the Date family and the history of the city. The café on the second floor is a good place to get refreshment before the walk to Zuihō-den. ✉ *¥400.* ☉ *Tues.–Sun. 9–4:45 (enter by 4:15); closed the day following national holidays and Dec. 28–Jan. 4.*

SS 30 Building. If you want a bird's-eye view of the city, 30 stories is as high as you'll get in Sendai. The top three floors are reserved for restaurants and viewing galleries. At night, riding up in the outside elevator, with the city lights descending below, is quite a thrill.

Tanabata. Sendai's big festival is held August 6–8, and, while similar festivals are held throughout Japan (usually on July 7), Sendai's is the largest, swelling the city to three times its normal size with Japanese tourists. The celebration stems from a poignant Chinese legend of a weaver girl and her boyfriend, a herdsman, represented by the stars Vega and Altair. Their excessive love for each other caused them to become idle, and the irate king of heaven exiled the two lovers to opposite sides of heaven. However, he permitted them to meet one day a year—that day is now celebrated as Tanabata, highlighted with a theatrical stage performance of the young lovers' anguish. For the festival, houses and streets are decorated with colorful paper and bamboo streamers fluttering from poles.

★ **Zuihō-den.** Burned during the firebombing in 1945, this mausoleum was reconstructed over a five-year period beginning in 1974. During the excavation, Date Masamune's well-preserved remains were found and have been reinterred in what appears to be a perfect replica of the original hall. Two other mausoleums for the remains of the second (Date

Tadamune) and third (Date Tsunamune) lords of Sendai were also reconstructed. These mausoleums, which cost in excess of ¥800 million to rebuild, are astounding in their craftsmanship and authenticity in the architectural style of the Momoyama period (16th century). Each mausoleum is the size of a small temple, and the exterior is inlaid with figures of people, birds, and flowers in natural colors all sheltered by elaborate curving roofs. Gold leaf is used extravagantly on the pillars and in the eaves of the roofs, creating a glinting golden aura. ⊠ ¥515. ⊙ *Daily 9–4.*

Take Bus 11 from JR Sendai Eki to the Otamaya-bashi bus stop. The mausoleum is a short walk up the hill.

Dining

The main cluster of restaurants is in the parallel streets Ichiban-chō, Inari-kōji, and Kokubun-chō, and most display their menus in their windows, along with the prices for each dish. Also, in JR eki, there are tempting arrays of prepared foods and numerous restaurants in the underground mall aptly named Restaurant Avenue.

$$$–$$$$ ✕ **Gintanabe Bekkan.** This is the place for fish in any form—sashimi, fried, boiled, baked, or grilled—and it is a favorite with local people. You can sit at the counter and order one item at a time or ask for a room in the back where complete courses are available with the catch of the day brought in from Pacific fishing ports. From the Ichiban-chō exit of Mitsukoshi department store, turn left, take a right at the first narrow street, walk two small blocks, turn left, and walk fifty yards. It is the restaurant with the tub-shaped fish tank. ⊠ 2-9-34 Kokubun-chō, ☎ 022/227–3478. AE, D, MC, V. Closed 2nd Sun. of month. No lunch.

$$$ ✕ **Santarō.** There is something for everyone at this elegant restaurant.
★ Known especially for delicious tempura, Santarō also serves *shabu-shabu*—thin slices of Sendai beef briefly simmered in broth—as well as sukiyaki, *fugu* (blowfish), and *kaiseki* (Kyōto-style set meals) courses. Tempura courses start at ¥4,000, sukiyaki courses start at ¥5,000, and shabu-shabu courses start at ¥5,000. To enjoy the refined atmosphere at a lower price, try weekday lunch specials for ¥1,000 to ¥3,000. Whenever you decide to go, you will not be disappointed in the service or the food. Just off Bansui-dōri several blocks south of Jōzen-ji-dōri. ⊠ 1-20 Tachi-machi, ☎ 022/224–1671. AE, D, MC, V. Closed during Obon in mid-Aug. and briefly at the new year.

$$–$$$ ✕ **Kakitoku.** Matsu-shima Bay is famous for its *kaki* (oysters), and even when they are unavailable locally, this shop brings in the best available. In business for more than 70 years, the place specializes in raw oysters, vinegared oysters, and fried oysters. For oyster lovers, this shop is a must. If you are not enamored with oysters, you can order steak or another entrées while your friends enjoy their shellfish. ⊠ 4-9-1 Ichiban-chō, ☎ 022/222–0785. AE, D, MC, V. Closed Mon.

$$ ✕ **Aji Tasuke.** This small shop, with a counter and several tables that
★ seat 30 maximum, is a local institution that serves excellent meals at inexpensive prices. Other shops with similar names also serve grilled gyūtan, but the master of this shop beats the others hands down. For lunch or dinner order *shokuji* (a meal) and ¥1,200 will get you the full set of grilled beef tongue and pickled cabbage, oxtail soup, and a bowl of barley mixed with rice. The clientele ranges from businessmen to bar hostesses, all drawn by the simple, delicious food. From the Ichiban-chō exit of Mitsukoshi department store turn left, walk to the first narrow street, turn right, turn left at the next corner, and Aji Tasuke is 50 yards down on the left next to a small shrine. ⊠ 4-4-13 Ichiban-chō, ☎ 022/225–4641. No credit cards. Closed Tues.

Lodging

$$$–$$$$ 🏨 **Hotel Metropolitan Sendai.** Adjacent to the railway station, this upscale business traveler's hotel has reasonably large guest rooms decorated in light colors. The 21st-floor Sky Lounge restaurant offers the best city view—and French food to go with it. Simpler fare at more reasonable prices is found in the coffee shop. ⊠ *1-1-1 Chūō-dōri, Sendai, Miyagi-ken 980,* ☎ *022/268–2525,* FAX *022/268–2521. 293 rooms, 3 suites, 4 Japanese-style rooms. 5 restaurants, coffee shop, indoor pool, exercise room. AE, DC, MC, V.*

$$$–$$$$ 🏨 **Sendai Kokusai Hotel.** This newest of Sendai's hotels (next to the
★ new SS 30 complex) immediately won attention as the town's leading hotel. The lobby glistens with marble and stainless steel, guest rooms are furnished in light pastels, and larger rooms have stucco arches to exaggerate their size. Fresh flowers add a touch of color. The hotel offers French, Chinese, and Japanese fare and a bar and is a short walk from the downtown restaurant area. ⊠ *4-6-1 Chūō, Aoba-ku, Sendai, Miyagi-ken 980,* ☎ *022/268–1112,* FAX *022/268–1113. 234 rooms. 10 restaurants, bar, coffee shop, sushi bar, shop. AE, DC, MC, V.*

$$–$$$ 🏨 **Sendai Hotel.** Pale colors and cheerful prints make up the decor at this modern hotel, popular with business travelers wishing to stay near the station. Foreign guests enjoy attentive service and get the English-language *Japan Times* newspaper every morning. There are Japanese, Chinese, Italian, and French restaurants on site, and the hotel is directly in front of the JR Sendai Eki. ⊠ *1-10-25 Chūō, Aoba-ku, Sendai, Miyagi-ken 980,* ☎ *022/225–5171,* FAX *022/268–9325. 113 rooms, mostly Japanese style. 4 restaurants, shops. AE, DC, MC, V.*

$$ 🏨 **Kōyō Grand Hotel.** With its objects of art from China and Europe mixed with Louis XV reproductions, this must be the most oddly furnished hotel in Japan. The total assemblage is a mismatch of statues, mounted deer heads, Regency upholstered furniture, gold painted chandeliers, and ceiling murals. Thankfully, the guest rooms have more simple and standard furniture—though with turn-of-the-century French reproductions—otherwise who knows what would happen in your dreams. The hotel has a small but good French restaurant and also a Chinese restaurant with Szechuan and Cantonese cooking. The Kōyō Grand is in front of the Hirose-dōri subway stop, or a 12-minute walk from the JR Sendai Eki. ⊠ *1-3-2 Hon-chō, Aoba-ku, Sendai, Miyagi-ken 980,* ☎ *022/267–5111,* FAX *022/265–2252. 149 Western-style rooms. 3 restaurants. AE, DC, MC, V.*

$$ 🏨 **Ryokan Aisaki.** This inn has been run by the same family since 1868,
★ but the present building is post–World War II. The hostelry is enjoyable for friendly companionship with other guests, and the owner welcomes foreigners. He speaks fluent English and often takes guests on sightseeing trips. Only two rooms have private baths, but the common bath does have the benefit of a sauna. Open until midnight, Ryokan Aisaki is behind Sendai Central Post Office, a 15-minute walk from JR Sendai Eki (five minutes by taxi). Meals, which are compulsory, are served in a dining room, and rates include the cost of two meals. ⊠ *5-6 Kitame-machi, Aoba-ku, Sendai, Miyagi-ken 980,* ☎ *022/264–0700,* FAX *022/227–6067. 15 rooms. Dining room, sauna. AE, V.*

Shopping

Bustling downtown Sendai is a shopper's paradise; the area is compact, and many of the stores and small shops are in or connected to the two main shopping arcades, **Ichiban-chō** and **Chūō-dōri.** Sendai is the unofficial capital of the Tōhoku region, and you can find many of the regional crafts—cherry-bark letter boxes, *washi* (hand-made paper) most notably—made outside of Miyagi Prefecture here.

Visitor Information

The **tourist information office** on the second floor of Sendai's JR eki has essential maps with bus routes to help you get to the main places in and around Sendai. More information in English is available at the Sendai International Center (☞ *above*). The center also operates an English-language hot line (☎ 022/224–1919) to answer questions about the city and its prefecture.

SIDE TRIPS FROM SENDAI

East to Matsu-shima

25 mins northeast of Sendai by JR.

The Japanese have named three places as their Three Big Scenic Wonders—Ama-no-hashidate on the Sea of Japan in Western Honshū, Miyajima in Hiroshima Bay, and Matsu-shima Bay. Hands down, Matsu-shima and its bay are the most popular coastal resort destinations in Tōhoku. Matsu-shima owes its distinction to the Japanese infatuation with oddly shaped rocks, which the bay has in abundance. Counts vary, but there are about 250 small, pine-clad islands scattered in the bay. Some are mere rocks with barely enough room for a couple of trees; others are large enough to shelter a few families. Each of the islets has a unique shape. Several have tunnels through them large enough to pass through in a rowboat. Its mass appeal aside, the bay is beautiful indeed, and it makes for a pleasant day's excursion from Sendai.

You can either go directly to Matsu-shima by train or opt for the scenic route by sea.

❻ On your way to Matsu-shima, we suggest that you stop at **Hon-Shiogama** to see its shrine and views of the bay. As the port city of Sendai, Shiogama itself has little appeal—except for one shrine, **Shiogama Jinja,** supposedly the home of guardian deities who look after mariners and expectant mothers. Its buildings, with bright orange-red exteriors and simple, natural wood interiors, are well worth the climb up the hill before you catch the boat to Matsu-shima. To reach Shiogama Jinja, on a wooded hill overlooking the town, turn left from the station and walk for about 10 minutes. Be warned that after passing through the main entrance, you have to clamber up 202 stone steps to get to the buildings. There are actually two shrines, Shiogama Jinja and **Shiwahiko Jinja.** The former is actually the second one you'll reach and is the main building of the complex; admission is free.

Two other reasons for the climb up to Shiogama Jinja are the view of Shiogama Bay and a 500-year-old Japanese holly tree on the grounds. Most days you'll recognize the tree by the crowds of Japanese taking photographs of themselves standing before it. A modern building near Shiwahiko Jinja houses swords, armor, and religious articles on its first floor and exhibits about fishing and salt manufacturing on its second. 🎫 ¥300. 🕐 Apr.–Nov., daily 8–5; Dec.–Mar., daily 9–4.

❼ Once you are in **Matsu-shima,** the key sights are within easy walking distance of each other. For maps and brochures, visit the tourist office at the end of the Matsushite Kaigan pier. The small temple of **Godai-dō** is just to the right as you step off the boat on the pier. Constructed at the behest of Date Masamune in 1609, this temple is on a tiny islet connected to the shore by two small arched bridges. Weathered by the sea and salt air, the small building's paint has peeled off, giving it an intimacy often lacking in other temples. Animals are carved in the timbers beneath the temple roof and among the complex supporting beams. If you have hopes of inspecting the temple's interior, you'll have a long wait: It is open to the public only during special ceremonies held once every 33 years, and the next opening is scheduled for 2006.

★ **Zuigan-ji,** Matsu-shima's main temple, dates from 828, but the present structure was built on Masamune's orders in 1609. Designated a National Treasure, Zuigan-ji is the most representative Zen temple in the Tōhoku region. The Main Hall is a large wood structure with ornately carved wood panels and paintings (faded with age) from the 17th century. Surrounding the temple are natural caves filled with Buddhist statues and memorial tablets that novices carved from the rock face as part of their training. The grounds surrounding the temple are full of trees, two of which are plum trees brought back from Korea in 1592 by Date Masamune after an unsuccessful military foray. Zuigan-ji is down the street from Godai-dō, across Route 45 and the central park. ☞ *¥500.* ⊙ *8–5; shorter hrs Oct.–Mar.*

For a glimpse at how people looked and dressed during Date Masamune's time, visit the wax museum, **Michinoku Date Masamune Rekishikan** (Date Masamune Historical Museum). With life-size figures, the museum displays scenes from the feudal period—battles, tea ceremonies, and processions. ⊠ *Rte. 45 (from Zuigan-ji, turn left and walk back toward the bay).* ☞ *¥1,000.* ⊙ *Daily 8:30–5.*

★ **Kanrantei,** translated as "Water Viewing Pavilion," was originally part of Fushimi-Momoyama-jō in Kyōto, but when that castle was demolished, it was moved to Edo (Tōkyō), before being shifted again to its present location in Matsu-shima by Date Tadamune, the great Masamune's eldest son. Here, the Date family held their tea parties for the next 270 years. Matsu-shima Hakubutsukan, next to Kanrantei, is a museum with a full collection of the Date family's armor, swords, pikes, and more genteel items, including an array of lacquerware. Kanrantei is on the south side of the harbor opposite Godaidō. ☞ *Kanrantei and museum ¥200.* ⊙ *Apr.–Oct., daily 8:30–5; Nov.–Mar., daily 8:30–4:30.*

From Godai-dō it is a short walk across the 250-yard pedestrian bridge near the Matsu-shima Century Hotel to **Fukurajima.** For the ¥150 toll, you can walk away from the crowds to enjoy a picnic or a brief nap while looking out across the bay from one of the islands.

Lodging

$$$$ 🏨 **Hotel Ichinobo.** An elegant, if somewhat pricey, hotel, this resort has a large garden consisting of a small man-made island connected by bridges which is lighted up at night. Rooms overlooking the bay—all do—are spacious, and the hotel's facilities are very attractively designed. ⊠ *1-4 Takagi Aza Hama, Matsu-shima-chō, Miyagi-ken 981,* ☎ *022/ 353–3331,* 🖷 *022/353–3339. 104 Japanese-style rooms, 20 Western-style rooms with toilet and bath. Restaurant, coffee shop, pool. AE, D, MC, V.*

$$$$ 🏨 **Matsu-shima Century Hotel.** In the heart of Matsu-shima, with an
★ excellent view of the bay, this luxury hotel has all of the amenities of an international resort hotel. Many of the rooms are lavish, and the meals include the best ingredients from the coastline and the deep Pacific. ⊠ *8 Sensui Aza Matsu-shima, Matsu-shima-chō, Miyagi-ken 981,* ☎ *022/354–4111,* 🖷 *022/354–4191. 192 rooms, Japanese style on the bay side, with some Western-style rooms on the mountain side. 2 restaurants, coffee shop, pool. AE, D, MC, V.*

Getting Around

For the 30-minute trip to **Hon-Shiogama Eki,** take the JR Senseki Line. Its platforms are reached from the Sendai Eki basement. The same train goes on to the Matsu-shima Kaigan Eki, so this itinerary may be done in reverse if you want to ferry straight to the island. Fares from Sendai are ¥320 to Hon-Shiogama and ¥400 to Matsu-shima Kaigan.

From April to November, between 9 AM and 3 PM, **sightseeing ferries** leave from Shiogama every 30 minutes for Matsu-shima (they run every hour from December to March). Whether you catch the gaudy "Chinese dragon" ferry or one that is less ostentatious, the route through the bay will be the same. So will the incessant and distracting loudspeaker naming (in Japanese) the islands. The first 10 minutes of the hour-long trip are dismal. Don't fret! Shiogama's ugly port and the oil refinery on the promontory soon give way to the beauty of Matsu-shima Bay and its islands. ⚐ *¥1,420 one-way, second class; ¥2,600 for the upper deck in first class. The dock is to the right (seaward side) of Hon-Shiogama Eki.*

West to Yamadera and Yamagata

Yamadera

❽ *By JR, 50 mins west of Sendai, 20 mins east of Yamagata.*

A delightful day trip from Sendai or Yamagata is Yamadera, more formally known as Risshaku-ji. Built 1,100 years ago, Yamadera's complex of temples with steeply pitched slate roofs on the slopes of Mt. Hoju is the largest one of the Tendai sect in northern Japan. It attracts some 700,000 pilgrims a year. The small town at the base of the hill has become very touristy with hotels and souvenir shops, but beyond the entrance to the temple grounds, a modicum of serenity prevails. Just inside the entrance and to the right is Kompon Chūdō, the temple where the sacred Flame of Belief has been burning constantly for 1,000 years—with, admittedly, one interruption: In 1521 a local lord called Tendo Yorinaga ransacked the complex and extinguished the flame, so that a replacement had to be brought from the original sacred fire at Mt. Hiei in Kyōto.

Near Kompon Chūdō there is a statue of the Japanese poet Matsuo Bashō (1644–94), who wrote extensively of his wanderings throughout Japan in 17-syllable haiku. The path continues on and up. Its 1,015 steps are well tended, and the ascent is relatively easy, but the path can be crowded during the summer and treacherous with snow in winter. On the way up, the best views are from the Niō-mon. Finally, after a steep ascent, you'll attain Okuno-in, a hall at the summit dedicated to the temple founder, Jikaku Daishi. After your descent, on the way back to the station, enjoy some refreshments at the shop to the right of the bridge, where you can sit and look out over the river. ⚐ *¥300.* ☽ *Sunrise–sunset (4:30 PM in winter, 7 PM in summer).*

LODGING

The train from Sendai to Yamadera passes through **Sakunami Onsen.** Sakunami is within the Sendai city limits, 40 minutes by train from the train station, close enough to make it an alternative overnight spot to a downtown hotel.

$$$$ ▦ **Iwamatsu Ryokan.** When this old Sakunami inn was renovated a decade ago, local regulars were worried that the management might change the open-air baths along the river and the wooden stairway leading to them. Fortunately, the Iwamatsu added the best of the new and kept the best of the old. Though called an inn, it is more of a hotel, with full amenities in a beautiful environment. Built along a cascade, the rooms look out on trees and the stream, and the regular Japanese baths, mixed-bathing open-air baths, and separate open-air baths for women, will make you want to relax in them forever. The original open-air bath is covered with a wooden roof, but it is at river level, allowing views of spring leaves, autumn foliage, or winter snow. Dinner is Japanese, with several local specialties. Breakfast is a buffet with a variety of Japanese and Western food that will fill anyone's plate. The inn has a shuttle bus service from JR Sakunami Eki. There is also regular bus service from Sendai Eki that stops in front of the inn. ✉ *16 Sakunami Motoki, Aoba-ku, Sendai-shi, Miyagi-ken 989,* ☎ *022/ 395–2211,* FAX *022/395–2020. 102 Japanese-style rooms. Restaurant, tea shop, hot springs, dance club. AE, MC, V.*

GETTING AROUND

To reach Yamadera, take the Senzan Line from Yamagata (20 minutes) or from Sendai (50 minutes). Sakunami Onsen is 40 minutes from Yamagata or Sendai on the JR Senzan Line.

Yamagata

9 *1 hr west of Sendai by JR.*

Yamagata, with a population of 240,000, is the capital of the prefecture of the same name. You're most likely to use Yamagata as a transportation hub than a destination in itself, but it is a friendly town that's working on its appeal to travelers. Yamagata Prefecture, incidentally, has at least one onsen in each of its 44 municipalities—the only 100% thermal Japanese prefecture.

10 Most people come to Yamagata for **Mt. Zaō,** where nearly 1.4 million alpine enthusiasts ski its 14 slopes and 11 runs between December and April. In summer hikers come, though in smaller numbers, to walk among the colored rocks and take in Zaō Okama, a caldera lake with a diameter of nearly 1,200 ft. Cable cars leave from **Zaō Onsen,** the mountain's resort town, one to climb 1,562 ft from the base lodge, which is 2,805 ft above sea level, another to make the final ascent, an additional 1,083 ft. Even nonskiers make the wintertime trip to see the *juhyō,* a phenomenon caused by heavy snow on the conifers. Layer after layer of snow covers the fir trees, creating weird, cylindrical figures that look like fairy-tale monsters.

Zaō Onsen is 19 km (12 mi) from Yamagata Eki—45 minutes by bus. In winter, there are direct buses between Tōkyō and Zaō Onsen.

Yamagata's main event is the **Hanagasa Festival** (Aug. 5–7), in which some 10,000 dancers from the entire area dance their way through the streets in traditional costume and *hanagasa,* hats so named for the safflowers used to decorate them. Floats are interspersed among the dancers, and stalls provide food and refreshments.

If you have an interest in pottery, take a trip to **Hirashimizu** on the outskirts of the city. This small enclave of traditional buildings and farmhouses is a step back in time and a sharp contrast to the modern urban sprawl of Yamagata. About six pottery families live here, each with its own kiln, each specializing in a particular style. Two of them, the Shichiemon and Hirayashi, offer pottery lessons, and participants can have the results fired and then mailed back home. The pottery of the Seiryugama family is the best known, and, with exhibitions of their wares in America and Europe, their prices are high. (Until now, the bus route to Hirashimizu has been a very confusing one for non-Japanese speakers, and taxis have been recommended as an easier means of getting there. However, at the time of this writing, Yamagata's prefectural government was preparing a new sightseeing guide with detailed instructions on reaching Hirashimizu by bus.)

Pick up free maps and brochures from the **tourist information office** opposite the ticket turnstiles inside the JR eki. ☎ *0236/31–7865.* ◷ *Weekdays 10–6, weekends 10–5.*

LODGING

$$–$$$ 🏨 **Hotel Castle.** A seven-minute walk from Yamagata Eki, the Castle is a modern, utilitarian hotel with small rooms. You'll find guests milling around the lobby area, where there is a coffee-tea lounge. ⊠ *2-7 Toka-machi 4-chōme, Yamagata, Yamagata-ken 990,* ☎ *0236/31–3311,* ℻ *0236/31–3373. 160 Western-style rooms. 3 restaurants, pub. AE, DC, MC, V.*

$$ 🏨 **Yamagata Washington Hotel.** This downtown Yamagata hotel is smart and efficient and has a friendly staff. The coffee shop is on the ground floor; reception and the Japanese restaurant are on the next floor; and the guest rooms are up above, from the third to eighth floors. Rooms are compact, with merely functional furnishings that are at least new. Bathrooms are the typical prefabricated plastic units. ⊠ *1-4-31 Nanoka-machi, Yamagata, Yamagata-ken 990,* ☎ *0236/25–1111,* ℻ *0236/24–1512. 227 rooms. Restaurant. AE, DC, MC, V.*

GETTING AROUND

To reach Yamagata from Tōkyō, the Shinkansen takes just under three hours. There is also direct train service on the JR Senzan Line from Sendai (about an hour). From west-coast towns, travel times to Yamagata by JR are as follows: 3½ hours from Niigata (Yonesaka Line); 2 hours, 20 minutes from Tsuruoka (Uetsu and Riku-u Sai lines); 3 hours from Akita (Ōu Line). The Tazawa-ko and Ōu lines (connecting in Ōmagari) provide access from Morioka in central Tōhoku.

Yamagata is also served by All Nippon Airways (ANA) flights from Tōkyō's Haneda Airport (50 minutes) and by Japan Air System (JAS) from Ōsaka (75 minutes). Yamagata's airport is 40 minutes by bus from the city center.

North to the Gorges and Hiraizumi

35 mins north of Sendai by Shinkansen, 95 mins by JR local.

East of Ichi-no-seki, the Iwai River flows through the naturally carved Geibikei Gorge, and one can either walk along the banks or travel upstream and take a boat through the gorge. Gembikei Gorge is west of Ichi-no-seki, and its proximity to the temples of Hiraizumi makes these two places a good combination for a full-day outing.

⑪ Flat-bottom boats, poled by two boatmen, ply the river for a 90-minute round-trip through **Geibikei Gorge.** The waters are peaceful and slow moving, relentlessly washing their way through silver-streaked cliffs. The high point of the trip is reaching the depths of the gorge, faced with 300-ft cliffs. Coming back downstream would be an anticlimax if it were not for the boatmen, who, with little to do but steer the boat, sing traditional songs. The boat trip, which costs ¥1,500, makes a marvelous rest from the temples of Hiraizumi.

★ ⑫ **Gembikei,** at a thousand yards long and less than 20 ft deep, is no less than a miniature gorge, but with all the features of the world's best gorges. Once, rushing water carved its path into solid rock; now it is quiet. Because of its small scale, you can walk its entire length and appreciate every detail of its web of sculptured patterns; the circular holes (called Jacob wells) scoured into the rock side become personal discoveries.

Takkoku-no-Iwaya is a cave with a small temple dedicated to Bishamonten, the Buddhist deity of warriors, at its entrance. To the side of the cave, etched into the rock face, are faint traces of an imposing image of Dainichi-Nyorai, a pose of Buddha said to have been carved in the 11th century. The current temple is a 1961 rendition of the 17th-century original. The cave is en route from Gembikei to Mōtsu-ji. 🎫 ¥300. 🕐 *Daily 8–5.*

⑬ In the 12th century, **Hiraizumi** came close to mirroring Kyōto as a cultural center. Hiraizumi was the family seat of the Fujiwara clan, who for three generations dedicated themselves to promoting peace and the arts. The fourth-generation lord became power hungry, and his ambition wiped out the Fujiwara dynasty. Little remains of the efflorescence of the first three generations of the Fujiwara clan, but what does—in particular Chūson-ji and the golden Konjiki-dō—is a tribute to Japan's past.

During the time of the Fujiwara clan, **Mōtsu-ji** was the most venerated temple in northern Honshū. The complex consisted of 40 temples and some 500 lodgings. Eight centuries later, only the foundations remain. The current buildings are of more recent vintage, including the local youth hostel. The Heian period Jodo-style (paradise-style) gardens, however, which were laid out according to the Buddhist principle some 700 years ago, have survived in good condition. The garden is especially beautiful June 20 through July 10 during the **Ayame (Iris) Festival.** The Hiraizumi Museum, with artifacts of the Fujiwara family, is beside the garden. 🎫 *Gardens and museum ¥800.* 🕐 *Daily 8–5.*

★ Now for Hiraizumi's major sight, **Chūson-ji.** Set amid thick woods, the temple was founded by the Fujiwara family in 1105. At that time, there were more than 40 buildings. In Chūson-ji's heyday the number reached 300. Unfortunately for the northern Fujiwara dream, war and a tremendous fire in 1337 destroyed all but two halls, Kyōzō and Konjiki-dō. The other buildings in the complex are reconstructions from the Edo period.

Of the two original buildings, **Kyōzō** is the less interesting. It once housed the greatest collection of Buddhist sutras (precepts), but fire destroyed many of them, and the remainder have been removed to the **Sankōzō Museum** next door.

The small but magnificent **Konjiki-dō** (Golden Hall) is considered one of Japan's most historic temples. Indeed, it was the first of Japan's National Treasures to be so designated. Konjiki-dō's exterior is black lacquer, and the interior is paneled with mother-of-pearl and gold leaf. In the Naijin (Inner Chamber) are three altars, each with 11 statues of Buddhist deities. The remains of the three rulers of the Fujiwara family—Kiyohira, Motohira, and Hidehira—are beneath the central altar.

To commemorate the grandeur that once was, two festivals are held every year, the spring and autumn **Fujiwara Festivals** (May 1–5 and Nov. 1–3). Costumed warriors mount the road up the temple slope on horseback. 🎫 *¥500 Chūson-ji and Sankōzō Museum.* 🕐 *Apr.–Oct., daily 8–5; Nov.–Mar., daily 8:30–4:30 (enter 30 mins before closing time).*

Getting Around

The Gorges. Travel east to **Geibikei** by changing to the Ofunato Line for a 30-minute ride to Higashiyama. However, the direct route is only about 21 km (13 mi), so a taxi (about ¥2,000) is much more convenient. There is little other than Geibikei to see along this route. Travel west from Ichi-no-seki to **Gembikei** by taxi (10 minutes) or by Iwate-ken Kotsu bus (22 minutes) to the end of the line. From there you are best off taking a taxi the 1½ km (1 mi) to Mōtsu-ji to begin your Hiraizumi visit.

Hiraizumi and the temples. From Hiraizumi Eki you can walk to the two major temples. If your time is short and you wish to limit your sightseeing to Mōtsu-ji and Chūson-ji, simply take the local train from

Sendai for the 100-minute run to Hiraizumi. To reach Mōtsu-ji, walk 1,000 yards up the street that leads directly away from the JR Hiraizumi Eki. For Chūson-ji, you can walk along a narrow road from Mōtsu-ji (30 minutes), take a taxi (¥950), or return to the JR eki and walk or take a short bus ride.

You can obtain maps at the **tourist office** on your right as you leave the JR Hiraizumi Eki. ☎ 0191/46–2110. ⊙ Apr.–Oct., daily 8:30–5; Nov.–Mar., daily 8:30–4:30; closed Dec. 29–Dec. 31.

From Hiraizumi, you can either return to Sendai and Tōkyō or continue to northern Tōhoku: to Morioka or travel to Hanamaki to turn east to Tōno and the coast.

NORTHERN TŌHOKU

The northern reaches of Tōhoku are distinguished by rugged people and rugged geography—from rocky cliffs along the ocean to volcanic peaks inland—which make for spectacular natural beauty. The Tōno Basin's farmland and the Pacific coastline to the east is easy to reach by train. At the seaside, a sightseeing boat will afford the best look at the work of waves on stone. The national parks of the central highlands are among the best places to view autumn foliage in late September. Oddly enough Morioka is still considered a castle town, even though its castle was destroyed in the mid-1800s. Morioka still does make its revered *nambutetsu* ironware.

The Tōno Basin

Allow two days for a turn through this traditional pastoral corner of Japan and the southern coastline. Tōno is rich in traditional ways and folklore, and the coast is an ever-changing landscape of cliffs, rock formations, and small coves.

Tōno
⑭ *2½ hrs north and east of Sendai by Shinkansen and JR local.*

The people of Tōno like their old ways. The town itself is not particularly remarkable, but the Tōno Basin has old buildings and historical remains that take us back to old Japan. In a peaceful, wooded area above the Atago Shrine southwest of downtown are the **Go-hyaku Rakan** (500 Disciples of Buddha) images carved by a priest on boulders in a shallow ravine. He wanted to appease the spirits of the quarter of Tōno's inhabitants who starved to death in the two-year famine of 1754–55.

The Tōno Basin is surrounded by forest-clad mountains, so the setting for this enclave of rusticity is picture-perfect. Along the valley on either side of Tōno, there are several *magariya* (L-shaped, thatched-roof Nambu-style farmhouses). A good representative is **Chiba-ke Magariya**, 13 km (8 mi) west of the JR eki. Families live in the long side of the L, and horses are kept in the short side.

North of Tōno, **Fukusen-ji** contains Japan's tallest wood Kannon (Goddess of Mercy), which was built by priest Yūzen Suriishi to boost morale after World War II. A long taxi ride northeast of town, there is a **suisha** (water mill), one of the few working ones left in Japan. **Kappa buchi** is a more reasonable bike or taxi ride northeast. It is a pool in a stream where *kappa*, supernatural amphibious creatures, live. They are said to drag people, horses, and cows into the water and to impregnate young girls, who then give birth to demi-kappas. The site is along the edge of the grounds of **Jōken-ji**, 6 km (4 mi) from the station, which is about as far as you need to go to see interesting countryside.

Stop in at **Denshō-en,** a Japanese folk-village museum where you can see a good Nambu magariya, complete with barn, storehouse, mill, and bath house. Be sure to go in the room at the back to see the **oshirasama,** a thousand small carved sticks upon which are placed votive clothes. These small god figures are said to be the god of silkworm cultivation and are able to predict the future. The museum is about 6½ km (4 mi) northeast of Tōno Eki. 🎫 *¥300.* ⊙ *Daily 9–4:30; closed last day of month and Dec. 28–Jan. 4.*

LODGING

$$$ 🏨 **Fukuzansō Inn.** Highly polished creaky floors characterize this friendly, old-fashioned ryokan, which is a five-minute walk from the JR Tōno Eki and is open 24 hours a day, 365 days a year. Rooms have a dressing room–closet area and a small enclosed balcony with table and chairs. Dinner, served in your room, consists mainly of seafood and Japanese vegetables. Country-style Japanese breakfast is served in the downstairs common room. No English is spoken, but the hospitality is all smiles; the staff lends bikes for sightseeing. ✉ *5-30 Chūō-dōri, Tōno-shi, Iwate-ken 028,* ☎ *0198/62–4120 or 0120/48–8588 toll-free. 18 rooms, none with bath. V.*

$$–$$$ 🏨 **Forukurōro Tōno.** If you decide to walk or bike around the sights
★ of this small town, you will be glad to stay at this new B&B, above the JR Tōno Eki, where the beds are comfortable, the rooms are simple but clean, and service is very friendly. Reservations are advised, but if you arrive in town without a place to stay, be sure to check here first. Because the last train comes through around 9:30 PM and the first around 6:30 AM, you will be able to get enough sleep. Rates include a light breakfast. ✉ *5-7 Shinkoku-chō, Tōno-shi, Iwate-ken 028,* ☎ *0198/ 62–0700,* 🖷 *0198-62-0800. 18 rooms with bath. No credit cards.*

$ 🏨 **Minshuku Magariya.** A highlight if you're planning to overnight in Tōno, this L-shaped farmhouse has been made into a family-run hotel—without the animals. Two meals including fish, chicken, and wild vegetable dishes are served, and after dinner one of the local elder ladies tells folktales. Surrounded by fields 7 km (4 mi) west of town, Magariya is best reached by a taxi from Tōno Station, unless you prefer the 20-minute walk from the nearest bus stop. ✉ *30-58-3 Niisato, Ayaori-chō, Tōno-shi, Iwate-ken 028,* ☎ *0198/62–4564. 16 rooms. No credit cards.*

GETTING AROUND

To reach the Tōno Basin from Sendai (or Hiraizumi if you stop there), take the Shinkansen to Shin-Hanamaki Eki, and then board a JR train to Tōno.

Distances between Tōno's sights are too far to walk. Unless you have a car, plan to rent a bicycle from a hotel, bicycle shop, or even the Tōno Tourist Office. A sightseeing taxi is a convenient way to see the faraway places, and even if the driver waits for you here and there, you can see a lot in one hour, which will cost about ¥6,000. To make the most of the Tōno experience, you should read Kunio Yanagita's *Tōno Mono-gatari,* translated into English by Robert Morse as *The Legends of Tōno.*

OFF THE BEATEN PATH   **TAKE –** If you do not go down to the Rikuchi coast from Tōno, consider renting a car or hiring a taxi to get to Take (*tah*-keh). It is especially worth considering if you are traveling at the end of July, when there is a delightful Shintō festival. The road from Tōno winds through picturesque hills to reach the village of Take, situated on the slopes of Mt. Haya-chine. For centuries Mt. Hayachine has been regarded as a sacred mountain, and every July 31–August 1 there is a festival at Hayachine Jinja. For two days the folkloric stories known collectively as *yamabushi-*

kagura are acted out in masked dance performances. The most colorful part of the festival is on August 1, when a procession of townspeople, wearing lion costumes and wooden lion masks, parades through the village en route from the main shrine to a lesser shrine nearby. Because the festival has grown in popularity, it is advisable to telephone local festival authorities (☎ 0198/48–5864) to secure accommodations. Note that some maps indicate Take only by the name of its shrine, Hayachine Jinja. The road from Take continues to Shiwa, a stop on the JR Tōhoku Line 20 minutes south of Morioka.

Morioka

⑮ *By Shinkansen 44 mins north of Ichinoseki, 50–100 mins north of Sendai.*

Morioka is a busy commercial and industrial city ringed by mountains. Westerners will be pleased by the generous amount of information written in English—on street signs and on the destination boards in the bus terminal, for example. Once Morioka had a fine castle built by the 26th Lord of Nambu in 1597, but it was destroyed in the Meiji Restoration and all that remains are its ruins. Its site is now **Iwate Kōen,** the focus of town and the place to escape the congestion of traffic and people in downtown Morioka. Because it is at the northernmost end of the Shinkansen Line, it has become a transfer point for destinations to northern Honshū and Hokkaidō.

If you arrive in town on June 15, stay around the front of the station around 12:15. That is when the parade of grandly decorated, bell-clad horses pass by during the festival called **Chagu-chagu Umakko.** The horses parade through the streets between 9:30 and 1:30, so just look for people gathering. To reach downtown Morioka take Bus 5 or 6 from the terminal in front of the JR eki.

Aside from horses, the major attraction of Morioka is its special craft, **nambutetsu.** The range of articles, from small wind bells to elaborate statues, is vast, but the most popular items are *nambutetsubin* (heavy iron kettles), which come in all shapes, weights, and sizes. Hundreds of shops throughout the city sell nambutetsu, but the main shopping streets are Saien-dōri and Ō-dōri, which pass Iwate Kōen.

Gozaku is the most interesting place to browse for nambutetsu. Across the river from Iwate Kōen, it is an area of small shops that look much as they did a century ago. To reach Gozaku from the park, use the **Nakan-ōhashi** and take the first main street on the left. A short way down, just past Hotel Saitō, you will find the large Nambu Iron shop and the narrow streets of the Gozaku section on your left. Beyond Gozaku is another bridge, **Yonoji-bashi.** At the street corner you'll see a very Western-looking firehouse, built in the 1920s and still in operation. The next bridge, Morioka's pride, is **Kamin-ōhashi,** one of the few decorated bridges in Japan. Eight specially crafted bronze railings were commissioned in 1609 and 10 bronze posts added two years later.

Whether you want to wander between connections or are in Morioka overnight, don't miss a visit to **Kōgensha,** a shop specializing in quality folk crafts such as lacquerware, kites, dyed fabrics, and pottery. The main shop is composed of several small buildings along a courtyard. Walk through the courtyard to a relaxing *kissaten* (coffee shop) and farther to the river. Along the wall to the left are poems by Miyazawa Kenji. To get to Kōgensha from Morioka Eki, walk left to the stoplight in front of the Metropolitan Hotel, turn right, and cross the river on **Asahi-bashi.** Take the first left into an artistically designed street that leads to the main shop 50 yards down on the left and a branch shop across the street that sells basketry and wooden bowls. ⊠ *2-18 Zaimoku-chō,* ☎ *019/622–2894.* ⊘ *Daily 10–6; closed the 15th of every month, several days in mid-Aug. and at year's end.*

★ If there is time to spare in Morioka, visit the **Hashimoto Bijutsukan,** which was created by Yaoji Hashimoto, himself an artist, from a traditional Nambu magariya rescued from a valley drowned by a dam. The building itself is worth a visit, and the works of Hashimoto and other Iwate-ken artists are an added pleasure, but you could skip the room exhibiting 19th-century paintings by French naturalists of the Barbizon school. There is also one room devoted to ironware and pottery in case you have not had your fill. The museum is a 25-minute bus ride from Morioka Eki. From mid-April to the end of November, Bus 8 goes up to the observation tower on Mt. Iwayama for a fee of ¥330; the museum is halfway up the small mountain. In winter, Bus 12 will drop you off within 10 minutes' walk of the museum if you ask the driver beforehand. Buses run infrequently, especially in winter, so verify the time of the return bus before you set out. ⊠ *¥700.* ⊘ *Daily 10–5; closed Dec. 29–Jan. 3.*

An alternative place to visit on the city's outskirts is the **Morioka Handiworks Square,** a tourist center that promotes the region's crafts (including the ubiquitous local ironware). Fourteen workshops allow you to watch Iwate-ken craftsmen at work in such varied fields as pottery, fabric dyeing, doll making, and bamboo work—and lessons are offered should you wish to participate. You'll also find a large shop, an exhibition hall, and yet another magariya farmhouse. Bus 10 from Morioka Eki is a 30-minute ride to the square. ⊠ *Exhibition hall ¥100.* ⊘ *Daily 8:40–5; closed Dec. 29–Jan. 3.*

The **tourist office,** Kankō Center, in the Train Square lounge on the south end of the second floor of Morioka Eki, has useful maps and other information on Morioka and Iwate Prefecture. The office can also help arrange accommodations. ☎ *019/625–2090.* ⊘ *Daily 8:30–7:30.*

Dining and Lodging

$$ ✕ **Azumaya.** Hearty *soba* (buckwheat noodles) comes from northern
★ Japanese grain, and Azumaya is Morioka's place to eat soba. *Wanko soba* courses start at ¥2,500, and a delicious tempura soba is only ¥1,200. The *maneki-neko,* beckoning cats, are mascots to ensure the customers will come again and again, and they seem to be doing their job. The main branch is in Gozaku, 10 minutes from the station by taxi, and a branch shop is across from the station on the far right corner next to the Tōhoku Bank, on the second floor above the fruit shop. ⊠ *1-8-3 Nakan-ōhashi-dōri,* ☎ *019-622–2252. No credit cards. Closed 1st and 3rd Tues. of month.*

$$ ✕ **Banya Nagasawa.** Everyone in town recommends this shop for its yellowtail, its charcoal grilled shellfish, such as scallops and abalone, and its own original sake. The place is across the street from the Mister Donut on Ō-dōri in the building next to the Kita Nippon Bank; take the elevator to the second floor. ⊠ *Kirihara Bldg., 2nd floor, 1-10-13 Ōdōri,* ☎ *019/622–2646. No credit cards. Closed Sun., mid-Aug., and a few days at year's end.*

$$ ✕ **Sawauchi Jinku.** Great for local Tōhoku food and atmosphere, this
★ shop serves wild vegetable dishes and country-style cooking with river fish, home-made sausages, tofu of various sorts, mushrooms, and local Ginga Kōgen Beer. Order one dish at a time or sets starting at ¥2,500. It is next to Morioka Tōkyō Kaijo Building. ⊠ *5-4 Kaiun-bashi-dōri,* ☎ *019/654–4860. No credit cards. Closed Sun., mid-Aug., and a few days at year's end.*

$$ ✕ **Steak House Wakana.** Good *teppanyaki*—fish and steaks prepared on a flat grill right in front of you—is the Wakana staple, and the restaurant claims to have the best beef in the city. Some English is spoken. This dining spot is a 15-minute walk from the station—cross the river, walk down Kaiun-bashi-dōri one block past the Kawatoku Department Store, turn right, and walk two blocks. ✉ *1-3-33 Ōsakawara,* ☎ *019/ 653–3333. AE, DC, MC, V. Closed Tues.*

$$$ ⛩ **Morioka Grand Hotel.** The most personable and smartest modern
★   hotel in town, the Grand is situated on a small hill on the edge of the city, 10 minutes by taxi from the station. Its views are broader, the air is cleaner, and its rooms are slightly larger than most those of other hotels in the area, but this is reflected in the price of the rooms, the most expensive in Morioka. There are both Japanese and Continental restaurants. Do not confuse this hotel with the cheaper Morioka Grand Hotel Annex. ✉ *1-10 Atagoshita, Morioka, Iwate-ken 020,* ☎ *019/625–2111,* 📠 *0196/22–4804. 36 rooms, 21 Western style. 2 restaurants. AE, DC, MC, V.*

$$–$$$ ⛩ **Hotel Metropolitan Morioka.** Morioka now has two hotels with the
★   same name where the staff is able to speak English. Just to the left of the station plaza, the older wing continues to provide clean, utilitarian rooms and good service. From the old wing, cross the street facing the hotel and walk one block to the new wing, where the rooms are larger and average ¥2,000 more. The Giovanni Café on the second floor of the new wing serves a reasonable breakfast and lunch for ¥1,200. Both wings have restaurants and a bar. As a guest, you can use the Central Fitness Club facilities for ¥500, including a 25-meter pool, a machine gym, a sauna, and a Jacuzzi. ✉ *Old wing: 1-44 Morioka Eki-mae-dōri, Morioka, Iwate-ken 020; new wing: 2-27 Morioka Eki-mae Kita-dōri;* ☎ *019/625–1211,* 📠 *019/625–1210. 134 rooms (old wing), 121 (new wing). 5 restaurants, 2 bars. AE, DC, MC, V.*

$ ⛩ **Ryokan Kumagai.** In a two-story wooden building, this simple hostelry is a member of the inexpensive Japanese Inn Group, offering basic tatami rooms. There is a small dining area where Japanese and Western breakfasts and Japanese dinners are optional. In traditional style, no rooms have private bath. Located between the station and center city, it is a 10-minute walk from the JR Morioka Eki—cross the river and walk along Kaiun-bashi-dōri two blocks and turn right (a gas station is on the left and a bank on the right). Cross over one block and the ryokan is on the left. ✉ *3-2-5 Ōsakawara, Morioka, Iwate-ken 020,* ☎ *019/651–3020. 11 rooms, none with private bath. Dining room. No credit cards.*

Getting Around

Morioka is the last stop on the Tōhoku Shinkansen Line: All trains continuing north, east, or west are "regular" JR trains. So while it can take less than an hour to travel between Sendai and Morioka, the same distance up to Aomori takes 2 hours and 20 minutes.

Should you wish to tour the city, the **Iwate Kankō Bus Company** has full-day, half-day, and evening "night-view" tours from Morioka Eki with Japanese-speaking guides. 🎫 *Full-day tour ¥5,400, departs 10 AM, returns at 4:30; ½-day tour ¥2,300, departs 9:30 and 1:30, returns 3 hrs later; night-view tour ¥4,000, departs 5 PM, returns 3 hrs later. Tours operate Apr. 20–Nov. 23; night-view tour July–Aug. only.*

Tazawa-ko (Lake Tazawa) and Kakunodate

The lake area of Tazawa-ko and traditional town of Kakunodate make for good side trips into Tōhoku's rugged interior from either Morioka or the west-coast city of Akita. For a little thermal relaxation, the old spa towns of Tama-gawa Onsen and Nyūtō Onsen lie just north of Tazawa-ko.

Tazawa-ko

★ ⑯ *1 hr west of Morioka by JR, 70 mins east of Akita by JR Express.*

At 1,390 ft, Tazawa-ko is Japan's deepest lake. Its blue waters in fact are too alkaline to support any fish. Like most of Japan's other lakes, Tazawa-ko sits in a volcanic cone, its shape a classic caldera. With its clear waters and forested slopes, it captures a mystical quality that appeals so much to the Japanese. In winter, the Tazawa-ko area is a popular and picturesque skiing destination, with the lake visible from the ski slopes. According to legend, the great beauty from Akita, Takko Hime, sleeps in the water's deep as a dragon. Apparently, that is why the lake never freezes over in winter. Takko Hime and her dragon husband churn the water with their passionate lovemaking. Or, perhaps, as scientists say, the water doesn't freeze because of a freshwater source that enters the bottom of the lake.

A boat takes 40-minute cruises on the lake from late April to November (¥1,150). There is also regular bus service around the lake (halfway around in winter), and bicycles are available for rent at the Tazawa-ko-han bus terminal. If you go by bike, you can take more time to appreciate the beauty of Takko Hime, whose bronze statue is on the western shore.

You will need to take a 15-minute bus ride (¥340) from the JR eki to the Tazawa-ko-han center on the lake shore, but first drop in at the tourist information office to the left of the JR eki for maps and bus schedules. ☎ *0187/34–0307.* ☉ *Daily 8:30–5:15; closed Jan. 1.*

A 30-minute bus ride from the JR Tazawa-ko Eki via Tazawa-ko-han takes you up to **Tazawa-ko Kōgen** northeast of Tazawa-ko for ¥580. The journey affords spectacular views of the lake, showing off the full dimensions of its caldera shape. The bus from Tazawa-ko continues
⑰ for another 15 minutes to **Nyūtō Onsen,** a collection of small, unspoiled, mountain hot-spring spas in some of the few traditional spa villages left in Tōhoku. Most of these villages have only one inn, so it is advisable to arrange accommodations before you arrive if you plan to stay the night (☞ Lodging, *below.*)

⑱ **Komagatake** stands a few miles east of Tazawa-ko. At 5,370 ft, it is the highest mountain in the area—and it is one of the easiest to climb. Between June and October, a bus from the Tazawa-ko Eki runs up to the eighth station, from which it takes an hour to hike to the summit. You'll walk through clusters of alpine flowers if you hike in June or July.

★ ⑲ Another traditional spa town, **Tama-gawa Onsen,** is north of Tazawa-ko on Route 341. The spa is quaint and delightfully old-fashioned, with mainly wood buildings surrounding the thermal springs. The elderly who come to take the waters are very serious about the curative qualities of the mineral waters. However, think twice before staying here overnight; the inn is a little ramshackle. There is frequent bus service between Tazawa-ko and Tama-gawa Onsen; the ride takes 90 minutes and costs ¥1,340.

DINING AND LODGING

$$$–$$$$ ✕▥ **Nyūtō Onsen** consists of six small spa villages, each with an inn, all generally within the same price range. Only Japanese-style rooms are available, and you must take your meals on site. No Western credit cards are accepted. Following are the telephone numbers for reservations at each of the village inns: **Tsurono Onsen** (☎ 0187/46–2139;

closed in winter), **Taeno-yu Onsen** (☎ 0187/46–2740), **Ogama Onsen** (☎ 0187/46–2438), **Kaniba Onsen** (☎ 0187/46–2021), **Magoroku Onsen** (☎ 0187/46–2224), **Kuro-yu Onsen** (☎ 0187/46–2214; closed in winter).

$$ ☷ **Tazawa-ko Prince.** A modern white hotel on the edge of the lake, the Tazawa-ko Prince has views of Komagatake. Choose from rooms that are large with a lake view, small with a lake view, or small with a mountain view. Aside from the main dining room, there is a garden room down near the lake. ✉ *Katajiri, Saimyo-ji, Nishikimura, Semboku-gun, Akita-ken 014,* ☎ *0187/47–2211,* FAX *0187/47–2104. Dining room, boating, game room, shops. AE, DC, MC, V.*

En Route Beyond Tama-gawa Onsen, the road joins the scenic, 27-km (17-mi) scenic Aspite Line toll road described below in the Hachimantai section. If you are making your way from Morioka to Hachimantai you can make the trip through Tazawa-ko and then up Route 341 instead of taking the train to Obuke and then boarding a bus.

Kakunodate

★ ⑳ *16 mins southwest of Tazawa-ko by JR.*

The small and delightful town of Kakunodate was founded in 1620 by the local lord, and it has remained an outpost of traditional Japan that, with cause, claims to be Tōhoku's little Kyōto. Within a 15-minute walk northwest from the station there are several samurai houses that date back to the founding of the town, all well preserved and maintained. The most renowned of the samurai houses is **Aoyagi**, with its sod-turf roof. The cherry tree in Aoyagi's garden is nearly three centuries old. The whole town is full of weeping cherry trees, more than 400 of them, and they are direct descendants of those imported from Kyōto three centuries ago. A number of them form a 2-km-long (1¼-mi-long) "tunnel" along the banks of Hinokinai-gawa. ☷ *Houses ¥500.* ☼ *Apr.–Nov., daily 8:30–5; Dec.–Mar., daily 9–4.*

If you have time, visit **Denshō-ken,** a hall in front of a cluster of samurai houses that serves as a museum and a workshop for cherry-bark handicrafts. ☷ *¥300.* ☼ *Apr.–Nov., daily 9–5; Dec.–Mar., Fri.–Wed. 9–4:30; closed Dec. 28–Jan. 4.*

LODGING

$$ ☷ **Forukurōro Kakunodate.** The JR people have converted part of Kakunodate Eki into an inexpensive B&B with clean rooms, each with private bath and toilet, a simple buffet breakfast, unbeatable convenience, and a low price. It is only 20 meters from the exit of the station. ✉ *14 Nakasugasawa, Iwaze-aza, Kakunodate-shi, Akita-ken 014,* ☎ *0187/53-2070. 26 rooms. No credit cards.*

$ ☷ **Hyakusuien.** This minshuku is in a converted 19th-century warehouse in Kakunodate, and during the winter, the drafts constantly remind you of this heritage. Hospitality is limited despite a brochure that welcomes guests enthusiastically. Meals are served in a large, cluttered room that holds a small charcoal open fire, a library of old books, and a shrine. Food, included in the price, is average. The tatami rooms are larger than those at some minshukus, but be prepared to hear the coughs and sputters of your neighbors through the thin walls. The bathroom facilities are clean but primitive, and like many traditional residences in rural Japan, they are not connected to a sewage or septic system. The minshuku is in the center of Kakunodate, a 10-minute walk from the JR eki, south of the post office. ✉ *31 Shimina Ka-machi, Kakunodate, Akita-ken 014,* ☎ *0187/55–5715,* FAX *0187/55–2767. 12 rooms with shared bath. No credit cards.*

Towada-Hachimantai National Park

★ *2 hrs northwest of Morioka by JR and bus.*

From Morioka, the main railway line runs north to Aomori via Hachinohe, circumventing Tōhoku's rugged interior, Hachimantai Kōgen. The mountains of Towada-Hachimantai National Park afford sweeping panoramas over the park's gorges and valleys—which form wrinkles in which natives seek shelter during the region's harsh winters—crystal-clear lakes like Towada-ko, gnarled and windswept trees, volcanic mountain cones, and the ubiquitous hot springs. Needless to say, winter weather conditions here are not conducive to extensive traveling. If you plan to travel here in winter, be sure to check beforehand which bus services are running and which roads are open.

Hachimantai Kōgen

㉑ **Higashi-Hachimantai** is the resort town where hikers and skiers begin their ascent into the upper reaches of the mountains. The nearby village of **Pūtaro Mura** consists of log cabins with private thermal pools. In this part of the park, you can either bring in your own food and cook in your cabin or eat in the attached restaurant. A few miles farther on is **Gozaisho Onsen**, a popular spa resort that can be a useful overnight stop. Because the large Hachimantai Kankō hotel is a bit iffy, the best place to stay is in one of the popular self-catering cabins of **Pūtaro Mura** (☞ *below*).

The left-hand fork of the road from Higashi-Hachimantai leads to **Matsukawa Onsen,** which is noted for its pure waters. You'll find the Kyounso Inn (☞ Lodging, *below*) in town. This spa town is on the backside of Mt. Iwate, amid the eerie barrenness left by the volcano's eruption in 1719.

You'll find the entrance to the **Aspite Line** past Gozaisho Onsen. This 27-km (17-mi) scenic toll road skirts Mt. Chausu (5,177 ft) and Mt. Hachimantai (5,295 ft). With every turn there is another view of evergreen-clad slopes and alpine flowers. The Aspite Line is closed November–April.

From Hachimantai-chōjō bus stop off the Aspite Line it is a 20-minute walk up a path to **Hachiman-numa** (marsh), originally a crater lake of a volcano. There is a paved esplanade around the crater, and in July and August alpine wildflowers are in peak bloom.

The road turns left (south) after Hachimantai-chōjō to **Toshichi Onsen.** The year-round spa town—elevation 4,593 ft at the foot of Mt. Mokko—is a popular spring skiing resort. On the north side of Toshichi is **Horaikyo**, a natural garden with dwarf pine trees and alpine plants scattered among strange rock formations. In early October, the autumn colors are resplendent.

Goshogake Onsen, noted for its abundance of hot water, is just before the western end of the Aspite Line. This spa and Toshichi are the best spas for overnight stays, especially Goshogake if you want to try *ondoru* (Korean-style) steam baths and box-type steam baths where only your head protrudes. Just outside of Goshogake is a mile-long nature trail highlighting the volcanic phenomena of the area, including *dorokazan* (muddy volcanoes) and *oyu-numa* (hot-water swamps).

After Goshogake Onsen, the toll road joins Route 341. A left turn here leads south to Lake Tazawa (☞ *above*). A right turn at the junction heads north for an hour's bus journey to the town of **Hachimantai,** where you can rejoin the JR Hanawa Line either to return to Obuke and Morioka or to travel north toward Towada-ko and Aomori.

LODGING

$-$$ ☒ **Matsu-kawa-so.** This ryokan is popular for its rustic flair and rejuvenating spa waters. It is simple, clean, and traditional, with highly polished wooden floors. Two meals are included, and all rooms are Japanese style. ⊠ *Matsu-kawa Onsen, Matsuo Mura, Iwate-gun, Iwate-ken 028,* ☎ *01957/8–2255. 35 rooms. Dining room, hot springs. No credit cards.*

$ ☒ **Kyoun-so Inn.** You'll find just the essentials at this little two-story wooden inn: small tatami rooms and traditional shared bathroom facilities. Optional meals are served in a communal room. Open-air hot springs are nearby, and the owners are always delighted to have a Westerner stay. ⊠ *Matsu-kawa Onsen, Matsuo Mura, Iwate-gun, Iwate-ken 028,* ☎ *01957/8–2256. 18 rooms. Dining room. AE, V.*

$ ☒ **Pūtaro Mura.** Cabins sleep anywhere from 2 to 12 in connecting cabins. The theme is self-entertainment and self-cooking—basic cooking utensils are provided and there is a food store—and if you are looking for a place to relax and hike, this is a good base. There's also an athletic course with ropes and bridges. Reservations are strongly advised. ⊠ *Hachimantai Onsen, Matsuo Mura, Iwate-ken 028,* ☎ *019/ 578–2277,* 𝔽𝔸𝕏 *019/578–3283. 66 cabins. Grocery, kitchens, miniature golf, 6 tennis courts. MC, V.*

Towada-ko

㉒ The area around **Towada-ko** is one of the most popular resorts in northern Tōhoku—almost crushingly so in autumn. If you choose one lake to visit, this should be it. The caldera lake fills a volcanic cone to depths of 1,096 ft, making it the third deepest in Japan. Towada-ko had no fish in it until Sadayuki Wainai stocked it with trout in 1903. The town of Towada-minami (Towada South) is 20 minutes north of Hachimantai on the JR Hanawa Line. From here, buses leave on the hour to Towada-ko; the bus fare is ¥1,110.

The road to Towada-ko snakes over **Hakka-toge** (pass), which affords some of the best views of the lake. Following a series of switchbacks, the road descends to circle the lakeshore, though the bus from Towada-Minami goes only part of the way around it. At the village resort of

㉓ **Yasumi-ya**—the word *yasumi* in the name means "holiday"—pleasure boats run across the lake to **Nenokuchi.** The one-hour trip on the boat, which costs ¥1,320, covers the most scenic parts of the lake. Boats run every 30 minutes from mid-April to early November, less frequently until January 31, then not at all until mid-April.

You can rent a bike at Yasumi-ya and Nenokuchi, but you are better off on foot. First you will want to walk along the lakeside at Yasumi-ya, especially to the right from the sightseeing boat pier. Go at least as far as the statue of two women, and if you are a rock-hopper continue on up the trail to the end of the peninsula. A short walk inland from the statue will take you to the impressively carved, weather-beaten Towada Shrine. Regular bus service from Yasumi-ya to Nenokuchi and beyond takes about 25 minutes.

An excellent choice for a walk is down the **Oirase** (oh-*ee*-ra-seh) cascades northeast from the lake at Nenokuchi. The carefully tended trail follows the stream for a total of 8.9 km (5.5 mi); 2 hours and 40 minutes). A two-lane road parallels the river; from it you can catch a bus at intervals of about 2 km (1 mi). The first stop is a 20-minute walk from the lake, and the second is another 50 minutes. Don't miss this easy trail, for it passes through one of the most pristine areas of Tōhoku. Be prepared for rain, take a map of the river and bus stops, and find out the bus schedule before you start out, and don't be daunted by the crowds of tourists, especially in autumn. Buses along the trail go north to Aomori and south to Nenokuchi and Yasumi-ya.

DINING AND LODGING

$$$$ ✕⌂ **Towada Kankō Hotel.** Yasumi-ya is dominated by rather old ho-
★ tels that cater to busloads of older people and high school excursions, but this hotel is a sophisticated place to make your base for enjoying the lake, which is steps away. Western-style rooms have comfortable beds and a separate tatami area. Kaiseki-style Japanese dinner is served in your room and includes *kiritampo-nabe* (grilled rice stick stew) and wild vegetables; Japanese-style breakfast is served in the dining room. ✉ *Towada-ko Yasumiya, Aomori-ken 018,* ☎ *0176/75–2111,* FAX *0176/75–2327. 72 rooms with private bath. Restaurant, bar, café, hot springs. AE, D, MC, V.*

GETTING AROUND

There are two ways to get from Morioka to the Hachimantai Kōgen: Take the JR Hanawa Line for a 43-minute ride to Ōbuke, 19 km (12 mi) from the plateau. From there, continue by bus 50 minutes to Higashi-Hachimantai. The faster way of reaching Higashi-Hachimantai is to take one of the seven daily buses directly from Morioka (1 hour, 50 minutes; from the Number 4 bus stop in front of the JR eki); the fare is ¥1,090. The bus's last stop is Hachimantai Kankō Hotel. Change buses in town for Matsu-kawa.

After exploring that area you can catch one of the 10 daily buses at Towada-minami, north of the plateau. From here you can take a bus to Towada-ko or connect in Ōdate to Hirosaki and Aomori. The total travel time is less than a day, but you should plan on spending at least one night en route to take in the remarkable scenery.

Hirosaki

★ ㉔ *1 hr, 40 mins north of Towada-minami by JR; 2 hrs, 20 mins north-west of Morioka by express bus, 4 hrs by JR.*

Hirosaki is one of northern Tōhoku's friendliest and most attractive cities, said to be the home of Japan's most beautiful women. Its major, and really only, sight is Hirosaki-jō, but the town has an intimacy that makes it appealing. Though the city is compact and walkable, finding your bearings in the ancient castle town might be difficult. Hirosaki's streets were laid out as confusingly as possible to disorient invaders before they could get to the battlements. So pick up a map at the tourist information office.

If you want to take in Hirosaki's nightlife, look for the small entertainment area just beyond the river as you head toward the castle, south of the two main streets, Chūō-dōri and Dote-machi; or, if you're still baffled by the town's geography, simply say the area's name, **Kaji-machi,** to any citizen and you'll be directed to its clutter of narrow streets. There are numerous choices for dining, from izakaya to restaurants with picture menus in their windows; and for after dinner there are coffeehouses, *nomi-ya* (pubs), and more expensive clubs.

Perhaps because of the large resident foreign population in Hirosaki, *gai-jin* are accepted, understood, and welcomed, seemingly more so than in other Tōhoku towns. You'll even find a **Kinokuniya** (☎ 0172/36–4511) bookshop with a selection of English-language books next to the Hotel Hokke Club on Dote-machi.

Hirosaki-jō, still the original, 400-year-old building, is a pleasant change from admirable replicas. Completed in 1611, it is perfectly proportioned in its compactness, and it is guarded by moats. The gates in the outlying grounds are also original, and when the more than 5,000 *someiyoshino* (cherry trees) blossom (festival, around Apr. 25–May 5) or the maples turn red in autumn (festival, late Oct.–mid-Nov.), the setting is marvelous. Winter snows mirror the castle's whiteness and give the grounds a sense of stillness and peace. A snow-lantern festival with illuminated ice sculptures is held in early February. The castle is on the northwestern end of town and across the river. ✉ ¥300. ⊙ *Daily 9–5; closed Nov. 23–Mar. 31.*

On the northeast corner of the castle grounds is the **Tsugaru Neputa Mura,** an exhibit of the giant drums and floats used in the summer festival. If you miss the real thing, come here to see the ten-meter fan-shaped floats lit from within. ✉ ¥500. ⊙ *Daily 9–5 (9–4 Dec.–Mar.).*

And don't miss the five-story pagoda, **Saishō-in,** by the river on the southwest edge of town. Built in 1672, it is the tallest pagoda in Japan supported by a single center beam.

At any time, Hirosaki makes for a pleasant overnight stay, but during the first week of August the city comes even more alive with its famous **Neputa Festival** (Aug. 1–7). Each night floats follow different routes through town, displaying scenes from Japanese and Chinese mythology represented by huge fanlike paintings that have faces on both sides. With lights inside the faces, the streets become an illuminated dreamscape. You'll have no trouble finding the route; just follow the throb of the four-meter-diameter drums.

Dining and Lodging

$$$$ ✕ **Suimeisō.** Kaiseki-style Japanese food with Aomori area ingredients make this upscale restaurant a favorite for special occasions. Sumeisō is near NHK, the national television station, just east of the castle grounds. ✉ *69 Motodera-chō,* ☎ *0172/32–8281. AE, D, MC, V.*

$$ ✕ **Yamauta.** Hirosaki's most interesting venue, a minute's walk from the station, Yamauta offers tasty Japanese food and live *shamisen* (a three-string banjo-like instrument) music every hour. The restaurant gets its musical character from its owner, who was once national shamisen champion and now uses the premises as a school for aspiring shamisen artists. Yamauta is closed one day a month; the day varies. ✉ *1-2-7 Ō-machi,* ☎ *0172/36–1835,* 𝖥𝖠𝖷 *0172/36–6115. No credit cards.*

$$–$$$$ 🏨 **Hotel New Castle.** A smart business hotel on a par with the Hokke Club (☞ *below*), the New Castle is fractionally more expensive, though no better. It is, however, a good alternative if the Hokke is full. The restaurant here offers formal and elegant Japanese meals. ✉ *24-1 Kamisayashi-machi, Hirosaki, Aomori-ken 036 (on the castle side, downtown Hirosaki),* ☎ *0172/36–1211,* 𝖥𝖠𝖷 *0172/36–1210. 59 rooms, mostly Western style. Restaurant. AE, DC, MC, V.*

$$ 🏨 **Hokke Club Hotel.** This modern, efficient hotel in the center of ★ town uses sparkling marble in its public rooms, which seem larger than they are due to an open design. Bedrooms tend to be small as well, so you may want to upgrade your room. Surrounded by shops and restaurants, the Hokke Club begins two flights up a moving escalator. The Kasen Japanese restaurant has excellent formal dining, and there is an American-style bar, called the Jolly Dog. ✉ *126 Dote-machi, Hirosaki, Aomori-ken 036,* ☎ *0172/34–3811,* 𝖥𝖠𝖷 *0172/32–0589. 65 rooms, mostly Western style. Restaurants, bar, tea shop. AE, DC, MC, V.*

Visitor Information

The **Hirosaki Sightseeing Information Center,** south of the castle grounds, displays local industry, crafts, and regional art, and provides tourist information; it is open daily and is free. There is also a **tourist informa-**

tion office (☎ 0172/32–0524) on the right side of the station as you go out; it is open daily 8:45–6, closed December 29–January 3.

Aomori

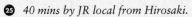 *40 mins by JR local from Hirosaki.*

Aomori is another of Tōhoku's prefectural capitals that have more appeal to their residents than to travelers. Foreign visitors used to stop here while waiting for the ferry to cross to Hokkaidō. Now, you can transfer to an express train and ride through the Seikan Undersea Tunnel (33.66 mi long, with 14.5 mi of it deep under the Tsugaru Straits) to Hokkaidō. The Seikan tunnel was the world's longest undersea tunnel until the Channel Tunnel linking Britain and France opened in 1994.

Aomori's marginal interest is temporarily dispelled by its **Nebuta Festival** (Aug. 3–7), which should not be confused with Hirosaki's Neputa Festival (residents of both places are greatly irritated when they are). Though both are held in early August—and both see large, illuminated floats being paraded through the streets at night and have an ancient mythology to do with a battle fought by the Tsugaru clan—there are important differences. Hirosaki's festival is rooted in the period before the battle and has a somber atmosphere with slowly beating drums. Aomori's celebrates the postbattle victory and is thus noisier and livelier. And while spectators in Hirosaki can only watch, at Aomori you can participate if you are willing to jump, yell, and generally lose your inhibitions.

If you are in Aomori at another time, you might take the JR bus from Gate 8 or 9 (¥440; 35 minutes) to **Nebuta-no-Sato** (Nebuta Museum) in the southeast part of town, where 10 of the figures used in Aomori's festival are stored and displayed. The JR bus that runs to Sukayu Onsen and the Hachimantai Plateau stops at Nebuta-no-Sato, so if you are coming from that spa, you may wish to get off and visit this museum before continuing into downtown Aomori. ⊡ ¥620. ◐ *July–Sept., daily 9–8 (except during Nebuta Festival in early Aug.); mid-Apr.–June and Oct.–Nov., daily 9–5:30.*

For those with historical curiosity, the **Sannai Maruyama Historical Site** is one of the largest sites yet found that date back 2,000-plus years to the Jōmon period. It has reconstructions of the large, raised buildings and an exhibition hall with clay figurines, lacquerware, and other items unearthed here. Admission is free, but you should inquire ahead about when exactly volunteer guides are offering tours. The site is accessible by bus from stop number 2 at the JR Aomori Eki (30 minutes). ☎ 0177/77–5077 *(Japanese only).* ◐ *Daily 9–4.*

Munakata Shikō Kinenkan, a museum dedicated to native son Munakata Shikō (1903–75), displays the wood-block prints, paintings, and calligraphy of this internationally known artist. The building itself is constructed in the attractive, rough-hewn wooden *azekura* style. Take a bus from the JR eki in the direction of Tsutsumi and get off at Shimin Bunka Senta-mae. Then walk back to the crossing and take a left. You will see the museum on the left. ⊡ ¥300. ◐ *Apr.–Oct., Tues.–Sun. 9:30–4:30; Nov.–Mar., Tues.–Sun. 9:30–4; closed last day of month (except Sat. and Sun.) and Dec. 27–Jan. 4. From Apr. to Oct., if a national holiday falls on Sun. or Mon., museum is closed Tues.*

Two other museums might pique your interest. **Aomori Kenritsu Kyōdokan** (Prefectural Museum) displays folk crafts and archaeological material. It is a 10-minute bus ride from bus stop 4 at the JR Aomori Eki or a 20-minute walk. Admission is ¥310. It's open

April–September, Tuesday–Sunday 9:30–4:30, and October–March, Tuesday–Sunday 9:30–4; it is closed December 28–January 4. The **Keikokan** (Museum of Folk Art) has a larger display of local crafts, including fine examples of Tsugaru-nuri (lacquerware), which achieves its hardness from 48 coats of lacquer. Dolls representing the Haneto dancing girls of the Nebuta Festival are also on display. The Keikokan is 25 minutes away from the JR eki by bus (board at Gate 3) on a busy highway of malls, arcades, and giant pachinko parlors, which makes it easy to miss: Watch for the Sanwa complex on your right, get off the bus three sets of traffic lights later, and you'll find the museum tucked away on the right side. Admission is ¥600. It's open 9:30–4:30 (enter by 4); closed Thursday November–April.

For a quick overview of Aomori there is the **ASPAM** (Asupamu) Building down by the waterfront, where the ferryboats once docked. The 15-story ultramodern eyesore is easy to recognize by its pyramid shape. Though the staff there speaks little English, a tourist information desk in the entrance lobby is very helpful in supplying details of the prefecture's attractions. An outside elevator whisks you 13 floors up to an enclosed observation deck, which is open after the lower floors are closed. There are a number of restaurants and exhibits on Aomori's tourist attractions and crafts inside the building. ▦ *¥400.* ☉ *Daily 9 AM–10 PM.*

Lodging

$$ ▦ **Aomori Grand Hotel.** Close to the station, this is the best place in town for an overnight stay. The lobby is somewhat personable, the lounge for morning coffee has superbly comfortable armchairs, and the Continental Bellevue restaurant on the 12th floor is an enjoyable place to spend an evening. Guest rooms tend to be small. ✉ *1-1-23 Shin-machi, Aomori-shi, Aomori-ken 030,* ☎ *0177/23–1011,* FAX *0177/34–0505. 139 rooms, mostly Western style. Restaurant. AE, DC, MC, V.*

Visitor Information

There is a tourist information center at the station (☎ 0177/22–7781), open daily 8:30–8, but most of the brochures are in Japanese.

OFF THE
BEATEN PATH

CAPE TAPPI – Northwest of Aomori is the cape on the Tsugaru Straits under which the JR Seikan Tunnel connects Honshū with Hokkaidō. This is the perfect place to enjoy sea urchin fresh from the sea, stroll along steep Nihon-kai cliffs, climb the stairs of national highway 339 to a windswept lighthouse, observe the power-generating Wind Park turbo fans, and generally get away from it all. Several JR trains per day on the Tsugaru Line pass through Kanita to Mimmaya (1 hour, 40 minutes), where you change to a bus that goes on to Tappi (30 minutes). There are minshuku with minimal facilities for an overnight, but you may prefer to return to the Aomori area by late bus.

OSORE-ZAN – As much as Aomori City might have its shortcomings, Aomori Prefecture possesses a great deal of natural beauty. If you have a day to spare, a worthwhile trip would be to this mountaintop in the center of the Shimokita Peninsula, the ax-shaped piece of land that juts from Aomori's northeastern corner. Osore-zan's temple, Entsū-ji, is dedicated to the spirits of dead children. The atmosphere of otherworldliness is heightened by its setting: the surrounding peaks, the neighboring dead lake, the steam from the hot springs, the desolate grounds that have been whitened by sulfuric rock, and the distinct sulfur smell that hangs in the air. Even eerier are some of the visitors: Crows often come to feed on the crackers and candles left at the shrines by mourning parents, and several blind old women frequent the site to offer their services as mediums for contacting the dead.

The trip to Osore-zan takes a little over three hours. Buses make the 35-minute trip between Osore-zan and Mutsu Bus Terminal, Mutsu being the main town of Shimokita Peninsula, from the end of April until the end of October. Bus fare is ¥690. Mutsu itself can be reached by bus from Aomori City in 2 hours and 40 minutes, costing ¥2,230, or by train to Nohe-ji, then bus. The distinct odor in Ozore-zan is sulfur escaping from vents around the lake and temple.

Sukayu Onsen

★ ㉖ *1 hr and 20 mins from the JR Aomori Eki by bus.*

Because Aomori's attractions are rather limited, you may prefer to overnight at Sukayu Onsen, near the Hakkoda Ropeway. One snag is that the last bus sets off at 3:30 PM, but if you can catch it, it's worth staying outside of the city.

It is known that more than 300 years ago a hunter shot and wounded a deer near here. Three days later he saw the deer again, miraculously healed. He realized that the deer had cured itself in the sulfur springs. Since then, people have been coming to Sukayu for the water's curative powers. The inn—and there is nothing but the inn—is a sprawling wooden building with highly polished creaking floors. The main bath, known as Sen-nin Buro (Thousand-person Bath), is made of *hiba* (Japanese cypress), a very strong wood. It is not segregated—men and women bathe together—but there are smaller baths that are segregated. Sen-nin Buro's two big tubs fill the bathhouse: One pool called Netsu-no-yu is 42° C, while the other, Shibu rokubu, is one degree hotter. The other two bathtubs, called Hie-no-yu, are for cooling off by pouring water on your head only so as not to wash the minerals off your body.

Lodging

$$$ ⊞ **Sukayu Onsen.** In a vast, rambling wood building in the mountains, ★ this traditional Japanese inn is one of the few left in the country where men and women are not separated in the main baths—except for the few hours it is set aside for women. In Sen-nin Buro, the sulfur mineral waters have been used for their curative powers for three centuries. Guest rooms are small and only thinly partitioned from each other, which light sleepers might find difficult. A fixed, multidish dinner is served in your room. Japanese breakfasts are served in a large dining room. There is no village nearby, but ski slopes and hiking trails are close. A taxi to the Onsen from Aomori takes 45 minutes. The staff does not speak English. ⊠ *Sukayu Onsen, Hakkoda-Sunchu, Aomori-ken 030,* ☎ *0177/38–6400,* ℻ *0177/38–6677. 134 rooms. Hot springs. AE, DC, MC, V.*

En Route If you are going straight to Hokkaidō, either take the train under, or the ferry across, the Tsugaru Straits to Hakodate.

TŌHOKU WEST COAST

So far, our travels have been on the central and Pacific sides of Tōhoku. The return journey travels south down the Nihon-kai side to Akita, then continues south to Tsuruoka and rises to the sacred elevations of Haguro-san.

Between Aomori and Akita, the train goes back through Hirosaki and past **Mt. Iwaki** (5,331 ft high), which dominates the countryside. A bus from Hirosaki travels to the foot of this mountain (40 minutes), from which you can take a sightseeing bus up the Iwaki Skyline toll road (open late Apr.–late Oct.) to the eighth station. The final ascent, with

the reward of a 360-degree view, is by a five-minute ropeway, followed
by a 30-minute walk to the summit.

South of Mt. Iwaki, straddling Aomori Prefecture's border with Akita,
are the **Shirakami Mountains,** home of the world's largest virgin beech-
wood forest. It is one of only two Japanese entries on UNESCO's list
of World Heritage Sites. Access to the mountains is provided by just
a few minor roads on their Aomori and Akita flanks, but they are a
rewarding place for adventuresome hikers. Once you're back on the
train, soon after Hirosaki and Mt. Iwaki, the mountains give way to
the rice fields and flat plains that surround Akita.

Akita

㉗ *2½ hrs from Aomori by JR express.*

Akita, another prefectural capital (population 300,000), is a relaxing
and friendly city, though not one loaded with sightseeing attractions.
Essentially, Akita is a built-up, commercial city whose major attraction for tourists is its famous **Kantō Festival** (Aug. 5–7), when young
men balance a 30-ft-long bamboo pole that supports as many as 50
lit paper lanterns on its eight crossbars. The area around Akita is said
to grow the best rice and have the purest water in Japan—the combination produces excellent dry sake.

If you have time between trains, walk west from the station for 10 minutes on Hiroko-ji-dōri to **Senshu Park,** once the site of the now-ruined
Kubota Castle and today a pleasant spot of greenery, with cherry blossoms and azaleas adding color in season. Aside from the prefectural
art museum, the Senshu Park includes the **Hirano Masakichi Bijutsukan,** with a noted collection of paintings by Tsuguji Fujita (1886–1968),
as well as works by van Gogh and Cézanne. The most eye-catching
exhibit is Fujita's *Events in Akita,* in which three of the local festivals
are merged together to form a single scene: painted on a single mon-
strous piece of canvas measuring 3.65 by 20.5 meters, Fujita painted
it in just 15 days and bragged that the feat would never be bettered—
now there's a way to make good art. The building itself is architecturally interesting for its Japanese palace-style roof covered with copper,
which slopes down and rolls outside at the edge. 🎫 ¥410. ☉ *May–
Sept., Tues.–Sun. 10–5:30; Oct.–Apr., Tues.–Sun. 10–5 (enter 30 mins
before closing); closed Dec. 28–Jan. 3.*

For regional arts and crafts and more information about the prefecture, visit the 12-story **Atorion Building,** a two-minute walk south
from the park on the other side of Hiroko-ji. A large shop in the basement, open daily 10–7, sells local crafts and souvenirs; elsewhere on
the premises are a prefectural tourist center, a concert hall, and an art
gallery, open daily 10–6, that shows the work of local artists as well
as oil paintings by Okada Kenzo, who achieved some fame in New York
after World War II. Six blocks west of the Atorion, across the Asahi-
gawa and slightly to the south, is Kawabata-dōri. This is where everyone comes in the evening to sample the regional hot-pot dishes
shottsuru-nabe (made with pickled sand fish) and *kiritampo nabe*
(grilled rice stick stew), drink *ji-zake* (locally-brewed sake), and find
entertainment at one of the many bars.

㉘ **Oga Peninsula**'s coastline is indented by strange rock formations and
reefs, its mountains are clad with Akita cedar, and its hills are carpeted
with green grass. At the neck of the peninsula is Mt. Kampu, whose
summit affords a panoramic view extending as far as Akita city. Nearby,
the town of Oga hosts a strange custom every December 31: Men dressed
in ferocious demon masks and coats of straw, carrying buckets and huge

knives, go from home to home issuing dire warnings against any loafers and good-for-nothings in the households. This ritual is reenacted for the public at the **Namahage Sedo Festival** on February 13–15 on the grounds of the local Shinzan Shrine.

Roads trace Oga's coastline, but public transport is infrequent. The easiest way to tour the peninsula, which is 30 km (19 mi) north and west of Akita, is by using Akita Chūō Kōtsū bus lines (☎ 0188/23–4411). Full-day tours costing ¥5,300 depart from Akita Eki, Oga Eki, and Oga Onsen from late April to early November. Tours are conducted in Japanese.

Dining and Lodging

$$ ✕ **Restaurant Bekkan Hama-no-ya.** This establishment is the local favorite for *hata-hata* (sand fish), a regional specialty that is especially good in winter. ⊠ *4-2-11 Ō-machi,* ☎ *0188/23–7481. MC, V.*

$$ ✕ **Suginoya.** A five-story restaurant serving everything from the traditional Akita Hanamaru course to more generic Japanese food, this place has something for everyone and every budget. The main shop is near the Red Cross Hospital. ⊠ *4-1-15 Naka-dōri,* ☎ *0188/35–5111. MC, V.*

$$$ 🏨 **Akita View Hotel.** This establishment has clean, fresh rooms and is the largest of the hotels in Akita. Located on the right side of a Seibu department store, seven minutes by foot from the JR eki, it is convenient to shopping but a 10-minute walk from downtown Akita. The staff will give you advice on what to see and do in the city and prefecture. An indoor pool adds to the hotel's appeal. ⊠ *2-6 Naka-dōri, Akita-shi, Akita-ken 010,* ☎ *0188/32–1111,* 🆕 *0188/33–6957. 115 Western-style rooms. 2 restaurants, bar, coffee shop, indoor pool, exercise room, shops. AE, DC, MC, V.*

$$–$$$ 🏨 **Akita Castle Hotel.** With the best location—opposite the moat, a 15-
★ minute walk from the train station—and the most professional service in Akita, the Castle Hotel has well-maintained rooms. Keep in mind that larger double rooms, normal American size, fall in the $$$ category, and the more commodious Japanese-style rooms (only three in the hotel) are the same price as the Western-style ones. The bar and the French restaurant have a park view, and there are Japanese and Chinese restaurants on site as well. ⊠ *1-3-5 Naka-dōri, Akita-shi, Akita-ken 010,* ☎ *0188/34–1141,* 🆕 *0188/34–5588. 182 rooms. 3 restaurants. AE, DC, MC, V.*

$ 🏨 **Kohama Ryokan.** This small inn is friendly, homey, and priced right. It is also conveniently located to the left of the square in front of the JR Akita Eki. The Japanese-style dinner using local fresh seafood is a bargain at ¥1,500, and a Continental breakfast is served. The owners also provide a photography service, whereby you can don traditional Japanese costumes and have your picture taken in front of a scenic mural. The ryokan has traditional shared baths. ⊠ *6-19-6 Naka-dōri, Akita-shi, Akita-ken 010,* ☎ *0188/32–5739. 10 rooms with shared bath. AE, V.*

Getting Around

Akita is now connected to Tōkyō by the Akita Shinkansen Ko-machi trains, making a 3-hour, 48-minute trip to Tōkyō and a 2-hour, 11-minute run to Sendai. The tourist information office is next to the entrance to the Shinkansen tracks at the station.

Tsuruoka and Haguro-san (Mt. Haguro)

2½ hrs from Akita by JR.

Heading south from Akita, you have two options: to head inland to Tazawa-ko (☞ *above*) or drop down the Nihon-kai coast to Tsuruoka and Haguro-san. There are five trains a day between Akita and Niigata; that trip takes 3 hours and 40–50 minutes.

㉙ South of Akita along the Nihon-kai coast, there are small fishing villages, notable only for the fact that few gai-jin, not to mention Nihonjin, stop over en route. The one exception is **Tsuruoka,** the religious center of Shugendo, an esoteric religious sect that combines Buddhism
★ with Shintoism. Tsuruoka is famous for its temple, **Zempo-ji,** which has a pagoda containing images of Buddha in every pose that could possibly be attributed to him. Tsuruoka also serves as the gateway to
㉚ **Haguro-san,** the most accessible of the three mountains in the Dewa-san range. All three mountains are sacred to the *yamabushi,* the popular name given to members of the Shugendo sect, but it is the thatched-roof shrine Dewa Sanzan Jinja, on the summit of Haguro-san, that attracts pilgrims throughout the year.

These days, most pilgrims take the easy way up to the summit—a direct bus from Tsuruoka Eki along the toll road. The old way, the one that the more devout or energetic take, is by bus from the JR eki or the Shoko Mall in Tsuruoka to Haguro's central bus stop; from there, they walk to the Zaishin Gate and then up the 2,446 stone steps to the summit. The climb is not for the faint at heart, but the route along avenues of 300-year-old cedar trees—with shafts of sunlight filtering through, the occasional waterfall, the tiny shrines, and the tea shop halfway up—is the reason for reaching the summit. Running alongside the steps is a trail of rock carvings, depicting such things as sake cups, gourds, lotus cups, and so on. According to legend, the lucky pilgrim who locates all 33 of the carvings will have a wish granted. The actual shrine, **Dewa Sanzan Jinja,** is not so impressive; you'll be glad to get on the bus to return to Tsuruoka, leaving behind on the slopes of Mt. Haguro the numerous small huts used by yamabushi pilgrims engaged in their penance. Once back in Tsuruoka, it is a 2-hour, 20-minute train ride to Yamagata.

Should you wish to spend the night in the Tsuruoka area, take the JR
㉛ express train 20 minutes south to **Atsumi Onsen,** a spa town where the curative waters are good for your skin as well as your digestive system. Facing the stormy Nihon-kai and backed by mountains, the small village exists in isolation. Unfortunately, it lost its old buildings in a fire that swept the valley in 1951, so virtually all of its buildings are new. One particularly hospitable ryokan is Tachibana-ya. To reach the village, use the bus from the JR Atsumi Onsen Eki; it's a 10-minute journey to town and costs ¥190.

Lodging

$$$$ 🏨 **Tachibana-ya.** Many traditional ryokan are reluctant to take reservations from gai-jin, especially if you do not speak Japanese. Not so with Tachibana-ya. This resort ryokan in the center of Atsumi Onsen welcomes gai-jin, and its accommodations are excellent. Guest rooms are spacious (12 tatami mats), with a separate dressing room that is large enough to serve as a second sleeping room, a small kitchen for the maid to prepare meals, a washroom, and a separate toilet with heated seat. Should you wish to bathe privately, there is also a *hinoki* (Japanese cypress-wood) bathtub with faucets tapped into the thermal springs. But best of all is a small terrace alcove off the main room with two large leather armchairs and a table. Sliding glass doors overlook a landscaped garden that surrounds a large pond filled with carp. The best rooms are on the ground floor—room Tokiwa 137 is especially nice. The hotel's buildings are angled so that rooms do not directly face each other, thus ensuring privacy. Service is extremely efficient and

friendly. Meals, served in your room, are a delight to the eye and palate. The common baths have been splendidly refurbished using natural stone and are filled with steaming water from the thermal springs. ✉ *Atsumi-machi-tei 3, Atsumi Onsen, Yamagata-ken 999,* ☎ *0235/ 43–2211,* ℻ *0235/43–3681. 67 Japanese-style rooms. Bar, coffee shop, mineral baths. AE, DC, MC, V.*

TŌHOKU A TO Z

Arriving and Departing

By Bus

While the Tōhoku Kyūkō Express Night Bus from Tōkyō to Sendai is inexpensive (¥6,210), it takes 7 hours and 10 minutes. It leaves Tōkyō Eki (Yaesu-guchi side, on the left as you walk along Yaesu-dōri, just before you get to the Matsuoka menswear shop) at 11 PM and arrives in Sendai at 6:10 AM. The bus from Sendai departs at 11 PM and arrives in Tōkyō at 6:10 AM.

By Car

The Tōhoku Expressway links Tōkyō with Aomori, but the cost of gas, tolls, and car rental makes driving expensive. It is also considerably slower to drive than to ride on the Shinkansen. Assuming you can clear metropolitan Tōkyō in 2 hours, the approximate driving time is 5 hours to Fukushima, 6 hours to Sendai, 8–10 hours to Morioka, and 10–11 hours to Aomori.

By Plane

Akita has four daily flights from Tōkyō's Haneda Airport by ANA (All Nippon Airways), which also operates flights from Nagoya. Two flights from Ōsaka International Airport and three flights from Sapporo are provided by JAS (Japan Air System).

Aomori has four daily flights from Tōkyō's Haneda Airport by JAS and one by ANA. Aomori also has two flights from Nagoya, three from Ōsaka, and two from Sapporo's Chitose Airport.

Morioka (whose Hanamaki Airport is 50 minutes by bus from downtown) has three flights from Ōsaka International Airport by JAS. There are also flights to Nagoya, Fukuoka, and Sapporo's Chitose Airport.

Sendai has fives daily flights from Ōsaka International Airport by ANA. There are also flights to Fukuoka, Nagoya, Hiroshima, and to Sapporo's Chitose Airport.

Yamagata has four daily flights from Tōkyō's Haneda Airport by ANA and three flights from Ōsaka International Airport by JAS. There are also two flights to Fukuoka and one flight to Sapporo.

By Train

The most efficient way to get to Tōhoku from Tōkyō is on the Tōhoku Shinkansen trains, all of which the JR Pass covers. The *Yamabiko,* which makes the fewest stops, and the slower *Aoba* Shinkansen, run to Sendai and Morioka; the *Tsubasa* runs to Yamagata; and the *Komachi* is the newest line, to Akita. There are 63 total Shinkansen runs a day from Tōkyō to Fukushima (1½ to slightly more than 2 hours), Sendai (2 hours to 2⅓ hours), Yamagata (2½ hours), Morioka (2¾ hours to 3½ hours), and Akita (3 hours, 50 minutes to 4½ hours). North of Morioka, conventional trains continue on to Aomori (an additional 2 hours, 10 minutes).

On Tōhoku's western side (facing the Sea of Japan), the train from Niigata takes 3 hours and 40–50 minutes to travel along the Sea of Japan coast to Akita, and an additional 3 hours to reach Aomori. From

Niigata inland to Yamagata, the train takes 3½ hours. (Niigata is connected to Tōkyō's Ueno Eki by the Jōetsu Shinkansen, which at its fastest makes the run in two hours.)

Getting Around

Transportation in rural Tōhoku was, until recently, limited, which is why Tōhoku still has been undiscovered by modern progress and tourists. However, that is changing rapidly. Now, using a combination of trains and buses, most of Tōhoku's hinterland is easily accessible, except in heavy winter snows.

By Boat

Three sightseeing boats are especially recommended: at Matsu-shima Bay, near Sendai; at Jodo-ga-hama up the Pacific coast; and at Towada-ko. Keep in mind that these boats offer constant commentary in Japanese over the loudspeaker; this can be particularly annoying if you do not understand what's being said.

By Bus

Buses take over where trains do not run, and, in most instances, they depart from JR train stations. Though English may not be widely spoken in Tōhoku, there is never any difficulty at train stations in finding someone to direct you to the appropriate bus.

In summer's tourist season, there are also scenic bus tours that run from major tourist areas. The local Japan Travel Bureau at the train station in each area, or at major hotels, will make arrangements.

By Car

Once you're in the locale you wish to explore, a car is ideal for getting around. All major towns have car-rental agencies. The Nippon-Hertz agency is the one most frequently represented. Bear in mind, though, that except on the Tōhoku Expressway, few road signs are in *romaji* (Japanese words rendered in English). However, major roads have route numbers. With a road map in which the towns are spelled in romaji and *kanji* (the Chinese characters used in Japanese writing), it becomes relatively easy to decipher the directional signs. **Note:** Maps are not provided by car-rental agencies; be sure to obtain bilingual maps in Tōkyō or Sendai.

By Train

Trains are fast and frequent on the north–south runs, and there is now Shinkansen service from Morioka west to Akita. On the main Shinkansen line north from Tōkyō, *Yamabiko* are the faster and *Aoba* the slower (because of more stops) trains. Elsewhere in Tōhoku, JR local trains are slower and less frequent (every two hours rather than every hour during the day) when they cross the region's mountainous spine. Most railways are owned by Japan Railways, so your JR Pass will work. Be aware that most trains stop running before midnight.

Contacts and Resources

Car Rental
Hertz Domestic Reservation Center, ☎ 0120/38–8002 toll-free.

Emergencies
Police, ☎ 110. **Ambulance,** ☎ 119.

Guided Tours
The **Japan Travel Bureau** has offices at every JR eki in each of the prefectural capitals and can assist in local tours, hotel reservations, and ticketing for onward travel. The phone numbers of the offices which

arrange guided tours in English are as follows: in **Tōkyō**, ☎ 03/5620–9500; in **Kyōto,** ☎ 075/8371–7891; in **Sendai,** ☎ 022/221–4422.

Visitor Information

In prefectural capitals, there are tourist information centers at all train stations. The largest and most helpful tourist center that gives information on all of Tōhoku and not just the local area is at **Morioka Eki** (☎ 019/625–2090). In **Sendai,** it might be a better idea to consult the International Center in Aobayama Kōen. The telephone numbers of each prefectural government tourist section are as follows: **Akita,** ☎ 0188/60–2266; **Aomori,** ☎ 0177/22–5080; **Fukushima,** ☎ 0245/21–3811; **Iwate,** ☎ 019/651–3111; **Miyagi,** ☎ 022/211–2743; and **Yamagata,** ☎ 0236/30–2373.

In **Tōkyō,** each prefecture also has an information center near Tōkyō Eki with a few English brochures and maps. The centers for **Akita** (☎ 03/3211–1775), **Iwate** (☎ 03/3231–2613), **Miyagi** (☎ 03/3231–0944), and **Yamagata** (☎ 03/3215–2222) are on the ninth floor of Tetsudō Kaikan (above Daimaru Department Store at the station's Yaesu exit; ✉ 1-9-1 Maru-no-uchi, Chiyoda-ku). The **Aomori** center is on the second floor of the nearby Kokusai Kankō Kaikàn (✉ 1-8-3 Marunouchi, Chiyoda-ku, ☎ 03/3216–6010), while **Fukushima**'s center (☎ 03/3214–2789) is one floor higher in the same building.

JAPAN TRAVEL PHONE
This nationwide service for English-language assistance or travel information is available seven days a week, 9–5. Dial toll-free 0088/222–800 or 0120/222–800 for information on eastern Japan. When using a yellow, blue, or green public phone (do not use the red phones), insert a ¥10 coin, which will be returned. There are different numbers for callers in Tōkyō (3503–4400) and Kyōto (371–5649), and in those cities the service costs ¥10 per three minutes.

15 Hokkaidō

Hokkaidō is Japan untamed. It can be said about the rest of Japan that cities dominate the countryside—not so in Hokkaidō. Its cities and towns are outposts of modern urban humanity that wild mountains, virgin forests, sapphire lakes, and surf-beaten shores keep at bay. Hokkaidō is Japan's last frontier, and the attitudes of the inhabitants are akin to those of the pioneers of the American West— or any other last places.

By Nigel Fisher

Updated by
Michael
O'Connell

T IS NO SMALL MARK of its remoteness that Hokkaidō was not even mentioned in books until the 7th century. Then for the next millennium it was written off as the place of the "hairy Ainu." The Ainu, indigenous inhabitants of Japan—possibly related to ethnic groups that populated Siberia—were always thought of as the inferior race by the Yamato Japanese, who arrived in Japan from the south via Kyūshū and founded Japan's imperial house. As the Yamato spread and expanded their empire from Kyūshū through Honshū, the peace-loving Ainu retreated north to Hokkaidō. There they lived, supporting themselves with their traditional pursuits of hunting and fishing. By the 16th century the Yamato had established themselves in the southern tip of Hokkaidō, and they soon began to make incursions into the island's interior.

With the Meiji Restoration in 1868, Japan changed its policy toward Hokkaidō and opened it up as the new frontier to be colonized by the Yamato Japanese. The Tōkyō government encouraged immigration from the rest of Japan but made no provision for the Ainu people. Indeed, the Ainu were given no choice but to assimilate themselves into the life and culture of the colonizers. Consequently, Ainu culture went into a sudden and near-terminal decline. It has been fashionable for academics in the 20th century to write them off as a "doomed" or even "extinct" race.

It should be noted, however, that in recent years there has been something of a revival in Ainu culture and activism. The number of full-blooded Ainu might be very small, but 24,000 people believe themselves to possess enough of the bloodline to have officially declared themselves "Ainu." Similarly, though the Ainu language has virtually disappeared as a native tongue, many people have begun to study it in a burgeoning number of college and evening courses. Ainu activism, meanwhile, received a boost when the United Nations made 1993 a Year of Indigenous Peoples, and the Ainu scored a propaganda victory in 1994 when their leading activist, Shigeru Kayano, was elected to Japan's House of Councillors—the first Ainu to reach such a prominent position. In May 1997, the national government passed belated legislation recognizing Ainu culture. Sadly, little of this may be obvious to tourists who head for Hokkaidō's (reconstructed) Ainu villages, many of which are tourist traps making money for Japanese entrepreneurs rather than for the Ainu themselves—these can be depressing places indeed.

The Ainu are not the only Japanese aborigines. Another race, the Moyoro, lived before the Ainu, but little is known about this mysterious people. Anthropological evidence found in the Moyoro Shell Mound on Hokkaidō's east coast, now displayed in the Abashiri Museum, supports the belief that Moyoro civilization came to an end in the 9th century.

One of the delights of traveling through Hokkaidō is meeting the people, who are known as Dosanko, after the sturdy draft horse introduced to the north. Since virtually all of the Japanese on this island are "immigrants to a new frontier," there is less emphasis placed on honoring tradition than there is on accomplishing the matter at hand. Dosanko are still very Japanese, sharing the same culture as the rest of Japan, but they are also open to new customs and other cultures. They have a great attachment to their island. In a 1993 survey conducted by the *Yomiuri Shimbun* (newspaper) to find out how positively the Japanese felt about their home prefectures, Hokkaidō received the most impressive score.

Hokkaidō as we know it was born during the Meiji Restoration (1868–1912), a time when the Japanese government turned to the West for new ideas. This island especially sought advice from America and Europe for its development. In the 1870s, some 63 foreign experts came here, including an American architect who designed the prefecture's principal city, Sapporo. Around the same time, agricultural experts from abroad were brought in to introduce dry-farming as a substitute for rice, which could not grow in the severe winter climate until hardy varieties were developed much later. This has left Dosanko with a peculiar fondness for Europeans. In Sapporo, Westerners are warmly received. In the countryside, Dosanko are shy, but hardly timid, in coming to the aid of Westerners.

Because Hokkaidō consists more of countryside than of cities—which implies language barriers that are more often than not bridged by the friendliness of locals—the number of gai-jin to come here has traditionally been small, compared to the many Japanese who come for winter skiing and summer hiking. At the same time, ongoing refurbishments at Sapporo's Chitose Airport have opened up the island to more international flights (from such places as Hong Kong and Honolulu), which in turn have brought more people. Because Hokkaidō is Japan's northernmost and least developed island, it is easy to romanticize it as a largely uncharted territory. That is mostly untrue, as road and rail networks crisscross Hokkaidō. Of course, wild beauty and open space still abound—from volcanic mountains and lakes to the marshlands of the red-crested tanchō-zuru (Japanese Crane) to the ice floes of the Ohotsuku-kai (Sea of Okhotsk) to the northerly isolation of Rishiri and Rebun islands.

Hokkaidō Glossary

Key Japanese words and suffixes in this chapter include -chō (street or block), -chōme (street), chūō (central, as in Central Street), dōri (avenue), eki (train station), gai-jin (foreigner), -kawa and -gawa (river), hantō (peninsula), higashi (east), izakaya (pub), -jima (island), -ken (prefecture), kita (north), -ko (lake, as in Tōya-ko, Lake Tōya), kōen ("ko-en," park), -ku (section or ward), kūkō (airport), minami (south), misaki (cape), Nihon-kai (Japan Sea), nishi (west), Ohotsuku-kai (Sea of Okhotsk), onsen (hot springs), ryūhyō (ice floes), sakura (cherry blossoms), san and zan (mountain), -shi (city or municipality), take and dake ("ta/da-keh," peak), tōge (pass), and yama (mountain).

Pleasures and Pastimes

Dining

The joy of Hokkaidō is its regional food. We strongly recommend that you eat at local Japanese restaurants whenever possible. Most that are reasonably priced will have a visual display of their menu in the window, which allows you to decide what you want before you enter. If you cannot order in Japanese and no English is spoken, lead the waiter to the window display and point, or try sketching for your server the Japanese character for the dish you want.

Hokkaidō is known for its seafood—the prefecture's name means "the Road to the Northern Sea." Sake (salmon), ika (squid), uni (sea urchin), nishin (herring), and kai (shellfish) are abundant, but the real treat is the fat, sweet scallop, kaibashira, collected from northernmost Wakkanai. The other great favorite is crab, which comes in three varieties: ke-gani (hairy crab), taraba-gani (king crab) and Nemuro's celebrated hanasaki-gani.

Jingisukan—Genghis Khan—is thin strips of mutton cooked in an iron skillet. Vegetables—usually onions, green peppers, and cabbage—are added to the sizzling mutton. It all gets dipped in a tangy brown sauce. Ramen (a Chinese noodle served in soup) is extremely popular and inexpensive.

Hokkaidō people pride themselves on their broad-mindedness, so it's not as great a crime here if you wear informal clothes in fancy restaurants as it would be in Honshū. Still, Japanese patrons will probably look immaculate, so avoid jeans and wear a tie if you don't want to feel conspicuous. Despite its modernity, Hokkaidō has its share of traditional tatami-mat restaurants; wear a decent pair of socks in case you have to remove your shoes. If you plan to tackle a Jingisukan barbecue, be warned that it's messy (though restaurants usually supply plastic aprons) and smelly enough to taint your clothes for days—don't wear your Sunday best.

CATEGORY	COST*
$$$$	over ¥6,000
$$$	¥4,000–¥6,000
$$	¥2,000–¥4,000
$	under ¥2,000

*per person, excluding drinks and service

Lodging

In the 1970s and '80s, accommodations in Hokkaidō consisted of modern, characterless hotels built for Japanese tour groups. Large, unattractively furnished sitting areas and spacious lobbies were the norm, with views the only redeeming factor. Invariably, prices depend on views and the size of public areas and guest rooms. As tourism in Hokkaidō has grown, more attractive and comfortable hotels have begun to appear.

Outside Sapporo and Hokkaidō's industrial and commercial cities, hot-spring hotels quote prices on a per-person basis with two meals, excluding service and tax, unless you specify otherwise. If you do not want dinner at your hotel, it is usually possible to renegotiate the price. On the average, food charges are 50%, per person, of the room cost. So, for example, if the double room is in the $$$ category (¥15,000–¥20,000), then add ¥15,000 to ¥20,000 for two meals for two people.

CATEGORY	COST*
$$$$	over ¥20,000
$$$	¥15,000–¥20,000
$$	¥10,000–¥15,000
$	under ¥10,000

*All prices are for a double room, excluding service and tax.

Outdoor Activities and Sports

Keeping in step with the seasons is the way to enjoy Hokkaidō, whether it is to savor a summer festival, take in the explosion of autumn colors, weave down an Olympic ski slope, or steam in an open-air hot spring. There are endless trails to hike and rivers, lakes, and oceans to fish.

Exploring Hokkaidō

With little visible past and newly born cities, Hokkaidō will provide a respite from the temples, shrines, and castles that populate itineraries in the rest of Japan. The island is a geological wonderland: Lava-seared mountains hide deeply carved ravines; hot springs, gushers, and steaming mud pools boil out of the ground; and crystal-clear caldera lakes fill the seemingly bottomless cones of volcanoes. Half of Hokkaidō is covered in forests. Wild, rugged coastlines hold back the sea, and all around the prefecture, islands surface offshore. Some are volcanic peaks poking their cones out of the ocean, and others were formed eons ago by the crunching of the earth's crust. The remnants of Hokkaidō's bear population, believed to number about 2,000, still roam the forests, snagging rabbits and scooping up fish from mountain streams, and deer wander the pastures, stealing fodder from cows. Hokkaidō's native crane, the *tanchō*, is especially magnificent, with a red-cap head and white body trimmed with black feathers. Look for it on the ¥1,000 note and in the marshes of Kushiro, east of Sapporo on the Pacific coast.

Numbers in the text correspond to numbers in the margin and on the Hokkaidō map.

Great Itineraries

Hokkaidō's expansiveness is daunting. Fortunately, the main sights—calderas, remote onsen, craggy coasts, dramatic climate—are everywhere. Rather than rushing to see everything, consider balancing the natural with the urban, the inland with the coastal, and figure seasonality of sights and activities more heavily than you would elsewhere in Japan. The historically minded should focus on the major cities of southern Hokkaidō. Wilderness lovers should venture east and center.

IF YOU HAVE 3 DAYS

Three days is just enough to take in a small slice of southern Hokkaidō. Fly into Chitose Kūkō outside of ⊞ **Sapporo** ②–㉚ and spend a day touring the city, finishing with the neon thrill of the Susukino nightlife district. The next day, head south and east on the JR to Tomikawa and then take a bus up to the Ainu village of **Nibutani** ㉚, backtracking to ⊞ **Shikotsu-ko** ㉛ for the night. That will position you for a final day around the caldera lake, either soaking in the scenery or going for a morning hike up the volcanic cones of Eniwa-dake or Tarumae-zan. Or, instead of two days between Nibutani and Shikotsu-ko, you could head west and south for **Niseko** ㉔ and a day's hiking or winter skiing. Overnight there and return to Sapporo on the third day on a coastal circuit around rocky Shakotan Hantō.

IF YOU HAVE 5 DAYS

Five days will allow a more in-depth tour of southern Hokkaidō or, if you skip Sapporo entirely, a dash around the central, eastern, or northern parts of the island. For the southern option, spend your first day in ⊞ **Sapporo** ②–㉚ or ⊞ **Hakodate** ①; then make a thorough loop through **Shikotsu-Tōya National Park,** detouring east to **Nibutani** ㉚ for its Ainu village. You could otherwise spend the last four days passing through ⊞ **Otaru** ㉑, then around the Shakotan Hantō on the way down to **Niseko** ㉔ for hiking or skiing. If you're hankering to leave civilization behind you, press north for the islands off the tip of Hokkaidō, **Rebun-tō** ㊾ and **Rishiri-tō** ㊼. It will take two days of travel round-trip unless you fly, but the tiny fishing villages and their fresh seafood, great hiking, and volcanic scenery will make for a singular experience of Japan.

IF YOU HAVE 7 DAYS

With a week, you can give yourself time in ⊞ **Sapporo** ②–㉚ or ⊞ **Hakodate** ① and one or two of the farther-flung parks. Skip the areas south of Sapporo and make your way through ⊞ **Asahikawa** ㊸ to the gorges and onsen of ⊞ **Daisetsu-zan National Park** ㊹ or the Northern Cape's **Wakkanai** ㊿ and the Nihon-kai islands. Or continue through Asahikawa and Daisetsu-zan National Park to ⊞ **Abashiri** ㉜, the wonders of the Ohotsuku-kai and ⊞ **Akan National Park** ㉟. Take five days or more to see all of eastern Hokkaidō, including a venture into the end-of-the-world wilds of **Shiretoko National Park** ㉞ and a stop at **Kushiro Shitsugen** ㊷ to see the rare and beautiful *tanchō-zuru*.

When to Tour Hokkaidō

Hokkaidō has Japan's most dramatic seasons. It is no accident that festivals predominate in the extreme seasons, summer and fall, which invigorate local and visitor alike. May and early summer bring lilacs and alpine flowers. The cherry trees in Hokkaidō are the last to offer up sakura in Japan, in late April and early May. Gloriously refreshing weather from May to October lures Japanese drowning in the muggy air of Honshū. Hotel accommodations become relatively difficult to find in summer, and the scenic areas become crowded with tour groups and Japanese families. September brings brief but spectacular golden foliage, reaching a peak in early October. Fall is as brief as it is crisp and striking, giving way to chilly drizzle in November and December— months to avoid. Winter makes travel more difficult (some minor roads are closed), and, especially on the east coast, weather is frigid. It is no less beautiful a time, however, with crisp white snow covering everything and ice floes crowding the Ohotsuku-kai.

HAKODATE

❶ *6¾ hrs north of Tōkyō by JR Shinkansen (to Morioka) and JR Express via the Seikan Tunnel, 2 hrs and 10 mins north of Aomori by JR Limited Express.*

When traveling by train from Honshū into Hokkaidō, you'll come first to Hakodate. It isn't the most fascinating of cities to see, but if you're tired of sitting on the train all the way from Tōkyō and want to do more than just stretch your legs in the station, there are a few things to take in on a short stop.

The Seikan Tunnel connects Honshū and Hokkaidō under the Tsugaru Straits, which was completed in 1988. As of 1997, an express ferry now makes the crossing in the same amount of time, at half the price. If you do opt for the convenience of the train, there is a railway station in the tunnel 400 ft beneath the sea, where there is a museum dedicated to the construction of the tunnel. You can get off the train here and take in the museum, then catch the next train 90 minutes later. However, because the first stop in Hokkaidō proper is Hakodate—with 3½ hours still to go on the train before you get to Sapporo—Hakodate may be a better place to stretch your legs.

Exploring Hakodate

In 1859 Hakodate was one of only three Japanese ports that the Meiji government opened to international trade. This heritage supplies the most interesting sights to see now. Old, sometimes rather decrepit, buildings with definite European- and American-style architecture cluster around the section of town known as **Moto-machi,** at the foot of Hakodate-yama. A useful place to start is the **Orthodox Church of the Resurrection,** which dates from 1859, when it served as the first Russian consulate in the city. Following a 1907 fire, it was rebuilt in Byzantine style in 1916. A large-scale restoration project was completed here in 1989, and the church has become something of an attraction for the city. To get to Moto-machi and the church from the JR eki, take Streetcar 5 to the Suehiro-chō stop and walk 10 minutes toward Mt. Hakodate, which rises above the city.

The **Bungakukan** (Literature Museum) provides information, some of it in English, about the city's most noted writers. Needless to say, none of these are household names in the West, but the museum is pleasant and also has a photographic display of the "eight most beautiful scenes in Hakodate"—evidence yet again of the Japanese mania for cataloging and ranking everything. (Quite how it was determined that there were eight such scenes is anyone's guess!) The Bungakukan is below the church, by the streetcar line. The **Hoppo Minzoku Shiryōkan** (Museum of Northern Peoples) gives a straightforward introduction to Hokkaidō's Ainu culture, though it's not nearly as detailed as other museums farther north, and the decor is rather spartan. The **Kyū Igirisu Ryōjikan**

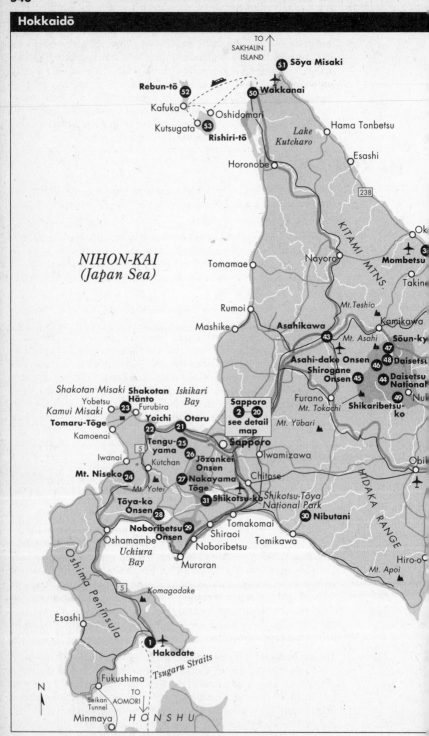

TO
SAKHALIN
ISLAND

51 **Sōya Misaki**

Rebun-tō **52**

Kafuka

50 **Wakkanai**

Oshidomari

Kutsugata **53**

Rishiri-tō

Horonobe

*Lake
Kutcharo*

Hama Tonbetsu

Esashi

238

KITAMI MTNS.

*NIHON-KAI
(Japan Sea)*

Tomamae

Nayoro

Ok

3
Mombetsu

Takine

Rumoi

Mt. Teshio

Kamikawa

Mashike

Asahikawa

43 *Mt. Asahi*

Sōun-ky

47

Daisetsu

48

Asahi-dake Onsen
**Shirogane
Onsen** **46**

45

44 **Daisetsu
National**

49 **Nu**

Shakotan Misaki

Yobetsu

**Shakotan
Hantō**

Furubira

*Ishikari
Bay*

**Shikaribetsu-
ko**

Kamui Misaki

23

Tomaru-Tōge

Yoichi

Otaru

Sapporo
2 – **20**
see detail
map

Furano
Mt. Tokachi

22

21

Kamoenai

5

**Tengu-
yama**

25

Sapporo

Mt. Yūbari

Iwanai

Kutchan

26 **Jōzankei
Onsen**

Iwamizawa

Obi

Mt. Niseko

24

27

**Nakayama
Tōge**

Chitose

HIDAKA

Mt. Yotei

31 **Shikotsu-ko**

*Shikotsu-Tōya
National Park*

RANGE

**Tōya-ko
Onsen**

28

Noboribetsu
Onsen **29**

Shiraoi

Tomakomai

30 **Nibutani**

Hiro-o

Oshamambe

*Uchiura
Bay*

Noboribetsu

Tomikawa

Mt. Apoi

Muroran

5

Komagadake

Esashi

1 **Hakodate**

Tsugaru Straits

N

Fukushima

TO
AOMORI

Seikan
Tunnel

Minmaya

H O N S H U

Oshima Peninsula

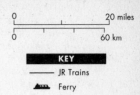

KEY
— JR Trains
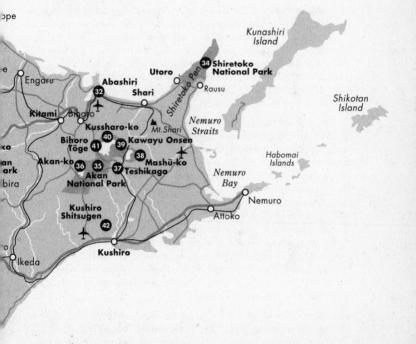

OHOTSUKU-KAI
(Sea of Okhotsk)

Kunashiri Island

Engaru

Utoro

34 Shiretoko National Park

Abashiri

Rausu

Shikotan Island

Kitami

Bihoro

Shari

Kussharo-ko

Mt. Shari

Nemuro Straits

Bihoro Tōge

40

41 **39** Kawayu Onsen

Akan-ko

36 **35** **37** Teshikaga

38 Mashū-ko

Habomai Islands

Akan National Park

Nemuro Bay

bira

Nemuro

Kushiro Shitsugen

Attoko

42

Kushiro

Ikeda

PACIFIC OCEAN

(British Consulate Building) farther up the hillside is now a museum devoted to the opening of the port in the 19th century. Architecturally, the consulate is picturesque, but the exhibits, alas, have no information in English. Just up the hill from the Igirisu Ryōjikan is the building that served as the city's public hall, now called the **Kyū Hakodate-ku Kokaido** (Old Hakodate Public Hall). With its classical columns and antebellum architecture, it looks as if it should be a manor house in America's Deep South. ✉ ¥840 *ticket includes Bungakukan, Hoppo Minzoku Shiryōkan, Kyū Igirisu Ryōjikan, and Kyū Hakodate-ku Kokaido.* ☽ *All four buildings Apr.–Oct., daily 9–7; Nov.–Mar., daily 9–5.*

★ Jutting out from the city like a spur, the once-volcanic **Hakodate-yama** rises to a height of 1,100 ft. Views of the city from its summit are especially good at night, with the darkness of the Tsugaru Straits on one side and the brilliant city lights accenting the small isthmus that connects the peak to the downtown. You can take a 20-minute bus ride to the top of Hakodate-yama from the JR eki, or for a more interesting trip, hop on Streetcar 2 or 5 to the Jūji-gai stop and then walk about seven minutes to the cable car for the three-minute ride up the mountain. The city claims that this cable car, with its capacity of 125 passengers, is the largest in Asia. A restaurant at the top is particularly appealing for its nighttime view. ✉ *Cable car ¥640 one-way, ¥1,160 round-trip.* ☽ *Apr. 26–Oct., daily 10–10; Nov.–Apr. 25, daily 10–9 (Apr. 26–May 5 and July 25–Aug. 20 opens 9 AM); road closed late Nov.–late Apr.*

In the center of the city is **Goryōkaku,** a Western-style fort completed in 1864. Its design is unusual for Japan, especially the five-pointed-star shape, which enabled its defenders to rake any attackers with murderous crossfire. In spite of all that protection, the Tokugawa shogunate's defenders were unable to hold out against the forces of the Meiji Restoration, and its walls were breached. Nothing of the interior of the castle remains, but there is a small museum with relics from the battle. Now the fort area is a park with some 4,000 cherry trees, which, when they bloom in late April, make the stopover in Hakodate worthwhile. There is also an observation tower in the park, but at ¥570 admission, it is not worth the climb for the view. Take Bus 12, 20, or 30 from JR Hakodate Eki's Gate B, or Streetcar 2 or 5 to the Goryōkaku Kōen-mae stop. From either stop, it is about a 10-minute walk to the fort. ☽ *May–Oct., daily 8–7; Nov.–Apr., daily 9–6.*

A number of buildings are being restored around the harbor, close to the Jūji-gai streetcar stop. One is **Hakodate Factory** (☎ 0138/22–5656), open every day from 9 to 9. It's a cross between a fish market, gourmet supermarket, bar, and restaurant. There are plenty of souvenirs for sale, but the sight of the dozens of crabs and other marine life crammed into the display tanks may put you off visiting the seafood restaurant upstairs. There are also a number of Western-style bars and cafés with funny English names like Very Very Beast, California Baby, and Comfortable Octopus.

If you get into Hakodate in the morning and only want a short stopover, visit the *asa-ichi,* a morning fish and vegetable market three minutes on foot south of the JR eki. In fact, it is more than just a market, with 400 shops selling anything from ke-gani (hairy crab) to sea urchin, asparagus to cherries. ☽ *Mon.–Sat. about 6 AM–noon, peaking at 8; the market takes place on occasional Sun. only.*

Should you need a bath before leaving Hakodate, take Streetcar 2 from the JR eki for a 15-minute ride, then a 5-minute walk, to **Yachigashira Onsen,** where a large public bathhouse accommodates 380 people. ✉ ¥320. ☽ *Apr.–Oct., daily 6 AM–9:30 PM; Nov.–Mar., daily 7 AM–9:30 PM; closed Jan. 1 and 2nd and 4th Fri. of month.*

The **Belongs Brewery** is near the JR eki and the asa-ichi. It serves locally brewed beer and has a plaza of restaurants. ⊙ *Daily 11 AM–10 PM.*

Lodging

$$ ☷ **Harborview Hotel.** Next to the JR Hakodate Eki and near buses to destinations within town, this hotel is very conveniently located. It maintains a fresh, cheerful ambience and a friendly staff. There is a pleasant coffee lounge and a sociable bar in the lobby. Guest rooms are standard Western style, furnished in light blue or peach—not particularly attractive but comfortable enough for an overnight. ⊠ *14-10 Wakamatsu-chō, Hakodate, Hokkaidō 040,* ☏ *0138/22–0111,* FAX *0138/23–0154. 190 rooms. 2 restaurants, bar, coffee shop. AE, DC, MC, V.*

$ ☷ **Auberge Kokian.** The reason for selecting this lodging is its central waterfront location, close to the historic sights. On the next street are several cafés and bars. The small tatami rooms are nothing special, with smudged walls and cracked plaster. The shared toilet facilities are basic, and for your bath you are told to hop on a tram for the 15-minute ride to the public baths at Yashigashira Onsen. Better than the accommodations is the restaurant, which has been spruced up so that even locals come in to dine (two meals are included in the room rate). ⊠ *13-2 Suehiro-chō, Hakodate, Hokkaidō 040,* ☏ *0138/26–5753,* FAX *0138/22–2710. 17 rooms. Restaurant. AE, MC, V.*

$ ☷ **Ryokan Hakodate.** This small house with tatami rooms is 10 minutes by foot from the JR eki. Only breakfast is served, either Japanese- or Continental-style. ⊠ *28-7 Omori-chō, Hakodate, Hokkaidō 040,* ☏ *0138/26–1255,* FAX *0138/26–1256. 15 rooms, 4 with bath. No credit cards.*

Visitor Information

To collect maps in English, stop at the **Information Office** (☏ 0138/23–5440) just to the right as you exit the JR Hakodate Eki. It's open April–October, daily 9–7, and November–March, daily 9–5.

Travel on **streetcars** ranges from ¥200 to ¥240 and on the municipal buses from ¥200 to ¥270. You can pick up a one-day bus-and-streetcar pass available from the tourist office for ¥1,000.

The **Hokuto Kōtsū** (Bus Company, ☏ 0138/57–7555) runs four-hour sightseeing tours of the city, leaving from the JR Hakodate Eki and covering most of the city sights for ¥4,500.

North to Sapporo

There are two train routes from Hakodate to Sapporo. The slow way breaks off at Oshamambe and skirts Niseko on its way past the coastal town of Otaru—allowing you to take a superb hike or detour around a rugged peninsula before you hit Sapporo. The fast way loops around Uchiura Bay before angling up to Sapporo. On this route, you can hop up to Tōya-ko (lake), Noboribetsu Onsen, or the Ainu village of Nibutani before continuing on to Sapporo. The Otaru and Tōya-ko areas are covered after Sapporo: ☞ *Otaru and Shakotan Hantō and Shikotsu-Tōya National Park, below.*

HOKKAIDŌ ROAD FOOD

Eki-ben—the classic station box lunch—is a must in Hokkaidō. Pick one up in JR Hakodate Eki: the local *nishin-migaki-bentō* consists of *nishin* (herring) boiled in a sweet, spicy sauce until the bones are soft enough to eat. Then, when your appetite returns at Mori Eki, about an hour north of Hakodate, try another well-known eki-ben, *ika-meshi,* a box lunch made by stuffing a whole *ika* (squid) with rice and cooking it in a sweet, spicy sauce. Each meal includes two or three ika.

SAPPORO

3½ hrs north of Hakodate by JR.

Sapporo is both Hokkaidō's capital and the island's premier city. With 1.7 million inhabitants, it is four times larger than Asahikawa, the prefecture's next-largest city. And, as Hokkaidō's unemployed from the economically depressed farms in the central plains and industrial and fishing towns on the coast migrate to Sapporo for work, it continues to expand. Though it is a large city, it is not confusing or congested. Chalk this up to an infusion of new-world, Western-style city planning. In 1870 the governor of Hokkaidō visited President Grant in the United States and requested that American advisers come to Hokkaidō to help design the capital on the site of an Ainu village. As a result, Sapporo was built on a 330-ft grid system with wide avenues and parks, and it is not the exotic and cultured city you expect to find in Japan— it is distinctly lacking in pre-Meiji historic sights. On the other hand, you can walk the sidewalks without being swept away in a surge of humanity. And though the city isn't pretty, it is easy to navigate.

By hosting the 1972 Winter Olympic Games, Sapporo launched itself as an international city and developed a cosmopolitan attitude. Developers built plenty of hotels and restaurants that are still up and running. Banks here are used to traveler's checks, and there is always someone on hand to help you out in English. Ultimately, though, Sapporo is best to use as a base from which to make excursions into the wild, dramatic countryside. If you want to explore the city, a day, perhaps two at the most, will do.

Numbers in the text correspond to numbers in the margin and on the Sapporo map.

A Good Walk

The comforting fact about Sapporo is the simplicity of the city's layout. East–west streets are called *jō,* and those running north–south are *chōme.* They are numbered consecutively, and each block is approximately 100 yards square. The cardinal points are used more often than elsewhere in Japan. North, south, east, and west are *kita, minami, higashi* and *nishi,* respectively. Ō-dōri Kōen divides the city in half north–south, and the Sosei-gawa separates east from west. Thus, the address Kita 1-jō Nishi 2 means one block north of Ō-dōri Park and two blocks west of the Sosei River, putting you at the Clock Tower.

A good place to start out on foot is **Nakajima Kōen** ② with its lake, rose garden, and two national cultural treasures: the 17th-century Japanese Hasso-an teahouse and Western-style Hoheikan. To get to the park, take the Namboku subway line to the Nakajima Kōen stop. You'll exit on the north edge of the park between the Park Hotel and Hotel Arthur Sapporo's white tower.

Head back to the Nakajima Kōen subway station and turn north on Eki-mai-dōri, leaving the park at your back. This avenue runs through the Susukino entertainment district before slicing Ō-dōri Park perpendicularly and being blocked by the JR eki. Save Susukino for the evening and take the time instead to explore the heart of Sapporo's downtown retail center, the **Chikagai** (downtown underground). Here, subterranean promenades form a "T" of shops and restaurants, intersecting at the Ō-dōri subway station, where the Namboku and Tozai subway lines cross.

The T's vertical leg is **Pole Town** ③, which extends north all the way from beneath the clock in the middle of Susukino crossing. The east–

west part of the T, **Aurora Town** ④, runs from below the TV Tower to West 5-chōme. Running perpendicular to Pole Town one block north of Susukino Crossing is a covered arcade called **Tanuki Koji** ⑤. Many years ago it was the city's main shopping street. Now Tanuki Koji has considerably lower prices than the area's department stores. It also provides welcome shelter from the snow during the lengthy winter.

Pole Town meets Aurora Town directly under **Ō-dōri Kōen** ⑥, a park in the median of a broad, east–west avenue. It is the site of a number of city events, including the Sapporo Snow Festival, which has made the city famous. The unappealing **TV Tower** ⑦ is at the east end of Ō-dōri Kōen. The best part of going to its top for the view is that you don't have to look at the tower itself. On Kita-Ichi-jō, one block north and one block west of the tower, Sapporo's landmark Russian-style **Tokei-dai** ⑧ is where Japanese tourists photograph each other to prove that they were in Sapporo.

Across the street from the Clock Tower, on the third floor of an office building fronted by the Royal Host restaurant, **Sapporo Kokusai Koryū Puraza** ⑨ is the best place in town to go for local information in English. In contrast, the **Hokkaidō Tourist Association Office** ⑩, on the other side of the Clock Tower, is not as useful a place for information, in part because the staff doesn't speak much English.

Back out on the streets of Sapporo, head west on Kita-Ichi-jō. Past the corner of Eki-mae-dōri, you'll come upon the entrance of the classical facade of the **Sapporo Grand Hotel** ⑪. It is yet another sign of Sapporo's late development and the importation of Western culture that Meiji leaders were so ardently pursuing in the late 19th century.

Just northwest of the Grand Hotel is a complex of municipal buildings, among them a large, redbrick building, the **Hokkaidō Kyū Hon-**

chosha ⑫, the Old Hokkaidō Government Building. West again from here, the **Shokubutsu-en** ⑬ is a good place to stroll amid a profusion of plants. The garden's greenhouse is on the south end of a pond.

Walk four blocks west of the gardens to see the paintings of artist Migishi Kotaro in the **Hokkaidō Migishi Kotaro Bijutsukan** ⑭. On the next block is the attractive **Hokkaidōritsu Kindai Bijutsukan** ⑮, which displays a more general collection of Japanese art.

Turn back toward the Botanical Gardens and head back downtown. The other sights listed below are best reached by subway or taxi.

TIMING

Sapporo's uncrowded streets and fresh air make one wonder how it can be Japan's fifth largest city. Not only does it lack the grade changes and dead ends that turn Tōkyō into a maddening labyrinth, it is also generously graced with parks that, unlike those of Tōkyō, include benches and welcoming green areas designed for lingering rather than just darting through. You can see the sights downtown on foot in about 2½ hours, not including time spent meandering, looking into museums, and shopping. Plan to spend an hour at each art museum, no more than a half hour for the other sites and at least a half hour at each park. In winter you can use the underground malls to cover large areas of downtown.

Sights to See

❹ **Aurora Town.** The east–west cap of the **Chikagai** "T" runs from below the ☞ TV Tower to West 5-chōme. Above ground are large department stores, while the subterranean malls are indispensable for navigating the downtown during the five-month winters. The underground restaurants are geared to tired shoppers looking for a chair and a cup of coffee. For real eating, head to the top of the department stores, or assemble a lunch from their basement food floors and picnic in ☞ Ō-dōri Kōen, to the north.

⑯ **Hokkaidō Daigaku** (Hokkaidō University). The Japanese are drawn to this spacious campus—Japan's largest—by a bust of Dr. Clark, the school's first president and a central figure in Hokkaidō's development. You are more likely to be impressed by the beautifully designed grounds, which make the campus another summer escape from urbanity to greenery and blossoming flowers. The school has 12,000 students. It is bordered on the west by Ishiyama-dōri, on the east by Nishi 5-chōme.

⑫ **Hokkaidō Kyū Honchōsha** (Old Hokkaidō Government Building). The grandest structure in Hokkaidō, this pleasing Western-style building was erected in 1888 and now contains exhibits displaying the early development of Hokkaidō. Its nickname, "Aka Renga," means "Ol' Red Brick." It is just northwest of the Grand Hotel in a complex of municipal buildings. 🎫 *Free.* ⊗ *Weekdays 9–5; closed Dec. 29–Jan. 1.*

⑭ **Hokkaidō Migishi Kotaro Bijutsukan** (Hokkaidō Kotaro Migishi Art Museum). This gallery was opened in 1983 for the sole purpose of hanging 235 oil and water-color paintings, drawings, and prints by native son Migishi, who died in 1934 at the age of 31. The museum was designed to reflect the many changes of style that characterize the artist's career. It is a few minutes walk north of the Nishi-jū-hat-chōme (West 18-chōme) Tōzai Line subway stop. ⊠ *Kita 1-jō Nishi 16.* ⊗ *Tues.– Sun. 10–5; closed Dec. 28–Jan. 4 and national holidays in winter only.*

⑩ **Hokkaidō Tourist Association Office.** Little English is spoken here, and the staff are limited in the amount of useful advice they have to offer, but maps and brochures in English are available. A collection of products, including crafts made in Hokkaidō, are for sale. The office is south across the street from the Clock Tower. ✉ *Keizai Center Bldg., Kita 1-jō Nishi 2, Chūō-ku*, ☎ *011/231–0941.* ⊘ *Weekdays 9–5; closed Dec. 29–Jan. 3.*

⓯ **Hokkaidōritsu Kindai Bijutsukan** (Hokkaidō Museum of Modern Art). This museum features local and foreign exhibits. Though not holding priceless works of art, it enables foreigners to see what in Japanese art is appreciated by the Japanese and, in that sense, what is worth visiting. The museum is a few minutes' walk north of the Nishi-jū-hat-chōme (West 18-chōme) Tōzai Line subway stop. ✉ *Kita 1-jō Nishi 17.* ≋ *¥250 for permanent exhibits only.* ⊘ *Tues.–Sun. 10–5; closed Dec. 28–Jan. 4 and national holidays in winter only.*

★ ⓱ **JR Sapporo Eki.** Underneath the JR station is another shopping mall with one section devoted to food stalls and restaurants. Recent expansion of the station has created a smart new shopping and restaurant complex known as **Paseo.** Other than coming here for its excellent tourist information counter, avoid the place. The restaurants are nothing but ambience, serving overpriced local specialties to undiscriminating tourists, and the shops carry expensive designer merchandise and souvenirs. For the real thing, try the unprepossessing but delicious Chinese restaurants and izakaya favored by commuters. Look in the underground westward passage up the stairs just beyond the north turnstile of Sapporo subway station (Namboku Line). A post office is on the East Concourse near the entrance for the JR platforms, and major banks and airline offices line Eki-mae-dōri, which runs south from the exit facing Ō-dōri Park. Here you can change your traveler's checks and confirm plane reservations.

❷ **Nakajima Kōen.** This city park has a couple of historic sights that, with its a small lake for boating (¥600 for 40 minutes) and beautiful rose garden, make it worth a visit. The easiest way to get there is by the Namboku Line subway to the Nakajima Kōen stop. You'll exit on the north edge of the park between the Park Hotel and Hotel Arthur Sapporo's white tower. The alternative is to walk here from the JR eki, heading due south along Eki-mae-dōri for 3 km (2 mi).

One of Nakajima Kōen's National Cultural Treasures is the 17th-century **Hasso-an** (Eight Windows) **teahouse,** harmoniously surrounded by a Japanese garden on the west side of the park. Virtually the only traditional Japanese structure in Hokkaidō, it stands in stark contrast to the new frontier style of architecture on the rest of the island. ≋ *Free.* ⊘ *Daily 9–4; closed Nov. 4–May 2.*

The other national treasure is **Hoheikan,** a stately if somewhat dilapidated Western-style building originally constructed as an imperial guest house. It is symbolic of the time when Hokkaidō was colonized by the Yamato Japanese and the Meiji government looked to the West as it built a modern nation state on top of its feudal predecessor. ≋ *Free.* ⊘ *Daily 9–5; closed Dec. 29–Jan. 3.*

On the west side of the park, one of Japan's finest concert halls stands in modern counterpoint to Hoheikan. **Sapporo Concert Hall,** opened in July 1997, has a 500-pipe organ and serves as a central facility to the city's Pacific Music Festival, held the last three weeks of July.

Also in Nakajima Kōen, the **Fuyu-no Supōtsu Hakubutsukan** (Museum of Winter Sports), on the east side of Nakajima Kōen, has modest exhibits related to the 1972 Sapporo Winter Olympic Games and domestic athletes. The reason to use the place is perk of three-day loans of cross-country skis (there are 100 pairs available; come between 8 AM and 9 PM). Just leave your I.D. at the lending office (the Aruku Sukii

Muryō Kashidashi-jō}, and off you go. ☎ 011/521–1039. 🖃 *Free.* ☉
*Dec. 16–Mar. 24, daily 10–8; closed Dec. 29–Jan. 3 and Mon. after
national holidays.*

❻ Ō-dōri Kōen. Pole Town meets Aurora Town directly under this broad,
345-ft-wide, east–west avenue park, which bisects the city center.
Here, in summer, office workers buy lunch from various food vendors
and take in the sun, so long absent during the winter months. That
makes it a good place to people-watch and try Hokkaidō corn on the
cob—an overpriced area specialty. First it's boiled, then roasted over
charcoal and, just before it is handed to you, given a dash of soy sauce.
Various events are held here in succession from July through August;
in February the park displays large, lifelike snow sculptures that the
Japanese Self-Defense Forces create for the Sapporo Snow Festival, which
has made the city famous (☞ Nightlife, *below*).

❸ Pole Town. The **Chikagai** (downtown underground) is the heart of Sapporo's downtown retail center. Here, subterranean promenades form
a "T" of shops and restaurants, intersecting at the Ō-dōri subway station, where the Namboku and Tozai subway lines cross. Pole Town is
the T's vertical leg, extending north all the way from beneath the clock
in the middle of Susukino crossing. ✉ *Minami 4-jō Nishi 4.*

★ ⑱ Sapporo Beer Garden and Museum. During the day, free tours through
the redbrick museum will acquaint you with the history and the modern brewing technology of Hokkaidō's most famous product. But the
real fun of coming here is the huge beer garden and the cavernous, three-
tier beer hall. You'll find that most of the action occurs in the evening
until closing at 9 PM in the hall, which is similar in atmosphere to a
German beer hall—it was a German, after all, who, upon finding wild
hops growing on Hokkaidō, taught locals how to make beer, but instead of bratwurst, its grilled-meat jingisukan is the highlight. It's Sapporo's favorite dish, and the irrepressible conviviality of the beer hall
is the perfect place to try it.

In summer, the beer garden is a gathering place day and evening, good
for seeing and meeting the Japanese at play. The *tabe-nomi-hodai* (all
you can eat and drink) menu means mugs of lager downed with gusto
amidst exclamations of *Kampai!*—Bottoms up! Around February,
snow sculpture and igloos festoon the site. The beer garden is about
a 15-minute walk east from JR Sapporo Eki, or a ¥1,000 taxi ride from
downtown. ✉ *Kita 7-jō Higashi 9. Museum:* ☎ *011/742–1531;* ☉
*Sept.–May, daily 9–5; June–Aug., daily 8:40–6 (enter 80 mins before
closing); closed Dec. 29–Jan. 5; reservations required; request a guide
who speaks some English. Beer garden:* ☎ *011/731–4368;* ☉ *Daily
11:30–9:30 (11:30–9 in winter); closed Dec. 31–Jan. 1.*

★ ⑲ Sapporo Factory. If you are more interested in shopping, eating, and
drinking than in trekking around to see the sights, Sapporo Factory
has enough boutiques, restaurants (the only good Mexican one in
Hokkaidō), and entertainment to fill an entire day. Small wonder its
promoters call it a "town within a city." The complex occupies several buildings—including an old Sapporo Beer brewery, which retains
its distinctive red brick and chimney—all but one linked by a second-
floor passageway. Among the venues are a 1,500-seat beer restaurant,
a wine cellar containing some 2,000 varieties of wine, an IMAX theater, and a space museum. Most striking of all, however, is the 275-ft-
high atrium, with an arching glass roof that shields an indoor garden
and terrace from the worst that Hokkaidō's climate can offer. It's the
largest structure of its type in Japan. In case you haven't gotten
enough—or heard enough about—onsen, **Sapporo Springs**, part of

the Factory, is yet another hot-spring pool and sauna. For ¥1,800 (for 3 hrs), or ¥2,700 (for the day), you can be pampered and invigorated in this steaming resort complex. It is open daily 10 AM to midnight (until 2 AM July and August). The Factory is east on Kita 2-jō in the Higashi 4 block. ⊠ *Kita 2-jō Higashi 4.* ☺ *Stores daily 10–8; restaurants daily 11–10; the American-style Nutberry Club closes at 3 am.*

⓫ **Sapporo Grand Hotel.** Classical European architecture appears so out of place in Japan, especially in modern Sapporo, that the columns and majestic lobby of the Sapporo Grand begin to make it even more of a landmark than the Clock Tower. The hotel has a bustling café looking out to the street, making it a convenient tea or coffee stop. ⊠ *Kita 1-jō Nishi 4, Chūō-ku,* ☎ *011/261–3311.*

❾ **Sapporo Kokusai Koryū Puraza** (Sapporo International Communication Plaza). Established to facilitate commercial and cultural relations with the world beyond Japan, this center is the best place—far better than the tourist office—for getting suggestions on travel in Hokkaidō and for meeting people who speak English. It is also a useful place to have something translated from Japanese into English. The center has a salon with books, newspapers, and brochures in English. Meant for informal socializing, it is also the place to ask foreign residents and Japanese about their favorite restaurants and night spots. It is across the street from the ☞ **Clock Tower,** on the third floor of an office building fronted by the Royal Host restaurant. ⊠ *Kita 1-jō Nishi 3, Chūō-ku,* ☎ *011/221–2105.* ☺ *Mon.–Sat. 9–5:30.*

Plaza i (☎ 011/211–3678, ℻ 011/219–0020), on the ground floor of the Kokusai Koryū Puraza building, is a volunteer-staffed tourist information service for Sapporo. The staff is extremely helpful in distributing free brochures, maps, and flyers on current happenings in town and will send and receive faxes if you need that. If they can't help you, they'll send you to the third-floor office. You may want to browse through its English-language books on Hokkaidō and other islands of Japan and take a look at the display of local crafts. ☺ *Daily 9–5:30; closed Dec. 29–Jan. 3.*

⓭ **Shokubutsu-en** (Botanical Gardens). With more than 5,000 plant varieties, the Shokobutsu-en makes for a cool retreat in the summer, both for its green space and its shade. 🎫 *Gardens ¥400, greenhouse ¥110 extra.* ☺ *Apr. 29–Sept., Tues.–Sun. 9–4; Oct.–Nov. 3, Tues.–Sun. 9–3:30; greenhouse only Nov. 4–Apr. 28, weekdays 10–3, Sat. 10–noon; closed Dec. 28–Jan. 4.*

⓴ **Susukino.** Sapporo's entertainment district is a nighttime reveler's paradise, with more than 5,000 bars and restaurants providing Japanese bacchanalian delights. As many of these boîtes stay open until 5 AM, save Susukino for last, if you have the yen (couldn't resist the pun) and the stamina. From Sapporo Factory, walk west to Ō-dōri before heading south down Eki-mae-dōri (☞ Nightlife, *below*).

❺ **Tanuki Koji.** A *tanuki* is a raccoon-dog, which in Japanese mythology is known for its cunning and shiftiness. The Tanuki Koji covered arcade got its name because it used to be frequented by prostitutes, who displayed similar characteristics when it came to relieving their clients of cash. Running perpendicular to Pole Town one block north of Susukino Crossing, its sides crowded with small shops selling clothing, footwear, electrical goods, records, and, inevitably, Ainu-inspired souvenirs of Hokkaidō, Tanuki Koji has considerably lower prices than the area's department stores. Adding some variety to the arcade is the presence of several coffee and ramen shops, and four cinemas. It is also the place to find Hokkaidō specialties—from melon confections to dried salmon and seaweed—as presents for Japanese friends on Honshū.

❽ Tokei-dai (Clock Tower). This is Sapporo's proper landmark. It was built in 1878 in Russian style, with a clock from Boston added three years later. Other than being on every Sapporo travel brochure, it is rather ordinary. Inside the building, a small museum recounts the local history of Sapporo and includes such items as horse-drawn trams. It would be more instructive, however, if it had information about the Ainu village that preceded present-day Sapporo, from which the city takes its name. The word *Sapporo* is derived from a combination of Ainu words meaning "a river running along a reed-filled plain." At press time, the Tokei-dai was closed for repairs and scheduled to reopen in September 1998. ▨ *Free.* ☉ *Tues.–Sun. 9–4; closed Dec. 29–Jan. 3 and day after national holidays.*

❼ TV Tower. At the east end of Ō-dōri Kōen, an unsightly metal frame stands 470 ft high. The Sapporo Tourist Association promotes it for the view from its observation platform, but views of the city are better, and free, from any of the high-rise hotels. ▨ *¥700.* ☉ *Summer, daily 9–9; winter, daily 9:30–6:30; closed Dec. 30–Jan. 2.*

Dining

Continental food is served in all major hotels in a formal dining room and/or a coffee shop. Invariably, the dining room looks to French cuisine for inspiration, and the food is always expensive. In addition to their Japanese restaurants, most large hotels have a Chinese restaurant. Most of Sapporo's restaurants, whatever their culinary origin, use visual displays for their menus. The greatest concentration of restaurants is in the entertainment district of Susukino, although other key locations are the downtown department stores and underneath the railway station. Hokkaidō is known for its *ramen,* a Chinese noodle served in broth, and Sapporo for its *miso,* fermented soybean broth. There are more than 1,000 ramen shops in the city, but do try to make it to **Ramen Yoko-chō,** in a small alley that runs perpendicular to the southern side of Susukino-dōri (Minami 4-jō). In the same area there are as many as three dozen tiny shops with counter service. If you prefer to eat in less cramped surroundings—but still cheaply and with quick and unfussy service—you might try one of the larger izakaya in Susukino: perhaps **Potato Circus,** on the fourth floor of the Urban Sapporo Building (✉ Minami 3, Nishi 4), or a member of the ubiquitous **Tsubohachi** chain. Their picture menus make life easy for even the most unrepentant monoglot English speaker.

$$$$ ✕ Ambrosia Room. On the penthouse floor of the Keio Plaza Hotel (☞ Lodging, *below*), this restaurant's extremely attentive and personable staff serves ambitious French fare. The view over the botanical gardens is perhaps more memorable than the cooking. ✉ *Keio Plaza Hotel, Kita 5-jō Nishi 7, Chūō-ku,* ☎ *011/271–0111. Jacket and tie. AE, DC, MC, V.*

$$$ ✕ Big Jug. In the Grand Hotel (☞ Lodging, *below*), this casual, beer hall–type brasserie is good for lunch, with a limited Continental menu and an opportunity to talk. It's popular with businessmen. ✉ *Sapporo Grand Hotel, Kita 1-jō Nishi 4, Chūō-ku,* ☎ *011/261–3311. AE, DC, MC, V.*

$$$ ✕ Yamatōya. You will find excellent sushi and sashimi here, with
★   counter service on the left and tatami seating on the right. Yamatōya is across the street from the JAL office downtown. ✉ *Koshiyama Bldg., basement, Kita 2-jō Nishi 3, Chūō-ku,* ☎ *011/251–5667. Reservations not accepted. MC, V. Closed Golden Week and New Year's.*

$$ ✕ **Izakaya Kuruma-ya.** Downstairs in Plaza 109 (on the south side of
★ the main east–west street in Susukino), this local tavern has the best
yakitori (chicken on skewers) in town. The elegant atmosphere makes
it popular with Japanese and foreigners, and there is an English-lan-
guage menu. Aside from yakitori, Karuma-ya also serves *oden* (diced
vegetables and tofu boiled in a soy-fish stock) as one of its specialties.
✉ *Minami 4-jō Nishi 5, Chūō-ku,* ☎ *011/512–9157. Reservations not
accepted. AE, DC, MC, V.*

$$ ✕ **Sapporo Beer Garden.** Jingusukan is popular here, though other Japanese dishes are also available. You'll find a festive atmosphere in ei-
ther the garden or the cavernous halls of the old brewery. ✉ *Kita 7-jō
Nishi 9, Higashi-ku,* ☎ *011/742–1531. AE, DC, MC, V.*

$$ ✕ **Sasa Sushi.** This small restaurant has a wide variety of sushi and is
extremely popular with local businessmen. Sit at the counter and you'll
likely strike up a conversation with fellow patrons. ✉ *Kita 2-jō Nishi
2, Chūō-ku (close to Hokkaidō Tourist Office),* ☎ *011/222–2897. Reser-
vations not accepted. No credit cards. Closed Sun.*

$$ ✕ **Shoya.** In the Plaza 109 building, this popular restaurant serves grilled
fish, but the side orders of sashimi and yakitori are also delicious. It's
a casual place where you are likely to strike up a conversation with
fellow diners. No English is spoken, but sign language suffices, and the
prices are not too high. ✉ *Minami 4-jō Nishi 5, Chūō-ku,* ☎ *011/512–
1241. Reservations not accepted. AE, DC, MC, V.*

$$ ✕ **Silo.** In its countrylike decor, with a menu to match, Silo serves only
Hokkaidō foods, including bear and deer. Some English is spoken. ✉
Hokusen Bldg., Minami 5-jō Nishi 3, Chūō-ku, ☎ *011/531–5837. AE,
DC, MC, V. Closed Sun.*

$$ ✕ **Yoyotei.** If you can't make it to the Sapporo Beer Garden (☞ *above*),
try a Jingusukan dinner here. Young waitresses in Bavarian dress and
a large open space try to re-create a German beer hall. ✉ *Matsuoka
Bldg., 5th floor, Minami 5-jō Nishi 4, Chūō-ku,* ☎ *011/241–8831. AE,
DC, MC, V.*

$ ✕ **Aji-no-tokei-dai.** Across from the Grand Hotel, Aji-no-tokei-dai is
a well-regarded ramen shop. You enter from street level—that bushy-
eyebrowed elderly gentleman slurping away in the photo, former prime
minister Tomiichi Murayama, ate here—and go downstairs into the
restaurant. Choose either the counter or a table, which you might share
with other diners if the restaurant is crowded. Though there are one
or two other items available, ramen is the specialty, and the steaming
noodles will set you back only ¥650–¥2,000. ✉ *Sanwa Ginkō (bank)
Bldg., Kita 1-jō Nishi 3,* ☎ *011/232–8171. Reservations not accepted.
No credit cards.*

$ ✕ **Tori.** On the first floor of the Sumire Hotel, just northeast of the Clock
Tower, this Japanese restaurant is easily the best lunch value in Sapporo. Try the *Chirashi Tekka* Ladies Set: sliced raw tuna over seasoned
rice, with two skewers of yakitori, fruit, salad, pickled vegetables, and
miso soup. The variety, quality, and ample portions of the sets make
this the ideal place to savor Japanese cooking. The only drawback is
the daunting menu, all in Japanese, and the absence of plastic food models to fall back on. Ask the helpful staff for one-word explanations of
the lunch sets (¥850), all of which are excellent. ✉ *Sumire Hotel, 1st
floor, Kita 1-jō Nishi 2,* ☎ *011/231–8324. Reservations not accepted.
AE, DC, MC, V.*

Lodging

$$$$ 🏨 **ANA Zennikku Hotel.** In the heart of the business center, three
blocks from the JR eki, this is Sapporo's tallest high-rise hotel (26 floors).
Shops and a coffee-pastry restaurant are on the ground floor, an open

lobby area with lounges and bars up an escalator. Rooms are spacious and brightly decorated. The Sky Restaurant and Sky Lounge have fine views. The hotel is convenient for ANA passengers because it runs buses to and from Chitose Airport. ⊠ *Kita 3-jō Nishi 1, Chūō-ku, Sapporo, Hokkaidō 060,* ☎ *011/221–4411,* ℻ *011/222–7624. 412 rooms, mostly Western style. 2 restaurants, 5 bars. AE, DC, MC, V.*

$$$$ 🏨 **Hotel Alpha Sapporo.** You can't beat this location if you want to walk to the downtown shopping area of the city and be close to Susukino's nightlife. Service is excellent, and the decor of warm rust-browns and reds makes it an inviting place to return to after a day of sightseeing. Though its copious facilities include a Japanese tea ceremony room and the Mitsukoshi Movie Theater, this is smaller than most of the other top hotels, which means that the hotel's staff will soon know you by name. Guest rooms tend to be ordinary, but they are larger than most other standard hotel rooms in Japan. Western rock bands playing one of Sapporo's very sporadic gigs usually stay here. The French restaurant Alsienne, in an elegant wood-paneled dining room, imports many of its ingredients from France. ⊠ *Minami 1-jō Nishi 5, Chūō-ku, Sapporo, Hokkaidō 060,* ☎ *011/221–2333,* ℻ *011/221–0819. 146 rooms. 3 restaurants, bar, tea room, indoor pool, beauty salon. AE, DC, MC, V.*

$$$$ 🏨 **Hotel Arthur Sapporo.** Located south of Susukino and at the northwest corner of Nakajima Park, this hotel opened in 1989, and although the guest-room carpeting needs to be replaced, the hotel has generally been well maintained. Rooms are reasonably large for Japan, and the dark-stained furniture gives them a European feel. Bathrooms have a hand-held shower, and the toilet is in a separate room that adjoins the alcove dressing area. The spacious lobby area has an open lounge where you can dine with views of the park. There are restaurants on the ground floor (with a dessert buffet), and the 4th (Italian), 5th, and 24th floors. The 25th floor has a bar and, oddly enough, a club called 21 Club. Not all staff members speak English, but they are eager to help gai-jin guests. ⊠ *Minami 10-jō Nishi 6, Chūō-ku, Sapporo, Hokkaidō 064,* ☎ *011/561–1000,* ℻ *011/521–5522. 229 Western-style rooms. 4 restaurants, bar, lobby lounge, beauty salon, nightclub, shop. AE, DC, MC, V.*

$$$$ 🏨 **Keio Plaza Hotel Sapporo.** A five-minute walk west of the JR eki, the Keio is a large, modern hotel with a vast, open-plan lobby. Because it stands between the botanical gardens and the Hokkaidō University campus, views from rooms on the upper floors are the best in town—and rooms are very spacious for a Japanese hotel. If you are not staying here, you can also take in the views from the Ambrosia (French) and Miyama (Japanese) restaurants on the 22nd floor. The 24-hour Jurin coffee shop, one of the few all-night restaurants in town, can be a welcome respite if you're an insomniac suffering from jet lag. There is also an izakaya and sushi bar, a tea lounge, and a delicatessen. The enthusiastic, helpful staff will always find someone to help out in English, if required. ⊠ *Kita 5-jō Nishi 7, Chūō-ku, Sapporo, Hokkaidō 060,* ☎ *011/271–0111,* ℻ *011/221–5450. 525 rooms, mostly Western style. 5 restaurants, coffee shop, sushi bar, tea room, health club, car rental, travel services. AE, DC, MC, V.*

$$$$ 🏨 **Sapporo Grand Hotel.** This is Sapporo's oldest established Western
★ hotel, centrally located on the main commercial street. Built in 1934 and renovated in 1984, the Grand is in the tradition of a great European hotel. It has a range of restaurants—Japanese, Chinese, French, and a pub, Big Jug (☞ *above*), popular for business lunches. Service is first-rate. Rooms in the new annex have a fresher, more modern air than those in the older wing. The hotel's numerous facilities, from a cake and coffee shop to elegant restaurants, create a more lively atmo-

sphere than you might expect from Sapporo's oldest hotel. ⊠ *Kita 1-jō Nishi 4 Chūō-ku, Sapporo, Hokkaidō 060,* ☎ *011/261–3311,* FAX *011/231–0388. 585 rooms, mostly Western style. 4 restaurants, coffee shop, shops. AE, DC, MC, V.*

$$$ 🏨 **Hotel Nikkō Chitose.** This is the best hotel in the Chitose area, south of the city, if you want to be near Sapporo's closest international airport, about 3 km (2 mi) away. It is owned by Japan Airlines in order to put up its flight crews. ⊠ *4-4-4 Hon-chō, Chitose-shi, Hokkaidō 066,* ☎ *0123/22–1121,* FAX *0123/22–1153. 258 rooms, mostly Western style. 3 restaurants. AE, DC, MC, V.*

$$–$$$ 🏨 **Fujiya Santus Hotel.** Although more than 15 years old, the Fujiya
★ Santus has kept up a fresh appearance. The staff is wonderfully friendly, and the smallness of the hotel adds to the personal warmth. Depending on the type of room you want and the time of year you want it, prices tend toward the low end of this category. The hotel is next to the botanical gardens, a pleasant location, but one that requires a 10-minute walk to the JR eki and downtown. ⊠ *Kita 3-jō Nishi 7, Chūō-ku, Sapporo, Hokkaidō 060,* ☎ *011/271–3344,* FAX *011/241–4182. 32 Western-style rooms, 8 Japanese-style rooms. Restaurant. MC, V.*

$$ 🏨 **Nakamuraya Ryokan.** This inn near the botanical gardens dates from 1898—ancient for Sapporo—though the current building is more recent. The six-tatami-mat rooms seem larger because of their spacious cupboards, built-in minibar, and wide window shelf. Most rooms have tiny private bathrooms. The staff are diffident with foreign guests but warm up after you've managed a few words in Japanese. The large communal bath is a welcome comfort in winter. When making reservations, explain that you saw a listing in the Japanese Inn Group brochure; otherwise you may be charged a higher rate. The Japanese dinner (¥3,000) is expansive, with a selection of fresh seafood from Hokkaidō's waters. ⊠ *Kita 3-jō Nishi 7, Chūō-ku, Sapporo, Hokkaidō 060,* ☎ *011/241–2111,* FAX *011/241–2118. 29 rooms, mostly Japanese style. Restaurant. AE, DC, MC, V.*

$ 🏨 **Hotel Public.** The best and swankiest (lots of marble) business hotel
★ in town, the Public has a friendly staff and Western-size beds, instead of the normal narrow ones found in other business hotels. The Public also has a reasonable restaurant–cum–coffee lounge and an izakaya. Though considerably west of the main attractions of central Sapporo, the hotel is next to the streetcar line, which can take you into town. ⊠ *Minami 1-jō Nishi 15, Chūō-ku, Sapporo, Hokkaidō 060,* ☎ *011/644–7711. 105 Western-style rooms. Restaurant. AE, DC, MC, V.*

Nightlife

★ **Susukino** is Sapporo's entertainment area, and it is the largest of its kind north of Tōkyō. More than 5,000 bars, restaurants, and nightclubs, all lit by lanterns and flashing signs, crowd into a compact area. It is mind-boggling and, in itself, justifies an overnight stay in Sapporo. Most bars stay open until the wee hours, some as late as 5 AM, though restaurants often close before midnight.

Just make sure that you know what kind of bar you're getting into before you enter. There are several kinds: clubs with many hostesses who make small talk (¥10,000 and up, proving that talk is *not* cheap); *sunakku* bars (the word sounds like "snack," which translates into fewer hostesses and expensive *ōdoburu*—hors d'oeuvres); izakaya, for different kinds of food and drink; bars with entertainment, either taped video music you can sing along with (karaoke bars) or live bands; and "soapland" and *herusu* ("health") massage parlors, which are generally off-limits to non-Japanese lacking an introduction. If at all possible, go to the clubs and *sunakku* with a Japanese-speaking acquaintance. If only for the drama of the streets, Susukino is worth an evening stroll—you're just as likely to bump into a businessman as a college student, Honshū tourist, hostess, Mafioso, or kimono-clad bar *mama-san*.

For agreeably mellow surroundings and a fine selection of cocktails and whiskies, try the popular **Blues Alley** in the basement of the Miyako Building (✉ Minami 3-jō Nishi 3). It's worth paying the ¥1,000 seating charge for the atmosphere, the nightly live performances, and the late hours. It's closed Sunday. Another Susukino bar that reflects the eclectic Japanese taste for foreign music and styles is the tiny but cozy **Anyway** (✉ Mimatsu Muraoka Bldg., 6th floor, Minami 5-jō Nishi 2), whose affable, Stetson-wearing owner is besotted with country-and-western and speaks English. There is a ¥3,000 door/live music charge.

Izakaya are well represented in Susukino, though one that has a menu with a distinctly Hokkaidō flavor is **Irohanihoheto,** on the second floor of the Bacchus Building (✉ Minami 5-jō Nishi 4). Wine lovers might prefer the **Wine Bar** (✉ New Hokusei Bldg., 9th floor, Minami 4-jō Nishi 3), which is reputed to be Sapporo's number one spot for young courting couples. Be warned, though, that you'll be hit by both a seating charge and a 10% service fee added to your bill.

Finally, for the adventurous, there is the district's strangest bar, **Susukino Rei-en** (cemetery; ✉ No. 2 Green Bldg., 8th floor, Minami 4-jō Nishi 3; ¥1,000 door charge), which has been furnished to resemble an Asian graveyard. Despite the awful-sounding concept, it is surprisingly comfortable. And the genial floor staff will entertain you with conjuring tricks when not serving drinks. Come before midnight if you like a good scare. Some menu items may put you off if you're not into vulgar humor.

Sapporo Snow Festival

★ Sapporo's best-known annual event, held in the first week of February, the **Sapporo Snow Festival** is the greatest of its kind. More than 300 lifelike sculptures, as large as 130 ft tall by 50 deep by 80 wide, are created each year. The festival began in 1950 with six statues that were carved to entertain local citizens, depressed by the aftermath of the war and the long winter nights. Now the event is so large that sculpture is displayed in three sections of the city: Ō-dōri Kōen (large sculpture and spectator events), Makomanai (mammoth creations and ice slides for children), and Susukino (magnificent ice sculpture lining Eki-mae-dōri). The festival attracts more than 2 million visitors each year, so book accommodations well in advance.

Sapporo A to Z

Arriving and Departing

BY CAR

Sapporo has two expressways. The Dō Expressway heads southeast to Chitose, then veers southwest to hug Hokkaidō's underside as far as Muroran. The Sasson Expressway links Otaru to the west with Asahikawa in the northeast.

BY PLANE

Sapporo's Chitose Kūkō, 40 km (25 mi) south of the city, is Hokkaidō's main airport. More than 32 domestic routes link Chitose to the rest of Japan, while flights from Chitose to other parts of Asia have been increasing. Eagerly awaited direct service to Europe is said to be in the works as of this writing. **Japan Airlines** (JAL; ☎ 011/231–4411 international, 011/231–0231 domestic), **All Nippon Airways** (ANA; ☎ 011/281–1212 international, 011/726–8800 domestic), and **Japan Air System** (JAS; ☎ 011/222–8111) all serve Chitose. The Hokkaidō Airport Terminal Company's number at Chitose is 0123/23–0111.

Between the Airport and Center City. Japan Railways (JR) runs frequently between the airport terminal and downtown Sapporo. (Shin Chitose Kūkō Eki is the final eastbound stop from Sapporo; do not get off at Chitose Eki if you want the airport.) The trip is usually made by rapid transit trains (¥1,040, 40 minutes). ANA runs a shuttle bus (¥800) that connects with its flights at Chitose and its hotel, the ANA Zenniku, in Sapporo, first stopping at the Ramada Renaissance and Sunroute hotels. Chūō Bus (¥800) runs a shuttle between the airport and Sapporo's Grand Hotel, also stopping at Ō-dōri Park, JR Sapporo Eki, and the Korakuen, Ryoton, and Keio Plaza hotels. Taxis are available, but the distance between Sapporo and the airport makes them ridiculously expensive.

BY TRAIN

All JR trains come into the central station, on the north side of downtown Sapporo. Trains arrive and depart for Honshū (sometimes involving a change of trains in Hakodate) about every two hours. As many as half a dozen trains per hour run to and from Otaru to the east. Every half hour from 7 AM to 10 PM there are trains heading north to Asahikawa in central Hokkaidō.

Getting Around

Sapporo is a walking city with wide sidewalks; it's easy to find your way around. The **International Information Corner** (☞ Contacts and Resources, *below*) at the Sapporo railway station has a city map, and most hotels have a smaller map marking their hotels and the major points of interest.

BY BUS

Bus fares begin at ¥200. Buses follow the grid system and stop running at midnight.

BY STREETCAR

Sapporo also has a streetcar service with a flat fare of ¥170. However, it is confined to a single line connecting the Susukino entertainment area with Moiwa-yama in the city's southwest corner (well away from the sights mentioned in this section) and has kept in business because of public affection rather than profitability. In an effort to scrape a little more money out of the service, the city has made its streetcars available for party-hire, and it is not uncommon to see the vehicles trundling across town with a crowd of revelers on board.

BY SUBWAY

Sapporo's subway is a pleasure. As in Toronto and Moscow, trains have rubber wheels that run quietly. Most signs include English. There are three lines: The **Namboku Line** runs south from the station past Susukino to Nakajima Park; the **Tōzai Line** bisects the city from east to west. These two cross at Ō-dōri Station. The third, the **Tōhō Line**, enters central Sapporo from the southeast of the city, then parallels the Namboku Line from Ō-dōri Station to the JR eki before branching off into the northeastern suburbs.

The basic fare, covering about three stations, is ¥200. There is a one-day open ticket for ¥1,000 that gives unlimited trips on the subway, bus, and streetcar (¥800 for the subway alone), while a ¥700 "eco" ticket (encouraging citizens to leave their cars at home for the day) covers the same three types of public transport on the 5th and 20th of every month. These tickets are available at any subway station, though the most central ticket window is at Ō-dōri Station Underground Commuter's Ticket Office, open January 4–December 29, daily 10–6. Prepaid "With You" cards (available from ¥1,000 at vending machines) eliminate the need to calculate your fare, which is automatically debited upon reaching your destination. The last trains set off around 11:30 and stop running at midnight.

BY TAXI
Taxi meters start at ¥550; an average fare, such as from the train station to Susukino, runs about ¥800.

Contacts and Resources

CONSULATE
U.S. Consulate. The consulate will process passports for American citizens; others applying for U.S. visas must do so in Tōkyō. ⊠ *Kita 1-jō Nishi 28, Chūō-ku,* ☎ *011/641–1115.*

DOCTORS AND DENTISTS
Sapporo City General Hospital (⊠ Kita 11-jō Nishi 13, ☎ 011/726–2211). **Hokkaidō University Hospital** (⊠ Kita 14-jō Nishi 5, ☎ 011/716–1161). The **Emergency Dental Clinic** (⊠ Minami 7-jō Nishi 10, ☎ 011/511–7774); open evenings only, 7–11.

EMERGENCIES
Police, ☎ 110. **Ambulance,** ☎ 119.

ENGLISH-LANGUAGE BOOKSTORES
Outside Sapporo, finding English-language books is difficult, so you may want to browse in Sapporo's two largest bookstores with (limited) books in English: **Kinokuniya** (⊠ Dai-ni Yuraku Bldg., 2nd floor, Minami 1-jō Nishi 1, ☎ 011/231–2131), on the south side of the TV Tower and accessible from Aurora Town; and **Maruzen** (⊠ Minami 1-jō, 4th floor, Nishi 3, ☎ 011/241–7251), one block south of Ō-dōri Park, adjoining Mitsukoshi department store above Ō-dōri subway station. The latter also sells small, interesting Japanese-style gifts in its basement that, by the standards of the neighboring large stores, are fairly well priced. You'll find smaller selections of books in **Asamiya Shoten** (⊠ Arche Bldg., 2nd level basement, Minami 3-jō Nishi 4, ☎ 011/241–3007), on the east side of Pole Town, and **Art Logos** (⊠ Parco Bldg., 7th floor, Minami 1-jō Nishi 3, ☎ 011/214–2301), across the street from Mitsukoshi. A sprawling **Tower Records** sells magazines in Japanese and English to trend-hungry young natives. It also has the requisite selection of CDs (⊠ Pivot Bldg., 7th floor, Minami 2-jō Nishi 4, ☎ 011/241–3851).

ROAD CONDITIONS
Information on road conditions in winter is available at ☎ 011/281–6511. However, as it is in Japanese, ask the staff at your hotel or Plaza i (☎ 011/211–3678) to call for you.

TRAVEL AGENCIES
Japan Travel Bureau. Coziness with Japan Airlines tends to make JTB push this carrier. For cheaper fares or additional flight times, specify other airlines. ☎ *011/241–6201.*

VISITOR INFORMATION
Look for copies of the magazine **Xene** in hotels and bookstores for its listings of local and Hokkaidō-wide events and festivals, as well as discount coupons, articles on Japanese issues, and a Japanese lesson. The most helpful places for information on Sapporo and Hokkaidō in general are the **International Information Corner** (Kokusai Jōhō Corner, ☎ 011/213–5062), open daily 9–5 and closed the second and fourth Wednesday of the month (second Wednesday only January and February and July–September), in the western portion of Lilac Paseo in the JR Sapporo Eki, and the Sapporo International Communication Plaza's tourist office, **Plaza i** (⊠ MN Bldg., ground floor, Kita 1-jō Nishi 3, Chūō-ku, ☎ 011/211–3678), which is open daily 9–5:30 and closed December 29–January 3.

Other offices that supply information include **Sapporo City Tourism Department Office** (⊠ Kita 1-jō Nishi 2, Chūō-ku, ☏ 011/211–2376), open weekdays 8:45–5:15, closed December 29–January 3; **Hokkaidō Tourist Association** (⊠ Keizai Center Bldg., Kita 2-jō Nishi 1, Chūō-ku, ☏ 011/231–0941), open weekdays 9–5; and **Sapporo Tourist Information Center** (⊠ Ō-dōri subway station, Ō-dōri Nishi 3-chōme, ☏ 011/232–7712), open daily 10–6, closed December 31–January 1.

OTARU AND THE SHAKOTAN HANTŌ

West of Sapporo, the Shakotan Hantō and its mysteriously shaped rocks jut fang-like into the yawning, bold blueness of the Nihon-kai. The peninsula is ideal for cliff-side drives and, in less precipitous stretches, walks down to the ocean. On the way, you might want to stop in the port city of Otaru. Then, inland, the Niseko resort area is dotted with cozy cottages and rustic open-air hot springs in which outdoor lovers unwind and refuel between days of skiing, hiking, or rafting. A quick circuit of the area takes one or two days to complete with a rented car, two days by public transport.

Otaru

㉑ *48 mins west of Sapporo by JR, 40 km (24 mi) west of Sapporo by car.*

Otaru is "famous for its canals and old Western-style buildings," according to the Hokkaidō Tourist Office. This image as a charming port city and romantic weekend retreat from Sapporo did occasion a tourist rush in the mid-1990s, but gai-jin are usually less impressed with what is essentially a commercial city in the shadow of Hokkaidō's capital. Nevertheless, Otaru's historical importance and peerless sushi make it worth a stop.

A number of 19th-century, wood-frame houses still stand—sandwiched between modern concrete structures—and a busy port area sees ferries departing for Niigata to the south and Russians arriving from the north. They come for black-market trade of seafood for consumer goods. Otaru once served as a more legitimate financial center, dubbed the Wall Street of the North. Its fortunes plunged with the decline of the fishery industry. Resourceful craftsmen turned from making glass buoys and lamps for squid fishing to fashioning the glass objets d'art now seen in boutiques on a lively strip 10 minutes by foot from the JR Otaru Eki in the **Otaru Canal** section.

Among numerous restaurants and cafés and restored turn-of-the-century buildings in the Otaru Canal section, the **Otaru Hakubutsukan** (City Museum), in a former warehouse, combines natural history exhibits with displays about the town's development since the 19th century. 🎟 *¥100 (extra may be charged for special exhibitions).* ☉ *Daily 9:30–5; closed day after national holidays.*

🐾 **Otaru Suizokukan,** Hokkaidō's only worthwhile aquarium, has a marine mammal show that thrills youngsters. To get there, ride the Suizokukan Yuki bus from the JR eki (Chūō bus platform 3) for 20 minutes to the last stop. 🎟 *¥1,300.* ☉ *Daily 9–5; closed Nov. 1–Apr. 6.*

Dining and Lodging
If you have any kind of a taste for fish, Otaru has two of Hokkaidō's best sashimi restaurants, **Uoisshin** (⊠ 1-11-10 Hanazono, ☏ 0134/32–5202) and **Isshintasuke** (⊠ 1-5-3 Hanazono, ☏ 0134/34–1790). Connoisseurs of sashimi from Sapporo will make a special trip to eat here, and, because frequent train service runs to and from Sapporo, you can do the same. Your Sapporo hotel will be happy to make reservations, which are essential.

$$$ 🏯 **Hasegawa Minshuku.** This popular but slightly overrated ryokan is just outside Otaru, on the way to the aquarium. The furnishings are worn, and the staff does not seem to be overjoyed at having foreigners. Japanese food is served in your room. ✉ *3-215, Shikutsu, Otaru, Hokkaidō 047,* ☎ *0134/22–5276. 10 rooms. No credit cards.*

$$ 🏯 **Otaru Kokusai Hotel.** Above a shopping arcade, this modern hotel is reached by an escalator from the main street. The lobby area is rather bare and uncomfortable, but guest rooms are cheerful, if small. The staff speaks a little English. ✉ *3-9-1 Inaho, Otaru, Hokkaidō 047,* ☎ *0134/33–2161,* 🅵🅰🆇 *0134/33–7744. 76 Western-style rooms, 4 Japanese-style rooms. 3 restaurants. AE, MC, V.*

Fishing

If you are interested in deep-sea fishing, inquire at the Otaru Tourist Office (☞ *below*).

Visitor Information

Otaru Tourist Office (☎ 0134/29–1333) is secreted away in a small wooden building to the left as you exit the JR eki. If you use the tourist office, open daily 9–6, have an attendant call to recheck any information she gives you, particularly business hours, as source materials are notoriously dated and hours for certain sights vary greatly by season.

Shakotan Hantō (Shakotan Peninsula)

Yoichi is 30 mins west of Otaru by JR local. Iwanai is 3 hrs and 40 mins southwest of Yoichi (95 km [59 mi]) on the coastal road by bus.

㉒ Some of Hokkaidō's best sandy beaches lie west of Otaru along the coast road leading to **Yoichi** (yo-ee-chee). After you pass the town, beaches soon give way to cliffs rising out of the sea.

★ ㉓ Yoichi marks the beginning of the **Shakotan Hantō.** Two mountain peaks, Yobetsu-dake (4,019 ft) and Shakotan-dake (4,258 ft), dominate the peninsula's interior. And there are two capes, Shakotan Misaki and Kamui Misaki, on its northern and western tips. Sentimental Japanese go to Kamui for sunsets over the Sea of Japan.

Shakotan typifies natural Hokkaidō. Cliffs stave off the endless surging sea; volcanic mountains dominate the interior. Thick forests blanket the slopes with dark, rich greens, and ravines crease the mountainsides. Shakotan Hantō has coastal scenery at its most dramatic.

The road from Yoichi circles the peninsula, keeping to the coast as much as the cliffs allow. At Yobetsu, near Kamui Misaki, it gets even more spectacular as it heads south to Iwanai.

If you are driving, Kamoenai presents the choice of continuing south or crossing the peninsula by taking the thrilling hairpin road (closed in winter) over **Tomaru Tōge** that skirts Yobetsu-dake (mountain) and returns to Furubira.

There are no hiking trails on Yobetsu-dake itself, but the neighboring Shakotan-dake (mountain) has a gentle round-trip climb of 3¼ hours. Buses run from the JR Otaru Eki and JR Yoichi Eki to the trail entrance.

Getting Around

To tour the northern coast of the peninsula by bus, take a **Chūō** line bus (☎ 011/272–1211) round-trip to Kamui Misaki. To continue from Kamui to Iwanai, catch a separate bus to Nishi-no-kawara, then another one to Iwanai. The ferry that used to run around the peninsula is no longer in operation.

En Route   From Iwanai a road cuts across the base of the peninsula back to Otaru. There is also the alternative, at Iwanai, to go south and combine this side trip with one through **Shikotsu-Tōya National Park** (☞ *below*).

Niseko

㉔   *60 km (36 mi) southwest of Otaru, 2 hrs and 10 mins by JR.*

For the best skiing in Hokkaidō, and perhaps Japan, head for Niseko, adjoining the town of **Kutchan**. The town itself has a sleepy charm—the real action is in the collection of peaks that have five ski areas and the stately **Yotei-zan**. Climbing this Fuji look-alike takes four hours. Two trails lead up the mountain: the more challenging Hirafu Course and the easier but still challenging Makkari Course. No matter your approach, you're bound to be taken by the summer wildflowers, as well as the vigorous elderly Japanese chomping on bamboo shoots that grow wild on the hills. A hut at the top of Yotei-zan provides crude lodging if you decide to hike up to see the next day's sunrise. To get to the trails, take the bus from the JR Kutchan Eki 20 minutes to Yotei To-zan-guchi (hiking trail entrance) for the Hirafu Course or 40 minutes to the Yotei Shinzan Kōen stop for the Makkari Course.

Several outfits also run river-rafting and mountain-biking excursions in the area. Inquire at the excellent tourist counter at the JR eki in town. The fastest way to get to Kutchan from Sapporo is by road or rail via Otaru. If you take a more overland route through Jōzankei Onsen, Kimobetsu, Rusutsu, and Makkari, smaller roads weave through more spectacular terrain.

Dining and Lodging

Three blocks from the station, in a weathered wooden building, **Yabutomi** is a venerable institution that serves superb *soba* (buckweat) noodles. Nearby **Kurowassan** (✉ Minami 3-jō Nishi 2) is another noodle shop, known for *imo udon*, a thicker gauge of noodle made of potato flour instead of the usual wheat.

If you are driving into the area, you might ask at the tourist office about staying at **pension cottages** with hot springs. If you are relying on public transport, try the modest **Minshuku Yamagoya** (✉ 1 Asahi, Kutchan, ☎ 0136/22–1164, FAX 0136/22–1165) in the center of town for ¥7,700 per night with two meals. **Hotel Yoteikaku**, behind the station, has more conventional modern accommodations for ¥7,000 per night, and a hot spring for ¥500.

Tengu-yama

★ **㉕**   *5 km (3 mi) southeast of Otaru.*

If you have the time and use of a car, instead of heading straight back to Sapporo through Jōzankei hot springs, take the picturesque detour that climbs Tengu-yama and continues among some of Hokkaidō's most scenic mountains. The road follows a ravine that winds its way up and around Tengu-yama before descending to Jōzankei. The forests and rock outcroppings make this trip especially beautiful in late spring, when patches of white snow are melting into crystal streams. Another good time for this journey is autumn, when golden leaves beautifully contrast with the dark green of the conifers.

A hiking trail adjoins Route 95, which skirts the waters of the Shiroigawa. Leave six hours for the intermediate-level climb from the cabin at the trailhead to the peak and back. Do not confuse this Tengu-yama with a hill of the same name just southwest of downtown Otaru. The far more scenic Tengu-yama is south and slightly east of Otaru.

To make the Mt. Tengu detour, return from Kutchan to Otaru, and then head toward Sapporo on the Sasson Expressway. Exit onto the Otaru–Jōzankei Highway 5 km (3 mi) east of Otaru. The road heads south through Asari-gawa Onsen and on past Tengu-yama. Buses between Otaru and Jōzankai cover this route less frequently than do those originating in Sapporo.

Jōzankei Onsen

❷❻ *43 km (27 mi) east of Tengu-yama, 1 hr south of Sapporo by bus (25 km [16 mi]).*

Because Jōzankei is actually within Sapporo's city limits, weekend day-trippers do crowd in. The resort town itself is wedged in a small valley in the foothills beneath the mountains of Shikotsu-Tōya National Park. Were it not for the modern, square-block hotels, the village would be beautiful. Unfortunately, while it has all the creature comforts of a resort with hot springs, developers managed to spoil the area with their monstrosities.

This year-round hot-spring resort attracts skiers from all over Japan in winter and Hokkaidō residents in summer for hiking and weekend camping. Skiing is in full swing by the beginning of December and lasts through May at **Sapporo Kokusai Ski Area** (☎ 001/598–4511). The ski area is 25 minutes by bus from the spa. A one-day lift ticket that includes night skiing costs ¥4,500.

One of the most unusual museums in Hokkaidō attests to Japan's legacy of peasant frankness about things sexual. The coyly named **Hihōkan** (House of Secret Treasures) is a museum devoted to Japan's tradition of erotica and sexual folk culture, including phallic and yonic objects formerly related to fertility rites. You can locate it by the huge statue of a crying Kannon, Buddhist deity of mercy, out front. ✉ *Rte. 230.* 📷 *¥1,500.* ☉ *Daily 9–7.*

SHIKOTSU-TŌYA NATIONAL PARK

Mountains, forests, refreshing caldera lakes, hot-spring resorts, and volcanoes—this outdoor circuit is virtually in Sapporo's backyard. At Tōya-ko, you can boat and fish and take in nightly, midsummer fireworks displays over the water. Noboribetsu Onsen claims to be Asia's largest hot-spring resort. And Shikotsu-ko is another caldera lake, this time with hiking on its nearby volcanic domes. There is also a detour east to Nibu-tani, which has one of Hokkaidō's best Ainu villages. For a quick tour of the area, plan two days by car and three by public transport.

For information on Jōzankei Onsen, *see* the end of the Otaru and the Shokotan Hantō, *above.*

Nakayama Tōge

★ ❷❼ *18 km (11 mi) south of Jōzankei Onsen, 90 mins south of Sapporo by bus.*

Once through Jōzankei Onsen, the twisting, winding road up through the ravine presages the high drama of the mountain pass ahead. The final ascent to 2,742 ft ends after a tunnel that opens out at Nakayama Tōge's sweeping panoramas of lonely mountains and peopled plains. In the distance, beyond the surrounding mountain peaks, the nearly perfect conical shape of **Yotei-zan** begs comparison to Fuji-san, but any native worth his or her salt would say that Mt. Yotei has no competition.

There is a souvenir shop to the side of the road at Nakayama Pass, with a restaurant called Potato Daishaku on its second floor where you can buy food and refreshments to help you catch your breath after the drive up—and before the descent. For those who like to go in style, this is also the site of Hokkaidō's priciest public toilet, a construction boondoggle that caused a stink when the million-dollar price tag was made public.

Tōya-ko (Lake Tōya)

★ *80 km (48 mi) southwest of Sapporo, 150 mins by bus.*

The road descends from Nakayama Tōge to Kimobetsu and Rusutsu, soon after which a flat stretch to Tōya-ko suddenly appears. The lake, in a collapsed volcanic cone, is almost circular. Just after your first glimpse of it, the inevitable crowd of small shops appears on either side of the road, though at least one of them is to be commended for the quality of the ice cream it sells. From here you get views that take in the northern circumference of the lake and its small islands, and the peaks of smaller volcanoes that pop up in the middle of the lake.

28 The spa town of **Tōya-ko Onsen,** on the southwestern edge of Tōya-ko, is the chief holiday center for this part of Shikotsu-Tōya Park. Consequently, it is loaded with hotels, inns, and souvenir shops. The hotels are open all year, but the busiest time is June through August, when Japanese families come in droves for trout fishing, hiking, boating, visiting Nakajima ("inner island")—the largest of the cluster of islands in the center of the lake, where there are fireworks nightly in summer—and, of course, taking the curative waters of the hot springs.

Tōya-ko Onsen is famous for its healing waters, but the geological wonder is **Shōwa Shin-zan,** which means "new mountain of the Shōwa era." Japan's latest volcano, it made its appearance in 1943, surprising everyone, but no one more than the farmer who witnessed its emergence from his wheat field. In the course of two years, it grew steadily until it reached its final height of 1,312 ft. The nearby **Abuta Kazan Kagakukan** (Volcanic Science Museum) chronicles both Shōwa Shinzan's development and the volcanic activity of the entire area.

Not to be outdone, **Usu-zan,** one peak over from Shōwa Shin-zan, erupted in 1977. It did so with flair, sending out 200 tremors an hour before blowing its top. This advance notice allowed local residents to flee and photographers to set up their cameras. Their photographs are shown amid sound effects of thunder and lightning at the Abuta Volcanic Science Museum, located between the lakeside and the foot of Usu-zan. The presentation is dramatic, realistic, and better seen after, rather than before, taking the cable car to the top of Usu-zan for the superb views of Tōya-ko.

Rowboats are available for rent for ¥1,000 per hour from the boat landing ⅙ mi north of the Tōya-ko bus terminal, where sightseeing boats also offer half-hour trips halfway around the lake for ¥930.

Lodging

$$–$$$ 🏨 **Tōya Park Hotel.** At this a sister hotel to the Tōya Park Sun Palace, the manager enjoys speaking English. Located at the head of the town and on a slight bluff, it has an unrestricted view of the lake. Only the Japanese-style guest rooms face the lake. ⊠ *Tōya-ko Onsen, Abutagun, Hokkaidō 049,* ☎ *0142/75–2445,* ℻ *01427/5–3918. 280 rooms, 140 Western style. 2 restaurants, hot springs, bowling, recreation room. AE, DC, MC, V.*

$ 🏨 **Nakanoshima.** This small hotel is around the lake 3 km (2 mi) west of Tōya-ko Onsen. No English is spoken, but the owners are happy to use sign language. There is a restaurant on the premises. ⊠ *Sobetsu Onsen, Sobetsu-chō, Hokkaidō 052,* ☎ *01427/5–4115,* FAX *01427/5– 2872. 26 rooms, mostly Western style. Restaurant. No credit cards.*

En Route   From Tōya-ko Onsen, the road continues around the lake through So-betsu Onsen, a quieter version of Tōya-ko Onsen. Here, take Route 453 away from the lake. A little farther on, the road forks—take the right-hand branch (closed in winter) southeast over the mountains to **Noboribetsu Onsen.** The 90-minute trip brings you over Orofure Tōge (3,051 ft), with its tremendous views of soaring mountains, hidden valleys, and, in the distance, Tōya-ko, Yotei-zan, Kuttara-ko, and the Pacific Ocean.

Noboribetsu Onsen

★ ㉙   *35 km (21 mi) east of Tōya-ko, 75 mins by bus; 2¼ hrs south of Sapporo by bus.*

Noboribetsu Onsen is the most famous spa in Hokkaidō, perhaps even in all of Japan. It's said that some 34,300 gallons of geologically heated water are pumped out every hour, making it the most prodigious hot spring in Asia. Its 11 types of water are said to cure ailments ranging from rheumatism to diabetes to menopause. Noboribetsu Onsen *is* a tourist town, so expect masses of hotels and souvenir shops. However, though the modern hotel architecture is decidedly an-aesthetic and out of tune with its mountain and forest surroundings, the village is not without charm. A stream runs through it, the main thoroughfare is cobblestone, and infernal gases billow from every street grate in winter. More important, the buildings do not block out the presence of the mountains. The onsen has undergone something of a gentrification in recent years, the cozier ryokan yielding to blockbuster hotels catering to busloads of visitors. For this reason, you might find yourself getting more for your yen if you arrange a tour from Sapporo.

Most hotels have their own baths, and the grandest of all are those at the **Dai-ichi Takimoto-kan.** This hotel is a monstrosity with 401 rooms, video-game halls, buffet dining rooms, and evening cabarets, but its 12 pools—men's and women's—have seven different waters of varying temperature. Signs above each pool are in Japanese. Because your knowledge of the language might leave you in the dark about just which minerals are in the waters—and what they will do for you—the solution is just to try them. These baths are worth the ¥2,000 non-occupant dipping fee even for non-hot-spring fanatics, if only for the view beyond the bathhouse's plate-glass window: It looks upon the steaming, volcanic gases of Jigokudani (☞ *below*). One floor beneath the baths, there is a swimming pool with a slide in case you like your water straight. The baths are open to non-occupants from 9 to 3; once inside you can stay until 5 PM.

★   **Jigokudani** (Valley of Hell) is a volcanic crater that looks like a bow-shaped valley. Boiling water spurts out of thousands of holes, sounding like the heartbeat of the earth itself—although, because of its strong sulfur smell, others have described it differently. Whereas hot springs elsewhere in Japan were used to dispose of zealous foreign missionaries during the equally zealous periods of xenophobia—Unzen on Kyūshū (☞ Chapter 13) is a notable example—Jigokudani's natural cauldrons once were favored by suicidal natives. The place is a couple hundred yards from the village.

The reconstructed Edo-period village of **Date Jidai Mura** is named for the members of the Date (*dah-teh*) clan who migrated here from Sendai after the fall of the shogunate. The complex includes samurai houses and geisha pleasure palaces watched over by actors attired in traditional garb. A visit here is probably not worth the hefty fee, except if you will miss the more traditional sites found in Honshū. The village is 5 km (3 mi) south of Noboribetsu Onsen. ☎ *0143/83–3311.* ⌑ *¥500 parking, ¥2,500 grounds only, ¥3,400 grounds and buildings.* ☉ *Apr.– Oct., daily 9–5; Nov.–Mar., daily 10–4.*

Do not confuse Noboribetsu Onsen with Noboribetsu, a city on the coast that is 13 minutes away by bus from the namesake spa town. Noboribetsu is an ugly industrial city on the JR Muroran Line. In fact, the whole coastal area from Date to Tomakomai is an industrial eyesore, sadly worsened by a sagging regional economy. Noboribetsu City is one hour and two minutes south of Sapporo by JR Limited Express. From the JR *eki*, a shuttle bus runs up to Noboribetsu Onsen.

Lodging

$$$$ 🏨 **Dai-ichi Takimoto-kan.** This huge, famous spa hotel may have as many as 1,200 guests at one time. They come to enjoy its thermal pools, the best and most famous throughout Japan. The hotel is very expensive, yet it has zero ambience. It is like a giant youth hostel and, invariably, fully booked. Service is efficiently impersonal, and you must hike from your bedroom to the lobby and to the thermal baths. One indication of the place's size is the English-language map available at reception to help you negotiate the labyrinth of buildings and passageways. An extension of the hotel has further increased the traffic to and from the baths. A vast dining room, the Food Plaza, serves average Japanese and Western food and stages nightclub variety acts. ⊠ *55 Noboribetsu Onsen, Noboribetsu, Hokkaidō 059,* ☎ *0143/84–2111,* 𝐅𝐀𝐗 *0143/ 84–2202. 401 rooms. 2 restaurants, hot springs, shops, recreation room. AE, DC, MC, V.*

$$$–$$$$ 🏨 **Akiyoshi Hotel.** This is a friendly, hospitable, modern ryokan in the
★ center of the village. Antiques and paintings are judiciously placed to give a balance between traditional hospitality and modern amenities. If you enjoy sleeping on tatami with a futon, this is the most personable hotel in town. Japanese food is served in rooms. ⊠ *Noboribetsu Onsen, Noboribetsu, Hokkaidō 059,* ☎ *0143/84–2261,* 𝐅𝐀𝐗 *0143/ 84–2263. 43 rooms. Hot springs. V.*

$$$–$$$$ 🏨 **Ryokan Hanaya.** A member of the Japanese Inn Group, this small
★ inn is less than 10 minutes on foot from the center of Noboribetsu. It has been very highly rated and is well kept. Meals provided in your room are exclusively *kaiseki,* aesthetically pleasing full-course meals of Japan's haute cuisine. Coming from the JR Noboribetsu Eki, take the bus to Noboribetsu Onsen and get off at the Hanaya-mae bus stop. ⊠ *134 Noboribetsu Onsen-machi, Noboribetsu, Hokkaidō 059,* ☎ *0143/84–2521,* 𝐅𝐀𝐗 *0143/84–2240. 22 rooms. AE, MC, V.*

$$$ 🏨 **Noboribetsu Grand Hotel.** This is another huge hotel with large, barren public rooms. Since it is at the bottom of the village and off to the side, its modern ugliness is well hidden. ⊠ *154 Noboribetsu Onsen, Noboribetsu, Hokkaidō 059,* ☎ *0143/84–2101,* 𝐅𝐀𝐗 *0143/84–2543. 174 Japanese-style rooms, 87 Western-style rooms. Restaurant, hot springs, shops. AE, DC, V.*

En Route Traveling along Route 36 from Noboribetsu toward Tomakomai, you pass through the coastal town of Shiraoi, where there's an Ainu museum and reconstructed Ainu village, Shiraoi Porota Kotan. However, the Ainu participants look dispirited and the bear cages miserable, making for a grim atmosphere. If you have a few hours to spare, rather than stopping here continue east along the coast from Tomakomai as far as the village of Tomikawa, where you can turn north along Route 237 to reach the village of Nibutani and the Ainu heartland.

A small railway line provides transport between Tomakomai and Tomikawa. To the right of the JR Tomikawa Eki you can catch a bus to take you the rest of the way. Don't make the mistake of getting off the bus too early, at the village of Biratori. Though it is described on brochures as a "village," Nibutani scarcely even qualifies as that—it is but a handful of buildings tucked away into the countryside several miles beyond Biratori.

Nibutani

★ ③⓪ *120 km (72 mi) east of Noboribetsu Onsen, 45 mins east of Tomiko-mai by JR then 30 mins by bus.*

Nibutani is one of the very last places in Hokkaidō with a sizable Ainu population—or at least part-Ainu, as the number of pure-blooded Ainu is very small now. Consequently, though the usual souvenir shops are much in evidence, there's some comfort in knowing your money has a better chance of finding its way into the pockets of proper Ainu, instead of someone trying to make a fistful of yen off of someone else's native heritage. The village has the excellent **Nibutani Ainu Bunka Hakubutsukan** (Nibutani Ainu Culture Museum), on the left side of the road. No information is given in English, but a selection of videos let you listen to the eerie sound of traditional Ainu chants and songs. ☎ 0145/72–2892. ▣ ¥300. ✆ Daily 9:30–4:30; closed Mon. Jan.–Mar., and Dec. 16–Jan. 15.

One minute away from Ainu Bunka Hakubutsukan on foot is a smaller museum, the **Kayano Shigeru Ainu Shiryōkan** (Shigeru Kayano Ainu Archive), which displays artifacts collected by Shigeru Kayano, the most prominent Ainu activist, who is now a member of Japan's House of Councillors. The surrounding rolling hills and spacious horse ranches make Nibutani a beguiling place to visit in summer, though it has been spoiled somewhat by the building of a new dam that put part of the area underwater. Unfortunately, much of the lost land was of sacred or economic value to the local Ainu. Keep in mind that only in 1997, with the passage of a law recognizing Ainu culture, did Japanese authorities begin to treat the group with anything approaching respect. ☎ 01457/2–3215. ▣ ¥300. ✆ Apr.–Nov., daily 9–5.

Shikotsu-ko (Lake Shikotsu)

★ ③① *50 mins south of Sapporo by bus.*

The last stop before returning to Sapporo should be Shikotsu-ko, the deepest lake in Hokkaidō—outfathomed only by Honshū's Tazawa-ko as the deepest in all of Japan. Swimmers should remember that although the beach shelves gently for 35 ft, it drops suddenly to an eventual depth of 1,191 ft. The lake's shape is a classic volcanic caldera, except that the rise of two volcanoes crumbled its peripheral walls on both north and south shores. Both the southern volcano, Tarumae-zan, and its northern counterpart, Eniwa-dake, remain active. They have fine hikes and summits with superb views of the lake, Eniwa-dake being the more challenging climb.

At the base of Mt. Eniwa is **Marukoma Onsen,** which has *rotemburo* (open-air thermal springs) along the lakeshore. Few experiences can compare to steaming in the waters to the sight of falling snow and the sound of the lake roiling just beyond the rotemburo wall.

Lodging

$$ ⛩ **Marukoma Onsen Ryokan.** Neither the building nor its interior furnishings have great aesthetic value. However, the lobby, lounges, and restaurant face the northwest shore of Shikotsu-ko. The tatami-style guest rooms have plain, modern, light-wood furnishings. If you have a room facing the lake and mountain, the view is splendid. Service is attentive and tolerant of foreigners, and dinner—served in your room—is above average. However, the real benefit of this ryokan is that besides the indoor thermal pool facing the water, there is a public rotemburo on the lake shore, as well as a private beach, within yards of the hotel. ✉ *Poropinai, Bangaichi, Shikotsu-ko, Chitose-shi, Hokkaidō 066,* ☎ *0123/25–2341. 60 Japanese-style rooms. Restaurant, bar, coffee shop, hot springs, recreation room. AE, DC, V.*

Getting Around

To reach Shikotsu-ko from Nibutani, take the freeway to Tomakomai and follow Route 276 to Shikotsu Onsen. Or take a train to JR Tomakomai Eki, from which Shikotsu-ko is a 40-minute bus ride.

From Shikotsu-ko, the quickest route back to Sapporo (by car or bus) is via Chitose and up the expressway. You could also return to Tomakomai by bus and take the JR train back westward in the direction of Hakodate, or take a bus to Chitose Kūkō, then the JR back to Sapporo.

Getting Around Shikotsu-Tōya National Park

You can see the park by car or by train and bus. If you want to pick just a couple of the area's sights, buses serve Tōya-ko Onsen, Noboribetsu Onsen, and Lake Shikotsu directly from Sapporo; in summer buses connect Tōya-ko and Noboribetsu Onsen.

By Bus

Direct bus service from Sapporo to Tōya-ko Onsen via Nakayama Tōge takes 2½ hours (¥2,550; reservations necessary). The **Chūō** (☎ 011/272–1211) and **Donan** (☎ 011/241–5143) coach lines also run from Sapporo to Noboribetsu Onsen; the trip takes 2¾ hours (¥1,700, reservations necessary). From June 1 to October 19 five buses per day make the 1¼-hour run between Tōya-ko Onsen and Noboribetsu Onsen via Orofure Tōge; only one bus runs per day the rest of the year (¥1,530, reservations necessary). Heavy snow keeps the road closed until spring.

By Car

The drive from Sapporo to Jōzankei is easy. Take the road that runs along the west side of the Botanical Gardens; it is a straight run to Jōzankei, less than an hour south of the city. There are sufficient signs in *romaji* (Japanese written in Roman script) throughout this area to give you directional confidence, and the route number, 230, is frequently displayed.

By Train

Tōya-ko Onsen and Noboribetsu Onsen are near the JR Sapporo–Hakodate Line. For Tōya-ko Onsen, disembark from the train at the JR Tōya Eki for a 15-minute bus ride to the lake. For Noboribetsu Onsen, disembark at Noboribetsu, and then take the Donan bus (a 13-minute ride) to the spa town.

EASTERN HOKKAIDŌ AND THE OHOTSUKU-KAI

The third side trip heads east to Abashiri on the Ohotsuku-kai, which makes a good base from which to head south to explore the mysterious lakes of Akan National Park; east out to the mountains and coastal scenery of Shiretoko National Park; or west to Hokkaidō's ice floe capital, Mombetsu. To see the great wetland breeding grounds for the striking and endangered tanchō-zuru, continue south from Akan National Park to Kushiro.

Abashiri

③② *350 km (210 mi) east of Sapporo, 5½ hrs east of Sapporo via Asahikawa by JR Limited Express.*

Abashiri is the principle Ohotsuku-kai town, but it is quite small. In winter, ryūhyō jam up on its shores and stretch out to sea as far as the eye can see. Two pleasure boats, **Aurora 1** and **Aurora 2,** give you a chance to inspect the ryūhyō at close quarters from mid-January to mid-April, for ¥3,000 (☎ 0152/43–6000). A museum at Mt. Tento—**Ohotsuku Ryūhyō Hakubutsukan**—explains the role of ice floes in nature. ☎ 0152/43–5951. ☞ ¥500. ⊙ *Apr.–Oct., daily 8–6; Nov.–Mar., daily 9–5; closed mid-Dec.–mid-Jan.*

A little farther inland, on the southeastern slope of Tento-zan, the **Hoppo Minzoku Hakubutsukan** (Hokkaidō Museum of Northern Peoples) contains artifacts belonging not only to the Ainu but also to indigenous cultures on the neighboring island of Sakhalin and in northern parts of America and Eurasia, such as the Inuit and the Lapps. If the museum's layout seems a little bizarre, it's because the building was designed to resemble the outline of a flying swan. The nodule housing the entrance lobby is fashioned like a conical tent. ☎ 0152/45–3883. ☞ ¥250. ⊙ *Tues.–Sun. 9:30–4:30; closed Dec. 29–Jan. 3.*

★ Down the hill from Tento-zan, toward Abashiri-ko, and a little closer to town, the **Abashiri Kangoku Hakubutsukan** (Prison Museum) recalls the days when convict labor was used to develop the region. Only the most heinous criminals were banished to this forbidding northern outpost, the Alcatraz of Japan. ☎ 0152/45–2411. ☞ ¥1,030. ⊙ *Apr.–Oct., daily 8–6, Nov.–Mar., daily 9–5.*

The **Abashiri Kyōdo Hakubutsukan** (Municipal Museum) houses a good collection of Ainu artifacts and anthropological findings taken from the nearby Moyoro Shell Mound that are believed to be relics from aboriginal people who predate the Ainu. It is located across the railroad tracks to the south of downtown, in the local park. ☎ 0152/43–3090. ☞ ¥100. ⊙ *May–Nov., daily 9–5; Nov.–Apr., daily 9–4; closed Dec. 31–Jan. 1 and some Mon.*

★ Another place worth visiting is **Tofutsu-ko,** just south of Abashiri. In winter, swans migrate from Siberia to hole up here. To get to the lake, take the train as far as Kitahama Eki and walk south for 10 minutes. Late June to late July, between Tofutsu-ko and the Ohotsuku-kai, the main attraction is the **Gensai Ka-en** (wildflower fields). Spread over 11 km (7 mi) of sand dunes and containing 50 species of flowers, this is where locals take their afternoon promenades.

Dining and Lodging

$$ ✕ **Nakazushi.** Sushi combinations of delicacies pulled fresh from the surrounding sea start at ¥2,000, including sea urchin, salmon roe over rice, and the famous Abashiri scallop. ⊠ *Minami 2-jō Nishi 2,* ☎ 0152/43–3447. *Closed two Wed. per month.*

$$$–$$$$ ▦ **Hotel Kanihonjin Yuaiso.** This hotel is perched on Tento-zan and overlooks Abashiri-ko. As you might expect from a hotel that calls itself the "Official Inn of Crab Lovers," the service is on the haughty side.

However, the restaurant menu includes dishes that give the crustacean a range of Western and Japanese treatments—10 different ones for the Kani-gozen (crab table d'hôte). The hotel is eight minutes by taxi from the JR eki. ✉ *Abashiri-shi, Ōagari 34, Hokkaidō 093,* ☎ *0152/43–0033,* FAX *0152/44–2468. 111 rooms. Restaurant, bar, karaoke room. AE, MC, V.*

$ 🖭 **Hotel Takeda Shimbashi.** This basic business hotel has the advantage of a convenient location just across from the train station. The proprietors speak some English and, though expectedly businesslike, are welcoming. The restaurant serves Japanese food, from soba to sushi to crab. ✉ *Shin-machi, Abashiri-shi, Hokkaidō 092,* ☎ *0152/43–4307,* FAX *0152/45–2091. 45 rooms. Restaurant. AE, DC, MC, V.*

Mombetsu

③ *90 km (54 mi) north of Abashiri.*

Mombetsu is a small port whose main industry is fishing the Ohotsuku-kai in summer. When the sea freezes in winter, Mombetsu is bitterly cold and surrounded by ice floes. The town has a couple of museums; a small, friendly entertainment section; a few shops on the main street; and a couple of hotels.

The icy waters of the Ohotsuku-kai wash the northeasternmost coast between Mombetsu and Wakkanai (☞ Central Hokkaidō and the Northern Cape, *below*), and it appropriately has a feeling of being at the end of the world. The people here make their living catching fish in summer. In winter the sea is frozen, and their livelihood depends on the success of the summer catch. The frigid Ohotsuku-kai waters produce *hokkai shima-ebi* (northern sea striped shrimp), the sweetest shrimp you'll ever taste, and ke-gani (best in June or July), which may look ugly, but its meat is so delicate that you'll have no trouble forgiving the creature's appearance. The coastline is relatively flat, and the drama is in its isolation rather than its scenery.

In hopes of increasing its interest to travelers, the city built **Okhotsk Tower,** a unique facility for the observation of ice floes. It bills itself as the only place in the world from which ice floes can be viewed from underwater and outlines the unusual conditions that conspire to bring such ice to this latitude, the southernmost reaches of ice floes in the northern hemisphere: Great volumes of fresh water from Siberia's Amur River empty into the shallow Ohotsuku-kai, diluting it to a salinity low enough to permit freezing. The tower stands at the end of a 1-km-long (½-mi-long) pier, on which there is also a seal pen. 🎫 *¥1,200.* ⊗ *Apr.–Oct., daily 9–6; Nov.–Mar., daily 9–4.*

You can also take a special boat, the ***Garinko Go,*** which in season acts as an icebreaker, pushing out through the floes. ☎ *01582/4–8000 (reservations and tickets).* 🎫 *¥1,500 summer, ¥3,000 winter.*

Mombetsu's **Ohotsuku Ryūhyō Kagaku Senta "Giza"** (Okhotsk Sea Ice Science Center "Giza") opened in 1991 as a multifunctional facility to promote understanding of ice floes. Its main feature is the Astrovision Hall, where spectacular views of sea ice are projected on a 360-degree dome, re-creating the experience of flying over the Okhotsk Sea when the ice floes are most impressive. There is also a low-temperature simulation room, where, clad in Eskimo-type clothing, you can experience the severe cold and wander around blocks of sea ice. ☎ *01582/3–5400.* 🎫 *¥250 (extra charges for Exhibition and Astrovision halls).* ⊗ *Tues.–Sun. 9:30–4:30.*

Mombetsu's municipal museum, **Mombetsu Kyōdo Hakubutsukan,** has examples of Hokkaidō's flora and fauna, some stone arrowheads, and ancient pottery. ☎ *01582/3–4236.* 🎫 *Free.* 🕐 *Tues.–Sun. 9–5:30.*

The road along the coast from Abashiri to Mombetsu is dotted with small summer resort hotels, especially along the shores of **Saroma-ko,** a brackish lagoon renowned for scallop aquaculture. The large body of water is almost locked in by two sand pits. However, all you can really take in here are the sea to the right and distant mountains to the left.

Thirty minutes southwest of Mombetsu (via Route 273), the town of **Takinoue** is famous for its Shiba-zakura Festival (May 1–June 1), when the surrounding hills bloom with *shiba-zakura* ("moss pink," or phlox), a flower that forms a delicate pink carpet. Japanese drumming booms out, a photo contest draws shutterbugs hoping to capture the fantasy of the season, and a sideshow contest picks a Miss Phlox, a.k.a Phlox Cinderella. Many of the villages on the coast between Mombetsu and Wakkanai host smaller versions of the same festival.

Dining and Lodging

Mombetsu's entertainment area, three streets up from the Harbor View Hotel (☞ *below*), is small, but there are plenty of bars that serve food and one or two modest discotheques (try the New Jazz Club). There are fewer restaurants than bars. While many eateries have visual displays in their windows to indicate prices and the type of food served, the bars do not. Count on about ¥5,000 per person in one of the bars that have hostesses with whom customers are expected to talk—in Japanese, not English. Prices can climb steeply, so establish the costs before you gulp too much whiskey.

$$ 🏯 **Togiya Ryokan.** This extremely friendly, old-fashioned inn is not elegant, but it has the warmth of rural Japan. No English is spoken, but mama-san does wonders with your use of a dictionary. Good Japanese family fare (fish—raw and grilled) is served in your room. There are no private baths, but good, deep Japanese baths are offered. The inn is on a small street, one block up from the harbor road. ⊠ *4 Minato-machi, Mombetsu, Hokkaidō 094,* ☎ *01582/3–3048. 15 rooms. No credit cards.*

$ 🏯 **Harbor View Hotel.** This is the best Western-style hotel in town. Even
★ though the Harbor View is modest, it is clean and comfortable. Request a room overlooking the harbor. Japanese and Western breakfasts are provided, while lunch or dinner might include grilled fish or shellfish. No English is spoken. The hotel is a half hour's drive from Ohotsuku-Mombetsu Airport; the trip from Memambetsu Airport takes one hour and 45 minutes. ⊠ *6 Minato-machi, Mombetsu, Hokkaidō 094,* ☎ *01582/4–6171. 35 Western-style rooms, 1 Japanese-style room. Restaurant. AE, DC, MC, V.*

En Route   If you would like to drive the 300 km (190 mi) from Mombetsu to Wakkanai, the road (Route 238) is a long one, but it has some redeeming features. The small coastal town of **Esashi** (north along Route 238) also hosts a *kani* (crab) festival in July, when the seafood available is particularly delicious. Farther north on Route 238, **Kutcharo-ko** is home in winter to large numbers of swans, who congregate around the unfrozen patches of water at its edges. And, of course, any winter traveler along this coast has a splendid chance to view the drift ice covering the sea.

If you want to head straight back to Sapporo from Mombetsu, follow the well-paved highway that cuts through the wooded mountain range to Asahikawa; this leg takes a little more than three hours by car or bus. Then, from Asahikawa, the train makes the 90-minute run to Sapporo.

Shiretoko Hantō (Shiretoko Peninsula)

Utoro is 74 km (46 mi) east of Abashiri, 45 mins by JR then 45 mins by bus.

★   A combination of somewhat difficult roads, changeable weather, and the local bear population—the last two of which aren't entirely agreeable to hikers—discourages all but the most adventurous of Japanese 34   tourists from coming to **Shiretoko National Park.** As a result, Shiretoko is the most remarkable of Japan's national parks, an untouched pocket of wilderness in this most industrialized and technologically advanced Asian nation. Twenty minutes east of Utoro by car is the **Shiretoko Go-ko** (five lakes) area, where a collection of small lakes cling like dew-drops perched above a precipitous northward drop into the ocean.

There is a sightseeing boat out of **Utoro** that runs out to the cape between April 28 and October 31. Catch the boat from the Fune Noriba (boat pier), about a 10 minutes' walk from the Utoro Onsen bus terminal. It costs ¥2,700 for the short tour, ¥6,000 for the long. There are five departures daily (fewer in the winter). As the boat skirts the shore and rounds the cape's tip, the views are impressive, with 600-ft cliffs breaking straight out of the sea and rugged mountains inland. In summer, you can also drive along the north shore to **Kamuiwakka Onsen** under Mt. Io. Along the shore are *rotemburo*, open-air hot springs. The pools are free—just take off your clothes and hop in.

To get to the peninsula, continue traveling southeast of Abashiri on the Kanno Line beyond Hama-Koshimizu. **Shari** is the end of the line and the jumping-off point for Shiretoko and its park. Most proper roads end about halfway along the peninsula. The final one terminates at Aidomari, with 30 km (19 mi) remaining before Shiretoko's tip. Bus service is erratic, and winter closes most of the area off to wheeled vehicles. To get to the park by public transport (summer only), take the 55-minute bus ride from Shari to Utoro.

Akan National Park

35   *170 km (102 mi) southeast of Mombetsu.*

Like Shikotsu-Tōya National Park, Akan National Park has some of Hokkaidō's most scenic lakes and mountains. And while the mountains are not as high as those in Daisetsu-zan (☞ *below*) they are no less imposing. In addition, Akan has three major lakes, each of which has a unique character. And, crucial to the success of any resort in Japan, the park has an abundance of thermal springs.

★ 36   The resort on the western side of **Akan-ko** is watched over by the smoking volcanoes **Me-Akan** and **O-Akan** (Mr. and Mrs. Akan). The lake itself is famous for *marimo*—spherical colonies of green algae that may be as small as a Ping-Pong ball or as large as a soccer ball (the latter taking up to 500 years to form). Marimo are rare, and the only other areas they can be found are Yamanaka-ko (lake) near Fuji-san and in a few lakes in North America, Siberia, and Switzerland. These strange plants act much like submarines, photosynthesizing by absorbing carbon dioxide from the water and then rising to the surface, where they exhale oxygen and sink. They also serve as weather indicators, rising closer to the surface when bright sunshine increases photosynthesis than when inclement weather portends and light levels drop. Akan-ko is especially beautiful in winter when it freezes over and the surrounding mountains are covered with snow. A popular sport from January to March is skating between the *wakasagi* (pond-smelt) fishermen. The wakasagi are hooked from ice holes and laid on the ice to freeze immediately. Their freshness makes them popular minced and eaten raw, though some people prefer to fry them.

Akan Kanko Kisen (☎ 0154/67–2511) runs a sightseeing boat (¥1, 120) around the lake. It lands on the lake side of the Hotel New Daitō and at a pier five minutes on foot northwest of the Hotel Yamaura.

The town of **Akan-kohan** is the resort area. This small village has expanded around the lake as new hotels go up. As is true in so much of Hokkaidō, these hotels are not very attractive. The key is to obtain a room over the lake so that you are looking at nature and not architectural calamities. The village center is kitschily dressed up for tourists and cluttered with souvenir shops with endless rows of carved bears, which are numerous here because a small Ainu population lives in the village, and the common commercial mythology is to connect native people and native animals.

Lodging

$$$–$$$$ 🏨 **Hotel Yamaura.** On the lake front at the south end of the village, the Yamaura has its own onsen. Half of the rooms are Japanese style, the others being a hybrid of Western and Japanese styles. All have private bathrooms. Prices, which include two Japanese-style meals, range from ¥12,000 to ¥20,000. Some staff members speak English. ⊠ *Akan-kohan Onsen, Akan-chō, Akan-gun, Hokkaidō 085, ☎ 0154/ 67–2311, ℻ 0154/67–2330. 92 rooms. 2 restaurants, hot springs, hot tub, sauna. AE, DC, V.*

$$$–$$$$ 🏨 **New Akan Hotel.** In Japanese eyes, this establishment is the most
★   prestigious in the area. It does have an ideal location on Akan-ko, but it tends toward sterility and vastness. Its newer annex is called Shangri-La, with the number of rooms totaling 370. Despite the hotel's size, there are only a few English speakers among its staff. There are Western- and Japanese-style restaurants. ⊠ *Akan-kohan Onsen, Akan-chō, Akan-gun, Hokkaidō 085, ☎ 0154/67–2121, ℻ 0154/67–3339. 271 Japanese-style rooms, 99 Western-style rooms. 2 restaurants, hot springs, shops. AE, DC, MC, V.*

$$ 🏨 **Hotel Park In.** Because this small hotel is not on the lake—it's just
★   off the main road that skirts the village—you'll have to request a room on the top floor to get a view of the lake and mountains. There are Japanese- and Western-style rooms; the Japanese restaurant, which attracts a local clientele, is especially good with its grilled fish. The owners are very friendly. ⊠ *Akan-kohan Onsen, Akan-chō, Akan-gun, Hokkaidō 085, ☎ 0154/67–3211, ℻ 0154/67–2752. 11 Western-style rooms, 5 Japanese-style rooms. No credit cards.*

En Route   From Akan the road to Teshikaga runs along the Akan Traverse. The distance is 51 km (32 mi) and has more than its share of scenery. The road winds past O-Akan, and at one point you can look over the dropoff to the right and its volcanic cone almost seems at eye level. It's not a road to be driven at night—not only are the views obscured, there is also the possibility of encountering a bear. And there is an even greater risk of smashing into a deer mesmerized by the glare of your headlights. The local bus between Akan and Teshikaga takes this road and stops at the Sokodai, an observation lookout, though only to collect and drop off passengers.

Elsewhere in Akan National Park

③⑦   **Teshikaga** is a small resort town with a few Japanese inns. Its JR eki goes under the name of Mashū. Mashū Onsen is nearby, and Mashū-ko itself is a 20-minute drive—35 minutes by bus to the nearest observation point—from Teshikaga.

★ ❸❽ **Mashū-ko** is ringed by 656-ft-high rock walls. Curiously, no water has been found either to enter or leave the lake, so what goes on in its 695-ft depths is anybody's guess. Perhaps that mystery and the dark blue water combine to exert a strange hypnotic effect and are what cause tourists to stare endlessly down from the cliffs into the lake. These cliff sides are incredibly steep and have few or no footholds. You may live longer if you forgo the pleasure of inspecting the water's clarity, said to be clear to a depth of 115 ft. Instead of climbing, consider taking in the lake from its two observation spots on the west rim. You'll recognize them by the parking lots and the buildings housing souvenir and food stands.

❸❾ **Kawayu Onsen,** lined with relatively expensive hotels (with mostly Japanese-style rooms), is for those who believe in the curative value of hot springs. Kawayu is not particularly attractive. However, just before the spa is **Iō-zan** (ee-*oh*-zan), an active volcano that emits sulfurous steam from vents in two ravines. There is a parking lot and souvenir and grocery store just off the road. Buy a couple of fresh eggs from the store, and then walk up to one of the saucepan-size pools and boil them. Kawayu is 14 km (9 mi) out of Mashū-ko.

❹❿ **Kussharo-ko** (sometimes spelled Kutcharo and not to be confused with similarly named lakes in northern and southern Hokkaidō) is Akan National Park's largest lake. Once it had a nearly perfect caldera shape, but other volcanoes have since sprung up and caused its shores to become flat and less dramatic. It is, however, an ideal area for camping and is popular with families who come for boating and paddling in the water. There are also a couple of natural hot springs that can be used free of charge. One other tourist attraction has been enthusiastically promoted in recent years—perhaps with an eye on the profits being made on the shores of Scotland's Loch Ness: "Kusshie," a creature said to inhabit the lake's depths. The lake is at its finest in the autumn, when the different shades of gold and green on the trees extend from the lakeshore into the higher mountain altitudes. From Kawayu, the road hugs the eastern side of the lake and connects with Route 243 to the south.

❹❶ At the northwest end of the lake, the road climbs up the mountains through **Bihoro Tōge,** affording the last great view of Akan National Park's mountains and the green waters of Kussharo-ko below. At Bihoro the road swings west back toward Kitami and Asahikawa, or northeast to Abashiri.

En Route An alternative exit from Akan National Park is to return from the lake to Kawayu Onsen and continue 3 km (2 mi) to a "T" junction and the JR Kawayu Eki. There, you can take a train or Route 391 either north or south: back to Abashiri or on to the great marsh at Kushiro.

Kushiro

60 km (36 mi) south of Teshikaga, 70 mins by JR.

Despite its romantic moniker "the City of Fog," Kushiro is a port town of no great appeal that used to be known for its rather seedy entertainment area for sailors and tourists coming in off the Tōkyō ferry. The city has been trying to reinvent itself as a base for nature conservation and tourism. Downtown, part of the old waterfront has been restored and now has a complex called, mysteriously, MOO-EGG, which contains souvenir shops and food stalls, cafés, a small botanical garden, and a popular ice cream stand. Even the entertainment district has some revamped bars with traditional fireplaces where fish is cooked to order.

★ ㊷   North and west of Kushiro (35 minutes by bus) is **Kushiro Shitsugen** (marsh), which constitutes 60% of Japan's marshland and was the world's first wetland designated for protection under the 1995 Ramsar Convention. It is the home of the red-crested tanchō-zuru. These cranes were ruthlessly hunted at the beginning of this century and were even believed to be extinct, until a handful of survivors were discovered in 1924. They have slowly regenerated and now number about 650. The crane—long-legged, long-billed, with a white body trimmed in black and a scarlet cap on its head—is a symbol of long life and happiness. Although said to live a thousand years, the birds nonetheless have made it to a rather impressive 80 in zoos. They pair for life, which has also made them the symbol of an ideal couple—they are frequently cited in Japanese wedding speeches. In March or April, females lay two eggs. The male and female play an equal role in looking after the eggs and, later, the chicks.

It is difficult to recommend a trip to see the cranes in summer: The birds are busy rearing their chicks and go deep into the swamps, where you can see them only through binoculars. Only a few are on view at an artificial breeding park, and these are kept behind a fence. In the winter, when they come for food handouts (especially near the village of Tsurui), they are easier to spot and no less beautiful in the snowy landscape.

Lodging

$ ⚏ **Kushiro Pacific Hotel.** This hotel is recommended mainly for its central location (five minutes by taxi from the train station). The staff is efficient, some English is spoken, and the rather small rooms are clean. Chinese and Western food is served in the restaurant. ⊠ *2-6 Sakae-chō, Kushiro, Hokkaidō 085,* ☎ *0154/24–8811,* ℻ *0154/23–9191. 132 rooms, mostly Western style. Restaurant. AE, MC, V.*

Getting Around Eastern Hokkaidō and the Ohotsuku-kai

The significant distance from Sapporo to Abashiri and Kushiro makes it advisable to take a train out, then rent a car or take a bus to get to the surrounding parks and towns.

By Bus

There are buses to Akan-ko from Kushiro and Kitami. You can also catch a bus from Lake Akan to Abashiri if you change buses in the town of Bihiro. A small number of bicycles are available for rent at the Akan Bus Terminal and at Akan View Hotel (☎ 0154/67–3131).

By Car

From Kitami, west of Abashiri, a road heads south to the small town of Tsubetsu, where it joins Route 240, entering Akan National Park near Akan-ko. From the southern part of Daisetsu-zan National Park at Nukabira, a road to Kamishihoro continues to Ashoro, which connects with Route 241; this runs directly to Akan. Coastal highway 238 skirts Saroma-ko between Mombetsu and Abashiri. Highway 244 continues east to Shari, from which 334 heads onto the Shiretoko Hantō until it dead-ends in the wilds of the national park.

By Train

Frequent service runs from Sapporo to Abashiri, and on to Shari (at the foot of the Shiretoko Hantō), and Teshikaga (the gateway to Akan National Park).

CENTRAL HOKKAIDŌ AND THE NORTHERN CAPE

This final jaunt to the Hokkaidō hinterlands is a voyage of exemplaries, taking in Japan's largest national park, its northernmost points, and the island's highest mountain. After ascending the breathtaking Daisetsu-zan range in central Hokkaidō, get ready for the trek to the northernmost cape, Sōya Misaki, and the stark beauty of Rishiri and Rebun islands.

Asahikawa

43 *120 km (82 mi) northwest of Sapporo.*

Asahikawa, Hokkaidō's second largest city, is the principal entrance to Daisetsu-zan National Park. The city is vast and sprawling, even though the first pioneers didn't establish a base here until as late as 1885. Now 365,000 people reside in an area of 750 square km (300 square mi). The endless suburbs are depressing, but the center of town is small, easy to navigate, and friendly. Several international hotels, including the sparkling Palace Hotel (☞ Lodging, *below*), are in the downtown center, close to the pedestrian shopping mall, the first such car-free mall in Japan, and the nightly scene of restaurants, izakaya, and bars. Asahikawa's major attractions are the Ainu Kinenkan and the Ice Festival in February.

The **Kawamura Kaneto Ainu Kinenkan** (memorial hall) is a reasonably good Ainu museum, though slightly ramshackle. However, like the Kayano Shigeru Ainu Shiryōkan in Nibutani (☞ Tōya-Shikotsu National Park, *above*), it does have the moral advantage of being run by a genuine Ainu, a man called Kaneto Kawamura, whose family has lived in the Asahikawa area for seven generations. There's a feeling that the museum really does exist to educate people about Ainu culture, rather than to exploit it for money. To get here, take Bus 24 (¥160) from the JR eki to Ainu Kinenkan-mae. ☎ 0166/51–2461. ☞ ¥500. ☉ May–Sept., daily 8:30–6; Oct.–Apr., daily 9–5.

Don't confuse the Ainu Kinenkan with the **Densho-no-Kotan** (traditional village), a re-creation of an Ainu village, with Ainu artifacts and tools, in Ainu Bunka-no-Mori (cultural forest) at Arashiyama Shizen Kōen (nature park). Take Bus 3 (¥190) from the JR eki and get off at Hoppo-yaso-en. ☎ 0166/52–1541. ☞ ¥300. ☉ Daily 9–5; closed winter, though it will open on request.

The **Ice Festival** is Asahikawa's smaller version of Sapporo's Snow Festival (200 sculptures, compared with the 300 at Sapporo). Here, the celebration has the feeling of a country fair.

Lodging

$$$ 🏨 **Palace Hotel.** Decorated with mock marble, the public spaces here
★ are brightly lit and airy, with potted plants separating the registration area from the lounge. The Palace is located downtown, one block from the New Hokkai. Some English is spoken. One of its restaurants, Lila, serves French fare (jacket required). ✉ 7-jō 6-chōme, Asahikawa, Hokkaidō 070, ☎ 0166/25–8811, ℻ 0116/25–8200. 265 rooms, mostly Western style. 3 restaurants, coffee shop. AE, DC, MC, V.

$$ 🏨 **Toyo Hotel.** Opposite the Palace Hotel (☞ above) on the main street, this small hotel has rooms with white and gray decor. The Toyo is used to serving Japanese guests but is friendly and helpful to Westerners. No English is spoken. There is a Japanese restaurant in the hotel. ✉ 7-jō

7-*chōme*, *Asahikawa, Hokkaidō 070,* ☎ *0166/22–7575,* FAX *0116/23–
1733. 104 rooms, mostly Western style. Restaurant. AE, DC, MC, V.*

En Route   Several roads lead from Asahikawa into Daisetsu-zan National Park,
but only one runs completely through the park, from north to south:
Asahikawa to Sōun-kyō, then on to Obihiro. Other roads, mainly
from the west, start into the mountains here and there but eventually
dead-end.

Daisetsu-zan National Park

㊹   *30 km (18 mi) east of Asahikawa.*

The geographical center of Hokkaidō and the largest of Japan's parks,
Daisetsu-zan National Park (*Daisetsu-zan* means "great snow mountains") contains the very essence of rugged Hokkaidō: vast plains,
soaring mountain peaks, hidden gorges, cascading waterfalls, wildflowers, forests, hiking trails, wilderness, and, of course, an onsen.
Daisetsu-zan refers to the park's five major peaks, whose combined
altitudes approach 6,560 ft. Their presence dominates the area and channels human entry into the park.

Daisetsu-zan West

On the west side of the park, the spa towns of Asahi-dake Onsen and
Shirogane Onsen serve as hiking centers in summer and ski resorts in
㊺   winter. **Shirogane Onsen,** at 2,461 ft, has had especially good skiing
since its mountain, Tokachi-dake, erupted in 1962, creating a good blanket of lava and a superb ski bowl. It erupted again in 1988.

㊻   At **Asahi-dake Onsen,** you can take a cable car up Asahi-dake,
Hokkaidō's highest mountain, to an altitude of 5,250 ft, and hike for
two hours to the 7,513-ft summit. In late spring and early summer, the
slopes are carpeted with alpine flowers. Die-hard skiers come here for
Japan's longest ski season.

Sōun-kyō

As you follow the main route through the park, the first place to go is
★ **㊼**   **Sōun-kyō** (*so-un-kyo*—*kyō* meaning "gorge"). The 24-km (15-mi)
ravine extends into the park from its northeast entrance and is doubtless the most scenic wonder. For an 8-km (5-mi) stretch, sheer cliff walls
rise on both sides of the canyon as the road winds into the mountains.
Sōun-kyō Onsen is halfway up. How the Japanese are able to abuse
natural splendor with ugly resort hotels is almost beyond belief. But
they do, and Sōun-kyō Onsen is yet another example. The Choyotei
Hotel is a particular concrete eyesore. Sitting on a bluff, the hotel dominates what otherwise would be a dramatic view of the gorge. Of
course hotel guests have magnificent views—not only of the gorge but
also of other concrete hotels.

Resting precariously on the side of the gorge are a couple of grocery
stores, some houses, and a few inns and restaurants, plus the inevitable
souvenir shops that make up the village of Sōun-kyō. There is also the
small **Sōun-kyō Hakubutsukan** (☎ 01658/5–3427), open 9–5, which
has exhibits on the formation of the Daisetsu range. Admission is
¥200. Activities take place in resort hotels, not in the village, and during the day most people are out on trails hiking through the park. One
popular, if easy, trip combines a seven-minute gondola (ropeway) ride
(¥1,500 round-trip) with a 15-minute chair-lift ride (¥500 round-trip)
up Kuro-dake for great views of Daisetsu-zan. For even finer views,
including one of Sōun-kyō, take the hour's walk to the very top. In
July and/or August the mountain is covered with alpine wildflowers.

You can also rent a bicycle from the Sōun-kyō bus terminal for ¥1,500 per day and pedal through the gorge. Bicycling has the advantage over driving of avoiding the main road's dark, viewless tunnels—the bike path skirts the gorge. The bike paths are also good for walks.

For good or ill, you have no option but to stay in Sōun-kyō Onsen if you want to stay in this part of the park. For assistance in finding lodging, contact the **Sōun-kyō Tourist Accommodation Office** (☎ 01658/5–3350). Rates tend to be 20% lower in winter. You can also try the small **youth hostel** (☎ 01658/5–3418). Drop by the **Sōun-kyō Tourist Information Center** (☎ 01658/2–1811) for maps.

LODGING

$$$ 🏨 **Choyotei.** Perched on a bluff halfway up the side of the gorge, this hotel has the best views—and, because of this, spoils some of Sōun-kyō's beauty. Its corner window in the huge foyer lounge looks straight down the gorge; however, the hotel itself is a mammoth eyesore, cold and sterile in the modern Japanese style. While rooms that face the gorge may merit the hotel's price, a room at the back looks onto a parking lot, another ugly building, and cliff walls. ⊠ *Sōun-kyō Onsen, Kamikawa-chō, Kamikawa, Hokkaidō 078,* ☎ *01658/5–3241. 272 rooms, mostly Japanese style. Bar, hot springs, shops, recreation room. AE, DC, MC, V.*

$$ 🏨 **Mount View Hotel.** This hotel has the nicest design around and an
★ air of freshness to it. It was built as a modern interpretation of an alpine inn, and the decor is in cheerful, warm pastels. Unfortunately, the hotel is down by the road and has limited views. Nevertheless, it has taste, which the other hotels lack. Western- and Japanese-style meals are available. ⊠ *Sōun-kyō Onsen, Hokkaidō 078,* ☎ *01658/5–3011. 69 Western-style rooms, 28 Japanese-style rooms. Hot springs. V.*

$ 🏨 **Pension Yukara.** This small inn is better priced than many others in Sōun-kyō Onsen, and though no English is spoken, the owners are hospitable to gai-jin. You'll find air-conditioning in summer and hot springs to soak in year-round. Western-style meals with Hokkaidō ingredients are included in the price. The management is happy to present picnic *onigiri* (rice balls) if you're planning to hit hiking trails early. The inn has Japanese-style shared baths. You can make reservations through the Welcome Inn association. ⊠ *Sōun-kyō Onsen, Hokkaidō 078,* ☎ *01658/5–3216. 4 Western-style rooms, 3 Japanese-style rooms. Dining room, hot springs. AE, V.*

GETTING AROUND

Sōun-kyō is less than two hours southeast of Asahikawa by car. You can catch a bus directly to Sōun-kyō Onsen in front of Asahikawa's JR eki. If you are using a Japan Rail Pass, you can save money by taking the JR train to Kamikawa Eki and transferring to the Dohoku bus for the 30-minute run to Sōun-kyō.

Daisetsu-ko and Shikaribetsu-ko

The picturesque, twin **Ryusei-no-taki** (Shooting-Star Falls) and **Ginga-no-taki** (Milky Way Falls) are 3 km (2 mi) up the road from Sōun-kyō Onsen. Neither is especially dramatic, but because they are a pair, separated by a buttresslike node called Buddhist Rock, they fit well into the Japanese natural aesthetic. The road continues past the falls, following the Ishi-kawa through perpendicular cliffs and fluted rock columns until it reaches the dammed-up **Daisetsu-ko.** The dam is a feat of engineering, its walls constructed only of earth and rubble. In itself, it has no visual merit, but islands appear to float in the lake behind it, surrounded by a backdrop of conifer-clad mountains.

At Daisetsu-ko the road divides. The right fork, Route 273, turns south and traverses the rough wilderness and least-visited part of the park. The road has been upgraded to avoid closure in winter, but there are no public buses. If you do not have a car, you must hitchhike as far as Nukabira, where you can catch buses and trains. This dramatic route climbs up and over **Mikuni Tōge** before it drops into lush valleys and through small ghost towns. In one such town, **Mitsumata**, stop in at the only restaurant, where you will be enthusiastically welcomed with a dish of *shika soba*—buckwheat noodles and deer meat. So fortified, it is an easy 18-km (11-mi) run into Nukabira and civilization. Nu-

49 kabira is a quiet spa town close to **Shikaribetsu-ko,** the park's only natural lake. Toward the end of December, the lake freezes over and an igloo village is built on the 3-ft-thick ice, in preparation for the Shikaribetsu Kotan Matsuri (village festival), which runs from mid-January to the end of February. The festival celebrates the dramatic Okhotsk winter, with an open-air bath erected on the ice and hot-air balloons taking people up and dotting the shimmering icy landscape with color.

En Route   Back at Daisetsu-ko, the left fork, Route 39, veers east to Kitami and Abashiri on the Ohotsuku-kai. The road is well paved, and buses make frequent trips between Sōun-kyō Onsen and Kitami. As spectacular as the route south, this road to Kitami climbs over the forested mountains and breaks through the peaks at Sekihoku Tōge. This pass road is short. Nineteen km (12 mi) from the lake it leaves Daisetsu-zan National Park to descend into flat fields of peppermint that sparkle white and purple in summer.

The road continues to Kitami and Abashiri on Hokkaidō's east coast. South of Kitami is Akan National Park (☞ *above*).

The Northern Cape

Wakkanai is 320 km (192 mi) north of Sapporo, 5¾ hrs by JR Limited Express, 65 mins by plane.

50 **Wakkanai** is a working-class town that subsists on farming the scrubland and fishing the cold waters for Alaska pollack and Atka mackerel when the sea is not packed with ice floes. It is an isolated outpost of humanity. Winter nights are long, and in summer there is a feeling of poetic solitude that comes from the eerie quality of the northern lights. From Wakkanai Park, on a ridge west of the city, there is a commanding view of Sakhalin, an island taken over by the Russians at the end of World War II. Several monuments in this park are dedicated to the days when Sakhalin was part of Japan. One commemorates nine female telephone operators who committed suicide at their post office in Maoka (on Sakhalin) when the island changed hands.

Few travelers come as far as Wakkanai for the town itself. You're likely to do the same and stick around long enough to catch one of the three ferries that make the daily two-hour crossing to the islands of Rebun-tō and Rishiri-tō. *Higashi-Nihon Ferry,* ☎ *0162/23–3780. To Rebun:* ☒ *¥3,710 1st class, ¥2,060 2nd class. To Rishiri: ¥3,300 1st class, ¥1,850 2nd class.*

Sōya Misaki

51 Halfway between Wakkanai and **Sōya Misaki,** the mountains push out toward the sea. Russia's Sakhalin Island stands out across the frigid waters. Sōya Misaki is at the northernmost limits of Japan. This lonely but significant spot is the site of several monuments marking the end of Japan's territory, as well as a memorial to the Korean airliner downed by the Soviet military north of here in 1982. If you happen to be rounding Sōya Misaki on the way to Wakkanai after a trip up

Hokkaidō's east coast, your first glimpse of Rishiri Island and its volcano on the horizon will come soon after rounding the cape. A public bus makes the hour-long run between Wakkanai and Cape Sōya six times a day.

Rebun-tō and Rishiri-tō

★ ㊼ **Rebun-tō** is the older of these two Nihon-kai islands, created by an upward thrust of the earth's crust. The long, fairly skinny island is oriented north–south. Along the east coast there are numerous fishing villages where men bring their catch, some of which is made into *nukaboke* (pollack covered in rice-bran paste), while women rake in the edible yellow-green *kombu* (kelp), which is often used in making soup broth, from the shore. On the west coast, cliffs stave off the surging waters of Nihon-kai. Inland, during the short summer months, wild alpine flowers, 300 species in all, blanket the mountain meadows. Momo-iwa is a 820-ft-high mound whose name means "peach rock." It is 2 km (1 mi) west of the ferry landing. Here, the wildflowers are in such profusion in mid-June that one fears to walk, for each step seems to crush a dozen delicate of them, including the white-pointed *usuyokiso,* which is found only on Rebun. Its name roughly translates as "dusting of snow."

Buses stop at the trailhead to the Kitosu Course (midway down the eastern side of the island) and the Nairo Course (10 km [6 mi] north). Bamboo and low-lying pines predominate. Leave 1¼ hours to cover the 4½-km (3-mi) loop to the top of 1,600-ft Rebun-dake, which overlooks rolling hills and the ocean beyond. Another hike, the Eight-Hour Course, covers the island from top to bottom on the west coast, passing along the way cliffs, waterfalls, and tiny seasonal villages. You can take on the whole course or half of it. Buses also go to Sukoton Misaki, a lovely cape on the west side of the island with a cove that is popular with anglers.

★ ㊽ **Rishiri-tō** is the result of a submarine volcano whose cone now towers 5,640 ft out of the water. The scenery is wilder than on Rebun-tō, and, though it is a larger island, Rishiri-tō has fewer inhabitants. The ruggedness of the terrain makes it harder to support life and figures for hardier climbing—sometimes too hardy: The Oniwaki Course was closed after a climber suffered a fatal misstep. The intermediate Kutsugata Course (4 hrs to the top), on the west side of the island, will take you past patches of buttercup-like *botan kimbai,* vibrant purple *hakusan chidori,* and numerous bird species.

To get the lay of the island, it is a good idea to take one of the regularly scheduled buses, which make a complete circle of the island in two hours. From May 1 to November 30, there are six a day between 6 AM and 6 PM that go both clockwise and counterclockwise. Fewer make the circuit the rest of the year. Get off at any of the several tourist stops along the way, and take the hiking routes laid out to the major scenic spots. Once you break above Rishiri-zan's tree line, at about 3,000 ft, the alpine panoramas of wildflowers, the cone-shape mountain, and wide expanses of sea are astonishing.

There is **ferry service** between Kafuka on Rebun-tō and Oshidomari and Kutsugata on Rishiri-tō (¥1,240 1st class, ¥720 2nd class). From Oshidomari on Rishiri-tō, the ferry to Wakkanai takes one hour and 40 minutes.

DINING AND LODGING

$$–$$$ ✕ **Sakatsubo.** Famous for sea urchin, this restaurant serves two varieties: *murasaki uni* (purple sea urchin) and *bafun* uni ("horse turd" urchin). Despite its inauspicious name, the latter is more prized and is

served as *domburi* (over steamed rice) from ¥3,500. The *unigiri* (sea urchin–filled rice balls) go for ¥400. ✉ *Kafuka, Rebun-chō, Hokkaidō 097,* ☎ *01638/6–1894. No credit cards.*

$ 🏠 **Hera-san no Uchi.** "Hera's House," as the name translates, typifies the warm, casual atmosphere that makes Hokkaidō so loved by Japanese hippies. Mr. Hera refuses to use artificial or frozen foods for the two meals that come with the ¥8,000 rooms, and he welcomes travelers of every nation. Bicycles are also available for rent. The house is at the entrance to the Peshi Misaki hiking trail. ✉ *Rishiri-Fuji Machi, Oshidomari, Rishiri-chō, Hokkaidō 097,* ☎ *01638/2–2361. 8 rooms with shared bath. No credit cards.*

$ 🏠 **Pension Uni.** This sky-blue building is one of few accommodations on Rebun-tō. Rooms come with bathrooms, and the two meals included in the rate feature ingredients that were swimming only hours before. ✉ *Tonnai, Kafuka, Rebun-chō, Hokkaidō 097,* ☎ *01638/6–1541. 10 rooms. No credit cards.*

HOKKAIDŌ A TO Z

Arriving and Departing

By Ferry

The least expensive form of travel to Hokkaidō is to take a ferry from Honshū. From Tōkyō to Kushiro (32 hrs), the luxury ferryboat *Sabrina Blue Zephyr* sails three or four times weekly and is operated by the Kinkai Yusen Company (☎ 0154/52–4890), with rates of ¥26,300 first class, ¥13,100 tourist class. From Tōkyō to Tomakomai (32½ hrs), three other large ferries are operated by the Blue Highway Line (☎ 0144/34–3121), with fares of ¥2,510 Cabin A, ¥16,780 sleeper. The same company also operates an overnight ferry (15 hrs) from Sendai to Tomakomai. Higashi-nihon Ferries' express *Unicorn,* between Aomori and Hakodate, debuted in 1997 with two round-trips daily. It takes two hours, as does the train, but costs only ¥2,130. At press time, some companies were still considering price changes in conjunction with a recent consumption tax increase.

By Plane

Japan Airlines (JAL), Japan Air System (JAS), and All Nippon Airways (ANA) link Hokkaidō to Honshū by direct flights from Tōkyō's Haneda Kūkō to Hakodate, Sapporo (Chitose), Asahikawa, Memambetsu (Abashiri), Nakashibetsu (Nemuro), Obihiro, and Kushiro. There are also two flights a day from Tōkyō's Narita international airport, which eliminates the need for the long Haneda–Narita transfer if you're skipping Tōkyō proper. Many other major cities on Honshū (including Sendai, Aomori, Akita, Niigata, Nagoya, Ōsaka, and Hiroshima) have flights to Sapporo, as do five places in the Asian and Pacific neighborhood (Seoul, Hong Kong, Guam, Saipan, and Honolulu).

The cost by air from Tōkyō to Sapporo is ¥24,600, compared with ¥21,380 by train. Some air travelers arriving in Japan on European flights can, with a change of planes at Tōkyō, fly at no extra charge to Sapporo. If you are flying from overseas to Sapporo via Tōkyō, book the domestic portion when you buy your international ticket; otherwise you will have to fork out for what is, per mile, the most expensive domestic ticket in the world, despite the fact that this is also the most heavily trafficked domestic route in the world. At press time, a start-up was planning to offer discount service to battle the price gauging on the Tōkyō–Sapporo route. Although the plan is welcome, it remains to be seen whether or not it will get off the ground.

Sapporo's airport is Chitose, 40 km (25 mi) south of Sapporo. Frequent trains and buses connect the city with the airport (☞ Sapporo, *above*).

By Train

With the 55-km (34-mi) Seikan Tunnel permitting train travel between Hokkaidō and Honshū, the train journey from Tōkyō to Sapporo can take as little as 10 hours, 41 minutes, allowing for a train-changing time of 17 minutes; this trip involves a combination of the Shinkansen train to Morioka (2 hrs, 36 mins), the northernmost point on the Tōhoku Shinkansen Line, and a change to an express train for the remaining journey to Hakodate (4 hrs, 8 mins) and then to Sapporo (3 hrs, 45 mins). Alternatively, there is the Blue Train (the blue-colored long-distance sleeper) from Tōkyō to Sapporo, which takes about 15 hours. The Japan Rail Pass covers the train fare in either case, but an additional charge is made for a sleeping compartment (¥13,350) or a bunk (¥6,300) on the Blue Train. (On the express train, you must pay an express fee of ¥3,150 regardless of how you choose to sleep.)

Getting Around

By Car

Cars are easy to rent. The Nippon-Hertz agency has offices in central Sapporo (✉ Minami 5 Nishi 1, Chūō-ku), at Chitose airport, and at the Hakodate Eki and JR Asahikawa Eki. For the most part, the Japanese are cautious drivers and obey the rules of the road, though a combination of wide, straight roads, light traffic, treacherous weather conditions, and Honshū visitors' unfamiliarity with all of the above gives Hokkaidō the worst accident figures in Japan. International traffic signs are used and are easy to understand. Directional signs are often sufficiently given in *romaji* (Japanese written in Roman script) to enable non-Japanese readers to navigate, and all major roads have route numbers. Also, the Dosanko are extremely helpful in giving instructions and directions to Western travelers. The limitation to renting a car is the expense. A day's rental is about ¥14,500 (not including tax), including 220 free km, after which you are charged ¥20 per km. Gas and tolls on the few expressways are three times as costly as in the United States. The best plan is, wherever possible, to travel long distances by public transport and then rent a car for local trips.

By Plane

The two domestic airlines—Japan Air System (JAS) and Nippon Kinkyori Airways—connect Sapporo with Hakodate, Kushiro, Wakkanai, and the smaller Memambetsu, Naka-Shibetsu, and Ohotsuku-Mombetsu airports in eastern Hokkaidō. There is also daily service between Wakkanai and both Rebun and Rishiri islands. Because its schedule suffers occasional interruptions, check flights before you get to Sapporo.

By Train and Bus

Japan Railways (JR) has routes connecting most of the major cities. For the most part, trains travel on less scenic routes and are simply efficient means to reach the areas that you want to explore. Buses cover most of the major routes through the scenic areas, and all the excursions in this chapter may be accomplished by bus.

Contacts and Resources

Emergencies

Police, ☎ 110. **Ambulance,** ☎ 119.

Guided Tours

The **Japan Travel Bureau** (☎ 03/5620–9500) runs tours of Hokkaidō from Tōkyō, lasting from a few to several days. These include airfare, hotel, and meals and stop at major cities and scenic areas. Bookings should be made at least 10 days in advance.

Visitor Information

The Japan National Tourist Organization's **Tourist Information Center** (TIC) in Tōkyō (✉ Tōkyō Kotsu Kaikan Bldg., 2-10-1 Yūraku-chō, Chiyoda-ku) has free maps and brochures on Hokkaidō. Also, the **Hokkaidō Tourist Association** has an office in Tōkyō, on the second floor of the Kokusai Kankō Kaikan Building (✉ Marunouchi 1-8-3, Chiyoda-ku), near the Yaesu exit of Tōkyō Eki. Within Hokkaidō, the best place for travel information is in Sapporo (☞ Sapporo, *above*).

Other important regional tourist information centers include **Akan Lake** (☎ 0154/67–2254), **Noboribetsu Onsen** (☎ 0143/84–2068), **Sōunkyō Onsen** (☎ 01658/5–1811), and **Lake Tōya** (☎ 01427/5–2446).

There are bus and train travel information centers at all the major train stations. The main Hokkaidō office of the **Japan Travel Bureau,** in Sapporo, is where you are most likely to find English spoken (☎ 011/241–6201).

The **Japan Travel Phone** (the nationwide service for English-language assistance or travel information) is available from 9 to 5, seven days a week. Dial toll-free 0088/22–2800 or 0120/222–800 for information on eastern Japan. When using a yellow, blue, or green public phone (do not use the red phones), insert a ¥10 coin, which will be returned. There are different numbers for callers in Tōkyō (☎ 3503–4400) and Kyōto (☎ 371–5649); in those cities, the service costs ¥10 per three minutes.

AN ENGLISH-JAPANESE TRAVELER'S VOCABULARY

Japanese sounds and spellings differ in principle from those of the West. We build words letter by letter, and one letter can sound different depending where it appears in a word. For example, we see *ta* as two letters, and *ta* could be pronounced three ways, as in *tat, tall,* and *tale.* For the Japanese, *ta* is one character, and it is pronounced one way: *tah.*

The *hiragana* and *katakana* (tables of sounds) are the rough equivalents of our alphabet. There are four types of syllables within these tables: the single vowels *a, i, u, e,* and *o,* in that order; vowel-consonant pairs like *ka, ni, hu,* or *ro;* the single consonant *n,* which punctuates the upbeats of the word for bullet train, *Shinkansen* (shee-n-*ka*-n-se-n); and compounds like *kya, chu,* and *ryo.* Remember that these compounds are one syllable. Thus Tōkyō, the capital city, has only two syllables—*tō* and *kyō*—not three. Likewise pronounce Kyōtō *kyō-tō*, not *kee-oh-to.*

Japanese vowels are pronounced as follows: *a*–ah, *i*–ee, *u*–oo, *e*–eh, *o*–oh. The Japanese *r* is rolled so that it sounds like a bounced *d.*

No diphthongs. Paired vowels in Japanese words are not slurred together, as in our words *coin, brain,* or *stein.* The Japanese separate them, as in *mae* (*ma*-eh), whch means in front of; *kōen* (*ko*-en), which means park; *byōin* (*byo*-een), which means hospital; and *tokei* (to-*keh*-ee), which means clock or watch.

Macrons. Many Japanese words, when rendered in *romaji* (roman letters), require macrons over vowels to indicate correct pronunciation, as in Tōkyō. When you see these macrons, double the length of the vowel, as if you're saying it twice: to-o-*kyo*-o. Likewise, when you see double consonants, as in the city name Nikkō, linger on the Ks—as in "bookkeeper"—and on the O.

Emphasis. Some books state that the Japanese emphasize all syllables in their words equally. This is not true. Take the words *sayōnara* and *Hiroshima.* Americans are likely to stress the downbeats: sa-yo-*na*-ra and hi-ro-*shi*-ma. The Japanese actually emphasize the second beat in each case: sa-*yō*-na-ra (note the macron) and hi-*ro*-shi-ma. Metaphorically speaking, the Japanese don't so much stress syllables as pause over them or race past them: Emphasis is more a question of speed than weight. In the vocabulary below, we indicate emphasis by italicizing the syllable that you should stress.

Three interesting pronunciations are in the vocabulary below. The word *desu* roughly means "is." It looks like it has two syllables, but the Japanese race past the final *u* and just say "dess." Likewise, some verbs end in -*masu,* which is pronounced "mahss." Similarly, the character *shi* is often quickly pronounced "sh," as in the phrase meaning "pleased to meet you:" ha-ji-me-*mash(i)*-te. Just like *desu* and -*masu,* what look like two syllables, in this case *ma* and *shi,* are pronounced *mahsh.*

Hyphens. Throughout *Fodor's Japan,* we have hyphenated certain words to help you recognize meaningful patterns. This isn't conventional; it is practical. For example, *Eki-mae-dōri,* which literally means "Station Front Avenue," turns into a blur when rendered Ekimaedōri. And in the Kyōto chapter, where you'll run across a number of sight names that end in -*jingū* or -*jinja* or -*taisha,* you'll soon catch on to their meaning: Shintō shrine.

Chapter glossaries. In the same spirit, we have added glossaries to each chapter to signal important words that appear in the city or region in question. From studying the Japanese language, we have found that knowing these few words and suffixes adds meaning to reading about Japan and makes asking directions from Japanese people a whole lot more productive.

Basics　基本的表現

Yes/No	*ha-i/ii*-e	はい／いいえ
Please	o-ne-*gai* shi-masu	お願いします
Thank you (very much)	(*dō*-mo) a-*ri*-ga-to go-*zai*-ma su	（どうも）ありがとう ございます
You're welcome	*dō* i-ta-shi-ma-shi-te	どういたしまして
Excuse me	su-mi-ma-*sen*	すみません
Sorry	go-*men* na-*sai*	ごめんなさい
Good morning	o-*ha*-yō *go*-zai-ma-su	お早うございます
Good day/afternoon	kon-*ni*-chi-wa	こんにちは
Good evening	kom-*ban*-wa	こんばんは
Good night	o-*ya*-su-mi na-*sai*	おやすみなさい
Goodbye	sa-*yō*-na-ra	さようなら
Mr./Mrs./Miss	-san	ー さん
Pleased to meet you	*ha*-ji-me-*mashi*-te	はじめまして
How do you do?	*dō*-zo yo-*ro*-shi-ku	どうぞよろしく

Numbers　数

The first reading is used for reading numbers, as in telephone numbers, and the second is often used for counting things.

1	*i*-chi / hi-*to*-tsu	一／一つ	17	*jū*-shi-chi	十七
2	ni / fu-*ta*-tsu	二／二つ	18	*jū*-ha-chi	十八
3	san / *mit*-tsu	三／三つ	19	*jū*-kyū	十九
4	shi / *yot*-tsu	四／四つ	20	*ni*-jū	二十
5	go / i-*tsu*-tsu	五／五つ	21	*ni*-jū-i-chi	二十一
6	ro-ku / *mut*-tsu	六／六つ	30	*san*-jū	三十
7	*na*-na / *na*-na-tsu	七／七つ	40	*yon*-jū	四十
8	*ha*-chi / *yat*-tsu	八／八つ	50	*go*-jū	五十
9	kyū / *ko*-ko-no-*tsu*	九／九つ	60	*ro*-ku-jū	六十
10	jū / tō	十／十	70	na-na-jū	七十
11	*jū*-i-chi	十一	80	*ha*-chi-jū	八十
12	*jū*-ni	十二	90	kyū-jū	九十
13	*jū*-san	十三	100	*hya*-ku	百
14	*jū*-yon	十四	1000	sen	千
15	*jū*-go	十五	10,000	*i*-chi-man	一万
16	*jū*-ro-ku	十六	100,000	*jū*-man	十万

Days of the Week　曜日

Sunday	*ni*-chi *yō*-bi	日曜日
Monday	*ge*-tsu *yō*-bi	月曜日
Tuesday	*ka* *yō*-bi	火曜日
Wednesday	*su*-i *yō*-bi	水曜日
Thursday	*mo*-ku *yō*-bi	木曜日
Friday	*kin* *yō*-bi	金曜日
Saturday	*dō* *yō*-bi	土曜日

Months 月

January	*i*-chi *ga*-tsu	一月
February	*ni* ga-tsu	二月
March	*san* ga-tsu	三月
April	*shi* ga-tsu	四月
May	*go* ga-tsu	五月
June	*ro*-ku *ga*-tsu	六月
July	*shi*-chi *ga*-tsu	七月
August	*ha*-chi *ga*-tsu	八月
September	*ku* ga-tsu	九月
October	*jū* ga-tsu	十月
November	*jū*-i-chi *ga*-tsu	十一月
December	*jū*-ni *ga*-tsu	十二月

Useful Expressions, Questions, and Answers   よく使われる表現

Do you speak English?	*ei*-go ga wa-*ka*-ri-ma-su *ka*	英語が。わかりますか
I don't speak Japanese.	*ni*-hon-go ga wa-*ka*-ri-ma-*sen*	日本語がわかりません。
I don't understand.	wa-*ka*-ri-ma-*sen*	わかりません。
I understand.	wa-*ka*-ri-ma-shi-*ta*	わかりました。
I don't know.	*shi*-ri-ma-*sen*	知りません。
I'm American (British).	wa-*ta*-shi wa a-*me*-ri-ka (i-*gi*-ri-su) jin *desu*	私はアメリカ（イギリス）人です。
What's your name?	o-*na*-ma-e wa *nan* desu *ka*	お名前は何ですか。
My name is . . .	. . . to *mo*-shi-*ma*-su	. . . . .と申します。
What time is it?	*i*-ma *nan*-ji desu *ka*	今何時ですか。
How?	*dō* yat-te	どうやって。
When?	*i*-tsu	いつ。
Yesterday/today/tomorrow	ki-*nō*/kyō/*ashi*-ta	きのう／きょう／あした
This morning	*ke*-sa	けさ
This afternoon	*kyō* no *go*-go	きょうの午後
Tonight	*kom*-ban	こんばん
Excuse me, what?	su-*mi*-ma-*sen*, *nan* desu *ka*	すみません、何ですか。
What is this/that?	*ko*-re/*so*-re wa *nan* desu *ka*	これ／それは何ですか。
Why?	*na*-ze desu *ka*	なぜですか。
Who?	*da*-re desu *ka*	だれですか。
I am lost.	*mi*-chi ni ma-yo-i-*mash*-ta	道に迷いました。
Where is [place]	[place] wa *do*-ko desu *ka*	. . . . .はどこですか。
Train station?	e-ki	駅
Subway station?	chi-*ka*-te-tsu-no eki	地下鉄の駅
Bus stop?	*ba*-su *no*-ri-*ba*	バス乗り場
Taxi stand?	*ta*-ku-shi-i *no*-ri-*ba*	タクシー乗り場
Airport?	kū-kō	空港

Post office?	*yū*-bin-*kyo*-ku	郵便局
Bank?	*gin*-kō	銀行
the [name] hotel?	[name] ho-*te*-ru	ホテル
Elevator?	e-re-bē-tā	エレベーター
Where are the restrooms?	*to*-i-re wa *do*-ko desu *ka*	トイレは どこですか。
Here/there/over there	*ko*-ko/*so*-ko/*a*-so-ko	ここ／そこ／あそこ
Left/right	hi-*da*-ri/*mi*-gi	左／右
Straight ahead	mas-*su*-gu	まっすぐ
Is it near (far)?	chi-*ka*-i (*to*-i) desu *ka*	近い（遠い）ですか。
Are there any rooms?	*he*-ya ga a-ri-masu *ka*	部屋がありますか。
I'd like [item]	[item] ga ho-*shi*-i no desu ga	…がほしいの ですが。
Newspaper	*shim*-bun	新聞
Stamp	*kit*-te	切手
Key	*ka*-gi	鍵
I'd like to buy [item]	[item] o kai-*ta*-i no desu ke do	…を買いたいの ですけど。
a ticket to [event]	[event] *ma*-de no *kip*-pu	…までの切符
Map	*chi*-zu	地図
How much is it?	i-*ku*-ra desu *ka*	いくらですか。
It's expensive (cheap).	ta-*ka*-i (ya-*su*-i) de su *ne*	高い（安い）ですね。
A little (a lot)	su-*ko*-shi (*ta*-ku-san)	少し（たくさん）
More/less	*mot*-to o-ku/su-ku-*na*-ku	もっと多く／少なく
Enough/too much	*jū*-bun/o-su-*gi*-ru	十分／多すぎる
I'd like to exchange . . .	. . . *ryō*-ga e shi-*te* i-*ta*-da-ke-masu *ka*	…両替して 頂けますか。
dollars to yen	*do*-ru o *en* ni	ドルを円に
pounds to yen	*pon*-do o *en* ni	ポンドを円に
How do you say . . . in Japanese?	ni-*hon*-go de . . . wa *dō* i-i-masu *ka*	日本語で…は どう言いますか。
I am ill/sick.	wa-*ta*-shi wa *byō*-ki de su	私は病気です。
Please call a doctor.	i-sha o *yon*-de ku-da-*sa*-i	医者を呼んで 下さい。
Please call the police.	ke-i-sa-tsu o *yon*-de ku-da-*sa*-i	警察を 呼んで下さい。
Help!	*ta*-su-*ke*-te	助けて！

Restaurants　レストラン

Basics and Useful Expressions　よく使われる表現

A bottle of . . .	. . . *ip*-pon	…一本
A glass/cup of . . .	. . . *ip*-pai	…一杯
Ashtray	*ha*-i-*za*-ra	灰皿
Plate	*sa*-ra	皿
Bill/check	kan-*jō*	かんじょう

English	Romaji	Japanese
Bread	pan	パン
Breakfast	*chō*-sho-ku	朝食
Butter	ba-*tā*	バター
Cheers!	kam-*pai*	乾杯！
Chopsticks	*ha*-shi	箸
Cocktail	*ka*-ku-*te*-ru	カクテル
Dinner	*yū*-sho-ku	夕食
Excuse me!	su-mi-ma-*sen*	すみません
Fork	*fō*-ku	フォーク
I am diabetic.	wa-*ta*-shi wa tō-*nyō*-byō de su	私は糖尿病です
I am dieting.	*da*-i-et-to *chū* desu	ダイエット中です。
I am a vegetarian.	sa-i-*sho*-ku *shū*-gi-sha de-su	菜食主義者です。
I cannot eat [item]	[item] wa *ta*-be-ra-re-ma-*sen*	.....は食べられません。
I'd like to order.	*chū*-mon o shi-*tai* desu	注文をしたいです。
I'd like [item]	[item] o o-ne-*gai*-shi-ma su	.....をお願いします。
I'm hungry.	o-na-ka ga *su*-i-te i-*ma* su	お腹が空いています。
I'm thirsty.	*no*-do ga ka-*wa*-i-te i-*ma* su	喉が渇いています。
It's tasty (not good)	o-i-shi-i (ma-*zu*-i) desu	おいしい（まずい）です。
Knife	*na*-i-fu	ナイフ
Lunch	*chū*-sho-ku	昼食
Menu	me-nyū	メニュー
Napkin	*na*-pu-*kin*	ナプキン
Pepper	ko-*shō*	こしょう
Please give me [item]	[item] o ku-da-*sa*-i	.....を下さい。
Salt	*shi*-o	塩
Set menu	*te*-i-sho-ku	定食
Spoon	su-*pūn*	スプーン
Sugar	sa-to	砂糖
Wine list	*wa*-i-n *ri*-su-*to*	ワインリスト
What do you recommend?	o-su-su-me *ryō*-ri wa *nan* desu ka	お勧め料理は何ですか。

Meat Dishes　肉料理

Japanese	Romaji	Description
焼き肉	yaki-niku	Thinly sliced beef and liver are marinated then barbecued over an open fire at the table.
すき焼き	suki-yaki	Thinly sliced beef, green onions, mushrooms, thin noodles, and cubes of tōfu are simmered in a large iron pan in front of you. These ingredients are cooked in a mixture of soy sauce, mirin (cooking wine), and a little sugar. You are given a saucer of raw egg to cool the suki-yaki morsels

before eating. Using chopsticks, you help yourself to anything on your side of the pan and dip it into the egg and then eat. Best enjoyed in a group.

しゃぶしゃぶ	shabu-shabu	Extremely thin slices of beef are plunged for an instant into boiling water flavored with soup stock and then dipped into a thin sauce and eaten.
肉じゃが	niku-jaga	Beef and potatoes stewed together with soy sauce.
ステーキ	sutēki	steak
ハンバーグ	hambāgu	Hamburger pattie served with sauce.
トンカツ	tonkatsu	Breaded deep fried pork cutlets.
しょうが焼	shōga-yaki	Pork cooked with ginger.
酢豚	subuta	Sweet and sour pork, originally a Chinese dish.
からあげ	kara-age	deep-fried without batter
焼き鳥	yaki-tori	Pieces of chicken, white meat, liver, skin, etc., threaded on skewers with green onions and marinated in sweet soy sauce and grilled.
親子どんぶり	oyako-domburi	Literally, "mother and child bowl"—chicken and egg in broth over rice.
他人どんぶり	tanin-domburi	Literally, "strangers in a bowl"—similar to oyako domburi, but with beef instead of chicken.
ロール・キャベツ	rōru kyabetsu	Rolled cabbage; beef or pork rolled in cabbage and cooked.
はやしライス	hayashi raisu	Beef flavored with tomato and soy sauce with onions and peas over rice.
カレーライス	karē-raisu	Curried rice. A thick curry gravy typically containing beef is poured over white rice.
カツカレー	katsu-karē	Curried rice with tonkatsu.
お好み焼き	okonomi-yaki	Sometimes called a Japanese pancake, this is made from a batter of flour, egg, cabbage, and meat or seafood, grilled then covered with green onions and a special sauce.
シュウマイ	shūmai	Shrimp or pork wrapped in a light dough and steamed.
ギョウザ	gyōza	Pork spiced with ginger and garlic in a Chinese wrapper and fried or steamed.

Seafood Dishes　魚貝類料理

焼き魚	yaki-zakana	broiled fish
塩焼	shio-yaki	Fish sprinkled with salt and broiled until crisp.
さんま	samma	saury pike
いわし	iwashi	sardines

しゃけ	shake	salmon
照り焼き	teri-yaki	Fish basted in soy sauce and broiled.
ぶり	buri	yellowtail
煮魚	nizakana	stewed fish
さばのみそ煮	saba no miso ni	Mackerel stewed with soy-bean paste.
揚げ魚	age-zakana	fried fish
かれいフライ	karei furai	deep-fried flounder
刺身	sashimi	Very fresh raw fish. Served sliced thin on a bed of white radish with a saucer of soy sauce and horseradish. Eaten by dipping fish into soy sauce mixed with horseradish.
まぐろ	maguro	tuna
あまえび	ama-ebi	sweet shrimp
いか	ika	squid
たこ	tako	octopus
あじ	aji	horse mackerel
さわら	sawara	Spanish mackerel
しめさば	shimesaba	Mackerel marinated in vinegar.
かつおのたたき	katsuo no tataki	Bonito cooked just slightly on the surface. Eaten with cut green onions and thin soy sauce.
どじょうの 柳川なべ	dojo no yanagawa nabe	Loach cooked with burdock root and egg in an earthen dish. Considered a delicacy.
うな重	una-jū	Eel marinated in a slightly sweet soy sauce is charcoal-broiled and served over rice. Considered a delicacy.
天重	ten-jū	Deep fried prawns served over rice with sauce.
海老フライ	ebi furai	Deep fried breaded prawns.
あさりの酒蒸し	asari no sakamushi	Clams steamed with rice wine.

Sushi　寿司

寿司	sushi	Basically, sushi is rice, fish, and vegetables. The rice is delicately seasoned with vinegar, salt, and sugar. There are basically three types of sushi: nigiri, chirashi, and maki.
にぎり寿司	nigiri zushi	The rice is formed into a bite-sized cake and topped with various raw or cooked fish. The various types are usually named after the fish, but not all are fish. Nigiri zushi is eaten by picking up the cakes with chopsticks or the fingers, dipping the fish side in soy sauce, and eating.

ちらし寿司	chirashi zushi	In chirashi zushi, a variety of seafood is arranged on the top of the rice and served in a bowl.
巻き寿司	maki zushi	Raw fish and vegetables or other morsels are rolled in sushi rice and wrapped in dried seaweed. Some popular varieties are listed here.
まぐろ	maguro	tuna
とろ	toro	fatty tuna
たい	tai	red snapper
さば	saba	mackerel
こはだ	kohada	gizzard shad
さけ	sake	salmon
はまち	hamachi	yellowtail
ひらめ	hirame	flounder
あじ	aji	horse mackerel
たこ	tako	octopus
あなご	anago	sea eel
えび	ebi	shrimp
甘えび	ama-ebi	sweet shrimp
いか	ika	squid
みる貝	miru-gai	giant clam
あおやぎ	aoyagi	round clam
卵	tamago	egg
かずのこ	kazunoko	herring roe
かに	kani	crab
ほたて貝	hotate-gai	scallop
うに	uni	sea urchin
いくら	ikura	salmon roe
鉄火巻	tekka-maki	tuna roll
かっぱ巻	kappa-maki	cucumber roll
新香巻	shinko-maki	shinko roll (shinko is a type of pickle)
カリフォルニア巻	kariforunia-maki	California roll, containing crab-meat and avocado. This was invented in the U.S. but was re-exported to Japan and is gaining popularity there.
うに	uni	Sea urchin on rice wrapped with seaweed.
いくら	ikura	Salmon roe on rice wrapped with seaweed.
太巻	futo-maki	Big roll with egg and pickled vegetables.

Vegetable Dishes   野菜料理

おでん	oden	Often sold by street vendors at festivals and in parks, etc., this is vegetables, octopus, or egg in a thick batter and boiled.
天ぷら	tempura	Vegetables, shrimp, or fish deep fried in a light batter. Eaten by dipping into a thin sauce containing grated white radish.
野菜サラダ	yasai sarada	vegetable salad
大学いも	daigaku imo	fried yams in a sweet syrup
野菜いため	yasai itame	"stir-fried" vegetables
きんぴらごぼう	kimpira gobō	Carrots and burdock root, fried with soy sauce.
煮もの	nimono	vegetables simmered in a soy- and sake-based sauce
かぼちゃ	kabocha	pumpkin
さといも	satoimo	taro root
たけのこ	takenoko	bamboo shoots
ごぼう	gobō	burdock root
れんこん	renkon	lotus root
酢のもの	sumono	Vegetables seasoned with ginger.
きゅうり	kyūri	cucumber
和えもの	aemono	Vegetables dressed with sauces.
ねぎ	tamanegi	onions
おひたし	ohitashi	Boiled vegetables with soy sauce and dried shaved bonito or sesame seeds.
ほうれん草	hōrenso	spinach
漬物	tsukemono	Japanese pickles. Made from white radish, eggplant or other vegetables. Considered essential to the Japanese meal.

Egg Dishes   卵料理

ベーコン・エッグ	bēkon-eggu	bacon and eggs
ハム・エッグ	hamu-eggu	ham and eggs
スクランブル・エッグ	sukuramburu eggu	scrambled eggs
ゆで卵	yude tamago	boiled eggs
目玉焼	medama-yaki	fried eggs, sunny-side up
オムレツ	omuretsu	omelet
オムライス	omuraisu	Omelet with rice inside, often eaten with ketchup.
茶わんむし	chawan mushi	Vegetables, shrimp, etc., steamed in egg custard.

Tōfu Dishes 豆腐料理

Tōfu, also called bean curd, is a white, high-protein food with the consistency of soft gelatin.

冷やっこ	hiya-yakko	Cold tōfu with soy sauce and grated ginger.
湯どうふ	yu-dōfu	boiled tōfu
あげだしどうふ	agedashi dōfu	Lightly fried plain tōfu dipped in soy sauce and grated ginger.
マーボーどうふ	mābō dōfu	Tōfu and ground pork in a spicy red sauce. Originally a Chinese dish.
とうふの田楽	tōfu no dengaku	Tōfu broiled on skewers and flavored with miso.

Rice Dishes ごはん料理

ごはん	gohan	steamed white rice
おにぎり	onigiri	Triangular balls of rice with fish or vegetables inside and wrapped in a type of seaweed.
おかゆ	okayu	rice porridge
チャーハン	chāhan	Fried rice; includes vegetables and pork.
ちまき	chimaki	A type of onigiri made with sweet rice.
パン	pan	Bread, but usually rolls with a meal.

Soups 汁もの

みそ汁	miso shiru	Miso soup. A thin broth containing tōfu, mushrooms, or other morsels in a soup flavored with miso or soy-bean paste. The morsels are taken out of the bowl and the soup is drunk straight from the bowl without a spoon.
すいもの	suimono	Soy sauce flavored soup, often including fish and tofu.
とん汁	tonjiru	Pork soup with vegetables.

Noodles 麺類

うどん	udon	Wide flour noodles in broth. Can be lunch in a light broth or a full dinner called *nabe-yaki udon* when meat, chicken, egg, and vegetables are added.
そば	soba	Buckwheat noodles. Served in a broth like udon or, during the summer, cold on a bamboo mesh and called *zaru soba*.
ラーメン	rāmen	Chinese noodles in broth, often with *chashu* or roast pork. Broth is soy sauce or miso flavored.
そう麺	sōmen	Very thin wheat noodles, usually served cold with a tsuyu or thin sauce. Eaten in summer.

ひやむぎ	hiyamugi	Similar to somen, but thicker.
やきそば	yaki-soba	Noodles fried with beef and cabbage, garnished with pickled ginger and vegetables.
スパゲッティ	supagetti	Spaghetti. There are many interesting variations on this dish, notably spaghetti in soup, often with seafood.

Fruit　果実

アーモンド	āmondo	almonds
あんず	anzu	apricot
バナナ	banana	banana
ぶどう	budō	grapes
グレープフルーツ	gurēpufurūtsu	grapefruit
干しぶどう	hoshi-budō	raisins
いちご	ichigo	strawberries
いちじく	ichijiku	figs
かき	kaki	persimmons
キーウィ	kiiui	kiwi
ココナツ	kokonatsu	coconut
くり	kuri	chestnuts
くるみ	kurumi	walnuts
マンゴ	mango	mango
メロン	meron	melon
みかん	mikan	tangerine (mandarin orange)
桃	momo	peach
梨	nashi	pear
オレンジ	orenji	orange
パイナップル	painappuru	pineapple
パパイヤ	papaiya	papaya
ピーナッツ	piinattsu	peanuts
プルーン	purūn	prunes
レモン	remon	lemon
りんご	ringo	apple
さくらんぼ	sakurambo	cherry
西瓜	suika	watermelon

Dessert　デザート類

アイスクリーム	aisukuriimu	ice cream
プリン	purin	caramel pudding
グレープ	kurēpu	crepes
ケーキ	kēki	cake
シャーベット	shābetto	sherbet
アップルパイ	appuru pai	apple pie
ようかん	yokan	sweet bean paste jelly

コーヒーゼリー	kōhii zeri	coffee-flavored gelatin
和菓子	wagashi	Japanese sweets

Drinks　飲物

Alcoholic　酒類

ビール	biiru	beer
生ビール	nama biiru	draft beer
カクテル	kakuteru	cocktail
ウィスキー	uisukii	whisky
スコッチ	sukocchi	scotch
バーボン	bābon	bourbon
日本酒（酒） あつかん ひや	nihonshu (sake) atsukan hiya	Sake, a wine brewed from rice. warmed sake cold sake
焼酎	shōchū	Spirit distilled from potatoes.
チューハイ	chūhai	Shōchū mixed with soda water and flavored with lemon juice or other flavors.
ワイン 赤 白 ロゼ	wain aka shiro roze	wine red white rose
シャンペン	shampen	champagne
ブランデー	burandē	brandy

Non-alcoholic　その他の飲物

コーヒー	kōhii	coffee
アイスコーヒー	aisu kōhii	iced coffee
日本茶	nihon cha	Japanese green tea
紅茶	kō-cha	black tea
レモンティー	remon tii	tea with lemon
ミルクティー	miruku tii	tea with milk
アイスティー	aisu tii	iced tea
ウーロン茶	ūron cha	oolong tea
ジャスミン茶	jasumin cha	jasmine tea
牛乳／ミルク	gyūnyū/miruku	milk
ココア	kokoa	hot chocolate
レモンスカッシュ	remon sukasshu	carbonated lemon soft drink
ミルクセーキ	miruku sēki	milk shake
ジュース	jūsu	juice, but can also mean any soft drink
レモネード	remonēdo	lemonade

More Useful Phrases   よく使われる表現

Temple	otera/odera/-ji/-in/-dō	堂／寺
Shrine	jinja/jingū/-gū/-dō/taisha	神社／神宮／大社
Castle	-jō	城
Park	kōen	公園
River	kawa/gawa	川
Bridge	hashi/bashi	橋
Museum	hakubutsukan	博物館
Zoo	dōbutsu-en	動物園
Botanical gardens	shokubutsu-en	植物園
Island	shima/jima/tō	島
Slope	saka/zaka	坂
Hill	oka	丘
Lake	-ko	湖
Bay	-wan	湾
Plain	hara/bara/taira/daira	平
Peninsula	hantō	半島
Mountain	yama/-san/-take	山
Cape	misaki/saki	岬
Sea	kai/nada	海
Gorge	kyōkoku	峡谷
Plateau	kōgen	高原
Train line	sen	線
Prefecture	-ken/-fu	県／府
Ward	-ku	区
Exit	deguchi/-guchi	出口
Street, avenue	dōri/-dō/michi	道
main road	kaidō/kōdō	街道／公道
In front of	mae	前
North	kita	北
South	minami	南
East	higashi	東
West	nishi	西
Shop, store	mise/-ya	店
Hot-spring spa	onsen	温泉

INDEX

WHEREVER YOU TRAVEL, *H*ELP IS NEVER FAR AWAY.

From planning your trip to providing travel assistance along the way, American Express® Travel Service Offices are always there to help you do more.

Japan

Okinawa Tourist Service (R)
2-3 Matsuo 1-Chome
Naha-Shi, Okinawa
Naha City
98/862-1116

Okinawa Tourist Service (R)
3-1-9 Kubota
Okinawa City
98/933-1152

American Express TFS
4-30-16, Ogikubo, Suginami-Ku
Tokyo
3/3220-6200

do more AMERICAN EXPRESS

Travel

http://www.americanexpress.com/travel

American Express Travel Service Offices are located throughout Japan.